CORPORATION LIMITED LIABILITY ENTITIES AND PARTNERSHIPS

Statutory and Documentary Supplement for
Hazen & Markham's Corporations
and Other Business Enterprises
Cases and Materials

2019–2020 EDITION

THOMAS LEE HAZEN

Cary C. Boshamer Distinguished Professor of Law
The University of North Carolina at Chapel Hill

JERRY W. MARKHAM

Professor of Law
Florida International University

WEST
ACADEMIC
PUBLISHING

© West, a Thomson business 2003–2008
© 2009–2012 Thomson Reuters
© 2013 LEG, Inc. d/b/a West Academic Publishing
© 2014–2018 LEG, Inc. d/b/a West Academic
© 2019 LEG, Inc. d/b/a West Academic
    444 Cedar Street, Suite 700
    St. Paul, MN 55101
    1-877-888-1330

Printed in the United States of America

ISBN: 978-1-64242-948-0

[No claim of copyright is made for official U.S. government statutes, rules or regulations.]

PREFACE

This statutory supplement is designed for use in law school courses covering corporations, other limited liability entities, and partnerships. The supplement contains the Uniform Partnership Act, the Revised Uniform Partnership Act, and the Revised Uniform Limited Partnership Act. It also contains the Delaware Limited Liability Company Act, the Delaware Corporate law, and the Model Business Corporation Act which was supplied by the American Bar Association along with the official comments.

The foregoing statutes are reproduced in their entirety. There are also selections from the federal securities laws that relate to subjects covered in a basic corporations course. In addition, this supplement contains some sample corporate documents to provide a glimpse of articles of incorporation, bylaws, and corporate minutes. This supplement is current through March 2019.

Some instructors may want to supplement the material herein with state-specific laws or with additional SEC rules and forms. The SEC rules and forms are readily available on the official SEC website (www.sec.gov).

We hope you will find this compilation useful. We welcome any suggestions for future editions.

THOMAS LEE HAZEN
JERRY W. MARKHAM

April 2019

SUMMARY OF CONTENTS

CORPORATIONS, OTHER LIMITED LIABILITY ENTITIES AND PARTNERSHIPS

Statutory and Documentary Supplement for
Hazen & Markham's Corporations
and Other Business Enterprises
Cases and Materials

2019–2020 EDITION

UNIFORM PARTNERSHIP ACT (1914) ("UPA")

Table of Sections

PART I. PRELIMINARY PROVISIONS

PART II. NATURE OF PARTNERSHIP

PART III. RELATIONS OF PARTNERS TO PERSONS DEALING WITH THE PARTNERSHIP

PART IV. RELATIONS OF PARTNERS TO ONE ANOTHER

PART V. PROPERTY RIGHTS OF A PARTNER

PART VI. DISSOLUTION AND WINDING UP

Commissioners' Prefatory Note

The subject of a uniform law on partnership was taken up by the Conference of Commissioners on Uniform State Laws in 1902, and the Committee on Commercial Law was instructed to employ an expert and prepare a draft to be submitted to the next annual Conference. (See Am. Bar Assn. Report for 1902, p. 477.) At the meeting in 1903 the committee reported that it had secured the services of James Barr Ames, Dean of the Law School of Harvard University, as expert to draft the act. (See Am. Bar Assn. Report for 1903, p. 501.)

In 1905 the Committee on Commercial Law reported progress on this subject, and a resolution was passed by the Conference, directing that a draft be prepared upon the mercantile theory. (See Am. Bar Assn. Reports, 1905, pp. 731–738.) And in 1909 the committee reported that it had in its hands a draft of an act on this subject, which draft was recommitted to the committee for revision and amendment, with directions to report to the next Conference for discussion and action. (See Report, C.U.S.L., 1906, p. 40.)

In 1907 the matter was brought before the Conference and postponed until the 1908 meeting. (See Report, C.U.S.L., 1907, p. 93.) In 1908 the matter was discussed by the Conference. (See Am. Bar Assn. Reports, 1908, pp. 983, 1048.) And in 1909 the Second Tentative Draft of the Partnership Act was introduced and discussed. (See p. 1081 of Am. Bar Assn. Reports for 1909.)

In 1910 the committee reported that on account of the death of Dean Ames no progress had been made, but that Dr. Wm. Draper Lewis, then Dean and now Professor of Law at the Law School of the University of Pennsylvania, and Mr. James B. Lichtenberger, of the Philadelphia Bar, had prepared a draft of a partnership act on the so-called entity idea, with the aid of the various drafts and notes of Dean Ames, and that they had also submitted a draft of a proposed uniform act, embodying the theory that a partnership is an aggregate of individuals associated in business, which is that at present accepted in nearly all the states of the Union. (See Report, C.U.S.L., 1910, p. 142.) Dean Lewis expressed his belief that with certain modifications the aggregate or common law theory should be adopted. A resolution was passed by the Conference that any action that might have theretofore been adopted by it, tending to limit the Committee on Commercial Law in its consideration of the partnership law to what is known as the entity theory, be rescinded and that the committee be allowed and directed to consider the subject of partnership at large as though no such resolution had been adopted by the Conference. (See p. 52.)

In the fall of 1910 the committee invited to a Conference, held in Philadelphia, all the teachers of, and writers on, partnerships, besides several other lawyers known to have made a special study of the subject. There was a large attendance. For two days the members of the committee and their guests discussed the theory on which the proposed act should be drawn. At the conclusion of the discussion the experts present recommended that the act be drawn on the aggregate or common law theory, with the modification that the partners be treated as owners of partnership property holding by a special tenancy which should be called tenancy in partnership. (See section 25 of the act recommended.) Accordingly, at the meeting of the Conference in the summer of 1911, the committee reported that, after hearing the discussion of experts, it had voted that Dean Lewis be requested to prepare a draft of a partnership act on the so-called common law theory. (See Report, C.U.S.L., 1911, p. 149.)

The committee reported another draft of the act to the Conference at its session in 1912, drawn on the aggregate or common law theory, with the modification referred to. At this session the Conference spent several days in the discussion of the act, again referring it to the Committee on Commercial Law for their further consideration. (See Report, C.U.S.L., 1912, p. 67.)

The Committee on Commercial Law held a meeting in New York on March 29, 1913, and took up the draft of the act referred back to it by the Conference, and after careful consideration of the amendments suggested by the Conference, prepared their seventh draft, which was, at their annual session in the summer of 1913, submitted to the Conference. The Conference again spent several days in discussing the act and again referred it to the Committee on Commercial Law, this time mainly for protection in form.

The Committee on Commercial Law assembled in the City of New York, September 21, 1914, and had before them a new draft of the act, which had been carefully prepared by Dr. Wm. Draper Lewis with valuable suggestions submitted by Charles E. Shepard, Esq., one of the commissioners from the State of Washington, and others interested in the subject. The committee reported the Eighth Draft to the Conference which, on October 14, 1914, passed a resolution recommending the act for adoption to the legislatures of all the States.

Uniformity of the law of partnerships is constantly becoming more important, as the number of firms increases which not only carry on business in more than one state, but have among the members residents of different states.

It is however, proper here to emphasize the fact that there are other reasons, in addition to the advantages which will result from uniformity, for the adoption of the act now issued by the Commissioners. There is probably no other subject connected with our business law in which a greater number of instances can be found where, in matters of almost daily occurrence, the law is uncertain. This uncertainty is due, not only to conflict between the decisions of different states, but more to the general lack of consistency in legal theory. In several of the sections, but especially in those which relate to the rights of the partner and his separate creditors in partnership property, and to the rights of firm creditors where the personnel of the partnership has been changed without liquidation of partnership affairs, there exists an almost hopeless confusion of theory and practice, making the actual administration of the law difficult and often inequitable.

Another difficulty of the present partnership law is the scarcity of authority on matters of considerable importance in the daily conduct and in the winding up of partnership affairs. In any one state it is often impossible to find an authority on a matter of comparatively frequent occurrence, while not infrequently an exhaustive research of the reports of the decisions of all the states and the federal courts fails to reveal a single authority throwing light on the question. The existence of a statute stating in detail the rights of the partners inter se during the carrying on of the partnership business, and on the winding up of partnership affairs, will be a real practical advantage of moment to the business world. The notes which are printed in connection with this edition of the Act were prepared by Dr. Wm. Draper Lewis, the draftsman. They are designed to point out the few changes in the law which the adoption of the act will effect, and the many confusions and uncertainties which it will end.

WALTER GEORGE SMITH,

Chairman, Committee on Commercial Law.

PART I.   PRELIMINARY PROVISIONS

§ 1.   Name of Act

This act may be cited as Uniform Partnership Act.

§ 2.   Definition of Terms

In this act, "Court" includes every court and judge having jurisdiction in the case.

"Business" includes every trade, occupation, or profession.

"Person" includes individuals, partnerships, corporations, and other associations.

"Bankrupt" includes bankrupt under the Federal Bankruptcy Act [11 U.S.C.A. § 1 et seq.] or insolvent under any state insolvent act.

"Conveyance" includes every assignment, lease, mortgage, or encumbrance.

"Real property" includes land and any interest or estate in land.

§ 3.   Interpretation of Knowledge and Notice

(1) A person has "knowledge" of a fact within the meaning of this act not only when he has actual knowledge thereof, but also when he has knowledge of such other facts as in the circumstances shows bad faith.

(2) A person has "notice" of a fact within the meaning of this act when the person who claims the benefit of the notice:

     (a) States the fact to such person, or

     (b) Delivers through the mail, or by other means of communication, a written statement of the fact to such person or to a proper person at his place of business or residence.

§ 4.   Rules of Construction

(1) The rule that statutes in derogation of the common law are to be strictly construed shall have no application to this act.

(2) The law of estoppel shall apply under this act.

(3) The law of agency shall apply under this act.

(4) This act shall be so interpreted and construed as to effect its general purpose to make uniform the law of those states which enact it.

(5) This act shall not be construed so as to impair the obligations of any contract existing when the act goes into effect, nor to affect any action or proceedings begun or right accrued before this act takes effect.

§ 5.   Rules for Cases Not Provided for in This Act

In any case not provided for in this act the rules of law and equity, including the law merchant, shall govern.

PART II.   NATURE OF PARTNERSHIP

§ 6.   Partnership Defined

(1) A partnership is an association of two or more persons to carry on as co-owners a business for profit.

(2) But any association formed under any other statute of this state, or any statute adopted by authority, other than the authority of this state, is not a partnership under this act, unless such association would have been a partnership in this state prior to the adoption of this act; but this act shall apply to limited partnerships except in so far as the statutes relating to such partnerships are inconsistent herewith.

§ 7. Rules for Determining the Existence of a Partnership

In determining whether a partnership exists, these rules shall apply:

(1) Except as provided by section 16 persons who are not partners as to each other are not partners as to third persons.

(2) Joint tenancy, tenancy in common, tenancy by the entireties, joint property, common property, or part ownership does not of itself establish a partnership, whether such co-owners do or do not share any profits made by the use of the property.

(3) The sharing of gross returns does not of itself establish a partnership, whether or not the persons sharing them have a joint or common right or interest in any property from which the returns are derived.

(4) The receipt by a person of a share of the profits of a business is prima facie evidence that he is a partner in the business, but no such inference shall be drawn if such profits were received in payment:

(a) As a debt by installments or otherwise,

(b) As wages of an employee or rent to a landlord,

(c) As an annuity to a widow or representative of a deceased partner,

(d) As interest on a loan, though the amount of payment vary with the profits of the business,

(e) As the consideration for the sale of a good-will of a business or other property by installments or otherwise.

§ 8. Partnership Property

(1) All property originally brought into the partnership stock or subsequently acquired by purchase or otherwise, on account of the partnership, is partnership property.

(2) Unless the contrary intention appears, property acquired with partnership funds is partnership property.

(3) Any estate in real property may be acquired in the partnership name. Title so acquired can be conveyed only in the partnership name.

(4) A conveyance to a partnership in the partnership name, though without words of inheritance, passes the entire estate of the grantor unless a contrary intent appears.

PART III. RELATIONS OF PARTNERS TO PERSONS DEALING WITH THE PARTNERSHIP

§ 9. Partner Agent of Partnership as to Partnership Business

(1) Every partner is an agent of the partnership for the purpose of its business, and the act of every partner, including the execution in the partnership name of any instrument, for apparently carrying on in the usual way the business of the partnership of which he is a member binds the partnership, unless the partner so acting has in fact no authority to act for the partnership in the

particular matter, and the person with whom he is dealing has knowledge of the fact that he has no such authority.

(2) An act of a partner which is not apparently for the carrying on of the business of the partnership in the usual way does not bind the partnership unless authorized by the other partners.

(3) Unless authorized by the other partners or unless they have abandoned the business, one or more but less than all the partners have no authority to:

(a) Assign the partnership property in trust for creditors or on the assignee's promise to pay the debts of the partnership,

(b) Dispose of the good-will of the business,

(c) Do any other act which would make it impossible to carry on the ordinary business of a partnership,

(d) Confess a judgment,

(e) Submit a partnership claim or liability to arbitration or reference.

(4) No act of a partner in contravention of a restriction on authority shall bind the partnership to persons having knowledge of the restriction.

§ 10.   Conveyance of Real Property of the Partnership

(1) Where title to real property is in the partnership name, any partner may convey title to such property by a conveyance executed in the partnership name; but the partnership may recover such property unless the partner's act binds the partnership under the provisions of paragraph (1) of section 9, or unless such property has been conveyed by the grantee or a person claiming through such grantee to a holder for value without knowledge that the partner, in making the conveyance, has exceeded his authority.

(2) Where title to real property is in the name of the partnership, a conveyance executed by a partner, in his own name, passes the equitable interest of the partnership, provided the act is one within the authority of the partner under the provisions of paragraph (1) of section 9.

(3) Where title to real property is in the name of one or more but not all the partners, and the record does not disclose the right of the partnership, the partners in whose name the title stands may convey title to such property, but the partnership may recover such property if the partners' act does not bind the partnership under the provisions of paragraph (1) of section 9, unless the purchaser or his assignee, is a holder for value, without knowledge.

(4) Where the title to real property is in the name of one or more or all the partners, or in a third person in trust for the partnership, a conveyance executed by a partner in the partnership name, or in his own name, passes the equitable interest of the partnership, provided the act is one within the authority of the partner under the provisions of paragraph (1) of section 9.

(5) Where the title to real property is in the names of all the partners a conveyance executed by all the partners passes all their rights in such property.

§ 11.   Partnership Bound by Admission of Partner

An admission or representation made by any partner concerning partnership affairs within the scope of his authority as conferred by this act is evidence against the partnership.

§ 12.   Partnership Charged With Knowledge of or Notice to Partner

Notice to any partner of any matter relating to partnership affairs, and the knowledge of the partner acting in the particular matter, acquired while a partner or then present to his mind, and the knowledge of any other partner who reasonably could and should have communicated it to the acting partner, operate as notice to or knowledge of the partnership, except in the case of a fraud on the partnership committed by or with the consent of that partner.

§ 13. Partnership Bound by Partner's Wrongful Act

Where, by any wrongful act or omission of any partner acting in the ordinary course of the business of the partnership or with the authority of his co-partners, loss or injury is caused to any person, not being a partner in the partnership, or any penalty is incurred, the partnership is liable therefor to the same extent as the partner so acting or omitting to act.

§ 14. Partnership Bound by Partner's Breach of Trust

The partnership is bound to make good the loss:

(a)   Where one partner acting within the scope of his apparent authority receives money or property of a third person and misapplies it; and

(b)   Where the partnership in the course of its business receives money or property of a third person and the money or property so received is misapplied by any partner while it is in the custody of the partnership.

§ 15. Nature of Partner's Liability

All partners are liable

(a)   Jointly and severally for everything chargeable to the partnership under sections 13 and 14.

(b)   Jointly for all other debts and obligations of the partnership; but any partner may enter into a separate obligation to perform a partnership contract.

§ 16. Partner by Estoppel

(1)   When a person, by words spoken or written or by conduct, represents himself, or consents to another representing him to any one, as a partner in an existing partnership or with one or more persons not actual partners, he is liable to any such person to whom such representation has been made, who has, on the faith of such representation, given credit to the actual or apparent partnership, and if he has made such representation or consented to its being made in a public manner he is liable to such person, whether the representation has or has not been made or communicated to such person so giving credit by or with the knowledge of the apparent partner making the representation or consenting to its being made.

(a)   When a partnership liability results, he is liable as though he were an actual member of the partnership.

(b)   When no partnership liability results, he is liable jointly with the other persons, if any, so consenting to the contract or representation as to incur liability, otherwise separately.

(2)   When a person has been thus represented to be a partner in an existing partnership, or with one or more persons not actual partners, he is an agent of the persons consenting to such representation to bind them to the same extent and in the same manner as though he were a partner in fact, with respect to persons who rely upon the representation. Where all the members of the existing partnership consent to the representation, a partnership act or obligation results; but in all other cases it is the joint act or obligation of the person acting and the persons consenting to the representation.

§ 17.   Liability of Incoming Partner

A person admitted as a partner into an existing partnership is liable for all the obligations of the partnership arising before his admission as though he had been a partner when such obligations were incurred, except that this liability shall be satisfied only out of partnership property.

PART IV. RELATIONS OF PARTNERS TO ONE ANOTHER

§ 18.   Rules Determining Rights and Duties of Partners

The rights and duties of the partners in relation to the partnership shall be determined, subject to any agreement between them, by the following rules:

(a)   Each partner shall be repaid his contributions, whether by way of capital or advances to the partnership property and share equally in the profits and surplus remaining after all liabilities, including those to partners, are satisfied; and must contribute towards the losses, whether of capital or otherwise, sustained by the partnership according to his share in the profits.

(b)   The partnership must indemnify every partner in respect of payments made and personal liabilities reasonably incurred by him in the ordinary and proper conduct of its business, or for the preservation of its business or property.

(c)   A partner, who in aid of the partnership makes any payment or advance beyond the amount of capital which he agreed to contribute, shall be paid interest from the date of the payment or advance.

(d)   A partner shall receive interest on the capital contributed by him only from the date when repayment should be made.

(e)   All partners have equal rights in the management and conduct of the partnership business.

(f)   No partner is entitled to remuneration for acting in the partnership business, except that a surviving partner is entitled to reasonable compensation for his services in winding up the partnership affairs.

(g)   No person can become a member of a partnership without the consent of all the partners.

(h)   Any difference arising as to ordinary matters connected with the partnership business may be decided by a majority of the partners; but no act in contravention of any agreement between the partners may be done rightfully without the consent of all the partners.

§ 19.   Partnership Books

The partnership books shall be kept, subject to any agreement between the partners, at the principal place of business of the partnership, and every partner shall at all times have access to and may inspect and copy any of them.

§ 20.   Duty of Partners to Render Information

Partners shall render on demand true and full information of all things affecting the partnership to any partner or the legal representative of any deceased partner or partner under legal disability.

§ 21.   Partner Accountable as a Fiduciary

(1)   Every partner must account to the partnership for any benefit, and hold as trustee for it any profits derived by him without the consent of the other partners from any transaction connected with the formation, conduct, or liquidation of the partnership or from any use by him of its property.

(2) This section applies also to the representatives of a deceased partner engaged in the liquidation of the affairs of the partnership as the personal representatives of the last surviving partner.

§ 22. Right to an Account

Any partner shall have the right to a formal account as to partnership affairs:

(a) If he is wrongfully excluded from the partnership business or possession of its property by his co-partners,

(b) If the right exists under the terms of any agreement,

(c) As provided by section 21,

(d) Whenever other circumstances render it just and reasonable.

§ 23. Continuation of Partnership Beyond Fixed Term

(1) When a partnership for a fixed term or particular undertaking is continued after the termination of such term or particular undertaking without any express agreement, the rights and duties of the partners remain the same as they were at such termination, so far as is consistent with a partnership at will.

(2) A continuation of the business by the partners or such of them as habitually acted therein during the term, without any settlement or liquidation of the partnership affairs, is prima facie evidence of a continuation of the partnership.

PART V. PROPERTY RIGHTS OF A PARTNER

§ 24. Extent of Property Rights of a Partner

The property rights of a partner are (1) his rights in specific partnership property, (2) his interest in the partnership, and (3) his right to participate in the management.

§ 25. Nature of a Partner's Right in Specific Partnership Property

(1) A partner is co-owner with his partners of specific partnership property holding as a tenant in partnership.

(2) The incidents of this tenancy are such that:

(a) A partner, subject to the provisions of this act and to any agreement between the partners, has an equal right with his partners to possess specific partnership property for partnership purposes; but he has no right to possess such property for any other purpose without the consent of his partners.

(b) A partner's right in specific partnership property is not assignable except in connection with the assignment of rights of all the partners in the same property.

(c) A partner's right in specific partnership property is not subject to attachment or execution, except on a claim against the partnership. When partnership property is attached for a partnership debt the partners, or any of them, or the representatives of a deceased partner, cannot claim any right under the homestead or exemption laws.

(d) On the death of a partner his right in specific partnership property vests in the surviving partner or partners, except where the deceased was the last surviving partner, when his right in such property vests in his legal representative. Such surviving partner or partners, or the legal representative of the last surviving partner, has no right to possess the partnership property for any but a partnership purpose.

(e) A partner's right in specific partnership property is not subject to dower, curtesy, or allowances to widows, heirs, or next of kin.

§ 26.   Nature of Partner's Interest in the Partnership

A partner's interest in the partnership is his share of the profits and surplus, and the same is personal property.

§ 27.   Assignment of Partner's Interest

(1) A conveyance by a partner of his interest in the partnership does not of itself dissolve the partnership, nor, as against the other partners in the absence of agreement, entitle the assignee, during the continuance of the partnership, to interfere in the management or administration of the partnership business or affairs, or to require any information or account of partnership transactions, or to inspect the partnership books; but it merely entitles the assignee to receive in accordance with his contract the profits to which the assigning partner would otherwise be entitled.

(2) In case of a dissolution of the partnership, the assignee is entitled to receive his assignor's interest and may require an account from the date only of the last account agreed to by all the partners.

§ 28.   Partner's Interest Subject to Charging Order

(1) On due application to a competent court by any judgment creditor of a partner, the court which entered the judgment, order, or decree, or any other court, may charge the interest of the debtor partner with payment of the unsatisfied amount of such judgment debt with interest thereon; and may then or later appoint a receiver of his share of the profits, and of any other money due or to fall due to him in respect of the partnership, and make all other orders, directions, accounts and inquiries which the debtor partner might have made, or which the circumstances of the case may require.

(2) The interest charged may be redeemed at any time before foreclosure, or in case of a sale being directed by the court may be purchased without thereby causing a dissolution:

(a) With separate property, by any one or more of the partners, or

(b) With partnership property, by any one or more of the partners with the consent of all the partners whose interests are not so charged or sold.

(3) Nothing in this act shall be held to deprive a partner of his right, if any, under the exemption laws, as regards his interest in the partnership.

PART VI. DISSOLUTION AND WINDING UP

§ 29.   Dissolution Defined

The dissolution of a partnership is the change in the relation of the partners caused by any partner ceasing to be associated in the carrying on as distinguished from the winding up of the business.

§ 30.   Partnership Not Terminated by Dissolution

On dissolution the partnership is not terminated, but continues until the winding up of partnership affairs is completed.

§ 31.   Causes of Dissolution

Dissolution is caused:

(1) Without violation of the agreement between the partners,

(a) By the termination of the definite term or particular undertaking specified in the agreement,

(b) By the express will of any partner when no definite term or particular undertaking is specified,

(c) By the express will of all the partners who have not assigned their interests or suffered them to be charged for their separate debts, either before or after the termination of any specified term or particular undertaking,

(d) By the expulsion of any partner from the business bona fide in accordance with such a power conferred by the agreement between the partners;

(2) In contravention of the agreement between the partners, where the circumstances do not permit a dissolution under any other provision of this section, by the express will of any partner at any time;

(3) By any event which makes it unlawful for the business of the partnership to be carried on or for the members to carry it on in partnership;

(4) By the death of any partner;

(5) By the bankruptcy of any partner or the partnership;

(6) By decree of court under section 32.

§ 32.   Dissolution by Decree of Court

(1) On application by or for a partner the court shall decree a dissolution whenever:

(a) A partner has been declared a lunatic in any judicial proceeding or is shown to be of unsound mind,

(b) A partner becomes in any other way incapable of performing his part of the partnership contract,

(c) A partner has been guilty of such conduct as tends to affect prejudicially the carrying on of the business,

(d) A partner wilfully or persistently commits a breach of the partnership agreement, or otherwise so conducts himself in matters relating to the partnership business that it is not reasonably practicable to carry on the business in partnership with him,

(e) The business of the partnership can only be carried on at a loss,

(f) Other circumstances render a dissolution equitable.

(2) On the application of the purchaser of a partner's interest under sections 27 or 28:

(a) After the termination of the specified term or particular undertaking,

(b) At any time if the partnership was a partnership at will when the interest was assigned or when the charging order was issued.

§ 33.   General Effect of Dissolution on Authority of Partner

Except so far as may be necessary to wind up partnership affairs or to complete transactions begun but not then finished, dissolution terminates all authority of any partner to act for the partnership,

(1) With respect to the partners,

(a) When the dissolution is not by the act, bankruptcy or death of a partner; or

(b)   When the dissolution is by such act, bankruptcy or death of a partner, in cases where section 34 so requires.

(2)   With respect to persons not partners, as declared in section 35.

§ 34.   Right of Partner to Contribution From Co-partners After Dissolution

Where the dissolution is caused by the act, death or bankruptcy of a partner, each partner is liable to his co-partners for his share of any liability created by any partner acting for the partnership as if the partnership had not been dissolved unless

(a)   The dissolution being by act of any partner, the partner acting for the partnership had knowledge of the dissolution, or

(b)   The dissolution being by the death or bankruptcy of a partner, the partner acting for the partnership had knowledge or notice of the death or bankruptcy.

§ 35.   Power of Partner to Bind Partnership to Third Persons After Dissolution

(1)   After dissolution a partner can bind the partnership except as provided in Paragraph (3).

(a)   By any act appropriate for winding up partnership affairs or completing transactions unfinished at dissolution;

(b)   By any transaction which would bind the partnership if dissolution had not taken place, provided the other party to the transaction

I.   Had extended credit to the partnership prior to dissolution and had no knowledge or notice of the dissolution; or

II.   Though he had not so extended credit, had nevertheless known of the partnership prior to dissolution, and, having no knowledge or notice of dissolution, the fact of dissolution had not been advertised in a newspaper of general circulation in the place (or in each place if more than one) at which the partnership business was regularly carried on.

(2)   The liability of a partner under Paragraph (1b) shall be satisfied out of partnership assets alone when such partner had been prior to dissolution

(a)   Unknown as a partner to the person with whom the contract is made; and

(b)   So far unknown and inactive in partnership affairs that the business reputation of the partnership could not be said to have been in any degree due to his connection with it.

(3)   The partnership is in no case bound by any act of a partner after dissolution

(a)   Where the partnership is dissolved because it is unlawful to carry on the business, unless the act is appropriate for winding up partnership affairs; or

(b)   Where the partner has become bankrupt; or

(c)   Where the partner has no authority to wind up partnership affairs; except by a transaction with one who

I.   Had extended credit to the partnership prior to dissolution and had no knowledge or notice of his want of authority; or

II.   Had not extended credit to the partnership prior to dissolution, and, having no knowledge or notice of his want of authority, the fact of his want of authority has not been advertised in the manner provided for advertising the fact of dissolution in Paragraph (1bII).

(4)   Nothing in this section shall affect the liability under Section 16 of any person who after dissolution represents himself or consents to another representing him as a partner in a partnership engaged in carrying on business.

§ 36.   Effect of Dissolution on Partner's Existing Liability

(1)   The dissolution of the partnership does not of itself discharge the existing liability of any partner.

(2)   A partner is discharged from any existing liability upon dissolution of the partnership by an agreement to that effect between himself, the partnership creditor and the person or partnership continuing the business; and such agreement may be inferred from the course of dealing between the creditor having knowledge of the dissolution and the person or partnership continuing the business.

(3)   Where a person agrees to assume the existing obligations of a dissolved partnership, the partners whose obligations have been assumed shall be discharged from any liability to any creditor of the partnership who, knowing of the agreement, consents to a material alteration in the nature or time of payment of such obligations.

(4)   The individual property of a deceased partner shall be liable for all obligations of the partnership incurred while he was a partner but subject to the prior payment of his separate debts.

§ 37.   Right to Wind Up

Unless otherwise agreed the partners who have not wrongfully dissolved the partnership or the legal representative of the last surviving partner, not bankrupt, has the right to wind up the partnership affairs; provided, however, that any partner, his legal representative or his assignee, upon cause shown, may obtain winding up by the court.

§ 38.   Rights of Partners to Application of Partnership Property

(1)   When dissolution is caused in any way, except in contravention of the partnership agreement, each partner, as against his co-partners and all persons claiming through them in respect of their interests in the partnership, unless otherwise agreed, may have the partnership property applied to discharge its liabilities, and the surplus applied to pay in cash the net amount owing to the respective partners. But if dissolution is caused by expulsion of a partner, bona fide under the partnership agreement and if the expelled partner is discharged from all partnership liabilities, either by payment or agreement under section 36(2), he shall receive in cash only the net amount due him from the partnership.

(2)   When dissolution is caused in contravention of the partnership agreement the rights of the partners shall be as follows:

(a)   Each partner who has not caused dissolution wrongfully shall have,

I.   All the rights specified in paragraph (1) of this section, and

II.   The right, as against each partner who has caused the dissolution wrongfully, to damages for breach of the agreement.

(b)   The partners who have not caused the dissolution wrongfully, if they all desire to continue the business in the same name, either by themselves or jointly with others, may do so, during the agreed term for the partnership and for that purpose may possess the partnership property, provided they secure the payment by bond approved by the court, or pay to any partner who has caused the dissolution wrongfully, the value of his interest in the partnership at the dissolution, less any damages recoverable under clause (2aII) of this section, and in like manner indemnify him against all present or future partnership liabilities.

(c)   A partner who has caused the dissolution wrongfully shall have:

I.   If the business is not continued under the provisions of paragraph (2b) all the rights of a partner under paragraph (1), subject to clause (2aII), of this section,

II.   If the business is continued under paragraph (2b) of this section the right as against his co-partners and all claiming through them in respect of their interests in the

13

partnership, to have the value of his interest in the partnership, less any damages caused to his co-partners by the dissolution, ascertained and paid to him in cash, or the payment secured by bond approved by the court, and to be released from all existing liabilities of the partnership; but in ascertaining the value of the partner's interest the value of the good-will of the business shall not be considered.

§ 39.   Rights Where Partnership Is Dissolved for Fraud or Misrepresentation

Where a partnership contract is rescinded on the ground of the fraud or misrepresentation of one of the parties thereto, the party entitled to rescind is, without prejudice to any other right, entitled,

(a)   To a lien on, or a right of retention of, the surplus of the partnership property after satisfying the partnership liabilities to third persons for any sum of money paid by him for the purchase of an interest in the partnership and for any capital or advances contributed by him; and

(b)   To stand, after all liabilities to third persons have been satisfied, in the place of the creditors of the partnership for any payments made by him in respect of the partnership liabilities; and

(c)   To be indemnified by the person guilty of the fraud or making the representation against all debts and liabilities of the partnership.

§ 40.   Rules for Distribution

In settling accounts between the partners after dissolution, the following rules shall be observed, subject to any agreement to the contrary:

(a)   The assets of the partnership are:

     I.   The partnership property,

     II.   The contributions of the partners necessary for the payment of all the liabilities specified in clause (b) of this paragraph.

(b)   The liabilities of the partnership shall rank in order of payment, as follows:

     I.   Those owing to creditors other than partners,

     II.   Those owing to partners other than for capital and profits,

     III.   Those owing to partners in respect of capital,

     IV.   Those owing to partners in respect of profits.

(c)   The assets shall be applied in order of their declaration in clause (a) of this paragraph to the satisfaction of the liabilities.

(d)   The partners shall contribute, as provided by section 18(a) the amount necessary to satisfy the liabilities; but if any, but not all, of the partners are insolvent, or, not being subject to process, refuse to contribute, the other partners shall contribute their share of the liabilities, and, in the relative proportions in which they share the profits, the additional amount necessary to pay the liabilities.

(e)   An assignee for the benefit of creditors or any person appointed by the court shall have the right to enforce the contributions specified in clause (d) of this paragraph.

(f)   Any partner or his legal representative shall have the right to enforce the contributions specified in clause (d) of this paragraph, to the extent of the amount which he has paid in excess of his share of the liability.

(g)   The individual property of a deceased partner shall be liable for the contributions specified in clause (d) of this paragraph.

(h) When partnership property and the individual properties of the partners are in possession of a court for distribution, partnership creditors shall have priority on partnership property and separate creditors on individual property, saving the rights of lien or secured creditors as heretofore.

(i) Where a partner has become bankrupt or his estate is insolvent the claims against his separate property shall rank in the following order:

I. Those owing to separate creditors,

II. Those owing to partnership creditors,

III. Those owing to partners by way of contribution.

§ 41. Liability of Persons Continuing the Business in Certain Cases

(1) When any new partner is admitted into an existing partnership, or when any partner retires and assigns (or the representative of the deceased partner assigns) his rights in partnership property to two or more of the partners, or to one or more of the partners and one or more third persons, if the business is continued without liquidation of the partnership affairs, creditors of the first or dissolved partnership are also creditors of the partnership so continuing the business.

(2) When all but one partner retire and assign (or the representative of a deceased partner assigns) their rights in partnership property to the remaining partner, who continues the business without liquidation of partnership affairs, either alone or with others, creditors of the dissolved partnership are also creditors of the person or partnership so continuing the business.

(3) When any partner retires or dies and the business of the dissolved partnership is continued as set forth in paragraphs (1) and (2) of this section, with the consent of the retired partners or the representative of the deceased partner, but without any assignment of his right in partnership property, rights of creditors of the dissolved partnership and of the creditors of the person or partnership continuing the business shall be as if such assignment had been made.

(4) When all the partners or their representatives assign their rights in partnership property to one or more third persons who promise to pay the debts and who continue the business of the dissolved partnership, creditors of the dissolved partnership are also creditors of the person or partnership continuing the business.

(5) When any partner wrongfully causes a dissolution and the remaining partners continue the business under the provisions of section 38(2b), either alone or with others, and without liquidation of the partnership affairs, creditors of the dissolved partnership are also creditors of the person or partnership continuing the business.

(6) When a partner is expelled and the remaining partners continue the business either alone or with others, without liquidation of the partnership affairs, creditors of the dissolved partnership are also creditors of the person or partnership continuing the business.

(7) The liability of a third person becoming a partner in the partnership continuing the business, under this section, to the creditors of the dissolved partnership shall be satisfied out of partnership property only.

(8) When the business of a partnership after dissolution is continued under any conditions set forth in this section the creditors of the dissolved partnership, as against the separate creditors of the retiring or deceased partner or the representative of the deceased partner, have a prior right to any claim of the retired partner or the representative of the deceased partner against the person or partnership continuing the business, on account of the retired or deceased partner's interest in the dissolved partnership or on account of any consideration promised for such interest or for his right in partnership property.

(9) Nothing in this section shall be held to modify any right of creditors to set aside any assignment on the ground of fraud.

(10) The use by the person or partnership continuing the business of the partnership name, or the name of a deceased partner as part thereof, shall not of itself make the individual property of the deceased partner liable for any debts contracted by such person or partnership.

§ 42.   Rights of Retiring or Estate of Deceased Partner When the Business Is Continued

When any partner retires or dies, and the business is continued under any of the conditions set forth in section 41 (1, 2, 3, 5, 6), or section 38(2b) without any settlement of accounts as between him or his estate and the person or partnership continuing the business, unless otherwise agreed, he or his legal representative as against such persons or partnership may have the value of his interest at the date of dissolution ascertained, and shall receive as an ordinary creditor an amount equal to the value of his interest in the dissolved partnership with interest, or, at his option or at the option of his legal representative, in lieu of interest, the profits attributable to the use of his right in the property of the dissolved partnership; provided that the creditors of the dissolved partnership as against the separate creditors, or the representative of the retired or deceased partner, shall have priority on any claim arising under this section, as provided by section 41(8) of this act.

§ 43.   Accrual of Actions

The right to an account of his interest shall accrue to any partner, or his legal representative, as against the winding up partners or the surviving partners or the person or partnership continuing the business, at the date of dissolution, in the absence of any agreement to the contrary.

PART VII. MISCELLANEOUS PROVISIONS

§ 44.   When Act Takes Effect

This act shall take effect on the . . . . day of . . . . one thousand nine hundred and . . . .

§ 45.   Legislation Repealed

All acts or parts of acts inconsistent with this act are hereby repealed.

UNIFORM PARTNERSHIP ACT (1997) ("RUPA")

Table of Sections

ARTICLE 1. GENERAL PROVISIONS

ARTICLE 2. NATURE OF PARTNERSHIP

ARTICLE 3. RELATIONS OF PARTNERS TO PERSONS DEALING WITH PARTNERSHIP

ARTICLE 4. RELATIONS OF PARTNERS TO EACH OTHER AND TO PARTNERSHIP

UNIFORM PARTNERSHIP ACT (1997)

ARTICLE 10. FOREIGN LIMITED LIABILITY PARTNERSHIP

ARTICLE 11. MERGER, INTEREST EXCHANGE, CONVERSIONS, AND DOMESTICATION

PART 1. GENERAL PROVISIONS

PART 2. MERGER

PART 3. INTEREST EXCHANGE

ARTICLE 1
GENERAL PROVISIONS

§ 101.　Short Title

This [Act] may be cited as the Uniform Partnership Act.

§ 102.　Definitions

In this [Act]:

(1)　"Business" includes every trade, occupation, and profession.

(2)　"Contribution", except in the phrase "right of contribution", means property or a benefit described in Section 403 which is provided by a person to a partnership to become a partner or in the person's capacity as a partner.

(3)　"Debtor in bankruptcy" means a person that is the subject of:

(A)　an order for relief under Title 11 of the United States Code or a comparable order under a successor statute of general application; or

(B)　a comparable order under federal, state, or foreign law governing insolvency.

(4)　"Distribution" means a transfer of money or other property from a partnership to a person on account of a transferable interest or in a person's capacity as a partner. The term:

(A)　includes:

(i)　a redemption or other purchase by a partnership of a transferable interest; and

    (ii) a transfer to a partner in return for the partner's relinquishment of any right to participate as a partner in the management or conduct of the partnership's business or have access to records or other information concerning the partnership's business; and

    (B) does not include amounts constituting reasonable compensation for present or past service or payments made in the ordinary course of business under a bona fide retirement plan or other bona fide benefits program.

    (5) "Foreign limited liability partnership" means a foreign partnership whose partners have limited liability for the debts, obligations, or other liabilities of the foreign partnership under a provision similar to Section 306(c).

    (6) "Foreign partnership" means an unincorporated entity formed under the law of a jurisdiction other than this state which would be a partnership if formed under the law of this state. The term includes a foreign limited liability partnership.

    (7) "Jurisdiction", used to refer to a political entity, means the United States, a state, a foreign country, or a political subdivision of a foreign country.

    (8) "Jurisdiction of formation" means the jurisdiction whose law governs the internal affairs of an entity.

    (9) "Limited liability partnership," except in the phrase "foreign limited liability partnership" and in [Article] 11, means a partnership that has filed a statement of qualification under Section 901 and does not have a similar statement in effect in any other jurisdiction.

    (10) "Partner" means a person that:

    (A) has become a partner in a partnership under Section 402 or was a partner in a partnership when the partnership became subject to this [Act] under Section 110; and

    (B) has not dissociated as a partner under Section 601.

    (11) "Partnership," except in [Article 11], means an association of two or more persons to carry on as co-owners a business for profit formed under this [Act] or that becomes subject to this [Act] under [Article] 11 or Section 110. The term includes a limited liability partnership.

    (12) "Partnership agreement" means the agreement, whether or not referred to as a partnership agreement and whether oral, implied, in a record, or in any combination thereof, of all the partners of a partnership concerning the matters described in Section 105(a). The term includes the agreement as amended or restated.

    (13) "Partnership at will" means a partnership in which the partners have not agreed to remain partners until the expiration of a definite term or the completion of a particular undertaking.

    (14) "Person" means an individual, business, corporation, nonprofit corporation, partnership, limited partnership, limited liability company, [general cooperative association,] limited cooperative association, unincorporated nonprofit association, statutory trust, business trust, common-law business trust, estate, trust, association, joint venture, public corporation, government or governmental subdivision, agency, or instrumentality, or any other legal or commercial entity.

    (15) "Principal office" means the principal executive office of a partnership or a foreign limited liability partnership, whether or not the office is located in this state.

    (16) "Property" means all property, whether real, personal, or mixed or tangible or intangible, or any right or interest therein.

    (17) "Record", used as a noun, means information that is inscribed on a tangible medium or that is stored in an electronic or other medium and is retrievable in perceivable form.

(18) "Registered agent" means an agent of a limited liability partnership or foreign limited liability partnership which is authorized to receive service of any process, notice, or demand required or permitted by law to be served on the partnership.

(19) "Registered foreign limited liability partnership" means a foreign limited liability partnership that is registered to do business in this state pursuant to a statement of registration filed by the [Secretary of State].

(20) "Sign" means, with present intent to authenticate or adopt a record:

    (A)   to execute or adopt a tangible symbol; or

    (B)   to attach to or logically associate with the record an electronic symbol, sound, or process.

(21) "State" means a state of the United States, the District of Columbia, Puerto Rico, the United States Virgin Islands, or any territory or insular possession subject to the jurisdiction of the United States.

(22) "Transfer" includes:

    (A)   an assignment;

    (B)   a conveyance;

    (C)   a sale;

    (D)   a lease;

    (E)   an encumbrance, including a mortgage or security interest;

    (F)   a gift; and

    (G)   a transfer by operation of law.

(23) "Transferable interest" means the right, as initially owned by a person in the person's capacity as a partner, to receive distributions from a partnership, whether or not the person remains a partner or continues to own any part of the right. The term applies to any fraction of the interest, by whomever owned.

(24) "Transferee" means a person to which all or part of a transferable interest has been transferred, whether or not the transferor is a partner.

§ 103. Knowledge; Notice

(a)   A person knows a fact if the person:

    (1)   has actual knowledge of it; or

    (2)   is deemed to know it under subsection (d)(1) or law other than this [Act].

(b)   A person has notice of a fact if the person:

    (1)   has reason to know the fact from all the facts known to the person at the time in question; or

    (2)   is deemed to have notice of the fact under subsection (d)(2).

(c)   Subject to Section 117(f), a person notifies another person of a fact by taking steps reasonably required to inform the other person in ordinary course, whether or not those steps cause the other person to know the fact.

(d)   A person not a partner is deemed:

    (1)   to know of a limitation on authority to transfer real property as provided in Section 303(g); and

(2)   to have notice of:

     (A)   a person's dissociation as a partner 90 days after a statement of dissociation under Section 704 becomes effective; and

     (B)   a partnership's:

         (i)   dissolution 90 days after a statement of dissolution under Section 802 becomes effective;

         (ii)   termination 90 days after a statement of termination under Section 802 becomes effective; and

         (iii)   participation in a merger, interest exchange, conversion, or domestication, 90 days after articles of merger, interest exchange, conversion, or domestication under [Article] 11 become effective.

(e)   A partner's knowledge or notice of a fact relating to the partnership is effective immediately as knowledge of or notice to the partnership, except in the case of a fraud on the partnership committed by or with the consent of that partner.

§ 104.   Governing Law

The internal affairs of a partnership and the liability of a partner as a partner for a debt, obligation, or other liability of the partnership are governed by:

(1)   in the case of a limited liability partnership, the law of this state; and

(2)   in the case of a partnership that is not a limited liability partnership, the law of the jurisdiction in which the partnership has its principal office.

§ 105.   Partnership Agreement; Scope, Function, and Limitations

(a)   Except as otherwise provided in subsections (c) and (d), the partnership agreement governs:

(1)   relations among the partners as partners and between the partners and the partnership;

(2)   the business of the partnership and the conduct of that business; and

(3)   the means and conditions for amending the partnership agreement.

(b)   To the extent the partnership agreement does not provide for a matter described in subsection (a), this [Act] governs the matter.

(c)   A partnership agreement may not:

(1)   vary the law applicable under Section 104(1);

(2)   vary the provisions of Section 110;

(3)   vary the provisions of Section 307;

(4)   unreasonably restrict the duties and rights under Section 408, but the partnership agreement may impose reasonable restrictions on the availability and use of information obtained under that section and may define appropriate remedies, including liquidated damages, for a breach of any reasonable restriction on use;

(5)   alter or eliminate the duty of loyalty or the duty of care, except as otherwise provided in subsection (d);

(6)   eliminate the contractual obligation of good faith and fair dealing under Section 409(d), but the partnership agreement may prescribe the standards, if not manifestly unreasonable, by which the performance of the obligation is to be measured;

(7)   unreasonably restrict the right of a person to maintain an action under Section 410(b);

(8)   relieve or exonerate a person from liability for conduct involving bad faith, willful or intentional misconduct, or knowing violation of law;

(9)   vary the power of a person to dissociate as a partner under Section 602(a), except to require that the notice under Section 601(1) to be in a record;

(10) vary the grounds for expulsion specified in Section 601(5);

(11) vary the causes of dissolution specified in Section 801(4) or (5);

(12) vary the requirement to wind up the partnership's business as specified in Section 802(a), (b)(1), and (d);

(13) vary the right of a partner under Section 901(f) to vote on or consent to a cancellation of a statement of qualification;

(14) vary the right of a partner to approve a merger, interest exchange, conversion, or domestication under Section 1123(a)(2), 1133(a)(2), 1143(a)(2), or 1153(a)(2);

(15) vary the required contents of a plan of merger under Section 1122(a), plan of interest exchange under Section 1132(a), plan of conversion under Section 1142(a), or plan of domestication under Section 1152(a);

(16) vary any requirement, procedure, or other provision of this [Act] pertaining to:

(A)   registered agents; or

(B)   the [Secretary of State], including provisions pertaining to records authorized or required to be delivered to the [Secretary of State] for filing under this [Act]; or

(17) except as otherwise provided in Sections 106 and 107(b), restrict the rights under this [Act] of a person other than a partner.

(d)   Subject to subsection (c)(8), without limiting other terms that may be included in a partnership agreement, the following rules apply:

(1)   The partnership agreement may:

(A)   specify the method by which a specific act or transaction that would otherwise violate the duty of loyalty may be authorized or ratified by one or more disinterested and independent persons after full disclosure of all material facts; and

(B)   alter the prohibition in Section 406(a)(2) so that the prohibition requires only that the partnership's total assets not be less than the sum of its total liabilities.

(2)   To the extent the partnership agreement expressly relieves a partner of a responsibility that the partner would otherwise have under this [Act] and imposes the responsibility on one or more other partners, the agreement also may eliminate or limit any fiduciary duty of the partner relieved of the responsibility which would have pertained to the responsibility.

(3)   If not manifestly unreasonable, the partnership agreement may:

(A)   alter or eliminate the aspects of the duty of loyalty stated in Section 409(b);

(B)   identify specific types or categories of activities that do not violate the duty of loyalty;

(C)   alter the duty of care, but may not authorize conduct involving bad faith, willful or intentional misconduct, or knowing violation of law; and

(D)   alter or eliminate any other fiduciary duty.

(e)   The court shall decide as a matter of law whether a term of a partnership agreement is manifestly unreasonable under subsection (c)(6) or (d)(3). The court:

(1) shall make its determination as of the time the challenged term became part of the partnership agreement and by considering only circumstances existing at that time; and

(2) may invalidate the term only if, in light of the purposes and business of the partnership, it is readily apparent that:

(A) the objective of the term is unreasonable; or

(B) the term is an unreasonable means to achieve the term's objective.

§ 106. Partnership Agreement; Effect on Partnership and Person Becoming Partner; Preformation Agreement

(a) A partnership is bound by and may enforce the partnership agreement, whether or not the partnership has itself manifested assent to the agreement.

(b) A person that becomes a partner is deemed to assent to the partnership agreement.

(c) Two or more persons intending to become the initial partners of a partnership may make an agreement providing that upon the formation of the partnership the agreement will become the partnership agreement.

§ 107. Partnership Agreement; Effect on Third Parties and Relationship to Records Effective on Behalf of Partnership

(a) A partnership agreement may specify that its amendment requires the approval of a person that is not a party to the agreement or the satisfaction of a condition. An amendment is ineffective if its adoption does not include the required approval or satisfy the specified condition.

(b) The obligations of a partnership and its partners to a person in the person's capacity as a transferee or person dissociated as a partner are governed by the partnership agreement. Subject only to a court order issued under Section 504(b)(2) to effectuate a charging order, an amendment to the partnership agreement made after a person becomes a transferee or is dissociated as a partner:

(1) is effective with regard to any debt, obligation, or other liability of the partnership or its partners to the person in the person's capacity as a transferee or person dissociated as a partner; and

(2) is not effective to the extent the amendment:

(A) imposes a new debt, obligation, or other liability on the transferee or person dissociated as a partner; or

(B) prejudices the rights under Section 701 of a person that dissociated as a partner before the amendment was made.

(c) If a record delivered by a partnership to the [Secretary of State] for filing becomes effective and contains a provision that would be ineffective under Section 105(c) or (d)(3) if contained in the partnership agreement, the provision is ineffective in the record.

(d) Subject to subsection (c), if a record delivered by a partnership to the [Secretary of State] for filing becomes effective and conflicts with a provision of the partnership agreement:

(1) the agreement prevails as to partners, persons dissociated as partners, and transferees; and

(2) the record prevails as to other persons to the extent they reasonably rely on the record.

§ 108. Signing of Records to Be Delivered for Filing to [Secretary of State]

(a) A record delivered to the [Secretary of State] for filing pursuant to this [Act] must be signed as follows:

(1)   Except as otherwise provided in paragraphs (2) and (3), a record signed by a partnership must be signed by a person authorized by the partnership.

(2)   A record filed on behalf of a dissolved partnership that has no partner must be signed by the person winding up the partnership's business under Section 802(c) or a person appointed under Section 802(d) to wind up the business.

(3)   A statement of denial by a person under Section 304 must be signed by that person.

(4)   Any other record delivered on behalf of a person to the [Secretary of State] for filing must be signed by that person.

(b)   A record filed under this [Act] may be signed by an agent. Whenever this [Act] requires a particular individual to sign a record and the individual is deceased or incompetent, the record may be signed by a legal representative of the individual.

(c)   A person that signs a record as an agent or legal representative affirms as a fact that the person is authorized to sign the record.

§ 109.   Liability for Inaccurate Information in Filed Record

(a)   If a record delivered to the [Secretary of State] for filing under this [Act] and filed by the [Secretary of State] contains inaccurate information, a person that suffers loss by reliance on the information may recover damages for the loss from:

(1)   a person that signed the record, or caused another to sign it on the person's behalf, and knew the information to be inaccurate at the time the record was signed; and

(2)   subject to subsection (b), a partner if:

(A)   the record was delivered for filing on behalf of the partnership; and

(B)   the partner knew or had notice of the inaccuracy for a reasonably sufficient time before the information was relied upon so that, before the reliance, the partner reasonably could have:

(i)   effected an amendment under Section 901(f);

(ii)   filed a petition under Section 112; or

(iii)   delivered to the [Secretary of State] for filing a statement of change under Section 909 or a statement of correction under Section 116.

(b)   To the extent the partnership agreement expressly relieves a partner of responsibility for maintaining the accuracy of information contained in records delivered on behalf of the partnership to the [Secretary of State] for filing under this [Act] and imposes that responsibility on one or more other partners, the liability stated in subsection (a)(2) applies to those other partners and not to the partner that the partnership agreement relieves of the responsibility.

(c)   An individual who signs a record authorized or required to be filed under this [Act] affirms under penalty of perjury that the information stated in the record is accurate.

§ 110.   Application to Existing Relationships

(a)   Before [all-inclusive date], this [Act] governs only:

(1)   a partnership formed on or after [the effective date of this [Act]]; and

(2)   except as otherwise provided in subsection (c), a partnership formed before [the effective date of this [Act]] which elects, in the manner provided in its partnership agreement or by law for amending the partnership agreement, to be subject to this [Act].

(b)   Except as otherwise provided in subsection (c), on and after [all-inclusive date] this [Act] governs all partnerships.

(c)   With respect to a partnership that elects pursuant to subsection (a)(2) to be subject to this [Act], after the election takes effect the provisions of this [Act] relating to the liability of the partnership's partners to third parties apply:

(1)   before [all-inclusive date], to:

(A)   a third party that had not done business with the partnership in the year before the election took effect; and

(B)   a third party that had done business with the partnership in the year before the election took effect only if the third party knows or has been notified of the election; and

(2)   on and after [all-inclusive date], to all third parties, but those provisions remain inapplicable to any obligation incurred while those provisions were inapplicable under paragraph (1)(B).

Legislative Note:

For states that have previously enacted UPA (1997): For these states this section is unnecessary. There is no need for a delayed effective date, even with regard to pre-existing partnerships. (Presumably, the "linkage" issue [discussed below] was addressed when UPA (1997) was enacted.)

For states that have not previously enacted UPA (1997): Each enacting jurisdiction should consider whether: (i) this act makes material changes to the "default" (or "gap filler") rules of the predecessor statute; and (ii) if so, whether Subsection (c) should carry forward any of those rules for pre-existing partnerships. In this assessment, the focus is on pre-existing partnerships that have left default rules in place, whether advisedly or not. The central question is whether, for such partnerships, expanding Subsection (c) is necessary to prevent material changes to the partners' "deal."

The "all-inclusive" date should be at least one year after the effective date of this act, Section 1206, but no more than two years.

The "linkage" issue—for states that still have ULPA (1976) or ULPA (1976/1985) in effect: These states should enact ULPA (2001) (Last Amended 2013) to take effect in conjunction with this act. If not, a state's current limited partnership act must be amended to link to this act.

§ 111.   Delivery of Record

(a)   Except as otherwise provided in this [Act], permissible means of delivery of a record include delivery by hand, mail, conventional commercial practice, and electronic transmission.

(b)   Delivery to the [Secretary of State] is effective only when a record is received by the [Secretary of State].

§ 112.   Signing and Filing Pursuant to Judicial Order

(a)   If a person required by this [Act] to sign a record or deliver a record to the [Secretary of State] for filing under this [Act] does not do so, any other person that is aggrieved may petition [the appropriate court] to order:

(1)   the person to sign the record;

(2)   the person to deliver the record to the [Secretary of State] for filing; or

(3)   the [Secretary of State] to file the record unsigned.

(b)   If a petitioner under subsection (a) is not the partnership or foreign limited liability partnership to which the record pertains, the petitioner shall make the partnership or foreign partnership a party to the action.

(c)   A record filed under subsection (a)(3) is effective without being signed.

§ 113. Filing Requirements

(a) To be filed by the [Secretary of State] pursuant to this [Act], a record must be received by the [Secretary of State], comply with this [Act], and satisfy the following:

(1) The filing of the record must be required or permitted by this [Act].

(2) The record must be physically delivered in written form unless and to the extent the [Secretary of State] permits electronic delivery of records.

(3) The words in the record must be in English, and numbers must be in Arabic or Roman numerals, but the name of an entity need not be in English if written in English letters or Arabic or Roman numerals.

(4) The record must be signed by a person authorized or required under this [Act] to sign the record.

(5) The record must state the name and capacity, if any, of each individual who signed it, either on behalf of the individual or the person authorized or required to sign the record, but need not contain a seal, attestation, acknowledgment, or verification.

(b) If law other than this [Act] prohibits the disclosure by the [Secretary of State] of information contained in a record delivered to the [Secretary of State] for filing, the [Secretary of State] shall file the record if the record otherwise complies with this [Act] but may redact the information.

(c) When a record is delivered to the [Secretary of State] for filing, any fee required under this [Act] and any fee, tax, interest, or penalty required to be paid under this [Act] or law other than this [Act] must be paid in a manner permitted by the [Secretary of State] or by that law.

(d) The [Secretary of State] may require that a record delivered in written form be accompanied by an identical or conformed copy.

(e) The [Secretary of State] may provide forms for filings required or permitted to be made by this [Act], but, except as otherwise provided in subsection (f), their use is not required.

(f) The [Secretary of State] may require that a cover sheet for a filing be on a form prescribed by the [Secretary of State].

§ 114. Effective Date and Time

Except as otherwise provided in Section 115 and subject to Section 116(c), a record filed under this [Act] is effective:

(1) on the date and at the time of its filing by the [Secretary of State], as provided in Section 117(b);

(2) on the date of filing and at the time specified in the record as its effective time, if later than the time under paragraph (1);

(3) at a specified delayed effective date and time, which may not be more than 90 days after the date of filing; or

(4) if a delayed effective date is specified, but no time is specified, at 12:01 a.m. on the date specified, which may not be more than 90 days after the date of filing.

§ 115. Withdrawal of Filed Record Before Effectiveness

(a) Except as otherwise provided in Sections 1124, 1134, 1144, and 1154, a record delivered to the [Secretary of State] for filing may be withdrawn before it takes effect by delivering to the [Secretary of State] for filing a statement of withdrawal.

(b) A statement of withdrawal must:

(1)   be signed by each person that signed the record being withdrawn, except as otherwise agreed by those persons;

(2)   identify the record to be withdrawn; and

(3)   if signed by fewer than all the persons that signed the record being withdrawn, state that the record is withdrawn in accordance with the agreement of all the persons that signed the record.

(c)   On filing by the [Secretary of State] of a statement of withdrawal, the action or transaction evidenced by the original record does not take effect.

§ 116.   Correcting Filed Record

(a)   A person on whose behalf a filed record was delivered to the [Secretary of State] for filing may correct the record if:

(1)   the record at the time of filing was inaccurate;

(2)   the record was defectively signed; or

(3)   the electronic transmission of the record to the [Secretary of State] was defective.

(b)   To correct a filed record, a person on whose behalf the record was delivered to the [Secretary of State] must deliver to the [Secretary of State] for filing a statement of correction.

(c)   A statement of correction:

(1)   may not state a delayed effective date;

(2)   must be signed by the person correcting the filed record;

(3)   must identify the filed record to be corrected;

(4)   must specify the inaccuracy or defect to be corrected; and

(5)   must correct the inaccuracy or defect.

(d)   A statement of correction is effective as of the effective date of the filed record that it corrects except for purposes of Section 103(d) and as to persons relying on the uncorrected filed record and adversely affected by the correction. For those purposes and as to those persons, the statement of correction is effective when filed.

§ 117.   Duty of [Secretary of State] to File; Review of Refusal to File; Delivery of Record by [Secretary of State]

(a)   The [Secretary of State] shall file a record delivered to the [Secretary of State] for filing which satisfies this [Act]. The duty of the [Secretary of State] under this section is ministerial.

(b)   When the [Secretary of State] files a record, the [Secretary of State] shall record it as filed on the date and at the time of its delivery. After filing a record, the [Secretary of State] shall deliver to the person that submitted the record a copy of the record with an acknowledgment of the date and time of filing and, in the case of a statement of denial, also to the partnership to which the statement pertains.

(c)   If the [Secretary of State] refuses to file a record, the [Secretary of State] shall, not later than [15] business days after the record is delivered:

(1)   return the record or notify the person that submitted the record of the refusal; and

(2)   provide a brief explanation in a record of the reason for the refusal.

(d)   If the [Secretary of State] refuses to file a record, the person that submitted the record may petition [the appropriate court] to compel filing of the record. The record and the explanation of the

[Secretary of State] of the refusal to file must be attached to the petition. The court may decide the matter in a summary proceeding.

(e)   The filing of or refusal to file a record does not:

(1)   affect the validity or invalidity of the record in whole or in part; or

(2)   create a presumption that the information contained in the record is correct or incorrect.

(f)   Except as otherwise provided by Section 909 or by law other than this [Act], the [Secretary of State] may deliver any record to a person by delivering it:

(1)   in person to the person that submitted it;

(2)   to the address of the person's registered agent;

(3)   to the principal office of the person; or

(4)   to another address the person provides to the [Secretary of State] for delivery.

§ 118.   Reservation of Power to Amend or Repeal

The [legislature of this state] has power to amend or repeal all or part of this [Act] at any time, and all limited liability partnerships and foreign limited liability partnerships subject to this [Act] are governed by the amendment or repeal.

§ 119.   Supplemental Principles of Law

Unless displaced by particular provisions of this [act], the principles of law and equity supplement this [Act].

ARTICLE 2
NATURE OF PARTNERSHIP

§ 201.   Partnership as Entity

(a)   A partnership is an entity distinct from its partners.

(b)   A partnership is the same entity regardless of whether the partnership has a statement of qualification in effect under Section 901.

§ 202.   Formation of Partnership

(a)   Except as otherwise provided in subsection (b), the association of two or more persons to carry on as co-owners a business for profit forms a partnership, whether or not the persons intend to form a partnership.

(b)   An association formed under a statute other than this [Act], a predecessor statute, or a comparable statute of another jurisdiction is not a partnership under this [Act].

(c)   In determining whether a partnership is formed, the following rules apply:

(1)   Joint tenancy, tenancy in common, tenancy by the entireties, joint property, common property, or part ownership does not by itself establish a partnership, even if the co-owners share profits made by the use of the property.

(2)   The sharing of gross returns does not by itself establish a partnership, even if the persons sharing them have a joint or common right or interest in property from which the returns are derived.

(3)   A person who receives a share of the profits of a business is presumed to be a partner in the business, unless the profits were received in payment:

(A)   of a debt by installments or otherwise;

(B)   for services as an independent contractor or of wages or other compensation to an employee;

(C)   of rent;

(D)   of an annuity or other retirement or health benefit to a deceased or retired partner or a beneficiary, representative, or designee of a deceased or retired partner;

(E)   of interest or other charge on a loan, even if the amount of payment varies with the profits of the business, including a direct or indirect present or future ownership of the collateral, or rights to income, proceeds, or increase in value derived from the collateral; or

(F)   for the sale of the goodwill of a business or other property by installments or otherwise.

§ 203. Partnership Property

Property acquired by a partnership is property of the partnership and not of the partners individually.

§ 204. When Property Is Partnership Property

(a)   Property is partnership property if acquired in the name of:

(1)   the partnership; or

(2)   one or more partners with an indication in the instrument transferring title to the property of the person's capacity as a partner or of the existence of a partnership but without an indication of the name of the partnership.

(b)   Property is acquired in the name of the partnership by a transfer to:

(1)   the partnership in its name; or

(2)   one or more partners in their capacity as partners in the partnership, if the name of the partnership is indicated in the instrument transferring title to the property.

(c)   Property is presumed to be partnership property if purchased with partnership assets, even if not acquired in the name of the partnership or of one or more partners with an indication in the instrument transferring title to the property of the person's capacity as a partner or of the existence of a partnership.

(d)   Property acquired in the name of one or more of the partners, without an indication in the instrument transferring title to the property of the person's capacity as a partner or of the existence of a partnership and without use of partnership assets, is presumed to be separate property, even if used for partnership purposes.

ARTICLE 3
RELATIONS OF PARTNERS TO PERSONS
DEALING WITH PARTNERSHIP

§ 301. Partner Agent of Partnership

Subject to the effect of a statement of partnership authority under Section 303, the following rules apply:

(1)   Each partner is an agent of the partnership for the purpose of its business. An act of a partner, including the signing of an instrument in the partnership name, for apparently carrying on in the ordinary course the partnership business or business of the kind carried on by the partnership binds the partnership, unless the partner did not have authority to act for the

partnership in the particular matter and the person with which the partner was dealing knew or had notice that the partner lacked authority.

(2)   An act of a partner which is not apparently for carrying on in the ordinary course the partnership's business or business of the kind carried on by the partnership binds the partnership only if the act was actually authorized by all the other partners.

§ 302.   Transfer of Partnership Property

(a)   Partnership property may be transferred as follows:

(1)   Subject to the effect of a statement of partnership authority under Section 303, partnership property held in the name of the partnership may be transferred by an instrument of transfer signed by a partner in the partnership name.

(2)   Partnership property held in the name of one or more partners with an indication in the instrument transferring the property to them of their capacity as partners or of the existence of a partnership, but without an indication of the name of the partnership, may be transferred by an instrument of transfer signed by the persons in whose name the property is held.

(3)   Partnership property held in the name of one or more persons other than the partnership, without an indication in the instrument transferring the property to them of their capacity as partners or of the existence of a partnership, may be transferred by an instrument of transfer signed by the persons in whose name the property is held.

(b)   A partnership may recover partnership property from a transferee only if it proves that signing of the instrument of initial transfer did not bind the partnership under Section 301 and:

(1)   as to a subsequent transferee who gave value for property transferred under subsection (a)(1) and (2), proves that the subsequent transferee knew or had been notified that the person who signed the instrument of initial transfer lacked authority to bind the partnership; or

(2)   as to a transferee who gave value for property transferred under subsection (a)(3), proves that the transferee knew or had been notified that the property was partnership property and that the person who signed the instrument of initial transfer lacked authority to bind the partnership.

(c)   A partnership may not recover partnership property from a subsequent transferee if the partnership would not have been entitled to recover the property, under subsection (b), from any earlier transferee of the property.

(d)   If a person holds all the partners' interests in the partnership, all of the partnership property vests in that person. The person may sign a record in the name of the partnership to evidence vesting of the property in that person and may file or record the record.

§ 303.   Statement of Partnership Authority

(a)   A partnership may deliver to the [Secretary of State] for filing a statement of partnership authority. The statement:

(1)   must include the name of the partnership and;

(A)   if the partnership is not a limited liability partnership, the street and mailing addresses of its principal office; or

(B)   if the partnership is a limited liability partnership, the name and street and mailing addresses of its registered agent;

(2)   with respect to any position that exists in or with respect to the partnership, may state the authority, or limitations on the authority, of all persons holding the position to:

    (A) sign an instrument transferring real property held in the name of the partnership; or

    (B) enter into other transactions on behalf of, or otherwise act for or bind, the partnership; and

(3) may state the authority, or limitations on the authority, of a specific person to:

    (A) sign an instrument transferring real property held in the name of the partnership; or

    (B) enter into other transactions on behalf of, or otherwise act for or bind, the partnership.

(b) To amend or cancel a statement of authority filed by the [Secretary of State], a partnership must deliver to the [Secretary of State] for filing an amendment or cancellation stating:

(1) the name of the partnership;

(2) if the partnership is not a limited liability partnership, the street and mailing addresses of the partnership's principal office;

(3) if the partnership is a limited liability partnership, the name and street and mailing addresses of its registered agent;

(4) the date the statement being affected became effective; and

(5) the contents of the amendment or a declaration that the statement is canceled.

(c) A statement of authority affects only the power of a person to bind a partnership to persons that are not partners.

(d) Subject to subsection (c) and Section 103(d)(1), and except as otherwise provided in subsections (f), (g), and (h), a limitation on the authority of a person or a position contained in an effective statement of authority is not by itself evidence of any person's knowledge or notice of the limitation.

(e) Subject to subsection (c), a grant of authority not pertaining to transfers of real property and contained in an effective statement of authority is conclusive in favor of a person that gives value in reliance on the grant, except to the extent that if the person gives value:

(1) the person has knowledge to the contrary;

(2) the statement has been canceled or restrictively amended under subsection (b); or

(3) a limitation on the grant is contained in another statement of authority that became effective after the statement containing the grant became effective.

(f) Subject to subsection (c), an effective statement of authority that grants authority to transfer real property held in the name of the partnership, a certified copy of which statement is recorded in the office for recording transfers of the real property, is conclusive in favor of a person that gives value in reliance on the grant without knowledge to the contrary, except to the extent that when the person gives value:

(1) the statement has been canceled or restrictively amended under subsection (b), and a certified copy of the cancellation or restrictive amendment has been recorded in the office for recording transfers of the real property; or

(2) a limitation on the grant is contained in another statement of authority that became effective after the statement containing the grant became effective, and a certified copy of the later-effective statement is recorded in the office for recording transfers of the real property.

(g) Subject to subsection (c), if a certified copy of an effective statement containing a limitation on the authority to transfer real property held in the name of a partnership is recorded in the office for recording transfers of that real property, all persons are deemed to know of the limitation.

(h) Subject to subsection (i), an effective statement of dissolution is a cancellation of any filed statement of authority for the purposes of subsection (f) and is a limitation on authority for purposes of subsection (g).

(i) After a statement of dissolution becomes effective, a partnership may deliver to the [Secretary of State] for filing and, if appropriate, may record a statement of authority that is designated as a post-dissolution statement of authority. The statement operates as provided in subsections (f) and (g).

(j) Unless canceled earlier, an effective statement of authority is canceled by operation of law five years after the date on which the statement, or its most recent amendment, becomes effective. The cancellation is effective without recording under subsection (f) or (g).

(k) An effective statement of denial operates as a restrictive amendment under this section and may be recorded by certified copy for purposes of subsection (f)(1).

§ 304. Statement of Denial

A person named in a filed statement of authority granting that person authority may deliver to the [Secretary of State] for filing a statement of denial that:

(1) provides the name of the partnership and the caption of the statement of authority to which the statement of denial pertains; and

(2) denies the grant of authority.

§ 305. Partnership Liable for Partner's Actionable Conduct

(a) A partnership is liable for loss or injury caused to a person, or for a penalty incurred, as a result of a wrongful act or omission, or other actionable conduct, of a partner acting in the ordinary course of business of the partnership or with the actual or apparent authority of the partnership.

(b) If, in the course of the partnership's business or while acting with actual or apparent authority of the partnership, a partner receives or causes the partnership to receive money or property of a person not a partner, and the money or property is misapplied by a partner, the partnership is liable for the loss.

§ 306. Partner's Liability

(a) Except as otherwise provided in subsections (b) and (c), all partners are liable jointly and severally for all debts, obligations, and other liabilities of the partnership unless otherwise agreed by the claimant or provided by law.

(b) A person that becomes a partner is not personally liable for a debt, obligation, or other liability of the partnership incurred before the person became a partner.

(c) A debt, obligation, or other liability of a partnership incurred while the partnership is a limited liability partnership is solely the debt, obligation, or other liability of the limited liability partnership. A partner is not personally liable, directly or indirectly, by way of contribution or otherwise, for a debt, obligation, or other liability of the limited liability partnership solely by reason of being or acting as a partner. This subsection applies:

(1) despite anything inconsistent in the partnership agreement that existed immediately before the vote or consent required to become a limited liability partnership under Section 901(b); and

(2) regardless of the dissolution of the limited liability partnership.

(d)   The failure of a limited liability partnership to observe formalities relating to the exercise of its powers or management of its business is not a ground for imposing liability on a partner for a debt, obligation, or other liability of the partnership.

(e)   The cancellation or administrative revocation of a limited liability partnership's statement of qualification does not affect the limitation in this section on the liability of a partner for a debt, obligation, or other liability of the partnership incurred while the statement was in effect.

§ 307.   Actions by and Against Partnership and Partners

(a)   A partnership may sue and be sued in the name of the partnership.

(b)   To the extent not inconsistent with Section 306 a partner may be joined in an action against the partnership or named in a separate action.

(c)   A judgment against a partnership is not by itself a judgment against a partner. A judgment against a partnership may not be satisfied from a partner's assets unless there is also a judgment against the partner.

(d)   A judgment creditor of a partner may not levy execution against the assets of the partner to satisfy a judgment based on a claim against the partnership unless the partner is personally liable for the claim under Section 306 and:

(1)   a judgment based on the same claim has been obtained against the partnership and a writ of execution on the judgment has been returned unsatisfied in whole or in part;

(2)   the partnership is a debtor in bankruptcy;

(3)   the partner has agreed that the creditor need not exhaust partnership assets;

(4)   a court grants permission to the judgment creditor to levy execution against the assets of a partner based on a finding that partnership assets subject to execution are clearly insufficient to satisfy the judgment, that exhaustion of partnership assets is excessively burdensome, or that the grant of permission is an appropriate exercise of the court's equitable powers; or

(5)   liability is imposed on the partner by law or contract independent of the existence of the partnership.

(e)   This section applies to any debt, liability, or other obligation of a partnership which results from a representation by a partner or purported partner under Section 308.

§ 308.   Liability of Purported Partner

(a)   If a person, by words or conduct, purports to be a partner, or consents to being represented by another as a partner, in a partnership or with one or more persons not partners, the purported partner is liable to a person to whom the representation is made, if that person, relying on the representation, enters into a transaction with the actual or purported partnership. If the representation, either by the purported partner or by a person with the purported partner's consent, is made in a public manner, the purported partner is liable to a person who relies upon the purported partnership even if the purported partner is not aware of being held out as a partner to the claimant. If partnership liability results, the purported partner is liable with respect to that liability as if the purported partner were a partner. If no partnership liability results, the purported partner is liable with respect to that liability jointly and severally with any other person consenting to the representation.

(b)   If a person is thus represented to be a partner in an existing partnership, or with one or more persons not partners, the purported partner is an agent of persons consenting to the representation to bind them to the same extent and in the same manner as if the purported partner were a partner, with respect to persons who enter into transactions in reliance upon the representation. If all the partners of the existing partnership consent to the representation, a

35

partnership act or obligation results. If fewer than all the partners of the existing partnership consent to the representation, the person acting and the partners consenting to the representation are jointly and severally liable.

(c)   A person is not liable as a partner merely because the person is named by another as a partner in a statement of partnership authority.

(d)   A person does not continue to be liable as a partner merely because of a failure to file a statement of dissociation or to amend a statement of partnership authority to indicate the person's dissociation as a partner.

(e)   Except as otherwise provided in subsections (a) and (b), persons who are not partners as to each other are not liable as partners to other persons.

ARTICLE 4
RELATIONS OF PARTNERS TO EACH OTHER AND TO PARTNERSHIP

§ 401.   Partner's Rights and Duties

(a)   Each partner is entitled to an equal share of the partnership distributions and, except in the case of a limited liability partnership, is chargeable with a share of the partnership losses in proportion to the partner's share of the distributions.

(b)   A partnership shall reimburse a partner for any payment made by the partner in the course of the partner's activities on behalf of the partnership, if the partner complied with this section and Section 409 in making the payment.

(c)   A partnership shall indemnify and hold harmless a person with respect to any claim or demand against the person and any debt, obligation, or other liability incurred by the person by reason of the person's former or present capacity as a partner, if the claim, demand, debt, obligation, or other liability does not arise from the person's breach of this section or Section 407 or 409.

(d)   In the ordinary course of its business, a partnership may advance reasonable expenses, including attorney's fees and costs, incurred by a person in connection with a claim or demand against the person by reason of the person's former or present capacity as a partner, if the person promises to repay the partnership if the person ultimately is determined not to be entitled to be indemnified under subsection (c).

(e)   A partnership may purchase and maintain insurance on behalf of a partner against liability asserted against or incurred by the partner in that capacity or arising from that status even if, under Section 105(c)(7), the partnership agreement could not eliminate or limit the person's liability to the partnership for the conduct giving rise to the liability.

(f)   A partnership shall reimburse a partner for an advance to the partnership beyond the amount of capital the partner agreed to contribute.

(g)   A payment or advance made by a partner which gives rise to a partnership obligation under subsection (b) or (f) constitutes a loan to the partnership which accrues interest from the date of the payment or advance.

(h)   Each partner has equal rights in the management and conduct of the partnership's business.

(i)   A partner may use or possess partnership property only on behalf of the partnership.

(j)   A partner is not entitled to remuneration for services performed for the partnership, except for reasonable compensation for services rendered in winding up the business of the partnership.

(k)   A difference arising as to a matter in the ordinary course of business of a partnership may be decided by a majority of the partners. An act outside the ordinary course of business of a partnership and an amendment to the partnership agreement may be undertaken only with the affirmative vote or consent of all the partners.

§ 402. Becoming Partner

(a) Upon formation of a partnership, a person becomes a partner under Section 202(a).

(b) After formation of a partnership, a person becomes a partner:

    (1) as provided in the partnership agreement;

    (2) as a result of a transaction effective under [Article] 11; or

    (3) with the affirmative vote or consent of all the partners.

(c) A person may become a partner without:

    (1) acquiring a transferable interest; or

    (2) making or being obligated to make a contribution to the partnership.

§ 403. Form of Contribution

A contribution may consist of property transferred to, services performed for, or another benefit provided to the partnership or an agreement to transfer property to, perform services for, or provide another benefit to the partnership.

§ 404. Liability for Contribution

(a) A person's obligation to make a contribution to a partnership is not excused by the person's death, disability, termination, or other inability to perform personally.

(b) If a person does not fulfill an obligation to make a contribution other than money, the person is obligated at the option of the partnership to contribute money equal to the value of the part of the contribution which has not been made.

(c) The obligation of a person to make a contribution may be compromised only by the affirmative vote or consent of all the partners. If a creditor of a limited liability partnership extends credit or otherwise acts in reliance on an obligation described in subsection (a) without knowledge or notice of a compromise under this subsection, the creditor may enforce the obligation.

§ 405. Sharing of and Right to Distributions Before Dissolution

(a) Any distribution made by a partnership before its dissolution and winding up must be in equal shares among partners, except to the extent necessary to comply with a transfer effective under Section 503 or charging order in effect under Section 504.

(b) Subject to Section 701, a person has a right to a distribution before the dissolution and winding up of a partnership only if the partnership decides to make an interim distribution.

(c) A person does not have a right to demand or receive a distribution from a partnership in any form other than money. Except as otherwise provided in Section 806, a partnership may distribute an asset in kind only if each part of the asset is fungible with each other part and each person receives a percentage of the asset equal in value to the person's share of distributions.

(d) If a partner or transferee becomes entitled to receive a distribution, the partner or transferee has the status of, and is entitled to all remedies available to, a creditor of the partnership with respect to the distribution. However, the partnership's obligation to make a distribution is subject to offset for any amount owed to the partnership by the partner or a person dissociated as partner on whose account the distribution is made.

§ 406. Limitations on Distributions by Limited Liability Partnership

(a)   A limited liability partnership may not make a distribution, including a distribution under Section 806, if after the distribution:

(1)   the partnership would not be able to pay its debts as they become due in the ordinary course of the partnership's business; or

(2)   the partnership's total assets would be less than the sum of its total liabilities plus the amount that would be needed, if the partnership were to be dissolved and wound up at the time of the distribution, to satisfy the preferential rights upon dissolution and winding up of partners and transferees whose preferential rights are superior to the rights of persons receiving the distribution.

(b)   A limited liability partnership may base a determination that a distribution is not prohibited under subsection (a) on:

(1)   financial statements prepared on the basis of accounting practices and principles that are reasonable in the circumstances; or

(2)   a fair valuation or other method that is reasonable under the circumstances.

(c)   Except as otherwise provided in subsection (e), the effect of a distribution under subsection (a) is measured:

(1)   in the case of a distribution as defined in Section 102(4)(A), as of the earlier of:

(A)   the date money or other property is transferred or debt is incurred by the limited liability partnership; or

(B)   the date the person entitled to the distribution ceases to own the interest or rights being acquired by the partnership in return for the distribution;

(2)   in the case of any other distribution of indebtedness, as of the date the indebtedness is distributed; and

(3)   in all other cases, as of the date:

(A)   the distribution is authorized, if the payment occurs not later than 120 days after that date; or

(B)   the payment is made, if the payment occurs more than 120 days after the distribution is authorized.

(d)   A limited liability partnership's indebtedness to a partner or transferee incurred by reason of a distribution made in accordance with this section is at parity with the partnership's indebtedness to its general, unsecured creditors, except to the extent subordinated by agreement.

(e)   A limited liability partnership's indebtedness, including indebtedness issued as a distribution, is not a liability for purposes of subsection (a) if the terms of the indebtedness provide that payment of principal and interest is made only if and to the extent that a payment of a distribution could then be made under this section. If the indebtedness is issued as a distribution, each payment of principal or interest is treated as a distribution, the effect of which is measured on the date the payment is made.

(f)   In measuring the effect of a distribution under Section 806, the liabilities of a dissolved limited liability partnership do not include any claim that has been disposed of under Section 807, 808, or 809.

§ 407. Liability for Improper Distributions by Limited Liability Partnership

(a)   Except as otherwise provided in subsection (b), if a partner of a limited liability partnership consents to a distribution made in violation of Section 406 and in consenting to the distribution fails to comply with Section 409, the partner is personally liable to the partnership for the amount of the distribution which exceeds the amount that could have been distributed without the violation of Section 406.

(b)   To the extent the partnership agreement of a limited liability partnership expressly relieves a partner of the authority and responsibility to consent to distributions and imposes that authority and responsibility on one or more other partners, the liability stated in subsection (a) applies to the other partners and not to the partner that the partnership agreement relieves of the authority and responsibility.

(c)   A person that receives a distribution knowing that the distribution violated Section 406 is personally liable to the limited liability partnership but only to the extent that the distribution received by the person exceeded the amount that could have been properly paid under Section 406.

(d)   A person against which an action is commenced because the person is liable under subsection (a) may:

(1)   implead any other person that is liable under subsection (a) and seek to enforce a right of contribution from the person; and

(2)   implead any person that received a distribution in violation of subsection (c) and seek to enforce a right of contribution from the person in the amount the person received in violation of subsection (c).

(e)   An action under this section is barred unless commenced not later than two years after the distribution.

§ 408.   Rights to Information of Partners and Persons Dissociated as Partner

(a)   A partnership shall keep its books and records, if any, at its principal office.

(b)   On reasonable notice, a partner may inspect and copy during regular business hours, at a reasonable location specified by the partnership, any record maintained by the partnership regarding the partnership's business, financial condition, and other circumstances, to the extent the information is material to the partner's rights and duties under the partnership agreement or this [Act].

(c)   The partnership shall furnish to each partner:

(1)   without demand, any information concerning the partnership's business, financial condition, and other circumstances which the partnership knows and is material to the proper exercise of the partner's rights and duties under the partnership agreement or this [act], except to the extent the partnership can establish that it reasonably believes the partner already knows the information; and

(2)   on demand, any other information concerning the partnership's business, financial condition, and other circumstances, except to the extent the demand or the information demanded is unreasonable or otherwise improper under the circumstances.

(d)   The duty to furnish information under subsection (c) also applies to each partner to the extent the partner knows any of the information described in subsection (c).

(e)   Subject to subsection (j), on 10 days' demand made in a record received by a partnership, a person dissociated as a partner may have access to information to which the person was entitled while a partner if:

(1)   the information pertains to the period during which the person was a partner;

(2)   the person seeks the information in good faith; and

(3)   the person satisfies the requirements imposed on a partner by subsection (b).

(f)   Not later than 10 days after receiving a demand under subsection (e), the partnership in a record shall inform the person that made the demand of:

(1)   the information that the partnership will provide in response to the demand and when and where the partnership will provide the information; and

(2)   the partnership's reasons for declining, if the partnership declines to provide any demanded information.

(g)   A partnership may charge a person that makes a demand under this section the reasonable costs of copying, limited to the costs of labor and material.

(h)   A partner or person dissociated as a partner may exercise the rights under this section through an agent or, in the case of an individual under legal disability, a legal representative. Any restriction or condition imposed by the partnership agreement or under subsection (j) applies both to the agent or legal representative and to the partner or person dissociated as a partner.

(i)   Subject to Section 505, the rights under this section do not extend to a person as transferee.

(j)   In addition to any restriction or condition stated in its partnership agreement, a partnership, as a matter within the ordinary course of its business, may impose reasonable restrictions and conditions on access to and use of information to be furnished under this section, including designating information confidential and imposing nondisclosure and safeguarding obligations on the recipient. In a dispute concerning the reasonableness of a restriction under this subsection, the partnership has the burden of proving reasonableness.

§ 409.   Standards of Conduct for Partners

(a)   A partner owes to the partnership and the other partners the duties of loyalty and care stated in subsections (b) and (c).

(b)   The fiduciary duty of loyalty of a partner includes the duties:

(1)   to account to the partnership and hold as trustee for it any property, profit, or benefit derived by the partner:

(A)   in the conduct or winding up of the partnership's business;

(B)   from a use by the partner of the partnership's property; or

(C)   from the appropriation of a partnership opportunity;

(2)   to refrain from dealing with the partnership in the conduct or winding up of the partnership business as or on behalf of a person having an interest adverse to the partnership; and

(3)   to refrain from competing with the partnership in the conduct of the partnership's business before the dissolution of the partnership.

(c)   The duty of care of a partner in the conduct or winding up of the partnership business is to refrain from engaging in grossly negligent or reckless conduct, willful or intentional misconduct, or a knowing violation of law.

(d)   A partner shall discharge the duties and obligations under this [act] or under the partnership agreement and exercise any rights consistently with the contractual obligation of good faith and fair dealing.

(e)   A partner does not violate a duty or obligation under this [act] or under the partnership agreement solely because the partner's conduct furthers the partner's own interest.

(f)   All the partners may authorize or ratify, after full disclosure of all material facts, a specific act or transaction by a partner that otherwise would violate the duty of loyalty.

(g)   It is a defense to a claim under subsection (b)(2) and any comparable claim in equity or at common law that the transaction was fair to the partnership.

(h)   If, as permitted by subsection (f) or the partnership agreement, a partner enters into a transaction with the partnership which otherwise would be prohibited by subsection (b)(2), the partner's rights and obligations arising from the transaction are the same as those of a person that is not a partner.

§ 410.   Actions by Partnership and Partners

(a)   A partnership may maintain an action against a partner for a breach of the partnership agreement, or for the violation of a duty to the partnership, causing harm to the partnership.

(b)   A partner may maintain an action against the partnership or another partner, with or without an accounting as to partnership business, to enforce the partner's rights and protect the partner's interests, including rights and interests under the partnership agreement or this [Act] or arising independently of the partnership relationship.

(c)   A right to an accounting on dissolution and winding up does not revive a claim barred by law.

§ 411.   Continuation of Partnership Beyond Definite Term or Particular Undertaking

(a)   If a partnership for a definite term or particular undertaking is continued, without an express agreement, after the expiration of the term or completion of the undertaking, the rights and duties of the partners remain the same as they were at the expiration or completion, so far as is consistent with a partnership at will.

(b)   If the partners, or those of them who habitually acted in the business during the term or undertaking, continue the business without any settlement or liquidation of the partnership, they are presumed to have agreed that the partnership will continue.

ARTICLE 5
TRANSFERABLE INTERESTS AND RIGHTS OF
TRANSFEREES AND CREDITORS

§ 501.   Partner Not Co-Owner of Partnership Property

A partner is not a co-owner of partnership property and has no interest in partnership property which can be transferred, either voluntarily or involuntarily.

§ 502.   Nature of Transferable Interest

A transferable interest is personal property.

§ 503.   Transfer of Transferable Interest

(a)   A transfer, in whole or in part, of a transferable interest:

(1)   is permissible;

(2)   does not by itself cause a person's dissociation as a partner or a dissolution and winding up of the partnership business; and

(3)   subject to Section 505, does not entitle the transferee to:

(A)   participate in the management or conduct of the partnership's business; or

(B)   except as otherwise provided in subsection (c), have access to records or other information concerning the partnership's business.

(b)   A transferee has the right to:

(1)   receive, in accordance with the transfer, distributions to which the transferor would otherwise be entitled; and

(2)   seek under Section 801(5) a judicial determination that it is equitable to wind up the partnership business.

(c)   In a dissolution and winding up of a partnership, a transferee is entitled to an account of the partnership's transactions only from the date of dissolution.

(d)   A partnership need not give effect to a transferee's rights under this section until the partnership knows or has notice of the transfer.

(e)   A transfer of a transferable interest in violation of a restriction on transfer contained in the partnership agreement is ineffective if the intended transferee has knowledge or notice of the restriction at the time of transfer.

(f)   Except as otherwise provided in Section 601(4)(B), if a partner transfers a transferable interest, the transferor retains the rights of a partner other than the transferable interest transferred and retains all the duties and obligations of a partner.

(g)   If a partner transfers a transferable interest to a person that becomes a partner with respect to the transferred interest, the transferee is liable for the partner's obligations under Sections 404 and 407 known to the transferee when the transferee becomes a partner.

§ 504.   Charging Order

(a)   On application by a judgment creditor of a partner or transferee, a court may enter a charging order against the transferable interest of the judgment debtor for the unsatisfied amount of the judgment. A charging order constitutes a lien on a judgment debtor's transferable interest and requires the partnership to pay over to the person to which the charging order was issued any distribution that otherwise would be paid to the judgment debtor.

(b)   To the extent necessary to effectuate the collection of distributions pursuant to a charging order in effect under subsection (a), the court may:

(1)   appoint a receiver of the distributions subject to the charging order, with the power to make all inquiries the judgment debtor might have made; and

(2)   make all other orders necessary to give effect to the charging order.

(c)   Upon a showing that distributions under a charging order will not pay the judgment debt within a reasonable time, the court may foreclose the lien and order the sale of the transferable interest. The purchaser at the foreclosure sale obtains only the transferable interest, does not thereby become a partner, and is subject to Section 503.

(d)   At any time before foreclosure under subsection (c), the partner or transferee whose transferable interest is subject to a charging order under subsection (a) may extinguish the charging order by satisfying the judgment and filing a certified copy of the satisfaction with the court that issued the charging order.

(e)   At any time before foreclosure under subsection (c), a partnership or one or more partners whose transferable interests are not subject to the charging order may pay to the judgment creditor the full amount due under the judgment and thereby succeed to the rights of the judgment creditor, including the charging order.

(f)   This [Act] does not deprive any partner or transferee of the benefit of any exemption law applicable to the transferable interest of the partner or transferee.

(g)   This section provides the exclusive remedy by which a person seeking in the capacity of a judgment creditor to enforce a judgment against a partner or transferee may satisfy the judgment from the judgment debtor's transferable interest.

§ 505. Power of Legal Representative of Deceased Partner

If a partner dies, the deceased partner's legal representative may exercise:

(1) the rights of a transferee provided in Section 503(c); and

(2) for purposes of settling the estate, the rights the deceased partner had under Section 408.

ARTICLE 6
DISSOCIATION

§ 601. Events Causing Dissociation

A person is dissociated as a partner when:

(1) the partnership knows or has notice of the person's express will to withdraw as a partner, but, if the person has specified a withdrawal date later than the date the partnership knew or had notice, on that later date;

(2) an event stated in the partnership agreement as causing the person's dissociation occurs;

(3) the person is expelled as a partner pursuant to the partnership agreement;

(4) the person is expelled as a partner by the affirmative vote or consent of all the other partners if:

(A) it is unlawful to carry on the partnership business with the person as a partner;

(B) there has been a transfer of all of the person's transferable interest in the partnership, other than:

(i) a transfer for security purposes; or

(ii) a charging order in effect under Section 504 which has not been foreclosed;

(C) the person is an entity and:

(i) the partnership notifies the person that it will be expelled as a partner because the person has filed a statement of dissolution or the equivalent, the person has been administratively dissolved, the person's charter or the equivalent has been revoked, or the person's right to conduct business has been suspended by the person's jurisdiction of formation; and

(ii) not later than 90 days after the notification, the statement of dissolution or the equivalent has not been withdrawn, rescinded, or revoked, or the person's charter or the equivalent or right to conduct business has not been reinstated; or

(D) the person is an unincorporated entity that has been dissolved and whose activities and affairs are being wound up;

(5) on application by the partnership or another partner, the person is expelled as a partner by judicial order because the person:

(A) has engaged or is engaging in wrongful conduct that has affected adversely and materially, or will affect adversely and materially the partnership's business;

(B) has committed willfully or persistently, or is committing willfully or persistently, a material breach of the partnership agreement or a duty or obligation under Section 409; or

(C) has engaged or is engaging in conduct relating to the partnership's business which makes it not reasonably practicable to carry on the business with the person as a partner;

(6)   the person:

(A)   becomes a debtor in bankruptcy;

(B)   signs an assignment for the benefit of creditors; or

(C)   seeks, consents to, or acquiesces in the appointment of a trustee, receiver, or liquidator of the person or of all or substantially all the person's property;

(7)   in the case of an individual:

(A)   the individual dies;

(B)   a guardian or general conservator for the individual is appointed; or

(C)   a court orders that the individual has otherwise become incapable of performing the individual's duties as a partner under this [Act] or the partnership agreement;

(8)   in the case of a person that is a testamentary or inter vivos trust or is acting as a partner by virtue of being a trustee of such a trust, the trust's entire transferable interest in the partnership is distributed;

(9)   in the case of a person that is an estate or is acting as a partner by virtue of being a personal representative of an estate, the estate's entire transferable interest in the partnership is distributed;

(10)   in the case of a person that is not an individual, the existence of the person terminates;

(11)   the partnership, participates in a merger under [Article] 11 and:

(A)   the partnership is not the surviving entity; or

(B)   otherwise as a result of the merger, the person ceases to be a partner;

(12)   the partnership participates in an interest exchange under [Article] 11 and, as a result of the interest exchange, the person ceases to be a partner;

(13)   the partnership participates in a conversion under [Article] 11;

(14)   the partnership participates in a domestication under [Article] 11 and, as a result of the domestication, the person ceases to be a partner; or

(15)   the partnership dissolves and completes winding up.

§ 602.   Power to Dissociate as Partner; Wrongful Dissociation

(a)   A person has the power to dissociate as a partner at any time, rightfully or wrongfully, by withdrawing as a partner by express will under Section 601(1).

(b)   A person's dissociation as a partner is wrongful only if the dissociation:

(1)   is in breach of an express provision of the partnership agreement; or

(2)   in the case of a partnership for a definite term or particular undertaking, occurs before the expiration of the term or the completion of the undertaking and:

(A)   the person withdraws as a partner by express will, unless the withdrawal follows not later than 90 days after another person's dissociation by death or otherwise under Section 601(6) through (10) or wrongful dissociation under this subsection;

(B)   the person is expelled as a partner by judicial order under Section 601(5);

(C)   the person is dissociated under Section 601(6); or

(D)   in the case of a person that is not a trust other than a business trust, an estate, or an individual, the person is expelled or otherwise dissociated because it willfully dissolved or terminated.

(c)   A person that wrongfully dissociates as a partner is liable to the partnership and to the other partners for damages caused by the dissociation. The liability is in addition to any debt, obligation, or other liability of the partner to the partnership or the other partners.

§ 603.   Effect of Dissociation

(a)   If a person's dissociation results in a dissolution and winding up of the partnership business, [Article] 8 applies; otherwise, [Article] 7 applies.

(b)   If a person is dissociated as a partner:

(1)   the person's right to participate in the management and conduct of the partnership's business terminates, except as otherwise provided in Section 802(c); and

(2)   the person's duties and obligations under Section 409 end with regard to matters arising and events occurring after the person's dissociation, except to the extent the partner participates in winding up the partnership's business pursuant to Section 802.

(c)   A person's dissociation does not of itself discharge the person from any debt, obligation, or other liability to the partnership or the other partners which the person incurred while a partner.

ARTICLE 7
PARTNER'S DISSOCIATION AS A PARTNER
WHEN BUSINESS NOT WOUND UP

§ 701.   Purchase of Interest of Person Dissociated as Partner

(a)   If a person is dissociated as a partner without the dissociation resulting in a dissolution and winding up of the partnership business under Section 801, the partnership shall cause the person's interest in the partnership to be purchased for a buyout price determined pursuant to subsection (b).

(b)   The buyout price of the interest of a person dissociated as a partner is the amount that would have been distributable to the person under Section 806(b) if, on the date of dissociation, the assets of the partnership were sold and the partnership were wound up, with the sale price equal to the greater of:

(1)   the liquidation value; or

(2)   the value based on a sale of the entire business as a going concern without the person.

(c)   Interest accrues on the buyout price from the date of dissociation to the date of payment, but damages for wrongful dissociation under Section 602(b), and all other amounts owing, whether or not presently due, from the person dissociated as a partner to the partnership, must be offset against the buyout price.

(d)   A partnership shall defend, indemnify, and hold harmless a person dissociated as a partner whose interest is being purchased against all partnership liabilities, whether incurred before or after the dissociation, except liabilities incurred by an act of the person under Section 702.

(e)   If no agreement for the purchase of the interest of a person dissociated as a partner is reached not later than 120 days after a written demand for payment, the partnership shall pay, or cause to be paid, in money to the person the amount the partnership estimates to be the buyout price and accrued interest, reduced by any offsets and accrued interest under subsection (c).

(f)   If a deferred payment is authorized under subsection (h), the partnership may tender a written offer to pay the amount it estimates to be the buyout price and accrued interest, reduced by any offsets under subsection (c), stating the time of payment, the amount and type of security for payment, and the other terms and conditions of the obligation.

(g)   The payment or tender required by subsection (e) or (f) must be accompanied by the following:

(1)   a statement of partnership assets and liabilities as of the date of dissociation;

(2)   the latest available partnership balance sheet and income statement, if any;

(3)   an explanation of how the estimated amount of the payment was calculated; and

(4)   written notice that the payment is in full satisfaction of the obligation to purchase unless, not later than 120 days after the written notice, the person dissociated as a partner commences an action to determine the buyout price, any offsets under subsection (c), or other terms of the obligation to purchase.

(h)   A person that wrongfully dissociates as a partner before the expiration of a definite term or the completion of a particular undertaking is not entitled to payment of any part of the buyout price until the expiration of the term or completion of the undertaking, unless the person establishes to the satisfaction of the court that earlier payment will not cause undue hardship to the business of the partnership. A deferred payment must be adequately secured and bear interest.

(i)   A person dissociated as a partner may maintain an action against the partnership, pursuant to Section 410(b)(2), to determine the buyout price of that person's interest, any offsets under subsection (c), or other terms of the obligation to purchase. The action must be commenced not later than 120 days after the partnership has tendered payment or an offer to pay or within one year after written demand for payment if no payment or offer to pay is tendered. The court shall determine the buyout price of the person's interest, any offset due under subsection (c), and accrued interest, and enter judgment for any additional payment or refund. If deferred payment is authorized under subsection (h), the court shall also determine the security for payment and other terms of the obligation to purchase. The court may assess reasonable attorney's fees and the fees and expenses of appraisers or other experts for a party to the action, in amounts the court finds equitable, against a party that the court finds acted arbitrarily, vexatiously, or not in good faith. The finding may be based on the partnership's failure to tender payment or an offer to pay or to comply with subsection (g).

§ 702. Power to Bind and Liability of Person Dissociated as Partner

(a)   After a person is dissociated as a partner without the dissociation resulting in a dissolution and winding up of the partnership business and before the partnership is merged out of existence, converted, or domesticated under [Article] 11, or dissolved, the partnership is bound by an act of the person only if:

(1)   the act would have bound the partnership under Section 301 before dissociation; and

(2)   at the time the other party enters into the transaction:

(A)   less than two years has passed since the dissociation; and

(B)   the other party does not know or have notice of the dissociation and reasonably believes that the person is a partner.

(b)   If a partnership is bound under subsection (a), the person dissociated as a partner which caused the partnership to be bound is liable:

(1)   to the partnership for any damage caused to the partnership arising from the obligation incurred under subsection (a); and

(2)   if a partner or another person dissociated as a partner is liable for the obligation, to the partner or other person for any damage caused to the partner or other person arising from the liability.

§ 703. Liability of Person Dissociated as Partner to Other Persons

(a)   Except as otherwise provided in subsection (b), a person dissociated as a partner is not liable for a partnership obligation incurred after dissociation.

(b)   A person that is dissociated as a partner is liable on a transaction entered into by the partnership after the dissociation only if:

(1)   a partner would be liable on the transaction; and

(2)   at the time the other party enters into the transaction:

(A)   less than two years has passed since the dissociation; and

(B)   the other party does not have knowledge or notice of the dissociation and reasonably believes that the person is a partner.

(c)   By agreement with a creditor of a partnership and the partnership, a person dissociated as a partner may be released from liability for a debt, obligation, or other liability of the partnership.

(d)   A person dissociated as a partner is released from liability for a debt, obligation, or other liability of the partnership if the partnership's creditor, with knowledge or notice of the person's dissociation but without the person's consent, agrees to a material alteration in the nature or time of payment of the debt, obligation, or other liability.

§ 704.   Statement of Dissociation

(a)   A person dissociated as a partner or the partnership may deliver to the [Secretary of State] for filing a statement of dissociation stating the name of the partnership and that the person has dissociated from the partnership.

(b)   A statement of dissociation is a limitation on the authority of a person dissociated as a partner for the purposes of Section 303.

§ 705.   Continued Use of Partnership Name

Continued use of a partnership name, or the name of a person dissociated as a partner as part of the partnership name, by partners continuing the business does not of itself make the person dissociated as a partner liable for an obligation of the partners or the partnership continuing the business.

ARTICLE 8
DISSOLUTION AND WINDING UP

§ 801.   Events Causing Dissolution

A partnership is dissolved, and its business must be wound up, upon the occurrence of any of the following:

(1)   in a partnership at will, the partnership knows or has notice of a person's express will to withdraw as a partner, other than a partner that has dissociated under Section 601(2) through (10), but, if the person has specified a withdrawal date later than the date the partnership knew or had notice, on the later date;

(2)   in a partnership for a definite term or particular undertaking:

(A)   within 90 days after a person's dissociation by death or otherwise under Section 601(6) through (10) or wrongful dissociation under Section 602(b), the affirmative vote or consent of at least half of the remaining partners to wind up the partnership business, for which purpose a person's rightful dissociation pursuant to Section 602(b)(2)(A) constitutes that partner's consent to wind up the partnership business;

(B)   the affirmative vote or consent of all the partners to wind up the partnership business; or

(C)   the expiration of the term or the completion of the undertaking;

(3)   an event or circumstance that the partnership agreement states causes dissolution;

(4)   on application by a partner, the entry by [the appropriate court] of an order dissolving the partnership on the grounds that:

(A)   the conduct of all or substantially all the partnership's business is unlawful;

(B)   the economic purpose of the partnership is likely to be unreasonably frustrated;

(C)   another partner has engaged in conduct relating to the partnership business which makes it not reasonably practicable to carry on the business in partnership with that partner; or

(D)   it is otherwise not reasonably practicable to carry on the partnership business in conformity with the partnership agreement;

(5)   on application by a transferee, the entry by [the appropriate court] of an order dissolving the partnership on the ground that it is equitable to wind up the partnership business:

(A)   after the expiration of the term or completion of the undertaking, if the partnership was for a definite term or particular undertaking at the time of the transfer or entry of the charging order that gave rise to the transfer; or

(B)   at any time, if the partnership was a partnership at will at the time of the transfer or entry of the charging order that gave rise to the transfer; or

(6)   the passage of 90 consecutive days during which the partnership does not have at least two partners.

§ 802. Winding Up

(a)   A dissolved partnership shall wind up its business and, except as otherwise provided in Section 803, the partnership continues after dissolution only for the purpose of winding up.

(b)   In winding up its business, the partnership:

(1)   shall discharge the partnership's debts, obligations, and other liabilities, settle and close the partnership's business, and marshal and distribute the assets of the partnership; and

(2)   may:

(A)   deliver to the [Secretary of State] for filing a statement of dissolution stating the name of the partnership and that the partnership is dissolved;

(B)   preserve the partnership business and property as a going concern for a reasonable time;

(C)   prosecute and defend actions and proceedings, whether civil, criminal, or administrative;

(D)   transfer the partnership's property;

(E)   settle disputes by mediation or arbitration;

(F)   deliver to the [Secretary of State] for filing a statement of termination stating the name of the partnership and that the partnership is terminated; and

(G)   perform other acts necessary or appropriate to the winding up.

(c)   A person whose dissociation as a partner resulted in dissolution may participate in winding up as if still a partner, unless the dissociation was wrongful.

(d)   If a dissolved partnership does not have a partner and no person has the right to participate in winding up under subsection (c), the personal or legal representative of the last person to have been a partner may wind up the partnership's business. If the representative does not exercise that right, a person to wind up the partnership's business may be appointed by the affirmative vote or consent of transferees owning a majority of the rights to receive distributions at the time the consent is to be effective. A person appointed under this subsection has the powers of a partner under Section 804 but is not liable for the debts, obligations, and other liabilities of the partnership solely by reason of having or exercising those powers or otherwise acting to wind up the partnership's business.

(e)   On the application of any partner or person entitled under subsection (c) to participate in winding up, the [appropriate court] may order judicial supervision of the winding up of a dissolved partnership, including the appointment of a person to wind up the partnership's business, if:

(1)   the partnership does not have a partner and within a reasonable time following the dissolution no person has been appointed under subsection (d); or

(2)   the applicant establishes other good cause.

§ 803.   Rescinding Dissolution

(a)   A partnership may rescind its dissolution, unless a statement of termination applicable to the partnership has become effective or [the appropriate court] has entered an order under Section 801(4) or (5) dissolving the partnership.

(b)   Rescinding dissolution under this section requires:

(1)   the affirmative vote or consent of each partner; and

(2)   if the partnership has delivered to the [Secretary of State] for filing a statement of dissolution and:

(A)   the statement has not become effective, delivery to the [Secretary of State] for filing of a statement of withdrawal under Section 115 applicable to the statement of dissolution; or

(B)   the statement of dissolution has become effective, delivery to the [Secretary of State] for filing of a statement of rescission stating the name of the partnership and that dissolution has been rescinded under this section.

(c)   If a partnership rescinds its dissolution:

(1)   the partnership resumes carrying on its business as if dissolution had never occurred;

(2)   subject to paragraph (3), any liability incurred by the partnership after the dissolution and before the rescission has become effective is determined as if dissolution had never occurred; and

(3)   the rights of a third party arising out of conduct in reliance on the dissolution before the third party knew or had notice of the rescission may not be adversely affected.

§ 804.   Power to Bind Partnership After Dissolution

(a)   A partnership is bound by a partner's act after dissolution which:

(1)   is appropriate for winding up the partnership business; or

(2)   would have bound the partnership under Section 301 before dissolution, if, at the time the other party enters into the transaction, the other party does not know or have notice of the dissolution.

(b)   A person dissociated as a partner binds a partnership through an act occurring after dissolution if:

(1)   at the time the other party enters into the transaction:

(A)   less than two years has passed since the dissociation; and

(B) the other party does not know or have notice of the dissociation and reasonably believes that the person is a partner; and

(2) the act:

(A) is appropriate for winding up the partnership's business; or

(B) would have bound the partnership under Section 301 before dissolution and at the time the other party enters into the transaction the other party does not know or have notice of the dissolution.

§ 805. Liability After Dissolution of Partner and Person Dissociated as Partner

(a) If a partner having knowledge of the dissolution causes a partnership to incur an obligation under Section 804(a) by an act that is not appropriate for winding up the partnership business, the partner is liable:

(1) to the partnership for any damage caused to the partnership arising from the obligation; and

(2) if another partner or person dissociated as a partner is liable for the obligation, to that other partner or person for any damage caused to that other partner or person arising from the liability.

(b) Except as otherwise provided in subsection (c), if a person dissociated as a partner causes a partnership to incur an obligation under Section 804(b), the person is liable:

(1) to the partnership for any damage caused to the partnership arising from the obligation; and

(2) if a partner or another person dissociated as a partner is liable for the obligation, to the partner or other person for any damage caused to the partner or other person arising from the obligation.

(c) A person dissociated as a partner is not liable under subsection (b) if:

(1) Section 802(c) permits the person to participate in winding up; and

(2) the act that causes the partnership to be bound under Section 804(b) is appropriate for winding up the partnership's business.

§ 806. Disposition of Assets in Winding Up; When Contributions Required

(a) In winding up its business, a partnership shall apply its assets, including the contributions required by this section, to discharge the partnership's obligations to creditors, including partners that are creditors.

(b) After a partnership complies with subsection (a), any surplus must be distributed in the following order, subject to any charging order in effect under Section 504:

(1) to each person owning a transferable interest that reflects contributions made and not previously returned, an amount equal to the value of the unreturned contributions; and

(2) among persons owning transferable interests in proportion to their respective rights to share in distributions immediately before the dissolution of the partnership.

(c) If a partnership's assets are insufficient to satisfy all its obligations under subsection (a), with respect to each unsatisfied obligation incurred when the partnership was not a limited liability partnership, the following rules apply:

(1) Each person that was a partner when the obligation was incurred and that has not been released from the obligation under Section 703(c) and (d) shall contribute to the partnership for the purpose of enabling the partnership to satisfy the obligation. The contribution due from each

of those persons is in proportion to the right to receive distributions in the capacity of a partner in effect for each of those persons when the obligation was incurred.

(2) If a person does not contribute the full amount required under paragraph (1) with respect to an unsatisfied obligation of the partnership, the other persons required to contribute by paragraph (1) on account of the obligation shall contribute the additional amount necessary to discharge the obligation. The additional contribution due from each of those other persons is in proportion to the right to receive distributions in the capacity of a partner in effect for each of those other persons when the obligation was incurred.

(3) If a person does not make the additional contribution required by paragraph (2), further additional contributions are determined and due in the same manner as provided in that paragraph.

(d) A person that makes an additional contribution under subsection (c)(2) or (3) may recover from any person whose failure to contribute under subsection (c)(1) or (2) necessitated the additional contribution. A person may not recover under this subsection more than the amount additionally contributed. A person's liability under this subsection may not exceed the amount the person failed to contribute.

(e) If a partnership does not have sufficient surplus to comply with subsection (b)(1), any surplus must be distributed among the owners of transferable interests in proportion to the value of the respective unreturned contributions.

(f) All distributions made under subsections (b) and (c) must be paid in money.

§ 807. Known Claims Against Dissolved Limited Liability Partnership

(a) Except as otherwise provided in subsection (d), a dissolved limited liability partnership may give notice of a known claim under subsection (b), which has the effect provided in subsection (c).

(b) A dissolved limited liability partnership may in a record notify its known claimants of the dissolution. The notice must:

(1) specify the information required to be included in a claim;

(2) state that a claim must be in writing and provide a mailing address to which the claim is to be sent;

(3) state the deadline for receipt of a claim, which may not be less than 120 days after the date the notice is received by the claimant;

(4) state that the claim will be barred if not received by the deadline; and

(5) unless the partnership has been throughout its existence a limited liability partnership, state that the barring of a claim against the partnership will also bar any corresponding claim against any partner or person dissociated as a partner which is based on Section 306.

(c) A claim against a dissolved limited liability partnership is barred if the requirements of subsection (b) are met and:

(1) the claim is not received by the specified deadline; or

(2) if the claim is timely received but rejected by the limited liability partnership:

(A) the partnership causes the claimant to receive a notice in a record stating that the claim is rejected and will be barred unless the claimant commences an action against the partnership to enforce the claim not later than 90 days after the claimant receives the notice; and

(B) the claimant does not commence the required action not later than 90 days after the claimant receives the notice.

(d)   This section does not apply to a claim based on an event occurring after the date of dissolution or a liability that on that date is contingent.

§ 808.   Other Claims Against Dissolved Limited Liability Partnership

(a)   A dissolved limited liability partnership may publish notice of its dissolution and request persons having claims against the partnership to present them in accordance with the notice.

(b)   A notice under subsection (a) must:

(1)   be published at least once in a newspaper of general circulation in the [county] in this state in which the dissolved limited liability partnership's principal office is located or, if the principal office is not located in this state, in the [county] in which the office of the partnership's registered agent is or was last located;

(2)   describe the information required to be contained in a claim, state that the claim must be in writing, and provide a mailing address to which the claim is to be sent;

(3)   state that a claim against the partnership is barred unless an action to enforce the claim is commenced not later than three years after publication of the notice; and

(4)   unless the partnership has been throughout its existence a limited liability partnership, state that the barring of a claim against the partnership will also bar any corresponding claim against any partner or person dissociated as a partner which is based on Section 306.

(c)   If a dissolved limited liability partnership publishes a notice in accordance with subsection (b), the claim of each of the following claimants is barred unless the claimant commences an action to enforce the claim against the partnership not later than three years after the publication date of the notice:

(1)   a claimant that did not receive notice in a record under Section 807;

(2)   a claimant whose claim was timely sent to the partnership but not acted on; and

(3)   a claimant whose claim is contingent at, or based on an event occurring after, the date of dissolution.

(d)   A claim not barred under this section or Section 807 may be enforced:

(1)   against a dissolved limited liability partnership, to the extent of its undistributed assets;

(2)   except as otherwise provided in Section 809, if assets of the partnership have been distributed after dissolution, against a partner or transferee to the extent of that person's proportionate share of the claim or of the partnership's assets distributed to the partner or transferee after dissolution, whichever is less, but a person's total liability for all claims under this paragraph may not exceed the total amount of assets distributed to the person after dissolution; and

(3)   against any person liable on the claim under Sections 306, 703, and 805

§ 809.   Court Proceedings

(a)   A dissolved limited liability partnership that has published a notice under Section 808 may file an application with [the appropriate court] in the [county] where the partnership's principal office is located or, if the principal office is not located in this state, where the office of its registered agent is or was last located, for a determination of the amount and form of security to be provided for payment of claims that are reasonably expected to arise after the date of dissolution based on facts known to the partnership and:

(1)   at the time of the application:

(A)   are contingent; or

(B)   have not been made known to the partnership; or

(2)   are based on an event occurring after the date of dissolution.

(b)   Security is not required for any claim that is or is reasonably anticipated to be barred under Section 807.

(c)   Not later than 10 days after the filing of an application under subsection (a), the dissolved limited liability partnership shall give notice of the proceeding to each claimant holding a contingent claim known to the partnership.

(d)   In any proceeding under this section, the court may appoint a guardian ad litem to represent all claimants whose identities are unknown. The reasonable fees and expenses of the guardian, including all reasonable expert witness fees, must be paid by the dissolved limited liability partnership.

(e)   A dissolved limited liability partnership that provides security in the amount and form ordered by the court under subsection (a) satisfies the partnership's obligations with respect to claims that are contingent, have not been made known to the partnership, or are based on an event occurring after the date of dissolution, and such claims may not be enforced against a partner or transferee on account of assets received in liquidation.

§ 810.   Liability of Partner and Person Dissociated as Partner When Claim Against Partnership Barred

If a claim against a dissolved partnership is barred under Section 807, 808, or 809, any corresponding claim under Section 306, 703, or 805 is also barred.

ARTICLE 9
LIMITED LIABILITY PARTNERSHIP

§ 901.   Statement of Qualification

(a)   A partnership may become a limited liability partnership pursuant to this section.

(b)   The terms and conditions on which a partnership becomes a limited liability partnership must be approved by the affirmative vote or consent necessary to amend the partnership agreement except, in the case of a partnership agreement that expressly addresses obligations to contribute to the partnership, the affirmative vote or consent necessary to amend those provisions.

(c)   After the approval required by subsection (b), a partnership may become a limited liability partnership by delivering to the [Secretary of State] for filing a statement of qualification. The statement must contain:

(1)   the name of the partnership which must comply with Section 902;

(2)   the street and mailing addresses of the partnership's principal office and, if different, the street address of an office in this state, if any;

(3)   the name and street and mailing addresses in this state of the partnership's registered agent; and

(4)   a statement that the partnership elects to become a limited liability partnership.

(d)   A partnership's status as a limited liability partnership remains effective, regardless of changes in the partnership, until it is canceled pursuant to subsection (f) or administratively revoked pursuant to Section 903.

(e)   The status of a partnership as a limited liability partnership and the protection against liability of its partners for the debts, obligations, or other liabilities of the partnership while it is a limited liability partnership is not affected by errors or later changes in the information required to be contained in the statement of qualification.

(f)   A limited liability partnership may amend or cancel its statement of qualification by delivering to the [Secretary of State] for filing a statement of amendment or cancellation. The statement must be approved by the affirmative vote or consent of all the partners and state the name of the limited liability partnership and in the case of:

    (1)   an amendment, state the text of the amendment; and

    (2)   a cancellation, state that the statement of qualification is canceled.

§ 902.   Permitted Names

(a)   The name of a partnership that is not a limited liability partnership may not contain the phrase "Registered Limited Liability Partnership" or "Limited Liability Partnership" or the abbreviation "R.L.L.P.", "L.L.P.", "RLLP", or "LLP".

(b)   The name of a limited liability partnership must contain the phrase "Registered Limited Liability Partnership" or "Limited Liability Partnership" or the abbreviation "R.L.L.P.", "L.L.P.", "RLLP", or "LLP".

(c)   Except as otherwise provided in subsection (f), the name of a limited liability partnership, and the name under which a foreign limited liability partnership may register to do business in this state, must be distinguishable on the records of the [Secretary of State] from any:

    (1)   name of an existing person whose formation required the filing of a record by the [Secretary of State] and which is not at the time administratively dissolved;

    (2)   name of a limited liability partnership whose statement of qualification is in effect;

    (3)   name under which a person that is registered to do business in this state by the filing of a record by the [Secretary of State];

    (4)   name that is reserved under Section 903 or other law of this state providing for the reservation of a name by a filing of a record by the [Secretary of State];

    (5)   name that is registered under Section 904 or other law of this state providing for the registration of a name by a filing of a record by the [Secretary of State]; and

    (6)   a name registered under [this state's assumed or fictitious name statute].

(d)   If a person consents in a record to the use of its name and submits an undertaking in a form satisfactory to the [Secretary of State] to change its name to a name that is distinguishable on the records of the [Secretary of State] from any name in any category of names in subsection (c), the name of the consenting person may be used by the person to which the consent was given.

(e)   Except as otherwise provided in subsection (f), in determining whether a name is the same as or not distinguishable on the records of the [Secretary of State] from the name of another person, words, phrases, or abbreviations indicating a type of entity, such as "corporation", "corp.", "incorporated", "Inc.", "professional corporation", "PC", "P.C.", "professional association", "PA", "P.A.", "Limited", "Ltd.", "limited partnership", "LP", "L.P.", "limited liability partnership", "LLP", "L.L.P.", "registered limited liability partnership", "RLLP", "R.L.L.P.", "limited liability limited partnership", "LLLP", "L.L.L.P.", "registered limited liability limited partnership", "RLLLP", "R.L.L.L.P.", "limited liability company", "LLC", or "L.L.C.", "limited cooperative association", "limited cooperative", "LCA", or "L.C.A." may not be taken into account.

(f)   A person may consent in a record to the use of a name that is not distinguishable on the records of the [Secretary of State] from its name except for the addition of a word, phrase, or abbreviation indicating the type of person as provided in subsection (e). In such a case, the person need not change its name pursuant to subsection (d).

(g)   The name of a limited liability partnership or foreign limited liability partnership may not contain the words [insert prohibited words or words that may be used only with approval by an appropriate state agency].

(h)   A limited liability partnership or foreign limited liability partnership may use a name that is not distinguishable from a name described in subsection (c)(1) through (6) if the partnership delivers to the [Secretary of State] a certified copy of a final judgment of a court of competent jurisdiction establishing the right of the partnership to use the name in this state.

§ 903.   Administrative Revocation of Statement of Qualification

(a)   The [Secretary of State] may commence a proceeding under subsection (b) to revoke the statement of qualification of a limited liability partnership administratively if the partnership does not:

(1)   pay any fee, tax, interest, or penalty required to be paid to the [Secretary of State] not later than [six months] after it is due;

(2)   deliver [an annual] [a biennial] report to the [Secretary of State] not later than [six months] after it is due; or

(3)   have a registered agent in this state for [60] consecutive days.

(b)   If the [Secretary of State] determines that one or more grounds exist for administratively revoking a statement of qualification, the [Secretary of State] shall serve the partnership with notice in a record of the [Secretary of State's] determination.

(c)   If a limited liability partnership, not later than [60] days after service of the notice under subsection (b), does not cure or demonstrate to the satisfaction of the [Secretary of State] the nonexistence of each ground determined by the [Secretary of State], the [Secretary of State] shall administratively revoke the statement of qualification by signing a statement of administrative revocation that recites the grounds for revocation and the effective date of the revocation. The [Secretary of State] shall file the statement and serve a copy on the partnership pursuant to Section 116.

(d)   An administrative revocation under subsection (c) affects only a partnership's status as a limited liability partnership and is not an event causing dissolution of the partnership.

(e)   The administrative revocation of a statement of qualification of a limited liability partnership does not terminate the authority of its registered agent.

§ 904.   Reinstatement

(a)   A partnership whose statement of qualification has been revoked administratively under Section 903 may apply to the [Secretary of State] for reinstatement of the statement of qualification [not later than [two] years after the effective date of the revocation]. The application must state:

(1)   the name of the partnership at the time of the administrative revocation of its statement of qualification and, if needed, a different name that satisfies Section 902;

(2)   the address of the principal office of the partnership and the name and street and mailing addresses of its registered agent;

(3)   the effective date of administrative revocation of the partnership's statement of qualification; and

(4)   that the grounds for revocation did not exist or have been cured.

(b)   To have its statement of qualification reinstated, a partnership must pay all fees, taxes, interest, and penalties that were due to the [Secretary of State] at the time of the administrative revocation and all fees, taxes, interest, and penalties that would have been due to the [Secretary of State] while the partnership's statement of qualification was revoked administratively.

(c)   If the [Secretary of State] determines that an application under subsection (a) contains the required information, is satisfied that the information is correct, and determines that all payments required to be made to the [Secretary of State] by subsection (b) have been made, the [Secretary of State] shall:

(1)   cancel the statement of revocation and prepare a statement of reinstatement that states the [Secretary of State's] determination and the effective date of reinstatement; and

(2)   file the statement of reinstatement and serve a copy on the partnership.

(d)   When reinstatement under this section has become effective, the following rules apply:

(1)   The reinstatement relates back to and takes effect as of the effective date of the administrative revocation.

(2)   The partnership's status as a limited liability partnership continues as if the revocation had not occurred.

(3)   The rights of a person arising out of an act or omission in reliance on the revocation before the person knew or had notice of the reinstatement are not affected.

§ 905. Judicial Review of Denial of Reinstatement

(a)   If the [Secretary of State] denies a partnership's application for reinstatement following administrative revocation of the partnership's statement of qualification, the [Secretary of State] shall serve the partnership with a notice in a record that explains the reasons for the denial.

(b)   A partnership may seek judicial review of denial of reinstatement in [the appropriate court] not later than [30] days after service of the notice of denial.

§ 906. Reservation of Name

(a)   A person may reserve the exclusive use of a name that complies with Section 902 by delivering an application to the [Secretary of State] for filing. The application must state the name and address of the applicant and the name to be reserved. If the [Secretary of State] finds that the name is available, the [Secretary of State] shall reserve the name for the applicant's exclusive use for [120] days.

(b)   The owner of a reserved name may transfer the reservation to another person by delivering to the [Secretary of State] a signed notice in a record of the transfer which states the name and address of the person to which the reservation is being transferred.

§ 907. Registration of Name

(a)   A foreign limited liability partnership not registered to do business in this state under [Article] 10 may register its name, or an alternate name adopted pursuant to Section 902, if the name is distinguishable on the records of the [Secretary of State] from the names that are not available under Section 902.

(b)   To register its name or an alternate name adopted pursuant to Section 902, a foreign limited liability partnership must deliver to the [Secretary of State] for filing an application stating the partnership's name, the jurisdiction and date of its formation, and any alternate name adopted pursuant to Section 902. If the [Secretary of State] finds that the name applied for is available, the [Secretary of State] shall register the name for the applicant's exclusive use.

(c)   The registration of a name under this section is effective for [one year] after the date of registration.

(d)   A foreign limited liability partnership whose name registration is effective may renew the registration for successive [one-year] periods by delivering, not earlier than [three months] before the expiration of the registration, to the [Secretary of State] for filing a renewal application that complies with this section. When filed, the renewal application renews the registration for a succeeding [one-year] period.

(e)   A foreign limited liability partnership whose name registration is effective may register as a foreign limited liability partnership under the registered name or consent in a signed record to the use of that name by another person that is not an individual.

§ 908.   Registered Agent

(a)   Each limited liability partnership and each registered foreign limited liability partnership shall designate and maintain a registered agent in this state. The designation of a registered agent is an affirmation of fact by the partnership or foreign partnership that the agent has consented to serve.

(b)   A registered agent for a limited liability partnership or registered foreign limited liability partnership must have a place of business in this state.

(c)   The only duties under this [Act] of a registered agent that has complied with this [Act] are:

(1)   to forward to the limited liability partnership or registered foreign limited liability partnership at the address most recently supplied to the agent by the partnership or foreign partnership any process, notice, or demand pertaining to the partnership or foreign partnership which is served on or received by the agent;

(2)   if the registered agent resigns, to provide the notice required by Section 907(c) to the partnership or foreign partnership at the address most recently supplied to the agent by the partnership or foreign partnership; and

(3)   to keep current the information with respect to the agent in the statement of qualification or foreign registration statement.

§ 909.   Change of Registered Agent or Address for Registered Agent by Limited Liability Partnership

(a)   A limited liability partnership or registered foreign limited liability partnership may change its registered agent or the address of its registered agent by delivering to the [Secretary of State] for filing a statement of change that states:

(1)   the name of the partnership or foreign partnership; and

(2)   the information that is to be in effect as a result of the filing of the statement of change.

(b)   The partners of a limited liability partnership need not approve the delivery to the [Secretary of State] for filing of:

(1)   a statement of change under this section; or

(2)   a similar filing changing the registered agent or registered office, if any, of the partnership in any other jurisdiction.

(c)   A statement of change under this section designating a new registered agent is an affirmation of fact by the limited liability partnership or registered foreign limited liability partnership that the agent has consented to serve.

(d)   As an alternative to using the procedure in this section, a limited liability partnership may amend its statement of qualification.

§ 910. Resignation of Registered Agent

(a)   A registered agent may resign as an agent for a limited liability partnership or registered foreign limited liability partnership by delivering to the [Secretary of State] for filing a statement of resignation that states:

(1)   the name of the partnership or foreign partnership;

(2)   the name of the agent;

(3)   that the agent resigns from serving as registered agent for the partnership or foreign partnership; and

(4)   the address of the partnership or foreign partnership to which the agent will send the notice required by subsection (c).

(b)   A statement of resignation takes effect on the earlier of:

(1)   the 31st day after the day on which it is filed by the [Secretary of State]; or

(2)   the designation of a new registered agent for the limited liability partnership or registered foreign limited liability partnership.

(c)   A registered agent promptly shall furnish to the limited liability partnership or registered foreign limited liability partnership notice in a record of the date on which a statement of resignation was filed.

(d)   When a statement of resignation takes effect, the registered agent ceases to have responsibility under this [Act] for any matter thereafter tendered to it as agent for the limited liability partnership or registered foreign limited liability partnership. The resignation does not affect any contractual rights the partnership or foreign partnership has against the agent or that the agent has against the partnership or foreign partnership.

(e)   A registered agent may resign with respect to a limited liability partnership or registered foreign limited liability partnership whether or not the partnership or foreign partnership is in good standing.

§ 911. Change of Name or Address by Registered Agent

(a)   If a registered agent changes its name or address, the agent may deliver to the [Secretary of State] for filing a statement of change that states:

(1)   the name of the limited liability partnership or registered foreign limited liability partnership represented by the registered agent;

(2)   the name of the agent as currently shown in the records of the [Secretary of State] for the partnership or foreign partnership;

(3)   if the name of the agent has changed, its new name; and

(4)   if the address of the agent has changed, its new address.

(b)   A registered agent promptly shall furnish notice to the represented limited liability partnership or registered foreign limited liability partnership of the filing by the [Secretary of State] of the statement of change and the changes made by the statement.

Legislative Note: Many registered agents act in that capacity for many entities, and the Model Registered Agents Act (2006) (Last Amended 2013) provides a streamlined method through which a commercial registered agent can make a single filing to change its information for all represented entities. The single filing does not prevent an enacting state from assessing filing fees on the basis of the number of entity records affected. Alternatively the fees can be set on an incremental sliding fee or capitated amount based upon potential economies of costs for a bulk filing.

§ 912. Service of Process, Notice, or Demand

(a) A limited liability partnership or registered foreign limited liability partnership may be served with any process, notice, or demand required or permitted by law by serving its registered agent.

(b) If a limited liability partnership or registered foreign limited liability partnership ceases to have a registered agent, or if its registered agent cannot with reasonable diligence be served, the partnership or foreign partnership may be served by registered or certified mail, return receipt requested, or by similar commercial delivery service, addressed to the partnership or foreign partnership at its principal office. The address of the principal office must be as shown in the partnership's or foreign partnership's most recent [annual] [biennial] report filed by the [Secretary of State]. Service is effected under this subsection on the earliest of:

(1) the date the partnership or foreign partnership receives the mail or delivery by the commercial delivery service;

(2) the date shown on the return receipt, if signed by the partnership or foreign partnership; or

(3) five days after its deposit with the United States Postal Service, or with the commercial delivery service, if correctly addressed and with sufficient postage or payment.

(c) If process, notice, or demand cannot be served on a limited liability partnership or registered foreign limited liability partnership pursuant to subsection (a) or (b), service may be made by handing a copy to the individual in charge of any regular place of business of the partnership or foreign partnership if the individual served is not a plaintiff in the action.

(d) Service of process, notice, or demand on a registered agent must be in a written record.

(e) Service of process, notice, or demand may be made by other means under law other than this [Act].

§ 913. [Annual] [Biennial] Report for [Secretary of State]

(a) A limited liability partnership or registered foreign limited liability partnership shall deliver to the [Secretary of State] for filing [an annual] [a biennial] report that states:

(1) the name of the partnership or registered foreign partnership;

(2) the name and street and mailing addresses of its registered agent in this state;

(3) the street and mailing addresses of its principal office;

(4) the name of at least one partner; and

(5) in the case of a foreign partnership, its jurisdiction of formation and any alternate name adopted under Section 1006.

(b) Information in the [annual] [biennial] report must be current as of the date the report is signed by the limited liability partnership or registered foreign limited liability partnership.

(c) The first [annual] [biennial] report must be delivered to the [Secretary of State] for filing after [January 1] and before [April 1] of the year following the calendar year in which the limited liability partnership's statement of qualification became effective or the registered foreign limited liability partnership registered to do business in this state. Subsequent [annual] [biennial] reports must be delivered to the [Secretary of State] for filing after [January 1] and before [April 1] of each [second] calendar year thereafter.

(d) If [an annual] [a biennial] report does not contain the information required by this section, the [Secretary of State] promptly shall notify the reporting limited liability partnership or registered foreign limited liability partnership in a record and return the report for correction.

(e) If [an annual] [a biennial] report contains the name or address of a registered agent which differs from the information shown in the records of the [Secretary of State] immediately before the report becomes effective, the differing information is considered a statement of change under Section 909.

ARTICLE 10
FOREIGN LIMITED LIABILITY PARTNERSHIP

§ 1001. Governing Law

(a) The law of the jurisdiction of formation of a foreign limited liability partnership governs:

(1) the internal affairs of the partnership; and

(2) the liability of a partner as partner for a debt, obligation, or other liability of the foreign partnership.

(b) A foreign limited liability partnership is not precluded from registering to do business in this state because of any difference between the law of its jurisdiction of formation and the law of this state.

(c) Registration of a foreign limited liability partnership to do business in this state does not authorize the foreign partnership to engage in any business or exercise any power that a limited liability partnership may not engage in or exercise in this state.

§ 1002. Registration to Do Business in This State

(a) A foreign limited liability partnership may not do business in this state until it registers with the [Secretary of State] under this [Article].

(b) A foreign limited liability partnership doing business in this state may not maintain an action or proceeding in this state unless it has registered to do business in this state.

(c) The failure of a foreign limited liability partnership to register to do business in this state does not impair the validity of a contract or act of the foreign partnership or preclude it from defending an action or proceeding in this state.

(d) A limitation on the liability of a partner of a foreign limited liability partnership is not waived solely because the foreign partnership does business in this state without registering to do business in this state.

(e) Section 1001(a) and (b) applies even if a foreign limited liability partnership fails to register under this [article].

§ 1003. Foreign Registration Statement

To register to do business in this state, a foreign limited liability partnership must deliver a foreign registration statement to the [Secretary of State] for filing. The statement must state:

(1) the name of the partnership and, if the name does not comply with Section 902, an alternate name adopted pursuant to Section 1006(a);

(2) that the partnership is a foreign limited liability partnership;

(3) the partnership's jurisdiction of formation;

(4) the street and mailing addresses of the partnership's principal office and, if the law of the partnership's jurisdiction of formation requires the partnership to maintain an office in that jurisdiction, the street and mailing addresses of the required office; and

(5) the name and street and mailing addresses of the partnership's registered agent in this state.

§ 1004. Amendment of Foreign Registration Statement

A registered foreign limited liability partnership shall deliver to the [Secretary of State] for filing an amendment to its foreign registration statement if there is a change in:

(1)   the name of the partnership;

(2)   the partnership's jurisdiction of formation;

(3)   an address required by Section 1003(4); or

(4)   the information required by Section 1003(5).

§ 1005. Activities Not Constituting Doing Business

(a)   Activities of a foreign limited liability partnership which do not constitute doing business in this state under this [Article] include:

(1)   maintaining, defending, mediating, arbitrating, or settling an action or proceeding;

(2)   carrying on any activity concerning its internal affairs, including holding meetings of its partners;

(3)   maintaining accounts in financial institutions;

(4)   maintaining offices or agencies for the transfer, exchange, and registration of securities of the partnership or maintaining trustees or depositories with respect to those securities;

(5)   selling through independent contractors;

(6)   soliciting or obtaining orders by any means if the orders require acceptance outside this state before they become contracts;

(7)   creating or acquiring indebtedness, mortgages, or security interests in property;

(8)   securing or collecting debts or enforcing mortgages or security interests in property securing the debts and holding, protecting, or maintaining property;

(9)   conducting an isolated transaction that is not in the course of similar transactions;

(10) owning, without more, property; and

(11) doing business in interstate commerce.

(b)   A person does not do business in this state solely by being a partner of a foreign limited liability partnership that does business in this state.

(c)   This section does not apply in determining the contacts or activities that may subject a foreign limited liability partnership to service of process, taxation, or regulation under law of this state other than this [Act].

§ 1006. Noncomplying Name of Foreign Limited Liability Partnership

(a)   A foreign limited liability partnership whose name does not comply with Section 902 may not register to do business in this state until it adopts, for the purpose of doing business in this state, an alternate name that complies with Section 902. A partnership that registers under an alternate name under this subsection need not comply with [this state's assumed or fictitious name statute]. After registering to do business in this state with an alternate name, a partnership shall do business in this state under:

(1)   the alternate name;

(2)   the partnership's name, with the addition of its jurisdiction of formation; or

(3)   a name the partnership is authorized to use under [this state's assumed or fictitious name statute].

(b)   If a registered foreign limited liability partnership changes its name to one that does not comply with Section 902, it may not do business in this state until it complies with subsection (a) by amending its registration to adopt an alternate name that complies with Section 902.

§ 1007. Withdrawal Deemed on Conversion to Domestic Filing Entity or Domestic Limited Liability Partnership

A registered foreign limited liability partnership that converts to a domestic limited liability partnership or to a domestic entity whose formation requires the delivery of a record to the [Secretary of State] for filing is deemed to have withdrawn its registration on the effective date of the conversion.

§ 1008. Withdrawal on Dissolution or Conversion to Nonfiling Entity Other than Limited Liability Partnership

(a)   A registered foreign limited liability partnership that has dissolved and completed winding up or has converted to a domestic or foreign entity whose formation does not require the public filing of a record, other than a limited liability partnership, shall deliver a statement of withdrawal to the [Secretary of State] for filing. The statement must state:

    (1)   in the case of a partnership that has completed winding up:

        (A)   its name and jurisdiction of formation;

        (B)   that the partnership surrenders its registration to do business in this state; and

    (2)   in the case of a partnership that has converted:

        (A)   the name of the converting partnership and its jurisdiction of formation;

        (B)   the type of entity to which the partnership has converted and its jurisdiction of formation;

        (C)   that the converted entity surrenders the converting partnership's registration to do business in this state and revokes the authority of the converting partnership's registered agent to act as registered agent in this state on behalf of the partnership or the converted entity; and

        (D)   a mailing address to which service of process may be made under subsection (b).

(b)   After a withdrawal under this section becomes effective, service of process in any action or proceeding based on a cause of action arising during the time the foreign limited liability partnership was registered to do business in this state may be made pursuant to Section 909.

§ 1009. Transfer of Registration

(a)   When a registered foreign limited liability partnership has merged into a foreign entity that is not registered to do business in this state or has converted to a foreign entity required to register with the [Secretary of State] to do business in this state, the foreign entity shall deliver to the [Secretary of State] for filing an application for transfer of registration. The application must state:

    (1)   the name of the registered foreign limited partnership before the merger or conversion;

    (2)   that before the merger or conversion the registration pertained to a foreign limited liability partnership;

    (3)   the name of the applicant foreign entity into which the foreign limited liability partnership has merged or to which it has been converted and, if the name does not comply with Section 902, an alternate name adopted pursuant to Section 1006(a);

    (4)   the type of entity of the applicant foreign entity and its jurisdiction of formation;

(5) the street and mailing addresses of the principal office of the applicant foreign entity and, if the law of that entity's jurisdiction of formation requires the entity to maintain an office in that jurisdiction, the street and mailing addresses of that office; and

(6) the name and street and mailing addresses of the applicant foreign entity's registered agent in this state.

(b) When an application for transfer of registration takes effect, the registration of the foreign limited liability limited partnership to do business in this state is transferred without interruption to the foreign entity into which the partnership has merged or to which it has been converted.

§ 1010. Termination of Registration

(a) The [Secretary of State] may terminate the registration of a registered foreign limited liability partnership in the manner provided in subsections (b) and (c) if the partnership does not:

(1) pay, not later than [60] days after the due date, any fee, tax, interest, or penalty required to be paid to the [Secretary of State] under this [Act] or law other than this [Act];

(2) deliver to the [Secretary of State] for filing, not later than [60] days after the due date, [an annual] [a biennial] report required under Section 913;

(3) have a registered agent as required by Section 908; or

(4) deliver to the [Secretary of State] for filing a statement of a change under Section 909 not later than [30] days after a change has occurred in the name or address of the registered agent.

(b) The [Secretary of State] may terminate the registration of a registered foreign limited liability partnership by:

(1) filing a notice of termination or noting the termination in the records of the [Secretary of State]; and

(2) delivering a copy of the notice or the information in the notation to the partnership's registered agent or, if the partnership does not have a registered agent, to the partnership's principal office.

(c) A notice or information in a notation under subsection (b) must include:

(1) the effective date of the termination, which must be at least [60] days after the date the [Secretary of State] delivers the copy; and

(2) the grounds for termination under subsection (a).

(d) The authority of a registered foreign limited liability partnership to do business in this state ceases on the effective date of the notice of termination or notation under subsection (b), unless before that date the partnership cures each ground for termination stated in the notice or notation. If the partnership cures each ground, the [Secretary of State] shall file a record so stating.

§ 1011. Withdrawal of Registration of Registered Foreign Limited Liability Partnership

(a) A registered foreign limited liability partnership may withdraw its registration by delivering a statement of withdrawal to the [Secretary of State] for filing. The statement of withdrawal must state:

(1) the name of the partnership and its jurisdiction of formation;

(2) that the partnership is not doing business in this state and that it withdraws its registration to do business in this state;

(3)   that the partnership revokes the authority of its registered agent to accept service on its behalf in this state; and

(4)   an address to which service of process may be made under subsection (b).

(b)   After the withdrawal of the registration of a foreign limited liability partnership, service of process in any action or proceeding based on a cause of action arising during the time the partnership was registered to do business in this state may be made pursuant to Section 909.

§ 1012. Action by [Attorney General]

The [Attorney General] may maintain an action to enjoin a foreign limited liability partnership from doing business in this state in violation of this [article].

ARTICLE 11
MERGER, INTEREST EXCHANGE, CONVERSIONS, AND DOMESTICATION
PART 1
GENERAL PROVISIONS

§ 1101. Definitions

In this [article]:

(1)   "Acquired entity" means the entity, all of one or more classes or series of interests of which are acquired in an interest exchange.

(2)   "Acquiring entity" means the entity that acquires all of one or more classes or series of interests of the acquired entity in an interest exchange.

(3)   "Conversion" means a transaction authorized by [Part] 4.

(4)   "Converted entity" means the converting entity as it continues in existence after a conversion.

(5)   "Converting entity" means the domestic entity that approves a plan of conversion pursuant to Section 1143 or the foreign entity that approves a conversion pursuant to the law of its jurisdiction of formation.

(6)   "Distributional interest" means the right under an unincorporated entity's organic law and organic rules to receive distributions from the entity.

(7)   "Domestic", with respect to an entity, means governed as to its internal affairs by the law of this state.

(8)   "Domesticated limited liability partnership" means a domesticating limited liability partnership as it continues in existence after a domestication.

(9)   "Domesticating limited liability partnership" means the domestic limited liability partnership that approves a plan of domestication pursuant to Section 1153 or the foreign limited liability partnership that approves a domestication pursuant to the law of its jurisdiction of formation.

(10) "Domestication" means a transaction authorized by [Part] 5.

(11) "Entity":

(A)   means:

(i)   a business corporation;

(ii) a nonprofit corporation;

(iii) a general partnership, including a limited liability partnership;

(iv) a limited partnership, including a limited liability limited partnership;

(v) a limited liability company;

[(vi) a general cooperative association;]

(vii) a limited cooperative association;

(viii) an unincorporated nonprofit association;

(ix) a statutory trust, business trust, or common-law business trust; or

(x) any other person that has:

(I) a legal existence separate from any interest holder of that person; or

(II) the power to acquire an interest in real property in its own name; and

(B) does not include:

(i) an individual;

(ii) a trust with a predominantly donative purpose or a charitable trust;

(iii) an association or relationship that is not an entity listed in subparagraph (A) and is not a partnership under the rules stated in [Section 202(c) of the Uniform Partnership Act (1997) (Last Amended 2013)] [Section 7 of the Uniform Partnership Act (1914)] or a similar provision of the law of another jurisdiction;

(iv) a decedent's estate; or

(v) a government or a governmental subdivision, agency, or instrumentality.

(12) "Filing entity" means an entity whose formation requires the filing of a public organic record. The term does not include a limited liability partnership.

(13) "Foreign", with respect to an entity, means an entity governed as to its internal affairs by the law of a jurisdiction other than this state.

(14) "Governance interest" means a right under the organic law or organic rules of an unincorporated entity, other than as a governor, agent, assignee, or proxy, to:

(A) receive or demand access to information concerning, or the books and records of, the entity;

(B) vote for or consent to the election of the governors of the entity; or

(C) receive notice of or vote on or consent to an issue involving the internal affairs of the entity.

(15) "Governor" means:

(A) a director of a business corporation;

(B) a director or trustee of a nonprofit corporation;

(C) a general partner of a general partnership;

(D) a general partner of a limited partnership;

(E) a manager of a manager-managed limited liability company;

(F) a member of a member-managed limited liability company;

[(G) a director of a general cooperative association;]

(H) a director of a limited cooperative association;

(I)   a manager of an unincorporated nonprofit association;

(J)   a trustee of a statutory trust, business trust, or common-law business trust; or

(K)   any other person under whose authority the powers of an entity are exercised and under whose direction the activities and affairs of the entity are managed pursuant to the organic law and organic rules of the entity.

(16) "Interest" means:

(A)   a share in a business corporation;

(B)   a membership in a nonprofit corporation;

(C)   a partnership interest in a general partnership;

(D)   a partnership interest in a limited partnership;

(E)   a membership interest in a limited liability company;

[(F)   a share in a general cooperative association;]

(G)   a member's interest in a limited cooperative association;

(H)   a membership in an unincorporated nonprofit association;

(I)   a beneficial interest in a statutory trust, business trust, or common-law business trust; or

(J)   a governance interest or distributional interest in any other type of unincorporated entity.

(17) "Interest Exchange" means a transaction authorized by [Part] 3.

(18) "Interest holder" means:

(A)   a shareholder of a business corporation;

(B)   a member of a nonprofit corporation;

(C)   a general partner of a general partnership;

(D)   a general partner of a limited partnership;

(E)   a limited partner of a limited partnership;

(F)   a member of a limited liability company;

[(G)   a shareholder of a general cooperative association;]

(H)   a member of a limited cooperative association;

(I)   a member of an unincorporated nonprofit association;

(J)   a beneficiary or beneficial owner of a statutory trust, business trust, or common-law business trust; or

(K)   any other direct holder of an interest.

(19) "Interest holder liability" means:

(A)   personal liability for a liability of an entity which is imposed on a person:

(i)   solely by reason of the status of the person as an interest holder; or

(ii)   by the organic rules of the entity which make one or more specified interest holders or categories of interest holders liable in their capacity as interest holders for all or specified liabilities of the entity; or

(B)   an obligation of an interest holder under the organic rules of an entity to contribute to the entity.

(20) "Merger" means a transaction authorized by [Part] 2.

(21) "Merging entity" means an entity that is a party to a merger and exists immediately before the merger becomes effective.

(22) "Organic law" means the law of an entity's jurisdiction of formation governing the internal affairs of the entity.

(23) "Organic rules" means the public organic record and private organic rules of an entity.

(24) "Plan" means a plan of merger, plan of interest exchange, plan of conversion, or plan of domestication.

(25) "Plan of conversion" means a plan under Section 1142.

(26) "Plan of domestication" means a plan under Section 1152.

(27) "Plan of interest exchange" means a plan under Section 1132.

(28) "Plan of merger" means a plan under Section 1122.

(29) "Private organic rules" means the rules, whether or not in a record, that govern the internal affairs of an entity, are binding on all its interest holders, and are not part of its public organic record, if any. The term includes:

(A)   the bylaws of a business corporation;

(B)   the bylaws of a nonprofit corporation;

(C)   the partnership agreement of a general partnership;

(D)   the partnership agreement of a limited partnership;

(E)   the operating agreement of a limited liability company;

[(F) the bylaws of a general cooperative association;]

(G)   the bylaws of a limited cooperative association;

(H)   the governing principles of an unincorporated nonprofit association; and

(I)   the trust instrument of a statutory trust or similar rules of a business trust or common-law business trust.

(30) "Protected agreement" means:

(A)   a record evidencing indebtedness and any related agreement in effect on [the effective date of this [Act]];

(B)   an agreement that is binding on an entity on [the effective date of this [Act]];

(C)   the organic rules of an entity in effect on [the effective date of this [Act]]; or

(D)   an agreement that is binding on any of the governors or interest holders of an entity on [the effective date of this [Act]].

(31) "Public organic record" means the record the filing of which by the [Secretary of State] is required to form an entity and any amendment to or restatement of that record. The term includes:

(A)   the articles of incorporation of a business corporation;

(B)   the articles of incorporation of a nonprofit corporation;

(C)   the certificate of limited partnership of a limited partnership;

(D)   the certificate of organization of a limited liability company;

[(E) the articles of incorporation of a general cooperative association;]

(F)   the articles of organization of a limited cooperative association; and

(G)   the certificate of trust of a statutory trust or similar record of a business trust.

(32) "Registered foreign entity" means a foreign entity that is registered to do business in this state pursuant to a record filed by the [Secretary of State].

(33) "Statement of conversion" means a statement under Section 1145.

(34) "Statement of domestication" means a statement under Section 1155.

(35) "Statement of interest exchange" means a statement under Section 1135.

(36) "Statement of merger" means a statement under Section 1125.

(37) "Surviving entity" means the entity that continues in existence after or is created by a merger.

(38) "Type of entity" means a generic form of entity:

(A)   recognized at common law; or

(B)   formed under an organic law, whether or not some entities formed under that organic law are subject to provisions of that law that create different categories of the form of entity.

§ 1102. Relationship of [Article] to Other Laws

(a)   This [article] does not authorize an act prohibited by, and does not affect the application or requirements of, law other than this [article].

(b)   A transaction effected under this [Act] may not create or impair a right, duty, or obligation of a person under the statutory law of this state relating to a change in control, takeover, business combination, control-share acquisition, or similar transaction involving a domestic merging, acquired, converting, or domesticating business corporation unless:

(1)   if the corporation does not survive the transaction, the transaction satisfies any requirements of the law; or

(2)   if the corporation survives the transaction, the approval of the plan is by a vote of the shareholders or directors which would be sufficient to create or impair the right, duty, or obligation directly under the law.

§ 1103. Required Notice or Approval

(a)   A domestic or foreign entity that is required to give notice to, or obtain the approval of, a governmental agency or officer of this state to be a party to a merger must give the notice or obtain the approval to be a party to an interest exchange, conversion, or domestication.

(b)   Property held for a charitable purpose under the law of this state by a domestic or foreign entity immediately before a transaction under this [article] becomes effective may not, as a result of the transaction, be diverted from the objects for which it was donated, granted, devised, or otherwise transferred unless, to the extent required by or pursuant to the law of this state concerning cy pres or other law dealing with nondiversion of charitable assets, the entity obtains an appropriate order of [the appropriate court] [the Attorney General] specifying the disposition of the property.

(c)   A bequest, devise, gift, grant, or promise contained in a will or other instrument of donation, subscription, or conveyance which is made to a merging entity that is not the surviving entity and which takes effect or remains payable after the merger inures to the surviving entity.

(d)   A trust obligation that would govern property if transferred to a nonsurviving entity applies to property that is transferred to the surviving entity under this section.

Legislative Note: As an alternative to enacting Subsection (a), a state may identify each of its regulatory laws that requires prior approval for a merger of a regulated entity, decide whether regulatory approval should be required for an interest exchange, conversion, or domestication, and make amendments as appropriate to those laws.

As with Subsection (a), an adopting state may choose to amend its various laws with respect to the nondiversion of charitable property to cover the various transactions authorized by this act as an alternative to enacting Subsection (b).

§ 1104. Nonexclusivity

The fact that a transaction under this [article] produces a certain result does not preclude the same result from being accomplished in any other manner permitted by law other than this [article].

§ 1105. Reference to External Facts

A plan may refer to facts ascertainable outside the plan if the manner in which the facts will operate upon the plan is specified in the plan. The facts may include the occurrence of an event or a determination or action by a person, whether or not the event, determination, or action is within the control of a party to the transaction.

§ 1106. Appraisal Rights

An interest holder of a domestic merging, acquired, converting, or domesticating partnership is entitled to contractual appraisal rights in connection with a transaction under this [article] to the extent provided in:

(1)   the partnership's organic rules; or

(2)   the plan.

[§ 1107. Excluded Entities and Transactions

(a)   The following entities may not participate in a transaction under this [article]:

(1)

(2).

(b)   This [article] may not be used to effect a transaction that:

(1)

(2).]

Legislative Note: Subsection (a) may be used by states that have special statutes restricted to the organization of certain types of entities. A common example is banking statutes that prohibit banks from engaging in transactions other than pursuant to those statutes.

Nonprofit entities may participate in transactions under this act with for-profit entities, subject to compliance with Section 1103. If a state desires, however, to exclude entities with a charitable purpose or to exclude other types of entities from the scope of this article, that may be done by referring to those entities in Subsection (a).

Subsection (b) may be used to exclude certain types of transactions governed by more specific statutes. A common example is the conversion of an insurance company from mutual to stock form. There may be other types of transactions that vary greatly among the states.

PART 2
MERGER

§ 1121. Merger Authorized

(a)   By complying with this [part]:

(1)   one or more domestic partnerships may merge with one or more domestic or foreign entities into a domestic or foreign surviving entity; and

(2)   two or more foreign entities may merge into a domestic partnership.

(b)   By complying with the provisions of this [part] applicable to foreign entities, a foreign entity may be a party to a merger under this [part] or may be the surviving entity in such a merger if the merger is authorized by the law of the foreign entity's jurisdiction of formation.

§ 1122. Plan of Merger

(a)   A domestic partnership may become a party to a merger under this [part] by approving a plan of merger. The plan must be in a record and contain:

(1)   as to each merging entity, its name, jurisdiction of formation, and type of entity;

(2)   if the surviving entity is to be created in the merger, a statement to that effect and the entity's name, jurisdiction of formation, and type of entity;

(3)   the manner of converting the interests in each party to the merger into interests, securities, obligations, money, other property, rights to acquire interests or securities, or any combination of the foregoing;

(4)   if the surviving entity exists before the merger, any proposed amendments to:

(A)   its public organic record, if any; or

(B)   its private organic rules that are, or are proposed to be, in a record;

(5)   if the surviving entity is to be created in the merger:

(A)   its proposed public organic record, if any; and

(B)   the full text of its private organic rules that are proposed to be in a record;

(6)   the other terms and conditions of the merger; and

(7)   any other provision required by the law of a merging entity's jurisdiction of formation or the organic rules of a merging entity.

(b)   In addition to the requirements of subsection (a), a plan of merger may contain any other provision not prohibited by law.

§ 1123. Approval of Merger

(a)   A plan of merger is not effective unless it has been approved:

(1)   by a domestic merging partnership, by all the partners of the partnership entitled to vote on or consent to any matter; and

(2)   in a record, by each partner of a domestic merging partnership which will have interest holder liability for debts, obligations, and other liabilities that are incurred after the merger becomes effective, unless:

(A)   the partnership agreement of the partnership provides in a record for the approval of a merger in which some or all of its partners become subject to interest holder liability by the affirmative vote or consent of fewer than all the partners; and

(B) the partner consented in a record to or voted for that provision of the partnership agreement or became a partner after the adoption of that provision.

(b) A merger involving a domestic merging entity that is not a partnership is not effective unless the merger is approved by that entity in accordance with its organic law.

(c) A merger involving a foreign merging entity is not effective unless the merger is approved by the foreign entity in accordance with the law of the foreign entity's jurisdiction of formation.

§ 1124. Amendment or Abandonment of Plan of Merger

(a) A plan of merger may be amended only with the consent of each party to the plan, except as otherwise provided in the plan.

(b) A domestic merging partnership may approve an amendment of a plan of merger:

(1) in the same manner as the plan was approved, if the plan does not provide for the manner in which it may be amended; or

(2) by its partners in the manner provided in the plan, but a partner that was entitled to vote on or consent to approval of the merger is entitled to vote on or consent to any amendment of the plan that will change:

(A) the amount or kind of interests, securities, obligations, money, other property, rights to acquire interests or securities, or any combination of the foregoing, to be received by the interest holders of any party to the plan;

(B) the public organic record, if any, or private organic rules of the surviving entity that will be in effect immediately after the merger be effective, except for changes that do not require approval of the interest holders of the surviving entity under its organic law or organic rules; or

(C) any other terms or conditions of the plan, if the change would adversely affect the partner in any material respect.

(c) After a plan of merger has been approved and before a statement of merger becomes effective, the plan may be abandoned as provided in the plan. Unless prohibited by the plan, a domestic merging partnership may abandon the plan in the same manner as the plan was approved.

(d) If a plan of merger is abandoned after a statement of merger has been delivered to the [Secretary of State] for filing and before the statement becomes effective, a statement of abandonment, signed by a party to the plan, must be delivered to the [Secretary of State] for filing before the statement of merger becomes effective. The statement of abandonment takes effect on filing, and the merger is abandoned and does not become effective. The statement of abandonment must contain:

(1) the name of each party to the plan of merger;

(2) the date on which the statement of merger was filed by the [Secretary of State]; and

(3) a statement that the merger has been abandoned in accordance with this section.

§ 1125. Statement of Merger; Effective Date of Merger

(a) A statement of merger must be signed by each merging entity and delivered to the [Secretary of State] for filing.

(b) A statement of merger must contain:

(1) the name, jurisdiction of formation, and type of entity of each merging entity that is not the surviving entity;

(2) the name, jurisdiction of formation, and type of entity of the surviving entity;

(3)   a statement that the merger was approved by each domestic merging entity, if any, in accordance with this [part] and by each foreign merging entity, if any, in accordance with the law of its jurisdiction of formation;

(4)   if the surviving entity exists before the merger and is a domestic filing entity, any amendment to its public organic record approved as part of the plan of merger;

(5)   if the surviving entity is created by the merger and is a domestic filing entity, its public organic record, as an attachment; and

(6)   if the surviving entity is created by the merger and is a domestic limited liability partnership, its statement of qualification, as an attachment.

(c)   In addition to the requirements of subsection (b), a statement of merger may contain any other provision not prohibited by law.

(d)   If the surviving entity is a domestic entity, its public organic record, if any, must satisfy the requirements of the law of this state, except that the public organic record does not need to be signed.

(e)   A plan of merger that is signed by all the merging entities and meets all the requirements of subsection (b) may be delivered to the [Secretary of State] for filing instead of a statement of merger and on filing has the same effect. If a plan of merger is filed as provided in this subsection, references in this [article] to a statement of merger refer to the plan of merger filed under this subsection.

(f)   If the surviving entity is a domestic partnership, the merger becomes effective when the statement of merger is effective. In all other cases, the merger becomes effective on the later of:

(1)   the date and time provided by the organic law of the surviving entity; and

(2)   when the statement is effective.

§ 1126. Effect of Merger

(a)   When a merger becomes effective:

(1)   the surviving entity continues or comes into existence;

(2)   each merging entity that is not the surviving entity ceases to exist;

(3)   all property of each merging entity vests in the surviving entity without transfer, reversion, or impairment;

(4)   all debts, obligations, and other liabilities of each merging entity are debts, obligations, and other liabilities of the surviving entity;

(5)   except as otherwise provided by law or the plan of merger, all the rights, privileges, immunities, powers, and purposes of each merging entity vest in the surviving entity;

(6)   if the surviving entity exists before the merger:

(A)   all its property continues to be vested in it without transfer, reversion, or impairment;

(B)   it remains subject to all its debts, obligations, and other liabilities; and

(C)   all its rights, privileges, immunities, powers, and purposes continue to be vested in it;

(7)   the name of the surviving entity may be substituted for the name of any merging entity that is a party to any pending action or proceeding;

(8)   if the surviving entity exists before the merger:

(A)   its public organic record, if any, is amended as provided in the statement of merger; and

(B)   its private organic rules that are to be in a record, if any, are amended to the extent provided in the plan of merger;

(9)   if the surviving entity is created by the merger, its private organic rules become effective and:

(A)   if it is a filing entity, its public organic record becomes effective; and

(B)   if it is a limited liability partnership, its statement of qualification becomes effective; and

(10) the interests in each merging entity which are to be converted in the merger are converted, and the interest holders of those interests are entitled only to the rights provided to them under the plan of merger and to any appraisal rights they have under Section 1106 and the merging entity's organic law.

(b)   Except as otherwise provided in the organic law or organic rules of a merging entity, the merger does not give rise to any rights that an interest holder, governor, or third party would have upon a dissolution, liquidation, or winding up of the merging entity.

(c)   When a merger becomes effective, a person that did not have interest holder liability with respect to any of the merging entities and becomes subject to interest holder liability with respect to a domestic entity as a result of the merger has interest holder liability only to the extent provided by the organic law of that entity and only for those debts, obligations, and other liabilities that are incurred after the merger becomes effective.

(d)   When a merger becomes effective, the interest holder liability of a person that ceases to hold an interest in a domestic merging partnership with respect to which the person had interest holder liability is subject to the following rules:

(1)   The merger does not discharge any interest holder liability under this [Act] to the extent the interest holder liability was incurred before the merger became effective.

(2)   The person does not have interest holder liability under this [Act] for any debt, obligation, or other liability that is incurred after the merger becomes effective.

(3)   This [Act] continues to apply to the release, collection, or discharge of any interest holder liability preserved under paragraph (1) as if the merger had not occurred and the surviving entity were the domestic merging entity.

(4)   The person has whatever rights of contribution from any other person as are provided by this [Act], law other than this [Act], or the partnership agreement of the domestic merging partnership with respect to any interest holder liability preserved under paragraph (1) as if the merger had not occurred.

(e)   When a merger has become effective, a foreign entity that is the surviving entity may be served with process in this state for the collection and enforcement of any debts, obligations, or other liabilities of a domestic merging partnership as provided in Section 119.

(f)   When a merger has become effective, the registration to do business in this state of any foreign merging entity that is not the surviving entity is canceled.

PART 3

INTEREST EXCHANGE

§ 1131. Interest Exchange Authorized

(a)   By complying with this [part]:

(1)   a domestic partnership may acquire all of one or more classes or series of interests of another domestic entity or a foreign entity in exchange for interests, securities, obligations,

money, other property, rights to acquire interests or securities, or any combination of the foregoing; or

(2)   all of one or more classes or series of interests of a domestic partnership may be acquired by another domestic entity or a foreign entity in exchange for interests, securities, obligations, money, other property, rights to acquire interests or securities, or any combination of the foregoing.

(b)   By complying with the provisions of this [part] applicable to foreign entities, a foreign entity may be the acquiring or acquired entity in an interest exchange under this [part] if the interest exchange is authorized by the law of the foreign entity's jurisdiction of formation.

(c)   If a protected agreement contains a provision that applies to a merger of a domestic partnership but does not refer to an interest exchange, the provision applies to an interest exchange in which the domestic partnership is the acquired entity as if the interest exchange were a merger until the provision is amended after [the effective date of this [Act]].

§ 1132. Plan of Interest Exchange

(a)   A domestic partnership may be the acquired entity in an interest exchange under this [part] by approving a plan of interest exchange. The plan must be in a record and contain:

(1)   the name of the acquired entity;

(2)   the name, jurisdiction of formation, and type of entity of the acquiring entity;

(3)   the manner of converting the interests in the acquired entity into interests, securities, obligations, money, other property, rights to acquire interests or securities, or any combination of the foregoing;

(4)   any proposed amendments to the partnership agreement that are, or are proposed to be, in a record of the acquired entity;

(5)   the other terms and conditions of the interest exchange; and

(6)   any other provision required by the law of this state or the partnership agreement of the acquired entity.

(b)   In addition to the requirements of subsection (a), a plan of interest exchange may contain any other provision not prohibited by law.

§ 1133. Approval of Interest Exchange

(a)   A plan of interest exchange is not effective unless it has been approved:

(1)   by all the partners of a domestic acquired partnership entitled to vote on or consent to any matter; and

(2)   in a record, by each partner of the domestic acquired partnership that will have interest holder liability for debts, obligations, and other liabilities that are incurred after the interest exchange becomes effective, unless:

(A)   the partnership agreement of the partnership provides in a record for the approval of an interest exchange or a merger in which some or all its partners become subject to interest holder liability by the affirmative vote or consent of fewer than all the partners; and

(B)   the partner consented in a record to or voted for that provision of the partnership agreement or became a partner after the adoption of that provision.

(b)   An interest exchange involving a domestic acquired entity that is not a partnership is not effective unless it is approved by the domestic entity in accordance with its organic law.

(c)   An interest exchange involving a foreign acquired entity is not effective unless it is approved by the foreign entity in accordance with the law of the foreign entity's jurisdiction of formation.

(d)   Except as otherwise provided in its organic law or organic rules, the interest holders of the acquiring entity are not required to approve the interest exchange.

§ 1134. Amendment or Abandonment of Plan of Interest Exchange

(a)   A plan of interest exchange may be amended only with the consent of each party to the plan, except as otherwise provided in the plan.

(b)   A domestic acquired partnership may approve an amendment of a plan of interest exchange:

(1)   in the same manner as the plan was approved, if the plan does not provide for the manner in which it may be amended; or

(2)   by its partners in the manner provided in the plan, but a partner that was entitled to vote on or consent to approval of the interest exchange is entitled to vote on or consent to any amendment of the plan that will change:

(A)   the amount or kind of interests, securities, obligations, money, other property, rights to acquire interests or securities, or any combination of the foregoing, to be received by any of the partners of the acquired partnership under the plan;

(B)   the partnership agreement of the acquired partnership that will be in effect immediately after the interest exchange becomes effective, except for changes that do not require approval of the partners of the acquired partnership under this [Act] or the partnership agreement; or

(C)   any other terms or conditions of the plan, if the change would adversely affect the partner in any material respect.

(c)   After a plan of interest exchange has been approved and before a statement of interest exchange becomes effective, the plan may be abandoned as provided in the plan. Unless prohibited by the plan, a domestic acquired partnership may abandon the plan in the same manner as the plan was approved.

(d)   If a plan of interest exchange is abandoned after a statement of interest exchange has been delivered to the [Secretary of State] for filing and before the statement becomes effective, a statement of abandonment, signed by the acquired partnership, must be delivered to the [Secretary of State] for filing before the statement of interest exchange becomes effective. The statement of abandonment takes effect on filing, and the interest exchange is abandoned and does not become effective. The statement of abandonment must contain:

(1)   the name of the acquired partnership;

(2)   the date on which the statement of interest exchange was filed by the [Secretary of State]; and

(3)   a statement that the interest exchange has been abandoned in accordance with this section.

§ 1135. Statement of Interest Exchange; Effective Date of Interest Exchange

(a)   A statement of interest exchange must be signed by a domestic acquired partnership and delivered to the [Secretary of State] for filing.

(b)   A statement of interest exchange must contain:

(1)   the name of the acquired partnership;

(2)   the name, jurisdiction of formation, and type of entity of the acquiring entity; and

(3) a statement that the plan of interest exchange was approved by the acquired partnership in accordance with this [part].

(c) In addition to the requirements of subsection (b), a statement of interest exchange may contain any other provision not prohibited by law.

(d) A plan of interest exchange that is signed by a domestic acquired partnership and meets all the requirements of subsection (b) may be delivered to the [Secretary of State] for filing instead of a statement of interest exchange and on filing has the same effect. If a plan of interest exchange is filed as provided in this subsection, references in this [article] to a statement of interest exchange refer to the plan of interest exchange filed under this subsection.

(e) An interest exchange becomes effective when the statement of interest exchange is effective.

§ 1136. Effect of Interest Exchange

(a) When an interest exchange in which the acquired entity is a domestic partnership becomes effective:

(1) the interests in the acquired partnership which are the subject of the interest exchange are converted, and the partners holding those interests are entitled only to the rights provided to them under the plan of interest exchange and to any appraisal rights they have under Section 1106;

(2) the acquiring entity becomes the interest holder of the interests in the acquired partnership stated in the plan of interest exchange to be acquired by the acquiring entity; and

(3) the provisions of the partnership agreement of the acquired partnership that are to be in a record, if any, are amended to the extent provided in the plan of interest exchange.

(b) Except as otherwise provided in the partnership agreement of a domestic acquired partnership, the interest exchange does not give rise to any rights that a partner or third party would have upon a dissolution, liquidation, or winding up of the acquired partnership.

(c) When an interest exchange becomes effective, a person that did not have interest holder liability with respect to a domestic acquired partnership and becomes subject to interest holder liability with respect to a domestic entity as a result of the interest exchange has interest holder liability only to the extent provided by the organic law of the entity and only for those debts, obligations, and other liabilities that are incurred after the interest exchange becomes effective.

(d) When an interest exchange becomes effective, the interest holder liability of a person that ceases to hold an interest in a domestic acquired partnership with respect to which the person had interest holder liability is subject to the following rules:

(1) The interest exchange does not discharge any interest holder liability under this [Act] to the extent the interest holder liability was incurred before the interest exchange became effective.

(2) The person does not have interest holder liability under this [Act] for any debt, obligation, or other liability that is incurred after the interest exchange becomes effective.

(3) This [Act] continues to apply to the release, collection, or discharge of any interest holder liability preserved under paragraph (1) as if the interest exchange had not occurred.

(4) The person has whatever rights of contribution from any other person as are provided by this [Act], law other than this [Act], or the partnership agreement of the domestic acquired partnership with respect to any interest holder liability preserved under paragraph (1) as if the interest exchange had not occurred.

PART 4

CONVERSION

§ 1141. Conversion Authorized

(a)   By complying with this [part], a domestic partnership may become:

(1)   a domestic entity that is a different type of entity; or

(2)   a foreign entity that is a different type of entity, if the conversion is authorized by the law of the foreign entity's jurisdiction of formation.

(b)   By complying with the provisions of this [part] applicable to foreign entities, a foreign entity that is not a foreign partnership may become a domestic partnership if the conversion is authorized by the law of the foreign entity's jurisdiction of formation.

(c)   If a protected agreement contains a provision that applies to a merger of a domestic partnership but does not refer to a conversion, the provision applies to a conversion of the partnership as if the conversion were a merger until the provision is amended after [the effective date of this [Act]].

§ 1142. Plan of Conversion

(a)   A domestic partnership may convert to a different type of entity under this [part] by approving a plan of conversion. The plan must be in a record and contain:

(1)   the name of the converting partnership;

(2)   the name, jurisdiction of formation, and type of entity of the converted entity;

(3)   the manner of converting the interests in the converting partnership into interests, securities, obligations, money, other property, rights to acquire interests or securities, or any combination of the foregoing;

(4)   the proposed public organic record of the converted entity if it will be a filing entity;

(5)   the full text of the private organic rules of the converted entity which are proposed to be in a record;

(6)   the other terms and conditions of the conversion; and

(7)   any other provision required by the law of this state or the partnership agreement of the converting partnership.

(b)   In addition to the requirements of subsection (a), a plan of conversion may contain any other provision not prohibited by law.

§ 1143. Approval of Conversion

(a)   A plan of conversion is not effective unless it has been approved:

(1)   by a domestic converting partnership, by all the partners of the partnership entitled to vote on or consent to any matter; and

(2)   in a record, by each partner of a domestic converting partnership which will have interest holder liability for debts, obligations, and other liabilities that are incurred after the conversion becomes effective, unless:

(A)   the partnership agreement of the partnership provides in a record for the approval of a conversion or a merger in which some or all of its partners become subject to interest holder liability by the affirmative vote or consent of fewer than all the partners; and

(B)   the partner voted for or consented in a record to that provision of the partnership agreement or became a partner after the adoption of that provision.

(b) A conversion involving a domestic converting entity that is not a partnership is not effective unless it is approved by the domestic converting entity in accordance with its organic law.

(c) A conversion of a foreign converting entity is not effective unless it is approved by the foreign entity in accordance with the law of the foreign entity's jurisdiction of formation.

§ 1144. Amendment or Abandonment of Plan of Conversion

(a) A plan of conversion of a domestic converting partnership may be amended:

(1) in the same manner as the plan was approved, if the plan does not provide for the manner in which it may be amended; or

(2) by its partners in the manner provided in the plan, but a partner that was entitled to vote on or consent to approval of the conversion is entitled to vote on or consent to any amendment of the plan that will change:

(A) the amount or kind of interests, securities, obligations, money, other property, rights to acquire interests or securities, or any combination of the foregoing, to be received by any of the partners of the converting partnership under the plan;

(B) the public organic record, if any, or private organic rules of the converted entity which will be in effect immediately after the conversion becomes effective, except for changes that do not require approval of the interest holders of the converted entity under its organic law or organic rules; or

(C) any other terms or conditions of the plan, if the change would adversely affect the partner in any material respect.

(b) After a plan of conversion has been approved by a domestic converting partnership and before a statement of conversion becomes effective, the plan may be abandoned as provided in the plan. Unless prohibited by the plan, a domestic converting partnership may abandon the plan in the same manner as the plan was approved.

(c) If a plan of conversion is abandoned after a statement of conversion has been delivered to the [Secretary of State] for filing and before the statement becomes effective, a statement of abandonment, signed by the converting entity, must be delivered to the [Secretary of State] for filing before the statement of conversion becomes effective. The statement of abandonment takes effect on filing, and the conversion is abandoned and does not become effective. The statement of abandonment must contain:

(1) the name of the converting partnership;

(2) the date on which the statement of conversion was filed by the [Secretary of State]; and

(3) a statement that the conversion has been abandoned in accordance with this section.

§ 1145. Statement of Conversion; Effective Date of Conversion

(a) A statement of conversion must be signed by the converting entity and delivered to the [Secretary of State] for filing.

(b) A statement of conversion must contain:

(1) the name, jurisdiction of formation, and type of entity of the converting entity;

(2) the name, jurisdiction of formation, and type of entity of the converted entity;

(3) if the converting entity is a domestic partnership, a statement that the plan of conversion was approved in accordance with this [part] or, if the converting entity is a foreign entity, a statement that the conversion was approved by the foreign entity in accordance with the law of its jurisdiction of formation;

(4) if the converted entity is a domestic filing entity, its public organic record, as an attachment; and

(5) if the converted entity is a domestic limited liability partnership, its statement of qualification, as an attachment.

(c) In addition to the requirements of subsection (b), a statement of conversion may contain any other provision not prohibited by law.

(d) If the converted entity is a domestic entity, its public organic record, if any, must satisfy the requirements of the law of this state, except that the public organic record does not need to be signed.

(e) A plan of conversion that is signed by a domestic converting partnership and meets all the requirements of subsection (b) may be delivered to the [Secretary of State] for filing instead of a statement of conversion and on filing has the same effect. If a plan of conversion is filed as provided in this subsection, references in this [article] to a statement of conversion refer to the plan of conversion filed under this subsection.

(f) If the converted entity is a domestic partnership, the conversion becomes effective when the statement of conversion is effective. In all other cases, the conversion becomes effective on the later of:

(1) the date and time provided by the organic law of the converted entity; and

(2) when the statement is effective.

§ 1146. Effect of Conversion

(a) When a conversion becomes effective:

(1) the converted entity is:

(A) organized under and subject to the organic law of the converted entity; and

(B) the same entity without interruption as the converting entity;

(2) all property of the converting entity continues to be vested in the converted entity without transfer, reversion, or impairment;

(3) all debts, obligations, and other liabilities of the converting entity continue as debts, obligations, and other liabilities of the converted entity;

(4) except as otherwise provided by law or the plan of conversion, all the rights, privileges, immunities, powers, and purposes of the converting entity remain in the converted entity;

(5) the name of the converted entity may be substituted for the name of the converting entity in any pending action or proceeding;

(6) if the converted entity is a limited liability partnership, its statement of qualification becomes effective;

(7) the provisions of the partnership agreement of the converted entity which are to be in a record, if any, approved as part of the plan of conversion become effective; and

(8) the interests in the converting entity are converted, and the interest holders of the converting entity are entitled only to the rights provided to them under the plan of conversion and to any appraisal rights they have under Section 1106.

(b) Except as otherwise provided in the partnership agreement of a domestic converting partnership, the conversion does not give rise to any rights that a partner or third party would have upon a dissolution, liquidation, or winding up of the converting entity.

(c) When a conversion becomes effective, a person that did not have interest holder liability with respect to the converting entity and becomes subject to interest holder liability with respect to a domestic entity as a result of the conversion has interest holder liability only to the extent provided by the organic law of the entity and only for those debts, obligations, and other liabilities that are incurred after the conversion becomes effective.

(d)　When a conversion becomes effective, the interest holder liability of a person that ceases to hold an interest in a domestic converting partnership with respect to which the person had interest holder liability is subject to the following rules:

(1)　The conversion does not discharge any interest holder liability under this [Act] to the extent the interest holder liability was incurred before the conversion became effective.

(2)　The person does not have interest holder liability under this [Act] for any debt, obligation, or other liability that is incurred after the conversion becomes effective.

(3)　This [Act] continues to apply to the release, collection, or discharge of any interest holder liability preserved under paragraph (1) as if the conversion had not occurred.

(4)　The person has whatever rights of contribution from any other person as are provided by this [Act], law other than this [Act], or the organic rules of the converting entity with respect to any interest holder liability preserved under paragraph (1) as if the conversion had not occurred.

(e)　When a conversion has become effective, a foreign entity that is the converted entity may be served with process in this state for the collection and enforcement of any of its debts, obligations, and other liabilities as provided in Section 119.

(f)　If the converting entity is a registered foreign entity, its registration to do business in this state is canceled when the conversion becomes effective.

(g)　A conversion does not require the entity to wind up its affairs and does not constitute or cause the dissolution of the entity.

PART 5
DOMESTICATION

§ 1151. Domestication Authorized

(a)　By complying with this [part], a domestic limited liability partnership may become a foreign limited liability partnership if the domestication is authorized by the law of the foreign jurisdiction.

(b)　By complying with the provisions of this [part] applicable to foreign limited liability partnerships, a foreign limited liability partnership may become a domestic limited liability partnership if the domestication is authorized by the law of the foreign limited liability partnership's jurisdiction of formation.

(c)　If a protected agreement contains a provision that applies to a merger of a domestic limited liability partnership but does not refer to a domestication, the provision applies to a domestication of the limited liability partnership as if the domestication were a merger until the provision is amended after [the effective date of this [Act]].

§ 1152. Plan of Domestication

(a)　A domestic limited liability partnership may become a foreign limited liability partnership in a domestication by approving a plan of domestication. The plan must be in a record and contain:

(1)　the name of the domesticating limited liability partnership;

(2)　the name and jurisdiction of formation of the domesticated limited liability partnership;

(3)　the manner of converting the interests in the domesticating limited liability partnership into interests, securities, obligations, money, other property, rights to acquire interests or securities, or any combination of the foregoing;

(4) the proposed statement of qualification of the domesticated limited liability partnership;

(5) the full text of the provisions of the partnership agreement of the domesticated limited liability partnership that are proposed to be in a record;

(6) the other terms and conditions of the domestication; and

(7) any other provision required by the law of this state or the partnership agreement of the domesticating limited liability partnership.

(b) In addition to the requirements of subsection (a), a plan of domestication may contain any other provision not prohibited by law.

§ 1153. Approval of Domestication

(a) A plan of domestication of a domestic domesticating limited liability partnership is not effective unless it has been approved:

(1) by all the partners entitled to vote on or consent to any matter; and

(2) in a record, by each partner that will have interest holder liability for debts, obligations, and other liabilities that are incurred after the domestication becomes effective, unless:

(A) the partnership agreement of the domesticating partnership in a record provides for the approval of a domestication or merger in which some or all of its partners become subject to interest holder liability by the affirmative vote or consent of fewer than all the partners; and

(B) the partner voted for or consented in a record to that provision of the partnership agreement or became a partner after the adoption of that provision.

(b) A domestication of a foreign domesticating limited liability partnership is not effective unless it is approved in accordance with the law of the foreign limited liability partnership's jurisdiction of formation.

§ 1154. Amendment or Abandonment of Plan of Domestication

(a) A plan of domestication of a domestic domesticating limited liability partnership may be amended:

(1) in the same manner as the plan was approved, if the plan does not provide for the manner in which it may be amended; or

(2) by its partners in the manner provided in the plan, but a partner that was entitled to vote on or consent to approval of the domestication is entitled to vote on or consent to any amendment of the plan that will change:

(A) the amount or kind of interests, securities, obligations, money, other property, rights to acquire interests or securities, or any combination of the foregoing, to be received by any of the partners of the domesticating limited liability partnership under the plan;

(B) the partnership agreement of the domesticated limited liability partnership that will be in effect immediately after the domestication becomes effective, except for changes that do not require approval of the partners of the domesticated limited liability partnership under its organic law or partnership agreement; or

(C) any other terms or conditions of the plan, if the change would adversely affect the partner in any material respect.

(b) After a plan of domestication has been approved by a domestic domesticating limited liability partnership and before a statement of domestication becomes effective, the plan may be abandoned as provided in the plan. Unless prohibited by the plan, a domestic domesticating limited liability partnership may abandon the plan in the same manner as the plan was approved.

(c)   If a plan of domestication is abandoned after a statement of domestication has been delivered to the [Secretary of State] for filing and before the statement becomes effective, a statement of abandonment, signed by the domesticating limited liability partnership, must be delivered to the [Secretary of State] for filing before the statement of domestication becomes effective. The statement of abandonment takes effect on filing, and the domestication is abandoned and does not become effective. The statement of abandonment must contain:

     (1)   the name of the domesticating limited liability partnership;

     (2)   the date on which the statement of domestication was filed by the [Secretary of State]; and

     (3)   a statement that the domestication has been abandoned in accordance with this section.

§ 1155. Statement of Domestication; Effective Date of Domestication

(a)   A statement of domestication must be signed by the domesticating limited liability partnership and delivered to the [Secretary of State] for filing.

(b)   A statement of domestication must contain:

     (1)   the name and jurisdiction of formation of the domesticating limited liability partnership;

     (2)   the name and jurisdiction of formation of the domesticated limited liability partnership;

     (3)   if the domesticating limited liability partnership is a domestic limited liability partnership, a statement that the plan of domestication was approved in accordance with this [part] or, if the domesticating limited liability partnership is a foreign limited liability partnership, a statement that the domestication was approved in accordance with the law of its jurisdiction of formation; and

     (4)   the statement of qualification of the domesticated limited liability partnership, as an attachment.

(c)   In addition to the requirements of subsection (b), a statement of domestication may contain any other provision not prohibited by law.

(d)   The statement of qualification of a domesticated domestic limited liability partnership must satisfy the requirements of this [Act], but the statement does not need to be signed.

(e)   A plan of domestication that is signed by a domesticating domestic limited liability partnership and meets all the requirements of subsection (b) may be delivered to the [Secretary of State] for filing instead of a statement of domestication and on filing has the same effect. If a plan of domestication is filed as provided in this subsection, references in this [article] to a statement of domestication refer to the plan of domestication filed under this subsection.

(f)   If the domesticated entity is a domestic partnership, the domestication becomes effective when the statement of domestication is effective. If the domesticated entity is a foreign partnership, the domestication becomes effective on the later of:

     (1)   the date and time provided in the organic law of the domesticated entity; and

     (2)   when the statement is effective.

§ 1156. Effect of Domestication

(a)   When a domestication becomes effective:

     (1)   the domesticated entity is:

  (A) organized under and subject to the organic law of the domesticated entity; and

  (B) the same entity without interruption as the domesticating entity;

 (2) all property of the domesticating entity continues to be vested in the domesticated entity without transfer, reversion, or impairment;

 (3) all debts, obligations, and other liabilities of the domesticating entity continue as debts, obligations, and other liabilities of the domesticated entity;

 (4) except as otherwise provided by law or the plan of domestication, all the rights, privileges, immunities, powers, and purposes of the domesticating entity remain in the domesticated entity;

 (5) the name of the domesticated entity may be substituted for the name of the domesticating entity in any pending action or proceeding;

 (6) the statement of qualification of the domesticated entity becomes effective;

 (7) the provisions of the partnership agreement of the domesticated entity that are to be in a record, if any, approved as part of the plan of domestication become effective; and

 (8) the interests in the domesticating entity are converted to the extent and as approved in connection with the domestication, and the partners of the domesticating entity are entitled only to the rights provided to them under the plan of domestication and to any appraisal rights they have under Section 1106.

(b) Except as otherwise provided in the organic law or partnership agreement of the domesticating limited liability partnership, the domestication does not give rise to any rights that a partner or third party would otherwise have upon a dissolution, liquidation, or winding up of the domesticating partnership.

(c) When a domestication becomes effective, a person that did not have interest holder liability with respect to the domesticating limited liability partnership and becomes subject to interest holder liability with respect to a domestic limited liability partnership as a result of the domestication has interest holder liability only to the extent provided by this [Act] and only for those debts, obligations, and other liabilities that are incurred after the domestication becomes effective.

(d) When a domestication becomes effective, the interest holder liability of a person that ceases to hold an interest in a domestic domesticating limited liability partnership with respect to which the person had interest holder liability is subject to the following rules:

 (1) The domestication does not discharge any interest holder liability under this [Act] to the extent the interest holder liability was incurred before the domestication became effective.

 (2) A person does not have interest holder liability under this [Act] for any debt, obligation, or other liability that is incurred after the domestication becomes effective.

 (3) This [Act] continues to apply to the release, collection, or discharge of any interest holder liability preserved under paragraph (1) as if the domestication had not occurred.

 (4) A person has whatever rights of contribution from any other person as are provided by this [Act], law other than this [Act], or the partnership agreement of the domestic domesticating limited liability partnership with respect to any interest holder liability preserved under paragraph (1) as if the domestication had not occurred.

(e) When a domestication becomes effective, a foreign limited liability partnership that is the domesticated partnership may be served with process in this state for the collection and enforcement of any of its debts, obligations, and other liabilities as provided in Section 119.

(f) If the domesticating limited liability partnership is a registered foreign entity, the registration of the partnership is canceled when the domestication becomes effective.

(g)　A domestication does not require a domestic domesticating limited liability partnership to wind up its business and does not constitute or cause the dissolution of the partnership.

ARTICLE 12
MISCELLANEOUS PROVISIONS

§ 1201. Uniformity of Application and Construction

In applying and construing this uniform act, consideration must be given to the need to promote uniformity of the law with respect to its subject matter among states that enact it.

§ 1202. Relation to Electronic Signatures in Global and National Commerce Act

This [Act] modifies, limits, and supersedes the Electronic Signatures in Global and National Commerce Act, 15 U.S.C. Section 7001 et seq., but does not modify, limit, or supersede Section 101(c) of that act, 15 U.S.C. Section 7001(c), or authorize electronic delivery of any of the notices described in Section 103(b) of that act, 15 U.S.C. Section 7003(b).

§ 1203. Savings Clause

This [Act] does not affect an action commenced, proceeding brought, or right accrued before [the effective date of this [Act]].

[§ 1204. Severability Clause

If any provision of this [Act] or its application to any person or circumstance is held invalid, the invalidity does not affect other provisions or applications of this [Act] which can be given effect without the invalid provision or application, and to this end the provisions of this [Act] are severable.]

Legislative Note: Include this section only if this state lacks a general severability statute or decision by the highest court of this state stating a general rule of severability.

§ 1205. Repeals

The following are repealed:

(1)　[the state partnership act as [amended, and as] in effect immediately before [the effective date of this [Act]]].

(2)　. . . .

(3)　. . . .

§ 1206. Effective Date

This [Act] takes effect . . . .

UNIFORM LIMITED PARTNERSHIP ACT (2001) ("RULPA")

WITH PREFATORY NOTE

Table of Sections

ARTICLE 1. GENERAL PROVISIONS

ARTICLE 2. FORMATION; CERTIFICATE OF LIMITED PARTNERSHIP AND OTHER FILINGS

UNIFORM LIMITED PARTNERSHIP ACT (2001)

ARTICLE 3. LIMITED PARTNERS

ARTICLE 4. GENERAL PARTNERS

ARTICLE 5. CONTRIBUTIONS AND DISTRIBUTIONS

ARTICLE 6. DISSOCIATION

ARTICLE 7. TRANSFERABLE INTERESTS AND RIGHTS OF TRANSFEREES AND CREDITORS

ARTICLE 8. DISSOLUTION AND WINDING UP

UNIFORM LIMITED PARTNERSHIP ACT (2001)

UNIFORM LIMITED PARTNERSHIP ACT (2001)

[PART] 3. INTEREST EXCHANGE

[PART] 4. CONVERSION

[PART] 5. DOMESTICATION

ARTICLE 12. MISCELLANEOUS PROVISIONS

PREFATORY NOTE

The Act's Overall Approach

The new Limited Partnership Act is a "stand alone" act, "de-linked" from both the original general partnership act ("UPA") and the Revised Uniform Partnership Act ("RUPA"). To be able to stand alone, the Limited Partnership incorporates many provisions from RUPA and some from the Uniform Limited Liability Company Act ("ULLCA"). As a result, the new Act is far longer and more complex than its immediate predecessor, the Revised Uniform Limited Partnership Act ("RULPA").

The new Act has been drafted for a world in which limited liability partnerships and limited liability companies can meet many of the needs formerly met by limited partnerships. This Act therefore targets two types of enterprises that seem largely beyond the scope of LLPs and LLCs: (i) sophisticated, manager-entrenched commercial deals whose participants commit for the long term, and (ii) estate planning arrangements (family limited partnerships). This Act accordingly assumes that, more often than not, people utilizing it will want:

- strong centralized management, strongly entrenched, and

- passive investors with little control over or right to exit the entity

UNIFORM LIMITED PARTNERSHIP ACT (2001)

The Act's rules, and particularly its default rules, have been designed to reflect these assumptions.

The Decision to "De-Link" and Create a Stand Alone Act

Unlike this Act, RULPA is not a stand-alone statute. RULPA was drafted to rest on and link to the UPA. RULPA Section 1105 states that "In any case not provided for in this [Act] the provisions of the Uniform Partnership Act govern." UPA Section 6(2) in turn provides that "this Act shall apply to limited partnerships except in so far as the statutes relating to such partnerships are inconsistent herewith." More particularly, RULPA Section 403 defines the rights, powers, restrictions and liabilities of a "general partner of a limited partnership" by equating them to the rights, powers, restrictions and liabilities of "a partner in a partnership without limited partners."

This arrangement has not been completely satisfactory, because the consequences of linkage are not always clear. *See, e.g., Frye v. Manacare Ltd.*, 431 So.2d 181, 183–84 (Fla. Dist. Ct. App. 1983) (applying UPA Section 42 in favor of a limited partner), *Porter v. Barnhouse*, 354 N.W.2d 227, 232–33 (Iowa 1984) (declining to apply UPA Section 42 in favor of a limited partner) and *Baltzell-Wolfe Agencies, Inc. v. Car Wash Investments No. 1, Ltd.*, 389 N.E.2d 517, 518–20 (Ohio App. 1978) (holding that neither the specific provisions of the general partnership statute nor those of the limited partnership statute determined the liability of a person who had withdrawn as general partner of a limited partnership). Moreover, in some instances the "not inconsistent" rules of the UPA can be inappropriate for the fundamentally different relations involved in a limited partnership.

In any event, the promulgation of RUPA unsettled matters. RUPA differs substantially from the UPA, and the drafters of RUPA expressly declined to decide whether RUPA provides a suitable base and link for the limited partnership statute. According to RUPA's Prefatory Note:

> Partnership law no longer governs limited partnerships pursuant to the provisions of RUPA itself. First, limited partnerships are not "partnerships" within the RUPA definition. Second, UPA Section 6(2), which provides that the UPA governs limited partnerships in cases not provided for in the Uniform Limited Partnership Act (1976) (1985) ("RULPA") has been deleted. No substantive change in result is intended, however. Section 1105 of RULPA already provides that the UPA governs in any case not provided for in RULPA, and thus the express linkage in RUPA is unnecessary. Structurally, it is more appropriately left to RULPA to determine the applicability of RUPA to limited partnerships. It is contemplated that the Conference will review the linkage question carefully, although no changes in RULPA may be necessary despite the many changes in RUPA.

The linkage question was the first major issue considered and decided by this Act's Drafting Committee. Since the Conference has recommended the repeal of the UPA, it made no sense to recommend retaining the UPA as the base and link for a revised or new limited partnership act. The Drafting Committee therefore had to choose between recommending linkage to the new general partnership act (i.e., RUPA) or recommending de-linking and a stand-alone act.

The Committee saw several substantial advantages to de-linking. A stand-alone statute would:

- be more convenient, providing a single, self-contained source of statutory authority for issues pertaining to limited partnerships;

- eliminate confusion as to which issues were solely subject to the limited partnership act and which required reference (i.e., linkage) to the general partnership act; and

- rationalize future case law, by ending the automatic link between the cases concerning partners in a general partnership and issues pertaining to general partners in a limited partnership.

Thus, a stand-alone act seemed likely to promote efficiency, clarity, and coherence in the law of limited partnerships.

In contrast, recommending linkage would have required the Drafting Committee to (1) consider each provision of RUPA and determine whether the provision addressed a matter provided for in RULPA; (2) for each RUPA provision which addressed a matter not provided for in RULPA, determine whether the provision stated an appropriate rule for limited partnerships; and (3) for each matter addressed both by RUPA and RULPA, determine whether RUPA or RULPA stated the better rule for limited partnerships.

That approach was unsatisfactory for at least two reasons. No matter how exhaustive the Drafting Committee's analysis might be, the Committee could not guarantee that courts and practitioners would reach the same conclusions. Therefore, in at least some situations linkage would have produced ambiguity. In addition, the Drafting Committee could not guarantee that all currently appropriate links would remain appropriate as courts begin to apply and interpret RUPA. Even if the Committee recommended linkage, RUPA was destined to be interpreted primarily in the context of general partnerships. Those interpretations might not make sense for limited partnership law, because the modern limited partnership involves fundamentally different relations than those involved in "the small, often informal, partnership" that is "[t]he primary focus of RUPA." RUPA, Prefatory Note.

The Drafting Committee therefore decided to draft and recommend a stand-alone act.

Availability of LLLP Status

Following the example of a growing number of States, this Act provides for limited liability limited partnerships. In a limited liability limited partnership ("LLLP"), no partner "whether general or limited" is liable on account of partner status for the limited partnership's obligations. Both general and limited partners benefit from a full, status-based liability shield that is equivalent to the shield enjoyed by corporate shareholders, LLC members, and partners in an LLP.

This Act is designed to serve preexisting limited partnerships as well as limited partnerships formed after the Act's enactment. Most of those preexisting limited partnership will not be LLLPs, and accordingly the Act does not prefer or presume LLLP status. Instead, the Act makes LLLP status available through a simple statement in the certificate of limited partnership. See Sections 102(9), 201(a)(4) and 404(c).

Liability Shield for Limited Partners

RULPA provides only a restricted liability shield for limited partners. The shield is at risk for any limited partner who "participates in the control of the business." RULPA Section 303(a). Although this "control rule" is subject to a lengthy list of safe harbors, RULPA Section 303(b), in a world with LLPs, LLCs and, most importantly, LLLPs, the rule is an anachronism. This Act therefore eliminates the control rule and provides a full, status-based shield against limited partner liability for entity obligations. The shield applies whether or not the limited partnership is an LLLP. See Section 303.

Transition Issues

Following RUPA's example, this Act provides (i) an effective date, after which all newly formed limited partnerships are subject to this Act; (ii) an optional period, during which limited partnerships formed under a predecessor statute may elect to become subject to this Act; and (iii) a mandatory date, on which all preexisting limited partnerships become subject to this Act by operation of law.

A few provisions of this Act differ so substantially from prior law that they should not apply automatically to a preexisting limited partnership. Section 1206(c) lists these provisions and states that each remains inapplicable to a preexisting limited partnership, unless the limited partnership elects for the provision to apply.

Comparison of RULPA and this Act

The following table compares some of the major characteristics of RULPA and this Act. In most instances, the rules involved are "default" rules—i.e., subject to change by the partnership agreement.

UNIFORM LIMITED PARTNERSHIP ACT (2001)

Characteristic	RULPA	This Act
relationship to general partnership act	linked, Sections 1105, 403; UPA Section 6(2)	de-linked (but many RUPA provisions incorporated)
permitted purposes	subject to any specified exceptions, "any business that a partnership without limited partners may carry on," Section 106	any lawful purpose, Section 104(b)
constructive notice via publicly filed documents	only that limited partnership exists and that designated general partners are general partners, Section 208	RULPA constructive notice provisions carried forward, Section 103(c), plus constructive notice, 90 days after appropriate filing, of: general partner dissociation and of limited partnership dissolution, termination, merger and conversion, Section 103(d)
duration	specified in certificate of limited partnership, Section 201(a)(4)	perpetual, Section 104(c); subject to change in partnership agreement
use of limited partner name in entity name	prohibited, except in unusual circumstances, Section 102(2)	permitted, Section 108(a)
annual report	none	required, Section 210
limited partner liability for entity debts	none unless limited partner "participates in the control of the business" and person "transact[s] business with the limited partnership reasonably believing . . . that the limited partner is a general partner," Section 303(a); safe harbor lists many activities that do not constitute participating in the control of the business, Section 303(b)	none, regardless of whether the limited partnership is an LLLP, "even if the limited partner participates in the management and control of the limited partnership," Section 303
limited partner duties	none specified	no fiduciary duties "solely by reason of being a limited partner," Section 305(a); each limited partner is obliged to "discharge duties . . . and exercise rights consistently with the obligation of good faith and fair dealing," Section 305(b)
partner access to information— required records/information	all partners have right of access; no requirement of good cause; Act does not state whether partnership agreement may limit access; Sections 105(b) and 305(1)	list of required information expanded slightly; Act expressly states that partner does not have to show good cause; Sections 304(a), 407(a); however, the partnership agreement may set reasonable restrictions on access to and use of required information, Section 110(b)(4), and limited partnership

		may impose reasonable restrictions on the use of information, Sections 304(g) and 407(f)
partner access to information—other information	limited partners have the right to obtain other relevant information "upon reasonable demand," Section 305(2); general partner rights linked to general partnership act, Section 403	for limited partners, RULPA approach essentially carried forward, with procedures and standards for making a reasonable demand stated in greater detail, plus requirement that limited partnership supply known material information when limited partner consent sought, Section 304; general partner access rights made explicit, following ULLCA and RUPA, including obligation of limited partnership and general partners to volunteer certain information, Section 407; access rights provided for former partners, Sections 304 and 407
general partner liability for entity debts	complete, automatic and formally inescapable, Section 403(b) (n.b.—in practice, most modern limited partnerships have used a general partner that has its own liability shield; e.g., a corporation or limited liability company)	LLLP status available via a simple statement in the certificate of limited partnership, Sections 102(9), 201(a)(4); LLLP status provides a full liability shield to all general partners, Section 404(c); if the limited partnership is not an LLLP, general partners are liable just as under RULPA, Section 404(a)
general partner duties	linked to duties of partners in a general partnership, Section 403	RUPA general partner duties imported, Section 408; general partner's non-compete duty continues during winding up, Section 408(b)(3)
allocation of profits, losses and distributions	provides separately for sharing of profits and losses, Section 503, and for sharing of distributions, Section 504; allocates each according to contributions made and not returned	eliminates as unnecessary the allocation rule for profits and losses; allocates distributions according to contributions made, Section 503 (n.b.—in the default mode, the Act's formulation produces the same result as RULPA formulation)
partner liability for distributions	recapture liability if distribution involved "the return of . . . contribution"; one year recapture liability if distribution rightful, Section 608(a); six year recapture liability if wrongful, Section 608(b)	following ULLCA Sections 406 and 407, the Act adopts the RMBCA approach to improper distributions, Sections 508 and 509
limited partner voluntary dissociation	theoretically, limited partner may withdraw on six months' notice unless partnership	no "right to dissociate as a limited partner before the termination of the limited partnership," Section

	agreement specifies a term for the limited partnership or withdrawal events for limited partner, Section 603; practically, virtually every partnership agreement specifies a term, thereby eliminating the right to withdraw (n.b.—due to estate planning concerns, several States have amended RULPA to prohibit limited partner withdrawal unless otherwise provided in the partnership agreement)	601(a); power to dissociate expressly recognized, Section 601(b)(1), but can be eliminated by the partnership agreement
limited partner involuntary dissociation	not addressed	lengthy list of causes, Section 601(b), taken with some modification from RUPA
limited partner dissociation—payout	"fair value . . . based upon [the partner's] right to share in distributions," Section 604	no payout; person becomes transferee of its own transferable interest, Section 602(3)
general partner voluntary dissociation	right exists unless otherwise provided in partnership agreement, Section 602; power exists regardless of partnership agreement, Section 602	RULPA rule carried forward, although phrased differently, Section 604(a); dissociation before termination of the limited partnership is defined as wrongful, Section 604(b)(2)
general partner involuntary dissociation	Section 402 lists causes	following RUPA, Section 603 expands the list of causes, including expulsion by court order, Section 603(5)
general partner dissociation—payout	"fair value . . . based upon [the partner's] right to share in distributions," Section 604, subject to offset for damages caused by wrongful withdrawal, Section 602	no payout; person becomes transferee of its own transferable interest, Section 605(5)
transfer of partner interest—nomenclature	"Assignment of Partnership Interest," Section 702	"Transfer of Partner's Transferable Interest," Section 702
transfer of partner interest—substance	economic rights fully transferable, but management rights and partner status are not transferable, Section 702	same rule, but Sections 701 and 702 follow RUPA's more detailed and less oblique formulation
rights of creditor of partner	limited to charging order, Section 703	essentially the same rule, but, following RUPA and ULLCA, the Act has a more elaborate provision that expressly extends to creditors of transferees, Section 703
dissolution by partner consent	requires unanimous written consent, Section 801(3)	requires consent of "all general partners and of limited partners

		owning a majority of the rights to receive distributions as limited partners at the time the consent is to be effective," Section 801(2)
dissolution following dissociation of a general partner	occurs automatically unless all partners agree to continue the business and, if there is no remaining general partner, to appoint a replacement general partner, Section 801(4)	if at least one general partner remains, no dissolution unless "within 90 days after the dissociation . . . partners owning a majority of the rights to receive distributions as partners" consent to dissolve the limited partnership; Section 801(3)(A); if no general partner remains, dissolution occurs upon the passage of 90 days after the dissociation, unless before that deadline limited partners owning a majority of the rights to receive distributions owned by limited partners consent to continue the business and admit at least one new general partner and a new general partner is admitted, Section 801(3)(B)
filings related to entity termination	certificate of limited partnership to be cancelled when limited partnership dissolves and begins winding up, Section 203	limited partnership may amend certificate to indicate dissolution, Section 803(b)(1), and may file statement of termination indicating that winding up has been completed and the limited partnership is terminated, Section 203
procedures for barring claims against dissolved limited partnership	none	following ULLCA Sections 807 and 808, the Act adopts the RMBCA approach providing for giving notice and barring claims, Sections 806 and 807
conversions and mergers	no provision	Article 11 permits conversions to and from and mergers with any "organization," defined as "a general partnership, including a limited liability partnership; limited partnership, including a limited liability limited partnership; limited liability company; business trust; corporation; or any other entity having a governing statute . . . [including] domestic and foreign entities regardless of whether organized for profit." Section 1101(8)
writing requirements	some provisions pertain only to written understandings; *see, e.g.*,	removes virtually all writing requirements; but does require that

Sections 401 (partnership agreement may "provide in writing for the admission of additional general partners"; such admission also permitted "with the written consent of all partners"), 502(a) (limited partner's promise to contribute "is not enforceable unless set out in a writing signed by the limited partner"), 801(2) and (3) (dissolution occurs "upon the happening of events specified in writing in the partnership agreement" and upon "written consent of all partners"), 801(4) (dissolution avoided following withdrawal of a general partner if "all partners agree in writing")	certain information be maintained in record form, Section 111

ARTICLE 1
GENERAL PROVISIONS

§ 101. Short Title

This [Act] may be cited as the Uniform Limited Partnership Act.

§ 102. Definitions

In this [Act]:

(1) "Certificate of limited partnership" means the certificate required by Section 201. The term includes the certificate as amended or restated.

(2) "Contribution", except in the phrase "right of contribution," means property or a benefit described in section 501 which is provided by a person to a limited partnership to become a partner or in the person's capacity as a partner.

(3) "Debtor in bankruptcy" means a person that is the subject of:

(A) an order for relief under Title 11 of the United States Code or a comparable order under a successor statute of general application; or

(B) a comparable order under federal, state, or foreign law governing insolvency.

(4) "Distribution" means a transfer of money or other property from a limited partnership to a person on account of a transferable interest or in the person's capacity as a partner. The term:

(A) includes:

(i) a redemption or other purchase by a limited partnership of a transferable interest; and

(ii) a transfer to a partner in return for the partner's relinquishment of any right to participate as a partner in the management or conduct of the partnership's activities and affairs or to have access to records or other information concerning the partnership's activities and affairs; and

(B) does not include amounts constituting reasonable compensation for present or past service or payments made in the ordinary course of business under a bona fide retirement plan or other bona fide benefits program.

(5) "Foreign limited liability limited partnership" means a foreign limited partnership whose general partners have limited liability for the debts, obligations, or other liabilities of the foreign partnership under a provision similar to Section 404(c).

(6) "Foreign limited partnership" means an unincorporated entity formed under the law of a jurisdiction other than this state which would be a limited partnership if formed under the law of this state. The term includes a foreign limited liability limited partnership.

(7) "General partner" means a person that:

(A) has become a general partner under Section 401 or was a general partner in a partnership when the partnership became subject to this [Act] under section 112; and

(B) has not dissociated as a general partner under Section 603.

(8) "Jurisdiction", used to refer to a political entity, means the United States, a state, a foreign country, or a political subdivision of a foreign country.

(9) "Jurisdiction of formation" means the jurisdiction whose law governs the internal affairs of an entity.

(10) "Limited liability limited partnership", except in the phrase "foreign limited liability limited partnership" and in [Article] 11, means a limited partnership whose certificate of limited partnership states that the partnership is a limited liability limited partnership.

(11) "Limited partner" means a person that:

(A) has become a limited partner under Section 301 or was a limited partner in a limited partnership when the partnership became subject to this [Act] under Section 112; and

(B) has not dissociated under Section 601.

(12) "Limited partnership", except in the phrase "foreign limited partnership" and in [Article] 11, means an entity formed under this [Act] or which becomes subject to this [Act] under [Article] 11 or Section 112. The term includes a limited liability limited partnership.

(13) "Partner" means a limited partner or general partner.

(14) "Partnership agreement" means the agreement, whether or not referred to as a partnership agreement and whether oral, implied, in a record, or in any combination thereof, of all the partners of a limited partnership concerning the matters described in Section 105(a). The term includes the agreement as amended or restated.

(15) "Person" means an individual, business corporation, nonprofit corporation, partnership, limited partnership, limited liability company, [general cooperative association,] limited cooperative association, unincorporated nonprofit association, statutory trust, business trust, common-law business trust, estate, trust, association, joint venture, public corporation, government or governmental subdivision, agency, or instrumentality, or any other legal or commercial entity.

(16) "Principal office" means the principal executive office of a limited partnership or foreign limited partnership, whether or not the office is located in this state.

(17) "Property" means all property, whether real, personal, or mixed or tangible or intangible, or any right or interest therein.

(18) "Record", used as a noun, means information that is inscribed on a tangible medium or that is stored in an electronic or other medium and is retrievable in perceivable form.

(19) "Registered agent" means an agent of a limited partnership or foreign limited partnership which is authorized to receive service of any process, notice, or demand required or permitted by law to be served on the partnership.

(20) "Registered foreign limited partnership" means a foreign limited partnership that is registered to do business in this state pursuant to a statement of registration filed by the [Secretary of State].

(21) "Required information" means the information that a limited partnership is required to maintain under Section 108.

(22) "Sign" means, with present intent to authenticate or adopt a record:

(A) to execute or adopt a tangible symbol; or

(B) to attach or logically associate with the record an electronic symbol, sound, or process.

(23) "State" means a state of the United States, the District of Columbia, Puerto Rico, the United States Virgin Islands, or any territory or insular possession subject to the jurisdiction of the United States.

(24) "Transfer" includes:

(A) an assignment;

(B) a conveyance;

(C) a sale;

(D) a lease;

(E) an encumbrance, including a mortgage or security interest;

(F) a gift; and

(G) a transfer by operation of law.

(25) "Transferable interest" means the right, as initially owned by a person in the person's capacity as a partner, to receive distributions from a limited partnership, whether or not the person remains a partner or continues to own any part of the right. The term applies to any fraction of the interest, by whomever owned.

(26) "Transferee" means a person to which all or part of a transferable interest has been transferred, whether or not the transferor is a partner. The term includes a person that owns a transferable interest under Section 602(a)(3) or 605(a)(4).

§ 103. Knowledge; Notice

(a) A person knows a fact if the person:

(1) has actual knowledge of it; or

(2) is deemed to know it under law other than this [Act].

(b) A person has notice of a fact if the person:

(1) has reason to know the fact from all the facts known to the person at the time in question; or

(2) is deemed to have notice of the fact under subsection (c) or (d).

(c) A certificate of limited partnership on file in the office of the [Secretary of State] is notice that the partnership is a limited partnership and the persons designated in the certificate as general partners are general partners. Except as otherwise provided in subsection (d), the certificate is not notice of any other fact.

(d)   A person not a partner is deemed to have notice of:

(1)   a person's dissociation as a general partner 90 days after an amendment to the certificate of limited partnership which states that the other person has dissociated becomes effective or 90 days after a statement of dissociation pertaining to the other person becomes effective, whichever occurs first;

(2)   a limited partnership's:

(A)   dissolution 90 days after an amendment to the certificate of limited partnership stating that the limited partnership is dissolved becomes effective;

(B)   termination 90 days after a statement of termination under Section 802(b)(2)(F) becomes effective; and

(C)   participation in a merger, interest exchange, conversion, or domestication, 90 days after articles of merger, interest exchange, conversion, or domestication under [Article] 11 become effective.

(e)   Subject to Section 210(f), a person notifies another person of a fact by taking steps reasonably required to inform the other person in ordinary course, whether or not those steps cause the other person to know the fact.

(f)   A general partner's knowledge or notice of a fact relating to the limited partnership is effective immediately as knowledge of or notice to the partnership, except in the case of a fraud on the partnership committed by or with the consent of the general partner. A limited partner's knowledge or notice of a fact relating to the partnership is not effective as knowledge of or notice to the partnership.

§ 104.   Governing Law

The law of this state governs:

(1)   the internal affairs of a limited partnership; and

(2)   the liability of a partner as partner for a debt, obligation, or other liability of a limited partnership.

§ 105.   Partnership Agreement; Scope, Function, and Limitations

(a)   Except as otherwise provided in subsections (c) and (d), the partnership agreement governs:

(1)   relations among the partners as partners and between the partners and the limited partnership;

(2)   the activities and affairs of the partnership and the conduct of those activities and affairs; and

(3)   the means and conditions for amending the partnership agreement.

(b)   To the extent the partnership agreement does not provide for a matter described in subsection (a), this [act] governs the matter.

(c)   A partnership agreement may not:

(1)   vary the law applicable under Section 104;

(2)   vary a limited partnership's capacity under Section 111 to sue and be sued in its own name;

(3)   vary any requirement, procedure, or other provision of this [act] pertaining to:

(A)   registered agents; or

(B) the [Secretary of State], including provisions pertaining to records authorized or required to be delivered to the [Secretary of State] for filing under this [act];

(4) vary the provisions of Section 204;

(5) vary the right of a general partner under Section 406(b)(2) to vote on or consent to an amendment to the certificate of limited partnership which deletes a statement that the limited partnership is a limited liability limited partnership;

(6) alter or eliminate the duty of loyalty or the duty of care except as otherwise provided in subsection (d);

(7) eliminate the contractual obligation of good faith and fair dealing under Sections 305(a) and 409(d), but the partnership agreement may prescribe the standards, if not manifestly unreasonable, by which the performance of the obligation is to be measured;

(8) relieve or exonerate a person from liability for conduct involving bad faith, willful or intentional misconduct, or knowing violation of law;

(9) vary the information required under Section 108 or unreasonably restrict the duties and rights under Section 304 or 407, but the partnership agreement may impose reasonable restrictions on the availability and use of information obtained under those sections and may define appropriate remedies, including liquidated damages, for a breach of any reasonable restriction on use;

(10) vary the grounds for expulsion specified in Section 603(5)(B);

(11) vary the power of a person to dissociate as a general partner under Section 604(a), except to require that the notice under Section 603(1) be in a record;

(12) vary the causes of dissolution specified in Section 801(a)(6);

(13) vary the requirement to wind up the partnership's activities and affairs as specified in Section 802(a), (b)(1), and (d);

(14) unreasonably restrict the right of a partner to maintain an action under [Article] 9;

(15) vary the provisions of Section 905, but the partnership agreement may provide that the partnership may not have a special litigation committee;

(16) vary the right of a partner to approve a merger, interest exchange, conversion, or domestication under Section 1123(a)(2), 1133(a)(2), 1143(a)(2), or 1153(a)(2);

(17) vary the required contents of a plan of merger under Section 1122(a), plan of interest exchange under Section 1132(a), plan of conversion under Section 1142(a), or plan of domestication under Section 1152(a); or

(18) except as otherwise provided in Sections 106 and 107(b), restrict the rights under this [act] of a person other than a partner.

(d) Subject to subsection (c)(8), without limiting other terms that may be included in a partnership agreement, the following rules apply:

(1) The partnership agreement may:

(A) specify the method by which a specific act or transaction that would otherwise violate the duty of loyalty may be authorized or ratified by one or more disinterested and independent persons after full disclosure of all material facts; and

(B) alter the prohibition in Section 504(a)(2) so that the prohibition requires only that the partnership's total assets not be less than the sum of its total liabilities.

(2) If not manifestly unreasonable, the partnership agreement may:

(A) alter or eliminate the aspects of the duty of loyalty stated in Section 409(b);

    (B)   identify specific types or categories of activities that do not violate the duty of loyalty;

    (C)   alter the duty of care, but may not authorize conduct involving bad faith, willful or intentional misconduct, or knowing violation of law; and

    (D)   alter or eliminate any other fiduciary duty.

(e)   The court shall decide as a matter of law whether a term of a partnership agreement is manifestly unreasonable under subsection (c)(7) or (d)(2). The court:

    (1)   shall make its determination as of the time the challenged term became part of the partnership agreement and by considering only circumstances existing at that time; and

    (2)   may invalidate the term only if, in light of the purposes, activities, and affairs of the limited partnership, it is readily apparent that:

    (A)   the objective of the term is unreasonable; or

    (B)   the term is an unreasonable means to achieve its objective.

§ 106. Partnership Agreement; Effect on Limited Partnership and Person Becoming Partner; Preformation Agreement

(a)   A limited partnership is bound by and may enforce the partnership agreement, whether or not the partnership has itself manifested assent to the agreement.

(b)   A person that becomes a partner is deemed to assent to the partnership agreement.

(c)   Two or more persons intending to become the initial partners of a limited partnership may make an agreement providing that upon the formation of the partnership the agreement will become the partnership agreement.

§ 107. Partnership Agreement; Effect on Third Parties and Relationship to Records Effective on Behalf of Limited Partnership

(a)   A partnership agreement may specify that its amendment requires the approval of a person that is not a party to the agreement or the satisfaction of a condition. An amendment is ineffective if its adoption does not include the required approval or satisfy the specified condition.

(b)   The obligations of a limited partnership and its partners to a person in the person's capacity as a transferee or person dissociated as a partner are governed by the partnership agreement. Subject only to a court order issued under Section 703(b)(2) to effectuate a charging order, an amendment to the partnership agreement made after a person becomes a transferee or is dissociated as a partner:

    (1)   is effective with regard to any debt, obligation, or other liability of the partnership or its partners to the person in the person's capacity as a transferee or person dissociated as a partner; and

    (2)   is not effective to the extent the amendment imposes a new debt, obligation, or other liability on the transferee or person dissociated as a partner.

(c)   If a record delivered by a limited partnership to the [Secretary of State] for filing becomes effective and contains a provision that would be ineffective under Section 105(c) or (d)(2) if contained in the partnership agreement, the provision is ineffective in the record.

(d)   Subject to subsection (c), if a record delivered by a limited partnership to the [Secretary of State] for filing becomes effective and conflicts with a provision of the partnership agreement:

    (1)   the agreement prevails as to partners, persons dissociated as partners, and transferees; and

    (2)   the record prevails as to other persons to the extent they reasonably rely on the record.

§ 108. Required Information

A limited partnership shall maintain at its principal office the following information:

(1)   a current list showing the full name and last known street and mailing address of each partner, separately identifying the general partners, in alphabetical order, and the limited partners, in alphabetical order;

(2)   a copy of the initial certificate of limited partnership and all amendments to and restatements of the certificate, together with signed copies of any powers of attorney under which any certificate, amendment, or restatement has been signed;

(3)   a copy of any filed articles of merger, interest exchange, conversion, or domestication;

(4)   a copy of the partnership's federal, state, and local income tax returns and reports, if any, for the three most recent years;

(5)   a copy of any partnership agreement made in a record and any amendment made in a record to any partnership agreement;

(6)   a copy of any financial statement of the partnership for the three most recent years;

(7)   a copy of the three most recent [annual] [biennial] reports delivered by the partnership to the [Secretary of State] pursuant to Section 212;

(8)   a copy of any record made by the partnership during the past three years of any consent given by or vote taken of any partner pursuant to this [act] or the partnership agreement; and

(9)   unless contained in a partnership agreement made in a record, a record stating:

(A)   a description and statement of the agreed value of contributions other than money made and agreed to be made by each partner;

(B)   the times at which, or events on the happening of which, any additional contributions agreed to be made by each partner are to be made;

(C)   for any person that is both a general partner and a limited partner, a specification of what transferable interest the person owns in each capacity; and

(D)   any events upon the happening of which the partnership is to be dissolved and its activities and affairs wound up.

§ 109. Dual Capacity

A person may be both a general partner and a limited partner. A person that is both a general and limited partner has the rights, powers, duties, and obligations provided by this [act] and the partnership agreement in each of those capacities. When the person acts as a general partner, the person is subject to the obligations, duties, and restrictions under this [act] and the partnership agreement for general partners. When the person acts as a limited partner, the person is subject to the obligations, duties, and restrictions under this [act] and the partnership agreement for limited partners.

§ 110. Nature, Purpose, and Duration of Limited Partnership

(a)   A limited partnership is an entity distinct from its partners. A limited partnership is the same entity regardless of whether its certificate states that the limited partnership is a limited liability limited partnership.

(b)   A limited partnership may have any lawful purpose, regardless of whether for profit.

(c)   A limited partnership has perpetual duration.

§ 111. Powers

A limited partnership has the capacity to sue and be sued in the name of the partnership and the power to do all things necessary or convenient to carry on the partnership's activities and affairs.

§ 112. Application to Existing Relationships

(a) Before [all-inclusive date], this [act] governs only:

(1) a limited partnership formed on or after [the effective date of this [act]]; and

(2) except as otherwise provided in subsections (c) and (d), a limited partnership formed before [the effective date of this [act]] which elects, in the manner provided in its partnership agreement or by law for amending the partnership agreement, to be subject to this [act].

(b) Except as otherwise provided in subsections (c) and (d), on and after [all-inclusive date] this [act] governs all limited partnerships.

(c) With respect to a limited partnership formed before [the effective date of this [act]], the following rules apply except as the partners otherwise elect in the manner provided in the partnership agreement or by law for amending the partnership agreement:

(1) Section 110(c) does not apply and the limited partnership has whatever duration it had under the law applicable immediately before [the effective date of this [act]].

(2) the limited partnership is not required to amend its certificate of limited partnership to comply with Section 201(b)(5).

(3) Sections 601 and 602 do not apply and a limited partner has the same right and power to dissociate from the limited partnership, with the same consequences, as existed immediately before [the effective date of this [act]].

(4) Section 603(4) does not apply.

(5) Section 603(5) does not apply and a court has the same power to expel a general partner as the court had immediately before [the effective date of this [act]].

(6) Section 801(a)(3) does not apply and the connection between a person's dissociation as a general partner and the dissolution of the limited partnership is the same as existed immediately before [the effective date of this [act]].

(d) With respect to a limited partnership that elects pursuant to subsection (a)(2) to be subject to this [act], after the election takes effect the provisions of this [act] relating to the liability of the limited partnership's general partners to third parties apply:

(1) before [all-inclusive date], to:

(A) a third party that had not done business with the limited partnership in the year before the election took effect; and

(B) a third party that had done business with the limited partnership in the year before the election took effect only if the third party knows or has been notified of the election; and

(2) on and after [all-inclusive date], to all third parties, but those provisions remain inapplicable to any obligation incurred while those provisions were inapplicable under paragraph (1)(B).

Legislative Note: *Subsection 112(c) presupposes that this act is replacing ULPA (1976) (Last Amended 1985). If this act is replacing a substantially different limited partnership act, the enacting jurisdiction should consider whether: (i) this act makes material changes to the "default" (or "gap filler") rules of the predecessor statute; and (ii) if so, whether Subsection (c) should carry forward any of those rules for pre-existing limited partnerships. In this assessment, the focus is on pre-existing limited partnerships* *that have left default rules in place, whether advisedly or not. The central question is whether, for such limited partnerships, expanding Subsection (c) is necessary to prevent material changes to the partners' "deal."*

In an enacting jurisdiction that has previously amended its existing limited partnership statute to provide for limited liability limited partnerships (LLLPs), this act should include transition provisions specifically applicable to pre-existing limited liability limited partnerships. The precise wording of those provisions must depend on the wording of the State's previously enacted LLLP provisions. However, the following principles apply generally:

1.   In Sections 806(b)(5) and 807(b)(4) (notice by dissolved limited partnership to claimants), the phrase "the limited partnership has been throughout its existence a limited liability limited partnership" should be revised to encompass a limited partnership that was a limited liability limited partnership under the State's previously enacted LLLP provisions.

2.   Section 112(d) should provide that, if a pre-existing limited liability limited partnership elects to be subject to this act, this act's provisions relating to the liability of general partners to third parties apply immediately to all third parties, regardless of whether a third party has previously done business with the limited liability limited partnership.

3.   A pre-existing limited liability limited partnership that elects to be subject to this act should have to comply with Sections 201(b)(5) (requiring the certificate of limited partnership to state whether the limited partnership is a limited liability limited partnership) and 114(c) (establishing name requirements for a limited liability limited partnership).

4.   As for Section 112(b) (providing that, after a transition period, this act applies to all preexisting limited partnerships):

a.   if a State's previously enacted LLLP provisions have requirements essentially the same as Sections 201(b)(5) and 114(c), pre-existing limited liability limited partnerships should automatically retain LLLP status under this act.

b.   if a State's previously enacted LLLP provisions have name requirements essentially the same as Section 114(c) and provide that a public filing other than the certificate of limited partnership establishes a limited partnership's status as a limited liability limited partnership:

i.   that filing can be deemed to an amendment to the certificate of limited partnership to comply with Section 201(b)(5), and

ii.   pre-existing limited liability limited partnerships should automatically retain LLLP status under this act.

c.   if a State's previously enacted LLLP provisions do not have name requirements essentially the same as Section 114(c), it will be impossible both to enforce Section 114(c) and provide for automatic transition to LLLP status under this act.

It is recommended that the "all-inclusive" date should be at least one year after the effective date of this act, Section 1206, but no more than two years.

§ 113.   Supplemental Principles of Law

Unless displaced by particular provisions of this [Act], the principles of law and equity supplement this [Act].

§ 114.   Permitted Names

(a)   The name of a limited partnership may contain the name of any partner.

(b)   The name of a limited partnership that is not a limited liability limited partnership must contain the phrase "limited partnership" or the abbreviation "LP" or "L.P." and may not contain the phrase "limited liability limited partnership" or the abbreviation "LLLP" or "L.L.L.P.".

(c)   The name of a limited liability limited partnership must contain the phrase "limited liability limited partnership" or the abbreviation "LLLP" or "L.L.L.P." and must not contain the abbreviation "LP" or "L.P.".

(d)   Except as otherwise provided in subsection (g), the name of a limited partnership, and the name under which a foreign limited partnership may register to do business in this state, must be distinguishable on the records of the [Secretary of State] from any:

(1)   name of an existing person whose formation required the filing of a record by the [Secretary of State] and which is not at the time administratively dissolved;

(2)   name of a limited liability partnership whose statement of qualification is in effect;

(3)   name under which a person is registered to do business in this state by the filing of a record by the [Secretary of State];

(4)   name reserved under Section 115 or other law of this state providing for the reservation of a name by the filing of a record by the [Secretary of State];

(5)   name registered under Section 116 or other law of this state providing for the registration of a name by the filing of a record by the [Secretary of State]; and

(6)   name registered under [this state's assumed or fictitious name statute].

(e)   If a person consents in a record to the use of its name and submits an undertaking in a form satisfactory to the [Secretary of State] to change its name to a name that is distinguishable on the records of the [Secretary of State] from any name in any category of names in subsection (d), the name of the consenting person may be used by the person to which the consent was given.

(f)   Except as otherwise provided in subsection (g), in determining whether a name is the same as or not distinguishable on the records of the [Secretary of State] from the name of another person, words, phrases, or abbreviations indicating the type of person, such as "corporation", "corp.", "incorporated", "Inc.", "professional corporation", "PC", "P.C.", "professional association", "PA", "P.A.", "Limited", "Ltd.", "limited partnership", "LP", "L.P.", "limited liability partnership", "LLP", "L.L.P.", "registered limited liability partnership", "RLLP", "R.L.L.P.", "limited liability limited partnership", "LLLP", "L.L.L.P.", "registered limited liability limited partnership", "RLLLP", "R.L.L.L.P.", "limited liability company", "LLC", "L.L.C.", "limited cooperative association", "limited cooperative", "LCA", or "L.C.A." may not be taken into account.

(g)   A person may consent in a record to the use of a name that is not distinguishable on the records of the [Secretary of State] from its name except for the addition of a word, phrase, or abbreviation indicating the type of person as provided in subsection (f). In such a case, the person need not change its name pursuant to subsection (e).

(h)   The name of a limited partnership or foreign limited partnership may not contain the words [insert prohibited words or words that may be used only with approval by an appropriate state agency].

(i)   A limited partnership or foreign limited partnership may use a name that is not distinguishable from a name described in subsection (d)(1) through (6) if the partnership delivers to the [Secretary of State] a certified copy of a final judgment of a court of competent jurisdiction establishing the right of the partnership to use the name in state.

§ 115. Reservation of Name

(a)   A person may reserve the exclusive use of a name that complies with Section 114 by delivering an application to the [Secretary of State] for filing. The application must state the name and address of the applicant and the name to be reserved. If the [Secretary of State] finds that the name is available, the [Secretary of State] shall reserve the name for the applicant's exclusive use for [120] days.

(b)   The owner of a reserved name may transfer the reservation to another person by delivering to the [Secretary of State] a signed notice in a record of the transfer which states the name and address of the person to which the reservation is being transferred.

§ 116.   Registration of Name

(a)   A foreign limited partnership not registered to do business in this state under [Article] 10 may register its name, or an alternate name adopted pursuant to Section 1006, if the name is distinguishable on the records of the [Secretary of State] from the names that are not available under Section 114.

(b)   To register its name or an alternate name adopted pursuant to Section 1006, a foreign limited partnership must deliver to the [Secretary of State] for filing an application stating the partnership's name, the jurisdiction and date of its formation, and any alternate name adopted pursuant to Section 1006. If the [Secretary of State] finds that the name applied for is available, the [Secretary of State] shall register the name for the applicant's exclusive use.

(c)   The registration of a name under this section is effective for [one year] after the date of registration.

(d)   A foreign limited partnership whose name registration is effective may renew the registration for successive [one-year] periods by delivering, not earlier than [three months] before the expiration of the registration, to the [Secretary of State] for filing a renewal application that complies with this section. When filed, the renewal application renews the registration for a succeeding [one-year] period.

§ 117.   Registered Agent

(a)   Each limited partnership and each registered foreign limited partnership shall designate and maintain a registered agent in this state. The designation of a registered agent is an affirmation of fact by the limited partnership or registered foreign limited partnership that the agent has consented to serve.

(b)   A registered agent for a limited partnership or registered foreign limited partnership must have a place of business in this state.

(c)   The only duties under this [act] of a registered agent that has complied with this [act] are:

(1)   to forward to the limited partnership or registered foreign limited partnership at the address most recently supplied to the agent by the partnership or foreign partnership any process, notice, or demand pertaining to the partnership or foreign partnership which is served on or received by the agent;

(2)   if the registered agent resigns, to provide the notice required by Section 119(c) to the partnership or foreign partnership at the address most recently supplied to the agent by the partnership or foreign partnership; and

(3)   to keep current the information with respect to the agent in the certificate of limited partnership.

§ 118.   Change of Registered Agent or Address for Registered Agent by Limited Partnership

(a)   A limited partnership or registered foreign limited partnership may change its registered agent or the address of its registered agent by delivering to the [Secretary of State] for filing a statement of change that states:

(1)   the name of the partnership or foreign partnership; and

(2)   the information that is to be in effect as a result of the filing of the statement of change.

(b)   The general or limited partners of a limited partnership need not approve the [delivery to the Secretary of State] for filing of:

(1)   a statement of change under this section; or

(2)   a similar filing changing the registered agent or registered office, if any, of the partnership in any other jurisdiction.

(c)   A statement of change under this section designating a new registered agent is an affirmation of fact by the limited partnership or registered foreign limited partnership that the agent has consented to serve.

(d)   As an alternative to using the procedure in this section, a limited partnership may amend its certificate of limited partnership.

§ 119.   Resignation of Registered Agent

(a)   A registered agent may resign as an agent for a limited partnership or registered foreign limited partnership by delivering to the [Secretary of State] for filing a statement of resignation that states:

(1)   the name of the partnership or foreign partnership;

(2)   the name of the agent;

(3)   that the agent resigns from serving as registered agent for the partnership or foreign partnership; and

(4)   the address of the partnership or foreign partnership to which the agent will send the notice required by subsection (c).

(b)   A statement of resignation takes effect on the earlier of:

(1)   the 31st day after the day on which it is filed by the [Secretary of State]; or

(2)   the designation of a new registered agent for the limited partnership or registered foreign limited partnership.

(c)   A registered agent promptly shall furnish to the limited partnership or registered foreign limited partnership notice in a record of the date on which a statement of resignation was filed.

(d)   When a statement of resignation takes effect, the registered agent ceases to have responsibility under this [act] for any matter thereafter tendered to it as agent for the limited partnership or registered foreign limited partnership. The resignation does not affect any contractual rights the partnership or foreign partnership has against the agent or that the agent has against the partnership or foreign partnership.

(e)   A registered agent may resign with respect to a limited partnership or registered foreign limited partnership whether or not the partnership or foreign partnership is in good standing.

§ 120.   Change of Name or Address by Registered Agent

(a)   If a registered agent changes its name or address, the agent may deliver to the [Secretary of State] for filing a statement of change that states:

(1)   the name of the limited partnership or registered foreign limited partnership represented by the registered agent;

(2)   the name of the agent as currently shown in the records of the [Secretary of State] for the partnership or foreign partnership;

(3)   if the name of the agent has changed, its new name; and

(4)   if the address of the agent has changed, its new address.

(b)   A registered agent promptly shall furnish notice to the represented limited partnership or registered foreign limited partnership of the filing by the [Secretary of State] of the statement of change and the changes made by the statement.

Legislative Note: Many registered agents act in that capacity for many entities, and the Model Registered Agents Act (2006) (Last Amended 2013) provides a streamlined method through which a commercial registered agent can make a single filing to change its information for all represented entities. The single filing does not prevent an enacting state from assessing filing fees on the basis of the number of entity records affected. Alternatively the fees can be set on an incremental sliding fee or capitated amount based upon potential economies of costs for a bulk filing.

§ 121.   Service of Process, Notice, or Demand

(a)   A limited partnership or registered foreign limited partnership may be served with any process, notice, or demand required or permitted by law by serving its registered agent.

(b)   If a limited partnership or registered foreign limited partnership ceases to have a registered agent, or if its registered agent cannot with reasonable diligence be served, the partnership or foreign partnership may be served by registered or certified mail, return receipt requested, or by similar commercial delivery service, addressed to the partnership or foreign partnership at its principal office. The address of the principal office must be as shown in the partnership's or foreign partnership's most recent [annual] [biennial] report filed by the [Secretary of State]. Service is effected under this subsection on the earliest of:

(1)   the date the partnership or foreign partnership receives the mail or delivery by the commercial delivery service;

(2)   the date shown on the return receipt, if signed by the partnership or foreign partnership; or

(3)   five days after its deposit with the United States Postal Service, or with the commercial delivery service, if correctly addressed and with sufficient postage or payment.

(c)   If process, notice, or demand cannot be served on a limited partnership or registered foreign limited partnership pursuant to subsection (a) or (b), service may be made by handing a copy to the individual in charge of any regular place of business or activity of the partnership or foreign partnership if the individual served is not a plaintiff in the action.

(d)   Service of process, notice, or demand on a registered agent must be in a written record.

(e)   Service of process, notice, or demand may be made by other means under law other than this [Act].

§ 122.   Delivery of Record

(a)   Except as otherwise provided in this [act], permissible means of delivery of a record include delivery by hand, mail, conventional commercial practice, and electronic transmission.

(b)   Delivery to the [Secretary of State] is effective only when a record is received by the [Secretary of State].

§ 123.   Reservation of Power to Amend or Repeal

The [legislature of this state] has power to amend or repeal all or part of this [act] at any time, and all limited partnerships and foreign limited partnerships subject to this [act] are governed by the amendment or repeal.

ARTICLE 2
FORMATION; CERTIFICATE OF LIMITED
PARTNERSHIP AND OTHER FILINGS

§ 201.　Formation of Limited Partnership; Certificate of Limited Partnership

(a)　To form a limited partnership, a person must deliver a certificate of limited partnership to the [Secretary of State] for filing.

(b)　A certificate of limited partnership must state:

(1)　the name of the limited partnership, which must comply with Section 114;

(2)　the street and mailing addresses of the partnership's principal office;

(3)　the name and street and mailing addresses in this state of the partnership's registered agent;

(4)　the name and street and mailing addresses of each general partner; and

(5)　whether the limited partnership is a limited liability limited partnership.

(c)　A certificate of limited partnership may contain statements as to matters other than those required by subsection (b), but may not vary or otherwise affect the provisions specified in Section 105(c) and (d) in a manner inconsistent with that section.

(d)　A limited partnership is formed when:

(1)　the certificate of limited partnership becomes effective;

(2)　at least two persons have become partners;

(3)　at least one person has become a general partner; and

(4)　at least one person has become a limited partner.

§ 202.　Amendment or Restatement of Certificate of Limited Partnership

(a)　A certificate of limited partnership may be amended or restated at any time.

(b)　To amend its certificate of limited partnership, a limited partnership must deliver to the [Secretary of State] for filing an amendment stating:

(1)　the name of the partnership;

(2)　the date of filing of its initial certificate; and

(3)　the text of the amendment.

(c)　To restate its certificate of limited partnership, a limited partnership must deliver to the [Secretary of State] for filing a restatement, designated as such in its heading.

(d)　A limited partnership shall promptly deliver to the [Secretary of State] for filing an amendment to a certificate of limited partnership to reflect:

(1)　the admission of a new general partner;

(2)　the dissociation of a person as a general partner; or

(3)　the appointment of a person to wind up the limited partnership's activities under Section 802(c) or (d).

(e)　If a general partner knows that any information in a filed certificate of limited partnership was inaccurate when the certificate was filed or has become inaccurate due to changed circumstances, the general partner shall promptly:

(1)　cause the certificate to be amended; or

(2)   if appropriate, deliver to the [Secretary of State] for filing a statement of change under Section 118 or a statement of correction under Section 209.

§ 203.   Signing of Records to Be Delivered for Filing to [Secretary of State]

(a)   A record delivered to the [Secretary of State] for filing pursuant to this [Act] must be signed as follows:

(1)   An initial certificate of limited partnership must be signed by all general partners listed in the certificate.

(2)   An amendment to the certificate of limited partnership adding or deleting a statement that the limited partnership is a limited liability limited partnership must be signed by all general partners listed in the certificate.

(3)   An amendment to the certificate of limited partnership designating as general partner a person admitted under Section 801(a)(3)(B) following the dissociation of a limited partnership's last general partner must be signed by that person.

(4)   An amendment to the certificate of limited partnership required by Section 802(c) following the appointment of a person to wind up the dissolved limited partnership's activities and affairs must be signed by that person.

(5)   Any other amendment to the certificate of limited partnership must be signed by:

(A)   at least one general partner listed in the certificate;

(B)   each person designated in the amendment as a new general partner; and

(C)   each person that the amendment indicates has dissociated as a general partner, unless:

(i)   the person is deceased or a guardian or general conservator has been appointed for the person and the amendment so states; or

(ii)   the person has previously delivered to the [Secretary of State] for filing a statement of dissociation.

(6)   A restated certificate of limited partnership must be signed by at least one general partner listed in the certificate, and, to the extent the restated certificate effects a change under any other paragraph of this subsection, the certificate must be signed in a manner that satisfies that paragraph.

(7)   A statement of termination must be signed by all general partners listed in the certificate of limited partnership or, if the certificate of a dissolved limited partnership lists no general partners, by the person appointed pursuant to Section 802(c) or (d) to wind up the dissolved limited partnership's activities and affairs.

(8)   Any other record delivered by a limited partnership to the [Secretary of State] for filing must be signed by at least one general partner listed in the certificate of limited partnership.

(9)   A statement by a person pursuant to Section 605(a)(3) stating that the person has dissociated as a general partner must be signed by that person.

(10)   A statement of negation by a person pursuant to Section 306 must be signed by that person.

(11)   Any other record delivered on behalf of a person to the [Secretary of State] for filing must be signed by that person.

(b)   Any record delivered for filing under this [act] may be signed by an agent. Whenever this [act] requires a particular individual to sign a record and the individual is deceased or incompetent, the record may be signed by a legal representative of the individual.

(c)   A person that signs a record as an agent or legal representative thereby affirms as a fact that the person is authorized to sign the record.

§ 204.   Signing and Filing Pursuant to Judicial Order

(a)   If a person required by this [Act] to sign a record or deliver a record to the [Secretary of State] for filing under this [Act] does not do so, any other person that is aggrieved may petition [the appropriate court] to order:

     (1)   the person to sign the record;

     (2)   the person to deliver the record to the [Secretary of State] for filing; or

     (3)   the [Secretary of State] to file the record unsigned.

(b)   If a petitioner under subsection (a) is not the limited partnership or foreign limited partnership to which the record pertains, the petitioner shall make the partnership or foreign partnership a party to the action.

(c)   A record filed under subsection (a)(3) is effective without being signed.

§ 205.   Liability for Inaccurate Information in Filed Record

(a)   If a record delivered to the [Secretary of State] for filing under this [Act] and filed by the [Secretary of State] contains inaccurate information, a person that suffers loss by reliance on the information may recover damages for the loss from:

     (1)   a person that signed the record, or caused another to sign it on the person's behalf, and knew the information to be inaccurate at the time the record was signed; and

     (2)   a general partner if:

         (A)   the record was delivered for filing on behalf of the partnership; and

         (B)   the general partner knew or had notice of the inaccuracy for a reasonably sufficient time before the information was relied upon so that, before the reliance, the general partner reasonably could have:

             (i)   effected an amendment under Section 202;

             (ii)   filed a petition under Section 204; or

             (iii)   delivered to the [Secretary of State] for filing a statement of change under Section 118 or a statement of correction under Section 209.

(b)   An individual who signs a record authorized or required to be filed under this [Act] constitutes affirms under penalty of perjury that the information stated in the record is accurate.

§ 206.   Filing Requirements

(a)   To be filed by the [Secretary of State] pursuant to this [Act], a record must be received by the [Secretary of State], must comply with this [act], and satisfy the following:

     (1)   The filing of the record must be required or permitted by this [act].

     (2)   The record must be physically delivered in written form unless and to the extent the [Secretary of State] permits electronic delivery of records.

     (3)   The words in the record must be in English, and numbers must be in Arabic or Roman numerals, but the name of an entity need not be in English if written in English letters or Arabic or Roman numerals.

     (4)   The record must be signed by a person authorized or required under this [act] to sign the record.

(5)   The record must state the name and capacity, if any, of each individual who signed it, either on behalf of the individual or the person authorized or required to sign the record, but need not contain a seal, attestation, acknowledgment, or verification.

(b)   If law other than this [act] prohibits the disclosure by the [Secretary of State] of information contained in a record delivered to the [Secretary of State] for filing, the [Secretary of State] shall file the record if the record otherwise complies with this [act] but may redact the information.

(c)   When a record is delivered to the [Secretary of State] for filing, any fee required under this [act] and any fee, tax, interest, or penalty required to be paid under this [act] or law other than this [act] must be paid in a manner permitted by the [Secretary of State] or by that law.

(d)   The [Secretary of State] may require that a record delivered in written form be accompanied by an identical or conformed copy.

(e)   The [Secretary of State] may provide forms for filings required or permitted to be made by this [act], but, except as otherwise provided in subsection (f), their use is not required.

(f)   The [Secretary of State] may require that a cover sheet for a filing be on a form prescribed by the [Secretary of State].

§ 207.   Effective Date and Time

Except as otherwise provided in Section 208 and subject to Section 209(d), a record filed under this [Act] is effective:

(1)   on the date and at the time of its filing by the [Secretary of State], as provided in Section 210(b);

(2)   on the date of filing and at the time specified in the record as its effective time, if later than the time under paragraph (1);

(3)   at a specified delayed effective date and time, which may not be more than 90 days after the date of filing; or

(4)   if a delayed effective date is specified, but no time is specified, at 12:01 a.m. on the date specified, which may not be more than 90 days after the date of filing.

§ 208.   Withdrawal of Filed Record Before Effectiveness

(a)   Except as otherwise provided in Sections 1124, 1134, 1144, and 1154, a record delivered to the [Secretary of State] for filing may be withdrawn before it takes effect by delivering to the [Secretary of State] for filing a statement of withdrawal.

(b)   A statement of withdrawal must:

(1)   be signed by each person that signed the record being withdrawn, except as otherwise agreed by those persons;

(2)   identify the record to be withdrawn; and

(3)   if signed by fewer than all the persons that signed the record being withdrawn, state that the record is withdrawn in accordance with the agreement of all the persons that signed the record.

(c)   On filing by the [Secretary of State] of a statement of withdrawal, the action or transaction evidenced by the original record does not take effect.

§ 209.   Correcting Filed Record

(a)   A person on whose behalf a filed record was delivered to the [Secretary of State] for filing may correct the record if:

    (1)   the record at the time of filing was inaccurate;

    (2)   the record was defectively signed; or

    (3)   the electronic transmission of the record to the [Secretary of State] was defective.

    (b)   To correct a filed record, a person on whose behalf the record was delivered to the [Secretary of State] must deliver to the [Secretary of State] for filing a statement of correction.

    (c)   A statement of correction:

    (1)   may not state a delayed effective date;

    (2)   must be signed by the person correcting the filed record;

    (3)   must identify the filed record to be corrected;

    (4)   must specify the inaccuracy or defect to be corrected; and

    (5)   must correct the inaccuracy or defect.

    (d)   A statement of correction is effective as of the effective date of the filed record that it corrects except for the purposes of Section 103(d) and as to persons relying on the uncorrected record and adversely affected by the correction. For those purposes and as to those persons, the statement of correction is effective when filed.

§ 210. Duty of [Secretary of State] to File; Review of Refusal to File; Delivery of Record by [Secretary of State]

    (a)   The [Secretary of State] shall file a record delivered to the [Secretary of State] for filing which satisfies this [act]. The duty of the [Secretary of State] under this section is ministerial.

    (b)   When the [Secretary of State] files a record, the [Secretary of State] shall record it as filed on the date and at the time of its delivery. After filing a record, the [Secretary of State] shall deliver to the person that submitted the record a copy of the record with an acknowledgment of the date and time of filing.

    (c)   If the [Secretary of State] refuses to file a record, the [Secretary of State] shall, not later than [15] business days after the record is delivered:

    (1)   return the record or notify the person that submitted the record of the refusal; and

    (2)   provide a brief explanation in a record of the reason for the refusal.

    (d)   If the [Secretary of State] refuses to file a record, the person that submitted the record may petition [the appropriate court] to compel filing of the record. The record and the explanation of the [Secretary of State] of the refusal to file must be attached to the petition. The court may decide the matter in a summary proceeding.

    (e)   The filing of or refusal to file a record does not:

    (1)   affect the validity or invalidity of the record in whole or in part; or

    (2)   create a presumption that the information contained in the record is correct or incorrect.

    (f)   Except as otherwise provided by Section 121 or by law other than this [act], the [Secretary of State] may deliver any record to a person by delivering it:

    (1)   in person to the person that submitted it;

    (2)   to the address of the person's registered agent;

    (3)   to the principal office of the person; or

    (4)   to another address the person provides to the [Secretary of State] for delivery.

§ 211. Certification of Good Standing or Registration

(a)   On request of any person, the [Secretary of State] shall issue a certificate of good standing for a limited partnership or a certificate of registration for a registered foreign limited partnership.

(b)   A certificate under subsection (a) must state:

(1)   the limited partnership's name or the registered foreign limited partnership's name used in this state;

(2)   in the case of a limited partnership:

(A)   that a certificate of limited partnership has been filed and has taken effect;

(B)   the date the certificate became effective;

(C)   the period of the partnership's duration if the records of the [Secretary of State] reflect that its period of duration is less than perpetual; and

(D)   that:

(i)   no statement of administrative dissolution, or statement of termination has been filed;

(ii)   the records of the [Secretary to State] do not otherwise reflect that the partnership has been dissolved or terminated; and

(iii)   a proceeding is not pending under Section 811;

(3)   in the case of a registered foreign limited partnership, that it is registered to do business in this state;

(4)   that all fees, taxes, interest, and penalties owed to this state by the limited partnership or the foreign partnership and collected through the [Secretary of State] have been paid, if:

(A)   payment is reflected in the records of the [Secretary of State]; and

(B)   nonpayment affects the good standing or registration of the partnership or foreign partnership;

(5)   that the most recent [annual] [biennial] report required by Section 212 has been delivered to the [Secretary of State] for filing; and

(6)   other facts reflected in the records of the [Secretary of State] pertaining to the limited partnership or foreign limited partnership which the person requesting the certificate reasonably requests.

(c)   Subject to any qualification stated in the certificate, a certificate issued by the [Secretary of State] under subsection (a) may be relied upon as conclusive evidence of the facts stated in the certificate.

§ 212. [Annual] [Biennial] Report for [Secretary of State]

(a)   A limited partnership or registered foreign limited partnership shall deliver to the [Secretary of State] for filing [an annual] [a biennial] report that states:

(1)   the name of the partnership or foreign partnership;

(2)   the name and street and mailing addresses of its registered agent in this state;

(3)   the street and mailing addresses of its principal office;

(4)   the name of at least one general partner; and

(5)   in the case of a foreign partnership, its jurisdiction of formation and any alternate name adopted under Section 1006(a).

(b) Information in the [annual] [biennial] report must be current as of the date the report is signed by the limited partnership or registered foreign limited partnership

(c) The first [annual] [biennial] report must be delivered to the [Secretary of State] for filing after [January 1] and before [April 1] of the year following the calendar year in which the limited partnership's certificate of limited partnership became effective or the registered foreign limited partnership registered to do business in this state. Subsequent [annual] [biennial] reports must be delivered to the [Secretary of State] for filing after [January 1] and before [April 1] of each [second] calendar year thereafter.

(d) If [an annual] [a biennial] report does not contain the information required by this section, the [Secretary of State] promptly shall notify the reporting limited partnership or registered foreign limited partnership in a record and return the report for correction

(e) If [an annual] [a biennial] report contains the name or address of a registered agent which differs from the information shown in the records of the [Secretary of State] immediately before the report becomes effective, the differing information is considered a statement of change under Section 118.

ARTICLE 3
LIMITED PARTNERS

§ 301. Becoming Limited Partner

(a) Upon formation of a limited partnership, a person becomes a limited partner as agreed among the persons that are to be the initial partners.

(b) After formation, a person becomes a limited partner:

(1) as provided in the partnership agreement;

(2) as the result of a transaction effective under [Article] 11;

(3) with the affirmative vote or consent of all the partners; or

(4) as provided in Section 801(a)(4) or (a)(5).

(c) A person may become a limited partner without:

(1) acquiring a transferable interest; or

(2) making or being obligated to make a contribution to the limited partnership.

§ 302. No Agency Power of Limited Partner as Limited Partner

(a) A limited partner is not an agent of a limited partnership solely by reason of being a limited partner.

(b) A person's status as a limited partner does not prevent or restrict law other than this [Act] from imposing liability on a limited partnership because of the person's conduct.

§ 303. No Liability as Limited Partner for Limited Partnership Obligations

(a) A debt, obligation, or other liability of a limited partnership is not the debt, obligation, or other liability of a limited partner. A limited partner is not personally liable, directly or indirectly, by way of contribution or otherwise, for a debt, obligation, or other liability of the partnership solely by reason of being or acting as a limited partner, even if the limited partner participates in the management and control of the limited partnership. This subsection applies regardless of the dissolution of the partnership.

(b)   The failure of a limited partnership to observe formalities relating to the exercise of its powers or management of its activities and affairs is not a group for imposing liability on a limited partner for a debt, obligation, or other liability of the partnership. *ground*

§ 304. Rights to Information of Limited Partner and Person Dissociated as Limited Partner

(a)   On 10 days' demand, made in a record received by the limited partnership, a limited partner may inspect and copy required information during regular business hours in the limited partnership's principal office. The limited partner need not have any particular purpose for seeking the information.

(b)   During regular business hours and at a reasonable location specified by the limited partnership, a limited partner may inspect and copy information regarding the activities, affairs, financial condition, and circumstances of the limited partnership as is just and reasonable if:

(1)   the limited partner seeks the information for a purpose reasonably related to the partner's interest as a limited partner;

(2)   the limited partner makes a demand in a record received by the limited partnership, describing with reasonable particularity the information sought and the purpose for seeking the information; and

(3)   the information sought is directly connected to the limited partner's purpose.

(c)   Not later than 10 days after receiving a demand pursuant to subsection (b), the limited partnership shall inform in a record the limited partner that made the demand of:

(1)   what information the partnership will provide in response to the demand and when and where the partnership will provide the information; and

(2)   the partnership's reasons for declining, if the partnership declines to provide any demanded information.

(d)   Whenever this [Act] or a partnership agreement provides for a limited partner to vote on or give or withhold consent to a matter, before the vote is cast or consent is given or withheld, the limited partnership shall, without demand, provide the limited partner with all information that is known to the partnership and is material to the limited partner's decision.

(e)   Subject to subsection (j), on 10 days' demand made in a record received by a limited partnership, a person dissociated as a limited partner may have access to information to which the person was entitled while a limited partner if:

(1)   the information pertains to the period during which the person was a limited partner;

(2)   the person seeks the information in good faith; and

(3)   the person satisfies the requirements imposed on a limited partner by subsection (b).

(f)   A limited partnership shall respond to a demand made pursuant to subsection (e) in the manner provided in subsection (c).

(g)   A limited partnership may charge a person that makes a demand under this section reasonable costs of copying, limited to the costs of labor and material.

(h)   A limited partner or person dissociated as a limited partner may exercise the rights under this section through an agent or, in the case of an individual under legal disability, a legal representative. Any restriction or condition imposed by the partnership agreement or under subsection (j) applies both to the agent or legal representative and to the limited partner or person dissociated as a limited partner.

(i)   Subject to Section 704, the rights under this section do not extend to a person as transferee.

(j)   In addition to any restriction or condition stated in its partnership agreement, a limited partnership, as a matter within the ordinary course of its activities and affairs, may impose reasonable restrictions and conditions on access to and use of information to be furnished under this section, including designating information confidential and imposing nondisclosure and safeguarding obligations on the recipient. In a dispute concerning the reasonableness of a restriction under this subsection, the partnership has the burden of proving reasonableness.

§ 305.   Limited Duties of Limited Partners

(a)   A limited partner shall discharge any duties to the partnership and the other partners under the partnership agreement and exercise any rights under this [Act] or partnership agreement consistently with the contractual obligation of good faith and fair dealing.

(b)   Except as otherwise provided in subsection (a), a limited partner does not have any duty to the limited partnership or to any other partner solely by reason of acting as a limited partner.

(c)   If a limited partner enters into a transaction with a limited partnership, the limited partner's rights and obligations arising from the transaction are the same as those of a person that is not a partner.

§ 306.   Person Erroneously Believing Self to be Limited Partner

(a)   Except as otherwise provided in subsection (b), a person that makes an investment in a business enterprise and erroneously but in good faith believes that the person has become a limited partner in the enterprise is not liable for the enterprise's obligations by reason of making the investment, receiving distributions from the enterprise, or exercising any rights of or appropriate to a limited partner, if, on ascertaining the mistake, the person:

     (1)   causes an appropriate certificate of limited partnership, amendment, or statement of correction to be signed and delivered to the [Secretary of State] for filing; or

     (2)   withdraws from future participation as an owner in the enterprise by signing and delivering to the [Secretary of State] for filing a statement of negation under this section.

(b)   A person that makes an investment described in subsection (a) is liable to the same extent as a general partner to any third party that enters into a transaction with the enterprise, believing in good faith that the person is a general partner, before the [Secretary of State] files a statement of negation, certificate of limited partnership, amendment, or statement of correction to show that the person is not a general partner.

(c)   If a person makes a diligent effort in good faith to comply with subsection (a)(1) and is unable to cause the appropriate certificate of limited partnership, amendment, or statement of correction to be signed and delivered to the [Secretary of State] for filing, the person has the right to withdraw from the enterprise pursuant to subsection (a)(2) even if the withdrawal would otherwise breach an agreement with others that are or have agreed to become co-owners of the enterprise.

ARTICLE 4
GENERAL PARTNERS

§ 401.   Becoming General Partner

(a)   Upon formation of a limited partnership, a person becomes a general partner as agreed among the persons that are to be the initial partners.

(b)   After formation of a limited partnership, a person becomes a general partner:

     (1)   as provided in the partnership agreement;

     (2)   as the result of a transaction effective under [Article] 11;

(3)   with the affirmative vote or consent of all the partners; or

(4)   as provided in Section 801(a)(3)(B).

(c)   A person may become a general partner without:

(1)   acquiring a transferable interest; or

(2)   making or being obligated to make a contribution to the partnership.

§ 402. General Partner Agent of Limited Partnership

(a)   Each general partner is an agent of the limited partnership for the purposes of its activities and affairs. An act of a general partner, including the signing of a record in the partnership's name, for apparently carrying on in the ordinary course the partnership's activities and affairs or activities and affairs of the kind carried on by the partnership binds the partnership, unless the general partner did not have authority to act for the partnership in the particular matter and the person with which the general partner was dealing knew or had notice that the general partner lacked authority.

(b)   An act of a general partner which is not apparently for carrying on in the ordinary course the limited partnership's activities and affairs or activities and affairs of the kind carried on by the partnership binds the partnership only if the act was actually authorized by all the other partners.

§ 403. Limited Partnership Liable for General Partner's Actionable Conduct

(a)   A limited partnership is liable for loss or injury caused to a person, or for a penalty incurred, as a result of a wrongful act or omission, or other actionable conduct, of a general partner acting in the ordinary course of activities and affairs of the partnership or with the actual or apparent authority of the partnership.

(b)   If, in the course of a limited partnership's activities and affairs or while acting with actual or apparent authority of the partnership, a general partner receives or causes the partnership to receive money or property of a person not a partner, and the money or property is misapplied by a general partner, the partnership is liable for the loss.

§ 404. General Partner's Liability

(a)   Except as otherwise provided in subsections (b) and (c), all general partners are liable jointly and severally for all debts, obligations, and other liabilities of the limited partnership unless otherwise agreed by the claimant or provided by law.

(b)   A person that becomes a general partner is not personally liable for a debt, obligation, or other liability of the limited partnership incurred before the person became a general partner.

(c)   A debt, obligation, or other liability of a limited partnership incurred while the partnership is a limited liability limited partnership is solely the debt, obligation, or other liability of the limited liability limited partnership. A general partner is not personally liable, directly or indirectly, by way of contribution or otherwise, for a debt, obligation, or other liability of the limited liability limited partnership solely by reason of being or acting as a general partner. This subsection applies:

(1)   despite anything inconsistent in the partnership agreement that existed immediately before the vote or consent required to become a limited liability limited partnership under Section 406(b)(2); and

(2)   regardless of the dissolution of the partnership.

(d)   The failure of a limited liability limited partnership to observe formalities relating to the exercise of its powers or management of its activities and affairs is not a ground for imposing liability on a general partner for a debt, obligation, or other liability of the partnership.

(e)   An amendment of a certificate of limited partnership which deletes a statement that the limited partnership is a limited liability limited partnership does not affect the limitation in this section on the liability of a general partner for a debt, obligation, or other liability of the limited partnership incurred before the amendment became effective.

§ 405.   Actions by and Against Partnership and Partners

(a)   To the extent not inconsistent with Section 404, a general partner may be joined in an action against the limited partnership or named in a separate action.

(b)   A judgment against a limited partnership is not by itself a judgment against a general partner. A judgment against a partnership may not be satisfied from a general partner's assets unless there is also a judgment against the general partner.

(c)   A judgment creditor of a general partner may not levy execution against the assets of the general partner to satisfy a judgment based on a claim against the limited partnership, unless the partner is personally liable for the claim under Section 404 and:

(1)   a judgment based on the same claim has been obtained against the limited partnership and a writ of execution on the judgment has been returned unsatisfied in whole or in part;

(2)   the partnership is a debtor in bankruptcy;

(3)   the general partner has agreed that the creditor need not exhaust partnership assets;

(4)   a court grants permission to the judgment creditor to levy execution against the assets of a general partner based on a finding that partnership assets subject to execution are clearly insufficient to satisfy the judgment, that exhaustion of assets is excessively burdensome, or that the grant of permission is an appropriate exercise of the court's equitable powers; or

(5)   liability is imposed on the general partner by law or contract independent of the existence of the partnership.

§ 406.   Management Rights of General Partner

(a)   Each general partner has equal rights in the management and conduct of the limited partnership's activities and affairs. Except as otherwise provided in this [Act], any matter relating to the activities and affairs of the partnership is decided exclusively by the general partner or, if there is more than one general partner, by a majority of the general partners.

(b)   The affirmative vote or consent of all the partners is required to:

(1)   amend the partnership agreement;

(2)   amend the certificate of limited partnership to add or delete a statement that the limited partnership is a limited liability limited partnership; and

(3)   sell, lease, exchange, or otherwise dispose of all, or substantially all, of the limited partnership's property, with or without the good will, other than in the usual and regular course of the limited partnership's activities and affairs.

(c)   A limited partnership shall reimburse a general partner for an advance to the partnership beyond the amount of capital the general partner agreed to contribute.

(d)   A payment or advance made by a general partner which gives rise to a limited partnership obligation under subsection (c) or Section 408(a) constitutes a loan to the limited partnership which accrues interest from the date of the payment or advance.

(e)   A general partner is not entitled to remuneration for services performed for the limited partnership.

§ 407. Rights to Information of General Partner and Person Dissociated as General Partner

(a)   A general partner may inspect and copy required information during regular business hours in the limited partnership's principal office, without having any particular purpose for seeking the information.

(b)   On reasonable notice, a general partner may inspect and copy during regular business hours, at a reasonable location specified by the limited partnership, any record maintained by the partnership regarding the partnership's activities, affairs, financial condition, and other circumstances, to the extent the information is material to the general partner's rights and duties under the partnership agreement or this [Act].

(c)   A limited partnership shall furnish to each general partner:

(1)   without demand, any information concerning the partnership's activities, affairs, financial condition, and other circumstances which the partnership knows and is material to the proper exercise of the general partner's rights and duties under the partnership agreement or this [Act], except to the extent the partnership can establish that it reasonably believes the general partner already knows the information; and

(2)   on demand, any other information concerning the partnership's activities, affairs, financial condition, and other circumstances, except to the extent the demand or the information demanded is unreasonable or otherwise improper under the circumstances.

(d)   The duty to furnish information under subsection (c) also applies to each general partner to the extent the general partner knows any of the information described in subsection (b).

(e)   Subject to subsection (j), on 10 days' demand made in a record received by a limited partnership, a person dissociated as a general partner may have access to the information and records described in subsections (a) and (b) at the locations specified in those subjections if:

(1)   the information or record pertains to the period during which the person was a general partner;

(2)   the person seeks the information or record in good faith; and

(3)   the person satisfies the requirements imposed on a limited partner by Section 304(b).

(f)   A limited partnership shall respond to a demand made pursuant to subsection (e) in the manner provided in Section 304(c).

(g)   A limited partnership may charge a person that makes a demand under this section the reasonable costs of copying, limited to the costs of labor and material.

(h)   A general partner or person dissociated as a general partner may exercise the rights under this section through an agent or, in the case of an individual under legal disability, a legal representative. Any restriction or condition imposed by the partnership agreement or under subsection (j) applies both to the agent or legal representative and to the general partner or person dissociated as a general partner.

(i)   The rights under this section do not extend to a person as transferee, but if:

(1)   a general partner dies, Section 704 applies; and

(2)   an individual dissociates as a general partner under Section 603(6)(B) or (C), the legal representative of the individual may exercise the rights under subsection (c) of a person dissociated as a general partner.

(j)   In addition to any restriction or condition stated in its partnership agreement, a limited partnership, as a matter within the ordinary course of its activities and affairs, may impose reasonable restrictions and conditions on access to and use of information to be furnished under this section, including designating information confidential and imposing nondisclosure and safeguarding obligations on the recipient. In a dispute concerning the reasonableness of a restriction under this subsection, the partnership has the burden of proving reasonableness.

§ 408. Reimbursement; Indemnification; Advancement; and Insurance

(a)   A limited partnership shall reimburse a general partner for any payment made by the general partner in the course of the general partner's activities on behalf of the partnership, if the general partner complied with Sections 406, 409, and 504 in making the payment.

(b)   A limited partnership shall indemnify and hold harmless a person with respect to any claim or demand against the person and any debt, obligation, or other liability incurred by the person by reason of the person's former or present capacity as a general partner, if the claim, demand, debt, obligation, or other liability does not arise from the person's breach of Section 406, 409, or 504.

(c)   In the ordinary course of its activities and affairs, a limited partnership may advance reasonable expenses, including attorney's fees and costs, incurred by a person in connection with a claim or demand against the person by reason of the person's former or present capacity as a general partner, if the person promises to repay the partnership if the person ultimately is determined not to be entitled to be indemnified under subsection (b).

(d)   A limited partnership may purchase and maintain insurance on behalf of a general partner against liability asserted against or incurred by the general partner in that capacity or arising from that status even if, under Section 105(c)(8), the partnership agreement could not eliminate or limit the person's liability to the partnership for the conduct giving rise to the liability.

§ 409. Standards of Conduct for General Partners

(a)   A general partner owes to the limited partnership and, subject to Section 901, the other partners the duties of loyalty and care stated in subsections (b) and (c).

(b)   The fiduciary duty of loyalty of a general partner includes the duties:

(1)   to account to the limited partnership and hold as trustee for it any property, profit, or benefit derived by the general partner:

(A)   in the conduct or winding up of the partnership's activities and affairs;

(B)   from a use by the general partner of the partnership's property; or

(C)   from the appropriation of a partnership opportunity;

(2)   to refrain from dealing with the partnership in the conduct or winding up of the partnership's activities and affairs as or on behalf of a person having an interest adverse to the partnership; and

(3)   to refrain from competing with the partnership in the conduct or winding up of the partnership's activities and affairs.

(c)   The duty of care a general partner in the conduct and winding up of the limited partnership's activities and affairs is to refrain from engaging in grossly negligent or reckless conduct, willful or intentional misconduct, or knowing violation of law.

(d)   A general partner shall discharge the duties and obligations under this [Act] or under the partnership agreement and exercise any rights consistently with the contractual obligation of good faith and fair dealing.

(e)   A general partner does not violate a duty or obligation under this [Act] or under the partnership agreement solely because the general partner's conduct furthers the general partner's own interest.

(f)   All the partners of a limited partnership may authorize or ratify, after full disclosure of all material facts, a specific act or transaction by a general partner that otherwise would violate the duty of loyalty.

(g)   It is a defense to a claim under subsection (b)(2) and any comparable claim in equity or at common law that the transaction was fair to the limited partnership.

(h)   If, as permitted by subsection (f) or the partnership agreement, a general partner enters into a transaction with the limited partnership which otherwise would be prohibited by subsection (b)(2), the general partner's rights and obligations arising from the transaction are the same as those of a person that is not a general partner.

ARTICLE 5
CONTRIBUTIONS AND DISTRIBUTIONS

§ 501.   Form of Contribution

A contribution may consist of property transferred to, services performed for, or another benefit provided to the limited partnership or an agreement to transfer property to, perform services for, or provide another benefit to the partnership.

§ 502.   Liability for Contribution

(a)   A person's obligation to make a contribution to a limited partnership is not excused by the person's death, disability, termination, or provide another benefit to the partnership.

(b)   If a person does not fulfill an obligation to make a contribution other than money, the person is obligated at the option of the limited partnership to contribute money equal to the value, as stated in the required information, of the part of the contribution which has not been made.

(c)   The obligation of a person to make a contribution may be compromised only by the affirmative vote or consent of all the partners. If a creditor of a limited partnership extends credit or otherwise acts in reliance on an obligation described in subsection (a) without knowledge or notice of a compromise under this subsection, the creditor may enforce the obligation.

§ 503.   Sharing of and Right to Distributions Before Dissolution

(a)   Any distribution made by a limited partnership before its dissolution and winding up must be shared among the partners on the basis of the value, as stated in the required information when the limited partnership decides to make the distribution, of the contributions the limited partnership has received from each partner, except to the extent necessary to comply with a transfer effective under Section 702 or charging order in effect under Section 703.

(b)   A person has a right to a distribution before the dissolution and winding up of a limited partnership only if the partnership decides to make an interim distribution. A person's dissociation does not entitle the person to a distribution.

(c)   A person does not have a right to demand or receive a distribution from a limited partnership in any form other than money. Except as otherwise provided in Section 810(f), a partnership may distribute an asset in kind only if each part of the asset is fungible with each other part and each person receives a percentage of the asset equal in value to the person's share of distributions.

(d)   If a partner or transferee becomes entitled to receive a distribution, the partner or transferee has the status of, and is entitled to all remedies available to, a creditor of the limited partnership with respect to the distribution. However, the partnership's obligation to make a distribution is subject to offset for any amount owed to the partnership by the partner or a person dissociated as a partner on whose account the distribution is made.

§ 504. Limitations on Distribution

(a)   A limited partnership may not make a distribution, including a distribution under Section 810, if after the distribution:

(1)   the partnership would not be able to pay its debts as they become due in the ordinary course of the partnership's activities and affairs; or

(2)   the partnership's total assets would be less than the sum of its total liabilities plus the amount that would be needed, if the partnership were to be dissolved and wound up at the time of the distribution, to satisfy the preferential rights upon dissolution and winding up of partners and transferees whose preferential rights are superior to the rights of persons receiving the distribution.

(b)   A limited partnership may base a determination that a distribution is not prohibited under subsection (a) on:

(1)   financial statements prepared on the basis of accounting practices and principles that are reasonable in the circumstances; or

(2)   a fair valuation or other method that is reasonable under the circumstances.

(c)   Except as otherwise provided in subsection (e), the effect of a distribution under subsection (a) is measured:

(1)   in the case of a distribution as defined in Section 102(4)(A), as of the earlier of:

(A)   the date money or other property is transferred or debt is incurred by the limited partnership; or

(B)   the date the person entitled to the distribution ceases to own the interest or right being acquired by the partnership in return for the distribution;

(2)   in the case of any other distribution of indebtedness, as of the date the indebtedness is distributed; and

(3)   in all other cases, as of the date:

(A)   the distribution is authorized, if the payment occurs not later than 120 days after that date; or

(B)   the payment is made, if the payment occurs more than 120 days after the distribution is authorized.

(d)   A limited partnership's indebtedness to a partner or transferee incurred by reason of a distribution made in accordance with this section is at parity with the partnership's indebtedness to its general, unsecured creditors, except to the extent subordinated by agreement.

(e)   A limited partnership's indebtedness, including indebtedness issued as a distribution, is not a liability for purposes of subsection (a) if the terms of the indebtedness provide that payment of principal and interest is made only if and to the extent that payment of a distribution could then be made under this section. If the indebtedness is issued as a distribution, each payment of principal or interest is treated as a distribution, the effect of which is measured on the date the payment is made.

(f)   In measuring the effect of a distribution under Section 810, the liabilities of a dissolved limited partnership do not include any claim that has been disposed of under Section 806, 807, or 808.

§ 505. Liability for Improper Distributions

(a)   If a general partner consents to a distribution made in violation of Section 504 and in consenting to the distribution fails to comply with Section 409, the general partner is personally liable to the limited partnership for the amount of the distribution which exceeds the amount that could have been distributed without the violation of Section 504.

(b)   A person that receives a distribution knowing that the distribution violated Section 504 is personally liable to the limited partnership but only to the extent that the distribution received by the person exceeded the amount that could have been properly paid under Section 504.

(c)   A general partner against which an action is commenced because the general partner is liable under subsection (a) may:

(1)   implead any other person that is liable under subsection (a) and seek to enforce a right of contribution from the person; and

(2)   implead any person that received a distribution in violation of subsection (b) and seek to enforce a right of contribution from the person in the amount the person received in violation of subsection (b).

(d)   An action under this section is barred unless commenced not later than two years after the distribution.

ARTICLE 6
DISSOCIATION

§ 601.   Dissociation as Limited Partner

(a)   A person does not have a right to dissociate as a limited partner before the completion of the winding up of the limited partnership.

(b)   A person is dissociated as a limited partner when:

(1)   the limited partnership knows or has notice of the person's express will to withdraw as a limited partner, but, if the person has specified a withdrawal date later than the date the partnership knew or had notice, on that later date;

(2)   an event stated in the partnership agreement as causing the person's dissociation as a limited partner occurs;

(3)   the person is expelled as a limited partner pursuant to the partnership agreement;

(4)   the person is expelled as a limited partner by the affirmative vote or consent of the other partners if:

(A)   it is unlawful to carry on the limited partnership's activities and affairs with the person as a limited partner;

(B)   there has been a transfer of all the person's transferable interest in the partnership, other than:

(i)   a transfer for security purposes; or

(ii)   a charging order in effect under Section 703 which has not been foreclosed;

(C)   the person is an entity and:

(i)   the partnership notifies the person that it will be expelled as a limited partner because the person has filed a statement of dissolution or the equivalent, the person has been administratively dissolved, the person's charter or the equivalent has been revoked, or the person's right to conduct business has been suspended by the person's jurisdiction of formation; and

(ii)   not later than 90 days after the notification, the statement of dissolution or the equivalent has not been withdrawn, rescinded, or revoked, the person has not been reinstated, or the person's charter or the equivalent or right to conduct business has not been reinstated; or

(D)   the person is an unincorporated entity that has been dissolved and whose activities and affairs are being wound up;

(5)   on application by the limited partnership or a partner in a direct action under Section 901, the person is expelled as a limited partner by judicial order because the person:

(A)   has engaged or is engaging in wrongful conduct that has affected adversely and materially, or will affect adversely and materially, the partnership's activities and affairs;

(B)   has committed willfully or persistently, or is committing willfully and persistently, a material breach of the partnership agreement or the contractual obligation of good faith and fair dealing under Section 305(a); or

(C)   has engaged or is engaging in conduct relating to the partnership's activities and affairs which makes it not reasonably practicable to carry on the activities and affairs with the person as a limited partner;

(6)   in the case of an individual, the individual dies;

(7)   in the case of a person that is a testamentary or inter vivos trust or is acting as a limited partner by virtue of being a trustee of such a trust, the trust's entire transferable interest in the limited partnership is distributed;

(8)   in the case of a person that is an estate or is acting as a limited partner by virtue of being a personal representative of an estate, the estate's entire transferable interest in the limited partnership is distributed;

(9)   in the case of a person that is not an individual, the existence of the person terminates;

(10)   the limited partnership participates in a merger under [Article] 11, and:

(A)   the partnership is not the surviving entity; or

(B)   otherwise as a result of the merger, the person ceases to be a limited partner;

(11)   the limited partnership participates in an interest exchange under [Article] 11 and, as a result of the interest exchange, the person ceases to be a limited partner;

(12)   the limited partnership participates in a conversion under [Article] 11;

(13)   the limited partnership participates in a domestication under [Article] 11 and, as a result of the domestication, the person ceases to be a limited partner; or

(14)   the limited partnership dissolves and completes winding up.

§ 602.   Effect of Dissociation as Limited Partner

(a)   If a person is dissociated as a limited partner:

(1)   subject to Section 704, the person does not have further rights as a limited partner;

(2)   the person's contractual obligation of good faith and fair dealing as a limited partner under Section 305(a) ends with regard to matters arising and events occurring after the person's dissociation; and

(3)   subject to Section 704 and [Article] 11, any transferable interest owned by the person in the person's capacity as a limited partner immediately before dissociation is owned by the person as a mere transferee.

(b)   A person's dissociation as a limited partner does not of itself discharge the person from any debt, obligation, or other liability to the limited partnership or the other partners which the person incurred while a limited partner.

§ 603. Dissociation as General Partner

A person is dissociated as a general partner when:

(1)   the limited partnership knows or has notice of the person's express will to withdraw as a general partner, but, if the person has specified a withdrawal date later than the date the partnership knew or had notice, on that later date;

(2)   an event stated in the partnership agreement as causing the person's dissociation as a general partner occurs;

(3)   the person is expelled as a general partner pursuant to the partnership agreement;

(4)   the person is expelled as a general partner by the affirmative vote or consent of all the other partners if:

(A)   it is unlawful to carry on the limited partnership's activities and affairs with the person as a general partner;

(B)   there has been a transfer of all or substantially all of the person's transferable interest in the limited partnership, other than:

(i)   a transfer for security purposes; or

(ii)   a charging order in effect under Section 703 which has not been foreclosed;

(C)   the person is an entity and:

(i)   the partnership notifies the person that it will be expelled as a general partner because the person has filed a statement of dissolution or the equivalent, the person has been administratively dissolved, the person's charter or the equivalent has been revoked, or the person's right to conduct business has been suspended by the person's jurisdiction of formation; and

(ii)   not later than 90 days after the notification, the statement of dissolution or the equivalent has not been withdrawn, rescinded, or revoked, the person has not been reinstated, or the person's charter or the equivalent or right to conduct business has not been reinstated; or

(D)   the person is an unincorporated entity that has been dissolved and whose activities and affairs are being wound up;

(5)   on application by the limited partnership or a partner in a direct action under Section 901, the person is expelled as a general partner by judicial order because the person:

(A)   has engaged or is engaging in wrongful conduct that has affected adversely and materially, or will affect adversely and materially, the partnership's activities and affairs;

(B)   has committed willfully or persistently, or is committing willfully or persistently, a material breach of the partnership agreement or a duty or obligation under Section 409; or

(C)   has engaged or is engaging in conduct relating to the partnership's activities and affairs which makes it not reasonably practicable to carry on the activities and affairs of the limited partnership with the person as a general partner;

(6)   in the case of an individual:

(A)   the individual dies;

(B)   a guardian or general conservator for the individual is appointed; or

(C)   a court orders that the individual has otherwise become incapable of performing the individual's duties as a general partner under this [act] or the partnership agreement;

(7)   the person:

   (A)   becomes a debtor in bankruptcy;

   (B)   executes an assignment for the benefit of creditors; or

   (C)   seeks, consents to, or acquiesces in the appointment of a trustee, receiver, or liquidator of the person or of all or substantially all the person's property;

(8)   in the case of a person that is a testamentary or inter vivos trust or is acting as a general partner by virtue of being a trustee of such a trust, the trust's entire transferable interest in the limited partnership is distributed;

(9)   in the case of a person that is an estate or is acting as a general partner by virtue of being a personal representative of an estate, the estate's entire transferable interest in the limited partnership is distributed;

(10)   in the case of a person that is not an individual, the existence of the person terminates;

(11)   the limited partnership participates in a merger under [Article] 11 and:

   (A)   the partnership is not the surviving entity; or

   (B)   otherwise as a result of the merger, the person ceases to be a general partner;

(12)   the limited partnership participates in an interest exchange under [Article] 11 and, as a result of the interest exchange, the person ceases to be a general partner;

(13)   the limited partnership participates in a conversion under [Article] 11;

(14)   the limited partnership participates in a domestication under [Article] 11 and, as a result of the domestication, the person ceases to be a general partner; or

(15)   the limited partnership dissolves and completes winding up.

§ 604.   Person's Power to Dissociate as General Partner; Wrongful Dissociation

(a)   A person has the power to dissociate as a general partner at any time, rightfully or wrongfully, by express will pursuant to Section 603(1).

(b)   A person's dissociation as a general partner is wrongful only if the dissociation:

   (1)   is in breach of an express provision of the partnership agreement; or

   (2)   occurs before the completion of the winding up of the limited partnership, and:

      (A)   the person withdraws as a general partner by express will;

      (B)   the person is expelled as a general partner by judicial determination under Section 603(5);

      (C)   the person is dissociated as a general partner under Section 603(7); or

      (D)   in the case of a person that is not a trust other than a business trust, an estate, or an individual, the person is expelled or otherwise dissociated as a general partner because it willfully dissolved or terminated.

(c)   A person that wrongfully dissociates as a general partner is liable to the limited partnership and, subject to Section 901, to the other partners for damages caused by the dissociation. The liability is in addition to any debt, obligation, or other liability of the general partner to the partnership or the other partners.

§ 605.   Effect of Dissociation as General Partner

(a)   Upon a person's dissociation as a general partner:

(1)   the person's right to participate as a general partner in the management and conduct of the partnership's activities terminates;

(2)   the person's duties and obligations as a general partner under Section 409 end with regard to matters arising and events occurring after the person's dissociation;

(3)   the person may sign and deliver to the [Secretary of State] for filing a statement of dissociation pertaining to the person and, at the request of the limited partnership, shall sign an amendment to the certificate of limited partnership which states that the person has dissociated as a general partner; and

(4)   subject to Section 704 and [Article] 11, any transferable interest owned by the person immediately before dissociation in the person's capacity as a general partner is owned by the person solely as a transferee.

(b)   A person's dissociation as a general partner does not of itself discharge the person from any debt, obligation, or other liability to the limited partnership or the other partners which the person incurred while a general partner.

§ 606.   Power to Bind and Liability of Person Dissociated as General Partner

(a)   After a person is dissociated as a general partner and before the limited partnership is merged out of existence, converted, or domesticated under [Article] 11, or dissolved, the partnership is bound by an act of the person only if:

(1)   the act would have bound the limited partnership under Section 402 before the dissociation; and

(2)   at the time the other party enters into the transaction:

(A)   less than two years has passed since the dissociation; and

(B)   the other party does not know or have notice of the dissociation and reasonably believes that the person is a general partner.

(b)   If a limited partnership is bound under subsection (a), the person dissociated as a general partner which caused the limited partnership to be bound is liable:

(1)   to the limited partnership for any damage caused to the partnership arising from the obligation incurred under subsection (a); and

(2)   if a general partner or another person dissociated as a general partner is liable for the obligation, to the general partner or other person for any damage caused to the general partner or other person arising from the liability.

§ 607.   Liability of Person Dissociated as General Partner to Other Persons

(a)   A person's dissociation as a general partner does not of itself discharge the person's liability as a general partner for an obligation of the limited partnership incurred before dissociation. Except as otherwise provided in subsections (b) and (c), the person is not liable for a limited partnership's obligation incurred after dissociation.

(b)   A person whose dissociation as a general partner results in a dissolution and winding up of the limited partnership's activities and affairs is liable on an obligation incurred by the partnership under Section 805 to the same extent as a general partner under Section 404.

(c)   A person that has dissociated as a general partner but whose dissociation did not result in a dissolution and winding up of the limited partnership's activities is liable on a transaction entered into by the limited partnership after the dissociation only if:

(1)   a general partner would be liable on the transaction; and

(2)   at the time the other party enters into the transaction:

    (A)   less than two years has passed since the dissociation; and

    (B)   the other party does not have notice of the dissociation and reasonably believes that the person is a general partner.

(d)   By agreement with a creditor of a limited partnership and the limited partnership, a person dissociated as a general partner may be released from liability for a debt, obligation, or other liability of the partnership.

(e)   A person dissociated as a general partner is released from liability for a debt, obligation, or other liability of the limited partnership if the partnership's creditor, with knowledge or notice of the person's dissociation as a general partner but without the person's consent, agrees to a material alteration in the nature or time of payment of the debt, obligation, or other liability.

ARTICLE 7
TRANSFERABLE INTERESTS AND RIGHTS
OF TRANSFEREES AND CREDITORS

§ 701.   Nature of Transferable Interest

A transferable interest is personal property.

§ 702.   Transfer of Transferable Interest

(a)   A transfer, in whole or in part, of a partner's transferable interest:

(1)   is permissible;

(2)   does not by itself cause the partner's dissociation or a dissolution and winding up of the limited partnership's activities; and

(3)   subject to Section 704, does not entitle the transferee to:

    (A)   participate in the management or conduct of the partnership's activities and affairs; or

    (B)   except as otherwise provided in subsection (c), have access to required information, records, or other information concerning the partnership's activities and affairs.

(b)   A transferee has a right to receive, in accordance with the transfer, distributions to which the transferor would otherwise be entitled.

(c)   In a dissolution and winding up of a limited partnership, a transferee is entitled to an account of the partnership's transactions only from the date of dissolution.

(d)   A transferable interest may be evidenced by a certificate of the interest issued by a limited partnership in a record, and, subject to this section, the interest represented by the certificate may be transferred by a transfer of the certificate.

(e)   A limited partnership need not give effect to a transferee's rights under this section until the partnership knows or has notice of the transfer.

(f)   A transfer of a transferable interest in violation of a restriction on transfer contained in the partnership agreement is ineffective if the intended transferee has knowledge or notice of the restriction at the time of transfer.

(g)   Except as otherwise provided in Sections 601(b)(4)(B) and 603(4)(B), if a general or limited partner transfers a transferable interest, the transferor retains the rights of a general or limited partner other than the transferable interest transferred and retains all the duties and obligations of a general or limited partner.

(h)   If a general or limited partner transfers a transferable interest to a person that becomes a general or limited partner with respect to the transferred interest, the transferee is liable for the transferor's obligations under Sections 502 and 505 known to the transferee when the transferee becomes a partner.

§ 703.   Charging Order

(a)   On application by a judgment creditor of a partner or transferee, a court may enter a charging order against the transferable interest of the judgment debtor for the unsatisfied amount of the judgment. A charging order constitutes a lien on a judgment debtor's transferable interest and requires the limited partnership to pay over to the person to which the charging order was issued any distribution that otherwise would be paid to the judgment debtor.

(b)   To the extent necessary to effectuate the collection of distributions pursuant to a charging order in effect under subsection (a), the court may:

(1)   appoint a receiver of the distributions subject to the charging order, with the power to make all inquiries the judgment debtor might have made; and

(2)   make all other orders necessary to give effect to the charging order.

(c)   Upon a showing that distributions under a charging order will not pay the judgment debt within a reasonable time, the court may foreclose the lien and order the sale of the transferable interest. The purchaser at the foreclosure sale obtains only the transferable interest, does not thereby become a partner, and is subject to Section 702.

(d)   At any time before foreclosure under subsection (c), the partner or transferee whose transferable interest is subject to a charging order under subsection (a) may extinguish the charging order by satisfying the judgment and filing a certified copy of the satisfaction with the court that issued the charging order.

(e)   At any time before foreclosure under subsection (c), a limited partnership or one or more partners whose transferable interests are not subject to the charging order may pay to the judgment creditor the full amount due under the judgment and thereby succeed to the rights of the judgment creditor, including the charging order.

(f)   This [Act] does not deprive any partner or transferee of the benefit of any exemption law applicable to the transferable interest of the partner or transferee.

(g)   This section provides the exclusive remedy by which a person seeking in the capacity of a judgment creditor to enforce a judgment against a partner or transferee may satisfy the judgment from the judgment debtor's transferable interest.

§ 704.   Power of Legal Representative of Deceased Partner

If a partner dies, the deceased partner's legal representative may exercise:

(1)   the rights of a transferee provided in Section 702(c); and

(2)   for the purposes of settling the estate, the rights of a current limited partner under Section 304.

ARTICLE 8
DISSOLUTION AND WINDING UP

§ 801.   Events Causing Dissolution

(a)   A limited partnership is dissolved, and its activities and affairs must be wound up upon the occurrence of any of the following:

(1)   an event or circumstance that the partnership agreement states causes dissolution;

(2)   the affirmative vote or consent of all general partners and of limited partners owning a majority of the rights to receive distributions as limited partners at the time the vote or consent is to be effective;

(3)   after the dissociation of a person as a general partner:

(A)   if the limited partnership has at least one remaining general partner, the affirmative vote or consent to dissolve the limited partnership not later than 90 days after the dissociation by partners owning a majority of the rights to receive distributions as partners at the time the vote or consent is to be effective; or

(B)   if the partnership does not have a remaining general partner, the passage of 90 days after the dissociation, unless before the end of the period:

(i)   consent to continue the activities and affairs of the partnership and admit at least one general partner is given by limited partners owning a majority of the rights to receive distributions as limited partners at the time the consent is to be effective; and

(ii)   at least one person is admitted as a general partner in accordance with the consent;

(4)   the passage of 90 consecutive days after the dissociation of the partnership's last limited partner, unless before the end of the period the partnership admits at least one limited partner;

(5)   the passage of 90 consecutive days during which the partnership has only one partner, unless before the end of the period:

(A)   the partnership admits at least one person as a partner;

(B)   if the previously sole remaining partner is only a general partner, the partnership admits the person as a limited partner; and

(C)   if the previously sole remaining partner is only a limited partner, the partnership admits a person as a general partner;

(6)   on application by a partner, the entry by [the appropriate court] of an order dissolving the partnership on the grounds that:

(A)   the conduct of all or substantially all the partnership's activities and affairs is unlawful; or

(B)   it is not reasonably practicable to carry on the partnership's activities and affairs in conformity with the certificate of limited partnership and partnership agreement; or

(7)   the signing and filing of a statement of administrative dissolution by the [Secretary of State] under Section 811.

(b)   If an event occurs that imposes a deadline on a limited partnership under subsection (a) and before the partnership has met the requirements of the deadline, another event occurs that imposes a different deadline on the partnership under subsection (a):

(1)   the occurrence of the second event does not affect the deadline caused by the first event; and

(2)   the partnership's meeting of the requirements of the first deadline does not extend to the second deadline.

§ 802. Winding Up

(a)   A dissolved limited partnership shall wind up its activities and affairs and, except as otherwise provided in Section 803, the partnership continues after dissolution only for the purpose of winding up.

(b)   In winding up its activities and affairs, the limited partnership:

(1)   shall discharge the partnership's debts, obligations, and other liabilities, settle and close the partnership's activities and affairs, and marshal and distribute the assets of the partnership; and

(2)   may

(A)   amend its certificate of limited partnership to state that the partnership is dissolved;

(B)   preserve the partnership activities, affairs, and property as a going concern for a reasonable time;

(C)   prosecute and defend actions and proceedings, whether civil, criminal, or administrative;

(D)   transfer the partnership's property;

(E)   settle disputes by mediation or arbitration;

(F)   deliver to the [Secretary of State] for filing a statement of termination stating the name of the partnership and that the partnership is terminated; and

(G)   perform other acts necessary or appropriate to the winding up.

(c)   If a dissolved limited partnership does not have a general partner, a person to wind up the dissolved limited partnership's activities and affairs may be appointed by the affirmative vote or consent of limited partners owning a majority of the rights to receive distributions as limited partners at the time the vote or consent is to be effective. A person appointed under this subsection:

(1)   has the powers of a general partner under Section 804 but is not liable for the debts, obligations, and other liabilities of the partnership solely by reason of having or exercising those powers or otherwise acting to wind up the dissolved partnership's activities and affairs; and

(2)   shall deliver promptly to the [Secretary of State] for filing an amendment to the partnership's certificate of limited partnership stating:

(A)   that the partnership does not have a general partner;

(B)   the name and street and mailing address of the person; and

(C)   that the person has been appointed pursuant to this subsection to wind up the partnership.

(d)   On the application of a partner, the [appropriate court] may order judicial supervision of the winding up, including the appointment of a person to wind up the partnership's activities and affairs, if:

(1)   the partnership does not have a general partner and within a reasonable time following the dissolution no person has been appointed pursuant to subsection (c); or

(2)   the applicant establishes other good cause.

§ 803. Rescinding Dissolution

(a)   A limited partnership may rescind its dissolution, unless a statement of termination applicable to the partnership has become effective, [the appropriate court] has entered an order under Section 801(a)(6) dissolving the partnership, or the [Secretary of State] has dissolved the partnership under Section 811.

(b)   Rescinding dissolution under this section requires:

(1)   the affirmative vote or consent of each partner; and

(2)　if the limited partnership has delivered to the [Secretary of State] for filing an amendment to the certificate of limited partnership stating that the partnership is dissolved and:

　　(A)　the amendment has not become effective, delivery to the [Secretary of State] for filing a statement of withdrawal under Section 208 applicable to the amendment; or

　　(B)　the amendment has become effective, delivery to the [Secretary of State] for filing an amendment to the certificate of limited partnership stating that dissolution has been rescinded under this section.

(c)　If a limited partnership rescinds its dissolution:

　　(1)　the partnership resumes carrying on its activities and affairs as if dissolution had never occurred;

　　(2)　subject to paragraph (3), any liability incurred by the partnership after the dissolution and before the rescission has become effective is determined as if dissolution had never occurred; and

　　(3)　the rights of a third party arising out of conduct in reliance on the dissolution before the third party knew or had notice of the rescission may not be adversely affected.

§ 804.　Power to Bind Partnership After Dissolution

(a)　A limited partnership is bound by a general partner's act after dissolution which:

　　(1)　is appropriate for winding up the limited partnership's activities and affairs; or

　　(2)　would have bound the limited partnership under Section 402 before dissolution, if, at the time the other party enters into the transaction, the other party does not have notice of the dissolution.

(b)　A person dissociated as a general partner binds a limited partnership through an act occurring after dissolution if:

　　(1)　at the time the other party enters into the transaction:

　　　　(A)　less than two years has passed since the dissociation; and

　　　　(B)　the other party does not know or have notice of the dissociation and reasonably believes that the person is a general partner; and

　　(2)　the act:

　　　　(A)　is appropriate for winding up the limited partnership's activities and affairs; or

　　　　(B)　would have bound the limited partnership under Section 402 before dissolution and at the time the other party enters into the transaction the other party does not have notice of the dissolution.

§ 805.　Liability After Dissolution of General Partner and Person Dissociated as General Partner

(a)　If a general partner having knowledge of the dissolution causes a limited partnership to incur an obligation under Section 804(a) by an act that is not appropriate for winding up the partnership's activities and affairs, the general partner is liable:

　　(1)　to the partnership for any damage caused to the partnership arising from the obligation; and

　　(2)　if another general partner or a person dissociated as a general partner is liable for the obligation, to that other general partner or person for any damage caused to that other general partner or person arising from the liability.

(b) If a person dissociated as a general partner causes a limited partnership to incur an obligation under Section 804(b), the person is liable:

(1) to the partnership for any damage caused to the partnership arising from the obligation; and

(2) if a general partner or another person dissociated as a general partner is liable for the obligation, to the general partner or other person for any damage caused to the general partner or other person arising from the obligation.

§ 806. Known Claims Against Dissolved Limited Partnership

(a) Except as otherwise provided in subsection (d), a dissolved limited partnership may give notice of a known claim under subsection (b), which has the effect provided in subsection (c).

(b) A dissolved limited partnership may in a record notify its known claimants of the dissolution. The notice must:

(1) specify the information required to be included in a claim;

(2) state that a claim must be in writing and provide a mailing address to which the claim is to be sent;

(3) state the deadline for receipt of the claim, which may not be less than 120 days after the date the notice is received by the claimant;

(4) state that the claim will be barred if not received by the deadline; and

(5) unless the limited partnership has been throughout its existence a limited liability limited partnership, state that the barring of a claim against the partnership will also bar any corresponding claim against any general partner or person dissociated as a general partner which is based on Section 404.

(c) A claim against a dissolved limited partnership is barred if the requirements of subsection (b) are met and:

(1) the claim is not received by the specified deadline; or

(2) if the claim is timely received but rejected by the partnership:

(A) the partnership causes the claimant to receive a notice in a record stating that the claim is rejected and will be barred unless the claimant commences an action against the partnership to enforce the claim not later than 90 days after the claimant receives the notice; and

(B) the claimant does not commence the required action not later than 90 days after the claimant receives the notice.

(d) This section does not apply to a claim based on an event occurring after the effective date of dissolution or a liability that is contingent.

§ 807. Other Claims Against Dissolved Limited Partnership

(a) A dissolved limited partnership may publish notice of its dissolution and request persons having claims against the partnership to present them in accordance with the notice.

(b) A notice under subsection (a) must:

(1) be published at least once in a newspaper of general circulation in the [county] in this state in which the dissolved limited partnership's principal office is located or, if the principal office is not located in this State, in the [county] in which the office of the partnership's registered agent is or was last located;

(2)   describe the information required to be contained in a claim, state that the claim must be in writing, and provide a mailing address to which the claim is to be sent;

(3)   state that a claim against the partnership is barred unless an action to enforce the claim is commenced not later than three years after publication of the notice; and

(4)   unless the limited partnership has been throughout its existence a limited liability limited partnership, state that the barring of a claim against the partnership will also bar any corresponding claim against any general partner or person dissociated as a general partner which is based on Section 404.

(c)   If a dissolved limited partnership publishes a notice in accordance with subsection (b), the claim of each of the following claimants is barred unless the claimant commences an action to enforce the claim against the partnership not later than three years after the publication date of the notice:

(1)   a claimant that did not receive notice in a record under Section 806;

(2)   a claimant whose claim was timely sent to the partnership but not acted on; and

(3)   a claimant whose claim is contingent at, or based on an event occurring after, the date of dissolution.

(d)   A claim not barred under this section may be enforced:

(1)   against the dissolved limited partnership, to the extent of its undistributed assets;

(2)   except as otherwise provided in Section 808, if the assets have been distributed after dissolution, against a partner or transferee to the extent of that person's proportionate share of the claim or the partnership's assets distributed to the partner or transferee after dissolution, whichever is less, but a person's total liability for all claims under this paragraph may not exceed the total amount of assets distributed to the person after dissolution; and

(3)   against any person liable on the claim under Sections 404 and 607.

§ 808.   Court Proceedings

(a)   A dissolved limited partnership that has published a notice under Section 807 may file an application with [the appropriate court] in the [county] where the partnership's principal office is located or, if the principal office is not located in this state, where the office of its registered agent is or was last located, for a determination of the amount and form of security to be provided for payment of claims that are contingent, have not been made known to the partnership, or are based on an event occurring after the date of dissolution but which, based on the facts known to the partnership, are reasonably expected to arise after the date of dissolution. Security is not required for any claim that is or is reasonably anticipated to be barred under Section 807.

(b)   Not later than 10 days after the filing of an application under subsection (a), the dissolved limited partnership shall give notice of the proceeding to each claimant holding a contingent claim known to the partnership.

(c)   In a proceeding brought under this section, the court may appoint a guardian ad litem to represent all claimants whose identities are unknown. The reasonable fees and expenses of the guardian, including all reasonable expert witness fees, must be paid by the dissolved limited partnership.

(d)   A dissolved limited partnership that provides security in the amount and form ordered by the court under subsection (a) satisfies the partnership's obligations with respect to claims that are contingent, have not been made known to the partnership, or are based on an event occurring after the date of dissolution, and such claims may not be enforced against a partner or transferee on account of assets received in liquidation.

§ 809. Liability of General Partner and Person Dissociated as General Partner When Claim Against Limited Partnership Barred

If a claim against a dissolved limited partnership is barred under Section 806, 807, or 808, any corresponding claim under Section 404 or 607 is also barred.

§ 810. Disposition of Assets in Winding Up; When Contributions Required

(a) In winding up its activities and affairs, a limited partnership shall apply its assets, including the contributions required by this section, to discharge the partnership's obligations to creditors, including partners that are creditors.

(b) After a limited partnership complies with subsection (a), any surplus must be distributed in the following order, subject to any charging order in effect under Section 703:

(1) to each person owning a transferable interest that reflects contributions made and not previously returned, an amount equal to the value of the unreturned contributions; and

(2) among persons owning transferable interests in proportion to their respective rights to share in distributions immediately before the dissolution of the partnership.

(c) If a limited partnership's assets are insufficient to satisfy all of its obligations under subsection (a), with respect to each unsatisfied obligation incurred when the partnership was not a limited liability limited partnership, the following rules apply:

(1) Each person that was a general partner when the obligation was incurred and that has not been released from the obligation under Section 607 shall contribute to the partnership for the purpose of enabling the partnership to satisfy the obligation. The contribution due from each of those persons is in proportion to the right to receive distributions in the capacity of a general partner in effect for each of those persons when the obligation was incurred.

(2) If a person does not contribute the full amount required under paragraph (1) with respect to an unsatisfied obligation of the partnership, the other persons required to contribute by paragraph (1) on account of the obligation shall contribute the additional amount necessary to discharge the obligation. The additional contribution due from each of those other persons is in proportion to the right to receive distributions in the capacity of a general partner in effect for each of those other persons when the obligation was incurred.

(3) If a person does not make the additional contribution required by paragraph (2), further additional contributions are determined and due in the same manner as provided in that paragraph.

(d) A person that makes an additional contribution under subsection (c)(2) or (3) may recover from any person whose failure to contribute under subsection (c)(1) or (2) necessitated the additional contribution. A person may not recover under this subsection more than the amount additionally contributed. A person's liability under this subsection may not exceed the amount the person failed to contribute.

(e) All distributions made under subsections (b) and (c) must be paid in money.

§ 811. Administrative Dissolution

(a) The [Secretary of State] may commence a proceeding under subsection (b) to dissolve a limited partnership administratively if the partnership does not:

(1) pay any fee, tax, interest, or penalty required to be paid to the [Secretary of State]not later than [six months] after it is due;

(2) deliver [an annual] [a biennial] report to the [Secretary of State] not later than [six months] after it is due; or

(3)   have a registered agent in this state for [60] consecutive days.

(b)   If the [Secretary of State] determines that a ground exists for administratively dissolving a limited partnership, the [Secretary of State] shall serve the partnership with notice in a record of the [Secretary of State's] determination.

(c)   If a limited partnership, not later than [60] days after service of the notice under subsection (b), does not cure or demonstrate to the satisfaction of the [Secretary of State] the nonexistence of each ground determined by the [Secretary of State], the [Secretary of State] shall administratively dissolve the partnership by signing a statement of administrative dissolution that recites the grounds for dissolution and the effective date of dissolution. The [Secretary of State] shall file the statement and serve a copy on the partnership pursuant to Section 121.

(d)   A limited partnership that is administratively dissolved continues in existence as an entity but may carry on any activities except as necessary to wind up its activities and affairs and liquidate its assets under Sections 802, 806, 807, 808, and 810, or to apply for reinstatement under Section 812.

(e)   The administrative dissolution of a limited partnership does not terminate the authority of its registered agent.

§ 812. Reinstatement

(a)   A limited partnership that has been administratively dissolved under Section 811 may apply to the [Secretary of State] for reinstatement [not later than [two] years after the effective date of dissolution]. The application must state:

(1)   the name of the partnership at the time of its administrative dissolution and, if needed, a different name that satisfies Section 114;

(2)   the address of the principal office of the partnership and the name and street and mailing addresses of its registered agent;

(3)   the effective date of the partnership's administrative dissolution; and

(4)   that the grounds for dissolution did not exist or have been cured.

(b)   To be reinstated, a limited partnership must pay all fees, taxes, interest, and penalties that were due to the [Secretary of State] at the time of the partnership's administrative dissolution and all fees, taxes, interest, and penalties that would have been due to the [Secretary of State] while the partnership was administratively dissolved.

(c)   If the [Secretary of State] determines that an application under subsection (a) contains the required information, is satisfied that the information is correct, and determines that all payments required to be made to the [Secretary of State] by subsection (b) have been made, the [Secretary of State] shall:

(1)   cancel the statement of administrative dissolution and prepare a statement of reinstatement that states the [Secretary of State's] determination and the effective date of reinstatement; and

(2)   file the statement of reinstatement and serve a copy on the limited partnership.

(d)   When reinstatement under this section has become effective, the following rules apply:

(1)   The reinstatement relates back to and takes effect as of the effective date of the administrative dissolution.

(2)   The limited partnership resumes carrying on its activities and affairs as if the administrative dissolution had not occurred.

(3)   The rights of a person arising out of an act or omission in reliance on the dissolution before the person knew or had notice of the reinstatement are not affected.

§ 813. Judicial Review of Denial of Reinstatement

(a) If the [Secretary of State] denies a limited partnership's application for reinstatement following administrative dissolution, the [Secretary of State] shall serve the limited partnership with a notice in the record that explains the reasons for the denial.

(b) A limited partnership may seek judicial review of denial of reinstatement in [the appropriate court] not later than [30] days after service of the notice of denial.

ARTICLE 9
ACTIONS BY PARTNERS

§ 901. Direct Action by Partner

(a) Subject to subsection (b), a partner may maintain a direct action against another partner or the limited partnership, with or without an accounting as to the partnership's activities and affairs, to enforce the rights and otherwise protect the partner's interests, including rights and interests under the partnership agreement or this [Act] or arising independently of the partnership relationship.

(b) A partner maintaining a direct action under this section must plead and prove an actual or threatened injury that is not solely the result of an injury suffered or threatened to be suffered by the limited partnership.

(c) A right to an accounting on a dissolution and winding up does not revive a claim barred by law.

§ 902. Derivative Action

A partner may maintain a derivative action to enforce a right of a limited partnership if:

(1) the partner first makes a demand on the general partners, requesting that they cause the limited partnership to bring an action to enforce the right, and the general partners do not bring the action within a reasonable time; or

(2) a demand under paragraph (1) would be futile.

§ 903. Proper Plaintiff

A derivative action to enforce a right of a limited partnership may be maintained only by a person that is a partner at the time the action is commenced and:

(1) was a partner when the conduct giving rise to the action occurred; or

(2) whose status as a partner devolved on the person by operation of law or pursuant to the terms of the partnership agreement from a person that was a partner at the time of the conduct.

§ 904. Pleading

In a derivative action, the complaint must state with particularity:

(1) the date and content of plaintiff's demand and the response to the demand by the general partner; or

(2) why demand should be excused as futile.

§ 905. Special Litigation Committee

(a) If a limited partnership is named as or made a party in a derivative proceeding, the partnership may appoint a special litigation committee to investigate the claims asserted in the proceeding and determine whether pursuing the action is in the best interests of the partnership. If the partnership appoints a special litigation committee, on motion by the committee made in the name of the partnership, except for good cause shown, the court shall stay discovery for the time reasonably necessary to permit to committee to make its investigation. This subsection does not prevent the court from:

(1)   enforcing a person's right to information under Section 304 or 407; or

(2)   granting extraordinary relief in the form of a temporary restraining order or preliminary injunction.

(b)   A special litigation committee must be composed of one or more disinterested and independent individuals, who may be partners.

(c)   A special litigation committee may be appointed:

(1)   by a majority of the general partners not named as parties in the proceeding; or

(2)   if all general partners are named as parties in the proceeding, by a majority of the general partners named as defendants.

(d)   After appropriate investigation, a special litigation committee may determine that it is in the best interests of the limited partnership that the proceeding:

(1)   continue under the control of the plaintiff;

(2)   continue under the control of the committee;

(3)   be settled on terms approved by the committee; or

(4)   be dismissed.

(e)   After making a determination under subsection (d), a special litigation committee shall file with the court a statement of its determination and its report supporting its determination and shall serve each party with a copy of the determination and report. The court shall determine whether the members of the committee were disinterested and independent and whether the committee conducted its investigation and made its recommendation in good faith, independently, and with reasonable care, with the committee having the burden of proof. If the court finds that the members of the committee were disinterested and independent and that the committee acted in good faith, independently, and with reasonable care, the court shall enforce the determination of the committee. Otherwise, the court shall dissolve the stay of discovery entered under subsection (a) and allow the action to continue under the control of the plaintiff.

§ 906.   Proceeds and Expenses

(a)   Except as otherwise provided in subsection (b):

(1)   any proceeds or other benefits of a derivative action, whether by judgment, compromise, or settlement, belong to the limited partnership and not to the plaintiff; and

(2)   if the plaintiff receives any proceeds, the derivative plaintiff shall remit them immediately to the partnership.

(b)   If a derivative action is successful in whole or in part, the court may award the plaintiff reasonable expenses, including reasonable attorney's fees and costs, from the recovery of the limited partnership.

(c)   A derivative action on behalf of a limited partnership may not be voluntarily dismissed or settled without the court's approval.

ARTICLE 10
FOREIGN LIMITED PARTNERSHIPS

§ 1001. Governing Law

(a)   The law of the jurisdiction of formation of a foreign limited partnership governs:

    (1)   the internal affairs of the partnership;

    (2)   the liability of a partner as partner for a debt, obligation, or other liability of the partnership; and

    (3)   the liability of a series of the partnership.

(b)   A foreign limited partnership is not precluded from registering to do business in this state because of any difference between the law of its jurisdiction of formation and the law of this state.

(c)   Registration of a foreign limited partnership to do business in this state does not authorize the foreign partnership to engage in any activities or affairs or exercise any power that a limited partnership may not engage in or exercise in this State.

§ 1002. Registration to do Business in this State

(a)   A foreign limited partnership may not do business in this State until it registers with the [Secretary of State] under this [article].

(b)   A foreign limited partnership doing business in this State may not maintain an action or proceeding in this State unless it is registered to do business in this State.

(c)   The failure of a foreign limited partnership to register to do business in this State does not impair the validity of a contract or act of the partnership or preclude it from defending an action or proceeding in this State.

(d)   A limitation on the liability of a general partner or limited partner of a foreign limited partnership is not waived solely because the partnership does business in this State without registering to do business in this State.

(e)   Section 1001(a) and (b) applies even if the foreign limited partnership fails to register under this [article].

§ 1003. Foreign Registration Statement

To register to do business in this State, a foreign limited partnership must deliver a foreign registration statement to the [Secretary of State] for filing. The statement must state:

    (1)   the name of the partnership and, if the name does not comply with Section 114, an alternate name adopted pursuant to Section 1006(a);

    (2)   that the partnership is a foreign limited partnership;

    (3)   the partnership's jurisdiction of formation;

    (4)   the street and mailing addresses of the partnership's principal office and, if the law of the partnership's jurisdiction of formation requires the partnership to maintain an office in that jurisdiction, the street and mailing addresses of the required office; and

    (5)   the name and street and mailing addresses of the partnership's registered agent in this state.

§ 1004. Amendment of Foreign Registration Statement

A registered foreign limited partnership shall deliver to the [Secretary of State] for filing an amendment to its foreign registration statement if there is a change in:

    (1)   the name of the partnership;

    (2)   the partnership's jurisdiction of formation;

    (3)   an address required by Section 1003(4); or

    (4)   the information required by Section 1003(5).

§ 1005. Activities Not Constituting Doing Business

    (a)   Activities of a foreign limited partnership which do not constitute doing business in this State under this [article] include:

    (1)   maintaining, defending, mediating, arbitrating, or settling an action or proceeding;

    (2)   carrying on any activity concerning its internal affairs, including holding meetings of its partners;

    (3)   maintaining accounts in financial institutions;

    (4)   maintaining offices or agencies for the transfer, exchange, and registration of the securities of the partnership or maintaining trustees or depositories with respect to those securities;

    (5)   selling through independent contractors;

    (6)   soliciting or obtaining orders by any means if the orders require acceptance outside this State before they become contracts;

    (7)   creating or acquiring indebtedness, mortgages, or security interests in property;

    (8)   securing or collecting debts or enforcing mortgages or other security interests in property securing the debts and holding, protecting, or maintaining property;

    (9)   conducting an isolated transaction that is not in the course of similar transactions;

    (10) owning, without more, property; and

    (11) doing business in interstate commerce.

    (b)   A person does not do business in this State solely by being a partner of a foreign limited partnership that does business in this State.

    (c)   This section does not apply in determining the contacts or activities that may subject a foreign limited partnership to service of process, taxation, or regulation under law of this State other than this [act].

§ 1006. Noncomplying Name of Foreign Limited Partnership

    (a)   A foreign limited partnership whose name does not comply with Section 114 may not register to do business in this State until it adopts, for the purpose of doing business in this State, an alternate name that complies with Section114. A partnership that registers under an alternate name under this subsection need not comply with [this State's assumed or fictitious name statute]. After registering to do business in this State with an alternate name, a partnership shall do business in this State under:

    (1)   the alternate name;

    (2)   the partnership's name, with the addition of its jurisdiction of formation; or

    (3)   a name the partnership is authorized to use under [this State's assumed or fictitious name statute].

    (b)   If a foreign limited partnership changes its name to one that does not comply with Section 114, it may not do business in this State until it complies with subsection (a) by amending its registration to adopt an alternate name that complies with Section 114.

§ 1007. Withdrawal Deemed on Conversion to Domestic Filing Entity or Domestic Limited Liability Partnership

A registered foreign limited partnership that converts to a domestic limited liability partnership or to a domestic entity whose formation requires delivery of a record to the [Secretary of State] for filing is deemed to have withdrawn its registration on the effective date of the conversion.

§ 1008. Withdrawal on Dissolution or Conversion to Nonfiling Entity Other than Limited Liability Partnership

(a)   A registered foreign limited liability partnership that has dissolved and completed winding up or has converted to a domestic or foreign entity whose formation does not require the public filing of a record, other than a limited liability partnership, shall deliver a statement of withdrawal to the [Secretary of State] for filing. The statement must state:

   (1)   in the case of a partnership that has completed winding up:

      (A)   its name and jurisdiction of formation;

      (B)   that the partnership surrenders its registration to do business in this State; and

   (2)   in the case of a partnership that has converted:

      (A)   the name of the converting partnership and its jurisdiction of formation;

      (B)   the type of entity to which the partnership has converted and its jurisdiction of formation;

      (C)   that the converted entity surrenders the converting partnership's registration to do business in this State and revokes the authority of the converting partnership's registered agent to act as registered agent in this State on behalf of the partnership or the converted entity; and

      (D)   a mailing address to which service of process may be made under subsection (b).

(b)   After a withdrawal under this section becomes effective, service of process in any action or proceeding based on a cause of action arising during the time the foreign limited liability partnership was registered to do business in this State may be made pursuant to Section 909.

§ 1009. Transfer of Registration

(a)   When a registered foreign limited liability partnership has merged into a foreign entity that is not registered to do business in this State or has converted to a foreign entity required to register with the [Secretary of State] to do business in this State, the foreign entity shall deliver to the [Secretary of State] for filing an application for transfer of registration. The application must state:

   (1)   the name of the registered foreign limited partnership before the merger or conversion;

   (2)   that before the merger or conversion the registration pertained to a foreign limited liability partnership;

   (3)   the name of the applicant foreign entity into which the foreign limited liability partnership has merged or to which it has been converted and, if the name does not comply with Section 902, an alternate name adopted pursuant to Section 1006(a);

   (4)   the type of entity of the applicant foreign entity and its jurisdiction of formation;

   (5)   the street and mailing addresses of the principal office of the applicant foreign entity and, if the law of that entity's jurisdiction of formation requires the entity to maintain an office in that jurisdiction, the street and mailing address of that office; and

   (6)   the name and street and mailing addresses of the applicant foreign entity's registered agent in this State.

(b)   When an application for transfer of registration takes effect, the registration of the foreign limited liability partnership to do business in this State is transferred without interruption to the foreign entity into which the partnership has merged or to which it has been converted.

§ 1010. Termination of Registration

(a)   The [Secretary of State] may terminate the registration of a registered foreign limited liability partnership in the manner provided in subsections (b) and (c) if the partnership does not:

(1)   pay, not later than [60] days after the due date, any fee, tax, interest, or penalty required to be paid to the [Secretary of State] under this [act] or law other than this [act];

(2)   deliver to the [Secretary of State] for filing, not later than [60] days after the due date, [an annual] [a biennial] report required under Section 913;

(3)   have a registered agent as required by Section 908; or

(4)   deliver to the [Secretary of State] for filing a statement of a change under Section 909 not later than [30] days after a change has occurred in the name or address of the registered agent.

(b)   The [Secretary of State] may terminate the registration of a registered foreign limited liability partnership by:

(1)   filing a notice of termination or noting the termination in the records of the [Secretary of State]; and

(2)   delivering a copy of the notice or the information in the notation to the partnership's registered agent or, if the partnership does not have a registered agent, to the partnership's principal office.

(c)   A notice or information in a notation under subsection (b) must include:

(1)   the effective date of the termination, which must be at least [60] days after the date the [Secretary of State] delivers the copy; and

(2)   the grounds for termination under subsection (a).

(d)   The authority of a registered foreign limited liability partnership to do business in this State ceases on the effective date of the notice of termination or notation under subsection (b), unless before that date the partnership cures each ground for termination stated in the notice or notation. If the partnership cures each ground, the [Secretary of State] shall file a record so stating.

§ 1011. Withdrawal of Registration of Registered Foreign Limited Liability Partnership

(a)   A registered foreign limited liability partnership may withdraw its registration by delivering a statement of withdrawal to the [Secretary of State] for filing. The statement of withdrawal must state:

(1)   the name of the partnership and its jurisdiction of formation;

(2)   that the partnership is not doing business in this State and that it withdraws its registration to do business in this State;

(3)   that the partnership revokes the authority of its registered agent to accept service on its behalf in this State; and

(4)   an address to which service of process may be made under subsection (b).

(b)   After withdrawal of the registration of a foreign limited liability partnership, service of process in any action or proceeding based on a cause of action arising during the time the partnership was registered to do business in this State may be made pursuant to Section 909.

§ 1012. Action by [Attorney General]

The [Attorney General] may maintain an action to enjoin a foreign limited partnership from doing business in this State in violation of this [article].

ARTICLE 11
MERGER, INTEREST EXCHANGE, CONVERSION, AND DOMESTICATION

§ 1101. Definitions

In this [article]:

(1) "Acquired entity" means the entity, all of one or more classes or series of interests of which are acquired in an interest exchange.

(2) "Acquiring Entity" means the entity that acquires all of one or more classes or series of interests of the acquired entity in an interest exchange.

(3) "Conversion" means a transaction authorized by [Part] 4.

(4) "Converted Entity" means the converting entity as it continues in existence after conversion.

(5) "Converting entity" means the domestic entity that approves a plan of conversion pursuant to Section 1143 or the foreign entity that approves a conversion pursuant to the law of its jurisdiction of formation.

(6) "Distributional interest" means the right under an unincorporated entity's organic law and organic rules to receive distributions from the entity.

(7) "Domestic," with respect to an entity, means governed as to its internal affairs by the law of this State.

(8) "Domesticated limited partnership" means the domesticating limited partnership as it continues in existence after domestication.

(9) "Domesticating limited partnership" means the domestic limited partnership that approves a plan of domestication pursuant to Section 1153 or the foreign limited partnership that approves a domestication pursuant to the law of its jurisdiction of formation.

(10) "Domestication" means a transaction authorized by [Part] 5.

(11) "Entity":

    (A) means:

        (i) a business corporation;

        (ii) a nonprofit corporation;

        (iii) a general partnership, including a limited liability partnership;

        (iv) a limited partnership, including the limited liability limited partnership

        (v) a limited liability company;

        [(vi) a general cooperative association;]

        (vii) a limited cooperative association;

        (viii) an unincorporated nonprofit association;

        (ix) a statutory trust, business trust, or common-law business trust; or

        (x) any other person that has:

            (I) a legal existence separate from any interest holder of that person; or

        (II)   the power to acquire an interest in real property in its own name; and

    (B)   does not include:

        (i)   an individual;

        (ii)   a trust with a predominantly donative purpose or a charitable trust;

        (iii)   an association or relationship that is not an entity listed in subparagraph A and is not a partnership under the rules stated in [Section 202(c) of the Uniform Partnership Act (1997) (Lasted Amended 2013)] [Section 7 of the Uniform Partnership Act (1914)] or a similar provision of the law of another jurisdiction;

        (iv)   a decedent's estate; or

        (v)   a government or a governmental subdivision, agency, or instrumentality.

(12)   "Filing entity" means an entity whose formation requires the filing of a public organic record. The term does not include a limited liability partnership.

(13)   "Foreign", with respect to an entity, means an entity governed as to its internal affairs by the law of a jurisdiction other than this State.

(14)   "Governance interest" means a right under the organic law or organic rules of an unincorporated entity, other than as a governor, agent, assignee, or proxy, to:

    (A)   receive or demand access to information concerning, or the books and records of, the entity;

    (B)   vote for or consent to the election of the governors of the entity; or

    (C)   receive notice of or vote on or consent to an issue involving the internal affairs of the entity.

(15)   "Governor" means:

    (A)   a director of a business corporation;

    (B)   a director or trustee of a nonprofit corporation;

    (C)   a general partner of a general partnership;

    (D)   a general partner of a limited partnership;

    (E)   a manager of a manager-managed limited liability company;

    (F)   a member of a member-managed limited liability company;

    [(G)   a director of a general cooperative association;]

    (H)   a director of a limited cooperative association;

    (I)   a manager of an unincorporated nonprofit association;

    (J)   a trustee of a statutory trust, business trust, or common-law business trust; or

    (K)   any other person under whose authority the powers of an entity are exercised and under whose direction the activities and affairs of the entity are managed pursuant to the organic law and organic rules of the entity.

(16)   "Interest" means:

    (A)   a share in a business corporation;

    (B)   a membership in a nonprofit corporation;

    (C)   a partnership interest in a general partnership;

    (D)   a partnership interest in a limited partnership;

(E)   a membership interest in a limited liability company;

[(F)   a share in a general cooperative association;]

(G)   a member's interest in a limited cooperative association;

(H)   a membership in an unincorporated nonprofit association;

(I)   a beneficial interest in a statutory trust, business trust, or common-law business trust; or

(J)   a governance interest or distributional interest in any other type of unincorporated entity.

(17) "Interest exchange" means a transaction authorized by [Part] 3.

(18) "Interest holder means:

(A)   a shareholder of a business corporation;

(B)   a member of a nonprofit corporation;

(C)   a general partner of a general partnership;

(D)   a general partner of a limited partnership;

(E)   a limited partner of a limited partnership;

(F)   a member of a limited liability company;

[(G)   a shareholder of a general cooperative association;]

(H)   a member of a limited cooperative association;

(I)   a member of an unincorporated nonprofit association;

(J)   a beneficiary or beneficial owner of a statutory trust, business trust, or common-law business trust; or

(K)   any other direct holder of an interest.

(19) "Interest holder liability" means:

(A)   personal liability for a liability of an entity which is imposed on a person:

(i)   solely by reason of the status of the person as an interest holder; or

(ii) by the organic rules of the entity which make one or more specified interest holders or categories of interest holders liable in their capacity as interest holders for all or specified liabilities of the entity; or

(B)   an obligation of an interest holder under the organic rules of an entity to contribute to the entity.

(20) "Merger" means a transaction authorized by [Part] 2.

(21) "Merging entity" means an entity that is a party to a merger and exists immediately before the merger becomes effective.

(22) "Organic law" means the law of an entity's jurisdiction of formation governing the internal affairs of the entity.

(23) "Organic rules" means the public organic record and private organic rules of an entity.

(24) "Plan" means a plan of merger, plan of interest exchange, plan of conversion, or plan of domestication.

(25) "Plan of conversion" means a plan under Section 11142.

(26) "Plan of domestication" means a plan under Section 1152.

(27) "Plan of interest exchange" means a plan under Section 1132.

(28) "Plan of merger" means a plan under Section 1122.

(29) "Private organic rules" means the rules, whether or not in a record, that govern the internal affairs of an entity, are binding on all its interest holders, and are not part of its public organic record, if any. The term includes:

(A)   the bylaws of a business corporation;

(B)   the bylaws of a nonprofit corporation;

(C)   the partnership agreement of a general partnership;

(D)   the partnership agreement of a limited partnership;

(E)   the operating agreement of a limited liability company;

[(F)   the bylaws of a general cooperative association;]

(G)   the bylaws of a limited cooperative association;

(H)   the governing principles of an unincorporated nonprofit association; and

(I)   the trust instrument of a statutory trust or similar rules of a business trust or a common-law business trust.

(30) "Protected agreement" means:

(A)   a record evidencing indebtedness and any related agreement in effect on [the effective date of this [act]];

(B)   an agreement that is binding on an entity on [the effective date of this [act]];

(C)   the organic rules of an entity in effect on [the effective date of this [act]];

(D)   an agreement that is binding on any of the governors or interest holders of an entity on [the effective date of this [act]].

(31) "Public organic record" means the record the filing of which by the [Secretary of State] is required to form an entity and any amendment to or restatement of that record. The term includes:

(A)   the articles of incorporation of a business corporation;

(B)   the articles of incorporation of a nonprofit corporation;

(C)   the certificate of limited partnership of a limited partnership;

(D)   the certificate of organization of a limited liability company;

[(E)   the articles of incorporation of a general cooperative association;]

(F)   the articles of organization of a limited cooperative association; and

(G)   the certificate of trust of a statutory trust or similar record of a business trust.

(32) "Registered foreign entity" means a foreign entity that is registered to do business in this State pursuant to a record filed by the [Secretary of State].

(33) "Statement of conversion" means a statement under Section 1145.

(34) "Statement of domestication" means a statement under Section 1155.

(35) "Statement of interest exchange" means a statement under Section 1135.

(36) "Statement of merger" means a statement under Section 1125.

(37) "Surviving entity" means the entity that continues in existence after or is created by a merger.

(38) "Type of entity" means a generic form of entity:

(A)   recognized at common law; or

(B)   formed under an organic law, whether or not some entities formed under that organic law are subject to provisions of that law that create different categories of the form of entity.

§ 1102. Relationship of [Article] to Other Laws

(a)   This [article] does not authorize an act prohibited by, and does not affect the application or requirements of, law other than this [article].

(b)   A transaction effected under this [article] may not create or impair a right, duty, or obligation of a person under the statutory law of this state relating to a change in control, takeover, business combination, control-share acquisition, or similar transaction involving a domestic merging, acquired, converting, or domesticating business corporation unless:

(1)   if the corporation does not survive the transaction, the transaction satisfies any requirements of the law; or

(2)   if the corporation survives the transaction, the approval of the plan is by a vote of the shareholders or directors which would be sufficient to create or impair the right, duty, or obligation directly under the law.

§ 1103. Required Notice or Approval

(a)   A domestic or foreign entity that is required to give notice to, or obtain the approval of, a governmental agency or officer of this state to be a party to a merger must give the notice or obtain the approval to be a party to an interest exchange, conversion, or domestication.

(b)   Property held for a charitable purpose under the law of this state by a domestic or foreign entity immediately before a transaction under this [article] becomes effective may not, as a result of the transaction, be diverted from the objects for which it was donated, granted, devised, or otherwise transferred unless, to the extent required by or pursuant to the law of this state concerning cy pres or other law dealing with nondiversion of charitable assets, the entity obtains an appropriate order of [the appropriate court] [the Attorney General] specifying the disposition of the property.

(c)   A bequest, devise, gift, grant, or promise contained in a will or other instrument of donation, subscription, or conveyance which is made to a merging entity that is not the surviving entity and which takes effect or remains payable after the merger inures to the surviving entity.

(d)   A trust obligation that would govern property if transferred to a nonsurviving entity applies to property that is transferred to the surviving entity under this section.

§ 1104. Nonexclusivity

The fact that a transaction under this [article] produces a certain result does not preclude the same result from being accomplished in any other manner permitted by law other than this [article].

§ 1105. Reference to External Facts

A plan may refer to facts ascertainable outside the plan if the manner in which the facts will operate upon the plan is specified in the plan. The facts may include the occurrence of an event or a determination or action by a person, whether or not the event, determination, or action is within the control of a party to the transaction.

§ 1106. Appraisal Rights

An interest holder of a domestic merging, acquired, converting, or domesticating limited partnership is entitled to contractual appraisal rights in connection with a transaction under this [article] to the extent provided in:

(1)   the partnership agreement; or

(2)   the plan.

§ 1107. Excluded Entities and Transactions

(a)   The following entities may not participate in a transaction under this [article]:

(1)

(2)

(b)   This [article] may not be used to effect a transaction that:

(1)

(2)

[PART] 2

MERGER

§ 1121. Merger Authorized

(a)   By complying with this [part]:

(1)   one or more domestic limited partnerships may merge with one or more domestic or foreign entities into a domestic or foreign surviving entity; and

(2)   two or more foreign entities may merge into a domestic limited partnership.

(b)   By complying with the provisions of this [part] applicable to foreign entities, a foreign entity may be a party to a merger under this [part] or may be the surviving entity in such a merger if the merger is authorized by the law of the foreign entity's jurisdiction of formation.

§ 1122. Plan of Merger

(a)   A domestic limited partnership may become a party to a merger under this [part] by approving a plan of merger. The plan must be in a record and contain:

(1)   as to each merging entity, its name, jurisdiction of formation, and type of entity;

(2)   if the surviving entity is to be created in the merger, a statement to that effect and the entity's name, jurisdiction of formation, and type of entity;

(3)   the manner of converting the interests in each party to the merger into interests, securities, obligations, money, other property, rights to acquire interests or securities, or any combination of the foregoing;

(4)   if the surviving entity exists before the merger, any proposed amendments to:

(A)   its public organic record, if any; and

(B)   its private organic rules that are, or are proposed to be, in a record;

(5)   if the surviving entity is to be created in the merger:

(A)   its proposed public organic record, if any; and

(B)   the full text of its private organic rules that are proposed to be in a record;

(6)   the other terms and conditions of the merger; and

(7)   any other provision required by the law of a merging entity's jurisdiction of formation or the organic rules of a merging entity.

(b)   In addition to the requirements of subsection (a), a plan of merger may contain any other provision not prohibited by law.

§ 1123. Approval of Merger

(a)   A plan of merger is not effective unless it has been approved:

(1)   by a domestic merging limited partnership, by all the partners of the partnership entitled to vote on or consent to any matter; and

(2)   in a record, by each partner of a domestic merging limited partnership which will have interest holder liability for debts, obligations, and other liabilities that are incurred after the merger becomes effective, unless:

(A)   the partnership agreement of the partnership provides in a record for the approval of a merger in which some or all of its partners become subject to interest holder liability by the affirmative vote or consent of fewer than all the partners; and

(B)   the partner consented in a record to or voted for that provision of the partnership agreement or became a partner after the adoption of that provision.

(b)   A merger involving a domestic merging entity that is not a limited partnership is not effective unless the merger is approved by that entity in accordance with its organic law.

(c)   A merger involving a foreign merging entity is not effective unless the merger is approved by the foreign entity in accordance with the law of the foreign entity's jurisdiction of formation.

§ 1124. Amendment or Abandonment of Plan of Merger

(a)   A plan of merger may be amended only with the consent of each party to the plan, except as otherwise provided in the plan.

(b)   A domestic merging limited partnership may approve an amendment of a plan of merger:

(1)   in the same manner as the plan was approved, if the plan does not provide for the manner in which it may be amended; or

(2)   by its partners in the manner provided in the plan, but a partner that was entitled to vote on or consent to approval of the merger is entitled to vote on or consent to any amendment of the plan that will change:

(A)   the amount or kind of interests, securities, obligations, money, other property, rights to acquire interests or securities, or any combination of the foregoing, to be received by the interest holders of any party to the plan;

(B)   the public organic record, if any, or private organic rules of the surviving entity that will be in effect immediately after the merger becomes effective, except for changes that do not require approval of the interest holders of the surviving entity under its organic law or organic rules; or

(C)   any other terms or conditions of the plan, if the change would adversely affect the partner in any material respect.

(c)   After a plan of merger has been approved and before a statement of merger becomes effective, the plan may be abandoned as provided in the plan. Unless prohibited by the plan, a domestic merging limited partnership may abandon the plan in the same manner as the plan was approved.

(d) If a plan of merger is abandoned after a statement of merger has been delivered to the [Secretary of State] for filing and before the statement becomes effective, a statement of abandonment, signed by a party to the plan, must be delivered to the [Secretary of State] for filing before the statement of merger becomes effective. The statement of abandonment takes effect on filing, and the merger is abandoned and does not become effective. The statement of abandonment must contain:

    (1) the name of each party to the plan of merger;

    (2) the date on which the statement of merger was filed by the [Secretary of State]; and

    (3) a statement that the merger has been abandoned in accordance with this section.

§ 1125. Statement of Merger; Effective Date of Merger

(a) A statement of merger must be signed by each merging entity and delivered to the [Secretary of State] for filing.

(b) A statement of merger must contain:

    (1) the name, jurisdiction of formation, and type of entity of each merging entity that is not the surviving entity;

    (2) the name, jurisdiction of formation, and type of entity of the surviving entity;

    (3) a statement that the merger was approved by each domestic merging entity, if any, in accordance with this [part] and by each foreign merging entity, if any, in accordance with the law of its jurisdiction of formation;

    (4) if the surviving entity exists before the merger and is a domestic filing entity, any amendment to its public organic record approved as part of the plan of merger;

    (5) if the surviving entity is created by the merger and is a domestic filing entity, its public organic record, as an attachment; and

    (6) if the surviving entity is created by the merger and is a domestic limited liability partnership, its statement of qualification, as an attachment.

(c) In addition to the requirements of subsection (b), a statement of merger may contain any other provision not prohibited by law.

(d) If the surviving entity is a domestic entity, its public organic record, if any, must satisfy the requirements of the law of this state, except that the public organic record does not need to be signed.

(e) A plan of merger that is signed by all the merging entities and meets all the requirements of subsection (b) may be delivered to the [Secretary of State] for filing instead of a statement of merger and on filing has the same effect. If a plan of merger is filed as provided in this subsection, references in this [article] to a statement of merger refer to the plan of merger filed under this subsection.

(f) If the surviving entity is a domestic limited partnership, the merger becomes effective when the statement of merger is effective. In all other cases, the merger becomes effective on the later of:

    (1) the date and time provided by the organic law of the surviving entity; and

    (2) when the statement is effective.

§ 1126. Effect of Merger

(a) When a merger becomes effective:

    (1) the surviving entity continues or comes into existence;

    (2) each merging entity that is not the surviving entity ceases to exist;

    (3) all property of each merging entity vests in the surviving entity without transfer, reversion, or impairment;

(4)   all debts, obligations, and other liabilities of each merging entity are debts, obligations, and other liabilities of the surviving entity;

(5)   except as otherwise provided by law or the plan of merger, all the rights, privileges, immunities, powers, and purposes of each merging entity vest in the surviving entity;

(6)   if the surviving entity exists before the merger:

(A)   all its property continues to be vested in it without transfer, reversion, or impairment;

(B)   it remains subject to all its debts, obligations, and other liabilities; and

(C)   all its rights, privileges, immunities, powers, and purposes continue to be vested in it;

(7)   the name of the surviving entity may be substituted for the name of any merging entity that is a party to any pending action or proceeding;

(8)   if the surviving entity exists before the merger:

(A)   its public organic record, if any, is amended to the extent provided in the statement of merger; and

(B)   its private organic rules that are to be in a record, if any, are amended to the extent provided in the plan of merger;

(9)   if the surviving entity is created by the merger, its private organic rules become effective and:

(A)   if it is a filing entity, its public organic record becomes effective; and

(B)   if it is a limited liability partnership, its statement of qualification becomes effective; and

(10) the interests in each merging entity which are to be converted in the merger are converted, and the interest holders of those interests are entitled only to the rights provided to them under the plan of merger and to any appraisal rights they have under Section 1106 and the merging entity's organic law.

(b)   Except as otherwise provided in the organic law or organic rules of a merging entity, the merger does not give rise to any rights that an interest holder, governor, or third party would have upon a dissolution, liquidation, or winding up of the merging entity.

(c)   When a merger becomes effective, a person that did not have interest holder liability with respect to any of the merging entities and becomes subject to interest holder liability with respect to a domestic entity as a result of the merger has interest holder liability only to the extent provided by the organic law of that entity and only for those debts, obligations, and other liabilities that are incurred after the merger becomes effective.

(d)   When a merger becomes effective, the interest holder liability of a person that ceases to hold an interest in a domestic merging limited partnership with respect to which the person had interest holder liability is subject to the following rules:

(1)   The merger does not discharge any interest holder liability under this [act] to the extent the interest holder liability was incurred before the merger became effective.

(2)   The person does not have interest holder liability under this [act] for any debt, obligation, or other liability that is incurred after the merger becomes effective.

(3)   This [act] continues to apply to the release, collection, or discharge of any interest holder liability preserved under paragraph (1) as if the merger had not occurred.

(4)   The person has whatever rights of contribution from any other person as are provided by this [act], law other than this [act], or the partnership agreement of the domestic merging limited partnership with respect to any interest holder liability preserved under paragraph (1) as if the merger had not occurred.

(e)   When a merger becomes effective, a foreign entity that is the surviving entity may be served with process in this state for the collection and enforcement of any debts, obligations, or other liabilities of a domestic merging limited partnership as provided in Section 121.

(f)   When a merger becomes effective, the registration to do business in this state of any foreign merging entity that is not the surviving entity is canceled.

[PART] 3
INTEREST EXCHANGE

§ 1131. Interest Exchange Authorized

(a)   By complying with this [part]:

(1)   a domestic limited partnership may acquire all of one or more classes or series of interests of another domestic entity or a foreign entity in exchange for interests, securities, obligations, money, other property, rights to acquire interests or securities, or any combination of the foregoing; or

(2)   all of one or more classes or series of interests of a domestic limited partnership may be acquired by another domestic entity or a foreign entity in exchange for interests, securities, obligations, money, other property, rights to acquire interests or securities, or any combination of the foregoing.

(b)   By complying with the provisions of this [part] applicable to foreign entities, a foreign entity may be the acquiring or acquired entity in an interest exchange under this [part] if the interest exchange is authorized by the law of the foreign entity's jurisdiction of formation.

(c)   If a protected agreement contains a provision that applies to a merger of a domestic limited partnership but does not refer to an interest exchange, the provision applies to an interest exchange in which the domestic limited partnership is the acquired entity as if the interest exchange were a merger until the provision is amended after [the effective date of this [act]].

§ 1132. Plan of Interest Exchange

(a)   A domestic limited partnership may be the acquired entity in an interest exchange under this [part] by approving a plan of interest exchange. The plan must be in a record and contain:

(1)   the name of the acquired entity;

(2)   the name, jurisdiction of formation, and type of entity of the acquiring entity;

(3)   the manner of converting the interests in the acquired entity into interests, securities, obligations, money, other property, rights to acquire interests or securities, or any combination of the foregoing;

(4)   any proposed amendments to:

(A)   the certificate of limited partnership of the acquired entity; and

(B)   the partnership agreement of the acquired entity that are, or are proposed to be, in a record;

(5)   the other terms and conditions of the interest exchange; and

(6)   any other provision required by the law of this state or the partnership agreement of the acquired entity.

(b)   In addition to the requirements of subsection (a), a plan of interest exchange may contain any other provision not prohibited by law.

§ 1133. Approval of Interest Exchange

(a)   A plan of interest exchange is not effective unless it has been approved:

(1)   by all the partners of a domestic acquired limited partnership entitled to vote on or consent to any matter; and

(2)   in a record, by each partner of the domestic acquired limited partnership that will have interest holder liability for debts, obligations, and other liabilities that are incurred_after the interest exchange becomes effective, unless:

(A)   the partnership agreement of the partnership provides in a record for the approval of an interest exchange or a merger in which some or all its partners become subject to interest holder liability by the affirmative vote or consent of fewer than all of the partners; and

(B)   the partner consented in a record to or voted for that provision of the partnership agreement or became a partner after the adoption of that provision.

(b)   An interest exchange involving a domestic acquired entity that is not a limited partnership is not effective unless it is approved by the domestic entity in accordance with its organic law.

(c)   An interest exchange involving a foreign acquired entity is not effective unless it is approved by the foreign entity in accordance with the law of the foreign entity's jurisdiction of formation.

(d)   Except as otherwise provided in its organic law or organic rules, the interest holders of the acquiring entity are not required to approve the interest exchange.

§ 1134. Amendment or Abandonment of Plan of Interest Exchange

(a)   A plan of interest exchange may be amended only with the consent of each party to the plan, except as otherwise provided in the plan.

(b)   A domestic acquired limited partnership may approve an amendment of a plan of interest exchange:

(1)   in the same manner as the plan was approved, if the plan does not provide for the manner in which it may be amended; or

(2)   by its partners in the manner provided in the plan, but a partner that was entitled to vote on or consent to approval of the interest exchange is entitled to vote on or consent to any amendment of the plan that will change:

(A)   the amount or kind of interests, securities, obligations, money, other property, rights to acquire interests or securities, or any combination of the foregoing, to be received by any of the partners of the acquired partnership under the plan;

(B)   the certificate of limited partnership or partnership agreement of the acquired partnership that will be in effect immediately after the interest exchange becomes effective, except for changes that do not require approval of the partners of the acquired partnership under this [act] or the partnership agreement; or

(C)   any other terms or conditions of the plan, if the change would adversely affect the partner in any material respect.

(c)   After a plan of interest exchange has been approved and before a statement of interest exchange becomes effective, the plan may be abandoned as provided in the plan. Unless prohibited by the plan, a domestic acquired limited partnership may abandon the plan in the same manner as the plan was approved.

(d)   If a plan of interest exchange is abandoned after a statement of interest exchange has been delivered to the [Secretary of State] for filing and before the statement becomes effective, a statement of abandonment, signed by the acquired limited partnership, must be delivered to the [Secretary of State] for filing before the statement of interest exchange becomes effective. The statement of abandonment takes effect on filing, and the interest exchange is abandoned and does not become effective. The statement of abandonment must contain:

(1)   the name of the acquired partnership;

(2)   the date on which the statement of interest exchange was filed by the [Secretary of State]; and

(3)   a statement that the interest exchange has been abandoned in accordance with this section.

§ 1135. Statement of Interest Exchange; Effective Date of Interest Exchange

(a)   A statement of interest exchange must be signed by a domestic acquired limited partnership and delivered to the [Secretary of State] for filing.

(b)   A statement of interest exchange must contain:

(1)   the name of the acquired limited partnership;

(2)   the name, jurisdiction of formation, and type of entity of the acquiring entity;

(3)   a statement that the plan of interest exchange was approved by the acquired limited partnership in accordance with this [part]; and

(4)   any amendments to the acquired limited partnership's certificate of limited partnership approved as part of the plan of interest exchange.

(c)   In addition to the requirements of subsection (b), a statement of interest exchange may contain any other provision not prohibited by law.

(d)   A plan of interest exchange that is signed by a domestic acquired limited partnership and meets all the requirements of subsection (b) may be delivered to the [Secretary of State] for filing instead of a statement of interest exchange and on filing has the same effect. If a plan of interest exchange is filed as provided in this subsection, references in this [article] to a statement of interest exchange refer to the plan of interest exchange filed under this subsection.

(e)   An interest exchange becomes effective when the statement of interest exchange is effective.

§ 1136. Effect of Interest Exchange

(a)   When an interest exchange in which the acquired entity is a domestic limited partnership becomes effective:

(1)   the interests in the acquired partnership which are the subject of the interest exchange are converted, and the partners holding those interests are entitled only to the rights provided to them under the plan of interest exchange and to any appraisal rights they have under Section 1106;

(2)   the acquiring entity becomes the interest holder of the interests in the acquired partnership stated in the plan of interest exchange to be acquired by the acquiring entity;

(3)   the certificate of limited partnership of the acquired partnership is amended to the extent provided in the statement of interest exchange; and

(4)   the provisions of the partnership agreement of the acquired partnership that are to be in a record, if any, are amended to the extent provided in the plan of interest exchange.

(b)   Except as otherwise provided in the certificate of limited partnership or partnership agreement of a domestic acquired limited partnership, the interest exchange does not give rise to any rights that a partner or third party would have upon a dissolution, liquidation, or winding up of the acquired partnership.

(c)   When an interest exchange becomes effective, a person that did not have interest holder liability with respect to a domestic acquired limited partnership and becomes subject to interest holder liability with respect to a domestic entity as a result of the interest exchange has interest holder liability only to the extent provided by the organic law of the entity and only for those debts, obligations, and other liabilities that are incurred after the interest exchange becomes effective.

(d)   When an interest exchange becomes effective, the interest holder liability of a person that ceases to hold an interest in a domestic acquired limited partnership with respect to which the person had interest holder liability is subject to the following rules:

(1)   The interest exchange does not discharge any interest holder liability under this [act] to the extent the interest holder liability was incurred before the interest exchange became effective.

(2)   The person does not have interest holder liability under this [act] for any debt, obligation, or other liability that is incurred after the interest exchange becomes effective.

(3)   This [act] continues to apply to the release, collection, or discharge of any interest holder liability preserved under paragraph (1) as if the interest exchange had not occurred.

(4)   The person has whatever rights of contribution from any other person as are provided by this [act], law other than this [act], or the partnership agreement of the domestic acquired partnership with respect to any interest holder liability preserved under paragraph (1) as if the interest exchange had not occurred.

[PART] 4
CONVERSION

§ 1141. Conversion Authorized

(a)   By complying with this [part], a domestic limited partnership may become:

(1)   a domestic entity that is a different type of entity; or

(2)   a foreign entity that is a different type of entity, if the conversion is authorized by the law of the foreign entity's jurisdiction of formation.

(b)   By complying with the provisions of this [part] applicable to foreign entities, a foreign entity that is not a foreign limited partnership may become a domestic limited partnership if the conversion is authorized by the law of the foreign entity's jurisdiction of formation.

(c)   If a protected agreement contains a provision that applies to a merger of a domestic limited partnership but does not refer to a conversion, the provision applies to a conversion of the partnership as if the conversion were a merger until the provision is amended after [the effective date of this [act]].

§ 1142. Plan of Conversion

(a)   A domestic limited partnership may convert to a different type of entity under this [part] by approving a plan of conversion. The plan must be in a record and contain:

(1)   the name of the converting limited partnership;

(2)   the name, jurisdiction of formation, and type of entity of the converted entity;

(3)   the manner of converting the interests in the converting limited partnership into interests, securities, obligations, money, other property, rights to acquire interests or securities, or any combination of the foregoing;

(4)   the proposed public organic record of the converted entity if it will be a filing entity;

(5)   the full text of the private organic rules of the converted entity which are proposed to be in a record;

(6)   the other terms and conditions of the conversion; and

(7)   any other provision required by the law of this state or the partnership agreement of the converting limited partnership.

(b)   In addition to the requirements of subsection (a), a plan of conversion may contain any other provision not prohibited by law.

§ 1143. Approval of Conversion

(a)   A plan of conversion is not effective unless it has been approved:

(1)   by a domestic converting limited partnership, by all the partners of the limited partnership entitled to vote on or consent to any matter; and

(2)   in a record, by each partner of a domestic converting limited partnership which will have interest holder liability for debts, obligations, and other liabilities that are incurred after the conversion becomes effective, unless:

(A)   the partnership agreement of the partnership provides in a record for the approval of a conversion or a merger in which some or all of its partners become subject to interest holder liability by the affirmative vote or consent of fewer than all the partners; and

(B)   the partner voted for or consented in a record to that provision of the partnership agreement or became a partner after the adoption of that provision.

(b)   A conversion involving a domestic converting entity that is not a limited partnership is not effective unless it is approved by the domestic converting entity in accordance with its organic law.

(c)   A conversion of a foreign converting entity is not effective unless it is approved by the foreign entity in accordance with the law of the foreign entity's jurisdiction of formation.

§ 1144. Amendment or Abandonment of Plan of Conversion

(a)   A plan of conversion of a domestic converting limited partnership may be amended:

(1)   in the same manner as the plan was approved, if the plan does not provide for the manner in which it may be amended; or

(2)   by its partners in the manner provided in the plan, but a partner that was entitled to vote on or consent to approval of the conversion is entitled to vote on or consent to any amendment of the plan that will change:

(A)   the amount or kind of interests, securities, obligations, money, other property, rights to acquire interests or securities, or any combination of the foregoing, to be received by any of the partners of the converting partnership under the plan;

(B)   the public organic record, if any, or private organic rules of the converted entity which will be in effect immediately after the conversion becomes effective, except for changes that do not require approval of the interest holders of the converted entity under its organic law or organic rules; or

(C)   any other terms or conditions of the plan, if the change would adversely affect the partner in any material respect.

(b) After a plan of conversion has been approved by a domestic converting limited partnership and before a statement of conversion becomes effective, the plan may be abandoned as provided in the plan. Unless prohibited by the plan, a domestic converting limited partnership may abandon the plan in the same manner as the plan was approved.

(c) If a plan of conversion is abandoned after a statement of conversion has been delivered to the [Secretary of State] for filing and before the statement becomes effective, a statement of abandonment, signed by the converting entity, must be delivered to the [Secretary of State] for filing before the statement of conversion becomes effective. The statement of abandonment takes effect on filing, and the conversion is abandoned and does not become effective. The statement of abandonment must contain:

(1) the name of the converting limited partnership;

(2) the date on which the statement of conversion was filed by the [Secretary of State]; and

(3) a statement that the conversion has been abandoned in accordance with this section.

§ 1145. Statement of Conversion; Effective Date of Conversion

(a) A statement of conversion must be signed by the converting entity and delivered to the [Secretary of State] for filing.

(b) A statement of conversion must contain:

(1) the name, jurisdiction of formation, and type of entity of the converting entity;

(2) the name, jurisdiction of formation, and type of entity of the converted entity;

(3) if the converting entity is a domestic limited partnership, a statement that the plan of conversion was approved in accordance with this [part] or, if the converting entity is a foreign entity, a statement that the conversion was approved by the foreign entity in accordance with the law of its jurisdiction of formation;

(4) if the converted entity is a domestic filing entity, its public organic record, as an attachment; and

(5) if the converted entity is a domestic limited liability partnership, its statement of qualification, as an attachment.

(c) In addition to the requirements of subsection (b), a statement of conversion may contain any other provision not prohibited by law.

(d) If the converted entity is a domestic entity, its public organic record, if any, must satisfy the requirements of the law of this state, except that the public organic record does not need to be signed.

(e) A plan of conversion that is signed by a domestic converting limited partnership and meets all the requirements of subsection (b) may be delivered to the [Secretary of State] for filing instead of a statement of conversion and on filing has the same effect. If a plan of conversion is filed as provided in this subsection, references in this [article] to a statement of conversion refer to the plan of conversion filed under this subsection.

(f) If the converted entity is a domestic limited partnership, the conversion becomes effective when the statement of conversion is effective. In all other cases, the conversion becomes effective on the later of:

(1) the date and time provided by the organic law of the converted entity; and

(2) when the statement is effective.

§ 1146. Effect of Conversion

(a) When a conversion becomes effective:

    (1)   the converted entity is:

        (A)   organized under and subject to the organic law of the converted entity; and

        (B)   the same entity without interruption as the converting entity;

    (2)   all property of the converting entity continues to be vested in the converted entity without transfer, reversion, or impairment;

    (3)   all debts, obligations, and other liabilities of the converting entity continue as debts, obligations, and other liabilities of the converted entity;

    (4)   except as otherwise provided by law or the plan of conversion, all the rights, privileges, immunities, powers, and purposes of the converting entity remain in the converted entity;

    (5)   the name of the converted entity may be substituted for the name of the converting entity in any pending action or proceeding;

    (6)   the certificate of limited partnership of the converted entity becomes effective;

    (7)   the provisions of the partnership agreement of the converted entity which are to be in a record, if any, approved as part of the plan of conversion become effective; and

    (8)   the interests in the converting entity are converted, and the interest holders of the converting entity are entitled only to the rights provided to them under the plan of conversion and to any appraisal rights they have under Section 1106.

(b)   Except as otherwise provided in the partnership agreement of a domestic converting limited partnership, the conversion does not give rise to any rights that a partner or third party would have upon a dissolution, liquidation, or winding up of the converting entity.

(c)   When a conversion becomes effective, a person that did not have interest holder liability with respect to the converting entity and becomes subject to interest holder liability with respect to a domestic entity as a result of the conversion has interest holder liability only to the extent provided by the organic law of the entity and only for those debts, obligations, and other liabilities that are incurred after the conversion becomes effective.

(d)   When a conversion becomes effective, the interest holder liability of a person that ceases to hold an interest in a domestic converting limited partnership with respect to which the person had interest holder liability is subject to the following rules:

    (1)   The conversion does not discharge any interest holder liability under this [act] to the extent the interest holder liability was incurred before the conversion became effective.

    (2)   The person does not have interest holder liability under this [act] for any debt, obligation, or other liability that is incurred after the conversion becomes effective.

    (3)   This [act] continues to apply to the release, collection, or discharge of any interest holder liability preserved under paragraph (1) as if the conversion had not occurred.

    (4)   The person has whatever rights of contribution from any other person as are provided by this [act], law other than this [act], or the organic rules of the converting entity with respect to any interest holder liability preserved under paragraph (1) as if the conversion had not occurred.

(e)   When a conversion becomes effective, a foreign entity that is the converted entity may be served with process in this state for the collection and enforcement of any of its debts, obligations, and other liabilities as provided in Section 121.

(f)   If the converting entity is a registered foreign entity, its registration to do business in this state is canceled when the conversion becomes effective.

(g)   A conversion does not require the entity to wind up its affairs and does not constitute or cause the dissolution of the entity.

[PART] 5

DOMESTICATION

§ 1151. Domestication Authorized

(a)   By complying with this [part], a domestic limited partnership may become a foreign limited partnership if the domestication is authorized by the law of the foreign jurisdiction.

(b)   By complying with the provisions of this [part] applicable to foreign limited partnerships, a foreign limited partnership may become a domestic limited partnership if the domestication is authorized by the law of the foreign limited partnership's jurisdiction of formation.

(c)   If a protected agreement contains a provision that applies to a merger of a domestic limited partnership but does not refer to a domestication, the provision applies to a domestication of the limited partnership as if the domestication were a merger until the provision is amended after [the effective date of this [act]].

§ 1152. Plan of Domestication

(a)   A domestic limited partnership may become a foreign limited partnership in a domestication by approving a plan of domestication. The plan must be in a record and contain:

(1)   the name of the domesticating limited partnership;

(2)   the name and jurisdiction of formation of the domesticated limited partnership;

(3)   the manner of converting the interests in the domesticating limited partnership into interests, securities, obligations, money, other property, rights to acquire interests or securities, or any combination of the foregoing;

(4)   the proposed certificate of limited partnership of the domesticated limited partnership;

(5)   the full text of the provisions of the partnership agreement of the domesticated limited partnership, that are proposed to be in a record;

(6)   the other terms and conditions of the domestication; and

(7)   any other provision required by the law of this state or the partnership agreement of the domesticating limited partnership.

(b)   In addition to the requirements of subsection (a), a plan of domestication may contain any other provision not prohibited by law.

§ 1153. Approval of Domestication

(a)   A plan of domestication of a domestic domesticating limited partnership is not effective unless it has been approved:

(1)   by all the partners entitled to vote on or consent to any matter; and

(2)   in a record, by each partner that will have interest holder liability for debts, obligations, and other liabilities that are incurred after the domestication becomes effective, unless:

(A)   the partnership agreement of the domesticating partnership in a record provides for the approval of a domestication or merger in which some or all of its partners become subject to interest holder liability by the affirmative vote or consent of fewer than all the partners; and

(B)   the partner voted for or consented in a record to that provision of the partnership agreement or became a partner after the adoption of that provision.

(b)   A domestication of a foreign domesticating limited partnership is not effective unless it is approved in accordance with the law of the foreign limited partnership's jurisdiction of formation.

§ 1154. Amendment or Abandonment of Plan of Domestication

(a)   A plan of domestication of a domestic domesticating limited partnership may be amended:

(1)   in the same manner as the plan was approved, if the plan does not provide for the manner in which it may be amended; or

(2)   by its partners in the manner provided in the plan, but a partner that was entitled to vote on or consent to approval of the domestication is entitled to vote on or consent to any amendment of the plan that will change:

(A)   the amount or kind of interests, securities, obligations, money, other property, rights to acquire interests or securities, or any combination of the foregoing, to be received by any of the partners of the domesticating limited partnership under the plan;

(B)   the certificate of limited partnership or partnership agreement of the domesticated limited partnership that will be in effect immediately after the domestication becomes effective, except for changes that do not require approval of the partners of the domesticated limited partnership under its organic law or partnership agreement; or

(C)   any other terms or conditions of the plan, if the change would adversely affect the partner in any material respect.

(b)   After a plan of domestication has been approved by a domestic domesticating limited partnership and before a statement of domestication becomes effective, the plan may be abandoned as provided in the plan. Unless prohibited by the plan, a domestic domesticating limited partnership may abandon the plan in the same manner as the plan was approved.

(c)   If a plan of domestication is abandoned after a statement of domestication has been delivered to the [Secretary of State] for filing and before the statement becomes effective, a statement of abandonment, signed by the domesticating limited partnership, must be delivered to the [Secretary of State] for filing before the statement of domestication becomes effective. The statement of abandonment takes effect on filing, and the domestication is abandoned and does not become effective. The statement of abandonment must contain:

(1)   the name of the domesticating limited partnership;

(2)   the date on which the statement of domestication was filed by the [Secretary of State]; and

(3)   a statement that the domestication has been abandoned in accordance with this section.

§ 1155. Statement of Domestication; Effective Date of Domestication

(a)   A statement of domestication must be signed by the domesticating limited partnership and delivered to the [Secretary of State] for filing.

(b)   A statement of domestication must contain:

(1)   the name and jurisdiction of formation of the domesticating limited partnership;

(2)   the name and jurisdiction of formation of the domesticated limited partnership;

(3)   if the domesticating limited partnership is a domestic limited partnership, a statement that the plan of domestication was approved in accordance with this [part] or, if the domesticating limited partnership is a foreign limited partnership, a statement that the domestication was approved in accordance with the law of its jurisdiction of formation; and

(4)   the certificate of limited partnership of the domesticated limited partnership, as an attachment.

(c)   In addition to the requirements of subsection (b), a statement of domestication may contain any other provision not prohibited by law.

(d)   The certificate of limited partnership of a domesticated domestic limited partnership must satisfy the requirements of this [act], but the certificate does not need to be signed.

(e)   A plan of domestication that is signed by a domesticating domestic limited partnership and meets all the requirements of subsection (b) may be delivered to the [Secretary of State] for filing instead of a statement of domestication and on filing has the same effect. If a plan of domestication is filed as provided in this subsection, references in this [article] to a statement of domestication refer to the plan of domestication filed under this subsection.

(f)   If the domesticated entity is a domestic limited partnership, the domestication becomes effective when the statement of domestication is effective. If the domesticated entity is a foreign limited partnership, the domestication becomes effective on the later of:

(1)   the date and time provided by the organic law of the domesticated entity; and

(2)   when the statement is effective.

§ 1156. Effect of Domestication

(a)   When a domestication becomes effective:

(1)   the domesticated entity is:

(A)   organized under and subject to the organic law of the domesticated entity; and

(B)   the same entity without interruption as the domesticating entity;

(2)   all property of the domesticating entity continues to be vested in the domesticated entity without transfer, reversion, or impairment;

(3)   all debts, obligations, and other liabilities of the domesticating entity continue as debts, obligations, and other liabilities of the domesticated entity;

(4)   except as otherwise provided by law or the plan of domestication, all the rights, privileges, immunities, powers, and purposes of the domesticating entity remain in the domesticated entity;

(5)   the name of the domesticated entity may be substituted for the name of the domesticating entity in any pending action or proceeding;

(6)   the certificate of limited partnership of the domesticated entity becomes effective;

(7)   the provisions of the partnership agreement of the domesticated entity that are to be in a record, if any, approved as part of the plan of domestication become effective; and

(8)   the interests in the domesticating entity are converted to the extent and as approved in connection with the domestication, and the partners of the domesticating entity are entitled only to the rights provided to them under the plan of domestication and to any appraisal rights they have under Section 1106.

(b)   Except as otherwise provided in the organic law or partnership agreement of the domesticating limited partnership, the domestication does not give rise to any rights that an partner or third party would have upon a dissolution, liquidation, or winding up of the domesticating partnership.

(c)   When a domestication becomes effective, a person that did not have interest holder liability with respect to the domesticating limited partnership and becomes subject to interest holder liability with respect to a domestic limited partnership as a result of the domestication has interest holder liability only to the extent provided by this [act] and only for those debts, obligations, and other liabilities that are incurred after the domestication becomes effective.

(d)   When a domestication becomes effective, the interest holder liability of a person that ceases to hold an interest in a domestic domesticating limited partnership with respect to which the person had interest holder liability is subject to the following rules:

(1)   The domestication does not discharge any interest holder liability under this [act] to the extent the interest holder liability was incurred before the domestication became effective.

(2)   A person does not have interest holder liability under this [act] for any debt, obligation, or other liability that is incurred after the domestication becomes effective.

(3)   This [act] continues to apply to the release, collection, or discharge of any interest holder liability preserved under paragraph (1) as if the domestication had not occurred.

(4)   A person has whatever rights of contribution from any other person as are provided by this [act], law other than this [act], or the partnership agreement of the domestic domesticating limited partnership with respect to any interest holder liability preserved under paragraph (1) as if the domestication had not occurred.

(e)   When a domestication becomes effective, a foreign limited partnership that is the domesticated partnership may be served with process in this state for the collection and enforcement of any of its debts, obligations, and other liabilities as provided in Section 121.

(f)   If the domesticating limited partnership is a registered foreign entity, the registration of the partnership is canceled when the domestication becomes effective.

(g)   A domestication does not require a domestic domesticating limited partnership to wind up its affairs and does not constitute or cause the dissolution of the partnership.

ARTICLE 12
MISCELLANEOUS PROVISIONS

§ 1201. Uniformity of Application and Construction

In applying and construing this Uniform Act, consideration must be given to the need to promote uniformity of the law with respect to its subject matter among States that enact it.

§ 1202. Relation to Electronic Signatures in Global and National Commerce Act

This [act] modifies, limits, and supersedes the Electronic Signatures in Global and National Commerce Act, 15 U.S.C. Section 7001 et seq., but does not modify, limit, or supersede Section 101(c) of that act, 15 U.S.C. Section 7001(c), or authorize electronic delivery of any of the notices described in Section 103(b) of that act, 15 U.S.C. Section 7003(b).

§ 1203. Savings Clause

This [act] does not affect an action commenced, proceeding brought, or right accrued before [the effective date of this [act]].

§ 1204. Severability Clause

If any provision of this [act] or its application to any person or circumstance is held invalid, the invalidity does not affect other provisions or applications of this [act] which can be given effect without the invalid provision or application, and to this end the provisions of this [act] are severable.]

§ 1205. Repeals

Effective [all-inclusive date], the following acts and parts of acts are repealed: [the State Limited Partnership Act as amended and in effect immediately before the effective date of this [Act]].

§ 1206. Effective Date

This [act] takes effect . . . .

DELAWARE LIMITED LIABILITY COMPANY ACT

(Title 6 Del. Stat.)

Table of Sections

CHAPTER 18. LIMITED LIABILITY COMPANY ACT

SUBCHAPTER I. GENERAL PROVISIONS

SUBCHAPTER II. FORMATION; CERTIFICATE OF FORMATION

DELAWARE LIMITED LIABILITY COMPANY ACT

SUBCHAPTER III. MEMBERS

SUBCHAPTER IV. MANAGERS

SUBCHAPTER V. FINANCE

SUBCHAPTER VI. DISTRIBUTIONS AND RESIGNATION

SUBCHAPTER VII. ASSIGNMENT OF LIMITED LIABILITY COMPANY INTERESTS

SUBCHAPTER VIII. DISSOLUTION

DELAWARE LIMITED LIABILITY COMPANY ACT

SUBCHAPTER IX. FOREIGN LIMITED LIABILITY COMPANIES

SUBCHAPTER X. DERIVATIVE ACTIONS

SUBCHAPTER XI. MISCELLANEOUS

SUBCHAPTER XII. STATUTORY PUBLIC BENEFIT
LIMITED LIABILITY COMPANIES

CHAPTER 18. LIMITED LIABILITY COMPANY ACT

SUBCHAPTER I
GENERAL PROVISIONS

§ 18–101. Definitions

As used in this chapter unless the context otherwise requires:

(1) "Bankruptcy" means an event that causes a person to cease to be a member as provided in § 18–304 of this title.

(2) "Certificate of formation" means the certificate referred to in § 18–201 of this title, and the certificate as amended.

(3) "Contribution" means any cash, property, services rendered or a promissory note or other obligation to contribute cash or property or to perform services, which a person contributes to a limited liability company in the person's capacity as a member.

(4) "Foreign limited liability company" means a limited liability company formed under the laws of any state or under the laws of any foreign country or other foreign jurisdiction. When used in this title in reference to a foreign limited liability company, the terms "limited liability company agreement," "limited liability company interest," "manager" or "member" shall mean a limited liability company agreement, limited liability company interest, manager or member, respectively, under the laws of the state or foreign country or other foreign jurisdiction under which the foreign limited liability company is formed.

(5) "Knowledge" means a person's actual knowledge of a fact, rather than the person's constructive knowledge of the fact.

(6) "Limited liability company" and "domestic limited liability company" means a limited liability company formed under the laws of the State of Delaware and having 1 or more members.

(7) "Limited liability company agreement" means any agreement (whether referred to as a limited liability company agreement, operating agreement or otherwise), written, oral or implied, of the member or members as to the affairs of a limited liability company and the conduct of its business. A member or manager of a limited liability company or an assignee of a limited liability company interest is bound by the limited liability company agreement whether or not the member or manager or assignee executes the limited liability company agreement. A limited liability company is not required to execute its limited liability company agreement. A limited liability company is bound by its limited liability company agreement whether or not the limited liability company executes the limited liability company agreement. A limited liability company agreement of a limited liability company having only 1 member shall not be unenforceable by reason of there being only 1 person who is a party to the limited liability company agreement. A limited liability company agreement is not subject to any statute of frauds (including § 2714 of this title). A limited liability company agreement may provide rights to any person, including a person who is not a party to the limited liability company agreement, to the extent set forth therein. A written limited liability company agreement or another written agreement or writing:

a.   May provide that a person shall be admitted as a member of a limited liability company, or shall become an assignee of a limited liability company interest or other rights or powers of a member to the extent assigned:

1.   If such person (or a representative authorized by such person orally, in writing or by other action such as payment for a limited liability company interest) executes the limited liability company agreement or any other writing evidencing the intent of such person to become a member or assignee; or

2.   Without such execution, if such person (or a representative authorized by such person orally, in writing or by other action such as payment for a limited liability company interest) complies with the conditions for becoming a member or assignee as set forth in the limited liability company agreement or any other writing; and

b.   Shall not be unenforceable by reason of its not having been signed by a person being admitted as a member or becoming an assignee as provided in paragraph (7)(a) of this section, or by reason of its having been signed by a representative as provided in this chapter.

(8)   "Limited liability company interest" means a member's share of the profits and losses of a limited liability company and a member's right to receive distributions of the limited liability company's assets.

(9)   "Liquidating trustee" means a person carrying out the winding up of a limited liability company.

(10)   "Manager" means a person who is named as a manager of a limited liability company in, or designated as a manager of a limited liability company pursuant to, a limited liability company agreement or similar instrument under which the limited liability company is formed.

(11)   "Member" means a person who is admitted to a limited liability company as a member as provided in § 18–301 of this title.

(12)   "Person" means a natural person, partnership (whether general or limited), limited liability company, trust (including a common law trust, business trust, statutory trust, voting trust or any other form of trust), estate, association (including any group, organization, co-tenancy plan, board, council or committee), corporation, government (including a country, state, county or any other governmental subdivision, agency or instrumentality), custodian, nominee or any other individual or entity (or series thereof) in its own or any representative capacity, in each case, whether domestic or foreign.

(13)   "Personal representative" means, as to a natural person, the executor, administrator, guardian, conservator or other legal representative thereof and, as to a person other than a natural person, the legal representative or successor thereof.

(14)   "Protected series" means a designated series of members, managers, limited liability company interests or assets that is established in accordance with § 18–215(b) of this title.

(15)   "Registered series" means a designated series of members, managers, limited liability company interests or assets that is formed in accordance with § 18–218 of this title.

(16)   "Series" means a designated series of members, managers, limited liability company interests or assets that is a protected series or a registered series, or that is neither a protected series nor a registered series.

(17)   "State" means the District of Columbia or the Commonwealth of Puerto Rico or any state, territory, possession or other jurisdiction of the United States other than the State of Delaware.

§ 18–102. Name Set Forth in Certificate

The name of each limited liability company as set forth in its certificate of formation:

(1)   Shall contain the words "Limited Liability Company" or the abbreviation "L.L.C." or the designation "LLC";

(2)   May contain the name of a member or manager;

(3)   Must be such as to distinguish it upon the records in the office of the Secretary of State from the name on such records of any corporation, partnership, limited partnership, statutory trust, limited liability company or registered series reserved, registered, formed or organized under the laws of the State of Delaware or qualified to do business or registered as a foreign

corporation, foreign limited partnership, foreign statutory trust, foreign partnership, or foreign limited liability company in the State of Delaware; provided however, that a limited liability company may register under any name which is not such as to distinguish it upon the records in the office of the Secretary of State from the name on such records of any domestic or foreign corporation, partnership, limited partnership, statutory trust, registered series or foreign limited liability company reserved, registered, formed or organized under the laws of the State of Delaware with the written consent of the other corporation, partnership, limited partnership, statutory trust, registered series or foreign limited liability company, which written consent shall be filed with the Secretary of State; provided further, that, if on July 31, 2011 a limited liability company is registered (with the consent of another limited liability company) under a name which is not such as to distinguish it upon the records in the office of the Secretary of State from the name on such records of such other domestic limited liability company, it shall not be necessary for any such limited liability company to amend its certificate of formation to comply with this subsection;

(4)   May contain the following words: "Company," "Association," "Club," "Foundation," "Fund," "Institute," "Society," "Union," "Syndicate," "Limited," "Public Benefit" or "Trust" (or abbreviations of like import); and

(5)   Shall not contain the word "bank," or any variation thereof, except for the name of a bank reporting to and under the supervision of the State Bank Commissioner of this State or a subsidiary of a bank or savings association (as those terms are defined in the Federal Deposit Insurance Act, as amended, at 12 U.S.C. § 1813), or a limited liability company regulated under the Bank Holding Company Act of 1956, as amended, 12 U.S.C. § 1841 et seq., or the Home Owners' Loan Act, as amended, 12 U.S.C. § 1461 et seq.; provided, however, that this section shall not be construed to prevent the use of the word "bank," or any variation thereof, in a context clearly not purporting to refer to a banking business or otherwise likely to mislead the public about the nature of the business of the limited liability company or to lead to a pattern and practice of abuse that might cause harm to the interests of the public or this State as determined by the Division of Corporations in the Department of State.

§ 18–103.   Reservation of Name

(a)   The exclusive right to the use of a name may be reserved by:

(1)   Any person intending to organize a limited liability company under this chapter and to adopt that name;

(2)   Any person intending to form a registered series of a limited liability company under this chapter and to adopt that name in accordance with § 18–218(e) of this title;

(3)   Any domestic limited liability company or any foreign limited liability company registered in the State of Delaware which, in either case, proposes to change its name;

(4)   Any foreign limited liability company intending to register in the State of Delaware and adopt that name; and

(5)   Any person intending to organize a foreign limited liability company and intending to have it register in the State of Delaware and adopt that name.

(b)   The reservation of a specified name shall be made by filing with the Secretary of State an application, executed by the applicant, specifying the name to be reserved and the name and address of the applicant. If the Secretary of State finds that the name is available for use by a domestic or foreign limited liability company, the Secretary shall reserve the name for the exclusive use of the applicant for a period of 120 days. Once having so reserved a name, the same applicant may again reserve the same name for successive 120-day periods. The right to the exclusive use of a reserved name may be transferred to any other person by filing in the office of the Secretary of State a notice of the transfer, executed by the applicant for whom the name was reserved, specifying the name to be transferred and the name and address of the transferee. The reservation of a specified name may be canceled by filing with the Secretary of State a notice of cancellation, executed by the applicant or transferee, specifying the name reservation to be canceled and the name and address of the applicant or transferee. Unless the Secretary of State finds that any application, notice of transfer, or notice of cancellation filed with the Secretary of State as required by this subsection does not conform to law, upon receipt of all filing fees required by law the Secretary shall prepare and return to the person who filed such instrument a copy of the filed instrument with a notation thereon of the action taken by the Secretary of State.

(c)   A fee as set forth in § 18–1105(a)(1) of this title shall be paid at the time of the initial reservation of any name, at the time of the renewal of any such reservation and at the time of the filing of a notice of the transfer or cancellation of any such reservation.

§ 18–104.   Registered Office; Registered Agent

(a)   Each limited liability company shall have and maintain in the State of Delaware:

(1)   A registered office, which may but need not be a place of its business in the State of Delaware; and

(2)   A registered agent for service of process on the limited liability company, having a business office identical with such registered office, which agent may be any of

a.   A limited liability company itself,

b.   An individual resident in the State of Delaware,

c.   A domestic limited liability company (other than the limited liability company itself), a domestic corporation, a domestic partnership (whether general (including a limited liability partnership) or limited (including a limited liability limited partnership)), or a domestic statutory trust, or

d.   A foreign corporation, a foreign partnership (whether general (including a limited liability partnership) or limited (including a limited liability limited partnership)), a foreign limited liability company, or a foreign statutory trust.

(b)   A registered agent may change the address of the registered office of the limited liability company(ies) for which it is registered agent to another address in the State of Delaware by paying a fee as set forth in § 18–1105(a)(2) of this title and filing with the Secretary of State a certificate, executed by such registered agent, setting forth the address at which such registered agent has maintained the registered office for each of the limited liability companies for which it is a registered agent, and further certifying to the new address to which each such registered office will be changed on a given day, and at which new address such registered agent will thereafter maintain the registered office for each of the limited liability companies for which it is a registered agent. Upon the filing of such certificate, the Secretary of State shall furnish to the registered agent a certified copy of the same under the Secretary's hand and seal of office, and thereafter, or until further change of address, as authorized by law, the registered office in the State of Delaware of each of the limited liability companies for which the agent is a registered agent shall be located at the new address of the registered agent thereof as given in the certificate. In the event of a change of name of any person acting as a registered agent of a limited liability company, such registered agent shall file with the Secretary of State a certificate executed by such registered agent setting forth the new name of such registered agent, the name of such registered agent before it was changed, and the address at which such registered agent has maintained the registered office for each of the limited liability companies for which it is a registered agent, and shall pay a fee as set forth in § 18–1105(a)(2) of this title. Upon the filing of such certificate, the Secretary of State shall furnish to the registered agent a certified copy of the certificate under the Secretary of State's own hand and seal of office. A change of name of any person acting as a registered agent of a limited liability company as a result of a merger or consolidation of the registered agent with or into another person which succeeds to its assets and liabilities by operation of law shall be deemed a change of name for purposes of this section. Filing a certificate under this section shall be deemed to be an amendment of the certificate of formation of each limited liability company affected thereby, and each such limited liability company shall not be required to take any further action with respect thereto to amend its certificate of formation under § 18–202 of this title. Any registered agent filing a certificate under this section shall promptly, upon such filing, deliver a copy of any such certificate to each limited liability company affected thereby.

(c)　The registered agent of 1 or more limited liability companies may resign and appoint a successor registered agent by paying a fee as set forth in § 18–1105(a)(2) of this title and filing a certificate with the Secretary of State stating that it resigns and the name and address of the successor registered agent. There shall be attached to such certificate a statement of each affected limited liability company ratifying and approving such change of registered agent. Upon such filing, the successor registered agent shall become the registered agent of such limited liability companies as have ratified and approved such substitution, and the successor registered agent's address, as stated in such certificate, shall become the address of each such limited liability company's registered office in the State of Delaware. The Secretary of State shall then issue a certificate that the successor registered agent has become the registered agent of the limited liability companies so ratifying and approving such change and setting out the names of such limited liability companies. Filing of such certificate of resignation shall be deemed to be an amendment of the certificate of formation of each limited liability company affected thereby, and each such limited liability company shall not be required to take any further action with respect thereto to amend its certificate of formation under § 18–202 of this title.

(d)　The registered agent of 1 or more limited liability companies may resign without appointing a successor registered agent by paying a fee as set forth in § 18–1105(a)(2) of this title and filing a certificate of resignation with the Secretary of State, but such resignation shall not become effective until 30 days after the certificate is filed. The certificate shall contain a statement that written notice of resignation was given to each affected limited liability company at least 30 days prior to the filing of the certificate by mailing or delivering such notice to the limited liability company at its address last known to the registered agent and shall set forth the date of such notice. After receipt of the notice of the resignation of its registered agent, the limited liability company for which such registered agent was acting shall obtain and designate a new registered agent, to take the place of the registered agent so resigning. If such limited liability company fails to obtain and designate a new registered agent as aforesaid prior to the expiration of the period of 30 days after the filing by the registered agent of the certificate of resignation, the certificate of formation of such limited liability company shall be canceled. After the resignation of the registered agent shall have become effective as provided in this section and if no new registered agent shall have been obtained and designated in the time and manner aforesaid, service of legal process against each limited liability company (and each protected series and each registered series thereof) for which the resigned registered agent had been acting shall thereafter be upon the Secretary of State in accordance with § 18–105 of this title.

(e)　Every registered agent shall:

(1)　If an entity, maintain a business office in the State of Delaware which is generally open, or if an individual, be generally present at a designated location in the State of Delaware, at sufficiently frequent times to accept service of process and otherwise perform the functions of a registered agent;

(2)　If a foreign entity, be authorized to transact business in the State of Delaware;

(3)　Accept service of process and other communications directed to the limited liability companies (and any protected series or registered series thereof) and foreign limited liability companies for which it serves as registered agent and forward same to the limited liability company or foreign limited liability company to which the service or communication is directed; and

(4)   Forward to the limited liability companies and foreign limited liability companies for which it serves as registered agent the statement for the annual tax for such limited liability company (and each registered series thereof) or such foreign limited liability company, as applicable, as described in § 18–1107 of this title or an electronic notification of same in a form satisfactory to the Secretary of State.

(f)   Any registered agent who at any time serves as registered agent for more than 50 entities (a "Commercial Registered Agent"), whether domestic or foreign, shall satisfy and comply with the following qualifications:

(1)   A natural person serving as a Commercial Registered Agent shall:

a.   Maintain a principal residence or a principal place of business in the State of Delaware;

b.   Maintain a Delaware business license;

c.   Be generally present at a designated location within the State of Delaware during normal business hours to accept service of process and otherwise perform the functions of a registered agent as specified in subsection (e) of this section; and

d.   Provide the Secretary of State upon request with such information identifying and enabling communication with such Commercial Registered Agent as the Secretary of State shall require.

(2)   A domestic or foreign corporation, a domestic or foreign partnership (whether general (including a limited liability partnership) or limited (including a limited liability limited partnership)), a domestic or foreign limited liability company, or a domestic or foreign statutory trust serving as a Commercial Registered Agent shall:

a.   Have a business office within the State of Delaware which is generally open during normal business hours to accept service of process and otherwise perform the functions of a registered agent as specified in subsection (e) of this section;

b.   Maintain a Delaware business license;

c.   Have generally present at such office during normal business hours an officer, director or managing agent who is a natural person; and

d.   Provide the Secretary of State upon request with such information identifying and enabling communication with such Commercial Registered Agent as the Secretary of State shall require.

(3)   For purposes of this subsection and paragraph (i)(2)a. of this section, a Commercial Registered Agent shall also include any registered agent which has an officer, director or managing agent in common with any other registered agent or agents if such registered agents at any time during such common service as officer, director or managing agent collectively served as registered agents for more than 50 entities, whether domestic or foreign.

(g)   Every domestic limited liability company and every foreign limited liability company qualified to do business in the State of Delaware shall provide to its registered agent and update from time to time as necessary the name, business address and business telephone number of a natural person who is a member, manager, officer, employee or designated agent of the domestic or foreign limited liability company who is then authorized to receive communications from the registered agent. Such person shall be deemed the communications contact for the domestic or foreign limited liability company. A domestic limited liability company, upon receipt of a request by the communications contact delivered in writing or by electronic transmission, shall provide the communications contact with the name, business address and business telephone number of a natural person who has access to the record required to be maintained pursuant to § 18–305(h) of this title. Every registered agent shall retain (in paper or electronic form) the above information concerning the current communications contact for each domestic limited liability company and each foreign limited liability company for which that registered agent serves as registered agent. If the domestic or foreign limited liability company fails to provide the registered agent with a current communications contact, the registered agent may resign as the registered agent for such domestic or foreign limited liability company pursuant to this section. For purposes of this subsection, the term "electronic transmission" means any form of communication not directly involving the physical transmission of paper, including the use of, or participation in, 1 or more electronic networks or databases (including 1 or more distributed electronic networks or databases), that creates a record that may be retained, retrieved and reviewed by a recipient thereof and that may be directly reproduced in paper form by such a recipient through an automated process.

(h)   The Secretary of State is authorized to issue such rules and regulations as may be necessary or appropriate to carry out the enforcement of subsections (e), (f) and (g) of this section, and to take actions reasonable and necessary to assure registered agents' compliance with subsections (e), (f) and (g) of this section. Such actions may include refusal to file documents submitted by a registered agent.

(i)   Upon application of the Secretary of State, the Court of Chancery may enjoin any person or entity from serving as a registered agent or as an officer, director or managing agent of a registered agent.

(1)   Upon the filing of a complaint by the Secretary of State pursuant to this section, the Court may make such orders respecting such proceeding as it deems appropriate, and may enter such orders granting interim or final relief as it deems proper under the circumstances.

(2)   Any 1 or more of the following grounds shall be a sufficient basis to grant an injunction pursuant to this section:

a.   With respect to any registered agent who at any time within 1 year immediately prior to the filing of the Secretary of State's complaint is a Commercial Registered Agent, failure after notice and warning to comply with the qualifications set forth in subsection (e) of this section and/or the requirements of subsection (f) or (g) of this section above;

b.   The person serving as a registered agent, or any person who is an officer, director or managing agent of an entity registered agent, has been convicted of a felony or any crime which includes an element of dishonesty or fraud or involves moral turpitude; or

c.   The registered agent has engaged in conduct in connection with acting as a registered agent that is intended to or likely to deceive or defraud the public.

(3)   With respect to any order the Court enters pursuant to this section with respect to an entity that has acted as a registered agent, the Court may also direct such order to any person who has served as an officer, director or managing agent of such registered agent. Any person who, on or after January 1, 2007, serves as an officer, director or managing agent of an entity acting as a registered agent in the State of Delaware shall be deemed thereby to have consented to the appointment of such registered agent as agent upon whom service of process may be made in any action brought pursuant to this section, and service as an officer, director or managing agent of an entity acting as a registered agent in the State of Delaware shall be a signification of the consent of such person that any process when so served shall be of the same legal force and validity as if served upon such person within the State of Delaware, and such appointment of the registered agent shall be irrevocable.

(4)   Upon the entry of an order by the Court enjoining any person or entity from acting as a registered agent, the Secretary of State shall mail or deliver notice of such order to each affected domestic or foreign limited liability company:

a.   That has specified the address of a place of business in a record of the Secretary of State, to the address specified, or

b.   An address of which the Secretary of State has obtained from the domestic or foreign limited liability company's former registered agent, to the address obtained.

If such a domestic limited liability company fails to obtain and designate a new registered agent within 30 days after such notice is given, the certificate of formation of such limited liability company shall be canceled. If such a foreign limited liability company fails to obtain and designate a new registered agent within 30 days after such notice is given, such foreign limited liability company shall not be permitted to do business in the State of Delaware and its registration shall be canceled. If any other domestic limited liability company fails to obtain and designate a new registered agent within 60 days after entry of an order by the Court enjoining such limited liability company's registered agent from acting as a registered agent, the certificate of formation of such limited liability company shall be canceled. If any other affected foreign limited liability company fails to obtain and designate a new registered agent within 60 days after entry of an order by the Court enjoining such foreign limited liability company's registered agent from acting as a registered agent, such foreign limited liability company shall not be permitted to do business in the State of Delaware and its registration shall be canceled. If the Court enjoins a person or entity from acting as a registered agent as provided in this section and no new registered agent shall have been obtained and designated in the time and manner aforesaid, service of legal process against the domestic or foreign limited liability company for which the registered agent had been acting shall thereafter be upon the Secretary of State in accordance with § 18–105 or § 18–911 of this title. The Court of Chancery may, upon application of the Secretary of State on notice to the former registered agent, enter such orders as it deems appropriate to give the Secretary of State access to information in the former registered agent's possession in order to facilitate communication with the domestic or foreign limited liability companies the former registered agent served.

(j)   The Secretary of State is authorized to make a list of registered agents available to the public, and to establish such qualifications and issue such rules and regulations with respect to such listing as the Secretary of State deems necessary or appropriate.

(k)   As contained in any certificate of formation, application for registration as a foreign limited liability company, or other document filed in the office of the Secretary of State under this chapter, the address of a registered agent or registered office shall include the street, number, city and postal code.

§ 18–105.   Service of Process on Domestic Limited Liability Companies and Series Thereof

(a)   Service of legal process upon any domestic limited liability company or any protected series or registered series thereof shall be made by delivering a copy personally to any manager of the limited liability company in the State of Delaware, or the registered agent of the limited liability company in the State of Delaware, or by leaving it at the dwelling house or usual place of abode in the State of Delaware of any such manager or registered agent (if the registered agent be an individual), or at the registered office or other place of business of the limited liability company in the State of Delaware. If service of legal process is made upon the registered agent of the limited liability company in the State of Delaware on behalf of any such protected series or registered series, such process shall include the name of the limited liability company and the name of such protected series or registered series. If the registered agent be a corporation, service of process upon it as such may be made by serving, in the State of Delaware, a copy thereof on the president, vice-president, secretary, assistant secretary or any director of the corporate registered agent. Service by copy left at the dwelling house or usual place of abode of a manager or registered agent, or at the registered office or other place of business of the limited liability company in the State of Delaware, to be effective, must be delivered thereat at least 6 days before the return date of the process, and in the presence of an adult person, and the officer serving the process shall distinctly state the manner of service in the officer's return thereto. Process returnable forthwith must be delivered personally to the manager or registered agent.

(b)   In case the officer whose duty it is to serve legal process cannot by due diligence serve the process in any manner provided for by subsection (a) of this section, it shall be lawful to serve the process against the limited liability company or any protected series or registered series thereof upon the Secretary of State, and such service shall be as effectual for all intents and purposes as if made in any of the ways provided for in subsection (a) of this section. If service of legal process is made upon the Secretary of State on behalf of any such protected series or registered series, such process shall include the name of the limited liability company and the name of such protected series or registered series. Process may be served upon the Secretary of State under this subsection by means of electronic transmission but only as prescribed by the Secretary of State. The Secretary of State is authorized to issue such rules and regulations with respect to such service as the Secretary of State deems necessary or appropriate. In the event that service is effected through the Secretary of State in accordance with this subsection, the Secretary of State shall forthwith notify the limited liability company by letter, directed to the limited liability company at its address as it appears on the records relating to such limited liability company on file with the Secretary of State or, if no such address appears, at its last registered office. Such letter shall be sent by a mail or courier service that includes a record of mailing or deposit with the courier and a record of delivery evidenced by the signature of the recipient. Such letter shall enclose a copy of the process and any other papers served on the Secretary of State pursuant to this subsection. It shall be the duty of the plaintiff in the event of such service to serve process and any other papers in duplicate, to notify the Secretary of State that service is being effected pursuant to this subsection, and to pay the Secretary of State the sum of $50 for the use of the State of Delaware, which sum shall be taxed as part of the costs in the proceeding if the plaintiff shall prevail therein. The Secretary of State shall maintain an alphabetical record of any such service setting forth the name of the plaintiff and defendant, the title, docket number and nature of the proceeding in which process has been served upon the Secretary, the fact that service has been effected pursuant to this subsection, the return date thereof, and the day and hour when the service was made. The Secretary of State shall not be required to retain such information for a period longer than 5 years from the Secretary's receipt of the service of process.

§ 18–106.   Nature of Business Permitted; Powers

(a)   A limited liability company may carry on any lawful business, purpose or activity, whether or not for profit, with the exception of the business of banking as defined in § 126 of Title 8.

(b)   A limited liability company shall possess and may exercise all the powers and privileges granted by this chapter or by any other law or by its limited liability company agreement, together with any powers incidental thereto, including such powers and privileges as are necessary or convenient to the conduct, promotion or attainment of the business, purposes or activities of the limited liability company.

(c)   Notwithstanding any provision of this chapter to the contrary, without limiting the general powers enumerated in subsection (b) of this section, a limited liability company shall, subject to such standards and restrictions, if any, as are set forth in its limited liability company agreement, have the power and authority to make contracts of guaranty and suretyship, and enter into interest rate, basis, currency, hedge or other swap agreements, or cap, floor, put, call, option, exchange or collar agreements, derivative agreements or other agreements similar to any of the foregoing.

(d)   Unless otherwise provided in a limited liability company agreement, a limited liability company has the power and authority to grant, hold or exercise a power of attorney, including an irrevocable power of attorney.

§ 18–107.   Business Transactions of Member or Manager With the Limited Liability Company

Except as provided in a limited liability company agreement, a member or manager may lend money to, borrow money from, act as a surety, guarantor or endorser for, guarantee or assume 1 or more obligations of, provide collateral for, and transact other business with, a limited liability company and, subject to other applicable law, has the same rights and obligations with respect to any such matter as a person who is not a member or manager.

§ 18–108. Indemnification

Subject to such standards and restrictions, if any, as are set forth in its limited liability company agreement, a limited liability company may, and shall have the power to, indemnify and hold harmless any member or manager or other person from and against any and all claims and demands whatsoever.

§ 18–109. Service of Process on Managers and Liquidating Trustees

(a) A manager or a liquidating trustee of a limited liability company may be served with process in the manner prescribed in this section in all civil actions or proceedings brought in the State of Delaware involving or relating to the business of the limited liability company or a violation by the manager or the liquidating trustee of a duty to the limited liability company, or any member of the limited liability company, whether or not the manager or the liquidating trustee is a manager or a liquidating trustee at the time suit is commenced. A manager's or a liquidating trustee's serving as such constitutes such person's consent to the appointment of the registered agent of the limited liability company (or, if there is none, the Secretary of State) as such person's agent upon whom service of process may be made as provided in this section. Such service as a manager or a liquidating trustee shall signify the consent of such manager or liquidating trustee that any process when so served shall be of the same legal force and validity as if served upon such manager or liquidating trustee within the State of Delaware and such appointment of the registered agent (or, if there is none, the Secretary of State) shall be irrevocable. As used in this subsection (a) and in subsections (b), (c) and (d) of this section, the term "manager" refers (i) to a person who is a manager as defined in § 18–101(10) of this title and (ii) to a person, whether or not a member of a limited liability company, who, although not a manager as defined in § 18–101(10) of this title, participates materially in the management of the limited liability company; provided however, that the power to elect or otherwise select or to participate in the election or selection of a person to be a manager as defined in § 18–101(10) of this title shall not, by itself, constitute participation in the management of the limited liability company.

(b) Service of process shall be effected by serving the registered agent (or, if there is none, the Secretary of State) with 1 copy of such process in the manner provided by law for service of writs of summons. In the event service is made under this subsection upon the Secretary of State, the plaintiff shall pay to the Secretary of State the sum of $50 for the use of the State of Delaware, which sum shall be taxed as part of the costs of the proceeding if the plaintiff shall prevail therein. In addition, the Prothonotary or the Register in Chancery of the court in which the civil action or proceeding is pending shall, within 7 days of such service, deposit in the United States mails, by registered mail, postage prepaid, true and attested copies of the process, together with a statement that service is being made pursuant to this section, addressed to such manager or liquidating trustee at the registered office of the limited liability company and at the manager's or liquidating trustee's address last known to the party desiring to make such service.

(c) In any action in which any such manager or liquidating trustee has been served with process as hereinabove provided, the time in which a defendant shall be required to appear and file a responsive pleading shall be computed from the date of mailing by the Prothonotary or the Register in Chancery as provided in subsection (b) of this section; however, the court in which such action has been commenced may order such continuance or continuances as may be necessary to afford such manager or liquidating trustee reasonable opportunity to defend the action.

(d) In a written limited liability company agreement or other writing, a manager or member may consent to be subject to the nonexclusive jurisdiction of the courts of, or arbitration in, a specified jurisdiction, or the exclusive jurisdiction of the courts of the State of Delaware, or the exclusivity of arbitration in a specified jurisdiction or the State of Delaware, and to be served with legal process in the manner prescribed in such limited liability company agreement or other writing. Except by agreeing to arbitrate any arbitrable matter in a specified jurisdiction or in the State of Delaware, a member who is not a manager may not waive its right to maintain a legal action or proceeding in the courts of the State of Delaware with respect to matters relating to the organization or internal affairs of a limited liability company.

(e)   Nothing herein contained limits or affects the right to serve process in any other manner now or hereafter provided by law. This section is an extension of and not a limitation upon the right otherwise existing of service of legal process upon nonresidents.

(f)   The Court of Chancery and the Superior Court may make all necessary rules respecting the form of process, the manner of issuance and return thereof and such other rules which may be necessary to implement this section and are not inconsistent with this section.

§ 18–110.   Contested Matters Relating to Managers; Contested Votes

(a)   Upon application of any member or manager, the Court of Chancery may hear and determine the validity of any admission, election, appointment, removal or resignation of a manager of a limited liability company, and the right of any person to become or continue to be a manager of a limited liability company, and, in case the right to serve as a manager is claimed by more than 1 person, may determine the person or persons entitled to serve as managers; and to that end make such order or decree in any such case as may be just and proper, with power to enforce the production of any books, papers and records of the limited liability company relating to the issue. In any such application, the limited liability company shall be named as a party and service of copies of the application upon the registered agent of the limited liability company shall be deemed to be service upon the limited liability company and upon the person or persons whose right to serve as a manager is contested and upon the person or persons, if any, claiming to be a manager or claiming the right to be a manager; and the registered agent shall forward immediately a copy of the application to the limited liability company and to the person or persons whose right to serve as a manager is contested and to the person or persons, if any, claiming to be a manager or the right to be a manager, in a postpaid, sealed, registered letter addressed to such limited liability company and such person or persons at their post-office addresses last known to the registered agent or furnished to the registered agent by the applicant member or manager. The Court may make such order respecting further or other notice of such application as it deems proper under these circumstances.

(b)   Upon application of any member or manager, the Court of Chancery may hear and determine the result of any vote of members or managers upon matters as to which the members or managers of the limited liability company, or any class or group of members or managers, have the right to vote pursuant to the limited liability company agreement or other agreement or this chapter (other than the admission, election, appointment, removal or resignation of managers). In any such application, the limited liability company shall be named as a party and service of the application upon the registered agent of the limited liability company shall be deemed to be service upon the limited liability company, and no other party need be joined in order for the Court to adjudicate the result of the vote. The Court may make such order respecting further or other notice of such application as it deems proper under these circumstances.

(c)   As used in this section, the term 'manager' refers to a person:

   a.   Who is a manager as defined in § 18–101(10) of this title and

   b.   Whether or not a member of a limited liability company, who, although not a manager as defined in § 18–101(10) of this title, participates materially in the management of the limited liability company;

provided however, that the power to elect or otherwise select or to participate in the election or selection of a person to be a manager as defined in § 18–101(10) of this title shall not, by itself, constitute participation in the management of the limited liability company.

(d)   Nothing herein contained limits or affects the right to serve process in any other manner now or hereafter provided by law. This section is an extension of and not a limitation upon the right otherwise existing of service of legal process upon nonresidents.

§ 18–111. Interpretation and Enforcement of Limited Liability Company Agreement

Any action to interpret, apply or enforce the provisions of a limited liability company agreement, or the duties, obligations or liabilities of a limited liability company to the members or managers of the limited liability company, or the duties, obligations or liabilities among members or managers and of members or managers to the limited liability company, or the rights or powers of, or restrictions on, the limited liability company, members or managers, or any provision of this chapter, or any other instrument, document, agreement or certificate contemplated by any provision of this chapter may be brought in the Court of Chancery.

As used in this section, the term 'manager' refers to a person:

(1) Who is a manager as defined in § 18–101(10) of this title, and

(2) Whether or not a member of a limited liability company, who, although not a manager as defined in § 18–101(10) of this title, participates materially in the management of the limited liability company; provided however, that the power to elect or otherwise select or to participate in the election or selection of a person to be a manager as defined in § 18–101(10) of this title shall not, by itself, constitute participation in the management of the limited liability company.

§ 18–112. Judicial Cancellation of Certificate of Formation; Proceedings

(a) Upon motion by the Attorney General, the Court of Chancery shall have jurisdiction to cancel the certificate of formation of any domestic limited liability company for abuse or misuse of its limited liability company powers, privileges or existence. The Attorney General shall proceed for this purpose in the Court of Chancery.

(b) The Court of Chancery shall have power, by appointment of trustees, receivers or otherwise, to administer and wind up the affairs of any domestic limited liability company whose certificate of formation shall be canceled by the Court of Chancery under this section, and to make such orders and decrees with respect thereto as shall be just and equitable respecting its affairs and assets and the rights of its members and creditors.

SUBCHAPTER II
FORMATION; CERTIFICATE OF FORMATION

§ 18–201. Certificate of Formation

(a) In order to form a limited liability company, 1 or more authorized persons must execute a certificate of formation. The certificate of formation shall be filed in the office of the Secretary of State and set forth:

(1) The name of the limited liability company;

(2) The address of the registered office and the name and address of the registered agent for service of process required to be maintained by § 18–104 of this title; and

(3) Any other matters the members determine to include therein.

(b) A limited liability company is formed at the time of the filing of the initial certificate of formation in the office of the Secretary of State or at any later date or time specified in the certificate of formation if, in either case, there has been substantial compliance with the requirements of this section. A limited liability company formed under this chapter shall be a separate legal entity, the existence of which as a separate legal entity shall continue until cancellation of the limited liability company's certificate of formation.

(c) The filing of the certificate of formation in the office of the Secretary of State shall make it unnecessary to file any other documents under Chapter 31 of this title.

(d)   A limited liability company agreement shall be entered into or otherwise existing either before, after or at the time of the filing of a certificate of formation and, whether entered into or otherwise existing before, after or at the time of such filing, may be made effective as of the effective time of such filing or at such other time or date as provided in or reflected by the limited liability company agreement.

(e)   A certificate of formation substantially complies with § 18–201(a)(2) of this title if it contains the name of the registered agent and the address of the registered office even if the certificate of formation does not expressly designate such person as the registered agent or such address as the registered office or the address of the registered agent.

§ 18–202.   Amendment to Certificate of Formation

(a)   A certificate of formation is amended by filing a certificate of amendment thereto in the office of the Secretary of State. The certificate of amendment shall set forth:

(1)   The name of the limited liability company; and

(2)   The amendment to the certificate of formation.

(b)   A manager or, if there is no manager, then any member who becomes aware that any statement in a certificate of formation was false when made, or that any matter described has changed making the certificate of formation false in any material respect, shall promptly amend the certificate of formation.

(c)   A certificate of formation may be amended at any time for any other proper purpose.

(d)   Unless otherwise provided in this chapter or unless a later effective date or time (which shall be a date or time certain) is provided for in the certificate of amendment, a certificate of amendment shall be effective at the time of its filing with the Secretary of State.

§ 18–203.   Cancellation of Certificate

(a)   A certificate of formation shall be canceled upon the dissolution and the completion of winding up of a limited liability company, or as provided in § 18–104(d) or § 18–104(i)(4) or § 18–1108 of this title, or upon the filing of a certificate of merger or consolidation or a certificate of ownership and merger if the limited liability company is not the surviving or resulting entity in a merger or consolidation or upon the future effective date or time of a certificate of merger or consolidation or a certificate of ownership and merger if the limited liability company is not the surviving or resulting entity in a merger or consolidation, or upon the filing of a certificate of transfer or upon the future effective date or time of a certificate of transfer, or upon the filing of a certificate of conversion to non-Delaware entity or upon the future effective date or time of a certificate of conversion to non-Delaware entity. A certificate of cancellation shall be filed in the office of the Secretary of State to accomplish the cancellation of a certificate of formation upon the dissolution and the completion of winding up of a limited liability company and shall set forth:

(1)   The name of the limited liability company;

(2)   The date of filing of its certificate of formation;

(3)   If the limited liability company has formed 1 or more registered series whose certificate of registered series has not been canceled prior to the filing of the certificate of cancellation, the name of each such registered series;

(4)   The future effective date or time (which shall be a date or time certain) of cancellation if it is not to be effective upon the filing of the certificate; and

(5)   Any other information the person filing the certificate of cancellation determines.

(b)   A certificate of cancellation that is filed in the office of the Secretary of State prior to the dissolution or the completion of winding up of a limited liability company may be corrected as an erroneously executed certificate of cancellation by filing with the office of the Secretary of State a certificate of correction of such certificate of cancellation in accordance with § 18–211 of this title.

(c)   The Secretary of State shall not issue a certificate of good standing with respect to a limited liability company (or any registered series thereof) if its certificate of formation is canceled.

§ 18–204.   Execution

(a)   Each certificate required by this subchapter to be filed in the office of the Secretary of State shall be executed by 1 or more authorized persons or, in the case of a certificate of conversion to limited liability company or certificate of limited liability company domestication, by any person authorized to execute such certificate on behalf of the other entity or non-United States entity, respectively, except that a certificate of merger or consolidation filed by a surviving or resulting other business entity shall be executed by any person authorized to execute such certificate on behalf of such other business entity.

(b)   Unless otherwise provided in a limited liability company agreement, any person may sign any certificate or amendment thereof or enter into a limited liability company agreement or amendment thereof by an agent, including an attorney-in-fact. An authorization, including a power of attorney, to sign any certificate or amendment thereof or to enter into a limited liability company agreement or amendment thereof need not be in writing, need not be sworn to, verified or acknowledged, and need not be filed in the office of the Secretary of State, but if in writing, must be retained by the limited liability company.

(c)   For all purposes of the laws of the State of Delaware, unless otherwise provided in a limited liability company agreement, a power of attorney or proxy with respect to a limited liability company granted to any person shall be irrevocable if it states that it is irrevocable and it is coupled with an interest sufficient in law to support an irrevocable power or proxy. Such irrevocable power of attorney or proxy, unless otherwise provided therein or in a limited liability company agreement, shall not be affected by subsequent death, disability, incapacity, dissolution, termination of existence or bankruptcy of, or any other event concerning, the principal. A power of attorney or proxy with respect to matters relating to the organization, internal affairs or termination of a limited liability company or granted by a person as a member or an assignee of a limited liability company interest or by a person seeking to become a member or an assignee of a limited liability company interest and, in either case, granted to the limited liability company, a manager or member thereof, or any of their respective officers, directors, managers, members, partners, trustees, employees or agents shall be deemed coupled with an interest sufficient in law to support an irrevocable power or proxy. The provisions of this subsection shall not be construed to limit the enforceability of a power of attorney or proxy that is part of a limited liability company agreement.

(d)   The execution of a certificate by a person who is authorized by this chapter to execute such certificate constitutes an oath or affirmation, under the penalties of perjury in the third degree, that, to the best of such person's knowledge and belief, the facts stated therein are true.

§ 18–205.   Execution, Amendment or Cancellation by Judicial Order

(a)   If a person required to execute a certificate required by this subchapter fails or refuses to do so, any other person who is adversely affected by the failure or refusal may petition the Court of Chancery to direct the execution of the certificate. If the Court finds that the execution of the certificate is proper and that any person so designated has failed or refused to execute the certificate, it shall order the Secretary of State to record an appropriate certificate.

(b)   If a person required to execute a limited liability company agreement or amendment thereof fails or refuses to do so, any other person who is adversely affected by the failure or refusal may petition the Court of Chancery to direct the execution of the limited liability company agreement or amendment thereof. If the Court finds that the limited liability company agreement or amendment thereof should be executed and that any person required to execute the limited liability company agreement or amendment thereof has failed or refused to do so, it shall enter an order granting appropriate relief.

§ 18–206.   Filing

(a)   The signed copy of the certificate of formation and of any certificates of amendment, correction, amendment of a certificate with a future effective date or time, termination of a certificate with a future effective date or time or cancellation (or of any judicial decree of amendment or cancellation), and of any certificate of merger or consolidation, any certificate of ownership and merger, any restated certificate, any corrected certificate, any certificate of conversion to limited liability company, any certificate of conversion to a non-Delaware entity, any certificate of transfer, any certificate of transfer and domestic continuance, any certificate of limited liability company domestication, and of any certificate of revival shall be delivered to the Secretary of State. A person who executes a certificate as an agent or fiduciary need not exhibit evidence of that person's authority as a prerequisite to filing. Any signature on any certificate authorized to be filed with the Secretary of State under any provision of this chapter may be a facsimile, a conformed signature or an electronically transmitted signature. Upon delivery of any certificate, the Secretary of State shall record the date and time of its delivery. Unless the Secretary of State finds that any certificate does not conform to law, upon receipt of all filing fees required by law the Secretary of State shall:

(1)   Certify that the certificate of formation, the certificate of amendment, the certificate of correction, the certificate of amendment of a certificate with a future effective date or time, the certificate of termination of a certificate with a future effective date or time, the certificate of cancellation (or of any judicial decree of amendment or cancellation), the certificate of merger or consolidation, the certificate of ownership and merger, the restated certificate, the corrected certificate, the certificate of conversion to limited liability company, the certificate of conversion to a non-Delaware entity, the certificate of transfer, the certificate of transfer and domestic continuance, the certificate of limited liability company domestication or the certificate of revival has been filed in the Secretary of State's office by endorsing upon the signed certificate the word "Filed," and the date and time of the filing. This endorsement is conclusive of the date and time of its filing in the absence of actual fraud. Except as provided in paragraph (a)(5) or (a)(6) of this section, such date and time of filing of a certificate shall be the date and time of delivery of the certificate;

(2)   File and index the endorsed certificate;

(3)   Prepare and return to the person who filed it or that person's representative a copy of the signed certificate, similarly endorsed, and shall certify such copy as a true copy of the signed certificate; and

(4)   Cause to be entered such information from the certificate as the Secretary of State deems appropriate into the Delaware Corporation Information System or any system which is a successor thereto in the office of the Secretary of State, and such information and a copy of such certificate shall be permanently maintained as a public record on a suitable medium. The Secretary of State is authorized to grant direct access to such system to registered agents subject to the execution of an operating agreement between the Secretary of State and such registered agent. Any registered agent granted such access shall demonstrate the existence of policies to ensure that information entered into the system accurately reflects the content of certificates in the possession of the registered agent at the time of entry.

(5)   Upon request made upon or prior to delivery, the Secretary of State may, to the extent deemed practicable, establish as the date and time of filing of a certificate a date and time after its delivery. If the Secretary of State refuses to file any certificate due to an error, omission or other imperfection, the Secretary of State may hold such certificate in suspension, and in such event, upon delivery of a replacement certificate in proper form for filing and tender of the required fees within 5 business days after notice of such suspension is given to the filer, the Secretary of State shall establish as the date and time of filing of such certificate the date and

time that would have been the date and time of filing of the rejected certificate had it been accepted for filing. The Secretary of State shall not issue a certificate of good standing with respect to any limited liability company or registered series with a certificate held in suspension pursuant to this subsection. The Secretary of State may establish as the date and time of filing of a certificate the date and time at which information from such certificate is entered pursuant to paragraph (a)(4) of this section if such certificate is delivered on the same date and within 4 hours after such information is entered.

(6) If:

a. Together with the actual delivery of a certificate and tender of the required fees, there is delivered to the Secretary of State a separate affidavit (which in its heading shall be designated as an affidavit of extraordinary condition) attesting, on the basis of personal knowledge of the affiant or a reliable source of knowledge identified in the affidavit, that an earlier effort to deliver such certificate and tender such fees was made in good faith, specifying the nature, date and time of such good faith effort and requesting that the Secretary of State establish such date and time as the date and time of filing of such certificate; or

b. Upon the actual delivery of a certificate and tender of the required fees, the Secretary of State in the Secretary of the State's own discretion provides a written waiver of the requirement for such an affidavit stating that it appears to the Secretary of State that an earlier effort to deliver such certificate and tender such fees was made in good faith and specifying the date and time of such effort; and

c. The Secretary of State determines that an extraordinary condition existed at such date and time, that such earlier effort was unsuccessful as a result of the existence of such extraordinary condition, and that such actual delivery and tender were made within a reasonable period (not to exceed 2 business days) after the cessation of such extraordinary condition, then the Secretary of State may establish such date and time as the date and time of filing of such certificate. No fee shall be paid to the Secretary of State for receiving an affidavit of extraordinary condition. For purposes of this subsection, an extraordinary condition means: any emergency resulting from an attack on, invasion or occupation by foreign military forces of, or disaster, catastrophe, war or other armed conflict, revolution or insurrection or rioting or civil commotion in, the United States or a locality in which the Secretary of State conducts its business or in which the good faith effort to deliver the certificate and tender the required fees is made, or the immediate threat of any of the foregoing; or any malfunction or outage of the electrical or telephone service to the Secretary of State's office, or weather or other condition in or about a locality in which the Secretary of State conducts its business, as a result of which the Secretary of State's office is not open for the purpose of the filing of certificates under this chapter or such filing cannot be effected without extraordinary effort. The Secretary of State may require such proof as it deems necessary to make the determination required under this paragraph (a)(6)c., and any such determination shall be conclusive in the absence of actual fraud. If the Secretary of State establishes the date and time of filing of a certificate pursuant to this subsection, the date and time of delivery of the affidavit of extraordinary condition or the date and time of the Secretary of State's written waiver of such affidavit shall be endorsed on such affidavit or waiver and such affidavit or waiver, so endorsed, shall be attached to the filed certificate to which it relates. Such filed certificate shall be effective as of the date and time established as the date and time of filing by the Secretary of State pursuant to this subsection, except as to those persons who are substantially and adversely affected by such establishment and, as to those persons, the certificate shall be effective from the date and time endorsed on the affidavit of extraordinary condition or written waiver attached thereto.

(b) Notwithstanding any other provision of this chapter, any certificate filed under this chapter shall be effective at the time of its filing with the Secretary of State or at any later date or time (not later than a time on the 180th day after the date of its filing if such date of filing is on or after January 1, 2012) specified in the certificate. Upon the filing of a certificate of amendment (or judicial decree of amendment), certificate of correction, corrected certificate or restated certificate in the office of the Secretary of State, or upon the future effective date or time of a certificate of amendment (or judicial decree thereof) or restated certificate, as provided for therein, the certificate of formation or certificate of registered series shall be amended, corrected or restated as set forth therein. Upon the filing of a certificate of cancellation (or a judicial decree thereof), or a certificate of merger or consolidation or certificate of ownership and merger which acts as a certificate of cancellation or a certificate of transfer, or a certificate of conversion to a non-Delaware entity, or a certificate of conversion of registered series to protected series, or upon the future effective date or time of a certificate of cancellation (or a judicial decree thereof) or of a certificate of merger or consolidation or certificate of ownership and merger which acts as a certificate of cancellation or a certificate of transfer, or a certificate of conversion to a non-Delaware entity, as provided for therein, or as specified in § 18–104(d), § 18–104(i)(4), § 18–112 or § 18–1108 of this title, the certificate of formation or certificate of registered series, as applicable, is canceled. Upon the filing of a certificate of limited liability company domestication or upon the future effective date or time of a certificate of limited liability company domestication, the entity filing the certificate of limited liability company domestication is domesticated as a limited liability company with the effect provided in § 18–212 of this title. Upon the filing of a certificate of conversion to limited liability company or upon the future effective date or time of a certificate of conversion to limited liability company, the entity filing the certificate of conversion to limited liability company is converted to a limited liability company with the effect provided in § 18–214 of this title. Upon the filing of a certificate of conversion of protected series to registered series, or upon the future effective date or time of a certificate of conversion of protected series to registered series, the protected series with respect to which such filing is made is converted to a registered series with the effect provided in § 18–219 of this title. Upon the filing of a certificate of conversion of registered series to protected series, or upon the future effective date or time of a certificate of conversion of registered series to protected series, the registered series filing such certificate is converted to a protected series with the effect provided in § 18–220 of this title. Upon the filing of a certificate of revival, a limited liability company or a registered series is revived with the effect provided in § 18–1109 or § 18–1110 of this title. Upon the filing of a certificate of transfer and domestic continuance, or upon the future effective date or time of a certificate of transfer and domestic continuance, as provided for therein, the limited liability company filing the certificate of transfer and domestic continuance shall continue to exist as a limited liability company of the State of Delaware with the effect provided in § 18–213 of this title.

(c)   If any certificate filed in accordance with this chapter provides for a future effective date or time and if, prior to such future effective date or time set forth in such certificate, the transaction is terminated or its terms are amended to change the future effective date or time or any other matter described in such certificate so as to make such certificate false or inaccurate in any respect, such certificate shall, prior to the future effective date or time set forth in such certificate, be terminated or amended by the filing of a certificate of termination or certificate of amendment of such certificate, executed in accordance with § 18–204 of this title, which shall identify the certificate which has been terminated or amended and shall state that the certificate has been terminated or the manner in which it has been amended. Upon the filing of a certificate of amendment of a certificate with a future effective date or time, the certificate identified in such certificate of amendment is amended. Upon the filing of a certificate of termination of a certificate with a future effective date or time, the certificate identified in such certificate of termination is terminated.

(d)   A fee as set forth in § 18–1105(a)(3) of this title shall be paid at the time of the filing of a certificate of formation, a certificate of registered series of amendment, a certificate of correction, a certificate of amendment of a certificate with a future effective date or time, a certificate of termination of a certificate with a future effective date or time, a certificate of cancellation, a certificate of merger or consolidation, a certificate of ownership and merger, a restated certificate, a corrected certificate, a certificate of conversion to limited liability company, a certificate of conversion to a non-Delaware entity, a certificate of conversion of protected series to registered series, a certificate of conversion of registered series to protected series, a certificate of transfer, a certificate of transfer and domestic continuance, a certificate of limited liability company domestication or a certificate of revival.

(e)   The Secretary of State, acting as agent, shall collect and deposit in a separate account established exclusively for that purpose, a courthouse municipality fee with respect to each filed instrument and shall thereafter monthly remit funds from such account to the treasuries of the municipalities designated in § 301 of Title 10. Said fees shall be for the purposes of defraying certain costs incurred by such municipalities in hosting the primary locations for the Delaware Courts. The fee to such municipalities shall be $20 for each instrument filed with the Secretary of State in accordance with this section. The municipality to receive the fee shall be the municipality designated in § 301 of Title 10 in the county in which the limited liability company's registered office in this State is, or is to be, located, except that a fee shall not be charged for a document filed in accordance with subchapter IX of this chapter.

(f)   A fee as set forth in § 18–1105(a)(4) of this title shall be paid for a certified copy of any paper on file as provided for by this chapter, and a fee as set forth in § 18–1105(a)(5) of this title shall be paid for each page copied.

(g)   Notwithstanding any other provision of this chapter, it shall not be necessary for any limited liability company or foreign limited liability company to amend its certificate of formation, its application for registration as a foreign limited liability company, or any other document that has been filed in the office of the Secretary of State prior to August 1, 2011, to comply with § 18–104(k) of this title; notwithstanding the foregoing, any certificate or other document filed under this chapter on or after August 1, 2011 and changing the address of a registered agent or registered office shall comply with § 18–104(k) of this title.

§ 18–207.   Notice

The fact that a certificate of formation is on file in the office of the Secretary of State is notice that the entity formed in connection with the filing of the certificate of formation is a limited liability company formed under the laws of the State of Delaware and is notice of all other facts set forth therein which are required to be set forth in a certificate of formation by § 18–201(a)(1) and (2) or § 18–1202 of this title and which are permitted to be set forth in a certificate of formation by § 18–215(b) or § 18–218(b) of this title. The fact that a certificate of registered series is on file in the office of the Secretary of State is notice that the registered series named in such certificate of registered series has been formed pursuant to § 18–218 of this title and is notice of all other facts set forth therein which are required to be set forth in a certificate of registered series by § 18–218(d) of this title.

§ 18–208.   Restated Certificate

(a)   Restated certificate of formation.—

(1)   A limited liability company may, whenever desired, integrate into a single instrument all of the provisions of its certificate of formation which are then in effect and operative as a result of there having theretofore been filed with the Secretary of State 1 or more certificates or other instruments pursuant to any of the sections referred to in this subchapter, and it may at the same time also further amend its certificate of formation by adopting a restated certificate of formation.

(2)   If a restated certificate of formation merely restates and integrates but does not further amend the initial certificate of formation, as theretofore amended or supplemented by any instrument that was executed and filed pursuant to any of the sections in this subchapter, it shall be specifically designated in its heading as a "Restated Certificate of Formation" together with such other words as the limited liability company may deem appropriate and shall be executed by an authorized person and filed as provided in § 18–206 of this title in the office of the Secretary of State. If a restated certificate restates and integrates and also further amends in any respect the certificate of formation, as theretofore amended or supplemented, it shall be specifically designated in its heading as an "Amended and Restated Certificate of Formation" together with

such other words as the limited liability company may deem appropriate and shall be executed by at least 1 authorized person, and filed as provided in § 18–206 of this title in the office of the Secretary of State.

(3)   A restated certificate of formation shall state, either in its heading or in an introductory paragraph, the limited liability company's present name, and, if it has been changed, the name under which it was originally filed, and the date of filing of its original certificate of formation with the Secretary of State, and the future effective date or time (which shall be a date or time certain) of the restated certificate if it is not to be effective upon the filing of the restated certificate. A restated certificate shall also state that it was duly executed and is being filed in accordance with this section. If a restated certificate only restates and integrates and does not further amend a limited liability company's certificate of formation, as theretofore amended or supplemented and there is no discrepancy between those provisions and the restated certificate, it shall state that fact as well.

(4)   Upon the filing of a restated certificate of formation with the Secretary of State, or upon the future effective date or time of a restated certificate of formation as provided for therein, the initial certificate of formation, as theretofore amended or supplemented, shall be superseded; thenceforth, the restated certificate of formation, including any further amendment or changes made thereby, shall be the certificate of formation of the limited liability company, but the original effective date of formation shall remain unchanged.

(5)   Any amendment or change effected in connection with the restatement and integration of the certificate of formation shall be subject to any other provision of this chapter, not inconsistent with this section, which would apply if a separate certificate of amendment were filed to effect such amendment or change.

(b)   Restated certificate of registered series.

(1)   A registered series of a limited liability company may, whenever desired, integrate into a single instrument all of the provisions of its certificate of registered series which are then in effect and operative as a result of there having theretofore been filed with the Secretary of State 1 or more certificates or other instruments pursuant to any of the sections referred to in this subchapter, and it may at the same time also further amend its certificate of registered series by adopting a restated certificate of registered series.

(2)   If a restated certificate of registered series merely restates and integrates but does not further amend the initial certificate of registered series, as theretofore amended or supplemented by any instrument that was executed and filed pursuant to any of the sections in this subchapter, it shall be specifically designated in its heading as a "Restated Certificate of Registered Series" together with such other words as the registered series may deem appropriate and shall be executed by an authorized person and filed as provided in § 18–206 of this title in the office of the Secretary of State. If a restated certificate restates and integrates and also further amends in any respect the certificate of registered series as theretofore amended or supplemented, it shall be specifically designated in its heading as an "Amended and Restated Certificate of Registered Series" together with such other words as the registered series may deem appropriate and shall be executed by at least 1 authorized person, and filed as provided in § 18–206 of this title in the office of the Secretary of State.

(3)   A restated certificate of registered series shall state, either in its heading or in an introductory paragraph, the name of the limited liability company, the present name of the registered series, and, if the name of the registered series has been changed, the name under which it was originally filed, and the date of filing of its original certificate of registered series with the Secretary of State, and the future effective date or time (which shall be a date or time certain) of the restated certificate of registered series if it is not to be effective upon the filing of the restated certificate of registered series. A restated certificate shall also state that it was duly executed and is being filed in accordance with this section. If a restated certificate only restates

and integrates and does not further amend a certificate of registered series, as theretofore amended or supplemented and there is no discrepancy between those provisions and the restated certificate, it shall state that fact as well.

(4)   Upon the filing of a restated certificate of registered series with the Secretary of State, or upon the future effective date or time of a restated certificate of registered series as provided for therein, the initial certificate of registered series, as theretofore amended or supplemented, shall be superseded; thenceforth, the restated certificate of registered series, including any further amendment or changes made thereby, shall be the certificate of registered series of such registered series, but the original effective date of formation of the registered series, as applicable, shall remain unchanged.

(5)   Any amendment or change effected in connection with the restatement and integration of a certificate of registered series shall be subject to any other provision of this chapter, not inconsistent with this section, which would apply if a separate certificate of amendment were filed to effect such amendment or change.

§ 18–209.   Merger and Consolidation

(a)   As used in this section and in §§ 18–204, 18–217, 18–219, 18–220 and 18–221 of this title, "other business entity" means a corporation, a statutory trust, a business trust, an association, a real estate investment trust, a common-law trust, or any other incorporated or unincorporated business or entity, including a partnership (whether general (including a limited liability partnership) or limited (including a limited liability limited partnership)), and a foreign limited liability company, but excluding a domestic limited liability company. As used in this section and in §§ 18–210 and 18–301 of this title, "plan of merger" means a writing approved by a domestic limited liability company, in the form of resolutions or otherwise, that states the terms and conditions of a merger under subsection (i) of this section.

(b)   Pursuant to an agreement of merger or consolidation, 1 or more domestic limited liability companies may merge or consolidate with or into 1 or more domestic limited liability companies or 1 or more other business entities formed or organized under the laws of the State of Delaware or any other state or the United States or any foreign country or other foreign jurisdiction, or any combination thereof, with such domestic limited liability company or other business entity as the agreement shall provide being the surviving or resulting domestic limited liability company or other business entity. Unless otherwise provided in the limited liability company agreement, an agreement of merger or consolidation or a plan of merger shall be approved by each domestic limited liability company which is to merge or consolidate by members who own more than 50 percent of the then current percentage or other interest in the profits of the domestic limited liability company owned by all of the members. In connection with a merger or consolidation hereunder, rights or securities of, or interests in, a domestic limited liability company or other business entity which is a constituent party to the merger or consolidation may be exchanged for or converted into cash, property, rights or securities of, or interests in, the surviving or resulting domestic limited liability company or other business entity or, in addition to or in lieu thereof, may be exchanged for or converted into cash, property, rights or securities of, or interests in, a domestic limited liability company or other business entity which is not the surviving or resulting limited liability company or other business entity in the merger or consolidation, may remain outstanding or may be canceled. Notwithstanding prior approval, an agreement of merger or consolidation or a plan of merger may be terminated or amended pursuant to a provision for such termination or amendment contained in the agreement of merger or consolidation or plan of merger. Unless otherwise provided in a limited liability company agreement, a limited liability company whose original certificate of formation was filed with the Secretary of State and effective on or prior to July 31, 2015, shall continue to be governed by the second sentence of this subsection as in effect on July 31, 2015.

(c)   Except in the case of a merger under subsection (i) of this section, if a domestic limited liability company is merging or consolidating under this section, the domestic limited liability company or other business entity surviving or resulting in or from the merger or consolidation shall file a certificate of merger or consolidation executed by 1 or more authorized persons on behalf of the domestic limited liability company when it is the surviving or resulting entity in the office of the Secretary of State. The certificate of merger or consolidation shall state:

(1)   The name, jurisdiction of formation or organization and type of entity of each of the domestic limited liability companies and other business entities which is to merge or consolidate;

(2)   That an agreement of merger or consolidation has been approved and executed by each of the domestic limited liability companies and other business entities which is to merge or consolidate;

(3)   The name of the surviving or resulting domestic limited liability company or other business entity;

(4)   In the case of a merger in which a domestic limited liability company is the surviving entity, such amendments, if any, to the certificate of formation of the surviving domestic limited liability company to change its name, registered office or registered agent as are desired to be effected by the merger;

(5)   The future effective date or time (which shall be a date or time certain) of the merger or consolidation if it is not to be effective upon the filing of the certificate of merger or consolidation;

(6)   That the agreement of merger or consolidation is on file at a place of business of the surviving or resulting domestic limited liability company or other business entity, and shall state the address thereof;

(7)   That a copy of the agreement of merger or consolidation will be furnished by the surviving or resulting domestic limited liability company or other business entity, on request and without cost, to any member of any domestic limited liability company or any person holding an interest in any other business entity which is to merge or consolidate; and

(8)   If the surviving or resulting entity is not a domestic limited liability company, or a corporation, partnership (whether general (including a limited liability partnership) or limited (including a limited liability limited partnership)) or statutory trust organized under the laws of the State of Delaware, a statement that such surviving or resulting other business entity agrees that it may be served with process in the State of Delaware in any action, suit or proceeding for the enforcement of any obligation of any domestic limited liability company which is to merge or consolidate, irrevocably appointing the Secretary of State as its agent to accept service of process in any such action, suit or proceeding and specifying the address to which a copy of such process shall be mailed to it by the Secretary of State. Process may be served upon the Secretary of State under this subsection by means of electronic transmission but only as prescribed by the Secretary of State. The Secretary of State is authorized to issue such rules and regulations with respect to such service as the Secretary of State deems necessary or appropriate. In the event of service hereunder upon the Secretary of State, the procedures set forth in § 18–911(c) of this title shall be applicable, except that the plaintiff in any such action, suit or proceeding shall furnish the Secretary of State with the address specified in the certificate of merger or consolidation provided for in this section and any other address which the plaintiff may elect to furnish, together with copies of such process as required by the Secretary of State, and the Secretary of State shall notify such surviving or resulting other business entity at all such addresses furnished by the plaintiff in accordance with the procedures set forth in § 18–911(c) of this title.

(d)   Unless a future effective date or time is provided in a certificate of merger or consolidation, or in the case of a merger under subsection (i) of this section in a certificate of ownership and merger, in which event a merger or consolidation shall be effective at any such future effective date or time, a merger or consolidation shall be effective upon the filing in the office of the Secretary of State of a certificate of merger or consolidation or a certificate of ownership and merger.

(e)   A certificate of merger or consolidation or a certificate of ownership and merger shall act as a certificate of cancellation for a domestic limited liability company which is not the surviving or resulting entity in the merger or consolidation. A certificate of merger that sets forth any amendment in accordance with paragraph (c)(4) of this section shall be deemed to be an amendment to the certificate of formation of the limited liability company, and the limited liability company shall not be required to take any further action to amend its certificate of formation under § 18–202 of this title with respect to such amendments set forth in the certificate of merger. Whenever this section requires the filing of a certificate of merger or consolidation, such requirement shall be deemed satisfied by the filing of an agreement of merger or consolidation containing the information required by this section to be set forth in the certificate of merger or consolidation.

(f)   An agreement of merger or consolidation or a plan of merger approved in accordance with subsection (b) of this section may:

(1)   Effect any amendment to the limited liability company agreement; or

(2)   Effect the adoption of a new limited liability company agreement, for a limited liability company if it is the surviving or resulting limited liability company in the merger or consolidation.

Any amendment to a limited liability company agreement or adoption of a new limited liability company agreement made pursuant to the foregoing sentence shall be effective at the effective time or date of the merger or consolidation and shall be effective notwithstanding any provision of the limited liability company agreement relating to amendment or adoption of a new limited liability company agreement, other than a provision that by its terms applies to an amendment to the limited liability company agreement or the adoption of a new limited liability company agreement, in either case, in connection with a merger or consolidation. The provisions of this subsection shall not be construed to limit the accomplishment of a merger or of any of the matters referred to herein by any other means provided for in a limited liability company agreement or other agreement or as otherwise permitted by law, including that the limited liability company agreement of any constituent limited liability company to the merger or consolidation (including a limited liability company formed for the purpose of consummating a merger or consolidation) shall be the limited liability company agreement of the surviving or resulting limited liability company.

(g)   When any merger or consolidation shall have become effective under this section, for all purposes of the laws of the State of Delaware, all of the rights, privileges and powers of each of the domestic limited liability companies and other business entities that have merged or consolidated, and all property, real, personal and mixed, and all debts due to any of said domestic limited liability companies and other business entities, as well as all other things and causes of action belonging to each of such domestic limited liability companies and other business entities, shall be vested in the surviving or resulting domestic limited liability company or other business entity, and shall thereafter be the property of the surviving or resulting domestic limited liability company or other business entity as they were of each of the domestic limited liability companies and other business entities that have merged or consolidated, and the title to any real property vested by deed or otherwise, under the laws of the State of Delaware, in any of such domestic limited liability companies and other business entities, shall not revert or be in any way impaired by reason of this chapter; but all rights of creditors and all liens upon any property of any of said domestic limited liability companies and other business entities shall be preserved unimpaired, and all debts, liabilities and duties of each of the said domestic limited liability companies and other business entities that have merged or consolidated shall thenceforth attach to the surviving or resulting domestic limited liability company or other business entity, and may be enforced against it to the same extent as if said debts, liabilities and duties had been incurred or contracted by it. Unless otherwise agreed, a merger or consolidation of a domestic limited liability company, including a domestic limited liability company which is not the surviving or resulting entity in the merger or consolidation, shall not require such domestic limited liability company to wind up its affairs under § 18–803 of this title or pay its liabilities and distribute its assets under § 18–804 of this title and the merger or consolidation shall not constitute a dissolution of such limited liability company.

(h)   A limited liability company agreement may provide that a domestic limited liability company shall not have the power to merge or consolidate as set forth in this section.

(i)   In any case in which (i) at least 90% of the outstanding shares of each class of the stock of a corporation or corporations (other than a corporation which has in its certificate of incorporation the provision required by § 251(g)(7)(i) of Title 8), of which class there are outstanding shares that, absent § 267(a) of Title 8, would be entitled to vote on such merger, is owned by a domestic limited liability company, (ii) 1 or more of such corporations is a corporation of the State of Delaware, and (iii) any corporation that is not a corporation of the State of Delaware is a corporation of any other state or the District of Columbia or another jurisdiction, the laws of which do not forbid such merger, the domestic limited liability company having such stock ownership may either merge the corporation or corporations into itself and assume all of its or their obligations, or merge itself, or itself and 1 or more of such corporations, into 1 of the other corporations, pursuant to a plan of merger. If a domestic limited liability company is causing a merger under this subsection, the domestic limited liability company shall file a certificate of ownership and merger executed by 1 or more authorized persons on behalf of the domestic limited liability company in the office of the Secretary of State. The certificate of ownership and merger shall certify that such merger was authorized in accordance with the domestic limited liability company's limited liability company agreement and this chapter, and if the domestic limited liability company shall not own all the outstanding stock of all the corporations that are parties to the merger, shall state the terms and conditions of the merger, including the securities, cash, property, or rights to be issued, paid, delivered or granted by the surviving domestic limited liability company or corporation upon surrender of each share of the corporation or corporations not owned by the domestic limited liability company, or the cancellation of some or all of such shares. If a corporation surviving a merger under this subsection is not a corporation organized under the laws of the State of Delaware, then the terms and conditions of the merger shall obligate such corporation to agree that it may be served with process in the State of Delaware in any proceeding for enforcement of any obligation of the domestic limited liability company or any obligation of any constituent corporation of the State of Delaware, as well as for enforcement of any obligation of the surviving corporation, including any suit or other proceeding to enforce the right of any stockholders as determined in appraisal proceedings pursuant to § 262 of Title 8, and to irrevocably appoint the Secretary of State as its agent to accept service of process in any such suit or other proceedings, and to specify the address to which a copy of such process shall be mailed by the Secretary of State. Process may be served upon the Secretary of State under this subsection by means of electronic transmission but only as prescribed by the Secretary of State. The Secretary of State is authorized to issue such rules and regulations with respect to such service as the Secretary of State deems necessary or appropriate. In the event of such service upon the Secretary of State in accordance with this subsection, the Secretary of State shall forthwith notify such surviving corporation thereof by letter, directed to such surviving corporation at its address so specified, unless such surviving corporation shall have designated in writing to the Secretary of State a different address for such purpose, in which case it shall be mailed to the last address so designated. Such letter shall be sent by a mail or courier service that includes a record of mailing or deposit with the courier and a record of delivery evidenced by the signature of the recipient. Such letter shall enclose a copy of the process and any other papers served on the Secretary of State pursuant to this subsection. It shall be the duty of the plaintiff in the event of such service to serve process and any other papers in duplicate, to notify the Secretary of State that service is being effected pursuant to this subsection and to pay the Secretary of State the sum of $50 for the use of the State of Delaware, which sum shall be taxed as part of the costs in the proceeding, if the plaintiff shall prevail therein. The Secretary of State shall maintain an alphabetical record of any such service setting forth the name of the plaintiff and the defendant, the title, docket number and nature of the proceeding in which process has been served, the fact that service has been effected pursuant to this subsection, the return date thereof, and the day and hour service was made. The Secretary of State shall not be required to retain such information longer than 5 years from receipt of the service of process.

§ 18–210. Contractual Appraisal Rights

A limited liability company agreement or an agreement of merger or consolidation or a plan of merger may provide that contractual appraisal rights with respect to a limited liability company interest or another interest in a limited liability company shall be available for any class or group or series of members or limited liability company interests in connection with any amendment of a limited liability company agreement, any merger or consolidation in which the limited liability company is a constituent party to the merger or consolidation, any conversion of the limited liability company to another business form, any transfer to or domestication or continuance in any jurisdiction by the limited liability company, or the sale of all or substantially all of the limited liability company's assets. The Court of Chancery shall have jurisdiction to hear and determine any matter relating to any such appraisal rights.

§ 18–211. Certificate of Correction

(a) Whenever any certificate authorized to be filed with the office of the Secretary of State under any provision of this chapter has been so filed and is an inaccurate record of the action therein referred to, or was defectively or erroneously executed, such certificate may be corrected by filing with the office of the Secretary of State a certificate of correction of such certificate. The certificate of correction shall specify the inaccuracy or defect to be corrected, shall set forth the portion of the certificate in corrected form, and shall be executed and filed as required by this chapter. The certificate of correction shall be effective as of the date the original certificate was filed, except as to those persons who are substantially and adversely affected by the correction, and as to those persons the certificate of correction shall be effective from the filing date.

(b) In lieu of filing a certificate of correction, a certificate may be corrected by filing with the Secretary of State a corrected certificate which shall be executed and filed as if the corrected certificate were the certificate being corrected, and a fee equal to the fee payable to the Secretary of State for a certificate of correction as prescribed by § 18–1105 of this title shall be paid and collected by the Secretary of State for the use of the State of Delaware in connection with the filing of the corrected certificate. The corrected certificate shall be specifically designated as such in its heading, shall specify the inaccuracy or defect to be corrected and shall set forth the entire certificate in corrected form. A certificate corrected in accordance with this section shall be effective as of the date the original certificate was filed, except as to those persons who are substantially and adversely affected by the correction and as to those persons the certificate as corrected shall be effective from the filing date.

§ 18–212. Domestication of Non-United States Entities

(a) As used in this section and in § 18–204 of this title, "non-United States entity" means a foreign limited liability company (other than 1 formed under the laws of a state) or a corporation, a statutory trust, a business trust, an association, a real estate investment trust, a common-law trust or any other incorporated or unincorporated business or entity, including a partnership (whether general (including a limited liability partnership) or limited (including a limited liability limited partnership)) formed, incorporated, created or that otherwise came into being under the laws of any foreign country or other foreign jurisdiction (other than any state).

(b) Any non-United States entity may become domesticated as a limited liability company in the State of Delaware by complying with subsection (g) of this section and filing in the office of the Secretary of State in accordance with § 18–206 of this title:

(1) A certificate of limited liability company domestication that has been executed in accordance with § 18–204 of this title; and

(2) A certificate of formation that complies with § 18–201 of this title and has been executed by 1 or more authorized persons in accordance with § 18–204 of this title.

Each of the certificates required by this subsection (b) shall be filed simultaneously in the office of the Secretary of State and, if such certificates are not to become effective upon their filing as permitted by § 18–206(b) of this title, then each such certificate shall provide for the same effective date or time in accordance with § 18–206(b) of this title.

(c)   The certificate of limited liability company domestication shall state:

(1)   The date on which and jurisdiction where the non-United States entity was first formed, incorporated, created or otherwise came into being;

(2)   The name of the non-United States entity immediately prior to the filing of the certificate of limited liability company domestication;

(3)   The name of the limited liability company as set forth in the certificate of formation filed in accordance with subsection (b) of this section;

(4)   The future effective date or time (which shall be a date or time certain) of the domestication as a limited liability company if it is not to be effective upon the filing of the certificate of limited liability company domestication and the certificate of formation;

(5)   The jurisdiction that constituted the seat, siege social, or principal place of business or central administration of the non-United States entity, or any other equivalent thereto under applicable law, immediately prior to the filing of the certificate of limited liability company domestication; and

(6)   That the domestication has been approved in the manner provided for by the document, instrument, agreement or other writing, as the case may be, governing the internal affairs of the non-United States entity and the conduct of its business or by applicable non-Delaware law, as appropriate.

(d)   Upon the filing in the office of the Secretary of State of the certificate of limited liability company domestication and the certificate of formation or upon the future effective date or time of the certificate of limited liability company domestication and the certificate of formation, the non-United States entity shall be domesticated as a limited liability company in the State of Delaware and the limited liability company shall thereafter be subject to all of the provisions of this chapter, except that notwithstanding § 18–201 of this title, the existence of the limited liability company shall be deemed to have commenced on the date the non-United States entity commenced its existence in the jurisdiction in which the non-United States entity was first formed, incorporated, created or otherwise came into being.

(e)   The domestication of any non-United States entity as a limited liability company in the State of Delaware shall not be deemed to affect any obligations or liabilities of the non-United States entity incurred prior to its domestication as a limited liability company in the State of Delaware, or the personal liability of any person therefor.

(f)   The filing of a certificate of limited liability company domestication shall not affect the choice of law applicable to the non-United States entity, except that from the effective date or time of the domestication, the law of the State of Delaware, including the provisions of this chapter, shall apply to the non-United States entity to the same extent as if the non-United States entity had been formed as a limited liability company on that date.

(g)   Prior to the filing of a certificate of limited liability company domestication with the Office of the Secretary of State, the domestication shall be approved in the manner provided for by the document, instrument, agreement or other writing, as the case may be, governing the internal affairs of the non-United States entity and the conduct of its business or by applicable non-Delaware law, as appropriate, and a limited liability company agreement shall be approved by the same authorization required to approve the domestication.

(h)   When any domestication shall have become effective under this section, for all purposes of the laws of the State of Delaware, all of the rights, privileges and powers of the non-United States entity that has been domesticated, and all property, real, personal and mixed, and all debts due to such non-United States entity, as well as all other things and causes of action belonging to such non-United States entity, shall remain vested in the domestic limited liability company to which such non-United States entity has been domesticated (and also in the non-United States entity, if and for so long as the non-United States entity continues its existence in the foreign jurisdiction in which it was existing immediately prior to the domestication) and shall be the property of such domestic limited liability company (and also of the non-United States entity, if and for so long as the non-United States entity continues its existence in the foreign jurisdiction in which it was existing immediately prior to the domestication), and the title to any real property vested by deed or otherwise in such non-United States entity shall not revert or be in any way impaired by reason of this chapter; but all rights of creditors and all liens upon any property of such non-United States entity shall be preserved unimpaired, and all debts, liabilities and duties of the non-United States entity that has been domesticated shall remain attached to the domestic limited liability company to which such non-United States entity has been domesticated (and also to the non-United States entity, if and for so long as the non-United States entity continues its existence in the foreign jurisdiction in which it was existing immediately prior to the domestication), and may be enforced against it to the same extent as if said debts, liabilities and duties had originally been incurred or contracted by it in its capacity as a domestic limited liability company. The rights, privileges, powers and interests in property of the non-United States entity, as well as the debts, liabilities and duties of the non-United States entity, shall not be deemed, as a consequence of the domestication, to have been transferred to the domestic limited liability company to which such non-United States entity has domesticated for any purpose of the laws of the State of Delaware.

(i) When a non-United States entity has become domesticated as a limited liability company pursuant to this section, for all purposes of the laws of the State of Delaware, the limited liability company shall be deemed to be the same entity as the domesticating non-United States entity and the domestication shall constitute a continuation of the existence of the domesticating non-United States entity in the form of a domestic limited liability company. Unless otherwise agreed, for all purposes of the laws of the State of Delaware, the domesticating non-United States entity shall not be required to wind up its affairs or pay its liabilities and distribute its assets, and the domestication shall not be deemed to constitute a dissolution of such non-United States entity. If, following domestication, a non-United States entity that has become domesticated as a limited liability company continues its existence in the foreign country or other foreign jurisdiction in which it was existing immediately prior to domestication, the limited liability company and such non-United States entity shall, for all purposes of the laws of the State of Delaware, constitute a single entity formed, incorporated, created or otherwise having come into being, as applicable, and existing under the laws of the State of Delaware and the laws of such foreign country or other foreign jurisdiction.

(j) In connection with a domestication hereunder, rights or securities of, or interests in, the non-United States entity that is to be domesticated as a domestic limited liability company may be exchanged for or converted into cash, property, rights or securities of, or interests in, such domestic limited liability company or, in addition to or in lieu thereof, may be exchanged for or converted into cash, property, rights or securities of, or interests in, another domestic limited liability company or other entity, may remain outstanding or may be canceled.

§ 18–213. Transfer or Continuance of Domestic Limited Liability Companies

(a) Upon compliance with this section, any limited liability company may transfer to or domesticate or continue in any jurisdiction, other than any state, and, in connection therewith, may elect to continue its existence as a limited liability company in the State of Delaware.

(b) If the limited liability company agreement specifies the manner of authorizing a transfer or domestication or continuance described in subsection (a) of this section, the transfer or domestication or continuance shall be authorized as specified in the limited liability company agreement. If the limited liability company agreement does not specify the manner of authorizing a transfer or domestication or continuance described in subsection (a) of this section and does not prohibit such a transfer or domestication or continuance, the transfer or domestication or continuance shall be authorized in the same manner as is specified in the limited liability company agreement for authorizing a merger or consolidation that involves the limited liability company as a constituent party to the merger or consolidation. If the limited liability company agreement does not specify the manner of authorizing a transfer or domestication or continuance described in subsection (a) of this section or a merger or consolidation that involves the limited liability company as a constituent party and does not prohibit such a transfer or domestication or continuance, the transfer or domestication or continuance shall be authorized by the approval by members who own more than 50 percent of the then current percentage or other interest in the profits of the domestic limited liability company owned by all of the members. If a transfer or domestication or continuance described in subsection (a) of this section shall be authorized as provided in this subsection (b), a certificate of transfer if the limited liability company's existence as a limited liability company of the State of Delaware is to cease, or a certificate of transfer and domestic continuance if the limited liability company's existence as a limited liability company in the State of Delaware is to continue, executed in accordance with § 18–204 of this title, shall be filed in the office of the Secretary of State in accordance with § 18–206 of this title. The certificate of transfer or the certificate of transfer and domestic continuance shall state:

(1)   The name of the limited liability company and, if it has been changed, the name under which its certificate of formation was originally filed;

(2)   The date of the filing of its original certificate of formation with the Secretary of State;

(3)   The jurisdiction to which the limited liability company shall be transferred or in which it shall be domesticated or continued and the name of the entity or business form formed, incorporated, created or that otherwise comes into being as a consequence of the transfer of the limited liability company to, or its domestication or continuance in, such foreign jurisdiction;

(4)   The future effective date or time (which shall be a date or time certain) of the transfer to or domestication or continuance in the jurisdiction specified in paragraph (b)(3) of this section if it is not to be effective upon the filing of the certificate of transfer or the certificate of transfer and domestic continuance;

(5)   That the transfer or domestication or continuance of the limited liability company has been approved in accordance with this section;

(6)   In the case of a certificate of transfer, (i) that the existence of the limited liability company as a limited liability company of the State of Delaware shall cease when the certificate of transfer becomes effective, and (ii) the agreement of the limited liability company that it may be served with process in the State of Delaware in any action, suit or proceeding for enforcement of any obligation of the limited liability company arising while it was a limited liability company of the State of Delaware, and that it irrevocably appoints the Secretary of State as its agent to accept service of process in any such action, suit or proceeding;

(7)   The address (which may not be that of the limited liability company's registered agent without the written consent of the limited liability company's registered agent, such consent to be filed with the certificate of transfer) to which a copy of the process referred to in paragraph (b)(6) of this section shall be mailed to it by the Secretary of State. Process may be served upon the Secretary of State under paragraph (b)(6) of this section by means of electronic transmission but only as prescribed by the Secretary of State. The Secretary of State is authorized to issue such rules and regulations with respect to such service as the Secretary of State deems necessary or appropriate. In the event of service hereunder upon the Secretary of State, the procedures set forth in § 18–911(c) of this title shall be applicable, except that the plaintiff in any such action, suit or proceeding shall furnish the Secretary of State with the address specified in this subsection and any other address that the plaintiff may elect to furnish, together with copies of such process as required by the Secretary of State, and the Secretary of State shall notify the limited liability company that has transferred or domesticated or continued out of the State of Delaware at all

such addresses furnished by the plaintiff in accordance with the procedures set forth in § 18–911(c) of this title; and

(8) In the case of a certificate of transfer and domestic continuance, that the limited liability company will continue to exist as a limited liability company of the State of Delaware after the certificate of transfer and domestic continuance becomes effective.

Unless otherwise provided in a limited liability company agreement, a limited liability company whose original certificate of formation was filed with the Secretary of State and effective on or prior to July 31, 2015, shall continue to be governed by the third sentence of this subsection as in effect on July 31, 2015.

(c) Upon the filing in the office of the Secretary of State of the certificate of transfer or upon the future effective date or time of the certificate of transfer and payment to the Secretary of State of all fees prescribed in this chapter, the Secretary of State shall certify that the limited liability company has filed all documents and paid all fees required by this chapter, and thereupon the limited liability company shall cease to exist as a limited liability company of the State of Delaware. Such certificate of the Secretary of State shall be prima facie evidence of the transfer or domestication or continuance by such limited liability company out of the State of Delaware.

(d) The transfer or domestication or continuance of a limited liability company out of the State of Delaware in accordance with this section and the resulting cessation of its existence as a limited liability company of the State of Delaware pursuant to a certificate of transfer shall not be deemed to affect any obligations or liabilities of the limited liability company incurred prior to such transfer or domestication or continuance or the personal liability of any person incurred prior to such transfer or domestication or continuance, nor shall it be deemed to affect the choice of law applicable to the limited liability company with respect to matters arising prior to such transfer or domestication or continuance. Unless otherwise agreed, the transfer or domestication or continuance of a limited liability company out of the State of Delaware in accordance with this section shall not require such limited liability company to wind up its affairs under § 18–803 of this title or pay its liabilities and distribute its assets under § 18–804 of this title and shall not be deemed to constitute a dissolution of such limited liability company.

(e) If a limited liability company files a certificate of transfer and domestic continuance, after the time the certificate of transfer and domestic continuance becomes effective, the limited liability company shall continue to exist as a limited liability company of the State of Delaware, and the laws of the State of Delaware, including this chapter, shall apply to the limited liability company to the same extent as prior to such time. So long as a limited liability company continues to exist as a limited liability company of the State of Delaware following the filing of a certificate of transfer and domestic continuance, the continuing domestic limited liability company and the entity or business form formed, incorporated, created or that otherwise came into being as a consequence of the transfer of the limited liability company to, or its domestication or continuance in, a foreign country or other foreign jurisdiction shall, for all purposes of the laws of the State of Delaware, constitute a single entity formed, incorporated, created or otherwise having come into being, as applicable, and existing under the laws of the State and the laws of such foreign country or other foreign jurisdiction.

(f) In connection with a transfer or domestication or continuance of a domestic limited liability company to or in another jurisdiction pursuant to subsection (a) of this section, rights or securities of, or interests in, such limited liability company may be exchanged for or converted into cash, property, rights or securities of, or interests in, the entity or business form in which the limited liability company will exist in such other jurisdiction as a consequence of the transfer or domestication or continuance or, in addition to or in lieu thereof, may be exchanged for or converted into cash, property, rights or securities of, or interests in, another entity or business form, may remain outstanding or may be canceled.

(g) When a limited liability company has transferred or domesticated or continued out of the State of Delaware pursuant to this section, the transferred or domesticated or continued entity or business form shall, for all purposes of the laws of the State of Delaware, be deemed to be the same entity as the limited liability company and shall constitute a continuation of the existence of such limited liability company in the form of the transferred or domesticated or continued entity or business form. When any transfer or domestication or continuance of a limited liability company out of the State of Delaware shall have become effective under this section, for all purposes of the laws of the State of Delaware, all of the rights, privileges and powers of the limited liability company that has transferred or domesticated or continued, and all property, real, personal and mixed, and all debts due to such limited liability company, as well as all other things and causes of action belonging to such limited liability company, shall remain vested in the transferred or domesticated or continued entity or business form (and also in the limited liability company that has transferred, domesticated or continued, if and for so long as such limited liability company continues its existence as a domestic limited liability company) and shall be the property of such transferred or domesticated or continued entity or business form (and also of the limited liability company that has transferred, domesticated or continued, if and for so long as such limited liability company continues its existence as a domestic limited liability company), and the title to any real property vested by deed or otherwise in such limited liability company shall not revert or be in any way impaired by reason of this chapter; but all rights of creditors and all liens upon any property of such limited liability company shall be preserved unimpaired, and all debts, liabilities and duties of the limited liability company that has transferred or domesticated or continued shall remain attached to the transferred or domesticated or continued entity or business form (and also to the limited liability company that has transferred, domesticated or continued, if and for so long as such limited liability company continues its existence as a domestic limited liability company), and may be enforced against it to the same extent as if said debts, liabilities and duties had originally been incurred or contracted by it in its capacity as the transferred or domesticated or continued entity or business form. The rights, privileges, powers and interests in property of the limited liability company that has transferred or domesticated or continued, as well as the debts, liabilities and duties of such limited liability company, shall not be deemed, as a consequence of the transfer or domestication or continuance out of the State of Delaware, to have been transferred to the transferred or domesticated or continued entity or business form for any purpose of the laws of the State of Delaware.

(h) A limited liability company agreement may provide that a domestic limited liability company shall not have the power to transfer, domesticate or continue as set forth in this section.

§ 18–214. Conversion of Certain Entities to a Limited Liability Company

(a) As used in this section, and in § 18–204 of this title, the term "other entity" means a corporation, a statutory trust, a business trust, an association, a real estate investment trust, a common-law trust or any other incorporated or unincorporated business or entity, including a partnership (whether general (including a limited liability partnership) or limited (including a limited liability limited partnership)) or a foreign limited liability company.

(b) Any other entity may convert to a domestic limited liability company by complying with subsection (h) of this section and filing in the office of the Secretary of State in accordance with § 18–206 of this title:

(1) A certificate of conversion to limited liability company that has been executed in accordance with § 18–204 of this title; and

(2) A certificate of formation that complies with § 18–201 of this title and has been executed by 1 or more authorized persons in accordance with § 18–204 of this title.

Each of the certificates required by this subsection (b) shall be filed simultaneously in the office of the Secretary of State and, if such certificates are not to become effective upon their filing as permitted by § 18–206(b) of this title, then each such certificate shall provide for the same effective date or time in accordance with § 18–206(b) of this title.

(c) The certificate of conversion to limited liability company shall state:

(1) The date on which and jurisdiction where the other entity was first created, incorporated, formed or otherwise came into being and, if it has changed, its jurisdiction immediately prior to its conversion to a domestic limited liability company;

(2) The name and type of entity of the other entity immediately prior to the filing of the certificate of conversion to limited liability company;

(3) The name of the limited liability company as set forth in its certificate of formation filed in accordance with subsection (b) of this section; and

(4) The future effective date or time (which shall be a date or time certain) of the conversion to a limited liability company if it is not to be effective upon the filing of the certificate of conversion to limited liability company and the certificate of formation.

(d) Upon the filing in the office of the Secretary of State of the certificate of conversion to limited liability company and the certificate of formation or upon the future effective date or time of the certificate of conversion to limited liability company and the certificate of formation, the other entity shall be converted into a domestic limited liability company and the limited liability company shall thereafter be subject to all of the provisions of this chapter, except that notwithstanding § 18–201 of this title, the existence of the limited liability company shall be deemed to have commenced on the date the other entity commenced its existence in the jurisdiction in which the other entity was first created, formed, incorporated or otherwise came into being.

(e) The conversion of any other entity into a domestic limited liability company shall not be deemed to affect any obligations or liabilities of the other entity incurred prior to its conversion to a domestic limited liability company or the personal liability of any person incurred prior to such conversion.

(f) When any conversion shall have become effective under this section, for all purposes of the laws of the State of Delaware, all of the rights, privileges and powers of the other entity that has converted, and all property, real, personal and mixed, and all debts due to such other entity, as well as all other things and causes of action belonging to such other entity, shall remain vested in the domestic limited liability company to which such other entity has converted and shall be the property of such domestic limited liability company, and the title to any real property vested by deed or otherwise in such other entity shall not revert or be in any way impaired by reason of this chapter; but all rights of creditors and all liens upon any property of such other entity shall be preserved unimpaired, and all debts, liabilities and duties of the other entity that has converted shall remain attached to the domestic limited liability company to which such other entity has converted, and may be enforced against it to the same extent as if said debts, liabilities and duties had originally been incurred or contracted by it in its capacity as a domestic limited liability company. The rights, privileges, powers and interests in property of the other entity, as well as the debts, liabilities and duties of the other entity, shall not be deemed, as a consequence of the conversion, to have been transferred to the domestic limited liability company to which such other entity has converted for any purpose of the laws of the State of Delaware.

(g) Unless otherwise agreed, for all purposes of the laws of the State of Delaware, the converting other entity shall not be required to wind up its affairs or pay its liabilities and distribute its assets, and the conversion shall not be deemed to constitute a dissolution of such other entity. When an other entity has been converted to a limited liability company pursuant to this section, for all purposes of the laws of the State of Delaware, the limited liability company shall be deemed to be the same entity as the converting other entity and the conversion shall constitute a continuation of the existence of the converting other entity in the form of a domestic limited liability company.

(h) Prior to filing a certificate of conversion to limited liability company with the office of the Secretary of State, the conversion shall be approved in the manner provided for by the document, instrument, agreement or other writing, as the case may be, governing the internal affairs of the other entity and the conduct of its business or by applicable law, as appropriate and a limited liability company agreement shall be approved by the same authorization required to approve the conversion.

(i)   In connection with a conversion hereunder, rights or securities of or interests in the other entity which is to be converted to a domestic limited liability company may be exchanged for or converted into cash, property, or rights or securities of or interests in such domestic limited liability company or, in addition to or in lieu thereof, may be exchanged for or converted into cash, property, or rights or securities of or interests in another domestic limited liability company or other entity, may remain outstanding or may be canceled.

(j)   The provisions of this section shall not be construed to limit the accomplishment of a change in the law governing, or the domicile of, an other entity to the State of Delaware by any other means provided for in a limited liability company agreement or other agreement or as otherwise permitted by law, including by the amendment of a limited liability company agreement or other agreement.

§ 18–215.   Series of Members, Managers, Limited Liability Company Interests or Assets

(a)   A limited liability company agreement may establish or provide for the establishment of 1 or more designated series of members, managers, limited liability company interests or assets. Any such series may have separate rights, powers or duties with respect to specified property or obligations of the limited liability company or profits and losses associated with specified property or obligations, and any such series may have a separate business purpose or investment objective. No provision of subsection (b) of this section or § 18–218 of this title shall be construed to limit the application of the principle of freedom of contract to a series that is not a protected series or a registered series. Other than pursuant to §§ 18–219, 18–220 and 18–221, a series may not merge, convert or consolidate pursuant to any section of this title or any other statute of this State.

(b)   A series established in accordance with the following sentence is a protected series. Notwithstanding anything to the contrary set forth in this chapter or under other applicable law, in the event that a limited liability company agreement establishes or provides for the establishment of 1 or more series, and to the extent the records maintained for any such series account for the assets associated with such series separately from the other assets of the limited liability company, or any other series thereof, and if the limited liability company agreement so provides, and if notice of the limitation on liabilities of a series as referenced in this subsection is set forth in the certificate of formation of the limited liability company, then the debts, liabilities, obligations and expenses incurred, contracted for or otherwise existing with respect to such series shall be enforceable against the assets of such series only, and not against the assets of the limited liability company generally or any other series thereof, and, unless otherwise provided in the limited liability company agreement, none of the debts, liabilities, obligations and expenses incurred, contracted for or otherwise existing with respect to the limited liability company generally or any other series thereof shall be enforceable against the assets of such series. Neither the preceding sentence nor any provision pursuant thereto in a limited liability company agreement or certificate of formation shall (i) restrict a protected series or limited liability company on behalf of a protected series from agreeing in the limited liability company agreement or otherwise that any or all of the debts, liabilities, obligations and expenses incurred, contracted for or otherwise existing with respect to the limited liability company generally or any other series thereof shall be enforceable against the assets of such protected series or (ii) restrict a limited liability company from agreeing in the limited liability company agreement or otherwise that any or all of the debts, liabilities, obligations and expenses incurred, contracted for or otherwise existing with respect to a protected series shall be enforceable against the assets of the limited liability company generally. Assets associated with a protected series may be held directly or indirectly, including in the name of such series, in the name of the limited liability company, through a nominee or otherwise. Records maintained for a protected series that reasonably identify its assets, including by specific listing, category, type, quantity, computational or allocational formula or procedure (including a percentage or share of any asset or assets) or by any other method where the identity of such assets is objectively determinable, will be deemed to account for the assets associated with such series separately from the other assets of the limited liability company, or any other series thereof. Notice in a certificate of formation of the limitation on liabilities of a protected series as referenced in this subsection shall be sufficient for all purposes of this subsection whether or not the limited liability company has established any protected series when such notice is included in the certificate of formation, and there shall be no requirement that any specific protected series of the limited liability company be referenced in such notice. The fact that a certificate of formation that contains the foregoing notice of the limitation on liabilities of a protected series is on file in the office of the Secretary of State shall constitute notice of such limitation on liabilities of a protected series. As used in this chapter, a reference to assets of a protected series includes assets associated with such series, a reference to assets associated with a protected series includes assets of such series, a reference to members or managers of a protected series includes members or managers associated with a protected series includes members or managers of such series. The following shall apply to a protected series:

(1) A protected series may carry on any lawful business, purpose or activity, whether or not for profit, with the exception of the business of banking as defined in § 126 of Title 8. Unless otherwise provided in a limited liability company agreement, a protected series shall have the power and capacity to, in its own name, contract, hold title to assets (including real, personal and intangible property), grant liens and security interests, and sue and be sued.

(2) Except as otherwise provided by this chapter, no member or manager of a protected series shall be obligated personally for any debt, obligation or liability of such series, whether arising in contract, tort or otherwise, solely by reason of being a member or acting as manager of such series. Notwithstanding the preceding sentence, under a limited liability company agreement or under another agreement, a member or manager may agree to be obligated personally for any or all of the debts, obligations and liabilities of 1 or more protected series.

(3) A limited liability company agreement may provide for classes or groups of members or managers associated with a protected series having such relative rights, powers and duties as the limited liability company agreement may provide, and may make provision for the future creation in the manner provided in the limited liability company agreement of additional classes or groups of members or managers associated with such series having such relative rights, powers and duties as may from time to time be established, including rights, powers and duties senior to existing classes and groups of members or managers associated with such series. A limited liability company agreement may provide for the taking of an action, including the amendment of the limited liability company agreement, without the vote or approval of any member or manager or class or group of members or managers, including an action to create under the provisions of the limited liability company agreement a class or group of a protected series of limited liability company interests that was not previously outstanding. A limited liability company agreement may provide that any member or class or group of members associated with a protected series shall have no voting rights.

(4) A limited liability company agreement may grant to all or certain identified members or managers or a specified class or group of the members or managers associated with a protected series the right to vote separately or with all or any class or group of the members or managers associated with such series, on any matter. Voting by members or managers associated with a protected series may be on a per capita, number, financial interest, class, group or any other basis.

(5) Unless otherwise provided in a limited liability company agreement, the management of a protected series shall be vested in the members associated with such series in proportion to the then current percentage or other interest of members in the profits of such series owned by all of the members associated with such series, the decision of members owning more than 50 percent of the said percentage or other interest in the profits controlling; provided, however, that if a limited liability company agreement provides for the management of a protected series, in whole or in part, by a manager, the management of such series, to the extent so provided, shall be vested in the manager who shall be chosen in the manner provided in the limited liability company agreement. The manager of a protected series shall also hold the offices and have the responsibilities accorded to the manager as set forth in a limited liability company agreement. A

protected series may have more than 1 manager. Subject to § 18–602 of this title, a manager shall cease to be a manager with respect to a protected series as provided in a limited liability company agreement. Except as otherwise provided in a limited liability company agreement, any event under this chapter or in a limited liability company agreement that causes a manager to cease to be a manager with respect to a protected series shall not, in itself, cause such manager to cease to be a manager of the limited liability company or with respect to any other series thereof.

(6) Notwithstanding § 18–606 of this title, but subject to paragraphs (b)(7) and (b)(10) of this section, and unless otherwise provided in a limited liability company agreement, at the time a member of a protected series becomes entitled to receive a distribution with respect to such series, the member has the status of, and is entitled to all remedies available to, a creditor of such series, with respect to the distribution. A limited liability company agreement may provide for the establishment of a record date with respect to allocations and distributions with respect to a protected series.

(7) Notwithstanding § 18–607(a) of this title, a limited liability company may make a distribution with respect to a protected series. A limited liability company shall not make a distribution with respect to a protected series to a member to the extent that at the time of the distribution, after giving effect to the distribution, all liabilities of such series, other than liabilities to members on account of their limited liability company interests with respect to such series and liabilities for which the recourse of creditors is limited to specified property of such series, exceed the fair value of the assets associated with such series, except that the fair value of property of such series that is subject to a liability for which the recourse of creditors is limited shall be included in the assets associated with such series only to the extent that the fair value of that property exceeds that liability. For purposes of the immediately preceding sentence, the term "distribution" shall not include amounts constituting reasonable compensation for present or past services or reasonable payments made in the ordinary course of business pursuant to a bona fide retirement plan or other benefits program. A member who receives a distribution in violation of this paragraph (b)(7), and who knew at the time of the distribution that the distribution violated this paragraph (b)(7), shall be liable to the protected series for the amount of the distribution. A member who receives a distribution in violation of this paragraph (b)(7), and who did not know at the time of the distribution that the distribution violated this paragraph (b)(7), shall not be liable for the amount of the distribution. Subject to § 18–607(c) of this title, which shall apply to any distribution made with respect to a protected series under this paragraph (b)(7), this paragraph (b)(7) shall not affect any obligation or liability of a member under an agreement or other applicable law for the amount of a distribution.

(8) Unless otherwise provided in the limited liability company agreement, a member shall cease to be associated with a protected series and to have the power to exercise any rights or powers of a member with respect to such series upon the assignment of all of the member's limited liability company interest with respect to such series. Except as otherwise provided in a limited liability company agreement, any event under this chapter or a limited liability company agreement that causes a member to cease to be associated with a protected series shall not, in itself, cause such member to cease to be associated with any other series or terminate the continued membership of a member in the limited liability company or cause the termination of the protected series, regardless of whether such member was the last remaining member associated with such series.

(9) Subject to § 18–801 of this title, except to the extent otherwise provided in the limited liability company agreement, a protected series may be terminated and its affairs wound up without causing the dissolution of the limited liability company. The termination of a protected series shall not affect the limitation on liabilities of such series provided by this subsection (b). A protected series is terminated and its affairs shall be wound up upon the dissolution of the limited liability company under § 18–801 of this title or otherwise upon the first to occur of the following:

     a.   At the time specified in the limited liability company agreement;

b. Upon the happening of events specified in the limited liability company agreement;

c. Unless otherwise provided in the limited liability company agreement, upon the vote or consent members associated with such series who own more than 2/3 of the then-current percentage or other interest in the profits of the series of such limited liability company owned by all of the members associated with such series; or

d. The termination of such series under paragraph (b)(11) of this section.

Unless otherwise provided in a limited liability company agreement, a limited liability company whose original certificate of formation was filed with the Secretary of State and effective on or prior to July 31, 2015, shall continue to be governed by paragraph (k)(3) of this section as in effect on July 31,2015.

(10) Notwithstanding § 18–803(a) of this title, unless otherwise provided in the limited liability company agreement, a manager associated with a protected series who has not wrongfully terminated such series or, if none, the members associated with such series or a person approved by the members associated with such series, in either case, by members who own more than 50 percent of the then current percentage or other interest in the profits of such series owned by all of the members associated with such series, may wind up the affairs of such series; but the Court of Chancery, upon cause shown, may wind up the affairs of a protected series upon application of any member or manager associated with such series, or the member's personal representative or assignee, and in connection therewith, may appoint a liquidating trustee. The persons winding up the affairs of a protected series may, in the name of the limited liability company and for and on behalf of the limited liability company and such series, take all actions with respect to such series as are permitted under § 18–803(b) of this title. The persons winding up the affairs of a protected series shall provide for the claims and obligations of such series and distribute the assets of such series as provided in § 18–804 of this title, which section shall apply to the winding up and distribution of assets of a protected series. Actions taken in accordance with this paragraph (b)(10) shall not affect the liability of members and shall not impose liability on a liquidating trustee. Unless otherwise provided in a limited liability company agreement, a limited liability company whose original certificate of formation was filed with the Secretary of State and effective on or prior to July 31, 2015, shall continue to be governed by the first sentence of this paragraph (b)(10) as in effect on July 31, 2015.

(11) On application by or for a member or manager associated with a protected series, the Court of Chancery may decree termination of such series whenever it is not reasonably practicable to carry on the business of such series in conformity with a limited liability company agreement.

(12) For all purposes of the laws of the State of Delaware, a protected series is an association, regardless of the number of members or managers, if any, of such series.

(c) If a foreign limited liability company that is registering to do business in the State of Delaware in accordance with § 18–902 of this title is governed by a limited liability company agreement that establishes or provides for the establishment of designated series of members, managers, limited liability company interests or assets having separate rights, powers or duties with respect to specified property or obligations of the foreign limited liability company or profits and losses associated with specified property or obligations, that fact shall be so stated on the application for registration as a foreign limited liability company. In addition, the foreign limited liability company shall state on such application whether the debts, liabilities and obligations incurred, contracted for or otherwise existing with respect to a particular series, if any, shall be enforceable against the assets of such series only, and not against the assets of the foreign limited liability company generally or any other series thereof, and whether any of the debts, liabilities, obligations and expenses incurred, contracted for or otherwise existing with respect to the foreign limited liability company generally or any other series thereof shall be enforceable against the assets of such series.

§ 18–216.   Approval of Conversion of a Limited Liability Company

(a)   Upon compliance with this section, a domestic limited liability company may convert to a corporation, a statutory trust, a business trust, an association, a real estate investment trust, a common-law trust or any other incorporated or unincorporated business or entity, including a partnership (whether general (including a limited liability partnership) or limited (including a limited liability limited partnership)) or a foreign limited liability company.

(b)   If the limited liability company agreement specifies the manner of authorizing a conversion of the limited liability company, the conversion shall be authorized as specified in the limited liability company agreement. If the limited liability company agreement does not specify the manner of authorizing a conversion of the limited liability company and does not prohibit a conversion of the limited liability company, the conversion shall be authorized in the same manner as is specified in the limited liability company agreement for authorizing a merger or consolidation that involves the limited liability company as a constituent party to the merger or consolidation. If the limited liability company agreement does not specify the manner of authorizing a conversion of the limited liability company or a merger or consolidation that involves the limited liability company as a constituent party and does not prohibit a conversion of the limited liability company, the conversion shall be authorized by the approval by members who own more than 50 percent of the then current percentage or other interest in the profits of the domestic limited liability company owned by all of the members. Unless otherwise provided in a limited liability company agreement, a limited liability company whose original certificate of formation was filed with the Secretary of State and effective on or prior to July 31, 2015, shall continue to be governed by the third sentence of this subsection as in effect on July 31, 2015.

(c)   Unless otherwise agreed, the conversion of a domestic limited liability company to another entity or business form pursuant to this section shall not require such limited liability company to wind up its affairs under § 18–803 of this title or pay its liabilities and distribute its assets under § 18–804 of this title, and the conversion shall not constitute a dissolution of such limited liability company. When a limited liability company has converted to another entity or business form pursuant to this section, for all purposes of the laws of the State of Delaware, the other entity or business form shall be deemed to be the same entity as the converting limited liability company and the conversion shall constitute a continuation of the existence of the limited liability company in the form of such other entity or business form.

(d)   In connection with a conversion of a domestic limited liability company to another entity or business form pursuant to this section, rights or securities of or interests in the domestic limited liability company which is to be converted may be exchanged for or converted into cash, property, rights or securities of or interests in the entity or business form into which the domestic limited liability company is being converted or, in addition to or in lieu thereof, may be exchanged for or converted into cash, property, rights or securities of or interests in another entity or business form, may remain outstanding or may be canceled.

(e)   If a limited liability company shall convert in accordance with this section to another entity or business form organized, formed or created under the laws of a jurisdiction other than the State of Delaware, a certificate of conversion to non-Delaware entity executed in accordance with § 18–204 of this title, shall be filed in the office of the Secretary of State in accordance with § 18–206 of this title. The certificate of conversion to non-Delaware entity shall state:

(1)   The name of the limited liability company and, if it has been changed, the name under which its certificate of formation was originally filed;

(2)   The date of filing of its original certificate of formation with the Secretary of State;

(3)   The jurisdiction in which the entity or business form, to which the limited liability company shall be converted, is organized, formed or created, and the name of such entity or business form;

(4)   The future effective date or time (which shall be a date or time certain) of the conversion if it is not to be effective upon the filing of the certificate of conversion to non-Delaware entity;

(5)   That the conversion has been approved in accordance with this section;

(6)   The agreement of the limited liability company that it may be served with process in the State of Delaware in any action, suit or proceeding for enforcement of any obligation of the limited liability company arising while it was a limited liability company of the State of Delaware, and that it irrevocably appoints the Secretary of State as its agent to accept service of process in any such action, suit or proceeding;

(7)   The address to which a copy of the process referred to in paragraph (e)(6) of this section shall be mailed to it by the Secretary of State. Process may be served upon the Secretary of State under paragraph (e)(6) of this section by means of electronic transmission but only as prescribed by the Secretary of State. The Secretary of State is authorized to issue such rules and regulations with respect to such service as the Secretary of State deems necessary or appropriate. In the event of service hereunder upon the Secretary of State, the procedures set forth in § 18–911(c) of this title shall be applicable, except that the plaintiff in any such action, suit or proceeding shall furnish the Secretary of State with the address specified in this subdivision and any other address that the plaintiff may elect to furnish, together with copies of such process as required by the Secretary of State, and the Secretary of State shall notify the limited liability company that has converted out of the State of Delaware at all such addresses furnished by the plaintiff in accordance with the procedures set forth in § 18–911(c) of this title.

(f)   Upon the filing in the office of the Secretary of State of the certificate of conversion to non-Delaware entity or upon the future effective date or time of the certificate of conversion to non-Delaware entity and payment to the Secretary of State of all fees prescribed in this chapter, the Secretary of State shall certify that the limited liability company has filed all documents and paid all fees required by this chapter, and thereupon the limited liability company shall cease to exist as a limited liability company of the State of Delaware. Such certificate of the Secretary of State shall be prima facie evidence of the conversion by such limited liability company out of the State of Delaware.

(g)   The conversion of a limited liability company out of the State of Delaware in accordance with this section and the resulting cessation of its existence as a limited liability company of the State of Delaware pursuant to a certificate of conversion to non-Delaware entity shall not be deemed to affect any obligations or liabilities of the limited liability company incurred prior to such conversion or the personal liability of any person incurred prior to such conversion, nor shall it be deemed to affect the choice of law applicable to the limited liability company with respect to matters arising prior to such conversion.

(h)   When any conversion shall have become effective under this section, for all purposes of the laws of the State of Delaware, all of the rights, privileges and powers of the limited liability company that has converted, and all property, real, personal and mixed, and all debts due to such limited liability company, as well as all other things and causes of action belonging to such limited liability company, shall remain vested in the other entity or business form to which such limited liability company has converted and shall be the property of such other entity or business form, and the title to any real property vested by deed or otherwise in such limited liability company shall not revert or be in any way impaired by reason of this chapter; but all rights of creditors and all liens upon any property of such limited liability company shall be preserved unimpaired, and all debts, liabilities and duties of the limited liability company that has converted shall remain attached to the other entity or business form to which such limited liability company has converted, and may be enforced against it to the same extent as if said debts, liabilities and duties had originally been incurred or contracted by it in its capacity as such other entity or business form. The rights, privileges, powers and interests in property of the limited liability company that has converted, as well as the debts, liabilities and duties of such limited liability company, shall not be deemed, as a consequence of the conversion, to have been transferred to the other entity or business form to which such limited liability company has converted for any purpose of the laws of the State of Delaware.

(i)　A limited liability company agreement may provide that a domestic limited liability company shall not have the power to convert as set forth in this section.

§ 18–217.　Division of a Limited Liability Company

(a)　As used in this section and §§ 18–203 and 18–1203:

(1)　"Dividing company" means the domestic limited liability company that is effecting a division in the manner provided in this section.

(2)　"Division" means the division of a dividing company into 2 or more domestic limited liability companies in accordance with this section.

(3)　"Division company" means a surviving company, if any, and each resulting company.

(4)　"Division contact" means, in connection with any division, a natural person who is a Delaware resident, any division company in such division or any other domestic limited liability company or other business entity as defined in § 18–209 of this title formed or organized under the laws of the State of Delaware, which division contact shall maintain a copy of the plan of division for a period of 6 years from the effective date of the division and shall comply with paragraph (g)(3) of this section.

(5)　"Organizational documents" means the certificate of formation and limited liability company agreement of a domestic limited liability company.

(6)　"Resulting company" means a domestic limited liability company formed as a consequence of a division.

(7)　"Surviving company" means a dividing company that survives the division.

(b)　Pursuant to a plan of division, any domestic limited liability company may, in the manner provided in this section, be divided into 2 or more domestic limited liability companies. The division of a domestic limited liability company in accordance with this section and, if applicable, the resulting cessation of the existence of the dividing company pursuant to a certificate of division shall not be deemed to affect the personal liability of any person incurred prior to such division with respect to matters arising prior to such division, nor shall it be deemed to affect the validity or enforceability of any obligations or liabilities of the dividing company incurred prior to such division; provided, that such obligations and liabilities shall be allocated to and vested in, and valid and enforceable obligations of, such division company or companies to which such obligations and liabilities have been allocated pursuant to the plan of division, as provided in subsection (*l*) of this section. Each resulting company in a division shall be formed in compliance with the requirements of this chapter and subsection (i) of this section.

(c)　If the limited liability company agreement of the dividing company specifies the manner of adopting a plan of division, the plan of division shall be adopted as specified in the limited liability company agreement. If the limited liability company agreement of the dividing company does not specify the manner of adopting a plan of division and does not prohibit a division of the limited liability company, the plan of division shall be adopted in the same manner as is specified in the limited liability company agreement for authorizing a merger or consolidation that involves the limited liability company as a constituent party to the merger or consolidation. If the limited liability company agreement of the dividing company does not specify the manner of adopting a plan of division or authorizing a merger or consolidation that involves the limited liability company as a constituent party and does not prohibit a division of the limited liability company, the adoption of a plan of division shall be authorized by the approval by members who own more than 50 percent of the then current percentage or other interest in the profits of the dividing company owned by all of the members. Notwithstanding prior approval, a plan of division may be terminated or amended pursuant to a provision for such termination or amendment contained in the plan of division.

(d)   Unless otherwise provided in a plan of division, the division of a domestic limited liability company pursuant to this section shall not require such limited liability company to wind up its affairs under § 18–803 of this title or pay its liabilities and distribute its assets under § 18–804 of this title, and the division shall not constitute a dissolution of such limited liability company.

(e)   In connection with a division under this section, rights or securities of, or interests in, the dividing company may be exchanged for or converted into cash, property, rights or securities of, or interests in, the surviving company or any resulting company or, in addition to or in lieu thereof, may be exchanged for or converted into cash, property, rights or securities of, or interests in, a domestic limited liability company or any other business entity which is not a division company or may be canceled or remain outstanding (if the dividing company is a surviving company).

(f)   A plan of division adopted in accordance with subsection (c) of this section:

(1)   May effect any amendment to the limited liability company agreement of the dividing company if it is a surviving company in the division; or

(2)   May effect the adoption of a new limited liability company agreement for the dividing company if it is a surviving company in the division; and

(3)   Shall effect the adoption of a new limited liability company agreement for each resulting company.

Any amendment to a limited liability company agreement or adoption of a new limited liability company agreement for the dividing company, if it is a surviving company in the division, or adoption of a new limited liability company agreement for each resulting company made pursuant to the foregoing sentence shall be effective at the effective time or date of the division. Any amendment to a limited liability company agreement or adoption of a limited liability company agreement for the dividing company, if it is a surviving company in the division, shall be effective notwithstanding any provision in the limited liability company agreement of the dividing company relating to amendment or adoption of a new limited liability company agreement, other than a provision that by its terms applies to an amendment to the limited liability company agreement or the adoption of a new limited liability company agreement, in either case, in connection with a division, merger or consolidation.

(g)   If a domestic limited liability company is dividing under this section, the dividing company shall adopt a plan of division which shall set forth:

(1)   The terms and conditions of the division, including:

a.   Any conversion or exchange of the limited liability company interests of the dividing company into or for limited liability company interests or other securities or obligations of any division company or cash, property or rights or securities or obligations of or interests in any other business entity or domestic limited liability company which is not a division company, or that the limited liability company interests of the dividing company shall remain outstanding or be canceled, or any combination of the foregoing; and

b.   The allocation of assets, property, rights, series, debts, liabilities and duties of the dividing company among the division companies;

(2)   The name of each resulting company and, if the dividing company will survive the division, the name of the surviving company;

(3)   The name and business address of a division contact which shall have custody of a copy of the plan of division. The division contact, or any successor division contact, shall serve for a period of 6 years following the effective date of the division. During such 6 year period the division contact shall provide, without cost, to any creditor of the dividing company, within 30 days following the division contact's receipt of a written request from any creditor of the dividing company, the name and business address of the division company to which the claim of such creditor was allocated pursuant to the plan of division; and

(4)   Any other matters that the dividing company determines to include therein.

(h)   If a domestic limited liability company divides under this section, the surviving company, if there be one, or any other division company shall file a certificate of division executed by 1 or more authorized persons on behalf of such division company in the office of the Secretary of State in accordance with § 18–204 of this title and a certificate of formation that complies with § 18–201 of this title for each resulting company executed by one or more authorized persons in accordance with § 18–204 of this title. The certificate of division shall state:

(1)   The name of the dividing company and, if it has been changed, the name under which its certificate of formation was originally filed and whether the dividing company is a surviving company;

(2)   The date of filing of the dividing company's original certificate of formation with the Secretary of State;

(3)   The name of each division company;

(4)   The name and business address of the division contact required by paragraph (g)(3) of this section;

(5)   The future effective date or time (which shall be a date or time certain) of the division if it is not to be effective upon the filing of the certificate of division;

(6)   That the division has been approved in accordance with this section;

(7)   That the plan of division is on file at a place of business of such division company as is specified therein, and shall state the address thereof; and

(8)   That a copy of the plan of division will be furnished by such division company as is specified therein, on request and without cost, to any member of the dividing company.

(i)   The certificate of division and each certificate of formation for each resulting company required by subsection (h) of this section shall be filed simultaneously in the office of the Secretary of State and, if such certificates are not to become effective upon their filing as permitted by § 18–206(b) of this title, then each such certificate shall provide for the same effective date or time in accordance with § 18–206(b) of this title. Concurrently with the effective date or time of a division, the limited liability company agreement of each resulting company shall become effective.

(j)   A certificate of division shall act as a certificate of cancellation for a dividing company which is not a surviving company.

(k)   A limited liability company agreement may provide that a domestic limited liability company shall not have the power to divide as set forth in this section.

(*l*)   Upon the division of a domestic limited liability company becoming effective:

(1)   The dividing company shall be subdivided into the distinct and independent resulting companies named in the plan of division, and, if the dividing company is not a surviving company, the existence of the dividing company shall cease.

(2)   For all purposes of the laws of the State of Delaware, all of the rights, privileges and powers, and all the property, real, personal and mixed, of the dividing company and all debts due on whatever account to it, as well as all other things and other causes of action belonging to it, shall without further action be allocated to and vested in the applicable division company in such a manner and basis and with such effect as is specified in the plan of division, and the title to any real property or interest therein allocated to and vested in any division company shall not revert or be in any way impaired by reason of the division.

(3)   Each division company shall, from and after effectiveness of the certificate of division, be liable as a separate and distinct domestic limited liability company for such debts, liabilities and duties of the dividing company as are allocated to such division company pursuant to the plan of division in the manner and on the basis provided in paragraph (g)(1)b. of this section.

(4)   Each of the debts, liabilities and duties of the dividing company shall without further action be allocated to and be the debts, liabilities and duties of such division company as is specified in the plan of division as having such debts, liabilities and duties allocated to it, in such a manner and basis and with such effect as is specified in the plan of division, and no other division company shall be liable therefor, so long as the plan of division does not constitute a fraudulent transfer under applicable law, and all liens upon any property of the dividing company shall be preserved unimpaired, and all debts, liabilities and duties of the dividing company shall remain attached to the division company to which such debts, liabilities and duties have been allocated in the plan of division, and may be enforced against such division company to the same extent as if said debts, liabilities and duties had originally been incurred or contracted by it in its capacity as a domestic limited liability company.

(5)   In the event that any allocation of assets, debts, liabilities and duties to division companies in accordance with a plan of division is determined by a court of competent jurisdiction to constitute a fraudulent transfer, each division company shall be jointly and severally liable on account of such fraudulent transfer notwithstanding the allocations made in the plan of division; provided, however, the validity and effectiveness of the division are not otherwise affected thereby.

(6)   Debts and liabilities of the dividing company that are not allocated by the plan of division shall be the joint and several debts and liabilities of all of the division companies.

(7)   It shall not be necessary for a plan of division to list each individual asset, property, right, series, debt, liability or duty of the dividing company to be allocated to a division company so long as the assets, property, rights, series, debts, liabilities or duties so allocated are reasonably identified by any method where the identity of such assets, property, rights, series, debts, liabilities or duties is objectively determinable.

(8)   The rights, privileges, powers and interests in property of the dividing company that have been allocated to a division company, as well as the debts, liabilities and duties of the dividing company that have been allocated to such division company pursuant to a plan of division, shall remain vested in each such division company and shall not be deemed, as a result of the division, to have been assigned or transferred to such division company for any purpose of the laws of the State of Delaware.

(9)   Any action or proceeding pending against a dividing company may be continued against the surviving company as if the division did not occur and against any resulting company to which the asset, property, right, series, debt, liability or duty associated with such action or proceeding was allocated pursuant to the plan of division by adding or substituting such resulting company as a party in the action or proceeding.

(m)   In applying the provisions of this chapter on distributions, a direct or indirect allocation of property or liabilities in a division is not deemed a distribution for purposes of this chapter.

(n)   The provisions of this section shall not be construed to limit the means of accomplishing a division by any other means provided for in a limited liability company agreement or other agreement or as otherwise permitted by this chapter or as otherwise permitted by law.

(o)   All limited liability companies formed on or after August 1, 2018 shall be governed by this section. All limited liability companies formed prior to August 1, 2018 shall be governed by this section; provided, that if the dividing company is a party to any written contract, indenture or other agreement entered into prior to August 1, 2018 that, by its terms, restricts, conditions or prohibits the consummation of a merger or consolidation by the dividing company with or into another party, or the transfer of assets by the dividing company to another party, then such restriction, condition or prohibition shall be deemed to apply to a division as if it were a merger, consolidation or transfer of assets, as applicable.

§ 18–218.   Registered Series of Members, Managers, Limited Liability Company Interests or Assets

(a)   If a limited liability company agreement provides for the establishment or formation of 1 or more series, then a registered series may be formed by complying with this § 18–218. A limited liability company agreement does not need to use the term registered when referencing series or refer to this § 18–218, and a reference in a limited liability company agreement for a registered series, including a registered series resulting from the conversion of a protected series to a registered series, may continue to refer to § 18–215 of this title, which reference shall be deemed a reference to this § 18–218 with respect to such registered series. A registered series is formed by the filing of a certificate of registered series in the office of the Secretary of State.

(b)   Notice of the limitation on liabilities of a registered series as referenced in subsection (c) of this section shall be set forth in the certificate of formation of the limited liability company. Notice in a certificate of formation of the limitation on liabilities of a registered series as referenced in subsection (c) of this section shall be sufficient for all purposes of this subsection whether or not the limited liability company has formed any registered series when such notice is included in the certificate of formation, and there shall be no requirement that (i) any specific registered series of the limited liability company be referenced in such notice, (ii) such notice use the term registered when referencing series or include a reference to this § 18–218, or (iii) the certificate of formation be amended if it includes a reference to § 18–215 of this title. Any reference to § 18–215 of this title in a certificate of formation of a limited liability company that has one or more registered series shall be deemed a reference to this § 18–218 with respect to such registered series. The fact that a certificate of formation that contains the foregoing notice of the limitation on liabilities of a series is on file in the office of the Secretary of State shall constitute notice of such limitation on liabilities of a registered series.

(c)   Notwithstanding anything to the contrary set forth in this chapter or under other applicable law, to the extent the records maintained for a registered series account for the assets associated with such series separately from the other assets of the limited liability company, or any other series thereof, then the debts, liabilities, obligations and expenses incurred, contracted for or otherwise existing with respect to such series shall be enforceable against the assets of such series only, and not against the assets of the limited liability company generally or any other series thereof, and, unless otherwise provided in the limited liability company agreement, none of the debts, liabilities, obligations and expenses incurred, contracted for or otherwise existing with respect to the limited liability company generally or any other series thereof shall be enforceable against the assets of such series. Neither the preceding sentences nor any provision pursuant thereto in a limited liability company agreement, certificate of formation or certificate of registered series shall (i) restrict a registered series or limited liability company on behalf of a registered series from agreeing in the limited liability company agreement or otherwise that any or all of the debts, liabilities, obligations and expenses incurred, contracted for or otherwise existing with respect to the limited liability company generally or any other series thereof shall be enforceable against the assets of such registered series or (ii) restrict a limited liability company from agreeing in the limited liability company agreement or otherwise that any or all of the debts, liabilities, obligations and expenses incurred, contracted for or otherwise existing with respect to a registered series shall be enforceable against the assets of the limited liability company generally. Assets associated with a registered series may be held directly or indirectly, including in the name of such series, in the name of the limited liability company, through a nominee or otherwise. Records maintained for a registered series that reasonably identify its assets, including by specific listing, category, type, quantity, computational or allocational formula or procedure (including a percentage or share of any asset or assets) or by any other method where the identity of such assets is objectively determinable, will be deemed to account for the assets associated with such series separately from the other assets of the limited liability company, or any other series thereof. As used in this chapter, a reference to assets of a registered series includes assets associated with such series, a reference to assets associated with a registered series includes assets of such series, a reference to members or managers of a registered series includes members or managers associated with such series, and a reference to members or managers associated with a registered series includes members or managers of such series. The following shall apply to a registered series:

(1)   A registered series may carry on any lawful business, purpose or activity, whether or not for profit, with the exception of the business of banking as defined in § 126 of Title 8. Unless otherwise provided in a limited liability company agreement, a registered series shall have the power and capacity to, in its own name, contract, hold title to assets (including real, personal and intangible property), grant liens and security interests, and sue and be sued.

(2)   Except as otherwise provided by this chapter, no member or manager of a registered series shall be obligated personally for any debt, obligation or liability of such series, whether arising in contract, tort or otherwise, solely by reason of being a member or acting as manager of such series. Notwithstanding the preceding sentence, under a limited liability company agreement or under another agreement, a member or manager may agree to be obligated personally for any or all of the debts, obligations and liabilities of 1 or more registered series.

(3)   A limited liability company agreement may provide for classes or groups of members or managers associated with a registered series having such relative rights, powers and duties as the limited liability company agreement may provide, and may make provision for the future creation in the manner provided in the limited liability company agreement of additional classes or groups of members or managers associated with such series having such relative rights, powers and duties as may from time to time be established, including rights, powers and duties senior to existing classes and groups of members or managers associated with such series. A limited liability company agreement may provide for the taking of an action, including the amendment of the limited liability company agreement, without the vote or approval of any member or manager or class or group of members or managers, including an action to create under the provisions of the limited liability company agreement a class or group of a registered series of limited liability company interests that was not previously outstanding. A limited liability company agreement may provide that any member or class or group of members associated with a registered series shall have no voting rights.

(4)   A limited liability company agreement may grant to all or certain identified members or managers or a specified class or group of the members or managers associated with a registered series the right to vote separately or with all or any class or group of the members or managers associated with such series, on any matter. Voting by members or managers associated with a registered series may be on a per capita, number, financial interest, class, group or any other basis.

(5)   Unless otherwise provided in a limited liability company agreement, the management of a registered series shall be vested in the members associated with such series in proportion to the then current percentage or other interest of members in the profits of such series owned by all of the members associated with such series, the decision of members owning more than 50 percent of the said percentage or other interest in the profits controlling; provided, however, that if a limited liability company agreement provides for the management of a registered series, in whole or in part, by a manager, the management of such series, to the extent so provided, shall be vested in the manager who shall be chosen in the manner provided in the limited liability company agreement. The manager of a registered series shall also hold the offices and have the responsibilities accorded to the manager as set forth in a limited liability company agreement. A registered series may have more than 1 manager. Subject to § 18–602 of this title, a manager shall cease to be a manager with respect to a registered series as provided in a limited liability company agreement. Except as otherwise provided in a limited liability company agreement, any event under this chapter or in a limited liability company agreement that causes a manager to cease to be a manager with respect to a registered series shall not, in itself, cause such manager to cease to be a manager of the limited liability company or with respect to any other series thereof.

(6)   Notwithstanding § 18–606 of this title, but subject to paragraphs (c)(7) and (c)(10) of this section, and unless otherwise provided in a limited liability company agreement, at the time a member of a registered series becomes entitled to receive a distribution with respect to such series, the member has the status of, and is entitled to all remedies available to, a creditor of such series, with respect to the distribution. A limited liability company agreement may provide for the establishment of a record date with respect to allocations and distributions with respect to a registered series.

(7)   Notwithstanding § 18–607(a) of this title, a limited liability company may make a distribution with respect to a registered series. A limited liability company shall not make a distribution with respect to a registered series to a member to the extent that at the time of the distribution, after giving effect to the distribution, all liabilities of such series, other than liabilities to members on account of their limited liability company interests with respect to such series and liabilities for which the recourse of creditors is limited to specified property of such series, exceed the fair value of the assets associated with such series, except that the fair value of property of such series that is subject to a liability for which the recourse of creditors is limited shall be included in the assets associated with such series only to the extent that the fair value of that property exceeds that liability. For purposes of the immediately preceding sentence, the term "distribution" shall not include amounts constituting reasonable compensation for present or past services or reasonable payments made in the ordinary course of business pursuant to a bona fide retirement plan or other benefits program. A member who receives a distribution in violation of this subsection, and who knew at the time of the distribution that the distribution violated this subsection, shall be liable to the registered series for the amount of the distribution. A member who receives a distribution in violation of this subsection, and who did not know at the time of the distribution that the distribution violated this subsection, shall not be liable for the amount of the distribution. Subject to § 18–607(c) of this title, which shall apply to any distribution made with respect to a registered series under this subsection, this subsection shall not affect any obligation or liability of a member under an agreement or other applicable law for the amount of a distribution.

(8)   Unless otherwise provided in the limited liability company agreement, a member shall cease to be associated with a registered series and to have the power to exercise any rights or powers of a member with respect to such series upon the assignment of all of the member's limited liability company interest with respect to such series. Except as otherwise provided in a limited liability company agreement, any event under this chapter or a limited liability company agreement that causes a member to cease to be associated with a registered series shall not, in itself, cause such member to cease to be associated with any other series or terminate the continued membership of a member in the limited liability company or cause the dissolution of the registered series, regardless of whether such member was the last remaining member associated with such series.

(9)   Subject to § 18–801 of this title, except to the extent otherwise provided in the limited liability company agreement, a registered series may be dissolved and its affairs wound up without causing the dissolution of the limited liability company. The dissolution of a registered series shall not affect the limitation on liabilities of such series provided by this subsection (c). A registered series is dissolved and its affairs shall be wound up upon the dissolution of the limited liability company under § 18–801 of this title or otherwise upon the first to occur of the following:

    a.   At the time specified in the limited liability company agreement;

    b.   Upon the happening of events specified in the limited liability company agreement;

    c.   Unless otherwise provided in the limited liability company agreement, upon the vote or consent of members associated with such series who own more than 2/3 of the then-current percentage or other interest in the profits of such series of the limited liability company owned by all of the members associated with such series; or

    d.   The dissolution of such series under paragraph (c)(11) of this section.

   (10) Notwithstanding § 18–803(a) of this title, unless otherwise provided in the limited liability company agreement, a manager associated with a registered series who has not wrongfully dissolved such series or, if none, the members associated with such series or a person approved by the members associated with such series, in either case, by members who own more than 50 percent of the then current percentage or other interest in the profits of such series owned by all of the members associated with such series, may wind up the affairs of such series; but the Court of Chancery, upon cause shown, may wind up the affairs of a registered series upon application of any member or manager associated with such series, or the member's personal representative or assignee, and in connection therewith, may appoint a liquidating trustee. The persons winding up the affairs of a registered series may, in the name of the limited liability company and for and on behalf of the limited liability company and such series, take all actions with respect to such series as are permitted under § 18–803(b) of this title. The persons winding up the affairs of a registered series shall provide for the claims and obligations of such series and distribute the assets of such series as provided in § 18–804 of this title, which section shall apply to the winding up and distribution of assets of a registered series. Actions taken in accordance with this subsection shall not affect the liability of members and shall not impose liability on a liquidating trustee.

   (11) On application by or for a member or manager associated with a registered series, the Court of Chancery may decree dissolution of such series whenever it is not reasonably practicable to carry on the business of such series in conformity with a limited liability company agreement.

   (12) For all purposes of the laws of the State of Delaware, a registered series is an association, regardless of the number of members or managers, if any, of such series.

  (d) In order to form a registered series of a limited liability company, a certificate of registered series must be filed in accordance with this subsection.

   (1) A certificate of registered series:

     a.   Shall set forth:

       1.   The name of the limited liability company; and

       2.   The name of the registered series.

     b.   May include any other matter that the members of such registered series determine to include therein.

   (2) A certificate of registered series shall be executed in accordance with § 18–204 of this title and shall be filed in the office of the Secretary of State in accordance with § 18–206 of this title. A certificate of registered series shall be effective as of the effective time of such filing unless a later effective date or time (which shall be a date or time certain) is provided for in the certificate of registered series. A certificate of registered series is not an amendment to the certificate of formation of the limited liability company. The filing of a certificate of registered series in the office of the Secretary of State shall make it unnecessary to file any other documents under Chapter 31 of this title.

   (3) A certificate of registered series is amended by filing a certificate of amendment thereto in the office of the Secretary of State. The certificate of amendment shall set forth:

     a.   The name of the limited liability company;

     b.   The name of the registered series; and

     c.   The amendment to the certificate of registered series.

   (4) A manager of a registered series or, if there is no manager, then any member of a registered series who becomes aware that any statement in a certificate of registered series filed with respect to such registered series was false when made, or that any matter described therein

has changed making the certificate of registered series false in any material respect, shall promptly amend the certificate of registered series.

(5) A certificate of registered series may be amended at any time for any other proper purpose.

(6) Unless otherwise provided in this chapter or unless a later effective date or time (which shall be a date or time certain) is provided for in the certificate of amendment, a certificate of amendment shall be effective at the time of its filing with the Secretary of State.

(7) A certificate of registered series shall be canceled upon the cancellation of the certificate of formation of the limited liability company named in the certificate of registered series, or upon the filing of a certificate of cancellation of the certificate of registered series or upon the future effective date or time of a certificate of cancellation of the certificate of registered series, or as provided in § 18–1108(b) of this title, or upon the filing of a certificate of merger or consolidation if the registered series is not the surviving or resulting registered series in a merger or consolidation or upon the future effective date or time of a certificate of merger or consolidation if the registered series is not the surviving or resulting registered series in a merger or consolidation, or upon the filing of a certificate of conversion to protected series or upon the future effective date or time of a certificate of conversion to a protected series. A certificate of cancellation of the certificate of registered series may be filed at any time, and shall be filed, in the office of the Secretary of State to accomplish the cancellation of a certificate of registered series upon the dissolution of a registered series for which a certificate of registered series was filed and completion of the winding up of such registered series. A certificate of cancellation of the certificate of registered series shall set forth:

     a.   The name of the limited liability company;

     b.   The name of the registered series;

     c.   The date of filing of the certificate of registered series;

     d.   The future effective date or time (which shall be a date or time certain) of cancellation if it is not to be effective upon the filing of the certificate of cancellation; and

     e.   Any other information the person filing the certificate of cancellation of the certificate of registered series determines.

(8) A certificate of cancellation of the certificate of registered series that is filed in the office of the Secretary of State prior to the dissolution or the completion of winding up of a registered series may be corrected as an erroneously executed certificate of cancellation of the certificate of registered series by filing with the office of the Secretary of State a certificate of correction of such certificate of cancellation of the certificate of registered series in accordance with § 18–211 of this title.

(9) The Secretary of State shall not issue a certificate of good standing with respect to a registered series if its certificate of registered series is canceled or the limited liability company has ceased to be in good standing.

(e) The name of each registered series as set forth in its certificate of registered series:

(1) Shall begin with the name of the limited liability company, including any word, abbreviation or designation required by § 18–102 of this title;

(2) May contain the name of a member or manager;

(3) Must be such as to distinguish it upon the records in the office of the Secretary of State from the name on such records of any corporation, partnership, limited partnership, statutory trust, limited liability company or registered series reserved, registered, formed or organized under the laws of the State of Delaware or qualified to do business or registered as a foreign corporation, foreign limited partnership, foreign statutory trust, foreign partnership or foreign

limited liability company in the State of Delaware; provided, however, that a registered series may register under any name which is not such as to distinguish it upon the records in the office of the Secretary of State from the name on such records of any domestic or foreign corporation, partnership, limited partnership, statutory trust, registered series or foreign limited liability company reserved, registered, formed or organized under the laws of the State of Delaware with the written consent of the other corporation, partnership, limited partnership, statutory trust, registered series or foreign limited liability company, which written consent shall be filed with the Secretary of State;

(4)   May contain the following words: "Company," "Association," "Club," "Foundation," "Fund," "Institute," "Society," "Union," "Syndicate," "Limited," "Public Benefit" or "Trust" (or abbreviations of like import); and

(5)   Shall not contain the word "bank," or any variation thereof, except for the name of a bank reporting to and under the supervision of the State Bank Commissioner of this State or a subsidiary of a bank or savings association (as those terms are defined in the Federal Deposit Insurance Act, as amended, at 12 U.S.C. § 1813), or a limited liability company regulated under the Bank Holding Company Act of 1956, as amended, 12 U.S.C. § 1841 et seq., or the Home Owners' Loan Act, as amended, 12 U.S.C. § 1461 et seq.; provided, however, that this section shall not be construed to prevent the use of the word "bank," or any variation thereof, in a context clearly not purporting to refer to a banking business or otherwise likely to mislead the public about the nature of the business of the limited liability company or the registered series, or to lead to a pattern and practice of abuse that might cause harm to the interests of the public or this State as determined by the Division of Corporations in the Department of State.

§ 18–219.   Approval of Conversion of a Protected Series of a Domestic Limited Liability Company to a Registered Series of Such Domestic Limited Liability Company

(a)   A protected series of a domestic limited liability company may convert to a registered series of such domestic limited liability company by complying with this section and filing in the office of the Secretary of State in accordance with § 18–206 of this title:

(1)   A certificate of conversion of protected series to registered series that has been executed in accordance with § 18–204 of this title; and

(2)   A certificate of registered series that complies with § 18–218(d) of this title and has been executed by 1 or more authorized persons in accordance with § 18–204 of this title.

Each of the certificates required by this subsection (a) shall be filed simultaneously in the office of the Secretary of State and, if such certificates are not to become effective upon their filing as permitted by § 18–206(b) of this title, then each such certificate shall provide for the same effective date or time in accordance with § 18–206(b) of this title.

An existing series may not become a registered series other than pursuant to this section.

(b)   If the limited liability company agreement specifies the manner of authorizing a conversion of a protected series of such limited liability company to a registered series of such limited liability company, the conversion of a protected series to a registered series shall be authorized as specified in the limited liability company agreement. If the limited liability company agreement does not specify the manner of authorizing a conversion of a protected series of such limited liability company to a registered series of such limited liability company and does not prohibit a conversion of a protected series to a registered series, the conversion shall be authorized by members of such protected series who own more than 50 percent of the then current percentage or other interest in the profits of such protected series owned by all of the members of such protected series.

(c)   Unless otherwise agreed, the conversion of a protected series of a limited liability company to a registered series of such limited liability company pursuant to this section shall not require such limited liability company or such protected series of such limited liability company to wind up its affairs under § 18–803 or § 18–215 of this title or pay its liabilities and distribute its assets under § 18–804 or § 18–215 of this title, and the conversion of a protected series of a limited liability company to a registered series of such limited liability company shall not constitute a dissolution of such limited liability company or a termination of such protected series. When a protected series of a limited liability company has converted to a registered series of such limited liability company pursuant to this section, for all purposes of the laws of the State of Delaware, the registered series shall be deemed to be the same series as the converting protected series and the conversion shall constitute a continuation of the existence of the protected series in the form of such registered series.

(d)   In connection with a conversion of a protected series of a limited liability company to a registered series of such limited liability company pursuant to this section, rights or securities of or interests in the protected series which is to be converted may be exchanged for or converted into cash, property, rights or securities of or interests in the registered series into which the protected series is being converted or, in addition to or in lieu thereof, may be exchanged for or converted into cash, property, rights or securities of or interests in any other business entity, may remain outstanding or may be canceled.

(e)   If a protected series shall convert to a registered series in accordance with this section, a certificate of conversion executed in accordance with § 18–204 of this title shall be filed in the office of the Secretary of State in accordance with § 18–206 of this title. The certificate of conversion to a registered series shall state:

(1)   The name of the limited liability company and, if it has been changed, the name under which its certificate of formation was originally filed;

(2)   The name of the protected series and, if it has been changed, the name of the protected series as originally established;

(3)   The name of the registered series as set forth in its certificate of registered series filed in accordance with subsection (a) of this section;

(4)   The date of filing of the original certificate of formation of the limited liability company with the Secretary of State;

(5)   The date on which the protected series was established;

(6)   The future effective date or time (which shall be a date or time certain) of the conversion if it is not to be effective upon the filing of the certificate of conversion to a registered series; and

(7)   That the conversion has been approved in accordance with this section.

(f)   A copy of the certificate of conversion to a registered series certified by the Secretary of State shall be prima facie evidence of the conversion by such protected series to a registered series of such limited liability company.

(g)   When any conversion shall have become effective under this section, for all purposes of the laws of the State of Delaware, all of the rights, privileges and powers of the protected series that has converted, and all property, real, personal and mixed, and all debts due to such protected series, as well as all other things and causes of action belonging to such protected series, shall remain vested in the registered series to which such protected series has converted and shall be the property of such registered series, and the title to any real property vested by deed or otherwise in such protected series shall not revert or be in any way impaired by reason of this chapter; but all rights of creditors and all liens upon any property of such protected series shall be preserved unimpaired, and all debts, liabilities and duties of the protected series that has converted shall remain attached to the registered series to which such protected series has converted, and may be enforced against it to the same extent as if said debts, liabilities and duties had originally been incurred or contracted by it in its capacity as such registered series. The rights, privileges, powers and interests in property of the protected series that has converted, as well as the debts, liabilities and duties of such protected series, shall not be deemed, as a consequence of the conversion, to have been transferred to the registered series to which such protected series of such limited liability company has converted for any purpose of the laws of the State of Delaware.

(h) A limited liability company agreement may provide that a protected series of a limited liability company shall not have the power to convert to a registered series of such limited liability company as set forth in this section.

§ 18–220. Approval of Conversion of a Registered Series of a Domestic Limited Liability Company to a Protected Series of Such Domestic Limited Liability Company

(a) Upon compliance with this section, a registered series of a domestic limited liability company may convert to a protected series of such domestic limited liability company. An existing registered series may not become a protected series other than pursuant to this section.

(b) If the limited liability company agreement specifies the manner of authorizing a conversion of a registered series of such limited liability company to a protected series of such limited liability company, the conversion of a registered series to a protected series shall be authorized as specified in the limited liability company agreement. If the limited liability company agreement does not specify the manner of authorizing a conversion of a registered series of such limited liability company to a protected series of such limited liability company and does not prohibit a conversion of a registered series to a protected series, the conversion shall be authorized by members of such registered series who own more than 50 percent of the then current percentage or other interest in the profits of such registered series owned by all of the members of such registered series.

(c) Unless otherwise agreed, the conversion of a registered series of a limited liability company to a protected series of such limited liability company pursuant to this section shall not require such limited liability company or such registered series of such limited liability company to wind up its affairs under § 18–803 or § 18–218 of this title or pay its liabilities and distribute its assets under § 18–804 or § 18–218 of this title, and the conversion of a registered series of a limited liability company to a protected series of such limited liability company shall not constitute a dissolution of such limited liability company or of such registered series. When a registered series of a limited liability company has converted to a protected series of such limited liability company pursuant to this section, for all purposes of the laws of the State of Delaware, the protected series shall be deemed to be the same series as the converting registered series and the conversion shall constitute a continuation of the existence of the registered series in the form of such protected series.

(d) In connection with a conversion of a registered series of a limited liability company to protected series of such limited liability company pursuant to this section, rights or securities of or interests in the registered series which is to be converted may be exchanged for or converted into cash, property, rights or securities of or interests in the protected series into which the registered series is being converted or, in addition to or in lieu thereof, may be exchanged for or converted into cash, property, rights or securities of or interests in any other business entity, may remain outstanding or may be canceled.

(e) If a registered series shall convert to a protected series in accordance with this section, a certificate of conversion executed in accordance with § 18–204 of this title shall be filed in the office of the Secretary of State in accordance with § 18–206 of this title. The certificate of conversion to a protected series shall state:

(1) The name of the limited liability company and, if it has been changed, the name under which its certificate of formation was originally filed;

(2) The date of filing of the original certificate of formation of the limited liability company with the Secretary of State;

(3)   The name of the registered series and, if it has been changed, the name under which its certificate of registered series was originally filed;

(4)   The date of filing of its original certificate of registered series with the Secretary of State;

(5)   The future effective date or time (which shall be a date or time certain) of the conversion if it is not to be effective upon the filing of the certificate of conversion to a registered series; and

(6)   That the conversion has been approved in accordance with this section.

(f)   Upon the filing in the office of the Secretary of State of the certificate of conversion to a protected series or upon the future effective date or time of the certificate of conversion to a protected series and payment to the Secretary of State of all fees prescribed in this chapter, the Secretary of State shall certify that the registered series has filed all documents and paid all fees required by this chapter. Such certificate of the Secretary of State shall be prima facie evidence of the conversion by such registered series to a protected series of such limited liability company.

(g)   When any conversion shall have become effective under this section, for all purposes of the laws of the State of Delaware, all of the rights, privileges and powers of the registered series that has converted, and all property, real, personal and mixed, and all debts due to such registered series, as well as all other things and causes of action belonging to such registered series, shall remain vested in the protected series to which such registered series has converted and shall be the property of such protected series, and the title to any real property vested by deed or otherwise in such registered series shall not revert or be in any way impaired by reason of this chapter; but all rights of creditors and all liens upon any property of such registered series shall be preserved unimpaired, and all debts, liabilities and duties of the registered series that has converted shall remain attached to the protected series to which such registered series has converted, and may be enforced against it to the same extent as if said debts, liabilities and duties had originally been incurred or contracted by it in its capacity as such protected series. The rights, privileges, powers and interests in property of the registered series that has converted, as well as the debts, liabilities and duties of such registered series, shall not be deemed, as a consequence of the conversion, to have been transferred to the protected series to which such registered series of such limited liability company has converted for any purpose of the laws of the State of Delaware.

(h)   A limited liability company agreement may provide that a registered series of a limited liability company shall not have the power to convert to a protected series of such limited liability company as set forth in this section.

§ 18–221.   Merger and Consolidation of Registered Series

(a)   Pursuant to an agreement of merger or consolidation, 1 or more registered series may merge or consolidate with or into 1 or more other registered series of the same limited liability company with such registered series as the agreement shall provide being the surviving or resulting registered series. Unless otherwise provided in the limited liability company agreement, an agreement of merger or consolidation shall be approved by each registered series which is to merge or consolidate by members of such registered series who own more than 50 percent of the then current percentage or other interest in the profits of such registered series owned by all of the members of such registered series. In connection with a merger or consolidation hereunder, rights or securities of, or interests in, a registered series which is a constituent party to the merger or consolidation may be exchanged for or converted into cash, property, rights or securities of, or interests in, the surviving or resulting registered series or, in addition to or in lieu thereof, may be exchanged for or converted into cash, property, rights or securities of, or interests in, a domestic limited liability company or other business entity which is not the surviving or resulting registered series in the merger or consolidation, may remain outstanding or may be canceled. Notwithstanding prior approval, an agreement of merger or consolidation may be terminated or amended pursuant to a provision for such termination or amendment contained in the agreement of merger or consolidation.

(b)   If a registered series is merging or consolidating under this section, the registered series surviving or resulting in or from the merger or consolidation shall file a certificate of merger or consolidation executed by 1 or more authorized persons on behalf of the registered series when it is the surviving or resulting registered series in the office of the Secretary of State. The certificate of merger or consolidation shall state:

(1)   The name of each registered series which is to merge or consolidate and the name of the limited liability company that formed such registered series;

(2)   That an agreement of merger or consolidation has been approved and executed by or on behalf of each registered series which is to merge or consolidate;

(3)   The name of the surviving or resulting registered series;

(4)   Such amendment, if any, to the certificate of registered series of the registered series that is the surviving or resulting registered series to change the name of the surviving registered series, as is desired to be effected by the merger;

(5)   The future effective date or time (which shall be a date or time certain) of the merger or consolidation if it is not to be effective upon the filing of the certificate of merger or consolidation;

(6)   That the agreement of merger or consolidation is on file at a place of business of the surviving or resulting registered series or the limited liability company that formed such registered series, and shall state the address thereof; and

(7)   That a copy of the agreement of merger or consolidation will be furnished by the surviving or resulting registered series, on request and without cost, to any member of any registered series which is to merge or consolidate.

(c)   Unless a future effective date or time is provided in a certificate of merger or consolidation, a merger or consolidation pursuant to this section shall be effective upon the filing in the office of the Secretary of State of a certificate of merger or consolidation.

(d)   A certificate of merger or consolidation shall act as a certificate of cancellation of the certificate of registered series of the registered series which is not the surviving or resulting registered series in the merger or consolidation. A certificate of merger or consolidation that sets forth any amendment in accordance with paragraph (b)(4) of this section shall be deemed to be an amendment to the certificate of registered series of the surviving or resulting registered series, and no further action shall be required to amend the certificate of registered series of the surviving or resulting registered series under § 18–218 of this title with respect to such amendments set forth in the certificate of merger or consolidation. Whenever this section requires the filing of a certificate of merger or consolidation, such requirement shall be deemed satisfied by the filing of an agreement of merger or consolidation containing the information required by this section to be set forth in the certificate of merger or consolidation.

(e)   An agreement of merger or consolidation approved in accordance with subsection (a) of this section may effect any amendment to the limited liability company agreement relating solely to the registered series that are constituent parties to the merger or consolidation.

Any amendment to a limited liability company agreement relating solely to the registered series that are constituent parties to the merger or consolidation made pursuant to the foregoing sentence shall be effective at the effective time or date of the merger or consolidation and shall be effective notwithstanding any provision of the limited liability company agreement relating to amendment of the limited liability company agreement, other than a provision that by its terms applies to an amendment to the limited liability company agreement in connection with a merger or consolidation. The provisions of this subsection shall not be construed to limit the accomplishment of a merger or of any of the matters referred to herein by any other means provided for in a limited liability company agreement or other agreement or as otherwise permitted by law, including that the limited liability company agreement relating to any constituent registered series to the merger or consolidation (including a registered series formed for the purpose of consummating a merger or consolidation) shall be the limited liability company agreement of the surviving or resulting registered series.

(f)   When any merger or consolidation shall have become effective under this section, for all purposes of the laws of the State of Delaware, all of the rights, privileges and powers of each of the registered series that have merged or consolidated, and all property, real, personal and mixed, and all debts due to any of said registered series, as well as all other things and causes of action belonging to each of such registered series, shall be vested in the surviving or resulting registered series, and shall thereafter be the property of the surviving or resulting registered series as they were of each of the registered series that have merged or consolidated, and the title to any real property vested by deed or otherwise, under the laws of the State of Delaware, in any of such registered series, shall not revert or be in any way impaired by reason of this chapter; but all rights of creditors and all liens upon any property of any of said registered series shall be preserved unimpaired, and all debts, liabilities and duties of each of the said registered series that have merged or consolidated shall thenceforth attach to the surviving or resulting registered series, and may be enforced against it to the same extent as if said debts, liabilities and duties had been incurred or contracted by it. Unless otherwise agreed, a merger or consolidation of a registered series of a limited liability company, including a registered series which is not the surviving or resulting registered series in the merger or consolidation, shall not require such registered series to wind up its affairs under § 18–218 of this title, or pay its liabilities and distribute its assets under § 18–218 of this title and the merger or consolidation shall not constitute a dissolution of such registered series.

(g)   A limited liability company agreement may provide that a registered series of such limited liability company shall not have the power to merge or consolidate as set forth in this section.

SUBCHAPTER III
MEMBERS

§ 18–301. Admission of Members

(a)   In connection with the formation of a limited liability company, a person is admitted as a member of the limited liability company upon the later to occur of:

(1)   The formation of the limited liability company; or

(2)   The time provided in and upon compliance with the limited liability company agreement or, if the limited liability company agreement does not so provide, when the person's admission is reflected in the records of the limited liability company.

(b)   After the formation of a limited liability company, a person is admitted as a member of the limited liability company:

(1)   In the case of a person who is not an assignee of a limited liability company interest, including a person acquiring a limited liability company interest directly from the limited liability company and a person to be admitted as a member of the limited liability company without acquiring a limited liability company interest in the limited liability company at the time provided in and upon compliance with the limited liability company agreement or, if the limited liability company agreement does not so provide, upon the consent of all members and when the person's admission is reflected in the records of the limited liability company;

(2)   In the case of an assignee of a limited liability company interest, as provided in § 18–704(a) of this title and at the time provided in and upon compliance with the limited liability company agreement or, if the limited liability company agreement does not so provide, when any such person's permitted admission is reflected in the records of the limited liability company; or

(3)   In the case of a person being admitted as a member of a surviving or resulting limited liability company pursuant to a merger or consolidation approved in accordance with § 18–209(b)

of this title, as provided in the limited liability company agreement of the surviving or resulting limited liability company or in the agreement of merger or consolidation or plan of merger, and in the event of any inconsistency, the terms of the agreement of merger or consolidation or plan of merger shall control; and in the case of a person being admitted as a member of a limited liability company pursuant to a merger or consolidation in which such limited liability company is not the surviving or resulting limited liability company in the merger or consolidation, as provided in the limited liability company agreement of such limited liability company.

(c) In connection with the domestication of a non-United States entity (as defined in § 18–212 of this title) as a limited liability company in the State of Delaware in accordance with § 18–212 of this title or the conversion of an other entity (as defined in § 18–214 of this title) to a domestic limited liability company in accordance with § 18–214 of this title, a person is admitted as a member of the limited liability company as provided in the limited liability company agreement.

(d) A person may be admitted to a limited liability company as a member of the limited liability company and may receive a limited liability company interest in the limited liability company without making a contribution or being obligated to make a contribution to the limited liability company. Unless otherwise provided in a limited liability company agreement, a person may be admitted to a limited liability company as a member of the limited liability company without acquiring a limited liability company interest in the limited liability company. Unless otherwise provided in a limited liability company agreement, a person may be admitted as the sole member of a limited liability company without making a contribution or being obligated to make a contribution to the limited liability company or without acquiring a limited liability company interest in the limited liability company.

(e) Unless otherwise provided in a limited liability company agreement or another agreement, a member shall have no preemptive right to subscribe to any additional issue of limited liability company interests or another interest in a limited liability company.

§ 18–302. Classes and Voting

(a) A limited liability company agreement may provide for classes or groups of members having such relative rights, powers and duties as the limited liability company agreement may provide, and may make provision for the future creation in the manner provided in the limited liability company agreement of additional classes or groups of members having such relative rights, powers and duties as may from time to time be established, including rights, powers and duties senior to existing classes and groups of members. A limited liability company agreement may provide for the taking of an action, including the amendment of the limited liability company agreement, without the vote or approval of any member or class or group of members, including an action to create under the provisions of the limited liability company agreement a class or group of limited liability company interests that was not previously outstanding. A limited liability company agreement may provide that any member or class or group of members shall have no voting rights.

(b) A limited liability company agreement may grant to all or certain identified members or a specified class or group of the members the right to vote separately or with all or any class or group of the members or managers, on any matter. Voting by members may be on a per capita, number, financial interest, class, group or any other basis.

(c) A limited liability company agreement may set forth provisions relating to notice of the time, place or purpose of any meeting at which any matter is to be voted on by any members, waiver of any such notice, action by consent without a meeting, the establishment of a record date, quorum requirements, voting in person or by proxy, or any other matter with respect to the exercise of any such right to vote.

(d) Unless otherwise provided in a limited liability company agreement, meetings of members may be held by means of conference telephone or other communications equipment by means of which all persons participating in the meeting can hear each other, and participation in a meeting pursuant to this subsection shall constitute presence in person at the meeting. Unless otherwise provided in a limited liability company agreement, on any matter that is to be voted on, consented to or approved by members, the members may take such action without a meeting, without prior notice and without a vote if consented to or approved, in writing, by electronic transmission or by any other means permitted by law, by members having not less than the minimum number of votes that would be necessary to authorize or take such action at a meeting at which all members entitled to vote thereon were present and voted. Unless otherwise provided in a limited liability company agreement, if a person (whether or not then a member) consenting as a member to any matter provides that such consent will be effective at a future time (including a time determined upon the happening of an event), then such person shall be deemed to have consented as a member at such future time so long as such person is then a member. Unless otherwise provided in a limited liability company agreement, on any matter that is to be voted on by members, the members may vote in person or by proxy, and such proxy may be granted in writing, by means of electronic transmission or as otherwise permitted by applicable law. Unless otherwise provided in a limited liability company agreement, a consent transmitted by electronic transmission by a member or by a person or persons authorized to act for a member shall be deemed to be written and signed for purposes of this subsection. For purposes of this subsection, the term "electronic transmission" means any form of communication not directly involving the physical transmission of paper, including the use of, or participation in, 1 or more electronic networks or databases (including 1 or more distributed electronic networks or databases), that creates a record that may be retained, retrieved and reviewed by a recipient thereof and that may be directly reproduced in paper form by such a recipient through an automated process.

(e)   If a limited liability company agreement provides for the manner in which it may be amended, including by requiring the approval of a person who is not a party to the limited liability company agreement or the satisfaction of conditions, it may be amended only in that manner or as otherwise permitted by law, including as permitted by § 18–209(f) of this title (provided that the approval of any person may be waived by such person and that any such conditions may be waived by all persons for whose benefit such conditions were intended). Unless otherwise provided in a limited liability company agreement, a supermajority amendment provision shall only apply to provisions of the limited liability company agreement that are expressly included in the limited liability company agreement. As used in this section, "supermajority amendment provision" means any amendment provision set forth in a limited liability company agreement requiring that an amendment to a provision of the limited liability company agreement be adopted by no less than the vote or consent required to take action under such latter provision.

(f)   If a limited liability company agreement does not provide for the manner in which it may be amended, the limited liability company agreement may be amended with the approval of all of the members or as otherwise permitted by law, including as permitted by § 18–209(f) of this title. This subsection shall only apply to a limited liability company whose original certificate of formation was filed with the Secretary of State on or after January 1, 2012.

§ 18–303.   Liability to 3rd Parties

(a)   Except as otherwise provided by this chapter, the debts, obligations and liabilities of a limited liability company, whether arising in contract, tort or otherwise, shall be solely the debts, obligations and liabilities of the limited liability company, and no member or manager of a limited liability company shall be obligated personally for any such debt, obligation or liability of the limited liability company solely by reason of being a member or acting as a manager of the limited liability company.

(b)   Notwithstanding the provisions of subsection (a) of this section, under a limited liability company agreement or under another agreement, a member or manager may agree to be obligated personally for any or all of the debts, obligations and liabilities of the limited liability company.

§ 18–304. Events of Bankruptcy

A person ceases to be a member of a limited liability company upon the happening of any of the following events:

(1)   Unless otherwise provided in a limited liability company agreement, or with the consent of all members, a member:

a.   Makes an assignment for the benefit of creditors;

b.   Files a voluntary petition in bankruptcy;

c.   Is adjudged a bankrupt or insolvent, or has entered against the member an order for relief, in any bankruptcy or insolvency proceeding;

d.   Files a petition or answer seeking for the member any reorganization, arrangement, composition, readjustment, liquidation, dissolution or similar relief under any statute, law or regulation;

e.   Files an answer or other pleading admitting or failing to contest the material allegations of a petition filed against the member in any proceeding of this nature;

f.   Seeks, consents to or acquiesces in the appointment of a trustee, receiver or liquidator of the member or of all or any substantial part of the member's properties; or

(2)   Unless otherwise provided in a limited liability company agreement, or with the consent of all members, 120 days after the commencement of any proceeding against the member seeking reorganization, arrangement, composition, readjustment, liquidation, dissolution or similar relief under any statute, law or regulation, if the proceeding has not been dismissed, or if within 90 days after the appointment without the member's consent or acquiescence of a trustee, receiver or liquidator of the member or of all or any substantial part of the member's properties, the appointment is not vacated or stayed, or within 90 days after the expiration of any such stay, the appointment is not vacated.

§ 18–305. Access to and Confidentiality of Information; Records

(a)   Each member of a limited liability company, in person or by attorney or other agent, has the right, subject to such reasonable standards (including standards governing what information and documents are to be furnished at what time and location and at whose expense) as may be set forth in a limited liability company agreement or otherwise established by the manager or, if there is no manager, then by the members, to obtain from the limited liability company from time to time upon reasonable demand for any purpose reasonably related to the member's interest as a member of the limited liability company:

(1)   True and full information regarding the status of the business and financial condition of the limited liability company;

(2)   Promptly after becoming available, a copy of the limited liability company's federal, state and local income tax returns for each year;

(3)   A current list of the name and last known business, residence or mailing address of each member and manager;

(4)   A copy of any written limited liability company agreement and certificate of formation and all amendments thereto, together with executed copies of any written powers of attorney pursuant to which the limited liability company agreement and any certificate and all amendments thereto have been executed;

(5)   True and full information regarding the amount of cash and a description and statement of the agreed value of any other property or services contributed by each member and

which each member has agreed to contribute in the future, and the date on which each became a member; and

(6)　Other information regarding the affairs of the limited liability company as is just and reasonable.

(b)　Each manager shall have the right to examine all of the information described in subsection (a) of this section for a purpose reasonably related to the position of manager.

(c)　The manager of a limited liability company shall have the right to keep confidential from the members, for such period of time as the manager deems reasonable, any information which the manager reasonably believes to be in the nature of trade secrets or other information the disclosure of which the manager in good faith believes is not in the best interest of the limited liability company or could damage the limited liability company or its business or which the limited liability company is required by law or by agreement with a 3rd party to keep confidential.

(d)　A limited liability company may maintain its records in other than a written form, including on, by means of, or in the form of any information storage device, method, or 1 or more electronic networks or databases (including 1 or more distributed electronic networks or databases), if such form is capable of conversion into written form within a reasonable time.

(e)　Any demand under this section shall be in writing and shall state the purpose of such demand. In every instance where an attorney or other agent shall be the person who seeks the right to obtain the information described in subsection (a) of this section, the demand shall be accompanied by a power of attorney or such other writing which authorizes the attorney or other agent to so act on behalf of the member.

(f)　Any action to enforce any right arising under this section shall be brought in the Court of Chancery. If the limited liability company refuses to permit a member, or attorney or other agent acting for the member, to obtain or a manager to examine the information described in subsection (a) of this section or does not reply to the demand that has been made within 5 business days (or such shorter or longer period of time as is provided for in a limited liability company agreement but not longer than 30 business days) after the demand has been made, the demanding member or manager may apply to the Court of Chancery for an order to compel such disclosure. The Court of Chancery is hereby vested with exclusive jurisdiction to determine whether or not the person seeking such information is entitled to the information sought. The Court of Chancery may summarily order the limited liability company to permit the demanding member to obtain or manager to examine the information described in subsection (a) of this section and to make copies or abstracts therefrom, or the Court of Chancery may summarily order the limited liability company to furnish to the demanding member or manager the information described in subsection (a) of this section on the condition that the demanding member or manager first pay to the limited liability company the reasonable cost of obtaining and furnishing such information and on such other conditions as the Court of Chancery deems appropriate. When a demanding member seeks to obtain or a manager seeks to examine the information described in subsection (a) of this section, the demanding member or manager shall first establish:

(1)　That the demanding member or manager has complied with the provisions of this section respecting the form and manner of making demand for obtaining or examining of such information, and

(2)　That the information the demanding member or manager seeks is reasonably related to the member's interest as a member or the manager's position as a manager, as the case may be. The Court of Chancery may, in its discretion, prescribe any limitations or conditions with reference to the obtaining or examining of information, or award such other or further relief as the Court of Chancery may deem just and proper. The Court of Chancery may order books, documents and records, pertinent extracts therefrom, or duly authenticated copies thereof, to be brought within the State of Delaware and kept in the State of Delaware upon such terms and conditions as the order may prescribe.

(g)   The rights of a member or manager to obtain information as provided in this section may be restricted in an original limited liability company agreement or in any subsequent amendment approved or adopted by all of the members or in compliance with any applicable requirements of the limited liability company agreement. The provisions of this subsection shall not be construed to limit the ability to impose restrictions on the rights of a member or manager to obtain information by any other means permitted under this chapter.

(h)   A limited liability company shall maintain a current record that identifies the name and last known business, residence or mailing address of each member and manager.

§ 18–306.   Remedies for Breach of Limited Liability Company Agreement by Member

A limited liability company agreement may provide that:

(1)   A member who fails to perform in accordance with, or to comply with the terms and conditions of, the limited liability company agreement shall be subject to specified penalties or specified consequences; and

(2)   At the time or upon the happening of events specified in the limited liability company agreement, a member shall be subject to specified penalties or specified consequences.

Such specified penalties or specified consequences may include and take the form of any penalty or consequence set forth in § 18–502(c) of this title.

SUBCHAPTER IV
MANAGERS

§ 18–401.   Admission of Managers

A person may be named or designated as a manager of the limited liability company as provided in § 18–101(10) of this title.

§ 18–402.   Management of Limited Liability Company

Unless otherwise provided in a limited liability company agreement, the management of a limited liability company shall be vested in its members in proportion to the then current percentage or other interest of members in the profits of the limited liability company owned by all of the members, the decision of members owning more than 50 percent of the said percentage or other interest in the profits controlling; provided however, that if a limited liability company agreement provides for the management, in whole or in part, of a limited liability company by a manager, the management of the limited liability company, to the extent so provided, shall be vested in the manager who shall be chosen in the manner provided in the limited liability company agreement. The manager shall also hold the offices and have the responsibilities accorded to the manager by or in the manner provided in a limited liability company agreement. Subject to § 18–602 of this title, a manager shall cease to be a manager as provided in a limited liability company agreement. A limited liability company may have more than 1 manager. Unless otherwise provided in a limited liability company agreement, each member and manager has the authority to bind the limited liability company.

§ 18–403.   Contributions by a Manager

A manager of a limited liability company may make contributions to the limited liability company and share in the profits and losses of, and in distributions from, the limited liability company as a member. A person who is both a manager and a member has the rights and powers, and is subject to the restrictions and liabilities, of a manager and, except as provided in a limited liability company agreement, also has the rights and powers, and is subject to the restrictions and liabilities, of a member to the extent of the manager's participation in the limited liability company as a member.

§ 18–404.   Classes and Voting

(a)   A limited liability company agreement may provide for classes or groups of managers having such relative rights, powers and duties as the limited liability company agreement may provide, and may make provision for the future creation in the manner provided in the limited liability company agreement of additional classes or groups of managers having such relative rights, powers and duties as may from time to time be established, including rights, powers and duties senior to existing classes and groups of managers. A limited liability company agreement may provide for the taking of an action, including the amendment of the limited liability company agreement, without the vote or approval of any manager or class or group of managers, including an action to create under the provisions of the limited liability company agreement a class or group of limited liability company interests that was not previously outstanding.

(b)   A limited liability company agreement may grant to all or certain identified managers or a specified class or group of the managers the right to vote, separately or with all or any class or group of managers or members, on any matter. Voting by managers may be on a per capita, number, financial interest, class, group or any other basis.

(c)   A limited liability company agreement may set forth provisions relating to notice of the time, place or purpose of any meeting at which any matter is to be voted on by any manager or class or group of managers, waiver of any such notice, action by consent without a meeting, the establishment of a record date, quorum requirements, voting in person or by proxy, or any other matter with respect to the exercise of any such right to vote.

(d)   Unless otherwise provided in a limited liability company agreement, meetings of managers may be held by means of conference telephone or other communications equipment by means of which all persons participating in the meeting can hear each other, and participation in a meeting pursuant to this subsection shall constitute presence in person at the meeting. Unless otherwise provided in a limited liability company agreement, on any matter that is to be voted on, consented to or approved by managers, the managers may take such action without a meeting, without prior notice and without a vote if consented to or approved, in writing, by electronic transmission or by any other means permitted by law, by managers having not less than the minimum number of votes that would be necessary to authorize or take such action at a meeting at which all managers entitled to vote thereon were present and voted. Unless otherwise provided in a limited liability company agreement, if a person (whether or not then a manager) consenting as a manager to any matter provides that such consent will be effective at a future time (including a time determined upon the happening of an event), then such person shall be deemed to have consented as a manager at such future time so long as such person is then a manager. Unless otherwise provided in a limited liability company agreement, on any matter that is to be voted on by managers, the managers may vote in person or by proxy, and such proxy may be granted in writing, by means of electronic transmission or as otherwise permitted by applicable law. Unless otherwise provided in a limited liability company agreement, a consent transmitted by electronic transmission by a manager or by a person or persons authorized to act for a manager shall be deemed to be written and signed for purposes of this subsection. For purposes of this subsection, the term "electronic transmission" means any form of communication not directly involving the physical transmission of paper, including the use of, or participation in, 1 or more electronic networks or databases (including 1 or more distributed electronic networks or databases), that creates a record that may be retained, retrieved and reviewed by a recipient thereof and that may be directly reproduced in paper form by such a recipient through an automated process.

§ 18–405. Remedies for Breach of Limited Liability Company Agreement by Manager

A limited liability company agreement may provide that:

(1) A manager who fails to perform in accordance with, or to comply with the terms and conditions of, the limited liability company agreement shall be subject to specified penalties or specified consequences; and

(2) At the time or upon the happening of events specified in the limited liability company agreement, a manager shall be subject to specified penalties or specified consequences.

§ 18–406. Reliance on Reports and Information by Member or Manager

A member, manager or liquidating trustee of a limited liability company shall be fully protected in relying in good faith upon the records of the limited liability company and upon information, opinions, reports or statements presented by another manager, member or liquidating trustee, an officer or employee of the limited liability company, or committees of the limited liability company, members or managers, or by any other person as to matters the member, manager or liquidating trustees reasonably believes are within such other person's professional or expert competence including information, opinions, reports or statements as to the value and amount of the assets, liabilities, profits or losses of the limited liability company, or the value and amount of assets or reserves or contracts, agreements or other undertakings that would be sufficient to pay claims and obligations of the limited liability company or to make reasonable provision to pay such claims and obligations, or any other facts pertinent to the existence and amount of assets from which distributions to members or creditors might properly be paid.

§ 18–407. Delegation of Rights and Powers to Manage

Unless otherwise provided in the limited liability company agreement, a member or manager of a limited liability company has the power and authority to delegate to 1 or more other persons any or all of the member's or manager's, as the case may be, rights, powers and duties to manage and control the business and affairs of the limited liability company. Any such delegation may be to agents, officers and employees of a member or manager or the limited liability company, and by a management agreement or another agreement with, or otherwise to, other persons. Unless otherwise provided in the limited liability company agreement, such delegation by a member or manager shall be irrevocable if it states that it is irrevocable. Unless otherwise provided in the limited liability company agreement, such delegation by a member or manager of a limited liability company shall not cause the member or manager to cease to be a member or manager, as the case may be, of the limited liability company or cause the person to whom any such rights, powers and duties have been delegated to be a member or manager, as the case may be, of the limited liability company. No other provision of this chapter shall be construed to restrict a member's or manager's power and authority to delegate any or all of its rights, powers and duties to manage and control the business and affairs of the limited liability company.

SUBCHAPTER V
FINANCE

§ 18–501. Form of Contribution

The contribution of a member to a limited liability company may be in cash, property or services rendered, or a promissory note or other obligation to contribute cash or property or to perform services.

§ 18–502.   Liability for Contribution

(a)   Except as provided in a limited liability company agreement, a member is obligated to a limited liability company to perform any promise to contribute cash or property or to perform services, even if the member is unable to perform because of death, disability or any other reason. If a member does not make the required contribution of property or services, the member is obligated at the option of the limited liability company to contribute cash equal to that portion of the agreed value (as stated in the records of the limited liability company) of the contribution that has not been made. The foregoing option shall be in addition to, and not in lieu of, any other rights, including the right to specific performance, that the limited liability company may have against such member under the limited liability company agreement or applicable law.

(b)   Unless otherwise provided in a limited liability company agreement, the obligation of a member to make a contribution or return money or other property paid or distributed in violation of this chapter may be compromised only by consent of all the members. Notwithstanding the compromise, a creditor of a limited liability company who extends credit, after the entering into of a limited liability company agreement or an amendment thereto which, in either case, reflects the obligation, and before the amendment thereof to reflect the compromise, may enforce the original obligation to the extent that, in extending credit, the creditor reasonably relied on the obligation of a member to make a contribution or return. A conditional obligation of a member to make a contribution or return money or other property to a limited liability company may not be enforced unless the conditions of the obligation have been satisfied or waived as to or by such member. Conditional obligations include contributions payable upon a discretionary call of a limited liability company prior to the time the call occurs.

(c)   A limited liability company agreement may provide that the interest of any member who fails to make any contribution that the member is obligated to make shall be subject to specified penalties for, or specified consequences of, such failure. Such penalty or consequence may take the form of reducing or eliminating the defaulting member's proportionate interest in a limited liability company, subordinating the member's limited liability company interest to that of nondefaulting members, a forced sale of that limited liability company interest, forfeiture of the defaulting member's limited liability company interest, the lending by other members of the amount necessary to meet the defaulting member's commitment, a fixing of the value of the defaulting member's limited liability company interest by appraisal or by formula and redemption or sale of the limited liability company interest at such value, or other penalty or consequence.

§ 18–503.   Allocation of Profits and Losses

The profits and losses of a limited liability company shall be allocated among the members, and among classes or groups of members, in the manner provided in a limited liability company agreement. If the limited liability company agreement does not so provide, profits and losses shall be allocated on the basis of the agreed value (as stated in the records of the limited liability company) of the contributions made by each member to the extent they have been received by the limited liability company and have not been returned.

§ 18–504.   Allocation of Distributions

Distributions of cash or other assets of a limited liability company shall be allocated among the members, and among classes or groups of members, in the manner provided in a limited liability company agreement. If the limited liability company agreement does not so provide, distributions shall be made on the basis of the agreed value (as stated in the records of the limited liability company) of the contributions made by each member to the extent they have been received by the limited liability company and have not been returned.

§ 18–505. Defense of Usury Not Available

No obligation of a member or manager of a limited liability company to the limited liability company, or to a member or manager of the limited liability company, arising under the limited liability company agreement or a separate agreement or writing, and no note, instrument or other writing evidencing any such obligation of a member or manager, shall be subject to the defense of usury, and no member or manager shall interpose the defense of usury with respect to any such obligation in any action.

SUBCHAPTER VI
DISTRIBUTIONS AND RESIGNATION

§ 18–601. Interim Distributions

Except as provided in this subchapter, to the extent and at the times or upon the happening of the events specified in a limited liability company agreement, a member is entitled to receive from a limited liability company distributions before the member's resignation from the limited liability company and before the dissolution and winding up thereof.

§ 18–602. Resignation of Manager

A manager may resign as a manager of a limited liability company at the time or upon the happening of events specified in a limited liability company agreement and in accordance with the limited liability company agreement. A limited liability company agreement may provide that a manager shall not have the right to resign as a manager of a limited liability company. Notwithstanding that a limited liability company agreement provides that a manager does not have the right to resign as a manager of a limited liability company, a manager may resign as a manager of a limited liability company at any time by giving written notice to the members and other managers. If the resignation of a manager violates a limited liability company agreement, in addition to any remedies otherwise available under applicable law, a limited liability company may recover from the resigning manager damages for breach of the limited liability company agreement and offset the damages against the amount otherwise distributable to the resigning manager.

§ 18–603. Resignation of Member

A member may resign from a limited liability company only at the time or upon the happening of events specified in a limited liability company agreement and in accordance with the limited liability company agreement. Notwithstanding anything to the contrary under applicable law, unless a limited liability company agreement provides otherwise, a member may not resign from a limited liability company prior to the dissolution and winding up of the limited liability company. Notwithstanding anything to the contrary under applicable law, a limited liability company agreement may provide that a limited liability company interest may not be assigned prior to the dissolution and winding up of the limited liability company.

Unless otherwise provided in a limited liability company agreement, a limited liability company whose original certificate of formation was filed with the Secretary of State and effective on or prior to July 31, 1996, shall continue to be governed by this section as in effect on July 31, 1996.

§ 18–604. Distribution Upon Resignation

Except as provided in this subchapter, upon resignation any resigning member is entitled to receive any distribution to which such member is entitled under a limited liability company agreement and, if not otherwise provided in a limited liability company agreement, such member is entitled to receive, within a reasonable time after resignation, the fair value of such member's limited liability company interest as of the date of resignation based upon such member's right to share in distributions from the limited liability company.

227

§ 18–605.   Distribution in Kind

Except as provided in a limited liability company agreement, a member, regardless of the nature of the member's contribution, has no right to demand and receive any distribution from a limited liability company in any form other than cash. Except as provided in a limited liability company agreement, a member may not be compelled to accept a distribution of any asset in kind from a limited liability company to the extent that the percentage of the asset distributed exceeds a percentage of that asset which is equal to the percentage in which the member shares in distributions from the limited liability company. Except as provided in the limited liability company agreement, a member may be compelled to accept a distribution of any asset in kind from a limited liability company to the extent that the percentage of the asset distributed is equal to a percentage of that asset which is equal to the percentage in which the member shares in distributions from the limited liability company.

§ 18–606.   Right to Distribution

Subject to §§ 18–607 and 18–804 of this title, and unless otherwise provided in a limited liability company agreement, at the time a member becomes entitled to receive a distribution, the member has the status of, and is entitled to all remedies available to, a creditor of a limited liability company with respect to the distribution. A limited liability company agreement may provide for the establishment of a record date with respect to allocations and distributions by a limited liability company.

§ 18–607.   Limitations on Distribution

(a)   A limited liability company shall not make a distribution to a member to the extent that at the time of the distribution, after giving effect to the distribution, all liabilities of the limited liability company, other than liabilities to members on account of their limited liability company interests and liabilities for which the recourse of creditors is limited to specified property of the limited liability company, exceed the fair value of the assets of the limited liability company, except that the fair value of property that is subject to a liability for which the recourse of creditors is limited shall be included in the assets of the limited liability company only to the extent that the fair value of that property exceeds that liability. For purposes of this subsection (a), the term "distribution" shall not include amounts constituting reasonable compensation for present or past services or reasonable payments made in the ordinary course of business pursuant to a bona fide retirement plan or other benefits program.

(b)   A member who receives a distribution in violation of subsection (a) of this section, and who knew at the time of the distribution that the distribution violated subsection (a) of this section, shall be liable to a limited liability company for the amount of the distribution. A member who receives a distribution in violation of subsection (a) of this section, and who did not know at the time of the distribution that the distribution violated subsection (a) of this section, shall not be liable for the amount of the distribution. Subject to subsection (c) of this section, this subsection shall not affect any obligation or liability of a member under an agreement or other applicable law for the amount of a distribution.

(c)   Unless otherwise agreed, a member who receives a distribution from a limited liability company shall have no liability under this chapter or other applicable law for the amount of the distribution after the expiration of 3 years from the date of the distribution unless an action to recover the distribution from such member is commenced prior to the expiration of the said 3-year period and an adjudication of liability against such member is made in the said action.

SUBCHAPTER VII
ASSIGNMENT OF LIMITED LIABILITY COMPANY INTERESTS

§ 18–701.   Nature of Limited Liability Company Interest

A limited liability company interest is personal property. A member has no interest in specific limited liability company property.

§ 18–702.   Assignment of Limited Liability Company Interest

(a)   A limited liability company interest is assignable in whole or in part except as provided in a limited liability company agreement. The assignee of a member's limited liability company interest shall have no right to participate in the management of the business and affairs of a limited liability company except as provided in a limited liability company agreement or, unless otherwise provided in the limited liability company agreement, upon the vote or consent of all of the members of the limited liability company.

(b)   Unless otherwise provided in a limited liability company agreement:

(1)   An assignment of a limited liability company interest does not entitle the assignee to become or to exercise any rights or powers of a member;

(2)   An assignment of a limited liability company interest entitles the assignee to share in such profits and losses, to receive such distribution or distributions, and to receive such allocation of income, gain, loss, deduction, or credit or similar item to which the assignor was entitled, to the extent assigned; and

(3)   A member ceases to be a member and to have the power to exercise any rights or powers of a member upon assignment of all of the member's limited liability company interest. Unless otherwise provided in a limited liability company agreement, the pledge of, or granting of a security interest, lien or other encumbrance in or against, any or all of the limited liability company interest of a member shall not cause the member to cease to be a member or to have the power to exercise any rights or powers of a member.

(c)   Unless otherwise provided in a limited liability company agreement, a member's interest in a limited liability company may be evidenced by a certificate of limited liability company interest issued by the limited liability company. A limited liability company agreement may provide for the assignment or transfer of any limited liability company interest represented by such a certificate and make other provisions with respect to such certificates. A limited liability company shall not have the power to issue a certificate of limited liability company interest in bearer form.

(d)   Unless otherwise provided in a limited liability company agreement and except to the extent assumed by agreement, until an assignee of a limited liability company interest becomes a member, the assignee shall have no liability as a member solely as a result of the assignment.

(e)   Unless otherwise provided in the limited liability company agreement, a limited liability company may acquire, by purchase, redemption or otherwise, any limited liability company interest or other interest of a member or manager in the limited liability company. Unless otherwise provided in the limited liability company agreement, any such interest so acquired by the limited liability company shall be deemed canceled.

§ 18–703.   Member's Limited Liability Company Interest Subject to Charging Order

(a)   On application by a judgment creditor of a member or of a member's assignee, a court having jurisdiction may charge the limited liability company interest of the judgment debtor to satisfy the judgment. To the extent so charged, the judgment creditor has only the right to receive any distribution or distributions to which the judgment debtor would otherwise have been entitled in respect of such limited liability company interest.

(b)　A charging order constitutes a lien on the judgment debtor's limited liability company interest.

(c)　This chapter does not deprive a member or member's assignee of a right under exemption laws with respect to the judgment debtor's limited liability company interest.

(d)　The entry of a charging order is the exclusive remedy by which a judgment creditor of a member or a member's assignee may satisfy a judgment out of the judgment debtor's limited liability company interest and attachment, garnishment, foreclosure or other legal or equitable remedies are not available to the judgment creditor, whether the limited liability company has 1 member or more than 1 member.

(e)　No creditor of a member or of a member's assignee shall have any right to obtain possession of, or otherwise exercise legal or equitable remedies with respect to, the property of the limited liability company.

(f)　The Court of Chancery shall have jurisdiction to hear and determine any matter relating to any such charging order.

§ 18–704.　Right of Assignee to Become Member

(a)　An assignee of a limited liability company interest may become a member:

(1)　As provided in the limited liability company agreement; or

(2)　Unless otherwise provided in the limited liability company agreement, upon the vote or consent of all of the members of the limited liability company.

(3) Unless otherwise provided in the limited liability company agreement by a specific reference to this subsection or otherwise provided in connection with the assignment, upon the voluntary assignment by the sole member of the limited liability company of all of the limited liability company interests in the limited liability company to a single assignee. An assignment will be voluntary for purposes of this subsection if it is consented to by the member at the time of the assignment and is not effected by foreclosure or other similar legal process.

(b)　An assignee who has become a member has, to the extent assigned, the rights and powers, and is subject to the restrictions and liabilities, of a member under a limited liability company agreement and this chapter. Notwithstanding the foregoing, unless otherwise provided in a limited liability company agreement, an assignee who becomes a member is liable for the obligations of the assignor to make contributions as provided in § 18–502 of this title, but shall not be liable for the obligations of the assignor under subchapter VI of this chapter. However, the assignee is not obligated for liabilities, including the obligations of the assignor to make contributions as provided in § 18–502 of this title, unknown to the assignee at the time the assignee became a member and which could not be ascertained from a limited liability company agreement.

(c)　Whether or not an assignee of a limited liability company interest becomes a member, the assignor is not released from liability to a limited liability company under subchapters V and VI of this chapter.

§ 18–705.　Powers of Estate of Deceased or Incompetent Member

If a member who is an individual dies or a court of competent jurisdiction adjudges the member to be incompetent to manage the member's person or property, the member's personal representative may exercise all of the member's rights for the purpose of settling the member's estate or administering the member's property, including any power under a limited liability company agreement of an assignee to become a member. If a member is a corporation, trust or other entity and is dissolved or terminated, the powers of that member may be exercised by its personal representative.

SUBCHAPTER VIII
DISSOLUTION

§ 18–801. Dissolution

(a) A limited liability company is dissolved and its affairs shall be wound up upon the first to occur of the following:

(1) At the time specified in a limited liability company agreement, but if no such time is set forth in the limited liability company agreement, then the limited liability company shall have a perpetual existence;

(2) Upon the happening of events specified in a limited liability company agreement;

(3) Unless otherwise provided in a limited liability company agreement, upon the vote or consent members who own more than 2/3 of the then-current percentage or other interest in the profits of the limited liability company owned by all of the members;

(4) At any time there are no members; provided, that the limited liability company is not dissolved and is not required to be wound up if:

a. Unless otherwise provided in a limited liability company agreement, within 90 days or such other period as is provided for in the limited liability company agreement after the occurrence of the event that terminated the continued membership of the last remaining member, the personal representative of the last remaining member agrees to continue the limited liability company and to the admission of the personal representative of such member or its nominee or designee to the limited liability company as a member, effective as of the occurrence of the event that terminated the continued membership of the last remaining member; provided, that a limited liability company agreement may provide that the personal representative of the last remaining member shall be obligated to agree to continue the limited liability company and to the admission of the personal representative of such member or its nominee or designee to the limited liability company as a member, effective as of the occurrence of the event that terminated the continued membership of the last remaining member, or

b. A member is admitted to the limited liability company in the manner provided for in the limited liability company agreement, effective as of the occurrence of the event that terminated the continued membership of the last remaining member, within 90 days or such other period as is provided for in the limited liability company agreement after the occurrence of the event that terminated the continued membership of the last remaining member, pursuant to a provision of the limited liability company agreement that specifically provides for the admission of a member to the limited liability company after there is no longer a remaining member of the limited liability company.

(5) The entry of a decree of judicial dissolution under § 18–802 of this title.

Unless otherwise provided in a limited liability company agreement, a limited liability company whose original certificate of formation was filed with the Secretary of State and effective on or prior to July 31, 2015, shall continue to be governed by paragraph (a)(3) of this section as in effect on July 31, 2015.

(b) Unless otherwise provided in a limited liability company agreement, the death, retirement, resignation, expulsion, bankruptcy or dissolution of any member or the occurrence of any other event that terminates the continued membership of any member shall not cause the limited liability company to be dissolved or its affairs to be wound up, and upon the occurrence of any such event, the limited liability company shall be continued without dissolution.

§ 18–802. Judicial Dissolution

On application by or for a member or manager the Court of Chancery may decree dissolution of a limited liability company whenever it is not reasonably practicable to carry on the business in conformity with a limited liability company agreement.

§ 18–803. Winding Up

(a)   Unless otherwise provided in a limited liability company agreement, a manager who has not wrongfully dissolved a limited liability company or, if none, the members or a person approved by the members, in either case, by members who own more than 50 percent of the then current percentage or other interest in the profits of the limited liability company owned by all of the members, may wind up the limited liability company's affairs; but the Court of Chancery, upon cause shown, may wind up the limited liability company's affairs upon application of any member or manager, or the member's personal representative or assignee, and in connection therewith, may appoint a liquidating trustee. Unless otherwise provided in a limited liability company agreement, a limited liability company whose original certificate of formation was filed with the Secretary of State and effective on or prior to July 31, 2015, shall continue to be governed by this subsection as in effect on July 31, 2015.

(b)   Upon dissolution of a limited liability company and until the filing of a certificate of cancellation as provided in § 18–203 of this title, the persons winding up the limited liability company's affairs may, in the name of, and for and on behalf of, the limited liability company, prosecute and defend suits, whether civil, criminal or administrative, gradually settle and close the limited liability company's business, dispose of and convey the limited liability company's property, discharge or make reasonable provision for the limited liability company's liabilities, and distribute to the members any remaining assets of the limited liability company, all without affecting the liability of members and managers and without imposing liability on a liquidating trustee.

§ 18–804. Distribution of Assets

(a)   Upon the winding up of a limited liability company, the assets shall be distributed as follows:

(1)   To creditors, including members and managers who are creditors, to the extent otherwise permitted by law, in satisfaction of liabilities of the limited liability company (whether by payment or the making of reasonable provision for payment thereof) other than liabilities for which reasonable provision for payment has been made and liabilities for distributions to members and former members under § 18–601 or § 18–604 of this title;

(2)   Unless otherwise provided in a limited liability company agreement, to members and former members in satisfaction of liabilities for distributions under § 18–601 or § 18–604 of this title; and

(3)   Unless otherwise provided in a limited liability company agreement, to members first for the return of their contributions and second respecting their limited liability company interests, in the proportions in which the members share in distributions.

(b)   A limited liability company which has dissolved:

(1)   Shall pay or make reasonable provision to pay all claims and obligations, including all contingent, conditional or unmatured contractual claims, known to the limited liability company;

(2)   Shall make such provision as will be reasonably likely to be sufficient to provide compensation for any claim against the limited liability company which is the subject of a pending action, suit or proceeding to which the limited liability company is a party; and

(3)   Shall make such provision as will be reasonably likely to be sufficient to provide compensation for claims that have not been made known to the limited liability company or that have not arisen but that, based on facts known to the limited liability company, are likely to arise or to become known to the limited liability company within 10 years after the date of dissolution.

If there are sufficient assets, such claims and obligations shall be paid in full and any such provision for payment made shall be made in full. If there are insufficient assets, such claims and obligations shall be paid or provided for according to their priority and, among claims of equal priority, ratably to the extent of assets available therefor. Unless otherwise provided in the limited liability company agreement, any remaining assets shall be distributed as provided in this chapter. Any liquidating trustee winding up a limited liability company's affairs who has complied with this section shall not be personally liable to the claimants of the dissolved limited liability company by reason of such person's actions in winding up the limited liability company.

(c) A member who receives a distribution in violation of subsection (a) of this section, and who knew at the time of the distribution that the distribution violated subsection (a) of this section, shall be liable to the limited liability company for the amount of the distribution. For purposes of the immediately preceding sentence, the term "distribution" shall not include amounts constituting reasonable compensation for present or past services or reasonable payments made in the ordinary course of business pursuant to a bona fide retirement plan or other benefits program. A member who receives a distribution in violation of subsection (a) of this section, and who did not know at the time of the distribution that the distribution violated subsection (a) of this section, shall not be liable for the amount of the distribution. Subject to subsection (d) of this section, this subsection shall not affect any obligation or liability of a member under an agreement or other applicable law for the amount of a distribution.

(d) Unless otherwise agreed, a member who receives a distribution from a limited liability company to which this section applies shall have no liability under this chapter or other applicable law for the amount of the distribution after the expiration of 3 years from the date of the distribution unless an action to recover the distribution from such member is commenced prior to the expiration of the said 3-year period and an adjudication of liability against such member is made in the said action.

(e) Section 18–607 of this title shall not apply to a distribution to which this section applies.

§ 18–805. Trustees or Receivers for Limited Liability Companies; Appointment; Powers; Duties

When the certificate of formation of any limited liability company formed under this chapter shall be canceled by the filing of a certificate of cancellation pursuant to § 18–203 of this title, the Court of Chancery, on application of any creditor, member or manager of the limited liability company, or any other person who shows good cause therefor, at any time, may either appoint 1 or more of the managers of the limited liability company to be trustees, or appoint 1 or more persons to be receivers, of and for the limited liability company, to take charge of the limited liability company's property, and to collect the debts and property due and belonging to the limited liability company, with the power to prosecute and defend, in the name of the limited liability company, or otherwise, all such suits as may be necessary or proper for the purposes aforesaid, and to appoint an agent or agents under them, and to do all other acts which might be done by the limited liability company, if in being, that may be necessary for the final settlement of the unfinished business of the limited liability company. The powers of the trustees or receivers may be continued as long as the Court of Chancery shall think necessary for the purposes aforesaid.

§ 18–806. Revocation of Dissolution

If a limited liability company agreement provides the manner in which a dissolution may be revoked, it may be revoked in that manner and, unless a limited liability company agreement prohibits revocation of dissolution, then notwithstanding the occurrence of an event set forth in § 18–801(a)(1), (2), (3) or (4) of this title, the limited liability company shall not be dissolved and its affairs shall not be wound up if, prior to the filing of a certificate of cancellation in the office of the Secretary of State, the limited liability company is continued, effective as of the occurrence of such event:

(1)　In the case of dissolution effected by the vote or consent of the members or other persons, pursuant to such vote or consent (and the approval of any members or other persons whose approval is required under the limited liability company agreement to revoke a dissolution contemplated by this paragraph);

(2)　In the case of dissolution under § 18–801(a)(1) or (2) of this title (other than a dissolution effected by the vote or consent of the members or other persons or the occurrence of an event that causes the last remaining member to cease to be a member), pursuant to such vote or consent that, pursuant to the terms of the limited liability company agreement, is required to amend the provision of the limited liability company agreement effecting such dissolution (and the approval of any members or other persons whose approval is required under the limited liability company agreement to revoke a dissolution contemplated by this paragraph); and

(3)　In the case of dissolution effected by the occurrence of an event that causes the last remaining member to cease to be a member, pursuant to the vote or consent of the personal representative of the last remaining member of the limited liability company or the assignee of all of the limited liability company interests in the limited liability company (and the approval of any other persons whose approval is required under the limited liability company agreement to revoke a dissolution contemplated by this paragraph).

If there is no remaining member of the limited liability company and the personal representative of the last remaining member or the assignee of all of the limited liability company interests in the limited liability company votes in favor of or consents to the continuation of the limited liability company, such personal representative or such assignee, as applicable, shall be required to agree to the admission of a nominee or designee as a member, effective as of the occurrence of the event that terminated the continued membership of the last remaining member. The provisions of this section shall not be construed to limit the accomplishment of a revocation of dissolution by other means permitted by law.

SUBCHAPTER IX
FOREIGN LIMITED LIABILITY COMPANIES

§ 18–901.　Law Governing

(a)　Subject to the Constitution of the State of Delaware:

(1)　The laws of the state, territory, possession, or other jurisdiction or country under which a foreign limited liability company is organized govern its organization and internal affairs and the liability of its members and managers; and

(2)　A foreign limited liability company may not be denied registration by reason of any difference between those laws and the laws of the State of Delaware.

(b)　A foreign limited liability company shall be subject to § 18–106 of this title.

§ 18–902.　Registration Required; Application

Before doing business in the State of Delaware, a foreign limited liability company shall register with the Secretary of State. In order to register, a foreign limited liability company shall submit to the Secretary of State:

(1)　A copy executed by an authorized person of an application for registration as a foreign limited liability company, setting forth:

a.　The name of the foreign limited liability company and, if different, the name under which it proposes to register and do business in the State of Delaware;

b.　The state, territory, possession or other jurisdiction or country where formed, the date of its formation and a statement from an authorized person that, as of the date of filing, the foreign limited liability company validly exists as a limited liability company under the laws of the jurisdiction of its formation;

        c.   The nature of the business or purposes to be conducted or promoted in the State of Delaware;

        d.   The address of the registered office and the name and address of the registered agent for service of process required to be maintained by § 18–904(b) of this title;

        e.   A statement that the Secretary of State is appointed the agent of the foreign limited liability company for service of process under the circumstances set forth in § 18–910(b) of this title; and

        f.   The date on which the foreign limited liability company first did, or intends to do, business in the State of Delaware.

    (2)   A certificate, as of a date not earlier than 6 months prior to the filing date, issued by an authorized officer of the jurisdiction of its formation evidencing its existence. If such certificate is in a foreign language, a translation thereof, under oath of the translator, shall be attached thereto.

    (3)   A fee as set forth in § 18–1105(a)(6) of this title shall be paid.

§ 18–903. Issuance of Registration

    (a)   If the Secretary of State finds that an application for registration conforms to law and all requisite fees have been paid, the Secretary shall:

    (1)   Certify that the application has been filed by endorsing upon the original application the word "Filed", and the date and hour of the filing. This endorsement is conclusive of the date and time of its filing in the absence of actual fraud;

    (2)   File and index the endorsed application.

    (b)   The Secretary of State shall prepare and return to the person who filed the application or the person's representative a copy of the original signed application, similarly endorsed, and shall certify such copy as a true copy of the original signed application.

    (c)   The filing of the application with the Secretary of State shall make it unnecessary to file any other documents under Chapter 31 of this title.

§ 18–904. Name; Registered Office; Registered Agent

    (a)   A foreign limited liability company may register with the Secretary of State under any name (whether or not it is the name under which it is registered in the jurisdiction of its formation) that includes the words "Limited Liability Company" or the abbreviation "L.L.C." or the designation "LLC" and that could be registered by a domestic limited liability company; provided however, that a foreign limited liability company may register under any name which is not such as to distinguish it upon the records in the office of the Secretary of State from the name on such records of any domestic or foreign corporation, partnership, statutory trust, limited liability company or limited partnership reserved, registered, formed or organized under the laws of the State of Delaware with the written consent of the other corporation, partnership, statutory trust, limited liability company or limited partnership, which written consent shall be filed with the Secretary of State.

    (b)   Each foreign limited liability company shall have and maintain in the State of Delaware:

    (1)   A registered office which may but need not be a place of its business in the State of Delaware; and

    (2)   A registered agent for service of process on the foreign limited liability company, having a business office identical with such registered office, which agent may be any of:

    a.   An individual resident in the State of Delaware,

    b.   A domestic limited liability company, a domestic corporation, a domestic partnership (whether general (including a limited liability partnership) or limited (including a limited liability limited partnership)) or a domestic statutory trust, or

    c.   A foreign corporation, a foreign partnership (whether general (including a limited liability partnership) or limited (including a limited liability limited partnership)), a foreign limited liability company (other than the foreign limited liability company itself), or a foreign statutory trust.

    (c)   A registered agent may change the address of the registered office of the foreign limited liability company or companies for which the agent is registered agent to another address in the State of Delaware by paying a fee as set forth in § 18–1105(a)(7) of this title and filing with the Secretary of State a certificate, executed by such registered agent, setting forth the address at which such registered agent has maintained the registered office for each of the foreign limited liability companies for which it is a registered agent, and further certifying to the new address to which each such registered office will be changed on a given day, and at which new address such registered agent will thereafter maintain the registered office for each of the foreign limited liability companies for which it is registered agent. Upon the filing of such certificate, the Secretary of State shall furnish to the registered agent a certified copy of the same under the Secretary's hand and seal of office, and thereafter, or until further change of address, as authorized by law, the registered office in the State of Delaware of each of the foreign limited liability companies for which the agent is a registered agent shall be located at the new address of the registered agent thereof as given in the certificate. In the event of a change of name of any person acting as a registered agent of a foreign limited liability company, such registered agent shall file with the Secretary of State a certificate, executed by such registered agent, setting forth the new name of such registered agent, the name of such registered agent before it was changed and the address at which such registered agent has maintained the registered office for each of the foreign limited liability companies for which it is registered agent, and shall pay a fee as set forth in § 18–1105(a)(7) of this title. Upon the filing of such certificate, the Secretary of State shall furnish to the registered agent a certified copy of the same under the Secretary of State's own hand and seal of office. A change of name of any person acting as a registered agent of a foreign limited liability company as a result of the merger or consolidation of the registered agent, with or into another person which succeeds to its assets and liabilities by operation of law, shall be deemed a change of name for purposes of this section. Filing a certificate under this section shall be deemed to be an amendment of the application of each foreign limited liability company affected thereby and each such foreign limited liability company shall not be required to take any further action with respect thereto, to amend its application under § 18–905 of this title. Any registered agent filing a certificate under this section shall promptly, upon such filing, deliver a copy of any such certificate to each foreign limited liability company affected thereby.

    (d)   The registered agent of 1 or more foreign limited liability companies may resign and appoint a successor registered agent by paying a fee as set forth in § 18–1105(a)(7) of this title and filing a certificate with the Secretary of State, stating that it resigns and the name and address of the successor registered agent. There shall be attached to such certificate a statement of each affected foreign limited liability company ratifying and approving such change of registered agent. Upon such filing, the successor registered agent shall become the registered agent of such foreign limited liability companies as have ratified and approved such substitution and the successor registered agent's address, as stated in such certificate, shall become the address of each such foreign limited liability company's registered office in the State of Delaware. The Secretary of State shall then issue a certificate that the successor registered agent has become the registered agent of the foreign limited liability companies so ratifying and approving such change and setting out the names of such foreign limited liability companies. Filing of such certificate of resignation shall be deemed to be an amendment of the application of each foreign limited liability company affected thereby and each such foreign limited liability company shall not be required to take any further action with respect thereto to amend its application under § 18–905 of this title.

(e)   The registered agent of 1 or more foreign limited liability companies may resign without appointing a successor registered agent by paying a fee as set forth in § 18–1105(a)(7) of this title and filing a certificate of resignation with the Secretary of State, but such resignation shall not become effective until 30 days after the certificate is filed. The certificate shall contain a statement that written notice of resignation was given to each affected foreign limited liability company at least 30 days prior to the filing of the certificate by mailing or delivering such notice to the foreign limited liability company at its address last known to the registered agent and shall set forth the date of such notice. After receipt of the notice of the resignation of its registered agent, the foreign limited liability company for which such registered agent was acting shall obtain and designate a new registered agent to take the place of the registered agent so resigning. If such foreign limited liability company fails to obtain and designate a new registered agent as aforesaid prior to the expiration of the period of 30 days after the filing by the registered agent of the certificate of resignation, such foreign limited liability company shall not be permitted to do business in the State of Delaware and its registration shall be canceled. After the resignation of the registered agent shall have become effective as provided in this section and if no new registered agent shall have been obtained and designated in the time and manner aforesaid, service of legal process against each foreign limited liability company for which the resigned registered agent had been acting shall thereafter be upon the Secretary of State in accordance with § 18–911 of this title.

§ 18–905.   Amendments to Application

If any statement in the application for registration of a foreign limited liability company was false when made or any arrangements or other facts described have changed, making the application false in any respect, the foreign limited liability company shall promptly file in the office of the Secretary of State a certificate, executed by an authorized person, correcting such statement, together with a fee as set forth in § 18–1105(a)(6) of this title.

§ 18–906.   Cancellation of Registration

A foreign limited liability company may cancel its registration by filing with the Secretary of State a certificate of cancellation, executed by an authorized person, together with a fee as set forth in § 18–1105(a)(6) of this title. The registration of a foreign limited liability company shall be canceled as provided in §§ 18–104(i)(4), 18–904(e) and 18–1107(h) of this title. A cancellation does not terminate the authority of the Secretary of State to accept service of process on the foreign limited liability company with respect to causes of action arising out of the doing of business in the State of Delaware.

§ 18–907.   Doing Business Without Registration

(a)   A foreign limited liability company doing business in the State of Delaware may not maintain any action, suit or proceeding in the State of Delaware until it has registered in the State of Delaware, and has paid to the State of Delaware all fees and penalties for the years or parts thereof, during which it did business in the State of Delaware without having registered.

(b)   The failure of a foreign limited liability company to register in the State of Delaware does not impair:

(1)   The validity of any contract or act of the foreign limited liability company;

(2)   The right of any other party to the contract to maintain any action, suit or proceeding on the contract; or

(3)   Prevent the foreign limited liability company from defending any action, suit or proceeding in any court of the State of Delaware.

(c)   A member or a manager of a foreign limited liability company is not liable for the obligations of the foreign limited liability company solely by reason of the limited liability company's having done business in the State of Delaware without registration.

(d)   Any foreign limited liability company doing business in the State of Delaware without first having registered shall be fined and shall pay to the Secretary of State $200 for each year or part thereof during which the foreign limited liability company failed to register in the State of Delaware.

§ 18–908.   Foreign Limited Liability Companies Doing Business Without Having Qualified; Injunctions

The Court of Chancery shall have jurisdiction to enjoin any foreign limited liability company, or any agent thereof, from doing any business in the State of Delaware if such foreign limited liability company has failed to register under this subchapter or if such foreign limited liability company has secured a certificate of the Secretary of State under § 18–903 of this title on the basis of false or misleading representations. Upon the motion of the Attorney General or upon the relation of proper parties, the Attorney General shall proceed for this purpose by complaint in any county in which such foreign limited liability company is doing or has done business.

§ 18–909.   Execution; Liability

Section 18–204(d) of this title shall be applicable to foreign limited liability companies as if they were domestic limited liability companies.

§ 18–910.   Service of Process on Registered Foreign Limited Liability Companies

(a)   Service of legal process upon any foreign limited liability company shall be made by delivering a copy personally to any managing or general agent or manager of the foreign limited liability company in the State of Delaware or the registered agent of the foreign limited liability company in the State of Delaware, or by leaving it at the dwelling house or usual place of abode in the State of Delaware of any such managing or general agent, manager or registered agent (if the registered agent be an individual), or at the registered office or other place of business of the foreign limited liability company in the State of Delaware. If the registered agent be a corporation, service of process upon it as such may be made by serving, in the State of Delaware, a copy thereof on the president, vice-president, secretary, assistant secretary or any director of the corporate registered agent. Service by copy left at the dwelling house or usual place of abode of any managing or general agent, manager or registered agent, or at the registered office or other place of business of the foreign limited liability company in the State of Delaware, to be effective must be delivered thereat at least 6 days before the return date of the process, and in the presence of an adult person, and the officer serving the process shall distinctly state the manner of service in the officer's return thereto. Process returnable forthwith must be delivered personally to the managing or general agent, manager or registered agent.

(b)   In case the officer whose duty it is to serve legal process cannot by due diligence serve the process in any manner provided for by subsection (a) of this section, it shall be lawful to serve the process against the foreign limited liability company upon the Secretary of State, and such service shall be as effectual for all intents and purposes as if made in any of the ways provided for in subsection (a) of this section. Process may be served upon the Secretary of State under this subsection by means of electronic transmission but only as prescribed by the Secretary of State. The Secretary of State is authorized to issue such rules and regulations with respect to such service as the Secretary of State deems necessary or appropriate. In the event that service is effected through the Secretary of State in accordance with this subsection, the Secretary of State shall forthwith notify the foreign limited liability company by letter, directed to the foreign limited liability company at its last registered office. Such letter shall be sent by a mail or courier service that includes a record of mailing or deposit with the courier and a record of delivery evidenced by the signature of the recipient. Such letter shall enclose a copy of the process and any other papers served on the Secretary of State pursuant to this subsection. It shall be the duty of the plaintiff in the event of such service to serve process and any other papers in duplicate, to notify the Secretary of State that service is being effected pursuant to this subsection, and to pay to the Secretary of State the sum of $50 for the use of the State of Delaware, which sum shall be taxed as a part of the costs in the proceeding if the plaintiff shall prevail therein. The Secretary of State shall maintain an alphabetical record of any such service setting forth the name of the plaintiff and defendant, the title, docket number and nature of the proceeding in which process has been served upon the Secretary, the fact that service has been effected pursuant to this subsection, the return date thereof and the day and hour when the service was made. The Secretary of State shall not be required to retain such information for a period longer than 5 years from the Secretary's receipt of the service of process.

§ 18–911.   Service of Process on Unregistered Foreign Limited Liability Companies

(a) Any foreign limited liability company which shall do business in the State of Delaware without having registered under § 18–902 of this title shall be deemed to have thereby appointed and constituted the Secretary of State of the State of Delaware its agent for the acceptance of legal process in any civil action, suit or proceeding against it in any state or federal court in the State of Delaware arising or growing out of any business done by it within the State of Delaware. The doing of business in the State of Delaware by such foreign limited liability company shall be a signification of the agreement of such foreign limited liability company that any such process when so served shall be of the same legal force and validity as if served upon an authorized manager or agent personally within the State of Delaware. Process may be served upon the Secretary of State under this subsection by means of electronic transmission but only as prescribed by the Secretary of State. The Secretary of State is authorized to issue such rules and regulations with respect to such service as the Secretary of State deems necessary or appropriate.

(b) Whenever the words "doing business," "the doing of business" or "business done in this State," by any such foreign limited liability company are used in this section, they shall mean the course or practice of carrying on any business activities in the State of Delaware, including, without limiting the generality of the foregoing, the solicitation of business or orders in the State of Delaware.

(c) In the event of service upon the Secretary of State in accordance with subsection (a) of this section, the Secretary of State shall forthwith notify the foreign limited liability company thereof by letter, directed to the foreign limited liability company at the address furnished to the Secretary of State by the plaintiff in such action, suit or proceeding. Such letter shall be sent by a mail or courier service that includes a record of mailing or deposit with the courier and a record of delivery evidenced by the signature of the recipient. Such letter shall enclose a copy of the process and any other papers served upon the Secretary of State. It shall be the duty of the plaintiff in the event of such service to serve process and any other papers in duplicate, to notify the Secretary of State that service is being made pursuant to this subsection, and to pay to the Secretary of State the sum of $50 for the use of the State of Delaware, which sum shall be taxed as part of the costs in the proceeding, if the plaintiff shall prevail therein. The Secretary of State shall maintain an alphabetical record of any such process setting forth the name of the plaintiff and defendant, the title, docket number and nature of the proceeding in which process has been served upon the Secretary, the return date thereof, and the day and hour when the service was made. The Secretary of State shall not be required to retain such information for a period longer than 5 years from the receipt of the service of process.

§ 18–912.   Activities Not Constituting Doing Business

(a) Activities of a foreign limited liability company in the State of Delaware that do not constitute doing business for the purpose of this subchapter include:

(1) Maintaining, defending or settling an action or proceeding;

(2) Holding meetings of its members or managers or carrying on any other activity concerning its internal affairs;

(3) Maintaining bank accounts;

(4)   Maintaining offices or agencies for the transfer, exchange or registration of the limited liability company's own securities or maintaining trustees or depositories with respect to those securities;

(5)   Selling through independent contractors;

(6)   Soliciting or obtaining orders, whether by mail or through employees or agents or otherwise, if the orders require acceptance outside the State of Delaware before they become contracts;

(7)   Selling, by contract consummated outside the State of Delaware, and agreeing, by the contract, to deliver into the State of Delaware, machinery, plants or equipment, the construction, erection or installation of which within the State of Delaware requires the supervision of technical engineers or skilled employees performing services not generally available, and as part of the contract of sale agreeing to furnish such services, and such services only, to the vendee at the time of construction, erection or installation;

(8)   Creating, as borrower or lender, or acquiring indebtedness with or without a mortgage or other security interest in property;

(9)   Collecting debts or foreclosing mortgages or other security interests in property securing the debts, and holding, protecting and maintaining property so acquired;

(10) Conducting an isolated transaction that is not 1 in the course of similar transactions;

(11) Doing business in interstate commerce; and

(12) Doing business in the State of Delaware as an insurance company.

(b)   A person shall not be deemed to be doing business in the State of Delaware solely by reason of being a member or manager of a domestic limited liability company or a foreign limited liability company.

(c)   This section does not apply in determining whether a foreign limited liability company is subject to service of process, taxation or regulation under any other law of the State of Delaware.

SUBCHAPTER X
DERIVATIVE ACTIONS

§ 18–1001. Right to Bring Action

A member or an assignee of a limited liability company interest may bring an action in the Court of Chancery in the right of a limited liability company to recover a judgment in its favor if managers or members with authority to do so have refused to bring the action or if an effort to cause those managers or members to bring the action is not likely to succeed.

§ 18–1002. Proper Plaintiff

In a derivative action, the plaintiff must be a member or an assignee of a limited liability company interest at the time of bringing the action and:

(1)   At the time of the transaction of which the plaintiff complains; or

(2)   The plaintiff's status as a member or an assignee of a limited liability company interest had devolved upon the plaintiff by operation of law or pursuant to the terms of a limited liability company agreement from a person who was a member or an assignee of a limited liability company interest at the time of the transaction.

§ 18–1003. Complaint

In a derivative action, the complaint shall set forth with particularity the effort, if any, of the plaintiff to secure initiation of the action by a manager or member or the reasons for not making the effort.

§ 18–1004. Expenses

If a derivative action is successful, in whole or in part, as a result of a judgment, compromise or settlement of any such action, the court may award the plaintiff reasonable expenses, including reasonable attorney's fees, from any recovery in any such action or from a limited liability company.

SUBCHAPTER XI
MISCELLANEOUS

§ 18–1101. Construction and Application of Chapter and Limited Liability Company Agreement

(a)   The rule that statutes in derogation of the common law are to be strictly construed shall have no application to this chapter.

(b)   It is the policy of this chapter to give the maximum effect to the principle of freedom of contract and to the enforceability of limited liability company agreements.

(c)   To the extent that, at law or in equity, a member or manager or other person has duties (including fiduciary duties) to a limited liability company or to another member or manager or to another person that is a party to or is otherwise bound by a limited liability company agreement, the member's or manager's or other person's duties may be expanded or restricted or eliminated by provisions in the limited liability company agreement; provided, that the limited liability company agreement may not eliminate the implied contractual covenant of good faith and fair dealing.

(d)   Unless otherwise provided in a limited liability company agreement, a member or manager or other person shall not be liable to a limited liability company or to another member or manager or to another person that is a party to or is otherwise bound by a limited liability company agreement for breach of fiduciary duty for the member's or manager's or other person's good faith reliance on the provisions of the limited liability company agreement.

(e)   A limited liability company agreement may provide for the limitation or elimination of any and all liabilities for breach of contract and breach of duties (including fiduciary duties) of a member, manager or other person to a limited liability company or to another member or manager or to another person that is a party to or is otherwise bound by a limited liability company agreement; provided, that a limited liability company agreement may not limit or eliminate liability for any act or omission that constitutes a bad faith violation of the implied contractual covenant of good faith and fair dealing.

(f)   Unless the context otherwise requires, as used herein, the singular shall include the plural and the plural may refer to only the singular. The use of any gender shall be applicable to all genders. The captions contained herein are for purposes of convenience only and shall not control or affect the construction of this chapter.

(g)   Sections 9–406 and 9–408 of this title do not apply to any interest in a limited liability company, including all rights, powers and interests arising under a limited liability company agreement or this chapter. This provision prevails over §§ 9–406 and 9–408 of this title.

(h)   Action validly taken pursuant to one provision of this chapter shall not be deemed invalid solely because it is identical or similar in substance to an action that could have been taken pursuant to some other provision of this chapter but fails to satisfy one or more requirements prescribed by such other provision.

(i)   A limited liability company agreement that provides for the application of Delaware law shall be governed by and construed under the laws of the State of Delaware in accordance with its terms.

(j)   The provisions of this chapter shall apply whether a limited liability company has 1 member or more than 1 member.

§ 18–1102. Short Title

This chapter may be cited as the "Delaware Limited Liability Company Act."

§ 18–1103. Severability

If any provision of this chapter or its application to any person or circumstances is held invalid, the invalidity does not affect other provisions or applications of the chapter which can be given effect without the invalid provision or application, and to this end, the provisions of this chapter are severable.

§ 18–1104. Cases Not Provided for in This Chapter

In any case not provided for in this chapter, the rules of law and equity, including the rules of law and equity relating to fiduciary duties and the law merchant, shall govern.

§ 18–1105. Fees

(a)   No document required to be filed under this chapter shall be effective until the applicable fee required by this section is paid. The following fees shall be paid to and collected by the Secretary of State for the use of the State of Delaware:

(1)   Upon the receipt for filing of an application for reservation of name, an application for renewal of reservation or a notice of transfer or cancellation of reservation pursuant to § 18–103(b) of this title, a fee in the amount of $75.

(2)   Upon the receipt for filing of a certificate under § 18–104(b) of this title, a fee in the amount of $200, upon the receipt for filing of a certificate under § 18–104(c) of this title, a fee in the amount of $200, and upon the receipt for filing of a certificate under § 18–104(d) of this title, a fee in the amount of $2 for each limited liability company whose registered agent has resigned by such certificate.

(3)   Upon the receipt for filing of a certificate of formation under § 18–201 of this title or a certificate of registered series under § 18–218 of this title, a fee in the amount of $70 and upon the receipt for filing of a certificate of limited liability company domestication under § 18–212 of this title, a certificate of transfer or a certificate of transfer and domestic continuance under § 18–213 of this title, a certificate of conversion to limited liability company under § 18–214 of this title, a certificate of conversion to a non-Delaware entity under § 18–216 of this title, a certificate of amendment under § 18–202 or § 18–218(d)(3) of this title (except as otherwise provided in paragraph (a)(11) of this section), a certificate of cancellation under § 18–203 or § 18–218(d)(7) of this title, a certificate of merger or consolidation or a certificate of ownership and merger under § 18–209 of this title, a restated certificate of formation or a restated certificate of registered series under § 18–208 of this title, a certificate of amendment of a certificate with a future effective date or time under § 18–206(c) of this title, a certificate of termination of a certificate with a future effective date or time under § 18–206(c) of this title, a certificate of correction under § 18–211 of this title, a certificate of division under § 18–217 of this title, a certificate of conversion of protected series to registered series under § 18–219 of this title, a certificate of conversion of registered series to protected series under § 18–220 of this title, a certificate of merger or consolidation under § 18–221 of this title or a certificate of revival under § 18–1109 or § 18–1110 of this title, a fee in the amount of $180, plus, in the case of a certificate of cancellation under

§ 18–203 of this title, a fee in the amount of $50 for each registered series of the limited liability company named in the certificate of cancellation.

(4) For certifying copies of any paper on file as provided for by this chapter, a fee in the amount of $50 for each copy certified.

(5) The Secretary of State may issue photocopies or electronic image copies of instruments on file, as well as instruments, documents and other papers not on file, and for all such photocopies or electronic image copies, whether certified or not, a fee of $10 shall be paid for the 1st page and $2 for each additional page. Notwithstanding Delaware's Freedom of Information Act (Chapter 100 of Title 29) or other provision of law granting access to public records, the Secretary of State upon request shall issue only photocopies or electronic image copies of public records in exchange for the fees described in this section, and in no case shall the Secretary of State be required to provide copies (or access to copies) of such public records (including without limitation bulk data, digital copies of instruments, documents and other papers, databases or other information) in an electronic medium or in any form other than photocopies or electronic image copies of such public records in exchange, as applicable, for the fees described in this section or § 2318 of Title 29 for each such record associated with a file number.

(6) Upon the receipt for filing of an application for registration as a foreign limited liability company under § 18–902 of this title, a certificate under § 18–905 of this title or a certificate of cancellation under § 18–906 of this title, a fee in the amount of $200.

(7) Upon the receipt for filing of a certificate under § 18–904(c) of this title, a fee in the amount of $200, upon the receipt for filing of a certificate under § 18–904(d) of this title, a fee in the amount of $200, and upon the receipt for filing of a certificate under § 18–904(e) of this title, a fee in the amount of $2 for each foreign limited liability company whose registered agent has resigned by such certificate.

(8) For preclearance of any document for filing, a fee in the amount of $250.

(9) For preparing and providing a written report of a record search, a fee in the amount of $50.

(10) For issuing any certificate of the Secretary of State, including but not limited to a certificate of good standing with respect to a limited liability company or a registered series thereof, other than a certification of a copy under paragraph (a)(4) of this section, a fee in the amount of $50, except that for issuing any certificate of the Secretary of State that recites all of the filings with the Secretary of State of a limited liability company or all of the filings of any registered series or that lists all of the registered series formed by a limited liability company, a fee of $175 shall be paid for each such certificate.

(11) For receiving and filing and/or indexing any certificate, affidavit, agreement or any other paper provided for by this chapter, for which no different fee is specifically prescribed, a fee in the amount of $200. For filing any instrument submitted by a limited liability company or foreign limited liability company that only changes the registered office or registered agent and is specifically captioned as a certificate of amendment changing only the registered office or registered agent, a fee in the amount of $50 provided that no fee shall be charged pursuant to § 18–206 (e) of this title.

(12) The Secretary of State may in the Secretary of State's own discretion charge a fee of $60 for each check received for payment of any fee that is returned due to insufficient funds or the result of a stop payment order.

(b) In addition to those fees charged under subsection (a) of this section, there shall be collected by and paid to the Secretary of State the following:

(1) For all services described in subsection (a) of this section that are requested to be completed within 30 minutes on the same day as the day of the request, an additional sum of up

to $7,500 and for all services described in subsection (a) of this section that are requested to be completed within 1 hour on the same day as the day of the request, an additional sum of up to $1,000 and for all services described in subsection (a) of this section that are requested to be completed within 2 hours on the same day of the request, an additional sum of up to $500;

(2)   For all services described in subsection (a) of this section that are requested to be completed within the same day as the day of the request, an additional sum of up to $300; and

(3)   For all services described in subsection (a) of this section that are requested to be completed within a 24-hour period from the time of the request, an additional sum of up to $150.

The Secretary of State shall establish (and may from time to time amend) a schedule of specific fees payable pursuant to this subsection.

(c)   The Secretary of State may in his or her discretion permit the extension of credit for the fees required by this section upon such terms as the secretary shall deem to be appropriate.

(d)   The Secretary of State shall retain from the revenue collected from the fees required by this section a sum sufficient to provide at all times a fund of at least $500, but not more than $1,500, from which the secretary may refund any payment made pursuant to this section to the extent that it exceeds the fees required by this section. The funds shall be deposited in a financial institution which is a legal depository of State of Delaware moneys to the credit of the Secretary of State and shall be disbursable on order of the Secretary of State.

(e)   Except as provided in this section, the fees of the Secretary of State shall be as provided in § 2315 of Title 29.

§ 18–1106. Reserved Power of State of Delaware to Alter or Repeal Chapter

All provisions of this chapter may be altered from time to time or repealed and all rights of members and managers are subject to this reservation. Unless expressly stated to the contrary in this chapter, all amendments of this chapter shall apply to limited liability companies and members and managers whether or not existing as such at the time of the enactment of any such amendment.

§ 18–1107. Taxation of Limited Liability Companies and Registered Series

(a)   For purposes of any tax imposed by the State of Delaware or any instrumentality, agency or political subdivision of the State of Delaware, a domestic limited liability company or a foreign limited liability company qualified to do business in the State of Delaware shall be classified as a partnership unless classified otherwise for federal income tax purposes, in which case the domestic or foreign limited liability company shall be classified in the same manner as it is classified for federal income tax purposes. For purposes of any tax imposed by the State of Delaware or any instrumentality, agency or political subdivision of the State of Delaware, a member or an assignee of a member of a domestic limited liability company or a foreign limited liability company qualified to do business in the State of Delaware shall be treated as either a resident or nonresident partner unless classified otherwise for federal income tax purposes, in which case the member or assignee of a member shall have the same status as such member or assignee of a member has for federal income tax purposes.

(b)   Every domestic limited liability company and every foreign limited liability company registered to do business in the State of Delaware shall pay an annual tax, for the use of the State of Delaware, in the amount of $300. There shall be paid by or on behalf of each registered series of a domestic limited liability company an annual tax, for use of the State of Delaware, in the amount of $75 per registered series.

(c)   The annual tax for a domestic limited liability company shall be due and payable on the first day of June following the close of the calendar year or upon the cancellation of a certificate of formation. The annual tax for a registered series shall be due and payable on the first day of June following the close of the calendar year or upon the cancellation of a certificate of registered series. The annual tax for a foreign limited liability company shall be due and payable on the first day of June following the close of the calendar year or upon the cancellation of the certificate of registration. The Secretary of State shall receive the annual tax and pay over all taxes collected to the Department of Finance of the State of Delaware. If the annual tax remains unpaid after the due date, the tax shall bear interest at the rate of 1 and one-half percent for each month or portion thereof until fully paid.

(d)   The Secretary of State shall, at least 60 days prior June 1 of each year, cause to be mailed to each domestic limited liability company and each registered series thereof and each foreign limited liability company required to comply with the provisions of this section in care of its registered agent in the State of Delaware an annual statement for the tax to be paid hereunder.

(e)   In the event of neglect, refusal or failure on the part of any domestic limited liability company, registered series or foreign limited liability company to pay the annual tax to be paid hereunder on or before June 1 in any year, such domestic limited liability company or foreign limited liability company shall pay the sum of $200, and such registered series shall pay the sum of $50, to be recovered by adding that amount to the annual tax and such additional sum shall become a part of the tax and shall be collected in the same manner and subject to the same penalties.

(f)   In case any domestic limited liability company, registered series or foreign limited liability company shall fail to pay the annual tax due within the time required by this section, and in case the agent in charge of the registered office of any domestic limited liability company or foreign limited liability company upon whom process against such domestic limited liability company any protected series or registered series thereof or foreign limited liability company may be served shall die, resign, refuse to act as such, remove from the State of Delaware or cannot with due diligence be found, it shall be lawful while default continues to serve process against such domestic limited liability company or any protected series or registered series thereof or foreign limited liability company upon the Secretary of State. Such service upon the Secretary of State shall be made in the manner and shall have the effect stated in § 18–105 of this title in the case of a domestic limited liability company or any protected series or registered series thereof and § 18–910 of this title in the case of a foreign limited liability company and shall be governed in all respects by said sections.

(g)   The annual tax shall be a debt due from a domestic limited liability company, registered series or foreign limited liability company to the State of Delaware, for which an action at law may be maintained after the same shall have been in arrears for a period of 1 month. The tax shall also be a preferred debt in the case of insolvency.

(h)   A domestic limited liability company that neglects, refuses or fails to pay the annual tax when due shall cease to be in good standing as a domestic limited liability company and all registered series thereof shall also cease to be in good standing. A registered series that neglects, refuses or fails to pay the annual tax when due shall cease to be in good standing as a registered series. A foreign limited liability company that neglects, refuses or fails to pay the annual tax when due shall cease to be registered as a foreign limited liability company in the State of Delaware.

(i)   A domestic limited liability company or registered series that has ceased to be in good standing or a foreign limited liability company that has ceased to be registered by reason of the failure by the limited liability company, registered series or foreign limited liability company to pay an annual tax shall be restored to and have the status of a domestic limited liability company or registered series in good standing or a foreign limited liability company that is registered in the State of Delaware upon the payment of the annual tax and all penalties and interest thereon for each year for which such domestic limited liability company, registered series or foreign limited liability company neglected, refused or failed to pay an annual tax.

(j)   On the motion of the Attorney General or upon request of the Secretary of State, whenever any annual tax due under this chapter from any domestic limited liability company, registered series, or foreign limited liability company shall have remained in arrears for a period of 3 months after the tax shall have become payable, the Attorney General may apply to the Court of Chancery, by petition in the name of the State of Delaware, on 5 days' notice to such domestic limited liability company, registered series or foreign limited liability company, which notice may be served in such manner as the Court may direct, for an injunction to restrain such domestic limited liability company, registered series or foreign limited liability company from the transaction of any business within the State of Delaware or elsewhere, until the payment of the annual tax, and all penalties and interest due thereon and the cost of the application which shall be fixed by the Court. The Court of Chancery may grant the injunction, if a proper case appears, and upon granting and service of the injunction, such domestic limited liability company, registered series or foreign limited liability company thereafter shall not transact any business until the injunction shall be dissolved.

(k) A domestic limited liability company that has ceased to be in good standing by reason of the domestic limited liability company's neglect, refusal or failure to pay an annual tax shall remain a domestic limited liability company formed under this chapter, and each registered series thereof shall remain a registered series formed under this chapter, and each protected series thereof shall remain a protected series established under this chapter. A registered series that has ceased to be in good standing by reason of the registered series' neglect, refusal or failure to pay an annual tax shall remain a registered series formed under this chapter. The Secretary of State shall not accept for filing any certificate (except a certificate of resignation of a registered agent when a successor registered agent is not being appointed) required or permitted by this chapter to be filed in respect of any domestic limited liability company, registered series or foreign limited liability company if such domestic limited liability company, registered series or foreign limited liability company has neglected, refused or failed to pay an annual tax, and shall not issue any certificate of good standing with respect to such domestic limited liability company, registered series or foreign limited liability company, unless or until such domestic limited liability company, registered series or foreign limited liability company shall have been restored to and have the status of a domestic limited liability company or registered series in good standing or a foreign limited liability company duly registered in the State of Delaware.

(*l*) A domestic limited liability company that has ceased to be in good standing (and each protected series and registered series thereof), a registered series that has ceased to be in good standing, or a foreign limited liability company that has ceased to be registered in the State of Delaware by reason of the domestic limited liability company's, registered series' or foreign limited liability company's neglect, refusal or failure to pay an annual tax may not maintain any action, suit or proceeding in any court of the State of Delaware until such domestic limited liability company, registered series or foreign limited liability company has been restored to and has the status of a domestic limited liability company, registered series or foreign limited liability company in good standing or duly registered in the State of Delaware. An action, suit or proceeding may not be maintained in any court of the State of Delaware by any successor or assignee of such domestic limited liability company (or any protected series or registered series thereof), registered series, or foreign limited liability company on any right, claim or demand arising out the transaction of business by such domestic limited liability company (or any protected series or registered series thereof) after the domestic limited liability company or registered series has ceased to be in good standing or a foreign limited liability company that has ceased to be registered in the State of Delaware until such domestic limited liability company, registered series or foreign limited liability company, or any person that has acquired all or substantially all of its assets, has paid any annual tax then due and payable, together with penalties and interest thereon.

(m) The neglect, refusal or failure of a domestic limited liability company, registered series or foreign limited liability company to pay an annual tax shall not impair the validity of any contract, deed, mortgage, security interest, lien or act of such domestic limited liability company or any protected series or registered series thereof or foreign limited liability company or prevent such domestic limited liability company or any protected series or registered series thereof or foreign limited liability company from defending any action, suit or proceeding with any court of the State of Delaware.

(n) A member or manager of a domestic limited liability company, registered series or foreign limited liability company is not liable for the debts, obligations or liabilities of such domestic limited liability company, registered series or foreign limited liability company solely by reason of the neglect, refusal or failure of such domestic limited liability company, registered series or foreign limited liability company to pay an annual tax or by reason of such domestic limited liability company, registered series or foreign limited liability company ceasing to be in good standing or duly registered. A protected series or registered series of a domestic limited liability company is not liable for the debts, obligations or liabilities of such domestic limited liability company or any other series thereof solely by reason of the neglect, refusal or failure of such domestic limited liability company to pay an annual tax or by reason of such domestic limited liability company ceasing to be in good standing.

§ 18–1108. Cancellation of Certificate of Formation or Certificate of Registered Series for Failure to Pay Taxes

(a)   The certificate of formation of a domestic limited liability company shall be canceled if the annual tax due under § 18–1107 of this title for the domestic limited liability company is not paid for a period of 3 years from the date it is due, such cancellation to be effective on the third anniversary of such due date.

(b)   The certificate of registered series shall be canceled if the annual tax due under § 18–1107 of this title is not paid for a period of 3 years from the date it is due, such cancellation to be effective on the third anniversary of such due date.

(c)   A list of those domestic limited liability companies and registered series whose certificates of formation or certificates of registered series were canceled on June 1 of such calendar year pursuant to § 18–1108(a) or § 18–1108(b) of this title shall be filed in the office of the Secretary of State. On or before October 31 of each calendar year, the Secretary of State shall publish such list on the Internet or on a similar medium for a period of 1 week and shall advertise the website or other address where such list can be accessed in at least 1 newspaper of general circulation in the State of Delaware.

§ 18–1109. Revival of Domestic Limited Liability Company

(a)   A domestic limited liability company whose certificate of formation has been canceled pursuant to § 18–104(d) or § 18–104(i)(4) or § 18–1108(a) of this title may be revived by filing in the office of the Secretary of State a certificate of revival accompanied by the payment of the fee required by § 18–1105(a)(3) of this title and payment of the annual tax due under § 18–1107 of this title and all penalties and interest thereon due at the time of the cancellation of its certificate of formation. The certificate of revival shall set forth:

(1)   The name of the limited liability company at the time its certificate of formation was canceled and, if such name is not available at the time of revival, the name under which the limited liability company is to be revived;

(2)   The date of filing of the original certificate of formation of the limited liability company;

(3)   The address of the limited liability company's registered office in the State of Delaware and the name and address of the limited liability company's registered agent in the State of Delaware;

(4)   A statement that the certificate of revival is filed by 1 or more persons authorized to execute and file the certificate of revival to revive the limited liability company; and

(5)   Any other matters the persons executing the certificate of revival determine to include therein.

(b)   The certificate of revival shall be deemed to be an amendment to the certificate of formation of the limited liability company, and the limited liability company shall not be required to take any further action to amend its certificate of formation under § 18–202 of this title with respect to the matters set forth in the certificate of revival.

(c)   Upon the filing of a certificate of revival, a limited liability company and all registered series thereof that have been formed and whose certificate of registered series has not been canceled prior to the cancellation of the certificate of formation shall be revived with the same force and effect as if its certificate of formation had not been canceled pursuant to § 18–104(d), § 18–104(i)(4), or § 18–1108(a) of this title. Such revival shall validate all contracts, acts, matters and things made, done and performed by the limited liability company, its members, managers, employees and agents during the time when its certificate of formation was canceled pursuant to § 18–104(d), § 18–104(i)(4) or § 18–1108(a) of this title, with the same force and effect and to all intents and purposes as if the certificate of formation had remained in full force and effect. All real and personal property, and all rights and interests, which belonged to the limited liability company at the time its certificate of formation was canceled pursuant to § 18–104(d), § 18–104(i)(4) or § 18–1108(a) of this title or which were acquired by the limited liability company following the cancellation of its certificate of formation pursuant to § 18–104(d), § 18–104(i)(4) or § 18–1108(a) of this title, and which were not disposed of prior to the time of its revival, shall be vested in the limited liability company after its revival as fully as they were held by the limited liability company at, and after, as the case may be, the time its certificate of formation was canceled pursuant to § 18–104(d), § 18–104(i)(4) or § 18–1108(a) of this title. After its revival, the limited liability company shall be as exclusively liable for all contracts, acts, matters and things made, done or performed in its name and on its behalf by its members, managers, employees and agents prior to its revival as if its certificate of formation had at all times remained in full force and effect.

§ 18–1110. Revival of a Registered Series

(a)   A registered series whose certificate of registered series has been canceled pursuant to § 18–1108(b) of this title may be revived by filing in the office of the Secretary of State a certificate of revival accompanied by the payment of the fee required by § 18–1105(a)(3) of this title and payment of the annual tax due under § 18–1107 of this title and all penalties and interest thereon due at the time of the cancellation of its certificate of registered series. The certificate of revival shall set forth:

(1)   The name of the limited liability company at the time the certificate of registered series was canceled and, if such name has changed, the name of the limited liability company at the time of revival of the registered series;

(2)   The name of the registered series at the time the certificate of registered series was canceled and, if such name is not available at the time of revival, the name under which the registered series is to be revived;

(3)   The date of filing of the original certificate of registered series;

(4)   A statement that the certificate of revival is filed by 1 or more persons authorized to execute and file the certificate of revival to revive the registered series; and

(5)   Any other matters the persons executing the certificate of revival determine to include therein.

(b)   The certificate of revival shall be deemed to be an amendment to the certificate of registered series, and no further actions shall be required to amend its certificate of registered series under § 18–218(d)(3) of this title with respect to the matters set forth in the certificate of revival.

(c)   Upon the filing of a certificate of revival, a registered series shall be revived with the same force and effect as if its certificate of registered series had not been canceled pursuant to § 18–1108(b) of this title. Such revival shall validate all contracts, acts, matters and things made, done and performed by the registered series, its members, managers, employees and agents during the time when its certificate of registered series was canceled pursuant to § 18–1108(b) of this title, with the same force and effect and to all intents and purposes as if the certificate of registered series had remained in full force and effect. All real and personal property, and all rights and interests, which belonged to the registered series at the time its certificate of registered series was canceled pursuant to § 18–1108(b) of this title or which were acquired by the registered series following the cancellation of its certificate of registered series pursuant to § 18–1108(b) of this title, and which were not disposed of prior to the time of its revival, shall be vested in the registered series after its revival as fully as they were held by the registered series at, and after, as the case may be, the time its certificate of registered series was canceled pursuant to § 18–1108(b) of this title. After its revival, the registered series shall be as exclusively liable for all contracts, acts, matters and things made, done or performed in its name and on its behalf by its members, managers, employees and agents prior to its revival as if its certificate of registered series had at all times remained in full force and effect.

SUBCHAPTER XII
STATUTORY PUBLIC BENEFIT LIMITED LIABILITY COMPANIES

§ 18–1201. Law Applicable to Statutory Public Benefit Limited Liability Companies; How Formed

This subchapter applies to all statutory public benefit limited liability companies, as defined in § 18–1202 of this title. If a limited liability company elects to become a statutory public benefit limited liability company under this subchapter in the manner prescribed in this subchapter, it shall be subject in all respects to the provisions of this chapter, except to the extent this subchapter imposes additional or different requirements, in which case such requirements shall apply, and notwithstanding § 18–1101 of this title or any other provision of this title, such requirements imposed by this subchapter may not be altered in the limited liability company agreement.

§ 18–1202. Statutory Public Benefit Limited Liability Company Defined; Contents of Certificate of Formation and Limited Liability Company Agreement

(a) A "statutory public benefit limited liability company" is a for-profit limited liability company formed under and subject to the requirements of this chapter that is intended to produce a public benefit or public benefits and to operate in a responsible and sustainable manner. To that end, a statutory public benefit limited liability company shall be managed in a manner that balances the members' pecuniary interests, the best interests of those materially affected by the limited liability company's conduct, and the public benefit or public benefits set forth in its certificate of formation. A statutory public benefit limited liability company shall state in the heading of its certificate of formation that it is a statutory public benefit limited liability company and shall set forth 1 or more specific public benefits to be promoted by the limited liability company in its certificate of formation. The limited liability company agreement of a statutory public benefit limited liability company may not contain any provision inconsistent with this subchapter.

(b) "Public benefit" means a positive effect (or reduction of negative effects) on 1 or more categories of persons, entities, communities or interests (other than members in their capacities as members) including, but not limited to, effects of an artistic, charitable, cultural, economic, educational, environmental, literary, medical, religious, scientific or technological nature. "Public benefit provisions" means the provisions of a limited liability company agreement contemplated by this subchapter.

§ 18–1203. Certain Amendments and Mergers; Votes Required

Notwithstanding any other provision of this chapter, a statutory public benefit limited liability company may not, without the approval of members who own at least ²/₃ of the then-current percentage or other interest in the profits of the limited liability company owned by all members:

(1) Amend its certificate of formation to delete or amend a provision required by § 18–1202(a) of this title;

(2) Merge or consolidate with or into another entity or divide into 2 or more domestic limited liability companies if, as a result of such merger, consolidation or division, the limited liability company interests in such limited liability company would become, or be converted into or exchanged for the right to receive, limited liability company interests or other equity interests in a domestic or foreign limited liability company or other entity that is not a statutory public benefit limited liability company or similar entity, the certificate of formation or limited liability

company agreement (or similar governing document) of which does not contain provisions identifying a public benefit or public benefits comparable in all material respects to those set forth in the certificate of formation of such limited liability company as contemplated by § 18–1202(a) of this title; or

(3)   Cease to be a statutory public benefit limited liability company under the provisions of this subchapter.

§ 18–1204. Duties of Members or Managers

(a)   The members or managers or other persons with authority to manage or direct the business and affairs of a statutory public benefit limited liability company shall manage or direct the business and affairs of the statutory public benefit limited liability company in a manner that balances the pecuniary interests of the members, the best interests of those materially affected by the limited liability company's conduct, and the specific public benefit or public benefits set forth in its certificate of formation. Unless otherwise provided in a limited liability company agreement, no member, manager or other person with authority to manage or direct the business and affairs of the statutory public benefit limited liability company shall have any liability for monetary damages for the failure to manage or direct the business and affairs of the statutory public benefit limited liability company as provided in this subsection.

(b)   A member or manager of a statutory public benefit limited liability company or any other person with authority to manage or direct the business and affairs of the statutory public benefit limited liability company shall not, by virtue of the public benefit provisions or § 18–1202(a) of this title, have any duty to any person on account of any interest of such person in the public benefit or public benefits set forth in its certificate of formation or on account of any interest materially affected by the limited liability company's conduct and, with respect to a decision implicating the balance requirement in subsection (a) of this section, will be deemed to satisfy such person's fiduciary duties to members and the limited liability company if such person's decision is both informed and disinterested and not such that no person of ordinary, sound judgment would approve.

§ 18–1205. Periodic Statements and Third-Party Certification

A statutory public benefit limited liability company shall no less than biennially provide its members with a statement as to the limited liability company's promotion of the public benefit or public benefits set forth in its certificate of formation and as to the best interests of those materially affected by the limited liability company's conduct. The statement shall include:

(1)   The objectives that have been established to promote such public benefit or public benefits and interests;

(2)   The standards that have been adopted to measure the limited liability company's progress in promoting such public benefit or public benefits and interests;

(3)   Objective factual information based on those standards regarding the limited liability company's success in meeting the objectives for promoting such public benefit or public benefits and interests; and

(4)   An assessment of the limited liability company's success in meeting the objectives and promoting such public benefit or public benefits and interests.

§ 18–1206. Derivative Suits

Members of a statutory public benefit limited liability company or assignees of limited liability company interests in a statutory public benefit limited liability company owning individually or collectively, as of the date of instituting such derivative suit, at least 2% of the then-current percentage or other interest in the profits of the limited liability company or, in the case of a limited liability company with limited liability company interests listed on a national securities exchange, the lesser of such percentage or limited liability company interests of at least $2,000,000 in market value, may maintain a derivative lawsuit to enforce the requirements set forth in § 18–1204(a) of this title.

§ 18–1207. No Effect on Other Limited Liability Companies

This subchapter shall not affect a statute or rule of law that is applicable to a limited liability company that is not a statutory public benefit limited liability company.

§ 18–1208. Accomplishment by Other Means

The provisions of this subchapter shall not be construed to limit the accomplishment by any other means permitted by law of the formation or operation of a limited liability company that is formed or operated for a public benefit (including a limited liability company that is designated as a public benefit limited liability company) that is not a statutory public benefit limited liability company.

MODEL BUSINESS CORPORATION ACT

Table of Sections

CHAPTER 1. GENERAL PROVISIONS

SUBCHAPTER A. SHORT TITLE AND RESERVATION OF POWER

SUBCHAPTER B. FILING DOCUMENTS

SUBCHAPTER C. SECRETARY OF STATE

SUBCHAPTER D. DEFINITIONS

SUBCHAPTER E. RATIFICATION OF DEFECTIVE CORPORATE ACTIONS

CHAPTER 2. INCORPORATION

MODEL BUSINESS CORPORATION ACT

MODEL BUSINESS CORPORATION ACT

CHAPTER 7. SHAREHOLDERS

SUBCHAPTER A. MEETINGS

SUBCHAPTER B. VOTING

SUBCHAPTER C. VOTING TRUSTS AND AGREEMENTS

SUBCHAPTER D. DERIVATIVE PROCEEDINGS

SUBCHAPTER E. JUDICIAL PROCEEDINGS

CHAPTER 8. DIRECTORS AND OFFICERS

SUBCHAPTER A. BOARD OF DIRECTORS

MODEL BUSINESS CORPORATION ACT

MODEL BUSINESS CORPORATION ACT

CHAPTER 9. DOMESTICATION AND CONVERSION

SUBCHAPTER A. PRELIMINARY PROVISIONS

SUBCHAPTER B. DOMESTICATION

SUBCHAPTER C. CONVERSION

CHAPTER 10. AMENDMENT OF ARTICLES OF INCORPORATION AND BYLAWS

SUBCHAPTER A. AMENDMENT OF ARTICLES OF INCORPORATION

SUBCHAPTER B. AMENDMENT OF BYLAWS

CHAPTER 11. MERGERS AND SHARE EXCHANGE

MODEL BUSINESS CORPORATION ACT

CHAPTER 1: GENERAL PROVISIONS

SUBCHAPTER A
SHORT TITLE AND RESERVATION OF POWER

§ 1.01. Short Title

This Act shall be known and may be cited as the "[name of state] Business Corporation Act."

Cross-References

Application of Act to existing domestic corporations, see § 17.01.

Application of Act to existing foreign corporations, see § 17.02.

Saving provisions, see § 17.03.

Official Comment

The short title provided by section 1.01 creates a convenient name for the state's business corporation act.

§ 1.02. Reservation of Power to Amend or Repeal

The [name of state legislature] has power to amend or repeal all or part of this Act at any time and all domestic and foreign corporations subject to this Act are governed by the amendment or repeal.

Cross-References

Application of Act to existing domestic corporations, see § 17.01.

Application of Act to existing foreign corporations, see § 17.02.

Saving provisions, see § 17.03.

Official Comment

The purpose of section 1.02 is to avoid any possible argument that a corporation has contractual or vested rights in any specific statutory provision and to ensure that the state may in the future modify its corporation statutes as it deems appropriate and require existing corporations to comply with the statutes as modified.

All articles of incorporation and foreign registration statements are subject to the reservation of power set forth in section 1.02. Further, corporations "governed" by this Act—which includes all corporations formed or qualified or registered under earlier general incorporation statutes that contain such a reservation of power—are also subject to the reservation of power of section 1.02 and bound by subsequent amendments to the Act.

SUBCHAPTER B
FILING DOCUMENTS

§ 1.20. Requirements for Documents; Extrinsic Facts

(a)   A document must satisfy the requirements of this section, and of any other section that adds to or varies these requirements, to be entitled to filing by the secretary of state.

(b)   This Act must require or permit filing the document in the office of the secretary of state.

(c)   The document must contain the information required by this Act and may contain other information.

(d)   The document must be typewritten or printed or, if electronically transmitted, it must be in a format that can be retrieved or reproduced in typewritten or printed form.

(e)   The document must be in the English language. A corporate name need not be in English if written in English letters or Arabic or Roman numerals.

(f)   The document must be signed:

(1)   by the chairman of the board of directors of a domestic or foreign corporation, by its president, or by another of its officers;

(2)   if directors have not been selected or the corporation has not been formed, by an incorporator; or

(3) if the corporation is in the hands of a receiver, trustee, or other court-appointed fiduciary, by that fiduciary.

(g) The person executing the document shall sign it and state beneath or opposite the person's signature the person's name and the capacity in which the document is signed. The document may but need not contain a corporate seal, attestation, acknowledgment, or verification.

(h) If the secretary of state has prescribed a mandatory form for the document under section 1.21(a), the document must be in or on the prescribed form.

(i) The document must be delivered to the office of the secretary of state for filing. Delivery may be made by electronic transmission if and to the extent permitted by the secretary of state. If it is filed in typewritten or printed form and not transmitted electronically, the secretary of state may require one exact or conformed copy to be delivered with the document.

(j) When the document is delivered to the office of the secretary of state for filing, the correct filing fee, and any franchise tax, license fee, or penalty required by this Act or other law to be paid at the time of delivery for filing must be paid or provision for payment made in a manner permitted by the secretary of state.

(k) Whenever a provision of this Act permits any of the terms of a plan or a filed document to be dependent on facts objectively ascertainable outside the plan or filed document, the following provisions apply:

(1) The manner in which the facts will operate upon the terms of the plan or filed document must be set forth in the plan or filed document.

(2) The facts may include:

(i) any of the following that is available in a nationally recognized news or information medium either in print or electronically: statistical or market indices, market prices of any security or group of securities, interest rates, currency exchange rates, or similar economic or financial data;

(ii) a determination or action by any person or body, including the corporation or any other party to a plan or filed document; or

(iii) the terms of, or actions taken under, an agreement to which the corporation is a party, or any other agreement or document.

(3) As used in this subsection (k):

(i) "filed document" means a document filed by the secretary of state under any provision of this Act except chapter 15 or section 16.21; and

(ii) "plan" means a plan of domestication, conversion, merger, or share exchange.

(4) The following provisions of a plan or filed document may not be made dependent on facts outside the plan or filed document:

(i) the name and address of any person required in a filed document;

(ii) the registered office of any entity required in a filed document;

(iii) the registered agent of any entity required in a filed document;

(iv) the number of authorized shares and designation of each class or series of shares;

(v) the effective date of a filed document; and

(vi) any required statement in a filed document of the date on which the underlying transaction was approved or the manner in which that approval was given.

(5) If a provision of a filed document is made dependent on a fact ascertainable outside of the filed document, and that fact is neither ascertainable by reference to a source described in

subsection (k)(2)(i) or a document that is a matter of public record, nor have the affected shareholders received notice of the fact from the corporation, then the corporation shall file with the secretary of state articles of amendment to the filed document setting forth the fact promptly after the time when the fact referred to is first ascertainable or thereafter changes. Articles of amendment under this subsection (k)(5) are deemed to be authorized by the authorization of the original filed document to which they relate and may be filed by the corporation without further action by the board of directors or the shareholders.

Cross-References

Corporate name, see ch. 4 and § 15.06.

Correcting filed document, see § 1.24.

Effective time and date of filing, see § 1.23.

"Electronic transmission" defined, see § 1.40.

Filing fees, see § 1.22.

Forms, see § 1.21.

Penalty for signing false document, see § 1.29.

Registration statement for foreign corporation, see § 15.03.

Secretary of state's filing duty, see § 1.25.

"Sign" defined, see § 1.40.

Official Comment

Section 1.20 standardizes the filing requirements for all documents expressly required or permitted by the Act to be filed by the secretary of state; it does not authorize or direct the secretary of state to accept or reject for filing other documents relating to corporations and does not address documents required or permitted to be filed under other statutes. In a few instances, other sections of the Act impose additional requirements which must also be complied with if the document in question is to be filed.

The filing requirements of chapter 1 are intended to minimize both the number of documents to be processed by the secretary of state and the number of disputes between persons seeking to file documents and the secretary of state as to the legal efficacy of documents.

1.   Form

The Act permits a document to be filed in typewritten or printed form through physical delivery to the secretary of state or (if permitted by the secretary of state) by electronic transmission, which is broadly defined in section 1.40. Section 1.21 permits the secretary of state to prescribe forms, but the secretary of state may only make mandatory those forms listed in section 1.21(a). As a result, the secretary of state may not reject other documents on the basis of form if they contain the information called for by the specific statutory requirement and meet the minimal formal requirements of this section. See section 1.25.

2.   Signing

Section 1.40 defines "sign" and "signing," and section 1.20(f) states who must sign a document. The Act does not require that documents be acknowledged or verified as a condition for filing. Requirements such as these serve little purpose in connection with documents filed under the Act because section 1.29 makes it a criminal offense for any person to sign a document for filing with knowledge that it contains false information. On the other hand, many organizations, like lenders or title companies, may desire that specific documents include acknowledgments, verifications, or seals. Section 1.20(g) therefore provides that these additional forms of authentication do not affect the eligibility of the document for filing.

3.   Copies

For purposes of section 1.20(i), an "exact" copy is a reproduction of the signed original document, and a "conformed" copy is a copy on which the existence of signatures is entered or noted on the copy. However, a person submitting "duplicate originals" meets any requirement for a conformed copy because the secretary of state may treat the duplicate original as a "conformed copy."

4. Reference to Extrinsic Facts

Section 1.20(k) applies where the Act permits any of the terms of a filed document or a plan to be made dependent on facts outside the document or plan. Common examples are references to an interest rate such as the federal funds rate or to securities market prices. Section 1.20(k)(2) also provides that the facts on which a filed document or plan may be made dependent include facts within the control of the corporation to make clear that those facts do not need to occur independently. In addition to a determination or action by the corporation, references to extrinsic facts may also include references to determinations or actions by the board of directors, a committee of the board, an officer, employee or agent of the corporation, or any other person.

If the terms of a filed document or plan are made dependent on an agreement or other document as authorized by section 1.20(k)(2)(iii), care should be taken to identify the agreement or document in a manner that satisfies the objectively ascertainable standard, and the manner in which the terms or events under it are to operate must be specified. Consideration should also be given to the intended effects of an amendment to the agreement or document. A simple reference to an agreement will presumably include subsequent amendments, although a reference to the same agreement as in effect on a specified date presumably will not.

Chapters 9 and 11 generally require the board of directors to adopt a plan of domestication, conversion, merger or share exchange, and section 6.21 requires the board to determine the adequacy of consideration for shares to be issued by the corporation.

§ 1.21. Forms

(a) The secretary of state may prescribe and furnish on request forms for: (i) an application for a certificate of existence or certificate of registration, (ii) a foreign corporation's registration statement, (iii) a foreign corporation's statement of withdrawal, (iv) a foreign corporation's transfer of registration statement, and (v) the annual report. If the secretary of state so requires, use of these forms is mandatory.

(b) The secretary of state may prescribe and furnish on request forms for other documents required or permitted to be filed by this Act but their use is not mandatory.

Cross-References

Annual report, see § 16.21.

Certificate of existence or registration, see § 1.28.

Filing requirements, see § 1.20.

Foreign registration statement, see § 15.03.

Statement of withdrawal, see § 15.09.

Transfer of foreign registration statement, see § 15.10.

Official Comment

The Act does not vest the secretary of state with general authority to establish mandatory forms for use under the Act. However, certain types of reports and requests for documents may be processed efficiently only if uniform forms are used. Applications for certificates of existence or registration, for example, should require specific information located at specific places on the form. Similarly, processing of large-volume, largely routine filings is expedited if standardized forms are required. Also, the disclosure requirements of the annual report may be administered on a systematic basis if a standardized form is mandated. Section 1.21(a) recognizes that these considerations may exist in limited cases.

§ 1.22. Filing, Service, and Copying Fees

(a)   The secretary of state shall collect the following fees when the documents described in this subsection are delivered to the secretary of state for filing:

Document	Fee
Articles of incorporation	$_____.
Application for use of indistinguishable name	$_____.
Application for reserved name	$_____.
Notice of transfer of reserved name	$_____.
Application for registered name	$_____.
Application for renewal of registered name	$_____.
Corporation's statement of change of registered agent or registered office or both	$_____.
Agent's statement of change of registered office for each affected corporation not to exceed a total of $_____	$_____.
Agent's statement of resignation	No fee.
Articles of domestication	$_____.
Articles of conversion	$_____.
Amendment of articles of incorporation	$_____.
Restatement of articles of incorporation with amendment of articles	$_____.
Restatement of articles of incorporation without amendment of articles	$_____.
Articles of merger or share exchange	$_____.
Articles of dissolution	$_____.
Articles of revocation of dissolution	$_____.
Certificate of administrative dissolution	No fee.
Application for reinstatement following administrative dissolution	$_____.
Certificate of reinstatement	No fee.
Certificate of judicial dissolution	No fee.
Foreign registration statement	$_____.
Amendment of foreign registration statement	$_____.
Statement of withdrawal	$_____.
Transfer of foreign registration statement	$_____.
Notice of termination of registration	No fee.
Annual report	$_____.
Articles of correction	$_____.
Articles of validation	$_____.
Application for certificate of existence or registration	$_____.
Any other document required or permitted to be filed by this Act	$_____.

(b)   The secretary of state shall collect a fee of $ _____ each time process is served on the secretary of state under this Act. The party to a proceeding causing service of process is entitled to recover this fee as costs if such party prevails in the proceeding.

(c)   The secretary of state shall collect the following fees for copying and certifying the copy of any filed document relating to a domestic or foreign corporation:

$ _____ a page for copying; and

$ _____ for the certificate.

Cross-References

Agent's change of registered office, see § 5.02.

Agent's resignation, see § 5.03.

Amendment of articles of incorporation, see §§ 10.06 and 10.08.

Annual report, see § 16.21.

Articles of conversion, see § 9.33.

Articles of domestication, see § 9.22.

Articles of merger or share exchange, see § 11.06.

Articles of validation, see § 1.51.

Corporation's change of registered agent or office, see § 5.02.

Correction of filed document, see § 1.24.

Dissolution:

administrative, see § 14.21.

judicial, see § 14.30.

reinstatement, see § 14.22.

revocation, see § 14.04.

voluntary, see §§ 14.01 through 14.09.

Evidentiary effect of certified copy, see § 1.27.

Existence, see § 1.28.

Foreign registration statement, see § 15.03.

Incorporation, see § 2.03.

Name of corporation, see § 4.01.

Notice of termination of registration, see § 15.11.

Registered name, see § 4.03.

Renewal of registered name, see § 4.03.

Reserved name, see § 4.02.

Restated articles of incorporation, see § 10.07.

Service on secretary of state, see §§ 5.04, 9.24, 9.35, 11.07, 15.07 and 15.09.

Statement of withdrawal, see §§ 15.07 and 15.09.

Transfer of foreign registration statement, see § 15.10.

Transfer of registered name, see § 4.03.

Official Comment

Section 1.22 establishes in a single section the filing fees for all documents that may be filed under the Act. The dollar amounts for each document should be inserted by each state as it adopts the Act.

The list of documents in section 1.22 includes all documents that are authorized to be filed with the secretary of state under the Act. The catch-all in the last item of the list will apply to any document for which a state does not establish a specific filing fee.

The provision relating to a registered agent's statement of change of registered office contains a maximum fee for filing a change of address of a registered agent. Since corporation service companies serve as registered agents for thousands of corporations in many jurisdictions, their change of address may require a very large number of filings. The fee is broadly based on the number of corporations affected but a maximum fee is specified to reflect that as the number of changes increases the cost per change should decrease.

§ 1.23.　Effective Date of Filed Document

(a)　Except to the extent otherwise provided in section 1.24(c) and subchapter E of this chapter, a document accepted for filing is effective:

(1)　on the date and at the time of filing, as provided in section 1.25(b);

(2)　on the date of filing and at the time specified in the document as its effective time if later than the time under subsection (a)(1);

(3)　at a specified delayed effective date and time which may not be more than 90 days after filing; or

(4)　if a delayed effective date is specified, but no time is specified, at 12:01 a.m. on the date specified, which may not be more than 90 days after the date of filing.

(b)　If a filed document does not specify the time zone or place at which a date or time or both is to be determined, the date or time or both at which it becomes effective shall be those prevailing at the place of filing in this state.

Cross-References

"Effective date" defined, see § 1.40.

Filing requirements, see § 1.20.

Official Comment

Section 1.23 provides definitive rules governing when a filed document becomes effective. The definition of effective date in section 1.40 ties in with this section so that throughout the Act the term "effective date" of a filed document means the effective date and time determined pursuant to section 1.23. The Act does not generally distinguish between the effective date of a filed document and the effectiveness of what the document is accomplishing. However, in a few instances where filings in more than one jurisdiction are required, the Act distinguishes between the effective date of the document and the effectiveness of a transaction being effected by the document. See sections 9.22(d) and 9.33(d) regarding certain domestications and conversions and section 11.06(e) regarding certain mergers.

Section 1.41 deals with the effectiveness of notices and other communications and does not use or define the term "effective date."

§ 1.24.　Correcting Filed Document

(a)　A document filed by the secretary of state pursuant to this Act may be corrected if (i) the document contains an inaccuracy, (ii) the document was defectively signed, attested, sealed, verified, or acknowledged, or (iii) the electronic transmission was defective.

(b)　A document is corrected:

(1) by preparing articles of correction that

(i) describe the document (including its filing date) or attach a copy of it to the articles of correction,

(ii) specify the inaccuracy or defect to be corrected, and

(iii) correct the inaccuracy or defect; and

(2) by delivering the articles of correction to the secretary of state for filing.

(c) Articles of correction are effective on the effective date of the document they correct except as to persons relying on the uncorrected document and adversely affected by the correction. As to those persons, articles of correction are effective when filed.

Cross-References

Effective time and date of filing, see § 1.23.

"Electronic transmission" defined, see § 1.40.

Filing requirements, see § 1.20.

Official Comment

Section 1.24 permits making corrections in filed documents without redelivering the entire document or submitting formal articles of amendment. This correction procedure has two advantages: (i) delivering articles of correction may be less expensive than delivering the document or filing articles of amendment, and (ii) articles of correction do not alter the effective date of the underlying document being corrected.

If no filing is made because of a defect in transmission or delivery, articles of correction may not be used to make a retroactive filing. Therefore, a corporation making an electronic filing should take steps to confirm that the filing was received by the secretary of state.

A provision in a document setting an effective date under section 1.23 may be corrected under this section, but the corrected effective date cannot be before the date of filing of the document or more than 90 days thereafter.

§ 1.25. Filing Duty of Secretary of State

(a) If a document delivered to the office of the secretary of state for filing satisfies the requirements of section 1.20, the secretary of state shall file it.

(b) The secretary of state files a document by recording it as filed on the date and time of receipt. After filing a document, the secretary of state shall return to the person who delivered the document for filing a copy of the document with an acknowledgement of the date and time of filing.

(c) If the secretary of state refuses to file a document, it shall be returned to the person who delivered the document for filing within five days after the document was delivered, together with a brief, written explanation of the reason for the refusal.

(d) The secretary of state's duty to file documents under this section is ministerial. The secretary of state's filing or refusing to file a document does not create a presumption that: (i) the document does or does not conform to the requirements of the Act; or (ii) the information contained in the document is correct or incorrect.

Cross-References

Appeal from refusal to file document, see § 1.26.

Effective time and date of filing, see § 1.23.

Filing requirements, see § 1.20.

Powers of secretary of state, see § 1.30.

Official Comment

Section 1.25 limits the discretion of the secretary of state to a ministerial role in reviewing the contents of documents. If the document submitted contains the information required by section 1.20 and the applicable provision of the Act (and if a mandatory form has been prescribed under section 1.21(a), the document is in that form), the secretary of state under section 1.25 must file it even though it contains additional provisions the secretary of state may believe are irrelevant or not authorized by the Act or by general legal principles. Persons adversely affected by provisions in a document may test their validity in a proceeding appropriate for that purpose. Similarly, the attorney general of the state may also question the validity of provisions of documents accepted for filing by the secretary of state in an independent suit brought for that purpose. In neither case should any presumption or inference be drawn about the validity of a provision from the fact that the secretary of state accepted the document for filing.

§ 1.26. Appeal from Secretary of State's Refusal to File Document

(a)   If the secretary of state refuses to file a document delivered for filing, the person that delivered the document for filing may petition [name or describe court] to compel its filing. The document and the explanation of the secretary of state of the refusal to file must be attached to the petition. The court may decide the matter in a summary proceeding.

(b)   The court may order the secretary of state to file the document or take other action the court considers appropriate.

(c)   The court's final decision may be appealed as in other civil proceedings.

Cross-References

Filing fees, see § 1.22.

Filing requirements, see § 1.20.

Secretary of state's filing duty, see § 1.25.

Official Comment

The identity of the specific court with jurisdiction to hear proceedings under section 1.26 must be supplied by each state when enacting this section. This may be a court of general civil jurisdiction or a court of relevant specialized jurisdiction. Other sections of the Act also contemplate that the court with jurisdiction over substantive corporate matters will be designated in the statute. See, for example, section 7.03, relating to the ordering of a shareholders' meeting after the corporation fails to hold such a meeting.

The phrase "summary proceeding" in section 1.26(a) refers to a class of cases where the court takes action on an expedited basis and decides the case on a limited record given the narrowness of the issues involved. See section 1.25.

The Act does not address either the burden of proof or the standard for review in judicial proceedings challenging action of the secretary of state. It is contemplated that these matters will be governed by general principles of judicial review of agency action.

§ 1.27. Evidentiary Effect of Certified Copy of Filed Document

A certificate from the secretary of state delivered with a copy of a document filed by the secretary of state is conclusive evidence that the original document is on file with the secretary of state.

Cross-References

Certifying fee, see § 1.22.

Forms, see § 1.21.

Official Comment

Upon payment of the fees specified in section 1.22(c), the secretary of state may be requested to certify that a specific document has been filed. The limited effect of the certificate is consistent with the ministerial filing obligation imposed on the secretary of state under the Act.

§ 1.28. Certificate of Existence or Registration

(a)   Any person may apply to the secretary of state to furnish a certificate of existence for a domestic corporation or a certificate of registration for a foreign corporation.

(b)   A certificate of existence sets forth:

(1)   the domestic corporation's corporate name;

(2)   that the domestic corporation is duly incorporated under the law of this state, the date of its incorporation, and the period of its duration if less than perpetual;

(3)   that all fees, taxes, and penalties owed to this state have been paid, if

(i)   payment is reflected in the records of the secretary of state, and

(ii)   nonpayment affects the existence of the domestic corporation;

(4)   that its most recent annual report required by section 16.21 has been filed with the secretary of state;

(5)   that articles of dissolution have not been filed;

(6)   that the corporation is not administratively dissolved and a proceeding is not pending under section 14.21; and

(7)   other facts of record in the office of the secretary of state that may be requested by the applicant.

(c)   A certificate of registration sets forth:

(1)   the foreign corporation's name used in this state;

(2)   that the foreign corporation is registered to do business in this state;

(3)   that all fees, taxes, and penalties owed to this state have been paid, if

(i)   payment is reflected in the records of the secretary of state, and

(ii)   nonpayment affects the registration of the foreign corporation;

(4)   that its most recent annual report required by section 16.21 has been filed with the secretary of state; and

(5)   other facts of record in the office of the secretary of state that may be requested by the applicant.

(d)   Subject to any qualification stated in the certificate, a certificate of existence or registration issued by the secretary of state may be relied upon as conclusive evidence of the facts stated in the certificate.

Cross-References

Filing fees, see § 1.22.

Filing requirements, see § 1.20.

Foreign registration statement, see § 15.03.

Forms, see § 1.21.

Official Comment

Section 1.28 establishes a procedure by which any person may obtain a conclusive certificate from the secretary of state that a particular domestic corporation is in existence or that a particular foreign corporation is registered to do business in the state. The secretary of state is to make the judgment whether the corporation is in existence or is registered to do business from public records only and is not expected to make a more extensive investigation. In appropriate cases, the secretary of state may issue a certificate subject to specified qualifications.

Sections 1.28(b)(3) and 1.28(c)(3) refer only to fees, taxes and penalties collected by the secretary of state or collected by other agencies and reported to the secretary of state. In some states the secretary of state may ascertain from other agencies that franchise or other taxes have been paid and include this information in the certificate. In states where this procedure does not unduly delay the issuance of certificates, section 1.28 may be revised appropriately. Sections 1.28(b)(3) and 1.28(c)(3) relate only to fees, taxes and penalties to the extent their nonpayment affects the existence or registration to do business of the corporation.

§ 1.29. Penalty for Signing False Document

(a)   A person commits an offense by signing a document that the person knows is false in any material respect with intent that the document be delivered to the secretary of state for filing.

(b)   An offense under this section is a [_____] misdemeanor [punishable by a fine of not to exceed $ _____].

Cross-References

"Sign" defined, see § 1.40.

Official Comment

As provided in section 1.40, "sign" includes any manual, facsimile, conformed, or electronic signature. Section 1.29(b) is keyed to the classification of offenses provided by the Model Penal Code. If a state has not adopted this classification, the dollar amount of the fine should be substituted for the misdemeanor classification.

SUBCHAPTER C
SECRETARY OF STATE

§ 1.30. Powers

The secretary of state has the power reasonably necessary to perform the duties required of the secretary of state by this Act.

Cross-References

Administrative dissolution, see § 14.20.

Administrative termination of registration, see § 15.11.

Secretary of state's filing duty, see § 1.25.

Official Comment

Section 1.30 is intended to grant the secretary of state the authority necessary for the efficient performance of the filing and other duties imposed on the secretary of state by the Act but is not intended as a grant of general authority to establish public policy. The most important aspects of a modern corporation statute relate to the creation and maintenance of relationships among persons interested in or involved with a corporation; these relationships should be a matter of concern to the parties involved and not subject to regulation or interpretation by the secretary of state. Further, even in situations involving claims that the corporation has been formed or is being operated for purposes that may violate the public policies of the state, the secretary of state is usually not the governmental official that determines the scope of public policy through administration of the secretary of state's filing responsibilities under the Act.

Rather, the attorney general may seek to enjoin the illegal conduct or to dissolve involuntarily the offending corporation.

SUBCHAPTER D
DEFINITIONS

§ 1.40. Act Definitions

In this Act, unless otherwise specified:

"Articles of incorporation" means the articles of incorporation described in section 2.02, all amendments to the articles of incorporation, and any other documents permitted or required to be delivered for filing by a domestic business corporation with the secretary of state under any provision of this Act that modify, amend, supplement, restate or replace the articles of incorporation. After an amendment of the articles of incorporation or any other document filed under this Act that restates the articles of incorporation in their entirety, the articles of incorporation shall not include any prior documents. When used with respect to a foreign corporation or a domestic or foreign nonprofit corporation, the "articles of incorporation" of such an entity means the document of such entity that is equivalent to the articles of incorporation of a domestic business corporation.

"Authorized shares" means the shares of all classes a domestic or foreign corporation is authorized to issue.

"Beneficial shareholder" means a person who owns the beneficial interest in shares, which may be a record shareholder or a person on whose behalf shares are registered in the name of an intermediary or nominee.

"Conspicuous" means so written, displayed, or presented that a reasonable person against whom the writing is to operate should have noticed it.

"Corporation," "domestic corporation," "business corporation" or "domestic business corporation" means a corporation for profit, which is not a foreign corporation, incorporated under this Act.

"Deliver" or "delivery" means any method of delivery used in conventional commercial practice, including delivery by hand, mail, commercial delivery, and, if authorized in accordance with section 1.41, by electronic transmission.

"Distribution" means a direct or indirect transfer of cash or other property (except a corporation's own shares) or incurrence of indebtedness by a corporation to or for the benefit of its shareholders in respect of any of its shares. A distribution may be in the form of a payment of a dividend; a purchase, redemption, or other acquisition of shares; a distribution of indebtedness; a distribution in liquidation; or otherwise.

"Document" means (i) any tangible medium on which information is inscribed, and includes handwritten, typed, printed or similar instruments, and copies of such instruments, or (ii) an electronic record.

"Domestic," with respect to an entity, means an entity governed as to its internal affairs by the law of this state.

"Effective date," when referring to a document accepted for filing by the secretary of state, means the time and date determined in accordance with section 1.23.

"Electronic" means relating to technology having electrical, digital, magnetic, wireless, optical, electromagnetic, or similar capabilities.

"Electronic record" means information that is stored in an electronic or other nontangible medium and is retrievable in paper form through an automated process used in conventional commercial practice, unless otherwise authorized in accordance with section 1.41(j).

"Electronic transmission" or "electronically transmitted" means any form or process of communication not directly involving the physical transfer of paper or another tangible medium, which (i) is suitable for the retention, retrieval, and reproduction of information by the recipient, and (ii) is retrievable in paper form by the recipient through an automated process used in conventional commercial practice, unless otherwise authorized in accordance with section 1.41(j).

"Eligible entity" means a domestic or foreign unincorporated entity or a domestic or foreign nonprofit corporation.

"Eligible interests" means interests or memberships.

"Employee" includes an officer but not a director. A director may accept duties that make the director also an employee.

"Entity" includes domestic and foreign business corporation; domestic and foreign nonprofit corporation; estate; trust; domestic and foreign unincorporated entity; and state, United States, and foreign government.

"Expenses" means reasonable expenses of any kind that are incurred in connection with a matter.

"Filing entity" means an unincorporated entity, other than a limited liability partnership, that is of a type that is created by filing a public organic record or is required to file a public organic record that evidences its creation.

"Foreign," with respect to an entity, means an entity governed as to its internal affairs by the organic law of a jurisdiction other than this state.

"Foreign corporation" or "foreign business corporation" means a corporation incorporated under a law other than the law of this state which would be a business corporation if incorporated under the law of this state.

"Foreign nonprofit corporation" means a corporation incorporated under a law other than the law of this state which would be a nonprofit corporation if incorporated under the law of this state.

"Foreign registration statement" means the foreign registration statement described in section 15.03.

"Governmental subdivision" includes authority, county, district, and municipality.

"Governor" means any person under whose authority the powers of an entity are exercised and under whose direction the activities and affairs of the entity are managed pursuant to the organic law governing the entity and its organic rules.

"Includes" and "including" denote a partial definition or a nonexclusive list.

"Individual" means a natural person.

"Interest" means either or both of the following rights under the organic law governing an unincorporated entity:

>   (i)   the right to receive distributions from the entity either in the ordinary course or upon liquidation; or

>   (ii)   the right to receive notice or vote on issues involving its internal affairs, other than as an agent, assignee, proxy or person responsible for managing its business and affairs.

"Interest holder" means a person who holds of record an interest.

"Interest holder liability" means:

>   (i)   personal liability for a debt, obligation, or other liability of a domestic or foreign corporation or eligible entity that is imposed on a person:

(A) solely by reason of the person's status as a shareholder, member or interest holder; or

(B) by the articles of incorporation of the domestic corporation or the organic rules of the eligible entity or foreign corporation that make one or more specified shareholders, members, or interest holders, or categories of shareholders, members, or interest holders, liable in their capacity as shareholders, members, or interest holders for all or specified liabilities of the corporation or eligible entity; or

(ii) an obligation of a shareholder, member, or interest holder under the articles of incorporation of a domestic corporation or the organic rules of an eligible entity or foreign corporation to contribute to the entity.

For purposes of the foregoing, except as otherwise provided in the articles of incorporation of a domestic corporation or the organic law or organic rules of an eligible entity or a foreign corporation, interest holder liability arises under clause (i) when the corporation or eligible entity incurs the liability.

"Jurisdiction of formation" means the state or country the law of which includes the organic law governing a domestic or foreign corporation or eligible entity.

"Means" denotes an exhaustive definition.

"Membership" means the rights of a member in a domestic or foreign nonprofit corporation.

"Merger" means a transaction pursuant to section 11.02.

"Nonfiling entity" means an unincorporated entity that is of a type that is not created by filing a public organic record.

"Nonprofit corporation" or "domestic nonprofit corporation" means a corporation incorporated under the laws of this state and subject to the provisions of the [name of state] Nonprofit Corporation Act.

"Organic law" means the statute governing the internal affairs of a domestic or foreign business or nonprofit corporation or unincorporated entity.

"Organic rules" means the public organic record and private organic rules of a domestic or foreign corporation or eligible entity.

"Person" includes an individual and an entity.

"Principal office" means the office (in or out of this state) so designated in the annual report or foreign registration statement where the principal executive offices of a domestic or foreign corporation are located.

"Private organic rules" means (i) the bylaws of a domestic or foreign business or nonprofit corporation or (ii) the rules, regardless of whether in writing, that govern the internal affairs of an unincorporated entity, are binding on all its interest holders, and are not part of its public organic record, if any. Where private organic rules have been amended or restated, the term means the private organic rules as last amended or restated.

"Proceeding" includes civil suit and criminal, administrative, and investigatory action.

"Public organic record" means (i) the articles of incorporation of a domestic or foreign business or nonprofit corporation or (ii) the document, if any, the filing of which is required to create an unincorporated entity, or which creates the unincorporated entity and is required to be filed. Where a public organic record has been amended or restated, the term means the public organic record as last amended or restated.

"Record date" means the date fixed for determining the identity of the corporation's shareholders and their shareholdings for purposes of this Act. Unless another time is specified when the record date is fixed, the determination shall be made as of the close of business at the principal office of the corporation on the date so fixed.

"Record shareholder" means (i) the person in whose name shares are registered in the records of the corporation or (ii) the person identified as the beneficial owner of shares in a beneficial ownership certificate pursuant to section 7.23 on file with the corporation to the extent of the rights granted by such certificate.

"Registered foreign corporation" means a foreign corporation registered to do business in the state pursuant to chapter 15.

"Secretary" means the corporate officer to whom the board of directors has delegated responsibility under section 8.40(c) to maintain the minutes of the meetings of the board of directors and of the shareholders and for authenticating records of the corporation.

"Share exchange" means a transaction pursuant to section 11.03.

"Shareholder" means a record shareholder.

"Shares" means the units into which the proprietary interests in a domestic or foreign corporation are divided.

"Sign" or "signature" means, with present intent to authenticate or adopt a document:

(i)   to execute or adopt a tangible symbol to a document, and includes any manual, facsimile, or conformed signature; or

(ii)   to attach to or logically associate with an electronic transmission an electronic sound, symbol, or process, and includes an electronic signature in an electronic transmission.

"State," when referring to a part of the United States, includes a state and commonwealth (and their agencies and governmental subdivisions) and a territory and insular possession (and their agencies and governmental subdivisions) of the United States.

"Subscriber" means a person who subscribes for shares in a corporation, whether before or after incorporation.

"Type of entity" means a generic form of entity:

(i)   recognized at common law; or

(ii)   formed under an organic law, regardless of whether some entities formed under that law are subject to provisions of that law that create different categories of the form of entity.

"Unincorporated entity" means an organization or artificial legal person that either has a separate legal existence or has the power to acquire an estate in real property in its own name and that is not any of the following: a domestic or foreign business or nonprofit corporation, a series of a limited liability company or of another type of entity, an estate, a trust, a state, United States, or foreign government. The term includes a general partnership, limited liability company, limited partnership, business trust, joint stock association and unincorporated nonprofit association.

"United States" includes district, authority, bureau, commission, department, and any other agency of the United States.

"Unrestricted voting trust beneficial owner" means, with respect to any shareholder rights, a voting trust beneficial owner whose entitlement to exercise the shareholder right in question is not inconsistent with the voting trust agreement.

"Voting group" means all shares of one or more classes or series that under the articles of incorporation or this Act are entitled to vote and be counted together collectively on a matter at a meeting of shareholders. All shares entitled by the articles of incorporation or this Act to vote generally on the matter are for that purpose a single voting group.

"Voting power" means the current power to vote in the election of directors.

"Voting trust beneficial owner" means an owner of a beneficial interest in shares of the corporation held in a voting trust established pursuant to section 7.30(a).

"Writing" or "written" means any information in the form of a document.

Cross-References

Annual report, see § 16.21.

Nominee shares, see § 7.23.

Notice, see § 1.41.

Special definitions:

"acquired entity," see § 11.01.

"acquiring entity," see § 11.01.

"affiliate," see § 13.01.

"beneficial shareholder," see § 13.01.

"claim," see § 14.06.

"control," see § 8.60.

"conversion," see § 9.01.

"converted entity," see § 9.01.

"converting entity," see § 9.01.

"corporation," see §§ 5.01, 8.50 and 13.01.

"derivative proceeding," see § 7.40.

"director's conflicting interest transaction," see § 8.60.

"domesticated corporation," see § 9.01.

"domesticating corporation," see § 9.01.

"domestication," see § 9.01.

"enactment date," see § 9.01.

"fair to the corporation," see § 8.60.

"fair value," see § 13.01.

"foreign corporation," see § 7.47 and ch. 15.

"interest," see § 13.01.

"interested transaction," see § 13.01.

"liability," see § 8.50.

"material financial interest," see § 8.60.

"merger," see § 11.01.

"new interest holder liability," see §§ 10.03 and 11.01.

"officer," see § 8.50.

"official capacity," see § 8.50.

"outstanding shares," see § 6.03.

"party," see § 8.50.

"party to a merger," see § 11.01.

"preferred shares," see § 13.01.

"proceeding," see § 8.50.

"protected agreement," see § 9.01.

"qualified director," see § 1.43.

"record shareholder," see § 13.01.

"related person," see § 8.60.

"relevant time," see § 8.60.

"required disclosure," see § 8.60.

"senior executive," see § 13.01.

"share exchange," see § 11.01.

"shareholder," see §§ 7.03, 7.40, 7.48, 13.01, 14.30 and 16.02.

"shares," see §§ 6.27 and 6.30.

"survivor," see § 11.01.

Official Comment

Section 1.40 contains definitions of terms used generally throughout the Act. Other subchapters and sections of the Act contain specialized definitions that are applicable only to those subchapters or sections.

Beneficial Shareholder

Because various provisions of the Act allow beneficial owners of shares to take actions as a shareholder even in the absence of a beneficial ownership certificate under section 7.23, the term "beneficial shareholder" has been defined in section 1.40.

The definition does not specify what interests are necessary for a person to be a beneficial shareholder, but consistent with section 8–207(a) of the Uniform Commercial Code, the Act contemplates that the corporation is entitled to treat the beneficial shareholder as having the full bundle of economic and voting rights associated with the shares. For this reason, the beneficial owner of shares in a voting trust has been defined separately in section 1.40 as a "voting trust beneficial owner."

Unlike section 7.23, which provides for a procedure to specify a beneficial owner in a beneficial ownership certificate, the definition of "beneficial shareholder" does not prescribe a procedure for establishing beneficial ownership. Where a court proceeding is involved, as it is, for example, in sections 7.41 (derivative proceeding), 13.30 (appraisal rights), and 14.30 (judicial dissolution), the court can determine what is necessary to establish beneficial ownership. In other situations, custom and practice and the reasonable requirements of the corporation should apply. Thus, a certification of a broker-dealer or other financial institution or a current account statement from such an institution often is sufficient to establish beneficial ownership. In the case of a public corporation, a filing with the Securities and Exchange Commission identifying beneficial ownership might be sufficient.

When shares of a public corporation are held, as explained in the Official Comment to section 7.23, indirectly in street name with a broker-dealer or other financial institution, which may in turn have the shares on deposit with Depository Trust Company ("DTC") as a clearing agency, a reference to shares in this Act is technically a reference to a "securities entitlement" under section 8–102(a)(17) of the Uniform Commercial Code, which is an undivided interest in a mass of shares held by the financial intermediary or on deposit with DTC. Nevertheless, the Act continues for convenience to refer to the interests as "shares," and thus references to shares should be read to include securities entitlements with respect to those shares.

Conspicuous

"Conspicuous" is defined in section 1.40 and is comparable to section 1–201(10) of the Uniform Commercial Code. The test is whether attention can reasonably be expected to be elicited.

Corporation, Domestic Corporation, Domestic Business Corporation, Business Corporation and Foreign Corporation

"Corporation," "domestic corporation," "business corporation," and "domestic business corporation," as defined in section 1.40, all mean the same thing and may be used interchangeably. The word "corporation," when used alone, refers only to a domestic corporation. In some instances, the phrase "domestic corporation" has been used to contrast it with a foreign corporation, a term also defined in section 1.40. The phrase "domestic business corporation" has been used on occasion to contrast it with a domestic nonprofit corporation. "Corporation" has been given special meanings in sections 5.01, 8.50 and 13.01.

Distribution

Section 1.40 defines "distribution" to include all transfers of cash or other property made by a corporation to any shareholder in respect of the corporation's shares, except mere changes in the unit of interest such as share dividends and share splits. Thus, a "distribution" includes the payment of a dividend, a purchase by a corporation of its own shares, a distribution of evidences of indebtedness or promissory notes of the corporation, and a distribution in voluntary or involuntary liquidation. If a corporation incurs indebtedness to shareholders in connection with a distribution (as in the case of a distribution of a debt instrument or an installment purchase of shares), the creation, incurrence, or distribution of the indebtedness is the event which constitutes the distribution rather than the subsequent payment of the debt by the corporation, except in the situation addressed in section 6.40(g).

The term "indirect" in the definition of "distribution" is intended to address transactions like the repurchase of parent company shares by a subsidiary whose actions are controlled by the parent. It also is intended to address any other transaction in which the substance is clearly the same as a typical dividend or share repurchase, no matter how structured or labeled.

The test for validity of distributions other than distributions in liquidation is set forth in section 6.40, and for distributions in liquidation in chapter 14.

Electronic Transmission

The terms "electronic," "electronic record," "electronic transmission" and "electronically transmitted" incorporate into the Act terminology from the Uniform Electronic Transmissions Act ("UETA") and the federal Electronic Signatures in Global and National Commerce Act ("E-Sign"). See Official Comment to section 1.41, Note on the Relationship Between Act Provisions on Electronic Technology and UETA and E-Sign. Electronic records and transmissions are intended to be broadly construed.

Entity

The term "entity," defined in section 1.40, appears in the definition of "person" in section 1.40 and covers all types of artificial persons. Estates and trusts and general partnerships are included even though they may not, in some jurisdictions, be considered artificial persons. "Trust," by itself, means a nonbusiness trust, such as a traditional testamentary or inter vivos trust. The term "entity" is broader than the term "unincorporated entity" which is also defined in section 1.40. See also the definitions in section 1.40 of "governmental subdivision," "state," and "United States." A form of co-ownership of property or sharing of returns from property that is not a partnership under the Uniform Partnership Act will not be an "unincorporated entity."

Expenses

The Act provides in a number of contexts that expenses relating to a proceeding incurred by a person shall or may be paid by another, through indemnification or by court order in specific contexts. See, for example, sections 7.46, 7.48, 8.53(a), 8.54, 13.31, 14.32(e), 16.04(c) and 16.05(c). Other than the requirement that expenses must be reasonable in the circumstances, the type or character of the expenses is not limited. Examples include such things as fees and disbursements of counsel, experts of all kinds, and jury and similar litigation consultants; travel, lodging, transcription, reproduction, photographic, video recording, communication, and delivery costs, whether included in the disbursements of counsel, experts, or consultants, or directly incurred; court costs; and premiums for posting required bonds.

Interest Holder Liability

The term "interest holder liability" is used in the context of provisions in chapters 9 and 11 that describe the effects on the personal liability of shareholders, members and interest holders when the entity in which they hold shares, memberships or interests is the subject of a transaction under those chapters. The term is also used in section 2.02 and chapter 10 with respect to the articles of incorporation and certain amendments to them. The term includes only liabilities that are imposed solely because of the person's status as a shareholder, member or interest holder, or by the organic rules of an entity on shareholders, members or interest holders. Liabilities that a shareholder, member or interest holder incurs by contract (other than a contract that is part of an entity's organic rules, such as a partnership agreement) are not included. Thus, for example, if a state's business corporation law were to make shareholders personally liable for unpaid wages, that liability would be an "interest holder liability." If, on the other hand, a shareholder were to contractually guarantee payment of an obligation of a corporation, that liability would not be an "interest holder liability."

Membership

"Membership" is defined in section 1.40 to refer only to the rights of a member in a nonprofit corporation. Although the owners of a limited liability company are generally referred to as "members," for purposes of the Act they are referred to as "interest holders" and what they own in the limited liability company is referred to in the Act as an "interest."

Organic Rules, Public Organic Record and Private Organic Rules

The term "organic rules" in section 1.40 includes both public organic records and private organic rules. The term "public organic record" includes such documents as the articles of incorporation of a business or nonprofit corporation, the certificate of limited partnership of a limited partnership, the articles of organization or certificate of formation of a limited liability company, the deed of trust of a business trust and comparable documents, however denominated, that are publicly filed to create other types of unincorporated entities. An election of limited liability partnership status is not of itself a public organic record because it does not create the underlying general or limited partnership by filing the election, although the election may be made part of the public organic record of the partnership by its organic law. The term "private organic rules" includes corporate bylaws, a partnership agreement of a general or limited partnership, an operating agreement of a limited liability company and comparable agreements, however denominated, of unincorporated types of other entities. Private organic rules of unincorporated entities are not required by the Act to be in writing, and therefore would include oral partnership agreements and oral operating agreements.

Person

The term "person" is defined in section 1.40 to include an individual or an entity. In the case of an individual the Act assumes that the person is competent to act in the matter under general state law independent of the corporation statute.

Principal Office

Many corporations maintain numerous offices, but there is usually one office, sometimes colloquially referred to as the home office or headquarters, where the principal corporate officers are located. The corporation must designate its principal office address in the annual report required by section 16.21, and a foreign corporation must also do so in its foreign registration statement. To clarify which corporate office is the principal office, the Act defines the office designated by the corporation in the annual report (or foreign registration statement) as the principal office of the corporation.

Secretary

The term "secretary" is defined in section 1.40 because the Act does not require the corporation to maintain any specific or titled officers. See section 8.40. However, some corporate officer, however titled, must perform the functions described in this definition, and various sections of the Act refer to that officer as the "secretary."

Shareholder and Record Shareholder

The term "shareholder" is usually used in the Act to mean a "record shareholder" as defined in section 1.40, but section 1.40 contemplates that definitions may be expanded or limited by the Act for purposes of specific provisions. The definition of "record shareholder" in section 1.40 includes a beneficial owner of shares named in a beneficial ownership certificate under section 7.23, but only to the extent of the rights granted the beneficial owner in the certificate—for example, the right to receive notice of, and vote at, shareholders' meetings. Various substantive sections of the Act also permit holders of voting trust certificates or beneficial owners of shares (not subject to a beneficial ownership certificate under section 7.23) to exercise some of the rights of a "shareholder." See, for example, section 7.40, which relates to derivative proceedings. Separate definitions of "voting trust beneficial owner," "unrestricted voting trust beneficial owner" and "beneficial shareholder" also appear in section 1.40.

Sign or Signature

The definition of "sign" or "signature" incorporates into the Act concepts and terminology from UETA and the federal E-Sign. Thus, the terms "sign" and "signature" include not only traditional forms of signing, such as manual, facsimile, or conformed signatures, but also electronic signatures in electronic transmissions. The intent of the Act is that any manifestation of an intention to sign or authenticate a document be accepted, although electronic transmissions having electronic signatures must comply with the requirements in the definition of "electronic transmission," including being retrievable in paper form by the recipient through an automated process unless otherwise authorized in accordance with section 1.41(j).

Unincorporated Entity

The term "unincorporated entity" is a subset of the broader term "entity" and includes an unincorporated nonprofit association. The Uniform Unincorporated Nonprofit Association Act gives an unincorporated nonprofit association the power to acquire an estate in real property and thus an unincorporated nonprofit association organized in a state that has adopted that act will be an "unincorporated entity." At common law, an unincorporated nonprofit association was not a legal entity and did not have the power to acquire real property.

As used in the definition of unincorporated entity, "business trust" includes any trust carrying on a business, such as a Massachusetts business trust, real estate investment trust, or other common law or statutory business trust. The term "unincorporated entity" (and thus the term "eligible entity") expressly excludes series of limited liability companies or of other types of entities, and estates and trusts (*i.e.*, trusts that are not business trusts), regardless of whether they would be considered artificial persons under the governing jurisdiction's law, to make it clear that they are not eligible to participate in a conversion under chapter 9 or a merger or share exchange under chapter 11.

Voting Group

Section 1.40 defines "voting group" for purposes of the Act as a matter of convenient reference. When the definition refers to shares entitled to vote "generally" on a matter, it signifies all shares entitled to vote together on the matter by the articles of incorporation or the Act, regardless of whether they also have the right to be counted or tabulated separately. "Voting groups" are thus the basic units of collective voting by shareholders, and voting by voting groups may provide essential protection to one or more classes or series of shares against actions that are detrimental to the rights or interests of that class or series.

The determination of which shares form part of a single voting group must be made from the provisions of the articles of incorporation and of the Act. In a few instances under the Act, the board of directors may establish the right to vote by voting groups. On most matters to be voted on by shareholders, only a single voting group, consisting of a class of voting or common shares, will be involved, and action on such a matter is effective when approved by that voting group pursuant to section 7.25. In other circumstances, the vote of multiple groups may be required. See sections 7.25 and 7.26.

Voting Power

Application of the definition of "voting power" turns on whether the relevant shares carry the power to vote in the election of directors as of the time for voting on the relevant transaction. If shares carry the power to vote in the election of directors only under a certain contingency, as is often the case with preferred stock, the shares would not carry voting power within the meaning of section 1.40 unless the contingency has occurred, and then only during the period when the voting rights are in effect. Shares that carry the power to vote for any directors as of the time to vote on the relevant transaction have the current power to vote in the election of directors within the meaning of the definition, even if the shares do not carry the power to vote for all directors.

Voting Trust Beneficial Owner and Unrestricted Voting Trust Beneficial Owner

Section 1.40 has a separate definition of "voting trust beneficial owner" because the number of such owners and value of their shares can enter into determinations under sections 13.02(b)(1) and 14.30(b)(ii). It also has a separate definition of "unrestricted voting trust beneficial owner" because rights are given under some provisions of the Act for a beneficial owner of shares deposited in a voting trust established under section 7.30 to take actions as a shareholder. These owners have the economic interest in the shares but the voting rights have been given to the voting trustee. In addition to the typical grant of voting rights, section 7.30 permits the voting trust agreement to confer on the voting trustee the right otherwise to act with respect to the shares, and thus could vest in the trustee the exclusive right to exercise statutory shareholder rights. The term "unrestricted voting trust beneficial owner" is used to distinguish from this possible limitation. If the voting trust agreement grants the trustee the exclusive right to act with respect to the shareholder right in question, then the voting trustee, and not the voting trust beneficial owner, may exercise those rights.

Writing or Written

"Writing" or "written" means information in the form of a "document," which in turn means any tangible medium on which information is inscribed, such as a paper instrument, as well as an electronic record. Thus, under the Act a written consent of shareholders under section 7.04, for example, may be in the form of paper or an electronic record.

§ 1.41. Notices and Other Communications

(a)   A notice under this Act must be in writing unless oral notice is reasonable in the circumstances. Unless otherwise agreed between the sender and the recipient, words in a notice or other communication under this Act must be in English.

(b)   A notice or other communication may be given by any method of delivery, except that electronic transmissions must be in accordance with this section. If the methods of delivery are impracticable, a notice or other communication may be given by means of a broad non-exclusionary distribution to the public (which may include a newspaper of general circulation in the area where published; radio, television, or other form of public broadcast communication; or other methods of distribution that the corporation has previously identified to its shareholders).

(c)   A notice or other communication to a domestic corporation or to a foreign corporation registered to do business in this state may be delivered to the corporation's registered agent at its registered office or to the secretary at the corporation's principal office shown in its most recent annual report or, in the case of a foreign corporation that has not yet delivered an annual report, in its foreign registration statement.

(d)   A notice or other communications may be delivered by electronic transmission if consented to by the recipient or if authorized by subsection (j).

(e)   Any consent under subsection (d) may be revoked by the person who consented by written or electronic notice to the person to whom the consent was delivered. Any such consent is deemed revoked if (i) the corporation is unable to deliver two consecutive electronic transmissions given by the corporation in accordance with such consent, and (ii) such inability becomes known to the secretary or an assistant secretary or to the transfer agent, or other person responsible for the giving of notice or other communications; provided, however, the inadvertent failure to treat such inability as a revocation shall not invalidate any meeting or other action.

(f)   Unless otherwise agreed between the sender and the recipient, an electronic transmission is received when:

(1)   it enters an information processing system that the recipient has designated or uses for the purposes of receiving electronic transmissions or information of the type sent, and from which the recipient is able to retrieve the electronic transmission; and

(2)   it is in a form capable of being processed by that system.

(g)   Receipt of an electronic acknowledgement from an information processing system described in subsection (f)(1) establishes that an electronic transmission was received but, by itself, does not establish that the content sent corresponds to the content received.

(h)   An electronic transmission is received under this section even if no person is aware of its receipt.

(i)   A notice or other communication, if in a comprehensible form or manner, is effective at the earliest of the following:

(1)   if in a physical form, the earliest of when it is actually received, or when it is left at:

(i)   a shareholder's address shown on the corporation's record of shareholders maintained by the corporation under section 16.01(d);

(ii)   a director's residence or usual place of business; or

(iii)   the corporation's principal office;

(2)   if mailed postage prepaid and correctly addressed to a shareholder, upon deposit in the United States mail;

(3)   if mailed by United States mail postage prepaid and correctly addressed to a recipient other than a shareholder, the earliest of when it is actually received, or:

(i)   if sent by registered or certified mail, return receipt requested, the date shown on the return receipt signed by or on behalf of the addressee; or

(ii)   five days after it is deposited in the United States mail;

(4)   if an electronic transmission, when it is received as provided in subsection (f); and

(5)   if oral, when communicated.

(j)   A notice or other communication may be in the form of an electronic transmission that cannot be directly reproduced in paper form by the recipient through an automated process used in conventional commercial practice only if (i) the electronic transmission is otherwise retrievable in perceivable form, and (ii) the sender and the recipient have consented in writing to the use of such form of electronic transmission.

(k)   If this Act prescribes requirements for notices or other communications in particular circumstances, those requirements govern. If articles of incorporation or bylaws prescribe requirements for notices or other communications, not inconsistent with this section or other provisions of this Act, those requirements govern. The articles of incorporation or bylaws may authorize or require delivery of notices of meetings of directors by electronic transmission.

(*l*)   In the event that any provisions of this Act are deemed to modify, limit, or supersede the federal Electronic Signatures in Global and National Commerce Act, 15 U.S.C. §§ 7001 *et seq.*, the provisions of this Act shall control to the maximum extent permitted by section 102(a)(2) of that federal act.

Cross-References

Annual report, see § 16.21.

"Deliver" defined, see § 1.40.

"Electronic transmission" defined, see § 1.40.

Householding, see § 1.44.

"Principal office":

　defined, see § 1.40.

　designated in annual report, see § 16.21.

　designated in foreign registration statement, see § 15.03.

Record of shareholders, see § 16.01.

"Secretary" defined, see § 1.40.

Special notice requirements:

　derivative proceedings, see § 7.40.

　resignation of registered agent, see § 5.03.

　service on corporation, see § 5.04.

"Writing" defined, see § 1.40.

Official Comment

Section 1.41 establishes rules for determining how notices and other communications may be given and when they are effective for a variety of purposes under the Act. Not only do the rules of section 1.41 apply to the delivery of notices of meetings of shareholders and directors and other similar notices, they apply as well to director and shareholder consents, demands to hold meetings, proxies, demands to commence derivative actions, demands to inspect books and records, assertions of appraisal rights, and other communications to and from the corporation.

Note on the Relationship Between Act Provisions on Electronic Technology and UETA and E-Sign

The provisions of the Act relating to electronic records, electronic transmissions and related matters, found principally in the definitions in section 1.40, are set against the backdrop of the Uniform Electronic Transmissions Act ("UETA") and the federal Electronic Signatures in Global and National Commerce Act ("E-Sign"). A brief description of certain aspects of UETA and E-Sign is useful to understand the Act's electronic technology provisions.

UETA adopted definitions for the terms electronic, electronic records, electronic signatures, records, transactions, and the like, as well as provisions governing the use of those terms. UETA applies to "transactions," which are defined to mean actions between two or more persons "relating to the conduct of business [or] commercial . . . affairs." UETA §§ 2(16) and 3(a). The reach of the term "transactions" in the context of a comprehensive business corporation act is unclear. For example, although obtaining a proxy from a shareholder that is voting on a cash-out merger would likely constitute a "transaction," the unilateral act by a corporation of sending notice of an annual meeting at which no significant action is proposed might not.

If UETA applies, it establishes certain statutory norms for the validity of electronic signatures, electronic records, etc. However, UETA also provides that it applies only to transactions between parties each of which has agreed to conduct transactions by electronic means, and that such agreement is determined from the context and surrounding circumstances, including the parties' conduct. *Id.* § 5(b).

E-Sign, codified at 15 U.S.C. §§ 7001 *et seq.*, in turn adopted the substance of UETA's principal definitions, including electronic, electronic signature, record, and transaction, as well as many of the operative provisions of UETA. The applicability of E-Sign, like UETA, turns on whether a "transaction" is involved. *Id.* § 7001(a). Like UETA, E-Sign's applicability also depends upon the parties consenting to transact business by electronic means. *Id.* § 7001(b)(2).

Importantly, E-Sign contains a federal preemption provision that itself excepts certain state adoptions of UETA. Thus, in general terms, section 7002(a) of E-Sign allows a state statute to modify, limit, or supersede the provisions of E-Sign section 7001 only if (i) it is a state enactment of the version of UETA approved in 1999, and (ii) the state's enactment of UETA does not contain any state exceptions, or "carve outs," other than those contained in the 1999 version of UETA § 3(b)(4). If, for example, a state enactment of UETA carved out that state's general business corporation law from the applicability of UETA, a carve out that is not contained in the 1999 version of UETA § 3(b)(4), and that business corporation law was deemed to be inconsistent with E-Sign, the offending provisions of the business corporation law would be preempted. *Id.* § 7002(a)(1).

Note one aspect of the definition of "record" in both UETA and E-Sign: they both provide that information that is stored in an electronic medium must simply be "retrievable in perceivable form." This is in contrast to states that require not only that an electronic transmission may be retained, retrieved, and reviewed but also requires that it "may be directly reproduced in paper form by [the] recipient through an automated process." The former would include, *e.g.*, a voicemail, a text message, and an electronic page, although the latter would not.

Against that backdrop, the Act's electronic technology provisions align, in all material respects, with the terminology and concepts of UETA and E-Sign. However, the Act does not adopt wholesale the vocabulary and concepts of UETA and E-Sign for the following reasons:

- Such wholesale changes would have involved amendments to the black letter in over 50 sections of the Act. Given that more than half the states in the United States have state corporation laws based in large measure on the Act, an approach to electronic technology that would require so many statutory changes in each state would have been extremely burdensome.

- The vocabulary of UETA and E-Sign, particularly the definition of "record" and "sign," although technically precise, are not written in the same style as the Act, do not use its terminology, and are less understandable to the ordinary reader. And if engrafted directly into the full body of the Act, the result would have been a major change from well-understood, obvious, and traditional terminology (*e.g.*, a "unanimous written consent") to a comparatively awkward and less intuitively obvious terminology (*e.g.,* a "consent in the form of a record").

- The Act rejects the concept that a voicemail or a text message alone should, as a default matter, have the same status as a paper document. In so doing, the Act implicitly acknowledges the corruptibility and/or inaccessibility of electronic data.

The Act instead adopts an approach that involves incorporating into the definitions in section 1.40, the principal electronic technology vocabulary and concepts of UETA and E-Sign, in ways that do not require substantial changes throughout the Act.

Thus, the Act's electronic technology provisions:

- define "document" "writing" and "written," to include electronic records;

- define "deliver" and "delivery" to include electronic transmissions if properly authorized;

- use definitions of "electronic" and "electronic record" that borrow heavily from UETA and E-Sign;

- define "electronic transmission" and "electronically transmitted" to incorporate UETA and E-Sign vocabulary and concepts;

- require that electronic records and electronic transmissions be retrievable in paper form through an automated process used in conventional commercial practice, unless specifically authorized in accordance with section 1.41(j), thereby establishing the default rule that, until they are used in conventional commercial practice, voicemails and text messages are not generally recognized as valid, absent a specific consent (parties may, however, consent to their use); and

- define "sign" or "signature" to incorporate technical E-Sign and UETA terminology, while retaining common terminology such as "any manual, facsimile, or conformed signature."

This approach is pragmatic, addresses the vast majority of recurring questions involving electronic transmissions and records, and yet enables parties who wish to do so to consent specifically to use electronic records or transmissions that are merely "retrievable in perceivable form."

As for the preemption issue under E-Sign, the Act's electronic technology provisions are consistent in all material respects with E-Sign and UETA. Although the Act's basic provision has the additional requirement that electronic records or transmissions be retrievable in paper form through an automated process, section 1.41(j) permits parties to agree to the broader "retrievable in perceivable form" formulation found in E-Sign and UETA, and accordingly the Act's provisions are consistent with those laws. Section 1.41(*l*) implements E-Sign section 7002(a)(2), which exempts from the federal preemption provisions of E-Sign certain state laws that modify, limit, or supersede E-Sign, and that also make specific reference to E-Sign.

Note that corporations desiring to conduct transactions by electronic means must also comply with the requirements of UETA or E-Sign, as applicable, to ensure the legal effect, validity, and enforceability of its transactions and records. For example, E-Sign contains specific provisions regarding accuracy, authenticity, accessibility, and retention of electronic records. Compliance with these statutes will require that corporations address certain technical issues, including system security and procedures.

* * *

1.   *General*

The rules set forth in section 1.41 permit many other sections of the Act to be phrased simply in terms of giving or delivering notice without repeating details with respect to how notice should be given and when it is effective. If all methods of delivery used in conventional commercial practice and electronic transmission in accordance with section 1.41 are impracticable, section 1.41(b) provides for alternate methods of communication.

2.   *Rules Governing Use of Electronic Transmissions*

Electronic records and transmissions are effective under the Act if in accordance with section 1.41. The definition of writing in section 1.40 includes a document, which is defined in section 1.40 to include an electronic record. Section 1.40 then defines the terms "deliver" or "delivery" to include delivery by hand, mail, commercial delivery, or by electronic transmission if authorized in accordance with section 1.41. Authorization of notices or other communications delivered by electronic transmission is governed by sections 1.41(d) and 1.41(j), which require the consent of the recipient.

Assuming consent, section 1.41 then establishes a number of rules with respect to electronic transmissions and records. Subsection (e) provides that any consent to the use of electronic transmissions may be revoked at any time. Subsection (e) also establishes a default rule in cases of failed electronic deliveries: a consent under section 1.41(d) is deemed revoked if the corporation is unable to deliver two consecutive electronic transmissions and the inability becomes known to specified corporate officers or agents. Subsection (f), based on UETA § 15(b), establishes basic rules, which can be varied by the sender and recipient, for when an electronic transmission is "received." An electronic transmission is received, even if the recipient's electronic filters, firewalls, or other similar systems effectively block the transmission, because a recipient who consents to the use of electronic transmissions is responsible for any such filters or firewalls that block access to them. Subsection (g), based on UETA § 15(f), provides legal certainty regarding an electronic acknowledgment, but only addresses the fact of receipt, not the quality of the content or whether it was "opened" or read. Subsection (h), based on UETA § 15(h), establishes that an electronic transmission is received even if the recipient or individual is unaware of its receipt, just as a written notice physically delivered to a person's correct address is duly delivered even if the addressee is not aware of its delivery or declines to open the envelope.

Section 1.41(j) requires specific consent to the use of the electronic transmissions that are only "retrievable in perceivable form" and that cannot be directly reproduced in paper form through an automated process used in conventional commercial practice. See the Official Comment to section 1.40. Such consent between the sender and recipient must be in writing, except with respect to notices of meetings to directors, which may be in the articles of incorporation or bylaws.

3.   *When Notices or Other Communications Are Effective*

Section 1.41(i) establishes rules governing when notices or communications are deemed to be legally effective, serially addressing delivery in physical form, regular mail sent to shareholders and to other recipients, registered or certified mail, electronic transmissions, and oral communications.

§ 1.42. Number of Shareholders

(a)   For purposes of this Act, the following identified as a shareholder in a corporation's current record of shareholders constitutes one shareholder:

(1)   three or fewer co-owners;

(2)   a corporation, partnership, trust, estate, or other entity; and

(3)   the trustees, guardians, custodians, or other fiduciaries of a single trust, estate, or account.

(b)   For purposes of this Act, shareholdings registered in substantially similar names constitute one shareholder if it is reasonable to believe that the names represent the same person.

Cross-References

"Entity" defined, see § 1.40.

Market exception to appraisal rights, see § 13.02.

Record of shareholders, see §§ 7.20 and 16.01.

"Shareholder" defined, see § 1.40.

Shareholder proceeding for judicial dissolution, see § 14.30.

Voting trusts, see § 7.30.

Official Comment

The Act generally avoids provisions that are based on the number of shareholders of a corporation, since these provisions may encourage individual shareholders to divide or combine their holdings for private strategic advantage. But the number of shareholders is important in determining: (i) whether the market exception to appraisal rights is available under section 13.02(b)(2) and (ii) whether a shareholder may bring a proceeding for judicial dissolution under section 14.30(a)(2).

§ 1.43. Qualified Director

(a)   A "qualified director" is a director who, at the time action is to be taken under:

(1)   section 2.02(b)(6), is not a director (i) to whom the limitation or elimination of the duty of an officer to offer potential business opportunities to the corporation would apply, or (ii) who has a material relationship with any other person to whom the limitation or elimination would apply;

(2)   section 7.44, does not have (i) a material interest in the outcome of the proceeding, or (ii) a material relationship with a person who has such an interest;

(3)   section 8.53 or 8.55, (i) is not a party to the proceeding, (ii) is not a director as to whom a transaction is a director's conflicting interest transaction or who sought a disclaimer of the corporation's interest in a business opportunity under section 8.70, which transaction or disclaimer is challenged in the proceeding, and (iii) does not have a material relationship with a director described in either clause (i) or clause (ii) of this subsection (a)(3);

(4)   section 8.62, is not a director (i) as to whom the transaction is a director's conflicting interest transaction, or (ii) who has a material relationship with another director as to whom the transaction is a director's conflicting interest transaction; or

(5)   section 8.70, is not a director who (i) pursues or takes advantage of the business opportunity, directly, or indirectly through or on behalf of another person, or (ii) has a material relationship with a director or officer who pursues or takes advantage of the business opportunity, directly, or indirectly through or on behalf of another person.

(b)   For purposes of this section:

(1)　"material relationship" means a familial, financial, professional, employment or other relationship that would reasonably be expected to impair the objectivity of the director's judgment when participating in the action to be taken; and

(2)　"material interest" means an actual or potential benefit or detriment (other than one which would devolve on the corporation or the shareholders generally) that would reasonably be expected to impair the objectivity of the director's judgment when participating in the action to be taken.

(c)　The presence of one or more of the following circumstances shall not automatically prevent a director from being a qualified director:

(1)　nomination or election of the director to the current board by any director who is not a qualified director with respect to the matter (or by any person that has a material relationship with that director), acting alone or participating with others;

(2)　service as a director of another corporation of which a director who is not a qualified director with respect to the matter (or any individual who has a material relationship with that director), is or was also a director; or

(3)　with respect to action to be taken under section 7.44, status as a named defendant, as a director against whom action is demanded, or as a director who approved the conduct being challenged.

Cross-References

Advance for expenses, see § 8.53.

Business opportunities, see § 8.70.

Determination and authorization of indemnification, see § 8.55.

Directors' action in director's conflicting interest transaction, see § 8.62.

Dismissal of derivative proceeding, see § 7.44.

Official Comment

The definition of the term "qualified director" identifies those directors: (i) who may take action on the dismissal of a derivative proceeding (section 7.44); (ii) who are eligible to make, in the first instance, the authorization and determination required in connection with the decision on a request for advance for expenses (section 8.53(c)) or for indemnification (sections 8.55(b) and (c)); (iii) who may authorize a director's conflicting interest transaction (section 8.62); (iv) who may disclaim the corporation's interest in a business opportunity (section 8.70(a)); and (v) who may make applicable the limitation or elimination of a duty of an officer to offer the corporation business opportunities before the officer or a related person of the officer pursues or takes the opportunity (section 2.02(b)(6)).

Although the term "qualified director" embraces the concept of independence, it does so only in relation to the director's interest or involvement in the specific situations to which the definition applies. The judicial decisions that have examined the qualifications of directors for such purposes have generally required that directors be both *disinterested,* in the sense of not having exposure to an actual or potential benefit or detriment arising out of the action being taken (as opposed to an actual or potential benefit or detriment to the corporation or all shareholders generally), and *independent,* in the sense of having no personal or other relationship with an interested director (*e.g.,* a director who is a party to a transaction with the corporation) that presents a reasonable likelihood that the director's objectivity will be impaired. The "qualified director" concept embraces both of those requirements, and its application is situation-specific; that is, "qualified director" determinations will depend upon the directly relevant facts and circumstances, and the disqualification of a director to act arises from factors that would reasonably be expected to impair the objectivity of the director's judgment. On the other hand, the concept does not suggest that a "qualified director" has or should have special expertise to act on the matter in question.

1. *Disqualification Due to Conflicting Interest*

The "qualified director" concept prescribes significant disqualifications, depending upon the purpose for which a director might be considered eligible to participate in the action to be taken. These disqualifications include the following:

- In the case of action under a provision adopted under the authority of section 2.02(b)(6) to limit or eliminate any duty of an officer to offer the corporation business opportunities, the definition excludes any director who is also an officer and to whom the provision would apply.

- In the case of action on dismissal of a derivative proceeding under section 7.44, the definition excludes any director who has a material interest in the outcome of the proceeding, such as where the proceeding involves a challenge to the validity of a transaction in which the director has a material financial interest.

- In the case of action to approve indemnification or advance of funds for expenses, the definition excludes any director who is a party to the proceeding (see section 8.50 for the definition of "party" and for the definition of "proceeding").

- In the case of action to approve a director's conflicting interest transaction, the definition excludes any director whose interest, knowledge or status results in the transaction being treated as a "director's conflicting interest transaction." See section 8.60 for the definition of "director's conflicting interest transaction."

- In the case of action under section 8.70(a) to disclaim corporate interest in a business opportunity, the definition excludes any director who directly or indirectly pursues or takes advantage of the business opportunity, or who has a material relationship with another director or officer who does so.

Whether a director has a material interest in the outcome of a proceeding in which the director does not have a conflicting personal interest is heavily fact-dependent. At one end of the spectrum, if a claim against a director is clearly frivolous or is not supported by particularized and well-pleaded facts, the director should not be deemed to have a "material interest in the outcome of the proceeding" within the meaning of section 1.43(a)(2), even though the director is named as a defendant. At the other end of the spectrum, a director normally should be deemed to have a "material interest in the outcome of the proceeding" within the meaning of section 1.43(a)(2) if a claim against the director is supported by particularized and well-pleaded facts which, if true, would be likely to give rise to a significant adverse outcome against the director.

2. *Disqualification Due to Relationships with Interested Persons*

In each context in which the "qualified director" definition applies, it also excludes any director who has a "material relationship" with another director (or, with respect to a provision applying to an officer under section 2.02(b)(6) or section 8.70, a "material relationship" with that officer) who is not disinterested for one or more of the reasons outlined in the preceding paragraph. Any relationship with such a person, whether the relationship is familial, financial, professional, employment or otherwise, is a "material relationship," as that term is defined in section 1.43(b)(1), if it would reasonably be expected to impair the objectivity of the director's judgment when voting or otherwise participating in action to be taken on a matter referred to in section 1.43(a). The determination of whether there is a "material relationship" should be based on the practicalities of the situation rather than on formalistic considerations. For example, a director employed by a corporation controlled by another director should be regarded as having an employment relationship with that director. On the other hand, a casual social acquaintance with another director should not be regarded as a disqualifying relationship.

The term "qualified director" is distinct from the generic term "independent director," which is not used in the Act. As a result, a director who might typically be viewed as an "independent director" may in some circumstances not be a "qualified director," and vice versa. See also the Official Comment to section 8.01.

3. *Elimination of Automatic Disqualification in Certain Circumstances*

Section 1.43(c) addresses three categories of circumstances that, if present alone or together, do not automatically prevent a director from being a qualified director:

- Subsection (c)(1) makes it clear that the participation of nonqualified directors (or interested shareholders or other interested persons) in the nomination or election of a director does not automatically prevent the director so nominated or elected from being qualified. Special litigation committees acting with regard to derivative litigation often consist of directors nominated or elected (after the alleged wrongful acts) by directors named as defendants in the action. In other settings, directors who are seeking indemnification, or who are interested in a director's conflicting interest transaction, may have participated in the nomination or election of an individual director who is otherwise a "qualified director."

- Subsection (c)(2) provides, in a similar fashion, that the mere fact that an individual director is or was a director of another corporation—on the board of which a director who is not a "qualified director" also serves or has served—does not automatically prevent qualification to act.

- Subsection (c)(3) confirms a number of decisions, involving dismissal of derivative proceedings, in which the court rejected a disqualification claim predicated on the mere fact that a director had been named as a defendant, was an individual against whom action has been demanded, or had approved the action being challenged. These cases have held that, where a director's approval of the challenged action is at issue, approval does not automatically make the director ineligible to act. On the other hand, for example, director approval of a challenged transaction, in combination with other particularized facts showing that the director's ability to act objectively on a proposal to dismiss a derivative proceeding is impaired by a material conflicting personal interest in the transaction, disqualifies a director from acting on the proposal to dismiss the proceeding.

The effect of section 1.43(c), while significant, is limited. It merely precludes an automatic inference of director disqualification from the circumstances specified in that subsection.

§ 1.44. Householding

(a) A corporation has delivered written notice or any other report or statement under this Act, the articles of incorporation or the bylaws to all shareholders who share a common address if:

    (1) the corporation delivers one copy of the notice, report or statement to the common address;

    (2) the corporation addresses the notice, report or statement to those shareholders either as a group or to each of those shareholders individually or to the shareholders in a form to which each of those shareholders has consented; and

    (3) each of those shareholders consents to delivery of a single copy of such notice, report or statement to the shareholders' common address.

(b) Any such consent described in subsections (a)(2) or (a)(3) shall be revocable by any of such shareholders who deliver written notice of revocation to the corporation. If such written notice of revocation is delivered, the corporation shall begin providing individual notices, reports or other statements to the revoking shareholder no later than 30 days after delivery of the written notice of revocation.

(c) Any shareholder who fails to object by written notice to the corporation, within 60 days of written notice by the corporation of its intention to deliver single copies of notices, reports or statements to shareholders who share a common address as permitted by subsection (a), shall be deemed to have consented to receiving such single copy at the common address; provided that the notice of intention explains that consent may be revoked and the method for revoking.

Cross-References

"Deliver" defined, see § 1.40.

Notices and other communications, see § 1.41.

Official Comment

The proxy rules under the Securities Exchange Act of 1934 permit publicly held corporations to meet their obligation to deliver proxy statements and annual reports to shareholders who share a common address by delivery of a single copy of such materials to the common address under certain conditions. This practice is known as "householding." This section permits a corporation comparable flexibility to household the written notice of shareholders' meetings as well as any other written notices, reports or statements required to be delivered to shareholders under the Act or the corporation's articles of incorporation or bylaws. Ability to household such notices, reports or statements would not, of course, eliminate the practical necessity of delivering to a common address sufficient copies of any accompanying document requiring individual shareholder signature or other action, such as a proxy card or consent.

To meet the conditions of section 1.44(a), the written notice, report or statement must be delivered to the common address. Address means a street address, a post office box number, an electronic mail address, a facsimile telephone number or another similar destination to which paper or electronic transmission may be sent. Whether consent is explicit or implicit, it is revocable at any time as provided in section 1.44(b).

To be effective, the written notice of intention to household notices, reports or other statements permitted by section 1.44(b) must explain that affirmative or implied consent may be revoked and the method for revoking.

SUBCHAPTER E
RATIFICATION OF DEFECTIVE CORPORATE ACTIONS

§ 1.45. Definitions

In this subchapter:

"Corporate action" means any action taken by or on behalf of the corporation, including any action taken by the incorporator, the board of directors, a committee of the board of directors, an officer or agent of the corporation or the shareholders.

"Date of the defective corporate action" means the date (or the approximate date, if the exact date is unknown) the defective corporate action was purported to have been taken.

"Defective corporate action" means (i) any corporate action purportedly taken that is, and at the time such corporate action was purportedly taken would have been, within the power of the corporation, but is void or voidable due to a failure of authorization, and (ii) an overissue.

"Failure of authorization" means the failure to authorize, approve or otherwise effect a corporate action in compliance with the provisions of this Act, the articles of incorporation or bylaws, a corporate resolution or any plan or agreement to which the corporation is a party, if and to the extent such failure would render such corporate action void or voidable.

"Overissue" means the purported issuance of:

    (i)   shares of a class or series in excess of the number of shares of a class or series the corporation has the power to issue under section 6.01 at the time of such issuance; or

    (ii)   shares of any class or series that is not then authorized for issuance by the articles of incorporation.

"Putative shares" means the shares of any class or series (including shares issued upon exercise of rights, options, warrants or other securities convertible into shares of the corporation, or interests with respect to such shares) that were created or issued as a result of a defective corporate action, that (i) but for any failure of authorization would constitute valid shares, or (ii) cannot be determined by the board of directors to be valid shares.

"Valid shares" means the shares of any class or series that have been duly authorized and validly issued in accordance with this Act, including as a result of ratification or validation under this subchapter.

"Validation effective time" with respect to any defective corporate action ratified under this subchapter means the later of:

(i)   the time at which the ratification of the defective corporate action is approved by the shareholders, or if approval of shareholders is not required, the time at which the notice required by section 1.49 becomes effective in accordance with section 1.41; and

(ii)   the time at which any articles of validation filed in accordance with section 1.51 become effective.

The validation effective time shall not be affected by the filing or pendency of a judicial proceeding under section 1.52 or otherwise, unless otherwise ordered by the court.

Cross-References

Authorized shares, see § 6.01.

Corporate powers, see § 3.02.

Issuance of shares, see § 6.21.

Lack of power to act, see § 3.04.

Share rights, options, warrants and awards, see § 6.24.

Official Comment

The definitions of "corporate action," "defective corporate action" and "failure of authorization" are intentionally broad so as to permit ratification of any corporate action purportedly taken that would have been within the power granted to a corporation under the Act.

The term "defective corporate action" includes an "overissue" of shares and other defects in share issuances that could cause shares to be treated as void. For purposes of determining which shares are overissued, only those shares issued in excess of the number of shares permitted to be issued under section 6.01 of the Act would be deemed overissued shares. If it cannot be determined from the records of the corporation which shares were issued before others, all shares included in an issuance that is or results in an overissue would be overissued shares.

§ 1.46.   Defective Corporate Actions

(a)   A defective corporate action shall not be void or voidable if ratified in accordance with section 1.47 or validated in accordance with section 1.52.

(b)   Ratification under section 1.47 or validation under section 1.52 shall not be deemed to be the exclusive means of ratifying or validating any defective corporate action, and the absence or failure of ratification in accordance with this subchapter shall not, of itself, affect the validity or effectiveness of any corporate action properly ratified under common law or otherwise, nor shall it create a presumption that any such corporate action is or was a defective corporate action or void or voidable.

(c)   In the case of an overissue, putative shares shall be valid shares effective as of the date originally issued or purportedly issued upon:

(1)   the effectiveness under this subchapter and under chapter 10 of an amendment to the articles of incorporation authorizing, designating or creating such shares; or

(2)   the effectiveness of any other corporate action under this subchapter ratifying the authorization, designation or creation of such shares.

Cross-References

Amendment of articles of incorporation by board of directors and shareholders, see § 10.03.

Authorized shares, see § 6.01.

Correcting filed documents, see § 1.24.

Official Comment

Subchapter E provides a statutory ratification procedure for corporate actions that may not have been properly authorized and shares that may have been improperly issued. The statutory ratification procedure is designed to supplement common law ratification. Corporate actions ratified under this subchapter remain subject to equitable review.

Examples of defective corporate actions subject to ratification include the failure of the incorporator to validly appoint an initial board of directors, corporate action taken in the absence of board resolutions authorizing the action, the failure to obtain the requisite shareholder approval of a corporate action, issuance of shares in the absence of evidence that consideration payable to the corporation for shares was received, the failure to comply with appraisal requirements and the issuance of shares without complying with preemptive rights. The ratification procedure is intended to be available only where there is objective evidence that a corporate action was defectively implemented. For example, subchapter E would permit ratification of shares previously issued but subsequently determined to have been issued improperly. It would not permit the corporation to issue shares retroactively as of an earlier date, however, where there is no objective evidence that those shares had previously been issued. Objective evidence may include resolutions, issuance of share certificates, subscription or share purchase agreements, entries in a share ledger or other correspondence indicating that shares were issued or intended to have been issued.

Section 1.46(a) does not distinguish between void and voidable actions. Instead it provides that any defective corporate action that is ratified in accordance with section 1.47 or validated under section 1.52 shall not be void or voidable. Section 1.47 is not the exclusive means by which a defective corporate action may be ratified. Thus, the general common law doctrine of ratification, as applied to a board of directors' adoption of actions taken by officers who may not have had the actual authority to take such actions, continues to be an effective mode of ratification. Section 1.46(b) makes clear that the corporation's ratification of a defective corporate action that is voidable but not void using common law methods of ratification rather than under section 1.47 will not, standing alone, affect the validity of the action or create a presumption that the action is not valid. In addition, ratification under subchapter E is distinct from correction of an already filed document under section 1.24.

Section 1.46(c) provides that an overissue can be remedied by the adoption of articles of amendment or other corporate action that has the effect of authorizing, designating or creating shares of a series or class, such that the putative shares that resulted in the overissue are deemed to be validly issued from the date of original issuance. This provision enables a corporation to cure an overissue occurring when shares have been duly authorized but are issued before articles of amendment are filed. It also permits a corporation to remedy an overissue even if it cannot specifically identify the putative shares.

§ 1.47. Ratification of Defective Corporate Actions

(a)   To ratify a defective corporate action under this section (other than the ratification of an election of the initial board of directors under subsection (b)), the board of directors shall take action ratifying the action in accordance with section 1.48, stating:

(1)   the defective corporate action to be ratified and, if the defective corporate action involved the issuance of putative shares, the number and type of putative shares purportedly issued;

(2)   the date of the defective corporate action;

(3)   the nature of the failure of authorization with respect to the defective corporate action to be ratified; and

(4)   that the board of directors approves the ratification of the defective corporate action.

(b)   In the event that a defective corporate action to be ratified relates to the election of the initial board of directors of the corporation under section 2.05(a)(2), a majority of the persons who, at the time of the ratification, are exercising the powers of directors may take an action stating:

(1)   the name of the person or persons who first took action in the name of the corporation as the initial board of directors of the corporation;

(2)   the earlier of the date on which such persons first took such action or were purported to have been elected as the initial board of directors; and

(3)   that the ratification of the election of such person or persons as the initial board of directors is approved.

(c)   If any provision of this Act, the articles of incorporation or bylaws, any corporate resolution or any plan or agreement to which the corporation is a party in effect at the time action under subsection (a) is taken requires shareholder approval or would have required shareholder approval at the date of the occurrence of the defective corporate action, the ratification of the defective corporate action approved in the action taken by the directors under subsection (a) shall be submitted to the shareholders for approval in accordance with section 1.48.

(d)   Unless otherwise provided in the action taken by the board of directors under subsection (a), after the action by the board of directors has been taken and, if required, approved by the shareholders, the board of directors may abandon the ratification at any time before the validation effective time without further action of the shareholders.

Cross-References

Organization of corporation, see § 2.05.

Requirement for and functions of board of directors, see § 8.01.

Official Comment

The information required by section 1.47(a)(1) regarding the listing of putative shares may be satisfied by attaching a table, including a capitalization table, listing the putative shares. Section 1.47(b) permits the ratification of the initial election of the board of directors by the persons who are acting as the current board of directors, recognizing that if the corporation's initial board of directors was defectively appointed, there may be no effective method of ratification because a duly elected board of directors does not exist.

§ 1.48. Action on Ratification

(a)   The quorum and voting requirements applicable to a ratifying action by the board of directors under section 1.47(a) shall be the quorum and voting requirements applicable to the corporate action proposed to be ratified at the time such ratifying action is taken.

(b)   If the ratification of the defective corporate action requires approval by the shareholders under section 1.47(c), and if the approval is to be given at a meeting, the corporation shall notify each holder of valid and putative shares, regardless of whether entitled to vote, as of the record date for notice of the meeting and as of the date of the occurrence of defective corporate action, provided that notice shall not be required to be given to holders of valid or putative shares whose identities or addresses for notice cannot be determined from the records of the corporation. The notice must state that the purpose, or one of the purposes, of the meeting, is to consider ratification of a defective corporate action and must be accompanied by (i) either a copy of the action taken by the board of directors in accordance with section 1.47(a) or the information required by sections 1.47(a)(1) through (a)(4), and (ii) a statement that any claim that the ratification of such defective corporate action and any putative shares issued as a result of such defective corporate action should not be effective, or should be effective only on certain conditions, shall be brought within 120 days from the applicable validation effective time.

(c)   Except as provided in subsection (d) with respect to the voting requirements to ratify the election of a director, the quorum and voting requirements applicable to the approval by the shareholders required by section 1.47(c) shall be the quorum and voting requirements applicable to the corporate action proposed to be ratified at the time of such shareholder approval.

(d) The approval by shareholders to ratify the election of a director requires that the votes cast within the voting group favoring such ratification exceed the votes cast opposing such ratification of the election at a meeting at which a quorum is present.

(e) Putative shares on the record date for determining the shareholders entitled to vote on any matter submitted to shareholders under section 1.47(c) (and without giving effect to any ratification of putative shares that becomes effective as a result of such vote) shall neither be entitled to vote nor counted for quorum purposes in any vote to approve the ratification of any defective corporate action.

(f) If the approval under this section of putative shares would result in an overissue, in addition to the approval required by section 1.47, approval of an amendment to the articles of incorporation under chapter 10 to increase the number of shares of an authorized class or series or to authorize the creation of a class or series of shares so there would be no overissue shall also be required.

Cross-References

Notices and other communications, see § 1.41.

Quorum and voting requirements for the board of directors, see § 8.24.

Quorum and voting requirements for voting groups, see § 7.25.

Official Comment

Notwithstanding the shareholder notice required by section 1.48(b), only valid shares are entitled to vote on the ratification action or counted for quorum purposes. The retroactive effect of a ratification of putative shares does not invalidate the quorum or voting result of the ratification.

For matters other than the election of directors, the quorum and voting requirements applicable to shareholder approval of ratification are the quorum and voting requirements applicable to the corporate action being ratified at the time of such approval. For example, if the defective corporate action being ratified is an amendment to the articles of incorporation, whether in connection with an overissue or otherwise, the vote required would be governed by section 10.03. If the defective corporate action involves a merger, the vote required would be the vote required by section 11.04.

§ 1.49. Notice Requirements

(a) Unless shareholder approval is required under section 1.47(c), prompt notice of an action taken under section 1.47 shall be given to each holder of valid and putative shares, regardless of whether entitled to vote, as of (i) the date of such action by the board of directors and (ii) the date of the defective corporate action ratified, provided that notice shall not be required to be given to holders of valid and putative shares whose identities or addresses for notice cannot be determined from the records of the corporation.

(b) The notice must contain (i) either a copy of the action taken by the board of directors in accordance with section 1.47(a) or (b) or the information required by sections 1.47(a)(1) through (a)(4) or sections 1.47(b)(1) through (b)(3), as applicable, and (ii) a statement that any claim that the ratification of the defective corporate action and any putative shares issued as a result of such defective corporate action should not be effective, or should be effective only on certain conditions, shall be brought within 120 days from the applicable validation effective time.

(c) No notice under this section is required with respect to any action required to be submitted to shareholders for approval under section 1.47(c) if notice is given in accordance with section 1.48(b).

(d) A notice required by this section may be given in any manner permitted by section 1.41 and, for any corporation subject to the reporting requirements of Section 13 or 15(d) of the Securities Exchange Act of 1934, may be given by means of a filing or furnishing of such notice with the United States Securities and Exchange Commission.

Cross References

> Corporate records, see § 16.01.
>
> Householding, see § 1.44.
>
> Notices and other communications, see § 1.41.

§ 1.50. Effect of Ratification

From and after the validation effective time, and without regard to the 120-day period during which a claim may be brought under section 1.52:

> (a)   Each defective corporate action ratified in accordance with section 1.47 shall not be void or voidable as a result of the failure of authorization identified in the action taken under section 1.47(a) or (b) and shall be deemed a valid corporate action effective as of the date of the defective corporate action;

> (b)   The issuance of each putative share or fraction of a putative share purportedly issued pursuant to a defective corporate action identified in the action taken under section 1.47 shall not be void or voidable, and each such putative share or fraction of a putative share shall be deemed to be an identical share or fraction of a valid share as of the time it was purportedly issued; and

> (c)   Any corporate action taken subsequent to the defective corporate action ratified in accordance with this subchapter in reliance on such defective corporate action having been validly effected and any subsequent defective corporate action resulting directly or indirectly from such original defective corporate action shall be valid as of the time taken.

Official Comment

Ratification is effective as of the validation effective time and is not dependent on the expiration of the 120-day time period in which an action challenging the ratification must be brought. The ratification of a defective corporate action has the additional effect of ratifying corporate actions that are defective as a result of the original defective corporate action. For example, an overissue which results in subsequent director elections being invalid calls into question all actions by the invalidly elected board members. The ratification of the overissue, however, would cure any such additional defects.

§ 1.51. Filings

(a)   If the defective corporate action ratified under this subchapter would have required under any other section of this Act a filing in accordance with this Act, then, regardless of whether a filing was previously made in respect of such defective corporate action and in lieu of a filing otherwise required by this Act, the corporation shall file articles of validation in accordance with this section, and such articles of validation shall serve to amend or substitute for any other filing with respect to such defective corporate action required by this Act.

(b)   The articles of validation must set forth:

> (1)   the defective corporate action that is the subject of the articles of validation (including, in the case of any defective corporate action involving the issuance of putative shares, the number and type of putative shares issued and the date or dates upon which such putative shares were purported to have been issued);

> (2)   the date of the defective corporate action;

> (3)   the nature of the failure of authorization in respect of the defective corporate action;

> (4)   a statement that the defective corporate action was ratified in accordance with section 1.47, including the date on which the board of directors ratified such defective corporate action and the date, if any, on which the shareholders approved the ratification of such defective corporate action; and

(5)   the information required by subsection (c).

(c)   The articles of validation must also contain the following information:

(1)   if a filing was previously made in respect of the defective corporate action and no changes to such filing are required to give effect to the ratification of such defective corporate action in accordance with section 1.47, the articles of validation must set forth (i) the name, title and filing date of the filing previously made and any articles of correction to that filing and (ii) a statement that a copy of the filing previously made, together with any articles of correction to that filing, is attached as an exhibit to the articles of validation;

(2)   if a filing was previously made in respect of the defective corporate action and such filing requires any change to give effect to the ratification of such defective corporate action in accordance with section 1.47, the articles of validation must set forth (i) the name, title and filing date of the filing previously made and any articles of correction to that filing and (ii) a statement that a filing containing all of the information required to be included under the applicable section or sections of the Act to give effect to such defective corporate action is attached as an exhibit to the articles of validation, and (iii) the date and time that such filing is deemed to have become effective; or

(3)   if a filing was not previously made in respect of the defective corporate action and the defective corporate action ratified under section 1.47 would have required a filing under any other section of the Act, the articles of validation must set forth (i) a statement that a filing containing all of the information required to be included under the applicable section or sections of the Act to give effect to such defective corporate action is attached as an exhibit to the articles of validation, and (ii) the date and time that such filing is deemed to have become effective.

Cross-References

Correcting filed documents, see § 1.24.

Effective time and date of filing, see § 1.23.

Official Comment

Section 1.51 requires that in the event any filing is or would have been required under the Act to effect the defective corporate action, such filing (if no filing was previously made), such corrected filing (if correction to a previous filing is required), or such original filing (if no correction to a previous filing is required) be attached as an exhibit to the articles of validation. This is intended to provide a clear public record of the actions relating to the ratification.

§ 1.52. Judicial Proceedings Regarding Validity of Corporate Actions

(a)   Upon application by the corporation, any successor entity to the corporation, a director of the corporation, any shareholder, beneficial shareholder or unrestricted voting trust beneficial owner of the corporation, including any such shareholder, beneficial shareholder or unrestricted voting trust beneficial owner as of the date of the defective corporate action ratified under section 1.47, or any other person claiming to be substantially and adversely affected by a ratification under section 1.47, the [name or describe court] may:

(1)   determine the validity and effectiveness of any corporate action or defective corporate action;

(2)   determine the validity and effectiveness of any ratification under section 1.47;

(3)   determine the validity of any putative shares; and

(4)   modify or waive any of the procedures specified in section 1.47 or 1.48 to ratify a defective corporate action.

(b)   In connection with an action under this section, the court may make such findings or orders, and take into account any factors or considerations, regarding such matters as it deems proper under the circumstances.

(c)   Service of process of the application under subsection (a) on the corporation may be made in any manner provided by statute of this state or by rule of the applicable court for service on the corporation, and no other party need be joined in order for the court to adjudicate the matter. In an action filed by the corporation, the court may require notice of the action be provided to other persons specified by the court and permit such other persons to intervene in the action.

(d)   Notwithstanding any other provision of this section or otherwise under applicable law, any action asserting that the ratification of any defective corporate action and any putative shares issued as a result of such defective corporate action should not be effective, or should be effective only on certain conditions, shall be brought within 120 days of the validation effective time.

Cross-References

"Beneficial shareholder" defined, see § 1.40.

"Shareholder" defined, see § 1.40.

"Unrestricted voting trust beneficial owner" defined, see § 1.40.

Official Comment

Section 1.52 confers plenary jurisdiction on a designated court to hear and determine claims regarding the validity of any corporate action or any shares, rights, options or warrants. The court's jurisdiction is not limited to reviewing corporate actions ratified or purportedly ratified under section 1.47, and includes the ability of a corporation or other permitted person to obtain a declaration regarding the validity of any corporate actions or shares that are potentially defective. In determining the validity of a corporate action or reviewing a corporate action ratified under section 1.47, the court may consider any factors or considerations it deems proper under the circumstances. These might include whether the person originally taking the defective corporate action believed that the action complied with corporate requirements, whether the corporation and board of directors has treated the defective corporate action as a valid action, whether any person has acted in reliance on the public record that such defective corporate action was valid and whether any person will be or was harmed by the ratification of the defective corporate action or will be harmed by the failure to ratify or validate the defective corporate action.

CHAPTER 2: INCORPORATION

§ 2.01. Incorporators

One or more persons may act as the incorporator or incorporators of a corporation by delivering articles of incorporation to the secretary of state for filing.

Cross-References

Effective time and date of filing, see § 1.23.

Filing requirements, see § 1.20.

Organization of corporation, see § 2.05.

"Person" defined, see § 1.40.

Official Comment

The only functions of incorporators under the Act are (i) to sign the articles of incorporation, (ii) to deliver them to the secretary of state for filing, and (iii) to complete the formation of the corporation to the extent set forth in section 2.05. "Person" is defined in section 1.40 and includes both individuals and entities.

The Act does not require that articles of incorporation be acknowledged or verified. See the Official Comment to section 1.20 with respect to execution and filing requirements.

§ 2.02. Articles of Incorporation

(a) The articles of incorporation must set forth:

(1) a corporate name for the corporation that satisfies the requirements of section 4.01;

(2) the number of shares the corporation is authorized to issue;

(3) the street and mailing addresses of the corporation's initial registered office and the name of its initial registered agent at that office; and

(4) the name and address of each incorporator.

(b) The articles of incorporation may set forth:

(1) the names and addresses of the individuals who are to serve as the initial directors;

(2) provisions not inconsistent with law regarding:

(i) the purpose or purposes for which the corporation is organized;

(ii) managing the business and regulating the affairs of the corporation;

(iii) defining, limiting, and regulating the powers of the corporation, its board of directors, and shareholders;

(iv) a par value for authorized shares or classes of shares; or

(v) the imposition of interest holder liability on shareholders;

(3) any provision that under this Act is required or permitted to be set forth in the bylaws;

(4) a provision eliminating or limiting the liability of a director to the corporation or its shareholders for money damages for any action taken, or any failure to take any action, as a director, except liability for (i) the amount of a financial benefit received by a director to which the director is not entitled; (ii) an intentional infliction of harm on the corporation or the shareholders; (iii) a violation of section 8.32; or (iv) an intentional violation of criminal law;

(5) a provision permitting or making obligatory indemnification of a director for liability as defined in section 8.50 to any person for any action taken, or any failure to take any action, as a director, except liability for (i) receipt of a financial benefit to which the director is not entitled, (ii) an intentional infliction of harm on the corporation or its shareholders, (iii) a violation of section 8.32, or (iv) an intentional violation of criminal law; and

(6) a provision limiting or eliminating any duty of a director or any other person to offer the corporation the right to have or participate in any, or one or more classes or categories of, business opportunities, before the pursuit or taking of the opportunity by the director or other person; provided that any application of such a provision to an officer or a related person of that officer (i) also requires approval of that application by the board of directors, subsequent to the effective date of the provision, by action of qualified directors taken in compliance with the same procedures as are set forth in section 8.62, and (ii) may be limited by the authorizing action of the board.

(c) The articles of incorporation need not set forth any of the corporate powers enumerated in this Act.

(d) Provisions of the articles of incorporation may be made dependent upon facts objectively ascertainable outside the articles of incorporation in accordance with section 1.20(k).

(e) As used in this section, "related person" has the meaning specified in section 8.60.

Cross-References

Amendment of articles of incorporation, see ch. 10A.

Classes of shares, see § 6.01.

Corporate powers, see § 3.02.

Duration of corporate existence, see § 3.02.

Filing requirements, see § 1.20.

Incorporators, see § 2.01.

Indemnification, see ch. 8E.

"Interest holder liability" defined, see § 1.40.

Liability of shareholders, see § 6.22.

Powers, see § 3.02.

Purposes, see § 3.01.

Restated articles of incorporation, see § 10.07.

Official Comment

1. Introduction

A corporation will have perpetual duration unless a special provision is included in its articles of incorporation providing for a shorter period. See section 3.02. Similarly, a corporation with articles of incorporation which do not contain a purpose clause will have the purpose of engaging in any lawful business under section 3.01(a). The option of providing a narrower purpose clause is also preserved in sections 2.02(b)(2)(i) and 3.01, with the effect described in the Official Comment to section 3.01.

2. Required Provisions

If a single class of shares is authorized, only the number of shares authorized need be stated; if more than one class of shares is authorized, however, both the number of authorized shares of each class and a description of the rights of each class must be included. See the Official Comment to sections 6.01 and 6.02. It is unnecessary to specify par value, expected minimum capitalization, or contemplated issue price.

The corporation's initial registered office and agent must be included, and a mailing address alone, such as a post office box, is not sufficient since the registered office is the designated location for service of process. See chapter 5.

No reference need be made to a variety of other matters such as preemptive rights. See section 6.30 and its Official Comment. Generally, no substantive effect should be given to the absence of a specific reference to such matters in section 2.02. They are referred to in other sections of the Act that usually provide an "opt in" privilege. See particularly the list of optional provisions set forth in parts 4 and 5 of this Official Comment.

3. Optional Provisions

Section 2.02(b) allows the articles of incorporation to contain optional provisions deemed sufficiently important to be of public record or subject to amendment only by the processes applicable to amendments of articles of incorporation.

A. BUSINESS OR AFFAIRS

Provisions relating to the business or affairs of the corporation that may be included in the articles may be subdivided into four general classes:

- provisions that under the Act may be elected only by specific inclusion in the articles of incorporation (a list of these provisions is set forth in part 4 of this Official Comment);

- provisions that under the Act may be elected by specific inclusion in either the articles of incorporation or the bylaws, as listed in part 5 of this Official Comment;

- other provisions not referred to in the Act, including any provision that the Act requires or permits to be set forth in the bylaws (see section 2.02(b)(3)); and

- other provisions that are inconsistent with one or more provisions of the Act but are nonetheless permitted by section 7.32 for inclusion in a shareholders' agreement, if the requirements of that section are met.

B. CORPORATE POWERS

Section 2.02(c) makes it unnecessary to set forth any corporate powers in the articles of incorporation in view of the broad grant of power in section 3.02. This grant of power, however, may be overbroad for particular corporations; if so, it may be qualified or narrowed by appropriate provisions in the articles of incorporation.

C. PAR VALUE

Although par value is no longer a mandatory statutory concept under the Act, section 2.02(b)(2)(iv) permits optional "par value" provisions with regard to shares. Other than being permitted by section 2.02(b)(2)(iv), however, "par value" is not mentioned in the Act. Special provisions may be included to give effect or meaning to "par value" essentially as a matter of contract between the parties. These provisions, whether appearing in the articles of incorporation or in other documents, have only the effect any permissible contractual provision has in the absence of a prohibition by statute. Provisions in the articles of incorporation establishing an optional par value may also be of use to corporations which are to be qualified or registered in foreign jurisdictions that compute franchise or other taxes upon the basis of par value.

For a general discussion of capitalization, see the Official Comment to section 6.21.

D. SHAREHOLDER LIABILITY

The basic tenet of corporation law is that shareholders are not liable for the corporation's liabilities by reason of their status as shareholders. Section 2.02(b)(2)(v) nevertheless permits a corporation to impose that liability under specified circumstances if that is desirable. If no provision of this type is included, shareholders have no liability for corporate liabilities except to the extent they become liable by reason of their own conduct or acts. See section 6.22(b).

E. LIMITATIONS OF DIRECTOR LIABILITY

Section 2.02(b)(4) authorizes the inclusion of a provision in the articles of incorporation eliminating or limiting, with certain exceptions, the liability of the directors to the corporation or its shareholders for money damages. This section is optional rather than self-executing and does not apply to equitable relief. Likewise, nothing in section 2.02(b)(4) in any way affects the right of the shareholders to remove directors, under section 8.08(a), with or without cause. The phrase "as a director" emphasizes that section 2.02(b)(4) applies to a director's actions or failures to take action in the director's capacity as a director and not in any other capacity, such as officer, employee or controlling shareholder. However, it is not intended to exclude coverage of conduct by individuals, even though they are also officers, employees or controlling shareholders, to the extent they are acting in their capacity as directors.

Shareholders are given considerable latitude in limiting directors' liability for money damages. The statutory exceptions to permitted limitations of director liability are few and narrow and are discussed below.

Financial Benefit

Corporate law subjects transactions from which a director could benefit personally to special scrutiny. The financial benefits exception is limited to the amount of the benefit actually received. Thus, liability for punitive damages could be eliminated, except in cases of intentional infliction of harm or for violation of criminal law (as described below) where, in a particular case (for example, theft), punitive damages may be available. The benefit must be financial rather than in less easily measured and more conjectural forms, such as business goodwill, personal reputation, or social ingratiation. The phrase "received by a director" is not intended to be a "bright line." As a director's conduct moves toward the edge of what may be exculpated, the director should bear the risk of miscalculation. Depending upon the circumstances, a director may be deemed to have received a benefit that the director caused to be directed to another person, for example, a relative, friend, or affiliate.

What constitutes a financial benefit "to which the director is not entitled" is left to judicial development. For example, a director is entitled to reasonable compensation for the performance of services or to an increase in the value of stock or stock options held by the director; on the other hand, a director is not entitled to a bribe, a kick-back, or the profits from a corporate opportunity improperly taken by the director. See section 8.70 as to procedures for disclaiming the corporation's interest in a business opportunity by action of qualified directors or shareholders. See section 2.02(b)(6) for optional provisions permitted in the articles of incorporation to limit or eliminate, in advance, any duty of directors and others to bring business opportunities to the corporation. If the corporation declines the opportunity after it has been presented to the corporation by the director in accordance with the provisions of section 8.70(a)(1)(i) or (ii), or if a provision under section 2.02(b)(6) limits or eliminates the duty to bring the particular opportunity to the corporation, the corporation will have no right to participate in any financial benefit arising from the opportunity if the director pursues or takes the opportunity.

Intentional Infliction of Harm

There may be situations in which a director intentionally causes harm to the corporation even though the director does not receive any improper benefit. The use of the word "intentional," rather than a less precise term such as "knowing," is meant to refer to the specific intent to perform, or fail to perform, the acts with actual knowledge that the director's action, or failure to act, will cause harm, rather than a general intent to perform the acts which cause the harm.

Unlawful Distributions

Section 8.32(a) indicates a strong policy in favor of liability for unlawful distributions approved by directors who have not complied with the standards of conduct of section 8.30. Accordingly, the exception in section 2.02(b)(4)(iii) prohibits the shareholders from eliminating or limiting the liability of directors for a violation of section 8.32.

Intentional Violation of Criminal Law

Even though a director committing a crime may intend to benefit the corporation, the shareholders should not be permitted to exculpate the director for any harm caused by an intentional violation of criminal law, including, for example, fines and legal expenses of the corporation in defending a criminal prosecution. The use of the word "intentional," rather than a less precise term such as "knowing," is meant to refer to the specific intent to perform, or fail to perform, the acts with actual knowledge that the director's action, or failure to act, constitutes a violation of criminal law.

F. DIRECTOR INDEMNIFICATION

Section 2.02(b)(5) specifically prohibits provisions for indemnification of director liability arising out of improper financial benefit received by a director, an intentional infliction of harm on the corporation or the shareholders, an unlawful distribution or an intentional violation of criminal law. These excepted liabilities parallel those a corporation is not permitted to limit or eliminate under section 2.02(b)(4). See "E. Limitations of Director Liability" above. Officers are not included in the language of section 2.02(b)(5) because the expansion of indemnification for directors that section permits must be set forth in the articles of incorporation as required by section 8.51(a)(2); section 8.56 allows a similar expansion of indemnification for officers to be set forth also in the bylaws, resolutions or contracts.

G. BUSINESS OPPORTUNITIES

Section 2.02 (b)(6) authorizes the inclusion of a provision in the articles of incorporation to limit or eliminate, in advance, the duty of a director or other person to bring a business opportunity to the corporation. The limitation or elimination may be blanket in nature and apply to any business opportunities, or it may extend only to one or more specified classes or categories of business opportunities. The adoption of such a provision constitutes a curtailment of the duty of loyalty which includes the doctrine of corporate opportunity. If such a provision is included in the articles, taking advantage of a business opportunity covered by the provision of the articles without offering it to the corporation will not expose the director or other person to whom it is made applicable either to monetary damages or to equitable or any other relief in favor of the corporation upon compliance with the requirements of section 2.02(b)(6).

This provision may be useful, for example, in the context of a private equity investor that wishes to have a nominee on the board but conditions its investment on an advance limitation or elimination of the corporate opportunity doctrine because of the uncertainty over the application of the corporate opportunity doctrine inherent when investments are made in multiple enterprises in specific industries. Another example is a joint venture in corporate form where the participants in the joint venture want to be sure that the corporate opportunity doctrine would not apply to their activities outside the joint venture.

The focus of the advance limitation or elimination is on the duty of the director which extends indirectly to the investor through the application of the related party definition in section 8.60. This provision also permits extension of the limitation or elimination of the duty to any other persons who might be deemed to have a duty to offer business opportunities to the corporation. For example, courts have held that the corporate opportunity doctrine extends to officers of the corporation. Although officers may be included in a provision under this subsection, the limitation or elimination of corporate opportunity obligations of officers must be addressed by the board of directors in specific cases or by the directors' authorizing provisions in employment agreements or other contractual arrangements with such officers. Accordingly, section 2.02(b)(6) requires that the application of an advance limitation or elimination of the duty to offer a business opportunity to the corporation to any person who is an officer of the corporation or a related person of an officer also requires action by the board of directors acting through qualified directors. This action must be taken subsequent to the inclusion of the provision in the articles of incorporation and may limit the application. This means that if the advance limitation or elimination of the duty of an officer to offer business opportunities to the corporation is included in the articles by an amendment recommended by the directors and approved by the shareholders, that recommendation of the directors does not serve as the required authorization by qualified directors; rather, separate authorization by qualified directors after the amendment is included in the articles is necessary to apply the provision to a particular officer or any related person of that officer. See sections 1.43(a)(1) and 8.60 for the definition of "qualified directors" and "related persons," respectively.

Whether a provision for advance limitation or elimination of duty in the articles of incorporation should be a broad "blanket" provision or one more tailored to specific categories or classes of transactions deserves careful consideration given the particular circumstances of the corporation.

Limitation or elimination of the duty of a director or officer to present a business opportunity to the corporation does not limit or eliminate the director's or officer's duty not to make unauthorized use of corporate property or information or to compete unfairly with the corporation.

4. *List of Options in the Act That May Be Elected Only in the Articles of Incorporation*

A. OPTIONS WITH RESPECT TO DIRECTORS

- Board of directors may be dispensed with entirely, § 7.32, or its functions may be restricted, § 8.01.
- Power to compensate directors may be restricted or eliminated, § 8.11.
- Election of directors by cumulative voting may be authorized, § 7.28.
- Election of directors by greater than plurality vote may be authorized, § 7.28.
- Directors may be elected by classes or series of shares, § 8.04.
- Director's term may be limited by failure to receive specified vote for election, § 8.05.
- Power to remove directors without cause may be restricted or eliminated, § 8.08.
- Terms of directors may be staggered so that all directors are not elected in the same year, § 8.06.
- Power to fill vacancies may be limited to the shareholders, § 8.10.
- Power to indemnify directors, officers, and employees may be limited, §§ 8.50 through 8.59.
- Prohibition on adoption of bylaw provision under § 10.22.

B. OPTIONS WITH RESPECT TO SHAREHOLDERS

- Action by shareholders may be taken without a meeting, § 7.04.
- Special voting groups of shareholders may be authorized, § 7.25.
- Elimination or restriction of separate voting groups for mergers and share exchanges, § 11.04, and for domestications, § 9.21.

- Quorum for voting groups of shareholders may be increased or reduced, §§ 7.25, 7.26, and 7.27.

- Quorum for voting by voting groups of shareholders may be prescribed, see § 7.26.

- Greater than majority vote may be required for action by voting groups of shareholders, § 7.27.

C.   OPTIONS WITH RESPECT TO SHARES

- Shares may be divided into classes and classes into series, §§ 6.01 and 6.02.

- Cumulative voting for directors may be permitted, § 7.28.

- Distributions may be restricted, § 6.40.

- Share dividends may be restricted, § 6.23.

- Voting rights of classes or series of shares may be limited or denied, § 6.01.

- Classes or series of shares may be given more or less than one vote per share, § 7.21.

- Terms of a class or series of shares may vary among holders of the same class or series, so long as such variations are expressly set forth in the articles, § 6.01.

- The board of directors may allocate authorized but unissued shares of a class or series of shares to another class or series without shareholder approval, § 6.02.

- Shares may be redeemed at the option of the corporation or the shareholder, § 6.01.

- Reissue of acquired or redeemed shares may be prohibited, § 6.31.

- Shareholders may be given preemptive rights to acquire unissued shares, § 6.30.

- Redemption preferences may be ignored in determining lawfulness of distributions, § 6.40.

5. *List of Options in the Act That May Be Elected Either in the Articles of Incorporation or in the Bylaws*

A.   OPTIONS WITH RESPECT TO DIRECTORS

- Number of directors may be fixed or changed within limits, § 8.03.

- Qualifications for directors may be prescribed, § 8.02.

- Notice of regular or special meetings of board of directors may be prescribed, § 8.22.

- Power of board of directors to act without meeting may be restricted, § 8.21.

- Quorum for meeting of board of directors may be increased or decreased (down to one-third) from majority, § 8.24.

- Action at meeting of board of directors may require a greater than majority vote, § 8.24.

- Power of directors to participate in meeting without being physically present may be prohibited, § 8.20.

- Board of directors may create board committees and specify their powers, § 8.25.

- Board of directors may create safe harbor for consideration of corporate opportunities, § 8.70.

- Power of board of directors to amend bylaws may be restricted, §§ 10.20 and 10.21.

- Election of directors may be governed by the optional rules under section 10.22.

B.   OPTIONS WITH RESPECT TO SHARES

- Shares may be issued without certificates, § 6.26.

- Procedure for treating beneficial owner of street name shares as record owner may be prescribed, § 7.23.

- Transfer of shares may be restricted, § 6.27.

§ 2.03. Incorporation

(a) Unless a delayed effective date is specified, the corporate existence begins when the articles of incorporation are filed.

(b) The secretary of state's filing of the articles of incorporation is conclusive proof that the incorporators satisfied all conditions precedent to incorporation except in a proceeding by the state to cancel or revoke the incorporation or involuntarily dissolve the corporation.

Cross-References

Effective time and date of filing, see § 1.23.

Evidentiary effect of certified copy of filed document, see § 1.27.

Filing requirements, see § 1.20.

Liability for preincorporation transactions, see § 2.04.

Official Comment

Section 2.03(a) fixes the beginning of corporate existence as the date and time the articles are filed by the secretary of state, as provided in section 1.23, unless the articles of incorporation provide that the corporation's existence will begin at a time later than the time of filing, to the extent permitted by section 1.23.

Under section 2.03(b) the filing of the articles of incorporation is conclusive proof that all conditions precedent to incorporation have been met, except in specified proceedings brought by the state.

See Chapter 1, which contains rules for the filing and effective dates of documents, all of which are applicable to articles of incorporation and other documents.

§ 2.04. Liability for Preincorporation Transactions

All persons purporting to act as or on behalf of a corporation, knowing there was no incorporation under this Act, are jointly and severally liable for all liabilities created while so acting.

Cross-References

Incorporation, see § 2.03.

"Person" defined, see § 1.40.

Official Comment

Ordinarily, only the filing of articles of incorporation should create the privilege of limited liability. Situations may arise, however, in which the protection of limited liability arguably should be recognized even though the simple incorporation process established by the Act has not been completed.

As a result, the Act imposes liability only on persons who act as or on behalf of corporations "knowing" that no corporation exists. In addition, section 2.04 does not foreclose the possibility that persons who urge defendants to execute contracts in the corporate name knowing that no steps to incorporate have been taken may be estopped to impose personal liability on individual defendants. This estoppel may be based on the inequity perceived when persons, unwilling or reluctant to enter into a commitment under their own name, are persuaded to use the name of a nonexistent corporation, and then are sought to be held personally liable under section 2.04 by the party advocating execution in the name of the corporation.

§ 2.05. Organization of Corporation

(a) After incorporation:

(1) if initial directors are named in the articles of incorporation, the initial directors shall hold an organizational meeting, at the call of a majority of the directors, to complete the organization of the corporation by appointing officers, adopting bylaws, and carrying on any other business brought before the meeting; or

(2)   if initial directors are not named in the articles of incorporation, the incorporator or incorporators shall hold an organizational meeting at the call of a majority of the incorporators:

(i)   to elect initial directors and complete the organization of the corporation; or

(ii)   to elect a board of directors who shall complete the organization of the corporation.

(b)   Action required or permitted by this Act to be taken by incorporators at an organizational meeting may be taken without a meeting if the action taken is evidenced by one or more written consents describing the action taken and signed by each incorporator.

(c)   An organizational meeting may be held in or out of this state.

Cross-References

Director action without meeting, see § 8.21.

Incorporators, see § 2.01.

Official Comment

Following incorporation, the organization of a new corporation must be completed so that it may engage in business. This usually requires adoption of bylaws, the appointment of officers and agents, the raising of equity capital by the issuance of shares to the participants in the venture, and the election of directors.

Section 2.05 allows alternative methods of completing the organization of the corporation. First, section 2.05(a)(1) contemplates that if initial directors are named in the articles of incorporation, the persons so named will organize the corporation. Second, section 2.05(a)(2) provides alternative methods for completing the organization of the corporation if initial directors are not named in the articles of incorporation. The incorporators may themselves complete the organization, or they may simply meet to elect a board of directors who are then to complete the organization. In routine incorporations, the first alternative is often elected, although in more complex situations when prompt business decisions must be made, the second alternative will be chosen and the completion of the organization will be turned over to the board of directors that will continue to serve the organization beyond its incorporation.

Section 2.05(b) is limited to incorporators because section 8.21 permits action by written consent by the board of directors.

§ 2.06. Bylaws

(a)   The incorporators or board of directors of a corporation shall adopt initial bylaws for the corporation.

(b)   The bylaws of a corporation may contain any provision that is not inconsistent with law or the articles of incorporation.

(c)   The bylaws may contain one or both of the following provisions:

(1)   a requirement that if the corporation solicits proxies or consents with respect to an election of directors, the corporation include in its proxy statement and any form of its proxy or consent, to the extent and subject to such procedures or conditions as are provided in the bylaws, one or more individuals nominated by a shareholder in addition to individuals nominated by the board of directors; and

(2)   a requirement that the corporation reimburse the expenses incurred by a shareholder in soliciting proxies or consents in connection with an election of directors, to the extent and subject to such procedures and conditions as are provided in the bylaws, provided that no bylaw so adopted shall apply to elections for which any record date precedes its adoption.

(d)   Notwithstanding section 10.20(b)(2), the shareholders in amending, repealing, or adopting a bylaw described in subsection (c) may not limit the authority of the board of directors to amend or repeal any condition or procedure set forth in or to add any procedure or condition to such a bylaw to provide for a reasonable, practical, and orderly process.

Cross-References

Amendment of bylaws, see §§ 10.20, 10.21 and 10.22.

Emergency bylaws, see § 2.07.

"Expenses" defined, see § 1.40.

Organizing corporation, see § 2.05.

Official Comment

The responsibility for adopting the original bylaws is placed on the person or persons completing the organization of the corporation. Section 2.06(b) permits any bylaw provision that is not inconsistent with law or the articles of incorporation. This limitation precludes bylaw provisions that limit the managerial authority of directors established by section 8.01(b). For a list of provisions that may be included in the bylaws, see the Official Comment to section 2.02.

The power to amend or repeal bylaws, or adopt new bylaws after the organization of the corporation is completed, is addressed in sections 10.20, 10.21 and 10.22.

Section 2.06(c) expressly authorizes bylaws that require the corporation to include individuals nominated by shareholders for election as directors in its proxy statement and proxy cards (or consents) and that require the reimbursement by the corporation of expenses incurred by a shareholder in soliciting proxies (or consents) in an election of directors, in each case subject to such procedures or conditions as may be provided in the bylaws. Expenses reimbursed under section 2.06(c)(2) must be reasonable as contemplated in the definition of expenses set forth in section 1.40.

Examples of the procedures and conditions that may be included in bylaws contemplated by section 2.06(c) include provisions that relate to the ownership of shares (including requirements as to the duration of ownership); informational requirements; restrictions on the number of directors to be nominated or on the use of the provisions by shareholders seeking to acquire control; provisions requiring the nominating shareholder to indemnify the corporation; limitations on reimbursement based on the amount spent by the corporation or the proportion of votes cast for the nominee; and limitations concerning the election of directors by cumulative voting.

Section 2.06(c) clarifies that proxy access and expense reimbursement provisions do not infringe upon the scope of authority granted to the board of directors of a corporation under section 8.01(b). Section 2.06(c) underscores the model of corporate governance embodied by the Act and reflected in section 8.01, but recognizes that different corporations may wish to grant shareholders varying rights in selecting directors through the election process.

Section 2.06(d) limits the rule set forth in section 10.20(b)(2) that shareholder adopted bylaws may limit the authority of directors to amend bylaws, by specifying that such a limit will not apply absolutely to conditions and procedures set forth in access or reimbursement bylaws authorized by section 2.06(c). Section 2.06(d) allows directors to ensure that such bylaws adequately provide for a reasonable, practical, and orderly process, but is not intended to allow the board of directors to frustrate the purpose of a shareholder-adopted proxy access or expense reimbursement provision.

§ 2.07. Emergency Bylaws

(a) Unless the articles of incorporation provide otherwise, the board of directors may adopt bylaws to be effective only in an emergency defined in subsection (d). The emergency bylaws, which are subject to amendment or repeal by the shareholders, may make all provisions necessary for managing the corporation during the emergency, including:

   (1)   procedures for calling a meeting of the board of directors;

   (2)   quorum requirements for the meeting; and

   (3)   designation of additional or substitute directors.

(b) All provisions of the regular bylaws not inconsistent with the emergency bylaws remain effective during the emergency. The emergency bylaws are not effective after the emergency ends.

(c)   Corporate action taken in good faith in accordance with the emergency bylaws:

     (1)   binds the corporation; and

     (2)   may not be used to impose liability on a director, officer, employee, or agent of the corporation.

(d)   An emergency exists for purposes of this section if a quorum of the board of directors cannot readily be assembled because of some catastrophic event.

Cross-References

Amendment of bylaws, see §§ 10.20 and 10.21.

Bylaws, see § 2.06.

Emergency powers without bylaw provision, see § 3.03.

Official Comment

The adoption of emergency bylaws in advance of an emergency not only clarifies lines of command and responsibility but also tends to ensure continuity of responsibility. The board of directors may be authorized by the emergency bylaws, for example, to designate the officers or other persons, in order of seniority and subject to various conditions, who may be deemed to be directors during the emergency.

The definition of "emergency" adopted by section 2.07(d) includes any catastrophic event that makes it difficult or impossible for a quorum of the board of directors to be assembled. To encourage corporations to adopt emergency bylaws, section 2.07(c) broadly validates all corporate actions taken "in good faith" pursuant to them and immunizes all directors, officers, employees, and agents of the corporation from liability as a result of these actions. The phrase "action taken in good faith in accordance with the emergency bylaws" is designed to conform to the standard for immunity elsewhere in the Act.

A corporation that does not adopt emergency bylaws under this section may nevertheless exercise the powers described in section 3.03 in the event of an emergency as defined in section 2.07(d).

§ 2.08.   Forum Selection Provisions

(a)   The articles of incorporation or the bylaws may require that any or all internal corporate claims shall be brought exclusively in any specified court or courts of this state and, if so specified, in any additional courts in this state or in any other jurisdictions with which the corporation has a reasonable relationship.

(b)   A provision of the articles of incorporation or bylaws adopted under subsection (a) shall not have the effect of conferring jurisdiction on any court or over any person or claim, and shall not apply if none of the courts specified by such provision has the requisite personal and subject matter jurisdiction. If the court or courts of this state specified in a provision adopted under subsection (a) do not have the requisite personal and subject matter jurisdiction and another court of this state does have such jurisdiction, then the internal corporate claim may be brought in such other court of this state, notwithstanding that such other court of this state is not specified in such provision, and in any other court specified in such provision that has the requisite jurisdiction.

(c)   No provision of the articles of incorporation or the bylaws may prohibit bringing an internal corporate claim in the courts of this state or require such claims to be determined by arbitration.

(d)   "Internal corporate claim" means, for the purposes of this section, (i) any claim that is based upon a violation of a duty under the laws of this state by a current or former director, officer, or shareholder in such capacity, (ii) any derivative action or proceeding brought on behalf of the corporation, (iii) any action asserting a claim arising pursuant to any provision of this Act or the articles of incorporation or bylaws, or (iv) any action asserting a claim governed by the internal affairs doctrine that is not included in (i) through (iii) above.

Cross-References

Derivative proceedings, see ch. 7D.

Official Comment

Section 2.08(a) authorizes a provision in either the articles of incorporation or the bylaws creating an exclusive forum or forums for the adjudication of internal corporate claims. Under section 2.08(a), the provision must specify at least one court of this state (*i.e.*, a state court rather than a federal court). The provision may also include additional specified courts or all courts of this state or courts in this state (such as federal courts) or in one or more additional jurisdictions with a reasonable relationship to the corporation. In addition, the provision may prioritize among the specified courts. For example, the provision may specify that the claim shall be brought exclusively in a particular court of this state unless such court does not have the requisite personal and subject matter jurisdiction, in which case the claim shall be brought in other specified courts.

Under the last sentence of section 2.08(b), an internal corporate claim will always be permitted to be brought in at least one court of this state unless there is no court of this state that has the requisite personal and subject matter jurisdiction. For example, if the articles of incorporation or the bylaws provide that an internal corporate claim may only be brought in a specified court of this state and in the courts of another state with a reasonable relationship to the corporation, and the specified court of this state does not have the requisite personal and subject matter jurisdiction, then the claim can be brought in any other court of this state that does have the requisite jurisdiction or in the courts of the specified other state (so long as those courts have the requisite jurisdiction). Similarly, if the articles of incorporation or the bylaws provide that an internal corporate claim may only be brought in a specified court of this state and in the federal courts in this state, and the specified court of this state does not have the requisite personal and subject matter jurisdiction, then the claim can be brought in any other court of this state that does have the requisite jurisdiction or in the federal courts in this state (so long as the federal court has the requisite jurisdiction). In each of the foregoing examples, (i) if the specified court of this state does have the requisite personal and subject matter jurisdiction, then such court would be the only court of this state in which the internal corporate claim could be brought, and (ii) if no court of this state has the requisite personal and subject matter jurisdiction, then the courts of the other state (in the first example) or the federal courts in this state (in the second example) would become the exclusive forum for such internal corporate claim, in each case so long as such court has the requisite jurisdiction.

If no court of this state has the requisite personal and subject matter jurisdiction, and none of the other courts, if any, specified in the provision of the articles of incorporation or the bylaws has the requisite jurisdiction, then the provision will have no effect and the internal corporate claim may be brought in any court that does have the requisite jurisdiction.

CHAPTER 3: PURPOSES AND POWERS

§ 3.01. Purposes

(a) Every corporation incorporated under this Act has the purpose of engaging in any lawful business unless a more limited purpose is set forth in the articles of incorporation.

(b) A corporation engaging in a business that is subject to regulation under another statute of this state may incorporate under this Act only if permitted by, and subject to all limitations of, the other statute.

Cross-References

Statement of purpose in articles of incorporation, see § 2.02.

Official Comment

The choice of an "any lawful business" clause has become nearly universal in states that permit the clause. Even if the articles of incorporation limit lines of business in which the corporation may engage, the limited scope of the ultra vires concept in litigation between the corporation and outsiders means that a third person entering into a transaction that violates the restrictions in the purpose clause may be able to enforce the transaction in accordance with its terms if the third person was unaware of the narrow purpose clause when entering into the transaction. See the Official Comment to section 3.04.

Many corporations may also find it desirable to supplement a general purpose clause with an additional statement of business purposes. This may be necessary for licensing or for qualification or registration purposes in some states.

Section 3.01(b) recognizes that certain state statutes may preclude incorporation under the Act or limit the purpose of or otherwise regulate the business or affairs of corporations formed to, or actually engaging in, certain lines of business.

- Some of these statutes, particularly those relating to banking and insurance, establish a separate incorporation process and incorporating agency. These special incorporating statutes may refer to or incorporate by reference portions of the Act. Other statutes provide for incorporation for the purpose of practicing a profession.

- Other statutes may permit incorporation under the Act if the corporation imposes restrictions or limitations in its articles of incorporation; these restrictions may relate to the business in which the corporation may engage, its manner of internal governance, or the persons who may or may not be shareholders and participate in the venture. The language of section 3.01(b) is designed to cover all these multiple variations.

- Other types of entities, such as nonprofit corporations, cooperatives, and unions, usually may not incorporate under the Act. Special statutes may apply to these entities, such as the Model Nonprofit Corporation Act.

§ 3.02. General Powers

Unless its articles of incorporation provide otherwise, every corporation has perpetual duration and succession in its corporate name and has the same powers as an individual to do all things necessary or convenient to carry out its business and affairs, including power:

(a) to sue and be sued, complain and defend in its corporate name;

(b) to have a corporate seal, which may be altered at will, and to use it, or a facsimile of it, by impressing or affixing it or in any other manner reproducing it;

(c) to make and amend bylaws, not inconsistent with its articles of incorporation or with the laws of this state, for managing the business and regulating the affairs of the corporation;

(d) to purchase, receive, lease, or otherwise acquire, and own, hold, improve, use, and otherwise deal with, real or personal property, or any legal or equitable interest in property, wherever located;

(e) to sell, convey, mortgage, pledge, lease, exchange, and otherwise dispose of all or any part of its property;

(f) to purchase, receive, subscribe for, or otherwise acquire, own, hold, vote, use, sell, mortgage, lend, pledge, or otherwise dispose of, and deal in and with shares or other interests in, or obligations of, any other entity;

(g) to make contracts and guarantees, incur liabilities, borrow money, issue its notes, bonds, and other securities and obligations (which may be convertible into or include the option to purchase other securities of the corporation), and secure any of its obligations by mortgage or pledge of any of its property, franchises, or income;

(h) to lend money, invest and reinvest its funds, and receive and hold real and personal property as security for repayment;

(i) to be a promoter, partner, member, associate, or manager of any partnership, joint venture, trust, or other entity;

(j) to conduct its business, locate offices, and exercise the powers granted by this Act within or without this state;

(k) to elect directors and appoint officers, employees, and agents of the corporation, define their duties, fix their compensation, and lend them money and credit;

(*l*) to pay pensions and establish pension plans, pension trusts, profit sharing plans, share bonus plans, share option plans, and benefit or incentive plans for any or all of its current or former directors, officers, employees, and agents;

(m) to make donations for the public welfare or for charitable, scientific, or educational purposes;

(n) to transact any lawful business that will aid governmental policy; and

(o) to make payments or donations, or do any other act, not inconsistent with law, that furthers the business and affairs of the corporation.

Cross-References

Compensation of directors, see § 8.11.

Disposition of assets, see ch. 12.

"Employee" defined, see § 1.40.

"Entity" defined, see § 1.40.

Foreign corporations, see § 15.01.

Indemnification, see ch. 8E.

Lack of power to act, see § 3.04.

Share rights, options, warrants and awards, see § 6.24.

Official Comment

The general philosophy of section 3.02 is that corporations formed under the Act should be automatically authorized to engage in all acts and have all powers that an individual may have. Because broad grants of power of this nature may not be desired in some corporations, section 3.02 generally authorizes articles of incorporation to deny or limit specific powers to a corporation.

The powers of a corporation under the Act exist independently of whether a corporation has a broad or narrow purpose clause. A corporation with a narrow purpose clause nevertheless has the same powers as an individual to do all things necessary or convenient to carry out its business. Many actions are therefore within the corporation's powers even if they do not directly affect the limited purpose for which the corporation is formed. For example, a corporation may generally make charitable contributions without regard to the purpose for which the charity will use the funds or may invest money in shares of other corporations without regard to whether the corporate purpose of the other corporation is broader or narrower than the limited purpose clause of the investing corporation. In some instances, however, a limited or narrow purpose clause may be considered to be a restriction on corporate powers as well as a restriction on purposes. Since the same ultra vires rule is applicable to corporations that exceed their purposes or powers (see the Official Comment to section 3.04), it is not necessary to determine whether a narrow purpose clause also limits the powers of the corporation but simply whether the purpose of the transaction in question is consistent with the purpose clause. These issues do not arise in corporations with an "any lawful business" purpose clause.

§ 3.03. Emergency Powers

(a) In anticipation of or during an emergency defined in subsection (d), the board of directors of a corporation may:

(1) modify lines of succession to accommodate the incapacity of any director, officer, employee, or agent; and

(2) relocate the principal office, designate alternative principal offices or regional offices, or authorize the officers to do so.

(b) During an emergency defined in subsection (d), unless emergency bylaws provide otherwise:

 (1) notice of a meeting of the board of directors need be given only to those directors whom it is practicable to reach and may be given in any practicable manner; and

 (2) one or more officers of the corporation present at a meeting of the board of directors may be deemed to be directors for the meeting, in order of rank and within the same rank in order of seniority, as necessary to achieve a quorum.

(c) Corporate action taken in good faith during an emergency under this section to further the ordinary business affairs of the corporation:

 (1) binds the corporation; and

 (2) may not be used to impose liability on a director, officer, employee, or agent.

(d) An emergency exists for purposes of this section if a quorum of the board of directors cannot readily be assembled because of some catastrophic event.

Cross-References

Corporate powers, see § 3.02.

Emergency bylaws, see § 2.07.

Notices and other communications, see § 1.41.

Notice of directors' meeting, see § 8.22.

"Principal office" defined, see § 1.40.

Official Comment

Section 3.03 should be read in conjunction with section 2.07, which authorizes a corporation to adopt emergency bylaws. Section 3.03 grants every corporation limited powers to act in an emergency even though it has failed to adopt emergency bylaws under section 2.07.

§ 3.04. Lack of Power to Act

(a) Except as provided in subsection (b), the validity of corporate action may not be challenged on the ground that the corporation lacks or lacked power to act.

(b) A corporation's power to act may be challenged:

 (1) in a proceeding by a shareholder against the corporation to enjoin the act;

 (2) in a proceeding by the corporation, directly, derivatively, or through a receiver, trustee, or other legal representative, against an incumbent or former director, officer, employee, or agent of the corporation; or

 (3) in a proceeding by the attorney general under section 14.30.

(c) In a shareholder's proceeding under subsection (b)(1) to enjoin an unauthorized corporate act, the court may enjoin or set aside the act, if equitable and if all affected persons are parties to the proceeding, and may award damages for loss (other than anticipated profits) suffered by the corporation or another party because of enjoining the unauthorized act.

Cross-References

Corporate powers, see § 3.02.

Corporate purposes, see § 3.01.

Derivative proceedings, see ch. 7D.

"Employee" defined, see § 1.40.

"Proceeding" defined, see § 1.40.

Official Comment

Under section 3.04, it is unnecessary for persons dealing with a corporation to inquire into limitations on its purpose or powers that may appear in its articles of incorporation. A person who is unaware of these limitations when dealing with the corporation is not bound by them. The phrase in section 3.04(a) that the "validity of corporate action may not be challenged on the ground that the corporation lacks or lacked power to act" applies equally to the use of the doctrine as a sword or as a shield: a third person may no more avoid an undesired contract with a corporation on the ground the corporation was without authority to make the contract than a corporation may defend a suit on a contract on the ground that the contract is ultra vires.

The language of section 3.04 extends beyond contracts and conveyances of property; "corporate action" of any kind cannot be challenged on the ground of ultra vires. For this reason it makes no difference whether a limitation in articles of incorporation is considered to be a limitation on a purpose or a limitation on a power; both are equally subject to section 3.04. Corporate action also includes inaction or refusal to act. The common law of ultra vires distinguished between executory contracts, partially executed contracts, and fully executed ones; section 3.04 treats all corporate action the same—except to the extent described in section 3.04(b)—and the same rules apply to all contracts no matter at what stage of performance.

Section 3.04, however, does not validate corporate conduct that is made illegal or unlawful by statute or common law decision. This conduct is subject to whatever sanction, criminal or civil, that is provided by the statute or decision. Whether illegal corporate conduct is voidable or rescindable depends on the applicable statute or substantive law and is not affected by section 3.04.

Section 3.04 also does not address the validity of essentially intra vires conduct that is not approved by appropriate corporate action. It does not deal, for example, with the enforceability of an executory contract to sell substantially all the assets of a corporation not in the ordinary course of business that was not approved by the shareholders as required by section 12.02. This type of transaction is not beyond the purposes or powers of the corporation; it simply has not been approved by the corporate authorities as required by law. Similarly, section 3.04 does not deal with whether a corporation is bound by the action of a corporate agent if the action requires, but has not received, approval by the board of directors. Whether the corporation is bound by this action depends on the law of agency, particularly the scope of apparent authority and whether the third person knew or should have known of the defect in the corporate approval process. These actions may be ultra vires with respect to the agent's authority but they are not ultra vires with respect to the corporation and are not controlled by section 3.04.

Similarly, corporate action is not ultra vires under section 3.04 merely because it constitutes a breach of duty. For example, a misuse of corporate assets for personal purposes by an officer or director is a breach of duty and may be enjoined. Similarly, in some circumstances a lien on corporate assets and a contract entered into by the corporation may be cancelled or enjoined if they constitute breaches of duty and the third person is charged with knowledge that they were improper. These transactions, however, are not ultra vires with respect to the corporation, and cannot be attacked under section 3.04. They may be enjoined because of breach of the duty, not because the transaction exceeds the powers or purposes of the corporation.

Section 3.04(b) permits challenges to the corporation's lack of power in three limited classes of cases:

- In a suit by a shareholder against the corporation to enjoin an ultra vires act. This suit, however, is subject to the requirements of section 3.04(c). Section 3.04(c) authorizes a court to enjoin or set aside an ultra vires act or grant other relief that may be necessary to protect the interests of all affected persons, including the interests of third persons who deal with the corporation. Under this subsection an ultra vires act may be enjoined only if all "affected parties" are parties to the suit. The requirement that the action be "equitable" generally means that only third persons dealing with a corporation while specifically aware that the corporation's action was ultra vires will be enjoined. The general phrase "if equitable" is used because of the possibility that other circumstances may exist in which it may be equitable to refuse to enforce an ultra vires contract. Further, if enforcement of the contract is enjoined, either the third person or the corporation may in the discretion of the court be awarded damages from the other for loss (excluding anticipated profits).

- In a suit by the corporation, either directly or through a legal representative, against incumbent or former officers or directors for authorizing or causing the corporation to engage in an ultra vires act. Again, this section does not address whether there is liability for causing the corporation to enter into an ultra vires act; it simply preserves the power of the corporation to assert that certain corporate action was ultra vires.

- In a suit by the attorney general under section 14.30. This provision does not answer the question whether a corporation may be dissolved or enjoined by the attorney general for committing an ultra vires act; it simply preserves the power of the state to assert that certain corporate action was ultra vires.

CHAPTER 4: NAME

§ 4.01. Corporate Name

(a) A corporate name:

(1)   must contain the word "corporation," "incorporated," "company," or "limited," or the abbreviation "corp.," "inc.," "co.," or "ltd.," or words or abbreviations of like import in another language; and

(2)   may not contain language stating or implying that the corporation is organized for a purpose other than that permitted by section 3.01 and its articles of incorporation.

(b)   Except as authorized by subsections (c) and (d), a corporate name must be distinguishable upon the records of the secretary of state from:

(1)   the corporate name of a corporation incorporated in this state which is not administratively dissolved;

(2)   a corporate name reserved or registered under section 4.02 or 4.03 or any similar provision of the law of this state;

(3)   the name of a foreign corporation registered to do business in this state or an alternate name adopted by a foreign corporation registered to do business in this state because its corporate name is unavailable;

(4)   the corporate name of a nonprofit corporation incorporated in this state which is not administratively dissolved;

(5)   the name of a foreign nonprofit corporation registered to do business in this state or an alternate name adopted by a foreign nonprofit corporation registered to conduct activities in this state because its real name is unavailable;

(6)   the name of a domestic filing entity or limited liability partnership which is not administratively dissolved;

(7)   the name of a foreign unincorporated entity registered to do business in this state or an alternate name adopted by such an entity registered to conduct activities in this state because its real name is unavailable; and

(8)   an assumed name registered under [state's assumed name statute].

(c)   A corporation may apply to the secretary of state for authorization to use a name that is not distinguishable upon the secretary of state's records from one or more of the names described in subsection (b). The secretary of state shall authorize use of the name applied for if:

(1)   the other corporation or unincorporated entity consents to the use in writing and submits an undertaking in form satisfactory to the secretary of state to change its name to a name that is distinguishable upon the records of the secretary of state from the name of the applying corporation; or

(2)   the applicant delivers to the secretary of state a certified copy of the final judgment of a court of competent jurisdiction establishing the applicant's right to use the name applied for in this state.

(d)   This Act does not control the use of fictitious names.

Cross-References

Corporate and alternate name for foreign corporations, see § 15.06.

Effective time and date of filing, see § 1.23.

"Filing entity" defined, see § 1.40.

Filing fees, see § 1.22.

Filing requirements, see § 1.20.

Registered name, see § 4.03.

Reserved name, see § 4.02.

Statement of name in articles of incorporation, see § 2.02.

Official Comment

Section 4.01 establishes two basic name requirements: the name must (i) indicate "corporateness," and (ii) be distinguishable upon the records of the secretary of state.

1.   Indication of Corporateness

Although the words "company" and "limited" are commonly used by partnerships, limited partnerships or limited liability companies, and therefore do not uniquely indicate corporateness, their use by corporations is widespread and is therefore permitted in section 4.01(a).

2.   Names That Are "Distinguishable upon the Records of the Secretary of State"

Section 4.01 is based on the fundamental premise that each corporation should have a sufficiently distinctive name so that it may be distinguished from other corporations and entities upon the records of the secretary of state. The Act should not be a partial substitute for a general assumed name, unfair competition or antifraud statute. As a result, the Act does not restrict the power of a corporation to adopt or use an assumed or fictitious name with the same freedom as an individual or impose a requirement that an "official" name not be "deceptively similar" to another corporate name. Principles of unfair competition, not the Act, provide the limits on the competitive use of similar names.

The principal justifications for requiring a distinguishable official name are (i) to prevent confusion within the secretary of state's office and the tax office and (ii) to permit accuracy in naming and serving corporate defendants in litigation. Thus, confusion in an absolute or linguistic sense is the appropriate test under the Act, not the competitive relationship between the corporations, which is the test for fraud or unfair competition. Corporate names that differ only in the words used to indicate corporateness are generally not distinguishable. Thus, if ABC Corporation is in existence, the names "ABC Inc.," "ABC Co." or "ABC Corp." should not be viewed as distinguishable. Similarly, minor variations between names that are unlikely to be noticed, such as the substitution of a "," for a "." or the substitution of an Arabic numeral for a word, such as "2" for "Two," or the substitution of a lower case letter for a capital, such as "d" for "D," generally should not be viewed as being distinguishable.

The secretary of state does not generally police the unfair competitive use of names and, indeed, usually has no resources to do so. For example, assume that "ABC Corporation" operates a retail furniture store in Albany, New York, and another group wants to use the same name to engage in a business involving imports of textiles in New York City. An attempt to incorporate a second "ABC Corporation" (or a very close variant such as "ABC Corp." or "ABC Inc.") should be rejected because the names are not distinguishable upon the records of the secretary of state. If the second group uses a distinguishable official name, like "ABD Corporation," the Act does not prohibit it from assuming the fictitious name "ABC Corporation" to import goods in New York City, although it must file the assumed name certificate required by New York law. In these situations, the secretary of state will usually not know in what business or in what geographical area

"ABC Corporation" is active or what name ABD Corporation is actually using in its business. Unless filings under the assumed name statute become part of the secretary of state's corporate records, the secretary of state simply maintains an alphabetical list of corporate names as they appear from corporate records and decides whether a proposed name is distinguishable from other corporate names by comparing the proposed name with those on the list.

3.   *Fictitious, Assumed or Alternate Names*

The secretary of state becomes involved with fictitious, assumed or alternate names only in the situation where a foreign corporation, planning to do business in a state, discovers that its corporate name is not available in that state. To register to do business it must adopt an alternate name that complies with section 4.01. See section 15.06. The alternate name is thereafter unavailable to others to the same extent as any other name described in section 4.01(b) is unavailable.

4.   *Consent to Use*

The authority of the secretary of state in section 4.01(c)(1) to accept a name that is indistinguishable from the name of another corporation may be important in a number of contexts, such as an acquisition transaction where a new corporation is to take over the business of an existing corporation without a change in corporate name. The secretary of state may require the undertaking described in section 4.01(c)(1) to specify the new name to be adopted and the time period within which the change will be made. Such requirements imposed on the undertaking should be consistent with the limited role of the secretary of state in the administration of section 4.01.

§ 4.02.   Reserved Name

(a)   A person may reserve the exclusive use of a corporate name, including a fictitious or alternate name for a foreign corporation whose corporate name is not available, by delivering an application to the secretary of state for filing. The application must set forth the name and address of the applicant and the name proposed to be reserved. If the secretary of state finds that the corporate name applied for is available, the secretary of state shall reserve the name for the applicant's exclusive use for a nonrenewable 120-day period.

(b)   The owner of a reserved corporate name may transfer the reservation to another person by delivering to the secretary of state a signed notice of the transfer that states the name and address of the transferee.

Cross-References

Alternate name for foreign corporations, see § 15.06.

Availability of names, § 4.01.

Consent to use corporate name, see § 4.01.

Effective time and date of filing, see § 1.23.

Filing requirements, see § 1.20.

Registered name, see § 4.03.

Official Comment

The "reservation" of a corporate name is basically a device to simplify the formation of a new corporation or the registration of a foreign corporation. By reserving a name, the persons considering such formation or registration can order stationery, prepare documents, etc., on the assumption that the reserved name will be available. Reference to a specific intent to form a new corporation is not required by the statute, however, because a secretary of state is not equipped and should not be asked to determine whether the requisite intent actually exists. For the same reason, "any person" is permitted to reserve a corporate name without reference to specific classes of persons who might wish to reserve a corporate name for various purposes. To use the name to register to do business under section 15.06 or incorporate, the name must comply with section 4.01.

Reasons to reserve a corporate name include:

- formation of a new domestic corporation;

- formation of a corporation in another state and the registration of that new corporation in this state; and

- a foreign corporation planning to do business in this state. The name reserved may be the foreign corporation's corporate name (if that name is available) or another name. The foreign corporation may thereafter use the reserved name as the name of a subsidiary it incorporates in this state or, if its corporate name is unavailable, as an alternate name for its registration under section 15.03.

Only a single, one-time 120-day reservation is provided for in section 4.02, although after that period expires, the name becomes available again and anyone may reserve the name. Nothing prevents the formation of an inactive corporation specifically to hold the desired name if a longer period of reservation is desired than the 120-day period specified by section 4.02.

§ 4.03. Registered Name

(a) A foreign corporation may register its corporate name (or its corporate name with the addition of any word or abbreviation listed in section 4.01(a)(1) if necessary for the corporate name to comply with section 4.01(a)(1)) if the name is distinguishable upon the records of the secretary of state from the corporate names that are not available under section 4.01(b).

(b) A foreign corporation registers its corporate name (or its corporate name with any addition permitted by subsection (a)) by delivering to the secretary of state for filing an application setting forth that name, the state or country and date of its incorporation, and a brief description of the nature of the business which is to be conducted in this state.

(c) The name is registered for the applicant's exclusive use upon the effective date of the application and for the remainder of the calendar year, unless renewed.

(d) A foreign corporation whose name registration is effective may renew it for successive years by delivering to the secretary of state for filing a renewal application, which complies with the requirements of subsection (b), between October 1 and December 31 of the preceding year. The renewal application when filed renews the registration for the following calendar year.

(e) A foreign corporation whose name registration is effective may thereafter (i) register to do business as a foreign corporation under the registered name (if it complies with section 4.01(a)(2)) or (ii) consent in writing to the use of that name by a domestic corporation thereafter incorporated under this Act or by another foreign corporation. The registration terminates when the domestic corporation is incorporated or the foreign corporation registers to do business under that name.

Cross-References

Alternate name for foreign corporations, see § 15.06.

Certificate of existence or foreign registration, see §§ 1.28 and 15.03.

Consent to use corporate name, see § 4.01.

Effective time and date of filing, see § 1.23.

Filing requirements, see § 1.20.

Reserved name, see § 4.02.

"State" defined, see § 1.40.

Official Comment

The "registration" of a corporate name is basically a device by which a foreign corporation, not registered to do business in the state, can preserve the right to use its unique corporate name if it decides later to register in the state. In effect, registration ensures corporate name availability in areas of potential future expansion.

Section 4.03 is limited to this purpose and is not for the preservation of trademarks, trade names, or possible assumed names. For this reason, generally only corporate names of foreign corporations may be registered (with the exception described below). A broader approach would create issues better resolved under a trademark or similar statute, or by litigation under unfair competition principles, and might impose duties on secretaries of state that they are generally not equipped to handle, or could handle only at increased cost.

Registration of a name other than the corporate name is permitted if the corporate name of a foreign corporation does not comply with section 4.01(a)(1) solely because it does not contain the words "corporation," "incorporated," "company" or "limited," or an abbreviation of one of these words. In that case, the corporation may add one of these words or abbreviations and register its corporate name as so modified. To use the name to register to do business under section 15.06, the name must comply with section 4.01. See also the Official Comment to section 4.01.

Confusion sometimes exists between "reservation" of names under section 4.02 and "registration" of names under section 4.03. A foreign corporation that is planning to register as a foreign corporation and finds that its name is available in the state may either reserve or register the name. Often a foreign corporation will have to decide whether to register in the state or to create a domestic subsidiary. This may be decided after the exclusive right to use the corporate name in the state is obtained either by reservation or by registration. If the corporation reserves its name, that name will be kept for 120 days and then become available again; if the corporation registers its name, that name will be kept for the remainder of the calendar year, unless renewed. That is the foreign corporation's choice. If a foreign corporation registers its name and then elects to form a domestic or foreign subsidiary, the written consent procedure of section 4.03(e) allows the secretary of state to ascertain that the domestic subsidiary is related to the foreign corporation and that use of the registered name by that subsidiary is acceptable to the foreign parent.

If a foreign corporation's corporate name is unavailable, a foreign corporation may reserve any available name—including one that is assumed or fictitious rather than the corporation's corporate name—for 120 days under section 4.02, but it may not register this type of name in light of the policy against allowing the name provisions of the Act to be used for purposes broader than the "unique name" issue. Nevertheless, a foreign corporation that wishes to be certain that a particular fictitious or assumed name will be available in the future may create an inactive domestic subsidiary with the desired name to preserve its future availability.

CHAPTER 5: OFFICE AND AGENT

§ 5.01. Registered Office and Agent of Domestic and Registered Foreign Corporations

(a) Each corporation shall continuously maintain in this state:

   (1) a registered office that may be the same as any of its places of business; and

   (2) a registered agent, which may be:

   (i) an individual who resides in this state and whose business office is identical with the registered office; or

   (ii) a domestic or foreign corporation or eligible entity whose business office is identical with the registered office and, in the case of a foreign corporation or foreign eligible entity, is registered to do business in this state.

(b) As used in this chapter, "corporation" means both a domestic corporation and a registered foreign corporation.

Cross-References

Annual report, see § 16.21.

Changing registered office or agent, see § 5.02.

Effect of dissolution of corporation, see § 14.05.

"Eligible entity" defined, see § 1.40.

Foreign corporation:

> defined, see § 1.40.

> generally, see ch. 15.

Involuntary dissolution for failure to appoint and maintain registered agent or office, see § 14.20.

Naming registered agent and office in articles of incorporation, see § 2.02.

"Registered foreign corporation" defined, see § 1.40.

Resignation of registered agent, see § 5.03.

Service on corporation, see § 5.04.

Official Comment

The requirements that a corporation organized under the Act or a registered foreign corporation continuously maintain a registered office and a registered agent at that office are based on the premises that at all times such a corporation should have an office where it may be found and a registered agent at that office to receive any notice or process required or permitted by law to be served. The street and mailing addresses of the registered office must appear in the public records maintained by the secretary of state. A mailing address alone, such as a post office box, is not sufficient since the registered office is the designated location for service of process. See section 2.02. The registered office may be a "legal" rather than a "business" office.

Many corporations designate their registered office to be a business office of the corporation and a corporate officer at that office to be the registered agent. Because most of the communication to the registered agent at the registered office deals with legal matters, however, corporations sometimes designate their regular legal counsel or the counsel's nominee as their registered agent and the counsel's office as the registered office of the corporation.

The registered agent need not be an individual. Corporation service businesses often provide, as a commercial service, registered offices and registered agents at the office of the corporation service business.

§ 5.02. Change of Registered Office or Registered Agent

(a) A corporation may change its registered office or registered agent by delivering to the secretary of state for filing a statement of change that sets forth:

(1) the name of the corporation;

(2) the street and mailing addresses of its current registered office;

(3) if the current registered office is to be changed, the street and mailing addresses of the new registered office;

(4) the name of its current registered agent;

(5) if the current registered agent is to be changed, the name of the new registered agent and the new agent's written consent (either on the statement or attached to it) to the appointment; and

(6) that after the change or changes are made, the street and mailing addresses of its registered office and of the business office of its registered agent will be identical.

(b) If the street or mailing address of a registered agent's business office changes, the agent shall change the street or mailing address of the registered office of any corporation for which the agent is the registered agent by delivering a signed written notice of the change to the corporation and delivering to the secretary of state for filing a signed statement that complies with the requirements of subsection (a) and states that the corporation has been notified of the change.

Cross-References

"Corporation" defined for purposes of ch. 5, see § 5.01.

Deletion of initial agent and office from articles of incorporation, see § 10.05.

"Deliver" defined, see § 1.40.

Effect of dissolution of corporation, see § 14.05.

Effective time and date of filing, see § 1.23.

Filing requirements, see § 1.20.

Involuntary dissolution for failure to file notice of change of registered agent or office, see § 14.20.

Notices and other communications, see § 1.41.

Registered foreign corporation subject to ch. 5, see § 5.01.

Resignation of registered agent, see § 5.03.

Official Comment

Changes of registered office or registered agent are usually routine matters which do not affect the rights of shareholders. The purpose of section 5.02 is to permit these changes without an amendment of the articles of incorporation or an approval of the board of directors or of the shareholders.

§ 5.03. Resignation of Registered Agent

(a) A registered agent may resign as agent for a corporation by delivering to the secretary of state for filing a statement of resignation signed by the agent which states:

    (1) the name of the corporation;

    (2) the name of the agent;

    (3) that the agent resigns from serving as registered agent for the corporation; and

    (4) the address of the corporation to which the agent will deliver the notice required by subsection (c).

(b) A statement of resignation takes effect on the earlier of:

    (1) 12:01 a.m. on the 31st day after the day on which it is filed by the secretary of state; or

    (2) the designation of a new registered agent for the corporation.

(c) A registered agent promptly shall deliver to the corporation notice of the date on which a statement of resignation was delivered to the secretary of state for filing.

(d) When a statement of resignation takes effect, the person that resigned ceases to have responsibility under this Act for any matter thereafter tendered to it as agent for the corporation. The resignation does not affect any contractual rights the corporation has against the agent or that the agent has against the corporation.

(e) A registered agent may resign with respect to a corporation regardless of whether the corporation is in good standing.

Cross-References

Annual report, see § 16.21.

Change of registered agent, see § 5.02.

"Corporation" defined for purposes of ch. 5, see § 5.01.

"Deliver" defined, see § 1.40.

Effect of dissolution of corporation, see § 14.05.

Effective time and date of filing, see § 1.23.

Filing requirements, see § 1.20.

Official Comment

Section 5.03 permits the discontinuation of the registered office as well as the resignation of the agent and sets forth procedures for doing so.

§ 5.04. Service on Corporation

(a)   A corporation's registered agent is the corporation's agent for service of process, notice, or demand required or permitted by law to be served on the corporation.

(b)   If a corporation has no registered agent, or the agent cannot with reasonable diligence be served, the corporation may be served by registered or certified mail, return receipt requested, addressed to the secretary at the corporation's principal office. Service is perfected under this subsection at the earliest of:

(1)   the date the corporation receives the mail;

(2)   the date shown on the return receipt, if signed on behalf of the corporation; or

(3)   five days after its deposit in the United States mail, as evidenced by the postmark, if mailed postpaid and correctly addressed.

(c)   If process, notice, or demand (i) cannot be served on a corporation pursuant to subsection (a) or (b), or (ii) is to be served on a registered foreign corporation that has withdrawn its registration pursuant to section 15.07 or 15.09, or the registration of which has been terminated pursuant to section 15.11, then the secretary of state shall be an agent of the corporation upon whom process, notice, or demand may be served. Service of any process, notice, or demand on the secretary of state as agent for a corporation may be made by delivering to the secretary of state duplicate copies of the process, notice, or demand. If process, notice, or demand is served on the secretary of state, the secretary of state shall forward one of the copies by registered or certified mail, return receipt requested, to the corporation at the last address shown in the records of the secretary of state. Service is effected under this subsection (c) at the earliest of:

(1)   the date the corporation receives the process, notice, or demand;

(2)   the date shown on the return receipt, if signed on behalf of the corporation; or

(3)   five days after the process, notice, or demand is deposited with the United States mail by the secretary of state.

(d)   This section does not prescribe the only means, or necessarily the required means, of serving a corporation.

Cross-References

Annual report, see § 16.21.

"Corporation" defined for purposes of ch. 5, see § 5.01.

"Notice" defined, see § 1.41.

"Principal office":

>   defined, see § 1.40.

>   designated in annual report, see § 16.21.

Registered foreign corporations:

>   defined, see § 1.40.

>   subject to ch. 5, see § 5.01.

Registered office and agent:

>   disclosed in annual report, see § 16.21.

>   required, see § 5.01.

"Secretary" defined, see § 1.40.

Official Comment

By providing for service by registered or certified mail addressed to the secretary at the principal office if the corporation has no registered agent or the registered agent cannot be found, section 5.04 alleviates the problem of service on an agent that is no longer serving the corporation or registered foreign corporation.

Because section 5.04(c) does not prescribe the exclusive means of serving a corporation or registered foreign corporation, service may also be perfected under civil practice statutes, under rules of civil procedure, or under statutes that provide special service requirements applicable to certain types of corporations.

CHAPTER 6: SHARES AND DISTRIBUTIONS

SUBCHAPTER A
SHARES

§ 6.01. Authorized Shares

(a)   The articles of incorporation must set forth any classes of shares and series of shares within a class, and the number of shares of each class and series, that the corporation is authorized to issue. If more than one class or series of shares is authorized, the articles of incorporation must prescribe a distinguishing designation for each class or series and, before the issuance of shares of a class or series, describe the terms, including the preferences, rights, and limitations, of that class or series. Except to the extent varied as permitted by this section, all shares of a class or series must have terms, including preferences, rights, and limitations, that are identical with those of other shares of the same class or series.

(b)   The articles of incorporation must authorize:

>   (1)   one or more classes or series of shares that together have full voting rights, and

>   (2)   one or more classes or series of shares (which may be the same class, classes or series as those with voting rights) that together are entitled to receive the net assets of the corporation upon dissolution.

(c)   The articles of incorporation may authorize one or more classes or series of shares that:

>   (1)   have special, conditional, or limited voting rights, or no right to vote, except to the extent otherwise provided by this Act;

>   (2)   are redeemable or convertible as specified in the articles of incorporation:

>>   (i)   at the option of the corporation, the shareholder, or another person or upon the occurrence of a specified event;

>>   (ii)   for cash, indebtedness, securities, or other property; and

(iii) at prices and in amounts specified or determined in accordance with a formula;

(3) entitle the holders to distributions calculated in any manner, including dividends that may be cumulative, noncumulative, or partially cumulative; or

(4) have preference over any other class or series of shares with respect to distributions, including distributions upon the dissolution of the corporation.

(d) Terms of shares may be made dependent upon facts objectively ascertainable outside the articles of incorporation in accordance with section 1.20(k).

(e) Any of the terms of shares may vary among holders of the same class or series so long as such variations are expressly set forth in the articles of incorporation.

(f) The description of the preferences, rights, and limitations of classes or series of shares in subsection (c) is not exhaustive.

Cross-References

Amendment of articles of incorporation, see ch. 10A.

Certificateless shares, see § 6.26.

Certificates for shares, see § 6.25.

Classes and series of shares, see §§ 6.01 and 6.02.

Consideration for shares, see § 6.21.

Distributions, see § 6.40.

Extrinsic facts, see § 1.20.

Fractional shares, see § 6.04.

Options, see § 6.24.

Outstanding shares, see § 6.03.

Preemptive rights, see § 6.30.

Redemption, see § 6.31.

Voting by nonvoting shares, see § 10.04.

Voting by voting groups of shares, see §§ 1.40, 7.25 and 7.26.

Voting rights, see § 7.21.

Official Comment

1. *Section 6.01(a)*

Section 6.01(a) requires that the articles of incorporation prescribe the classes and series of shares and the number of shares of each class and series that the corporation is authorized to issue. If the articles of incorporation authorize the issue of only one class of shares, no designation or description of the shares is required, it being understood that these shares have both the power to vote and the power to receive the net assets of the corporation upon dissolution. See section 6.01(b). Shares with both of these characteristics are usually referred to as "common shares" but no specific designation is required by the Act. The articles of incorporation may set forth the number of shares authorized and permit the board of directors under section 6.02 to allocate the authorized shares among designated classes or series of shares.

The preferences, rights and limitations of each class or series of shares constitute the "contract" of the holders of those classes and series of shares with respect to the holders' interest in the corporation and must be set forth in sufficient detail reasonably to define their interest. The terms, including the preferences, rights and limitations, of shares with one or more special or preferential rights which may be authorized are further described in section 6.01(c).

If more than one class or series is authorized (or if only one class or series is originally authorized but at some future time one or more other classes or series of shares are added by amendment), the terms, including the preferences, rights and limitations of each class, classes or series of shares, including the class, classes or series that possess the fundamental characteristics of voting and residual equity financial interests, must be described before shares of those classes or series are issued. If both fundamental characteristics are placed exclusively in a single class of shares, that class may be described simply as "common shares" or by statements such as the "shares have the general distribution and voting rights," the "shares have all the rights of common shares," or the "shares have all rights not granted to the class A shares."

If the articles of incorporation create classes or series of shares that divide these fundamental rights among two or more classes or series of shares, it is necessary that the rights be clearly allocated among the classes and series. Specificity is required only to the extent necessary to differentiate the relative rights of the respective classes and series. For example, where one class or series has a liquidation preference over another, it is necessary to specify only the preferential liquidation right of that class or series; in the absence of a contrary provision in the articles of incorporation, the remaining class or series would be entitled to receive the net assets remaining after the liquidation preference has been satisfied. More than one class or series of shares may be designated as "common shares;" however, each must have a "distinguishing designation" under section 6.01(a), *e.g.*, "nonvoting common shares" or "class A common shares," and the rights of the classes and series must be described. For example, if a corporation authorizes two classes of shares with equal rights to share in all distributions and with identical voting rights except that one class is entitled exclusively to elect one director and the second class is entitled exclusively to elect a second director, the two classes may be designated, *e.g.*, as "Class A common" and "Class B common." What is required is language that makes the allocation of these rights clear.

Rather than describing the terms of each class or series of shares in the articles of incorporation, the corporation may delegate to the board of directors under section 6.02 the power to establish the terms of a class of shares or a series within a class if no shares of that class or series have previously been issued. Those terms, however, must be set forth in an amendment to the articles of incorporation that is effective before the shares are issued.

2.   Section 6.01(b)

Section 6.01(b) requires that every corporation authorize one or more classes or series of shares that in the aggregate have the two fundamental characteristics of full voting rights and the right to receive the net assets of the corporation upon its dissolution. The phrase "full voting rights" refers to the right to vote on all matters for which voting is required by either the Act or the articles of incorporation.

The two fundamental characteristics need not be placed in a single class or series of shares but may be divided as desired. It is nevertheless essential that the corporation always have authorized shares having in the aggregate these two characteristics, and section 6.03 requires that shares having in the aggregate these characteristics always be outstanding.

3.   Section 6.01(c)

Section 6.01(c) provides a non-exhaustive list of the principal features that are customarily incorporated into classes or series of shares.

A.   IN GENERAL

Section 6.01(c) authorizes creation of classes or series of shares with a range of preferences, rights and limitations as further described below. The Act permits the creation of shares convertible into, or redeemable in exchange for, cash, other property, or shares or debt securities of the corporation ranking senior to the shares, at the option of either the holder or the corporation. Such a conversion or redemption is subject to the restrictions on distributions under section 6.40.

B.   VOTING OF SHARES

Any class or series of shares may be granted multiple or fractional votes per share without limitation. See section 7.21. Shares of any class or series may also be made nonvoting "except to the extent otherwise provided by this Act." This "except" clause refers to the provisions in the Act that permit shares which are designated to be nonvoting to vote as separate voting groups on amendments to articles of incorporation and other organic changes in the corporation that directly affect that class or series (see sections 7.26 and 10.04). In addition, shares may be given voting rights that are limited or conditional (*e.g.*, voting rights triggered by the failure to pay specified dividends).

C. REDEMPTION AND CONVERSION OF SHARES

Section 6.01(c)(2) permits redemption for any class or series of shares and thereby permits the creation of redeemable or callable shares without limitation (subject only to the provisions that the class, classes or series of shares described in section 6.01(b) must always be authorized and that at least one or more shares which together have those rights must be outstanding under section 6.03).

The prices to be paid upon the redemption of shares under section 6.01(c)(2) and the amounts to be redeemed may be fixed in the articles of incorporation or "determined in accordance with a formula." The formula could be self contained or, pursuant to the provisions of section 6.01(d), could be determined by reference to extrinsic data or events. This permits the redemption price and the amounts to be redeemed to be established on the basis of matters external to the corporation, such as the purchase price of other shares, the level of market reference rates, the effective interest rate at which the corporation may obtain short or long-term financing, the consumer price index or a designated currency ratio.

All redemptions of shares are subject to the restrictions on distributions set forth in section 6.40. See section 6.03(b).

Section 6.01(c)(2) also permits shares of any class or series to be made convertible into shares of any other class or series or into cash, indebtedness, securities, or other property of the corporation or another person.

D. EXTRINSIC FACTS

Section 6.01(d) permits the creation of classes or series of shares with terms that are dependent upon facts objectively ascertainable outside the articles of incorporation. See section 1.20(k) and the related Official Comment for an explanation of the meaning of the phrase "facts objectively ascertainable" and the requirement for the filing of articles of amendment under the circumstances set forth in that section. Terms that depend upon reference to extrinsic facts may include dividend rates that vary according to some external index or event. Because such a "variable rate" class or series of shares would be intended to respond to current market conditions, it would most often be used with "blank check" provisions in the articles of incorporation with the terms of shares set by the board of directors immediately before issuance. See the Official Comment to section 6.02. Note that section 6.21 requires the board to determine the adequacy of consideration received or to be received by the corporation before issuing shares. If shares with terms to be determined by reference to extrinsic facts are to be authorized for issuance, the board should take care to establish appropriately defined parameters for such terms.

E. VARIATION AMONG HOLDERS

Section 6.01(e) permits the creation of classes or series of shares with terms that may vary among holders of the same class or series of shares. An example of such variation would be a provision that shares held by a bank or bank holding company in excess of a certain percentage would not have voting rights. In addition, section 6.24(b) expressly permits the issuance of rights, options or warrants for the purchase of shares or other securities of the corporation that contain terms and conditions which vary the rights of the holders of such rights, warrants or options based on a holder's ownership of, or offer to acquire, a specified number or percentage of the outstanding shares or other securities of the corporation.

4. Examples of Classes or Series of Shares Permitted by Section 6.01

Section 6.01 is enabling rather than restrictive given that corporations often find it necessary to create new classes or series of shares for a variety of reasons, for instance in connection with raising debt or equity capital. Classes or series of shares may also be used in connection with desired control relationships among the participants in a venture. Under section 7.21, only securities classified as "shares" in the articles of incorporation can have the power to vote.

Examples of such classes and series of shares include:

- Shares of one class or series may be authorized to elect a specified number of directors while shares of a second class or series may be authorized to elect the same or a different number of directors.

- Shares of one class or series may be entitled to vote as a separate voting group on certain transactions, but shares of two or more classes or series may be only entitled to vote together as a single voting group on the election of directors and other matters.

- Shares of one class or series may be nonvoting or may be given multiple or fractional votes per share.

- Shares of one class or series may be entitled to different dividend rights or rights on dissolution than shares of another class or series.

- Shares of one class or series may be created to include some characteristics of debt securities.

A corporation has power to issue debt securities under section 3.02. Although 6.01 authorizes the creation of interests that usually will be classed as "equity" rather than "debt," it is permissible to create classes or series of securities under section 6.01 that have some of the characteristics of debt securities. These securities are often referred to as "hybrid securities." Section 6.01 does not limit the development of hybrid securities, and equity securities may be created under the Act that embody any characteristics of debt. As noted above, however, the Act restricts the power to vote to securities classified as "shares" in the articles of incorporation.

§ 6.02. Terms of Class or Series Determined by Board of Directors

(a) If the articles of incorporation so provide, the board of directors is authorized, without shareholder approval, to:

(1) classify any unissued shares into one or more classes or into one or more series within a class;

(2) reclassify any unissued shares of any class into one or more classes or into one or more series within one or more classes; or

(3) reclassify any unissued shares of any series of any class into one or more classes or into one or more series within a class.

(b) If the board of directors acts pursuant to subsection (a), it shall determine the terms, including the preferences, rights, and limitations, to the same extent permitted under section 6.01, of:

(1) any class of shares before the issuance of any shares of that class, or

(2) any series within a class before the issuance of any shares of that series.

(c) Before issuing any shares of a class or series created under this section, the corporation shall deliver to the secretary of state for filing articles of amendment setting forth the terms determined under subsection (a).

Cross-References

Amendment of articles of incorporation, see ch. 10A.

Class or series of shares as voting group, see §§ 1.40, 7.25, 7.26 and 10.04.

Distributions, see § 6.40.

Effective time and date of filing, see § 1.23.

Filing requirements, see § 1.20.

Terms of shares, see § 6.01.

Voting by voting group, see §§ 7.25 and 7.26.

"Voting group" defined, see § 1.40.

Official Comment

Section 6.02 permits the board of directors, if authority to do so is contained in the articles of incorporation, to determine the terms of a class of shares or of a series of shares within a class to meet corporate needs, including current requirements of the securities markets or the flexibility needed for acquisitions, without the necessity of holding a shareholders' meeting to amend the articles of incorporation. If given that authority, the board of directors may create new series within a class and may also determine the terms of a class or series if there are no outstanding shares of that class or series.

A provision in the articles of incorporation authorizing shares to be issued in different classes or series with terms to be set by the board of directors is sometimes referred to as a "blank check" provision. The power to make the terms of shares so created dependent on facts objectively ascertainable outside the articles of incorporation and to vary their terms among holders of the same class or series extends to all the permitted provisions set forth in section 6.01(c).

Sections 6.02(a) and (b) make it clear that the board of directors has the same broad flexibility with regard to setting the terms of a class or series under this section as is permitted under section 6.01(c). Section 6.02(c) requires a filing to amend the articles of incorporation so there will be a public record of the class or series which the corporation intends to issue. The amendment does not require shareholder action. See section 10.05(h).

§ 6.03. Issued and Outstanding Shares

(a) A corporation may issue the number of shares of each class or series authorized by the articles of incorporation. Shares that are issued are outstanding shares until they are reacquired, redeemed, converted, or cancelled.

(b) The reacquisition, redemption, or conversion of outstanding shares is subject to the limitations of subsection (c) and to section 6.40.

(c) At all times that shares of the corporation are outstanding, one or more shares that together have full voting rights and one or more shares that together are entitled to receive the net assets of the corporation upon dissolution must be outstanding.

Cross-References

Cancellation of shares, see § 6.21.

Certificateless shares, see § 6.26.

Certificates for shares, see § 6.25.

Classes and series of shares, see §§ 6.01 and 6.02.

Consideration for shares, see § 6.21.

Reacquisition of shares, see § 6.31.

Redemption of shares, see §§ 6.01 and 6.31.

Share dividends, see § 6.23.

Voting by voting groups, see §§ 1.40, 7.25 and 7.26.

"Voting group" defined, see § 1.40.

Official Comment

The determination of the number of shares to be issued under section 6.03 is usually made by the board of directors but may be reserved by the articles of incorporation to the shareholders. The only requirements are that no class or series of shares be overissued and that one or more shares of a class, classes or series that together have full voting rights and one or more shares of a class, classes or series that together are entitled to the net assets of the corporation upon dissolution at all times must be outstanding.

The corporation may acquire outstanding shares pursuant to a voluntary transaction between a shareholder and the corporation. Also, shares may be made subject to transfer restrictions that may result in contractual obligations by the corporation to reacquire shares. See section 6.27. Further, the corporation may reacquire shares pursuant to a right of redemption (or an obligation to redeem) established in the articles of incorporation. See section 6.01(c)(2). All voluntary or contractual reacquisitions are subject to the limitations set forth in section 6.03(c) and to section 6.40.

The provisions of the Act are consistent with the specialized class of corporation known as the open-end investment company, which permits unlimited redemptions of shares at net asset value at the request of shareholders. Sections 6.01 and 6.03 permit the classes or series of shares with voting and dissolution rights to be made redeemable without limitation. The requirement of section 6.03(c) that at least one share be outstanding is also consistent with an unlimited right of redemption since that section only applies while there are shares outstanding.

§ 6.04. Fractional Shares

(a)   A corporation may issue fractions of a share or in lieu of doing so may:

(1)   pay in cash the value of fractions of a share;

(2)   issue scrip in registered or bearer form entitling the holder to receive a full share upon surrendering enough scrip to equal a full share; or

(3)   arrange for disposition of fractional shares by the holders of such shares.

(b)   Each certificate representing scrip must be conspicuously labeled "scrip" and must contain the information required by section 6.25(b).

(c)   The holder of a fractional share is entitled to exercise the rights of a shareholder, including the rights to vote, to receive dividends and to receive distributions upon dissolution. The holder of scrip is not entitled to any of these rights unless the scrip provides for them.

(d)   The board of directors may authorize the issuance of scrip subject to any condition, including that:

(1)   the scrip will become void if not exchanged for full shares before a specified date; and

(2)   the shares for which the scrip is exchangeable may be sold and the proceeds paid to the scripholders.

Cross-References

Issuance of shares, see § 6.21.

Official Comment

Fractional shares may arise from a share dividend that, as applied to a particular holder, does not produce an even multiple of shares. They may also result from other corporate actions, such as fractional stock splits, reverse splits, and reclassifications and mergers. Although corporations are authorized to issue fractional shares, which are vested proportionately with the same rights as full shares, the creation of fractional shares may create administrative difficulties, particularly for voting and dividend purposes.

Section 6.04 authorizes handling fractional shares in the following ways:

- The corporation may pay in cash the value of the fractional shares.

- The corporation may issue scrip instead of fractional shares. Unless otherwise specified in the scrip, scrip confers none of the substantive rights of shareholders, but only authorizes holders to combine scrip certificates in amounts aggregating a full share and then to exchange them for a full share. This aggregation must occur within the time and subject to the conditions set initially by the board of directors and stated in the scrip certificate. To protect shareholders against forfeiture of their interest, it is usually provided that the shares represented by scrip certificates not exchanged by the expiration date are to be sold and the proceeds held, either indefinitely or for a stated period, for the benefit of the scripholders and paid to them on surrender of their scrip certificates.

- The corporation may authorize the immediate sale of all fractional share interests, typically by an agent on behalf of the holders, thereby avoiding the expense and delay of other methods of dealing with fractional shares. Although this procedure denies shareholders the benefit of any subsequent rise in the market price of the shares, it protects them against any subsequent decline and ensures them of recognition based on market prices at the time of the transaction.

Under section 6.04, fractional shares may be certificated or uncertificated. There is no difference in treatment of certificated or uncertificated shares for this purpose. See sections 6.25 and 6.26.

SUBCHAPTER B
ISSUANCE OF SHARES

§ 6.20. Subscription for Shares Before Incorporation

(a) A subscription for shares entered into before incorporation is irrevocable for six months unless the subscription agreement provides a longer or shorter period or all the subscribers agree to revocation.

(b) The board of directors may determine the payment terms of subscriptions for shares that were entered into before incorporation, unless the subscription agreement specifies them. A call for payment by the board of directors must be uniform so far as practicable as to all shares of the same class or series, unless the subscription agreement specifies otherwise.

(c) Shares issued pursuant to subscriptions entered into before incorporation are fully paid and nonassessable when the corporation receives the consideration specified in the subscription agreement.

(d) If a subscriber defaults in payment of cash or property under a subscription agreement entered into before incorporation, the corporation may collect the amount owed as any other debt. Alternatively, unless the subscription agreement provides otherwise, the corporation may rescind the agreement and may sell the shares if the debt remains unpaid for more than 20 days after the corporation delivers a written demand for payment to the subscriber.

Cross-References

Consideration for shares, see § 6.21.

Notices and other communications, see § 1.41.

Official Comment

Because of the uncertainty of the legal enforceability of preincorporation agreements to purchase shares, section 6.20 provides a simple set of rules applicable to the enforcement of preincorporation subscriptions by the corporation after its formation. It does not address the extent to which preincorporation subscriptions may constitute a contract between or among subscribers, and other subscribers may enforce whatever contract rights they have without regard to section 6.20.

Section 6.20(a) provides as a default that preincorporation subscriptions are irrevocable for six months but the subscription agreement may provide otherwise or all the subscribers to shares may agree otherwise. If the corporation accepts the subscription during the period of irrevocability, the subscription becomes a contract binding on both the subscribers and the corporation. The terms of this contract are set forth in sections 6.20(b) and (d).

Section 6.20(c) provides that shares issued pursuant to preincorporation subscriptions are fully paid and nonassessable when the corporation receives the subscription price. The liability of the subscriber to pay the purchase price is addressed in section 6.22. Section 6.20 does not address the liability of transferees of shares for any unpaid subscription price, or the power of the corporation to cancel for nonpayment shares that have been issued before payment of the full subscription price. Issued shares represented by unpaid subscriptions are subject to cancellation for nonpayment to the same extent as shares issued for promissory notes or shares issued before the consideration therefor is paid. See the Official Comment to sections 6.21 and 6.22.

§ 6.21. Issuance of Shares

(a) The powers granted in this section to the board of directors may be reserved to the shareholders by the articles of incorporation.

(b) The board of directors may authorize shares to be issued for consideration consisting of any tangible or intangible property or benefit to the corporation, including cash, promissory notes, services performed, contracts for services to be performed, or other securities of the corporation.

(c) Before the corporation issues shares, the board of directors shall determine that the consideration received or to be received for shares to be issued is adequate. That determination by the board of directors is conclusive insofar as the adequacy of consideration for the issuance of shares relates to whether the shares are validly issued, fully paid, and nonassessable.

(d) When the corporation receives the consideration for which the board of directors authorized the issuance of shares, the shares issued therefor are fully paid and nonassessable.

(e) The corporation may place in escrow shares issued for a contract for future services or benefits or a promissory note, or make other arrangements to restrict the transfer of the shares, and may credit distributions in respect of the shares against their purchase price, until the services are performed, the benefits are received, or the note is paid. If the services are not performed, the benefits are not received, or the note is not paid, the shares escrowed or restricted and the distributions credited may be cancelled in whole or part.

(f)(1) An issuance of shares or other securities convertible into or rights exercisable for shares in a transaction or a series of integrated transactions requires approval of the shareholders, at a meeting at which a quorum consisting of a majority (or such greater number as the articles of incorporation may prescribe) of the votes entitled to be cast on the matter exists, if:

(i) the shares, other securities, or rights are to be issued for consideration other than cash or cash equivalents, and

(ii) the voting power of shares that are issued and issuable as a result of the transaction or series of integrated transactions will comprise more than 20% of the voting power of the shares of the corporation that were outstanding immediately before the transaction.

(2) In this subsection:

(i) For purposes of determining the voting power of shares issued and issuable as a result of a transaction or series of integrated transactions, the voting power of shares or other securities convertible into or rights exercisable for shares shall be the greater of (A) the voting power of the shares to be issued, or (B) the voting power of the shares that would be outstanding after giving effect to the conversion of convertible shares and other securities and the exercise of rights to be issued.

(ii) A series of transactions is integrated only if consummation of one transaction is made contingent on consummation of one or more of the other transactions.

Cross-References

Certificateless shares, see § 6.26.

Certificates for shares, see § 6.25.

Committees of board of directors, see § 8.25.

Liability of subscribers and shareholders, see § 6.22.

Par value shares, see § 2.02.

Preincorporation subscriptions for shares, see § 6.20.

Share dividends, see § 6.23.

Share options, see § 6.24.

Share transfer restrictions, see § 6.27.

"Voting power" defined, see § 1.40.

Official Comment

Because a statutory structure embodying "par value" and "stated capital" concepts does not protect creditors and senior security holders from payments to junior security holders, section 6.21 does not use these concepts.

1. Consideration

Because shares need not have a par value under section 6.21, there is no minimum price at which shares must be issued. Section 6.21(b) specifically validates "any tangible or intangible property or benefit to the corporation," as consideration for the present issue of shares, specifically including contracts for future services (including promoters' services) and promissory notes. The term "benefit" should be broadly construed also to include, for example, a reduction of a liability, a release of a claim, or intangible gain obtained by a corporation. Business judgment should determine what kind of property or benefit should be obtained for shares, and a determination by the directors meeting the requirements of section 8.30 to accept a specific kind of property or benefit for shares should be accepted and not circumscribed by artificial or arbitrary rules.

2. Board Determination of Adequacy

Protection of shareholders against abuse of the power granted to the board of directors to determine that shares should be issued for intangible property or benefit is provided by the requirements of section 8.30 applicable to a determination that the consideration received for shares is adequate.

In many instances, property or benefit received by the corporation will be of uncertain value; if the board of directors determines that the issuance of shares for the property or benefit is an appropriate transaction, that is sufficient under section 6.21. The board of directors does not have to make an explicit "adequacy" determination by formal resolution; that determination may be inferred from a determination to authorize the issuance of shares for a specified consideration. Likewise, section 6.21 does not require the board of directors to determine an exact value of the consideration to be entered on the books of the corporation.

The second sentence of section 6.21(c) describes the effect of the determination by the board of directors that consideration is adequate for the issuance of shares. That determination, without more, is conclusive to the extent that adequacy is relevant to the question whether the shares are validly issued, fully paid, and nonassessable. Whether shares are validly issued may depend on compliance with corporate procedural requirements, such as issuance within the amount authorized in the articles of incorporation or holding a directors' meeting upon proper notice and with a quorum present. The Act does not address the remedies that may be available for issuances that are subject to challenge. See subchapter E of chapter 1 regarding ratification of defective issuance of shares.

The Act also does not address whether validly issued shares may thereafter be cancelled on the grounds of fraud or bad faith if the shares are in the hands of the original shareholder or other persons who were aware of the circumstances under which they were issued when they acquired the shares. It also leaves to the Uniform Commercial Code other questions relating to the rights of persons other than the person acquiring the shares from the corporation. See the Official Comment to section 6.22.

Section 6.21(e) permits shares issued for contracts for future services or benefits or for promissory notes to be placed in escrow, or their transfer otherwise restricted, until the services are performed, the benefits are received or the notes are paid. In addition, any distributions on such shares may be credited against payment, or other agreed performance, of the consideration for the shares. Under section 6.21(e), if the corporation has restricted the transfer of the shares or placed them in escrow, it may cancel the shares and any credited distributions, in whole or in part, in the event of a failure of performance. This remedy is in the nature of a partial or complete rescission, and therefore rescission principles would be applicable.

Section 6.21 addresses only the corporation's cancellation remedy. It does not address whether other remedies may be available to the corporation, including a right to a deficiency against the nonperforming shareholder, or whether the shareholder may have any rights where the value of the shares subject to cancellation exceeds the value of the obligation remaining unperformed.

If the shares are issued without being restricted as provided in section 6.21(e), they are validly issued in so far as the adequacy of consideration is concerned. See section 6.22 and its Official Comment.

Section 6.24(c) provides express authority for delegation by the board of directors to officers for the issuance of shares as compensatory awards within limitations established by the board.

3.   *Shareholder Approval Requirement for Certain Issuances*

The shareholder approval requirement of section 6.21(f) is generally patterned after the listing standards of national securities exchanges. The calculation of the 20% compares the maximum number of votes entitled to be cast by the shares to be issued or that could be outstanding after giving effect to the conversion of convertible securities and the exercise of rights being issued, with the actual number of votes entitled to be cast by outstanding shares before the transaction.

In making the 20% determination under section 6.21(f), shares that are issuable in a transaction of any kind, including a merger, share exchange, or acquisition of assets, on a contingent basis are counted as shares or securities to be issued as a result of the transaction. On the other hand, shares that are issuable under antidilution clauses, such as those designed to take account of future share splits or share dividends, are not counted as shares or securities to be issued as a result of the transaction, because they are issuable only as a result of a later corporate action authorizing the split or dividend. If a transaction involves an earn-out provision, under which the total amount of shares or securities to be issued will depend on future earnings or other performance measures, the maximum amount of shares or securities that can be issued under the earn-out must be included in the determination.

If the number of shares to be issued or issuable is not fixed, but is subject to a formula, the application of the test in section 6.21(f)(2)(i) requires a calculation of the maximum amount that could be issued under the formula, whether stated as a range or otherwise, in the governing agreement. Even if ultimate issuance of the maximum amount is unlikely, a vote will be required if the maximum amount would result in an issuance of more than 20% of the voting power of shares outstanding immediately before the transaction.

Shares that have or would have only contingent voting rights when issued or issuable are not shares that carry voting power for purposes of the calculation under section 6.21(f).

The vote required to approve issuances that fall within section 6.21(f) is the basic voting rule under the Act, set forth in section 7.25, that more shares must be voted in favor of the issuance than are voted against. This is the same voting rule that applies under chapter 9 for domestications and conversions, chapter 10 for amendments of the articles of incorporation, chapter 11 for mergers and share exchanges, chapter 12 for dispositions of assets that require shareholder approval, and chapter 14 for voluntary dissolutions. The quorum rule under section 6.21(f) is also the same as the quorum rule under chapters 9, 10, 11, 12, and 14.

Section 6.21(f) does not apply to an issuance for cash or cash equivalents, regardless of whether in connection with a public offering. "Cash equivalents" are generally short-term investments that are both readily convertible to known amounts of cash and present insignificant risk of changes in interest rates. Shares that are issued partly for cash or cash equivalents and partly for other consideration are "issued for consideration other than cash or cash equivalents" within the meaning of section 6.21(f).

The term "rights" in section 6.21(f) includes warrants, options, and rights of exchange, whether at the option of the holder, the corporation, or another person. The term "voting power" is defined in section 1.40 as the current power to vote in the election of directors. See also the Official Comment to that section. Because transactions are integrated within the meaning of section 6.21(f) only where consummation of one transaction is made contingent on consummation of one or more of the other transactions, transactions are not integrated for purposes of section 6.21(f) merely because they are proximate in time or because the kind of consideration for which the corporation issues shares is similar in each transaction.

Section 6.21(f) only applies to issuances for consideration. Accordingly, section 6.21(f) does not require shareholder approval for share dividends or for shareholder rights plans. See section 6.23 and its Official Comment.

Illustrations of the application of section 6.21(f) follow:

1. C corporation, which has 2,000,000 shares of Class A voting common stock outstanding (carrying one vote per share), proposes to issue 600,000 shares of authorized but unissued Class B nonvoting common stock in exchange for a business owned by D Corporation. The proposed issuance does not require shareholder approval under section 6.21(f) because the Class B shares do not carry voting power.

2. The facts being otherwise as stated in Illustration 1, C proposes to issue 600,000 additional shares of its Class A voting common stock. The proposed issuance requires shareholder approval under section 6.21(f) because the voting power carried by the shares to be issued will comprise more than 20% of the voting power of C's shares outstanding immediately before the issuance.

3. The facts being otherwise as stated in Illustration 1, C proposes to issue 400,000 shares of authorized but unissued voting preferred stock, each share of which carries one vote and is convertible into 1.5 shares of Class A voting common stock. The proposed issuance requires shareholder approval under section 6.21(f). Although the voting power of the preferred shares to be issued will not comprise more than 20% of the voting power of C's shares outstanding immediately before the issuance, the voting power of the shares issuable upon conversion of the preferred shares will carry more than 20% of such voting power.

4. The facts being otherwise as stated in Illustration 1, C proposes to issue 200,000 shares of its Class A voting common stock, and 100,000 shares of authorized but unissued nonvoting preferred stock, each share of which is convertible into 2.5 shares of C's Class A voting common stock. The proposed issuance requires shareholder approval under section 6.21(f) because the voting power of the Class A shares to be issued, after giving effect to the common stock that is issuable upon conversion of the preferred shares, would comprise more than 20% of the voting power of C's outstanding shares immediately before the issuance.

5. The facts being otherwise as stated in Illustration 4, each share of the preferred stock is convertible into 1.2 shares of the Class A voting common stock. The proposed issuance does not require shareholder approval under section 6.21(f) because neither the voting power of the shares to be issued at the outset (200,000) nor the voting power of the shares that would be outstanding after giving effect to the common stock issuable upon conversion of the preferred shares (a total of 320,000) constitutes more than 20% of the voting power of C's outstanding shares immediately before the issuance.

6. The facts being otherwise as stated in Illustration 1, C proposes to acquire businesses from Corporations G, H, and I for 200,000, 300,000, and 400,000 shares of Class A voting common stock, respectively, within a short period of time. None of the transactions is conditioned on the negotiation or completion of the other transactions. The proposed issuance of voting shares does not require shareholder approval, because the three transactions are not integrated within the meaning of section 6.21(f), and none of the transactions individually involves the issuance of more than 20% of the voting power of C's outstanding shares immediately before each issuance.

§ 6.22. Liability of Shareholders

(a) A purchaser from a corporation of the corporation's own shares is not liable to the corporation or its creditors with respect to the shares except to pay the consideration for which the shares were authorized to be issued or specified in the subscription agreement.

(b) A shareholder of a corporation is not personally liable for any liabilities of the corporation (including liabilities arising from acts of the corporation) except (i) to the extent provided in a provision of the articles of incorporation permitted by section 2.02(b)(2)(v), and (ii) that a shareholder may become personally liable by reason of the shareholder's own acts or conduct.

Cross-References

Articles of incorporation, see § 2.02.

Consideration for shares, see § 6.21.

Subscriptions for shares, see § 6.20.

Official Comment

The sole obligation of a purchaser of shares from the corporation is to pay the consideration determined by the board of directors (or the consideration specified in the subscription agreement, in the case of preincorporation subscriptions). Upon the transfer to the corporation of the consideration so determined or specified, the shareholder has no further responsibility to the corporation or its creditors "with respect to the shares," although the shareholder may have continuing obligations under a contract or promissory note entered into in connection with the acquisition of shares.

Section 6.22(a) deals only with the responsibility for payment by the purchaser of shares from the corporation. The Act leaves to the Uniform Commercial Code questions with respect to the rights of subsequent purchasers of shares if the consideration is not paid when due. See sections 8–202 and 8–302 of the Uniform Commercial Code.

Section 6.22(b) sets forth the basic rule of nonliability of shareholders for corporate acts or debts that underlies corporation law. Unless such liability is provided for in the articles of incorporation (see section 2.02(b)(2)(v)), shareholders are not liable for corporate obligations, although the last clause of section 6.22(b) recognizes that such liability may be assumed voluntarily or by other conduct.

§ 6.23. Share Dividends

(a) Unless the articles of incorporation provide otherwise, shares may be issued pro rata and without consideration to the corporation's shareholders or to the shareholders of one or more classes or series of shares. An issuance of shares under this subsection is a share dividend.

(b) Shares of one class or series may not be issued as a share dividend in respect of shares of another class or series unless (i) the articles of incorporation so authorize, (ii) a majority of the votes entitled to be cast by the class or series to be issued approve the issue, or (iii) there are no outstanding shares of the class or series to be issued.

(c) The board of directors may fix the record date for determining shareholders entitled to a share dividend, which date may not be retroactive. If the board of directors does not fix the record date for determining shareholders entitled to a share dividend, the record date is the date the board of directors authorizes the share dividend.

Cross-References

Classes and series of shares, see §§ 6.01 and 6.02.

Consideration for shares, see § 6.21.

"Distribution" defined, see § 1.40.

Distributions, see § 6.40.

Fractional shares, see § 6.04.

Record date for distributions, see § 6.40.

Official Comment

A share dividend is solely a paper transaction: no assets are received by the corporation for the shares and any "dividend" paid in shares does not involve the distribution of property by the corporation to its shareholders. Section 6.23 therefore recognizes that such a transaction involves the issuance of shares "without consideration," and section 1.40 excludes it from the definition of a "distribution."

§ 6.24. Share Rights, Options, Warrants and Awards

(a) A corporation may issue rights, options, or warrants for the purchase of shares or other securities of the corporation. The board of directors shall determine (i) the terms and conditions upon which the rights, options, or warrants are issued and (ii) the terms, including the consideration for which the shares or other securities are to be issued. The authorization by the board of directors for the corporation to issue such rights, options, or warrants constitutes authorization of the issuance of the shares or other securities for which the rights, options or warrants are exercisable.

(b)   The terms and conditions of such rights, options or warrants may include restrictions or conditions that:

(1)   preclude or limit the exercise, transfer or receipt of such rights, options or warrants by any person or persons owning or offering to acquire a specified number or percentage of the outstanding shares or other securities of the corporation or by any transferee or transferees of any such person or persons, or

(2)   invalidate or void such rights, options, or warrants held by any such person or persons or any such transferee or transferees.

(c)   The board of directors may authorize one or more officers to (i) designate the recipients of rights, options, warrants, or other equity compensation awards that involve the issuance of shares and (ii) determine, within an amount and subject to any other limitations established by the board of directors and, if applicable, the shareholders, the number of such rights, options, warrants, or other equity compensation awards and the terms of such rights, options, warrants or awards to be received by the recipients, provided that an officer may not use such authority to designate himself or herself or any other persons as the board of directors may specify as a recipient of such rights, options, warrants, or other equity compensation awards.

Cross-References

Committees of board of directors, see § 8.25.

Compensation, see § 3.02.

Consideration for shares, see § 6.21.

Director's conflicting interest transactions, see ch. 8F.

Distributions, see § 6.40.

Official Comment

Section 6.24 specifically authorizes the creation of rights, options and warrants and confirms the broad discretion of the board of directors in determining the consideration to be received by the corporation for their issuance, including the creation of compensation plans for directors, officers, agents, and employees.

Section 6.24(a) does not require shareholder approval of rights, options, warrants or compensation plans. Of course, prior shareholder approval may be sought as a discretionary matter, or required to comply with the rules of national securities exchanges or to acquire federal income tax benefits that may be conditioned upon shareholder approval of such plans.

Section 6.24(b) confirms that the issuance of rights, options or warrants as part of a shareholder rights plan is permitted. The permissible scope of shareholder rights plans may, however, be limited by the courts.

Section 6.24(c) provides express authority for the delegation to officers of the designation of recipients of compensatory awards involving the issuance of shares, either directly or upon exercise of rights to acquire shares, and the determination of the amount and other terms of the awards, subject to any applicable limitations established by the board of directors or the shareholders. A board of directors (or a board committee with authority delegated to it under section 8.25, typically a compensation committee) may decide whether to exercise the authority under section 6.24(c) and, to the extent it does so, the board must specify the total amount that may be awarded and may impose any other limits it desires as part of the board's oversight of the award process. A board or committee delegating authority under section 6.24(c) would typically include appropriate limits. These limits might include, for example, the amount or range of shares to be awarded to different classes of employees, the timing and pricing of awards, and the vesting terms or other variable provisions of awards.

§ 6.25. Form and Content of Certificates

(a)   Shares may, but need not, be represented by certificates. Unless this Act or another statute expressly provides otherwise, the rights and obligations of shareholders are identical regardless of whether their shares are represented by certificates.

(b)   At a minimum each share certificate must state on its face:

(1)   the name of the corporation and that it is organized under the law of this state;

(2)   the name of the person to whom issued; and

(3)   the number and class of shares and the designation of the series, if any, the certificate represents.

(c)   If the corporation is authorized to issue different classes of shares or series of shares within a class, the front or back of each certificate must summarize (i) the preferences, rights, and limitations applicable to each class and series, (ii) any variations in preferences, rights, and limitations among the holders of the same class or series, and (iii) the authority of the board of directors to determine the terms of future classes or series. Alternatively, each certificate may state conspicuously on its front or back that the corporation will furnish the shareholder this information on request in writing and without charge.

(d)   Each share certificate must be signed by two officers designated in the bylaws.

(e)   If the person who signed a share certificate no longer holds office when the certificate is issued, the certificate is nevertheless valid.

Cross-References

Certificateless shares, see § 6.26.

Classes and series of shares, see §§ 6.01 and 6.02.

"Conspicuous" defined, see § 1.40.

Descriptions of classes, see § 6.01.

Officers, see § 8.40.

Share transfer restrictions, see § 6.27.

Official Comment

Section 6.25 sets forth the minimum requirements for share certificates. Shares without certificates are permitted under section 6.25(a) upon compliance with section 6.26. There are no differences in the rights and obligations of shareholders by reason of shares being represented by certificates or not being represented by certificates, other than mechanical differences, such as the means by which instructions for transfer are communicated to the issuer, necessitated by the use or nonuse of certificates.

All signatures on a share certificate may be facsimiles. See the definition of "sign" in section 1.40. This recognizes that a purchaser of publicly traded shares will rarely be in a position to determine whether a manual signature on a stock certificate is in fact the authorized signature of an officer or the transfer agent or registrar.

§ 6.26. Shares Without Certificates

(a)   Unless the articles of incorporation or bylaws provide otherwise, the board of directors of a corporation may authorize the issuance of some or all of the shares of any or all of its classes or series without certificates. The authorization does not affect shares already represented by certificates until they are surrendered to the corporation.

(b)   Within a reasonable time after the issuance or transfer of shares without certificates, the corporation shall deliver to the shareholder a written statement of the information required on certificates by sections 6.25(b) and (c), and, if applicable, section 6.27.

Cross-References

Certificates for shares, see § 6.25.

Information on share certificates, see § 6.25.

Share transfer restrictions, see § 6.27.

Official Comment

Section 6.26(a) authorizes the creation of shares without certificates either by original issue or in substitution for shares previously represented by certificates. This section gives the board of directors the widest discretion so that a particular class and series of shares might be entirely represented by certificates, entirely uncertificated, or represented partly by each. A corporation may not treat as uncertificated, and accordingly transferable on its books without due presentation of a certificate, any shares for which a certificate is outstanding.

The statement required by section 6.26(b) ensures that holders of shares without certificates will receive from the corporation the same information that the holders of certificates receive when certificates are issued. There is no requirement that this information be delivered to purchasers of shares without certificates before purchase.

§ 6.27. Restriction on Transfer of Shares

(a)   The articles of incorporation, the bylaws, an agreement among shareholders, or an agreement between shareholders and the corporation may impose restrictions on the transfer or registration of transfer of shares of the corporation. A restriction does not affect shares issued before the restriction was adopted unless the holders of the shares are parties to the restriction agreement or voted in favor of the restriction.

(b)   A restriction on the transfer or registration of transfer of shares is valid and enforceable against the holder or a transferee of the holder if the restriction is authorized by this section and its existence is noted conspicuously on the front or back of the certificate or is contained in the information statement required by section 6.26(b). Unless so noted or contained, a restriction is not enforceable against a person without knowledge of the restriction.

(c)   A restriction on the transfer or registration of transfer of shares is authorized:

(1)   to maintain the corporation's status when it is dependent on the number or identity of its shareholders;

(2)   to preserve exemptions under federal or state securities law; or

(3)   for any other reasonable purpose.

(d)   A restriction on the transfer or registration of transfer of shares may:

(1)   obligate the shareholder first to offer the corporation or other persons (separately, consecutively, or simultaneously) an opportunity to acquire the restricted shares;

(2)   obligate the corporation or other persons (separately, consecutively, or simultaneously) to acquire the restricted shares;

(3)   require the corporation, the holders of any class or series of its shares, or other persons to approve the transfer of the restricted shares, if the requirement is not manifestly unreasonable; or

(4)   prohibit the transfer of the restricted shares to designated persons or classes of persons, if the prohibition is not manifestly unreasonable.

(e)   For purposes of this section, "shares" includes a security convertible into or carrying a right to subscribe for or acquire shares.

Cross-References

Certificateless shares, see § 6.26.

Certificates for shares, see § 6.25.

Classes and series of shares, see §§ 6.01 and 6.02.

"Conspicuous" defined, see § 1.40.

Information statement, see § 6.26.

Official Comment

Share transfer restrictions are used by corporations for a variety of purposes. Section 6.27(c) enumerates certain purposes for which share transfer restrictions may be imposed, but does not limit the purposes given that section 6.27(c)(3) permits restrictions "for any other reasonable purpose." Examples of the "status" referred to in section 6.27(c)(1) include the subchapter S election under the Internal Revenue Code, and entitlement to a program or eligibility for a privilege administered by governmental agencies or national securities exchanges.

Examples of the uses of share transfer restrictions include:

- a corporation with few shareholders may impose share transfer restrictions to ensure that shareholders do not transfer their shares to a person not acceptable to the corporation or other shareholders;

- a corporation with few shareholders may impose share transfer restrictions to establish the value of the shares of deceased shareholders;

- a professional corporation may impose share transfer restrictions to ensure that its treatment of departing, retiring or deceased shareholders is consistent with rules applicable to the profession in question;

- a corporation may impose share transfer restrictions to ensure that its election of subchapter S treatment under the Internal Revenue Code will not be unexpectedly terminated; and

- a corporation issuing securities pursuant to an exemption from federal or state securities registration may impose share transfer restrictions to ensure that subsequent transfers of shares will not result in the loss of the exemption being relied upon.

Section 6.27(d) describes the types of restrictions that may be imposed. The types of restrictions referred to in sections 6.27(d)(1) (rights of first offer) and (d)(2) (buy-sell agreements) are imposed as a matter of contractual negotiation and do not prohibit the outright transfer of shares. Rather, they designate to whom shares or other securities must be offered at a price established in the agreement or by a formula or method agreed to in advance. By contrast, the restrictions described in clauses sections 6.27(d)(3) and (d)(4) may permanently limit the market for shares by disqualifying all or some potential purchasers. The restrictions imposed by these two provisions must not be "manifestly unreasonable."

SUBCHAPTER C
SUBSEQUENT ACQUISITION OF SHARES BY
SHAREHOLDERS AND CORPORATION

§ 6.30. Shareholders' Preemptive Rights

(a)   The shareholders of a corporation do not have a preemptive right to acquire the corporation's unissued shares except to the extent the articles of incorporation so provide.

(b)   A statement included in the articles of incorporation that "the corporation elects to have preemptive rights" (or words of similar effect) means that the following principles apply except to the extent the articles of incorporation expressly provide otherwise:

(1)   The shareholders of the corporation have a preemptive right, granted on uniform terms and conditions prescribed by the board of directors to provide a fair and reasonable opportunity to exercise the right, to acquire proportional amounts of the corporation's unissued shares upon the decision of the board of directors to issue them.

(2)   A preemptive right may be waived by a shareholder. A waiver evidenced by a writing is irrevocable even though it is not supported by consideration.

(3)   There is no preemptive right with respect to:

(i)   shares issued as compensation to directors, officers, employees or agents of the corporation, its subsidiaries or affiliates;

(ii)   shares issued to satisfy conversion or option rights created to provide compensation to directors, officers, employees or agents of the corporation, its subsidiaries or affiliates;

(iii)   shares authorized in the articles of incorporation that are issued within six months from the effective date of incorporation; or

(iv)   shares sold otherwise than for cash.

(4)   Holders of shares of any class or series without voting power but with preferential rights to distributions have no preemptive rights with respect to shares of any class or series.

(5)   Holders of shares of any class or series with voting power but without preferential rights to distributions have no preemptive rights with respect to shares of any class or series with preferential rights to distributions unless the shares with preferential rights are convertible into or carry a right to subscribe for or acquire the shares without preferential rights.

(6)   Shares subject to preemptive rights that are not acquired by shareholders may be issued to any person for a period of one year after being offered to shareholders at a consideration set by the board of directors that is not lower than the consideration set for the exercise of preemptive rights. An offer at a lower consideration or after the expiration of one year is subject to the shareholders' preemptive rights.

(c)   For purposes of this section, "shares" includes a security convertible into or carrying a right to subscribe for or acquire shares.

Cross-References

Articles of incorporation, see § 2.02.

Consideration for shares, see § 6.21.

Classes and series of shares, see §§ 6.01 and 6.02.

Share options, see § 6.24.

"Voting power" defined, see § 1.40.

Official Comment

Section 6.30(a) adopts an "opt in" provision for preemptive rights: unless an affirmative reference to these rights appears in the articles of incorporation, no preemptive rights exist.

Section 6.30(b) provides a standard model for preemptive rights if the corporation desires to exercise the "opt in" alternative of section 6.30(a). A corporation may qualify or limit any of the rules set forth in this section by express provisions in the articles of incorporation. The purposes of this standard model for preemptive rights are (i) to simplify drafting articles of incorporation and (ii) to provide a simple checklist of business considerations for the benefit of attorneys who are considering the inclusion of preemptive rights in articles of incorporation.

Section 6.30(b) establishes rules for most of the problems involving preemptive rights. Subsection (b)(1) defines the general scope of the preemptive right giving appropriate recognition to the discretion of the board of directors in establishing the terms and conditions for exercise of that right. Subsection (b)(2) creates rules with respect to the waiver of these rights. Subsection (b)(3) lists the principal exceptions to preemptive rights, including a six-month period during which initial capital can be raised by a newly-formed corporation without regard to the preemptive rights of persons who have previously acquired shares. Subsections (b)(4) and (b)(5) provide rules for problems created when preemptive rights are recognized in corporations with more than a single class or series of shares. These problems are discussed further below. Subsection (b)(6) defines the status of preemptive rights after a shareholder has elected not to exercise a proffered preemptive right.

Preemptive rights can protect the voting power and equity participation of shareholders. This combination of functions creates no problem in a corporation that has authorized only a single class of shares but may occasionally create problems in corporations with more complex capital structures. In many capital structures, the issuance of additional shares of one class or series typically does not adversely affect other classes or series. For example, the issuance of additional shares with voting power but without preferential rights normally does not affect either the limited voting power or equity participation of holders of shares with preferential rights; holders of shares with preferential equity participation rights but without voting power should therefore have no preemptive rights with respect to shares with voting power but without preferential rights. See sections 6.30(b)(4) and (b)(5). Classes or series of shares that may give rise to possible conflict between the protection of voting interests and equity participation when the board of directors desires to issue additional shares include classes or series of nonvoting shares without preferential rights and classes or series of shares with both voting power and preferential rights to distributions. These conflicts can be dealt with by specific provisions in the articles of incorporation.

§ 6.31. Corporation's Acquisition of Its Own Shares

(a)   A corporation may acquire its own shares, and shares so acquired constitute authorized but unissued shares.

(b)   If the articles of incorporation prohibit the reissue of the acquired shares, the number of authorized shares is reduced by the number of shares acquired.

Cross-References

Acquisition of own shares by corporation as "distribution," see § 1.40.

Amendment of articles of incorporation by board, see § 10.05.

Annual report, see § 16.21.

Distributions, see § 6.40.

Issued and outstanding shares, see § 6.03.

Liability for unlawful distributions, see § 8.32.

Voting entitlement of shares, see § 7.21.

Official Comment

Shares that are acquired by the corporation become authorized but unissued shares under section 6.31 unless the articles of incorporation prohibit reissue, in which event the shares are cancelled and the number of authorized shares is automatically reduced.

If the number of authorized shares of a class is reduced as a result of the operation of section 6.31(b), the board of directors should amend the articles of incorporation under section 10.05(f) to reflect that reduction. If there are no remaining authorized shares in a class as a result of the operation of section 6.31, the board should amend the articles of incorporation under section 10.05(g) to delete the class from the classes of shares authorized by the articles of incorporation.

SUBCHAPTER D
DISTRIBUTIONS

§ 6.40. Distributions to Shareholders

(a)　A board of directors may authorize and the corporation may make distributions to its shareholders subject to restriction by the articles of incorporation and the limitation in subsection (c).

(b)　The board of directors may fix the record date for determining shareholders entitled to a distribution, which date may not be retroactive. If the board of directors does not fix a record date for determining shareholders entitled to a distribution (other than one involving a purchase, redemption, or other acquisition of the corporation's shares), the record date is the date the board of directors authorizes the distribution.

(c)　No distribution may be made if, after giving it effect:

(1)　the corporation would not be able to pay its debts as they become due in the usual course of business; or

(2)　the corporation's total assets would be less than the sum of its total liabilities plus (unless the articles of incorporation permit otherwise) the amount that would be needed, if the corporation were to be dissolved at the time of the distribution, to satisfy the preferential rights upon dissolution of shareholders whose preferential rights are superior to those receiving the distribution.

(d)　The board of directors may base a determination that a distribution is not prohibited under subsection (c) either on financial statements prepared on the basis of accounting practices and principles that are reasonable in the circumstances or on a fair valuation or other method that is reasonable in the circumstances.

(e)　Except as provided in subsection (g), the effect of a distribution under subsection (c) is measured:

(1)　in the case of distribution by purchase, redemption, or other acquisition of the corporation's shares, as of the earlier of (i) the date cash or other property is transferred or debt to a shareholder is incurred by the corporation or (ii) the date the shareholder ceases to be a shareholder with respect to the acquired shares;

(2)　in the case of any other distribution of indebtedness, as of the date the indebtedness is distributed; and

(3)　in all other cases, as of (i) the date the distribution is authorized if the payment occurs within 120 days after the date of authorization or (ii) the date the payment is made if it occurs more than 120 days after the date of authorization.

(f)　A corporation's indebtedness to a shareholder incurred by reason of a distribution made in accordance with this section is at parity with the corporation's indebtedness to its general, unsecured creditors except to the extent subordinated by agreement.

(g)　Indebtedness of a corporation, including indebtedness issued as a distribution, is not considered a liability for purposes of determinations under subsection (c) if its terms provide that payment of principal and interest are made only if and to the extent that payment of a distribution to shareholders could then be made under this section. If such indebtedness is issued as a distribution, each payment of principal or interest is treated as a distribution, the effect of which is measured on the date the payment is actually made.

(h)　This section shall not apply to distributions in liquidation under chapter 14.

Cross-References

Director standards of conduct, see § 8.30.

"Distribution" defined, see § 1.40.

Distribution in liquidation, see § 14.05.

Liability for unlawful distributions, see § 8.32.

"Record date" defined, see § 1.40.

Redemption, see §§ 6.01 and 6.31.

Share dividends, see § 6.23.

Official Comment

1.   *The Scope of Section 6.40*

Section 6.40 imposes a single, uniform test on all distributions other than distributions in liquidation under chapter 14. Section 1.40 defines "distribution" broadly to include transfers of cash and other property (excluding a corporation's own shares) to a shareholder in respect of the corporation's shares. Examples of such transfers are cash or property dividends, payments by a corporation to purchase its own shares, and distributions of promissory notes or indebtedness. The financial provisions of the Act do not use the concept of surplus but do have restrictions on distributions built around both equity insolvency and balance sheet tests.

2.   *Equity Insolvency Test*

In most cases involving a corporation operating as a going concern in the normal course, it will be apparent from information generally available that no particular inquiry concerning the equity insolvency test in section 6.40(c)(1) is needed. Although neither a balance sheet nor an income statement can be conclusive as to this test, the existence of significant shareholders' equity and normal operating conditions are of themselves a strong indication that no issue should arise under that test. In the case of a corporation having regularly audited financial statements, the absence of any qualification in the most recent auditor's opinion as to the corporation's status as a "going concern," coupled with a lack of subsequent adverse events, would normally be decisive.

It is only when circumstances indicate that the corporation is encountering difficulties or is in an uncertain position concerning its liquidity and operations that the board of directors or, more commonly, the officers or others upon whom they may place reliance under section 8.30(d), may need to address the issue. Because of the overall judgment required in evaluating the equity insolvency test, no "bright line" test is provided. However, in determining whether the equity insolvency test has been met, certain judgments or assumptions as to the future course of the corporation's business are customarily justified, absent clear evidence to the contrary. These include the likelihood that (i) based on existing and contemplated demand for the corporation's products or services, it will be able to generate funds over a period of time sufficient to satisfy its existing and reasonably anticipated obligations as they mature, and (ii) indebtedness which matures in the near-term will be refinanced where, on the basis of the corporation's financial condition and future prospects and the general availability of credit to businesses similarly situated, it is reasonable to assume that such refinancing may be accomplished. To the extent that the corporation may be subject to asserted or unasserted contingent liabilities, reasonable judgments as to the likelihood, amount, and time of any recovery against the corporation, after giving consideration to the extent to which the corporation is insured or otherwise protected against loss, may be utilized. There may be occasions when it would be useful to consider a cash flow analysis, based on a business forecast and budget, covering a sufficient period of time to permit a conclusion that known obligations of the corporation can reasonably be expected to be satisfied over the period of time that they will mature.

In exercising their judgment, the directors are entitled to rely, as provided in section 8.30(e), on information, opinions, reports, and statements prepared by others. Ordinarily, they should not be expected to become involved in the details of the various analyses or market or economic projections that may be relevant.

3. Balance Sheet Test

The determination of a corporation's assets and liabilities for purposes of the balance sheet test of section 6.40(c)(2) and the choice of the permissible basis on which to do so are left to the judgment of its board of directors. In making a judgment under section 6.40(d), the board may rely as provided in section 8.30(e) upon information, opinions, reports, and statements, including financial statements and other financial data, prepared or presented by public accountants or others.

Section 6.40 does not utilize particular accounting terminology of a technical nature or specify particular accounting concepts. In making determinations under this section, the board of directors may make judgments about accounting matters.

In a corporation with subsidiaries, the board of directors may rely on unconsolidated statements prepared on the basis of the equity method of accounting as to the corporation's investee corporations, including corporate joint ventures and subsidiaries, although other evidence would be relevant in the total determination. The board of directors is entitled to rely as provided by section 8.30(e) upon reasonably current financial statements in determining whether the balance sheet test of section 6.40(c)(2) has been met, unless the board has knowledge that makes such reliance unwarranted. Section 6.40 does not mandate the use of generally accepted accounting principles; it only requires the use of accounting practices and principles that are reasonable in the circumstances. Although corporations subject to registration under the Securities Exchange Act of 1934 must, and many other corporations in fact do, use financial statements prepared on the basis of generally accepted accounting principles, a great number of smaller or closely held corporations do not. Some of these corporations maintain records solely on a tax accounting basis and their financial statements are of necessity prepared on that basis. Others prepare financial statements that substantially reflect generally accepted accounting principles but may depart from them in some respects (e.g., footnote disclosure). A statutory standard of reasonableness, rather than stipulating generally accepted accounting principles as the normative standard, is appropriate to achieve a reasonable degree of flexibility and to accommodate the needs of the many different types of business corporations which might be subject to these provisions, including in particular closely held corporations.

Section 6.40(d) specifically permits determinations to be made under section 6.40(c)(2) on the basis of a fair valuation or other method that is reasonable in the circumstances. The statute authorizes departures from historical cost accounting and permits the use of appraisal and current value methods to determine the amount available for distribution. No particular method of valuation is prescribed in the statute, as different methods may have validity depending upon the circumstances, including the type of enterprise and the purpose for which the determination is made. In most cases, a fair valuation method or a going concern basis would be appropriate if it is believed that the enterprise will continue as a going concern.

Ordinarily a corporation should not selectively revalue assets. It should consider the value of all of its material assets, regardless of whether they are reflected in the financial statements (e.g., a valuable executory contract). Likewise, all of a corporation's material obligations should be considered and revalued to the extent appropriate and possible. In any event, section 6.40(d) calls for the application under section 6.40(c)(2) of a method of determining the aggregate amount of assets and liabilities that is reasonable in the circumstances.

The phrase "other method that is reasonable in the circumstances means that under section 6.40(c)(2) a wide variety of methods may be considered reasonable in a particular case even if any such method might not be a "fair valuation" or "current value" method.

4. Relationship to the Federal Bankruptcy Code and Other Fraudulent Conveyance Statutes

The Act establishes the validity of distributions from the corporate law standpoint under section 6.40 and determines the potential liability of directors for improper distributions under sections 8.30 and 8.32. The federal bankruptcy laws and state fraudulent conveyance statutes, on the other hand, are designed to enable the trustee or other representative to recapture for the benefit of creditors funds distributed to others in some circumstances. Accordingly, the tests of section 6.40 are different from the tests for insolvency under those statutes.

5.   Preferential Dissolution Rights and the Balance Sheet Test

Section 6.40(c)(2) treats preferential dissolution rights of shares for distribution purposes as if they were liabilities for the sole purpose of determining the amount available for distributions. In making the calculation of the amount that must be added to the liabilities of the corporation to reflect the preferential dissolution rights, the assumption should be made that the preferential dissolution rights are to be established pursuant to the articles of incorporation as of the date of the distribution or proposed distribution. The amount so determined must include arrearages in preferential dividends if the articles of incorporation require that they be paid upon the dissolution of the corporation. In the case of shares having both preferential rights upon dissolution and other nonpreferential rights, only the preferential rights should be taken into account. The treatment of preferential dissolution rights of classes or series of shares set forth in section 6.40(c)(2) is applicable only to the balance sheet test and is not applicable to the equity insolvency test of section 6.40(c)(1). The treatment of preferential rights mandated by section 6.40(c)(2) may always be eliminated by an appropriate provision in the articles of incorporation.

6.   Application to Acquisition of Shares

In an acquisition of its shares, a corporation may transfer property or incur debt to the former holder of the shares. Share repurchase agreements involving payment for shares over a period of time are of special importance in closely held corporations. Section 6.40(e) provides a clear rule for this situation: the legality of the distribution must be measured at the time of the issuance or incurrence of the debt, not at a later date when the debt is actually paid, except as provided in section 6.40(g).

Section 6.40(g) provides that indebtedness need not be taken into account as a liability in determining whether the tests of section 6.40(c) have been met if the terms of the indebtedness provide that payments of principal or interest can be made only if and to the extent that payment of a distribution could then be made under section 6.40. This has the effect of making the holder of the indebtedness junior to all other creditors but senior to the holders of shares, not only during the time the corporation is operating but also upon dissolution and liquidation. It should be noted that the creation of such indebtedness, and the related limitations on payments of principal and interest, may create tax problems or raise other legal questions.

Although section 6.40(g) is applicable to all indebtedness meeting its tests, regardless of the circumstances of its issuance, it is anticipated that it will apply most frequently to permit the reacquisition of shares of the corporation at a time when the deferred purchase price exceeds the net worth of the corporation. This type of reacquisition may be necessary in the case of businesses in early stages of development or service businesses whose value derives principally from existing or prospective net income or cash flow rather than from net asset value. In such situations, net worth will usually be anticipated to grow over time from operations so that when payments in respect of the indebtedness are to be made the two insolvency tests will be satisfied. In the meantime, the fact that the indebtedness is outstanding will not prevent distributions that could be made under section 6.40(c) if the indebtedness were not counted in making the determination.

CHAPTER 7: SHAREHOLDERS

SUBCHAPTER A
MEETINGS

§ 7.01. Annual Meeting

    (a)   Unless directors are elected by written consent in lieu of an annual meeting as permitted by section 7.04, a corporation shall hold a meeting of shareholders annually at a time stated in or fixed in accordance with the bylaws at which directors shall be elected.

    (b)   Annual meetings may be held in or out of this state at the place stated in or fixed in accordance with the bylaws. If no place is so stated or fixed, annual meetings shall be held at the corporation's principal office.

    (c)   The failure to hold an annual meeting at the time stated in or fixed in accordance with a corporation's bylaws does not affect the validity of any corporate action.

Cross-References

Action without meeting, see § 7.04.

Annual election of directors, see § 8.03.

Court-ordered meeting, see § 7.03.

Director holdover terms, see § 8.05.

Notice of meeting, see § 7.05.

"Principal office":

defined, see § 1.40.

designated in annual report, see § 16.21.

Proxies, see § 7.22.

Quorum and voting requirements, see §§ 7.25 through 7.28.

Shareholders' list for meeting, see § 7.20.

Special meeting, see § 7.02.

Voting entitlement of shares, see § 7.21.

"Voting group" defined, see § 1.40.

Official Comment

The principal action to be taken at the annual meeting is the election of directors pursuant to section 8.03, but the purposes of the annual meeting are not limited by the Act. The requirement of section 7.01(a) that an annual meeting be held is phrased in mandatory terms to ensure that every shareholder entitled to participate in an annual meeting has the unqualified rights to (i) demand that an annual meeting be held and (ii) compel the holding of the meeting under section 7.03 if the corporation does not promptly hold the meeting and if the shareholders have not elected directors by written consent.

Many corporations, such as nonpublic subsidiaries and closely held corporations, do not regularly hold annual meetings and, if no shareholder objects or action has been taken by written consent, that practice creates no problem under section 7.01, because section 7.01(c) provides that failure to hold an annual meeting does not affect the validity of any corporate action. The shareholders may act by unanimous written consent under section 7.04 (or by less than unanimous written consent if the articles of incorporation so provide). Directors, once duly elected, remain in office until their successors are elected or they resign or are removed. See sections 8.05 and 8.07 through 8.09.

The time and place of the annual meeting may be "stated in or fixed in accordance with the bylaws." If the bylaws do not themselves state a time and place for the annual meeting, authority to fix them may be delegated to the board of directors or to a specified officer. This section thus gives corporations the flexibility to hold annual meetings in varying places at varying times as convenience may dictate.

If the bylaws do not fix, or state the method of fixing, the place of the meeting, the meeting must be held at the "principal office" of the corporation as defined in section 1.40, which may or may not be its registered office under section 5.01.

§ 7.02. Special Meeting

(a)   A corporation shall hold a special meeting of shareholders:

(1)   on call of its board of directors or the person or persons authorized to do so by the articles of incorporation or bylaws; or

(2)   if shareholders holding at least 10% of all the votes entitled to be cast on an issue proposed to be considered at the proposed special meeting sign, date, and deliver to the corporation one or more written demands for the meeting describing the purpose or purposes for

which it is to be held, provided that the articles of incorporation may fix a lower percentage or a higher percentage not exceeding 25% of all the votes entitled to be cast on any issue proposed to be considered. Unless otherwise provided in the articles of incorporation, a written demand for a special meeting may be revoked by a writing to that effect received by the corporation before the receipt by the corporation of demands sufficient in number to require the holding of a special meeting.

(b)   If not otherwise fixed under section 7.03 or 7.07, the record date for determining shareholders entitled to demand a special meeting shall be the first date on which a signed shareholder demand is delivered to the corporation. No written demand for a special meeting shall be effective unless, within 60 days of the earliest date on which such a demand delivered to the corporation as required by this section was signed, written demands signed by shareholders holding at least the percentage of votes specified in or fixed in accordance with subsection (a)(2) have been delivered to the corporation.

(c)   Special meetings of shareholders may be held in or out of this state at the place stated in or fixed in accordance with the bylaws. If no place is so stated or fixed, special meetings shall be held at the corporation's principal office.

(d)   Only business within the purpose or purposes described in the meeting notice required by section 7.05(c) may be conducted at a special meeting of shareholders.

Cross-References

> Action without meeting, see § 7.04.
>
> Annual meeting, see § 7.01.
>
> Court-ordered meeting, see § 7.03.
>
> "Deliver" defined, see § 1.40.
>
> Delivery to corporation, see § 1.41.
>
> Notice of meeting, see § 7.05.
>
> Objection to meeting or certain business at meeting, see § 7.06.
>
> "Principal office":
>
> > defined, see § 1.40.
> >
> > designated in annual report, see § 16.21.
>
> Quorum and voting requirements, see §§ 7.25 through 7.28.
>
> Shareholders' list for meeting, see § 7.20.
>
> Voting entitlement of shares, see § 7.21.
>
> "Voting group" defined, see § 1.40.
>
> Waiver of notice, see § 7.06.

Official Comment

Any meeting other than an annual meeting is a special meeting under section 7.02. The principal differences between an annual meeting and a special meeting are that at an annual meeting directors are elected and, subject to any applicable special notice requirement prescribed by the Act or by the articles of incorporation, any relevant issue pertaining to the corporation may be considered, while at a special meeting only matters within the specific purposes for which the meeting is called may be considered.

1.   Who May Call a Special Meeting

A special meeting may be called by the board of directors, a person or persons authorized to do so by the articles of incorporation or bylaws, or upon written demand by shareholders as described below.

Typically, the person or persons holding certain designated offices within the corporation, *e.g.*, the president, chairman of the board of directors, or chief executive officer, are given authority to call special meetings of the shareholders. In addition, the shareholders holding at least 10% of all the votes entitled to be cast on a proposed issue at the special meeting may require the corporation to hold a special meeting by signing, dating, and delivering one or more writings that demand a special meeting and set forth the purpose or purposes of the desired meeting. That percentage may be decreased or increased (but to not more than 25%) by a provision in the articles of incorporation fixing a different percentage. Shareholders demanding a special meeting do not have to sign a single document, but the writings signed must all describe essentially the same purpose or purposes. Revocations of written demands will be effective if delivered to the corporation in the manner contemplated by section 1.41 and received before the corporation receives the requisite number of demands requiring that a special meeting be called. Revocations received after that time will have no effect. Upon receipt of demands from holders with the requisite number of votes, the corporation (through an appropriate officer) must call the special meeting at a reasonable time and place. The shareholders' demand may suggest a time and place but the final decision on such matters belongs to the corporation. If no meeting is held within the time periods specified in section 7.03, a shareholder, as defined in section 7.03(c), who signed the demand may seek judicial relief under that section requiring that the meeting be held.

2. *The Business That May Be Conducted at a Special Meeting*

Section 7.05(c) provides that a notice of a special meeting must include a "description of the purpose or purposes for which the meeting is called." Section 7.02(d) states that only business that is "within" that purpose or those purposes may be conducted at the special meeting. The word "within" was chosen, rather than a broader phrase like "reasonably related to," to describe the relationship between the notice and the authorized business to assure a shareholder who does not attend a special meeting that new or unexpected matters will not be considered in the shareholder's absence.

§ 7.03. Court-Ordered Meeting

(a) The [name or describe court] may summarily order a meeting to be held:

(1) on application of any shareholder of the corporation if an annual meeting was not held or action by written consent in lieu of an annual meeting did not become effective within the earlier of six months after the end of the corporation's fiscal year or 15 months after its last annual meeting; or

(2) on application of one or more shareholders who signed a demand for a special meeting valid under section 7.02, if:

(i) notice of the special meeting was not given within 30 days after the first day on which the requisite number of such demands have been delivered to the corporation; or

(ii) the special meeting was not held in accordance with the notice.

(b) The court may fix the time and place of the meeting, determine the shares entitled to participate in the meeting, specify a record date or dates for determining shareholders entitled to notice of and to vote at the meeting, prescribe the form and content of the meeting notice, fix the quorum required for specific matters to be considered at the meeting (or direct that the shares represented at the meeting constitute a quorum for action on those matters), and enter other orders necessary to accomplish the purpose or purposes of the meeting.

(c) For purposes of subsection (a)(1), "shareholder" means a record shareholder, a beneficial shareholder, and an unrestricted voting trust beneficial owner.

Cross-References

Annual meeting, see § 7.01.

"Beneficial shareholder," "record shareholder" and "unrestricted voting trust beneficial owner" defined, see § 1.40.

Notice of meeting, see § 7.05.

Notices and other communications, see § 1.41.

Quorum and voting requirements, see §§ 7.25 through 7.28.

Shareholders' list for meeting, see § 7.20.

Voting entitlement, see § 7.21.

Official Comment

Section 7.03 provides the remedy for shareholders if the corporation refuses or fails to hold a shareholders' meeting as required by section 7.01 or 7.02. Because a meeting must be held within 60 days of the notice date under section 7.05, the maximum delay between the demand for a special meeting and the right to petition a court for a summary order is 90 days.

1.   *The Discretion of the Court to Order a Meeting*

The court has broad discretion under section 7.03 whether to order that a meeting be held, since the language of the statute is that the court "may summarily order" that a meeting be held. A court, for example, may refuse to order a special meeting if the specified purpose is repetitive of the purpose of a special meeting held in the recent past. Alternatively, the court may view the demand as a good faith request for reconsideration of an action taken in the recent past and may order a meeting to be held. Similarly, even though a demand for an annual meeting is not a formal prerequisite for an application for a summary order under this section, the court may withhold setting a time and date for the annual meeting for a reasonably short period to permit the corporation to do so.

2.   *Notice, Time, Place, and Quorum and Other Requirements*

If the court orders that a meeting be held, the court has wide discretion over the terms of the order, including the matters set forth in section 7.03(b). The discretion of the court with respect to quorum requirements prevents a holder of the majority of the votes (who may not desire that a meeting be held) from frustrating the court-ordered meeting by not attending to prevent the existence of a quorum. To prevent misunderstanding about a special quorum requirement, if one is imposed, it is appropriate for the court to order that the notice of the meeting state specifically and conspicuously that a special quorum requirement is applicable to the court-ordered meeting. The court may also enter orders overriding the articles of incorporation or bylaws relating to matters such as notice (including advance notice requirements), *and* time and place of the meeting.

3.   *Status as Annual Meeting*

The court may provide that a meeting it has ordered is to be the annual meeting. If so provided, the meeting should be viewed as compliance with section 7.01, precluding all other shareholder requests for an annual meeting for that year.

§ 7.04. Action Without Meeting

(a)   Action required or permitted by this Act to be taken at a shareholders' meeting may be taken without a meeting if the action is taken by all the shareholders entitled to vote on the action. The action must be evidenced by one or more written consents bearing the date of signature and describing the action taken, signed by all the shareholders entitled to vote on the action and delivered to the corporation for filing by the corporation with the minutes or corporate records.

(b)   The articles of incorporation may provide that any action required or permitted by this Act to be taken at a shareholders' meeting may be taken without a meeting, and without prior notice, if consents in writing setting forth the action so taken are signed by the holders of outstanding shares having not less than the minimum number of votes that would be required to authorize or take the action at a meeting at which all shares entitled to vote on the action were present and voted; provided, however, that if a corporation's articles of incorporation authorize shareholders to cumulate their votes when electing directors pursuant to section 7.28, directors may not be elected by less than unanimous written consent. A written consent must bear the date of signature of the shareholder who signs the consent and be delivered to the corporation for filing by the corporation with the minutes or corporate records.

(c)   If not otherwise fixed under section 7.07 and if prior action by the board of directors is not required respecting the action to be taken without a meeting, the record date for determining the shareholders entitled to take action without a meeting shall be the first date on which a signed written consent is delivered to the corporation. If not otherwise fixed under section 7.07 and if prior action by the board of directors is required respecting the action to be taken without a meeting, the record date shall be the close of business on the day the resolution of the board of directors taking such prior action is adopted. No written consent shall be effective to take the corporate action referred to therein unless, within 60 days of the earliest date on which a consent delivered to the corporation as required by this section was signed, written consents signed by sufficient shareholders to take the action have been delivered to the corporation. A written consent may be revoked by a writing to that effect delivered to the corporation before unrevoked written consents sufficient in number to take the corporate action have been delivered to the corporation.

(d)   A consent signed pursuant to the provisions of this section has the effect of a vote taken at a meeting and may be described as such in any document. Unless the articles of incorporation, bylaws or a resolution of the board of directors provides for a reasonable delay to permit tabulation of written consents, the action taken by written consent shall be effective when written consents signed by sufficient shareholders to take the action have been delivered to the corporation.

(e)   If this Act requires that notice of a proposed action be given to nonvoting shareholders and the action is to be taken by written consent of the voting shareholders, the corporation shall give its nonvoting shareholders written notice of the action not more than 10 days after (i) written consents sufficient to take the action have been delivered to the corporation, or (ii) such later date that tabulation of consents is completed pursuant to an authorization under subsection (d). The notice must reasonably describe the action taken and contain or be accompanied by the same material that, under any provision of this Act, would have been required to be sent to nonvoting shareholders in a notice of a meeting at which the proposed action would have been submitted to the shareholders for action.

(f)   If action is taken by less than unanimous written consent of the voting shareholders, the corporation shall give its nonconsenting voting shareholders written notice of the action not more than 10 days after (i) written consents sufficient to take the action have been delivered to the corporation, or (ii) such later date that tabulation of consents is completed pursuant to an authorization under subsection (d). The notice must reasonably describe the action taken and contain or be accompanied by the same material that, under any provision of this Act, would have been required to be sent to voting shareholders in a notice of a meeting at which the action would have been submitted to the shareholders for action.

(g)   The notice requirements in subsections (e) and (f) shall not delay the effectiveness of actions taken by written consent, and a failure to comply with such notice requirements shall not invalidate actions taken by written consent, provided that this subsection shall not be deemed to limit judicial power to fashion any appropriate remedy in favor of a shareholder adversely affected by a failure to give such notice within the required time period.

Cross-References

Acceptance of consents, see § 7.24.

"Deliver" defined, see § 1.40.

Notices and other communications, see § 1.41.

"Sign" defined, see § 1.40.

Voting entitlement of shares, see § 7.21.

Official Comment

Section 7.04(a) permits shareholders to act by unanimous written consent without holding a meeting. This applies to any shareholder action, including election of directors, approval of mergers, domestications, conversions, sales of the corporation's assets requiring shareholder approval, amendments of articles of incorporation, and dissolution. Unanimous written consent is generally obtainable only for matters on which there are relatively few shareholders entitled to vote and is thus generally not used by public corporations. Under section 7.04(b), however, a corporation may include in its articles of incorporation a provision that permits shareholder action by less than unanimous written consent except with respect to the election of directors by written consent where cumulative voting applies. See section 7.28. If the articles of incorporation permit action by less than unanimous written consent, they may also limit or otherwise specify the shareholder actions that may be approved by less than unanimous consent.

1. Form of Written Consent

To be effective, consents must be in writing, dated and sent to the corporation in any manner authorized by section 1.41, including electronic transmission if the applicable conditions of section 1.41 are met.

A shareholder or proxy may use an electronic transmission to consent to an action. If an electronic transmission is used to consent to an action, the corporation must be able to determine from the transmission the date of the signature and that the consent was authorized by the shareholder or a person authorized to act for the shareholder. See sections 1.40 ("electronic," "sign," and "signature") and 1.41(d).

In some cases, more votes may be required to approve an action by less than unanimous written consent than would be required to approve the same action at a meeting that is not attended by all shareholders. For example, for a corporation with 1,000 shares eligible to vote, unrevoked consents from the holders of at least 501 shares are necessary to take action by written consent under the default quorum and voting requirement provisions of section 7.25. In contrast, at a meeting at which the minimum quorum is present, the same action could be taken with the vote of the holders of 251 shares, or even fewer if not all shares present are voted. Where the Act or a corporation's articles of incorporation provide for a greater voting requirement, however, the number of shares required to consent to an action may be the same as the number of shares required to approve the action at a meeting of shareholders.

The phrase "one or more written consents" in section 7.04 makes it clear that shareholders do not need to sign the same document. To minimize the possibility that action by written consent will be authorized by action of persons who may no longer be shareholders at the time the action is taken, section 7.04(c) requires that all consents be signed within 60 days of the earliest signature date of the consents delivered to the corporation.

2. Notice to Nonconsenting Shareholders

When action is taken by less than unanimous written consent, section 7.04(f) requires that notice be given to nonconsenting shareholders entitled to vote on the matter. Section 7.04(e) also requires such notice to shareholders not entitled to vote on the matter if the Act requires that they be given notice of a proposed action. By requiring notice only after shareholder action has been taken, the Act preserves the practical utility of the less than unanimous written consent when action needs to be taken quickly, without the delay that would result from a mandatory prior notice requirement. A corporation may provide for advance notice in its articles of incorporation.

3. Revocation of Consent

Before shareholder action by written consent is effective, a shareholder may withdraw a consent by delivering a written revocation of the consent to the corporation.

§ 7.05. Notice of Meeting

(a) A corporation shall notify shareholders of the date, time, and place of each annual and special shareholders' meeting no fewer than 10 nor more than 60 days before the meeting date. If the board of directors has authorized participation by means of remote communication pursuant to section 7.09 for holders of any class or series of shares, the notice to the holders of such class or series of shares must describe the means of remote communication to be used. The notice must include the record date for determining the shareholders entitled to vote at the meeting, if such date is different from the record date for determining shareholders entitled to notice of the meeting. Unless this Act or the articles of incorporation require otherwise, the corporation is required to give notice only to shareholders entitled to vote at the meeting as of the record date for determining the shareholders entitled to notice of the meeting.

(b)   Unless this Act or the articles of incorporation require otherwise, the notice of an annual meeting of shareholders need not include a description of the purpose or purposes for which the meeting is called.

(c)   Notice of a special meeting of shareholders must include a description of the purpose or purposes for which the meeting is called.

(d)   If not otherwise fixed under section 7.03 or 7.07, the record date for determining shareholders entitled to notice of and to vote at an annual or special shareholders' meeting is the day before the first notice is delivered to shareholders.

(e)   Unless the bylaws require otherwise, if an annual or special shareholders' meeting is adjourned to a different date, time, or place, notice need not be given of the new date, time, or place if the new date, time, or place is announced at the meeting before adjournment. If a new record date for the adjourned meeting is or must be fixed under section 7.07, however, notice of the adjourned meeting shall be given under this section to shareholders entitled to vote at such adjourned meeting as of the record date fixed for notice of such adjourned meeting.

Cross-References

Annual meeting, see § 7.01.

"Deliver" defined, see § 1.40.

Notice otherwise required:

>   amendment of articles of incorporation, see § 10.03.

>   appraisal rights, see §§ 13.20 and 13.22.

>   conversion, see § 9.32.

>   disposition of assets, see § 12.02.

>   dissolution, see § 14.02.

>   domestication, see § 9.21.

>   merger and share exchange, see § 11.04.

Notices and other communications, see § 1.41.

Remote participation in shareholders' meetings, see § 7.09.

Special meeting, see § 7.02.

Waiver of notice, see § 7.06.

Official Comment

The Act does not require that the notice of an annual meeting refer to any specific purpose or purposes, and any matter appropriate for shareholder action may be considered. Section 7.05(b) recognizes, however, that other provisions of the Act or the corporation's articles of incorporation may require that specific reference to a proposed action appear in the notice of meeting. See sections 9.21, 9.32, 10.03, 11.04, 12.02, and 14.02. In addition, as a condition to relying upon shareholder action to establish the safe harbor protection of section 8.61(b), section 8.63 requires notice to shareholders providing information regarding any director's conflict of interest in a transaction. If the board of directors chooses, a notice of an annual meeting may contain references to purposes or proposals not required by statute. If a notice of an annual meeting refers specifically to one or more purposes, the meeting is not limited to those purposes. Although the corporation is not required to give notice of the purpose or purposes of an annual meeting unless the Act or the articles of incorporation so provide, a shareholder, in order to raise a matter at an annual meeting (for example, to nominate an individual for election as a director or to propose a resolution for adoption), may have to comply with any advance notice provisions in the corporation's articles of incorporation or bylaws. Such provisions might include requirements that shareholder nominations for election to the board of directors or resolutions intended to be voted on at the annual meeting be submitted in writing and received by the corporation a prescribed number of days in advance of the meeting.

The selection of the day before the notice is delivered as the catch-all record date under section 7.05(d) is intended to permit the corporation to deliver notices to shareholders on a given day without regard to any requests for transfer that may have been received during that day. For this reason, this section is consistent with the general principle set forth in section 7.07(b) that the board of directors may not fix a retroactive record date.

Section 7.05(e) provides rules for adjourned meetings and determines whether new notice must be given to shareholders. If a new record date is or must be fixed under section 7.07, the 10- to 60-day notice requirement and all other requirements of section 7.05 must be complied with because notice must be given to the persons who are shareholders as of the new record date. In such circumstances, a new quorum for the adjourned meeting must also be established. See section 7.25, which provides that if a quorum exists for a meeting, it is deemed to continue to exist automatically for an adjourned meeting unless a new record date is or must be set for the adjourned meeting.

§ 7.06.   Waiver of Notice

(a)   A shareholder may waive any notice required by this Act or the articles of incorporation or bylaws, before or after the date and time stated in the notice. The waiver must be in writing, be signed by the shareholder entitled to the notice, and be delivered to the corporation for filing by the corporation with the minutes or corporate records.

(b)   A shareholder's attendance at a meeting:

(1)   waives objection to lack of notice or defective notice of the meeting, unless the shareholder at the beginning of the meeting objects to holding the meeting or transacting business at the meeting; and

(2)   waives objection to consideration of a particular matter at the meeting that is not within the purpose or purposes described in the meeting notice, unless the shareholder objects to considering the matter when it is presented.

Cross-References

Acceptance of votes and other instruments, see § 7.24.

Action without meeting, see § 7.04.

Notice of meeting, see § 7.05.

Notices and other communications, see § 1.41.

Proxies, see § 7.22.

Remote participation in shareholders' meetings, see § 7.09.

"Sign" defined, see § 1.40.

Official Comment

A notice of shareholders' meeting serves two principal purposes: (i) it advises shareholders of the date, time, and place of the annual or special meeting, and (ii) in the case of a special shareholders' meeting (or an annual meeting at which fundamental changes may be made), it advises shareholders of the purposes of the meeting. Section 7.06(b)(1) provides that attendance at a meeting constitutes waiver of any failure to receive the notice or defects in the statement of the date, time, and place of any meeting. Defects waived by attendance for this purpose include a failure to send the notice altogether, delivery to the wrong address, a misstatement of the date, time, or place of the meeting, and a failure to notice the meeting within the time periods specified in section 7.05(a). If a shareholder believes that the defect in or failure of notice was in some way prejudicial, the shareholder must state at the beginning of the meeting an objection to holding the meeting or transacting any business or the objection is waived. If this objection is made, the corporation may correct the defect by sending proper notice to the shareholders for a subsequent meeting or by obtaining written waivers of notice from all shareholders who did not receive the notice required by section 7.05.

For purposes of this section, "attendance" at a meeting involves the presence of the shareholder in person or by proxy or, if authorized in accordance with section 7.09(b), the shareholder or proxy may attend by means of remote communication. A shareholder who attends a meeting solely for the purpose of objecting to the notice is counted as present for purposes of determining whether a quorum is present. See section 7.25 and its Official Comment.

In the case of special shareholders' meetings, or annual meetings at which certain fundamental corporate changes are considered, a second purpose of the notice is to inform shareholders of the matters to be considered at the meeting. An objection that a particular matter is not within the stated purposes of the meeting cannot be raised until the matter is presented. Thus section 7.06(b)(2) provides that a shareholder waives this kind of objection by failing to object when the matter is presented. If this objection is made, the corporation may correct the defect by sending proper notice to the shareholders for a subsequent meeting or obtaining written waivers of notice from all shareholders. Whether a specific matter is within a stated purpose of a meeting is ultimately a matter for judicial determination, typically in a suit to invalidate action taken at the meeting brought by a shareholder who was not present at the meeting or who was present at the meeting and preserved an objection under section 7.06(b).

The purpose of both waiver rules in section 7.06(b) is to require shareholders with technical objections to holding the meeting or considering a specific matter to raise them at the outset and not reserve them to be raised only if they are unhappy with the outcome of the meeting. The rules set forth in this section differ in some respects from the waiver rules for directors set forth in section 8.23 where a waiver is inferred if the director acquiesces in the action taken at a meeting even if the director raised a technical objection to the notice of a meeting at the outset.

Other sections of the Act require that shareholders who are not entitled to vote be given notice of meetings at which certain fundamental corporate changes are to be considered. See sections 9.21, 9.32, 10.03, 11.04, 12.02, and 14.02. To obtain an effective waiver of notice for these meetings under this section, waivers must be obtained from the nonvoting shareholders who are entitled to notice but not entitled to vote, as well as from the shareholders entitled to vote.

§ 7.07. Record Date for Meeting

(a) The bylaws may fix or provide the manner of fixing the record date or dates for one or more voting groups to determine the shareholders entitled to notice of a shareholders' meeting, to demand a special meeting, to vote, or to take any other action. If the bylaws do not fix or provide for fixing a record date, the board of directors may fix the record date.

(b) A record date fixed under this section may not be more than 70 days before the meeting or action requiring a determination of shareholders and may not be retroactive.

(c) A determination of shareholders entitled to notice of or to vote at a shareholders' meeting is effective for any adjournment of the meeting unless the board of directors fixes a new record date or dates, which it shall do if the meeting is adjourned to a date more than 120 days after the date fixed for the original meeting.

(d) If a court orders a meeting adjourned to a date more than 120 days after the date fixed for the original meeting, it may provide that the original record date or dates continues in effect or it may fix a new record date or dates.

(e) The record dates for a shareholders' meeting fixed by or in the manner provided in the bylaws or by the board of directors shall be the record date for determining shareholders entitled both to notice of and to vote at the shareholders' meeting, unless in the case of a record date fixed by the board of directors and to the extent not prohibited by the bylaws, the board, at the time it fixes the record date for shareholders entitled to notice of the meeting, fixes a later record date on or before the date of the meeting to determine the shareholders entitled to vote at the meeting.

Cross-References

Annual meeting, see § 7.01.

Court-ordered meeting, see § 7.03.

Other record date provisions:

> action without meeting, see § 7.04.

> distributions to shareholders, see § 6.40.

> liquidating distributions, see § 14.05.

> notice of meeting, see § 7.05.

> share dividends, see § 6.23.

> special meeting, see § 7.02.

"Voting group" defined, see § 1.40.

Official Comment

Section 7.07 authorizes the board of directors to fix record dates for determining shareholders entitled to take any action unless the bylaws themselves fix or otherwise provide for the fixing of a record date. A separate record date may be established for each voting group entitled to vote separately on a matter at a meeting, or a single record date may be established for all voting groups entitled to participate in the meeting. If neither the bylaws nor the board of directors fixes a record date for a specific action, the section of the Act that deals with that action itself fixes the record date. For example, section 7.05(d), relating to giving notice of a meeting, provides that the record date for determining who is entitled to notice of and to vote at a meeting (if not fixed by the directors or the bylaws) is the close of business on the day before the date the corporation first gives notice to shareholders of the meeting.

After a record date is fixed, if a new record date subsequently is or must be fixed under section 7.07, section 7.05 requires that new notice be given to the persons who are shareholders as of the new record date, and section 7.25 requires that a quorum be reestablished for that meeting.

Section 7.07(e) provides a board of directors with flexibility to align shareholders' voting and economic interests and addresses, in part, concerns over the separation of ownership and voting by permitting a board of directors to set a record date for voting closer to the meeting date. This provision does not restrict how close a record date for voting can be to the meeting date, but a board of directors would need to consider the practical issues in fixing the voting record date, including the requirement of section 7.20(c) that a list of shareholders entitled to vote be available at the meeting. The board may fix a separate record date for voting only at the time it fixes the record date for notice, and, as provided in section 7.05, notice of the separate record date must be included in the notice of meeting. If the board fixes separate record dates, section 16.02(e) provides for shareholders entitled to vote at the meeting who were not shareholders on the record date for notice to have access to the information provided by the corporation to shareholders in connection with the meeting. If the board does not fix separate record dates, the normal provisions for fixing a single record date for notice and voting will apply.

§ 7.08. Conduct of Meeting

(a)   At each meeting of shareholders, a chair shall preside. The chair shall be appointed as provided in the bylaws or, in the absence of such provision, by the board of directors.

(b)   The chair, unless the articles of incorporation or bylaws provide otherwise, shall determine the order of business and shall have the authority to establish rules for the conduct of the meeting.

(c)   Any rules adopted for, and the conduct of, the meeting shall be fair to shareholders.

(d)   The chair of the meeting shall announce at the meeting when the polls close for each matter voted upon. If no announcement is made, the polls shall be deemed to have closed upon the final adjournment of the meeting. After the polls close, no ballots, proxies or votes nor any revocations or changes to such ballots, proxies or votes may be accepted.

Cross-References

Annual meeting, see § 7.01.

Court-ordered meeting, see § 7.03.

Proxies, see § 7.22.

Special meeting, see § 7.02.

Official Comment

Section 7.08 provides that, at any meeting of the shareholders, there shall be a chair who shall preside over the meeting. Inherent in the chair's power in section 7.08(b) to establish rules for the conduct of the meeting is the authority to require that the order of business be observed and that any discussion or comments from shareholders or their proxies be confined to the business item under discussion. The rules for conduct of the meeting may cover such subjects as the proper means for obtaining the floor, who shall have the right to address the meeting, the manner in which shareholders will be recognized to speak, time limits per speaker, the number of times a shareholder may address the meeting, and the person to whom questions should be addressed. The chair should be fair in determining the order of business and in establishing rules for the conduct of the meeting so as not to unfairly foreclose the right of shareholders—subject to the Act, the articles of incorporation and the bylaws—to raise items which are properly a subject for shareholder discussion or action at some point in the meeting before adjournment.

The Act provides that only business within the purpose or purposes described in the meeting notice may be conducted at a special shareholders' meeting. See sections 7.02(d) and 7.05(c). In addition, in order to raise a matter at an annual meeting (for example, to nominate an individual for election as a director or to propose a resolution for adoption), a shareholder may be required to comply with any advance notice provision in the articles of incorporation or bylaws. See the Official Comment to section 7.05.

§ 7.09. Remote Participation in Shareholders' Meetings

(a) Shareholders of any class or series of shares may participate in any meeting of shareholders by means of remote communication to the extent the board of directors authorizes such participation for such class or series. Participation as a shareholder by means of remote communication shall be subject to such guidelines and procedures as the board of directors adopts, and shall be in conformity with subsection (b).

(b) Shareholders participating in a shareholders' meeting by means of remote communication shall be deemed present and may vote at such a meeting if the corporation has implemented reasonable measures:

(1) to verify that each person participating remotely as a shareholder is a shareholder; and

(2) to provide such shareholders a reasonable opportunity to participate in the meeting and to vote on matters submitted to the shareholders, including an opportunity to communicate, and to read or hear the proceedings of the meeting, substantially concurrently with such proceedings.

Official Comment

Section 7.09 permits shareholders to participate in annual and special shareholders' meetings by means of remote communication, such as over the Internet or through telephone conference calls, subject to the conditions set forth in section 7.09(b) and any other guidelines and procedures that the board of directors adopts. This would include the use of electronic ballots to the extent authorized by the board of directors. This authorization extends as well to anyone to whom such shareholder has granted a proxy appointment. Section 7.09(a) ensures that the board of directors has the sole discretion to determine whether to allow shareholders to participate by means of remote communication.

Section 7.09 allows the board of directors to limit participation by means of remote communication to all shareholders of a particular class or series, but does not permit the board of directors to limit such participation to particular shareholders within a class or series.

Section 7.09 is not intended to expand the rights to participate in meetings or otherwise alter the ability of the board of directors or the chair to conduct meetings, pursuant to section 7.08, in a manner that is fair. For example, many corporations limit shareholder comments and, if such practice is fair to shareholders consistent with section 7.08, such practice is not changed by section 7.09. The two requirements under section 7.09(b) reflect the minimum deemed necessary to safeguard the integrity of the shareholders' meeting. Section 7.09 specifically gives the board of directors the flexibility and discretion to adopt additional guidelines and procedures for allowing shareholders to participate in a meeting by means of remote communication.

To give corporations the flexibility to choose the most efficient means of remote communication, under section 7.09(a), the board of directors may require that shareholders communicate their desire to participate by a certain date and condition the provision of remote communication or the form of communication to be used on the affirmative response of a certain number or proportion of shareholders eligible to participate. If the board of directors authorizes shareholder participation by means of remote communication pursuant to this section, such authorization and the process for participating by remote means of communication must be included in the meeting notice required by section 7.05.

SUBCHAPTER B
VOTING

§ 7.20. Shareholders' List for Meeting

(a)   After fixing a record date for a meeting, a corporation shall prepare an alphabetical list of the names of all its shareholders who are entitled to notice of a shareholders' meeting. If the board of directors fixes a different record date under section 7.07(e) to determine the shareholders entitled to vote at the meeting, a corporation also shall prepare an alphabetical list of the names of all its shareholders who are entitled to vote at the meeting. A list must be arranged by voting group (and within each voting group by class or series of shares) and show the address of and number of shares held by each shareholder. Nothing contained in this subsection shall require the corporation to include on such list the electronic mail address or other electronic contact information of a shareholder.

(b)   The shareholders' list for notice shall be available for inspection by any shareholder, beginning two business days after notice of the meeting is given for which the list was prepared and continuing through the meeting, at the corporation's principal office or at a place identified in the meeting notice in the city where the meeting will be held. A shareholders' list for voting shall be similarly available for inspection promptly after the record date for voting. A shareholder, or the shareholder's agent or attorney, is entitled on written demand to inspect and, subject to the requirements of section 16.02(c), to copy a list, during regular business hours and at the shareholder's expense, during the period it is available for inspection.

(c)   The corporation shall make the list of shareholders entitled to vote available at the meeting, and any shareholder, or the shareholder's agent or attorney, is entitled to inspect the list at any time during the meeting or any adjournment.

(d)   If the corporation refuses to allow a shareholder, or the shareholder's agent or attorney, to inspect a shareholders' list before or at the meeting (or copy a list as permitted by subsection (b)), the [name or describe court], on application of the shareholder, may summarily order the inspection or copying at the corporation's expense and may postpone the meeting for which the list was prepared until the inspection or copying is complete.

(e)   Refusal or failure to prepare or make available the shareholders' list does not affect the validity of action taken at the meeting.

Cross-References

Annual meeting, see § 7.01.

Charge for providing copy, see § 16.03.

Inspection of corporate records, see ch. 16A.

Notices and other communications, see § 1.41.

Notice of meeting, see § 7.05.

"Principal office":

defined, see § 1.40.

designated in annual report, see § 16.21.

Proper purpose for copying, see § 16.02.

Record date, see § 7.07.

Record of shareholders, see § 16.01.

"Shareholder" defined, see § 1.40.

Special meeting, see § 7.02.

Voting entitlement of shares, see § 7.21.

"Voting group" defined, see § 1.40.

Official Comment

The list of shareholders required by section 7.20 must include the names, addresses and number of shares of those shareholders entitled to vote at the meeting. The list must also include the names, addresses and number of shares of holders of nonvoting shares if they are entitled to notice of the meeting by reason of the nature of the actions proposed to be taken at the meeting. See section 7.05 and its Official Comment.

1. *When the List Must Be Available*

Sections 7.20(b) and (c) govern when the list of shareholders must generally be available for inspection. The requirement of availability for continuous inspection permits the corporation and others soliciting votes to be on a relatively equal footing. If, however, notice of the meeting is waived by all the shareholders, the list need be available only at the meeting itself under section 7.20(c) unless one or more waivers are conditioned upon receipt of the list.

2. *Where the List Must Be Maintained*

Sections 7.20(b) and (c) also govern where the corporation must maintain the list. If the corporation changes the location of the meeting, it thus may correspondingly change the location of the list under section 7.20(b).

3. *The Form in Which the List Is Maintained*

Section 7.20 does not require the list of shareholders to be in any particular form. It may be maintained, for example, in electronic form. If the list is maintained in other than written form, however, suitable equipment must be provided so that a comprehensible list may be inspected by a shareholder as permitted by section 7.20.

4. *Consequences of Failing to Prepare the List or Refusal to Make It Available*

Section 7.20 creates a corporate obligation rather than an obligation imposed upon a corporate officer. If the corporation fails to prepare the list or refuses to permit a shareholder to inspect it, either before the meeting as required by section 7.20(b) or at the meeting itself as required by section 7.20(c), a shareholder may apply to the appropriate court for a summary order as contemplated by section 7.20(d). If the court orders a copy of the list to be provided to the shareholders, the copying is at the corporation's expense; if the corporation produces the list voluntarily pursuant to section 7.20(b) or (c), any inspection and copying are at the shareholder's expense.

This judicial remedy is the only sanction in the Act for violation of section 7.20 given that section 7.20(e) provides that the failure to prepare, maintain, or produce the list does not affect the validity of any action taken at the meeting.

5.   The Right to Obtain a Copy of the List

Section 7.20(b) permits shareholders to inspect the list without limitation, but permits the shareholder to copy the list only if the shareholder complies with the requirement of section 16.02(c) that the demand be made in good faith and for a proper purpose. The right to copy the list may be satisfied at the corporation's option, if reasonable, by furnishing to the shareholder a copy of the list upon payment of a reasonable charge. See sections 16.03(b) and (c). The distinction between inspection and copying set forth in section 7.20(b) reflects an accommodation between competing considerations of permitting shareholders access to the list before a meeting and possible misuse of the list.

6.   Relationship to Right to Inspect Corporate Records Generally

Section 7.20 creates a right of shareholders to inspect a list of shareholders in advance of and at a meeting that is independent of the right of shareholders to inspect corporate records under chapter 16. A shareholder may obtain the right to inspect the list of shareholders as provided in chapter 16 without regard to the provisions relating to the pendency of a meeting in section 7.20, and similarly the limitations of chapter 16 are not applicable to the right of inspection created by section 7.20 except to the extent the shareholder seeks to copy the list in advance of the meeting.

The right to inspect under chapter 16 is also broader in the sense that the shareholder may make or receive copies of the documents the shareholder is entitled to inspect. See section 16.03.

§ 7.21. Voting Entitlement of Shares

(a)   Except as provided in subsections (b) and (d) or unless the articles of incorporation provide otherwise, each outstanding share, regardless of class or series, is entitled to one vote on each matter voted on at a shareholders' meeting. Only shares are entitled to vote.

(b)   Shares of a corporation are not entitled to vote if they are owned by or otherwise belong to the corporation directly, or indirectly through an entity of which a majority of the voting power is held directly or indirectly by the corporation or which is otherwise controlled by the corporation.

(c)   Shares held by the corporation in a fiduciary capacity for the benefit of any person are entitled to vote unless they are held for the benefit of, or otherwise belong to, the corporation directly, or indirectly through an entity of which a majority of the voting power is held directly or indirectly by the corporation or which is otherwise controlled by the corporation.

(d)   Redeemable shares are not entitled to vote after delivery of written notice of redemption is effective and a sum sufficient to redeem the shares has been deposited with a bank, trust company, or other financial institution under an irrevocable obligation to pay the holders the redemption price on surrender of the shares.

(e)   For purposes of this section, "voting power" means the current power to vote in the election of directors of a corporation or to elect, select or appoint governors of another entity.

Cross-References

Acceptance of votes, see § 7.24.

Classes and series of shares, see §§ 6.01 and 6.02.

Cumulative voting, see § 7.28.

Director establishment of voting rights, see § 6.02.

"Governor" defined, see § 1.40.

Notices and other communications, see § 1.41.

Proxy voting, see § 7.22.

Redeemable shares, see § 6.01.

Shareholders' meetings, see §§ 7.01 through 7.03.

Status of shares belonging to the corporation, see § 6.31.

Voting by nominees, see § 7.23.

Voting by voting groups, see §§ 1.40, 7.25 and 7.26.

"Voting power" defined, see § 1.40.

Official Comment

1. Voting Power of Shares

Section 7.21(a) provides that each outstanding share, regardless of class or series, is entitled to one vote per share unless otherwise provided in the articles of incorporation. The articles of incorporation may provide for multiple or fractional votes per share and may provide that some classes or series of shares are nonvoting on some or all matters, or that some classes or series have a single vote per share or different multiple or fractional votes per share, or that some classes or series constitute one or more separate voting groups and are entitled to vote separately on the matter. To reflect the possibility that shares may have multiple or fractional votes per share, the provisions relating to quorums, voting, and similar matters in the Act are phrased in terms of votes represented by shares.

2. Voting Power of Nonshareholders

Under the last sentence of section 7.21(a), the power to vote may only be vested in shares. For example, bondholders may not be given the direct power to vote under the Act. They may, however, be given the power to vote by issuing them special classes or series of shares. See the Official Comment to section 7.22.

3. Circular Holdings

The purpose of the prohibition in section 7.21(b) is to prevent a board of directors or management from using a corporate investment to perpetuate itself in power. While shares acquired by a corporation cease to be outstanding under section 6.31, except as provided in that section, and therefore are not entitled to vote, other arrangements may be devised seeking to obtain the benefits of ownership without actually acquiring the shares at all or not acquiring the shares at the time the right to vote is determined. The concept of shares that "otherwise belong to" is included in addition to "owned by" to ensure that courts will have the flexibility to apply public policy considerations to arrangements under which shares are not technically "owned," or under which shares may or will be owned at a later time, but which have a similar effect. For example, if the corporation or a controlled entity has entered into a forward purchase contract for shares with the right to vote or direct the vote of the shares, a court could find that the shares belong to the corporation and are not entitled to be voted under section 7.21. Similarly, if the voting power is exercised by someone acting on behalf of the corporation or by a member of management of the corporation, a court could find that the shares otherwise belong to the corporation, and are not entitled to vote under section 7.21. Section 7.21(c), however, makes the prohibition of section 7.21(b) against voting of shares inapplicable to shares held in a fiduciary capacity where the beneficiaries are persons other than the corporation directly or through an entity controlled by the corporation.

4. Redeemable Shares

Redeemable shares are often redeemed in connection with a transaction such as a merger or the issuance of a new senior class or series of shares that requires shareholder approval. Section 7.21(d) avoids subjecting a transaction to approval by a class or series of redeemable shares that will be redeemed as a result of the transaction if adequate provision has been made to ensure that the holders of the redeemable shares will in fact receive the amount payable to them on redemption.

§ 7.22. Proxies

(a)   A shareholder may vote the shareholder's shares in person or by proxy.

(b)   A shareholder, or the shareholder's agent or attorney-in-fact, may appoint a proxy to vote or otherwise act for the shareholder by signing an appointment form, or by an electronic transmission. An electronic transmission must contain or be accompanied by information from which the recipient can determine the date of the transmission and that the transmission was authorized by the sender or the sender's agent or attorney-in-fact.

(c)   An appointment of a proxy is effective when a signed appointment form or an electronic transmission of the appointment is received by the inspector of election or the officer or agent of the corporation authorized to count votes. An appointment is valid for the term provided in the appointment form, and, if no term is provided, is valid for 11 months unless the appointment is irrevocable under subsection (d).

(d)   An appointment of a proxy is revocable unless the appointment form or electronic transmission states that it is irrevocable and the appointment is coupled with an interest. Appointments coupled with an interest include the appointment of:

(1)   a pledgee;

(2)   a person who purchased or agreed to purchase the shares;

(3)   a creditor of the corporation who extended it credit under terms requiring the appointment;

(4)   an employee of the corporation whose employment contract requires the appointment; or

(5)   a party to a voting agreement created under section 7.31.

(e)   The death or incapacity of the shareholder appointing a proxy does not affect the right of the corporation to accept the proxy's authority unless notice of the death or incapacity is received by the secretary or other officer or agent authorized to tabulate votes before the proxy exercises authority under the appointment.

(f)   An appointment made irrevocable under subsection (d) is revoked when the interest with which it is coupled is extinguished.

(g)   Unless it otherwise provides, an appointment made irrevocable under subsection (d) continues in effect after a transfer of the shares and a transferee takes subject to the appointment, except that a transferee for value of shares subject to an irrevocable appointment may revoke the appointment if the transferee did not know of its existence when acquiring the shares and the existence of the irrevocable appointment was not noted conspicuously on the certificate representing the shares or on the information statement for shares without certificates.

(h)   Subject to section 7.24 and to any express limitation on the proxy's authority stated in the appointment form or electronic transmission, a corporation is entitled to accept the proxy's vote or other action as that of the shareholder making the appointment.

Cross-References

Acceptance of proxy votes, see § 7.24.

Certificateless shares, see § 6.26.

"Conspicuous" defined, see § 1.40.

"Electronic transmission" defined, see § 1.40.

Information on share certificates, see § 6.25.

Notices and other communications, see § 1.41.

"Sign" defined, see § 1.40.

Official Comment

1. Nomenclature

The word "proxy" is often used ambiguously, sometimes referring to the grant of authority to vote, sometimes to the document granting the authority, and sometimes to the person to whom the authority is granted. In the Act, the word "proxy" is used only in the last sense; the terms "proxy appointment," "appointment form" and "electronic transmission" are used to describe the document or communication appointing the proxy; and the word "appointment" is used to describe the grant of authority to vote.

Sections 7.22(b) and 1.41(d) permit the practice by which shareholders who have been provided in proxy materials with a personal identification number may submit their vote and identifying number to a person who, acting as the shareholder's agent, causes that information to be transmitted, directly or indirectly, to the inspector of election.

Sections 1.41(f) through (i) govern when an electronic transmission is "received" and "effective." If the appointment form or electronic transmission contains an express limitation on the power to vote or direction as to how to vote the shares on a particular matter the corporation must count the votes in a manner consistent with that limitation or direction. See section 7.22(h).

2. Duration of Appointment

An appointment form that contains no expiration date is valid for 11 months unless it is irrevocable. See section 7.22(c). This ensures that in the normal course a new appointment will be solicited at least once every 12 months. An appointment form may validly specify its term if the parties agree, which may be longer or shorter than 11 months. An irrevocable appointment is valid for so long as it is irrevocable unless it terminates earlier in accordance with its terms.

The appointment of a proxy is essentially the appointment of an agent and is revocable in accordance with the principles of agency law unless it is "coupled with an interest." See section 7.22(d). An appointment may be revoked either expressly or by implication, as when a shareholder later signs a second appointment form inconsistent with an earlier one, or attends the meeting in person and seeks to vote on the shareholder's own behalf.

Although death or incapacity of the appointing shareholder revokes an agency appointment under common law principles, section 7.22(e) modifies the common law rule to provide that the corporation may accept the vote of the proxy until the appropriate corporate officer or agent receives notice of the shareholder's death or incapacity. In view of the widespread dispersal of shareholders in many corporations, it is not feasible for the corporation to learn of these events independently of notice. On the other hand, section 7.22(e) does not affect the validity of the appointment or its manner of exercise as between the proxy and the personal representatives of the decedent or incompetent.

3. Irrevocable Appointment of Proxies

Section 7.22(d) deals with the irrevocable appointment of a proxy. The general test adopted is the common law test that all appointments are revocable unless "coupled with an interest." Section 7.22(d) provides considerable certainty as it describes several accepted forms of relationship as examples of "proxies coupled with an interest." These examples are not exhaustive and other arrangements may also be "coupled with an interest."

Section 7.22(f) provides that an irrevocable appointment is revoked when the interest with which it was coupled is extinguished—for example, by repayment of the loan or release of the pledge.

Section 7.22(g) clarifies the default rule that an irrevocable appointment survives a transfer, but that the grantor may modify that rule. It also clarifies that both the appointment and the irrevocable nature of the appointment must conspicuously appear on the certificate or information statement to continue to be irrevocable against a transferee for value that does not know of the existence of the appointment.

§ 7.23. Shares Held by Intermediaries and Nominees

(a) A corporation's board of directors may establish a procedure under which a person on whose behalf shares are registered in the name of an intermediary or nominee may elect to be treated by the corporation as the record shareholder by filing with the corporation a beneficial ownership certificate. The terms, conditions, and limitations of this treatment shall be specified in the procedure. To the extent such person is treated under such procedure as having rights or privileges that the record shareholder otherwise would have, the record shareholder shall not have those rights or privileges.

(b) The procedure must specify:

(1) the types of intermediaries or nominees to which it applies;

(2) the rights or privileges that the corporation recognizes in a person with respect to whom a beneficial ownership certificate is filed;

(3) the manner in which the procedure is selected which must include that the beneficial ownership certificate be signed or assented to by or on behalf of the record shareholder and the person on whose behalf the shares are held;

(4) the information that must be provided when the procedure is selected;

(5) the period for which selection of the procedure is effective;

(6) requirements for notice to the corporation with respect to the arrangement; and

(7) the form and contents of the beneficial ownership certificate.

(c) The procedure may specify any other aspects of the rights and duties created by the filing of a beneficial ownership certificate.

Cross-Reference

"Shareholder" defined, see § 1.40.

Official Comment

Traditionally, a corporation recognizes only the person in whose name shares are registered as the owner of the shares. It is a common practice for persons purchasing shares of a public company to hold them in "street name" through a broker-dealer or other financial institution. In addition, a securities depository system exists under which financial institutions deposit securities with the depository, whose nominee becomes the registered owner of the shares or the "record shareholder." Transfers between depository participants are accomplished by book entry of the depository. As a result, there may be several entities interposed between the corporation and the beneficial owner.

The purpose of section 7.23 is to facilitate direct communication between the corporation and the beneficial owner by authorizing the corporation to create a procedure for bypassing the depository and its intermediary participants or other intermediaries and nominees. The adoption of this procedure is discretionary with each corporation and affirmative action by the corporation's board of directors is necessary to accomplish it. The procedure is also discretionary with the ultimate beneficial owner, who must elect, and the intermediary or nominee who holds on behalf of the beneficial owner as record shareholder, who must assent to, the applicable procedure established by the corporation.

The signature or assent of the record shareholder and the person or persons on whose behalf the shares are held, as required by section 7.23(b)(3), can be provided on behalf of any such person by another person authorized to do so. In a typical situation where the record shareholder is Cede & Co., the nominee of Depository Trust Company, and the shares are ultimately beneficially owned by a shareholder who has an account with a broker-dealer that is a participant in the Depository Trust Company, a beneficial ownership certificate could be signed by both the ultimate beneficial owner and the broker-dealer shown on the position list of Depository Trust Company, acting under authority granted to it by Cede & Co., as the record shareholder. The statute does not prescribe the notices that must be provided to the corporation, but provides that the procedure shall specify whatever notice provisions will be required. For example, the corporation may wish to include provisions for notice to it by the ultimate beneficial owner and the broker-dealer upon the sale or other disposition of the shares, which normally should be accompanied by notice to the corporation of termination or modification of the effect of the beneficial ownership certificate.

The corporation also may limit or qualify the procedure as it deems appropriate. For example, the corporation may:

- limit the procedure to certain classes of shareholders, such as depositories, broker-dealers and banks, and their nominees, or make the procedure available to all shareholders, and define requirements to be a beneficial owner eligible to use the procedure;

- permit a record shareholder and beneficial owner to adopt the procedure with respect to some but not all of the shares registered or held on behalf of the beneficial owner in the record shareholder's name (and in that case the record shareholder continues to be treated as the shareholder with respect to the balance);

- specify the purpose or purposes for which the beneficial ownership certificate is effective, *e.g.*, for giving notice of, and voting at, shareholders' meetings, for the distribution of proxy statements and annual reports, or for payment of cash dividends;

- specify the form of the beneficial ownership certificate, *e.g.*, a writing or an electronic record;

- specify the type of information that must be provided, *e.g.*, the name, address, and taxpayer identification number of the person for whose benefit a beneficial ownership certificate is filed, and the number of shares registered directly in the shareholder's name;

- establish deadlines for receipt of the beneficial ownership certificate in connection with the establishment of a record date by the corporation; or

- provide that a new beneficial ownership certificate is required in connection with each record date or that a beneficial ownership certificate as of a certain date may continue until changed by the certifying person or persons.

The validity of a procedure adopted under section 7.23 is to be determined by the terms of the section as in effect at the time the procedure is adopted.

The definition of "record shareholder" in section 1.40 includes beneficial owners to the extent they obtain the rights of record shareholders through the filing of a beneficial ownership certificate pursuant to the procedure authorized by section 7.23.

§ 7.24. Acceptance of Votes and Other Instruments

(a) If the name signed on a vote, ballot, consent, waiver, shareholder demand, or proxy appointment corresponds to the name of a shareholder, the corporation, if acting in good faith, is entitled to accept the vote, ballot, consent, waiver, shareholder demand, or proxy appointment and give it effect as the act of the shareholder.

(b) If the name signed on a vote, ballot, consent, waiver, shareholder demand, or proxy appointment does not correspond to the name of its shareholder, the corporation, if acting in good faith, is nevertheless entitled to accept the vote, ballot, consent, waiver, shareholder demand, or proxy appointment and give it effect as the act of the shareholder if:

(1) the shareholder is an entity and the name signed purports to be that of an officer or agent of the entity;

(2) the name signed purports to be that of an administrator, executor, guardian, or conservator representing the shareholder and, if the corporation requests, evidence of fiduciary status acceptable to the corporation has been presented with respect to the vote, ballot, consent, waiver, shareholder demand, or proxy appointment;

(3) the name signed purports to be that of a receiver or trustee in bankruptcy of the shareholder and, if the corporation requests, evidence of this status acceptable to the corporation has been presented with respect to the vote, ballot, consent, waiver, shareholder demand, or proxy appointment;

(4) the name signed purports to be that of a pledgee, beneficial owner, or attorney-in-fact of the shareholder and, if the corporation requests, evidence acceptable to the corporation of the signatory's authority to sign for the shareholder has been presented with respect to the vote, ballot, consent, waiver, shareholder demand, or proxy appointment; or

(5) two or more persons are the shareholder as co-tenants or fiduciaries and the name signed purports to be the name of at least one of the co-owners and the person signing appears to be acting on behalf of all the co-owners.

(c) The corporation is entitled to reject a vote, ballot, consent, waiver, shareholder demand, or proxy appointment if the person authorized to accept or reject such instrument, acting in good faith, has reasonable basis for doubt about the validity of the signature on it or about the signatory's authority to sign for the shareholder.

(d) Neither the corporation or any person authorized by it, nor an inspector of election appointed under section 7.29, that accepts or rejects a vote, ballot, consent, waiver, shareholder demand, or proxy appointment in good faith and in accordance with the standards of this section 7.24 or section 7.22(b) is liable in damages to the shareholder for the consequences of the acceptance or rejection.

(e) Corporate action based on the acceptance or rejection of a vote, ballot, consent, waiver, shareholder demand, or proxy appointment under this section is valid unless a court of competent jurisdiction determines otherwise.

(f) If an inspector of election has been appointed under section 7.29, the inspector of election also has the authority to request information and make determinations under subsections (a), (b), and (c). Any determination made by the inspector of election under those subsections is controlling.

Cross-References

Consents, see § 7.04.

Demand for special meeting, see § 7.02.

"Entity" defined, see § 1.40.

Officers, see § 8.40.

Proxies, see § 7.22.

"Shareholder" defined, see § 1.40.

"Sign" defined, see § 1.40.

Voting by nominees, see § 7.23.

Waiver of notice, see § 7.06.

Official Comment

Corporations are often asked to accept a written instrument as evidence of action by a shareholder. These instruments usually involve appointment forms for a proxy to vote the shares, but may also include ballots, waivers of notice, consents to action without a meeting, demands for a special meeting of shareholders, and other demands by shareholders. Usually the corporation or its officers will have no personal knowledge of the circumstances under which the instrument was executed and no way of verifying whether the signature on the instrument is in fact the signature of the shareholder. This problem is particularly acute in public corporations.

Section 7.24 establishes general rules permitting the corporation and any inspector of election appointed under section 7.29 to accept these instruments if they appear to be signed by the shareholder or by a person who has authority to sign the instrument for the shareholder and they are accompanied by whatever authenticating evidence is requested. Section 7.24 also establishes general rules for rejecting these instruments. The rules set forth in this section are not exclusive and may be supplemented by additional rules established by the corporation pursuant to section 2.06(b). If an inspector of election has been appointed under section 7.29, the inspector has the authority under section 7.24, as well as the corporation. If there is a difference in a determination by the corporation and the inspector, the inspector's determination controls as against the corporation.

A purpose of section 7.24 is to protect the corporation and any inspector of election from liability for damages to the shareholder if action is taken in accordance with the section. Under section 7.24(d) there is no liability to the shareholder if the corporation or inspector of election, acting in good faith, accepts an instrument that meets the requirements of section 7.24(a) or (b) or accepts an electronic transmission authorized by section 7.22(b), even if it turns out that the signature or transmission was invalid or unauthorized. Similarly, no liability exists if an instrument is rejected in accordance with section 7.24(c) because the corporation or inspector of election, again acting in good faith, has a "reasonable basis for doubt," even though it turns out that the instrument was properly signed by the shareholder. This protection extends to officers and other persons who are authorized by the corporation to accept or reject an instrument identified in section 7.24. Section 7.24 does not, however, address the question whether an action was properly taken or approved, and section 7.24(e) makes clear that the validity of corporate action is ultimately a matter for judicial resolution through review of the results of a vote in a suit to enjoin or compel corporate action. Section 7.49 provides a mechanism for seeking such judicial resolution. It is contemplated that any such proceeding will be brought promptly, typically before the corporate action is consummated or the corporation's position otherwise changes in reliance on the vote, and that any proceeding that is not brought promptly under the circumstances would normally be barred because of laches.

Similarly, section 7.24 does not address the liability of the proxy to the shareholder for exercising authority beyond that granted or for disobeying instructions. These matters are governed by the law of agency and not by section 7.24.

A corporation may wish to establish guidelines that it will follow in determining whether to accept a vote, ballot, consent, waiver, shareholder demand, or proxy appointment to provide consistency in the corporation's application of the general rules set forth in section 7.24.

§ 7.25. Quorum and Voting Requirements for Voting Groups

(a)   Shares entitled to vote as a separate voting group may take action on a matter at a meeting only if a quorum of those shares exists with respect to that matter. Unless the articles of incorporation provide otherwise, shares representing a majority of the votes entitled to be cast on the matter by the voting group constitutes a quorum of that voting group for action on that matter. Whenever this Act requires a particular quorum for a specified action, the articles of incorporation may not provide for a lower quorum.

(b)   Once a share is represented for any purpose at a meeting, it is deemed present for quorum purposes for the remainder of the meeting and for any adjournment of that meeting unless a new record date is or must be fixed for that adjourned meeting.

(c)   If a quorum exists, action on a matter (other than the election of directors) by a voting group is approved if the votes cast within the voting group favoring the action exceed the votes cast opposing the action, unless the articles of incorporation require a greater number of affirmative votes.

(d)   An amendment of the articles of incorporation adding, changing, or deleting a quorum or voting requirement for a voting group greater than specified in subsection (a) or (c) is governed by section 7.27.

(e)   The election of directors is governed by section 7.28.

(f)   Whenever a provision of this Act provides for voting of classes or series as separate voting groups, the rules provided in section 10.04(c) for amendments of the articles of incorporation apply to that provision.

Cross-References

Adjourned meeting record date, see § 7.07.

Election of directors, see § 7.28.

Multiple voting groups, see § 7.26.

Proxy voting, see § 7.22.

Record date, see § 7.07.

Remote participation in shareholders' meetings, see § 7.09.

Supermajority requirements, see § 7.27.

"Voting group" defined, see § 1.40.

Official Comment

Section 7.25 establishes general quorum and voting requirements for voting groups for purposes of the Act. As defined in section 1.40, a "voting group" consists of all shares of one or more classes or series that under the articles of incorporation or the Act are entitled to vote and be counted together collectively on a matter. Shares entitled to vote "generally" on a matter (that is, all shares entitled to vote on the matter by the articles of incorporation or the Act that do not expressly have the right to be counted separately) are a single voting group. On most matters coming before shareholders' meetings, only a single voting group, consisting of a class of voting shares, will be involved, and action on such a matter is effective when approved by that voting group pursuant to section 7.25. See section 7.26(a).

Section 7.25 covers quorum and voting requirements for all actions by the shareholders of a corporation with a single class of voting shares. It also covers quorum and voting requirements for a matter on which only a class or series of shares is entitled to vote under the articles of incorporation, for example, when a class with preferential rights may vote to elect directors because of a default in the payment of dividends (a vote which is often described as a "class vote"). Finally, section 7.25 also covers quorum and voting requirements for a matter on which both common and preferred shares or separate classes or series of common or preferred shares are entitled to vote, either together as a single voting group under the articles of incorporation or separately as two or more voting groups under either the articles of incorporation or the Act. See section 7.26(b).

1. Determination of Voting Groups under the Act

Under the Act, classes or series of shares are generally not entitled to vote separately by voting group except to the extent specifically authorized by the articles of incorporation. But sections 9.21, 9.32, 10.04, and 11.04 of the Act grant classes or series of shares the right to vote separately when fundamental changes are proposed that may adversely affect that class or series. Section 10.04(c) further provides that when two or more classes or series are affected by an amendment covered by section 10.04 in essentially the same way, the classes or series are grouped together and must vote as a single voting group rather than as multiple voting groups on the matter, unless otherwise provided in the articles of incorporation or required by the board of directors. Section 7.25(f) provides that the group voting rule of section 10.04(c), including the ability to vary that rule in the articles of incorporation or by action of the board of directors, also applies to the group voting provisions in sections 9.21, 9.32, and 11.04. Under the Act even a class or series of shares that is expressly described as nonvoting under the articles of incorporation may be entitled to vote separately on an amendment to the articles of incorporation that affects the class or series in a designated way. See section 10.04(d).

In addition to the provisions of the Act, separate voting by voting group may be authorized by the articles of incorporation (except that the statutory privilege of voting by separate voting groups cannot be diluted or reduced). On some matters, the board of directors may condition its submission of matters to shareholders on their approval by specific voting groups designated by the board of directors. Sections 7.25 and 7.26 establish the mechanics by which all voting by single or multiple voting groups is carried out.

In some situations, shares of a single class or series may be entitled to vote in two different voting groups. See the Official Comment to section 7.26.

2. Quorum and Voting Requirements in General

A corporation's determination of the voting groups entitled to vote, and the quorum and voting requirements applicable to that determination, should be determined separately for each matter coming before a meeting. As a result, different quorum and voting requirements may be applicable to different portions of a meeting, depending on the matter being considered. In the normal case where only a single voting group is entitled to vote on all matters coming before a meeting of shareholders, a single quorum and voting requirement will usually be applicable to the entire meeting. To reflect the possibility that shares may have multiple or fractional votes per share, the provisions relating to quorums are phrased in terms of votes represented by shares.

3.   Quorum Requirements for Action by Voting Group

Under Section 7.25(b), once a share is present at a meeting, it is deemed present for quorum purposes throughout the meeting. Thus, a voting group may continue to act despite the withdrawal of persons having the power to vote one or more shares.

The shares owned by a shareholder who comes to the meeting to object on grounds of lack of notice are considered present for purposes of determining the presence of a quorum. Similarly, shares owned by a shareholder who attends a meeting solely for purposes of raising the objection that a quorum is not present are considered present for purposes of determining the presence of a quorum. Attendance at a meeting, however, does not constitute a waiver of other objections to the meeting such as the lack of notice. Such waivers are governed by section 7.06(b).

If a new record date is set, new notice must be given to holders of shares of a voting group and a quorum must be established from within the holders of shares of that voting group as of the new record date.

4.   Voting Requirements for Approval by Voting Group

Section 7.25(c) provides that an action (other than the election of directors, which is governed by section 7.28) is approved by a voting group at a meeting at which a quorum is present if the votes cast in favor of the action exceed the votes cast opposing the action, unless the articles of incorporation require a greater number of votes. This default rule differs from a formulation appearing in some state statutes that an action is approved at a meeting at which a quorum is present if it receives the affirmative vote of a majority of the shares represented at that meeting. That formulation in effect treats abstentions as negative votes; the Act treats them truly as abstentions. For example, if a corporation (that has not, through the articles of incorporation, modified quorum and voting requirements) has 1,000 shares of a single class outstanding, each share entitled to cast one vote, a quorum consists of 501 shares; if 600 shares are represented at the meeting and the vote on a proposed action is 280 in favor, 225 opposed, and 95 abstaining, the action would not be approved in a state following the formulation that treats abstentions as negative votes because fewer than a majority of the 600 shares attending voted in favor of the action. Under section 7.25(c) the action would be approved and not be defeated by the 95 abstaining votes.

5.   Modification of Standard Requirements

The articles of incorporation may modify the quorum and voting requirements of section 7.25 for a single voting group or for all voting groups entitled to vote on any matter. The articles of incorporation may increase the quorum and voting requirements to any extent desired up to and including unanimity, subject to section 7.27. They may also require that shares of different classes or series are entitled to vote separately or together on specific issues or provide that actions are approved only if they receive the favorable vote of a majority of the shares of a voting group present at a meeting at which a quorum is present. The articles may also decrease the quorum requirement as desired, subject to section 7.25(a) and section 7.27.

§ 7.26. Action by Single and Multiple Voting Groups

(a)   If the articles of incorporation or this Act provide for voting by a single voting group on a matter, action on that matter is taken when voted upon by that voting group as provided in section 7.25.

(b)   If the articles of incorporation or this Act provide for voting by two or more voting groups on a matter, action on that matter is taken only when voted upon by each of those voting groups counted separately as provided in section 7.25. Action may be taken by different voting groups on a matter at different times.

Cross-References

Change of voting group requirements, see § 7.27.

Number of votes per share, see § 7.21.

Quorum and voting requirements, see § 7.25.

Supermajority requirements, see § 7.27.

Voting by voting groups on amendments of articles of incorporation, see § 10.04.

"Voting group" defined, see § 1.40.

Official Comment

Section 7.26(a) provides that when a matter is to be voted upon by a single voting group, action is taken when the voting group votes upon the action as provided in section 7.25. In most instances, a single voting group will consist of all the shares of the class or classes or series entitled to vote by the articles of incorporation. Voting by two or more voting groups as contemplated by section 7.26(b) is the exceptional case.

Implicit in section 7.26(b) are the concepts that (i) different quorum and voting requirements may be applicable to different matters considered at a single meeting and (ii) different quorum and voting requirements may be applicable to different voting groups voting on the same matter. See the Official Comment to section 7.25. Each group entitled to vote must independently meet the quorum and voting requirements established by section 7.25. If a quorum is present for one or more voting groups but not for all voting groups, section 7.26(b) provides that the voting groups for which a quorum is present may vote upon the matter, even though their vote alone will not be sufficient for the matter to be approved.

A single meeting, furthermore, may consider matters on which action by several voting groups is required and also matters on which only a single voting group may act. Action may be taken on the matters on which the single voting group may act even though no quorum is present to take action on other matters. For example, in a corporation with one class of nonvoting shares with preferential rights ("preferred shares") and one class of general voting shares without preferential rights ("common shares"), a matter to be considered at the annual meeting might be a proposed amendment to the articles of incorporation that reduces the cumulative dividend right of the preferred shares (a matter on which the preferred shares have a statutory right to vote as a separate voting group). Other matters to be considered might include the election of directors and the ratification of the appointment of an auditor, both matters on which the preferred shares may have no vote. If a quorum of the voting group consisting of the common shares but no quorum of the voting group consisting of the preferred shares is present, the common shares may proceed to elect directors and ratify the appointment of the auditor. The common shares voting group may also vote to approve the proposed amendment to the articles of incorporation, but that amendment will not be approved until the preferred shares voting group also votes to approve the amendment, which could occur at a different time.

Normally, each class or series of shares will participate in only a single voting group. But because holders of shares entitled by the articles of incorporation to vote generally on a matter are always entitled to vote in the voting group consisting of the general voting shares, in some instances classes or series of shares may be entitled to be counted in two voting groups. This will occur whenever a class or series of shares entitled to vote generally on a matter under the articles of incorporation is affected by the matter in a way that gives rise to the right to have its vote counted separately as an independent voting group under the Act. For example, assume that corporation Y has outstanding one class of common shares, 500 shares issued and outstanding, and one class of preferred shares, 100 shares issued and outstanding, that also have full voting rights under the articles of incorporation, *i.e.*, the preferred may vote for election of directors and on all other matters on which common may vote. The preferred and the common therefore are part of the general voting group. The directors propose to amend the articles of incorporation to change the preferential dividend rights of the preferred from cumulative to noncumulative. All shares are present at the meeting and they divide as follows on the proposal to adopt the amendment.

Yes	Common	230
	Preferred	80
No	Common	270
	Preferred	20

Both the preferred and the common are entitled to vote on the amendment to the articles of incorporation because they are part of a general voting group pursuant to the articles. But the vote of the preferred is also entitled to be counted separately on the proposal by section 10.04(a)(3). The result is that the proposal passes by a vote of 310 to 290 in the voting group consisting of the shares entitled to vote generally and 80 to 20 in the voting group consisting solely of the preferred shares.

In this situation, in the absence of a special quorum requirement, a meeting could approve the proposal to amend the articles of incorporation if—and only if—a quorum of each voting group is present, *i.e.*, at least 51 shares of preferred and 301 shares of common and preferred were represented at the meeting.

§ 7.27. Modifying Quorum or Voting Requirements

An amendment to the articles of incorporation that adds, changes, or deletes a quorum or voting requirement shall meet the same quorum requirement and be adopted by the same vote and voting groups required to take action under the quorum and voting requirements then in effect or proposed to be adopted, whichever is greater.

Cross-References

Amendment of articles of incorporation, see ch. 10A.

Quorum and voting requirements, see § 7.25.

Voting by voting group, see § 7.26.

"Voting group" defined, see § 1.40.

Official Comment

Section 7.27 permits the articles of incorporation to change the quorum or voting requirements for approval of an action by shareholders up to any desired amount so long as the change is adopted in accordance with the requirements of section 7.27. For example, a supermajority provision that requires an 80% affirmative vote of all eligible votes of a voting group present at the meeting may not be removed from the articles of incorporation or reduced in any way except by an 80% affirmative vote. If the 80% requirement is coupled with a quorum requirement for a voting group that shares representing two-thirds of the total votes must be present in person or by proxy, both the 80% voting requirement and the two-thirds quorum requirement are immune from reduction except at a meeting of the voting group at which the two-thirds quorum requirement is met and the reduction is approved by an 80% affirmative vote. If the proposal is to increase the 80% voting requirement to 90%, that proposal must be approved by a 90% affirmative vote at a meeting of the voting group at which the two-thirds quorum requirement is met; if the proposal is to increase the two-thirds quorum requirement to three-quarters without changing the 80% voting requirement, that proposal must be approved by an 80% affirmative vote at a meeting of the voting group at which a three-quarters quorum requirement is met.

§ 7.28. Voting for Directors; Cumulative Voting

(a) Unless otherwise provided in the articles of incorporation, directors are elected by a plurality of the votes cast by the shares entitled to vote in the election at a meeting at which a quorum is present.

(b) Shareholders do not have a right to cumulate their votes for directors unless the articles of incorporation so provide.

(c) A statement included in the articles of incorporation that "[all] [a designated voting group of] shareholders are entitled to cumulate their votes for directors" (or words of similar import) means that the shareholders designated are entitled to multiply the number of votes they are entitled to cast by the number of directors for whom they are entitled to vote and cast the product for a single candidate or distribute the product among two or more candidates.

(d) Shares otherwise entitled to vote cumulatively may not be voted cumulatively at a particular meeting unless:

(1) the meeting notice or proxy statement accompanying the notice states conspicuously that cumulative voting is authorized; or

(2)   a shareholder who has the right to cumulate the shareholder's votes gives notice to the corporation not less than 48 hours before the time set for the meeting of the shareholder's intent to cumulate votes during the meeting, and if one shareholder gives this notice all other shareholders in the same voting group participating in the election are entitled to cumulate their votes without giving further notice.

Cross-References

"Conspicuous" defined, see § 1.40.

Notice of meeting, see § 7.05.

Notices and other communications, see § 1.41.

Proxies, see § 7.22.

Quorum of shareholders, see § 7.25.

Voting for directors by voting group, see § 8.04.

"Voting group" defined, see § 1.40.

Official Comment

As used in section 7.28(a), election by a "plurality" means that the individuals with the largest number of votes are elected as directors up to the maximum number of directors to be chosen at the election. In elections in which several factions are competing within a voting group, an individual may be elected with votes of fewer than a majority of the votes cast. The articles of incorporation of the corporation may, however, provide a different vote requirement for the election of directors and the bylaws may also do so to the extent provided in section 10.22.

The entire board of directors may be elected by a single voting group or the articles of incorporation may provide that different voting groups are entitled to elect a designated number or fraction of the board of directors. See section 8.04. Elections are contested only within specific voting groups.

Under section 7.28(b), each corporation may determine whether to elect its directors by cumulative voting. If directors are elected by different voting groups, the articles of incorporation may provide that specified voting groups are entitled to vote cumulatively while others are not. Cumulative voting affects the manner in which votes may be cast by shares participating in the election but does not affect the plurality principle set forth in section 7.28(a).

If a corporation has determined to elect directors by cumulative voting, such directors may not be elected by written consent unless that consent is unanimous. See section 7.04(b).

Section 7.28(c) describes the mechanics of cumulative voting. By casting all of the shareholder's votes for a single candidate or a limited number of candidates, a minority shareholder's voting power with respect to a given candidate can be increased, and such shareholder may be able to elect one or more directors.

Section 7.28(d), which applies only if cumulative voting is potentially available under section 7.28(b), covers a notice designed to ensure that all shareholders participating in the election understand the rules and to avoid the distortions that may be created when some shareholders vote cumulatively while others do not. Cumulative voting will be employed if the notice of meeting or accompanying proxy statement conspicuously announces that a shareholder is entitled to cumulate votes or a shareholder who is entitled to vote gives notice to the corporation of such shareholder's intent to do so at least 48 hours before the meeting. If this notice is given by any shareholder, all other shareholders who are part of the same voting group are entitled to vote cumulatively without giving further notice.

§ 7.29. Inspectors of Election

(a)   A corporation that has a class of equity securities registered pursuant to section 12 of the Securities Exchange Act of 1934 shall, and any other corporation may, appoint one or more inspectors to act at a meeting of shareholders in connection with determining voting results. Each inspector shall verify in writing that the inspector will faithfully execute the duties of inspector with strict impartiality and according to the best of the inspector's ability. An inspector may be an officer or employee of the corporation. The inspectors may appoint or retain other persons to assist the inspectors in the performance of the duties of inspector under subsection (b), and may rely on information provided by such persons and other persons, including those appointed to tabulate votes, unless the inspectors believe reliance is unwarranted.

(b)   The inspectors shall:

     (1)   ascertain the number of shares outstanding and the voting power of each;

     (2)   determine the shares represented at a meeting;

     (3)   determine the validity of proxy appointments and ballots;

     (4)   count the votes; and

     (5)   make a written report of the results.

(c)   In performing their duties, the inspectors may examine (i) the proxy appointment forms and any other information provided in accordance with section 7.22(b), (ii) any envelope or related writing submitted with those appointment forms, (iii) any ballots, (iv) any evidence or other information specified in section 7.24 and (v) the relevant books and records of the corporation relating to its shareholders and their entitlement to vote, including any securities position list provided by a depository clearing agency.

(d)   The inspectors also may consider other information that they believe is relevant and reliable for the purpose of performing any of the duties assigned to them pursuant to subsection (b), including for the purpose of evaluating inconsistent, incomplete or erroneous information and reconciling information submitted on behalf of banks, brokers, their nominees or similar persons that indicates more votes being cast than a proxy authorized by the record shareholder is entitled to cast. If the inspectors consider other information allowed by this subsection, they shall in their report under subsection (b) specify the information considered by them, including the purpose or purposes for which the information was considered, the person or persons from whom they obtained the information, when the information was obtained, the means by which the information was obtained, and the basis for the inspectors' belief that such information is relevant and reliable.

(e)   Determinations of law by the inspectors of election are subject to de novo review by a court in a proceeding under section 7.49 or other judicial proceeding.

Cross-References

     Officers, see § 8.40.

     Proxies, see § 7.22.

Official Comment

"Street name" holdings, the use of a securities depository system and the involvement of intermediaries complicate the vote counting process. See Official Comment to section 7.23. This complexity limits the role of inspectors of election in the case of corporations subject to the federal proxy rules. Such inspectors have a limited role because federal law requires multiple steps to be taken by various parties before shares are voted. The inspectors may not have access to information pertaining to each of those steps or from each of the parties involved in the process, such as the voting instruction forms given by beneficial shareholders that lead to voting by the record shareholders. For these reasons, section 7.29 generally permits inspectors to rely on information provided by others.

The selection of inspectors of election should usually be made by responsible officers or by the directors, as authorized either generally or specifically in the corporation's bylaws. Alternate inspectors could also be designated to replace any inspector who is unable or fails to act. The requirement of a written report is to facilitate judicial review of determinations made by inspectors. The ability of inspectors to retain other persons to assist them does not limit the ability of the corporation also to appoint others, such as a vote tabulator to assist in the vote counting process.

In the case of corporations subject to the federal proxy rules, inspectors should generally be independent persons who are neither employees nor officers if there is a contested matter to be considered. The use of independent inspectors in these circumstances enhances shareholder perception of the fairness of the voting process, and the report of independent inspectors can be expected to be given greater evidentiary weight by any court reviewing a contested vote.

To determine the validity of proxy appointments and ballots, depending on the issues presented, the inspectors of election may be required to determine whether appointment forms have been validly executed by the record shareholder, to identify the latest executed appointment form and to determine whether the proxy cast more votes than the record shareholder was entitled to cast. The inspectors are expected to apply the provisions of chapter 7 regarding acceptance of proxy appointments and voting, including those in sections 7.08(d), 7.22(h), and 7.24. In the event of a challenge of any determination by the inspectors in a court of competent jurisdiction, including in a proceeding under section 7.49, the court should give such weight to determinations of fact by the inspectors as it deems appropriate, taking into account the relationship of the inspectors, if any, to the management of the company and other persons interested in the outcome of the vote, the evidence available to inspectors, whether their determinations appear to be consistent and reasonable, and such other circumstances as the court regards as relevant. As provided in section 7.29(e), the court may review de novo all determinations of law made by the inspectors.

Section 7.29(d) gives the inspectors broad discretion with respect to the information they may consider but does not require that they take any specific action with respect to such information other than to specify in their report the information they considered and the other details listed in section 7.29(d).

SUBCHAPTER C
VOTING TRUSTS AND AGREEMENTS

§ 7.30. Voting Trusts

(a) One or more shareholders may create a voting trust, conferring on a trustee the right to vote or otherwise act for them, by signing an agreement setting out the provisions of the trust (which may include anything consistent with its purpose) and transferring their shares to the trustee. When a voting trust agreement is signed, the trustee shall prepare a list of the names and addresses of all voting trust beneficial owners, together with the number and class of shares each transferred to the trust, and deliver copies of the list and agreement to the corporation at its principal office.

(b) A voting trust becomes effective on the date the first shares subject to the trust are registered in the trustee's name.

(c) Limits, if any, on the duration of a voting trust shall be as set forth in the voting trust. A voting trust that became effective when this Act provided a 10-year limit on its duration remains governed by the provisions of this section concerning duration then in effect, unless the voting trust is amended to provide otherwise by unanimous agreement of the parties to the voting trust.

Cross-References

Delivery to corporation, see § 1.41.

Inspection of shareholder lists, see § 7.20 and ch. 16A.

"Principal office":

> defined, see § 1.40.

> designated in annual report, see § 16.21.

"Shareholder" defined, see § 1.40.

Shares held by nominees, see § 7.23.

"Sign" defined, see § 1.40.

Voting agreements, see § 7.31.

"Voting trust beneficial owner" defined, see § 1.40.

Official Comment

A voting trust is a device by which one or more shareholders divorce the voting rights of their shares from the ownership, retaining the latter but transferring the former to one or more trustees in whom the voting rights of all the shareholders who are parties to the trust are pooled. Section 7.30(a) provides a straightforward procedure for the creation of an enforceable voting trust and does not impose narrow or technical requirements. Typically, the voting trust provides that all attributes of beneficial ownership other than the power to vote are retained by the voting trust beneficial owners. In addition, the voting trustees may issue to the voting trust beneficial owners voting trust certificates which may be transferable in the same way as shares. Section 7.30 does not limit the duration of a voting trust, consistent with section 7.32 governing shareholder agreements generally. Section 7.30 permits participants to specify limits but does not establish an automatic sunset provision as a matter of law. Section 7.30(c) addresses voting trusts entered into when the Act limited their duration to 10 years.

§ 7.31. Voting Agreements

(a)   Two or more shareholders may provide for the manner in which they will vote their shares by signing an agreement for that purpose. A voting agreement created under this section is not subject to the provisions of section 7.30.

(b)   A voting agreement created under this section is specifically enforceable.

Cross-References

Irrevocable proxies, see § 7.22.

"Sign" defined, see § 1.40.

Voting trust, see § 7.30.

Official Comment

Section 7.31(a) explicitly recognizes agreements among two or more shareholders as to the voting of shares and makes clear that these agreements are not subject to the rules relating to a voting trust. The only formal requirements are that they be in writing and signed by all the participating shareholders. In other respects their validity is to be judged like any other contract.

A voting agreement may provide its own enforcement mechanism, as by the appointment of a proxy to vote all shares subject to the agreement; the appointment may be made irrevocable under section 7.22. If no enforcement mechanism is provided, a court may order specific enforcement of the agreement and order the votes cast as the agreement contemplates. Section 7.31(b) recognizes that damages are not likely to be an appropriate remedy for breach of a voting agreement.

§ 7.32. Shareholder Agreements

(a)   An agreement among the shareholders of a corporation that complies with this section is effective among the shareholders and the corporation even though it is inconsistent with one or more other provisions of this Act in that it:

(1)   eliminates the board of directors or restricts the discretion or powers of the board of directors;

(2)   governs the authorization or making of distributions, regardless of whether they are in proportion to ownership of shares, subject to the limitations in section 6.40;

(3)   establishes who shall be directors or officers of the corporation, or their terms of office or manner of selection or removal;

(4)   governs, in general or in regard to specific matters, the exercise or division of voting power by or between the shareholders and directors or by or among any of them, including use of weighted voting rights or director proxies;

(5) establishes the terms and conditions of any agreement for the transfer or use of property or the provision of services between the corporation and any shareholder, director, officer or employee of the corporation or among any of them;

(6) transfers to one or more shareholders or other persons all or part of the authority to exercise the corporate powers or to manage the business and affairs of the corporation, including the resolution of any issue about which there exists a deadlock among directors or shareholders;

(7) requires dissolution of the corporation at the request of one or more of the shareholders or upon the occurrence of a specified event or contingency; or

(8) otherwise governs the exercise of the corporate powers or the management of the business and affairs of the corporation or the relationship among the shareholders, the directors and the corporation, or among any of them, and is not contrary to public policy.

(b) An agreement authorized by this section shall be:

(1) as set forth (i) in the articles of incorporation or bylaws and approved by all persons who are shareholders at the time of the agreement, or (ii) in a written agreement that is signed by all persons who are shareholders at the time of the agreement and is made known to the corporation; and

(2) subject to amendment only by all persons who are shareholders at the time of the amendment, unless the agreement provides otherwise.

(c) The existence of an agreement authorized by this section shall be noted conspicuously on the front or back of each certificate for outstanding shares or on the information statement required by section 6.26(b). If at the time of the agreement the corporation has shares outstanding represented by certificates, the corporation shall recall the outstanding certificates and issue substitute certificates that comply with this subsection. The failure to note the existence of the agreement on the certificate or information statement shall not affect the validity of the agreement or any action taken pursuant to it. Any purchaser of shares who, at the time of purchase, did not have knowledge of the existence of the agreement shall be entitled to rescission of the purchase. A purchaser shall be deemed to have knowledge of the existence of the agreement if its existence is noted on the certificate or information statement for the shares in compliance with this subsection and, if the shares are not represented by a certificate, the information statement is delivered to the purchaser at or before the time of purchase of the shares. An action to enforce the right of rescission authorized by this subsection shall be commenced within the earlier of 90 days after discovery of the existence of the agreement or two years after the time of purchase of the shares.

(d) If the agreement ceases to be effective for any reason, the board of directors may, if the agreement is contained or referred to in the corporation's articles of incorporation or bylaws, adopt an amendment to the articles of incorporation or bylaws, without shareholder action, to delete the agreement and any references to it.

(e) An agreement authorized by this section that limits the discretion or powers of the board of directors shall relieve the directors of, and impose upon the person or persons in whom such discretion or powers are vested, liability for acts or omissions imposed by law on directors to the extent that the discretion or powers of the directors are limited by the agreement.

(f) The existence or performance of an agreement authorized by this section shall not be a ground for imposing personal liability on any shareholder for the acts or debts of the corporation even if the agreement or its performance treats the corporation as if it were a partnership or results in failure to observe the corporate formalities otherwise applicable to the matters governed by the agreement.

(g) Incorporators or subscribers for shares may act as shareholders with respect to an agreement authorized by this section if no shares have been issued when the agreement is made.

(h) Limits, if any, on the duration of an agreement authorized by this section must be set forth in the agreement. An agreement that became effective when this Act provided for a 10-year limit on duration of shareholder agreements, unless the agreement provided otherwise, remains governed by the provisions of this section concerning duration then in effect.

Cross-Reference

Certificateless shares, see § 6.26.

Certificates for shares, see § 6.25.

"Conspicuous" defined, see § 1.40.

Standards of conduct for directors, see § 8.30.

Official Comment

Shareholders of some corporations, especially those that are closely held, frequently enter into agreements that govern the operation of the enterprise.

Section 7.32 provides, within the context of the traditional corporate structure, legal certainty to such agreements that embody various aspects of the business arrangement established by the shareholders to meet their business and personal needs. The subject matter of these arrangements includes governance of the entity, allocation of the economic return from the business, and other aspects of the relationships among shareholders, directors, and the corporation which are part of the business arrangement. Section 7.32 also recognizes that many of the corporate norms contained in the Act were designed with an eye towards corporations whose management and share ownership are distinct. These functions are often conjoined in some corporations, such as the close corporation. Thus, section 7.32 validates agreements among shareholders even when the agreements are inconsistent with the statutory norms contained in the Act.

Importantly, section 7.32 only addresses the parties to the shareholder agreement, their transferees, and the corporation, and does not have any binding legal effect on the state, creditors, or other third persons.

Section 7.32 supplements the other provisions of the Act. If an agreement is not in conflict with another section of the Act, no resort need be made to section 7.32 with its requirement of unanimity. For example, special provisions may be included in the articles of incorporation or bylaws with less than unanimous shareholder agreement so long as such provisions are not in conflict with other provisions of the Act. Similarly, section 7.32 would not have to be relied upon to validate typical buy-sell agreements among two or more shareholders or the covenants and other terms of a stock purchase agreement entered into in connection with the issuance of shares by a corporation.

1. Section 7.32(a)

An agreement authorized by section 7.32 is "not inconsistent with law" within the meaning of sections 2.02(b)(2) and 2.06(b) of the Act.

The range of agreements validated by section 7.32(a) is expansive though not unlimited. Section 7.32 defines the types of agreements that can be validated largely by illustration. The seven specific categories that are listed are designed to cover some of the most frequently used arrangements. There are numerous other arrangements that may be made, and section 7.32(a)(8) provides an additional category for any provisions that, in a manner inconsistent with any other provision of the Act, otherwise govern the exercise of the corporate powers or the management of the business and affairs of the corporation or the relationship between and among the shareholders, the directors, and the corporation or any of them, and are not contrary to public policy.

Section 7.32(a) validates virtually all types of shareholder agreements that, in practice, normally concern shareholders and their advisors. Given that breadth, any provision that may be contained in the articles of incorporation with a majority vote under sections 2.02(b)(2)(ii) and (iii), as well as under section 2.02(b)(4), may also be effective if contained in a shareholder agreement that complies with section 7.32.

The provisions of a shareholder agreement authorized by section 7.32(a) will often, in operation, conflict with the language of more than one section of the Act, and courts should in such cases construe all related sections of the Act flexibly and in a manner consistent with the underlying intent of the shareholder agreement. Thus, for example, in the case of an agreement that provides for weighted voting by directors, every reference in the Act to a majority or other proportion of directors should be construed to refer to a majority or other proportion of the votes of the directors.

Although the limits of section 7.32(a)(8) are left uncertain, there are provisions of the Act that may not be overridden if they reflect core principles of public policy with respect to corporate affairs. For example, a provision of a shareholder agreement that purports to eliminate all of the standards of conduct established under section 8.30 might be viewed as contrary to public policy and thus not validated under section 7.32(a)(8). Similarly, a provision that exculpates directors from liability more broadly than permitted by section 2.02(b)(4), or indemnifies them more broadly than permitted by section 2.02(b)(5), might not be validated under section 7.32 because of strong public policy reasons for the statutory limitations on the right to exculpate directors from liability and to indemnify them. The validity of some provisions may depend upon the circumstances. For example, a provision of a shareholder agreement that limited inspection rights under section 16.02 or the right to financial statements under section 16.20 might, as a general matter, be valid, but that provision might not be given effect if it prevented shareholders from obtaining information necessary to determine whether directors of the corporation have satisfied the standards of conduct under section 8.30. The foregoing are examples and are not intended to be exclusive.

As noted above, shareholder agreements otherwise validated by section 7.32 are not legally binding on the state, on creditors, or on other third parties. For example, an agreement that dispenses with the need to make corporate filings required by the Act would be ineffective. Similarly, an agreement among shareholders that provides that only the president has authority to enter into contracts for the corporation would not, without more, be binding against third parties, and ordinary principles of agency, including the concept of apparent authority, would continue to apply.

2.　*Section 7.32(b)*

Section 7.32 minimizes the formal requirements for a shareholder agreement so as not to restrict unduly the shareholders' ability to take advantage of the flexibility the section provides. Thus, it is not necessary to "opt in" to a special class of close corporations to obtain the benefits of section 7.32. An agreement can be validated under section 7.32 whether it is set forth in the articles of incorporation, the bylaws or in a separate agreement, and regardless of whether section 7.32 is specifically referenced in the agreement. Where the corporation has a single shareholder, the requirement of an "agreement among the shareholders" is satisfied by the unilateral action of the shareholder in establishing the terms of the agreement, evidenced by provisions in the articles of incorporation or bylaws, or in a writing signed by the sole shareholder. Although a writing signed by all the shareholders is not required where the agreement is contained in articles of incorporation or bylaws unanimously approved, it may be desirable to have all the shareholders actually sign the instrument to establish unequivocally their agreement. Similarly, although transferees are bound by a valid shareholder agreement, subject to section 7.32(c), it may be desirable to obtain the affirmative written assent of the transferee at the time of the transfer. Section 7.32(b) also establishes and permits amendments by less than unanimous agreement if the shareholder agreement so provides.

Section 7.32(b) requires unanimous shareholder approval of the shareholder agreement regardless of entitlement to vote. Unanimity is required because an agreement authorized by section 7.32 can effect material organic changes in the corporation's operation and structure, and in the rights and obligations of shareholders.

The requirement that the shareholder agreement be made known to the corporation is the predicate for the requirement in section 7.32(c) that share certificates or information statements be legended to note the existence of the agreement. No specific form of notification is required and the agreement need not be filed with the corporation. In the case of shareholder agreements in the articles of incorporation or bylaws, the corporation will necessarily have notice. In the case of a shareholder agreement outside the articles of incorporation or bylaws, the requirement of signatures by all of the shareholders should in virtually all cases be sufficient to make the corporation aware of the agreement, as one or more signatories will normally also be a director or an officer.

3.   Section 7.32(c)

Section 7.32(c) addresses the effect of a shareholder agreement on subsequent purchasers or transferees of shares. Typically, corporations with shareholder agreements also have restrictions on the transferability of the shares as authorized by section 6.27, thus lessening the practical effects of the problem in the context of voluntary transferees. Transferees of shares without knowledge of the agreement or those acquiring shares upon the death of an original participant in a close corporation may, however, be heavily affected. Weighing the burdens on transferees against the burdens on the remaining shareholders in the enterprise, section 7.32(c) affirms the continued validity of the shareholder agreement on all transferees, whether by purchase, gift, operation of law, or otherwise. Unlike restrictions on transfer, it may be impossible to enforce a shareholder agreement against less than all of the shareholders. Thus, under section 7.32, one who inherits shares subject to a shareholder agreement must continue to abide by the agreement. If that is not the desired result, care must be exercised at the initiation of the shareholder agreement to ensure a different outcome, such as providing for a buy-back upon death.

Where shares are transferred to a purchaser without knowledge of a shareholder agreement, the validity of the agreement is similarly unaffected, but the purchaser is afforded a rescission remedy against the seller. Under section 7.32(c), the time at which notice to a purchaser is relevant for purposes of determining entitlement to rescission is the time when a purchaser acquires the shares rather than when a commitment is made to acquire the shares. If the purchaser learns of the agreement after committing to purchase but before acquiring the shares, the purchaser may not proceed with the purchase and still obtain the benefit of the remedies in section 7.32(c). Under contract principles and the securities laws, a failure to disclose the existence of a shareholder agreement may constitute the omission of a material fact and may excuse performance of the commitment to purchase. The term "purchaser" includes a person acquiring shares upon initial issue or by transfer, and also includes a pledgee, for whom the time of purchase is the time the shares are pledged.

Section 7.32 addresses the underlying rights of shares and shareholders and the validity of shareholder action which redefines those rights, as contrasted with questions regarding entitlement to ownership of the security, competing ownership claims, and disclosure issues. Consistent with this dichotomy, the rights and remedies available to purchasers under section 7.32(c) are independent of those provided by contract law, Article 8 of the Uniform Commercial Code, the securities laws, and other laws outside the Act.

With respect to the related subject of restrictions on transferability of shares, note that section 7.32 does not directly address or validate such restrictions, which are governed instead by section 6.27 of the Act. However, if such restrictions are adopted as a part of a shareholder agreement that complies with the requirements of section 7.32, a court should apply the concept of reasonableness under section 6.27 in determining the validity of such restrictions.

Section 7.32(c) contains an affirmative requirement that the share certificate or information statement for the shares be legended to note the existence of a shareholder agreement. No specified form of legend is required, and a simple statement that "[t]he shares represented by this certificate are subject to a shareholder agreement" is sufficient. At that point, a purchaser must obtain a copy of the shareholder agreement from the transferor or proceed at the purchaser's peril. In the event a corporation fails to legend share certificates or information statements, a court may, in an appropriate case, imply a cause of action against the corporation in favor of an injured purchaser without knowledge of a shareholder agreement. The circumstances under which such a remedy would be implied, the proper measure of damages, and other attributes of and limitations on such an implied remedy are left to development in the courts.

A purchaser who has no actual knowledge of a shareholder agreement and is not charged with knowledge by virtue of a legend on the certificate or information statement has a rescission remedy against the transferor (which would be the corporation in the case of a new issue of shares).

If the shares are certificated and duly legended, a purchaser is charged with notice of the shareholder agreement even if the purchaser never saw the certificate. In the case of uncertificated shares, however, the purchaser is not charged with notice of the shareholder agreement unless a duly-legended information statement is delivered to the purchaser at or before the time of purchase. This different rule for uncertificated shares is intended to provide an additional safeguard to protect innocent purchasers, and is necessary because section 6.26(b) of the Act and Article 8 of the Uniform Commercial Code permit delivery of statements after a transfer of shares.

4. Section 7.32(d)

Section 7.32(d) recognizes that the terms of a shareholder agreement may provide for its termination upon the happening of a specified event or condition. An example may be when the corporation undergoes an initial public offering. This approach is consistent with the broad freedom of contract provided to participants in such enterprises.

5. Sections 7.32(e) through (g)

Section 7.32(e) provides a shift of liability from the directors to any person or persons in whom the discretion or powers otherwise exercised by the board of directors are vested under the shareholder agreement. A shareholder agreement which provides for such a shift of responsibility, with the concomitant shift of liability provided by subsection (e), could also provide for exculpation from that liability to the extent otherwise authorized by the Act. The transfer of liability provided by subsection (e) covers liabilities imposed on directors "by law," which is intended to include liabilities arising under the Act, the common law, and statutory law outside the Act.

Section 7.32(f) provides that shareholders shall not have personal liability for the debts of a corporation arising out of acts or omissions taken pursuant to a shareholder agreement validated by section 7.32. Section 7.32(g) authorizes shareholder agreements for corporations that are in the process of being organized and do not yet have shareholders.

6. Section 7.32(h)

Section 7.32 does not limit the duration of a shareholder agreement. This approach is consistent with the wide freedom of contract provided to participants in such enterprises. For agreements entered into during a time that section 7.32 provided for a 10-year term if no other time limit was specified, section 7.32(h) provides that its duration will be governed by the provisions of section 7.32 concerning duration in force at the time the agreement became effective. This would include, for example, both the default termination rule and the authority under former section 7.32(b)(2) that such an agreement's automatic 10-year term could be amended by all shareholders (unless the agreement had prohibited such amendment).

SUBCHAPTER D
DERIVATIVE PROCEEDINGS

§ 7.40. Subchapter Definitions

In this subchapter:

"Derivative proceeding" means a civil suit in the right of a domestic corporation or, to the extent provided in section 7.47, in the right of a foreign corporation.

"Shareholder" means a record shareholder, a beneficial shareholder, and an unrestricted voting trust beneficial owner.

Cross-References

"Beneficial shareholder," "record shareholder" and "unrestricted voting trust beneficial owner" defined, see § 1.40.

Shares held by nominees, see § 7.23.

Voting trusts, see § 7.30.

Official Comment

The definition of "shareholder," for purposes of chapter 7D, extends the right to bring a derivative proceeding to a beneficial shareholder and an unrestricted voting trust beneficial owner. The inclusion of beneficial shareholder and unrestricted voting trust beneficial owner recognizes that these persons have or hold on behalf of others an economic interest in the shares.

§ 7.41. Standing

A shareholder may not commence or maintain a derivative proceeding unless the shareholder (i) was a shareholder of the corporation at the time of the act or omission complained of or became a shareholder through transfer by operation of law from one who was a shareholder at that time and (ii) fairly and adequately represents the interests of the corporation in enforcing the right of the corporation.

Cross-References

"Derivative proceeding" defined, see § 7.40.

"Shareholder" defined, see § 7.40.

Official Comment

Section 7.41 requires (i) the plaintiff to be a shareholder and therefore does not permit, for example, creditors or holders of options, warrants, or conversion rights to commence a derivative proceeding, and (ii) that the plaintiff fairly and adequately represent the interests of *the corporation,* rather than *shareholders similarly situated* as provided in some rules of procedure, because the reference to the corporation more clearly reflects the nature of the derivative suit.

The introductory language of section 7.41 refers both to the commencement and maintenance of the proceeding to make it clear that the proceeding should be dismissed if, after commencement, the plaintiff ceases to be a shareholder or a fair and adequate representative. The latter would occur, for example, if the plaintiff were using the proceeding for personal advantage. If a plaintiff no longer has standing, courts have in a number of instances provided an opportunity for one or more other shareholders to intervene.

§ 7.42. Demand

No shareholder may commence a derivative proceeding until (i) a written demand has been made upon the corporation to take suitable action and (ii) 90 days have expired from the date delivery of the demand was made unless the shareholder has earlier been notified that the demand has been rejected by the corporation or unless irreparable injury to the corporation would result by waiting for the expiration of the 90-day period.

Cross-References

"Deliver" defined, see § 1.40.

"Derivative proceeding" defined, see § 7.40.

Notices and other communications, see § 1.41.

"Shareholder" defined, see § 7.40.

Official Comment

Section 7.42 requires a written demand for two reasons. First, even though no director may be "qualified" (see section 1.43), the demand will give the corporation the opportunity to re-examine the act complained of in the light of a potential lawsuit and take corrective action. Second, the provision eliminates the time and expense of litigating whether demand is required. Requiring a demand in all cases does not impose an onerous burden given the relatively short waiting period and that this period may be shortened if irreparable injury to the corporation would result by waiting for the expiration of the 90-day period.

1. Form of Demand

Section 7.42 specifies only that the demand shall be in writing. Detailed pleading is not required given that the corporation can contact the shareholder for clarification if there are any questions, and cases have noted that a demand which sets forth the facts concerning share ownership and is sufficiently specific should apprise the corporation of the action sought to be taken and the grounds for that action so that the demand can be evaluated.

2.   Upon Whom Demand Should Be Made

To ensure that the demand reaches the appropriate person for review, it should be addressed to the board of directors, chief executive officer, or secretary at the corporation's principal office. In most cases the board of directors will be the appropriate body to review the demand but there may be instances, such as a decision to sue a third party for an injury to the corporation, in which the taking of, or refusal to take, action would fall within the authority of an officer of the corporation.

3.   The 90-Day Period

The 90-day period in section 7.42 was chosen as a reasonable time within which the board of directors can meet, conduct the necessary inquiry into the charges, receive the results of the inquiry and make its decision. A fixed time period also eliminates litigation over what is or is not a reasonable time. If additional time is needed, the corporation may request counsel for the shareholder to delay filing suit until the inquiry has been completed or, if suit is commenced, the corporation can apply to the court for a stay under section 7.43.

Two exceptions are provided to the 90-day waiting period. The first exception is the situation where the shareholder has been notified of the rejection of the demand before the end of the 90 days. The standard under the second exception for irreparable injury to the corporation is intended to be the same as that governing the entry of a preliminary injunction. Other factors may also be considered, such as the possible expiration of the statute of limitations, although this would depend on the period of time during which the shareholder was aware of the grounds for the proceeding.

The shareholder bringing suit does not necessarily have to be the person making the demand. Only one demand need be made in order for the corporation to consider whether to take corrective action.

4.   Response by the Corporation

There is no obligation on the part of the corporation to respond to the demand. However, if the corporation, after receiving the demand, decides to institute litigation or, after a derivative proceeding has commenced, decides to assume control of the litigation, the shareholder's right to commence or control the proceeding normally ends unless it can be shown that the corporation will not adequately pursue the matter.

§ 7.43. Stay of Proceedings

If the corporation commences an inquiry into the allegations made in the demand or complaint, the court may stay any derivative proceeding for such period as the court deems appropriate.

Cross-References

Demand, see § 7.42.

"Derivative proceeding" defined, see § 7.40.

Official Comment

A stay may be appropriate where, for example, the complaint is filed 90 days after demand but the inquiry into matters raised by the demand has not been completed or where a demand has not been investigated but the corporation commences the inquiry after the complaint has been filed. In any case, the court will likely monitor the course of the inquiry to ensure that the corporation is proceeding expeditiously and in good faith.

§ 7.44. Dismissal

(a)   A derivative proceeding shall be dismissed by the court on motion by the corporation if one of the groups specified in subsection (b) or subsection (e) has determined in good faith, after conducting a reasonable inquiry upon which its conclusions are based, that the maintenance of the derivative proceeding is not in the best interests of the corporation.

(b)   Unless a panel is appointed pursuant to subsection (e), the determination in subsection (a) shall be made by:

(1)   a majority vote of qualified directors present at a meeting of the board of directors if the qualified directors constitute a quorum; or

(2)   a majority vote of a committee consisting of two or more qualified directors appointed by majority vote of qualified directors present at a meeting of the board of directors, regardless of whether such qualified directors constitute a quorum.

(c)   If a derivative proceeding is commenced after a determination has been made rejecting a demand by a shareholder, the complaint shall allege with particularity facts establishing either (1) that a majority of the board of directors did not consist of qualified directors at the time the determination was made or (2) that the requirements of subsection (a) have not been met.

(d)   If a majority of the board of directors consisted of qualified directors at the time the determination was made, the plaintiff shall have the burden of proving that the requirements of subsection (a) have not been met; if not, the corporation shall have the burden of proving that the requirements of subsection (a) have been met.

(e)   Upon motion by the corporation, the court may appoint a panel of one or more individuals to make a determination whether the maintenance of the derivative proceeding is in the best interests of the corporation. In such case, the plaintiff shall have the burden of proving that the requirements of subsection (a) have not been met.

Cross-References

Board of directors:

> committees, see § 8.25.

> meetings, see § 8.20.

> quorum and voting, see § 8.24.

Demand, see § 7.42.

"Derivative proceeding" defined, see § 7.40.

"Qualified director" defined, see § 1.43.

"Shareholder" defined, see § 7.40.

Official Comment

The procedures set forth in section 7.44 are not intended to be exclusive. Discretion is left with the courts to determine when a derivative action should be dismissed under circumstances other than those set forth in section 7.44. For example, as noted in the comment to section 7.42, there may be instances where a decision to commence an action falls within the authority of an officer of the corporation, depending upon the amount of the claim and the identity of the potential defendants.

1.   The Persons Making the Determination and Timing

The determination under section 7.44(b) that the maintenance of the proceeding is not in the best interests of the corporation can be made before commencement of the derivative action in response to a demand or after commencement of the action upon examination of the allegations of the complaint. Section 7.44(b) allows the determination to be made by "qualified directors" as defined in section 1.43. These provisions parallel the mechanics for authorizing an officer's pursuit of a business opportunity pursuant to a provision in the articles of incorporation (section 2.02(b)(6)), for determining entitlement to indemnification (section 8.55), for authorizing directors' conflicting interest transactions (section 8.62), and for renunciation of the corporation's interests in a business opportunity (section 8.70). Section 7.44(e) provides for the appointment of a panel only upon motion by the corporation. This would not, however, prevent the court on its own initiative from appointing a special master if permitted under applicable state rules of procedure.

This panel procedure may be desirable in a number of circumstances, particularly if there are no qualified directors available. In addition, even if there are qualified directors, they may not be in a position to conduct the inquiry.

2.　*Standards to Be Applied*

Section 7.44(a) contemplates that the court will examine the "good faith" of the persons making the determination. Both the determination and the inquiry in section 7.44(a) must be made in "good faith." Section 7.44(a) does not authorize the court to review the reasonableness of the determination to reject a demand or seek a dismissal. The "good faith" standard, which is also found in section 8.30 (general standards of conduct for directors) and 8.51 (authority to indemnify), is a subjective one, meaning "honestly or in an honest manner."

The word "inquiry"—rather than "investigation"—has been used to make it clear that the scope of the inquiry will depend upon the issues raised and the knowledge of the group making the determination with respect to those issues. In some cases, the issues may be within the knowledge of the group so that extensive additional investigation is not necessary. In other cases, the group may need to engage counsel and possibly other professionals to conduct an investigation and assist the group in its evaluation of the issues.

The phrase "upon which its conclusions are based" requires that the conclusions follow logically from the inquiry. The burden of convincing the court about this issue lies with whichever party has the burden under section 7.44(d). This phrase does not require the persons making the determination to prepare a written report that sets forth their determination and its bases, as circumstances will vary as to the need for such a report.

Section 7.44 is not intended to modify the general standards of conduct for directors set forth in section 8.30 but rather to make those standards more explicit in the derivative proceeding context. In this regard, the qualified directors making the determination would be entitled to rely on information and reports from other persons in accordance with section 8.30.

§ 7.45. Discontinuance or Settlement

A derivative proceeding may not be discontinued or settled without the court's approval. If the court determines that a proposed discontinuance or settlement will substantially affect the interests of the corporation's shareholders or a class or series of shareholders, the court shall direct that notice be given to the shareholders affected.

Cross-References

"Derivative proceeding" defined, see § 7.40.

"Shareholder" defined, see § 7.40.

Official Comment

Section 7.45's requirement that all proposed settlements and discontinuances receive judicial approval supports the proposition that a derivative suit is brought for the benefit of all shareholders and thus should not be settled privately.

By requiring that notice be given to all affected shareholders if the court determines that the proposed settlement may substantially affect their interests, section 7.45 permits the court to decide whether notice to shareholders (or holders of a class or series of shares) need be given. For example, the court may decide not to require notice of dismissal if, in the court's judgment, the proceeding is frivolous or has become moot. Section 7.45 also makes a distinction between classes or series of shareholders, an approach that could be used, for example, to eliminate the costs of notice to preferred shareholders where the settlement does not have an effect on their rights, such as their rights to dividends or a liquidation preference.

Section 7.45 does not address the issue of which party should bear the cost of giving this notice, which is left to the discretion of the court reviewing the proposed settlement.

§ 7.46. Payment of Expenses

On termination of the derivative proceeding the court may:

(1)   order the corporation to pay the plaintiff's expenses incurred in the proceeding if it finds that the proceeding has resulted in a substantial benefit to the corporation;

(2)   order the plaintiff to pay any defendant's expenses incurred in defending the proceeding if it finds that the proceeding was commenced or maintained without reasonable cause or for an improper purpose; or

(3)   order a party to pay an opposing party's expenses incurred because of the filing of a pleading, motion or other paper, if it finds that the pleading, motion or other paper (i) was not well grounded in fact, after reasonable inquiry, or warranted by existing law or a good faith argument for the extension, modification or reversal of existing law or (ii) was interposed for an improper purpose, such as to harass or cause unnecessary delay or needless increase in the cost of litigation.

Cross-References

"Derivative proceeding" defined, see § 7.40.

"Expenses" defined, see § 1.40.

Official Comment

The requirement in section 7.46(a) that the court may order the corporation to pay the plaintiff's expenses if it finds that the proceeding has resulted in a "substantial" benefit to the corporation, should discourage a plaintiff from proposing inconsequential matters to justify the payment of counsel fees. The provision does not specify the method for calculating attorneys' fees given that there is a substantial body of case law that delineates this issue, which usually includes taking into account the amount or character of the benefit to the corporation.

The standard under section 7.46(b) for the court to require the plaintiff to pay the defendants' expenses if the action was commenced without reasonable cause or for an improper purpose is intended to discourage proceedings brought for the sole purpose of obtaining early settlement payments by defendants to avoid significant defense costs, while also protecting plaintiffs whose suits have a reasonable foundation. This test is similar to but not identical to the test utilized in section 13.31, relating to dissenters' rights, where the standard for award of expenses is that dissenters "acted arbitrarily, vexatiously or not in good faith" in demanding a judicial appraisal of their shares. The derivative action situation is sufficiently different from the dissenters' rights situation to justify a different and less onerous test for imposing costs on the plaintiff.

Section 7.46(c) addresses other abuses in the conduct of derivative litigation which may occur on the part of the defendants and their counsel as well as by the plaintiffs and their counsel. This provision may be unnecessary if these abuses are already addressed under applicable rules of civil procedure.

§ 7.47. Applicability to Foreign Corporations

In any derivative proceeding in the right of a foreign corporation, the matters covered by this subchapter shall be governed by the laws of the jurisdiction of incorporation of the foreign corporation except for sections 7.43, 7.45, and 7.46.

Cross-References

"Derivative proceeding" defined, see § 7.40.

"Foreign corporation" defined, see § 1.40.

Foreign corporations, see ch. 15.

Official Comment

Section 7.47 clarifies the application of the provisions of chapter 7D to foreign corporations by setting forth a choice of law provision for derivative proceedings involving foreign corporations. It provides, subject to three exceptions, that the matters covered by the chapter 7D shall be governed by the laws of the jurisdiction of incorporation of the foreign corporation.

The three exceptions to the general rule are areas which are traditionally part of the forum's oversight of the litigation process: section 7.43, dealing with the ability of the court to stay proceedings; section 7.45, setting forth the procedure for settling a proceeding; and section 7.46, providing for the assessment of reasonable expenses (including counsel fees) in certain situations.

SUBCHAPTER E
JUDICIAL PROCEEDINGS

§ 7.48. Shareholder Action to Appoint a Custodian or Receiver

(a)   The [name or describe court] may appoint one or more persons to be custodians, or, if the corporation is insolvent, to be receivers, of and for a corporation in a proceeding by a shareholder where it is established that:

(1)   the directors are deadlocked in the management of the corporate affairs, the shareholders are unable to break the deadlock, and irreparable injury to the corporation is threatened or being suffered; or

(2)   the directors or those in control of the corporation are acting fraudulently and irreparable injury to the corporation is threatened or being suffered.

(b)   The court:

(1)   may issue injunctions, appoint a temporary custodian or temporary receiver with all the powers and duties the court directs, take other action to preserve the corporate assets wherever located, and carry on the business of the corporation until a full hearing is held;

(2)   shall hold a full hearing, after notifying all parties to the proceeding and any interested persons designated by the court, before appointing a custodian or receiver; and

(3)   has jurisdiction over the corporation and all of its property, wherever located.

(c)   The court may appoint an individual or domestic or foreign corporation (registered to do business in this state) as a custodian or receiver and may require the custodian or receiver to post bond, with or without sureties, in an amount the court directs.

(d)   The court shall describe the powers and duties of the custodian or receiver in its appointing order, which may be amended from time to time. Among other powers:

(1)   a custodian may exercise all of the powers of the corporation, through or in place of its board of directors, to the extent necessary to manage the business and affairs of the corporation; and

(2)   a receiver (i) may dispose of all or any part of the assets of the corporation wherever located, at a public or private sale, if authorized by the court; and (ii) may sue and defend in the receiver's own name as receiver in all courts of this state.

(e)   The court during a custodianship may redesignate the custodian a receiver, and during a receivership may redesignate the receiver a custodian, if doing so is in the best interests of the corporation.

(f)   The court from time to time during the custodianship or receivership may order compensation paid and expense disbursements or reimbursements made to the custodian or receiver from the assets of the corporation or proceeds from the sale of its assets.

(g)   In this section, "shareholder" means a record shareholder, a beneficial shareholder, and an unrestricted voting trust beneficial owner.

Cross-References

"Beneficial shareholder," "record shareholder" and "unrestricted voting trust beneficial owner" defined, see § 1.40.

"Expenses" defined, see § 1.40.

Official Comment

Section 7.48 provides procedures for shareholders to bring an action for the appointment of a custodian or receiver in two situations, both requiring a showing of actual or threatened irreparable injury, as specified in section 7.48(a)(1) and (2). These two grounds are narrower than those found in a shareholder's action for judicial dissolution of a nonpublic corporation under section 14.30(a)(2). See the Official Comment to section 14.30(a)(2). Section 7.48 is in addition to other shareholder remedies provided by the Act and could, for example, be relied upon by a shareholder of a nonpublic corporation in lieu of involuntary dissolution under section 14.30(a)(2).

Section 7.48(g) extends the right to seek court appointment of a custodian or receiver to a beneficial shareholder and an unrestricted voting trust beneficial owner. This recognizes that these persons have or hold on behalf of others an economic interest in the shares.

§ 7.49. Judicial Determination of Corporate Offices and Review of Elections and Shareholder Votes

(a) Upon application of or in a proceeding commenced by a person specified in subsection (b), the [name or describe court] may determine:

(1) the result or validity of the election, appointment, removal or resignation of a director or officer of the corporation;

(2) the right of an individual to hold the office of director or officer of the corporation;

(3) the result or validity of any vote by the shareholders of the corporation;

(4) the right of a director to membership on a committee of the board of directors; and

(5) the right of a person to nominate or an individual to be nominated as a candidate for election or appointment as a director of the corporation, and any right under a bylaw adopted pursuant to section 2.06(c) or any comparable right under any provision of the articles of incorporation, contract, or applicable law.

(b) An application or proceeding pursuant to subsection (a) of this section may be filed or commenced by any of the following persons:

(1) the corporation;

(2) any record shareholder, beneficial shareholder or unrestricted voting trust beneficial owner of the corporation;

(3) a director of the corporation, an individual claiming the office of director, or a director whose membership on a committee of the board of directors is contested, in each case who is seeking a determination of his or her right to such office or membership;

(4) an officer of the corporation or an individual claiming to be an officer of the corporation, in each case who is seeking a determination of his or her right to such office; and

(5) a person claiming a right covered by subsection (a)(5) and who is seeking a determination of such right.

(c) In connection with any application or proceeding under subsection (a), the following shall be named as defendants, unless such person made the application or commenced the proceeding:

(1) the corporation;

(2)   any individual whose right to office or membership on a committee of the board of directors is contested;

(3)   any individual claiming the office or membership at issue; and

(4)   any person claiming a right covered by subsection (a)(5) that is at issue.

(d)   In connection with any application or proceeding under subsection (a), service of process may be made upon each of the persons specified in subsection (c) either by:

(1)   service of process on the corporation addressed to such person in any manner provided by statute of this state or by rule of the applicable court for service on the corporation; or

(2)   service of process on the person in any manner provided by statute of this state or by rule of the applicable court.

(e)   When service of process is made upon a person other than the corporation by service upon the corporation pursuant to subsection (d)(1), the plaintiff and the corporation or its registered agent shall promptly provide written notice of such service, together with copies of all process and the application or complaint, to the person at the person's last known residence or business address, or as permitted by statute of this state or by rule of the applicable court.

(f)   In connection with any application or proceeding under subsection (a), the court shall dispose of the application or proceeding on an expedited basis and also may:

(1)   order such additional or further notice as the court deems proper under the circumstances;

(2)   order that additional persons be joined as parties to the proceeding if the court determines that such joinder is necessary for a just adjudication of matters before the court;

(3)   order an election or meeting be held in accordance with the provisions of section 7.03(b) or otherwise;

(4)   appoint a master to conduct an election or meeting;

(5)   enter temporary, preliminary or permanent injunctive relief;

(6)   resolve solely for the purpose of this proceeding any legal or factual issues necessary for the resolution of any of the matters specified in subsection (a), including the right and power of persons claiming to own shares to vote at any meeting of the shareholders; and

(7)   order such other relief as the court determines is equitable, just and proper.

(g)   It is not necessary to make shareholders a party to a proceeding or application pursuant to this section unless the shareholder is a required defendant under subsection (c)(4), relief is sought against the shareholder individually, or the court orders joinder pursuant to subsection (f)(2).

(h)   Nothing in this section limits, restricts, or abolishes the subject matter jurisdiction or powers of the court as existed before the enactment of this section, and an application or proceeding pursuant to this section is not the exclusive remedy or proceeding available with respect to the matters specified in subsection (a).

Cross-References

Notices and other communications, see § 1.41.

Officers, see § 8.40.

Qualifications for directors and nominations, see § 8.02.

"Registered agent" defined, see §§ 2.02, 5.01, 5.02, 5.03 and 16.21.

"Registered office" defined, see §§ 2.02, 5.01, 5.02 and 16.21.

"Shareholder" defined, see § 1.40.

Official Comment

Section 7.49 establishes a procedure for judicial resolution of disputes with respect to the identity of the corporation's directors or officers, the identity of the members of any committee of its board of directors, the validity of nominations for director or the results or validity of shareholder votes. It confers subject matter jurisdiction on the specified court to resolve these disputes. That jurisdiction may be exercised either in a new proceeding or by an application made in an already pending proceeding. Section 7.49 also requires an expedited review of disputes to prevent them from immobilizing the corporation.

1. The Court with Jurisdiction to Administer Section 7.49

Subject to any special rules that may be adopted by the specified court, a proceeding instituted pursuant to section 7.49 is governed by the otherwise applicable rules of civil procedure that apply in the specified court, including rules relating to the filing or initiation of an action, service of process, discovery, injunctive relief, motions, and judgments.

The grant of jurisdiction under section 7.49 is permissive, not mandatory. The court has the discretion to decline to resolve a matter, for example, because a justiciable controversy is not present, the court lacks jurisdiction over a party that the court determines is necessary to the resolution of the dispute, a prior action seeking the same relief is pending in another forum, or for other reasons generally applicable under the law of the enacting state. In view of the section's purpose to provide a prompt remedy for corporate governance disputes, the court ought to decline to exercise the jurisdiction provided under section 7.49 only in a rare and unusual case.

An action under section 7.49 should be promptly filed. A delay in resolving disputes concerning corporate governance can result in prejudice to the corporation and its shareholders. The doctrine of laches provides an appropriate basis for determining whether there has been an unreasonable delay in commencing an action, and that doctrine should be applicable to an action pursuant to this section.

2. The Matters or Disputes Covered

Section 7.49(a) specifies five types of disputes that the court will have jurisdiction to resolve. Section 7.49(a)(3) relates to disputes concerning the result or validity of any shareholder vote on any matter, which would include election of directors, a merger, dissolution, amendment to the articles of incorporation, or any other matter on which a shareholder vote is required or held. A shareholder vote would be taken at a meeting or by written consent. Section 7.49(a)(5) covers disputes concerning the right to nominate or be nominated for election or appointment as a director, which includes whether an individual meets any applicable qualifications to be nominated or serve as a director established under the authority of section 8.02. Section 7.49(a)(5) also extends to disputes concerning rights under a bylaw adopted pursuant to section 2.06(c) to have a nominee appear on the corporation's proxy appointment form or to be reimbursed for expenses incurred in a proxy contest or any comparable rights under any provision of the articles of incorporation, contracts, or applicable law.

The ability to resolve disputes under section 7.49 over who shall serve as a director or officer of the corporation is not intended to reach a dispute concerning an employment contract relating to one of those positions, such as a claim for money damages for breach of the contract, because resolution of a contractual dispute generally will not affect who is entitled to serve as a director or an officer.

3. Person Who May Initiate a Proceeding

Section 7.49(b) specifies that the corporation or a shareholder of the corporation has standing to seek resolution of any of the disputes covered by the section. The standing of any other person is limited to a dispute in which that person's rights are directly at issue. For example, directors or officers of the corporation, or an individual claiming the right to be a director or officer of the corporation, may only initiate a proceeding under section 7.49 with respect to a claim to resolve his or her right to such office or, in the case of directors, his or her right to membership on a committee of the board of directors. A director, officer, or an individual claiming the right to be a director or officer does not have standing as a director or officer to bring an action seeking the resolution of a contest over the right of some other director or officer to serve, the right of some other individual claiming some other office, or the result or validity of any shareholder vote unrelated to the individual's own election. Similarly, a person who has a disputed right to nominate someone for election will not have standing to initiate a proceeding under section 7.49 to resolve some other dispute covered by this section unless that person has standing to raise that other matter, such as where the person also is a shareholder. Similarly, a person who has a disputed right to nominate someone for election will not have standing to initiate a proceeding under section 7.49 to resolve some other dispute covered by this section unless that person has standing to raise that other matter separately, such as where the person also is a shareholder.

4.   *Necessary Defendants*

Section 7.49(c) specifies the persons that must be named as defendants in an action pursuant to section 7.49. The corporation whose affairs are at issue must always be named as a defendant in the action unless the corporation initiates the proceeding. If the corporation initiates a proceeding to resolve the result or validity of a shareholder vote, section 7.49(c) does not require that any particular person be named as a defendant. There is no assurance that whoever is named as the defendant will take a position adverse to the corporation. The court, therefore—pursuant to its power under section 7.49(f)(2)—may order that some adverse party be added as a defendant to assure that the requisite adversity between parties exists and that both sides of any dispute are fairly presented. Section 7.49(d) does not provide a method for serving process on a shareholder who is named as a defendant in an action under section 7.49. Consequently, any shareholder joined as a defendant either will be required to consent to the personal jurisdiction of the court or be subject to service of process pursuant to some other statute of the state or rule of the applicable court.

Section 7.49(g) provides that it is unnecessary to make shareholders a party except, among other circumstances, when relief is sought against any of the shareholders individually. A proceeding to resolve a shareholder vote, for instance, does not mean that relief is being sought against the shareholders individually, even where the vote of particular shareholders may be the determinative factor, so long as the resolution of any issues pertaining to that vote are solely for the purpose of resolving a governance issue under section 7.49 and are not binding on the shareholder individually. Nonetheless, the court has the power to order the joinder of a shareholder whose vote is at issue if the court determines the joinder is necessary for the just adjudication of the matter. If the shareholder is not subject to the personal jurisdiction of the court, the usual rules of the court will apply in determining whether the shareholder is an indispensable party whose absence requires the dismissal of the action. In determining whether such a shareholder is indispensable party whose absence requires the dismissal of the action, a relevant factor for the court to consider is that any judicial determinations—such as a resolution of share ownership—are solely for the purpose of resolving the result or validity of the vote or election and will not be binding on the absent shareholder for any other purpose.

5.   *Service of Process on and Notice to Required Defendants*

Section 7.49(d) provides the methods to serve process on those persons who are required to be joined as defendants under section 7.49(c) and, among other things, permits service upon specified persons by service upon the corporation. If service is accomplished by service on the corporation, notice must be provided to the defendant as required by section 7.49(e) and must be provided both by the plaintiff and by the corporation or its registered agent. This duplicative requirement is intended to increase the likelihood that the defendant receives actual notice of the filing of the lawsuit. Under section 7.49(f)(1), the court may require additional notice.

Section 7.49(e) does not specify the manner by which written notice must be delivered or communicated to the defendant. Section 1.41 contains various provisions dealing with notice and will be applicable to notice pursuant to section 7.49(e) except to the extent that section specifies certain requirements, in which case those requirements will govern. Although section 1.41 provides that notice must be in writing unless oral notice is reasonable under the circumstances, the requirement in subsection (e) that notice be in writing will govern. Section 1.41 also provides that electronic transmission constitutes written notice and contains various other provisions concerning notice.

6.   *Powers of the Court*

Section 7.49(f) lists various nonexclusive powers of the court in connection with a proceeding under section 7.49. Powers of the court provided by statute, rule, or applicable law may also be available in a proceeding under section 7.49. Section 7.49(f) requires that a proceeding be expedited, but the degree of expedition will be determined by the court and may vary depending upon the circumstances of the corporation and the nature of the dispute.

One of the powers granted to the court under section 7.49(f)(6) is to resolve legal or factual issues necessary to the resolution of the corporate governance dispute at issue. The resolution of the disputes specified in section 7.49(a) may require the court to resolve related legal or factual issues, such as whether a shareholder who voted the shares at a meeting is the rightful owner of the shares. However, the determination of such legal or factual matters must be "necessary" for the resolution of the dispute over which the court is granted subject matter jurisdiction in section 7.49(a), and the resolution of these issues must be "solely for the purpose of" the proceeding pursuant to this section. Consequently, for example, the resolution of the rightful owner of shares will be controlling with respect to a section 7.49 determination of the result of the shareholder vote, but that resolution will not be binding on the shareholder whose shares are at issue, unless that shareholder is properly subject to the personal jurisdiction of the court and is made a party to the proceeding. Such a shareholder would not, however, need to be made a party to the proceeding to determine whether the shares were properly voted or counted.

The types of legal or factual issues that it may be necessary for the court to determine to resolve a matter specified in section 7.49(a) may be quite varied. The proper scope of a proceeding under this section is a case-specific inquiry not subject to precise statutory rules. Those issues may include, for example, the interpretation of the bylaws or articles of incorporation, the validity of a share issuance, the validity of a proxy appointment, voting rights pursuant to a contract between shareholders, the power of a beneficial shareholder to direct the voting of shares, the right of the record shareholder to vote shares without direction from the beneficial shareholder, the voting rights of preferred shareholders, whether notice and quorum requirements have been met, and the propriety of the inspectors' tabulation of the vote.

The issues "necessary" to resolve a matter specified in section 7.49(a) may turn upon the type of claim or contest made or identified by the plaintiff in the action. A proceeding under section 7.49 must be pursued primarily to resolve a matter specified in subsection (a) and not to seek adjudication of an issue that is not covered by the section. Issues not covered by section 7.49 might include breach of duty claims against directors (unless those claims are central to the vote, election, appointment, or resignation at issue), claims that persons elected intend to breach their duties in the future, and breach of duty claims in connection with the approval of a particular transaction.

The court's power under sections 7.49(f)(1) and (2) to order additional or further notice may be used to assure that persons with a particular interest in the matter being adjudicated have notice of the proceeding and are given the opportunity to intervene. The court's power to order joinder of additional parties may be used to assure adversity of the parties or to join a person who is directly affected by the resolution of subsidiary legal or factual issues under section 7.49(f)(6).

Although the issues presented in a proceeding under section 7.49 may not require a new meeting or election, in some situations the court may be unable to determine the proper result without conducting a new election or meeting or the matter may be so uncertain that a new meeting or election is the fairest means of resolving the dispute. Sections 7.49(f)(3) and (4) permit the court to order a new meeting or election without necessarily determining that the prior meeting or election was invalid. The new meeting or election may be held in accordance with the provisions of section 7.03(b) or otherwise. Under section 7.03(b), the court, among other matters, may fix the time and place of the meeting, determine the shares entitled to participate in the meeting, specify the record date, prescribe the notice of the meeting, set the quorum and "enter other orders necessary to accomplish the purpose or purposes of the meeting." However, the court's power to control a new meeting or election is not limited to the powers specified in section 7.03(b).

The court might use its injunctive power under section 7.49(f)(5) to address a wide variety of circumstances. It might, for example, (i) enter a temporary or preliminary injunction against action outside the ordinary course unless the opposing parties consent to the action or the court approves, thereby maintaining the status quo until the proceeding can be resolved, (ii) delay a meeting or election until issues can be resolved in advance of the meeting, (iii) delay the closing of a transaction subject to a shareholder vote until the result of the vote is determined, or (iv) restrain a person from exercising the powers of a director or officer until the person's claim to office can be resolved. Once the dispute is resolved, the court may need to enter permanent injunctive relief to implement its decision.

Under section 7.49(f)(7), the court, for example, may consider relief to assure that the shareholder franchise is not improperly manipulated and that the vote of the shareholders is counted and implemented in accordance with the wishes of those entitled to vote or direct the voting of the shares.

CHAPTER 8: DIRECTORS AND OFFICERS

SUBCHAPTER A
BOARD OF DIRECTORS

§ 8.01. Requirement for and Functions of Board of Directors

(a)   Except as may be provided in an agreement authorized under section 7.32, each corporation shall have a board of directors.

(b)   Except as may be provided in an agreement authorized under section 7.32, and subject to any limitation in the articles of incorporation permitted by section 2.02(b), all corporate powers shall be exercised by or under the authority of the board of directors, and the business and affairs of the corporation shall be managed by or under the direction, and subject to the oversight, of the board of directors.

Cross-References

Director standards of conduct, see § 8.30.

Indemnification, see §§ 8.50 through 8.59.

Official Comment

As provided in Section 8.01(a), the board of directors is the traditional form of governance, but the shareholders of a corporation may, in an agreement that satisfies the requirements of section 7.32, dispense with a board of directors and structure the corporation's management and governance to address specific needs of the enterprise.

In section 8.01(b), the phrase "by or under the direction, and subject to the oversight, of" encompasses the varying functions of boards of directors of different corporations. In some corporations, particularly closely held corporations, the board of directors may be involved in the day-to-day business and affairs and it may be reasonable to describe management as being "by" the board of directors. In many other corporations, including most public corporations, the business and affairs are managed "under the direction, and subject to the oversight, of" the board of directors, and operational management is delegated to executive officers and other professional managers.

Section 8.01(b) often is considered to constitute the heart of the governance provisions of the Act. Giving the board of directors the power, and the responsibility, to oversee and direct the business of the corporation permits separation of ownership of the corporation from control of its oversight and direction. The Act's broad grant of authority and responsibility to the board of directors constitutes the rejection of the concept that the directors, having been elected by the shareholders, merely serve as agents to implement the will of the shareholders. See section 8.30.

Section 8.01(b), in providing for corporate powers to be exercised under the direction of the board of directors, allows the board of directors to delegate to appropriate officers, employees or agents of the corporation authority to exercise powers and perform functions not required by law to be exercised or performed by the board of directors itself. Although such delegation does not relieve the board of directors from its responsibility to oversee the business and affairs of the corporation, directors are not personally responsible for actions or omissions of officers, employees, or agents of the corporation so long as the directors have relied reasonably and in good faith upon these officers, employees, or agents. See sections 8.30 and 8.31 and their Official Comments.

The scope of the board's oversight responsibility will vary depending on the nature of the corporation and its business. At least for public corporations, the board's responsibilities generally include oversight of the following:

- business performance, plans and strategy;
- management's assessment of major risks to which the corporation is or may be exposed;
- the performance and compensation of executive officers;

- policies and practices to foster the corporation's compliance with law and ethical conduct;

- management's preparation of the corporation's financial statements;

- management's design and assessment of effectiveness of the corporation's internal controls;

- plans for the succession of the chief executive officer and other executive officers;

- the composition of the board and of board committees; and

- whether the corporation has information and reporting systems in place to provide directors with appropriate information in a timely manner.

In giving attention to the composition of the board, directors of public corporations should consider the corporation's processes for obtaining and evaluating the views of shareholders, including processes for considering individuals proposed by shareholders as nominees for election as directors. Directors of public corporations also should take into account the important role of independent directors. When ownership is separated from responsibility for oversight and direction, as is the case with public corporations, having nonmanagement independent directors who participate actively in the board's oversight functions increases the likelihood that actions taken by the board, if challenged, will be given deference by the courts. The listing standards of most public securities markets have requirements for independent directors to serve on boards; in many cases, they must constitute a majority of the board, and certain board committees must be composed entirely of independent directors. The listing standards have differing rules as to what constitutes an independent director. The Act does not attempt to define "independent director." Ordinarily, an independent director may not be a present or recent member of senior management and must be free of significant professional, financial or similar relationships with the corporation, and the director and members of the director's immediate family must be free of similar relationships with the corporation's senior management. Judgment is required to determine independence in light of the particular circumstances, subject to any specific requirements of a listing standard. The qualifications for disinterestedness required of directors for specific purposes under the Act are similar, but not necessarily identical, to those that are prerequisites to independence. For the requirements for a director to be considered disinterested and qualified to act in those specified situations, see section 1.43. An individual who is an independent director may not be eligible to act in a particular case under those other provisions of the Act. Conversely, a director who is not independent (for example, a member of management) may be disinterested and qualified to act in a particular case.

Section 8.01(b) recognizes that the powers of the board of directors may be limited by express provisions in the articles of incorporation and in an agreement among all shareholders under section 7.32. In an agreement under section 7.32, board powers also may be assigned to others. Because all of the shareholders must approve a section 7.32 agreement, the only restriction on limiting or assigning board powers is that any limitation or assignment must be provided for in sections 7.32(a)(1) through (a)(7) or must not be contrary to public policy under section 7.32(a)(8). In contrast, as is provided in section 2.02(b)(2), any limitation on board powers in the articles of incorporation cannot be "inconsistent with law." As a result of this difference in standards, any such limitation under section 2.02 should not, for example, be inconsistent with requirements of section 8.30 regarding standards of conduct for directors or otherwise preclude the directors from fulfilling their duties to the corporation.

§ 8.02. Qualifications of Directors

(a) The articles of incorporation or bylaws may prescribe qualifications for directors or for nominees for directors. Qualifications must be reasonable as applied to the corporation and be lawful.

(b) A requirement that is based on a past, prospective, or current action, or expression of opinion, by a nominee or director that could limit the ability of a nominee or director to discharge his or her duties as a director is not a permissible qualification under this section. Notwithstanding the foregoing, qualifications may include not being or having been subject to specified criminal, civil, or regulatory sanctions or not having been removed as a director by judicial action or for cause.

(c) A director need not be a resident of this state or a shareholder unless the articles of incorporation or bylaws so prescribe.

(d)   A qualification for nomination for director prescribed before a person's nomination shall apply to such person at the time of nomination. A qualification for nomination for director prescribed after a person's nomination shall not apply to such person with respect to such nomination.

(e)   A qualification for director prescribed before a director has been elected or appointed may apply only at the time an individual becomes a director or may apply during a director's term. A qualification prescribed after a director has been elected or appointed shall not apply to that director before the end of that director's term.

Cross-References

Election of directors, see §§ 8.03 through 8.06.

Judicial determination of corporate offices and review of elections and shareholder votes, see § 7.49.

Resignation of directors, see § 8.07.

Official Comment

Some corporations have adopted qualifications for individuals to be directors or to be nominated as directors. One use of qualifications may be by closely held corporations, to ensure representation and voting power on the board of directors. Other provisions of the Act also are designed to accomplish these purposes. See, for example, section 7.32 providing for shareholder agreements. See also section 2.02(b).

Qualifications may apply to all board members or to a specified percentage or number of directors. An example of a qualification applying to fewer than all directors would be a requirement that at least two directors must have specified business or professional experience or a particular educational degree or background. Careful consideration should be given to the intended effect of the application of any qualification that applies to fewer than all directors in the context of an election contest in which only some of the nominees satisfy this qualification. In the event that specified qualifications for some or all directors are not satisfied, remedial steps could be addressed in the articles of incorporation or bylaws, or can be left to other mechanisms available to a corporation and its board and shareholders, such as the provisions permitting changes in the number of directors and providing for the filling of vacancies on the board. See sections 8.03 and 8.10.

The purpose of section 8.02(a) is to permit qualifications that may benefit the corporation by enhancing the board's ability to perform its role effectively. However, this needs to be balanced against the risk that qualifications could be misused for entrenchment purposes by incumbents or for other improper purposes. To address these concerns, section 8.02(a) requires that qualifications must be reasonable as applied to the corporation and must be lawful. For example, a qualification that seeks to favor incumbent directors or distinguish between a director elected from the slate nominated by a corporation's board and a director elected as the result of being nominated by one or more shareholders, including under a bylaw adopted pursuant to section 2.06(c), would not ordinarily be reasonable and thus not ordinarily authorized by section 8.02(a). An example of a qualification that would not be lawful would be a requirement that is impermissibly discriminatory under the Civil Rights Act of 1964.

1.   Scope of Permitted Qualifications

Examples of qualifications that may be permissible under section 8.02 are eligibility requirements based on residence, shareholdings, age, length of service, experience, expertise, and professional licenses or certifications.

Under section 8.02(b) a qualification that is based on a past, current, or prospective action, or expression of opinion, by a nominee or director that could limit the ability of a nominee or director to discharge his or her duties as a director is not a permissible qualification. The discharge of duties of a director is referenced in section 8.30. A requirement based on a director's having voted for or against, or expressed an intent to vote for or against, a particular type of resolution, such as a resolution in favor of or against a bylaw pursuant to section 2.06(c) or a resolution in favor of or against a shareholder rights plan, would be impermissible.

A shareholder agreement that meets the requirements of section 7.32 could override the terms of section 8.02, including with respect to the requirement of reasonableness in section 8.02(a) and the limitation on permitted qualifications in section 8.02(b).

2. Timing and Applicability of Qualifications

Sections 8.02(d) and (e) prohibit "springing" qualifications. A qualification for a director that is prescribed during the term of that director shall, assuming it remains in effect, apply to that director upon the start of any additional term of that director.

To avoid ambiguity as to whether a qualification for director only applies at the start of a term or applies during the term, a qualification provision should provide clearly when it applies. In the event that a qualification provision does not so specify, customary principles of interpretation and construction will apply. Examples of qualifications the nature of which would generally indicate an intent that they apply throughout a term would be a citizenship or residence qualification or a qualification that a director have a particular license or government clearance.

A director who ceases to meet a qualification that applies during a term will not satisfy that qualification at that time. For example, if a bylaw provision that is in effect at the start of a director's term requires that all directors be residents of state X during their terms, and that director at the start of his or her term is a resident of state X but during the term becomes a resident of state Y, then that director would cease to satisfy the qualification and, therefore, cease to be a director at the time the director becomes a resident of state Y.

§ 8.03. Number and Election of Directors

(a) A board of directors shall consist of one or more individuals, with the number specified in or fixed in accordance with the articles of incorporation or bylaws.

(b) The number of directors may be increased or decreased from time to time by amendment to, or in the manner provided in, the articles of incorporation or bylaws.

(c) Directors are elected at the first annual shareholders' meeting and at each annual shareholders' meeting thereafter unless elected by written consent in lieu of an annual meeting as permitted by section 7.04 or unless their terms are staggered under section 8.06.

Cross-References

Annual shareholders' meeting, see § 7.01.

Classification of board of directors, see § 8.06.

Cumulative voting, see § 7.28.

Deadlocked board of directors as ground for dissolution, see § 14.30.

Staggered terms for directors, see § 8.06.

Terms of directors generally, see § 8.05.

Voting for directors, see § 7.28.

Official Comment

Section 8.03 prescribes rules for (i) the determination of the size of the board of directors of corporations, and (ii) changes in the number of directors once the board's size has been established.

1. Number of Directors

Under section 8.03(a), the size of the board of directors may be fixed initially in one or more of the fundamental corporate documents, or the decision as to the size of the initial board of directors may be made thereafter in the manner authorized in those documents.

2.   Changes in the Size of the Board of Directors

Section 8.03(b) provides a corporation with the freedom to design its articles of incorporation and bylaw provisions relating to the size of its board with a view to achieving the combination of flexibility for the board of directors and protection for shareholders that it deems appropriate. The articles of incorporation could provide for a specified number of directors or a board size within a range from a minimum to a maximum, or an unlimited size not fewer than one as determined by the board or the shareholders. If the shareholders or the board of directors want to change the specified size of the board, to change the range established for the size of the board or to change from a board size within a range or of unlimited size to a specified board size or vice versa, board of directors and shareholder action would be required to make those changes by amending the articles of incorporation. Alternatively, the bylaws could provide for a specified number of directors or a size within a stated range or unlimited size, with the number to be fixed by the board of directors. Any change would be made in the manner provided by the bylaws. The bylaws could permit amendment by the board of directors or the bylaws could require that any amendment, in whole or in part, be made only by the shareholders in accordance with section 10.20(a). Typically, the board of directors would be permitted to change the board size within the established range. If a corporation wishes to ensure that any change in the number of directors be approved by shareholders, then an appropriate restriction would have to be included in the articles of incorporation or bylaws.

The board's power to change the number of directors, like all other board powers, is subject to compliance with applicable standards governing director conduct. In particular, it may be inappropriate to change the size of the board for the primary purpose of maintaining control or defeating particular candidates for the board.

In many closely held corporations, shareholder approval for a change in the size of the board of directors may be readily accomplished if that is desired. In many closely held corporations a board of directors of a fixed size may be an essential part of a control arrangement. In these situations, an increase or decrease in the size of the board of directors by even a single member may significantly affect control. To maintain control arrangements dependent on a board of directors of a fixed size, the power of the board of directors to change its own size must be negated. This may be accomplished by fixing the size of the board of directors in the articles of incorporation or by expressly negating the power of the board of directors to change the size of the board, whether by amendment of the bylaws or otherwise. See section 10.20(a).

§ 8.04. Election of Directors by Certain Classes or Series of Shares

If the articles of incorporation or action by the board of directors pursuant to section 6.02 authorize dividing the shares into classes or series, the articles of incorporation may also authorize the election of all or a specified number of directors by the holders of one or more authorized classes or series of shares. A class or series (or multiple classes or series) of shares entitled to elect one or more directors is a separate voting group for purposes of the election of directors.

Cross-References

Classes and series of shares, see § 6.01.

Cumulative voting, see § 7.28.

Removal of directors, see §§ 8.08 and 8.09.

Voting by voting groups, see §§ 7.25 and 7.26.

Voting for directors, see § 7.28.

"Voting group" defined, see § 1.40.

Official Comment

Provisions allowing separate classes or series of shares each to elect a specified number of directors are often used in corporations to effect an agreed upon allocation of control, for example, to ensure representation on the board of directors by particular shareholders by issuing to those shareholders a class or series of shares entitled to elect one or more directors. Each class or series (or multiple classes or series) entitled to elect separately one or more directors constitutes a separate voting group for this purpose, and the quorum and voting requirements must be separately met by each voting group as provided in sections 7.25, 7.26 and 7.28.

§ 8.05. Terms of Directors Generally

(a) The terms of the initial directors of a corporation expire at the first shareholders' meeting at which directors are elected.

(b) The terms of all other directors expire at the next, or if their terms are staggered in accordance with section 8.06, at the applicable second or third, annual shareholders' meeting following their election, except to the extent (i) provided in section 10.22 if a bylaw electing to be governed by that section is in effect, or (ii) a shorter term is specified in the articles of incorporation in the event of a director nominee failing to receive a specified vote for election.

(c) A decrease in the number of directors does not shorten an incumbent director's term.

(d) The term of a director elected to fill a vacancy expires at the next shareholders' meeting at which directors are elected.

(e) Except to the extent otherwise provided in the articles of incorporation or under section 10.22 if a bylaw electing to be governed by that section is in effect, despite the expiration of a director's term, the director continues to serve until the director's successor is elected and qualifies or there is a decrease in the number of directors.

Cross-References

Annual shareholders' meeting, see § 7.01.

Court-ordered shareholders' meeting, see § 7.03.

Number of directors, see § 8.03.

Removal of directors, see §§ 8.08 and 8.09.

Resignation of directors, see § 8.07.

Staggered terms for directors, see § 8.06.

Vacancies on board of directors, see § 8.10.

Official Comment

Section 8.05 provides for the annual election of directors at the annual shareholders' meeting with the single exception that terms may be staggered as permitted in section 8.06.

Under section 8.05(d), if terms are staggered, the term of a director elected to fill a vacant term with more than a year to run is shorter than the term of the director's predecessor. The board of directors may take appropriate steps, by designation of short terms or otherwise, to return the rotation of election of directors to the original staggered terms established or fixed by the articles of incorporation or bylaws.

Section 8.05(e), with two exceptions, provides for "holdover" directors so that directorships do not automatically become vacant at the expiration of their terms. This means that the power of the board of directors to act continues uninterrupted even if an annual shareholders' meeting is not held or the shareholders are deadlocked or otherwise do not elect directors at the meeting. The articles of incorporation may modify or eliminate this holdover concept. Also, if a bylaw is adopted invoking section 10.22, the effect will be that directors who are elected by a plurality vote but receive more votes against than for their election will not hold over past the abbreviated 90-day term of office specified in section 10.22.

§ 8.06. Staggered Terms for Directors

The articles of incorporation may provide for staggering the terms of directors by dividing the total number of directors into two or three groups, with each group containing half or one-third of the total, as near as may be practicable. In that event, the terms of directors in the first group expire at the first annual shareholders' meeting after their election, the terms of the second group expire at the second annual shareholders' meeting after their election, and the terms of the third group, if any, expire at the third annual shareholders' meeting after their election. At each annual shareholders' meeting held thereafter, directors shall be elected for a term of two years or three years, as the case may be, to succeed those whose terms expire.

Cross-References

> Annual shareholders' meeting, see § 7.01.
>
> Cumulative voting, see § 7.28.
>
> Election of directors, see § 7.28.
>
> Number of directors, see § 8.03.
>
> Removal of directors, see §§ 8.08 and 8.09.
>
> Resignation of directors, see § 8.07.
>
> Terms of directors, see § 8.05.
>
> Vacancies on board of directors, see § 8.10.

Official Comment

Section 8.06 permits the practice of "classifying" the board or "staggering" the terms of directors. The requirement that these provisions be in the articles of incorporation ensures that, unless included in the corporation's original articles, a staggered board may only be implemented with shareholder approval.

§ 8.07. Resignation of Directors

(a)   A director may resign at any time by delivering a written notice of resignation to the board of directors or its chair, or to the secretary.

(b)   A resignation is effective as provided in section 1.41(i) unless the resignation provides for a delayed effectiveness, including effectiveness determined upon a future event or events. A resignation that is conditioned upon failing to receive a specified vote for election as a director may provide that it is irrevocable.

Cross-References

> "Deliver" defined, see § 1.40.
>
> Notices and other communications, see § 1.41.
>
> "Secretary" defined, see § 1.40.
>
> Vacancies on board of directors, see § 8.10.

Official Comment

In addition to permitting resignations effective at a date later than the date of delivery of the resignation, section 8.07(b) permits a director resignation to be conditioned upon "future events," which might include the director failing to achieve a specified vote for reelection, *e.g.*, more votes "for" than "against" coupled with board acceptance of the resignation. Corporations and individual directors may thus give effect, in a manner subsequently enforceable by the corporation, to voting standards for the election of directors that exceed the plurality default standard in section 7.28. Section 8.07(b) also makes it clear that such arrangements do not contravene public policy. The express reference to the failure to receive a specified vote is not to be construed to address or negate the possible validity of other appropriate conditions for an irrevocable resignation.

Under section 8.10, a vacancy that will occur at a specific later date by reason of a resignation effective at a later date may be filled before the vacancy occurs, but the new director may not take office until the vacancy occurs. Because the individual tendering that resignation is still a member of the board, he or she may participate in all decisions until the specified date, including the choice of his or her successor under section 8.10.

§ 8.08. Removal of Directors by Shareholders

(a) The shareholders may remove one or more directors with or without cause unless the articles of incorporation provide that directors may be removed only for cause.

(b) If a director is elected by a voting group of shareholders, only the shareholders of that voting group may participate in the vote to remove that director.

(c) A director may be removed if the number of votes cast to remove exceeds the number of votes cast not to remove the director, except to the extent the articles of incorporation or bylaws require a greater number; provided that if cumulative voting is authorized, a director may not be removed if, in the case of a meeting, the number of votes sufficient to elect the director under cumulative voting is voted against removal and, if action is taken by less than unanimous written consent, voting shareholders entitled to the number of votes sufficient to elect the director under cumulative voting do not consent to the removal.

(d) A director may be removed by the shareholders only at a meeting called for the purpose of removing the director and the meeting notice must state that removal of the director is a purpose of the meeting.

Cross-References

Cumulative voting, see § 7.28.

Election of directors by certain classes or series of shares, see § 8.04.

Election of directors, see § 7.28.

Notice of meeting, see § 7.05.

Quorum and voting requirements for voting groups, see § 7.25.

Removal of directors by judicial proceeding, see § 8.09.

Shareholders' meetings, see §§ 7.01 through 7.03.

"Voting group" defined, see § 1.40.

Official Comment

Section 8.08(a) provides a default rule that shareholders have the power to change the directors at will. However, that section permits the power to remove directors without cause to be eliminated by a provision in the articles of incorporation. Section 8.08(c) assures that a minority faction with sufficient votes to guarantee the election of a director under cumulative voting will be able to protect that director from removal by the remaining shareholders. In computing whether a director elected by cumulative voting is protected from removal under that section, the votes should be counted as though (i) the vote to remove the director occurred in an election to elect the number of directors normally elected by the relevant voting group along with the director whose removal is sought, (ii) the number of votes cast cumulatively against removal had been cast for election of the director, and (iii) all votes cast for removal of the director had been cast cumulatively in an efficient pattern for the election of a sufficient number of candidates so as to deprive the director whose removal is being sought of the director's office.

Although sections 8.08(b) and (c) have specific requirements with respect to removal of directors elected by particular voting groups or by cumulative voting, such directors nevertheless may be removed by court proceeding under section 8.09. Section 8.08(d) acknowledges the seriousness of director removal by requiring the meeting notice to state that removal of specific directors will be proposed. Section 8.08(d) governs removal of directors at a meeting of shareholders, but does not preclude removal by means of shareholder action by written consent under section 7.04. Unless cumulative voting is authorized, and in the absence of a greater vote requirement in the articles of incorporation or bylaws, removal of a director by less than unanimous written consent would require that a majority of the outstanding shares of the relevant voting group consent to the removal.

§ 8.09. Removal of Directors by Judicial Proceeding

(a)   The [name or describe court] may remove a director from office or may order other relief, including barring the director from reelection for a period prescribed by the court, in a proceeding commenced by or in the right of the corporation if the court finds that (i) the director engaged in fraudulent conduct with respect to the corporation or its shareholders, grossly abused the position of director, or intentionally inflicted harm on the corporation; and (ii) considering the director's course of conduct and the inadequacy of other available remedies, removal or such other relief would be in the best interest of the corporation.

(b)   A shareholder proceeding on behalf of the corporation under subsection (a) shall comply with all of the requirements of subchapter 7D, except clause (i) of section 7.41.

Cross-References

Derivative proceedings, see §§ 7.40 through 7.47.

Director standards of conduct, see § 8.30.

"Proceeding" defined, see § 1.40.

Removal of directors by shareholders, see § 8.08.

"Shareholder" defined, see § 1.40.

Official Comment

Section 8.09 is designed to operate in the limited circumstance where other remedies are inadequate to address serious misconduct by a director and it is impracticable for shareholders to invoke removal under section 8.08. A proceeding under section 8.09 may be brought by the corporation or by a shareholder suing derivatively. If an action is brought derivatively, all of the provisions of chapter 7D, including dismissal under section 7.44, are applicable to the action with the exception of the contemporaneous ownership requirement of clause (i) of section 7.41. This extraordinary remedy of judicial removal is only for the kind of misconduct described in clause (i) of section 8.09(a) and does not reach matters falling within an individual director's lawful exercise of business judgment.

The court may determine that the director's continuation in office is inimical to the best interest of the corporation. Judicial removal might be the most appropriate remedy if shareholder removal under section 8.08 is impracticable because of situations such as the following:

- The director charged with serious misconduct personally owns or controls sufficient shares to block removal.

- The director was elected by voting group or cumulative voting, and the shareholders with voting power to prevent removal will exercise that power despite the director's serious misconduct and without regard to what the court deems to be the best interest of the corporation.

- A shareholders' meeting to consider removal under section 8.08 will entail considerable expense and a period of delay that will be contrary to the corporation's best interest.

§ 8.10. Vacancy on Board of Directors

(a)   Unless the articles of incorporation provide otherwise, if a vacancy occurs on a board of directors, including a vacancy resulting from an increase in the number of directors:

(1)   the shareholders may fill the vacancy;

(2)   the board of directors may fill the vacancy; or

(3)   if the directors remaining in office are less than a quorum, they may fill the vacancy by the affirmative vote of a majority of all the directors remaining in office.

(b)   If the vacant office was held by a director elected by a voting group of shareholders, only the holders of shares of that voting group are entitled to vote to fill the vacancy if it is filled by the shareholders, and only the remaining directors elected by that voting group, even if less than a quorum, are entitled to fill the vacancy if it is filled by the directors.

(c) A vacancy that will occur at a specific later date (by reason of a resignation effective at a later date under section 8.07(b) or otherwise) may be filled before the vacancy occurs but the new director may not take office until the vacancy occurs.

Cross-References

Election of directors by certain classes or series of shares, see § 8.04.

Number of directors, see § 8.03.

Quorum and voting of directors, see § 8.24.

Removal of directors, see §§ 8.08 and 8.09.

Resignation of directors, see § 8.07.

Shareholders' meetings, see §§ 7.01 through 7.03.

Terms of directors, see § 8.05.

Voting by voting group, see §§ 7.25 and 7.26.

"Voting group" defined, see § 1.40.

Official Comment

Section 8.10(a)(3) allows the directors remaining in office to fill director vacancies even though they do not constitute a quorum. The test for the exercise of this power is whether the directors remaining in office are less than a quorum, not whether the directors seeking to act are less than a quorum. For example, on a board of six directors where a quorum is four, if there are two vacancies, they may not be filled under section 8.10(a)(3) at a "meeting" attended by only three directors. Even though the three directors are less than a quorum, section 8.10(a)(3) is not applicable because the number of directors remaining in office—four—is not less than a quorum.

Section 8.10(b) is part of the consistent treatment of directors elected by a voting group of shareholders. See sections 1.40, 7.25, 7.26, 7.28, 8.04 and 8.08(b).

Under section 8.10(c), the director in the office that will become vacant may participate in the selection of a successor. Such a vacancy typically arises when there is a resignation by a director that is effective at a later date; it may also arise in connection with retirements or with prospective amendments to bylaws. In a closely held corporation with a balance of power on the board of directors that was reached by agreement, a prospective resignation followed by the appointment of a successor under this section permits the board to act on the replacement before the change in balance of power the resignation would otherwise cause.

§ 8.11. Compensation of Directors

Unless the articles of incorporation or bylaws provide otherwise, the board of directors may fix the compensation of directors.

Cross-References

Committees of board of directors, see § 8.25.

Director's conflicting interest transaction, see ch. 8F.

Director standards of conduct, see § 8.30.

Official Comment

Section 8.11 reflects the view that director compensation is an appropriate function of the board of directors. Board action on directors' compensation and benefits is a director's conflicting interest transaction subject to chapter 8F. See Official Comment to section 8.61, Note on Directors' Compensation.

SUBCHAPTER B
MEETINGS AND ACTION OF THE BOARD

§ 8.20. Meetings

(a)   The board of directors may hold regular or special meetings in or out of this state.

(b)   Unless restricted by the articles of incorporation or bylaws, any or all directors may participate in any meeting of the board of directors through the use of any means of communication by which all directors participating may simultaneously hear each other during the meeting. A director participating in a meeting by this means is deemed to be present in person at the meeting.

Cross-References

Action without meeting, see § 8.21.

Notice of meeting, see § 8.22.

Quorum and voting, see § 8.24.

Waiver of meeting notice, see § 8.23.

Official Comment

Section 8.20 provides flexibility with respect to holding meetings of directors. Under section 8.20, a meeting in which any or all of the directors participate through any means of communication that complies with section 8.20(b) will meet the statutory requirements. Depending on the nature of the matters to be considered at the meeting, however, a board of directors may wish to consider whether holding an in-person meeting at which some or all directors are physically present provides greater opportunity for interchange.

§ 8.21. Action Without Meeting

(a)   Except to the extent that the articles of incorporation or bylaws require that action by the board of directors be taken at a meeting, action required or permitted by this Act to be taken by the board of directors may be taken without a meeting if each director signs a consent describing the action to be taken and delivers it to the corporation.

(b)   Action taken under this section is the act of the board of directors when one or more consents signed by all the directors are delivered to the corporation. The consent may specify a later time as the time at which the action taken is to be effective. A director's consent may be withdrawn by a revocation signed by the director and delivered to the corporation before delivery to the corporation of unrevoked written consents signed by all the directors.

(c)   A consent signed under this section has the effect of action taken at a meeting of the board of directors and may be described as such in any document.

Cross-References

Notices and other communications, see § 1.41.

Notice of meeting, see § 8.22.

Waiver of meeting notice, see § 8.23.

Official Comment

Directors may take action by written consent without a meeting only when approval of an action is unanimous. Accordingly, if a director abstains, is recused or withholds consent on an action, the action could not be authorized by consent, and a meeting would need to be held for the action to be approved.

§ 8.22. Notice of Meeting

(a)   Unless the articles of incorporation or bylaws provide otherwise, regular meetings of the board of directors may be held without notice of the date, time, place, or purpose of the meeting.

(b) Unless the articles of incorporation or bylaws provide for a longer or shorter period, special meetings of the board of directors shall be preceded by at least two days' notice of the date, time, and place of the meeting. The notice need not describe the purpose of the special meeting unless required by the articles of incorporation or bylaws.

Cross-References

Action without meeting, see § 8.21.

Meetings of board of directors, see §§ 8.20 and 8.21.

Notices and other communications, see § 1.41.

Waiver of meeting notice, see § 8.23.

Official Comment

Unlike regular meetings of the board of directors, special meetings always require notice, the timing of which may be varied by the articles of incorporation or bylaws. The notice may be written, or oral if oral notice is reasonable in the circumstances. See section 1.41(a). No statement of the purpose of any meeting of the board of directors is necessary in the notice unless required by the articles of incorporation or bylaws. These requirements differ from the requirements applicable to meetings of shareholders because of the fundamental differences in the roles and involvement of directors and shareholders.

§ 8.23. Waiver of Notice

(a) A director may waive any notice required by this Act, the articles of incorporation or the bylaws before or after the date and time stated in the notice. Except as provided by subsection (b), the waiver must be in writing, signed by the director entitled to the notice and delivered to the corporation for filing by the corporation with the minutes or corporate records.

(b) A director's attendance at or participation in a meeting waives any required notice to the director of the meeting unless the director at the beginning of the meeting (or promptly upon arrival) objects to holding the meeting or transacting business at the meeting and does not after objecting vote for or assent to action taken at the meeting.

Cross-References

Action without meeting, see § 8.21.

Meetings of board of directors, see § 8.20.

Notices and other communications, see § 1.41.

Notice of meeting, see § 8.22.

Official Comment

If a director actually attends the meeting, section 8.23(b) generally provides the director may not subsequently raise an objection based on lack of notice. If a director does wish to object, he or she must call attention to the lack of notice at the outset of the meeting or promptly upon arriving and not vote for any action taken at the meeting. That director may then attack the validity of any action taken at the meeting on the grounds of lack of notice, as may any other director who was not given notice and was not present at the meeting.

§ 8.24. Quorum and Voting

(a) Unless the articles of incorporation or bylaws provide for a greater or lesser number or unless otherwise expressly provided in this Act, a quorum of a board of directors consists of a majority of the number of directors specified in or fixed in accordance with the articles of incorporation or bylaws.

(b) The quorum of the board of directors specified in or fixed in accordance with the articles of incorporation or bylaws may not consist of less than one-third of the specified or fixed number of directors.

(c)　If a quorum is present when a vote is taken, the affirmative vote of a majority of directors present is the act of the board of directors unless the articles of incorporation or bylaws require the vote of a greater number of directors or unless otherwise expressly provided in this Act.

(d)　A director who is present at a meeting of the board of directors or a committee when corporate action is taken is deemed to have assented to the action taken unless: (i) the director objects at the beginning of the meeting (or promptly upon arrival) to holding it or transacting business at the meeting; (ii) the dissent or abstention from the action taken is entered in the minutes of the meeting; or (iii) the director delivers written notice of the director's dissent or abstention to the presiding officer of the meeting before its adjournment or to the corporation immediately after adjournment of the meeting. The right of dissent or abstention is not available to a director who votes in favor of the action taken.

Cross-References

Action without meeting, see § 8.21.

Committees of board of directors, see § 8.25.

Meetings of board of directors, see § 8.20.

Notices and other communications, see § 1.41.

Number of directors, see § 8.03.

Quorum for determination of advance for expenses, see § 8.53.

Quorum for determination and authorization of indemnification, see § 8.55.

Official Comment

In the absence of a provision in the articles of incorporation or bylaws, a quorum is a majority of the total number of directors specified (*e.g.*, "the number of directors shall be X") in or fixed (*e.g.*, "the number of directors shall be not less than Y or more than Z as determined by the board of directors") in accordance with the articles of incorporation or the bylaws.

Section 8.24(a) recognizes that the Act itself may provide for a different quorum in certain specified situations. See sections 8.53(c)(1) and 8.55(b)(1).

Section 8.24 allows the articles of incorporation or bylaws to decrease the required quorum (but not below one-third) or to increase the quorum or the vote necessary to take action up to and including unanimity. The articles of incorporation or bylaws may also establish quorum or voting requirements with respect to directors elected by voting groups of shareholders pursuant to section 8.04. The options to increase the quorum and vote requirements might be used, for example, in closely held corporations where a greater degree of participation is thought appropriate or where a minority participant in the venture seeks to obtain a veto power over corporate action.

The phrase "when the vote is taken" in section 8.24(c) is designed to make clear that the board of directors may act only when a quorum is present. If directors leave during the course of a meeting, the board of directors may not act after the number of directors present is reduced to less than a quorum.

If a director who is present at a meeting wishes to object or abstain with respect to action taken by the board of directors or a committee, that director must make his or her position clear in one of the ways described in section 8.24(d). If objection is made in the form of a written dissent under clause (iii) of section 8.24(d), it may be transmitted by any form of delivery authorized by the definition of that term in section 1.40, including electronic transmission, if authorized by section 1.41. Section 8.24(d) serves the important purpose of bringing the position of the dissenting director clearly to the attention of the other directors. The provision that a director who is present is deemed to have assented unless an objection is noted also prevents a director from later seeking to avoid responsibility because of unexpressed doubts about the wisdom of the action taken.

Section 8.24(d) applies only to directors who are present at the meeting. Directors who are not present are not deemed to have assented to any action taken at the meeting in their absence.

§ 8.25. Committees of the Board

(a)   Unless this Act, the articles of incorporation or the bylaws provide otherwise, a board of directors may establish one or more board committees composed exclusively of one or more directors to perform functions of the board of directors.

(b)   The establishment of a board committee and appointment of members to it shall be approved by the greater of (i) a majority of all the directors in office when the action is taken or (ii) the number of directors required by the articles of incorporation or bylaws to take action under section 8.24, unless, in either case, this Act or the articles of incorporation provide otherwise.

(c)   Sections 8.20 through 8.24 apply to board committees and their members.

(d)   A board committee may exercise the powers of the board of directors under section 8.01, to the extent specified by the board of directors or in the articles of incorporation or bylaws, except that a board committee may not:

(1)   authorize or approve distributions, except according to a formula or method, or within limits, prescribed by the board of directors;

(2)   approve or propose to shareholders action that this Act requires be approved by shareholders;

(3)   fill vacancies on the board of directors or, subject to subsection (e), on any board committees; or

(4)   adopt, amend, or repeal bylaws.

(e)   The board of directors may appoint one or more directors as alternate members of any board committee to replace any absent or disqualified member during the member's absence or disqualification. If the articles of incorporation, the bylaws, or the resolution creating the board committee so provide, the member or members present at any board committee meeting and not disqualified from voting may, by unanimous action, appoint another director to act in place of an absent or disqualified member during that member's absence or disqualification.

Cross-References

Amendment of articles of incorporation, see ch. 10A.

Amendment of bylaws, see ch. 10B.

Conversions, see ch. 9C.

Derivative proceedings, see §§ 7.40 through 7.47.

Director standards of conduct, see § 8.30.

Disposition of assets, see ch. 12.

Dissolution, see ch. 14.

"Distribution" defined, see § 1.40.

Distributions to shareholders, see § 6.40.

Domestications, see ch. 9B.

Functions of board of directors, see § 8.01.

Indemnification determination and authorization, see § 8.55.

Issuance of shares, see §§ 6.01 and 6.02.

Mergers and share exchanges, see ch. 11.

Quorum and voting, see § 8.24.

Reacquisition of shares, see §§ 6.03 and 6.31.

Vacancies on board of directors, see § 8.10.

Official Comment

Section 8.25 deals only with board committees authorized to perform functions of the board of directors. The board of directors or management, independently of section 8.25, may establish non-board committees composed in whole or in part of directors, employees, or others to address matters in ways that do not constitute performing functions required to be performed by the board of directors under section 8.01, including acting in an advisory capacity.

Under section 8.25(a), except as otherwise provided by the Act, the articles of incorporation or the bylaws, a board committee may consist of a single director. This accommodates situations in which only one director may be present or available to make a decision on short notice, as well as situations in which it is unnecessary or inconvenient to have more than one member on a board committee or where only one board member is disinterested or independent with respect to a matter. Various other sections of the Act require the participation or approval of at least two qualified directors in order for the decision of the board or committee to have effect. (For the definition of "qualified director," see section 1.43.) These include a determination that maintenance of a derivative suit is not in the corporation's best interests (section 7.44(b)(2)), a determination that indemnification is permissible (section 8.55(b)(1)), an approval of a director's conflicting interest transaction (section 8.62(a)), and disclaimer of the corporation's interest in a business opportunity (section 8.70(a)).

The requirement of section 8.25(b) that, unless the Act or the articles of incorporation otherwise provide, a board committee may be created only by the affirmative vote of a majority of the board of directors then in office, or, if greater, by the number of directors required to take action by the articles of incorporation or bylaws, reflects the importance of the decision to invest board committees with power to act under section 8.25. Sections 7.44(b), 8.55(b), 8.62(a) and 8.70 contain exceptions to this rule.

The limitations in section 8.25(d)(1) through (4) are based on the principle that the listed actions so substantially affect the rights of shareholders or are so fundamental to the governance of the corporation that they should be determined by the full board and not delegated to a committee. On the other hand, section 8.25(d) allows board committees to take many actions that may be material, such as the authorization of long-term debt and capital investment or the issuance of shares.

Although section 8.25(d)(1) generally makes nondelegable the decision whether to authorize or approve distributions, including dividends, it does permit the delegation to a board committee of power to approve a distribution pursuant to a formula or method or within limits prescribed by the board of directors. Therefore, the board of directors could set a dollar range and timeframe for a prospective dividend and delegate to a board committee the authority to determine the exact amount and record and payment dates of the dividend. The board of directors also could establish certain conditions to the payment of a distribution and delegate to a board committee the power to determine whether the conditions have been satisfied.

Section 8.25(e) is a rule of convenience that permits the board of directors or the other board committee members to replace an absent or disqualified member during the time that the member is absent or disqualified. Unless otherwise provided or unless a quorum is no longer present, replacement of an absent or disqualified member of a committee is not necessary to permit the other committee members to continue to perform their duties.

§ 8.26. Submission of Matters for Shareholder Vote

A corporation may agree to submit a matter to a vote of its shareholders even if, after approving the matter, the board of directors determines it no longer recommends the matter.

Cross-References

Action on a plan of:

       conversion, see § 9.32.

       domestication, see § 9.21.

       merger or share exchange, see § 11.04.

Amendment of articles, see § 10.03.

Disposition of assets, see § 12.02.

Dissolution, see § 14.02.

Official Comment

Section 8.26 authorizes a corporation to enter into an agreement, such as a merger agreement, containing a provision that requires a shareholder vote on the matter despite a subsequent change in the recommendation of the board of directors. Otherwise, a board is not required to submit a matter to the shareholders, even if it has been approved by the board. Section 8.26 also applies to the provisions of the Act that require the board of directors to approve a matter before recommending that the shareholders vote to approve it. Section 8.26 does not change the standards of conduct or liability applicable when considering whether to authorize such agreement by the corporation.

SUBCHAPTER C
DIRECTORS

§ 8.30. Standards of Conduct for Directors

(a) Each member of the board of directors, when discharging the duties of a director, shall act: (i) in good faith, and (ii) in a manner the director reasonably believes to be in the best interests of the corporation.

(b) The members of the board of directors or a board committee, when becoming informed in connection with their decision-making function or devoting attention to their oversight function, shall discharge their duties with the care that a person in a like position would reasonably believe appropriate under similar circumstances.

(c) In discharging board or board committee duties, a director shall disclose, or cause to be disclosed, to the other board or committee members information not already known by them but known by the director to be material to the discharge of their decision-making or oversight functions, except that disclosure is not required to the extent that the director reasonably believes that doing so would violate a duty imposed under law, a legally enforceable obligation of confidentiality, or a professional ethics rule.

(d) In discharging board or board committee duties, a director who does not have knowledge that makes reliance unwarranted is entitled to rely on the performance by any of the persons specified in subsection (f)(1) or subsection (f)(3) to whom the board may have delegated, formally or informally by course of conduct, the authority or duty to perform one or more of the board's functions that are delegable under applicable law.

(e) In discharging board or board committee duties, a director who does not have knowledge that makes reliance unwarranted is entitled to rely on information, opinions, reports, or statements, including financial statements and other financial data, prepared or presented by any of the persons specified in subsection (f).

(f) A director is entitled to rely, in accordance with subsection (d) or (e), on:

(1) one or more officers or employees of the corporation whom the director reasonably believes to be reliable and competent in the functions performed or the information, opinions, reports or statements provided;

(2) legal counsel, public accountants, or other persons retained by the corporation as to matters involving skills or expertise the director reasonably believes are matters (i) within the particular person's professional or expert competence, or (ii) as to which the particular person merits confidence; or

(3) a board committee of which the director is not a member if the director reasonably believes the committee merits confidence.

Cross-References

Committees of board of directors, see § 8.25.

Derivative proceedings, see §§ 7.40 through 7.47.

Director's conflicting interest transactions, see ch. 8F.

Functions of board of directors, see § 8.01.

Indemnification, see §§ 8.50 through 8.59.

Meetings of board of directors, see §§ 8.20 and 8.21.

Quorum of directors, see § 8.24.

Removal of directors, see §§ 8.08 and 8.09.

Standards of conduct for officers, see § 8.42.

Standards of liability for directors, see § 8.31.

Unlawful distributions, see § 8.32.

Official Comment

Section 8.30 sets standards of conduct for directors that focus on the manner in which directors make their decisions, not the correctness of the decisions made. Section 8.30 should be read in light of the basic role of directors set forth in section 8.01(b), which provides that the "business and affairs of a corporation shall be managed by or under the direction and subject to the oversight of the board of directors," as supplemented by various provisions of the Act assigning specific powers or responsibilities to the board. The standards of conduct for directors established by section 8.30 are analogous to those generally articulated by courts in evaluating director conduct, often referred to as the duties of care and loyalty.

Section 8.30 addresses standards of conduct—the level of performance expected of directors undertaking the role and responsibilities of the office of director. The section does not address the liability of a director, although exposure to liability may result from a failure to honor the standards of conduct required to be observed. The issue of director liability is addressed in sections 8.31 and 8.32. Section 8.30 does, however, play an important role in evaluating a director's conduct and the effectiveness of board action. It has relevance in assessing, under section 8.31, the reasonableness of a director's belief. Similarly, it has relevance in assessing a director's timely attention to appropriate inquiry when particular facts and circumstances of significant concern materialize. It also serves as a frame of reference for determining, under section 8.32(a), liability for an unlawful distribution. Finally, section 8.30 compliance may influence a court's analysis where injunctive relief against a transaction is being sought. Directors act both individually and collectively as a board in performing their functions and discharging their duties. Section 8.30 addresses actions in both capacities.

Under the standards of section 8.30, the board may delegate or assign to appropriate officers or employees of the corporation the authority or duty to exercise powers that the law does not require the board to retain. Because the directors are entitled to rely on these persons absent knowledge making reliance unwarranted, the directors will not be in breach of the standards under section 8.30 as a result of their delegatees' actions or omissions so long as the board acted in good faith and complied with the other standards of conduct set forth in section 8.30 in delegating responsibility and, where appropriate, monitoring performance of the duties delegated. In addition, subsections (d), (e) and (f) permit a director to rely on enumerated third parties for specified purposes, although reliance is prohibited when a director has knowledge that makes reliance unwarranted. Section 8.30(a)'s standards of good faith and reasonable belief in the best interests of the corporation also apply to a director's reliance under subsections (d), (e) and (f).

1.   Section 8.30(a)

Section 8.30(a) establishes the basic standards of conduct for all directors and its mandate governs all aspects of directors' conduct, including the requirements in other subsections. It includes concepts courts have used in defining the duty of loyalty. Two of the phrases used in section 8.30(a) deserve further comment:

- The phrase "reasonably believes" is both subjective and objective in character. Its first level of analysis is geared to what the particular director, acting in good faith, actually believes—not what objective analysis would lead another director (in a like position and acting in similar circumstances) to conclude. The second level of analysis is focused specifically on "reasonably." Although a director has wide discretion in gathering information and reaching conclusions, whether a director's belief is reasonable (*i.e.*, could—not would—a reasonable person in a like position and acting in similar circumstances, taking into account that director's knowledge and experience, have arrived at that belief) ultimately involves an overview that is objective in character.

- The phrase "best interests of the corporation" is key to an understanding of a director's duties. The term "corporation" is a surrogate for the business enterprise as well as a frame of reference encompassing the shareholder body. In determining the corporation's "best interests," the director has wide discretion in deciding how to weigh near-term opportunities versus long-term benefits as well as in making judgments where the interests of various groups of shareholders or other corporate constituencies may differ.

Section 8.30 operates as a "baseline" principle governing director conduct in circumstances uncomplicated by self-interest. The Act recognizes, however, that directors' personal interests may not always align with the corporation's best interests and provides procedures by which situations and transactions involving conflicts of interest can be processed. See subchapter D (derivative proceedings) of chapter 7 and subchapters E (indemnification and advance for expenses), F (directors' conflicting interest transactions), and G (business opportunities) of this chapter 8. Those procedures generally contemplate that the interested director will provide appropriate disclosure and will not be involved in taking action on the matter giving rise to the conflict of interest.

2. *Section 8.30(b)*

Section 8.30(b) establishes a general standard of care for directors in the context of their dealing with the board's decision-making and oversight functions. Although certain aspects will involve individual conduct (*e.g.*, preparation for meetings), these functions are generally performed by the board of directors through collective action, as recognized by the reference in subsection (b) to board and committee "members" and "their duties." In contrast with section 8.30(a)'s individual conduct mandate, section 8.30(b) has a two-fold thrust: it provides a standard of conduct for individual action and, more broadly, it states a conduct obligation—"shall discharge their duties"—concerning the degree of care to be used collectively by the directors when performing those functions. The standard is not what care a particular director might believe appropriate in the circumstances but what a person—in a like position and acting under similar circumstances—would reasonably believe to be appropriate. Thus, the degree of care that directors should employ under section 8.30(b) involves an objective standard.

The process by which a director becomes informed, in carrying out the decision-making and oversight functions, will vary. The directors' decision-making function is reflected in various sections of the Act, including: the issuance of shares (section 6.21); distributions (section 6.40); dismissal of derivative proceedings (section 7.44); indemnification (section 8.55); conflict of interest transaction authorization (section 8.62); articles of incorporation amendments (sections 10.02 and 10.03); bylaw amendments (section 10.20); mergers and share exchanges (section 11.04); asset dispositions (section 12.02); and dissolution (section 14.02). The directors' oversight function is established under section 8.01. In discharging the section 8.01 duties associated with the board's oversight function, the standard of care entails primarily a requirement of attention. In contrast with the board's decision-making function, which generally involves informed action at a point in time, the oversight function is concerned with a continuum and the attention of the directors accordingly involves participatory performance over a period of time.

Several of the phrases chosen to define the standard of conduct in section 8.30(b) deserve specific mention:

- The phrase "becoming informed," in the context of the decision-making function, refers to the process of gaining sufficient familiarity with the background facts and circumstances to make an informed judgment. Unless the circumstances would permit a reasonable director to conclude that he or she is already sufficiently informed, the standard of care requires every director to take steps to become informed about the background facts and circumstances before taking action on the matter at hand. The process typically involves review of written materials provided before or at the meeting and attention to or participation in the deliberations leading up to a vote. In addition to considering information and data on which a director is expressly entitled to rely under section 8.30(e), "becoming informed" can also involve consideration of information and data generated by other persons, for example, review of industry studies or research articles prepared by third parties. It can also involve direct communications, outside of the boardroom, with members of management or other directors. There is no one way for "becoming informed," and both the method and measure—"how to" and "how much"—are matters of reasonable judgment for the director to exercise.

- The phrase "devoting attention," in the context of the oversight function, refers to considering such matters as the corporation's information and reporting systems generally and not to an independent investigation into particular system inadequacies or noncompliance. Although directors typically give attention to future plans and trends as well as current activities, they should not be expected to anticipate any particular problems which the corporation may face except in those circumstances where something has occurred to make it obvious to the board that the corporation should be addressing a particular problem. The standard of care associated with the oversight function involves gaining assurances from management and advisers that appropriate systems have been established, such as those concerned with legal compliance, risk assessment or internal controls. Such assurances also should cover establishment of ongoing monitoring of the systems in place, with appropriate follow-up responses when alerted to the issues requiring attention.

- The reference to "person," without embellishment, is intended to avoid implying any qualifications, such as specialized expertise or experience requirements, beyond the basic attributes of common sense, practical wisdom, and informed judgment (however, see the last bullet below).

- The phrase "reasonably believe appropriate" refers to the array of possible options that a person possessing the basic attributes of common sense, practical wisdom and informed judgment would recognize to be available, in terms of the degree of care that might be appropriate, and from which a choice by such person would be made. The measure of care that such person might determine to be appropriate, in a given instance, would normally involve a selection from the range of options and any choice within the realm of reason would be an appropriate decision under the standard of care called for under section 8.30(b). However, a decision that is so removed from the realm of reason, or is so unreasonable, that it falls outside the permissible bounds of sound discretion, and thus is an abuse of discretion, will not satisfy the standard.

- The phrase "in a like position" recognizes that the "care" under consideration is that which would be used by the "person" if he or she were a director of the particular corporation.

- The combined phrase "in a like position . . . under similar circumstances" is intended to recognize that (i) the nature and extent of responsibilities will vary, depending upon such factors as the size, complexity, urgency, and location of activities carried on by the particular corporation, (ii) decisions must be made on the basis of the information known to the directors without the benefit of hindsight, and (iii) the special background, qualifications, and oversight responsibilities of a particular director may be relevant in evaluating that director's compliance with the standard of care.

3. *Section 8.30(c)*

A requirement to disclose to other directors information that a director knows to be material to the decision-making or oversight functions of the board of directors or a board committee is implicit in the standards of conduct set forth in sections 8.30(a) and (b), but section 8.30(c) makes this explicit. Thus, for example, when a member of the board of directors knows information that the director recognizes is material to a decision by the board but is not known to the other directors, the director is obligated to disclose that information to the other members of the board. Such disclosure can occur through direct statements in meetings of the board, or by any other timely means, including, for example, communicating the information to the chairman of the board or the chairman of a committee, or to the corporation's general counsel, and requesting that the recipient inform the other board or committee members of the information.

Section 8.30(c) recognizes that a duty of confidentiality to a third party can override a director's obligation to share with other directors information pertaining to a current corporate matter. In some circumstances, a duty of confidentiality to a third party may even prohibit disclosure of the nature or the existence of the duty itself. Ordinarily, however, a director who withholds material information based on a reasonable belief that a duty of confidentiality to a third party prohibits disclosure should advise the other directors of the existence and nature of that duty. Under the standards of conduct set forth in section 8.30(a), the withholding of material information may, depending on the nature of the material information and of the matter before the board of directors or a board committee, require that a director abstain or recuse himself or herself from all or a portion of the other directors' deliberation or vote on the matter to which the undisclosed information is material, or even resign as a director. See Official Comment to section 8.62.

In connection with a director's conflicting interest transaction, the required disclosure (as defined in section 8.60) that must be made under section 8.62(a) and the exceptions to the required disclosure in that context under section 8.62(b) have elements that parallel the disclosure obligation of directors under section 8.30(c). The demands of section 8.62, however, are more detailed and specific. They apply to just one situation—a director's conflicting interest transaction—while the requirements of section 8.30(c) apply generally to all other decision-making and oversight functions. For example, the specific requirements of section 8.62(a)(1) for deliberation and a vote outside the presence of the conflicted director are not imposed universally for all decision-making matters or for oversight matters that do not involve decisions. Although they may be different from the generally applicable provisions of section 8.30(c), the specific provisions of subchapter 8F control and are exclusive with respect to director conflicting interest transactions.

The requirement that a director disclose information to other directors as set forth in section 8.30(c) is different from any common law duty the board may have to cause the corporation to make disclosures to shareholders under certain circumstances. The Act does not seek to codify such a duty of disclosure, but leaves its existence and scope, the circumstances for its application, and the consequences of any failure to satisfy it, to be developed by courts on a case-by-case basis.

4. Section 8.30(d)

The delegation of authority and responsibility described in section 8.30(d) may take a variety of forms, including (i) formal action through a board resolution, (ii) implicit action through the election of corporate officers (*e.g.*, chief financial officer or controller) or the appointment of corporate managers (*e.g.*, credit manager), or (iii) informal action through a course of conduct (*e.g.*, involvement through corporate officers and managers in the management of a significant 50%-owned joint venture). Under section 8.30(d), a director may properly rely on those to whom authority has been delegated pursuant to section 8.30(d) respecting particular matters calling for specific action or attention in connection with the directors' decision-making function as well as matters on the board's continuing agenda, such as legal compliance and internal controls, in connection with the directors' oversight function. Delegation should be carried out in accordance with the standard of care set forth in section 8.30(b).

By identifying those persons upon whom a director may rely in connection with the discharge of duties, section 8.30(d) does not limit the ability of directors to delegate their powers under section 8.01(b) except where delegation is expressly prohibited by the Act or otherwise by applicable law. See section 8.25 and its Official Comment for discussion of delegation to committees of the authority of the board under section 8.01. By employing the concept of delegation, the Act does not limit the ability of directors to establish baseline principles as to management responsibilities. Specifically, section 8.01(b) provides that "all corporate powers shall be exercised by or under the authority of" the board, and a basic board function involves the allocation of management responsibilities and the related assignment (or delegation) of corporate powers. For example, a board can properly decide to retain a third party to assume responsibility for the administration of designated aspects of risk management for the corporation (*e.g.*, health insurance or disability claims).

Although the board of directors may delegate the authority or duty to perform one or more of its functions, delegation and reliance under section 8.30(d) may not alone constitute compliance with sections 8.30(a) and (b) and the action taken by the delegatee may not alone satisfy the directors or a noncommittee board member's section 8.01 responsibilities. On the other hand, failure of the board committee or the corporate officer or employee performing the function delegated to meet section 8.30(b)'s standard of care will not automatically result in violation by the board of section 8.01. Factors to be considered in determining whether a violation of section 8.01 has occurred will include the care used in the delegation to and supervision over the delegatee, and the amount of knowledge regarding the particular matter which is reasonably available to the particular director. Care in delegation and supervision includes appraisal of the capabilities and diligence of the delegatee in light of the subject and its relative importance and may be satisfied, in the usual case, by receipt of reports concerning the delegatee's activities. The enumeration of these factors is intended to emphasize that directors may not abdicate their responsibilities and avoid accountability simply by delegating authority to others. Rather, a director who is accountable for the acts of delegatees will fulfill the director's duties if the standards contained in section 8.30 are met.

5.   *Section 8.30(e)*

Reliance under section 8.30(e) on a report, statement, opinion, or other information is permitted only if the director has read or heard orally presented the information, opinion, report or statement in question, or took other steps to become generally familiar with it. A director must comply with the general standard of care of section 8.30(b) in making a judgment as to the reliability and competence of the source of information upon which the director proposes to rely or, as appropriate, that it otherwise merits confidence.

6.   *Section 8.30(f)*

In determining whether a corporate officer or employee is "reliable," for purposes of section 8.30(f)(1), the director would typically consider (i) the individual's background experience and scope of responsibility within the corporation in gauging the individual's familiarity and knowledge respecting the subject matter and (ii) the individual's record and reputation for honesty, care and ability in discharging responsibilities which he or she undertakes. In determining whether a person is "competent," the director would normally take into account the same considerations and, if expertise should be relevant, the director would consider the individual's technical skills as well. Recognition of the right of one director to rely on the expertise and experience of another director, in the context of board or committee deliberations, is unnecessary, for reliance on shared experience and wisdom of other board members is an implicit underpinning of collective board conduct. In relying on another member of the board, a director would quite properly take advantage of the colleague's knowledge and experience in becoming informed about the matter at hand before taking action; however, the director would be expected to exercise independent judgment when it comes time to vote.

Advisers on whom a director may rely under section 8.30(f)(2) include not only licensed professionals, such as lawyers, accountants, and engineers, but also those in other fields involving special experience and skills, such as investment bankers, geologists, management consultants, actuaries, and appraisers. The adviser could be an individual or an organization, such as a law or investment banking firm. Reliance on a nonmanagement director, who is specifically engaged (and, normally, additionally compensated) to undertake a special assignment or a particular consulting role, would fall within this outside adviser frame of reference. The concept of "expert competence" embraces a wide variety of qualifications and is not limited to the more precise and narrower recognition of experts under the Securities Act of 1933. In addition, a director may also rely on outside advisers where skills or expertise of a technical nature is not a prerequisite, or where the person's professional or expert competence has not been established, so long as the director reasonably believes the person merits confidence. For example, a board might choose to engage a private investigator to inquire into a particular matter (*e.g.*, follow up on rumors about a senior executive's alleged misconduct) and properly rely on the private investigator's report.

Section 8.30(f)(3) permits reliance on a board committee when it is submitting recommendations for action by the full board of directors as well as when it is performing supervisory or other functions in instances where neither the full board of directors nor the committee takes dispositive action. For example, the compensation committee typically reviews proposals and makes recommendations for action by the full board of directors. There also might be reliance upon an investigation undertaken by a board committee and reported to the full board, which forms the basis for a decision by the board of directors not to take dispositive action. Another example is reliance on a board committee, such as an audit committee with respect to the board's ongoing role of oversight of the accounting and auditing functions of the corporation. In addition, where reliance on information or materials prepared or presented by a board committee is not involved in connection with board action, a director may properly rely on oversight monitoring or dispositive action by a board committee (of which the director is not a member) empowered to act pursuant to authority delegated under section 8.25 or acting with the acquiescence of the board of directors. See the Official Comment to section 8.25. In parallel with section 8.30(f)(2)(ii), the concept of "confidence" is used instead of "competence" to avoid any inference that technical skills are a prerequisite. In the usual case, the appointment of committee members or the reconstitution of the membership of a standing committee (*e.g.*, the audit committee), following an annual shareholders' meeting, would alone manifest the noncommittee members' belief that the committee "merits confidence." Depending on the circumstances, the reliance contemplated by section 8.30(f)(3) is geared to the point in time when the board takes action or the period of time over which a committee is engaged in an oversight function; consequently, the judgment to be made (*i.e.*, whether a committee "merits confidence") will arise at varying points in time. Ordinarily, after making an initial judgment that a committee (of which a director is not a member) merits confidence, a director may continue to rely on that committee so long as the director has no reason to believe that confidence is no longer warranted.

7. Application to Officers

Section 8.30 generally deals only with directors. Section 8.42 and its Official Comment explain the extent to which the principles set forth in section 8.30 apply to officers.

§8.31. Standards of Liability for Directors

(a) A director shall not be liable to the corporation or its shareholders for any decision to take or not to take action, or any failure to take any action, as a director, unless the party asserting liability in a proceeding establishes that:

(1) no defense interposed by the director based on (i) any provision in the articles of incorporation authorized by section 2.02(b)(4) or by section 2.02(b)(6), (ii) the protection afforded by section 8.61 (for action taken in compliance with section 8.62 or section 8.63), or (iii) the protection afforded by section 8.70, precludes liability; and

(2) the challenged conduct consisted or was the result of:

(i) action not in good faith; or

(ii) a decision

(A) which the director did not reasonably believe to be in the best interests of the corporation, or

(B) as to which the director was not informed to an extent the director reasonably believed appropriate in the circumstances; or

(iii) a lack of objectivity due to the director's familial, financial or business relationship with, or a lack of independence due to the director's domination or control by, another person having a material interest in the challenged conduct,

(A) which relationship or which domination or control could reasonably be expected to have affected the director's judgment respecting the challenged conduct in a manner adverse to the corporation, and

(B) after a reasonable expectation to such effect has been established, the director shall not have established that the challenged conduct was reasonably believed by the director to be in the best interests of the corporation; or

(iv) a sustained failure of the director to devote attention to ongoing oversight of the business and affairs of the corporation, or a failure to devote timely attention, by making (or causing to be made) appropriate inquiry, when particular facts and circumstances of significant concern materialize that would alert a reasonably attentive director to the need for such inquiry; or

(v) receipt of a financial benefit to which the director was not entitled or any other breach of the director's duties to deal fairly with the corporation and its shareholders that is actionable under applicable law.

(b) The party seeking to hold the director liable:

    (1)   for money damages, shall also have the burden of establishing that:

        (i)   harm to the corporation or its shareholders has been suffered, and

        (ii)   the harm suffered was proximately caused by the director's challenged conduct; or

    (2)   for other money payment under a legal remedy, such as compensation for the unauthorized use of corporate assets, shall also have whatever persuasion burden may be called for to establish that the payment sought is appropriate in the circumstances; or

    (3)   for other money payment under an equitable remedy, such as profit recovery by or disgorgement to the corporation, shall also have whatever persuasion burden may be called for to establish that the equitable remedy sought is appropriate in the circumstances.

    (c)   Nothing contained in this section shall (i) in any instance where fairness is at issue, such as consideration of the fairness of a transaction to the corporation under section 8.61(b)(3), alter the burden of proving the fact or lack of fairness otherwise applicable, (ii) alter the fact or lack of liability of a director under another section of this Act, such as the provisions governing the consequences of an unlawful distribution under section 8.32 or a transactional interest under section 8.61, or (iii) affect any rights to which the corporation or a shareholder may be entitled under another statute of this state or the United States.

Cross-References

Business opportunities, see ch. 8G.

Derivative proceedings, see §§ 7.40 through 7.47.

Director's conflicting interest transactions, see ch. 8F.

Expanding indemnification by provision in articles of incorporation, see § 2.02.

Functions of board of directors, see § 8.01.

Indemnification and advance for expenses, see §§ 8.50 through 8.59.

Limiting director liability by provision in articles of incorporation, see § 2.02.

Removal of directors by judicial proceeding, see § 8.09.

Standards of conduct for directors, see § 8.30.

Unlawful distributions, see § 8.32.

Official Comment

Boards of directors and corporate managers make numerous decisions that involve the balancing of risks and benefits for the enterprise. Although some decisions turn out to have been unwise or the result of a mistake of judgment, it is not reasonable to impose liability for an informed decision made in good faith which with the benefit of hindsight turns out to be wrong or unwise. Therefore, as a general rule, a director is not exposed to personal liability for injury or damage caused by an unwise decision and conduct conforming with the standards of section 8.30 will almost always be protected regardless of the end result. Moreover, the fact that a director's performance fails to meet the standards of section 8.30 does not in itself establish personal liability for damages that the corporation or its shareholders may have suffered as a consequence. Nevertheless, a director can be held liable for misfeasance or nonfeasance in performing his or her duties. Section 8.31 sets forth the standards of liability of directors as distinct from the standards of conduct set forth in section 8.30.

Courts have developed the broad common law concept of the business judgment rule. Although formulations vary, in basic principle, a board of directors generally enjoys a presumption of sound business judgment and its decisions will not be disturbed by a court substituting its own notions of what is or is not sound business judgment if the board's decisions can be attributed to any rational business purpose. It is also presumed that, in making a business decision, directors act in good faith, on an informed basis, and in the honest belief that the action taken is in the best interests of the corporation. The elements of the business judgment rule and the circumstances for its application continue to be developed and refined by courts.

Accordingly, it would not be desirable to freeze the concept in a statute. Thus, section 8.31 does not codify the business judgment rule as a whole, although certain of its principal elements, relating to personal liability issues, are reflected in section 8.31(a)(2).

* * *

Note on Directors' Liability

A director's exposure to financial liability (*e.g.*, in a lawsuit for money damages suffered by the corporation or its shareholders claimed to have resulted from misfeasance or nonfeasance in connection with the performance of the director's duties) can be analyzed as follows:

- *Articles of incorporation limitations.* If the corporation's articles of incorporation contain a provision eliminating its directors' liability to the corporation or its shareholders for money damages, adopted pursuant to section 2.02(b)(4), there is no liability unless the director's conduct involves one of the exceptions prescribed in that section that preclude the elimination of liability. If the matter involves a director's taking of a business opportunity and an articles of incorporation provision has been adopted under section 2.02(b)(6) eliminating directors' duties with respect to those opportunities, there also will be no liability. See section 2.02 and its Official Comment.

- *Director's conflicting interest transaction safe harbor.* If the matter at issue involves a director's conflicting interest transaction (as defined in section 8.60) and a safe harbor procedure under section 8.61 involving action taken in compliance with section 8.62 or 8.63 has been properly implemented, there is no liability for the interested director arising out of the transaction. See subchapter 8F.

- *Business opportunities safe harbors.* Similarly, if the matter involves a director's pursuit or taking of a business opportunity, there is no liability for that director if (i) an applicable limitation or elimination of any duty to offer that business opportunity has been adopted pursuant to section 2.02(b)(6), or (ii) a safe harbor procedure under section 8.70 has been properly implemented, even if the articles of incorporation contain no provision under section 2.02(b)(6). See subchapter 8G.

- *Business judgment rule.* If a provision in the articles of incorporation adopted pursuant to section 2.02(b)(4) or (6) or a safe harbor procedure under section 8.61 or 8.70 does not shield the director's conduct from liability, the presumptions, standards of judicial review and procedural matters related to the business judgment rule may insulate the director from liability for conduct in connection with a corporate decision.

- *Damages and proximate cause.* If the business judgment rule does not shield the directors' decision-making from liability, as a general rule it must be established that money damages were suffered by the corporation or its shareholders and those damages resulted from and were legally caused by the challenged act or omission of the director.

- *Other liability for money payment.* Aside from a claim for damages, the director may have monetary liability for other reasons, for example, if corporate resources have been used without proper authorization, or a claim for disgorgement of short-swing trading profits under section 16(b) of the Securities Exchange Act of 1934.

- *Equitable profit recovery or disgorgement.* An equitable remedy compelling the disgorgement of the director's improper financial gain or entitling the corporation to profit recovery, where directors' duties have been breached, may require the payment of money by the director to the corporation.

- *Corporate indemnification.* If the director is monetarily liable, the director may be indemnified by the corporation for any payments made and expenses incurred, depending upon the circumstances. See subchapter 8E.

- *Insurance.* To the extent that corporate indemnification is not available, the director may be reimbursed for the money damages for which the director is accountable, together with proceeding-related expenses, if the claim and grounds for liability come within the coverage under directors' and officers' liability insurance that has been purchased by the corporation as authorized under section 8.57.

411

* * *

1.   Section 8.31(a)

A.   SECTION 8.31(a)(1)—AFFIRMATIVE DEFENSES

Under section 8.31(a)(1), if a provision in the articles of incorporation (i) (adopted pursuant to section 2.02(b)(4)) shelters the director from liability for money damages, or (ii) (adopted pursuant to section 2.02(b)(6)) limits or eliminates any duty to offer the particular business opportunity to the corporation, or if a safe harbor procedure under sections 8.61(b)(1) or (b)(2) or section 8.70(a)(1) shelters the director's conduct in connection with a conflicting interest transaction or the pursuit or taking of a business opportunity, and such defense applies to all claims in plaintiff's complaint, there is no need to consider further the application of section 8.31's standards of liability. In that event, the court would presumably grant the defendant director's motion for dismissal or summary judgment (or the equivalent) and the proceeding would be ended. If the defense applies to some but not all of plaintiff's claims, dismissal or summary judgment would presumably be granted with respect to those claims. Termination of the proceeding or dismissal of claims on the basis of a provision in the articles of incorporation or a safe harbor procedure will not automatically follow, however, if the party challenging the director's conduct can assert any of the valid bases for contesting the availability of the liability shelter. Absent such a challenge, the relevant shelter provision is self-executing and the individual director's exoneration from liability is automatic. Further, under both sections 8.61 and 8.70, the directors approving the conflicting interest transaction or approving a director's taking of the business opportunity will presumably be protected as well, because compliance with the relevant standards of conduct under section 8.30 is important for their action to be effective and because, as noted above, conduct meeting section 8.30's standards will almost always be protected.

If a claim of liability arising out of a challenged act or omission of a director is not resolved and disposed of under section 8.31(a)(1), section 8.31(a)(2) provides the basis for evaluating whether the conduct in question can be challenged. One of the elements in section 8.31(a)(2) must be established for a director to have liability under section 8.31.

B.   SECTION 8.31(a)(2)(I)—GOOD FAITH

It is a basic standard under section 8.31(a)(2)(i) that a director's conduct in performing his or her duties be in good faith. If a director's conduct can be successfully challenged pursuant to other clauses of section 8.31(a)(2), there is a substantial likelihood that the conduct in question will also present an issue of good faith implicating section 8.31(a)(2)(i). Similarly, if section 8.31(a)(2) included only subsection (i), much of the conduct with which the other clauses are concerned could still be considered under that subsection, on the basis that such conduct evidenced the director's lack of good faith. Where conduct has not been found deficient on other grounds, decision-making outside the bounds of reasonable judgment can give rise to an inference of bad faith. That form of conduct, sometimes characterized as "reckless indifference" or "deliberate disregard," giving rise to an inference of bad faith can also raise a question whether the director could have reasonably believed that the best interests of the corporation would be served. These issues could arise, for example, in approval of conflicting interest transactions. See the Official Comment to section 8.61.

C.   SECTION 8.31(a)(2)(II)—REASONABLE BELIEF

Liability under section 8.31(a)(2)(ii) turns on a director's reasonable belief with respect to the nature of his or her decision and the degree to which he or she has become informed. In each case, the director must have an actual subjective belief and, so long as it is his or her honest and good faith belief, a director has wide discretion. There is also an objective element to be met, in that the director's belief must also be reasonable. The inquiry is similar to that in section 8.30(a)—could a reasonable person in a like position and acting in similar circumstances have arrived at that belief? In the rare case where a decision respecting the corporation's best interests is so removed from the realm of reason (*e.g.*, corporate waste), or a belief as to the sufficiency of the director's preparation to make an informed judgment is so unreasonable as to fall outside the permissible bounds of sound discretion (*e.g.*, if the director has undertaken no preparation and is completely uninformed), the director's judgment will not be sustained.

D.   SECTION 8.31(a)(2)(III)—LACK OF OBJECTIVITY OR INDEPENDENCE

If the matter at issue involves a director's transactional interest, such as a "director's conflicting interest transaction" in which a "related person" is involved (see section 8.60), it will be governed by section

8.61; otherwise, a lack of objectivity due to a relationship's influence on the director's judgment will be evaluated, in the context of the pending challenge of director conduct, under section 8.31. If the matter at issue involves lack of independence, the proof of domination or control and its influence on the director's judgment will typically entail different (and perhaps more convincing) evidence than what may be involved in a lack of objectivity case. The variables are manifold, and the facts must be sorted out and weighed on a case-by-case basis. For example, the closeness or nature of the relationship with the person allegedly exerting influence on the director could be a factor. If the director is required under section 8.31(a)(2)(iii)(B) to establish that the action taken by him or her was reasonably believed to be in the best interests of the corporation, the inquiry will involve the elements of actual subjective belief and objective reasonableness similar to those found in section 8.31(a)(2)(ii) and section 8.30(a).

To call into question the director's objectivity or independence on the basis of a person's relationship with, or exertion of dominance over, the director, the person must have a material interest in the challenged conduct. In the typical case, analysis of another's interest would first consider the materiality of the transaction or conduct at issue—in most cases, any transaction or other action involving the attention of the board of directors or a board committee will cross the materiality threshold, but not always—and would then consider the materiality of that person's interest in the matter. The possibility that a director's judgment would be adversely affected by another's interest in a transaction or conduct that is not material, or another's immaterial interest in a transaction or conduct, is sufficiently remote that it should not be made subject to judicial review.

In situations where there may be a lack of objectivity, domination, a conflict of interest or divided loyalty, or even where there may be grounds for the issue to be raised, the better course to follow where board or committee action is required is usually for the director to disclose the facts and circumstances posing the possible issue, and then to withdraw from the meeting (or, in the alternative, to abstain from the deliberations and voting). The board members free of any possible taint may then take appropriate action as contemplated by section 8.30 (or section 8.61 if applicable). If this course is followed, the director's conduct respecting the matter in question should be beyond challenge.

E.   SECTION 8.31(a)(2)(IV)—FAILURE TO DEVOTE ATTENTION

The director's role involves two fundamental components: the decision-making function and the oversight function. In contrast with the decision-making function, which generally involves action taken at a point in time, the oversight function under section 8.01(b) involves ongoing monitoring of the corporation's business and affairs over a period of time. Although the facts will be outcome-determinative, deficient conduct involving a sustained failure to exercise oversight—where found actionable—has typically been characterized by the courts in terms of abdication and continued neglect by a director to devote attention, not a brief distraction or temporary interruption. Also embedded in the oversight function is the need to inquire when suspicions are aroused. This need to inquire is not a component of ongoing oversight, and does not entail proactive vigilance, but arises under section 8.31(a)(2)(iv) when, and only when, particular facts and circumstances of material concern (*e.g.*, evidence of embezzlement at a high level or the discovery of significant inventory shortages) surface.

F.   SECTION 8.31(a)(2)(V)—IMPROPER FINANCIAL BENEFIT AND OTHER BREACHES OF DUTIES

Subchapter 8F deals in detail with directors' transactional interests. Its coverage of those interests is exclusive and its safe harbor procedures for director's conflicting interest transactions (as defined)—providing shelter from legal challenges based on interest conflicts, when properly observed—will establish a director's entitlement to any financial benefit gained from the transactional event. A director's conflicting interest transaction that is not protected by the fairness standard set forth in section 8.61(b)(3), pursuant to which the conflicted director may establish the transaction to have been fair to the corporation, would often involve receipt of a financial benefit to which the director was not entitled (*i.e.*, the transaction was not "fair" to the corporation). Unauthorized use of corporate assets, such as aircraft or hotel suites, would also provide a basis for the proper challenge of a director's conduct. There can be other forms of improper financial benefit not involving a transaction with the corporation or use of its facilities, such as where a director profits from unauthorized use of proprietary information.

There is no materiality threshold that applies to a financial benefit to which a director is not properly entitled. The Act observes this principle in several places, for example, the exception to liability elimination prescribed in section 2.02(b)(4)(i) and the indemnification restriction in section 8.51(d)(2), as well as the liability standard in section 8.31(a)(2)(v).

The second clause of section 8.31(a)(2)(v) is, in part, a catchall provision that implements the intention to make section 8.31 a generally inclusive provision but, at the same time, to recognize the existence of other breaches of common-law principles that can give rise to liability for directors. As developed in the case law, these actionable breaches may include unauthorized use of corporate property or information (which as noted above, might also be characterized as receipt of an improper financial benefit), unfair competition with the corporation or the taking of a corporate opportunity. In the case of corporate opportunity, if the director is alleged to have wrongfully diverted a business opportunity as to which the corporation had a prior right, the Act provides two possible safe harbors. First, any duty to offer the business opportunity to the corporation may have been limited or eliminated pursuant to a provision in the articles of incorporation authorized by section 2.02(b)(6). Second, section 8.70(a)(1) provides a safe harbor procedure for a director who wishes to pursue or take advantage of a business opportunity, regardless of whether such opportunity would be characterized as a "corporate opportunity" under existing case law. Note that section 8.70(b) provides that the fact that a director did not employ the safe harbor procedure of section 8.70(a)(1) does not create an implication that the opportunity should have first been presented to the corporation or alter the burden of proof otherwise applicable to establish a breach of the director's duty to the corporation.

2. Section 8.31(b)

Whether a corporation or its shareholders have suffered harm and whether a particular director's conduct was the proximate cause of that harm may be affected by the collective nature of board action. Proper performance of the relevant duty through the action taken by the director's colleagues can overcome the consequences of his or her deficient conduct. For example, where a director's conduct can be challenged under section 8.31(a)(2)(ii)(B) by reason of having been uninformed about the decision or not reading the materials distributed before the meeting, or arriving late at the board meeting just in time for the vote but, nonetheless, voting in favor solely because the others were in favor—the favorable action by a quorum of properly informed directors would ordinarily protect the director against liability, either because there was no harm or the offending director's actions were not the proximate cause of the harm. Although the concept of "proximate cause" is a term of art that is basic to tort law, for purposes of section 8.31(b)(1), a useful approach for the concept's application would be that the challenged conduct must have been a "substantial factor in producing the harm."

3. Section 8.31(c)

Section 8.31(c) expressly disclaims any shift of the burden of proof otherwise applicable where the question of the fairness of a transaction or other challenged conduct is at issue. This is the case whether the question of fairness arises under another section of the Act, such as section 8.61, under existing case law, under a judicial requirement in a particular instance or otherwise. Similarly, section 8.31 does not affect liability under other sections of the Act. It also does not foreclose any rights of the corporation or its shareholders under other laws, for example, rights of shareholders or the corporation under applicable federal securities laws. In addition, directors can have liability to persons other than the corporation and its shareholders, such as liability to employee benefit plan participants and beneficiaries (who may or may not be shareholders), if the directors are determined to be fiduciaries under other applicable laws, to government agencies for regulatory violations or to individuals claiming damages for injury governed by tort-law concepts (*e.g.*, libel or slander). Section 8.31 is not intended to change the standards applicable under these other laws or legal principles.

§ 8.32. Directors' Liability for Unlawful Distributions

(a) A director who votes for or assents to a distribution in excess of what may be authorized and made pursuant to section 6.40(a) or 14.09(a) is personally liable to the corporation for the amount of the distribution that exceeds what could have been distributed without violating section 6.40(a) or 14.09(a) if the party asserting liability establishes that when taking the action the director did not comply with section 8.30.

(b) A director held liable under subsection (a) for an unlawful distribution is entitled to:

(1)   contribution from every other director who could be held liable under subsection (a) for the unlawful distribution; and

(2)   recoupment from each shareholder of the pro-rata portion of the amount of the unlawful distribution the shareholder accepted, knowing the distribution was made in violation of section 6.40(a) or 14.09(a).

(c)   A proceeding to enforce:

(1)   the liability of a director under subsection (a) is barred unless it is commenced within two years after the date (i) on which the effect of the distribution was measured under section 6.40(e) or (g), (ii) as of which the violation of section 6.40(a) occurred as the consequence of disregard of a restriction in the articles of incorporation, or (iii) on which the distribution of assets to shareholders under section 14.09(a) was made; or

(2)   contribution or recoupment under subsection (b) is barred unless it is commenced within one year after the liability of the claimant has been finally adjudicated under subsection (a).

Cross-References

Director duties in dissolution, see § 14.09.

Director standards of conduct, see § 8.30.

"Distribution" defined, see § 1.40.

Distributions to shareholders, see § 6.40.

Indemnification, see §§ 2.02 and 8.50 through 8.59.

Limiting director liability by provision in articles of incorporation, see § 2.02.

Official Comment

A director whose conduct, in voting for or assenting to a distribution, is challenged under section 8.32 will have no liability unless the complaining party establishes a breach of the relevant standards of section 8.30, for example a failure to act with the care required by section 8.30(b) or reliance on persons or information unwarranted under section 8.30(d) or (e). A shareholder (other than a director) who receives a payment not knowing of its invalidity is not subject to recoupment under subsection (b)(2). Although no attempt has been made in the Act to work out in detail the relationship between the right of recoupment from shareholders under subsection (b)(2) and the right of contribution from directors under subsection (b)(1), a court may equitably apportion the obligations and benefits arising from the application of the principles set forth in section 8.32.

Section 8.32(c) limits the time within which a proceeding may be commenced against a director for an unlawful distribution and the time within which a proceeding for contribution or recoupment may be made. The one-year period specified in subsection (c)(2) may end within or extend beyond the two-year period specified in subsection (c)(1).

SUBCHAPTER D
OFFICERS

§ 8.40. Officers

(a)   A corporation has the officers described in its bylaws or appointed by the board of directors in accordance with the bylaws.

(b)   The board of directors may elect individuals to fill one or more offices of the corporation. An officer may appoint one or more officers if authorized by the bylaws or the board of directors.

(c)   The bylaws or the board of directors shall assign to an officer responsibility for maintaining and authenticating the records of the corporation required to be kept under section 16.01(a).

(d)   The same individual may simultaneously hold more than one office in a corporation.

Cross-References

Agents of corporation, see § 3.02.

Bylaws, see § 2.06 and ch. 10B.

Contract rights of officers, see § 8.44.

Functions of officers, see § 8.41.

Officer as employee of corporation, see § 1.40.

Officer standards of conduct, see § 8.42.

Resignation and removal of officers, see § 8.43.

"Secretary" defined, see § 1.40.

Tenure of officers, see § 8.44.

Official Comment

Section 8.40 permits every corporation to designate the officers it will have. No particular officers are required.

The board of directors, as well as duly authorized officers, employees or agents, may also appoint other agents for the corporation. In addition, a board of directors has the intrinsic power to organize its own internal affairs, including designating officers of the board.

The officer who has the responsibility to maintain the minutes and authenticate the corporate records referred to in section 16.01(a) is referred to as the "secretary" of the corporation throughout the Act. See section 1.40. The person so designated has authority to bind the corporation by that officer's authentication under this section. This assignment of authority, traditionally vested in the corporate "secretary," allows third persons to rely on authenticated records without inquiry as to their truth or accuracy.

§ 8.41. Functions of Officers

Each officer has the authority and shall perform the functions set forth in the bylaws or, to the extent consistent with the bylaws, the functions prescribed by the board of directors or by direction of an officer authorized by the board of directors to prescribe the functions of other officers.

Cross-References

Bylaws, see § 2.06 and ch. 10B.

Officer as employee, see § 1.40.

Standards of conduct:

directors, see § 8.30.

officers, see § 8.42.

Official Comment

The methods of investing officers with formal authority in section 8.41 do not exhaust the sources of an officer's actual or apparent authority. Specific officers, particularly the chief executive officer, may have implied authority to take certain actions on behalf of a corporation merely by virtue of their positions. Officers may also be vested with apparent authority by reason of corporate conduct on which third persons reasonably rely.

In addition to express, implied, or apparent authority, a corporation is bound by unauthorized acts of officers if they are ratified by the board of directors. Generally, ratification may extend only to acts that could have been authorized as an original matter. Ratification may itself be express or implied and may in some cases serve as the basis of apparent authority.

§ 8.42. Standards of Conduct for Officers

(a) An officer, when performing in such capacity, has the duty to act:

(1) in good faith;

(2) with the care that a person in a like position would reasonably exercise under similar circumstances; and

(3) in a manner the officer reasonably believes to be in the best interests of the corporation.

(b) The duty of an officer includes the obligation:

(1) to inform the superior officer to whom, or the board of directors or the board committee to which, the officer reports of information about the affairs of the corporation known to the officer, within the scope of the officer's functions, and known to the officer to be material to such superior officer, board or committee; and

(2) to inform his or her superior officer, or another appropriate person within the corporation, or the board of directors, or a board committee, of any actual or probable material violation of law involving the corporation or material breach of duty to the corporation by an officer, employee, or agent of the corporation, that the officer believes has occurred or is likely to occur.

(c) In discharging his or her duties, an officer who does not have knowledge that makes reliance unwarranted is entitled to rely on:

(1) the performance of properly delegated responsibilities by one or more employees of the corporation whom the officer reasonably believes to be reliable and competent in performing the responsibilities delegated; or

(2) information, opinions, reports or statements, including financial statements and other financial data, prepared or presented by one or more employees of the corporation whom the officer reasonably believes to be reliable and competent in the matters presented or by legal counsel, public accountants, or other persons retained by the corporation as to matters involving skills or expertise the officer reasonably believes are matters (i) within the particular person's professional or expert competence or (ii) as to which the particular person merits confidence.

(d) An officer shall not be liable to the corporation or its shareholders for any decision to take or not to take action, or any failure to take any action, as an officer, if the duties of the office are performed in compliance with this section. Whether an officer who does not comply with this section shall have liability will depend in such instance on applicable law, including those principles of section 8.31 that have relevance.

Cross-References

Appointment of officers, see § 8.40.

Functions of officers, see § 8.41.

Indemnification, see §§ 8.50 through 8.59.

Resignation and removal of officers, see § 8.43.

Standards of conduct for directors, see § 8.30.

Standards of liability for directors, see § 8.31.

Official Comment

Under section 8.42(a), an officer, when performing in such officer's official capacity, has to meet standards of conduct generally specified for directors under section 8.30. This section is not intended to modify, diminish or qualify the duties or standards of conduct that may be imposed upon specific officers by other law or regulation.

Common law has generally recognized a duty on the part of officers and key employees to disclose to their superiors material information relevant to the affairs of the corporation. This duty is implicit in, and embraced under, the broader standard of section 8.42(a), but section 8.42(b) sets forth this disclosure obligation explicitly. Section 8.42(b)(1) specifies that business information shall be transmitted through the officer's regular reporting channels. Section 8.42(b)(2) specifies the reporting responsibility differently with respect to actual or probable material violations of law or material breaches of duty. The use of the term "appropriate" in subsection (b)(2) accommodates any normative standard that the corporation may have prescribed for reporting potential violations of law or duty to a specified person, such as an ombudsperson, ethics officer, internal auditor, general counsel or the like, as well as situations where there is no designated person but the officer's immediate superior is not appropriate (for example, because the officer believes that individual is complicit in the unlawful activity or breach of duty).

Section 8.42(b)(1) should not be interpreted so broadly as to discourage efficient delegation of functions. It addresses the flow of information to the board of directors and to superior officers necessary to enable them to perform their decision-making and oversight functions. See the Official Comment to section 8.31. The officer's duties under subsection (b) may not be negated by agreement; however, their scope under section 8.42(b)(1) may be shaped by prescribing the scope of an officer's functional responsibilities.

With respect to the duties under section 8.42(b)(2), codes of conduct or codes of ethics may prescribe the circumstances in which and mechanisms by which officers and employees may discharge their duty to report material information to superior officers or the board of directors, or to other designated persons.

The term "material" modifying violations of law or breaches of duty in section 8.42(b)(2) denotes a qualitative as well as quantitative standard. It relates not only to the potential direct financial impact on the corporation, but also to the nature of the violation or breach. For example, an embezzlement of $10,000, or even less, would be material because of the seriousness of the offense, even though the amount involved would ordinarily not be material to the financial position or results of operations of the corporation.

The duty under section 8.42(b)(2) is triggered by an officer's subjective belief that a material violation of law or breach of duty actually or probably has occurred or is likely to occur. This duty is not triggered by objective knowledge concepts, such as whether the officer should have concluded that such misconduct was occurring. The subjectivity of the trigger under subsection (b)(2), however, does not excuse officers from their obligations under subsection (a) to act in good faith and with due care in the performance of the functions assigned to them, including oversight duties within their respective areas of responsibility. There may be occasions when the principles applicable under section 8.30(c) limiting the duty of disclosure by directors where a duty of confidentiality is overriding may also apply to officers. See the Official Comment to section 8.30(c).

An officer's ability to rely on others in meeting the standards prescribed in section 8.42 may be more limited, depending upon the circumstances of the particular case, than the measure and scope of reliance permitted a director under section 8.30, in view of the greater obligation the officer may have to be familiar with the affairs of the corporation. The proper delegation of responsibilities by an officer, separate and apart from the exercise of judgment as to the delegatee's reliability and competence, is concerned with the procedure employed. This will involve, in the usual case, sufficient communication such that the delegatee understands the scope of the assignment and, in turn, manifests to the officer a willingness and commitment to undertake its performance. The entitlement to rely upon employees assumes that a delegating officer will maintain a sufficient level of communication with the officer's subordinates to fulfill his or her supervisory responsibilities. The definition of "employee" in section 1.40 includes an officer; accordingly, section 8.42 contemplates the delegation of responsibilities to other officers as well as to non-officer employees.

Although under section 8.42(d), performance meeting that section's standards of conduct will eliminate an officer's exposure to any liability to the corporation or its shareholders, failure by an officer to meet that section's standards will not automatically result in liability. Deficient performance of duties by an officer, depending upon the facts and circumstances, will normally be dealt with through intracorporate disciplinary procedures, such as reprimand, compensation adjustment, delayed promotion, demotion or discharge. These procedures may be subject to (and limited by) the terms of an officer's employment agreement. See section 8.44.

In some cases, failure to observe relevant standards of conduct can give rise to an officer's liability to the corporation or its shareholders. A court review of challenged conduct will involve an evaluation of the particular facts and circumstances in light of applicable law. In this connection, section 8.42(d) recognizes that relevant principles of section 8.31, such as duties to deal fairly with the corporation and its shareholders and the challenger's burden of establishing proximately caused harm, should be taken into account. In addition, the business judgment rule will normally apply to decisions within an officer's discretionary authority. Liability to others can also arise from an officer's own acts or omissions (*e.g.*, violations of law or tort claims) and, in some cases, an officer with supervisory responsibilities can have risk exposure in connection with the acts or omissions of others.

The Official Comment to section 8.30 supplements this Official Comment to the extent that it can be appropriately viewed as generally applicable to officers as well as directors.

§ 8.43. Resignation and Removal of Officers

(a)   An officer may resign at any time by delivering a written notice to the board of directors, or its chair, or to the appointing officer or the secretary. A resignation is effective as provided in section 1.41(i) unless the notice provides for a delayed effectiveness, including effectiveness determined upon a future event or events. If effectiveness of a resignation is stated to be delayed and the board of directors or the appointing officer accepts the delay, the board of directors or the appointing officer may fill the pending vacancy before the delayed effectiveness but the new officer may not take office until the vacancy occurs.

(b)   An officer may be removed at any time with or without cause by (i) the board of directors; (ii) the appointing officer, unless the bylaws or the board of directors provide otherwise; or (iii) any other officer if authorized by the bylaws or the board of directors.

(c)   In this section, "appointing officer" means the officer (including any successor to that officer) who appointed the officer resigning or being removed.

Cross-References

Contract rights of officers, see § 8.44.

"Deliver" defined, see § 1.40.

Notices and other communications, see § 1.41.

"Secretary" defined, see § 1.40.

Official Comment

In part because of the unlimited power of removal under section 8.43(b), a corporation may enter into an employment agreement with the holder of an office that gives the officer rights in the event of removal or failure to be reelected or reappointed to office. This type of contract is binding on the corporation even if the articles of incorporation or bylaws provide that officers are elected for a term shorter than the period of the employment contract. Such an employment agreement does not override the removal power set forth in section 8.43(b) and may give the officer the right to damages, but not specific performance, if employment is terminated before the end of the contract term.

Section 8.43(b) provides the corporation with the flexibility to determine when, if ever, an officer will be permitted to remove another officer. To the extent that the corporation wishes to permit an officer, other than the appointing officer, to remove another officer, the bylaws or a board resolution should set forth clearly the persons having removal authority.

A person may be removed from office irrespective of contract rights or the presence or absence of "cause" in a legal sense.

§ 8.44. Contract Rights of Officers

(a)   The election or appointment of an officer does not itself create contract rights.

(b)   An officer's removal does not affect the officer's contract rights, if any, with the corporation. An officer's resignation does not affect the corporation's contract rights, if any, with the officer.

Cross-References

Appointment of officers, see § 8.40.

Resignation and removal of officers, see § 8.43.

Official Comment

The removal of an officer with contract rights is without prejudice to the officer's rights in a proceeding seeking damages for breach of contract. See the Official Comment to section 8.43. Similarly, an officer with an employment contract who prematurely resigns may be in breach of his or her employment contract. The mere election or appointment of an officer for a term does not create a contractual obligation on the officer's part to complete the term.

SUBCHAPTER E
INDEMNIFICATION AND ADVANCE FOR EXPENSES

Introductory Comment

1.   Policy Issues Raised by Indemnification and Advance for Expenses

Indemnification (including advance for expenses) provides financial protection by the corporation for its directors against exposure to expenses and liabilities that may be incurred by them in connection with legal proceedings based on an alleged breach of duty in their service to or on behalf of the corporation.

The concept of indemnification recognizes that there will be situations in which even though the director does not satisfy all of the elements of the standard of conduct set forth in section 8.30(a) or the requirements of some other applicable law, the corporation should nevertheless be permitted (or required) to absorb the economic costs incurred by the director in any ensuing litigation.

Subchapter 8E is an integrated treatment of indemnification and advance for expenses and strikes a balance among important public policies. It would be difficult to persuade responsible persons to serve as directors if they were compelled to bear personally the cost of vindicating the propriety of their conduct in every instance in which it might be challenged. If permitted too broadly, however, indemnification may violate equally basic tenets of public policy. For example, a director who intentionally inflicts harm on the corporation should not expect to receive assistance from the corporation for legal or other expenses and should be required to satisfy from his or her personal assets not only any adverse judgment but also expenses incurred in connection with the proceeding. A similar policy issue is raised in connection with indemnification against liabilities or sanctions imposed under state or federal civil or criminal statutes. A shift of the economic cost of these liabilities from the individual director to the corporation by way of indemnification may in some instances frustrate the public policy of those statutes.

Some of the same policy considerations apply to the indemnification of officers and, in many cases, employees and agents. The indemnification of officers, whose duties are specified in section 8.42, is dealt with separately in section 8.56. The indemnification of employees and agents, whose duties are prescribed by sources of law other than corporation law (*e.g.*, contract and agency law), is beyond the scope of this subchapter. Section 8.58(d), however, makes clear that subchapter E does not limit a corporation's power to indemnify or advance expenses to employees and agents in accordance with applicable law.

2.   Relationship of Indemnification to Other Policies Established in the Act

Indemnification is closely related to the standards of conduct for directors and officers established elsewhere in chapter 8. The structure of the Act is based on the assumption that if a director acts consistently with the standards of conduct described in section 8.30 or with the standards of a liability-limitation provision in the articles of incorporation (as authorized by section 2.02(b)(4)), the director will not have exposure to liability to the corporation or to shareholders and any expenses necessary to establish a defense will be borne by the corporation (under section 8.52). The converse, however, is not necessarily true. The basic standards for indemnification set forth in section 8.51 for a civil action, in the absence of an indemnification provision in the articles of incorporation (as authorized by section 2.02(b)(5)), are good faith and reasonable belief that the conduct was in or not opposed to the best interests of the corporation. In some circumstances, a director or officer may be found to have violated a statutory or common law duty and yet be able to establish eligibility for indemnification under these standards of conduct. In addition, subchapter

E permits a director or officer who is held liable for violating a statutory or common law duty, but who does not meet the relevant standard of conduct, to petition a court to order indemnification under section 8.54 if the court determines that it would be fair and reasonable to do so.

§ 8.50. Subchapter Definitions

In this subchapter:

"Corporation" includes any domestic or foreign predecessor entity of a corporation in a merger.

"Director" or "officer" means an individual who is or was a director or officer, respectively, of a corporation or who, while a director or officer of the corporation, is or was serving at the corporation's request as a director, officer, manager, partner, trustee, employee, or agent of another entity or employee benefit plan. A director or officer is considered to be serving an employee benefit plan at the corporation's request if the individual's duties to the corporation also impose duties on, or otherwise involve services by, the individual to the plan or to participants in or beneficiaries of the plan. "Director" or "officer" includes, unless the context requires otherwise, the estate or personal representative of a director or officer.

"Liability" means the obligation to pay a judgment, settlement, penalty, fine (including an excise tax assessed with respect to an employee benefit plan), or expenses incurred with respect to a proceeding.

"Official capacity" means: (i) when used with respect to a director, the office of director in a corporation; and (ii) when used with respect to an officer, as contemplated in section 8.56, the office in a corporation held by the officer. "Official capacity" does not include service for any other domestic or foreign corporation or any joint venture, trust, employee benefit plan, or other entity.

"Party" means an individual who was, is, or is threatened to be made, a defendant or respondent in a proceeding.

"Proceeding" means any threatened, pending, or completed action, suit, or proceeding, whether civil, criminal, administrative, arbitrative, or investigative and whether formal or informal.

Cross-References

Effect of merger or share exchange, see § 11.07.

"Entity" defined, see § 1.40.

"Expenses" defined, see § 1.40.

Officers, see § 8.40.

Official Comment

The definitions set forth in section 8.50 apply only to subchapter E and have no application elsewhere in the Act, except for the use of "liability" in section 2.02(b)(5). The term "qualified director," which is used in sections 8.53 and 8.55, is defined in section 1.43.

1. Corporation

Subchapter E's definition of "corporation" includes predecessor entities that have been absorbed in mergers to negate any argument that a different result might be reached under section 11.07(a), which provides for the assumption of liabilities by operation of law upon a merger. The express responsibility of successor entities for the liabilities of their predecessors under this subchapter is broader than under section 11.07(a) and may impose liability on a successor although section 11.07(a) does not. The definition of "corporation" in section 8.50 is thus an essential aspect of the protection provided by this subchapter for persons eligible for indemnification.

2.   Director and Officer

A special definition of "director" and "officer" is included in subchapter E to cover individuals who are made parties to proceedings because they are or were directors or officers or, while serving as directors or officers, also serve or served at the corporation's request in another capacity for another entity. The purpose of the latter part of this definition is to give directors and officers the benefits of the protection of this subchapter while serving at the corporation's request in a responsible position for employee benefit plans, trade associations, nonprofit or charitable entities, domestic or foreign entities, or other kinds of profit or nonprofit ventures. To avoid misunderstanding, it is good practice from both the corporation's and director's or officer's viewpoint for this type of request to be evidenced by resolution, memorandum or other writing.

Even without such a formal action, the second sentence of the definition of "director" or "officer" in section 8.50 addresses the question of liabilities arising under the Employee Retirement Income Security Act of 1974 (ERISA). It makes clear that a director or officer who is serving as a fiduciary of an employee benefit plan is automatically viewed for purposes of this subchapter as having been requested by the corporation to act in that capacity. Special treatment is believed necessary because of ERISA's broad definition of "fiduciary" and the requirement that a "fiduciary" must discharge his or her duties "solely in the interest" of the participants and beneficiaries of the employee benefit plan. Decisions by a director or officer, who is serving as a fiduciary under the plan on questions regarding, for example, (i) eligibility for benefits, (ii) investment decisions, or (iii) interpretation of plan provisions respecting (a) qualifying service, (b) years of service, or (c) retroactivity, are all subject to the protections of this subchapter. See also the definition of "official capacity" in section 8.50.

In the last sentence of the definition of "director" or "officer" in section 8.50, the phrase "unless the context requires otherwise" is intended to clarify that the estate or personal representative does not have the right to participate in decisions by directors authorized in this subchapter.

3.   Liability

"Liability" is defined for convenience to avoid repeated references to recoverable items throughout the subchapter. Even though the definition of "liability" includes amounts paid in settlement or to satisfy a judgment, indemnification against certain types of settlements and judgments is not allowed under several provisions of subchapter E. For example, indemnification in suits brought by or in the right of the corporation is limited to expenses (see section 8.51(d)(1)), unless indemnification for a settlement is ordered by a court under section 8.54(a)(3).

The definition of "liability" permits the indemnification of "expenses." The definition of "expenses" in section 1.40 limits expenses to those that are reasonable. The result is that any portion of expenses which is not reasonable should not be advanced or indemnified. In contrast, amounts paid to settle or satisfy substantive claims are not subject to a reasonableness test. Since payment of these amounts is permissive—mandatory indemnification is available under section 8.52 only where the defendant is "wholly successful"—a limitation of "reasonableness" for settlements is inappropriate.

The definition of "liability" is intended to cover every type of monetary obligation that may be imposed upon a director, including civil penalties, restitution, and the levy of excise taxes under the Internal Revenue Code pursuant to ERISA.

4.   Official Capacity

The term "official capacity" is used in determining which of the two alternative standards of conduct set forth in section 8.51(a)(1)(ii) applies: If the action was taken in an "official capacity," the individual to be indemnified must have reasonably believed that he or she was acting in the best interests of the corporation. In contrast, if the action in question was not taken in an "official capacity," the individual need only have reasonably believed that the conduct was not opposed to the best interests of the corporation. See also the Official Comment to section 8.51(a).

5.   Party

The definition of "party" includes present and former parties in addition to individuals currently or formerly threatened with being made a party. An individual who is only called as a witness is not a "party" within this definition, but as specifically provided in section 8.58(e) payment or reimbursement of witness expenses is not limited by this subchapter.

6. Proceeding

The broad definition of "proceeding" ensures that the benefits of this subchapter will be available to directors in new and unexpected, as well as traditional, types of litigation or other adversarial matters, whether civil, criminal, administrative, or investigative. It also includes arbitration and other dispute resolution proceedings, appeals and petitions to review administrative actions.

§ 8.51. Permissible Indemnification

(a) Except as otherwise provided in this section, a corporation may indemnify an individual who is a party to a proceeding because the individual is a director against liability incurred in the proceeding if:

(1)(i) the director conducted himself or herself in good faith; and

(ii) the director reasonably believed:

(A) in the case of conduct in an official capacity, that his or her conduct was in the best interests of the corporation; and

(B) in all other cases, that his or her conduct was at least not opposed to the best interests of the corporation; and

(iii) in the case of any criminal proceeding, the director had no reasonable cause to believe his or her conduct was unlawful; or

(2) the director engaged in conduct for which broader indemnification has been made permissible or obligatory under a provision of the articles of incorporation (as authorized by section 2.02(b)(5)).

(b) A director's conduct with respect to an employee benefit plan for a purpose the director reasonably believed to be in the interests of the participants in, and the beneficiaries of, the plan is conduct that satisfies the requirement of subsection (a)(1)(ii)(B).

(c) The termination of a proceeding by judgment, order, settlement, or conviction, or upon a plea of nolo contendere or its equivalent, is not, of itself, determinative that the director did not meet the relevant standard of conduct described in this section.

(d) Unless ordered by a court under section 8.54(a)(3), a corporation may not indemnify a director:

(1) in connection with a proceeding by or in the right of the corporation, except for expenses incurred in connection with the proceeding if it is determined that the director has met the relevant standard of conduct under subsection (a); or

(2) in connection with any proceeding with respect to conduct for which the director was adjudged liable on the basis of receiving a financial benefit to which he or she was not entitled, regardless of whether it involved action in the director's official capacity.

Cross-References

Advance for expenses, see § 8.53.

"Corporation" defined, see § 8.50.

Court-ordered indemnification and advance for expenses, see § 8.54.

Derivative proceedings, see §§ 7.40 through 7.47.

Determination and authorization of indemnification, see § 8.55.

"Director" defined, see § 8.50.

Director's conflicting interest transaction, see ch. 8F.

Exclusivity of subchapter, see § 8.59.

"Expenses" defined, see § 1.40.

"Liability" defined, see § 8.50.

Limiting director liability by provision in articles of incorporation, see § 2.02.

Limits on indemnification, see § 8.58.

Mandatory indemnification, see § 8.52.

Obligatory indemnification, see §§ 2.02 and 8.58.

"Officer" defined, see § 8.50.

Officer indemnification, see § 8.56.

"Official capacity" defined, see § 8.50.

"Party" defined, see § 8.50.

"Proceeding" defined, see § 8.50.

Standards of conduct for directors, see § 8.30.

Standards of liability for directors, see § 8.31.

Official Comment

1.　Section 8.51(a)

The standards for indemnification of directors contained in section 8.51(a) define the limits of the conduct for which discretionary indemnification is permitted under the Act, except to the extent that court-ordered indemnification is available under section 8.54(a)(3). Conduct that falls within these limits does not automatically entitle directors to indemnification, although a corporation may obligate itself to indemnify directors to the maximum extent permitted by applicable law. See section 8.58(a). Absent such an obligatory provision, section 8.52 defines much narrower circumstances in which directors are entitled as a matter of right to indemnification.

The standards of conduct in section 8.51(a) are not dependent on the type of proceeding in which the claim arises. These standards are closely related, but not identical, to the standards of conduct imposed by section 8.30 on directors when discharging the duties of a director: good faith, reasonable belief that the best interests of the corporation are being served, and appropriate care (*i.e.*, that which a person in a like position would reasonably believe appropriate under similar circumstances). As in the case of section 8.30, where the concept of good faith is also used, section 8.51 provides no definition for that term. The concept involves a subjective test, which would permit indemnification for an unwise decision or "a mistake of judgment," even though made negligently by objective standards. Section 8.51 also requires, as does section 8.30, a "reasonable" belief that conduct when acting in the director's official capacity was in the corporation's best interests. It then adds a provision, not found in section 8.30, relating to criminal proceedings that requires the director to have had no "reasonable cause" to believe that the conduct was unlawful. These both involve objective standards applicable to the director's belief concerning the effect of the conduct in question. Conduct includes both acts and omissions.

In section 8.51(a)(1)(ii)(B), the words "at least" qualify "not opposed to" and make clear that this standard is for conduct other than in an official capacity. Although this provision deals with indemnification by the corporation, a director serving another entity at the request of the corporation remains subject to the provisions of the law governing service to that other entity, including provisions dealing with conflicts of interest. Compare sections 8.60 through 8.63. Should indemnification from the requesting corporation be sought by a director for acts done while serving another entity, which acts involved breach of a duty owed to that other entity, nothing in section 8.51(a)(1)(ii)(B) would preclude the requesting corporation from considering, in assessing its own best interests, whether the fact that its director had engaged in a violation of the duty owed to the other entity was in fact "opposed to" the interests of the indemnifying corporation.

If the relevant standards are met, section 8.51 also permits indemnification in connection with a proceeding involving an alleged failure to satisfy legal standards other than the standards of conduct in section 8.30, *e.g.*, violations of antitrust, environmental or securities laws.

In addition to indemnification under section 8.51(a)(1), section 8.51(a)(2) permits indemnification under the standard of conduct set forth in a provision of the articles of incorporation adopted pursuant to section 2.02(b)(5). Based on such a provision, section 8.51(a)(2) permits indemnification in connection with claims by third parties and, through section 8.56, applies to officers as well as directors. (This goes beyond the scope of a provision of the articles of incorporation adopted pursuant to section 2.02(b)(4), which can only limit liability of directors against claims by the corporation or its shareholders.) Section 8.51(a)(2) is subject to the prohibition of subsection (d)(1) against indemnification of settlements and judgments in derivative suits, except as ordered by a court under section 8.54(a)(3). It is also subject to the prohibition of subsection (d)(2) against indemnification for receipt of an improper financial benefit; however, this prohibition is already subsumed in the exception contained in section 2.02(b)(5)(i).

2. *Section 8.51(b)*

As discussed in the Official Comment to the definition of "director" or "officer" in section 8.50, ERISA requires that a "fiduciary" (as defined in ERISA) discharge the fiduciary's duties "solely in the interest" of the participants in and beneficiaries of an employee benefit plan. The standard in section 8.51(b) for indemnification of a director who is serving as a trustee or fiduciary for an employee benefit plan under ERISA is arguably an exception to the more general standard that conduct not in an official corporate capacity is indemnifiable if it is "at least not opposed to" the best interests of the corporation. However, a corporation that causes a director to undertake fiduciary duties in connection with an employee benefit plan should expect the director to act in the best interests of the plan's beneficiaries or participants. Thus, subsection (b) establishes and provides a standard for indemnification that is consistent with the statutory policies embodied in ERISA. See Official Comment to section 8.50(2).

3. *Section 8.51(c)*

Section 8.51(c) rejects the argument that indemnification is automatically improper whenever a proceeding has been concluded on a basis that does not exonerate the director claiming indemnification. However, any judicial determination of substantive liability should be taken into account in determining whether the standards of section 8.51(a) were met. By the same token, it is clear that the termination of a proceeding by settlement or plea of no contest should not of itself create a presumption either that conduct met or did not meet the relevant standard of subsection (a) since a settlement or nolo plea may be agreed to for many reasons unrelated to the merits of the claim. On the other hand, a final determination of non-liability (including one based on a liability-limitation provision adopted under section 2.02(b)(4)) or an acquittal in a criminal case automatically entitles the director to indemnification of expenses under section 8.52.

4. *Section 8.51(d)*

Section 8.51(d) does not permit indemnification of settlements and judgments in derivative proceedings which would give rise to a circularity in which the corporation receiving payment of damages by the director in the settlement or judgment (less attorneys' fees) would then immediately return the same amount to the director (including attorneys' fees) as indemnification. Thus, the corporation would be in a poorer economic position than if there had been no proceeding. Further, in many cases a director may be protected by a provision in the articles of incorporation under section 2.02(b)(4) limiting liability or because a proceeding was dismissed under section 7.44. The prohibition on indemnification of a settlement or a judgment in a derivative proceeding, however, does not extend to the related expenses incurred in the proceeding so long as the director meets the relevant standard of conduct set forth in section 8.51(a). In addition, indemnification and advance of expenses may be ordered by a court under section 8.54(a)(3) even if the relevant standard was not met.

Indemnification under section 8.51 is also prohibited if there has been an adjudication that a director received a financial benefit to which the director is not entitled, even if, for example, the director acted in a manner not opposed to the best interests of the corporation. For example, improper use of inside information for financial benefit should not be an action for which the corporation may elect to provide indemnification, even if the corporation was not thereby harmed. Given the express language of section 2.02(b)(5) establishing the limit of an indemnification provision contained in the articles of incorporation, a director found to have received an improper financial benefit would not be permitted indemnification under section 8.51(a)(2). Although it is unlikely that a director found to have received an improper financial benefit could meet the standard in section 8.51(a)(1)(ii)(B), this limitation is made explicit in section 8.51(d)(2). Section

8.54(a)(3) permits a director found liable in a proceeding referred to in section 8.51(d)(2) to petition a court for a judicial determination of entitlement to indemnification for expenses. The language of section 8.51(d)(2) parallels sections 2.02(b)(4)(i) and 2.02(b)(5)(i), and thus, the same standards should be used in interpreting the application of all three provisions. Although a settlement may create an obligation to pay money, it should not be construed for purposes of this subchapter as an adjudication of liability.

§ 8.52. Mandatory Indemnification

A corporation shall indemnify a director who was wholly successful, on the merits or otherwise, in the defense of any proceeding to which the director was a party because he or she was a director of the corporation against expenses incurred by the director in connection with the proceeding.

Cross-References

"Corporation" defined, see § 8.50.

Court-ordered indemnification, see § 8.54.

"Director" defined, see § 8.50.

"Expenses" defined, see § 1.40.

Limits on indemnification, see § 8.58.

"Party" defined, see § 8.50.

Permissible indemnification, see § 8.51.

"Proceeding" defined, see § 8.50.

Official Comment

Section 8.52 creates a right of indemnification in favor of the director who meets its requirements. Enforcement of this right by judicial proceeding is specifically contemplated by section 8.54(a)(1). Section 8.54(b) gives the director a right to recover expenses incurred in enforcing the director's right to indemnification under section 8.52.

The basic standard for mandatory indemnification is that the director has been "wholly successful, on the merits or otherwise," in the defense of the proceeding. A defendant is "wholly successful" only if the entire proceeding is disposed of on a basis which does not involve a finding of liability. A director who is precluded from mandatory indemnification by this requirement may still be entitled to permissible indemnification under section 8.51(a) or court-ordered indemnification under section 8.54(a)(3).

Although the standard "on the merits or otherwise" may result in an occasional defendant becoming entitled to indemnification because of procedural defenses not related to the merits, *e.g.*, the statute of limitations or disqualification of the plaintiff, it is unreasonable to require a defendant with a valid procedural defense to undergo a possibly prolonged and expensive trial on the merits to establish eligibility for mandatory indemnification.

§ 8.53. Advance for Expenses

(a) A corporation may, before final disposition of a proceeding, advance funds to pay for or reimburse expenses incurred in connection with the proceeding by an individual who is a party to the proceeding because that individual is a director if the director delivers to the corporation a signed written undertaking of the director to repay any funds advanced if (i) the director is not entitled to mandatory indemnification under section 8.52 and (ii) it is ultimately determined under section 8.54 or section 8.55 that the director is not entitled to indemnification.

(b) The undertaking required by subsection (a) must be an unlimited general obligation of the director but need not be secured and may be accepted without reference to the financial ability of the director to make repayment.

(c) Authorizations under this section shall be made:

(1) by the board of directors:

(i) if there are two or more qualified directors, by a majority vote of all the qualified directors (a majority of whom shall for such purpose constitute a quorum) or by a majority of the members of a committee consisting solely of two or more qualified directors appointed by such a vote; or

(ii) if there are fewer than two qualified directors, by the vote necessary for action by the board of directors in accordance with section 8.24(c), in which authorization directors who are not qualified directors may participate; or

(2) by the shareholders, but shares owned by or voted under the control of a director who at the time is not a qualified director may not be voted on the authorization.

Cross-References

Committees of board of directors, see § 8.25.

"Corporation" defined, see § 8.50.

Court-ordered advance for expenses, see § 8.54.

Determination and authorization of indemnification, see § 8.55.

"Director" defined, see § 8.50.

"Expenses" defined, see § 1.40.

Limits on indemnification and advance for expenses, see § 8.58.

Obligatory advance for expenses, see § 8.50.

"Party" defined, see § 8.50.

"Proceeding" defined, see § 8.50.

"Qualified director" defined, see § 1.43.

Quorum of directors, see § 8.24.

Standard for indemnification, see § 8.51.

Official Comment

Section 8.53 authorizes, but does not require, a corporation to advance or reimburse a director's reasonable expenses, subject to the delivery of the repayment undertaking required by subsection (a) and any limitations set forth in the articles of incorporation pursuant to section 8.58(d). The repayment undertaking required by section 8.53 is also required in connection with obligatory advancement pursuant to section 8.58(a).

Section 8.53 recognizes an important difference between indemnification and an advance for expenses: indemnification is retrospective and, therefore, enables the persons determining whether to indemnify to do so on the basis of known facts, including the outcome of the proceeding. Indemnification may include reimbursement for non-advanced expenses. Advance for expenses is necessarily prospective and, in situations where advancement is not obligatory, the individuals making the decision whether to authorize expense advancement generally have fewer known facts on which to base their decision.

Section 8.53 reflects a determination that it is sound public policy to permit the corporation to advance (by direct payment or by reimbursement) the defense expenses of a director so long as the director agrees to repay any amounts advanced if it is ultimately determined that the director is not entitled to indemnification. This policy is based upon the view that a person who serves an entity in a representative capacity should not be required to finance his or her own defense of actions taken in that capacity. Moreover, adequate legal representation often involves substantial expenses during the course of the proceeding and many individuals are willing to serve as directors only if they have the assurance that the corporation will advance these expenses. Accordingly, many corporations enter into contractual obligations (*e.g.*, by a provision in the articles of incorporation or bylaws or by individual agreements) to advance expenses for directors. See section 8.58(a).

A single written undertaking by the director pursuant to section 8.53(a) may cover all funds advanced from time to time in connection with a proceeding. The theory underlying section 8.53(b) is that wealthy directors should not be favored over directors whose financial resources are modest. The undertaking must be made by the director and not by a third party. If the director or the corporation wishes some third party to be responsible for the director's obligation in this regard, either is free to make those arrangements separately with the third party.

If advancement is not obligatory, the standards of section 8.30 should, in general, govern the decision of directors acting on a request for advancement. In making such a decision, the directors may consider any matters they deem appropriate and may condition the advance of expenses on compliance with any requirements they believe are appropriate, including, for example, an affirmation of a requesting director's good faith belief that he or she is entitled to indemnification under section 8.51.

A corporation may obligate itself pursuant to section 8.58(a) to advance for expenses under section 8.53 by means of a provision set forth in the articles of incorporation or bylaws, by a resolution of its board of directors or shareholders, or by an agreement. Unless provided otherwise, section 8.58(a) deems a general obligatory provision requiring indemnification to the fullest extent permitted by law to include advance for expenses to the fullest extent permitted by law, even if not specifically mentioned, subject to providing the required repayment undertaking. No other procedures are required or contemplated although obligatory arrangements may include notice and any other requirements that the directors believe are appropriate.

If advancement is not obligatory, the decision to advance expenses is required to be made only one time with respect to each proceeding rather than each time a request for payment of expenses is received by the corporation. However, the directors are free to reconsider the decision at any time (*e.g.*, upon a change in the financial ability of the corporation to pay the amounts in question). The decision as to the reasonableness of any expenses may be made by any officer or agent of the corporation duly authorized to do so.

The procedures set forth in section 8.53(c) for authorizing an advance for expenses parallel the procedures set forth in section 8.55(b) for selecting the person or persons to make the determination that indemnification is permissible. If the advance for expenses is not authorized by the shareholders under section 8.53(c)(2), the applicable procedure specified in subsection (c)(1) must be used.

Under subsection (c)(1)(ii), which is available only if subsection (c)(1)(i) is not available, the action of the board of directors must be taken in accordance with section 8.20 or section 8.21, as the case may be, and directors who are not qualified directors may participate in the vote. Allowing directors who at the time are not qualified directors to participate in the authorization decision, if there is no or only one qualified director, is based on the concept that, if there are not at least two qualified directors, then it is preferable to return the power to make the decision to the full board (even though it includes non-qualified directors) than to leave it with one qualified director.

Illustration 1: The board consists of 15 directors, four of whom are non-qualified directors. Of the 11 qualified directors, nine are present at the meeting at which the authorization is to be made (or the committee is to be appointed). Under subsection (c)(1)(i), a quorum is present and at least six of the nine qualified directors present at the board meeting must authorize any advance for expenses because six is an absolute majority of the 11 qualified directors. Alternatively, six of the nine qualified directors present at the board meeting may appoint a committee of two or more of the qualified directors (up to all 11) to decide whether to authorize the advance. Action by the committee would require a majority of the committee.

Illustration 2: The board consists of 15 directors, only one of whom is a qualified director. Subsection (c)(1)(i) is not available because the number of qualified directors is less than two. Accordingly, the decision must be made by the board under subsection (c)(1)(ii) (or, as is always permitted, by the shareholders under subsection (c)(2)).

With respect to shareholder authorizations under section 8.53(c)(2), the prohibition on voting shares owned by or voted under the control of directors who at the time are not qualified directors does not affect general rules as to the required presence of a quorum at the meeting.

The fact that there has been an advance for expenses does not determine whether a director is entitled to indemnification. A proceeding will often terminate without a judicial or other determination as to whether the director's conduct met the applicable standard of conduct in section 8.51. Nevertheless, the board of directors should make, or cause to be made, an affirmative determination of entitlement to indemnification at the conclusion of the proceeding. This decision should be made in accordance with the procedures set forth in section 8.55.

Judicial enforcement of rights granted by or pursuant to section 8.53 is specifically contemplated by section 8.54.

§ 8.54. Court-Ordered Indemnification and Advance for Expenses

(a)   A director who is a party to a proceeding because he or she is a director may apply for indemnification or an advance for expenses to the court conducting the proceeding or to another court of competent jurisdiction. After receipt of an application and after giving any notice it considers necessary, the court shall:

(1)   order indemnification if the court determines that the director is entitled to mandatory indemnification under section 8.52;

(2)   order indemnification or advance for expenses if the court determines that the director is entitled to indemnification or advance for expenses pursuant to a provision authorized by section 8.58(a); or

(3)   order indemnification or advance for expenses if the court determines, in view of all the relevant circumstances, that it is fair and reasonable (i) to indemnify the director, or (ii) to advance expenses to the director, even if, in the case of (i) or (ii), he or she has not met the relevant standard of conduct set forth in section 8.51(a), failed to comply with section 8.53 or was adjudged liable in a proceeding referred to in section 8.51(d)(1) or (d)(2), but if the director was adjudged so liable indemnification shall be limited to expenses incurred in connection with the proceeding.

(b)   If the court determines that the director is entitled to indemnification under subsection (a)(1) or to indemnification or advance for expenses under subsection (a)(2), it shall also order the corporation to pay the director's expenses incurred in connection with obtaining court-ordered indemnification or advance for expenses. If the court determines that the director is entitled to indemnification or advance for expenses under subsection (a)(3), it may also order the corporation to pay the director's expenses to obtain court-ordered indemnification or advance for expenses.

Cross-References

Advance for expenses, see § 8.53.

"Corporation" defined, see § 8.50.

"Director" defined, see § 8.50.

"Expenses" defined, see § 1.40.

Limits on indemnification and advance for expenses, see § 8.58.

Mandatory indemnification, see § 8.52.

Obligatory indemnification, see § 8.58.

"Party" defined, see § 8.50.

Permissible indemnification, see § 8.51.

"Proceeding" defined, see § 8.50.

Official Comment

In determining whether indemnification or expense advance would be "fair and reasonable" under section 8.54(a)(3), a court should give appropriate deference to an informed decision of a board of directors or committee made in good faith and based upon full information. Ordinarily, a court should not determine that it is "fair and reasonable" to order indemnification or expense advance where the director has not met conditions and procedures to which he or she agreed. A director seeking court-ordered indemnification or expense advance under section 8.54(a)(3) must show that there are facts peculiar to his or her situation that make it fair and reasonable to both the corporation and to the director to override an intra-corporate declination or any otherwise applicable statutory prohibition against indemnification, *e.g.*, sections 8.51(a) or (d).

Apart from the provisions of section 8.54(a)(3), there are no statutory outer limits on the court's power to order indemnification under that subsection. In an appropriate case, a court may wish to refer to the provisions of section 2.02(b)(4) establishing the outer limits of a liability-limiting provision in the articles of incorporation. It would be unusual for a court to provide indemnification going beyond the limits of section 2.02(b)(4), but the court is permitted to do so.

Among the factors a court may want to consider under section 8.54(a)(3) are the gravity of the offense, the financial impact upon the corporation, the occurrence of a change in control or, in the case of an advance for expenses, the inability of the director to finance a defense. A court may want to give special attention to certain other issues. For example, has the corporation joined in the application to the court for indemnification or an advance for expenses? This factor may be particularly important where under section 8.51(d) indemnification is not permitted for an amount paid in settlement of a proceeding brought by or in the right of the corporation. Also, in a case where indemnification would have been available under section 8.51(a)(2) if the corporation had adopted a provision authorized by section 2.02(b)(5), was the decision to adopt such a provision presented to and rejected by the shareholders and, if not, would exculpation of the director's conduct have resulted under a section 2.02(b)(4) provision? Additionally, in connection with considering indemnification for expenses under section 8.51(d)(2) in a proceeding in which a director was adjudged liable for receiving a financial benefit to which he or she was not entitled, was the financial benefit insubstantial—particularly in relation to the other aspects of the transaction involved—and what was the degree of the director's involvement in the transaction and the corporate decision to participate?

Under section 8.54(b), if a director successfully sues to enforce the right to indemnification under subsection (a)(1) or to indemnification or advance for expenses under subsection (a)(2), the court is required to order the corporation to pay the director's expenses in the enforcement proceeding. However, if a director successfully sues for indemnification or expense advancement under subsection (a)(3), the court may (but is not required to) order the corporation to pay those expenses. The basis for the distinction is that the corporation breached its obligation in the first two cases but not in the third.

Application for indemnification under section 8.54 may be made either to the court in which the proceeding was heard or to another court of appropriate jurisdiction. For example, a defendant in a criminal proceeding who has been convicted but believes that indemnification would be proper could apply either to the court which heard the criminal proceeding or bring an action against the corporation in another forum.

A decision by the board of directors not to oppose a request for indemnification is governed by the general standards of conduct of section 8.30. Even if the corporation does not oppose the request, the court must satisfy itself that the person seeking indemnification is entitled to or otherwise deserving of receiving it under section 8.54.

As provided in section 8.58(d), a corporation may limit the rights of a director under section 8.54 by a provision in the articles of incorporation. In the absence of such a provision, the court has general power to exercise the authority granted under this section.

§ 8.55. Determination and Authorization of Indemnification

(a)   A corporation may not indemnify a director under section 8.51 unless authorized for a specific proceeding after a determination has been made that indemnification is permissible because the director has met the relevant standard of conduct set forth in section 8.51.

(b)   The determination shall be made:

(1)   if there are two or more qualified directors, by the board of directors by a majority vote of all the qualified directors (a majority of whom shall for such purpose constitute a quorum), or

by a majority of the members of a committee of two or more qualified directors appointed by such a vote;

    (2) by special legal counsel:

        (i) selected in the manner prescribed in subsection (b)(1); or

        (ii) if there are fewer than two qualified directors, selected by the board of directors (in which selection directors who are not qualified directors may participate); or

    (3) by the shareholders, but shares owned by or voted under the control of a director who at the time is not a qualified director may not be voted on the determination.

(c) Authorization of indemnification shall be made in the same manner as the determination that indemnification is permissible except that if there are fewer than two qualified directors, or if the determination is made by special legal counsel, authorization of indemnification shall be made by those entitled to select special legal counsel under subsection (b)(2)(ii).

Cross-References

Advance for expenses, see § 8.53.

Committees of board of directors, see § 8.25.

"Corporation" defined, see § 8.50.

"Director" defined, see § 8.50.

"Party" defined, see § 8.50.

"Proceeding" defined, see § 8.50.

"Qualified director" defined, see § 1.43.

Quorum of directors, see § 8.24.

Standard for indemnification, see § 8.51.

Official Comment

Section 8.55 distinguishes between a "determination" that indemnification is permissible and an "authorization" of indemnification. A "determination" involves a decision by individuals or groups described in section 8.55(b) whether, under the circumstances, the person seeking indemnification has met the relevant standard of conduct under section 8.51 and is therefore eligible for indemnification. After a favorable determination has been made, the corporation must decide whether to authorize indemnification except to the extent that an obligatory provision under section 8.58(a) is applicable. Although special legal counsel may make the determination of eligibility for indemnification, counsel may not authorize the indemnification. A pre-existing obligation under section 8.58(a) to indemnify if the director is eligible for indemnification dispenses with the second-step decision to authorize indemnification.

Section 8.55(b) establishes procedures for selecting the person or persons who will make the determination of permissibility of indemnification. The committee of qualified directors referred to in subsection (b)(1) may include a committee to which has been delegated the power to determine whether to indemnify a director so long as the appointment and composition of the committee members comply with subsection (b)(1). In selecting special legal counsel under subsection (b)(2), directors who are parties to the proceeding may participate in the decision if there are insufficient qualified directors to satisfy subsection (b)(1). Directors who are not eligible to act as qualified directors may also participate in the decision to authorize indemnification on the basis of a favorable determination if necessary to permit action by the board of directors. The authorization of indemnification is the decision that results in payment of any amounts to be indemnified. This limited participation of non-qualified directors in the authorization decision is justified by the principle of necessity.

Under section 8.55(b)(*l*), the vote required when the qualified directors act as a group is an absolute majority of their number. A majority of the qualified directors constitutes a quorum for board action for this purpose. If there are not at least two qualified directors, then the determination of entitlement to indemnification must be made by special legal counsel or by the shareholders.

The phrase "special legal counsel" is not defined in the Act, and it is important that the process be sufficiently flexible to permit selection of counsel in light of the particular circumstances. In many instances, however, it may be important that "special legal counsel" be counsel having no prior professional relationship with those seeking indemnification, be retained for the specific purpose, and not be or have been either inside counsel or regular outside counsel to the corporation. Among other factors that may be considered are whether special legal counsel has any familial, financial or other relationship with any of those seeking indemnification that would, in the circumstances, reasonably be expected to exert an influence on counsel in making the determination.

In determinations of eligibility for indemnification by shareholders under section 8.55(b)(3), shares owned by or voted under the control of directors who at the time are not qualified directors may not be voted on the determination. This does not affect general rules as to the required presence of a quorum at the meeting in order for the determination to be made.

Section 8.55 is subject to section 8.58(a), which authorizes an arrangement obligating the corporation in advance to provide indemnification or to advance expenses. Although such an arrangement may effectively provide an authorization of indemnification, the determination requirements of sections 8.55(a) and (b) must still be satisfied.

§ 8.56. Indemnification of Officers

(a)   A corporation may indemnify and advance expenses under this subchapter to an officer who is a party to a proceeding because he or she is an officer

    (1)   to the same extent as a director; and

    (2)   if he or she is an officer but not a director, to such further extent as may be provided by the articles of incorporation or the bylaws, or by a resolution adopted or a contract approved by the board of directors or shareholders, except for

        (i)   liability in connection with a proceeding by or in the right of the corporation other than for expenses incurred in connection with the proceeding, or

        (ii)   liability arising out of conduct that constitutes

            (A)   receipt by the officer of a financial benefit to which he or she is not entitled,

            (B)   an intentional infliction of harm on the corporation or the shareholders, or

            (C)   an intentional violation of criminal law.

(b)   Subsection (a)(2) shall apply to an officer who is also a director if he or she is made a party to the proceeding based on an act or omission solely as an officer.

(c)   An officer who is not a director is entitled to mandatory indemnification under section 8.52, and may apply to a court under section 8.54 for indemnification or an advance for expenses, in each case to the same extent to which a director may be entitled to indemnification or advance for expenses under those sections.

Cross-References

Advance for expenses, see § 8.53.

"Corporation" defined, see § 8.50.

"Director" defined, see § 8.50.

"Expenses" defined, see § 1.40.

Indemnification of employees and agents, see § 8.58.

"Liability" defined, see § 8.50.

Limits on rights to indemnification and advance for expenses, see § 8.58.

Obligatory indemnification, see §§ 2.02 and 8.58.

"Officer" defined, see § 8.50.

Officer standards of conduct, see § 8.42.

"Party" defined, see § 8.50.

"Proceeding" defined, see § 8.50.

Official Comment

Section 8.56 correlates the general legal principles relating to the indemnification of officers of the corporation with the limitations on indemnification in subchapter E. This correlation may be summarized in general terms as follows.

- An officer of a corporation who is *not* a director may be indemnified by the corporation on a discretionary basis to the same extent as though he or she were a director, and, in addition, may have additional indemnification rights apart from subchapter E, subject to the limits set forth in section 8.56(a)(2).

- An officer who is *also* a director is entitled to the indemnification rights of a director, and if the conduct that is the subject of the proceeding was solely in his or her capacity as an officer, also to any of the rights of an officer who is not a director. See preceding bullet.

- An *officer* who is not a director has the right of mandatory indemnification granted to directors under section 8.52 and the right to apply for court-ordered indemnification under section 8.54. See section 8.56(c).

Section 8.56 does not deal with indemnification of employees and agents because the concerns of self-dealing that arise when directors provide for their own indemnification and expense advance (and sometimes for senior executive officers) are not present when directors (or officers) provide for indemnification and expense advance for employees and agents who are not directors or officers.

Although subchapter E is silent with respect to such employees and agents, they may be indemnified using broad grants of powers to corporations under section 3.02, including powers to make contracts, appoint and fix the compensation of employees and agents and to make payments furthering the business and affairs of the corporation. Many corporations use these powers to provide for employees and agents in the same provisions in the articles, bylaws or otherwise in which they provide for expense advance and indemnification for directors and officers. Indemnification may also be provided to protect employees or agents from liabilities incurred while serving at a corporation's request as a director, officer, partner, trustee, or agent of another commercial, charitable, or nonprofit venture.

Although employees and agents are not covered by subchapter E, the principles and procedures set forth in the subchapter for indemnification and advance for expenses for directors and officers may be helpful to counsel and courts in dealing with indemnification and expense advance for employees and agents.

Careful consideration should be given to extending mandatory maximum indemnification and expense advance to employees and agents. The same considerations that may favor mandatory maximum indemnification for directors and officers—*e.g.*, encouraging qualified individuals to serve—may not be present in the cases of employees and agents. Many corporations may prefer to retain the discretion to decide, on a case-by-case basis, whether to indemnify and advance expenses to employees and agents (and perhaps even officers, especially nonexecutive officers) rather than binding themselves in advance to do so.

1. Officers Who Are Not Directors

Although section 8.56 does not prescribe the standards governing the rights of officers to indemnification, subsection (a) does set outer limits beyond which the corporation may not indemnify. These limits for officers are substantially the same as the outer limits on the corporation's power to indemnify directors. Since officers are held to substantially the same standards of conduct as directors (see section 8.42), there does not appear to be any reasoned basis for granting officers greater indemnification rights as a substantive matter. Procedurally, however, there is an important difference. To permit greater flexibility, officers may be indemnified (within the above-mentioned limits) with respect to conduct that does not meet the standards set by section 8.51(a)(1) simply by authorization of the board of directors, whereas directors' indemnification can reach beyond those standards, as contemplated by section 8.51(a)(2), only with a provision included in the articles of incorporation pursuant to section 2.02(b)(5). This procedural difference reflects the reduced risk of self-dealing as to officers.

The broad authority in section 8.56(a)(2) to grant indemnification may be limited by appropriate provisions in the articles of incorporation. See section 8.58(c).

2.   Officers Who Are Also Directors

Section 8.56(b) provides, in effect, that an officer of the corporation who is also a director is subject to the same standards of indemnification as other directors and cannot avail himself or herself of the provisions of subsection (a) unless the act or omission that is the subject of the proceeding was committed solely in the capacity as an officer. Thus, a vice president for sales who is also a director and whose actions failed to meet section 8.51(a) standards could be indemnified provided that the conduct was within the limits of section 8.56(a)(2) and involved only his or her officer capacity.

This more flexible approach for situations where the individual is not acting as a director seems appropriate as a matter of fairness. There are many instances where officers who also serve as directors assume responsibilities and take actions in their non-director capacities for which indemnification may be appropriate.

For a director-officer to be indemnified under section 8.51 for conduct in the capacity as a director when he or she has not satisfied the standards of section 8.51(a), a provision in the articles of incorporation under section 2.02(b)(5) is required. If such a provision is included in the articles, the standards for indemnification are those specified in the articles of incorporation, subject to the limitations in section 2.02(b)(5). For a director-officer to be indemnified for conduct solely in the capacity as an officer, even though the director-officer has not satisfied the standards of section 8.56(a), only a bylaw or a resolution of the board of directors authorizing such indemnification is required, rather than a provision in the articles of incorporation. If such a bylaw or resolution is adopted, the standards for indemnification are those specified in section 8.56(a)(2). However, when a director-officer seeks indemnification or expense advance under sections 8.56(b) and (a)(2) on the basis of having acted solely in the capacity as an officer, indemnification or expense advance must be approved through the same procedures as set forth in section 8.55 or 8.53(c), as the case may be, for approval of indemnification or expense advance for a director when acting in the capacity of a director.

§ 8.57. Insurance

A corporation may purchase and maintain insurance on behalf of an individual who is a director or officer of the corporation, or who, while a director or officer of the corporation, serves at the corporation's request as a director, officer, partner, trustee, employee, or agent of another domestic or foreign corporation or a joint venture, trust, employee benefit plan, or other entity, against liability asserted against or incurred by the individual in that capacity or arising from the individual's status as a director or officer, regardless of whether the corporation would have power to indemnify or advance expenses to the individual against the same liability under this subchapter.

Cross-References

"Corporation" defined, see § 8.50.

"Director" defined, see § 8.50.

Employees and agents, see § 8.58.

"Expenses" defined, see § 1.40.

"Liability" defined, see § 8.50.

"Officer" defined, see § 8.50.

"Official capacity" defined, see § 8.50.

Standard for indemnification, see § 8.51.

Official Comment

In authorizing a corporation to purchase and maintain insurance on behalf of directors and officers, section 8.57 sets no limits on the type of insurance which a corporation may maintain or the type of persons who are covered. Insurance is not limited to claims against which a corporation is entitled to indemnify under this subchapter. Such insurance can provide protection to directors and officers in addition to the rights of indemnification created by or pursuant to subchapter E (as well as typically protecting the individual insureds against the corporation's failure to pay indemnification required or permitted by this subchapter) and can also provide a source of reimbursement for a corporation that indemnifies its directors and others for conduct covered by the insurance. On the other hand, policies typically do not cover uninsurable matters, such as actions involving dishonesty, self-dealing, bad faith, knowing violations of the securities laws, or other willful misconduct.

Although section 8.57 does not include employees and agents for the reasons stated in the Official Comment to section 8.58, the corporation has the power under section 3.02 to purchase and maintain insurance on their behalf. This power is confirmed in section 8.58(f).

§ 8.58. Variation by Corporate Action; Application of Subchapter

(a) A corporation may, by a provision in its articles of incorporation or bylaws or in a resolution adopted or a contract approved by the board of directors or shareholders, obligate itself in advance of the act or omission giving rise to a proceeding to provide indemnification in accordance with section 8.51 or advance funds to pay for or reimburse expenses in accordance with section 8.53. Any such obligatory provision shall be deemed to satisfy the requirements for authorization referred to in section 8.53(c) and in section 8.55(c). Any such provision that obligates the corporation to provide indemnification to the fullest extent permitted by law shall be deemed to obligate the corporation to advance funds to pay for or reimburse expenses in accordance with section 8.53 to the fullest extent permitted by law, unless the provision expressly provides otherwise.

(b) A right of indemnification or to advances for expenses created by this subchapter or under subsection (a) and in effect at the time of an act or omission shall not be eliminated or impaired with respect to such act or omission by an amendment of the articles of incorporation or bylaws or a resolution of the board of directors or shareholders, adopted after the occurrence of such act or omission, unless, in the case of a right created under subsection (a), the provision creating such right and in effect at the time of such act or omission explicitly authorizes such elimination or impairment after such act or omission has occurred.

(c) Any provision pursuant to subsection (a) shall not obligate the corporation to indemnify or advance expenses to a director of a predecessor of the corporation, pertaining to conduct with respect to the predecessor, unless otherwise expressly provided. Any provision for indemnification or advance for expenses in the articles of incorporation or bylaws, or a resolution of the board of directors or shareholders of a predecessor of the corporation in a merger or in a contract to which the predecessor is a party, existing at the time the merger takes effect, shall be governed by section 11.07(a)(4).

(d) Subject to subsection (b), a corporation may, by a provision in its articles of incorporation, limit any of the rights to indemnification or advance for expenses created by or pursuant to this subchapter.

(e) This subchapter does not limit a corporation's power to pay or reimburse expenses incurred by a director or an officer in connection with appearing as a witness in a proceeding at a time when he or she is not a party.

(f) This subchapter does not limit a corporation's power to indemnify, advance expenses to or provide or maintain insurance on behalf of an employee or agent.

Cross-References

> Advance for expenses, see § 8.53.
>
> "Corporation" defined, see § 8.50.
>
> "Director" defined, see § 8.50.
>
> Effect of amendments to articles of incorporation, see § 10.09.
>
> "Expenses" defined, see § 1.40.
>
> Indemnification, see §§ 8.51 through 8.56.
>
> Insurance, power to provide, see § 8.57.
>
> "Officer" defined, see § 8.50.
>
> "Party" defined, see § 8.50.
>
> Predecessor, see § 8.50.
>
> "Proceeding" defined, see § 8.50.

Official Comment

Section 8.58(a) authorizes a corporation to make obligatory the permissive provisions of subchapter E in advance of the conduct giving rise to the request for indemnification or advance for expenses. An obligatory provision satisfies the requirements for authorization in sections 8.53(c) and 8.55(c), but the requirements for determination of eligibility for indemnification in subsections (a) and (b) of those sections must still be met.

If a corporation provides for obligatory indemnification and not for obligatory advance for expenses, the provision should be reviewed to ensure that it properly reflects the intent in view of the third sentence of section 8.58(a). Also, a corporation should consider whether obligatory expense advance is intended for direct suits by the corporation as well as for derivative suits by shareholders in the right of the corporation. In the former case, assuming compliance with sections 8.53(a) and (b), the corporation could be required to fund the defense of a defendant director even where the board of directors has already concluded that the director has engaged in significant wrongdoing. See Official Comment to section 8.53.

Although section 8.58(d) permits a corporation to limit the right of the corporation to indemnify or advance expenses by a provision in its articles of incorporation, as provided in section 10.09, no such limitation will affect rights in existence when the provision becomes effective pursuant to section 1.23.

Subchapter E does not regulate the power of the corporation to indemnify or advance expenses to employees and agents. That subject is governed by the law of agency and related principles and frequently by contractual arrangements between the corporation and the employee or agent. Section 8.58(f) makes clear that, although indemnification, advance for expenses, and insurance for employees and agents are beyond the scope of subchapter E, the elaboration in subchapter E of standards and procedures for indemnification, expense advance, and insurance for directors and officers is not in any way intended to cast doubt on the power of the corporation to indemnify or advance expenses to or purchase and maintain insurance for employees and agents under section 3.02 or otherwise.

§ 8.59. Exclusivity of Subchapter

A corporation may provide indemnification or advance expenses to a director or an officer only as permitted by this subchapter.

Cross-References

> Advance for expenses, see § 8.53.
>
> "Corporation" defined, see § 8.50.
>
> "Director" defined, see § 8.50.

"Expenses" defined, see § 1.40.

"Officer" defined, see § 8.50.

Standards for indemnification, see §§ 8.51 through 8.56.

Official Comment

Subchapter E is the exclusive source for the power of a corporation to indemnify or advance expenses to a director or an officer.

Section 8.59 does not preclude provisions in the articles of incorporation, the bylaws, resolutions, or contracts designed to provide procedural machinery in addition to (but not inconsistent with) that provided by subchapter E. For example, a corporation may properly obligate the board of directors to consider and act expeditiously on an application for indemnification or advance for expenses or to cooperate in the procedural steps required to obtain a judicial determination under section 8.54.

SUBCHAPTER F
DIRECTOR'S CONFLICTING INTEREST TRANSACTIONS

Introductory Comment

1. Overview

There are four basic elements in subchapter F.

First, subchapter F defines, with bright-line rules, the transactions that are to be treated as director's conflicting interest transactions.

Second, subchapter F provides that a director's transaction that is not within the statutory definition of a director's conflicting interest transaction is not subject to judicial review for fairness on the ground that it involved a conflict of interest (although circumstances that fall outside the statutory definition may afford the basis for a legal attack on the transaction on some other ground), even if the transaction involves some sort of conflict lying outside the statutory definition, such as a remote familial relationship.

Third, subchapter F provides that if a director's conflicting interest transaction is properly approved by disinterested (or "qualified") directors or shareholders, the transaction is insulated from judicial review for fairness (although, again, it might be open to attack on some basis other than the conflict).

Fourth, subchapter F also provides that if a director's conflicting interest transaction is properly approved by disinterested (or "qualified") directors or shareholders, the conflicted director may not be subject to an award of damages or other sanctions (although the director could be subject to claims on some basis other than the conflict).

Bright-line provisions of any kind represent a trade-off between the benefits of certainty and the danger that some transactions or conduct that fall outside the area circumscribed by the bright-lines may be so similar to the transactions and conduct that fall within the area that different treatment may seem anomalous. Subchapter F reflects the judgment that in corporate matters, where planning is critical, the clear and important efficiency gains that result from certainty through defining director's conflicting interest transactions exceed any potential and uncertain efficiency losses that might follow from excluding other director's transactions from judicial review for fairness on conflict-of-interest grounds.

2. Scope of Subchapter F

Subchapter F addresses legal challenges based on director conflicts of interest only. Subchapter F does not undertake to define, regulate, or provide any form of procedure regarding other possible claims. For example, subchapter F does not address a claim that a controlling shareholder has violated a duty owed to the corporation or minority shareholders. So, although transactions between a corporation and a parent corporation or other controlling shareholder who owns less than all of its shares may give rise to the possibility of abuse of power by the controlling shareholder, subchapter F does not address proceedings brought on that basis because section 8.61 concerns only proceedings that are brought on the ground that a "director has an interest respecting the transaction."

Subchapter F applies only when there is a "transaction" by or with the corporation. For purposes of subchapter F, "transaction" generally connotes negotiations or consensual arrangements between the corporation and another party or parties that concern their respective and differing economic rights or interests—not a unilateral action by the corporation or a director. Whether safe harbor procedures of some kind might be available to the director and the corporation with respect to non-transactional matters is discussed in numbered part 3 of this Introductory Comment.

Subchapter F does not preclude the assertion of defenses, such as statute of limitations or failure of a condition precedent, that are based on grounds other than the defenses set forth in this subchapter.

The voting procedures and conduct standards prescribed in subchapter F deal solely with the complicating element presented by the director's conflicting interest in a transaction. A transaction that receives favorable directors' or shareholders' action complying with subchapter F may still fail to satisfy a different quorum requirement or to achieve a different vote than may be needed for substantive approval of the transaction under other applicable statutory provisions or under the articles of incorporation, and vice versa. (Under the Act, a corporation may set higher voting requirements and different quorum requirements in the articles of incorporation. See sections 2.02(b)(2) and 7.27). In addition, subchapter F does not shield misbehavior by a director or other person that is actionable under other provisions of the Act, such as section 8.31, or under other legal rules, regardless of whether the misbehavior is incident to a transaction with the corporation and regardless of whether the rule is one of corporate law.

Finally, certain corporate transactions or arrangements in which directors inherently have a special personal interest are of a unique character and are regulated by special procedural provisions of the Act. See sections 8.51 and 8.52 dealing with indemnification arrangements, and section 7.44 dealing with termination of derivative proceedings by board action. Any corporate transactions or arrangements affecting directors that are governed by such regulatory sections of the Act are not governed by subchapter F.

3. Nontransactional Situations Involving Interest Conflicts

A.   CORPORATE OR BUSINESS OPPORTUNITY

Subchapter F does not apply by its terms to corporate or business opportunities because no transaction between the corporation and the director is involved in the taking of an opportunity. However, subchapter 8G provides, in effect, that the safe harbor procedures of section 8.62 or 8.63 may be employed, at the interested director's election, to protect the taking of a business opportunity that might be challenged under the corporate opportunity doctrine. Also, section 2.02(b)(6) permits a corporation to include in its articles of incorporation a provision that limits or eliminates the duty to present a business opportunity to the corporation.

B.   OTHER SITUATIONS

Many other kinds of situations can give rise to divergent economic interests between a director and the corporation. For example, a director's personal financial interests can be affected by a nontransactional policy decision of the board of directors, such as where it decides to establish a divisional headquarters in the director's small hometown. In other situations, simple inaction by a board might work to a director's personal advantage, or a flow of ongoing business relationships between a director and the corporation may, without centering upon any discrete "transaction," raise questions of possible favoritism, unfair dealing, or undue influence. If a director decides to engage in business activity that directly competes with the corporation's own business, the economic interest in that competing activity ordinarily will conflict with the best interests of the corporation and put in issue the breach of the director's duties to the corporation. Basic conflicts and improprieties can also arise out of a director's personal appropriation of corporate assets or improper use of corporate proprietary or inside information.

The circumstances in which such nontransactional conflict situations should be brought to the board of directors or shareholders for clearance, and the legal effect, if any, of such clearance, are matters for development under the common law and lie outside the ambit of subchapter F. Although these nontransactional situations are not covered by the provisions of subchapter F, a court may well recognize that the subchapter F procedures provide a useful analogy for dealing with such situations.

* * *

Note on Terms in Official Comments

In the Official Comments to subchapter F, the director who has a conflicting interest is for convenience referred to as "the director" or "D," and the corporation of which he or she is a director is referred to as "the corporation" or "X Co." A subsidiary of the corporation is referred to as "S Co." Another corporation dealing with X Co. is referred to as "Y Co."

§ 8.60. Subchapter Definitions

In this subchapter:

"Control" (including the term "controlled by") means (i) having the power, directly or indirectly, to elect or remove a majority of the members of the board of directors or other governing body of an entity, whether through the ownership of voting shares or interests, by contract, or otherwise, or (ii) being subject to a majority of the risk of loss from the entity's activities or entitled to receive a majority of the entity's residual returns.

"Director's conflicting interest transaction" means a transaction effected or proposed to be effected by the corporation (or by an entity controlled by the corporation)

    (i)   to which, at the relevant time, the director is a party;

    (ii)   respecting which, at the relevant time, the director had knowledge and a material financial interest known to the director; or

    (iii)   respecting which, at the relevant time, the director knew that a related person was a party or had a material financial interest.

"Fair to the corporation" means, for purposes of section 8.61(b)(3), that the transaction as a whole was beneficial to the corporation, taking into appropriate account whether it was (i) fair in terms of the director's dealings with the corporation, and (ii) comparable to what might have been obtainable in an arm's length transaction, given the consideration paid or received by the corporation.

"Material financial interest" means a financial interest in a transaction that would reasonably be expected to impair the objectivity of the director's judgment when participating in action on the authorization of the transaction.

"Related person" means:

    (i)   the individual's spouse;

    (ii)   a child, stepchild, grandchild, parent, step parent, grandparent, sibling, step sibling, half sibling, aunt, uncle, niece or nephew (or spouse of any such person) of the individual or of the individual's spouse;

    (iii)   a natural person living in the same home as the individual;

    (iv)   an entity (other than the corporation or an entity controlled by the corporation) controlled by the individual or any person specified above in this definition;

    (v)   a domestic or foreign (A) business or nonprofit corporation (other than the corporation or an entity controlled by the corporation) of which the individual is a director, (B) unincorporated entity of which the individual is a general partner or a member of the governing body, or (C) individual, trust or estate for whom or of which the individual is a trustee, guardian, personal representative or like fiduciary; or

    (vi)   a person that is, or an entity that is controlled by, an employer of the individual.

"Relevant time" means (i) the time at which directors' action respecting the transaction is taken in compliance with section 8.62, or (ii) if the transaction is not brought before the board of directors (or a committee) for action under section 8.62, at the time the corporation (or an entity controlled by the corporation) becomes legally obligated to consummate the transaction.

"Required disclosure" means disclosure of (i) the existence and nature of the director's conflicting interest, and (ii) all facts known to the director respecting the subject matter of the transaction that a director free of such conflicting interest would reasonably believe to be material in deciding whether to proceed with the transaction.

Cross-References

Committees of board of directors, see § 8.25.

Director action, see §§ 8.20 and 8.21.

"Entity" defined, see § 1.40.

Indemnification and advance for expenses, see §§ 8.50 through 8.59.

"Proceeding" defined, see § 1.40.

Quorum and voting:

> by directors, see § 8.24.

> by shareholders, see §§ 7.25 through 7.27.

Shareholder action, see §§ 7.01 through 7.04.

Standards of conduct:

> directors, see § 8.30.

> officers, see § 8.42.

"Unincorporated entity" defined, see § 1.40.

Vote needed to approve transactions by shareholders:

> amendment to articles of incorporation, see § 10.03.

> conversions, see § 9.21.

> disposition of assets, see § 12.02.

> domestications, see § 9.32.

> generally, see §§ 7.25 and 7.26.

> mergers and share exchanges, see § 11.04.

"Voting group" defined, see § 1.40.

Official Comment

The definitions set forth in section 8.60 apply only to subchapter F and section 2.02(b)(6) and, where relevant to subchapter G. They have no application elsewhere in the Act. (For the meaning and use of certain terms used below, such as "D," "X Co." and "Y Co.," see the Note on Terms at the end of the Introductory Comment of subchapter F.)

1. Director's Conflicting Interest Transaction

The definition of "director's conflicting interest transaction" in section 8.60 is the core concept underlying subchapter F. The definition operates preclusively in that, as used in section 8.61, it denies the power of a court to invalidate transactions or otherwise to remedy conduct on the ground that the director has a conflict of interest if it falls outside the statutory definition of "director's conflicting interest transaction."

A. TRANSACTION

For purposes of subchapter F, "transaction" requires a bilateral (or multilateral) arrangement to which the corporation or an entity controlled by the corporation is a party. Subchapter F does not apply to transactions to which no such entity is a party. For example, a purchase or sale by the director of the corporation's shares on the open market or from or to a third party is not a "director's conflicting interest transaction" within the meaning of subchapter F.

B. PARTY TO THE TRANSACTION—THE CORPORATION OR A CONTROLLED ENTITY

In the usual case, the transaction would be effected by X Co. Assume, however, that X Co. controls the vote for directors of S Co. D wishes to sell a building D owns to X Co. and X Co. is willing to buy it. As a business matter, it makes no difference to X Co. whether it takes the title directly or indirectly through its subsidiary S Co. or some other entity that X Co. controls. The applicability of subchapter F does not depend upon that formal distinction, because the subchapter includes within its operative framework transactions by entities controlled by X Co. Thus, subchapter F would apply to a sale of the building by D to S Co.

C. PARTY TO THE TRANSACTION—THE DIRECTOR OR A RELATED PERSON

D can have a conflicting interest in only two ways.

First, a conflicting interest can arise under either clause (i) or (ii) of the definition of "director's conflicting interest transaction." This will be the case if, under clause (i), the transaction is between D and X Co. A conflicting interest also will arise under clause (ii) if D is not a party to the transaction, but knows about it and knows that he or she has a material financial interest in it. The personal economic stake of the director must be in the transaction itself—that is, the director's gain must flow directly from the transaction. A remote gain (for example, a future reduction in tax rates in the local community) is not enough to give rise to a conflicting interest under clause (ii) of the definition.

Second, a conflicting interest for D can arise under clause (iii) of the definition from the involvement in the transaction of a "related person" of D that is either a party to the transaction or has a "material financial interest" in it. "Related person" is defined in section 8.60.

Circumstances may arise where a director could have a conflicting interest under more than one clause of the definition. For example, if Y Co. is a party to or interested in the transaction with X Co. and Y Co. is a related person of D, the matter would fall under clause (iii), but D also may have a conflicting interest under clause (ii) if D's economic interest in Y Co. is sufficiently material and if the importance of the transaction to Y Co. is sufficiently material.

A director may have relationships and connections to persons and institutions that are not specified in clause (iii) of the definition. Such relationships and connections fall outside subchapter F because the categories of persons described in clause (iii) constitute the exclusive universe for purposes of subchapter F. For example, in a challenged transaction between X Co. and Y Co., suppose the court confronts the argument that D also is a major creditor of Y Co. and that creditor status in Y Co. gives D a conflicting interest. The court should rule that D's creditor status in Y Co. does not fit any category of the definition; and therefore, the conflict of interest claim must be rejected by reason of section 8.61(a). The result would be different if Y Co.'s debt to D were of such economic significance to D that it would either fall under clause (ii) of the definition or, if it placed D in control of Y Co., it would fall under clause (iii) (because Y Co. is a related person of D under clause (iv) of the definition). To explore the example further, if D is also a shareholder of Y Co., but D does not have a material financial interest in the transaction and does not control Y Co., no director's conflicting interest transaction arises and the transaction cannot be challenged on conflict of interest grounds. To avoid any appearance of impropriety, D, nonetheless, could consider recusal from the other directors' deliberations and voting on the transaction between X Co. and Y Co.

Any director's interest in a transaction that meets the criteria of the definition renders the transaction a "director's conflicting interest transaction." If the director's interest satisfies those criteria, subchapter F draws no distinction between a director's interest that clashes with the interests of the corporation and a director's interest that coincides with, or is parallel to, or even furthers the interests of the corporation.

Routine business transactions frequently occur between companies with overlapping directors. If X Co. and Y Co. have routine, frequent business dealings with terms dictated by competitive market forces, then even if a director of X Co. has a relevant relationship with Y Co., the transactions would almost always be defensible, regardless of approval by disinterested directors or shareholders, on the ground that they are "fair." For example, a common transaction involves a purchase of the corporation's products or services by Y Co., or perhaps by D or a related person, at prices normally charged by the corporation. In such circumstances, it usually will not be difficult for D to show that the transaction was on arms-length terms and was fair. Even a purchase by D of a product of X Co. at a usual "employee's discount," although technically assailable as a conflicting interest transaction, would customarily be viewed as a routine incident of the office of director and, thus, "fair" to the corporation.

2. *Control*

The definition of "control" in section 8.60 contains two independent clauses. The first clause addresses the ability to elect or remove a majority of the members of an entity's governing body. That power can arise, for example, from articles of incorporation or a shareholders' agreement. The second clause addresses economic interest in the entity and may include, among other circumstances, financial structures that do not have voting interests or a governing body in the traditional sense, such as special purpose entities.

3. *Relevant Time*

The definition of director's conflicting interest transaction requires that, except where he or she is a party, the director know of the transaction at the "relevant time" as defined in section 8.60. Where the director lacks such knowledge, the risk to the corporation that the director's judgment might be improperly influenced, or the risk of unfair dealing by the director, is not present. In a corporation of significant size, routine transactions in the ordinary course of business, which typically involve decision making at lower management levels, normally will not be known to the director and, if that is the case, will not meet the "knowledge" requirement of clauses (ii) or (iii) of the definition of director's conflicting interest transaction.

4. *Material Financial Interest*

The "interest" of a director or a related person in a transaction can be direct or indirect (*e.g.*, as an owner of an entity or a beneficiary of a trust or estate), but it must be financial for there to exist a "director's conflicting interest transaction." Thus, for example, an interest in a transaction between X Co. and a director's alma mater, or any other transaction involving X Co. and a party with which D might have emotional involvement but no financial interest, would not give rise to a director's conflicting interest transaction. Moreover, whether a financial interest is material does not turn on any assertion by the possibly conflicted director that the interest in question would not impair his or her objectivity if called upon to vote on the authorization of the transaction. Instead, assuming a court challenge asserting the materiality of the financial interest, the standard calls upon the trier of fact to determine whether the objectivity of the director would reasonably be expected to have been impaired by the financial interest when voting on the matter. Thus, the standard is objective, not subjective.

Under clause (ii) of the definition of "director's conflicting interest transaction," at the relevant time a director must have knowledge of his or her financial interest in the transaction in addition to knowing about the transaction itself. As a practical matter, a director could not be influenced by a financial interest about which that director had no knowledge. For example, the possibly conflicted director might know about X Co.'s transaction with Y Co., but might not know that his or her money manager recently established a significant position in Y Co. stock for the director's portfolio. In such circumstances, the transaction with Y Co. would not fall within clause (ii), notwithstanding the portfolio investment's significance. If the director did not know about the Y Co. portfolio investment, it could not reasonably be expected to impair the objectivity of that director's judgment.

Similarly, under clause (iii) of that definition, a director must know about his or her related person's financial interest in the transaction for the matter to give rise to a "material financial interest" as defined in section 8.60. If there is such knowledge and "interest" (*i.e.*, the financial interest could reasonably be expected to influence the director's judgment), then the matter involves a director's conflicting interest transaction.

5. *Related Person*

Six categories of "related person" of the director are set out in the definition of that term. These categories are specific, exclusive and preemptive.

The first three categories involve closely related family, or near-family, individuals as specified in clauses (i) through (iii). These clauses are exclusive insofar as family relationships are concerned and include adoptive relationships. The references to a "spouse" include a common law spouse. Clause (iii) covers personal, as opposed to business, relationships; for example, clause (iii) does not cover a lessee.

Regarding the subcategories of persons described in clause (v) from the perspective of X Co., certain of D's relationships with other entities and D's fiduciary relationships are always a sensitive concern, separate and apart from whether D has a financial interest in the transaction. Clause (v) reflects the policy judgment that D cannot escape D's legal obligation to act in the best interests of another person for whom D has such a relationship and, accordingly, that such a relationship (without regard to any financial interest on D's part) should cause the relevant entity to have "related person" status.

The term "employer" as used in clause (vi) is not separately defined but should be interpreted in light of the purpose of subchapter F. The relevant inquiry is whether D, because of an employment relationship with an employer who has a significant stake in the outcome of the transaction, is likely to be influenced to act in the interest of that employer rather than in the interest of X Co.

References in the foregoing to "director" or "D" include the term "officer" where relevant in section 2.02(b)(6) and section 8.70.

6. *Fair to the Corporation*

The term "fair" to the corporation in subchapter F has a special meaning. The transaction, viewed as a whole, must have been beneficial to the corporation.

In considering the "fairness" of the transaction, the court will be required to consider not only the market fairness of the terms of the deal—whether it is comparable to what might have been obtainable in an arm's length transaction—but also (as the board of directors would have been required to do) whether the transaction was one that was reasonably likely to yield favorable results (or reduce detrimental results). Thus, if a manufacturing company that lacks sufficient working capital allocates some of its scarce funds to purchase at a market price a sailing yacht owned by one of its directors, it will not be easy to persuade the court that the transaction was "fair" in the sense that it was reasonably made to further the business interests of the corporation. The fact that the price paid for the yacht was a "fair" market price, and that the full measure of disclosures made by the director is beyond challenge, may still not be enough to defend and uphold the transaction.

A. CONSIDERATION AND OTHER TERMS OF THE TRANSACTION

The fairness of the consideration and other transaction terms are to be judged at the relevant time. See section 8.61(b)(3). The relevant inquiry is whether the consideration paid or received by the corporation or the benefit expected to be realized by the corporation was adequate in relation to the obligations assumed or received or other consideration provided by or to the corporation. If the issue in a transaction is the "fairness" of a price, "fair" is not to be taken to imply that there is one single "fair" price, all others being "unfair." Generally a "fair" price is any price within a range that an unrelated party might have been willing to pay or willing to accept, as the case may be, for the relevant property, asset, service or commitment, following a normal arm's-length business negotiation. The same approach applies not only to gauging the fairness of price, but also to the fairness evaluation of any other key term of the deal.

Although the "fair" criterion used to assess the consideration under section 8.61(b)(3) is also a range rather than a point, the width of that range may be narrower than would be the case in an arm's-length transaction. For example, the quality and completeness of disclosures, if any, made by the conflicted director that bear upon the consideration in question are relevant in determining whether the consideration paid or received by the corporation, although otherwise commercially reasonable, was "fair" for purposes of section 8.61(b)(3).

B. PROCESS OF DECISION AND THE DIRECTOR'S CONDUCT

In some circumstances, the behavior of the director having the conflicting interest may affect the finding and content of "fairness." Fair dealing requires that the director make "required disclosure" at the "relevant time" (both as defined) even if the director plays no role in arranging or negotiating the terms of the transaction. One illustration of unfair dealing is the director's failure to disclose fully the director's interest or hidden defects known to the director regarding the transaction. Another illustration would be the exertion by the director of improper pressure upon the other directors or other parties that might be involved with the transaction. Whether a transaction can be successfully challenged by reason of deficient or improper conduct, notwithstanding the fairness of the economic terms, will turn on the court's evaluation of the conduct and its impact on the transaction.

7.   Required Disclosure

An important element of subchapter F's safe harbor procedures is that those acting for the corporation be able to make an informed judgment. As an example of "required disclosure" (as defined), if D knows that the land the corporation is proposing to buy from D is sinking into an abandoned coal mine, D must disclose not only D's interest in the transaction but also that the land is subsiding. As a director of X Co., D may not invoke the "buyer beware" doctrine. On the other hand, D does not have any obligation to reveal the price that D paid for the property 10 years ago, or the fact that D inherited the property, because that information is not material to the board's evaluation of the property and its business decision whether to proceed with the transaction. Further, although material facts respecting the subject of the transaction must be disclosed, D is not required to reveal personal or subjective information that bears upon D's negotiating position (such as, for example, D's urgent need for cash, or the lowest price D would be willing to accept). This is true even though such information would be highly relevant to the corporation's decision-making in that, if the information were known to the corporation, it could enable the corporation to hold out for more favorable terms.

§ 8.61. Judicial Action

(a)   A transaction effected or proposed to be effected by the corporation (or by an entity controlled by the corporation) may not be the subject of equitable relief, or give rise to an award of damages or other sanctions against a director of the corporation, in a proceeding by a shareholder or by or in the right of the corporation, on the ground that the director has an interest respecting the transaction, if it is not a director's conflicting interest transaction.

(b)   A director's conflicting interest transaction may not be the subject of equitable relief, or give rise to an award of damages or other sanctions against a director of the corporation, in a proceeding by a shareholder or by or in the right of the corporation, on the ground that the director has an interest respecting the transaction, if:

(1)   directors' action respecting the transaction was taken in compliance with section 8.62 at any time; or

(2)   shareholders' action respecting the transaction was taken in compliance with section 8.63 at any time; or

(3)   the transaction, judged according to the circumstances at the relevant time, is established to have been fair to the corporation.

Cross-References

Directors' action, see § 8.62.

"Director's conflicting interest transaction" defined, see § 8.60.

"Fair to the corporation" defined, see § 8.60.

"Related person" defined, see § 8.60.

"Relevant time" defined, see § 8.60.

"Required disclosure" defined, see § 8.60.

Shareholders' action, see § 8.63.

Standards of conduct for directors, see § 8.30.

Official Comment

Section 8.61 is the operational section of subchapter F, as it prescribes the judicial consequences of the other sections. In general terms:

- If the section 8.62 or 8.63 procedures are complied with, or if it is established that at the relevant time a director's conflicting interest transaction was fair to the corporation, then a director's conflicting interest transaction is immune from attack by a shareholder or the corporation on the ground of an interest of the director. However, if the transaction is vulnerable to attack on some other ground, observance of subchapter F's procedures does not make it less so.

- If a transaction is *not* a director's conflicting interest transaction as defined in section 8.60, then the transaction may *not* be enjoined, rescinded, or made the basis of other sanction on the ground of a conflict of interest of a director, regardless of whether it went through the procedures of subchapter F. In that sense, subchapter F is specifically intended to be both comprehensive and exclusive.

- If a director's conflicting interest transaction that was not at any time the subject of action taken in compliance with section 8.62 or 8.63 is challenged on grounds of the director's conflicting interest, and is not shown to be fair to the corporation, then the court may take such remedial action as it considers appropriate under the applicable law of the jurisdiction.

1. Section 8.61(a)

Section 8.61(a) makes clear that the bright-line definition of "director's conflicting interest transaction" is exclusive with respect to a court's review of a director's interest in a transaction. So, for example, a transaction will not constitute a director's conflicting interest transaction and, therefore, will not be subject to judicial review on the ground that a director had an interest in the transaction, where the transaction is made with a relative of a director who is not one of the relatives specified in the definition of "related person," or on the ground of an alleged interest other than a material financial interest, such as a financial interest of the director that is not material, as defined in section 8.60, or a nonfinancial interest. If, however, there is reason to believe that the fairness of a transaction involving D could be questioned, D should subject the transaction to the safe harbor procedures of subchapter F. The procedures of section 8.62 (and, to a lesser extent, section 8.63) may be used for many transactions that lie outside the definitions of section 8.60.

2. Section 8.61(b)

Section 8.61(b)(1) provides a defense in a proceeding challenging a director's conflicting interest transaction if the procedures of section 8.62 have been properly followed.

The plaintiff may challenge the availability of that defense based on a failure to meet the specific requirements of section 8.62 or to conform with general standards of director conduct. For example, a challenge addressed to section 8.62 compliance might question whether the acting directors were "qualified directors" or might dispute the quality and completeness of the disclosures made by D to the qualified directors. If such a challenge is successful, the board action is ineffective for purposes of section 8.61(b)(1) and both D and the transaction may be subject to the full range of remedies that might apply, absent the safe harbor, unless the fairness of the transaction can be established under section 8.61(b)(3). The fact that a transaction has been nominally passed through safe harbor procedures does not preclude a subsequent challenge based on any failure to meet the requirements of section 8.62. A challenge to the effectiveness of board action for purposes of section 8.61(b)(1) might also assert that, although the conflicted director's conduct in connection with the process of approval by qualified directors may have been consistent with the statute's expectations, the qualified directors dealing with the matter did not act in good faith or on reasonable inquiry. The kind of relief that may be appropriate when qualified directors have approved a transaction but have not acted in good faith or have failed to become reasonably informed—and, again, where the fairness of the transaction has not been established under section 8.61(b)(3)—will depend heavily on the facts of the individual case.

Section 8.61(b)(2) regarding shareholders' approval of the transaction is the matching piece to section 8.61(b)(1) regarding directors' approval.

The language "at any time" in these provisions permits the directors or the shareholders to ratify a director's conflicting interest transaction after the fact for purposes of subchapter F.

Section 8.61(b)(3) permits a showing that a director's conflicting interest transaction was fair to the corporation even if there was no compliance with section 8.62 or 8.63. Under section 8.61(b)(3) the interested director has the burden of establishing that the transaction was fair.

* * *

Note on Directors' Compensation

Although directors' fees and other forms of director compensation are typically set by the board of directors and are specifically authorized by section 8.11 of the Act, they do involve a director's conflicting interest transaction in which most if not all of the directors may not be qualified directors. Therefore, board action on directors' compensation and benefits would be subject to judicial sanction if they are not favorably acted upon by shareholders pursuant to section 8.63 or if they are not in the circumstances fair to the corporation pursuant to section 8.61(b)(3).

§ 8.62. Directors' Action

(a)   Directors' action respecting a director's conflicting interest transaction is effective for purposes of section 8.61(b)(1) if the transaction has been authorized by the affirmative vote of a majority (but no fewer than two) of the qualified directors who voted on the transaction, after required disclosure by the conflicted director of information not already known by such qualified directors, or after modified disclosure in compliance with subsection (b), provided that:

(1)   the qualified directors have deliberated and voted outside the presence of and without the participation by any other director; and

(2)   where the action has been taken by a board committee, all members of the committee were qualified directors, and either (i) the committee was composed of all the qualified directors on the board of directors or (ii) the members of the committee were appointed by the affirmative vote of a majority of the qualified directors on the board of directors.

(b)   Notwithstanding subsection (a), when a transaction is a director's conflicting interest transaction only because a related person described in clause (v) or (vi) of the definition of "related person" in section 8.60 is a party to or has a material financial interest in the transaction, the conflicted director is not obligated to make required disclosure to the extent that the director reasonably believes that doing so would violate a duty imposed under law, a legally enforceable obligation of confidentiality, or a professional ethics rule, provided that the conflicted director discloses to the qualified directors voting on the transaction:

(1)   all information required to be disclosed that is not so violative,

(2)   the existence and nature of the director's conflicting interest, and

(3)   the nature of the conflicted director's duty not to disclose the confidential information.

(c)   A majority (but no fewer than two) of all the qualified directors on the board of directors, or on the board committee, constitutes a quorum for purposes of action that complies with this section.

(d)   Where directors' action under this section does not satisfy a quorum or voting requirement applicable to the authorization of the transaction by reason of the articles of incorporation or bylaws or a provision of law, independent action to satisfy those authorization requirements shall be taken by the board of directors or a board committee, in which action directors who are not qualified directors may participate.

Cross-References

"Director's conflicting interest transaction" defined, see § 8.60.

Judicial action, see § 8.61.

"Qualified director" defined, see § 1.43.

"Related person" defined, see § 8.60.

"Relevant time" defined, see § 8.60.

"Required disclosure" defined, see § 8.60.

Shareholders' action, see § 8.63.

Standards of conduct for directors, see § 8.30.

Official Comment

Section 8.62 provides the procedure for action by the board of directors or by a board committee under subchapter F. In the normal course this section, together with section 8.61(b), will be the key method for addressing directors' conflicting interest transactions. Any discussion of section 8.62 must have in mind the requirements that directors act in good faith and on reasonable inquiry. See section 8.30. Director action that does not comply with those requirements, even if otherwise in compliance with section 8.62, will be subject to challenge and not be given effect under section 8.62. See the Official Comment to section 8.61(b).

1. Section 8.62(a)

The definition of "qualified director" in section 1.43(a)(4) excludes not only a director who is conflicted directly or because of a person specified in the categories of the "related person" definition in section 8.60, but also any director with a familial, financial, employment, professional or other relationship with *another director for whom the transaction is a director's conflicting interest transaction* that would be likely to impair the objectivity of the first director's judgment when participating in a vote on the transaction.

Action under section 8.62 may take the form of committee action meeting the requirements of subsection (a)(2). The requirements for effective committee action are intended to preclude the appointment as committee members of a favorably inclined minority from among all the qualified directors. With respect to required disclosure under subsection (a), if there is more than one conflicted director interested in the transaction, the need for required disclosure would apply to each.

2. Section 8.62(b)

Section 8.62(b) accommodates situations where a director who has a conflicting interest is not able to comply fully with the disclosure requirement of subsection (a) because of an extrinsic duty of confidentiality that such director reasonably believes to exist. The director may, for example, be prohibited from making full disclosure because of legal restrictions that happen to apply to the transaction (*e.g.*, grand jury seal or national security statute) or professional ethics rule (*e.g.*, attorney-client confidentiality). The most frequent use of subsection (b), however, will likely involve directors who have conflicting fiduciary obligations. If D is also a director of Y Co., D may have acquired confidential information from one or both directorships relevant to a transaction between X Co. and Y Co., that D cannot reveal to one without violating a fiduciary duty owed to the other. In such circumstances, subsection (b) enables the conflicting interest complication to be presented for consideration under subsection (a), and thereby enables X Co. (and Y Co.) and D to secure for the transaction the protection afforded by subchapter F even though D cannot, by reason of applicable law, confidentiality strictures or a professional ethics rule, make the full disclosure otherwise required.

To comply with section 8.62(b), D must meet all three requirements set forth in clauses (1), (2) and (3). D must then play no personal role in the board's (or committee's) ultimate deliberations or action. The purpose of subsection (b) is to make it clear that the provisions of subchapter F may be employed to "safe harbor" a transaction in circumstances where a conflicted director cannot, because of enforced fiduciary silence, disclose all the known facts. A director could, of course, encounter the same problem of mandated silence with regard to any matter that comes before the board; that is, the problem of forced silence is not linked at all to the problems of transactions involving a conflicting interest of a director. It could happen that at the same board meeting of X Co. at which D invokes subsection (b), another director who has no financial interest in the transaction might conclude that under applicable law he or she is bound to silence (because of attorney-client confidentiality, for example) and would under general principles of sound director conduct withdraw from participation in the board's deliberations and action. Of course, if D invokes subsection (b) and does not make disclosures that would otherwise be required under subsection (a) before leaving the meeting, the qualified directors may decline to act on the transaction out of concern that D knows (or may know) something they do not. On the other hand, if D is subject to an extrinsic duty of confidentiality but has no knowledge of material facts that should otherwise be disclosed, D would normally state just that and subsection (b) would be irrelevant. Having disclosed the existence and nature of the conflicting interest, D would thereby comply with the "required disclosure" as defined under section 8.60.

Although section 8.62(b) will apply to the recurring situation where transacting corporations have common directors (or where a director of one party is an officer of the other), it should not otherwise be read as attempting to address the scope, or mandate the consequences, of various silence-privileges.

Section 8.62(b) is available to D if a transaction is a director's conflicting interest transaction only because a related person described in clauses (v) or (vi) of the definition of that term in section 8.60 is a party to or has a material financial interest in the transaction. Its availability is so limited because in those instances a director owes a fiduciary duty to such a related person. If D or a related person of D other than a related person described in clauses (v) or (vi) of the definition of is a party to or has a material financial interest in the transaction, D's only options are satisfying the required disclosure obligation on an unrestricted basis, abandoning the transaction, or accepting the risk of establishing fairness under section 8.61(b)(3), if the transaction is challenged in a court proceeding.

Whenever a conflicted director proceeds in the manner provided in subsection (b), the other directors should recognize that the conflicted director may have information that, but for the narrow exception set forth in subsection (b), D would be required to reveal to the qualified directors who are acting on the transaction—information that could well indicate that the transaction would be either favorable or unfavorable for X Co.

3.   Section 8.62(d)

Subsection 8.62(d) underscores the fact that the directors' voting procedures and requirements set forth in subsections (a) through (c) address only the director's conflicting interest. Thus, in any case where the quorum or voting requirements for substantive approval of a transaction differ from the quorum or voting requirements for "safe harbor" protection under section 8.62, the directors may find it necessary to conduct (and record in the minutes of the proceedings) two separate votes—one for section 8.62 purposes and the other for substantive approval purposes.

§ 8.63. Shareholders' Action

(a)   Shareholders' action respecting a director's conflicting interest transaction is effective for purposes of section 8.61(b)(2) if a majority of the votes cast by the holders of all qualified shares are in favor of the transaction after (i) notice to shareholders describing the action to be taken respecting the transaction, (ii) provision to the corporation of the information referred to in subsection (b), and (iii) communication to the shareholders entitled to vote on the transaction of the information that is the subject of required disclosure, to the extent the information is not known by them. In the case of shareholders' action at a meeting, the shareholders entitled to vote shall be determined as of the record date for notice of the meeting.

(b)   A director who has a conflicting interest respecting the transaction shall, before the shareholders' vote, inform the secretary or other officer or agent of the corporation authorized to tabulate votes, in writing, of the number of shares that the director knows are not qualified shares under subsection (c), and the identity of the holders of those shares.

(c)   For purposes of this section: (i) "holder" means and "held by" refers to shares held by a record shareholder, a beneficial shareholder, and an unrestricted voting trust beneficial owner; and (ii) "qualified shares" means all shares entitled to be voted with respect to the transaction except for shares that the secretary or other officer or agent of the corporation authorized to tabulate votes either knows, or under subsection (b) is notified, are held by (A) a director who has a conflicting interest respecting the transaction or (B) a related person of the director (excluding a person described in clause (vi) of the definition of "related person" in section 8.60).

(d)   A majority of the votes entitled to be cast by the holders of all qualified shares constitutes a quorum for purposes of compliance with this section. Subject to the provisions of subsection (e), shareholders' action that otherwise complies with this section is not affected by the presence of holders, or by the voting, of shares that are not qualified shares.

(e)   If a shareholders' vote does not comply with subsection (a) solely because of a director's failure to comply with subsection (b), and if the director establishes that the failure was not intended to influence and did not in fact determine the outcome of the vote, the court may take such action respecting the transaction and the director, and may give such effect, if any, to the shareholders' vote, as the court considers appropriate in the circumstances.

(f)   Where shareholders' action under this section does not satisfy a quorum or voting requirement applicable to the authorization of the transaction by reason of the articles of incorporation or the bylaws or a provision of law, independent action to satisfy those authorization requirements shall be taken by the shareholders, in which action shares that are not qualified shares may participate.

Cross-References

"Beneficial shareholder," "record shareholder" and "unrestricted voting trust beneficial owner" defined, see § 1.40.

Directors' action, see § 8.62.

"Director's conflicting interest transaction" defined, see § 8.60.

Judicial action, see § 8.61.

"Related person" defined, see § 8.60.

"Required disclosure" defined, see § 8.60.

"Secretary" defined, see § 1.40.

Official Comment

Section 8.63 provides the machinery for shareholders' action that confers safe harbor protection for a director's conflicting interest transaction, just as section 8.62 provides the machinery for directors' action that confers subchapter F safe harbor protection for such a transaction.

1.   Section 8.63(a)

Section 8.63(a) specifies the procedure required to confer effective safe harbor protection for a director's conflicting interest transaction through a vote of shareholders. In advance of the vote, three steps must be taken: (i) shareholders must be given timely and adequate notice describing the transaction; (ii) D must disclose the information called for in subsection (b); and (iii) required disclosure (as defined in section 8.60) must be made to the shareholders entitled to vote. Shareholder action that complies with subsection (a) may be taken at any time, before or after the corporation becomes legally obligated to complete the transaction.

Section 8.63 does not contain a "limited disclosure" provision that is comparable to section 8.62(b). Thus, the safe harbor protection of subchapter F is not available through shareholder action under section 8.63 in a case where D either remains silent or makes less than required disclosure because of an extrinsic duty of confidentiality

2.   Section 8.63(b)

In many circumstances, the secretary or other person charged with counting votes on behalf of X Co. will have no way to know which of X Co.'s outstanding shares should be excluded from the vote. Section 8.63(b) (together with subsection (c)) therefore obligates a director who has a conflicting interest respecting the transaction, as a prerequisite to safe harbor protection by shareholder action, to provide information known to the director with respect to the shares that are not qualified.

If the person counting the votes knows, or is notified under subsection (b), that particular shares should be excluded but for some reason fails to exclude them from the count and their inclusion in the vote does not affect its outcome, the shareholders' vote will stand. If the improper inclusion determines the outcome, the shareholders' vote fails because it does not comply with subsection (a). Subsection (e) permits the court to take the appropriate action in cases where the notification under subsection (b) is defective but not determinative of the outcome of the vote.

3.   Section 8.63(c)

The definition of "qualified shares" in section 8.63(c) does not exclude shares held by entities or persons described in clause (vi) of the definition of "related person" in section 8.60, *i.e.*, a person that is, or is an entity that is controlled by, an employer of D. If D is an employee of Y Co., that fact does not prevent Y Co. from exercising its usual rights to vote any shares it may hold in X Co. D may be unaware of, and would not necessarily monitor, whether his or her employer holds X Co. shares. Moreover, D will typically have no control over his or her employer and how it may vote its X Co. shares.

4. Section 8.63(e)

If D did not provide the information required under section 8.63(b), on its face the shareholders' action is not in compliance with subsection (a) and D has no safe harbor under subsection (a). In the absence of that safe harbor, D can be put to the burden of establishing the fairness of the transaction under section 8.61(b)(3).

That result is proper where D's failure to inform was determinative of the vote results or, worse, was part of a deliberate effort on D's part to influence the outcome. If, however, D's omission was not motivated by D's effort to influence the integrity of the voting process (for example, it was the result of D's negligence), and the voting of the unreported shares was not determinative of the outcome of the vote, then the court should be free to fashion an appropriate response to the situation in light of all the considerations at the time of its decision.

Despite the presumption of regularity customarily accorded the secretary's record, a plaintiff may go behind the secretary's record for purposes of subsection (e).

5. Section 8.63(f)

Section 8.63(f) underscores that the shareholders' voting procedures and requirements set forth in subsections (a) through (e) treat only the director's conflicting interest. A transaction that receives a shareholders' vote that complies with subchapter F may well fail to achieve a different vote or quorum that may be required for substantive approval of the transaction under other applicable statutory provisions or provisions contained in X Co.'s articles of incorporation or bylaws, and vice versa. Thus, in any case where the quorum or voting requirements for substantive approval of a transaction differ from the quorum or voting requirements for "safe harbor" protection under section 8.63, the corporation may find it necessary to conduct (and record in the minutes of the proceedings) two separate shareholder votes—one for section 8.63 purposes and the other for substantive approval purposes (or, if appropriate, conduct two separate tabulations of one vote).

SUBCHAPTER G
BUSINESS OPPORTUNITIES

§ 8.70. Business Opportunities

(a) If a director or officer pursues or takes advantage of a business opportunity directly, or indirectly through or on behalf of another person, that action may not be the subject of equitable relief, or give rise to an award of damages or other sanctions against the director, officer or other person, in a proceeding by or in the right of the corporation on the ground that the opportunity should have first been offered to the corporation, if

(1) before the director, officer or other person becomes legally obligated respecting the opportunity the director or officer brings it to the attention of the corporation and either:

(i) action by qualified directors disclaiming the corporation's interest in the opportunity is taken in compliance with the same procedures as are set forth in section 8.62, or

(ii) shareholders' action disclaiming the corporation's interest in the opportunity is taken in compliance with the procedures set forth in section 8.63, in either case as if the decision being made concerned a director's conflicting interest transaction, except that, rather than making "required disclosure" as defined in section 8.60, the director or officer shall have made prior disclosure to those acting on behalf of the corporation of all material facts concerning the business opportunity known to the director or officer; or

(2) the duty to offer the corporation the business opportunity has been limited or eliminated pursuant to a provision of the articles of incorporation adopted (and where required, made effective by action of qualified directors) in accordance with section 2.02(b)(6).

(b)   In any proceeding seeking equitable relief or other remedies based upon an alleged improper pursuit or taking advantage of a business opportunity by a director or officer, directly, or indirectly through or on behalf of another person, the fact that the director or officer did not employ the procedure described in subsection (a)(1)(i) or (ii) before pursuing or taking advantage of the opportunity shall not create an implication that the opportunity should have been first presented to the corporation or alter the burden of proof otherwise applicable to establish that the director or officer breached a duty to the corporation in the circumstances.

Cross-References

Directors' action, see § 8.62.

"Qualified director" defined, see § 1.43.

Shareholders' action, see § 8.63.

Standards of conduct for directors, see § 8.30.

Standards of liability for directors, see § 8.31.

Standards of conduct for officers, see § 8.42.

Official Comment

Section 8.70(a)(1) provides a safe harbor for a director or officer weighing possible involvement with a prospective business opportunity that might constitute a "corporate opportunity." The phrase "directly, or indirectly through or on behalf of another person" recognizes the need to cover transactions pursued or effected either directly by the director or officer or indirectly through or on behalf of another person, which might be a related person as defined in section 8.60 or a person which is not a related person. By action of the board of directors or shareholders of the corporation under section 8.70(a)(1), the director or officer can obtain a disclaimer of the corporation's interest in the matter before proceeding with such involvement. In the alternative, the corporation may, among other things, (i) decline to disclaim its interest, (ii) delay a decision respecting granting a disclaimer pending receipt from the director or officer of additional information (or for any other reason), or (iii) attach conditions to the disclaimer it grants under section 8.70(a)(1).

The safe harbor provided under section 8.70(a)(1) may be utilized only for a specific business opportunity. A broader advance safe harbor for any, or one or more classes or categories of, business opportunities must meet the requirements of section 2.02(b)(6). Section 8.70(a)(2) confirms that if the duty of an officer or director to present an opportunity has been limited or eliminated by a provision in the articles of incorporation under section 2.02(b)(6) (and, in the case of officers, appropriate action by qualified directors as required by that section), a safe harbor exists in connection with the pursuit or taking of the opportunity. The common law doctrine of "corporate opportunity" has long been recognized as a part of the director's duty of loyalty and, under court decisions, extends to officers. See section 8.30(a) and its Official Comment. The doctrine recognizes that the corporation has a right prior to that of its directors or officers to act on certain business opportunities that come to the attention of the directors or officers. In such situations, a director or officer who acts on the opportunity for the benefit of the director or officer or another person without having first presented it to the corporation can be held to have "usurped" or "intercepted" a right of the corporation. A defendant director or officer who is found by a court to have violated the duty of loyalty in this regard, as well as related or other persons involved in the transaction, may be subject to damages or possible equitable remedies, including injunction, disgorgement or the imposition of a constructive trust in favor of the corporation. Although the doctrine's concept is easily described, whether it will be found to apply in a given case depends on the facts and circumstances of the particular situation and is thus frequently unpredictable.

In recognition that the corporation need not pursue every business opportunity of which it becomes aware, an opportunity coming within the doctrine's criteria that has been properly presented to and declined by the corporation may then be pursued or taken by the presenting director or officer without breach of the duty of loyalty.

The fact-intensive nature of the corporate opportunity doctrine resists statutory definition. Instead, subchapter G employs the broader notion of "business opportunity" that encompasses any opportunity, without regard to whether it would come within the judicial definition of a "corporate opportunity," as it may have been developed by courts in a jurisdiction. When properly employed, subchapter G provides a safe-harbor mechanism enabling a director or officer to pursue an opportunity directly, or indirectly through or on behalf of another person, free of possible challenge claiming conflict with the director's or officer's duty on the ground that the opportunity should first have been offered to the corporation. Section 8.70 is modeled on the safe-harbor and approval procedures of subchapter F pertaining to directors' conflicting interest transactions with, however, some modifications necessary to accommodate differences in the two matters addressed.

1. Section 8.70(a)(1)

Section 8.70(a)(1) describes the safe harbor available to a director or officer who elects to subject a business opportunity, regardless of whether the opportunity would be classified as a "corporate opportunity," to the disclosure and approval procedures set forth in that section. The safe harbor provided is as broad as that provided for a director's conflicting interest transaction in section 8.61. If the director or officer makes the prescribed disclosure of the facts specified and the corporation's interest in the opportunity is disclaimed by director action under subsection (a)(1)(i) or shareholder action under subsection (a)(1)(ii), the director or officer has foreclosed any claimed breach of the duty of loyalty and may not be subject to equitable relief, damages or other sanctions if the director or officer thereafter pursues or takes the opportunity for his or her own account or through or for the benefit of another person. As a general proposition, disclaimer by director action under subsection (a)(1)(i) must meet all of the requirements provided in section 8.62 with respect to a director's conflicting interest transaction and disclaimer by shareholder action under subsection (a)(1)(ii) must likewise meet all of the requirements for shareholder action under section 8.63. Note, however, several important differences.

First, in contrast to director or shareholder action under sections 8.62 and 8.63, which may be taken at any time, section 8.70(a)(1) requires that the director or officer present the opportunity and secure director or shareholder action disclaiming it *before* the director of officer or other person involved through or on behalf of the director or officer becomes legally obligated respecting the opportunity. The safe harbor concept contemplates that the corporation's decision maker will have full freedom of action in deciding whether the corporation should take over a proffered opportunity or disclaim the corporation's interest in it. If the director or officer could seek ratification after the legal obligation respecting the opportunity arises, the option of taking over the opportunity would, in most cases, be foreclosed to the corporation. The safe harbor's benefit is available only when the corporation can entertain the opportunity in a fully objective way.

The second difference relates to the necessary disclosure. Instead of employing section 8.60's definition of "required disclosure" which is incorporated in sections 8.62 and 8.63 and includes "the existence and nature of the director's conflicting interest," the disclosure obligation of section 8.70(a)(1) requires only that the director or officer reveal all material facts concerning the business opportunity known to the director or officer. The safe harbor procedure shields the director or officer even if a material fact regarding the business opportunity is not disclosed, so long as the proffering director or officer had no knowledge of that fact.

2. Section 8.70(b)

Section 8.70(b) reflects a fundamental difference between the coverage of subchapters F and G. Because subchapter F provides an exclusive definition of "director's conflicting interest transaction," any transaction meeting the definition that is not approved in accordance with the provisions of subchapter F is not entitled to its safe harbor. Unless the interested director can, upon challenge, establish the transaction's fairness, the director's conduct is presumptively actionable and subject to the full range of remedies that might otherwise be awarded by a court. In contrast, the concept of "business opportunity" under section 8.70 is not defined but is intended to be broader than what might be regarded as an actionable "corporate opportunity." This approach reflects the fact-intensive nature of the corporate opportunity doctrine, with the result that a director or officer may be inclined to seek safe harbor protection under section 8.70 before pursuing an opportunity that may or may not be a "corporate opportunity." Likewise, a director or officer may conclude that a business opportunity is not a "corporate opportunity" under applicable law and choose to pursue it without seeking a disclaimer by the corporation under subsection (a)(1). Accordingly, subsection (b) provides that a decision not to seek the safe harbor offered by subsection (a)(1) neither creates a negative implication nor alters the burden of proof in any subsequent proceeding seeking damages or equitable relief based upon an alleged improper taking of a "corporate opportunity."

CHAPTER 9: DOMESTICATION AND CONVERSION

Introductory Comment

This chapter provides procedures by which a domestic corporation may become a foreign corporation or a different form of domestic or foreign entity and, conversely, a foreign corporation or an eligible entity may become a domestic corporation. These procedures are:

- **Domestication.** The procedures in subchapter 9B permit a corporation to change its state of incorporation, thus allowing a domestic corporation to become a foreign corporation or a foreign corporation to become a domestic corporation.

- **Conversion.** The procedures in subchapter 9C permit a domestic corporation to become a domestic or foreign eligible entity and also permit a domestic or foreign eligible entity to become a domestic corporation.

The provisions of this chapter apply only if a domestic corporation is present either immediately before or immediately after a domestication or conversion.

Note on adoption: Some states may wish to generalize the provisions of this chapter so that they are not limited to transactions involving a domestic business corporation. For example, a state may wish to permit a domestic limited partnership to become a domestic limited liability company. The Model Entity Transactions Act prepared by the Uniform Law Commission is such a generalized statute. Some states have elected to include transactions that are described in chapter 9 as domestications in their definition of conversions and not to refer to domestication separately.

SUBCHAPTER A
PRELIMINARY PROVISIONS

§ 9.01. Definitions

As used in this chapter:

"Conversion" means a transaction pursuant to subchapter C.

"Converted entity" means the converting entity as it continues in existence after a conversion.

"Converting entity" means the domestic corporation or eligible entity that approves a plan of conversion pursuant to section 9.32 or the foreign eligible entity that approves a conversion pursuant to the organic law of the eligible entity.

"Domesticated corporation" means the domesticating corporation as it continues in existence after a domestication.

"Domesticating corporation" means the domestic corporation that approves a plan of domestication pursuant to section 9.21 or the foreign corporation that approves a domestication pursuant to the organic law of the foreign corporation.

"Domestication" means a transaction pursuant to subchapter B.

"Protected agreement" means:

(i) a document evidencing indebtedness of a domestic corporation or eligible entity and any related agreement in effect immediately before the enactment date;

(ii) an agreement that is binding on a domestic corporation or eligible entity immediately before the enactment date;

(iii) the articles of incorporation or bylaws of a domestic corporation or the organic rules of a domestic eligible entity, in each case in effect immediately before the enactment date; or

      (iv) an agreement that is binding on any of the shareholders, members, interest holders, directors or other governors of a domestic corporation or eligible entity, in their capacities as such, immediately before the enactment date.

For purposes of this definition and sections 9.20 and 9.30, "enactment date" means the first date on which the law of this state authorized a transaction having the effect of a domestication or a conversion, as applicable.

Note on adoption: When adopting the definition of "protected agreement," a state could consider setting out in the last sentence of the definition the actual dates when domestication and conversion statutes were first enacted in the state so those dates would be apparent on the face of the statute.

Cross-References

Articles of incorporation, see § 2.02.

"Corporation," "domestic" and "foreign" defined, see § 1.40.

"Document" defined, see § 1.40.

"Eligible entity" defined, see § 1.40.

"Entity" defined, see § 1.40.

"Governor" defined, see § 1.40.

"Interest holder" defined, see § 1.40.

"Membership" defined, see § 1.40.

"Organic law" and "organic rules" defined, see § 1.40.

Official Comment

Section 9.01 sets out definitions used in the Act's provisions on domestication and conversion. It defines "protected agreement" as those specified documents and agreements which were in effect before the laws of the state first provided for domestication or conversion transactions. A person contracting with a corporation or loaning it money, or which drafted and negotiated special rights relating to mergers or similar transactions, before the enactment of this chapter (or any similar predecessor law) should not be charged with the consequences of not having dealt with domestications and conversions. Sections 9.20(f) and 9.30(d) provide special rules dealing with protected agreements.

§ 9.02. Excluded Transactions [Optional]

This chapter may not be used to effect a transaction that:

      (a) [converts a company organized on the mutual principle to one organized on the basis of share ownership]; or

      (b) [other examples]

Note on adoption: A state should use this section to list those situations in which the state has enacted specific legislation governing the domestication or conversion of domestic corporations that engage in particular types of activities or that do business in a regulated industry. Mutual to share conversions (for instance, of an insurance company, bank, savings institution or credit union) are examples of such transactions.

Official Comment

The purpose of this section is to prohibit certain transactions that are subject to a separate statutory or legal framework from being effected under this chapter.

§ 9.03. Required Approvals [Optional]

If a domestic or foreign corporation or eligible entity may not be a party to a merger without the approval of the [attorney general], the [department of banking], the [department of insurance] or the [public utility commission], and the applicable statutes or regulations do not specifically deal with transactions under this chapter but do require such approval for mergers, a corporation or eligible entity shall not be a party to a transaction under this chapter without the prior approval of that agency or official.

Note on adoption: *Section 9.03 is an optional provision that should be considered in states where corporations or other entities that conduct regulated activities, such as banking, insurance or the provision of public utility services, are incorporated or organized under general laws instead of under special laws applicable only to entities conducting the regulated activity. If this section is used, the list of officials and agencies should be conformed to the laws of the enacting state.*

Official Comment

The purpose of section 9.03 is to ensure that transactions under chapter 9 will be effected only if required state governmental approvals have been obtained. If other state laws require such approvals in the case of mergers, but do not address approvals in the case of domestications and conversions, then section 9.03 requires that transactions under chapter 9 obtain the same regulatory approvals as mergers.

§ 9.04. Relationship of Chapter to Other Laws [Optional]

A transaction effected under this chapter may not create or impair a right, duty or obligation of a person under the statutory law of this state other than this chapter relating to a change in control, business combination, control-share acquisition, or similar transaction involving a domesticating or converting domestic corporation, unless the approval of the plan of domestication or conversion is by a vote of the shareholders or the board of directors which would be sufficient to create or impair the right, duty or obligation directly under that law.

Official Comment

This section protects the application of change of control statutes from being affected by a transaction under this chapter by requiring that the transaction be approved in a manner that would be sufficient to approve changing the application of the change of control statute. If a domestication or conversion is approved in that manner, there is no policy reason to prohibit the application of the change of control statute from being varied for the transaction. If the application of a change of control statute cannot be varied by action of an entity subject to it, then a transaction under this chapter will be permissible only if the change of control provision continues to apply after the transaction or the transaction itself is permissible under the change of control statute.

SUBCHAPTER B
DOMESTICATION

§ 9.20. Domestication

(a) By complying with the provisions of this subchapter applicable to foreign corporations, a foreign corporation may become a domestic corporation if the domestication is permitted by the organic law of the foreign corporation.

(b) By complying with the provisions of this subchapter, a domestic corporation may become a foreign corporation pursuant to a plan of domestication if the domestication is permitted by the organic law of the foreign corporation.

(c) The plan of domestication must include:

(1) the name of the domesticating corporation;

(2) the name and jurisdiction of formation of the domesticated corporation;

(3)   the manner and basis of reclassifying the shares of the domesticating corporation into shares or other securities, obligations, rights to acquire shares or other securities, cash, other property, or any combination of the foregoing;

(4)   the proposed articles of incorporation and bylaws of the domesticated corporation; and

(5)   the other terms and conditions of the domestication.

(d)   In addition to the requirements of subsection (c), a plan of domestication may contain any other provision not prohibited by law.

(e)   The terms of a plan of domestication may be made dependent upon facts objectively ascertainable outside the plan in accordance with section 1.20(k).

(f)   If a protected agreement of a domestic domesticating corporation in effect immediately before the domestication becomes effective contains a provision applying to a merger of the corporation and the agreement does not refer to a domestication of the corporation, the provision applies to a domestication of the corporation as if the domestication were a merger until such time as the provision is first amended after the enactment date.

Cross-References

Abandonment of domestication, see § 9.25.

Approval of plan, see § 9.21.

Articles of domestication, see § 9.22.

Articles of incorporation following domestication, see § 9.22.

"Domestic corporation" defined, see § 1.40.

Effect of domestication, see § 9.24.

"Enactment date" defined in definition of protected agreement, see § 9.01.

Excluded transactions, see § 9.02.

"Interest holder liability" defined, see § 1.40.

"Foreign corporation" defined, see § 1.40.

"Organic law" defined, see § 1.40.

"Protected agreement" defined, see § 9.01.

[Required approvals, see § 9.03.]

"Voting group" defined, see § 1.40.

Official Comment

1.   Applicability

This subchapter authorizes a foreign corporation to become a domestic corporation and a domestic corporation to become a foreign corporation. In each case, the domestication is authorized only if the laws of the foreign jurisdiction permit it. Whether and on what terms a foreign corporation is authorized to domesticate in this state are issues governed by the organic law of the foreign corporation, not by this subchapter. A foreign corporation is not required to have a valid registration to do business in this state under chapter 15 to domesticate in this state.

2.   Terms and Conditions of Domestication

This subchapter imposes no restrictions or limitations on the terms and conditions of a domestication, except for those set forth in section 9.23(a) with respect to certain amendments to the plan of domestication. The list in section 9.20(c) of required provisions in a plan of domestication is not exhaustive. Unlike a domestic corporation, a foreign corporation is not required to have a plan of domestication, although it must comply with the provisions of this subchapter applicable to foreign corporations.

3.   *Articles of Incorporation*

Under section 9.20(c)(4), a domestic corporation's plan of domestication must include that corporation's proposed articles of incorporation and bylaws, which should comply with the organic law of the foreign jurisdiction into which it is domesticating. In the case of a domestic corporation domesticating into a foreign jurisdiction, the Act places no separate limitations on the provisions that the proposed articles of incorporation and bylaws may contain, and they may be substantially identical to or completely different from those of the domesticating corporation. However, the content of the proposed articles may affect the approvals required for the plan of domestication. See the approval requirements in section 9.21(f) with respect to certain changes in the articles of incorporation, and section 9.21(g) with respect to interest holder liability with respect to the domesticated corporation.

4.   *Appraisal Rights*

This subchapter does not require that a shareholder in the domesticating corporation receive the same type or amount, or even any, shares of the domesticated corporation. However, a shareholder of a domestic corporation that domesticates into a foreign jurisdiction has appraisal rights if the shareholder does not receive shares in the domesticated corporation having terms as favorable to the shareholder in all material respects, and representing at least the same percentage interest of the total voting rights of the outstanding shares of the domesticated corporation, as the shares held by the shareholder before the domestication. See section 13.02(a)(6).

5.   *Protected Agreements*

Section 9.20(f) provides special rules for "protected agreements"—certain documents and agreements in effect before the date (defined as the "enactment date") of this chapter (or any similar predecessor statute).

§ 9.21. Action on a Plan of Domestication

In the case of a domestication of a domestic corporation into a foreign jurisdiction, the plan of domestication shall be adopted in the following manner:

(a)   The plan of domestication shall first be adopted by the board of directors.

(b)   The plan of domestication shall then be approved by the shareholders. In submitting the plan of domestication to the shareholders for approval, the board of directors shall recommend that the shareholders approve the plan, unless (i) the board of directors makes a determination that because of conflicts of interest or other special circumstances it should not make such a recommendation or (ii) section 8.26 applies. If either (i) or (ii) applies, the board shall inform the shareholders of the basis for its so proceeding.

(c)   The board of directors may set conditions for approval of the plan of domestication by the shareholders or the effectiveness of the plan of domestication.

(d)   If the approval of the shareholders is to be given at a meeting, the corporation shall notify each shareholder, regardless of whether entitled to vote, of the meeting of shareholders at which the plan of domestication is to be submitted for approval. The notice must state that the purpose, or one of the purposes, of the meeting is to consider the plan of domestication and must contain or be accompanied by a copy or summary of the plan. The notice must include or be accompanied by a copy of the articles of incorporation and the bylaws as they will be in effect immediately after the domestication.

(e)   Unless the articles of incorporation, or the board of directors acting pursuant to subsection (c), require a greater vote or a greater quorum, approval of the plan of domestication requires (i) the approval of the shareholders at a meeting at which a quorum exists consisting of a majority of the votes entitled to be cast on the plan, and, (ii) except as provided in subsection (f), the approval of each class or series of shares voting as a separate voting group at a meeting at which a quorum of the voting group exists consisting of a majority of the votes entitled to be cast on the plan by that voting group.

(f)   The articles of incorporation may expressly limit or eliminate the separate voting rights provided in subsection (e)(ii) as to any class or series of shares, except when the articles of incorporation of the foreign corporation resulting from the domestication include what would be in effect an amendment that would entitle the class or series to vote as a separate group under section 10.04 if it were a proposed amendment of the articles of incorporation of the domestic domesticating corporation.

(g)   If as a result of a domestication one or more shareholders of a domestic domesticating corporation would become subject to interest holder liability, approval of the plan of domestication shall require the signing in connection with the domestication, by each such shareholder, of a separate written consent to become subject to such interest holder liability, unless in the case of a shareholder that already has interest holder liability with respect to the domesticating corporation, the terms and conditions of the interest holder liability with respect to the domesticated corporation are substantially identical to those of the existing interest holder liability (other than for changes that eliminate or reduce such interest holder liability).

Cross-References

Abandonment of domestication, see § 9.23.

Contents of plan of domestication, see § 9.20.

"Domestic corporation" defined, see § 1.40.

"Interest holder liability" defined, see § 1.40.

"Organic law" defined, see § 1.40.

Submission of matters for shareholder vote, see § 8.26.

"Voting group" defined, see § 1.40.

Official Comment

1.   In General

Section 9.21 sets forth the rules for adoption and approval of a plan of domestication of a domestic corporation into a foreign jurisdiction. The manner in which the domestication of a foreign corporation into this state must be adopted and approved will be controlled by the organic law of the foreign corporation.

When submitting a plan of domestication to shareholders, the board of directors must recommend the transaction, subject to two exceptions in section 9.21(b). The board might exercise the exception under clause (i) where the number of directors having a conflicting interest makes it inadvisable for the board to recommend the domestication or where the board is evenly divided as to the merits of the domestication but is able to agree that shareholders should be permitted to consider it. Alternatively, the board of directors might exercise the exception under clause (ii), which recognizes that, under section 8.26, a board of directors may agree to submit a plan to a vote of shareholders even if, after approving the plan, the board of directors determines that it no longer recommends the plan.

Section 9.21(c) permits the board of directors to condition its submission of a plan of domestication to the shareholders or the effectiveness of the plan of domestication. Among the conditions that a board of directors might impose are that the plan will not be deemed approved (i) unless it is approved by a specified vote of the shareholders, or by one or more specified classes or series of shares, voting as a separate voting group, or by a specified percentage of disinterested shareholders or (ii) if shareholders holding more than a specified fraction of the outstanding shares assert appraisal rights.

Section 9.21(d) provides a notice requirement if a plan of domestication is to be considered by the shareholders at a meeting. Requirements concerning the timing and content of a notice of meeting are in section 7.05. Section 9.21(d) does not address the notice to be given to nonvoting or nonconsenting shareholders where the plan is approved without a meeting by written consent. However, that requirement is imposed by section 7.04.

2.   Quorum; Voting by Separate Groups

Section 9.21(e) sets forth quorum and voting requirements applicable to a shareholder vote to approve a plan of domestication. Section 9.21(e) also provides that each class or series has a right to vote on a plan of domestication as a separate voting group. See sections 7.25(f) and 10.04(c) for rules governing when separate classes or series vote together as a single voting group. Section 9.21(f) permits the articles of incorporation to expressly limit or eliminate separate voting as a voting group for any class or series of shares on a plan of domestication unless the articles of incorporation of the foreign domesticated corporation into which the corporation would be domesticated include what would be an amendment requiring separate group voting under section 10.04 if it had been done as an amendment of that domestic corporation's articles of incorporation. The requirement that such a limitation or elimination be "express" is meant to avoid any ambiguity that might arise from a provision in the articles of incorporation that denies voting rights to the class or series. In lieu of approval at a meeting, shareholder approval may be by written consent under the procedures set forth in section 7.04.

3.   Personal Liability of Shareholders

Section 9.21(g) applies only in situations where a shareholder of a domestic corporation is becoming subject to "interest holder liability," as defined in section 1.40, with respect to the domesticated corporation. Approval of a domestication that would have such a result generally requires the written consent of each such shareholder who becomes subject to such interest holder liability. The exception is the limited case where the shareholder has interest holder liability with respect to the domesticating corporation, and the terms and conditions of the shareholder's interest holder liability with respect to the domesticated corporation are substantially identical to those existing prior to the domestication. If, for example, a shareholder before the domestication has interest holder liability for certain borrowings and after the domestication would have interest holder liability for unpaid wages, the terms and conditions of the interest holder liability are not substantially identical, and the shareholder's written consent to become subject to that liability would be required for the domestication to be approved.

§ 9.22. Articles of Domestication; Effectiveness

(a)   After (i) a plan of domestication of a domestic corporation has been adopted and approved as required by this Act, or (ii) a foreign corporation that is the domesticating corporation has approved a domestication as required under its organic law, articles of domestication shall be signed by the domesticating corporation. The articles must set forth:

(1)   the name of the domesticating corporation and its jurisdiction of formation;

(2)   the name and jurisdiction of formation of the domesticated corporation; and

(3)   if the domesticating corporation is a domestic corporation, a statement that the plan of domestication was approved in accordance with this chapter or, if the domesticating corporation is a foreign corporation, a statement that the domestication was approved in accordance with its organic law.

(b)   If the domesticated corporation is a domestic corporation, the articles of domestication must attach articles of incorporation of the domesticated corporation that satisfy the requirements of section 2.02. Provisions that would not be required to be included in restated articles of incorporation may be omitted from the articles of incorporation attached to the articles of domestication.

(c)   The articles of domestication shall be delivered to the secretary of state for filing, and shall take effect at the effective date determined in accordance with section 1.23.

(d)   If the domesticated corporation is a domestic corporation, the domestication becomes effective when the articles of domestication are effective. If the domesticated corporation is a foreign corporation, the domestication becomes effective on the later of (i) the date and time provided by the organic law of the domesticated corporation, and (ii) when the articles of domestication are effective.

(e)   If the domesticating corporation is a foreign corporation that is registered to do business in this state under chapter 15, its registration statement shall be cancelled automatically when the domestication becomes effective.

Cross-References

"Domestic corporation" defined, see § 1.40.

"Domesticated corporation" defined, see § 9.01.

"Domesticating corporation" defined, see § 9.01.

Effect of domestication, see § 9.24.

Filing requirements, see § 1.20.

"Organic law" defined, see § 1.40.

[Required approvals, see § 9.03.]

Official Comment

The filing of articles of domestication makes the domestication a matter of public record. Where the domesticated corporation is a domestic corporation, it also makes its articles of incorporation a matter of public record.

The requirements for filing are set forth in section 1.20. Under section 1.23, the articles of domestication are effective on the date and at the time of filing unless a later effective date is specified in the articles within the limits provided in section 1.23. Under section 1.23, a delayed effective date may not be later than the 90th day after the date the document is filed. Section 9.22(d) provides when the domestication becomes effective.

§ 9.23. Amendment of Plan of Domestication; Abandonment

(a) A plan of domestication of a domestic corporation may be amended:

(1) in the same manner as the plan was approved, if the plan does not provide for the manner in which it may be amended; or

(2) in the manner provided in the plan, except that a shareholder that was entitled to vote on or consent to approval of the plan is entitled to vote on or consent to any amendment of the plan that will change:

(i) the amount or kind of shares or other securities, obligations, rights to acquire shares or other securities, cash, other property, or any combination of the foregoing, to be received by any of the shareholders of the domesticating corporation under the plan;

(ii) the articles of incorporation or bylaws of the domesticated corporation that will be in effect immediately after the domestication becomes effective, except for changes that do not require approval of the shareholders of the domesticated corporation under its organic law or its proposed articles of incorporation or bylaws as set forth in the plan; or

(iii) any of the other terms or conditions of the plan, if the change would adversely affect the shareholder in any material respect.

(b) After a plan of domestication has been adopted and approved by a domestic corporation as required by this subchapter, and before the articles of domestication have become effective, the plan may be abandoned by the corporation without action by its shareholders in accordance with any procedures set forth in the plan or, if no such procedures are set forth in the plan, in the manner determined by the board of directors.

(c) If a domestication is abandoned after the articles of domestication have been delivered to the secretary of state for filing but before the articles of domestication have become effective, articles of abandonment, signed by the domesticating corporation, must be delivered to the secretary of state for filing before the articles of domestication become effective. The articles of abandonment take effect upon filing, and the domestication shall be deemed abandoned and shall not become effective. The articles of abandonment must contain:

(1) the name of the domesticating corporation;

(2)   the date on which the articles of domestication were filed by the secretary of state; and

(3)   a statement that the domestication has been abandoned in accordance with this section.

Cross-References

"Domestic corporation" defined, see § 1.40.

"Domesticated corporation" defined, see § 9.01.

"Domesticating corporation" defined, see § 9.01.

"Organic law" defined, see § 1.40.

Official Comment

Section 9.23(a)(2) permits the plan of domestication to be amended in the manner provided in the plan, subject to certain cases requiring a shareholder vote on the amendment. If the plan has no provisions with respect to its amendment, it may be amended under section 9.23(a)(1) in the same manner as it was approved.

Under section 9.23(b), unless otherwise provided in the plan of domestication, a domestic corporation may abandon a domestication without shareholder approval, even though the transaction has been previously approved by the shareholders. The power of a foreign corporation to abandon a domestication will be determined by its organic law.

§ 9.24. Effect of Domestication

(a)   When a domestication becomes effective:

(1)   all property owned by, and every contract right possessed by, the domesticating corporation are the property and contract rights of the domesticated corporation without transfer, reversion or impairment;

(2)   all debts, obligations and other liabilities of the domesticating corporation are the debts, obligations and other liabilities of the domesticated corporation;

(3)   the name of the domesticated corporation may but need not be substituted for the name of the domesticating corporation in any pending proceeding;

(4)   the articles of incorporation and bylaws of the domesticated corporation become effective;

(5)   the shares of the domesticating corporation are reclassified into shares or other securities, obligations, rights to acquire shares or other securities, cash or other property in accordance with the terms of the domestication, and the shareholders of the domesticating corporation are entitled only to the rights provided to them by those terms and to any appraisal rights they may have under the organic law of the domesticating corporation; and

(6)   the domesticated corporation is:

(i)   incorporated under and subject to the organic law of the domesticated corporation;

(ii)   the same corporation without interruption as the domesticating corporation; and

(iii)   deemed to have been incorporated on the date the domesticating corporation was originally incorporated.

(b)   When a domestication of a domestic corporation into a foreign jurisdiction becomes effective, the domesticated corporation is deemed to:

(1)   appoint the secretary of state as its agent for service of process in a proceeding to enforce the rights of shareholders who exercise appraisal rights in connection with the domestication; and

(2)   agree that it will promptly pay the amount, if any, to which such shareholders are entitled under chapter 13.

(c)   Except as otherwise provided in the organic law or organic rules of a domesticating foreign corporation, the interest holder liability of a shareholder in a foreign corporation that is domesticated into this state who had interest holder liability in respect of such domesticating corporation before the domestication becomes effective shall be as follows:

(1)   The domestication does not discharge that prior interest holder liability with respect to any interest holder liabilities that arose before the domestication becomes effective.

(2)   The provisions of the organic law of the domesticating corporation shall continue to apply to the collection or discharge of any interest holder liabilities preserved by subsection (c)(1), as if the domestication had not occurred.

(3)   The shareholder shall have such rights of contribution from other persons as are provided by the organic law of the domesticating corporation with respect to any interest holder liabilities preserved by subsection (c)(1), as if the domestication had not occurred.

(4)   The shareholder shall not, by reason of such prior interest holder liability, have interest holder liability with respect to any interest holder liabilities that are incurred after the domestication becomes effective.

(d)   A shareholder who becomes subject to interest holder liability in respect of the domesticated corporation as a result of the domestication shall have such interest holder liability only in respect of interest holder liabilities that arise after the domestication becomes effective.

(e)   A domestication does not constitute or cause the dissolution of the domesticating corporation.

(f)   Property held for charitable purposes under the laws of this state by a domestic or foreign corporation immediately before a domestication shall not, as a result of the transaction, be diverted from the objects for which it was donated, granted, devised, or otherwise transferred except and to the extent permitted by or pursuant to the laws of this state addressing cy près or dealing with nondiversion of charitable assets.

(g)   A bequest, devise, gift, grant, or promise contained in a will or other instrument of donation, subscription, or conveyance which is made to the domesticating corporation and which takes effect or remains payable after the domestication inures to the domesticated corporation.

(h)   A trust obligation that would govern property if transferred to the domesticating corporation applies to property that is transferred to the domesticated corporation after the domestication takes effect.

Cross-References

Appraisal rights, see ch. 13.

"Domesticated corporation" defined, see § 9.01.

"Domesticating corporation" defined, see § 9.01.

"Interest holder liability" defined, see § 1.40.

"Organic law" and "organic rules" defined, see § 1.40.

Official Comment

The domesticated corporation is the same entity as the domesticating corporation, and it continues without interruption. It becomes a business corporation in the resulting jurisdiction with the same status as if it had been originally incorporated there. The domesticated corporation will have all of the powers, privileges and rights granted to corporations originally incorporated in that jurisdiction and will be subject to all of the duties, liabilities and limitations imposed on business corporations in that jurisdiction. Thus, a domestication is not a conveyance, transfer or assignment. It does not give rise to claims of reverter or impairment of title based on a prohibited conveyance, transfer or assignment. Nor does it give rise to a claim that a contract with the corporation is no longer in effect on the ground of nonassignability, unless the contract specifically provides that it does not survive domestication. See, however, section 9.20(f) and its Official Comment with respect to special rules regarding protected agreements. All pending proceedings involving the domesticating corporation are continued.

A domestic corporation domesticating into a foreign jurisdiction remains obligated to its shareholders who exercise appraisal rights to pay them the amount, if any, to which they are entitled under chapter 13. For this purpose, under section 9.24(b) the domesticated corporation is deemed to appoint the secretary of state as its agent for service of process in proceedings to enforce those rights.

Section 9.24(c) preserves the interest holder liability of shareholders of the domesticating foreign corporation only for interest holder liabilities to the extent they arise before the domestication becomes effective. Interest holder liability is not preserved for subsequent changes in an underlying liability, regardless of whether a change is voluntary or involuntary. Section 9.24(d) similarly provides that interest holder liability with respect to the domesticated corporation only relates to interest holder liabilities that arise after the domestication.

SUBCHAPTER C
CONVERSION

§ 9.30. Conversion

(a)   By complying with this chapter, a domestic corporation may become (i) a domestic eligible entity or (ii) a foreign eligible entity if the conversion is permitted by the organic law of the foreign entity.

(b)   By complying with this subchapter and applicable provisions of its organic law, a domestic eligible entity may become a domestic corporation. If procedures for the approval of a conversion are not provided by the organic law or organic rules of a domestic eligible entity, the conversion shall be adopted and approved in the same manner as a merger of that eligible entity. If the organic law or organic rules of a domestic eligible entity do not provide procedures for the approval of either a conversion or a merger, a plan of conversion may nonetheless be adopted and approved by the unanimous consent of all the interest holders of such eligible entity. In either such case, the conversion thereafter may be effected as provided in the other provisions of this subchapter; and for purposes of applying this chapter in such a case:

(1)   the eligible entity, its members or interest holders, eligible interests and organic rules taken together, shall be deemed to be a domestic business corporation, shareholders, shares and articles of incorporation, respectively and vice versa, as the context may require; and

(2)   if the business and affairs of the eligible entity are managed by a person or persons that are not identical to the members or interest holders, that person or persons shall be deemed to be the board of directors.

(c)   By complying with the provisions of this subchapter applicable to foreign entities, a foreign eligible entity may become a domestic corporation if the organic law of the foreign eligible entity permits it to become a business corporation in another jurisdiction.

(d)   If a protected agreement of a domestic converting corporation in effect immediately before the conversion becomes effective contains a provision applying to a merger of the corporation that is a converting entity and the agreement does not refer to a conversion of the corporation, the provision applies to a conversion of the corporation as if the conversion were a merger, until such time as the provision is first amended after the enactment date.

Cross-References

"Converted entity" defined, see § 9.01.

"Converting entity" defined, see § 9.01.

"Corporation," "business corporation," "domestic corporation" and "domestic business corporation" defined, see § 1.40.

"Domestic" and "eligible entity" defined, see § 1.40.

"Eligible interest" defined, see § 1.40.

"Enactment date" defined in definition of protected agreement, see § 9.01.

[Excluded transactions, see § 9.02.]

"Foreign" and "eligible entity" defined, see § 1.40.

"Interest holder" defined, see § 1.40.

"Membership" defined, see § 1.40.

"Organic law" and "organic rules" defined, see § 1.40.

"Protected agreement" defined, see § 9.01.

[Required approvals, see § 9.03.]

Official Comment

1.   Applicability

This subchapter authorizes a domestic corporation to become a domestic eligible entity. It also authorizes a domestic corporation to become a foreign eligible entity, but only if the conversion is permitted by the laws under which the foreign eligible entity will be organized. Further, this subchapter authorizes a domestic or foreign eligible entity to become a domestic corporation. Whether and on what terms a foreign eligible entity is authorized to convert is governed by its organic law. If a foreign eligible entity is so authorized, it must comply with the provisions of this subchapter applicable to foreign entities. For example, it must file articles of conversion under section 9.33(a), and section 9.33(b) requires its articles of incorporation to meet the requirements of section 2.02.

With respect to a domestic eligible entity, if the law under which it is organized does not expressly authorize it to convert to a domestic corporation, section 9.30(b) provides procedures for such an entity to adopt and effect a plan of conversion.

2.   Protected Agreements

Section 9.30(d) provides special rules about "protected agreements"—certain documents and agreements in effect before the date (defined as the "enactment date") of this chapter (or any similar predecessor statute).

§ 9.31. Plan of Conversion

(a)   A domestic corporation may convert to a domestic or foreign eligible entity under this subchapter by approving a plan of conversion. The plan of conversion must include:

(1)   the name of the converting corporation;

(2)   the name, jurisdiction of formation and type of entity of the converted entity;

(3)   the manner and basis of converting the shares of the domestic corporation into eligible interests or other securities, obligations, rights to acquire eligible interests or other securities, cash, other property, or any combination of the foregoing;

(4)   the other terms and conditions of the conversion; and

(5)   the full text, as it will be in effect immediately after the conversion becomes effective, of the organic rules of the converted entity which are to be in writing.

(b)   In addition to the requirements of subsection (a), a plan of conversion may contain any other provision not prohibited by law.

(c) The terms of a plan of conversion may be made dependent upon facts objectively ascertainable outside the plan in accordance with section 1.20(k).

Cross-References

Amendment or abandonment of plan of conversion, see § 9.34.

Application to domestic eligible entities, see § 9.30.

Approval of plan, see § 9.32.

Effect of conversion, see § 9.35.

"Eligible entity" defined, see § 1.40.

"Eligible interest" defined, see § 1.40.

"Organic rules" defined, see § 1.40.

Official Comment

This subchapter imposes no restrictions or limitations on the terms and conditions of a conversion, except for those set forth in section 9.34(a) with respect to certain amendments to the plan of conversion. Under section 9.31(a)(5), the plan of conversion must include the written organic rules of the converted entity, which should comply with the organic law governing the converted entity. The list in section 9.31(a) of required provisions in a plan of conversion is not exhaustive.

The conversion of a domestic corporation to a foreign eligible entity must be adopted and approved as provided in section 9.32. Shareholders of a domestic corporation that adopts and approves a plan of conversion have appraisal rights. See chapter 13.

§ 9.32. Action on a Plan of Conversion

In the case of a conversion of a domestic corporation to a domestic or foreign eligible entity, the plan of conversion shall be adopted in the following manner:

(a) The plan of conversion shall first be adopted by the board of directors.

(b) The plan of conversion shall then be approved by the shareholders. In submitting the plan of conversion to the shareholders for their approval, the board of directors must recommend that the shareholders approve the plan, unless (i) the board of directors makes a determination that because of conflicts of interest or other special circumstances it should not make such a recommendation, or (ii) section 8.26 applies. If either (i) or (ii) applies, the board of directors shall inform the shareholders of the basis for its so proceeding.

(c) The board of directors may set conditions for approval of the plan of conversion by the shareholders or the effectiveness of the plan of conversion.

(d) If the approval of the shareholders is to be given at a meeting, the corporation shall notify each shareholder, regardless of whether entitled to vote, of the meeting of shareholders at which the plan of conversion is to be submitted for approval. The notice must state that the purpose, or one of the purposes, of the meeting is to consider the plan of conversion and must contain or be accompanied by a copy or summary of the plan. The notice must include or be accompanied by a copy of the organic rules of the converted entity which are to be in writing as they will be in effect immediately after the conversion.

(e) Unless the articles of incorporation, or the board of directors acting pursuant to subsection (c), require a greater vote or a greater quorum, approval of the plan of conversion requires (i) the approval of the shareholders at a meeting at which a quorum exists consisting of a majority of the votes entitled to be cast on the plan, and (ii) the approval of each class or series of shares voting as a separate voting group at a meeting at which a quorum of the voting group exists consisting of a majority of the votes entitled to be cast on the plan by that voting group.

(f)   If as a result of the conversion one or more shareholders of the converting domestic corporation would become subject to interest holder liability, approval of the plan of conversion shall require the signing in connection with the transaction, by each such shareholder, of a separate written consent to become subject to such interest holder liability.

Cross-References

Abandonment of conversion, see § 9.34.

Application to domestic eligible entities, see § 9.30.

Contents of plan of conversion, see § 9.31.

"Eligible entity" defined, see § 1.40.

"Interest holder liability" defined, see § 1.40.

"Organic rules" defined, see § 1.40.

Submission of matters to shareholders, see § 8.26.

"Voting group" defined, see § 1.40.

Official Comment

1.   In General

This section sets forth the rules for adoption and approval of a plan of conversion by a domestic corporation. The manner in which the conversion of a foreign eligible entity to a domestic corporation must be adopted and approved will be controlled by the organic law of the foreign jurisdiction. The manner in which the conversion of a domestic eligible entity to a domestic corporation must be adopted and approved will be controlled by the organic law of the eligible entity, as supplemented by section 9.30(b), if applicable.

When submitting a plan of conversion to shareholders, the board of directors must recommend the transaction, subject to two exceptions in section 9.32(b). The board might exercise the exception under clause (i) where the number of directors having a conflicting interest makes it inadvisable for the board to recommend the conversion or where the board is evenly divided as to the merits of the conversion but is able to agree that shareholders should be permitted to consider it. Alternatively, the board of directors might exercise the exception in clause (ii), which recognizes that, under section 8.26, a board of directors may agree to submit a plan to a vote of shareholders even if, after approving the plan, the board of directors determines that it no longer recommends the plan.

Section 9.32(c) permits the board of directors to condition its submission of a plan of conversion to the shareholders or the effectiveness of the plan of conversion. Among the conditions that a board of directors might impose are that the plan will not be deemed approved (i) unless it is approved by a specified vote of the shareholders, or by one or more specified classes or series of shares, voting as a separate voting group, or by a specified percentage of disinterested shareholders or (ii) if shareholders holding more than a specified percentage of the outstanding shares assert appraisal rights.

Section 9.32(d) provides a notice requirement if a plan of conversion is to be considered by the shareholders at a meeting. Requirements concerning the timing and content of a notice of meeting are in section 7.05. Section 9.32(d) does not address the notice to be given to nonvoting or nonconsenting shareholders where the plan is approved without a meeting by written consent. However, that requirement is imposed by section 7.04.

2.   Quorum and Voting

Section 9.32(e) sets forth quorum and voting requirements applicable to a shareholder vote to approve a plan of conversion. It requires both the vote of the shareholders entitled to vote on the plan, and the vote of each class or series of shares voting as a separate voting group. See sections 7.25(f) and 10.04(c) for rules governing when separate classes or series vote together as a single voting group. In lieu of approval at a meeting, shareholder approval may be by written consent under the procedures set forth in section 7.04.

3. *Personal Liability of Shareholders*

Section 9.32(f) applies only in situations where a shareholder of a domestic corporation is becoming subject to "interest holder liability," as defined in section 1.40, with respect to the converted entity. Approval of a conversion that would have such a result requires the written consent of each such shareholder who becomes subject to such interest holder liability.

§ 9.33. Articles of Conversion; Effectiveness

(a)   After (i) a plan of conversion of a domestic corporation has been adopted and approved as required by this Act, or (ii) a domestic or foreign eligible entity that is the converting entity has approved a conversion as required under its organic law, articles of conversion shall be signed by the converting entity and must:

(1)   state the name, jurisdiction of formation, and type of entity of the converting entity;

(2)   state the name, jurisdiction of formation, and type of entity of the converted entity;

(3)   if the converting entity is (i) a domestic corporation, state that the plan of conversion was approved in accordance with this subchapter; or (ii) an eligible entity, (A) state that the conversion was approved by the eligible entity in accordance with its organic law or (B) if the converting entity is a domestic eligible entity the organic law of which does not provide for approval of the conversion, state that the conversion was approved by the domestic eligible entity in accordance with this subchapter; and

(4)   if the converted entity is (i) a domestic business corporation, or a domestic nonprofit corporation or filing entity, have attached the public organic record of the converted entity, except that provisions that would not be required to be included in a restated public organic record may be omitted; or (ii) a domestic limited liability partnership, have attached the filing required to become a limited liability partnership.

(b)   If the converted entity is a domestic corporation, its articles of incorporation must satisfy the requirements of section 2.02, except that provisions that would not be required to be included in restated articles of incorporation may be omitted from the articles of incorporation. If the converted entity is a domestic eligible entity, its public organic record, if any, must satisfy the requirements of the organic law of this state, except that the public organic record does not need to be signed.

(c)   The articles of conversion shall be delivered to the secretary of state for filing, and shall take effect at the effective date determined in accordance with section 1.23.

(d)   If a converted entity is a domestic entity, the conversion becomes effective when the articles of conversion are effective. With respect to a conversion in which the converted entity is a foreign eligible entity, the conversion itself shall become effective at the later of (i) the date and time provided by the organic law of that eligible entity, and (ii) when the articles of conversion become effective.

(e)   Articles of conversion under this section may be combined with any required conversion filing under the organic law of a domestic eligible entity that is the converting entity or converted entity if the combined filing satisfies the requirements of both this section and the other organic law.

(f)   If the converting entity is a foreign eligible entity that is registered to do business in this state under a provision of law similar to chapter 15, its registration statement or other type of foreign qualification shall be cancelled automatically on the effective date of its conversion.

Cross-References

"Domestic business corporation" and "domestic corporation" defined, see § 1.40.

"Domestic nonprofit corporation" defined, see § 1.40.

Effect of conversion, see § 9.35.

Effective time and date of filing, see § 1.23.

"Eligible entity" defined, see § 1.40.

"Filing entity" defined, see § 1.40.

Filing requirements, see § 1.20.

"Organic law" defined, see § 1.40.

"Public organic record" defined, see § 1.40.

[Required approvals, see § 9.03.]

Official Comment

The filing of articles of conversion makes the conversion a matter of public record. Where the converted entity is organized under the laws of this state, the filing also makes a public record of its articles of incorporation or public organic record.

The requirements for filing are set forth in section 1.20. Under section 1.23, the articles of conversion are effective on the date and at the time of filing unless a later effective date is specified in the articles within the limits provided in section 1.23. Under that section, a delayed effective date may not be later than the 90th day after the date the document is filed. Section 9.33(d) provides when the conversion becomes effective.

§ 9.34. Amendment of Plan of Conversion; Abandonment

(a)   A plan of conversion of a converting entity that is a domestic corporation may be amended:

(1)   in the same manner as the plan was approved, if the plan does not provide for the manner in which it may be amended; or

(2)   in the manner provided in the plan, except that shareholders that were entitled to vote on or consent to approval of the plan are entitled to vote on or consent to any amendment of the plan that will change:

(i)   the amount or kind of eligible interests or other securities, obligations, rights to acquire eligible interests or other securities, cash, other property, or any combination of the foregoing, to be received by any of the shareholders of the converting corporation under the plan;

(ii)   the organic rules of the converted entity that will be in effect immediately after the conversion becomes effective, except for changes that do not require approval of the eligible interest holders of the converted entity under its organic law or organic rules; or

(iii) any other terms or conditions of the plan, if the change would adversely affect such shareholders in any material respect.

(b)   After a plan of conversion has been approved by a converting entity that is a domestic corporation in the manner required by this subchapter and before the articles of conversion become effective, the plan may be abandoned by the corporation without action by its shareholders in accordance with any procedures set forth in the plan or, if no such procedures are set forth in the plan, in the manner determined by the board of directors.

(c)   If a conversion is abandoned after the articles of conversion have been delivered to the secretary of state for filing and before the articles of conversion become effective, articles of abandonment, signed by the converting entity, must be delivered to the secretary of state for filing before the articles of conversion become effective. The articles of abandonment take effect on filing, and the conversion is abandoned and does not become effective. The articles of abandonment must contain:

(1)   the name of the converting entity;

(2)   the date on which the articles of conversion were filed by the secretary of state; and

(3)   a statement that the conversion has been abandoned in accordance with this section.

Cross-References

"Domestic corporation" defined, see § 1.40.

"Eligible interests" defined, see § 1.40.

"Organic law" and "organic rules" defined, see § 1.40.

Official Comment

Section 9.34(a)(2) permits the plan of conversion to be amended in the manner provided in the plan, subject to certain cases requiring a shareholder vote on the amendment. If the plan has no provisions with respect to its amendment, it may be amended under section 9.34(a)(1) in the same manner as it was approved.

Under section 9.34(b), unless otherwise provided in the plan of conversion, a domestic corporation may abandon a conversion without shareholder approval, even though the transaction has been previously approved by the shareholders. The power of a foreign or domestic eligible entity to abandon a conversion will be determined by its organic law.

§ 9.35. Effect of Conversion

(a)   When a conversion becomes effective:

(1)   all property owned by, and every contract right possessed by, the converting entity remain the property and contract rights of the converted entity without transfer, reversion or impairment;

(2)   all debts, obligations and other liabilities of the converting entity remain the debts, obligations and other liabilities of the converted entity;

(3)   the name of the converted entity may but need not be substituted for the name of the converting entity in any pending action or proceeding;

(4)   if the converted entity is a filing entity or a domestic business corporation or a domestic or foreign nonprofit corporation, its public organic record and its private organic rules become effective;

(5)   if the converted entity is a nonfiling entity, its private organic rules become effective;

(6)   if the converted entity is a limited liability partnership, the filing required to become a limited liability partnership and its private organic rules become effective;

(7)   the shares or eligible interests of the converting entity are reclassified into shares, eligible interests or other securities, obligations, rights to acquire shares, eligible interests or other securities, cash, or other property in accordance with the terms of the conversion, and the shareholders or interest holders of the converting entity are entitled only to the rights provided to them by those terms and to any appraisal rights they may have under the organic law of the converting entity; and

(8)   the converted entity is:

(i)   incorporated or organized under and subject to the organic law of the converted entity;

(ii)   the same entity without interruption as the converting entity; and

(iii)   deemed to have been incorporated or otherwise organized on the date that the converting entity was originally incorporated or organized.

(b)   When a conversion of a domestic corporation to a foreign eligible entity becomes effective, the converted entity is deemed to:

(1)   appoint the secretary of state as its agent for service of process in a proceeding to enforce the rights of shareholders who exercise appraisal rights in connection with the conversion; and

(2)   agree that it will promptly pay the amount, if any, to which such shareholders are entitled under chapter 13.

(c)   Except as otherwise provided in the articles of incorporation of a domestic corporation or the organic law or organic rules of a foreign corporation or a domestic or foreign eligible entity, a shareholder or eligible interest holder who becomes subject to interest holder liability in respect of a domestic corporation or eligible entity as a result of the conversion shall have such interest holder liability only in respect of interest holder liabilities that arise after the conversion becomes effective.

(d)   Except as otherwise provided in the organic law or the organic rules of the eligible entity, the interest holder liability of an interest holder in a converting eligible entity that converts to a domestic corporation who had interest holder liability in respect of such converting eligible entity before the conversion becomes effective shall be as follows:

(1)   The conversion does not discharge that prior interest holder liability with respect to any interest holder liabilities that arose before the conversion became effective.

(2)   The provisions of the organic law of the eligible entity shall continue to apply to the collection or discharge of any interest holder liabilities preserved by subsection (d)(1), as if the conversion had not occurred.

(3)   The eligible interest holder shall have such rights of contribution from other persons as are provided by the organic law of the eligible entity with respect to any interest holder liabilities preserved by subsection (d)(1), as if the conversion had not occurred.

(4)   The eligible interest holder shall not, by reason of such prior interest holder liability, have interest holder liability with respect to any interest holder liabilities that arise after the conversion becomes effective.

(e)   A conversion does not require the converting entity to wind up its affairs and does not constitute or cause the dissolution or termination of the entity.

(f)   Property held for charitable purposes under the laws of this state by a corporation or a domestic or foreign eligible entity immediately before a conversion shall not, as a result of the transaction, be diverted from the objects for which it was donated, granted, devised, or otherwise transferred except and to the extent permitted by or pursuant to the laws of this state addressing cy près or dealing with nondiversion of charitable assets.

(g)   A bequest, devise, gift, grant, or promise contained in a will or other instrument of donation, subscription, or conveyance which is made to the converting entity and which takes effect or remains payable after the conversion inures to the converted entity.

(h)   A trust obligation that would govern property if transferred to the converting entity applies to property that is transferred to the converted entity after the conversion takes effect.

Cross-References

Appraisal rights, see ch. 13.

"Eligible entity" defined, see § 1.40.

"Eligible interest" defined, see § 1.40.

"Filing entity" defined, see § 1.40.

"Interest holder" defined, see § 1.40.

"Interest holder liability" defined, see § 1.40.

"Nonfiling entity" defined, see § 1.40.

"Organic law" and "organic rules" defined, see § 1.40.

"Private organic rules" defined, see § 1.40.

"Public organic record" defined, see § 1.40.

Official Comment

The converted entity is the same entity as the converting entity, and it continues without interruption. It becomes the new type of entity in the specified jurisdiction of formation with the same status as if it had been originally incorporated or organized there. The converted entity will be subject to the organic law for that entity in that jurisdiction and will be subject to all of the duties, liabilities and limitations imposed on such entities in that jurisdiction. Thus, a conversion is not a conveyance, transfer or assignment. It does not give rise to claims of reverter or impairment of title based on a prohibited conveyance, transfer or assignment. Nor does it give rise to a claim that a contract with the converting entity is no longer in effect on the ground of nonassignability, unless the contract specifically provides that it does not survive a conversion. See, however, section 9.30(d) and its Official Comment with respect to special rules regarding protected agreements. All pending proceedings involving the converting entity are continued.

A domestic corporation converting to a foreign entity remains obligated to its shareholders who exercise appraisal rights to pay them the amount, if any, to which they are entitled under chapter 13. For this purpose, under section 9.35(b)(1) that entity is deemed to appoint the secretary of state as its agent for service of process in proceedings to enforce those rights. Where the converted entity is a domestic other entity, it will be similarly liable to the shareholders of a domestic converting corporation pursuant to section 9.35(a)(2).

Section 9.35(c) provides that interest holder liability with respect to a domestic corporation or eligible entity that is the converted entity only relates to interest holder liabilities that arise after the conversion. Section 9.35(d) similarly preserves the interest holder liability of interest holders in an eligible entity that converts to a domestic corporation only for interest holder liabilities to the extent they arise before the conversion becomes effective. Interest holder liability is not preserved for subsequent changes in an underlying liability, regardless of whether a change is voluntary or involuntary.

CHAPTER 10: AMENDMENT OF ARTICLES OF INCORPORATION AND BYLAWS

SUBCHAPTER A
AMENDMENT OF ARTICLES OF INCORPORATION

§ 10.01. Authority to Amend

(a)   A corporation may amend its articles of incorporation at any time to add or change a provision that is required or permitted in the articles of incorporation as of the effective date of the amendment or to delete a provision that is not required to be contained in the articles of incorporation.

(b)   A shareholder of the corporation does not have a vested property right resulting from any provision in the articles of incorporation, including provisions relating to management, control, capital structure, dividend entitlement, or purpose or duration of the corporation.

Cross-References

Amendment:

> before issuance of shares, see § 10.02.

> by board of directors and shareholders, see § 10.03.

> by board of directors, see § 10.05.

> pursuant to court reorganization, see § 10.08.

Appraisal rights, see ch. 13.

Articles of incorporation, see § 2.02.

Effective date of amendment, see § 1.23.

Procedure for amendment, see §§ 10.02 through 10.07.

Restatement of articles, see § 10.07.

Share transfer restrictions, see § 6.27.

Voting by voting groups, see §§ 7.25, 7.26, and 10.04.

"Voting group" defined, see § 1.40.

Official Comment

Under section 10.01(a), the sole test for the permissibility of an amendment to the corporation's articles of incorporation is whether the provision could lawfully have been included in (or in the case of a deletion, omitted from) the articles of incorporation on the effective date of the amendment. The articles of incorporation need not make any reference to, or reserve, the express power to amend the articles of incorporation. Under the Act, a provision in the articles of incorporation is subject to amendment under section 10.01 even though the provision is described, referred to, or stated in a share certificate, a written information statement, or other document issued by the corporation that reflects provisions of the articles of incorporation. Certain amendments or liabilities, however, may not be enforceable against all shareholders without their consent. See, *e.g.*, section 6.27(a) with respect to transfer restrictions and section 9.32(e) with respect to interest holder liability after a conversion, section 10.03(f) with respect to new interest holder liability after an amendment of the articles of incorporation, and section 11.04(i) with respect to new interest holder liability after a merger or share exchange.

Section 10.01 does not override contracts by a corporation outside of its articles of incorporation. For example, a corporation might contract with a shareholder or a third party that it would not make particular amendments to its articles. If the corporation made such an amendment, it would be in breach of the contract even if the amendment were otherwise permitted by this section. A shareholder may also obtain protection against amendments by establishing procedures in the articles of incorporation or bylaws that limit the power of amendment without that shareholder's consent.

Section 10.01(b) expressly rejects the concept that an otherwise lawful amendment to the articles of incorporation might be restricted or invalidated because it modified particular rights conferred on shareholders by the original or prior version of the articles of incorporation. Similarly, under section 1.02, corporations and their shareholders are subject to subsequent amendments of the Act.

§ 10.02. Amendment Before Issuance of Shares

If a corporation has not yet issued shares, its board of directors, or its incorporators if it has no board of directors, may adopt one or more amendments to the corporation's articles of incorporation.

Cross-References

Articles of amendment, see § 10.06.

Effective date of amendment, see § 1.23.

Restated articles of incorporation, see § 10.07.

Official Comment

Section 10.02 allows the incorporators or the board to amend the articles of incorporation before any shares are issued.

§ 10.03. Amendment by Board of Directors and Shareholders

If a corporation has issued shares, an amendment to the articles of incorporation shall be adopted in the following manner:

    (a)   The proposed amendment shall first be adopted by the board of directors.

(b)   Except as provided in sections 10.05, 10.07, and 10.08, the amendment shall then be approved by the shareholders. In submitting the proposed amendment to the shareholders for approval, the board of directors shall recommend that the shareholders approve the amendment, unless (i) the board of directors makes a determination that because of conflicts of interest or other special circumstances it should not make such a recommendation, or (ii) section 8.26 applies. If either (i) or (ii) applies, the board must inform the shareholders of the basis for its so proceeding.

(c)   The board of directors may set conditions for the approval of the amendment by the shareholders or the effectiveness of the amendment.

(d)   If the amendment is required to be approved by the shareholders, and the approval is to be given at a meeting, the corporation shall notify each shareholder, regardless of whether entitled to vote, of the meeting of shareholders at which the amendment is to be submitted for approval. The notice must state that the purpose, or one of the purposes, of the meeting is to consider the amendment. The notice must contain or be accompanied by a copy of the amendment.

(e)   Unless the articles of incorporation, or the board of directors acting pursuant to subsection (c), require a greater vote or a greater quorum, approval of the amendment requires the approval of the shareholders at a meeting at which a quorum consisting of a majority of the votes entitled to be cast on the amendment exists, and, if any class or series of shares is entitled to vote as a separate group on the amendment, except as provided in section 10.04(c), the approval of each such separate voting group at a meeting at which a quorum of the voting group exists consisting of a majority of the votes entitled to be cast on the amendment by that voting group.

(f)   If as a result of an amendment of the articles of incorporation one or more shareholders of a domestic corporation would become subject to new interest holder liability, approval of the amendment requires the signing in connection with the amendment, by each such shareholder, of a separate written consent to become subject to such new interest holder liability, unless in the case of a shareholder that already has interest holder liability the terms and conditions of the new interest holder liability (i) are substantially identical to those of the existing interest holder liability, or (ii) are substantially identical to those of the existing interest holder liability (other than changes that eliminate or reduce such interest holder liability).

(g)   For purposes of subsection (f) and section 10.09, "new interest holder liability" means interest holder liability of a person resulting from an amendment of the articles of incorporation if (i) the person did not have interest holder liability before the amendment becomes effective, or (ii) the person had interest holder liability before the amendment becomes effective, the terms and conditions of which are changed when the amendment becomes effective.

Cross-References

"Interest holder liability" defined, see § 1.40.

Notices and other communications, see § 1.41.

Notice of shareholders' meeting, see § 7.05.

Quorum and voting requirements for shareholders, see §§ 7.25 and 7.27.

Restatement of articles of incorporation, see § 10.07.

Submission of matters to shareholders, see § 8.26.

Voting by voting group, see §§ 7.25, 7.26 and 10.04.

Voting entitlement of shares, see § 7.21.

"Voting group" defined, see § 1.40.

Official Comment

Section 10.03 governs amendments to the articles of incorporation after shares have been issued. Most such amendments will require a shareholder vote. When submitting an amendment to the articles of incorporation to shareholders, the board of directors must recommend the amendment, subject to two exceptions in section 10.03(b). The board might exercise the exception under clause (i) where the number of directors having a conflicting interest makes it inadvisable for the board to recommend the amendment or where the board is evenly divided as to the merits of the amendment but is able to agree that shareholders should be permitted to consider it. Alternatively, the board of directors might exercise the exception under clause (ii), which recognizes that, under section 8.26, a board of directors may agree to submit an amendment to a vote of shareholders even if, after approving the amendment, the board of directors determines that it no longer recommends the amendment.

Section 10.03(c) permits the board of directors to set conditions for its submission of an amendment to the shareholders or effectiveness of an amendment. Examples of conditions that a board might impose are that the amendment will not be deemed approved (i) unless it is approved by a specified vote of the shareholders, or by one or more specified classes or series of shares, voting as a separate voting group, or by a specified percentage of votes of disinterested shareholders, or (ii) if shareholders holding more than a specified number or percentage of outstanding shares assert appraisal rights.

Section 10.03(e) specifies quorum and voting requirements applicable to a shareholder vote to approve an amendment to the articles of incorporation. If the prescribed quorum exists, then under sections 7.25 and 7.26 the amendment will be approved if more votes are cast in favor of the amendment than against it by the voting group or separate voting groups entitled to vote on the amendment, unless the articles of incorporation or the board of directors acting pursuant to section 10.03(c) require a greater vote. In lieu of approval at a meeting, shareholder approval may be by written consent under the procedures set forth in section 7.04.

If an amendment would affect the voting or quorum requirements on future amendments, it must also be approved by the vote required by section 7.27.

§ 10.04. Voting on Amendments by Voting Groups

(a)   The holders of the outstanding shares of a class are entitled to vote as a separate voting group (if shareholder voting is otherwise required by this Act) on a proposed amendment to the articles of incorporation if the amendment would:

     (1)   effect an exchange or reclassification of all or part of the shares of the class into shares of another class;

     (2)   effect an exchange or reclassification, or create the right of exchange, of all or part of the shares of another class into shares of the class;

     (3)   change the rights, preferences, or limitations of all or part of the shares of the class;

     (4)   change the shares of all or part of the class into a different number of shares of the same class;

     (5)   create a new class of shares having rights or preferences with respect to distributions that are prior or superior to the shares of the class;

     (6)   increase the rights, preferences, or number of authorized shares of any class that, after giving effect to the amendment, have rights or preferences with respect to distributions that are prior or superior to the shares of the class;

     (7)   limit or deny an existing preemptive right of all or part of the shares of the class; or

     (8)   cancel or otherwise affect rights to distributions that have accumulated but not yet been authorized on all or part of the shares of the class.

(b)   If a proposed amendment would affect a series of a class of shares in one or more of the ways described in subsection (a), the holders of shares of that series are entitled to vote as a separate voting group on the proposed amendment.

(c)   If a proposed amendment that entitles the holders of two or more classes or series of shares to vote as separate voting groups under this section would affect those two or more classes or series in the same or a substantially similar way, the holders of shares of all the classes or series so affected shall vote together as a single voting group on the proposed amendment, unless otherwise provided in the articles of incorporation or added as a condition by the board of directors pursuant to section 10.03(c).

(d)   A class or series of shares is entitled to the voting rights granted by this section even if the articles of incorporation provide that the shares are nonvoting shares.

Cross-References

Authorized shares, see § 6.01.

Classes and series of shares, see §§ 6.01 and 6.02.

Share rights and limitations, see § 6.01.

Voting by voting groups, see §§ 7.25 and 7.26.

"Voting group" defined, see § 1.40.

Official Comment

Section 10.04(a) requires separate approval by voting groups for certain types of amendments to the articles of incorporation where the corporation has more than one class or series of shares outstanding. Even if a class or series of shares is described as "nonvoting" or the articles purport to make that class or series nonvoting "for all purposes," that class or series nonetheless has the voting rights provided by this section. Likewise, shares are entitled to vote as separate voting groups under this section even though the articles of incorporation purport to allow other classes or series of shares to vote as part of the same voting group. However, an amendment that does not require shareholder approval does not trigger the right to vote by voting groups under this section. This would include a determination by the board, pursuant to authority granted in the articles of incorporation, of the rights, preferences and limitations of any class before the issuance of any shares of that class, or of one or more series within a class before the issuance of any shares of that series. See sections 6.02(a) and (b).

The right to vote as a separate voting group provides a major protection for classes or series of shares with preferential rights, or classes or series of limited or nonvoting shares, against amendments that affect that class or series. This section, however, does not make the right to vote by a separate voting group dependent on an evaluation of whether the amendment is detrimental to that class or series; if the amendment is one of those described in section 10.04(a), the class or series is automatically entitled to vote as a separate voting group on the amendment.

An amendment that changes the number of shares owned by one or more shareholders of a class into a fraction of a share, through a "reverse split," falls within subsection (a)(4) and therefore requires approval by the class, voting as a separate voting group, whether the fractional share is to be issued or otherwise paid in cash under section 6.04. Sections 10.04(a)(5) and (6) refer to preferences with respect to distributions, including distributions in liquidation or dissolution. See section 1.40 and the Official Comment to section 1.40 under "Distributions."

Sections 7.25 and 7.26 set forth the mechanics of voting by multiple voting groups. Section 10.04(b) extends the privilege of voting as a separate voting group to a series of a class of shares if the series is affected in one or more of the ways described in subsection (a). Any distinguishing feature of a series, which an amendment affects or alters, should trigger the right of voting as a separate voting group for that series. However, if a proposed amendment that affects two or more classes or series of shares in the same or a substantially similar way, under subsection (c), the shares of all the class or series so affected must vote together, as a single voting group, unless otherwise provided in the articles of incorporation or a condition set by the board of directors pursuant to section 10.03(c).

The application of sections 10.04(b) and (c) may best be illustrated by the following examples, all of which assume there is no provision in the articles of incorporation providing otherwise and that the board has not set an additional voting condition.

First, assume there is a class of shares comprised of three series, each with different preferential dividend rights. A proposed amendment would reduce the rate of dividend applicable to the "Series A" shares and would change the dividend right of the "Series B" shares from a cumulative to a noncumulative right. The amendment would not affect the preferential dividend right of the "Series C" shares. Both Series A and B would be entitled to vote as separate voting groups on the proposed amendment; the holders of the Series C shares, not directly affected by the amendment, would not be entitled to vote unless the Series C shares are voting shares under the articles of incorporation, in which case the Series C shares would not vote as a separate voting group but would vote in the voting group consisting of all shares in the class, as well as in the voting group consisting of all shares with general voting rights under the articles of incorporation.

Second, if the proposed amendment would reduce the dividend right of Series A and change the dividend right of both Series B and C from a cumulative to a noncumulative right, the holders of Series A would be entitled to vote as a single voting group, and the holders of Series B and C would be required to vote together as a single, separate voting group.

Third, assume that a corporation has common stock and two classes of preferred stock. A proposed amendment would create a new class of senior preferred that would have priority in distribution rights over both the common stock and the existing classes of preferred stock. Because the creation of the new senior preferred would affect all three classes of stock in the same or a substantially similar way, all three classes would vote together as a single voting group on the proposed amendment.

§ 10.05. Amendment by Board of Directors

Unless the articles of incorporation provide otherwise, a corporation's board of directors may adopt amendments to the corporation's articles of incorporation without shareholder approval:

    (a)   to extend the duration of the corporation if it was incorporated at a time when limited duration was required by law;

    (b)   to delete the names and addresses of the initial directors;

    (c)   to delete the name and address of the initial registered agent or registered office, if a statement of change is on file with the secretary of state;

    (d)   if the corporation has only one class of shares outstanding:

        (1)   to change each issued and unissued authorized share of the class into a greater number of whole shares of that class; or

        (2)   to increase the number of authorized shares of the class to the extent necessary to permit the issuance of shares as a share dividend;

    (e)   to change the corporate name by substituting the word "corporation," "incorporated," "company," "limited," or the abbreviation "corp.," "inc.," "co.," or "ltd.," for a similar word or abbreviation in the name, or by adding, deleting, or changing a geographical attribution for the name;

    (f)   to reflect a reduction in authorized shares, as a result of the operation of section 6.31(b), when the corporation has acquired its own shares and the articles of incorporation prohibit the reissue of the acquired shares;

    (g)   to delete a class of shares from the articles of incorporation, as a result of the operation of section 6.31(b), when there are no remaining shares of the class because the corporation has acquired all shares of the class and the articles of incorporation prohibit the reissue of the acquired shares; or

    (h)   to make any change expressly permitted by section 6.02(a) or (b) to be made without shareholder approval.

Cross-References

Acquisition of shares, see § 6.31.

Classes and series of shares, see §§ 6.01 and 6.02.

Duration of corporate existence, see § 3.02.

Effective date of amendment, see § 1.23.

Name of corporation, see ch. 4.

Registered office and agent, see ch. 5.

Restatement of articles, see § 10.07.

Terms of class or series determined by board of directors, see § 6.02.

Official Comment

The amendments described in subsections (a) through (h) are so routine and ministerial in nature as not to require approval by shareholders. None affects the substantive rights of shareholders in any meaningful way. Although the board of directors' designation of the preferences, rights and limitations of a new class or series of shares under section 6.02 may have substantive effects, amendments of the articles of incorporation to set forth the terms of a new class or series are already permitted by section 6.02(c). Amendments provided for in this section may be included in restated articles of incorporation under section 10.07 or in articles of merger under chapter 11.

§ 10.06. Articles of Amendment

(a) After an amendment to the articles of incorporation has been adopted and approved in the manner required by this Act and by the articles of incorporation, the corporation shall deliver to the secretary of state for filing articles of amendment, which must set forth:

(1) the name of the corporation;

(2) the text of each amendment adopted, or the information required by section 1.20(k)(5);

(3) if an amendment provides for an exchange, reclassification, or cancellation of issued shares, provisions for implementing the amendment if not contained in the amendment itself, (which may be made dependent upon facts objectively ascertainable outside the articles of amendment in accordance with section 1.20(k)(5);

(4) the date of each amendment's adoption; and

(5) if an amendment:

(i) was adopted by the incorporators or board of directors without shareholder approval, a statement that the amendment was duly adopted by the incorporators or by the board of directors, as the case may be, and that shareholder approval was not required;

(ii) required approval by the shareholders, a statement that the amendment was duly approved by the shareholders in the manner required by this Act and by the articles of incorporation; or

(iii) is being filed pursuant to section 1.20(k)(5), a statement to that effect.

(b) Articles of amendment shall take effect at the effective date determined in accordance with section 1.23.

Cross-References

Amendment by:

board of directors and shareholders, see § 10.03.

board of directors, see § 10.05.

incorporators or initial directors, see § 10.02.

Effective date of amendment, see § 1.23.

Extrinsic facts, see § 1.20.

Filing requirements, see § 1.20.

Voting by voting groups, see §§ 7.25, 7.26 and 10.04.

"Voting group" defined, see § 1.40.

Official Comment

Section 10.06(a)(3) requires the articles of amendment to contain a statement of the manner in which an exchange, reclassification, or cancellation of issued shares is to be put into effect if not set forth in the amendment itself. This requirement avoids confusion as to how the amendment is to be put into effect and also permits the amendment itself to be limited to provisions of permanent applicability, with transitional provisions having no long-range effect appearing only in the articles of amendment. If such transitional provisions are not part of the amendment itself, they are not required to be in a restatement of the articles of incorporation pursuant to section 10.07.

§ 10.07. Restated Articles of Incorporation

(a) A corporation's board of directors may restate its articles of incorporation at any time, without shareholder approval, to consolidate all amendments into a single document.

(b) If the restated articles include one or more new amendments that require shareholder approval, the amendments shall be adopted and approved as provided in section 10.03.

(c) A corporation that restates its articles of incorporation shall deliver to the secretary of state for filing articles of restatement setting forth:

(1) the name of the corporation;

(2) the text of the restated articles of incorporation;

(3) a statement that the restated articles consolidate all amendments into a single document; and

(4) if a new amendment is included in the restated articles, the statements required under section 10.06 with respect to the new amendment.

(d) Duly adopted restated articles of incorporation supersede the original articles of incorporation and all amendments to the articles of incorporation.

(e) The secretary of state may certify restated articles of incorporation as the articles of incorporation currently in effect, without including the statements required by subsection (c)(4).

Cross-References

Amendment of articles of incorporation:

before issuance of shares, see § 10.02.

by board of directors, see § 10.05.

by board of directors and shareholders, see § 10.03.

Certified copies, see § 1.22.

Effective date of restatement, see § 1.23.

Filing requirements, see § 1.20.

Notices and other communications, see § 1.40.

Notice of shareholders' meeting, see § 7.05.

Official Comment

Restated articles of incorporation permit articles of incorporation that have been amended over time, or are being concurrently amended, to be consolidated into a single document. A restatement of a corporation's articles of incorporation is not an amendment, but only a consolidation of amendments. A corporation that is restating its articles may concurrently amend the articles, and include the new amendments in the restated articles. In such a case, the provisions of this chapter that govern amendments of the articles of incorporation would apply to the new amendments. If it is unclear whether a provision of a restatement of the articles of incorporation might be deemed to be an amendment, rather than a consolidation, the prudent course for the corporation is to treat that provision as an amendment, and follow the procedures that apply to amendments under this chapter.

§ 10.08. Amendment Pursuant to Reorganization

(a)   A corporation's articles of incorporation may be amended without action by the board of directors or shareholders to carry out a plan of reorganization ordered or decreed by a court of competent jurisdiction under the authority of a law of the United States.

(b)   The individual or individuals designated by the court shall deliver to the secretary of state for filing articles of amendment setting forth:

(1)   the name of the corporation;

(2)   the text of each amendment approved by the court;

(3)   the date of the court's order or decree approving the articles of amendment;

(4)   the title of the reorganization proceeding in which the order or decree was entered; and

(5)   a statement that the court had jurisdiction of the proceeding under federal statute.

(c)   This section does not apply after entry of a final decree in the reorganization proceeding even though the court retains jurisdiction of the proceeding for limited purposes unrelated to consummation of the reorganization plan.

Cross-References

Effective date of amendment, see § 1.23.

Filing requirements, see § 1.20.

"Proceeding" defined, see § 1.40.

Official Comment

Section 10.08 provides a simplified method of conforming corporate documents filed under state law with the federal statutes relating to corporate reorganization. If a federal court confirms a plan of reorganization that requires articles of amendment to be filed, those amendments may be prepared and filed by the persons designated by the court and the approval of neither the shareholders nor the board of directors is required.

§ 10.09. Effect of Amendment

(a)   An amendment to the articles of incorporation does not affect a cause of action existing against or in favor of the corporation, a proceeding to which the corporation is a party, or the existing rights of persons other than the shareholders. An amendment changing a corporation's name does not affect a proceeding brought by or against the corporation in its former name.

(b)   A shareholder who becomes subject to new interest holder liability in respect of the corporation as a result of an amendment to the articles of incorporation shall have that new interest holder liability only in respect of interest holder liabilities that arise after the amendment becomes effective.

(c)   Except as otherwise provided in the articles of incorporation of the corporation, the interest holder liability of a shareholder who had interest holder liability in respect of the corporation before the amendment becomes effective and has new interest holder liability after the amendment becomes effective shall be as follows:

(1)   The amendment does not discharge that prior interest holder liability with respect to any interest holder liabilities that arose before the amendment becomes effective.

(2)   The provisions of the articles of incorporation of the corporation relating to interest holder liability as in effect immediately prior to the amendment shall continue to apply to the collection or discharge of any interest holder liabilities preserved by subsection (c)(1), as if the amendment had not occurred.

(3)   The shareholder shall have such rights of contribution from other persons as are provided by the articles of incorporation relating to interest holder liability as in effect immediately prior to the amendment with respect to any interest holder liabilities preserved by subsection (c)(1), as if the amendment had not occurred.

(4)   The shareholder shall not, by reason of such prior interest holder liability, have interest holder liability with respect to any interest holder liabilities that arise after the amendment becomes effective.

Cross-References

Amendment after issuance of shares, see §§ 10.03 through 10.05.

Amendment before issuance of shares, see § 10.02.

Effective time and date of filing, see § 1.23.

"Interest holder liability" defined, see § 1.40.

"New interest holder liability" defined, see § 10.03.

"Proceeding" defined, see § 1.40.

Official Comment

Under section 10.09, amendments to articles of incorporation do not interrupt the corporate existence. Sections 10.09(b) and (c) govern the effects of amendments to the articles of incorporation that impose or change interest holder liability.

SUBCHAPTER B
AMENDMENT OF BYLAWS

§ 10.20. Authority to Amend

(a)   A corporation's shareholders may amend or repeal the corporation's bylaws.

(b)   A corporation's board of directors may amend or repeal the corporation's bylaws, unless:

(1)   the articles of incorporation, section 10.21 or, if applicable, section 10.22 reserve that power exclusively to the shareholders in whole or part; or

(2)   except as provided in section 2.06(d), the shareholders in amending, repealing, or adopting a bylaw expressly provide that the board of directors may not amend, repeal, or adopt that bylaw.

(c)   A shareholder of the corporation does not have a vested property right resulting from any provision in the bylaws.

Cross-References

Action by:

board of directors, see §§ 8.20 through 8.24.

shareholders, see §§ 7.01 through 7.04.

Bylaw provisions relating to the election of directors, see § 10.22.

Increase in quorum and voting requirements for directors, see § 10.21.

Official Comment

The power to amend or repeal bylaws is shared by the board of directors and the shareholders, unless that power is reserved exclusively to the shareholders by an appropriate provision in the articles of incorporation. Section 10.20(b)(1) permits the reservation of amendment power to the shareholders to be limited to specific articles or sections of the bylaws or to specific subjects or topics addressed in the bylaws.

The authority granted to the shareholders in section 10.20(b)(2) to prevent the board of directors from further changing a bylaw which the shareholders have amended, repealed, or adopted is expressly subject to section 2.06(d), which limits the authority of shareholders to restrict board action on bylaws with regard to procedures or conditions set forth in certain bylaws regulating the election of directors. See the Official Comment to section 2.06.

See section 10.21 and its Official Comment describing limitations on the power of directors to adopt or amend supermajority provisions in bylaws.

See section 10.22 and its Official Comment describing limitations on the power of directors to repeal a bylaw adopted by shareholders which elects the provisions of that section. Similar to section 10.01(b), section 10.21(c) expressly confirms that an amendment to the bylaws may not be restricted or invalidated because it modifies particular rights conferred on shareholders by the original or a prior version of the bylaws.

§ 10.21. Bylaw Increasing Quorum or Voting Requirement for Directors

(a) A bylaw that increases a quorum or voting requirement for the board of directors may be amended or repealed:

(1) if originally adopted by the shareholders, only by the shareholders, unless the bylaw otherwise provides; or

(2) if adopted by the board of directors, either by the shareholders or by the board of directors.

(b) A bylaw adopted or amended by the shareholders that increases a quorum or voting requirement for the board of directors may provide that it can be amended or repealed only by a specified vote of either the shareholders or the board of directors.

(c) Action by the board of directors under subsection (a) to amend or repeal a bylaw that changes a quorum or voting requirement for the board of directors shall meet the same quorum requirement and be adopted by the same vote required to take action under the quorum and voting requirement then in effect or proposed to be adopted, whichever is greater.

Cross-References

Modifying quorum and voting requirements for shareholders, see § 7.27.

Quorum and voting of directors, see § 8.24.

Official Comment

The bylaws may increase a quorum or voting requirement for the board over the requirement that would otherwise apply under the Act ("supermajority requirements"). See sections 8.24(a) and (c). These requirements may be amended or repealed by the board of directors or shareholders as provided in section 10.21.

§ 10.22. Bylaw Provisions Relating to the Election of Directors

(a)   Unless the articles of incorporation (i) specifically prohibit the adoption of a bylaw pursuant to this section, (ii) alter the vote specified in section 7.28(a), or (iii) provide for cumulative voting, a corporation may elect in its bylaws to be governed in the election of directors as follows:

(1)   each vote entitled to be cast may be voted for or against up to that number of candidates that is equal to the number of directors to be elected, or a shareholder may indicate an abstention, but without cumulating the votes;

(2)   to be elected, a nominee shall have received a plurality of the votes cast by holders of shares entitled to vote in the election at a meeting at which a quorum is present, provided that a nominee who is elected but receives more votes against than for election shall serve as a director for a term that shall terminate on the date that is the earlier of (i) 90 days from the date on which the voting results are determined pursuant to section 7.29(b)(5) or (ii) the date on which an individual is selected by the board of directors to fill the office held by such director, which selection shall be deemed to constitute the filling of a vacancy by the board to which section 8.10 applies. Subject to subsection (a)(3), a nominee who is elected but receives more votes against than for election shall not serve as a director beyond the 90-day period referenced above; and

(3)   the board of directors may select any qualified individual to fill the office held by a director who received more votes against than for election.

(b)   Subsection (a) does not apply to an election of directors by a voting group if (i) at the expiration of the time fixed under a provision requiring advance notification of director candidates, or (ii) absent such a provision, at a time fixed by the board of directors which is not more than 14 days before notice is given of the meeting at which the election is to occur, there are more candidates for election by the voting group than the number of directors to be elected, one or more of whom are properly proposed by shareholders. An individual shall not be considered a candidate for purposes of this subsection if the board of directors determines before the notice of meeting is given that such individual's candidacy does not create a bona fide election contest.

(c)   A bylaw electing to be governed by this section may be repealed:

(1)   if originally adopted by the shareholders, only by the shareholders, unless the bylaw otherwise provides;

(2)   if adopted by the board of directors, by the board of directors or the shareholders.

Cross References

Cumulative voting, see § 7.28.

Inspectors of election, see § 7.29.

Resignation of directors, see § 8.07.

Vacancy on board of directors, see § 8.10.

Voting for directors, see § 7.28.

Voting for directors by voting group, see § 8.04.

"Voting group" defined, see § 1.40.

Official Comment

Section 10.22 is effective only if a corporation elects in a bylaw to be governed by its terms. The provisions of section 10.22 effectively modify the term and holdover provisions of section 8.05 pursuant to a limited exception for section 10.22 that is recognized in section 8.05. Accordingly, a bylaw provision that would seek to alter the term and holdover provision of section 8.05 that varied in any manner from section 10.22 would not be effective.

1. Section 10.22(a)

The rule in subsection (a) is straightforward if the nominees for director equal the number of directorships up for election. In that case, and by way of example, the holder of a single share could vote either for or against each director. In the unusual case that section 10.22(a) were applicable to a contested election notwithstanding the provisions of section 10.22(b) (*e.g.*, in the absence of an advance notice bylaw, a contest arises as a result of candidates for director being proposed subsequent to the determination date under section 10.22(b)), the holder of a share would have to choose whether to indicate opposition to a slate by voting in favor of a candidate on the preferred slate or by voting against a candidate on the disfavored slate, or to abstain. Because it would be in the interests of all contestants to explain in their proxy materials that against votes would not be counted in favor of any candidate in a contested election, the rational voter in a contested election might be expected to vote in favor of all candidates on the preferred slate to promote a simple plurality victory rather than voting against candidates on the disfavored slate. Nothing in section 10.22 would prevent the holder of more than one share from voting differently with respect to each share held.

Section 10.22(a) specifically contemplates that a corporate ballot for the election of directors would provide for "against" votes. Although there is no prohibition in the Act against a corporation offering shareholders the opportunity to vote "against" candidates at any time, unless the corporation elects to be governed by section 10.22 or the articles of incorporation are amended to make such a vote meaningful, an "against" vote is given no effect under the Act.

Section 10.22(a)(2) does not conflict with or alter the plurality voting default standard. However, because section 10.22 shortens the term of a director who is elected but receives more votes against election than in favor of election, a vacancy will exist if no action is taken to fill the vacancy before the expiration of the shortened term. As contemplated by section 8.10, that vacancy may be filled by shareholders or by the board of directors, unless the articles of incorporation provide otherwise. In the alternative, action could be taken by amendment to, or in the manner provided in, the articles of incorporation or bylaws to reduce the size of the board of directors. See section 8.03.

Under section 8.05(d), the director appointed to fill the vacancy would be up for reelection at the next annual meeting, even if the term for that directorship would otherwise have been for more than one year, as in the case of a staggered board.

There is also no limitation in section 10.22 or elsewhere in the Act on the power of either the board of directors or shareholders to fill a vacancy with the person who held such directorship before the vacancy arose.

2. Section 10.22(b)

Under section 10.22(b), when there are more candidates for election as directors by a voting group (as defined in section 1.40) than director positions to be filled, the resulting election contest would not be subject to the voting regime under section 10.22(a). Instead, it would be conducted by means of a plurality vote under section 7.28(a). Such plurality voting is appropriate in that circumstance because shareholders will have a choice between competing candidates.

The timing provided in clauses (i) and (ii) of subsection (b) for determining when section 10.22(a) does not apply to an election assures that the voting regime that will apply will be known in advance of the giving of notice, and that the disclosure of the voting rules and the proxy appointment form will be clear and reflect the applicable voting regime. The determination of how many candidates there are to fill the number of director positions up for election may be made by the board of directors. The board's determination of whether an individual shall not be considered a candidate for purposes of section 10.22(b) because the candidacy does not create a bona fide election contest must be made before notice of the meeting is given. The board of directors might choose, for example, to exercise this authority to preserve the voting regime under section 10.22(a) when it is clear that an individual has designated himself or herself as a candidate without intending to solicit votes or for the purpose of frustrating the availability of the section 10.22(a) voting regime.

The contested or uncontested nature of the election can change following the date for determining the voting regime that will apply. For example, an election that is contested at that date could become uncontested if a candidate withdraws. Conversely, unless the bylaws require advance notice of director nomination, an uncontested election could become contested before the vote is taken but after notice of the meeting has been given because there is no limitation on the ability of shareholders to nominate candidates for directorships up until the time nominations are closed at the meeting. Section 10.22(b) does not authorize changing the voting regime in those circumstances.

CHAPTER 11: MERGERS AND SHARE EXCHANGE

Introductory Comment

Transactions Permitted

Chapter 11 deals with mergers and share exchanges. A merger is the traditional form for combining entities by operation of law, and the range of merger transactions chapter 11 permits is broad. In a merger, a domestic business corporation may merge with one or more of the following domestic or foreign entities: (i) business corporations; (ii) unincorporated entities (including limited liability companies, general and limited partnerships and business trusts); and (iii) nonprofit corporations (which are defined together with unincorporated entities as "eligible entities;" neither is included in the defined term "corporation"). These and other relevant terms used in this chapter are defined in sections 1.40 and 11.01.

The entity resulting from the merger may be one of the parties to the merger, or a new corporation or eligible entity created by the merger. Chapter 11 therefore may apply to a merger in which none of the parties is a domestic corporation, as long as the resulting entity (defined in section 11.01 as the "survivor") is a new domestic corporation. In the case of any merger involving a corporation or eligible entity organized under the laws of a foreign jurisdiction, the Act recognizes that whether and how those foreign entities may merge are matters governed by the law of the foreign jurisdiction.

Chapter 11 also permits share exchanges in which either (i) a domestic corporation acquires all of the shares or eligible interests of one or more classes or series of another domestic or foreign corporation or eligible entity, or (ii) all of the shares of one of more classes or series of a domestic corporation are acquired by another domestic or foreign corporation or eligible entity. As a result, in a share exchange, the existence of the acquired entity (the entity whose shares are acquired) continues. If enough shares or eligible interests are acquired, the acquired entity may become a subsidiary of the acquiring entity. Each of these transactions is a share exchange, even if it involves no shares and only "eligible interests" (which are defined in section 1.40 as specified rights in unincorporated entities and memberships in nonprofit corporations). A foreign corporation or eligible entity may only be the acquired entity in a share exchange if it is permitted by the law governing the foreign corporation or eligible entity.

Other chapters of the Act permit transactions that once could only be effected by merger. For example, chapter 9 provides for domestications, in which corporations can reincorporate in another jurisdiction, and conversions, in which corporations may convert to eligible entities. The Act's approach is generally to provide similar procedures for effecting any of these types of transactions and certain other fundamental actions, such as amendments to the articles of incorporation under chapter 10 and sales of assets outside the usual and regular course of business under chapter 12.

Requirements and Effects

Section 11.02 generally authorizes mergers and sets out requirements for their approval. For a domestic corporation, the requirements usually include a plan of merger, adopted by the board of directors and recommended by the board of directors to the shareholders, and approved by the shareholders. Section 11.03 has similar provisions for share exchanges and plans of share exchange. These sections permit the holders of shares or eligible interests of a party to a merger or of an acquired class or series in a share exchange to receive a broad range of consideration for their shares or interests. Section 11.04 sets out the approval requirements for domestic corporations that are parties to mergers or acquired entities in share exchanges, although section 11.05 has special rules for certain parent-subsidiary transactions. Section 11.06 relates to the preparation and filing of articles of merger and share exchange, and section 11.07 states the effects of those transactions. Finally, section 11.08 provides how mergers and share exchanges may be abandoned after they are adopted and approved. Dissenting shareholders in certain mergers and share exchanges and certain other fundamental actions have appraisal rights under chapter 13.

§ 11.01. Definitions

As used in this chapter:

"Acquired entity" means the domestic or foreign corporation or eligible entity that will have all of one or more classes or series of its shares or eligible interests acquired in a share exchange.

"Acquiring entity" means the domestic or foreign corporation or eligible entity that will acquire all of one or more classes or series of shares or eligible interests of the acquired entity in a share exchange.

"New interest holder liability" means interest holder liability of a person, resulting from a merger or share exchange, that is (i) in respect of an entity which is different from the entity in which the person held shares or eligible interests immediately before the merger or share exchange became effective; or (ii) in respect of the same entity as the one in which the person held shares or eligible interests immediately before the merger or share exchange became effective if (A) the person did not have interest holder liability immediately before the merger or share exchange became effective, or (B) the person had interest holder liability immediately before the merger or share exchange became effective, the terms and conditions of which were changed when the merger or share exchange became effective.

"Party to a merger" means any domestic or foreign corporation or eligible entity that will merge under a plan of merger but does not include a survivor created by the merger.

"Survivor" in a merger means the domestic or foreign corporation or eligible entity into which one or more other corporations or eligible entities are merged.

Cross-References

"Corporation," "domestic corporation," "business corporation" and "domestic business corporation" defined, see § 1.40.

"Eligible entity," "domestic" and "foreign" defined, see § 1.40.

"Eligible interest" defined, see § 1.40.

"Foreign corporation" and "foreign business corporation" defined, see § 1.40.

"Interest holder liability" defined, see § 1.40.

"Merger" defined, see § 1.40.

"Share exchange" defined, see § 1.40.

Official Comment

Section 11.01 defines the parties to a merger as the entities that merge. Thus the parties to a merger do not include, for example, a new corporation or entity created by the merger that is the survivor, even though it results from the merger, or a parent corporation or entity that issues its securities as part of the merger consideration but does not itself merge. The definition of "survivor" contemplates the possibility that the survivor may not exist prior to the merger, and not be a party to the merger, but rather be created by the merger of two or more other corporations or entities. In that case, the survivor will need to be specified as a new corporation or entity in the plan of merger.

Share exchange is defined in section 1.40 by reference to section 11.03, and the range of parties and types of consideration permitted in a transaction under that section is broad. It could include, for example, the acquisition by a corporation of eligible interests in a partnership for cash. While that transaction would not involve either the acquisition or issuance of a corporation's shares, it nevertheless falls within the definition of share exchange.

§ 11.02. Merger

(a)   By complying with this chapter:

(1)   one or more domestic business corporations may merge with one or more domestic or foreign business corporations or eligible entities pursuant to a plan of merger, resulting in a survivor; and

(2)   two or more foreign business corporations or domestic or foreign eligible entities may merge, resulting in a survivor that is a domestic business corporation created in the merger.

(b)   By complying with the provisions of this chapter applicable to foreign entities, a foreign business corporation or a foreign eligible entity may be a party to a merger with a domestic business corporation, or may be created as the survivor in a merger in which a domestic business corporation is a party, but only if the merger is permitted by the organic law of the foreign business corporation or eligible entity.

(c)   If the organic law or organic rules of a domestic eligible entity do not provide procedures for the approval of a merger, a plan of merger may nonetheless be adopted and approved by the unanimous consent of all of the interest holders of such eligible entity, and the merger may thereafter by effected as provided in the other provisions of this chapter; and for the purposes of applying this chapter in such a case:

(1)   the eligible entity, its members or interest holders, eligible interests and articles of incorporation or other organic rules taken together shall be deemed to be a domestic business corporation, shareholders, shares and articles of incorporation, respectively and vice versa as the context may require; and

(2)   if the business and affairs of the eligible entity are managed by a person or persons that are not identical to the members or interest holders, that group shall be deemed to be the board of directors.

(d)   The plan of merger must include:

(1)   as to each party to the merger, its name, jurisdiction of formation, and type of entity;

(2)   the survivor's name, jurisdiction of formation, and type of entity, and, if the survivor is to be created in the merger, a statement to that effect;

(3)   the terms and conditions of the merger;

(4)   the manner and basis of converting the shares of each merging domestic or foreign business corporation and eligible interests of each merging domestic or foreign eligible entity into shares or other securities, eligible interests, obligations, rights to acquire shares, other securities or eligible interests, cash, other property, or any combination of the foregoing;

(5)   the articles of incorporation of any domestic or foreign business or nonprofit corporation, or the public organic record of any domestic or foreign unincorporated entity, to be created by the merger, or if a new domestic or foreign business or nonprofit corporation or unincorporated entity is not to be created by the merger, any amendments to the survivor's articles of incorporation or other public organic record; and

(6)   any other provisions required by the laws under which any party to the merger is organized or by which it is governed, or by the articles of incorporation or organic rules of any such party.

(e)   In addition to the requirements of subsection (d), a plan of merger may contain any other provision not prohibited by law.

(f)   Terms of a plan of merger may be made dependent on facts objectively ascertainable outside the plan in accordance with section 1.20(k).

(g)   A plan of merger may be amended only with the consent of each party to the merger, except as provided in the plan. A domestic party to a merger may approve an amendment to a plan:

(1)   in the same manner as the plan was approved, if the plan does not provide for the manner in which it may be amended; or

(2)   in the manner provided in the plan, except that shareholders, members, or interest holders that were entitled to vote on or consent to approval of the plan are entitled to vote on or consent to any amendment of the plan that will change:

(i)   the amount or kind of shares or other securities, eligible interests, obligations, rights to acquire shares, other securities or eligible interests, cash, or other property to be received under the plan by the shareholders, members, or interest holders of any party to the merger;

(ii)   the articles of incorporation of any domestic or foreign business or nonprofit corporation, or the organic rules of any unincorporated entity, that will be the survivor of the merger, except for changes permitted by section 10.05 or by comparable provisions of the organic law of any such foreign corporation or domestic or foreign nonprofit corporation or unincorporated entity; or

(iii)   any of the other terms or conditions of the plan if the change would adversely affect such shareholders, members, or interest holders in any material respect.

Cross-References

Abandonment of merger, see § 11.08.

Amendment of articles of incorporation in merger, see § 11.06.

Amendment of articles of incorporation by board of directors, see § 10.05.

Appraisal rights, see ch. 13.

Approval of plan of merger, see § 11.04.

Articles of merger, see § 11.06.

"Corporation" and "domestic business corporation" defined, see § 1.40.

Effect of merger, see § 11.07.

"Eligible entity" defined, see § 1.40.

Extrinsic facts, see § 1.20.

"Foreign corporation" and "foreign business corporation" defined, see § 1.40.

"Interest holder" defined, see § 1.40.

"Membership" defined, see § 1.40.

Merger between parent and subsidiary or between subsidiaries, see § 11.05.

"Organic law" and "organic rules" defined, see § 1.40.

"Public organic record" defined, see § 1.40.

"Unincorporated entity" defined, see § 1.40.

Official Comment

1.   In General

Section 11.02 authorizes domestic corporations to merge with each other. It also authorizes one or more domestic corporations to merge with one or more foreign corporations or domestic or foreign eligible entities (such as limited liability companies or partnerships). In addition, it provides for the merger of two or more foreign corporations or foreign or domestic eligible entities, even if no domestic business corporation is a party to the merger, but only if the survivor is a domestic business corporation created by the merger.

2. *Applicability to Foreign Corporations and Eligible Entities and to Domestic Eligible Entities*

A foreign corporation or a foreign eligible entity may be a party to or be the survivor in a merger authorized by chapter 11 only if the merger is permitted by the laws under which the foreign corporation or eligible entity is organized. Whether and on what terms a foreign corporation or a foreign eligible entity is authorized to merge is governed by those laws. If a foreign corporation or eligible entity is so authorized, it must comply with the applicable provisions of chapter 11 in addition to the requirements of its own governing laws. For example, section 11.02(d) sets forth certain requirements for the contents of a plan of merger with a domestic corporation, and section 11.07(d) provides that upon a merger becoming effective, a foreign corporation or foreign eligible entity that is the survivor is deemed to appoint the secretary of state as its agent for service of process in a proceeding to enforce appraisal rights of shareholders of each domestic corporation that is a party to the merger.

With respect to a domestic eligible entity, if the law under which it is organized does not expressly authorize it to be a party to or survive a merger under chapter 11, section 11.02(c) provides procedures for such an entity to adopt and effect a plan of merger.

3. *Terms and Conditions of Merger*

Chapter 11 imposes no restrictions or limitations on the terms or conditions of a merger, except for those set forth in section 11.02(g). The list in section 11.02(d) of provisions in a plan of merger is not exhaustive.

4. *Amendments of Articles of Incorporation*

Under section 11.02, a corporation's articles of incorporation may be amended by a merger, and section 11.02(d)(5) provides that a plan of merger must include any such amendments. If the plan of merger is approved and the survivor is a domestic entity, section 11.07 provides that the amendments will become effective with the merger. If the plan includes amendments to the articles of incorporation of a surviving domestic corporation, section 11.04(f)(1)(ii), by reference to the voting requirements of section 10.04 relating to amendments of the articles of incorporation, may impose voting requirements by separate voting groups that would not otherwise apply.

Although the plan of merger must include any amendments to the articles of incorporation or public organic record of the survivor, the survivor's articles of incorporation or public organic record are not required to be included in the plan unless the survivor is created by the merger. However, if approval of the plan of merger by the shareholders of a domestic corporation is required under section 11.04, section 11.04(d) requires that its shareholders be furnished with a copy or summary of the articles of incorporation or public organic record of the survivor in connection with voting on approval.

§ 11.03. Share Exchange

(a) By complying with this chapter:

(1) a domestic corporation may acquire all of the shares of one or more classes or series of shares of another domestic or foreign corporation, or all of the eligible interests of one or more classes or series of interests of a domestic or foreign eligible entity, in exchange for shares or other securities, eligible interests, obligations, rights to acquire shares or other securities or eligible interests, cash, other property, or any combination of the foregoing, pursuant to a plan of share exchange; or

(2) all of the shares of one or more classes or series of shares of a domestic corporation may be acquired by another domestic or foreign corporation or eligible entity, in exchange for shares or other securities, eligible interests, obligations, rights to acquire shares or other securities or eligible interests, cash, other property, or any combination of the foregoing, pursuant to a plan of share exchange.

(b) A foreign corporation or eligible entity may be the acquired entity in a share exchange only if the share exchange is permitted by the organic law of that corporation or other entity.

(c) If the organic law or organic rules of a domestic eligible entity do not provide procedures for the approval of a share exchange, a plan of share exchange may be adopted and approved, and the share exchange effected, in accordance with the procedures, if any, for a merger. If the organic law or organic rules of a domestic eligible entity do not provide procedures for the approval of either a share exchange or a merger, a plan of share exchange may nonetheless be adopted and approved by the unanimous consent of all of the interest holders of such eligible entity whose interests will be exchanged under the plan of share exchange, and the share exchange may thereafter be effected as provided in the other provisions of this chapter; and for purposes of applying this chapter in such a case:

(1) the eligible entity, its interest holders, interests and articles of incorporation or other organic rules taken together shall be deemed to be a domestic business corporation, shareholders, shares and articles of incorporation, respectively and vice versa as the context may require; and

(2) if the business and affairs of the eligible entity are managed by a person or persons that are not identical to the members or interest holders, that person or those persons shall be deemed to be the board of directors.

(d) The plan of share exchange must include:

(1) the name of each domestic or foreign corporation or other eligible entity the shares or eligible interests of which will be acquired and the name of the domestic or foreign corporation or eligible entity that will acquire those shares or eligible interests;

(2) the terms and conditions of the share exchange;

(3) the manner and basis of exchanging shares of a domestic or foreign corporation or eligible interests in a domestic or foreign eligible entity the shares or eligible interests of which will be acquired under the share exchange for shares or other securities, eligible interests, obligations, rights to acquire shares, other securities, or eligible interests, cash, other property, or any combination of the foregoing; and

(4) any other provisions required by the organic law governing the acquired entity or its articles of incorporation or organic rules.

(e) Terms of a plan of share exchange may be made dependent on facts objectively ascertainable outside the plan in accordance with section 1.20(k).

(f) A plan of share exchange may be amended only with the consent of each party to the share exchange, except as provided in the plan. A domestic entity may approve an amendment to a plan:

(1) in the same manner as the plan was approved, if the plan does not provide for the manner in which it may be amended; or

(2) in the manner provided in the plan, except that shareholders, members, or interest holders that were entitled to vote on or consent to approval of the plan are entitled to vote on or consent to any amendment of the plan that will change:

(i) the amount or kind of shares or other securities, eligible interests, obligations, rights to acquire shares, other securities or eligible interests, cash, or other property to be received under the plan by the shareholders, members or interest holders of the acquired entity; or

(ii) any of the other terms or conditions of the plan if the change would adversely affect such shareholders, members or interest holders in any material respect.

Cross-References

Abandonment of share exchange, see § 11.08.

Appraisal rights, see ch. 13.

Approval of plan, see § 11.04.

Articles of share exchange, see § 11.06.

Classes and series of shares, see §§ 6.01 and 6.02.

"Corporation" and "domestic corporation" defined, see § 1.40.

Effect of share exchange, see § 11.07.

"Eligible entity" defined, see § 1.40.

Extrinsic facts, see § 1.20.

"Foreign corporation" defined, see § 1.40.

"Interest holder" defined, see § 1.40.

"Membership" defined, see § 1.40.

"Organic law" and "organic rules" defined, see § 1.40.

Official Comment

1. In General

It is often desirable to structure a corporate combination so that the separate existence of one or more parties to the combination does not cease although another corporation or other entity obtains ownership of the shares or interests of those parties. This objective is often particularly important in the formation of insurance and bank holding companies, but is not limited to those contexts. In the absence of the procedure authorized in section 11.03, this kind of result often can be accomplished only by a reverse triangular merger, which involves the formation by a corporation, A, of a new subsidiary, followed by a merger of that subsidiary into another party to the merger, B, effected through the exchange of A's securities for securities of B. Section 11.03 authorizes a more straightforward procedure to accomplish the same result.

Section 11.03 authorizes a share exchange—a transaction in which the acquiring entity acquires all of the shares or eligible interests of one or more classes or series of shares or eligible interests of the acquired entity. The shares or eligible interests of one or more other classes or series of the acquired entity may be excluded from the share exchange or may be included on different bases. Shares or eligible interests of the affected class or series of the acquired entity owned at the effective time of the share exchange by the acquiring entity (or any parent of the acquiring entity or by any wholly owned subsidiary of the acquiring entity or of any such parent, each as defined in section 11.04(k)), may also be excluded from the share exchange.

After the plan of share exchange is adopted and approved as required by section 11.04, it is binding on all holders of the shares or eligible interests of the class or series to be acquired. Section 11.03 does not limit the power of a domestic corporation to acquire shares of another corporation or interests in another entity in a transaction other than a share exchange. In contrast to mergers, the articles of incorporation or public organic record of a party to a share exchange may not be amended by a plan of share exchange. Such an amendment to the articles of incorporation may, however, be effected under chapter 10 as a separate element of a corporate combination that involves a share exchange.

2. Applicability to Foreign Corporations and Foreign and Domestic Eligible Entities

A foreign corporation or a foreign eligible entity may be an acquired entity in a share exchange authorized by chapter 11 only if the share exchange is permitted by the organic law of the foreign corporation or eligible entity. Whether and on what terms a foreign corporation or a foreign eligible entity is authorized to be a party to a share exchange is governed by its organic law. If a foreign corporation or eligible entity is so authorized, it must also comply with the applicable terms of chapter 11 in addition to the requirements of its organic law. For example, section 11.03(d) sets forth certain requirements for the content of a plan of share exchange.

With respect to a domestic eligible entity, if the law under which it is organized does not expressly authorize it to be a party to a share exchange under chapter 11, section 11.03(a) is intended to provide the necessary authority. In that case, section 11.03(c) provides procedures for adopting, approving and effecting a plan of share exchange.

3.   *Terms and Conditions of Share Exchange*

Chapter 11 imposes no restrictions or limitations on the terms or conditions of a share exchange, except for those contained in section 11.03(f), and the requirement in section 11.03(a) that the acquiring entity must acquire all the shares or eligible interests of the acquired class or series of shares or eligible interests. However, shares or interests of the acquired class or series owned at the effective time of the share exchange by the acquiring entity or any of its parents or their wholly owned subsidiaries may be excluded from the exchange. The list in section 11.03(d) of provisions in a plan of share exchange is not exhaustive.

§ 11.04. Action on a Plan of Merger or Share Exchange

In the case of a domestic corporation that is a party to a merger or the acquired entity in a share exchange, the plan of merger or share exchange shall be adopted in the following manner:

(a)   The plan of merger or share exchange shall first be adopted by the board of directors.

(b)   Except as provided in subsections (h), (j) and (*l*) and in section 11.05, the plan of merger or share exchange shall then be approved by the shareholders. In submitting the plan of merger or share exchange to the shareholders for approval, the board of directors shall recommend that the shareholders approve the plan or, in the case of an offer referred to in subsection (j)(2), that the shareholders tender their shares to the offeror in response to the offer, unless (i) the board of directors makes a determination that because of conflicts of interest or other special circumstances it should not make such a recommendation or (ii) section 8.26 applies. If either (i) or (ii) applies, the board shall inform the shareholders of the basis for its so proceeding.

(c)   The board of directors may set conditions for the approval of the plan of merger or share exchange by the shareholders or the effectiveness of the plan of merger or share exchange.

(d)   If the plan of merger or share exchange is required to be approved by the shareholders, and if the approval is to be given at a meeting, the corporation shall notify each shareholder, regardless of whether entitled to vote, of the meeting of shareholders at which the plan is to be submitted for approval. The notice must state that the purpose, or one of the purposes, of the meeting is to consider the plan and must contain or be accompanied by a copy or summary of the plan. If the corporation is to be merged into an existing foreign or domestic corporation or eligible entity, the notice must also include or be accompanied by a copy or summary of the articles of incorporation and bylaws or the organic rules of that corporation or eligible entity. If the corporation is to be merged with a domestic or foreign corporation or eligible entity and a new domestic or foreign corporation or eligible entity is to be created pursuant to the merger, the notice must include or be accompanied by a copy or a summary of the articles of incorporation and bylaws or the organic rules of the new corporation or eligible entity.

(e)   Unless the articles of incorporation, or the board of directors acting pursuant to subsection (c), require a greater vote or a greater quorum, approval of the plan of merger or share exchange requires the approval of the shareholders at a meeting at which a quorum exists consisting of a majority of the votes entitled to be cast on the plan, and, if any class or series of shares is entitled to vote as a separate group on the plan of merger or share exchange, the approval of each such separate voting group at a meeting at which a quorum of the voting group is present consisting of a majority of the votes entitled to be cast on the merger or share exchange by that voting group.

(f)   Subject to subsection (g), separate voting by voting groups is required:

(1)　on a plan of merger, by each class or series of shares that:

(i)　are to be converted under the plan of merger into shares, other securities, eligible interests, obligations, rights to acquire shares, other securities or eligible interests, cash, other property, or any combination of the foregoing; or

(ii)　are entitled to vote as a separate group on a provision in the plan that constitutes a proposed amendment to the articles of incorporation of a surviving corporation that requires action by separate voting groups under section 10.04;

(2)　on a plan of share exchange, by each class or series of shares included in the exchange, with each class or series constituting a separate voting group; and

(3)　on a plan of merger or share exchange, if the voting group is entitled under the articles of incorporation to vote as a voting group to approve a plan of merger or share exchange, respectively.

(g)　The articles of incorporation may expressly limit or eliminate the separate voting rights provided in subsections (f)(1)(i) and (f)(2) as to any class or series of shares, except when the plan of merger or share exchange (i) includes what is or would be in effect an amendment subject to subsection (f)(1)(ii), and (ii) will not effect a substantive business combination.

(h)　Unless the articles of incorporation otherwise provide, approval by the corporation's shareholders of a plan of merger is not required if:

(1)　the corporation will survive the merger;

(2)　except for amendments permitted by section 10.05, its articles of incorporation will not be changed;

(3)　each shareholder of the corporation whose shares were outstanding immediately before the effective date of the merger or share exchange will hold the same number of shares, with identical preferences, rights and limitations, immediately after the effective date of the merger; and

(4)　the issuance in the merger of shares or other securities convertible into or rights exercisable for shares does not require a vote under section 6.21(f).

(i)　If as a result of a merger or share exchange one or more shareholders of a domestic corporation would become subject to new interest holder liability, approval of the plan of merger or share exchange requires the signing in connection with the transaction, by each such shareholder, of a separate written consent to become subject to such new interest holder liability, unless in the case of a shareholder that already has interest holder liability with respect to such domestic corporation, (i) the new interest holder liability is with respect to a domestic or foreign corporation (which may be a different or the same domestic corporation in which the person is a shareholder), and (ii) the terms and conditions of the new interest holder liability are substantially identical to those of the existing interest holder liability (other than for changes that eliminate or reduce such interest holder liability).

(j)　Unless the articles of incorporation otherwise provide, approval by the shareholders of a plan of merger or share exchange is not required if:

(1)　the plan of merger or share exchange expressly (i) permits or requires the merger or share exchange to be effected under this subsection and (ii) provides that, if the merger or share exchange is to be effected under this subsection, the merger or share exchange will be effected as soon as practicable following the satisfaction of the requirement set forth in subsection (j)(6);

(2)　another party to the merger, the acquiring entity in the share exchange, or a parent of another party to the merger or the acquiring entity in the share exchange, makes an offer to purchase, on the terms provided in the plan of merger or share exchange, any and all of the outstanding shares of the corporation that, absent this subsection, would be entitled to vote on the plan of merger or share exchange, except that the offer may exclude shares of the corporation that are owned at the commencement of the offer by the corporation, the offeror, or any parent of the offeror, or by any wholly owned subsidiary of any of the foregoing;

(3)   the offer discloses that the plan of merger or share exchange provides that the merger or share exchange will be effected as soon as practicable following the satisfaction of the requirement set forth in subsection (j)(6) and that the shares of the corporation that are not tendered in response to the offer will be treated as set forth in subsection (j)(8);

(4)   the offer remains open for at least 10 days;

(5)   the offeror purchases all shares properly tendered in response to the offer and not properly withdrawn;

(6)   the shares listed below are collectively entitled to cast at least the minimum number of votes on the merger or share exchange that, absent this subsection, would be required by this chapter and by the articles of incorporation for the approval of the merger or share exchange by the shareholders and by any other voting group entitled to vote on the merger or share exchange at a meeting at which all shares entitled to vote on the approval were present and voted:

(i)   shares purchased by the offeror in accordance with the offer;

(ii)   shares otherwise owned by the offeror or by any parent of the offeror or any wholly owned subsidiary of any of the foregoing; and

(iii)   shares subject to an agreement that they are to be transferred, contributed or delivered to the offeror, any parent of the offeror, or any wholly owned subsidiary of any of the foregoing in exchange for shares or eligible interests in such offeror, parent or subsidiary;

(7)   the offeror or a wholly owned subsidiary of the offeror merges with or into, or effects a share exchange in which it acquires shares of, the corporation; and

(8)   each outstanding share of each class or series of shares of the corporation that the offeror is offering to purchase in accordance with the offer, and that is not purchased in accordance with the offer, is to be converted in the merger into, or into the right to receive, or is to be exchanged in the share exchange for, or for the right to receive, the same amount and kind of securities, eligible interests, obligations, rights, cash, or other property to be paid or exchanged in accordance with the offer for each share of that class or series of shares that is tendered in response to the offer, except that shares of the corporation that are owned by the corporation or that are described in clause (ii) or (iii) of subsection (j)(6) need not be converted into or exchanged for the consideration described in this subsection (j)(8).

(k)   As used in subsection (j):

(1)   "offer" means the offer referred to in subsection (j)(2);

(2)   "offeror" means the person making the offer;

(3)   "parent" of an entity means a person that owns, directly or indirectly (through one or more wholly owned subsidiaries), all of the outstanding shares of or eligible interests in that entity;

(4)   shares tendered in response to the offer shall be deemed to have been "purchased" in accordance with the offer at the earliest time as of which (i) the offeror has irrevocably accepted those shares for payment and (ii) either (A) in the case of shares represented by certificates, the offeror, or the offeror's designated depository or other agent, has physically received the certificates representing those shares or (B) in the case of shares without

certificates, those shares have been transferred into the account of the offeror or its designated depository or other agent, or an agent's message relating to those shares has been received by the offeror or its designated depository or other agent; and

(5)   "wholly owned subsidiary" of a person means an entity of or in which that person owns, directly or indirectly (through one or more wholly owned subsidiaries), all of the outstanding shares or eligible interests.

(*l*)   Unless the articles of incorporation otherwise provide,

(1)   approval of a plan of share exchange by the shareholders of a domestic corporation is not required if the corporation is the acquiring entity in the share exchange; and

(2)   shares not to be exchanged under the plan of share exchange are not entitled to vote on the plan.

Cross-References

Abandonment of merger or share exchange, see § 11.08.

Appraisal rights, see ch. 13.

"Corporation" and "domestic corporation" defined, see § 1.40.

"Eligible entity" defined, see § 1.40.

"Foreign corporation" defined, see § 1.40.

"Interest holder liability" defined, see § 1.40.

"New interest holder liability" defined, see § 11.01.

Notices and other communications, see § 1.41.

Notice of shareholders' meeting, see § 7.05.

"Organic rules" defined, see § 1.40.

Share issuances requiring shareholder approval, see § 6.21.

Submission of matters to shareholders, see § 8.26.

Supermajority quorum and voting requirements for shareholders, see § 7.27.

Voting by voting groups, see §§ 7.25 and 7.26.

Voting by voting group on amendment of articles of incorporation, see § 10.04.

Voting entitlement of shares, see § 7.21.

"Voting group" defined, see § 1.40.

"Voting power" defined, see § 1.40.

Written consent of shareholders, see § 7.04.

Official Comment

1.   In General

Subject to the exceptions set forth in section 11.04(b), a plan of merger must always be approved by the shareholders of a corporation that is a party to a merger and a plan of share exchange must always be approved by shareholders of the class or series that is being acquired in a share exchange. Under section 11.04(h) approval of a plan of merger by the shareholders of a surviving corporation is not required if the conditions stated in that section are satisfied. Under section 11.04(j), shareholder action by selling shares in a tender offer or exchange offer is accepted as an alternative to the traditional consent by voting if the conditions specified in section 11.04(j) are met.

Section 11.04(g), together with the appraisal rights provisions of chapter 13, is designed to assure that in transactions or actions that may occur under chapters 9, 10, 11 and 12, a shareholder has either a group voting right or an appraisal right.

Under section 10.04(c), and therefore under section 11.04(f)(1)(ii), if a change that requires voting by separate voting groups affects two or more classes or two or more series in the same or a substantially similar way, the relevant classes or series vote together, rather than separately, on the change, unless otherwise provided in the articles of incorporation or required by the board of directors. If separate voting by voting groups is required for a merger or a share exchange under section 11.04(f), it will not fall within the exception to shareholder approval provided by section 11.04(h). For the mechanics of voting where voting by voting groups is required under section 11.04(f), see sections 7.25 and 7.26 and the Official Comments to those sections.

If a merger would amend the articles of incorporation of a survivor that is a domestic corporation in such a way as to affect the voting requirements on future amendments, the transaction must also be approved by the vote required by section 7.27.

2.   Submission to the Shareholders

When submitting a plan of merger or share exchange to shareholders, the board of directors must recommend the transaction, subject to two exceptions in section 11.04(b). The board might exercise the exception under clause (i) where the number of directors having a conflicting interest makes it inadvisable for them to recommend the transaction or where the board is evenly divided as to the merits of the transaction but is able to agree that shareholders should be permitted to consider the transaction. Alternatively, the board of directors might exercise the exception in clause (ii), which recognizes that, under section 8.26, a board of directors may include a "force the vote" clause in a plan of merger or share exchange, agreeing to submit the plan to shareholders even if, after approving the plan, the board of directors determines that it no longer recommends the plan. Section 11.04(c) permits the board of directors to condition its submission of a plan of merger or share exchange to the shareholders or the effectiveness of a plan of merger or share exchange. Among the conditions that a board of directors might impose are that the plan will not be deemed approved (i) unless it is approved by a specified vote of the shareholders, or by one or more specified classes or series of shares, voting as a separate voting group, or by a specified percentage of disinterested shareholders or (ii) if shareholders holding more than a specified fraction of the outstanding shares assert appraisal rights.

Section 11.04(d) sets forth the notice requirements if a plan of merger or share exchange is to be considered by the shareholders at a meeting. Requirements concerning the timing and content of a notice of meeting are set out in section 7.05. Section 11.04(d) does not address the notice to be given to nonvoting or nonconsenting shareholders where the merger or share exchange is approved, without a meeting, by written consent. However, that requirement is imposed by section 7.04.

3.   Quorum and Voting

Section 11.04(e) sets forth quorum and voting requirements applicable to a shareholder vote to approve a plan of merger or share exchange. See sections 7.25(f) and 10.04(c) for rules governing when separate classes or series vote together as a single voting group. If a quorum is present, and subject to any greater vote required by the articles of incorporation or the board of directors pursuant to section 11.04(c), under sections 7.25 and 7.26 the plan will be approved if more votes are cast in favor of the plan than against it by the voting group or each separate voting group, as the case may be, entitled to vote on the plan. In lieu of action at a meeting, shareholder approval may be by written consent under the procedures set forth in section 7.04.

Section 11.04(g) authorizes limiting or eliminating separate voting as a voting group for a class or series of shares in a merger or share exchange by an express provision in the articles of incorporation. The authorization, however, does not apply to a plan of merger that includes amendments to the articles of incorporation of the survivor for which, under section 11.04(f)(1)(ii), a separate vote under section 10.04 is required. The authorization also would not apply if a plan of merger that is subject to section 11.04(f)(1)(i) or a share exchange that is subject to section 11.04(f)(2) has the same effect as an amendment to which section 10.04 would apply and the transaction has no substantive business combination effect, such as a reincorporation or recapitalization where there is no significant change in the enterprise on a consolidated basis. For example, if a corporation with preferred and common shares merges into a wholly-owned subsidiary with all shares being exchanged for common shares of the subsidiary, the authorization to eliminate the separate group vote of the preferred shares would not apply because the transaction would be in effect an amendment of the preferred stock without separate substance as a business combination. On the other hand, if the subsidiary (assuming it was significant) was only 60% owned and the holders of the remaining 40% were being cashed out in the merger, elimination of the separate group vote would be effective because the merger would have substance as a business combination. The requirement that a provision limiting or eliminating group voting rights on a merger or share exchange be "express" is meant to avoid any ambiguity that might arise from a provision that generally denies voting rights.

4.　Two-Step Transactions

Section 11.04(j) authorizes a two-step transaction meeting the requirements of that section to proceed without the shareholder vote that would otherwise be required by section 11.04(b). The first step is an offer to the shareholders to tender their shares in response to which enough shareholders tender so that, upon consummation of the offer, the offering party (and any parent or wholly owned subsidiary) owns or has the right to acquire shares with sufficient voting power to satisfy the shareholder approval that would otherwise be required to approve the plan of merger or share exchange pursuant to section 11.04. The second step is a merger or share exchange providing the remaining shareholders the same consideration as was offered to their class or series in the first step offer. The shareholder action in selling in response to the offer provides the necessary consent for the transaction, in lieu of a shareholder vote, if the other conditions set forth in section 11.04(j) are met. The requirements of section 11.04(j), together with sections 11.04(b), 13.20, 13.21 and 13.22, are intended to ensure that shareholders are not disadvantaged by the absence of a vote, and that they receive the same protection in terms of timing, director duties and appraisal rights that they would in a transaction approved by a shareholder vote. For example, section 11.04(b) requires, subject to limited exceptions, that the board of directors make a recommendation with respect to the offer that shareholders tender their shares. This ensures that there is a corporate action implicated by the offer, and that the same director duties will apply to the recommendation to tender into the offer as to conversion or exchange pursuant to a plan of merger or share exchange.

5.　Personal Liability of Shareholders

The approval provisions of section 11.04(i) apply only in situations where a shareholder is becoming subject to "new interest holder liability" as defined in section 11.01, for example, where a corporation is merging into a general partnership or a cap on the shareholder's interest holder liability is increased. The effect of a merger or share exchange on interest holder liability will be determined as provided in section 11.07(e).

§ 11.05. Merger Between Parent and Subsidiary or Between Subsidiaries

(a)　A domestic or foreign parent entity that owns shares of a domestic corporation which carry at least 90% of the voting power of each class and series of the outstanding shares of the subsidiary that has voting power may (i) merge the subsidiary into itself (if it is a domestic or foreign corporation or eligible entity) or into another domestic or foreign corporation or eligible entity in which the parent entity owns at least 90% of the voting power of each class and series of the outstanding shares or eligible interests which have voting power, or (ii) merge itself (if it is a domestic or foreign corporation or eligible entity) into such subsidiary, in either case without the approval of the board of directors or shareholders of the subsidiary, unless the articles of incorporation or organic rules of the parent entity or the articles of incorporation of the subsidiary corporation otherwise provide. Section 11.04(i) applies to a merger under this section. The articles of merger relating to a merger under this section do not need to be signed by the subsidiary.

(b)　A parent entity shall, within 10 days after the effective date of a merger approved under subsection (a), notify each of the subsidiary's shareholders that the merger has become effective.

(c)　Except as provided in subsections (a) and (b), a merger between a parent entity and a domestic subsidiary corporation shall be governed by the provisions of chapter 11 applicable to mergers generally.

Cross-References

Appraisal rights, see ch. 13.

Articles of merger, see § 11.06.

"Corporation" and "domestic corporation" defined, see § 1.40.

"Eligible entity" defined, see § 1.40.

"Foreign corporation" defined, see § 1.40.

"Organic rules" defined, see § 1.40.

"Voting power" defined, see § 1.40.

Official Comment

If the conditions of section 11.05 are met, no approval is required by the board of directors and the shareholders of a subsidiary that is merged into the parent or another subsidiary. In other respects, mergers between parents and 90%-owned subsidiaries are governed by the other provisions of chapter 11, including section 11.04(i).

§ 11.06. Articles of Merger or Share Exchange

(a)   After (i) a plan of merger has been adopted and approved as required by this Act, or (ii) if the merger is being effected under section 11.02(a)(2), the merger has been approved as required by the organic law governing the parties to the merger, then articles of merger shall be signed by each party to the merger except as provided in section 11.05(a). The articles must set forth:

(1)   the name, jurisdiction of formation, and type of entity of each party to the merger;

(2)   the name, jurisdiction of formation, and type of entity of the survivor;

(3)   if the survivor of the merger is a domestic corporation and its articles of incorporation are amended, or if a new domestic corporation is created as a result of the merger:

(i)   the amendments to the survivor's articles of incorporation; or

(ii)   the articles of incorporation of the new corporation;

(4)   if the survivor of the merger is a domestic eligible entity and its public organic record is amended, or if a new domestic eligible entity is created as a result of the merger:

(i)   the amendments to the public organic record of the survivor; or

(ii)   the public organic record of the new eligible entity;

(5)   if the plan of merger required approval by the shareholders of a domestic corporation that is a party to the merger, a statement that the plan was duly approved by the shareholders and, if voting by any separate voting group was required, by each such separate voting group, in the manner required by this Act and the articles of incorporation;

(6)   if the plan of merger or share exchange did not require approval by the shareholders of a domestic corporation that is a party to the merger, a statement to that effect;

(7)   as to each foreign corporation that is a party to the merger, a statement that the participation of the foreign corporation was duly authorized as required by its organic law;

(8)   as to each domestic or foreign eligible entity that is a party to the merger, a statement that the merger was approved in accordance with its organic law or section 11.02(c); and

(9)   if the survivor is created by the merger and is a domestic limited liability partnership, the filing required to become a limited liability partnership, as an attachment.

(b)　After a plan of share exchange in which the acquired entity is a domestic corporation or eligible entity has been adopted and approved as required by this Act, articles of share exchange shall be signed by the acquired entity and the acquiring entity. The articles shall set forth:

(1)　the name of the acquired entity;

(2)　the name, jurisdiction of formation, and type of entity of the domestic or foreign corporation or eligible entity that is the acquiring entity; and

(3)　a statement that the plan of share exchange was duly approved by the acquired entity by:

(i)　the required vote or consent of each class or series of shares or eligible interests included in the exchange; and

(ii)　the required vote or consent of each other class or series of shares or eligible interests entitled to vote on approval of the exchange by the articles of incorporation or organic rules of the acquired entity or section 11.03(c).

(c)　In addition to the requirements of subsection (a) or (b), articles of merger or share exchange may contain any other provision not prohibited by law.

(d)　The articles of merger or share exchange shall be delivered to the secretary of state for filing and, subject to subsection (e), the merger or share exchange shall take effect at the effective date determined in accordance with section 1.23.

(e)　With respect to a merger in which one or more foreign entities is a party or a foreign entity created by the merger is the survivor, the merger itself shall become effective at the later of:

(1)　when all documents required to be filed in foreign jurisdictions to effect the merger have become effective, or

(2)　when the articles of merger take effect.

(f)　Articles of merger filed under this section may be combined with any filing required under the organic law governing any domestic eligible entity involved in the transaction if the combined filing satisfies the requirements of both this section and the other organic law.

Cross-References

"Acquired entity" defined, see § 11.01.

"Acquiring entity" defined, see § 11.01.

Approval of merger or share exchange, see § 11.04.

"Corporation" and "domestic corporation" defined, see § 1.40.

"Eligible entity" defined, see § 1.40.

Filing requirements, see § 1.20.

"Foreign corporation" defined, see § 1.40.

Merger of parent and subsidiary, see § 11.05.

"Organic law" and "organic rules" defined, see § 1.40.

"Public organic record" defined, see § 1.40.

Voting by voting group, see §§ 7.25 and 7.26.

"Voting group" defined, see § 1.40.

Official Comment

The filing of articles of merger or share exchange makes the transaction a matter of public record. The requirements of filing are set forth in section 1.20. Under section 1.23, the articles are effective on the date and at the time of filing unless a later effective date is specified in the articles within the limits provided in section 1.23 under the authority of section 11.06(c). Under section 1.23, a delayed effective date may not be later than the 90th day after the date the document is filed.

If a merger involves a domestic eligible entity whose organic law also requires a filing to effect the transaction, section 11.06(f) permits the filings under that organic law and this section to be combined so that only one document need be delivered to the secretary of state for filing.

§ 11.07. Effect of Merger or Share Exchange

(a)   When a merger becomes effective:

(1)   the domestic or foreign corporation or eligible entity that is designated in the plan of merger as the survivor continues or comes into existence, as the case may be;

(2)   the separate existence of every domestic or foreign corporation or eligible entity that is a party to the merger, other than the survivor, ceases;

(3)   all property owned by, and every contract right possessed by, each domestic or foreign corporation or eligible entity that is a party to the merger, other than the survivor, are the property and contract rights of the survivor without transfer, reversion or impairment;

(4)   all debts, obligations and other liabilities of each domestic or foreign corporation or eligible entity that is a party to the merger, other than the survivor, are debts, obligations or liabilities of the survivor;

(5)   the name of the survivor may, but need not be, substituted in any pending proceeding for the name of any party to the merger whose separate existence ceased in the merger;

(6)   if the survivor is a domestic entity, the articles of incorporation and bylaws or the organic rules of the survivor are amended to the extent provided in the plan of merger;

(7)   the articles of incorporation and bylaws or the organic rules of a survivor that is a domestic entity and is created by the merger become effective;

(8)   the shares of each domestic or foreign corporation that is a party to the merger, and the eligible interests in an eligible entity that is a party to a merger, that are to be converted in accordance with the terms of the merger into shares or other securities, eligible interests, obligations, rights to acquire shares, other securities, or eligible interests, cash, other property, or any combination of the foregoing, are converted, and the former holders of such shares or eligible interests are entitled only to the rights provided to them by those terms or to any rights they may have under chapter 13 or the organic law governing the eligible entity or foreign corporation;

(9)   except as provided by law or the terms of the merger, all the rights, privileges, franchises, and immunities of each entity that is a party to the merger, other than the survivor, are the rights, privileges, franchises, and immunities of the survivor; and

(10) if the survivor exists before the merger:

(i)   all the property and contract rights of the survivor remain its property and contract rights without transfer, reversion, or impairment;

(ii)   the survivor remains subject to all its debts, obligations, and other liabilities; and

(iii) except as provided by law or the plan of merger, the survivor continues to hold all of its rights, privileges, franchises, and immunities.

(b)   When a share exchange becomes effective, the shares or eligible interests in the acquired entity that are to be exchanged for shares or other securities, eligible interests, obligations, rights to acquire shares, other securities or eligible interests, cash, other property, or any combination of the foregoing, are entitled only to the rights provided to them in the plan of share exchange or to any rights they may have under chapter 13 or under the organic law governing the acquired entity.

(c)   Except as otherwise provided in the articles of incorporation of a domestic corporation or the organic law governing or organic rules of a foreign corporation or a domestic or foreign eligible entity, the effect of a merger or share exchange on interest holder liability is as follows:

(1)   A person who becomes subject to new interest holder liability in respect of an entity as a result of a merger or share exchange shall have that new interest holder liability only in respect of interest holder liabilities that arise after the merger or share exchange becomes effective.

(2)   If a person had interest holder liability with respect to a party to the merger or the acquired entity before the merger or share exchange becomes effective with respect to shares or eligible interests of such party or acquired entity which were (i) exchanged in the merger or share exchange, (ii) were cancelled in the merger or (iii) the terms and conditions of which relating to interest holder liability were amended pursuant to the merger:

(i)   The merger or share exchange does not discharge that prior interest holder liability with respect to any interest holder liabilities that arose before the merger or share exchange becomes effective.

(ii)   The provisions of the organic law governing any entity for which the person had that prior interest holder liability shall continue to apply to the collection or discharge of any interest holder liabilities preserved by subsection (c)(2)(i), as if the merger or share exchange had not occurred.

(iii) The person shall have such rights of contribution from other persons as are provided by the organic law governing the entity for which the person had that prior interest holder liability with respect to any interest holder liabilities preserved by subsection (c)(2)(i), as if the merger or share exchange had not occurred.

(iv)   The person shall not, by reason of such prior interest holder liability, have interest holder liability with respect to any interest holder liabilities that arise after the merger or share exchange becomes effective.

(3)   If a person has interest holder liability both before and after a merger becomes effective with unchanged terms and conditions with respect to the entity that is the survivor by reason of owning the same shares or eligible interests before and after the merger becomes effective, the merger has no effect on such interest holder liability.

(4)   A share exchange has no effect on interest holder liability related to shares or eligible interests of the acquired entity that were not exchanged in the share exchange.

(d)   Upon a merger becoming effective, a foreign corporation, or a foreign eligible entity, that is the survivor of the merger is deemed to:

(1)   appoint the secretary of state as its agent for service of process in a proceeding to enforce the rights of shareholders of each domestic corporation that is a party to the merger who exercise appraisal rights; and

(2)   agree that it will promptly pay the amount, if any, to which such shareholders are entitled under chapter 13.

(e)   Except as provided in the organic law governing a party to a merger or in its articles of incorporation or organic rules, the merger does not give rise to any rights that an interest holder, governor, or third party would have upon a dissolution, liquidation, or winding up of that party. The merger does not require a party to the merger to wind up its affairs and does not constitute or cause its dissolution or termination.

(f)   Property held for a charitable purpose under the law of this state by a domestic or foreign corporation or eligible entity immediately before a merger becomes effective may not, as a result of the transaction, be diverted from the objects for which it was donated, granted, devised, or otherwise transferred except and to the extent permitted by or pursuant to the laws of this state addressing cy près or dealing with nondiversion of charitable assets.

(g)	A bequest, devise, gift, grant, or promise contained in a will or other instrument of donation, subscription, or conveyance which is made to an entity that is a party to a merger that is not the survivor and which takes effect or remains payable after the merger inures to the survivor.

(h)	A trust obligation that would govern property if transferred to a nonsurviving entity applies to property that is transferred to the survivor after a merger becomes effective.

Cross-References

Appraisal rights, see ch. 13.

"Corporation" and "domestic corporation" defined, see § 1.40.

Effective time and date of merger or share exchange, see §§ 1.23 and 11.06.

"Eligible entity" defined, see § 1.40.

"Foreign corporation" defined, see § 1.40.

"Governor" defined, see § 1.40.

"Organic law" and "organic rules" defined, see § 1.40.

"Interest holder liability" defined, see § 1.40.

"New interest holder liability" defined, see § 11.01.

"Proceeding" defined, see § 1.40.

Official Comment

Under section 11.07(a), in a merger the parties that merge become one. The survivor automatically becomes the owner of all real and personal property and becomes subject to all the liabilities, actual or contingent, of each other party to the merger. A merger is not a conveyance, transfer, or assignment. It does not give rise to claims of reverter or impairment of title based on a prohibited conveyance, transfer, or assignment. It does not give rise to a claim that a contract with a party to the merger is no longer in effect on the ground of nonassignability, unless the contract specifically addresses that issue. All pending proceedings involving either the survivor or a party whose separate existence ceased as a result of the merger are continued.

In contrast to a merger, a share exchange does not vest in the acquiring entity the assets of the acquired entity, or render the acquiring entity liable for the liabilities of the acquired entity. The statements in sections 11.07(a)(8) and 11.07(b) regarding the rights of former holders of shares or eligible interests are not intended to preclude an otherwise proper question concerning the validity of the merger or share exchange, or to override or otherwise affect any provisions of chapter 13 concerning the exclusiveness of rights under that chapter.

The deemed appointment and agreement in section 11.07(d) by a foreign survivor is based on the implied consent of such a foreign corporation, or foreign eligible entity, to the terms of chapter 11 by reason of entering into an agreement that is governed by this chapter.

Section 11.07(e) sets forth the impact of mergers and share exchanges on interest holder liability. Section 11.04(i) sets forth when approval of a merger or share exchange requires the consent of shareholders who would otherwise become subject to new interest holder liability.

§ 11.08. Abandonment of a Merger or Share Exchange

(a)	After a plan of merger or share exchange has been adopted and approved as required by this chapter, and before articles of merger or share exchange have become effective, the plan may be abandoned by a domestic business corporation that is a party to the plan without action by its shareholders in accordance with any procedures set forth in the plan of merger or share exchange or, if no such procedures are set forth in the plan, in the manner determined by the board of directors.

(b)   If a merger or share exchange is abandoned under subsection (a) after articles of merger or share exchange have been delivered to the secretary of state for filing but before the merger or share exchange has become effective, a statement of abandonment signed by all the parties that signed the articles of merger or share exchange shall be delivered to the secretary of state for filing before the articles of merger or share exchange become effective. The statement shall take effect on filing and the merger or share exchange shall be deemed abandoned and shall not become effective. The statement of abandonment must contain:

(1)   the name of each party to the merger or the names of the acquiring and acquired entities in a share exchange;

(2)   the date on which the articles of merger or share exchange were filed by the secretary of state; and

(3)   a statement that the merger or share exchange has been abandoned in accordance with this section.

Cross-References

Approval of merger or share exchange, see § 11.04.

"Corporation" and "domestic business corporation" defined, see § 1.40.

Effective time and date of filing, see § 1.23.

Filing requirements, see § 1.20.

Official Comment

Under section 11.08, unless otherwise provided in the plan of merger or share exchange, a domestic business corporation that is a party to a merger or share exchange may abandon the transaction without shareholder approval, even though the transaction has been previously approved by the shareholders. The power to abandon a transaction does not affect any contract rights that other parties may have. The power of a foreign business corporation or a domestic or foreign eligible entity to abandon a transaction will be determined by the organic law of the corporation or eligible entity, except as provided in sections 11.02(c) and 11.03(c).

CHAPTER 12: DISPOSITION OF ASSETS

§ 12.01. Disposition of Assets Not Requiring Shareholder Approval

No approval of the shareholders is required, unless the articles of incorporation otherwise provide:

(a)   to sell, lease, exchange, or otherwise dispose of any or all of the corporation's assets in the usual and regular course of business;

(b)   to mortgage, pledge, dedicate to the repayment of indebtedness (whether with or without recourse), or otherwise encumber any or all of the corporation's assets, regardless of whether in the usual and regular course of business;

(c)   to transfer any or all of the corporation's assets to one or more domestic or foreign corporations or other entities all of the shares or interests of which are owned by the corporation; or

(d)   to distribute assets pro rata to the holders of one or more classes or series of the corporation's shares.

Cross-References

Dissolution, see ch. 14.

"Distribution" defined, see § 1.40.

Distributions to shareholders, see § 6.40.

Shareholder approval of certain dispositions, see § 12.02.

Official Comment

Section 12.01 specifies dispositions for which shareholder approval is not required, and section 12.02 specifies dispositions requiring shareholder approval.

Examples of dispositions in the usual and regular course of business under section 12.01(a) include the sale of a building that was the corporation's only major asset where the corporation was formed for the purpose of constructing and selling that building, the sale by a corporation of its only major business where the corporation was formed to buy and sell businesses and the proceeds of the sale are to be reinvested in the purchase of a new business, or sales of assets by an open- or closed-end investment company the portfolio of which turns over many times in short periods.

No shareholder approval is required for a transaction involving a pro rata distribution because it comes within section 12.01(d). An example is a spin-off in which shares of a subsidiary are distributed pro rata to the holders of one or more classes or series of shares. On the other hand, a non pro rata distribution—for example, a split-off in which shares of a subsidiary are distributed only to some shareholders in exchange for some or all of their shares—would require shareholder approval under section 12.02(a) if the disposition would leave the corporation without a significant continuing business activity. When the transaction involves a distribution in liquidation—for example, when two or more subsidiaries (whether they have existed previously or are newly formed) representing all of a dissolved corporation's business activities are distributed to shareholders (sometimes referred to as a split-up)—the transaction will be governed by chapter 14 (dissolution), not by chapter 12.

§ 12.02. Shareholder Approval of Certain Dispositions

(a)   A sale, lease, exchange, or other disposition of assets, other than a disposition described in section 12.01, requires approval of the corporation's shareholders if the disposition would leave the corporation without a significant continuing business activity. A corporation will conclusively be deemed to have retained a significant continuing business activity if it retains a business activity that represented, for the corporation and its subsidiaries on a consolidated basis, at least (i) 25% of total assets at the end of the most recently completed fiscal year, and (ii) either 25% of either income from continuing operations before taxes or 25% of revenues from continuing operations, in each case for the most recently completed fiscal year.

(b)   To obtain the approval of the shareholders under subsection (a) the board of directors shall first adopt a resolution authorizing the disposition. The disposition shall then be approved by the shareholders. In submitting the disposition to the shareholders for approval, the board of directors shall recommend that the shareholders approve the disposition, unless (i) the board of directors makes a determination that because of conflicts of interest or other special circumstances it should not make such a recommendation, or (ii) section 8.26 applies. If either (i) or (ii) applies, the board shall inform the shareholders of the basis for its so proceeding.

(c)   The board of directors may set conditions for the approval by the shareholders of a disposition or the effectiveness of the disposition.

(d)   If a disposition is required to be approved by the shareholders under subsection (a), and if the approval is to be given at a meeting, the corporation shall notify each shareholder, regardless of whether entitled to vote, of the meeting of shareholders at which the disposition is to be submitted for approval. The notice must state that the purpose, or one of the purposes, of the meeting is to consider the disposition and must contain a description of the disposition, including the terms and conditions of the disposition and the consideration to be received by the corporation.

(e)   Unless the articles of incorporation or the board of directors acting pursuant to subsection (c) require a greater vote or a greater quorum, the approval of a disposition by the shareholders shall require the approval of the shareholders at a meeting at which a quorum exists consisting of a majority of the votes entitled to be cast on the disposition.

(f)   After a disposition has been approved by the shareholders under this chapter, and at any time before the disposition has been consummated, it may be abandoned by the corporation without action by the shareholders, subject to any contractual rights of other parties to the disposition.

(g)   A disposition of assets in the course of dissolution under chapter 14 is not governed by this section.

(h)   The assets of a direct or indirect consolidated subsidiary shall be deemed to be the assets of the parent corporation for the purposes of this section.

Cross-References

Appraisal rights, see ch. 13.

Disposition of assets not requiring shareholder approval, see § 12.01.

Dissolution, see ch. 14.

Modifying quorum or voting requirements, see § 7.27.

Notices and other communications, see § 1.41.

Notice of shareholders' meeting, see § 7.05.

Submission of matters for shareholder vote, see § 8.26.

Voting entitlement of shares, see § 7.21.

Official Comment

1.   In General

Section 12.02(a) requires shareholder approval for a sale, lease, exchange or other disposition of assets by a corporation that would leave the corporation without a significant continuing business activity, other than as provided in section 12.01. Whether a disposition leaves a corporation with a significant continuing business activity, within the meaning of section 12.02(a), depends on whether the corporation's remaining business activity is significant when compared to the corporation's business before the disposition. The 25% safe harbor provides a measure of certainty in making this determination. The safe-harbor test is applied to assets and to revenue or income for the fiscal year ended immediately before the decision by the board of directors to make the disposition in question.

If a corporation disposes of assets for the purpose of reinvesting the proceeds of the disposition in substantially the same business in a somewhat different form (for example, by selling the corporation's only plant for the purpose of buying or building a replacement plant), the disposition and reinvestment should be treated together, so that the transaction should not be deemed to leave the corporation without a significant continuing business activity.

In determining whether a disposition would leave a corporation without a significant continuing business activity, the test combines a parent corporation with subsidiaries that are or should be consolidated with it under applicable accounting principles. For example, if a corporation's only significant business is owned by a consolidated subsidiary, a sale of that business requires approval of the parent's shareholders under section 12.02. Correspondingly, if a corporation owns one significant business directly, and several other significant businesses through one or more wholly or almost wholly owned subsidiaries, a sale by the corporation of the single business it owns directly does not require shareholder approval under section 12.02 (for example, the 25% retention tests of section 12.02(a) are met).

If all or a large part of a corporation's assets are held for investment, the corporation actively manages those assets, and it has no other significant business, for purposes of chapter 12 the corporation should be considered to be in the business of investing in assets, so that a sale of most of those assets without a reinvestment should be considered a sale that would leave the corporation without a significant continuing business activity. In applying the 25% tests of section 12.02(a), an issue could arise if a corporation had more than one business activity, one or more of which might be traditional operating activities, such as manufacturing or distribution, and another of which might be considered managing investments in other securities or enterprises. If the activity constituting the management of investments is to be a continuing business activity as a result of the active engagement of the management of the corporation in that process and the 25% retention tests were met upon the disposition of the other businesses, shareholder approval would not be required.

A board of directors may determine that a retained continuing business falls within the 25% bright-line tests of the safe harbor in section 12.02(a) based either on accounting principles and practices that are reasonable in the circumstances or (in applying the asset test) on a fair valuation or other method that is reasonable in the circumstances in a manner similar to that described in section 6.40(d) and the Official Comment 4 to that section.

The use of the term "significant" and the specific 25% safe harbor test for purposes of this section do not imply a standard for the test of significance or materiality for any other purposes under the Act or otherwise.

2.   *Submission to Shareholders*

When submitting a proposal to shareholders for a disposition of assets, the board of directors must recommend the disposition, subject to two exceptions in section 12.02(b). The board might exercise the exception under clause (i) where the number of directors having a conflicting interest makes it inadvisable for the board to recommend the disposition or where the board is evenly divided as to the merits of the proposal but is able to agree that shareholders should be permitted to consider it. Alternatively, the board of directors might exercise the exception under clause (ii), which recognizes that, under section 8.26, a board of directors may agree to submit a proposal for a disposition to a vote of shareholders even if, after approving the proposal, the board of directors determines that it no longer recommends the proposal.

Section 12.02(c) permits the board of directors to condition its submission to the shareholders of a proposal for a disposition of assets or the effectiveness of the disposition. Among the conditions that a board of directors might impose are that the proposal will not be deemed approved: (i) unless it is approved by a specified percentage of the shareholders, or by one or more specified classes or series of shares, voting as a separate voting group, or by a specified percentage of disinterested shareholders; or (ii) if shareholders holding more than a specified fraction of the outstanding shares exercise appraisal rights.

3.   *Quorum and Voting*

Requirements concerning the timing and content of a notice of meeting, as required by section 12.02(d), are set out in section 7.05. Section 12.02(d) does not address the notice to be given to nonvoting or nonconsenting shareholders where the proposal is approved without a meeting by written consent. That requirement is imposed by section 7.04.

Section 12.02(e) sets forth quorum and voting requirements applicable to a shareholder vote to approve a disposition. In lieu of approval at a meeting, shareholder approval may be by written consent under the procedures set forth in section 7.04.

The Act does not mandate separate voting by voting groups on dispositions, because after a disposition under this chapter the rights of all classes or series of shares remain the same. Separate voting by voting groups may nevertheless be required if provided for in the articles of incorporation or by the board of directors, acting pursuant to section 12.02(c). Appraisal may be available to shareholders entitled to vote on the disposition. See chapter 13.

CHAPTER 13: APPRAISAL RIGHTS

SUBCHAPTER A
RIGHT TO APPRAISAL AND PAYMENT FOR SHARES

§ 13.01. Definitions

In this chapter:

"Affiliate" means a person that directly or indirectly through one or more intermediaries controls, is controlled by, or is under common control with another person or is a senior executive of such person. For purposes of section 13.02(b)(4), a person is deemed to be an affiliate of its senior executives.

"Corporation" means the domestic corporation that is the issuer of the shares held by a shareholder demanding appraisal and, for matters covered in sections 13.22 through 13.31, includes the survivor of a merger.

"Fair value" means the value of the corporation's shares determined:

(i) immediately before the effectiveness of the corporate action to which the shareholder objects;

(ii) using customary and current valuation concepts and techniques generally employed for similar businesses in the context of the transaction requiring appraisal; and

(iii) without discounting for lack of marketability or minority status except, if appropriate, for amendments to the articles of incorporation pursuant to section 13.02(a)(4).

"Interest" means interest from the date the corporate action becomes effective until the date of payment, at the rate of interest on judgments in this state on the effective date of the corporate action.

"Interested transaction" means a corporate action described in section 13.02(a), other than a merger pursuant to section 11.05, involving an interested person in which any of the shares or assets of the corporation are being acquired or converted. As used in this definition:

(i) "Interested person" means a person, or an affiliate of a person, who at any time during the one-year period immediately preceding approval by the board of directors of the corporate action:

(A) was the beneficial owner of 20% or more of the voting power of the corporation, other than as owner of excluded shares;

(B) had the power, contractually or otherwise, other than as owner of excluded shares, to cause the appointment or election of 25% or more of the directors to the board of directors of the corporation; or

(C) was a senior executive or director of the corporation or a senior executive of any affiliate of the corporation, and that senior executive or director will receive, as a result of the corporate action, a financial benefit not generally available to other shareholders as such, other than:

(I) employment, consulting, retirement, or similar benefits established separately and not as part of or in contemplation of the corporate action;

(II) employment, consulting, retirement, or similar benefits established in contemplation of, or as part of, the corporate action that are not more favorable than those existing before the corporate action or, if more favorable, that have been approved on behalf of the corporation in the same manner as is provided in section 8.62; or

(III) in the case of a director of the corporation who will, in the corporate action, become a director or governor of the acquiror or any of its affiliates, rights and benefits as a director or governor that are provided on the same basis as those afforded by the acquiror generally to other directors or governors of such entity or such affiliate.

(ii) "Beneficial owner" means any person who, directly or indirectly, through any contract, arrangement, or understanding, other than a revocable proxy, has or shares the power to vote, or to direct the voting of, shares; except that a member of a national securities exchange is not deemed to be a beneficial owner of securities held directly or indirectly by it on behalf of another person if the member is precluded by the rules of the exchange from voting without instruction on contested matters or matters that may affect substantially the rights or privileges of the holders of the securities to be voted. When two or more persons agree to act together for the purpose of voting their shares of the corporation, each member of the group formed thereby is deemed to have acquired beneficial ownership, as of the date of the agreement, of all shares having voting power of the corporation beneficially owned by any member of the group.

(iii) "Excluded shares" means shares acquired pursuant to an offer for all shares having voting power if the offer was made within one year before the corporate action for consideration of the same kind and of a value equal to or less than that paid in connection with the corporate action.

"Preferred shares" means a class or series of shares whose holders have preference over any other class or series of shares with respect to distributions.

"Senior executive" means the chief executive officer, chief operating officer, chief financial officer, and any individual in charge of a principal business unit or function.

"Shareholder" means a record shareholder, a beneficial shareholder, and a voting trust beneficial owner.

Cross-References

Directors' action on director's conflicting interest transaction, see § 8.62.

"Governor" defined, see § 1.40.

"Voting power" defined, see § 1.40.

Official Comment

1. Overview

Chapter 13 proceeds from the premise that judicial appraisal should be provided by statute only when two conditions co-exist. First, a proposed corporate action as approved by a majority will result in a fundamental change in the shares to be affected by the action. Second, uncertainty concerning the fair value of the affected shares may cause reasonable persons to differ about the fairness of the terms of the corporate action. Uncertainty is reduced, however, in the case of publicly traded shares. This explains both the market exception described below and the limits provided to that exception.

When these two conditions exist in connection with domestications and conversions under chapter 9, mergers and share exchanges under chapter 11, and dispositions of assets requiring shareholder approval under chapter 12, chapter 13 provides for appraisal rights. Each of these actions will result in a fundamental change in the shares that a disapproving shareholder may believe was not adequately compensated by the terms approved by the majority. Shareholders are not entitled to appraisal, however, if the change will not alter the terms of the class or series of securities that they hold. For example, statutory appraisal rights are not available for shares of any class or series of the surviving corporation in a merger that are not being changed in the merger or for shares of any class or series that is not included in a share exchange. Appraisal is also not triggered by a voluntary dissolution under chapter 14 because the dissolution does not affect liquidation rights of the shares of any class or series.

With the exception of reverse stock splits that result in cashing out some of the shares of a class or series, chapter 13 does not grant appraisal rights in connection with amendments to the articles of incorporation. This does not reflect a judgment that an amendment changing the terms of a particular class or series may not have significant economic effects. Rather, it reflects a judgment that distinguishing among different types of amendments for the purposes of statutory appraisal is necessarily arbitrary. Chapter 13 delineates in section 13.02(a)(5) a list of actions for which the corporation may voluntarily choose to provide appraisal. It also allows, under section 13.02(c), a provision in the articles of incorporation that eliminates, in whole or in part, statutory appraisal rights for preferred shares, subject to certain conditions.

Chapter 13 provides an exception to appraisal rights for publicly traded shares, referred to as the "market exception." This exception is available in those situations when shareholders are likely to receive fair value if they sell their shares in the market after the announcement of an appraisal-triggering transaction. For the market exception to apply under chapter 13, there must be a liquid market for the shares. The market exception does not apply where the appraisal-triggering action is a conflict transaction.

2. *Definitions*

Section 13.01 contains specialized definitions applicable only to chapter 13.

A.   CORPORATION

The definition of "corporation" in section 13.01 includes, for purposes of the post-transaction matters covered in sections 13.22 through 13.31, a successor entity in a merger where the corporation is not the surviving entity. The definition does not include an acquiring entity in a share exchange or disposition of assets because the corporation whose shares or assets were acquired continues in existence in both of these instances and remains responsible for the appraisal obligations. Whether a foreign corporation or other form of domestic or foreign entity is subject to appraisal rights in connection with any of these transactions depends upon the applicable law of the relevant jurisdiction.

B.   FAIR VALUE

Clause (i) of the definition of "fair value" in section 13.01 specifies that fair value is to be determined immediately before the effectiveness of the corporate action, which will be after the shareholder vote. Accordingly, section 13.01 permits consideration of changes in the value of the corporation's shares after the shareholder vote but before the effectiveness of the transaction, to the extent such changes are relevant. Similarly, in a two-step transaction culminating in a merger, fair value is determined immediately before the second step merger, taking into account any interim changes in value.

Clause (ii) of the definition of "fair value" in section 13.01 adopts the view that different transactions and different contexts may warrant different valuation methodologies. Customary valuation concepts and techniques will typically take into account numerous relevant factors, and will normally result in a range of values, not a particular single value. A court determining fair value under chapter 13 should give great deference to the aggregate consideration accepted or approved by a disinterested board of directors for an appraisal-triggering transaction.

Valuation discounts for lack of marketability or minority status are inappropriate in most appraisal actions, both because most transactions that trigger appraisal rights affect the corporation as a whole and because such discounts may give the majority the opportunity to take advantage of minority shareholders who have been forced against their will to accept the appraisal-triggering transaction. Clause (iii) of the definition of "fair value" adopts the view that appraisal should generally award a shareholder his or her proportional interest in the corporation after valuing the corporation as a whole, rather than the value of the shareholder's shares when valued alone.

C.   INTEREST

The specification of the rate of interest on judgments, rather than a more subjective rate, eliminates a possible issue of contention and should facilitate voluntary settlements. Other state law determines whether interest is compound or simple.

D.   INTERESTED TRANSACTION

The term "interested transaction" addresses two groups of conflict transactions: those in subsections (i)(A) and (B) of the definition, which involve large shareholders; and those in subsection (i)(C), which involve senior executives and directors. The phrase "involving an interested person" as applied to subsections (i)(A) and (B) denotes participation beyond merely voting or participating on the same basis as other holders of securities of the same or a similar class or series. When a transaction fits within the definition of an interested transaction there are two consequences: the market exception will not be applicable, and the exclusion of other remedies under section 13.40 will not be applicable unless certain disinterested approvals have been obtained.

The definition of "beneficial owner" in subsection (ii) of the definition of "interested transaction" is used to identify possible conflict situations by deeming each member of a group that agrees to vote in concert to be a beneficial owner of all the voting shares owned by the members of the group. (In contrast, the term "beneficial shareholder," as defined in section 1.40, is used to identify those persons entitled to appraisal rights.) When an acquisition is effected in two steps (a tender offer followed by a merger) within one year, and the consideration in the merger is of the same kind and of at least the same value as that in the tender offer, the two-step acquisition is properly considered a single transaction for purposes of identifying conflict transactions, regardless of whether the second-step merger is governed by section 11.04 or 11.05. Therefore the shares acquired in such an offer (defined as "excluded shares" in subsection (iii)) are excluded in subsections (i)(A) and (B) from the determination of whether a person is an "interested person" for purposes of the second-step merger.

A reverse split in which small shareholders are cashed out will constitute an interested transaction if there is an affiliate of the corporation who satisfies the test in subsections (i)(A) or (B). In that case, the corporation itself will be considered an affiliate of the large shareholder and fall within the definition of "interested person," such that when the corporation acquires and cashes out the shares of the small shareholders the acquisition will be an interested transaction.

Subsection (i)(C) applies to management buyouts because management's participation in the buyout group is itself "a financial benefit not generally available to other shareholders." It also applies to transactions involving other types of economic benefits (excluding benefits afforded to shareholders generally) afforded to senior executives (as defined in section 13.01) and directors in specified conflict situations, unless specific objective or procedural standards are met. It would also apply to less common situations, such as where the vote of a director is manipulated by providing the director with special consideration to secure his or her vote in favor of the transaction. Section 13.01 specifically defines the term "affiliate" to include an entity of which a person is a senior executive. As a result of this definition, if a senior executive of the corporation is to continue and is to receive enumerated employment and other financial benefits after the transaction, exempting the transaction from the category of "interested transactions" will depend on meeting one of the three conditions specified in subsection (i)(C), for example:

- If an individual has an arrangement under which benefits will be triggered on a "change of control," such as accelerated vesting of options, retirement benefits, deferred compensation and similar items, or is afforded the opportunity to retire or leave the employ of the enterprise with more favorable economic results than would be the case absent a change of control, the existence of these arrangements would not mean that the transaction is an interested transaction if the arrangements had been established as a general condition of the individual's employment or continued employment, rather than in contemplation of the particular transaction.

- If such arrangements are established as part of, or as a condition of, the transaction, the transaction will still not be considered an interested transaction if the arrangements are either not more favorable to the officer or director than those already in existence or, if they treat the director or officer more favorably, are approved by "qualified" directors (*i.e.*, meeting the standard specified in section 1.43), in the same manner as provided for conflicting interest transactions generally with the corporation under section 8.62. This category would include arrangements with the corporation that have been negotiated as part of, or as a condition to, the transaction or arrangements with the acquiring company or one or more of its other subsidiaries.

- If a person who is a director of the corporation and, in connection with the transaction, is to become a director of the acquiror or its parent, or to continue as a director of the corporation when it becomes a subsidiary of the acquiror, the transaction will not be considered an interested transaction as long as that person will not be treated more favorably as a director than are other persons who are serving in the same director positions.

E.   SENIOR EXECUTIVE

The definition of "senior executive" in section 13.01 encompasses the group of individuals in control of corporate information and the corporation's day-to-day operations. An employee of a subsidiary organization is a "senior executive" of the parent if the employee is "in charge of a principal business unit or function" of the parent and its subsidiaries on a combined or consolidated basis.

F.   SHAREHOLDER

The definition of "shareholder" in section 13.01 encompasses beneficial shareholders and voting trust beneficial owners. This recognizes that these persons have or hold on behalf of others an economic interest in the shares. Use of the term "beneficial shareholder" for this purpose is to be contrasted with the use of the term "beneficial owner" in subsection (ii) of the definition of "interested transaction" to identify possible conflict situations. The distinction between "record shareholder" and "beneficial shareholder" appears primarily in section 13.03, which establishes the manner in which beneficial shareholders, and record shareholders who are acting on behalf of beneficial shareholders, perfect appraisal rights.

§ 13.02. Right to Appraisal

(a)   A shareholder is entitled to appraisal rights, and to obtain payment of the fair value of that shareholder's shares, in the event of any of the following corporate actions:

(1)   consummation of a merger to which the corporation is a party (i) if shareholder approval is required for the merger by section 11.04, or would be required but for the provisions of section 11.04(j), except that appraisal rights shall not be available to any shareholder of the corporation with respect to shares of any class or series that remain outstanding after consummation of the merger, or (ii) if the corporation is a subsidiary and the merger is governed by section 11.05;

(2)   consummation of a share exchange to which the corporation is a party the shares of which will be acquired, except that appraisal rights shall not be available to any shareholder of the corporation with respect to any class or series of shares of the corporation that is not acquired in the share exchange;

(3)   consummation of a disposition of assets pursuant to section 12.02 if the shareholder is entitled to vote on the disposition, except that appraisal rights shall not be available to any shareholder of the corporation with respect to shares of any class or series if (i) under the terms of the corporate action approved by the shareholders there is to be distributed to shareholders in cash the corporation's net assets, in excess of a reasonable amount reserved to meet claims of the type described in sections 14.06 and 14.07, (A) within one year after the shareholders' approval of the action and (B) in accordance with their respective interests determined at the time of distribution, and (ii) the disposition of assets is not an interested transaction;

(4)   an amendment of the articles of incorporation with respect to a class or series of shares that reduces the number of shares of a class or series owned by the shareholder to a fraction of a share if the corporation has the obligation or right to repurchase the fractional share so created;

(5)   any other merger, share exchange, disposition of assets or amendment to the articles of incorporation, in each case to the extent provided by the articles of incorporation, bylaws or a resolution of the board of directors;

(6)   consummation of a domestication pursuant to section 9.20 if the shareholder does not receive shares in the foreign corporation resulting from the domestication that have terms as favorable to the shareholder in all material respects, and represent at least the same percentage interest of the total voting rights of the outstanding shares of the foreign corporation, as the shares held by the shareholder before the domestication;

(7)   consummation of a conversion of the corporation to a nonprofit corporation pursuant to section 9.30; or

(8)   consummation of a conversion of the corporation to an unincorporated entity pursuant to section 9.30.

(b)   Notwithstanding subsection (a), the availability of appraisal rights under subsections (a)(1), (2), (3), (4), (6) and (8) shall be limited in accordance with the following provisions:

(1)   Appraisal rights shall not be available for the holders of shares of any class or series of shares which is:

(i)   a covered security under section 18(b)(1)(A) or (B) of the Securities Act of 1933;

(ii)   traded in an organized market and has at least 2,000 shareholders and a market value of at least $20 million (exclusive of the value of such shares held by the corporation's subsidiaries, senior executives and directors and by any beneficial shareholder and any voting trust beneficial owner owning more than 10% of such shares); or

(iii)   issued by an open end management investment company registered with the Securities and Exchange Commission under the Investment Company Act of 1940 and which may be redeemed at the option of the holder at net asset value.

(2)   The applicability of subsection (b)(1) shall be determined as of:

(i)   the record date fixed to determine the shareholders entitled to receive notice of the meeting of shareholders to act upon the corporate action requiring appraisal rights or, in the case of an offer made pursuant to section 11.04(j), the date of such offer; or

(ii)   if there is no meeting of shareholders and no offer made pursuant to section 11.04(j), the day before the consummation of the corporate action or effective date of the amendment of the articles of incorporation, as applicable.

(3)   Subsection (b)(1) shall not be applicable and appraisal rights shall be available pursuant to subsection (a) for the holders of any class or series of shares (i) who are required by the terms of the corporate action requiring appraisal rights to accept for such shares anything other than cash or shares of any class or any series of shares of any corporation, or any other proprietary interest of any other entity, that satisfies the standards set forth in subsection (b)(1) at the time the corporate action becomes effective, or (ii) in the case of the consummation of a disposition of assets pursuant to section 12.02, unless the cash, shares, or proprietary interests received in the disposition are, under the terms of the corporate action approved by the shareholders, to be distributed to the shareholders, as part of a distribution to shareholders of the net assets of the corporation in excess of a reasonable amount to meet claims of the type described in sections 14.06 and 14.07, (A) within one year after the shareholders' approval of the action, and (B) in accordance with their respective interests determined at the time of the distribution.

(4)   Subsection (b)(1) shall not be applicable and appraisal rights shall be available pursuant to subsection (a) for the holders of any class or series of shares where the corporate action is an interested transaction.

(c)   Notwithstanding any other provision of section 13.02, the articles of incorporation as originally filed or any amendment to the articles of incorporation may limit or eliminate appraisal rights for any class or series of preferred shares, except that (i) no such limitation or elimination shall be effective if the class or series does not have the right to vote separately as a voting group (alone or as part of a group) on the action or if the action is a conversion under section 9.30, or a merger having a similar effect as a conversion in which the converted entity is an eligible entity, and (ii) any such limitation or elimination contained in an amendment to the articles of incorporation that limits or eliminates appraisal rights for any of such shares that are outstanding immediately before the effective date of such amendment or that the corporation is or may be required to issue or sell thereafter pursuant to any conversion, exchange or other right existing immediately before the effective date of such amendment shall not apply to any corporate action that becomes effective within one year after the effective date of such amendment if such action would otherwise afford appraisal rights.

Cross-References

Amendment of articles of incorporation, see ch. 10A.

Classes and series of shares, see §§ 6.01 and 6.02.

Conversion, see ch. 9C.

Disposition of assets, see ch. 12.

Domestication, see ch. 9B.

Effective time and date of amendment, see § 1.23.

"Eligible entity" defined, see § 1.40.

"Foreign corporation" defined, see § 1.40.

"Interested transaction" defined, see § 13.01.

Merger and share exchange, see ch. 11.

Merger of subsidiary, see § 11.05.

"Nonprofit corporation" defined, see § 1.40.

"Person" defined, see § 1.40.

"Preferred shares" defined, see § 13.01.

Record date, see § 7.07.

Redemption of shares, see §§ 6.01 and 6.31.

Share dividends, see § 6.23.

Share preferences, see §§ 6.01 and 6.02.

"Unincorporated entity" defined, see § 1.40.

Voting by voting groups, see §§ 1.40, 7.25 and 7.26.

"Voting power" defined, see § 1.40.

Voting rights, see § 7.21.

Official Comment

1.   Transactions Requiring Appraisal Rights

Section 13.02(a) establishes the scope of appraisal rights by identifying those transactions that afford this right. Statutory appraisal is made available only for corporate actions that will result in a fundamental change in the shares to be affected by the action and then only when uncertainty concerning the fair value of the affected shares may cause reasonable differences about the fairness of the terms of the corporate action. The transactions that satisfy both of these criteria are set forth in section 13.02(a), subject to the exceptions set forth in section 13.02(b). In a two-step transaction authorized by section 11.04(j), shareholders at the time of the second step merger could have appraisal rights even though there is no shareholder vote. Shareholders who tender in response to the offer in the first step of such a transaction would not have appraisal rights; their tendering in response to the offer has the same effect on appraisal rights as if they had voted for the transaction.

Under section 13.02(b)(4), the reasons for granting appraisal rights in a reverse stock split in which shares are cashed out are similar to those for granting such rights in cases of cash-out mergers, as both transactions could compel affected shareholders to accept cash for their investment in an amount established by the corporation. Appraisal is afforded only for those shareholders of a class or series whose interest is so affected by the amendment. As provided in section 12.02(g), a disposition of assets by a corporation in the course of dissolution under chapter 14 is governed by that chapter, not chapter 12, and thus does not implicate appraisal rights.

An express grant of voluntary appraisal rights under section 13.02(a)(5) overrides any of the exceptions to the availability of appraisal rights in section 13.02(a). Any voluntary grant of appraisal rights by the corporation to the holders of one or more of its classes or series of shares in connection with a corporate action will automatically make all of the provisions of chapter 13 applicable to the corporation and such holders regarding that corporate action.

2. Market Exception to Appraisal Rights

Chapter 13 provides a limited exception to appraisal rights for those situations where shareholders may either accept the appraisal-triggering corporate action or sell their shares in an organized market described in section 13.02(b)(1). For purposes of this chapter, the market exception is provided for a class or series of shares if two tests are satisfied: the market in which the shares are traded must be liquid, as described in section 13.02(b)(1), and the value of the shares established by the appraisal-triggering event must be the result of a process reasonably calculated to arrive at a price reflective of an arm's length transaction.

Because section 13.02(b)(3)(i) excludes from the market exception those transactions that require shareholders to accept anything other than cash or securities that also meet the liquidity tests of section 13.02(b)(1), shareholders are assured of receiving either appraisal rights, cash from the transaction, or shares or other proprietary interests in the survivor entity that are liquid. Section 13.02(b)(2) specifies the date on which the corporation must satisfy the requirements of section 13.02(b)(1) for the market exception to be applicable. Section 13.02(b)(4) recognizes that the market price of, or consideration for, shares of a corporation that proposes to engage in an interested transaction of the type listed in section 13.02(a) may be subject to influences where a corporation's management, controlling shareholders or directors have conflicting interests that could, if not dealt with appropriately, adversely affect the consideration that otherwise could have been expected. Section 13.02(b)(4) thus provides that the market exception will not apply in those instances where the transaction constitutes an interested transaction (as defined in section 13.01).

3. Elimination of Appraisal Rights for Preferred Shares

Section 13.02(c) permits the corporation to eliminate or limit appraisal rights that would otherwise be available for the holders of one or more series or classes of preferred shares provided that the standards in that section are met. Chapter 13 does not permit the corporation to eliminate or limit the appraisal rights of common shares.

§ 13.03. Assertion of Rights by Nominees and Beneficial Shareholders

(a)   A record shareholder may assert appraisal rights as to fewer than all the shares registered in the record shareholder's name but owned by a beneficial shareholder or a voting trust beneficial owner only if the record shareholder objects with respect to all shares of a class or series owned by the beneficial shareholder or the voting trust beneficial owner and notifies the corporation in writing of the name and address of each beneficial shareholder or voting trust beneficial owner on whose behalf appraisal rights are being asserted. The rights of a record shareholder who asserts appraisal rights for only part of the shares held of record in the record shareholder's name under this subsection shall be determined as if the shares as to which the record shareholder objects and the record shareholder's other shares were registered in the names of different record shareholders.

(b)   A beneficial shareholder and a voting trust beneficial owner may assert appraisal rights as to shares of any class or series held on behalf of the shareholder only if such shareholder:

(1)   submits to the corporation the record shareholder's written consent to the assertion of such rights no later than the date referred to in section 13.22(b)(2)(ii); and

(2)   does so with respect to all shares of the class or series that are beneficially owned by the beneficial shareholder or the voting trust beneficial owner.

Cross-References

"Beneficial shareholder," "record shareholder" and "voting trust beneficial owner" defined, see §§ 1.40 and 13.01.

Notice to the corporation, see § 1.41.

"Person" defined, see § 1.40.

"Shareholder" defined, see §§ 1.40 and 13.01.

Shares held by nominee, see § 7.23.

Voting agreements, see § 7.31.

Voting trusts, see § 7.30.

Official Comment

Section 13.03 addresses the relationship between those who are entitled to assert appraisal rights and the widespread practice of nominee or street name ownership of publicly traded shares. Generally, a shareholder must demand appraisal for all the shares of a class or series which the shareholder owns. If a record shareholder is a nominee for several beneficial shareholders, some of whom wish to demand appraisal and some of whom do not, section 13.03(a) permits the record shareholder to assert appraisal rights with respect to a portion of the shares held of record by the record shareholder but only with respect to all the shares beneficially owned by a single person. The same rule applies to shares held by voting trustees. A shareholder who owns shares in more than one class or series, however, may assert appraisal rights for only some rather than all classes or series that the shareholder owns.

Voting trustees hold shares on behalf of voting trust beneficial owners and may want to or be required to pass the decision on asserting appraisal rights on to the voting trust beneficial owners. To make appraisal rights effective without burdening record shareholders, beneficial shareholders and voting trust beneficial owners are allowed to assert their own claims as provided in section 13.03(b). After the corporation has received the form of consent required by section 13.03(b)(1), the corporation must deal with the beneficial shareholder, or, in the case of a voting trust, the voting trust beneficial owner.

SUBCHAPTER B
PROCEDURE FOR EXERCISE OF APPRAISAL RIGHTS

§ 13.20. Notice of Appraisal Rights

(a)   Where any corporate action specified in section 13.02(a) is to be submitted to a vote at a shareholders' meeting, the meeting notice (or where no approval of such action is required pursuant to section 11.04(j), the offer made pursuant to section 11.04(j)), must state that the corporation has concluded that appraisal rights are, are not or may be available under this chapter. If the corporation concludes that appraisal rights are or may be available, a copy of this chapter must accompany the meeting notice or offer sent to those record shareholders entitled to exercise appraisal rights.

(b)   In a merger pursuant to section 11.05, the parent entity shall notify in writing all record shareholders of the subsidiary who are entitled to assert appraisal rights that the corporate action became effective. Such notice shall be sent within 10 days after the corporate action became effective and include the materials described in section 13.22.

(c)   Where any corporate action specified in section 13.02(a) is to be approved by written consent of the shareholders pursuant to section 7.04:

(1)   written notice that appraisal rights are, are not or may be available shall be sent to each record shareholder from whom a consent is solicited at the time consent of such shareholder is first solicited and, if the corporation has concluded that appraisal rights are or may be available, the notice must be accompanied by a copy of this chapter; and

(2)   written notice that appraisal rights are, are not or may be available must be delivered together with the notice to nonconsenting and nonvoting shareholders required by sections 7.04(e) and (f), may include the materials described in section 13.22 and, if the corporation has concluded that appraisal rights are or may be available, must be accompanied by a copy of this chapter.

(d)   Where corporate action described in section 13.02(a) is proposed, or a merger pursuant to section 11.05 is effected, the notice referred to in subsection (a) or (c), if the corporation concludes that appraisal rights are or may be available, and in subsection (b) must be accompanied by:

(1)   financial statements of the corporation that issued the shares that may be subject to appraisal, consisting of a balance sheet as of the end of a fiscal year ending not more than 16 months before the date of the notice, an income statement for that year, and a cash flow statement for that year; provided that, if such financial statements are not reasonably available, the corporation shall provide reasonably equivalent financial information; and

(2)   the latest interim financial statements of such corporation, if any.

(e)   The right to receive the information described in subsection (d) may be waived in writing by a shareholder before or after the corporate action.

Cross-References

Availability of appraisal rights, see § 13.02.

"Beneficial shareholder," "record shareholder" and "voting trust beneficial owner" defined, see §§ 1.40 and 13.01.

Meeting notice, see § 7.05.

Merger of subsidiary, see § 11.05.

Notices and other communications, see § 1.41.

Shareholder action without a meeting, see § 7.04.

"Shareholder" defined, see §§ 1.40 and 13.01.

Shareholders' meetings, see §§ 7.01 through 7.03.

Official Comment

The notices required by sections 13.20(a), (b) and (c) are necessary because many shareholders do not know what appraisal rights they may have or how to assert them. Because appraisal is an "opt in" remedy, shareholders otherwise entitled to an appraisal of their shares by reason of corporate actions specified in section 13.02 must elect whether to seek that remedy or accept the results of that action.

Section 13.20(d) specifies certain disclosure requirements for corporate actions for which appraisal rights are provided. Disclosure of additional information may be necessary under common law disclosure duties.

By specifying certain disclosure requirements, section 13.20(d) reduces the risk, in the transactions to which it applies, of an uninformed shareholder decision whether to exercise appraisal rights. Section 13.31(b)(1) provides that a corporation may be liable for the fees and expenses of counsel and experts for the respective parties for failure to comply substantially with sections 13.20 and 13.24.

§ 13.21. Notice of Intent to Demand Payment and Consequences of Voting or Consenting

(a)   If a corporate action specified in section 13.02(a) is submitted to a vote at a shareholders' meeting, a shareholder who wishes to assert appraisal rights with respect to any class or series of shares:

(1)   shall deliver to the corporation, before the vote is taken, written notice of the shareholder's intent to demand payment if the proposed action is effectuated; and

(2)   shall not vote, or cause or permit to be voted, any shares of such class or series in favor of the proposed action.

(b)   If a corporate action specified in section 13.02(a) is to be approved by written consent, a shareholder who wishes to assert appraisal rights with respect to any class or series of shares shall not sign a consent in favor of the proposed action with respect to that class or series of shares.

(c)   If a corporate action specified in section 13.02(a) does not require shareholder approval pursuant to section 11.04(j), a shareholder who wishes to assert appraisal rights with respect to any class or series of shares (i) shall deliver to the corporation before the shares are purchased pursuant to the offer written notice of the shareholder's intent to demand payment if the proposed action is effected; and (ii) shall not tender, or cause or permit to be tendered, any shares of such class or series in response to such offer.

(d)   A shareholder who fails to satisfy the requirements of subsection (a), (b) or (c) is not entitled to payment under this chapter.

Cross-References

"Deliver" defined, see § 1.40.

Notices and other communications, see § 1.41.

Shareholder action without a meeting, see § 7.04.

Official Comment

Section 13.21 applies to all transactions requiring appraisal, except short-form mergers under section 11.05 in which shareholders of the subsidiary do not vote on the transaction but are nevertheless entitled to appraisal.

The notice from the shareholder required by section 13.21(a) enables the corporation, among other things, to estimate how much of a cash payment may be required by reference to the maximum number of shares for which appraisal may be sought. It also limits the number of persons to whom the corporation must give further notice during the remainder of the appraisal process.

§ 13.22. Appraisal Notice and Form

(a)   If a corporate action requiring appraisal rights under section 13.02(a) becomes effective, the corporation shall deliver a written appraisal notice and form required by subsection (b) to all shareholders who satisfy the requirements of sections 13.21(a), (b) or (c). In the case of a merger under section 11.05, the parent shall deliver an appraisal notice and form to all record shareholders who may be entitled to assert appraisal rights.

(b)   The appraisal notice shall be delivered no earlier than the date the corporate action specified in section 13.02(a) became effective, and no later than 10 days after such date, and must:

(1)   supply a form that (i) specifies the first date of any announcement to shareholders made before the date the corporate action became effective of the principal terms of the proposed corporate action, and (ii) if such announcement was made, requires the shareholder asserting appraisal rights to certify whether beneficial ownership of those shares for which appraisal rights are asserted was acquired before that date, and (iii) requires the shareholder asserting appraisal rights to certify that such shareholder did not vote for or consent to the transaction as to the class or series of shares for which appraisal is sought;

(2)   state:

(i)   where the form shall be sent and where certificates for certificated shares shall be deposited and the date by which those certificates must be deposited, which date may not be earlier than the date by which the corporation must receive the required form under subsection (b)(2)(ii);

(ii)   a date by which the corporation shall receive the form, which date may not be fewer than 40 nor more than 60 days after the date the subsection (a) appraisal notice is sent, and state that the shareholder shall have waived the right to demand appraisal with respect to the shares unless the form is received by the corporation by such specified date;

(iii)   the corporation's estimate of the fair value of the shares;

(iv)   that, if requested in writing, the corporation will provide, to the shareholder so requesting, within 10 days after the date specified in subsection (b)(2)(ii) the number of shareholders who return the forms by the specified date and the total number of shares owned by them; and

(v)   the date by which the notice to withdraw under section 13.23 shall be received, which date shall be within 20 days after the date specified in subsection (b)(2)(ii); and

(3)   be accompanied by a copy of this chapter.

Cross-References

After-acquired shares, see § 13.25.

"Deliver" defined, see § 1.40.

Merger of subsidiary, see § 11.05.

Notices and other communications, see § 1.41.

Official Comment

The purpose of section 13.22 is to require the corporation to provide shareholders with information and a form for perfecting appraisal rights.

Section 13.22(b)(1) requires that the corporation specify the date of the first announcement of the terms of the proposed corporate action. This date determines the rights of shareholder-transferees. Persons who became shareholders before that date are entitled to full appraisal rights, while persons who became shareholders on or after that date are entitled only to the more limited rights provided by section 13.25. See the Official Comments to sections 13.23 and 13.25. The date the principal terms of the transaction were announced by the corporation to shareholders may be the day the terms were communicated directly to the shareholders, included in a public filing with the Securities and Exchange Commission, published in a newspaper of general circulation that can be expected to reach the financial community, or any earlier date on which such terms were first announced by any other person or entity to such persons or sources. Any announcement to news media or to shareholders that relates to the proposed transaction but does not contain the principal terms of the transaction to be authorized at the shareholders' meeting is not considered to be an announcement for the purposes of section 13.22. If a corporation or other person does not make a public announcement of the terms of a proposed corporation action, the requirement of section 13.22(b)(1) is not applicable.

The information required by sections 13.22(b)(2)(iii) and (iv) is intended to help shareholders assess whether they wish to demand payment or to withdraw their demand for appraisal, although the information under section 13.22(b)(2)(iv) is required to be sent only to those shareholders from whom the corporation has received a written request.

§ 13.23. Perfection of Rights; Right to Withdraw

(a)   A shareholder who receives notice pursuant to section 13.22 and who wishes to exercise appraisal rights shall sign and return the form sent by the corporation and, in the case of certificated shares, deposit the shareholder's certificates in accordance with the terms of the notice by the date referred to in the notice pursuant to section 13.22(b)(2)(ii). In addition, if applicable, the shareholder shall certify on the form whether the beneficial owner of such shares acquired beneficial ownership of the shares before the date required to be set forth in the notice pursuant to section 13.22(b)(1)(i). If a shareholder fails to make this certification, the corporation may elect to treat the shareholder's shares as after-acquired shares under section 13.25. Once a shareholder deposits that shareholder's certificates or, in the case of uncertificated shares, returns the signed forms, that shareholder loses all rights as a shareholder, unless the shareholder withdraws pursuant to subsection (b).

(b)   A shareholder who has complied with subsection (a) may nevertheless decline to exercise appraisal rights and withdraw from the appraisal process by so notifying the corporation in writing by the date set forth in the appraisal notice pursuant to section 13.22(b)(2)(v). A shareholder who fails to so withdraw from the appraisal process may not thereafter withdraw without the corporation's written consent.

(c)   A shareholder who does not sign and return the form and, in the case of certificated shares, deposit that shareholder's share certificates where required, each by the date set forth in the notice described in section 13.22(b), shall not be entitled to payment under this chapter.

Cross-References

After-acquired shares, see § 13.25.

Notice of appraisal rights, see § 13.22.

Notices and other communications, see § 1.41.

Official Comment

In the case of a transaction involving a vote by shareholders, returning the signed form and, in the case of certificated shares, depositing the shares are the shareholder's confirmation of the intention expressed earlier under section 13.21(a) to pursue appraisal rights. In the case of a merger of a subsidiary under section 11.05, the form required by section 13.23 is the shareholder's first statement of this intention.

Information on the appraisal form regarding whether the beneficial shareholder acquired beneficial ownership of the shares before, on or after the date the transaction was announced permits the corporation to exercise its right under section 13.25 to defer payment of compensation for certain shares. The corporation may elect to proceed under section 13.25 with respect to those shareholders who were required to make the certification but did not do so.

Once a shareholder deposits that shareholder's shares as required by section 13.23(a), that shareholder loses all rights as a shareholder unless the shareholder withdraws from the appraisal process pursuant to section 13.23(b).

Under section 13.23(c), a shareholder who fails to comply with the requirements of section 13.23(a) loses all rights to pursue appraisal and obtain payment under this chapter. If a beneficial shareholder wishes to assert appraisal rights in place of the record shareholder, the beneficial shareholder must also comply with section 13.03(b).

§ 13.24. Payment

(a)   Except as provided in section 13.25, within 30 days after the form required by section 13.22(b)(2)(ii) is due, the corporation shall pay in cash to those shareholders who complied with section 13.23(a) the amount the corporation estimates to be the fair value of their shares, plus interest.

(b)   The payment to each shareholder pursuant to subsection (a) must be accompanied by:

(1)(i)   financial statements of the corporation that issued the shares to be appraised, consisting of a balance sheet as of the end of a fiscal year ending not more than 16 months before the date of payment, an income statement for that year, and a cash flow statement for that year; provided that, if such annual financial statements are not reasonably available, the corporation shall provide reasonably equivalent financial information, and (ii) the latest interim financial statements of such corporation, if any;

(2)   a statement of the corporation's estimate of the fair value of the shares, which estimate shall equal or exceed the corporation's estimate given pursuant to section 13.22(b)(2)(iii); and

(3)   a statement that shareholders described in subsection (a) have the right to demand further payment under section 13.26 and that if any such shareholder does not do so within the

time period specified in section 13.26(b), such shareholder shall be deemed to have accepted the payment under subsection (a) in full satisfaction of the corporation's obligations under this chapter.

Cross-References

After-acquired shares, see § 13.25.

"Fair value" defined, see § 13.01.

"Interest" defined, see § 13.01.

Notice of appraisal rights, see § 13.22.

Payment demand, see § 13.23.

Rejection of corporation's offer, see § 13.26.

Official Comment

Section 13.24 is applicable to shareholders who have complied with section 13.23(a) and to shareholders described in section 13.25(a) if the corporation so chooses. The corporation must, however, elect to treat all shareholders described in section 13.25(a) either under section 13.24 or under section 13.25; it may not treat some shareholders described in section 13.25(a) under section 13.24 but treat others under section 13.25.

The requirement of section 13.24 that the corporation pay its estimate of the fair value of the stock plus interest reflects a judgment that a difference of opinion over the total amount to be paid should not delay payment of the amount that is undisputed. Because a former shareholder must decide whether to accept that payment in full satisfaction, the corporation must include with the payment the information specified in section 13.24(b), which includes a reminder of the former shareholder's further rights.

Even though the information specified in section 13.24(b) was previously furnished under section 13.20(d) at the time notice of appraisal rights was given, it must still be furnished under section 13.24(b) at the time of payment. That information may need to be updated to satisfy the requirements of section 13.24(b).

§ 13.25. After-Acquired Shares

(a)   A corporation may elect to withhold payment required by section 13.24 from any shareholder who was required to, but did not certify that beneficial ownership of all of the shareholder's shares for which appraisal rights are asserted was acquired before the date set forth in the appraisal notice sent pursuant to section 13.22(b)(1).

(b)   If the corporation elected to withhold payment under subsection (a), it shall, within 30 days after the form required by section 13.22(b)(2)(ii) is due, notify all shareholders who are described in subsection (a):

(1)   of the information required by section 13.24(b)(1);

(2)   of the corporation's estimate of fair value pursuant to section 13.24(b)(2);

(3)   that they may accept the corporation's estimate of fair value, plus interest, in full satisfaction of their demands or demand appraisal under section 13.26;

(4)   that those shareholders who wish to accept such offer shall so notify the corporation of their acceptance of the corporation's offer within 30 days after receiving the offer; and

(5)   that those shareholders who do not satisfy the requirements for demanding appraisal under section 13.26 shall be deemed to have accepted the corporation's offer.

(c)   Within 10 days after receiving the shareholder's acceptance pursuant to subsection (b)(4), the corporation shall pay in cash the amount it offered under subsection (b)(2) plus interest to each shareholder who agreed to accept the corporation's offer in full satisfaction of the shareholder's demand.

(d)　Within 40 days after delivering the notice described in subsection (b), the corporation shall pay in cash the amount it offered to pay under subsection (b)(2) plus interest to each shareholder described in subsection (b)(5).

Cross-References

"Fair value" defined, see § 13.01.

"Interest" defined, see § 13.01.

Notices and other communications, see § 1.41.

Rejection of corporation's offer, see § 13.26.

Official Comment

If a public announcement of the proposed corporate action is made, section 13.25(a) gives the corporation the option not to make payment under section 13.24(a) to holders of shares acquired on or after the date of that announcement or to holders of shares who are required to but do not certify under section 13.23(a) when they acquired beneficial ownership. Instead, the corporation may give these shareholders an offer of payment which is conditioned on their agreement to accept it in full satisfaction of their claim.

The date used as a cut-off for determining the application of this section is when "the principal terms" of the proposed transaction are first announced to shareholders. See the Official Comment to section 13.22. The cut-off is not set at an earlier date, such as when the first public statement that the corporate action was under consideration was made, because the goal of this section is to discourage use of appraisal rights as a speculative device only after the principal terms of the proposed transaction are announced.

A shareholder may accept the offered payment in full satisfaction of that shareholder's claim; alternatively, a shareholder may reject the corporation's offer and demand a judicial determination under section 13.26 and payment of the amount so determined at the termination of the proceeding. A shareholder who does not satisfy the requirements of section 13.26 shall be deemed to have accepted the corporation's offer.

§ 13.26. Procedure if Shareholder Dissatisfied with Payment or Offer

(a)　A shareholder paid pursuant to section 13.24 who is dissatisfied with the amount of the payment shall notify the corporation in writing of that shareholder's estimate of the fair value of the shares and demand payment of that estimate (less any payment under section 13.24) plus interest. A shareholder offered payment under section 13.25 who is dissatisfied with that offer shall reject the offer and demand payment of the shareholder's stated estimate of the fair value of the shares plus interest.

(b)　A shareholder who fails to notify the corporation in writing of that shareholder's demand to be paid the shareholder's stated estimate of the fair value plus interest under subsection (a) within 30 days after receiving the corporation's payment or offer of payment under section 13.24 or section 13.25, respectively, waives the right to demand payment under this section and shall be entitled only to the payment made or offered pursuant to those respective sections.

Cross-References

After-acquired shares, see § 13.25.

"Fair value" defined, see § 13.01.

"Interest" defined, see § 13.01.

Judicial appraisal, see § 13.30.

Notices and other communications, see § 1.41.

Offer of payment for after-acquired shares, see § 13.25.

Other remedies, see § 13.40.

Payment for shares, see § 13.24.

Official Comment

A shareholder who is not content with the corporation's remittance under section 13.24, or offer of remittance under section 13.25, and wishes to pursue appraisal rights further must state in writing the amount the shareholder is willing to accept. A shareholder whose demand is deemed arbitrary, unreasonable or not in good faith, however, runs the risk of being assessed litigation expenses under section 13.31. These provisions are designed to encourage settlement without a judicial proceeding.

A shareholder to whom the corporation has made payment (or who has been offered payment under section 13.25) must make a supplemental demand within 30 days after receipt of the payment or offer of payment to permit the corporation to make an early decision on initiating appraisal proceedings. A failure to make such demand causes the shareholder to relinquish under section 13.26(b) anything beyond the amount the corporation paid or offered to pay.

SUBCHAPTER C
JUDICIAL APPRAISAL OF SHARES

§ 13.30. Court Action

(a)   If a shareholder makes demand for payment under section 13.26 which remains unsettled, the corporation shall commence a proceeding within 60 days after receiving the payment demand and petition the court to determine the fair value of the shares and accrued interest. If the corporation does not commence the proceeding within the 60-day period, it shall pay in cash to each shareholder the amount the shareholder demanded pursuant to section 13.26 plus interest.

(b)   The corporation shall commence the proceeding in the [name or describe court].

(c)   The corporation shall make all shareholders (regardless of whether they are residents of this state) whose demands remain unsettled parties to the proceeding as in an action against their shares, and all parties shall be served with a copy of the petition. Nonresidents may be served by registered or certified mail or by publication as provided by law.

(d)   The jurisdiction of the court in which the proceeding is commenced under subsection (b) is plenary and exclusive. The court may appoint one or more persons as appraisers to receive evidence and recommend a decision on the question of fair value. The appraisers shall have the powers described in the order appointing them, or in any amendment to it. The shareholders demanding appraisal rights are entitled to the same discovery rights as parties in other civil proceedings. There shall be no right to a jury trial.

(e)   Each shareholder made a party to the proceeding is entitled to judgment (i) for the amount, if any, by which the court finds the fair value of the shareholder's shares exceeds the amount paid by the corporation to the shareholder for such shares, plus interest, or (ii) for the fair value, plus interest, of the shareholder's shares for which the corporation elected to withhold payment under section 13.25.

Cross-References

After-acquired shares, see § 13.25.

"Fair value" defined, see § 13.01.

"Interest" defined, see § 13.01.

"Person" defined, see § 1.40.

"Proceeding" defined, see § 1.40.

Official Comment

Section 13.30 provides for judicial appraisal as the ultimate means of determining fair value. All demands for payment made under section 13.26 are to be resolved in a single proceeding brought in the court specified by section 13.30(b). All shareholders making demands under section 13.26 must be made parties, with service by publication authorized if necessary. Because the nature of the proceeding is similar to a proceeding in equity or for an accounting, section 13.30(d) provides that there is no right to a jury trial. The final judgment establishes not only the fair value of the shares in the abstract but also determines how much each shareholder who made a section 13.26 demand should receive.

§ 13.31. Court Costs and Expenses

(a)   The court in an appraisal proceeding commenced under section 13.30 shall determine all court costs of the proceeding, including the reasonable compensation and expenses of appraisers appointed by the court. The court shall assess the court costs against the corporation, except that the court may assess court costs against all or some of the shareholders demanding appraisal, in amounts which the court finds equitable, to the extent the court finds such shareholders acted arbitrarily, vexatiously, or not in good faith with respect to the rights provided by this chapter.

(b)   The court in an appraisal proceeding may also assess the expenses of the respective parties in amounts the court finds equitable:

(1)   against the corporation and in favor of any or all shareholders demanding appraisal if the court finds the corporation did not substantially comply with the requirements of sections 13.20, 13.22, 13.24, or 13.25; or

(2)   against either the corporation or a shareholder demanding appraisal, in favor of any other party, if the court finds the party against whom expenses are assessed acted arbitrarily, vexatiously, or not in good faith with respect to the rights provided by this chapter.

(c)   If the court in an appraisal proceeding finds that the expenses incurred by any shareholder were of substantial benefit to other shareholders similarly situated and that such expenses should not be assessed against the corporation, the court may direct that such expenses be paid out of the amounts awarded the shareholders who were benefited.

(d)   To the extent the corporation fails to make a required payment pursuant to sections 13.24, 13.25, or 13.26, the shareholder may sue directly for the amount owed, and to the extent successful, shall be entitled to recover from the corporation all expenses of the suit.

Cross-References

Appraisers, see § 13.30.

"Expenses" defined, see § 1.40.

Judicial appraisal, see § 13.30.

"Proceeding" defined, see § 1.40.

Official Comment

The purpose of the grants of discretion to the court under section 13.31 with respect to expenses of appraisal proceedings is to increase the incentives of both sides to proceed in good faith under this chapter to attempt to resolve their disagreement without the need of a formal judicial appraisal of the value of shares.

While subsections (a) through (c) allocate court costs and expenses in an appraisal proceeding, subsection (d) covers the situation where the corporation was obligated to make payment and did not meet this obligation.

SUBCHAPTER D
OTHER REMEDIES

§ 13.40. Other Remedies Limited

(a)   The legality of a proposed or completed corporate action described in section 13.02(a) may not be contested, nor may the corporate action be enjoined, set aside or rescinded, in a legal or equitable proceeding by a shareholder after the shareholders have approved the corporate action.

(b)   Subsection (a) does not apply to a corporate action that:

(1)   was not authorized and approved in accordance with the applicable provisions of:

(i)   chapter 9, 10, 11, or 12;

(ii)   the articles of incorporation or bylaws; or

(iii)   the resolution of the board of directors authorizing the corporate action;

(2)   was procured as a result of fraud, a material misrepresentation, or an omission of a material fact necessary to make statements made, in light of the circumstances in which they were made, not misleading;

(3)   is an interested transaction, unless it has been recommended by the board of directors in the same manner as is provided in section 8.62 and has been approved by the shareholders in the same manner as is provided in section 8.63 as if the interested transaction were a director's conflicting interest transaction; or

(4)   is approved by less than unanimous consent of the voting shareholders pursuant to section 7.04 if:

(i)   the challenge to the corporate action is brought by a shareholder who did not consent and as to whom notice of the approval of the corporate action was not effective at least 10 days before the corporate action was effected; and

(ii)   the proceeding challenging the corporate action is commenced within 10 days after notice of the approval of the corporate action is effective as to the shareholder bringing the proceeding.

Cross References

Directors' action respecting a director's conflicting interest transaction, see § 8.62.

"Director's conflicting interest transaction" defined, see § 8.60.

"Interested transaction" defined, see § 13.01.

Shareholders' action respecting a director's conflicting interest transaction, see § 8.63.

Official Comment

The principle underlying section 13.40 generally is that when the holders of a majority of the shares have approved a corporate change, the corporation should be permitted to proceed even if a minority considers the change unwise or disadvantageous. The existence of an appraisal remedy recognizes that shareholders may disagree about the financial consequences that a corporate action may have and that some may hold such strong views that they will want to vindicate them in a judicial proceeding. Accordingly, if an appraisal proceeding results in an award of additional consideration to the shareholders who pursued appraisal, no inference should be drawn that the judgment of the majority was wrong or that compensation is now owed to shareholders who did not seek appraisal. The limitations are not confined to cases where appraisal is available. The liquidity and reliability considerations that justify the market exception also justify imposing the same limitation on post-shareholder approval remedies that apply when appraisal is available.

Section 13.40 permits proceedings contesting the legality of a transaction, or seeking to enjoin, rescind or set aside the corporate action after the action has been approved by shareholders under the four circumstances described in section 13.40(b)(1). In the case of a corporate action that is an interested transaction, the same reasoning that supports the provision of appraisal rights in situations where the market exception would otherwise apply under section 13.02(b) also supports the approach in section 13.40(b)(3) not to preclude judicial review or relief in connection with such transactions, unless other strong safeguards are present. Those safeguards are drawn from the treatment of director conflicting interest transactions in sections 8.60 through 8.63. In those sections, a conflict of interest transaction may be protected if either qualified director or disinterested shareholder approval is obtained after required disclosure. Here, the protection is made available only if both those requirements are met. Absent compliance with those safeguards, the standard of review to be applied, and the extent of the relief that may be available is not addressed by this section.

The scope of section 13.40(b) is limited and does not otherwise affect applicable state law. Section 13.40(b) does not create any cause of action; it merely removes the bar to the types of post-transaction claims provided in section 13.40(a). Even then, whether the specific facts of a transaction subject to section 13.40(b) warrant invalidation or rescission is left to the discretion of the court. Similarly, section 13.40 leaves to applicable state law the question of remedies, such as injunctive relief, that may be available before the corporate action is approved by shareholders in light of other remedies that may be available after the transaction is approved or completed. Where post-shareholder approval claims outside the scope of section 13.40 are asserted, the availability of judicial review, the remedies (such as damages) that shareholders may have, and questions relating to election of remedies, will be determined by applicable state law. Section 13.40 addresses challenges only to the corporate action and does not address remedies, if any, that shareholders may have against directors or other persons as a result of the corporate action, even where subsection (b)(4) applies. See section 8.31 and the related Official Comment and the introductory Official Comment to chapter 8F under the heading "Scope of Subchapter F."

CHAPTER 14: DISSOLUTION

SUBCHAPTER A
VOLUNTARY DISSOLUTION

§ 14.01. Dissolution by Incorporators or Initial Directors

A majority of the incorporators or initial directors of a corporation that has not issued shares or has not commenced business may dissolve the corporation by delivering to the secretary of state for filing articles of dissolution that set forth:

    (a)   the name of the corporation;

    (b)   the date of its incorporation;

    (c)   either (i) that none of the corporation's shares has been issued or (ii) that the corporation has not commenced business;

    (d)   that no debt of the corporation remains unpaid;

    (e)   that the net assets of the corporation remaining after winding up have been distributed to the shareholders, if shares were issued; and

    (f)   that a majority of the incorporators or initial directors authorized the dissolution.

Cross-References

Claims against dissolved corporation, see §§ 14.06 and 14.07.

Dissolution by board of directors and shareholders, see § 14.02.

Effective date of dissolution, see § 14.03.

Effect of dissolution, see § 14.05.

Filing requirements, see § 1.20.

Incorporators, see § 2.01.

Initial directors, see § 2.05.

Revocation of dissolution, see § 14.04.

Official Comment

Under the Act, a corporation is dissolved on the effective date of its articles of dissolution. The Act uses the term "dissolution" in this specialized sense, and not to describe the final step in the liquidation of the corporate business. Section 14.05 provides that dissolution does not terminate the corporation's existence, but that section does require the corporation to wind up its affairs and liquidate.

Section 14.01 provides a simple method for voluntary dissolution if the corporation has not issued shares (even though it has commenced business) or if it has issued shares but has not commenced business. Section 14.01 takes these situations into account by requiring statements in the articles of dissolution that no debts remain unpaid and that the net assets of the corporation remaining after winding up have been distributed to the shareholders. Dissolution may be accomplished in either situation simply by a majority vote of the incorporators or initial directors.

§ 14.02. Dissolution by Board of Directors and Shareholders

(a) The board of directors may propose dissolution for submission to the shareholders by first adopting a resolution authorizing the dissolution.

(b) For a proposal to dissolve to be adopted, it shall then be approved by the shareholders. In submitting the proposal to dissolve to the shareholders for approval, the board of directors shall recommend that the shareholders approve the dissolution, unless (i) the board of directors determines that because of conflict of interest or other special circumstances it should make no recommendation or (ii) section 8.26 applies. If either (i) or (ii) applies, the board shall inform the shareholders of the basis for its so proceeding.

(c) The board of directors may set conditions for the approval of the proposal for dissolution by shareholders or the effectiveness of the dissolution.

(d) If the approval of the shareholders is to be given at a meeting, the corporation shall notify each shareholder, regardless of whether entitled to vote, of the meeting of shareholders at which the dissolution is to be submitted for approval. The notice must state that the purpose, or one of the purposes, of the meeting is to consider dissolving the corporation.

(e) Unless the articles of incorporation or the board of directors acting pursuant to subsection (c) require a greater vote, a greater quorum, or a vote by voting groups, adoption of the proposal to dissolve shall require the approval of the shareholders at a meeting at which a quorum exists consisting of a majority of the votes entitled to be cast on the proposal to dissolve.

Cross-References

Effect of dissolution, see § 14.05.

Modifying quorum or voting requirements, see § 7.27.

Notices and other communications, see § 1.41.

Notice of shareholders' meeting, see § 7.05.

Quorum at shareholders' meeting, see § 7.25.

Revocation of dissolution, see § 14.04.

Shareholder action without a meeting, see § 7.04.

Voting by voting group, see §§ 7.25 and 7.26.

Voting entitlement of shares, see § 7.21.

"Voting group" defined, see § 1.40.

Official Comment

When submitting a proposal to dissolve to shareholders, the board of directors must recommend the dissolution, subject to two exceptions in section 14.02(b). The board might exercise the exception under clause (i) where the number of directors having a conflicting interest makes it inadvisable for the board to recommend the proposal or where the board is evenly divided as to the merits of the proposal but is able to agree that shareholders should be permitted to consider it. Alternatively, the board of directors might exercise the exception under clause (ii), which recognizes that, under section 8.26, a board of directors may agree to submit a proposal to dissolve to a vote of shareholders even if, after approving the proposal, the board of directors determines that it no longer recommends the proposal.

Section 14.02(c) permits the board of directors to condition its submission to the shareholders of a proposal for dissolution or the effectiveness of the dissolution. Among the conditions that a board might impose are that the proposal will not be deemed approved unless it is approved by a specified percentage of the shareholders, or by one or more specified classes or series of shares, voting as a separate voting group, or by a specified percentage of disinterested shareholders.

Requirements concerning the timing and content of a notice of meeting, as required by section 14.02(d), are set out in section 7.05. Section 14.02(d) does not address the notice to be given to nonvoting or nonconsenting shareholders where the proposal is approved, without a meeting, by written consent. However, that requirement is imposed by section 7.04.

Section 14.02(e) sets forth the quorum and voting requirements applicable to a shareholder vote to approve a dissolution. In lieu of approval at a meeting, shareholder approval may be by written consent under the procedures set forth in section 7.04.

The Act does not mandate separate voting by voting groups or appraisal rights in relation to dissolution proposals because upon dissolution, the rights of all classes or series of shares are fixed by the articles of incorporation. Separate voting by voting groups may nevertheless be required if provided for in the articles of incorporation or by the board of directors, acting pursuant to section 14.02(c).

§ 14.03. Articles of Dissolution

(a)   At any time after dissolution is authorized, the corporation may dissolve by delivering to the secretary of state for filing articles of dissolution setting forth:

(1)   the name of the corporation;

(2)   the date that dissolution was authorized; and

(3)   if dissolution was approved by the shareholders, a statement that the proposal to dissolve was duly approved by the shareholders in the manner required by this Act and by the articles of incorporation.

(b)   The articles of dissolution shall take effect at the effective date determined in accordance with section 1.23. A corporation is dissolved upon the effective date of its articles of dissolution.

(c)   For purposes of this subchapter, "dissolved corporation" means a corporation whose articles of dissolution have become effective and includes a successor entity to which the remaining assets of the corporation are transferred subject to its liabilities for purposes of liquidation.

Cross-References

Dissolution by:

board of directors and shareholders, see § 14.02.

incorporators or initial directors, see § 14.01.

Effect of dissolution, see § 14.05.

Effective time and date of filing, see § 1.23.

Filing fees, see § 1.22.

Filing requirements, see § 1.20.

Revocation of dissolution, see § 14.04.

Voting by voting group, see §§ 7.25 and 7.26.

"Voting group" defined, see § 1.40.

Official Comment

Filing the articles of dissolution makes the decision to dissolve a matter of public record and establishes the time when the corporation must begin the process of winding up and cease carrying on its business except to the extent necessary for winding up. Under the Act, articles of dissolution may be filed at the commencement of winding up or at any time thereafter. This is the only filing required for voluntary dissolution; no filing is required to mark the completion of winding up as the existence of the corporation continues for certain purposes even after the business is wound up and the assets remaining after satisfaction of all creditors are distributed to the shareholders. No time limit for filing the articles of dissolution is specified, although filing must precede making distributions to shareholders unless there is compliance with section 6.40.

After the effective date of the articles of dissolution, the corporation is referred to as a "dissolved corporation," although its existence continues under section 14.05 for purposes of winding up. The inclusion of a successor entity within the definition of "dissolved corporation" under section 14.03(c) covers the situation where a liquidating trust or other successor liquidating entity is used to complete the liquidation.

§ 14.04. Revocation of Dissolution

(a)   A corporation may revoke its dissolution within 120 days after its effective date.

(b)   Revocation of dissolution shall be authorized in the same manner as the dissolution was authorized unless that authorization permitted revocation by action of the board of directors alone, in which event the board of directors may revoke the dissolution without shareholder action.

(c)   After the revocation of dissolution is authorized, the corporation may revoke the dissolution by delivering to the secretary of state for filing articles of revocation of dissolution, together with a copy of its articles of dissolution, that set forth:

(1)   the name of the corporation;

(2)   the effective date of the dissolution that was revoked;

(3)   the date that the revocation of dissolution was authorized;

(4)   if the corporation's board of directors (or incorporators) revoked the dissolution, a statement to that effect;

(5)   if the corporation's board of directors revoked a dissolution as authorized by the shareholders, a statement that revocation was permitted by action by the board of directors alone pursuant to that authorization; and

(6)   if shareholder action was required to revoke the dissolution, a statement that the revocation was duly approved by the shareholders in the manner required by this Act and by the articles of incorporation.

(d)   The articles of revocation of dissolution shall take effect at the effective date determined in accordance with section 1.23. Revocation of dissolution is effective upon the effective date of the articles of revocation of dissolution.

(e)   When the revocation of dissolution is effective, it relates back to and takes effect as of the effective date of the dissolution and the corporation resumes carrying on its business as if dissolution had never occurred.

Cross-References

Articles of dissolution, see § 14.03.

Dissolution by:

> board of directors and shareholders, see § 14.02.

> incorporators or initial directors, see § 14.01.

> shareholder action without a meeting, see § 7.04.

Effective date of dissolution, see § 14.03.

Effective time and date of filing, see § 1.23.

Filing requirements, see § 1.20.

Official Comment

Section 14.04 provides a procedure to revoke dissolution. Revocation generally requires the same authorization as the dissolution, although section 14.04(b) allows shareholders to authorize the board of directors to act alone in revoking dissolution. This authority could be useful, for example, in proposals to dissolve that are contingent upon the effectiveness of another transaction, such as a sale of corporate assets not in the ordinary course of business.

Articles of revocation of dissolution must be filed before resuming the business of the corporation. The information required in the articles of revocation parallels the information required in the articles of dissolution.

Effectiveness of articles of revocation of dissolution dates back to the effective date of the articles of dissolution and permits the corporation to resume its business without limitation.

§ 14.05. Effect of Dissolution

(a)   A corporation that has dissolved continues its corporate existence but the dissolved corporation may not carry on any business except that appropriate to wind up and liquidate its business and affairs, including:

> (1)   collecting its assets;

> (2)   disposing of its properties that will not be distributed in kind to its shareholders;

> (3)   discharging or making provision for discharging its liabilities;

> (4)   making distributions of its remaining assets among its shareholders according to their interests; and

> (5)   doing every other act necessary to wind up and liquidate its business and affairs.

(b)   Dissolution of a corporation does not:

> (1)   transfer title to the corporation's property;

> (2)   prevent transfer of its shares or securities;

> (3)   subject its directors or officers to standards of conduct different from those prescribed in chapter 8;

> (4)   change (i) quorum or voting requirements for its board of directors or shareholders; (ii) provisions for selection, resignation, or removal of its directors or officers or both; or (iii) provisions for amending its bylaws;

(5) prevent commencement of a proceeding by or against the corporation in its corporate name;

(6) abate or suspend a proceeding pending by or against the corporation on the effective date of dissolution; or

(7) terminate the authority of the registered agent of the corporation.

(c) A distribution in liquidation under this section may only be made by a dissolved corporation. For purposes of determining the shareholders entitled to receive a distribution in liquidation, the board of directors may fix a record date for determining shareholders entitled to a distribution in liquidation, which date may not be retroactive. If the board of directors does not fix a record date for determining shareholders entitled to a distribution in liquidation, the record date is the date the board of directors authorizes the distribution in liquidation.

Cross-References

Administrative dissolution, see §§ 14.20 through 14.23.

Claims against dissolved corporation, see §§ 14.06 and 14.07.

Deposit with state treasurer, see § 14.40.

Dissolution by:

board of directors and shareholders, see § 14.02.

incorporators or initial directors, see § 14.01.

"Dissolved corporation" defined, see § 14.03.

"Distribution" defined, see § 1.40.

Effective date of dissolution, see § 14.03.

Judicial dissolution, see §§ 14.30 through 14.34.

"Proceeding" defined, see § 1.40.

Quorum requirements:

board of directors, see § 8.24.

shareholders, see §§ 7.25 and 7.26.

Revocation of dissolution, see § 14.04.

Service on corporation, see § 5.04.

Official Comment

Although section 14.05(a) provides that dissolution does not terminate the corporate existence, it does require the corporation to wind up its affairs and liquidate its assets. After dissolution, the corporation may not carry on its business except as may be appropriate for winding up. Because distributions in liquidation that occur after dissolution are distinct from the pre-dissolution distributions governed by section 6.40, section 14.05(c) sets forth a separate provision for establishing a record date for determining shareholders entitled to receive a distribution in liquidation.

§ 14.06. Known Claims Against Dissolved Corporation

(a) A dissolved corporation may dispose of the known claims against it by notifying its known claimants in writing of the dissolution at any time after its effective date.

(b) The written notice must:

(1) describe information that must be included in a claim;

(2) provide a mailing address where a claim may be sent;

(3)   state the deadline, which may not be fewer than 120 days after the written notice is effective, by which the dissolved corporation shall receive the claim; and

(4)   state that the claim will be barred if not received by the deadline.

(c)   A claim against the dissolved corporation is barred:

(1)   if a claimant who was given written notice under subsection (b) does not deliver the claim to the dissolved corporation by the deadline; or

(2)   if a claimant whose claim was rejected by the dissolved corporation does not commence a proceeding to enforce the claim within 90 days after the rejection notice is effective.

(d)   For purposes of this section, "claim" does not include a contingent liability or a claim based on an event occurring after the effective date of dissolution.

Cross-References

Administrative dissolution, see § 14.21.

Decree of judicial dissolution, see § 14.33.

"Deliver" defined, see § 1.40.

"Dissolved corporation" defined, see § 14.03.

Effective date of dissolution, see § 14.03.

Effective date of notice, see § 1.41.

Notices and other communications, see § 1.41.

Other claims against dissolved corporation, see § 14.07.

"Proceeding" defined, see § 1.40.

Official Comment

Sections 14.06 and 14.07 provide a simplified system for handling claims against a dissolved corporation. Section 14.06 deals solely with known claims while section 14.07 deals with unknown or subsequently arising claims. Known claims may be unliquidated, but a claim that is contingent or has not yet matured (or in certain cases has matured but has not been asserted) is not a "claim" for purposes of section 14.06(d). For example, an unmatured liability under a guarantee, a potential default under a lease, or an unasserted claim based upon a defective product manufactured by the dissolved corporation would not be a "claim" under section 14.06.

Known claims are handled in section 14.06 through a process of written notice to claimants, which must provide the information described in section 14.06(b). See section 1.41 with respect to notices and communications generally. Section 14.06(c) then provides fixed deadlines by which known claims are barred under various circumstances. Section 14.06(c), however, does not bar a claim if the dissolved corporation does not act on it or fails to notify the claimant of the rejection of the claim. Section 14.07 bars certain claims not covered by section 14.06.

The principles of sections 14.06 and 14.07 do not lengthen statutes of limitation applicable under general state law. Thus, claims that are not barred under the foregoing rules—for example, if the corporation does not give notice to the claimant under section 14.06(a) or does not act on a claim—will nevertheless be subject to the general statute of limitations applicable to claims of that type. The Act does not require that a dissolved corporation take the actions set out in sections 14.06 and 14.07, but if it does not do so the protections those sections provide are not available to it.

§ 14.07. Other Claims Against Dissolved Corporation

(a)   A dissolved corporation may publish notice of its dissolution and request that persons with claims against the dissolved corporation present them in accordance with the notice.

(b)   The notice must:

(1)   be published (i) one time in a newspaper of general circulation in the county where the dissolved corporation's principal office (or, if none in this state, its registered office) is or was last located or (ii) be posted conspicuously for at least 30 days on the dissolved corporation's website;

(2)   describe the information that must be included in a claim and provide a mailing address where the claim may be sent; and

(3)   state that a claim against the dissolved corporation will be barred unless a proceeding to enforce the claim is commenced within three years after the publication of the notice.

(c)   If the dissolved corporation publishes a notice in accordance with subsection (b), the claim of each of the following claimants is barred unless the claimant commences a proceeding to enforce the claim against the dissolved corporation within three years after the publication date of the notice:

(1)   a claimant who was not given written notice under section 14.06;

(2)   a claimant whose claim was timely sent to the dissolved corporation but not acted on by the corporation;

(3)   a claimant whose claim is contingent or based on an event occurring after the effective date of dissolution.

(d)   A claim that is not barred by section 14.06(c) or section 14.07(c) may be enforced:

(1)   against the dissolved corporation, to the extent of its undistributed assets; or

(2)   except as provided in section 14.08(d), if the assets have been distributed in liquidation, against a shareholder of the dissolved corporation to the extent of the shareholder's pro rata share of the claim or the corporate assets distributed to the shareholder in liquidation, whichever is less, but a shareholder's total liability for all claims under this section may not exceed the total amount of assets distributed to the shareholder.

Cross-References

Administrative dissolution, see § 14.21.

Court proceedings, see § 14.08.

Decree of judicial dissolution, see § 14.33.

"Dissolved corporation" defined, see § 14.03.

"Distribution" defined, see § 1.40.

Effective date of dissolution, see § 14.03.

Known claims against dissolved corporation, see § 14.06.

Notices and other communications, see § 1.41.

"Principal office":

defined, see § 1.40.

designated in annual report, see § 16.21.

"Proceeding" defined, see § 1.40.

Registered office:

designated in annual report, see § 16.21.

required, see §§ 2.02 and 5.01.

Official Comment

Section 14.07 addresses the problems created by possible claims that might arise long after the dissolution process is completed and the corporate assets distributed to shareholders. One example would be claims based on personal injuries occurring after dissolution but caused by allegedly defective products sold before dissolution. The problems raised by such claims are difficult. On one hand, the application of a mechanical limitation period to a claim for injury that occurs after the period has expired may involve injustice to the plaintiff. On the other hand, to permit these suits generally makes it impossible ever to complete the winding up of the corporation, make suitable provision for creditors, and distribute the balance of the corporate assets to the shareholders.

The approach adopted in section 14.07 is to continue the liability of a dissolved corporation for subsequent claims for a period of three years after it publishes notice of dissolution. The three-year cut-off, although arbitrary, provides a reasonable compromise between the competing interests of potential injured plaintiffs, the ability of dissolved corporations to distribute remaining assets free of all claims, and the interests of shareholders in receiving those assets secure in the knowledge that they may not be reclaimed.

Directors must generally discharge or make provision for discharging the corporation's liabilities before distributing the remaining assets to the shareholders. See section 14.09(a). Under section 14.07(d)(1), unbarred claimants will continue to have recourse to the remaining assets of the dissolved corporation. Further, where unbarred claims arise after distributions have been made to shareholders in liquidation, section 14.07(d)(2) authorizes recovery against the shareholders receiving those distributions. That section limits recovery, however, to the smaller of the recipient shareholder's pro rata share of the claim or the total amount of assets received as liquidating distributions by the shareholder from the corporation. The provision encourages claimants seeking to recover distributions from shareholders to try to recover from the entire class of shareholders rather than concentrating only on the larger shareholders and protects the limited liability of shareholders. Shareholders also may be liable to directors for recoupment under section 8.32(b)(2).

§ 14.08. Court Proceedings

(a)   A dissolved corporation that has published a notice under section 14.07 may file an application with the [name or describe court] for a determination of the amount and form of security to be provided for payment of claims that are contingent or have not been made known to the dissolved corporation or that are based on an event occurring after the effective date of dissolution but that, based on the facts known to the dissolved corporation, are reasonably estimated to arise after the effective date of dissolution. Provision need not be made for any claim that is or is reasonably anticipated to be barred under section 14.07(c).

(b)   Within 10 days after the filing of the application, notice of the proceeding shall be given by the dissolved corporation to each claimant holding a contingent claim whose contingent claim is shown on the records of the dissolved corporation.

(c)   The court may appoint a guardian ad litem to represent all claimants whose identities are unknown in any proceeding brought under this section. The reasonable fees and expenses of such guardian, including all reasonable expert witness fees, shall be paid by the dissolved corporation.

(d)   Provision by the dissolved corporation for security in the amount and the form ordered by the court under section 14.08(a) shall satisfy the dissolved corporation's obligations with respect to claims that are contingent, have not been made known to the dissolved corporation or are based on an event occurring after the effective date of dissolution, and such claims may not be enforced against a shareholder who received assets in liquidation.

Cross-References

"Dissolved corporation" defined, see § 14.03.

Effective date of dissolution, see § 14.03.

Notices and other communications, see § 1.41.

"Proceeding" defined, see § 1.41.

Official Comment

Section 14.08 allows a dissolved corporation to initiate a court proceeding to establish the provision that should be made for contingent or unknown claims that are not reasonably expected to be barred after the three-year period in section 14.07(c). By following this procedure, a corporation removes the risk of director and shareholder liability for inadequate provision for claims.

Section 14.08 is designed to permit the court to adopt procedures appropriate to the circumstances. Estimates for contingent or unknown claims, such as product liability injury claims that might arise after dissolution, need only be made for those claims that the court determines are reasonably anticipated to be asserted within three years after dissolution.

The notice required by section 14.08(b) would include notice to holders of guarantees made by the corporation.

If the dissolved corporation provides for security for claims as set forth in section 14.08(d), that section protects shareholders who receive distributions against those claims, and section 14.09(b) similarly protects directors from liability for those distributions.

§ 14.09. Director Duties

(a) Directors shall cause the dissolved corporation to discharge or make reasonable provision for the payment of claims and make distributions in liquidation of assets to shareholders after payment or provision for claims.

(b) Directors of a dissolved corporation which has disposed of claims under section 14.06, 14.07, or 14.08 shall not be liable for breach of section 14.09(a) with respect to claims against the dissolved corporation that are barred or satisfied under section 14.06, 14.07 or 14.08.

Cross-References

Claims against dissolved corporation, see §§ 14.06 and 14.07.

Directors' liability for unlawful distributions, see § 8.32.

"Dissolved corporation" defined, see § 14.03.

"Distribution" defined, see § 1.40.

Notices and other communications, see § 1.41.

Proceeding to determine security for contingent claims, see § 14.08.

Official Comment

Section 14.09(a) establishes the duty of directors to discharge or make provision for claims and to make distributions of the remaining assets to shareholders. Section 14.09(b) protects directors of a dissolved corporation from liability under section 14.09(a) with respect to claims that are disposed of under section 14.06, 14.07 or 14.08. For example, directors need not make provision for claims of known creditors who are barred under section 14.06 by failure to file a claim or commence a proceeding within the specified times, for contingent claimants whose claims are barred by the three-year period after publication pursuant to section 14.07(c), or for claimants such as guarantors if provision for their claims has been approved by a court under section 14.08(d). Section 14.09(b) does not change the provision in section 8.32 that director liability is to the corporation.

SUBCHAPTER B
ADMINISTRATIVE DISSOLUTION

§ 14.20. Grounds for Administrative Dissolution

The secretary of state may commence a proceeding under section 14.21 to dissolve a corporation administratively if:

(a)　the corporation does not pay within 60 days after they are due any fees, taxes, interest or penalties imposed by this Act or other laws of this state;

(b)　the corporation does not deliver its annual report to the secretary of state within 60 days after it is due;

(c)　the corporation is without a registered agent or registered office in this state for 60 days or more;

(d)　the secretary of state has not been notified within 60 days that the corporation's registered agent or registered office has been changed, that its registered agent has resigned, or that its registered office has been discontinued; or

(e)　the corporation's period of duration stated in its articles of incorporation expires.

Cross-References

Annual report, see § 16.21.

Appeal from administrative dissolution, see § 14.23.

Duration of corporation, see § 3.02.

Judicial dissolution, see §§ 14.30 through 14.34.

Registered office and agent, see ch. 5.

Reinstatement following administrative dissolution, see § 14.22.

Official Comment

Under the Act, actual or threatened administrative dissolution is an effective enforcement mechanism for a variety of statutory obligations. The advantages of administrative dissolution in the circumstances outlined in this section are compelling: it not only reduces the number of records maintained by the secretary of state, but also avoids futile attempts to compel compliance by abandoned corporations and returns corporate names promptly to the status of available names. It is also less costly and requires fewer legal resources than judicial dissolution.

§ 14.21. Procedure for and Effect of Administrative Dissolution

(a)　If the secretary of state determines that one or more grounds exist under section 14.20 for dissolving a corporation, the secretary of state shall serve the corporation with written notice of such determination under section 5.04.

(b)　If the corporation does not correct each ground for dissolution or demonstrate to the reasonable satisfaction of the secretary of state that each ground determined by the secretary of state does not exist within 60 days after service of the notice under section 5.04, the secretary of state shall administratively dissolve the corporation by signing a certificate of dissolution that recites the ground or grounds for dissolution and its effective date. The secretary of state shall file the original of the certificate and serve a copy on the corporation under section 5.04.

(c)　A corporation administratively dissolved continues its corporate existence but may not carry on any business except that necessary to wind up and liquidate its business and affairs under section 14.05 and notify claimants under sections 14.06 and 14.07.

(d)　The administrative dissolution of a corporation does not terminate the authority of its registered agent.

Cross-References

Appeal from denial of reinstatement, see § 14.23.

Claims against dissolved corporation, see §§ 14.06 and 14.07.

Deposit with state treasurer, see § 14.40.

Perfection of service, see § 5.04.

Reinstatement following administrative dissolution, see § 14.22.

Service of process, see § 5.04.

Winding up, see § 14.05.

Official Comment

Some failures to comply with statutory requirements that give rise to administrative dissolution under section 14.20 occur because of oversight or inadvertence by officers of corporations that are carrying on business. Because such failures can usually be corrected promptly when brought to the corporation's attention, sections 14.21(a) and (b) provide for notice from the secretary of state and a 60-day grace period before the certificate of administrative dissolution is filed.

If a corporation is administratively dissolved, it may petition the secretary of state for reinstatement under section 14.22 and, if this is denied, it may appeal to the courts under section 14.23.

§ 14.22. Reinstatement Following Administrative Dissolution

(a) A corporation administratively dissolved under section 14.21 may apply to the secretary of state for reinstatement within two years after the effective date of dissolution. The application must:

(1) state the name of the corporation and the effective date of its administrative dissolution;

(2) state that the ground or grounds for dissolution either did not exist or have been eliminated;

(3) state that the corporation's name satisfies the requirements of section 4.01; and

(4) contain a certificate from the [taxing authority] reciting that all taxes owed by the corporation have been paid.

(b) If the secretary of state determines that the application contains the information required by subsection (a) and that the information is correct, the secretary of state shall cancel the certificate of dissolution and prepare a certificate of reinstatement that recites such determination and the effective date of reinstatement, file the original of the certificate, and serve a copy on the corporation under section 5.04.

(c) When the reinstatement is effective, it relates back to and takes effect as of the effective date of the administrative dissolution and the corporation resumes carrying on its business as if the administrative dissolution had never occurred.

Cross-References

Appeal from denial of reinstatement, see § 14.23.

Corporate name, see ch. 4.

Effective date of administrative dissolution, see § 14.21.

Filing requirements, see § 1.20.

Grounds for administrative dissolution, see § 14.20.

Official Comment

Section 14.22 provides a two-year period during which a corporation may seek reinstatement following administrative dissolution. This section is useful when a corporation through inadvertence or a failure to maintain a registered agent fails to receive or respond to the pre-dissolution notice of default required by section 14.21 and is administratively dissolved. A corporation that is reinstated pursuant to this section resumes carrying on its business as before dissolution.

To be eligible for reinstatement, a corporation must comply with all statutory requirements at the time it seeks reinstatement. It must establish, for example, that all taxes have been paid and that its name is available when it files the application for reinstatement.

§ 14.23. Appeal from Denial of Reinstatement

(a)   If the secretary of state denies a corporation's application for reinstatement following administrative dissolution, the secretary of state shall serve the corporation under section 5.04 with a written notice that explains the reason or reasons for denial.

(b)   The corporation may appeal the denial of reinstatement to the [name or describe court] within 30 days after service of the notice of denial is effected. The corporation appeals by petitioning the court to set aside the dissolution and attaching to the petition copies of the secretary of state's certificate of dissolution, the corporation's application for reinstatement, and the secretary of state's notice of denial.

(c)   The court may summarily order the secretary of state to reinstate the dissolved corporation or may take other action the court considers appropriate.

(d)   The court's final decision may be appealed as in other civil proceedings.

Cross-References

Grounds for administrative dissolution, see § 14.20.

Notices and other communications, see § 1.41.

Reinstatement following administrative dissolution, see § 14.22.

Service of process, see § 5.04.

Official Comment

Section 14.23 provides for an appeal from a decision by the secretary of state denying a petition for reinstatement. Because the Act does not specify who has the burden of proof on appeal and the standard for judicial review, these matters will be governed by general principles of judicial review of agency actions in this state.

SUBCHAPTER C
JUDICIAL DISSOLUTION

§ 14.30. Grounds for Judicial Dissolution

(a)   The [name or describe court or courts] may dissolve a corporation:

(1)   in a proceeding by the attorney general if it is established that:

(i)   the corporation obtained its articles of incorporation through fraud; or

(ii)   the corporation has continued to exceed or abuse the authority conferred upon it by law;

(2)   in a proceeding by a shareholder if it is established that:

(i)   the directors are deadlocked in the management of the corporate affairs, the shareholders are unable to break the deadlock, and irreparable injury to the corporation is threatened or being suffered, or the business and affairs of the corporation can no longer be conducted to the advantage of the shareholders generally, because of the deadlock;

(ii)   the directors or those in control of the corporation have acted, are acting, or will act in a manner that is illegal, oppressive, or fraudulent;

(iii)   the shareholders are deadlocked in voting power and have failed, for a period that includes at least two consecutive annual meeting dates, to elect successors to directors whose terms have expired; or

(iv)   the corporate assets are being misapplied or wasted;

(3)   in a proceeding by a creditor if it is established that:

(i)   the creditor's claim has been reduced to judgment, the execution on the judgment returned unsatisfied, and the corporation is insolvent; or

(ii)   the corporation has admitted in writing that the creditor's claim is due and owing and the corporation is insolvent;

(4)   in a proceeding by the corporation to have its voluntary dissolution continued under court supervision; or

(5)   in a proceeding by a shareholder if the corporation has abandoned its business and has failed within a reasonable time to liquidate and distribute its assets and dissolve.

(b)   Subsection (a)(2) shall not apply in the case of a corporation that, on the date of the filing of the proceeding, has a class or series of shares which is:

(i)   a covered security under section 18(b)(1)(A) or (B) of the Securities Act of 1933; or

(ii)   not a covered security, but is held by at least 300 shareholders and the shares outstanding have a market value of at least $20 million (exclusive of the value of such shares held by the corporation's subsidiaries, senior executives, directors and beneficial shareholders and voting trust beneficial owners owning more than 10% of such shares).

(c)   In subsection (a), "shareholder" means a record shareholder, a beneficial shareholder, and an unrestricted voting trust beneficial owner, and in subsection (b), "shareholder" means a record shareholder, a beneficial shareholder, and a voting trust beneficial owner.

Cross-References

Administrative dissolution, see §§ 14.20 through 14.23.

Appointment of custodian or receiver, see § 7.48.

"Beneficial owner," "record shareholder" and "unrestricted voting trust beneficial owner" defined, see § 1.40.

Director action, see §§ 8.20 through 8.24.

Election of directors, see § 8.03.

Lack of power to act, see § 3.04.

"Proceeding" defined, see § 1.40.

Purchase of shares in lieu of dissolution, see § 14.34.

Receiver or custodian, see §§ 14.31 and 14.32.

Revocation of incorporation by state, see § 2.03.

Shareholder voting, see §§ 7.25 through 7.27.

Terms of directors, see §§ 8.05 and 8.06.

Voluntary dissolution, see §§ 14.01 through 14.05.

Official Comment

Section 14.30 provides grounds for the judicial dissolution of a corporation at the request of the state, a shareholder, a creditor, or when a corporation that has commenced voluntary dissolution seeks judicial oversight. Judicial oversight may be useful to protect the corporation from suits by creditors or shareholders.

Under this section, the court has discretion as to whether dissolution is appropriate even though the specified grounds for judicial dissolution exist.

1. Involuntary Dissolution by State

Section 14.30(a)(1) provides a means by which the state may ensure compliance with the fundamentals of corporate existence and prevent abuse. That section limits the power of the state in this regard to grounds that are reasonably related to this objective.

2. Involuntary Dissolution by Shareholders

Section 14.30(a)(2) provides for involuntary dissolution at the request of a shareholder under circumstances involving deadlock or significant abuse of power by controlling shareholders or directors. Section 14.30(c) extends the ability to seek judicial dissolution under section 14.30(a)(2) to beneficial shareholders and unrestricted voting trust beneficial owners, as these persons have, or hold on behalf of others, an economic interest in the shares. The remedy of judicial dissolution is available only for shareholders of corporations that do not meet the tests in section 14.30(b). Even for those corporations to which section 14.30(a)(2) applies, however, the court can take into account the number of shareholders and the nature of the trading market for the shares in deciding whether to exercise its discretion to order dissolution. Shareholders of corporations that meet the tests of section 14.30(b) may often have the ability to sell their shares if they are dissatisfied with current management or may seek other remedies under the Act. See, for example, sections 7.48(a) and 8.09. The grounds for dissolution under section 14.30(a)(2) are broader than those required to be shown for the appointment of a custodian or receiver under section 7.48(a). The difference is attributable to the different focus of the two proceedings. Although some of the circumstances listed in 14.30(a)(2), such as deadlock, may implicate the welfare of the corporation as a whole, the primary focus is on the effect of actions by those in control on the value of the complaining shareholder's individual investment. For example, "oppressive" behavior in section 14.30(a)(2)(ii) generally describes action directed against a particular shareholder. In contrast, the focus of protection in an action to appoint a custodian or receiver under section 7.48(a) is the corporate entity, and the remedy is intended to protect the interests of all shareholders, creditors and others who may have an interest therein. In other instances, action that is "illegal" or "fraudulent" under section 14.30(a)(2)(ii) may be severely prejudicial to the interests of an individual shareholder, whereas conduct that is illegal with respect to the entire corporation may be remedied by other causes of action under the Act.

Section 14.30(a)(5) provides a basis for a shareholder to obtain involuntary dissolution in the event the corporation has abandoned its business, but those in control of the corporation have delayed unreasonably in either liquidating and distributing its assets or completing the necessary procedures to dissolve the corporation

3. Involuntary Dissolution by Creditors

Creditors may obtain involuntary dissolution only when the corporation is insolvent and only in the limited circumstances set forth in section 14.30(a)(3). Typically, a proceeding under the federal bankruptcy laws is an alternative in these situations.

4. Judicial Supervision of Dissolution

A corporation that has commenced voluntary dissolution may petition a court to supervise its dissolution. Such an action may be appropriate to permit the orderly liquidation of the corporate assets and to protect the corporation from a multitude of creditors' suits or suits by dissatisfied shareholders.

§ 14.31. Procedure for Judicial Dissolution

(a)   Venue for a proceeding by the attorney general to dissolve a corporation lies in [name or describe court]. Venue for a proceeding brought by any other party named in section 14.30(a) lies in [name or describe court].

(b)   It is not necessary to make shareholders parties to a proceeding to dissolve a corporation unless relief is sought against them individually.

(c)   A court in a proceeding brought to dissolve a corporation may issue injunctions, appoint a receiver or custodian during the proceeding with all powers and duties the court directs, take other action required to preserve the corporate assets wherever located, and carry on the business of the corporation until a full hearing can be held.

(d)   Within 10 days of the commencement of a proceeding to dissolve a corporation under section 14.30(a)(2), the corporation shall deliver to all shareholders, other than the petitioner, a notice stating that the shareholders are entitled to avoid the dissolution of the corporation by electing to purchase the petitioner's shares under section 14.34 and accompanied by a copy of section 14.34.

Cross-References

Receiver or custodian, see § 14.32.

Judicial dissolution:

grounds, see § 14.30(a)(2).

purchase of shares in lieu of, see § 14.34.

Notices and other communications, see § 1.41.

"Proceeding" defined, see § 1.40.

Official Comment

Section 14.31 designates the attorney general as the officer to bring suits for involuntary dissolution by the state. It also sets out procedures for judicial dissolution generally.

§ 14.32. Receivership or Custodianship

(a)   Unless an election to purchase has been filed under section 14.34, a court in a judicial proceeding brought to dissolve a corporation may appoint one or more receivers to wind up and liquidate, or one or more custodians to manage, the business and affairs of the corporation. The court shall hold a hearing, after notifying all parties to the proceeding and any interested persons designated by the court, before appointing a receiver or custodian. The court appointing a receiver or custodian has jurisdiction over the corporation and all of its property wherever located.

(b)   The court may appoint an individual or a domestic or foreign corporation or eligible entity as a receiver or custodian, which, if a foreign corporation or foreign eligible entity, must be registered to do business in this state. The court may require the receiver or custodian to post bond, with or without sureties, in an amount the court directs.

(c)   The court shall describe the powers and duties of the receiver or custodian in its appointing order, which may be amended from time to time. Among other powers:

(1)   the receiver (i) may dispose of all or any part of the assets of the corporation wherever located, at a public or private sale; and (ii) may sue and defend in the receiver's own name as receiver of the corporation in all courts of this state;

(2)   the custodian may exercise all of the powers of the corporation, through or in place of its board of directors, to the extent necessary to manage the affairs of the corporation in the best interests of its shareholders and creditors.

The receiver or custodian shall have such other powers and duties as the court may provide in the appointing order, which may be amended from time to time.

(d)   The court during a receivership may redesignate the receiver a custodian and during a custodianship may redesignate the custodian a receiver.

(e)   The court from time to time during the receivership or custodianship may order compensation paid and expenses paid or reimbursed to the receiver or custodian from the assets of the corporation or proceeds from the sale of the assets.

Cross-References

Appointment of custodian or receiver, see § 7.48.

"Expenses" defined, see § 1.40.

"Notice" defined, see § 1.41.

Receiver or custodian during the proceeding, see § 14.31.

Official Comment

Although the court always has discretion to appoint a receiver or custodian under section 14.31 (which would be temporary), an appointment under section 14.32 may not be made during the 90-day period the corporation or other shareholders are given in section 14.34 to file an election to purchase the shares of a shareholder who has commenced a proceeding seeking dissolution under section 14.30(a)(2). After that 90-day period has expired, the court may grant leave to file an election. If no such election is filed, or if the court declines to permit a later filing, the court may choose to appoint a receiver or custodian under section 14.32.

General statutes or rules of court may regulate the appointment of receivers or custodians and define their duties. Section 14.32 is designed to supplement these general provisions and grant the court power to take the steps it considers necessary to resolve the internal corporate problem or to effect liquidation of the corporation in an efficient manner.

§ 14.33. Decree of Dissolution

(a)　If after a hearing the court determines that one or more grounds for judicial dissolution described in section 14.30 exist, it may enter a decree dissolving the corporation and specifying the effective date of the dissolution, and the clerk of the court shall deliver a certified copy of the decree to the secretary of state for filing.

(b)　After entering the decree of dissolution, the court shall direct the winding-up and liquidation of the corporation's business and affairs in accordance with section 14.05 and the notification of claimants in accordance with sections 14.06 and 14.07.

Cross-References

Claims against a dissolved corporation, see §§ 14.06 and 14.07.

Deposit with state treasurer, see § 14.40.

Dissolution does not terminate authority of registered agent, see § 14.05.

"Proceeding" defined, see § 1.40.

Receiver or custodian, see §§ 14.31 and 14.32.

Secretary of state's filing duties, see § 1.25.

Winding up, see § 14.05.

Official Comment

A court decree ordering that a corporation be dissolved involuntarily has the same legal effect as articles of dissolution. Section 14.33 requires that the secretary of state receive and file a copy of the decree. Thereafter the corporation's business and affairs are to be wound up as provided in sections 14.05, 14.06 and 14.07.

§ 14.34. Election to Purchase in Lieu of Dissolution

(a)　In a proceeding under section 14.30(a)(2) to dissolve a corporation, the corporation may elect or, if it fails to elect, one or more shareholders may elect to purchase all shares owned by the petitioning shareholder at the fair value of the shares. An election pursuant to this section shall be irrevocable unless the court determines that it is equitable to set aside or modify the election.

(b)   An election to purchase pursuant to this section may be filed with the court at any time within 90 days after the filing of the petition under section 14.30(a)(2) or at such later time as the court in its discretion may allow. If the election to purchase is filed by one or more shareholders, the corporation shall, within 10 days thereafter, give written notice to all shareholders, other than the petitioner. The notice must state the name and number of shares owned by the petitioner and the name and number of shares owned by each electing shareholder and must advise the recipients of their right to join in the election to purchase shares in accordance with this section. Shareholders who wish to participate shall file notice of their intention to join in the purchase no later than 30 days after the effectiveness of the notice to them. All shareholders who have filed an election or notice of their intention to participate in the election to purchase thereby become parties to the proceeding and shall participate in the purchase in proportion to their ownership of shares as of the date the first election was filed, unless they otherwise agree or the court otherwise directs. After an election has been filed by the corporation or one or more shareholders, the proceeding under section 14.30(a)(2) may not be discontinued or settled, nor may the petitioning shareholder sell or otherwise dispose of his or her shares, unless the court determines that it would be equitable to the corporation and the shareholders, other than the petitioner, to permit such discontinuance, settlement, sale, or other disposition.

(c)   If, within 60 days of the filing of the first election, the parties reach agreement as to the fair value and terms of purchase of the petitioner's shares, the court shall enter an order directing the purchase of the petitioner's shares upon the terms and conditions agreed to by the parties.

(d)   If the parties are unable to reach an agreement as provided for in subsection (c), the court, upon application of any party, shall stay the proceedings under section 14.30(a)(2) and determine the fair value of the petitioner's shares as of the day before the date on which the petition under section 14.30(a)(2) was filed or as of such other date as the court deems appropriate under the circumstances.

(e)   Upon determining the fair value of the shares, the court shall enter an order directing the purchase upon such terms and conditions as the court deems appropriate, which may include payment of the purchase price in installments, where necessary in the interests of equity, provision for security to assure payment of the purchase price and any additional expenses as may have been awarded, and, if the shares are to be purchased by shareholders, the allocation of shares among them. In allocating the petitioner's shares among holders of different classes or series of shares, the court should attempt to preserve the existing distribution of voting rights among holders of different classes or series insofar as practicable and may direct that holders of a specific class or classes or series shall not participate in the purchase. Interest may be allowed at the rate and from the date determined by the court to be equitable, but if the court finds that the refusal of the petitioning shareholder to accept an offer of payment was arbitrary or otherwise not in good faith, no interest shall be allowed. If the court finds that the petitioning shareholder had probable grounds for relief under sections 14.30(a)(2)(ii) or (iv), it may award expenses to the petitioning shareholder.

(f)   Upon entry of an order under subsections (c) or (e), the court shall dismiss the petition to dissolve the corporation under section 14.30(a)(2), and the petitioning shareholder shall no longer have any rights or status as a shareholder of the corporation, except the right to receive the amounts awarded by the order of the court which shall be enforceable in the same manner as any other judgment.

(g)   The purchase ordered pursuant to subsection (e) shall be made within 10 days after the date the order becomes final.

(h)   Any payment by the corporation pursuant to an order under subsections (c) or (e), other than an award of expenses pursuant to subsection (e), is subject to the provisions of section 6.40.

Cross-References

Acquisition of own shares by corporation as distribution, see § 1.40.

"Expenses" defined, see § 1.40.

Judicial dissolution, see § 14.30.

Notice required, see § 14.31.

Official Comment

It is not always necessary to dissolve a corporation and liquidate its assets to provide relief for the situations covered in section 14.30(a)(2). Section 14.34 provides an alternative by means of which a dissolution proceeding under section 14.30(a)(2) can be terminated upon payment of the fair value of the petitioner's shares, allowing the corporation to continue in existence for the benefit of the remaining shareholders.

1.   Availability

There are two prerequisites to filing an election to purchase under section 14.34. First, a proceeding to dissolve the corporation under section 14.30(a)(2) must have been commenced. Second, the election may be made only by the corporation or by shareholders other than the shareholder who is seeking to dissolve the corporation under section 14.30(a)(2).

2.   Effect of Filing

The election to purchase is wholly voluntary, but it may only be made as a matter of right within 90 days after the filing of the petition under section 14.30(a)(2). After 90 days, leave of court is required to make an election to purchase.

Sections 14.34(a) and (b) include provisions with respect to the irrevocability of an election and the inability to discontinue a dissolution proceeding or dispose of shares following the filing of an election. These provisions are intended to reduce the risk that either the dissolution proceeding or the buyout election will be used other than in good faith, because under section 14.34 a petitioner using section 14.30(a)(2) becomes irrevocably committed to sell these shares pursuant to section 14.34 once an election is filed. The petitioning shareholder may not thereafter discontinue the dissolution proceeding or dispose of the petitioner's shares without permission of the court, which is specifically directed to consider whether such action would be equitable from the standpoint of the corporation and the other shareholders.

If the corporation or the other shareholders fail to elect to purchase the petitioner's shares within the first 90 days, they run the risk that the court will decline to accept a subsequent election and will, instead, allow the dissolution proceeding to go forward. The dissolution proceeding is not affected by the filing of an election; it will be stayed only upon an application to the court to determine the fair value of the petitioner's shares filed after the expiration of the 60-day negotiating period provided for in section 14.34(c).

Once an election is filed, it may be set aside or modified only for reasons that the court finds equitable. If the court sets aside the election, the corporation or the electing shareholders are released from their obligation to purchase the petitioner's shares. Under section 14.34(a), the court also has discretion to "modify" the election by releasing one or more electing shareholders without releasing the others.

3.   Election by Corporation or Shareholders

Because any change in the allocation of shareholdings may upset control or other arrangements that have been previously negotiated by the parties, the corporation's election to purchase is given preference during the 90-day period provided for in section 14.34(b). This preference does not affect the order of filing, and any shareholder may file an election (thus triggering the provisions of subsection (b)) as soon as the dissolution proceeding is commenced. If the corporation thereafter files an election within the 90-day period, its election takes precedence over any previously filed election by shareholders. An election by the corporation after 90 days may be filed only with the court's approval. Section 14.34 does not affect an agreement between the corporation and the other shareholders to participate jointly in the purchase of the petitioner's shares.

Section 14.34(b) requires the corporation to notify all other shareholders of their right to join in the purchase "in proportion to their ownership of shares as of the date the first election was filed." This may raise the question of whether shareholders of a class different from the class of shares owned by the petitioner may participate in the purchase. Given the wide variety of capital structures adopted by corporations, it is not possible to state a general rule that would be appropriate in all cases. Any allocation that is agreed to by the electing shareholders controls regardless of whether the other terms and conditions of the purchase are set by the parties' agreement pursuant to subsection (c) or are determined by the court pursuant to subsection (e). If electing shareholders cannot agree, the court, under subsection (e), must determine an allocation.

4. Court Order

If the parties come to terms within the 60-day negotiating period provided for in section 14.34(c), their agreement will be incorporated in an order of the court and will thereafter be enforceable as such. If the parties are unable to reach agreement, any party may apply to the court to determine the fair value of the shares. After the court makes that determination, section 14.34(e) requires it to enter an order directing the sale on such terms as the court finds appropriate. Section 14.34(e) does place some limitations on when the court may provide for installment payments or award interest or expenses and does state that the court should attempt to preserve the distribution of certain voting rights. Otherwise, the contents of the order under subsection (e) are subject to the court's discretion.

The entry of an order under section 14.34(c) or (e) requires the court to dismiss the dissolution proceeding under section 14.30(a)(2) and terminates all rights of the petitioner as a shareholder. Thus, the order also terminates all claims that the petitioner may have had in his or her capacity as a shareholder, and the value of such claims must either be asserted as part of the "fair value" of the petitioner's shares or forever lost. Under subsection (f), claims asserted by the petitioner in any nonshareholder capacity, such as claims for back wages or indemnification, are not affected by the entry of an order nor does the order affect any rights the petitioner may have as a creditor with respect to shares pledged as security for the purchase price. Otherwise, the order is enforceable only in the same manner as any other judgment, and the petitioner may not seek to reopen the proceedings in the event of a default.

After the entry of an order under section 14.34(c) or (e), the petitioner is a creditor with respect to the electing shareholders who participate in the purchase, but any payments to be made by the corporation, other than expenses awarded under section 14.34(e), fall within the definition of "distribution" and are subject to section 6.40.

SUBCHAPTER D
MISCELLANEOUS

§ 14.40. Deposit with State Treasurer

Assets of a dissolved corporation that should be transferred to a creditor, claimant, or shareholder of the corporation who cannot be found or who is not competent to receive them shall be reduced to cash and deposited with the state treasurer or other appropriate state official for safekeeping. When the creditor, claimant, or shareholder furnishes satisfactory proof of entitlement to the amount deposited, the state treasurer or other appropriate state official shall pay such person or his or her representative that amount.

Cross-References

Administrative dissolution, see § 14.20.

Claims against dissolved corporation, see §§ 14.06 and 14.07.

Judicial dissolution, see § 14.30.

Official Comment

Section 14.40 is a deposit provision, not an escheat provision. It does not provide for ultimate disposition of unclaimed funds. The handling and ultimate disposition of unclaimed funds by the state treasurer or other appropriate state official is to be determined by state law other than the Act.

CHAPTER 15: FOREIGN CORPORATIONS

§ 15.01. Governing Law

(a) The law of the jurisdiction of formation of a foreign corporation governs:

(1) the internal affairs of the foreign corporation; and

(2)   the interest holder liability of its shareholders.

(b)   A foreign corporation is not precluded from registering to do business in this state because of any difference between the law of the foreign corporation's jurisdiction of formation and the law of this state.

(c)   Registration of a foreign corporation to do business in this state does not permit the foreign corporation to engage in any business or affairs or exercise any power that a domestic corporation may not engage in or exercise in this state.

Cross-References

Application of Act to existing foreign corporation, see § 17.02.

Doing business without registration, see § 15.02.

"Foreign corporation" defined, see § 1.40.

Foreign registration statement, see § 15.03.

"Interest holder liability" defined, see § 1.40.

Powers of domestic corporation, see § 3.02.

Official Comment

Section 15.01 confirms that a foreign corporation is generally governed by the laws of its jurisdiction of formation. A foreign corporation registered in this state, however, may only engage in business or exercise powers in this state to the same extent as a domestic corporation.

§ 15.02. Registration to Do Business in This State

(a)   A foreign corporation may not do business in this state until it registers with the secretary of state under this chapter.

(b)   A foreign corporation doing business in this state may not maintain a proceeding in any court of this state until it is registered to do business in this state.

(c)   The failure of a foreign corporation to register to do business in this state does not impair the validity of a contract or act of the foreign corporation or preclude it from defending a proceeding in this state.

(d)   A limitation on the liability of a shareholder or director of a foreign corporation is not waived solely because the foreign corporation does business in this state without registering.

(e)   Section 15.01(a) applies even if a foreign corporation fails to register under this chapter.

Cross-References

Activities not constituting doing business, see § 15.05.

Foreign registration statement, see § 15.03.

"Proceeding" defined, see § 1.40.

Official Comment

Section 15.02(b) closes the courts of this state to suits brought by foreign corporations that should have registered. Section 15.02(c) makes clear, however, that the failure to register does not impair the validity of a foreign corporation's acts, and section 15.02(d) preserves the effectiveness of any liability shields applicable under the corporation's organic law. If a foreign corporation should have registered and failed to do so, it may still enforce its contracts in the courts of this state by registering.

Although section 15.02(b) prevents a foreign corporation that is not registered but should from maintaining a proceeding in this state, section 15.02(c) makes clear that the foreign corporation may still defend a proceeding. The distinction between "maintaining" and "defending" an action or proceeding is determined on the basis of whether affirmative relief is sought. Such a nonregistered foreign corporation may interpose any defense or permissive or mandatory counterclaim to defeat a claimed recovery, but may not obtain a judgment based on the counterclaim until it has registered.

§ 15.03. Foreign Registration Statement

To register to do business in this state, a foreign corporation shall deliver a foreign registration statement to the secretary of state for filing. The registration statement must be signed by the foreign corporation and state:

(a)   the corporate name of the foreign corporation and, if the name does not comply with section 4.01, an alternate name as required by section 15.06;

(b)   the foreign corporation's jurisdiction of formation;

(c)   the street and mailing addresses of the foreign corporation's principal office and, if the law of the foreign corporation's jurisdiction of formation requires the foreign corporation to maintain an office in that jurisdiction, the street and mailing addresses of that office;

(d)   the street and mailing addresses of the foreign corporation's registered office in this state and the name of its registered agent at that office;

(e)   the names and business addresses of its directors and principal officers; and

(f)   a brief description of the nature of its business to be conducted in this state.

Cross-References

Alternate name, see § 15.06.

Amendment to foreign registration statement, see § 15.04.

Annual report, see § 16.21.

Application of Act to existing qualified foreign corporation, see § 17.02.

Corporate name, see § 15.06 and ch. 4.

Filing requirements, see § 1.20.

"Principal office":

defined, see § 1.40.

designated in annual report, see § 16.21.

Registered office and agent, see ch. 5.

Official Comment

The foreign registration statement assures that certain basic information about the foreign corporation will be publicly available and that citizens of the state will have access to that information in their dealings with the foreign corporation. The foreign registration statement also provides information that facilitates service of process on the foreign corporation. A registered foreign corporation also must file an annual report as provided in section 16.21.

§ 15.04. Amendment of Foreign Registration Statement

A registered foreign corporation shall sign and deliver to the secretary of state for filing an amendment to its foreign registration statement if there is a change in:

(a)   its name or alternate name;

(b)   its jurisdiction of formation, unless its registration is deemed to have been withdrawn under section 15.08 or transferred under section 15.10; or

(c)   an address required by section 15.03(c).

Cross-References

Change of registered office or agent, see § 5.02.

Corporate name, see § 15.06 and ch. 4.

Filing requirements, see § 1.20.

Foreign registration statement, see § 15.03.

Resignation of registered agent, see § 5.03.

Official Comment

This section requires that certain information of record in the office of the secretary of state about a registered foreign corporation be kept current. Filings for changes in the foreign corporation's registered office or agent are required by sections 5.02 and 5.03, and need not be duplicated by an amendment to the registration statement.

§ 15.05. Activities Not Constituting Doing Business

(a) Activities of a foreign corporation that do not constitute doing business in this state for purposes of this chapter include:

(1) maintaining, defending, mediating, arbitrating, or settling a proceeding;

(2) carrying on any activity concerning the internal affairs of the foreign corporation, including holding meetings of its shareholders or board of directors;

(3) maintaining accounts in financial institutions;

(4) maintaining offices or agencies for the transfer, exchange, and registration of securities of the foreign corporation or maintaining trustees or depositories with respect to those securities;

(5) selling through independent contractors;

(6) soliciting or obtaining orders by any means if the orders require acceptance outside this state before they become contracts;

(7) creating or acquiring indebtedness, mortgages, or security interests in property;

(8) securing or collecting debts or enforcing mortgages or security interests in property securing the debts, and holding, protecting, or maintaining property so acquired;

(9) conducting an isolated transaction that is not in the course of similar transactions;

(10) owning, protecting and maintaining property; and

(11) doing business in interstate commerce.

(b) This section does not apply in determining the contacts or activities that may subject a foreign corporation to service of process, taxation, or regulation under the laws of this state other than this Act.

Cross-References

Corporate powers, see § 3.02.

Corporate purposes, see § 3.01.

Governing law, see § 15.01.

"Proceeding" defined, see § 1.40.

Official Comment

The Act does not attempt to formulate an exclusive definition of what constitutes doing business in this state. Rather, the concept is illustrated in a negative fashion by the non-exclusive list of examples in section 15.05(a) of activities that do not constitute doing business. In general terms, any conduct more regular, systematic, or extensive than that described in subsection (a) constitutes doing business and requires the foreign corporation to register to do business. Typical conduct requiring registration includes maintaining an office to conduct local intrastate business, selling personal property not in interstate commerce, entering into contracts relating to the local business or sales, and owning or using real estate for general purposes. The passive owning of real estate for investment purposes does not constitute doing business. See sections 15.05(a)(8) and (a)(10).

The description of "doing business" set forth in section 15.05(a) applies only under this chapter, and only to the question whether the foreign corporation's activities in this state are such that it must register under the Act. It is not applicable to other questions, such as whether the foreign corporation is amenable to service of process under state "long-arm" statutes or liable for state or local taxes. A foreign corporation that has registered (or is required to register) will generally be subject to suit and state taxation in this state, while a foreign corporation that is subject to service of process or state taxation in this state will not necessarily be required to register.

The following provides additional guidance with respect to some of the activities listed in section 15.05(a) that will not, in and of themselves, constitute doing business in this state.

1. *Engaging in Litigation and Other Proceedings*

Under section 15.05(a)(1), a foreign corporation is not doing business by maintaining, defending, mediating, arbitrating, or settling a proceeding, which as defined in section 1.40 includes civil suits and criminal, administrative, and investigatory actions. Accordingly, a foreign corporation is not doing business solely because it resorts to the courts of this state to, for example, collect indebtedness, enforce an obligation, recover possession of personal property, obtain the appointment of a receiver, intervene in a pending proceeding, bring a petition to compel arbitration, file an appeal bond, or pursue appellate remedies. Similarly, a foreign corporation is not required to register merely because it files a complaint with a governmental agency or participates in an administrative proceeding within this state.

2. *Internal Affairs*

As provided in section 15.05(a)(2), a foreign corporation does not do business in this state merely because it holds meetings of its shareholders or board of directors within this state. It also may maintain offices or agencies within this state relating solely to the transfer, exchange or registration of its securities without registering. Other activities relating to the internal affairs of the foreign corporation that do not constitute doing business under this section include having officers or representatives who reside within or are physically present in this state. While there, the officers or representatives may make executive decisions without imposing on the foreign corporation the requirement that it register, if these activities are not so regular and systematic as to cause the residence to be viewed as a business office.

3. *Sales through Independent Contractors*

Under section 15.05(a)(5), a foreign corporation need not register if it sells goods in this state through independent contractors. These transactions are viewed as transactions by the independent contractors, not by the foreign corporation itself, even if the foreign corporation sets some limits or rules for its contractors. If these limits or rules are sufficiently pervasive, however, the foreign corporation may be deemed to be selling for itself in intrastate commerce, and not through the independent contractors and therefore doing business in this state.

4. *Creating, Acquiring, or Collecting Debts*

The mere act of making a loan by a foreign corporation does not constitute doing business in the state in which the loan is made. On the same theory a foreign corporation may obtain security for the repayment of a loan, and foreclose or enforce the lien or security interest to collect the loan, without being deemed to be doing business. Similarly, a refunding or "roll over" of a loan or its adjustment or compromise does not involve doing business.

5. *Isolated Transactions*

The concept of doing business involves regular, repeated, and continuing business activities in this state. A single agreement or isolated transaction within the state does not constitute doing business. An isolated transaction does not constitute "doing business" regardless of how long the transaction takes to complete.

6.   *Interstate Transactions*

A foreign corporation is not doing business within the meaning of this chapter if it is transacting business in interstate commerce (section 15.05 (a)(11)) or soliciting or obtaining orders that must be accepted outside this state before they become contracts (section 15.05(a)(6)). These limitations reflect the provisions of the United States Constitution that grant to the United States Congress exclusive power over interstate commerce, and preclude states from imposing restrictions or conditions upon this commerce.

7.   *Other Activities*

Among other activities that do not give rise to the requirement that a registration statement be filed by a foreign corporation are the ownership of all the shares of a corporation that is engaged in activities in the state or as a limited partner in a limited partnership engaged in activities in the state, or taking ministerial actions such as filing financing statements or registering trademarks.

§ 15.06. Noncomplying Name of Foreign Corporation

(a)   A foreign corporation whose name does not comply with section 4.01 may not register to do business in this state until it adopts, for the purpose of doing business in this state, an alternate name that complies with section 4.01 by filing a foreign registration statement under section 15.03, or if applicable, a transfer of registration statement under section 15.10, setting forth that alternate name. A foreign corporation adopting an alternate name as provided in this subsection need not file under this state's assumed or fictitious name statute with respect that alternate name. After registering to do business in this state with an alternate name, a foreign corporation shall do business in this state under:

     (1)   the alternate name;

     (2)   the foreign corporation's name, with the addition of its jurisdiction of formation; or

     (3)   a name the foreign corporation is authorized to use under the assumed or fictitious name statute of this state.

(b)   If a registered foreign corporation changes its name after registration to a name that does not comply with section 4.01, it may not do business in this state until it complies with subsection (a) by amending its registration statement to adopt an alternate name that complies with section 4.01.

Cross-References

Amendment of foreign registration statement, see § 15.04.

Corporate names, see ch. 4.

Effective time and date of filing, see § 1.23.

Filing requirements, see § 1.20.

Foreign registration statement, see §15.03.

Registered name, see § 4.03.

Reserved name, see § 4.02.

Official Comment

A foreign corporation must register under its name if that name satisfies the requirements of section 4.01. If that name cannot be used because it does not comply with section 4.01, the foreign corporation may adopt and use an alternate name as provided in this section. Because the alternate name will be part of the records of the secretary of state by reason of the foreign registration statement, section 15.06(a) provides that an assumed or fictitious name filing with respect to the alternate name is not required. However, the assumed or fictitious name statute will apply to any other name under which the foreign corporation does business in this state.

A foreign corporation that registers to do business in this state may do business under a fictitious name to the same extent as a domestic corporation.

§ 15.07. Withdrawal of Registration of Registered Foreign Corporation

(a)   A registered foreign corporation may withdraw its registration by delivering a statement of withdrawal to the secretary of state for filing. The statement of withdrawal must be signed by the foreign corporation and state:

(1)   the name of the foreign corporation and its jurisdiction of formation;

(2)   that the foreign corporation is not doing business in this state and that it withdraws its registration to do business in this state;

(3)   that the foreign corporation revokes the authority of its registered agent in this state; and

(4)   an address to which process on the foreign corporation may be sent by the secretary of state under section 5.04(c).

(b)   After the withdrawal of the registration of a foreign corporation, service of process in any proceeding based on a cause of action arising during the time the entity was registered to do business in this state may be made as provided in section 5.04.

Cross-References

Administrative termination of foreign registration, see § 15.11.

Changing registered office or agent, see § 5.02.

Effective time and date of filing, see § 1.23.

Filing requirements, see § 1.20.

Foreign corporation included in definition of "corporation" for purposes of ch. 5, see § 5.01.

Registered office and agent, see ch. 5.

Resignation of registered agent, see § 5.03.

Service on foreign corporation, see § 5.04.

Official Comment

The statement of withdrawal must set forth an address where service of process may be sent to the foreign corporation by the secretary of state pursuant to section 5.04(c).

§ 15.08. Deemed Withdrawal upon Domestication or Conversion to Certain Domestic Entities

A registered foreign corporation that domesticates to a domestic business corporation or converts to a domestic nonprofit corporation or any type of domestic filing entity or to a domestic limited liability partnership is deemed to have withdrawn its registration on the effectiveness of such event.

Cross-References

Conversion, see ch. 9C.

Domestication, see ch. 9B.

"Filing entity" defined, see § 1.40.

Official Comment

When a registered foreign corporation has domesticated or converted to a domestic entity of the type set forth in this section, information about that entity in its capacity as a domestic entity will continue to be of record in the office of the secretary of state. At that point, there is no further reason for it to be registered and this section automatically treats its prior registration as withdrawn.

§ 15.09. Withdrawal upon Dissolution or Conversion to Certain Nonfiling Entities

(a)   A registered foreign corporation that has dissolved and completed winding up or has converted to a domestic or foreign nonfiling entity other than a limited liability partnership shall deliver to the secretary of state for filing a statement of withdrawal. The statement must be signed by the dissolved corporation or the converted domestic or foreign nonfiling entity and state:

(1)   in the case of a foreign corporation that has completed winding up:

(i)   its name and jurisdiction of formation;

(ii)   that the foreign corporation withdraws its registration to do business in this state and revokes the authority of its registered agent to accept service on its behalf; and

(iii)   an address to which process on the foreign corporation may be sent by the secretary of state under section 5.04(c); or

(2)   in the case of a foreign corporation that has converted to a domestic or foreign nonfiling entity other than a limited liability partnership:

(i)   the name of the converting foreign corporation and its jurisdiction of formation;

(ii)   the type of the nonfiling entity to which it has converted and its name and jurisdiction of formation;

(iii)   that it withdraws its registration to do business in this state and revokes the authority of its registered agent to accept service on its behalf; and

(iv)   an address to which process on the foreign corporation may be sent by the secretary of state under 5.04(c).

(b)   After the withdrawal of the registration of a foreign corporation, service of process in any proceeding based on a cause of action arising during the time the entity was registered to do business in this state may be made as provided in section 5.04.

Cross-References

Annual report, see § 16.21.

Change of registered agent, see § 5.02.

Conversion, see ch. 9C.

Effective time and date of filing, see § 1.23.

Filing requirements, see § 1.20.

Foreign corporation included in definition of "corporation" for purposes of ch. 5, see § 5.01.

"Nonfiling entity" defined, see § 1.40.

Registered agent, see §§ 5.01 and 5.02.

Service on foreign corporations, see § 5.04.

Official Comment

When a registered foreign corporation has dissolved and completed winding up, or has converted to a nonfiling entity other than a limited liability partnership, there is no further reason for information about it to appear in the records of the secretary of state. This section thus requires delivery of a statement of withdrawal for the purpose of removing the entity from the rolls of active entities.

§ 15.10. Transfer of Registration

(a)   If a registered foreign corporation merges into a nonregistered foreign corporation or converts to a foreign corporation required to register with the secretary of state to do business in this state, the foreign corporation shall deliver to the secretary of state for filing a transfer of registration statement. The transfer of registration statement must be signed by the surviving or converted foreign corporation and state:

(1)   the name of the registered foreign corporation and its jurisdiction of formation before the merger or conversion;

(2)   the name of the surviving or converted foreign corporation and its jurisdiction of formation after the merger or conversion and, if the name does not comply with section 4.01, an alternate name adopted pursuant to section 15.06; and

(3)   the following information regarding the surviving or converted foreign corporation after the merger or conversion:

(i)   the street and mailing addresses of the principal office of the foreign corporation and, if the law of the foreign corporation's jurisdiction of formation requires it to maintain an office in that jurisdiction, the street and mailing addresses of that office; and

(ii)   the street and mailing addresses of the foreign corporation's registered office in this state and the name of its registered agent at that office.

(b)   On the effective date of a transfer of registration statement as determined in accordance with section 1.23, the registration of the registered foreign corporation to do business in this state is transferred without interruption to the foreign corporation into which it has merged or to which it has been converted.

Cross-References

Annual report, see § 16.21.

Corporate name, see ch. 4.

Notices and other communications, see § 1.41.

"Principal office":

defined, see § 1.40.

designated in annual report, see § 16.21.

Service on foreign corporation, see § 5.04.

Official Comment

The purpose of this section is to clarify the status of the merged or converted registered foreign corporation in the public records of this state, and to reflect the status of the surviving or converted foreign corporation as a registered foreign corporation. A filing under this section has the effect of canceling the authority of the foreign corporation to do business in this state while at the same time reregistering it as the new foreign corporation. If the reregistered foreign corporation subsequently wishes to withdraw its registration to do business in this state, it may do so under section 15.07.

§ 15.11. Administrative Termination of Registration

(a)   The secretary of state may terminate the registration of a registered foreign corporation in the manner provided in subsections (b) and (c) if:

(1)   the foreign corporation does not pay within 60 days after they are due any fees, taxes, interest or penalties imposed by this Act or other laws of this state;

(2)   the foreign corporation does not deliver its annual report to the secretary of state within 60 days after it is due;

(3)   the foreign corporation is without a registered agent or registered office in this state for 60 days or more; or

(4)   the secretary of state has not been notified within 60 days that the foreign corporation's registered agent or registered office has been changed, that its registered agent has resigned, or that its registered office has been discontinued.

(b)   The secretary of state may terminate the registration of a registered foreign corporation by:

(1)   filing a certificate of termination; and

(2)   delivering a copy of the certificate of termination to the foreign corporation's registered agent or, if the foreign corporation does not have a registered agent, to the foreign corporation's principal office.

(c)   The certificate of termination must state:

(1)   the effective date of the termination, which must be not less than 60 days after the secretary of state delivers the copy of the certificate of termination as prescribed in subsection (b)(2); and

(2)   the grounds for termination under subsection (a).

(d)   The registration of a registered foreign corporation to do business in this state ceases on the effective date of the termination as set forth in the certificate of termination, unless before that date the foreign corporation cures each ground for termination stated in the certificate of termination. If the foreign corporation cures each ground, the secretary of state shall file a statement that the certificate of termination is withdrawn.

(e)   After the effective date of the termination as set forth in the certificate of termination, service of process in any proceeding based on a cause of action arising during the time the entity was registered to do business in this state may be made as provided in section 5.04.

Cross-References

Annual report, see § 16.21.

Activities not constituting doing business, see § 15.05.

Change of registered office or agent, see § 5.02.

"Deliver" defined, see § 1.40.

Effective time and date of filing, see § 1.23.

Foreign corporation included in definition of "corporation" for purposes of ch. 5, see § 5.01.

"Principal office" defined, see § 1.40.

Registered office and agent required, see § 5.01.

Resignation of registered agent, see § 5.01.

Service on foreign corporation, see § 5.04.

Official Comment

This section describes the circumstances under and manner in which the secretary of state may terminate the registration of a foreign corporation.

§ 15.12. Action by [Attorney General]

The [attorney general] may maintain an action to enjoin a foreign corporation from doing business in this state in violation of this Act.

Cross-References

Activities not constituting doing business in this state, see § 15.05.

Official Comment

Although the Act provides no fines or penalties for failure to register to do business when required, this section confirms that the [attorney general] can nevertheless bring an action to enforce the laws of the state.

CHAPTER 16: RECORDS AND REPORTS

SUBCHAPTER A
RECORDS

§ 16.01. Corporate Records

(a)   A corporation shall maintain the following records:

(1)   its articles of incorporation as currently in effect;

(2)   any notices to shareholders referred to in section 1.20(k)(5) specifying facts on which a filed document is dependent if those facts are not included in the articles of incorporation or otherwise available as specified in section 1.20(k)(5);

(3)   its bylaws as currently in effect;

(4)   all written communications within the past three years to shareholders generally;

(5)   minutes of all meetings of, and records of all actions taken without a meeting by, its shareholders, its board of directors, and board committees established under section 8.25;

(6)   a list of the names and business addresses of its current directors and officers; and

(7)   its most recent annual report delivered to the secretary of state under section 16.21.

(b)   A corporation shall maintain all annual financial statements prepared for the corporation for its last three fiscal years (or such shorter period of existence) and any audit or other reports with respect to such financial statements.

(c)   A corporation shall maintain accounting records in a form that permits preparation of its financial statements.

(d)   A corporation shall maintain a record of its current shareholders in alphabetical order by class or series of shares showing the address of, and the number and class or series of shares held by, each shareholder. Nothing contained in this subsection shall require the corporation to include in such record the electronic mail address or other electronic contact information of a shareholder.

(e)   A corporation shall maintain the records specified in this section in a manner so that they may be made available for inspection within a reasonable time.

Cross-References

Annual report of corporation, see § 16.21.

Articles of incorporation, see § 2.02.

Articles of amendment, see § 10.06.

Bylaws, see § 2.06 and ch. 10B.

Committees of board of directors, see § 8.25.

Directors' action without meeting, see § 8.21.

Inspection of corporate records, see §§ 16.02 and 16.04.

Meetings of board of directors, see § 8.20.

Officers, see § 8.40.

Restated articles of incorporation, see § 10.07.

Series of shares, see §§ 6.01 and 6.02.

Shareholders' action without meeting, see § 7.04.

Shareholders' meeting, see §§ 7.01 through 7.03.

Shareholders' voting list, see § 7.20.

Official Comment

1.　Records to be Maintained

Section 16.01(a) requires certain basic records to be maintained by the corporation. The Act does not generally specify how records must be maintained (other than in a manner so that they may be made available for inspection within a reasonable time), where they must be located or, with the exception of section 16.02(a), where they must be available. They may be maintained in one or more offices within or without the state and in some cases, such as shareholder records, may be maintained by agents of the corporation; indeed, in the case of records in intangible form, it may be impossible to determine where they are located.

2.　Minutes and Related Documents

Section 16.01(a) does not address the amount of detail that should appear in minutes or written actions. Minutes of meetings customarily include the formalities of notice, the time and place of the meeting, those in attendance, and the results of any votes. Minutes of meetings and written actions without a meeting show formal action taken. The extent to which further detail is included is a matter of judgment which may depend upon the circumstances. Section 7.04, which addresses written actions taken by shareholders, requires that written consents by shareholders be delivered to the corporation for filing with corporate records.

3.　Financial Statements and Accounting Records

The Act does not provide normative standards for the financial statements and accounting records to be prepared or maintained. The financial statements to be maintained under section 16.01(b) are those that the corporation prepares in the operation of its business, including in response to third party requirements. The form of the financial statements prepared by a corporation depends to some extent on the nature and complexity of the corporation's business and third party requirements such as those governing the preparation and filing of tax returns with applicable tax authorities. To accommodate the needs of the many different types of business corporations that may be subject to these provisions, including closely held corporations, the Act does not require that the corporation prepare and maintain financial statements on the basis of generally accepted accounting principles ("GAAP") if it is not otherwise required to prepare GAAP financial statements. The Act does not define what accounting records must be maintained or mandate how long they must be maintained. The accounting records to be maintained under section 16.01(c) depend upon the form of the corporation's financial statements. For example, annual tax returns filed with the relevant taxing authorities may be the only annual financial statements prepared by small businesses operating on a cash basis and, in those instances, the requisite accounting records to be maintained might consist of only a check register, vouchers and receipts.

4.　Shareholders' Lists

Section 16.01(d) requires the corporation to maintain such records of its shareholders as will permit it to compile a list of current shareholders when required. These records may vary from stubs from which certificates have been detached in the case of corporations with a few shareholders to elaborate electronic data in the case of large corporations whose shares are publicly traded. The record may be maintained by the corporation or an agent, who traditionally is the transfer agent but may be another agent. A corporation may maintain additional information regarding its shareholders, such as a list of nominees and nonobjecting beneficial owners if its shares are publicly traded.

§ 16.02. Inspection Rights of Shareholders

(a)   A shareholder of a corporation is entitled to inspect and copy, during regular business hours at the corporation's principal office, any of the records of the corporation described in section 16.01(a), excluding minutes of meetings of, and records of actions taken without a meeting by, the corporation's board of directors and board committees established under section 8.25, if the shareholder gives the corporation a signed written notice of the shareholder's demand at least five business days before the date on which the shareholder wishes to inspect and copy.

(b)   A shareholder of a corporation is entitled to inspect and copy, during regular business hours at a reasonable location specified by the corporation, any of the following records of the corporation if the shareholder meets the requirements of subsection (c) and gives the corporation a signed written notice of the shareholder's demand at least five business days before the date on which the shareholder wishes to inspect and copy:

    (1)   the financial statements of the corporation maintained in accordance with section 16.01(b);

    (2)   accounting records of the corporation;

    (3)   excerpts from minutes of any meeting of, or records of any actions taken without a meeting by, the corporation's board of directors and board committees maintained in accordance with section 16.01(a); and

    (4)   the record of shareholders maintained in accordance with section 16.01(d).

(c)   A shareholder may inspect and copy the records described in subsection (b) only if:

    (1)   the shareholder's demand is made in good faith and for a proper purpose;

    (2)   the shareholder's demand describes with reasonable particularity the shareholder's purpose and the records the shareholder desires to inspect; and

    (3)   the records are directly connected with the shareholder's purpose.

(d)   The corporation may impose reasonable restrictions on the confidentiality, use or distribution of records described in subsection (b).

(e)   For any meeting of shareholders for which the record date for determining shareholders entitled to vote at the meeting is different than the record date for notice of the meeting, any person who becomes a shareholder subsequent to the record date for notice of the meeting and is entitled to vote at the meeting is entitled to obtain from the corporation upon request the notice and any other information provided by the corporation to shareholders in connection with the meeting, unless the corporation has made such information generally available to shareholders by posting it on its website or by other generally recognized means. Failure of a corporation to provide such information does not affect the validity of action taken at the meeting.

(f)   The right of inspection granted by this section may not be abolished or limited by a corporation's articles of incorporation or bylaws.

(g)   This section does not affect:

    (1)   the right of a shareholder to inspect records under section 7.20 or, if the shareholder is in litigation with the corporation, to the same extent as any other litigant; or

    (2)   the power of a court, independently of this Act, to compel the production of corporate records for examination and to impose reasonable restrictions as provided in section 16.04(c), provided that, in the case of production of records described in subsection (b) of this section at the request of a shareholder, the shareholder has met the requirements of subsection (c).

(h)   For purposes of this section, "shareholder" means a record shareholder, a beneficial shareholder, and an unrestricted voting trust beneficial owner.

Cross-References

Articles of incorporation, see § 2.02.

"Beneficial owner," "record shareholder" and "unrestricted voting trust beneficial owner" defined, see § 1.40.

Bylaws, see § 2.06 and ch. 10B.

Committees of board of directors, see § 8.25.

Corporate records, see § 16.01.

Court-ordered inspection, see § 16.04.

"Deliver" defined, see § 1.40.

Directors' action without meeting, see § 8.21.

Effective date of notice, see § 1.41.

Meeting of board of directors, see § 8.20.

Notices and other communications, see § 1.41.

"Principal office":

> defined, see § 1.40.
>
> designated in annual report, see § 16.21.

"Shareholder" defined, see § 1.40.

Shareholders' action without meeting, see § 7.04.

Shareholders' list inspection, see § 7.20.

Shareholders' meeting, see §§ 7.01 through 7.03.

Voting trusts, see § 7.30.

Official Comment

1.   Section 16.02(a)

Under section 16.02(a), each shareholder is entitled to inspect all documents that deal with the shareholder's interest in the corporation. The right to inspection includes the right to make copies, as further described in section 16.03. Although some of these documents may also be a matter of public record in the office of the secretary of state, a shareholder should not be compelled to go to a public office that may be physically distant to examine the basic documents relating to the corporation. The "principal office" of the corporation is defined in section 1.40 to be the location of the executive offices of the corporation at its address as set forth by the corporation in its annual report required by section 16.21.

2.   Section 16.02(b)

In contrast to the right to inspect minutes of meetings of, and written actions taken without a meeting by, shareholders, a shareholder is entitled to inspect only excerpts of meetings of, and records of written actions taken by, the board of directors and board committees related to the purpose of the inspection. A shareholder is entitled to inspect the record of shareholders under section 16.02(b) without regard to the size or value of the shareholder's holding. This right is independent of the right to inspect a shareholders' list under section 7.20.

3.   Section 16.02(c)

Section 16.02(c) permits inspection of the financial statements and records described in section 16.02(b) by a shareholder only if the demand is made in good faith and for a "proper purpose." Although not defined in the Act, "proper purpose" under section 16.02(c) has been defined in case law to involve a purpose that is reasonably relevant to the demanding shareholder's interest as a shareholder.

Section 16.02(c) requires that a shareholder designate "with reasonable particularity" the purpose for the demand and the records he or she desires to inspect. Also, the records demanded must be "directly connected" with that purpose. If disputed by the corporation, the "connection" of the records to the shareholder's purpose may be determined by a court's examination of the records.

4. Section 16.02(d)

The reasonable restrictions on the confidentiality, use or distribution of financial statements and records permitted by section 16.02(d) allow for the protection of confidential or proprietary information in the corporation's records or sensitive matters that might be disclosed in a shareholder inspection. Such restrictions might include, for example, requiring the demanding shareholder to sign a confidentiality and use agreement. A similar provision is found in section 16.04(d) in connection with court ordered inspections.

5. Section 16.02(e)

Section 16.02(e) provides shareholders of a corporation the right to receive from the corporation the notice and other information provided by the corporation to shareholders in connection with a meeting if the record date for voting is subsequent to the record date for notice and the shareholder became entitled to vote after the record date for notice. This provision does not apply to information provided to shareholders by persons other than the corporation.

6. Sections 16.02(f) and (g)

The prohibition in section 16.02(f) does not apply to a shareholder agreement permissible under section 7.32. No inference should be drawn from the prohibition in section 16.02(f) as to whether other, unrelated sections of the Act may be modified by provisions in the articles of incorporation or bylaws.

Section 16.02(g) preserves whatever independent rights of inspection exist under the referenced sources and does not create any rights, either expressly or by implication. A shareholder also has the right to obtain financial statements under section 16.20.

§ 16.03. Scope of Inspection Right

(a)   A shareholder may appoint an agent or attorney to exercise the shareholder's inspection and copying rights under section 16.02.

(b)   The corporation may, if reasonable, satisfy the right of a shareholder to copy records under section 16.02 by furnishing to the shareholder copies by photocopy or other means chosen by the corporation, including furnishing copies through an electronic transmission.

(c)   The corporation may comply at its expense with a shareholder's demand to inspect the record of shareholders under section 16.02(b)(4) by providing the shareholder with a list of shareholders that was compiled no earlier than the date of the shareholder's demand.

(d)   The corporation may impose a reasonable charge to cover the costs of providing copies of documents to the shareholder, which may be based on an estimate of such costs.

Cross-References

Corporate records, see § 16.01.

Court-ordered inspection, see § 16.04.

"Electronic transmission" defined, see § 1.40.

Inspection right, see § 16.02.

Shareholders' list inspection, see § 7.20.

Official Comment

Section 16.03(a) provides that the rights of inspection and copying granted to shareholders in section 16.02 may be exercised by agents and attorneys of shareholders appointed by shareholders to conduct such inspection and copying. Providing the corporation with the right to choose among alternative delivery methods for copies in section 16.03(b), including by electronic transmissions, is intended to reduce burdens on the corporation. No consent by the shareholder is required under section 1.41 for the corporation to furnish copies to the shareholder under section 16.03 by electronic transmission.

Section 16.03(c) gives the corporation, at its option and expense, the right to provide a list of its shareholders instead of granting the right of inspection. Such a list must be compiled no earlier than the date of the written demand.

Section 16.03(d) permits the corporation to be reimbursed for the expense of providing copies of documents to a shareholder.

§ 16.04. Court-Ordered Inspection

(a)   If a corporation does not allow a shareholder who complies with section 16.02(a) to inspect and copy any records required by that section to be available for inspection, the [name or describe court] may summarily order inspection and copying of the records demanded at the corporation's expense upon application of the shareholder.

(b)   If a corporation does not within a reasonable time allow a shareholder who complies with section 16.02(b) to inspect and copy the records required by that section, the shareholder who complies with section 16.02(c) may apply to the [name or describe court] for an order to permit inspection and copying of the records demanded. The court shall dispose of an application under this subsection on an expedited basis.

(c)   If the court orders inspection and copying of the records demanded under section 16.02(b), it may impose reasonable restrictions on their confidentiality, use or distribution by the demanding shareholder and it shall also order the corporation to pay the shareholder's expenses incurred to obtain the order unless the corporation establishes that it refused inspection in good faith because the corporation had:

(1)   a reasonable basis for doubt about the right of the shareholder to inspect the records demanded; or

(2)   required reasonable restrictions on the confidentiality, use or distribution of the records demanded to which the demanding shareholder had been unwilling to agree.

Cross-References

Corporate records, see § 16.01.

"Expenses" defined, see § 1.40.

Service on corporation, see § 5.04.

Shareholders' list inspection, see § 7.20.

Voluntary inspection, see § 16.02.

Official Comment

Section 16.04 provides a judicial remedy if a corporation refuses to grant the right of inspection provided by section 16.02.

If the right of inspection under section 16.02(a) is invoked and the corporation refuses to grant inspection, the shareholder may seek a summary order compelling inspection at the corporation's expense. A summary order is appropriate since the right of inspection under section 16.02(a) is either automatic or subject only to a determination that the person is in fact a shareholder of the corporation. By contrast, if inspection is demanded under section 16.02(b), a number of matters may be at issue, including the shareholder's good faith and proper purpose for demands under section 16.02(c) or the reasonableness of the restrictions required by the corporation on the confidentiality, use or distribution of the records. Accordingly, section 16.04(b) directs the court to handle the proceeding "on an expedited basis" instead of in a summary proceeding. The purpose of this phrase is to discourage dilatory tactics to avoid or delay inspection without requiring the court to resolve these issues on a summary basis.

The principal sanction against unreasonable delay or refusal to grant inspection is provided by section 16.04(c), which imposes on the corporation the shareholder's expenses to obtain the order unless the corporation establishes that it refused inspection in good faith on the grounds specified in section 16.04(c)(1) or (2). For example, a corporation may point to conduct of the shareholder involving improper use of information obtained from the corporation in the past as indicating that reasonable doubt existed as to the shareholder's present purpose or by showing that the corporation refused inspection because the shareholder had been unwilling to agree to reasonable restrictions on the confidentiality, use or distribution of records demanded under section 16.02(b).

§ 16.05. Inspection Rights of Directors

(a)   A director of a corporation is entitled to inspect and copy the books, records and documents of the corporation at any reasonable time to the extent reasonably related to the performance of the director's duties as a director, including duties as a member of a board committee, but not for any other purpose or in any manner that would violate any duty to the corporation.

(b)   The [name or describe court] may order inspection and copying of the books, records and documents at the corporation's expense, upon application of a director who has been refused such inspection rights, unless the corporation establishes that the director is not entitled to such inspection rights. The court shall dispose of an application under this subsection on an expedited basis.

(c)   If an order is issued, the court may include provisions protecting the corporation from undue burden or expense, and prohibiting the director from using information obtained upon exercise of the inspection rights in a manner that would violate a duty to the corporation, and may also order the corporation to reimburse the director for the director's expenses incurred in connection with the application.

Cross-References

Corporate records, see § 16.01.

Court-ordered inspection, see § 16.04.

"Expenses" defined, see § 1.40.

Official Comment

The purpose of section 16.05(a) is to confirm the principle that a director always is entitled to inspect books, records and documents to the extent reasonably related to the performance of the director's duties, provided that the requested inspection is not for an improper purpose and the director's use of the information obtained would not violate any duty to the corporation. In addition, section 16.05 sets forth a remedy for the director in circumstances where the corporation improperly denies the right of inspection.

Section 16.05(b) provides for a court order on an expedited basis because there is a presumption that significant latitude and discretion should be granted to the director, and the corporation has the burden of establishing that the director is not entitled to inspection of the documents requested. There may be circumstances where the director's inspection right might be denied, for example, when it would be contrary to the interest of the corporation because of adversity with the director, and the courts have broad discretion to address these circumstances. Section 16.05 does not directly deal with the ability of a director to inspect records of a subsidiary of which he or she is not also a director. A director's ability to inspect records of a subsidiary generally should be exercised through the parent's rights or power and section 16.05(a) does not independently provide that right or power to a director of the parent. In the case of wholly-owned subsidiaries, a director's ability to inspect should approximate his or her rights with respect to the parent.

SUBCHAPTER B
REPORTS

§ 16.20. Financial Statements for Shareholders

(a)　Upon the written request of a shareholder, a corporation shall deliver or make available to such requesting shareholder by posting on its website or by other generally recognized means annual financial statements for the most recent fiscal year of the corporation for which annual financial statements have been prepared for the corporation. If financial statements have been prepared for the corporation on the basis of generally accepted accounting principles for such specified period, the corporation shall deliver or make available such financial statements to the requesting shareholder. If the annual financial statements to be delivered or made available to the requesting shareholder are audited or otherwise reported upon by a public accountant, the report shall also be delivered or made available to the requesting shareholder.

(b)　A corporation shall deliver, or make available and provide written notice of availability of, the financial statements required under subsection (a) to the requesting shareholder within five business days of delivery of such written request to the corporation.

(c)　A corporation may fulfill its responsibilities under this section by delivering the specified financial statements, or otherwise making them available, in any manner permitted by the applicable rules and regulations of the United States Securities and Exchange Commission.

(d)　Notwithstanding the provisions of subsections (a), (b) and (c) of this section:

(1)　as a condition to delivering or making available financial statements to a requesting shareholder, the corporation may require the requesting shareholder to agree to reasonable restrictions on the confidentiality, use and distribution of such financial statements; and

(2)　the corporation may, if it reasonably determines that the shareholder's request is not made in good faith or for a proper purpose, decline to deliver or make available such financial statements to that shareholder.

(e)　If a corporation does not respond to a shareholder's request for annual financial statements pursuant to this section in accordance with subsection (b) within five business days of delivery of such request to the corporation:

(1)　The requesting shareholder may apply to the [name or describe court] for an order requiring delivery of or access to the requested financial statements. The court shall dispose of an application under this subsection on an expedited basis.

(2)　If the court orders delivery or access to the requested financial statements, it may impose reasonable restrictions on their confidentiality, use or distribution.

(3)　In such proceeding, if the corporation has declined to deliver or make available such financial statements because the shareholder had been unwilling to agree to restrictions proposed by the corporation on the confidentiality, use and distribution of such financials statements, the corporation shall have the burden of demonstrating that the restrictions proposed by the corporation were reasonable.

(4)　In such proceeding, if the corporation has declined to deliver or make available such financial statements pursuant to section 16.20(d)(2), the corporation shall have the burden of demonstrating that it had reasonably determined that the shareholder's request was not made in good faith or for a proper purpose.

(5)　If the court orders delivery or access to the requested financial statements it shall order the corporation to pay the shareholder's expenses incurred to obtain such order unless the corporation establishes that it had refused delivery or access to the requested financial statements because the shareholder had refused to agree to reasonable restrictions on the confidentiality, use or distribution of the financial statements or that the corporation had reasonably determined that the shareholder's request was not made in good faith or for a proper purpose.

Cross-References

"Deliver" defined, see § 1.40.

"Expenses" defined, see § 1.40.

Inspection of records, see § 16.02.

Notices and other communications, see § 1.41.

"Shareholder" defined, see § 1.40.

Shareholder agreements, see § 7.32.

Official Comment

1. *Section 16.20(a)*

Although section 16.20 requires a corporation, upon the written request of a shareholder, to deliver or make available annual financial statements that have been prepared, it does not require a corporation to prepare financial statements. This recognizes that many small, closely held corporations do not regularly prepare formal financial statements unless required by banks, suppliers or other third parties.

Section 16.20 does not limit the financial statements to be delivered or made available to shareholders to financial statements prepared on the basis of generally accepted accounting principles. Many small corporations have never prepared financial statements on the basis of GAAP. "Cash basis" financial statements (often used in preparing the tax returns of small corporations) do not comply with GAAP. Smaller corporations that keep accrual basis records, and file their federal income tax returns on that basis, frequently do not make the adjustments that may be required to present their financial statements on a GAAP basis. Internally or externally prepared financial statements prepared on the basis of other accounting practices and principles that are reasonable in the circumstances, including tax returns filed with the U.S. Internal Revenue Service (if that is all that is prepared), will suffice for these types of corporations and they may satisfy their obligations under section 16.20 by delivering or making available the requested financial statements in whatever form that they have been prepared for other purposes. If a corporation does prepare financial statements on a GAAP basis for any purpose for the particular year, however, it must send or make available those statements to the requesting shareholder as provided by section 16.20(a).

The last sentence of section 16.20(a) requires that if the financial statements to be delivered or made available have been reported upon by a public accountant, that report must be furnished. Section 16.20(a) refers to a "public accountant." The same terminology is used in section 8.30 (standards of conduct for directors). In various states different terms are employed to identify those persons who are permitted under the state licensing requirements to act as professional accountants. Phrases like "independent public accountant," "certified public accountant," "public accountant," and others may be used. In adopting the term "public accountant," the Act uses the words in a general sense to refer to any class or classes of persons who, under the applicable requirements of a particular jurisdiction, are professionally entitled to practice accountancy.

Failure to comply with the requirements of section 16.20 does not adversely affect the existence or good standing of the corporation. Rather, failure to comply gives an aggrieved shareholder rights to compel compliance or to obtain damages, if they can be established, under general principles of law.

A shareholder may also seek access to the financial statements of the corporation through the inspection rights established in section 16.02.

2. *Section 16.20(d)*

In establishing restrictions with respect to confidentiality, use or distribution that are reasonable under the circumstances, a corporation may consider a number of factors, including the potential competitive harm to the corporation and its other shareholders that could result if the confidential financial information were used to compete with the corporation or disclosed to third parties such as competitors. As provided in section 16.20(d)(2), a corporation may withhold delivery or making available its financial statements to a requesting shareholder if it reasonably determines that the shareholder's request is not made in good faith and for a proper purpose.

3.   *Section 16.20(e)*

If a corporation fails to comply with section 16.20(b) in a timely manner the judicial remedy of 16.20(e) directs the court to handle the proceeding on an expedited basis to discourage dilatory tactics to avoid or delay delivery or access to financial statements, but does not require the court to resolve these issues on a summary basis. Section 16.20(e), like section 16.04, establishes a sanction against unreasonable delay or refusal to deliver or provide access to financial statements by imposing on the corporation the shareholder's expenses in obtaining the court's order unless the corporation can establish that the shareholder had been unwilling to agree to reasonable restrictions on the confidentiality, use or distribution of the requested financial statements or the corporation had reasonably determined that the shareholder's request was not made in good faith or for a proper purpose.

§ 16.21. Annual Report for Secretary of State

(a)   Each domestic corporation shall deliver to the secretary of state for filing an annual report that sets forth:

(1)   the name of the corporation;

(2)   the street and mailing address of its registered office and the name of its registered agent at that office in this state;

(3)   the street and mailing address of its principal office;

(4)   the names and business addresses of its directors and principal officers;

(5)   a brief description of the nature of its business;

(6)   the total number of authorized shares, itemized by class and series, if any, within each class; and

(7)   the total number of issued and outstanding shares, itemized by class and series, if any, within each class.

(b)   Each foreign corporation registered to do business in this state shall deliver to the secretary of state for filing an annual report that sets forth:

(1)   the name of the foreign corporation and, if the name does not comply with section 4.01, an alternate name as required by section 15.06;

(2)   the foreign corporation's jurisdiction of formation;

(3)   the street and mailing addresses of the foreign corporation's principal office and, if the law of the foreign corporation's jurisdiction of formation requires the foreign corporation to maintain an office in that jurisdiction, the street and mailing addresses of that office;

(4)   the street and mailing addresses of the foreign corporation's registered office in this state and the name of its registered agent at that office;

(5)   the names and business addresses of its directors and principal officers; and

(6)   a brief description of the nature of its business conducted in this state.

(c)   Information in the annual report must be current as of the date the annual report is signed on behalf of the corporation.

(d)   The first annual report shall be delivered to the secretary of state between January 1 and April 1 of the year following the calendar year in which a domestic corporation was incorporated or a foreign corporation was registered to do business. Subsequent annual reports shall be delivered to the secretary of state between January 1 and April 1 of the following calendar years.

(e)   If an annual report does not contain the information required by this section, the secretary of state shall promptly notify the reporting domestic or foreign corporation in writing and return the report to it for correction. If the report is corrected to contain the information required by this section and delivered to the secretary of state within 30 days after the notice from the secretary of state becomes effective as determined in accordance with section 1.41, it is deemed to be timely filed.

Cross-References

Administrative termination of registration to do business, see § 15.11.

Annual report form prescribed by secretary of state, see § 1.21.

Authorized shares, see § 2.02.

Effective time and date of filing, see § 1.23.

Filing fees, see § 1.22.

Filing requirements, see § 1.20.

Grounds for administrative dissolution, see § 14.20.

Issuance of shares, see §§ 6.01 through 6.03.

Notices and other communications, see § 1.41.

Officers, see § 8.40.

"Principal office" defined, see § 1.40.

Registered agent and registered office, see § 5.01.

Official Comment

The purpose of the annual report by a domestic corporation is to show the location of the principal office of the corporation, the names and business addresses of its directors and principal officers, the general nature of the corporation's business, and its capital structure. It permits members of the general public to ascertain the identity of the corporation and communicate directly with it. It also establishes the alternative to the registered office for service of process and related matters. The "principal office" of the corporation is defined in section 1.40 as the location of its principal executive offices as set forth in its annual report or foreign registration statement.

The reference to "principal officers" in sections 16.21(a)(4) and (b)(5) simplifies reporting requirements of corporations with very large numbers of employees who have some managerial responsibility and who, for business reasons, are designated as officers. The "principal officers" of a corporation include at least the chair of the board of directors, the chief executive officer, and the officers performing the traditional functions performed by the secretary and treasurer, no matter what their designation.

An annual report is also required of foreign corporations registered to do business in the state, and serves functions similar to those served with respect to domestic corporations. For both domestic and foreign corporations, the failure to file an annual report, like the failure to satisfy other mandatory requirements of the Act, is a ground for administrative dissolution of a domestic corporation or termination of the registration of a foreign corporation to do business. See sections 14.20 and 15.11.

CHAPTER 17: TRANSITION PROVISIONS

Note on Adoption of the Act

Chapter 17 addresses various transitional and interpretational issues that merit consideration by the legislature adopting the Act, especially as an entirety. This Note summarizes and explains some of those issues. Each adopting state will need to consider the differences between the Act and its existing corporation statute to determine if additional transitional provisions will be necessary.

Special Circumstances Warranting Delayed Effectiveness

The Act has been drafted to apply to domestic business corporations in existence on its effective date. See section 17.01. To the extent that some of the provisions of the Act differ in significant respects from earlier laws, it may be appropriate to delay the effective date of such provisions to give existing corporations adequate time to revise controlling corporate documents to take into account the provisions of the Act, or in unusual circumstances, to allow existing corporations to continue to be governed by a preexisting law until a later election to be governed by the pertinent provision of the Act. Two examples of such transitional problems are discussed below.

- Changes in Voting Requirements

The Act, unlike some corporation statutes, requires by virtue of section 7.25 only that votes cast in favor exceed votes cast against, in a meeting at which a quorum is present, to approve transactions such as mergers, sale of assets outside the usual and regular course of business, important amendments to the articles of incorporation, and dissolution. When considering adoption of the Act's voting requirements, it is important to recognize that specific control arrangements may have been established on the assumption that the existing statutory voting requirements would not be reduced. Rather than defeat those reasonable assumptions by effectively eliminating a shareholder's power to veto changes when there was a higher statutory vote requirement, a state that adopts the Act's lesser voting requirement may wish to consider "grandfathering" existing corporations and afford them an option to elect to be governed by the new requirement.

- Increased Power of the Board of Directors

The Act generally grants the board of directors authority to increase or decrease its own size without specific authority (section 8.03) unless the articles of incorporation restrict this power. Some corporation statutes do not grant this power to the board of directors unless express provision is made in the articles or bylaws. Corporations that have not granted this express power to the board of directors may in effect do so when they become subject to the Act, and a delayed effective date therefore may be appropriate.

Foreign Corporations

Although chapter 15 of the Act may change the rules applicable to foreign corporations in some states, these changes are not of a type that requires a transition period. It is therefore recommended that only a single effective date be provided for the application of the Act to foreign corporations and that delayed effective dates for specific provisions in this regard are unnecessary. See section 17.02.

Savings and Severability Provisions

The Act contains its own savings and severability provisions, in sections 17.03 and 17.04, respectively. If the state has a savings statute of general application, however, it may be unnecessary to adopt section 17.03. Likewise, if the state has a severability provision of general application, or if the state's highest court has established a general rule of severability, it may be unnecessary to adopt section 17.04.

Repeal

Although section 17.05 provides for repeal of previously enacted general corporation statutes that are specified, such repeal is generally unnecessary with regard to statutes providing special incorporation and regulatory provisions for corporations engaged in specific businesses, like banking and insurance. If these specialized statutes expressly incorporate by reference provisions from the general business corporation act, however, these statutes should be amended to refer specifically to the present Act rather than to an earlier statute; an appropriate provision would apply this Act to all these corporations except to the extent the specialized statute expressly provides that a different principle should apply.

§ 17.01. Application to Existing Domestic Corporations

This Act applies to all domestic corporations in existence on its effective date that were incorporated under any general statute of this state providing for incorporation of corporations for profit if power to amend or repeal the statute under which the corporation was incorporated was reserved.

Official Comment

The Act's application to all domestic corporations in existence on the effective date of the Act, as well as to all new domestic corporations formed after that date, avoids a confusing coexistence of different and overlapping rules of corporation law. The Act does not, however, supersede statutes governing nonprofit corporations or associations, nor does it apply to corporations formed for the purpose of engaging in a business for which the state has provided a separate incorporation procedure.

Section 17.01 applies the Act to all corporations to which that application is constitutionally permissible. In view of the universal adoption of "reservation of power" clauses in all states for more than a century, there are very few active domestic corporations to which the Act will not be applicable under this section.

§ 17.02. Application to Existing Foreign Corporations

A foreign corporation registered or authorized to do business in this state on the effective date of this Act is subject to this Act, is deemed to be registered to do business in this state, and is not required to file a foreign registration statement under this Act.

Official Comment

Section 17.02 makes the Act applicable on its effective date to all foreign corporations that are registered or authorized to do business in the state on that date without action by the foreign corporation.

§ 17.03. Saving Provisions

(a)   Except as to procedural provisions, this Act does not affect a pending action or proceeding or a right accrued before the effective date of this Act, and a pending civil action or proceeding may be completed, and a right accrued may be enforced, as if this Act had not become effective.

(b)   If a penalty or punishment for violation of a statute or rule is reduced by this Act, the penalty, if not already imposed, shall be imposed in accordance with this Act.

§ 17.04. Severability

If any provision of this Act or its application to any person or circumstance is held invalid by a court of competent jurisdiction, the invalidity does not affect other provisions or applications of this Act that can be given effect without the invalid provision or application.

§ 17.05. Repeal

The following laws and parts of laws are repealed: [to be inserted by the adopting state].

Official Comment

The Act is a complete substitute for earlier statutes of general applicability to business corporations and earlier statutes have been repealed.

DELAWARE GENERAL CORPORATION LAW

(Title 8 Del. Stat.)

Table of Sections

DELAWARE GENERAL CORPORATION LAW

§ 101. Incorporators; How Corporation Formed; Purposes

(a)   Any person, partnership, association or corporation, singly or jointly with others, and without regard to such person's or entity's residence, domicile or state of incorporation, may incorporate or organize a corporation under this chapter by filing with the Division of Corporations in the Department of State a certificate of incorporation which shall be executed, acknowledged and filed in accordance with § 103 of this title.

(b)   A corporation may be incorporated or organized under this chapter to conduct or promote any lawful business or purposes, except as may otherwise be provided by the Constitution or other law of this State.

(c)   Corporations for constructing, maintaining and operating public utilities, whether in or outside of this State, may be organized under this chapter, but corporations for constructing, maintaining and operating public utilities within this State shall be subject to, in addition to this chapter, the special provisions and requirements of Title 26 applicable to such corporations.

§ 102. Contents of Certificate of Incorporation

(a)   The certificate of incorporation shall set forth:

(1)   The name of the corporation, which

(i)   shall contain 1 of the words "association," "company," "corporation," "club," "foundation," "fund," "incorporated," "institute," "society," "union," "syndicate," or "limited," (or abbreviations thereof, with or without punctuation), or words (or abbreviations thereof, with or without punctuation) of like import of foreign countries or jurisdictions (provided they are written in roman characters or letters); provided, however, that the Division of Corporations in the Department of State may waive such requirement (unless it determines that such name is, or might otherwise appear to be, that of a natural person) if such corporation executes, acknowledges and files with the Secretary of State in accordance with § 103 of this title a certificate stating that its total assets, as defined in § 503(i) of this title, are not less than $10,000,000, or, in the sole discretion of the Division of Corporations in the

Department of State, if the corporation is both a nonprofit nonstock corporation and an association of professionals,

(ii)   shall be such as to distinguish it upon the records in the office of the Division of Corporations in the Department of State from the names that are reserved on such records and from the names on such records of each other corporation, partnership, limited partnership, limited liability company, registered series of a limited liability company or statutory trust organized or registered as a domestic or foreign corporation, partnership, limited partnership, limited liability company, registered series of a limited liability company or statutory trust under the laws of this State, except with the written consent of the person who has reserved such name or such other foreign corporation or domestic or foreign partnership, limited partnership, limited liability company, registered series of a limited liability company or statutory trust, executed, acknowledged and filed with the Secretary of State in accordance with § 103 of this title, or except that, without prejudicing any rights of the person who has reserved such name or such other foreign corporation or domestic or foreign partnership, limited partnership, limited liability company or statutory trust, the Division of Corporations in the Department of State may waive such requirement if the corporation demonstrates to the satisfaction of the Secretary of State that the corporation or a predecessor entity previously has made substantial use of such name or substantially similar name, that the corporation has made reasonable efforts to secure such written consent, and that such waiver is in the interest of the State.

(iii)   except as permitted by § 395 of this title, shall not contain the word "trust," and (iv) shall not contain the word "bank," or any variation thereof, except for the name of a bank reporting to and under the supervision of the State Bank Commissioner of this State or a subsidiary of a bank or savings association (as those terms are defined in the Federal Deposit Insurance Act, as amended, at 12 U.S.C. § 1813), or a corporation regulated under the Bank Holding Company Act of 1956, as amended, 12 U.S.C. § 1841 et seq., or the Home Owners' Loan Act, as amended, 12 U.S.C. § 1461 et seq.; provided, however, that this section shall not be construed to prevent the use of the word "bank," or any variation thereof, in a context clearly not purporting to refer to a banking business or otherwise likely to mislead the public about the nature of the business of the corporation or to lead to a pattern and practice of abuse that might cause harm to the interests of the public or the State as determined by the Division of Corporations in the Department of State;

(2)   The address (which shall be stated in accordance with § 131(c) of this title) of the corporation's registered office in this State, and the name of its registered agent at such address;

(3)   The nature of the business or purposes to be conducted or promoted. It shall be sufficient to state, either alone or with other businesses or purposes, that the purpose of the corporation is to engage in any lawful act or activity for which corporations may be organized under the General Corporation Law of Delaware, and by such statement all lawful acts and activities shall be within the purposes of the corporation, except for express limitations, if any;

(4)   If the corporation is to be authorized to issue only 1 class of stock, the total number of shares of stock which the corporation shall have authority to issue and the par value of each of such shares, or a statement that all such shares are to be without par value. If the corporation is to be authorized to issue more than 1 class of stock, the certificate of incorporation shall set forth the total number of shares of all classes of stock which the corporation shall have authority to issue and the number of shares of each class and shall specify each class the shares of which are to be without par value and each class the shares of which are to have par value and the par value of the shares of each such class. The certificate of incorporation shall also set forth a statement of the designations and the powers, preferences and rights, and the qualifications, limitations or restrictions thereof, which are permitted by § 151 of this title in respect of any class or classes of stock or any series of any class of stock of the corporation and the fixing of which by the certificate of incorporation is desired, and an express grant of such authority as it may then be desired to

grant to the board of directors to fix by resolution or resolutions any thereof that may be desired but which shall not be fixed by the certificate of incorporation. The foregoing provisions of this paragraph shall not apply to nonstock corporations. In the case of nonstock corporations, the fact that they are not authorized to issue capital stock shall be stated in the certificate of incorporation. The conditions of membership, or other criteria for identifying members, of nonstock corporations shall likewise be stated in the certificate of incorporation or the bylaws. Nonstock corporations shall have members, but failure to have members shall not affect otherwise valid corporate acts or work a forfeiture or dissolution of the corporation. Nonstock corporations may provide for classes or groups of members having relative rights, powers and duties, and may make provision for the future creation of additional classes or groups of members having such relative rights, powers and duties as may from time to time be established, including rights, powers and duties senior to existing classes and groups of members. Except as otherwise provided in this chapter, nonstock corporations may also provide that any member or class or group of members shall have full, limited, or no voting rights or powers, including that any member or class or group of members shall have the right to vote on a specified transaction even if that member or class or group of members does not have the right to vote for the election of the members of the governing body of the corporation. Voting by members of a nonstock corporation may be on a per capita, number, financial interest, class, group, or any other basis set forth. The provisions referred to in the 3 preceding sentences may be set forth in the certificate of incorporation or the bylaws. If neither the certificate of incorporation nor the bylaws of a nonstock corporation state the conditions of membership, or other criteria for identifying members, the members of the corporation shall be deemed to be those entitled to vote for the election of the members of the governing body pursuant to the certificate of incorporation or bylaws of such corporation or otherwise until thereafter otherwise provided by the certificate of incorporation or the bylaws;

(5) The name and mailing address of the incorporator or incorporators;

(6) If the powers of the incorporator or incorporators are to terminate upon the filing of the certificate of incorporation, the names and mailing addresses of the persons who are to serve as directors until the first annual meeting of stockholders or until their successors are elected and qualify.

(b) In addition to the matters required to be set forth in the certificate of incorporation by subsection (a) of this section, the certificate of incorporation may also contain any or all of the following matters:

(1) Any provision for the management of the business and for the conduct of the affairs of the corporation, and any provision creating, defining, limiting and regulating the powers of the corporation, the directors, and the stockholders, or any class of the stockholders, or the governing body, members, or any class or group of members of a nonstock corporation; if such provisions are not contrary to the laws of this State. Any provision which is required or permitted by any section of this chapter to be stated in the bylaws may instead be stated in the certificate of incorporation;

(2) The following provisions, in haec verba, (i), for a corporation other than a nonstock corporation, viz:

"Whenever a compromise or arrangement is proposed between this corporation and its creditors or any class of them and/or between this corporation and its stockholders or any class of them, any court of equitable jurisdiction within the State of Delaware may, on the application in a summary way of this corporation or of any creditor or stockholder thereof or on the application of any receiver or receivers appointed for this corporation under § 291 of Title 8 of the Delaware Code or on the application of trustees in dissolution or of any receiver or receivers appointed for this corporation under § 279 of Title 8 of the Delaware Code order a meeting of the creditors or class of creditors, and/or of the stockholders or class of stockholders of this corporation, as the case may be, to be summoned in such manner as the said court directs. If a majority in number representing three fourths in value of the creditors or class of creditors, and/or of the stockholders or class of stockholders of this corporation, as the case may be, agree to any compromise or arrangement and to any reorganization of this corporation as consequence of such compromise or arrangement, the said compromise or arrangement and the said reorganization shall, if sanctioned by the court to which the said application has been made, be binding on all the creditors or class of creditors, and/or on all the stockholders or class of stockholders, of this corporation, as the case may be, and also on this corporation"; or

(ii), for a nonstock corporation, viz:

"Whenever a compromise or arrangement is proposed between this corporation and its creditors or any class of them and/or between this corporation and its members or any class of them, any court of equitable jurisdiction within the State of Delaware may, on the application in a summary way of this corporation or of any creditor or member thereof or on the application of any receiver or receivers appointed for this corporation under § 291 of Title 8 of the Delaware Code or on the application of trustees in dissolution or of any receiver or receiver appointed for this corporation under § 279 of Title 8 of the Delaware Code order a meeting of the creditors or class of creditors, and/or of the members or class of members of this corporation, as the case may be, to be summoned in such manner as the said court directs. If a majority in number representing three fourths in value of the creditors or class of creditors, and/or of the members or class of members of this corporation, as the case may be, agree to any compromise or arrangement and to any reorganization of this corporation as consequence of such compromise or arrangement, the said compromise or arrangement and the said reorganization shall, if sanctioned by the court to which the said application has been made, be binding on all the creditors or class of creditors, and/or on all the members or class of members, of this corporation, as the case may be, and also on this corporation";

(3) Such provisions as may be desired granting to the holders of the stock of the corporation, or the holders of any class or series of a class thereof, the preemptive right to subscribe to any or all additional issues of stock of the corporation of any or all classes or series thereof, or to any securities of the corporation convertible into such stock. No stockholder shall have any preemptive right to subscribe to an additional issue of stock or to any security convertible into such stock unless, and except to the extent that, such right is expressly granted to such stockholder in the certificate of incorporation. All such rights in existence on July 3, 1967, shall remain in existence unaffected by this paragraph unless and until changed or terminated by appropriate action which expressly provides for the change or termination;

(4) Provisions requiring for any corporate action, the vote of a larger portion of the stock or of any class or series thereof, or of any other securities having voting power, or a larger number of the directors, than is required by this chapter;

(5) A provision limiting the duration of the corporation's existence to a specified date; otherwise, the corporation shall have perpetual existence;

(6) A provision imposing personal liability for the debts of the corporation on its stockholders to a specified extent and upon specified conditions; otherwise, the stockholders of a corporation shall not be personally liable for the payment of the corporation's debts except as they may be liable by reason of their own conduct or acts;

(7) A provision eliminating or limiting the personal liability of a director to the corporation or its stockholders for monetary damages for breach of fiduciary duty as a director, provided that such provision shall not eliminate or limit the liability of a director:

(i) For any breach of the director's duty of loyalty to the corporation or its stockholders;

(ii) for acts or omissions not in good faith or which involve intentional misconduct or a knowing violation of law;

(iii)   under § 174 of this title; or

(iv)   for any transaction from which the director derived an improper personal benefit. No such provision shall eliminate or limit the liability of a director for any act or omission occurring prior to the date when such provision becomes effective. All references in this paragraph to a director shall also be deemed to refer to such other person or persons, if any, who, pursuant to a provision of the certificate of incorporation in accordance with § 141(a) of this title, exercise or perform any of the powers or duties otherwise conferred or imposed upon the board of directors by this title.

(c)   It shall not be necessary to set forth in the certificate of incorporation any of the powers conferred on corporations by this chapter.

(d)   Except for provisions included pursuant to paragraphs (a)(1), (a)(2), (a)(5), (a)(6), (b)(2), (b)(5), (b)(7) of this section, and provisions included pursuant to paragraph (a)(4) of this section specifying the classes, number of shares, and par value of shares a corporation other than a nonstock corporation is authorized to issue, any provision of the certificate of incorporation may be made dependent upon facts ascertainable outside such instrument, provided that the manner in which such facts shall operate upon the provision is clearly and explicitly set forth therein. The term "facts," as used in this subsection, includes, but is not limited to, the occurrence of any event, including a determination or action by any person or body, including the corporation.

(e)   The exclusive right to the use of a name that is available for use by a domestic or foreign corporation may be reserved by or on behalf of:

(1)   Any person intending to incorporate or organize a corporation with that name under this chapter or contemplating such incorporation or organization;

(2)   Any domestic corporation or any foreign corporation qualified to do business in the State of Delaware, in either case, intending to change its name or contemplating such a change;

(3)   Any foreign corporation intending to qualify to do business in the State of Delaware and adopt that name or contemplating such qualification and adoption; and

(4)   Any person intending to organize a foreign corporation and have it qualify to do business in the State of Delaware and adopt that name or contemplating such organization, qualification and adoption.

The reservation of a specified name may be made by filing with the Secretary of State an application, executed by the applicant, certifying that the reservation is made by or on behalf of a domestic corporation, foreign corporation or other person described in paragraphs (e)(1)–(4) of this section above, and specifying the name to be reserved and the name and address of the applicant. If the Secretary of State finds that the name is available for use by a domestic or foreign corporation, the Secretary shall reserve the name for the use of the applicant for a period of 120 days. The same applicant may renew for successive 120-day periods a reservation of a specified name by filing with the Secretary of State, prior to the expiration of such reservation (or renewal thereof), an application for renewal of such reservation, executed by the applicant, certifying that the reservation is renewed by or on behalf of a domestic corporation, foreign corporation or other person described in paragraphs (e)(1)–(4) of this section above and specifying the name reservation to be renewed and the name and address of the applicant. The right to the exclusive use of a reserved name may be transferred to any other person by filing in the office of the Secretary of State a notice of the transfer, executed by the applicant for whom the name was reserved, specifying the name reservation to be transferred and the name and address of the transferee. The reservation of a specified name may be cancelled by filing with the Secretary of State a notice of cancellation, executed by the applicant or transferee, specifying the name reservation to be cancelled and the name and address of the applicant or transferee. Unless the Secretary of State finds that any application, application for renewal, notice of transfer, or notice of cancellation filed with the Secretary of State as required by this subsection does not conform to law, upon receipt of all filing fees required by law the Secretary of State shall prepare and return to the person who filed such instrument a copy of the filed instrument with a notation thereon of the action taken by the Secretary of State. A fee as set forth in § 391 of this title shall be paid at the time of the reservation of any name, at the time of the renewal of any such reservation and at the time of the filing of a notice of the transfer or cancellation of any such reservation.

(f) The certificate of incorporation may not contain any provision that would impose liability on a stockholder for the attorneys' fees or expenses of the corporation or any other party in connection with an internal corporate claim, as defined in § 115 of this title.

§ 103. Execution, Acknowledgment, Filing, Recording and Effective Date of Original Certificate of Incorporation and Other Instruments; Exceptions

(a) Whenever any instrument is to be filed with the Secretary of State or in accordance with this section or chapter, such instrument shall be executed as follows:

(1) The certificate of incorporation, and any other instrument to be filed before the election of the initial board of directors if the initial directors were not named in the certificate of incorporation, shall be signed by the incorporator or incorporators (or, in the case of any such other instrument, such incorporator's or incorporators' successors and assigns). If any incorporator is not available then any such other instrument may be signed, with the same effect as if such incorporator had signed it, by any person for whom or on whose behalf such incorporator, in executing the certificate of incorporation, was acting directly or indirectly as employee or agent, provided that such other instrument shall state that such incorporator is not available and the reason therefor, that such incorporator in executing the certificate of incorporation was acting directly or indirectly as employee or agent for or on behalf of such person, and that such person's signature on such instrument is otherwise authorized and not wrongful.

(2) All other instruments shall be signed:

a. By any authorized officer of the corporation; or

b. If it shall appear from the instrument that there are no such officers, then by a majority of the directors or by such directors as may be designated by the board; or

c. If it shall appear from the instrument that there are no such officers or directors, then by the holders of record, or such of them as may be designated by the holders of record, of a majority of all outstanding shares of stock; or

d. By the holders of record of all outstanding shares of stock.

(b) Whenever this chapter requires any instrument to be acknowledged, such requirement is satisfied by either:

(1) The formal acknowledgment by the person or 1 of the persons signing the instrument that it is such person's act and deed or the act and deed of the corporation, and that the facts stated therein are true. Such acknowledgment shall be made before a person who is authorized by the law of the place of execution to take acknowledgments of deeds. If such person has a seal of office such person shall affix it to the instrument.

(2) The signature, without more, of the person or persons signing the instrument, in which case such signature or signatures shall constitute the affirmation or acknowledgment of the signatory, under penalties of perjury, that the instrument is such person's act and deed or the act and deed of the corporation, and that the facts stated therein are true.

(c) Whenever any instrument is to be filed with the Secretary of State or in accordance with this section or chapter, such requirement means that:

(1) The signed instrument shall be delivered to the office of the Secretary of State;

(2)   All taxes and fees authorized by law to be collected by the Secretary of State in connection with the filing of the instrument shall be tendered to the Secretary of State; and

(3)   Upon delivery of the instrument, the Secretary of State shall record the date and time of its delivery. Upon such delivery and tender of the required taxes and fees, the Secretary of State shall certify that the instrument has been filed in the Secretary of State's office by endorsing upon the signed instrument the word "Filed", and the date and time of its filing. This endorsement is the "filing date" of the instrument, and is conclusive of the date and time of its filing in the absence of actual fraud. The Secretary of State shall file and index the endorsed instrument. Except as provided in paragraph (c)(4) of this section and in subsection (i) of this section, such filing date of an instrument shall be the date and time of delivery of the instrument.

(4)   Upon request made upon or prior to delivery, the Secretary of State may, to the extent deemed practicable, establish as the filing date of an instrument a date and time after its delivery. If the Secretary of State refuses to file any instrument due to an error, omission or other imperfection, the Secretary of State may hold such instrument in suspension, and in such event, upon delivery of a replacement instrument in proper form for filing and tender of the required taxes and fees within 5 business days after notice of such suspension is given to the filer, the Secretary of State shall establish as the filing date of such instrument the date and time that would have been the filing date of the rejected instrument had it been accepted for filing. The Secretary of State shall not issue a certificate of good standing with respect to any corporation with an instrument held in suspension pursuant to this subsection. The Secretary of State may establish as the filing date of an instrument the date and time at which information from such instrument is entered pursuant to paragraph (c)(8) of this section if such instrument is delivered on the same date and within 4 hours after such information is entered.

(5)   The Secretary of State, acting as agent for the recorders of each of the counties, shall collect and deposit in a separate account established exclusively for that purpose a county assessment fee with respect to each filed instrument and shall thereafter weekly remit from such account to the recorder of each of the said counties the amount or amounts of such fees as provided for in paragraph (c)(6) of this section or as elsewhere provided by law. Said fees shall be for the purposes of defraying certain costs incurred by the counties in merging the information and images of such filed documents with the document information systems of each of the recorder's offices in the counties and in retrieving, maintaining and displaying such information and images in the offices of the recorders and at remote locations in each of such counties. In consideration for its acting as the agent for the recorders with respect to the collection and payment of the county assessment fees, the Secretary of State shall retain and pay over to the General Fund of the State an administrative charge of 1 percent of the total fees collected.

(6)   The assessment fee to the counties shall be $24 for each 1-page instrument filed with the Secretary of State in accordance with this section and $9 for each additional page for instruments with more than 1 page. The recorder's office to receive the assessment fee shall be the recorder's office in the county in which the corporation's registered office in this State is, or is to be, located, except that an assessment fee shall not be charged for either a certificate of dissolution qualifying for treatment under § 391(a)(5)b of this title or a document filed in accordance with Subchapter XVI of this chapter.

(7)   The Secretary of State, acting as agent, shall collect and deposit in a separate account established exclusively for that purpose a courthouse municipality fee with respect to each filed instrument and shall thereafter monthly remit funds from such account to the treasuries of the municipalities designated in § 301 of Title 10. Said fees shall be for the purposes of defraying certain costs incurred by such municipalities in hosting the primary locations for the Delaware Courts. The fee to such municipalities shall be $20 for each instrument filed with the Secretary of State in accordance with this section. The municipality to receive the fee shall be the municipality designated in § 301 of Title 10 in the county in which the corporation's registered office in this State is, or is to be, located, except that a fee shall not be charged for a certificate of

dissolution qualifying for treatment under § 391(a)(5)b. of this title, a resignation of agent without appointment of a successor under § 136 of this title, or a document filed in accordance with subchapter XVI of this chapter.

(8)   The Secretary of State shall cause to be entered such information from each instrument as the Secretary of State deems appropriate into the Delaware Corporation Information System or any system which is a successor thereto in the office of the Secretary of State, and such information and a copy of each such instrument shall be permanently maintained as a public record on a suitable medium. The Secretary of State is authorized to grant direct access to such system to registered agents subject to the execution of an operating agreement between the Secretary of State and such registered agent. Any registered agent granted such access shall demonstrate the existence of policies to ensure that information entered into the system accurately reflects the content of instruments in the possession of the registered agent at the time of entry.

(d)   Any instrument filed in accordance with subsection (c) of this section shall be effective upon its filing date. Any instrument may provide that it is not to become effective until a specified time subsequent to the time it is filed, but such time shall not be later than a time on the 90th day after the date of its filing. If any instrument filed in accordance with subsection (c) of this section provides for a future effective date or time and if the transaction is terminated or its terms are amended to change the future effective date or time prior to the future effective date or time, the instrument shall be terminated or amended by the filing, prior to the future effective date or time set forth in such instrument, of a certificate of termination or amendment of the original instrument, executed in accordance with subsection (a) of this section, which shall identify the instrument which has been terminated or amended and shall state that the instrument has been terminated or the manner in which it has been amended.

(e)   If another section of this chapter specifically prescribes a manner of executing, acknowledging or filing a specified instrument or a time when such instrument shall become effective which differs from the corresponding provisions of this section, then such other section shall govern.

(f)   Whenever any instrument authorized to be filed with the Secretary of State under any provision of this title, has been so filed and is an inaccurate record of the corporate action therein referred to, or was defectively or erroneously executed, sealed or acknowledged, the instrument may be corrected by filing with the Secretary of State a certificate of correction of the instrument which shall be executed, acknowledged and filed in accordance with this section. The certificate of correction shall specify the inaccuracy or defect to be corrected and shall set forth the portion of the instrument in corrected form. In lieu of filing a certificate of correction the instrument may be corrected by filing with the Secretary of State a corrected instrument which shall be executed, acknowledged and filed in accordance with this section. The corrected instrument shall be specifically designated as such in its heading, shall specify the inaccuracy or defect to be corrected, and shall set forth the entire instrument in corrected form. An instrument corrected in accordance with this section shall be effective as of the date the original instrument was filed, except as to those persons who are substantially and adversely affected by the correction and as to those persons the instrument as corrected shall be effective from the filing date.

(g)   Notwithstanding that any instrument authorized to be filed with the Secretary of State under this title is when filed inaccurately, defectively or erroneously executed, sealed or acknowledged, or otherwise defective in any respect, the Secretary of State shall have no liability to any person for the preclearance for filing, the acceptance for filing or the filing and indexing of such instrument by the Secretary of State.

(h)   Any signature on any instrument authorized to be filed with the Secretary of State under this title may be a facsimile, a conformed signature or an electronically transmitted signature.

(i)(1) If:

a. Together with the actual delivery of an instrument and tender of the required taxes and fees, there is delivered to the Secretary of State a separate affidavit (which in its heading shall be designated as an "affidavit of extraordinary condition") attesting, on the basis of personal knowledge of the affiant or a reliable source of knowledge identified in the affidavit, that an earlier effort to deliver such instrument and tender such taxes and fees was made in good faith, specifying the nature, date and time of such good faith effort and requesting that the Secretary of State establish such date and time as the filing date of such instrument; or

b. Upon the actual delivery of an instrument and tender of the required taxes and fees, the Secretary of State in the Secretary's discretion provides a written waiver of the requirement for such an affidavit stating that it appears to the Secretary of State that an earlier effort to deliver such instrument and tender such taxes and fees was made in good faith and specifying the date and time of such effort; and

c. The Secretary of State determines that an extraordinary condition existed at such date and time, that such earlier effort was unsuccessful as a result of the existence of such extraordinary condition, and that such actual delivery and tender were made within a reasonable period (not to exceed 2 business days) after the cessation of such extraordinary condition, then the Secretary of State may establish such date and time as the filing date of such instrument. No fee shall be paid to the Secretary of State for receiving an affidavit of extraordinary condition.

(2) For purposes of this subsection, an "extraordinary condition" means: any emergency resulting from an attack on, invasion or occupation by foreign military forces of, or disaster, catastrophe, war or other armed conflict, revolution or insurrection, or rioting or civil commotion in, the United States or a locality in which the Secretary of State conducts its business or in which the good faith effort to deliver the instrument and tender the required taxes and fees is made, or the immediate threat of any of the foregoing; or any malfunction or outage of the electrical or telephone service to the Secretary of State's office, or weather or other condition in or about a locality in which the Secretary of State conducts its business, as a result of which the Secretary of State's office is not open for the purpose of the filing of instruments under this chapter or such filing cannot be effected without extraordinary effort. The Secretary of State may require such proof as it deems necessary to make the determination required under paragraph (i)(1)c. of this section, and any such determination shall be conclusive in the absence of actual fraud.

(3) If the Secretary of State establishes the filing date of an instrument pursuant to this subsection, the date and time of delivery of the affidavit of extraordinary condition or the date and time of the Secretary of State's written waiver of such affidavit shall be endorsed on such affidavit or waiver and such affidavit or waiver, so endorsed, shall be attached to the filed instrument to which it relates. Such filed instrument shall be effective as of the date and time established as the filing date by the Secretary of State pursuant to this subsection, except as to those persons who are substantially and adversely affected by such establishment and, as to those persons, the instrument shall be effective from the date and time endorsed on the affidavit of extraordinary condition or written waiver attached thereto.

(j) Notwithstanding any other provision of this chapter, it shall not be necessary for any corporation to amend its certificate of incorporation, or any other document, that has been filed prior to August 1, 2011, to comply with § 131(c) of this title, provided that any certificate or other document filed under this chapter on or after August 1, 2011, and changing the address of a registered office shall comply with § 131(c) of this title.

§ 104. Certificate of Incorporation; Definition

The term "certificate of incorporation," as used in this chapter, unless the context requires otherwise, includes not only the original certificate of incorporation filed to create a corporation but also all other certificates, agreements of merger or consolidation, plans of reorganization, or other instruments, howsoever designated, which are filed pursuant to § 102, §§ 133–136, § 151, §§ 241–243, § 245, §§ 251–258, §§ 263–264, § 267, § 303, or any other section of this title, and which have the effect of amending or supplementing in some respect a corporation's original certificate of incorporation.

§ 105. Certificate of Incorporation and Other Certificates; Evidence

A copy of a certificate of incorporation, or a restated certificate of incorporation, or of any other certificate which has been filed in the office of the Secretary of State as required by any provision of this title shall, when duly certified by the Secretary of State, be received in all courts, public offices and official bodies as prima facie evidence of:

(1)   Due execution, acknowledgment and filing of the instrument;

(2)   Observance and performance of all acts and conditions necessary to have been observed and performed precedent to the instrument becoming effective; and

(3)   Any other facts required or permitted by law to be stated in the instrument.

§ 106. Commencement of Corporate Existence

Upon the filing with the Secretary of State of the certificate of incorporation, executed and acknowledged in accordance with § 103 of this title, the incorporator or incorporators who signed the certificate, and such incorporator's or incorporators' successors and assigns, shall, from the date of such filing, be and constitute a body corporate, by the name set forth in the certificate, subject to § 103 (d) of this title and subject to dissolution or other termination of its existence as provided in this chapter.

§ 107. Powers of Incorporators

If the persons who are to serve as directors until the first annual meeting of stockholders have not been named in the certificate of incorporation, the incorporator or incorporators, until the directors are elected, shall manage the affairs of the corporation and may do whatever is necessary and proper to perfect the organization of the corporation, including the adoption of the original bylaws of the corporation and the election of directors.

§ 108. Organization Meeting of Incorporators or Directors Named in Certificate of Incorporation

(a)   After the filing of the certificate of incorporation an organization meeting of the incorporator or incorporators, or of the board of directors if the initial directors were named in the certificate of incorporation, shall be held, either within or without this State, at the call of a majority of the incorporators or directors, as the case may be, for the purposes of adopting bylaws, electing directors (if the meeting is of the incorporators) to serve or hold office until the first annual meeting of stockholders or until their successors are elected and qualify, electing officers if the meeting is of the directors, doing any other or further acts to perfect the organization of the corporation, and transacting such other business as may come before the meeting.

(b)   The persons calling the meeting shall give to each other incorporator or director, as the case may be, at least 2 days' written notice thereof by any usual means of communication, which notice shall state the time, place and purposes of the meeting as fixed by the persons calling it. Notice of the meeting need not be given to anyone who attends the meeting or who signs a waiver of notice either before or after the meeting.

(c)   Any action permitted to be taken at the organization meeting of the incorporators or directors, as the case may be, may be taken without a meeting if each incorporator or director, where there is more than 1, or the sole incorporator or director where there is only 1, signs an instrument which states the action so taken.

(d)   If any incorporator is not available to act, then any person for whom or on whose behalf the incorporator was acting directly or indirectly as employee or agent, may take any action that such incorporator would have been authorized to take under this section or § 107 of this title; provided that any instrument signed by such other person, or any record of the proceedings of a meeting in which such person participated, shall state that such incorporator is not available and the reason therefor, that such incorporator was acting directly or indirectly as employee or agent for or on behalf of such person, and that such person's signature on such instrument or participation in such meeting is otherwise authorized and not wrongful.

§ 109.   Bylaws

(a)   The original or other bylaws of a corporation may be adopted, amended or repealed by the incorporators, by the initial directors of a corporation other than a nonstock corporation or initial members of the governing body of a nonstock corporation if they were named in the certificate of incorporation, or, before a corporation other than a nonstock corporation has received any payment for any of its stock, by its board of directors. After a corporation other than a nonstock corporation has received any payment for any of its stock, the power to adopt, amend or repeal bylaws shall be in the stockholders entitled to vote. In the case of a nonstock corporation, the power to adopt, amend or repeal bylaws shall be in its members entitled to vote. Notwithstanding the foregoing, any corporation may, in its certificate of incorporation, confer the power to adopt, amend or repeal bylaws upon the directors or, in the case of a nonstock corporation, upon its governing body. The fact that such power has been so conferred upon the directors or governing body, as the case may be, shall not divest the stockholders or members of the power, nor limit their power to adopt, amend or repeal bylaws.

(b)   The bylaws may contain any provision, not inconsistent with law or with the certificate of incorporation, relating to the business of the corporation, the conduct of its affairs, and its rights or powers or the rights or powers of its stockholders, directors, officers or employees. The bylaws may not contain any provision that would impose liability on a stockholder for the attorneys' fees or expenses of the corporation or any other party in connection with an internal corporate claim, as defined in § 115 of this title.

§ 110.   Emergency Bylaws and Other Powers in Emergency

(a)   The board of directors of any corporation may adopt emergency bylaws, subject to repeal or change by action of the stockholders, which shall notwithstanding any different provision elsewhere in this chapter or in Chapters 3 [repealed] and 5 [repealed] of Title 26, or in Chapter 7 of Title 5, or in the certificate of incorporation or bylaws, be operative during any emergency resulting from an attack on the United States or on a locality in which the corporation conducts its business or customarily holds meetings of its board of directors or its stockholders, or during any nuclear or atomic disaster, or during the existence of any catastrophe, or other similar emergency condition, as a result of which a quorum of the board of directors or a standing committee thereof cannot readily be convened for action. The emergency bylaws may make any provision that may be practical and necessary for the circumstances of the emergency, including provisions that:

(1)   A meeting of the board of directors or a committee thereof may be called by any officer or director in such manner and under such conditions as shall be prescribed in the emergency bylaws;

(2)   The director or directors in attendance at the meeting, or any greater number fixed by the emergency bylaws, shall constitute a quorum; and

(3)   The officers or other persons designated on a list approved by the board of directors before the emergency, all in such order of priority and subject to such conditions and for such period of time (not longer than reasonably necessary after the termination of the emergency) as may be provided in the emergency bylaws or in the resolution approving the list, shall, to the extent required to provide a quorum at any meeting of the board of directors, be deemed directors for such meeting.

(b)   The board of directors, either before or during any such emergency, may provide, and from time to time modify, lines of succession in the event that during such emergency any or all officers or agents of the corporation shall for any reason be rendered incapable of discharging their duties.

(c)   The board of directors, either before or during any such emergency, may, effective in the emergency, change the head office or designate several alternative head offices or regional offices, or authorize the officers so to do.

(d)   No officer, director or employee acting in accordance with any emergency bylaws shall be liable except for willful misconduct.

(e)   To the extent not inconsistent with any emergency bylaws so adopted, the bylaws of the corporation shall remain in effect during any emergency and upon its termination the emergency bylaws shall cease to be operative.

(f)   Unless otherwise provided in emergency bylaws, notice of any meeting of the board of directors during such an emergency may be given only to such of the directors as it may be feasible to reach at the time and by such means as may be feasible at the time, including publication or radio.

(g)   To the extent required to constitute a quorum at any meeting of the board of directors during such an emergency, the officers of the corporation who are present shall, unless otherwise provided in emergency bylaws, be deemed, in order of rank and within the same rank in order of seniority, directors for such meeting.

(h)   Nothing contained in this section shall be deemed exclusive of any other provisions for emergency powers consistent with other sections of this title which have been or may be adopted by corporations created under this chapter.

§ 111.   Jurisdiction to Interpret, Apply, Enforce or Determine the Validity of Corporate Instruments and Provisions of This Title

(a)   Any civil action to interpret, apply, enforce or determine the validity of the provisions of:

(1)   The certificate of incorporation or the bylaws of a corporation;

(2)   Any instrument, document or agreement (i) by which a corporation creates or sells, or offers to create or sell, any of its stock, or any rights or options respecting its stock, or (ii) to which a corporation and 1 or more holders of its stock are parties, and pursuant to which any such holder or holders sell or offer to sell any of such stock, or (iii) by which a corporation agrees to sell, lease or exchange any of its property or assets, and which by its terms provides that 1 or more holders of its stock approve of or consent to such sale, lease or exchange;

(3)   Any written restrictions on the transfer, registration of transfer or ownership of securities under § 202 of this title;

(4)   Any proxy under § 212 or § 215 of this title;

(5)   Any voting trust or other voting agreement under § 218 of this title;

(6)   Any agreement, certificate of merger or consolidation, or certificate of ownership and merger governed by §§ 251–253, §§ 255–258, §§ 263–264, or § 267 of this title;

(7)   Any certificate of conversion under § 265 or § 266 of this title;

(8)   Any certificate of domestication, transfer or continuance under § 388, § 389 or § 390 of this title; or

(9)   Any other instrument, document, agreement, or certificate required by any provision of this title;

may be brought in the Court of Chancery, except to the extent that a statute confers exclusive jurisdiction on a court, agency or tribunal other than the Court of Chancery.

(b)   Any civil action to interpret, apply or enforce any provision of this title may be brought in the Court of Chancery.

§ 112.   Access to Proxy Solicitation Materials

The bylaws may provide that if the corporation solicits proxies with respect to an election of directors, it may be required, to the extent and subject to such procedures or conditions as may be provided in the bylaws, to include in its proxy solicitation materials (including any form of proxy it distributes), in addition to individuals nominated by the board of directors, 1 or more individuals nominated by a stockholder. Such procedures or conditions may include any of the following:

(1)   A provision requiring a minimum record or beneficial ownership, or duration of ownership, of shares of the corporation's capital stock, by the nominating stockholder, and defining beneficial ownership to take into account options or other rights in respect of or related to such stock;

(2)   A provision requiring the nominating stockholder to submit specified information concerning the stockholder and the stockholder's nominees, including information concerning ownership by such persons of shares of the corporation's capital stock, or options or other rights in respect of or related to such stock;

(3)   A provision conditioning eligibility to require inclusion in the corporation's proxy solicitation materials upon the number or proportion of directors nominated by stockholders or whether the stockholder previously sought to require such inclusion;

(4)   A provision precluding nominations by any person if such person, any nominee of such person, or any affiliate or associate of such person or nominee, has acquired or publicly proposed to acquire shares constituting a specified percentage of the voting power of the corporation's outstanding voting stock within a specified period before the election of directors;

(5)   A provision requiring that the nominating stockholder undertake to indemnify the corporation in respect of any loss arising as a result of any false or misleading information or statement submitted by the nominating stockholder in connection with a nomination; and

(6)   Any other lawful condition.

§ 113.   Proxy Expense Reimbursement

(a)   The bylaws may provide for the reimbursement by the corporation of expenses incurred by a stockholder in soliciting proxies in connection with an election of directors, subject to such procedures or conditions as the bylaws may prescribe, including:

(1)   Conditioning eligibility for reimbursement upon the number or proportion of persons nominated by the stockholder seeking reimbursement or whether such stockholder previously sought reimbursement for similar expenses;

(2)   Limitations on the amount of reimbursement based upon the proportion of votes cast in favor of one or more of the persons nominated by the stockholder seeking reimbursement, or upon the amount spent by the corporation in soliciting proxies in connection with the election;

(3)   Limitations concerning elections of directors by cumulative voting pursuant to § 214 of this title; or

(4)   Any other lawful condition.

(b)   No bylaw so adopted shall apply to elections for which any record date precedes its adoption.

§ 114.   Application of Chapter to Nonstock Corporations

(a)   Except as otherwise provided in subsections (b) and (c) of this section, the provisions of this chapter and of chapter 5 of this title shall apply to nonstock corporations in the manner specified in the following paragraphs (a)(1)–(4) of this section:

(1)   All references to stockholders of the corporation shall be deemed to refer to members of the corporation;

(2)   All references to the board of directors of the corporation shall be deemed to refer to the governing body of the corporation;

(3)   All references to directors or to members of the board of directors of the corporation shall be deemed to refer to members of the governing body of the corporation; and

(4)   All references to stock, capital stock, or shares thereof of a corporation authorized to issue capital stock shall be deemed to refer to memberships of a nonprofit nonstock corporation and to membership interests of any other nonstock corporation.

(b)   Subsection (a) of this section shall not apply to:

(1)   Sections 102(a)(4), (b)(1) and (2), 109(a), 114, 141, 154, 215, 228, 230(b), 241, 242, 253, 254, 255, 256, 257, 258, 271, 276, 311, 312, 313, 390, and 503 of this title, which apply to nonstock corporations by their terms;

(2)   Sections 102(f), 109(b) (last sentence), 151, 152, 153, 155, 156, 157(d), 158, 161, 162, 163, 164, 165, 166, 167, 168, 203, 211, 212, 213, 214, 216, 219, 222, 231, 243, 244, 251, 252, 267, 274, 275, 324, 364, 366(a), 391, and 502(a)(5) of this title; and

(3)   Subchapter XIV and subchapter XVI of this chapter.

(c)   In the case of a nonprofit nonstock corporation, subsection (a) of this section shall not apply to:

(1)   The sections and subchapters listed in subsection (b) of this section;

(2)   Sections 102(b)(3), 111(a)(2) and (3), 144(a)(2), 217, 218(a) and (b), and 262 of this title; and

(3)   Subchapter V, subchapter VI (other than §§ 204 and 205 of this title) and subchapter XV of this chapter.

(d)   For purposes of this chapter:

(1)   A "charitable nonstock corporation" is any nonprofit nonstock corporation that is exempt from taxation under § 501(c)(3) of the United States Internal Revenue Code [26 U.S.C. § 501(c)(3)], or any successor provisions.

(2)   A "membership interest" is, unless otherwise provided in a nonstock corporation's certificate of incorporation, a member's share of the profits and losses of a nonstock corporation, or a member's right to receive distributions of the nonstock corporation's assets, or both;

(3)   A "nonprofit nonstock corporation" is a nonstock corporation that does not have membership interests; and

(4)   A "nonstock corporation" is any corporation organized under this chapter that is not authorized to issue capital stock.

§ 115. Forum Selection Provisions

The certification of incorporation or the bylaws may require, consistent with applicable jurisdictional requirements, that any or all internal corporate claims shall be brought solely and exclusively in any or all of the courts in this State, and no provision of the certificate of incorporation or the bylaws may prohibit bringing such claims in the courts of this State. "Internal corporate claims" means claims, including claims in the right of the corporation, (i) that are based upon a violation of a duty by a current or former director or officer or stockholder in such capacity, or (ii) as to which this title confers jurisdiction upon the Court of Chancery.

§ 121. General Powers

(a)   In addition to the powers enumerated in § 122 of this title, every corporation, its officers, directors and stockholders shall possess and may exercise all the powers and privileges granted by this chapter or by any other law or by its certificate of incorporation, together with any powers incidental thereto, so far as such powers and privileges are necessary or convenient to the conduct, promotion or attainment of the business or purposes set forth in its certificate of incorporation.

(b)   Every corporation shall be governed by the provisions and be subject to the restrictions and liabilities contained in this chapter.

§ 122. Specific Powers

Every corporation created under this chapter shall have power to:

(1)   Have perpetual succession by its corporate name, unless a limited period of duration is stated in its certificate of incorporation;

(2)   Sue and be sued in all courts and participate, as a party or otherwise, in any judicial, administrative, arbitrative or other proceeding, in its corporate name;

(3)   Have a corporate seal, which may be altered at pleasure, and use the same by causing it or a facsimile thereof, to be impressed or affixed or in any other manner reproduced;

(4)   Purchase, receive, take by grant, gift, devise, bequest or otherwise, lease, or otherwise acquire, own, hold, improve, employ, use and otherwise deal in and with real or personal property, or any interest therein, wherever situated, and to sell, convey, lease, exchange, transfer or otherwise dispose of, or mortgage or pledge, all or any of its property and assets, or any interest therein, wherever situated;

(5)   Appoint such officers and agents as the business of the corporation requires and to pay or otherwise provide for them suitable compensation;

(6)   Adopt, amend and repeal bylaws;

(7)   Wind up and dissolve itself in the manner provided in this chapter;

(8)   Conduct its business, carry on its operations and have offices and exercise its powers within or without this State;

(9)   Make donations for the public welfare or for charitable, scientific or educational purposes, and in time of war or other national emergency in aid thereof;

(10) Be an incorporator, promoter or manager of other corporations of any type or kind;

(11) Participate with others in any corporation, partnership, limited partnership, joint venture or other association of any kind, or in any transaction, undertaking or arrangement which the participating corporation would have power to conduct by itself, whether or not such participation involves sharing or delegation of control with or to others;

(12) Transact any lawful business which the corporation's board of directors shall find to be in aid of governmental authority;

(13) Make contracts, including contracts of guaranty and suretyship, incur liabilities, borrow money at such rates of interest as the corporation may determine, issue its notes, bonds and other obligations, and secure any of its obligations by mortgage, pledge or other encumbrance of all or any of its property, franchises and income, and make contracts of guaranty and suretyship which are necessary or convenient to the conduct, promotion or attainment of the business of (a) a corporation all of the outstanding stock of which is owned, directly or indirectly, by the contracting corporation, or (b) a corporation which owns, directly or indirectly, all of the outstanding stock of the contracting corporation, or (c) a corporation all of the outstanding stock of which is owned, directly or indirectly, by a corporation which owns, directly or indirectly, all of the outstanding stock of the contracting corporation, which contracts of guaranty and suretyship shall be deemed to be necessary or convenient to the conduct, promotion or attainment of the business of the contracting corporation, and make other contracts of guaranty and suretyship which are necessary or convenient to the conduct, promotion or attainment of the business of the contracting corporation;

(14) Lend money for its corporate purposes, invest and reinvest its funds, and take, hold and deal with real and personal property as security for the payment of funds so loaned or invested;

(15) Pay pensions and establish and carry out pension, profit sharing, stock option, stock purchase, stock bonus, retirement, benefit, incentive and compensation plans, trusts and provisions for any or all of its directors, officers and employees, and for any or all of the directors, officers and employees of its subsidiaries;

(16) Provide insurance for its benefit on the life of any of its directors, officers or employees, or on the life of any stockholder for the purpose of acquiring at such stockholder's death shares of its stock owned by such stockholder.

(17) Renounce, in its certificate of incorporation or by action of its board of directors, any interest or expectancy of the corporation in, or in being offered an opportunity to participate in, specified business opportunities or specified classes or categories of business opportunities that are presented to the corporation or 1 or more of its officers, directors or stockholders.

§ 123. Powers Respecting Securities of Other Corporations or Entities

Any corporation organized under the laws of this State may guarantee, purchase, take, receive, subscribe for or otherwise acquire; own, hold, use or otherwise employ; sell, lease, exchange, transfer or otherwise dispose of; mortgage, lend, pledge or otherwise deal in and with, bonds and other obligations of, or shares or other securities or interests in, or issued by, any other domestic or foreign corporation, partnership, association or individual, or by any government or agency or instrumentality thereof. A corporation while owner of any such securities may exercise all the rights, powers and privileges of ownership, including the right to vote.

§ 124. Effect of Lack of Corporate Capacity or Power; Ultra Vires

No act of a corporation and no conveyance or transfer of real or personal property to or by a corporation shall be invalid by reason of the fact that the corporation was without capacity or power to do such act or to make or receive such conveyance or transfer, but such lack of capacity or power may be asserted:

(1) In a proceeding by a stockholder against the corporation to enjoin the doing of any act or acts or the transfer of real or personal property by or to the corporation. If the unauthorized acts or transfer sought to be enjoined are being, or are to be, performed or made pursuant to any contract to which the corporation is a party, the court may, if all of the parties to the contract are parties to the proceeding and if it deems the same to be equitable, set aside and enjoin the performance of such contract, and in so doing may allow to the corporation or to the other parties to the contract, as the case may be, such compensation as may be equitable for the loss or damage sustained by any of them which may result from the action of the court in setting aside and

enjoining the performance of such contract, but anticipated profits to be derived from the performance of the contract shall not be awarded by the court as a loss or damage sustained;

(2) In a proceeding by the corporation, whether acting directly or through a receiver, trustee or other legal representative, or through stockholders in a representative suit, against an incumbent or former officer or director of the corporation, for loss or damage due to such incumbent or former officer's or director's unauthorized act;

(3) In a proceeding by the Attorney General to dissolve the corporation, or to enjoin the corporation from the transaction of unauthorized business.

§ 125. Conferring Academic or Honorary Degrees

No corporation organized after April 18, 1945, shall have power to confer academic or honorary degrees unless the certificate of incorporation or an amendment thereof shall so provide and unless the certificate of incorporation or an amendment thereof prior to its being filed in the office of the Secretary of State shall have endorsed thereon the approval of the Department of Education of this State. No corporation organized before April 18, 1945, any provision in its certificate of incorporation to the contrary notwithstanding, shall possess the power aforesaid without first filing in the office of the Secretary of State a certificate of amendment so providing, the filing of which certificate of amendment in the office of the Secretary of State shall be subject to prior approval of the Department of Education, evidenced as hereinabove provided. Approval shall be granted only when it appears to the reasonable satisfaction of the Department of Education that the corporation is engaged in conducting a bona fide institution of higher learning, giving instructions in arts and letters, science or the professions, or that the corporation proposes, in good faith, to engage in that field and has or will have the resources, including personnel, requisite for the conduct of an institution of higher learning. Upon dissolution, all such corporations shall comply with § 8530 of Title 14. Notwithstanding any provision herein to the contrary, no corporation shall have the power to conduct a private business or trade school unless the certificate of incorporation or an amendment thereof, prior to its being filed in the office of the Secretary of State, shall have endorsed thereon the approval of the Department of Education pursuant to Chapter 85 of Title 14. Notwithstanding the foregoing provisions, any corporation conducting a law school, which has its principal place of operation in Delaware, and which intends to meet the standards of approval of the American Bar Association, may, after it has been in actual operation for not less than 1 year, retain at its own expense a dean or dean emeritus of a law school fully approved by the American Bar Association to make an on-site inspection and report concerning the progress of the corporation toward meeting the standards for approval by the American Bar Association. Such dean or dean emeritus shall be chosen by the Attorney General from a panel of 3 deans whose names are presented to the Attorney General as being willing to serve. One such dean on this panel shall be nominated by the trustees of said law school corporation; another dean shall be nominated by a committee of the Student Bar Association of said law school; and the other dean shall be nominated by a committee of lawyers who are parents of students attending such law school. If any of the above-named groups cannot find a dean, it may substitute 2 full professors of accredited law schools for the dean it is entitled to nominate, and in such a case if the Attorney General chooses 1 of such professors, such professor shall serve the function of a dean as herein prescribed. If the dean so retained shall report in writing that, in such dean's professional judgment, the corporation is attempting, in good faith, to comply with the standards for approval of the American Bar Association and is making reasonable progress toward meeting such standards, the corporation may file a copy of the report with the Secretary of Education and with the Attorney General. Any corporation which complies with these provisions by filing such report shall be deemed to have temporary approval from the State and shall be entitled to amend its certificate of incorporation to authorize the granting of standard academic law degrees. Thereafter, until the law school operated by the corporation is approved by the American Bar Association, the corporation shall file once during each academic year a new report, in the same manner as the first report. If, at any time, the corporation fails to file such a report, or if the dean retained to render such report states that, in such dean's opinion, the corporation is not continuing to make reasonable progress toward accreditation, the Attorney General, at the request of the Secretary of Education, may file a complaint in the Court of Chancery to suspend said temporary approval and degree-granting power until a further report is filed by a dean or dean emeritus of an accredited law school that the school has resumed its progress towards meeting the standards for approval. Upon approval of the law school by the American Bar Association, temporary approval shall become final, and shall no longer be subject to suspension or vacation under this section.

§ 126.   Banking Power Denied

(a)   No corporation organized under this chapter shall possess the power of issuing bills, notes, or other evidences of debt for circulation as money, or the power of carrying on the business of receiving deposits of money.

(b)   Corporations organized under this chapter to buy, sell and otherwise deal in notes, open accounts and other similar evidences of debt, or to loan money and to take notes, open accounts and other similar evidences of debt as collateral security therefor, shall not be deemed to be engaging in the business of banking.

§ 127.   Private Foundation; Powers and Duties

A corporation of this State which is a private foundation under the United States internal revenue laws and whose certificate of incorporation does not expressly provide that this section shall not apply to it is required to act or to refrain from acting so as not to subject itself to the taxes imposed by 26 U.S.C. § 4941 (relating to taxes on self-dealing), § 4942 (relating to taxes on failure to distribute income), § 4943 (relating to taxes on excess business holdings), § 4944 (relating to taxes on investments which jeopardize charitable purpose), or § 4945 (relating to taxable expenditures), or corresponding provisions of any subsequent United States internal revenue law.

§ 131.   Registered Office in State; Principal Office or Place of Business in State

(a)   Every corporation shall have and maintain in this State a registered office which may, but need not be, the same as its place of business.

(b)   Whenever the term "corporation's principal office or place of business in this State" or "principal office or place of business of the corporation in this State," or other term of like import, is or has been used in a corporation's certificate of incorporation, or in any other document, or in any statute, it shall be deemed to mean and refer to, unless the context indicates otherwise, the corporation's registered office required by this section; and it shall not be necessary for any corporation to amend its certificate of incorporation or any other document to comply with this section.

(c)   As contained in any certificate of incorporation or other document filed with the Secretary of State under this chapter, the address of a registered office shall include the street, number, city, county and postal code.

§ 132.   Registered Agent in State; Resident Agent

(a)   Every corporation shall have and maintain in this State a registered agent, which agent may be any of:

(1)   The corporation itself;

(2)   An individual resident in this State;

(3)   A domestic corporation (other than the corporation itself), a domestic partnership (whether general (including a limited liability partnership) or limited (including a limited liability limited partnership)), a domestic limited liability company or a domestic statutory trust; or

(4)   A foreign corporation, a foreign partnership (whether general (including a limited liability partnership) or limited (including a limited liability limited partnership)), a foreign limited liability company or a foreign statutory trust.

(b)   Every registered agent for a domestic corporation or a foreign corporation shall:

(1)   If an entity, maintain a business office in this State which is generally open, or if an individual, be generally present at a designated location in this State, at sufficiently frequent times to accept service of process and otherwise perform the functions of a registered agent;

(2)   If a foreign entity, be authorized to transact business in this State;

(3)   Accept service of process and other communications directed to the corporations for which it serves as registered agent and forward same to the corporation to which the service or communication is directed;

(4)   Forward to the corporations for which it serves as registered agent the annual report required by § 502 of this title or an electronic notification of same in a form satisfactory to the Secretary of State ("Secretary"); and

(5)   Satisfy and adhere to regulations established by the Secretary regarding the verification of both the identity of the entity's contacts and individuals for which the registered agent maintains a record for the reduction of risk of unlawful business purposes.

(c)   Any registered agent who at any time serves as registered agent for more than 50 entities (a "commercial registered agent"), whether domestic or foreign, shall satisfy and comply with the following qualifications.

(1)   A natural person serving as a commercial registered agent shall:

a.   Maintain a principal residence or a principal place of business in this State;

b.   Maintain a Delaware business license;

c.   Be generally present at a designated location within this State during normal business hours to accept service of process and otherwise perform the functions of a registered agent as specified in subsection (b) of this section;

d.   Provide the Secretary upon request with such information identifying and enabling communication with such commercial registered agent as the Secretary shall require; and

e.   Satisfy and adhere to regulations established by the Secretary regarding the verification of both the identity of the entity's contacts and individuals for which the natural person maintains a record for the reduction of risk of unlawful business purposes.

(2)   A domestic or foreign corporation, a domestic or foreign partnership (whether general (including a limited liability partnership) or limited (including a limited liability limited partnership)), a domestic or foreign limited liability company, or a domestic or foreign statutory trust serving as a commercial registered agent shall:

a.   Have a business office within this State which is generally open during normal business hours to accept service of process and otherwise perform the functions of a registered agent as specified in subsection (b) of this section;

b.   Maintain a Delaware business license;

c.   Have generally present at such office during normal business hours an officer, director or managing agent who is a natural person;

d.   Provide the Secretary upon request with such information identifying and enabling communication with such commercial registered agent as the Secretary shall require; and

e.   Satisfy and adhere to regulations established by the Secretary regarding the verification of both the identity of the entity's contacts and individuals for which it maintains a record for the reduction of risk of unlawful business purposes.

(3)   For purposes of this subsection and paragraph (f)(2)a, of this section, a commercial registered agent shall also include any registered agent which has an officer, director or managing agent in common with any other registered agent or agents if such registered agents at any time during such common service as officer, director or managing agent collectively served as registered agents for more than 50 entities, whether domestic or foreign.

(d)   Every corporation formed under the laws of this State or qualified to do business in this State shall provide to its registered agent and update from time to time as necessary the name, business address and business telephone number of a natural person who is an officer, director, employee, or designated agent of the corporation, who is then authorized to receive communications from the registered agent. Such person shall be deemed the communications contact for the corporation. Every registered agent shall retain (in paper or electronic form) the above information concerning the current communications contact for each corporation for which he, she or it serves as a registered agent. If the corporation fails to provide the registered agent with a current communications contact, the registered agent may resign as the registered agent for such corporation pursuant to 136 of this title.

(e)   The Secretary is fully authorized to issue such regulations, as may be necessary or appropriate to carry out the enforcement of subsections (b), (c) and (d) of this section, and to take actions reasonable and necessary to assure registered agents' compliance with subsections (b), (c) and (d) of this section. Such actions may include refusal to file documents submitted by a registered agent, including the refusal to file any documents regarding an entity's formation.

(f)   Upon application of the Secretary, the Court of Chancery may enjoin any person or entity from serving as a registered agent or as an officer, director or managing agent of a registered agent.

(1)   Upon the filing of a complaint by the Secretary pursuant to this section, the Court may make such orders respecting such proceeding as it deems appropriate, and may enter such orders granting interim or final relief as it deems proper under the circumstances.

(2)   Any one or more of the following grounds shall be a sufficient basis to grant an injunction pursuant to this section:

a.   With respect to any registered agent who at any time within 1 year immediately prior to the filing of the Secretary's complaint is a commercial registered agent, failure after notice and warning to comply with the qualifications set forth in subsection (b) of this section and/or the requirements of subsection (c) or (d) of this section above;

b.   The person serving as a registered agent, or any person who is an officer, director or managing agent of an entity registered agent, has been convicted of a felony or any crime which includes an element of dishonesty or fraud or involves moral turpitude;

c.   The registered agent has engaged in conduct in connection with acting as a registered agent that is intended to or likely to deceive or defraud the public.

(3)   With respect to any order the court enters pursuant to this section with respect to an entity that has acted as a registered agent, the court may also direct such order to any person who has served as an officer, director, or managing agent of such registered agent. Any person who, on or after January 1, 2007, serves as an officer, director, or managing agent of an entity acting as a registered agent in this State shall be deemed thereby to have consented to the appointment of such registered agent as agent upon whom service of process may be made in any action brought pursuant to this section, and service as an officer, director, or managing agent of an entity acting as a registered agent in this State shall be a signification of the consent of such person that any process when so served shall be of the same legal force and validity as if served upon such person within this State, and such appointment of the registered agent shall be irrevocable.

(4)   Upon the entry of an order by the Court enjoining any person or entity from acting as a registered agent, the Secretary shall mail or deliver notice of such order to each affected

corporation at the address of its principal place of business as specified in its most recent franchise tax report or other record of the Secretary. If such corporation is a domestic corporation and fails to obtain and designate a new registered agent within 30 days after such notice is given, the Secretary shall declare the charter of such corporation forfeited. If such corporation is a foreign corporation, and fails to obtain and designate a new registered agent within 30 days after such notice is given, the Secretary shall forfeit its qualification to do business in this State. If the court enjoins a person or entity from acting as a registered agent as provided in this section and no new registered agent shall have been obtained and designated in the time and manner aforesaid, service of legal process against the corporation for which the registered agent had been acting shall thereafter be upon the Secretary in accordance with § 321 of this title. The Court of Chancery may, upon application of the Secretary on notice to the former registered agent, enter such orders as it deems appropriate to give the Secretary access to information in the former registered agent's possession in order to facilitate communication with the corporations the former registered agent served.

(g)   The Secretary is authorized to make a list of registered agents available to the public, and to establish such qualifications and issue such rules and regulations with respect to such listing as the Secretary deems necessary or appropriate.

(h)   Whenever the term "resident agent" or "resident agent in charge of a corporation's principal office or place of business in this State," or other term of like import which refers to a corporation's agent required by statute to be located in this State, is or has been used in a corporation's certificate of incorporation, or in any other document, or in any statute, it shall be deemed to mean and refer to, unless the context indicates otherwise, the corporation's registered agent required by this section; and it shall not be necessary for any corporation to amend its certificate of incorporation or any other document to comply with this section.

§ 133.   Change of Location of Registered Office; Change of Registered Agent

Any corporation may, by resolution of its board of directors, change the location of its registered office in this State to any other place in this State. By like resolution, the registered agent of a corporation may be changed to any other person or corporation including itself. In either such case, the resolution shall be as detailed in its statement as is required by § 102(a)(2) of this title. Upon the adoption of such a resolution, a certificate certifying the change shall be executed, acknowledged, and filed in accordance with § 103 of this title.

§ 134.   Change of Address or Name of Registered Agent

(a)   A registered agent may change the address of the registered office of the corporation or corporations for which the agent is a registered agent to another address in this State by filing with the Secretary of State a certificate, executed and acknowledged by such registered agent, setting forth the address at which such registered agent has maintained the registered office for each of the corporations for which it is a registered agent, and further certifying to the new address to which each such registered office will be changed on a given day, and at which new address such registered agent will thereafter maintain the registered office for each of the corporations for which it is a registered agent. Thereafter, or until further change of address, as authorized by law, the registered office in this State of each of the corporations for which the agent is a registered agent shall be located at the new address of the registered agent thereof as given in the certificate.

(b)   In the event of a change of name of any person or corporation acting as registered agent in this State, such registered agent shall file with the Secretary of State a certificate, executed and acknowledged by such registered agent, setting forth the new name of such registered agent, the name of such registered agent before it was changed, and the address at which such registered agent has maintained the registered office for each of the corporations for which it acts as a registered agent. A change of name of any person or corporation acting as a registered agent as a result of a merger or consolidation of the registered agent, with or into another person or corporation which succeeds to its assets by operation of law, shall be deemed a change of name for purposes of this section.

§ 135. Resignation of Registered Agent Coupled With Appointment of Successor

The registered agent of 1 or more corporations may resign and appoint a successor registered agent by filing a certificate with the Secretary of State, stating the name and address of the successor agent, in accordance with § 102(a)(2) of this title. There shall be attached to such certificate a statement of each affected corporation ratifying and approving such change of registered agent. Each such statement shall be executed and acknowledged in accordance with § 103 of this title. Upon such filing, the successor registered agent shall become the registered agent of such corporations as have ratified and approved such substitution and the successor registered agent's address, as stated in such certificate, shall become the address of each such corporation's registered office in this State. The Secretary of State shall then issue a certificate that the successor registered agent has become the registered agent of the corporations so ratifying and approving such change and setting out the names of such corporations.

§ 136. Resignation of Registered Agent Not Coupled With Appointment of Successor

(a) The registered agent of 1 or more corporations may resign without appointing a successor by filing a certificate of resignation with the Secretary of State, but such resignation shall not become effective until 30 days after the certificate is filed. The certificate shall be executed and acknowledged by the registered agent, shall contain a statement that written notice of resignation was given to each affected corporation at least 30 days prior to the filing of the certificate by mailing or delivering such notice to the corporation at its address last known to the registered agent and shall set forth the date of such notice.

(b) After receipt of the notice of the resignation of its registered agent, provided for in subsection (a) of this section, the corporation for which such registered agent was acting shall obtain and designate a new registered agent to take the place of the registered agent so resigning in the same manner as provided in § 133 of this title for change of registered agent. If such corporation, being a corporation of this State, fails to obtain and designate a new registered agent as aforesaid prior to the expiration of the period of 30 days after the filing by the registered agent of the certificate of resignation, the Secretary of State shall declare the charter of such corporation forfeited. If such corporation, being a foreign corporation, fails to obtain and designate a new registered agent as aforesaid prior to the expiration of the period of 30 days after the filing by the registered agent of the certificate of resignation, the Secretary of State shall forfeit its authority to do business in this State.

(c) After the resignation of the registered agent shall have become effective as provided in this section and if no new registered agent shall have been obtained and designated in the time and manner aforesaid, service of legal process against the corporation for which the resigned registered agent had been acting shall thereafter be upon the Secretary of State in accordance with § 321 of this title.

§ 141. Board of Directors; Powers; Number, Qualifications, Terms and Quorum; Committees; Classes of Directors; Nonstock Corporations; Reliance Upon Books; Action Without Meeting; Removal

(a) The business and affairs of every corporation organized under this chapter shall be managed by or under the direction of a board of directors, except as may be otherwise provided in this chapter or in its certificate of incorporation. If any such provision is made in the certificate of incorporation, the powers and duties conferred or imposed upon the board of directors by this chapter shall be exercised or performed to such extent and by such person or persons as shall be provided in the certificate of incorporation.

(b) The board of directors of a corporation shall consist of 1 or more members, each of whom shall be a natural person. The number of directors shall be fixed by, or in the manner provided in, the bylaws, unless the certificate of incorporation fixes the number of directors, in which case a change in the number of directors shall be made only by amendment of the certificate. Directors need not be stockholders unless so required by the certificate of incorporation or the bylaws. The certificate of incorporation or bylaws may prescribe other qualifications for directors. Each director shall hold office until such director's successor is elected and qualified or until such director's earlier resignation or removal. Any director may resign at any time upon notice given in writing or by electronic transmission to the corporation. A resignation is effective when the resignation is delivered unless the resignation specifies a later effective date or an effective date determined upon the happening of an event or events. A resignation which is conditioned upon the director failing to receive a specified vote for reelection as a director may provide that it is irrevocable. A majority of the total number of directors shall constitute a quorum for the transaction of business unless the certificate of incorporation or the bylaws require a greater number. Unless the certificate of incorporation provides otherwise, the bylaws may provide that a number less than a majority shall constitute a quorum which in no case shall be less than 1/3 of the total number of directors. The vote of the majority of the directors present at a meeting at which a quorum is present shall be the act of the board of directors unless the certificate of incorporation or the bylaws shall require a vote of a greater number.

(c)(1)   All corporations incorporated prior to July 1, 1996, shall be governed by this paragraph (c)(1) of this section, provided that any such corporation may by a resolution adopted by a majority of the whole board elect to be governed by paragraph (c)(2) of this section, in which case this paragraph (c)(1) of this section shall not apply to such corporation. All corporations incorporated on or after July 1, 1996, shall be governed by paragraph (c)(2) of this section. The board of directors may, by resolution passed by a majority of the whole board, designate 1 or more committees, each committee to consist of 1 or more of the directors of the corporation. The board may designate 1 or more directors as alternate members of any committee, who may replace any absent or disqualified member at any meeting of the committee. The bylaws may provide that in the absence or disqualification of a member of a committee, the member or members present at any meeting and not disqualified from voting, whether or not the member or members present constitute a quorum, may unanimously appoint another member of the board of directors to act at the meeting in the place of any such absent or disqualified member. Any such committee, to the extent provided in the resolution of the board of directors, or in the bylaws of the corporation, shall have and may exercise all the powers and authority of the board of directors in the management of the business and affairs of the corporation, and may authorize the seal of the corporation to be affixed to all papers which may require it; but no such committee shall have the power or authority in reference to amending the certificate of incorporation (except that a committee may, to the extent authorized in the resolution or resolutions providing for the issuance of shares of stock adopted by the board of directors as provided in § 151(a) of this title, fix the designations and any of the preferences or rights of such shares relating to dividends, redemption, dissolution, any distribution of assets of the corporation or the conversion into, or the exchange of such shares for, shares of any other class or classes or any other series of the same or any other class or classes of stock of the corporation or fix the number of shares of any series of stock or authorize the increase or decrease of the shares of any series), adopting an agreement of merger or consolidation under § 251, § 252, § 254, § 255, § 256, § 257, § 258, § 263 or § 264 of this title, recommending to the stockholders the sale, lease or exchange of all or substantially all of the corporation's property and assets, recommending to the stockholders a dissolution of the corporation or a revocation of a dissolution, or amending the bylaws of the corporation; and, unless the resolution, bylaws or certificate of incorporation expressly so provides, no such committee shall have the power or authority to declare a dividend, to authorize the issuance of stock or to adopt a certificate of ownership and merger pursuant to § 253 of this title.

(2)   The board of directors may designate 1 or more committees, each committee to consist of 1 or more of the directors of the corporation. The board may designate 1 or more directors as alternate members of any committee, who may replace any absent or disqualified member at any meeting of the committee. The bylaws may provide that in the absence or disqualification of a member of a committee, the member or members present at any meeting and not disqualified from voting, whether or not such member or members constitute a quorum, may unanimously appoint another member of the board of directors to act at the meeting in the place of any such

absent or disqualified member. Any such committee, to the extent provided in the resolution of the board of directors, or in the bylaws of the corporation, shall have and may exercise all the powers and authority of the board of directors in the management of the business and affairs of the corporation, and may authorize the seal of the corporation to be affixed to all papers which may require it; but no such committee shall have the power or authority in reference to the following matter: (i) approving or adopting, or recommending to the stockholders, any action or matter (other than the election or removal of directors) expressly required by this chapter to be submitted to stockholders for approval or (ii) adopting, amending or repealing any bylaw of the corporation.

(3) Unless otherwise provided in the certificate of incorporation, the bylaws or the resolution of the board of directors designating the committee, a committee may create 1 or more subcommittees, each subcommittee to consist of 1 or more members of the committee, and delegate to a subcommittee any or all of the powers and authority of the committee. Except for references to committees and members of committees in subsection (c) of this section, every reference in this chapter to a committee of the board of directors or a member of a committee shall be deemed to include a reference to a subcommittee or member of a subcommittee.

(4) A majority of the directors then serving on a committee of the board of directors or on a subcommittee of a committee shall constitute a quorum for the transaction of business by the committee or subcommittee, unless the certificate of incorporation, the bylaws, a resolution of the board of directors or a resolution of a committee that created the subcommittee requires a greater or lesser number, provided that in no case shall a quorum be less than 1/3 of the directors then serving on the committee or subcommittee. The vote of the majority of the members of a committee or subcommittee present at a meeting at which a quorum is present shall be the act of the committee or subcommittee, unless the certificate of incorporation, the bylaws, a resolution of the board of directors or a resolution of a committee that created the subcommittee requires a greater number.

(d) The directors of any corporation organized under this chapter may, by the certificate of incorporation or by an initial bylaw, or by a bylaw adopted by a vote of the stockholders, be divided into 1, 2 or 3 classes; the term of office of those of the first class to expire at the first annual meeting held after such classification becomes effective; of the second class 1 year thereafter; of the third class 2 years thereafter; and at each annual election held after such classification becomes effective, directors shall be chosen for a full term, as the case may be, to succeed those whose terms expire. The certificate of incorporation or bylaw provision dividing the directors into classes may authorize the board of directors to assign members of the board already in office to such classes at the time such classification becomes effective. The certificate of incorporation may confer upon holders of any class or series of stock the right to elect 1 or more directors who shall serve for such term, and have such voting powers as shall be stated in the certificate of incorporation. The terms of office and voting powers of the directors elected separately by the holders of any class or series of stock may be greater than or less than those of any other director or class of directors. In addition, the certificate of incorporation may confer upon 1 or more directors, whether or not elected separately by the holders of any class or series of stock, voting powers greater than or less than those of other directors. Any such provision conferring greater or lesser voting power shall apply to voting in any committee, unless otherwise provided in the certificate of incorporation or bylaws. If the certificate of incorporation provides that 1 or more directors shall have more or less than 1 vote per director on any matter, every reference in this chapter to a majority or other proportion of the directors shall refer to a majority or other proportion of the votes of the directors.

(e) A member of the board of directors, or a member of any committee designated by the board of directors, shall, in the performance of such member's duties, be fully protected in relying in good faith upon the records of the corporation and upon such information, opinions, reports or statements presented to the corporation by any of the corporation's officers or employees, or committees of the board of directors, or by any other person as to matters the member reasonably believes are within such other person's professional or expert competence and who has been selected with reasonable care by or on behalf of the corporation.

(f)   Unless otherwise restricted by the certificate of incorporation or bylaws, any action required or permitted to be taken at any meeting of the board of directors or of any committee thereof may be taken without a meeting if all members of the board or committee, as the case may be, consent thereto in writing, or by electronic transmission and the writing or writings or electronic transmission or transmissions are filed with the minutes of proceedings of the board, or committee. Such filing shall be in paper form if the minutes are maintained in paper form and shall be in electronic form if the minutes are maintained in electronic form. Any person (whether or not then a director) may provide, whether through instruction to an agent or otherwise, that a consent to action will be effective at a future time (including a time determined upon the happening of an event), no later than 60 days after such instruction is given or such provision is made and such consent shall be deemed to have been given for purposes of this subsection at such effective time so long as such person is then a director and did not revoke the consent prior to such time. Any such consent shall be revocable prior to its becoming effective.

(g)   Unless otherwise restricted by the certificate of incorporation or bylaws, the board of directors of any corporation organized under this chapter may hold its meetings, and have an office or offices, outside of this State.

(h)   Unless otherwise restricted by the certificate of incorporation or bylaws, the board of directors shall have the authority to fix the compensation of directors.

(i)   Unless otherwise restricted by the certificate of incorporation or bylaws, members of the board of directors of any corporation, or any committee designated by the board, may participate in a meeting of such board, or committee by means of conference telephone or other communications equipment by means of which all persons participating in the meeting can hear each other, and participation in a meeting pursuant to this subsection shall constitute presence in person at the meeting.

(j)   The certificate of incorporation of any nonstock corporation may provide that less than 1/3 of the members of the governing body may constitute a quorum thereof and may otherwise provide that the business and affairs of the corporation shall be managed in a manner different from that provided in this section. Except as may be otherwise provided by the certificate of incorporation, this section shall apply to such a corporation, and when so applied, all references to the board of directors, to members thereof, and to stockholders shall be deemed to refer to the governing body of the corporation, the members thereof and the members of the corporation, respectively; and all references to stock, capital stock, or shares thereof shall be deemed to refer to memberships of a nonprofit nonstock corporation and to membership interests of any other nonstock corporation.

(k)   Any director or the entire board of directors may be removed, with or without cause, by the holders of a majority of the shares then entitled to vote at an election of directors, except as follows:

(1)   Unless the certificate of incorporation otherwise provides, in the case of a corporation whose board is classified as provided in subsection (d) of this section, stockholders may effect such removal only for cause; or

(2)   In the case of a corporation having cumulative voting, if less than the entire board is to be removed, no director may be removed without cause if the votes cast against such director's removal would be sufficient to elect such director if then cumulatively voted at an election of the entire board of directors, or, if there be classes of directors, at an election of the class of directors of which such director is a part.

Whenever the holders of any class or series are entitled to elect 1 or more directors by the certificate of incorporation, this subsection shall apply, in respect to the removal without cause of a director or directors so elected, to the vote of the holders of the outstanding shares of that class or series and not to the vote of the outstanding shares as a whole.

§ 142. Officers; Titles, Duties, Selection, Term; Failure to Elect; Vacancies

(a)   Every corporation organized under this chapter shall have such officers with such titles and duties as shall be stated in the bylaws or in a resolution of the board of directors which is not inconsistent with the bylaws and as may be necessary to enable it to sign instruments and stock certificates which comply with §§ 103(a)(2) and 158 of this title. One of the officers shall have the duty to record the proceedings of the meetings of the stockholders and directors in a book to be kept for that purpose. Any number of offices may be held by the same person unless the certificate of incorporation or bylaws otherwise provide.

(b)   Officers shall be chosen in such manner and shall hold their offices for such terms as are prescribed by the bylaws or determined by the board of directors or other governing body. Each officer shall hold office until such officer's successor is elected and qualified or until such officer's earlier resignation or removal. Any officer may resign at any time upon written notice to the corporation.

(c)   The corporation may secure the fidelity of any or all of its officers or agents by bond or otherwise.

(d)   A failure to elect officers shall not dissolve or otherwise affect the corporation.

(e)   Any vacancy occurring in any office of the corporation by death, resignation, removal or otherwise, shall be filled as the bylaws provide. In the absence of such provision, the vacancy shall be filled by the board of directors or other governing body.

§ 143. Loans to Employees and Officers; Guaranty of Obligations of Employees and Officers

Any corporation may lend money to, or guarantee any obligation of, or otherwise assist any officer or other employee of the corporation or of its subsidiary, including any officer or employee who is a director of the corporation or its subsidiary, whenever, in the judgment of the directors, such loan, guaranty or assistance may reasonably be expected to benefit the corporation. The loan, guaranty or other assistance may be with or without interest, and may be unsecured, or secured in such manner as the board of directors shall approve, including, without limitation, a pledge of shares of stock of the corporation. Nothing in this section contained shall be deemed to deny, limit or restrict the powers of guaranty or warranty of any corporation at common law or under any statute.

§ 144. Interested Directors; Quorum

(a)   No contract or transaction between a corporation and 1 or more of its directors or officers, or between a corporation and any other corporation, partnership, association, or other organization in which 1 or more of its directors or officers, are directors or officers, or have a financial interest, shall be void or voidable solely for this reason, or solely because the director or officer is present at or participates in the meeting of the board or committee which authorizes the contract or transaction, or solely because any such director's or officer's votes are counted for such purpose, if:

(1)   The material facts as to the director's or officer's relationship or interest and as to the contract or transaction are disclosed or are known to the board of directors or the committee, and the board or committee in good faith authorizes the contract or transaction by the affirmative votes of a majority of the disinterested directors, even though the disinterested directors be less than a quorum; or

(2)   The material facts as to the director's or officer's relationship or interest and as to the contract or transaction are disclosed or are known to the stockholders entitled to vote thereon, and the contract or transaction is specifically approved in good faith by vote of the stockholders; or

(3)   The contract or transaction is fair as to the corporation as of the time it is authorized, approved or ratified, by the board of directors, a committee or the stockholders.

(b)   Common or interested directors may be counted in determining the presence of a quorum at a meeting of the board of directors or of a committee which authorizes the contract or transaction.

§ 145.   Indemnification of Officers, Directors, Employees and Agents; Insurance

(a)   A corporation shall have power to indemnify any person who was or is a party or is threatened to be made a party to any threatened, pending or completed action, suit or proceeding, whether civil, criminal, administrative or investigative (other than an action by or in the right of the corporation) by reason of the fact that the person is or was a director, officer, employee or agent of the corporation, or is or was serving at the request of the corporation as a director, officer, employee or agent of another corporation, partnership, joint venture, trust or other enterprise, against expenses (including attorneys' fees), judgments, fines and amounts paid in settlement actually and reasonably incurred by the person in connection with such action, suit or proceeding if the person acted in good faith and in a manner the person reasonably believed to be in or not opposed to the best interests of the corporation, and, with respect to any criminal action or proceeding, had no reasonable cause to believe the person's conduct was unlawful. The termination of any action, suit or proceeding by judgment, order, settlement, conviction, or upon a plea of nolo contendere or its equivalent, shall not, of itself, create a presumption that the person did not act in good faith and in a manner which the person reasonably believed to be in or not opposed to the best interests of the corporation, and, with respect to any criminal action or proceeding, had reasonable cause to believe that the person's conduct was unlawful.

(b)   A corporation shall have power to indemnify any person who was or is a party or is threatened to be made a party to any threatened, pending or completed action or suit by or in the right of the corporation to procure a judgment in its favor by reason of the fact that the person is or was a director, officer, employee or agent of the corporation, or is or was serving at the request of the corporation as a director, officer, employee or agent of another corporation, partnership, joint venture, trust or other enterprise against expenses (including attorneys' fees) actually and reasonably incurred by the person in connection with the defense or settlement of such action or suit if the person acted in good faith and in a manner the person reasonably believed to be in or not opposed to the best interests of the corporation and except that no indemnification shall be made in respect of any claim, issue or matter as to which such person shall have been adjudged to be liable to the corporation unless and only to the extent that the Court of Chancery or the court in which such action or suit was brought shall determine upon application that, despite the adjudication of liability but in view of all the circumstances of the case, such person is fairly and reasonably entitled to indemnity for such expenses which the Court of Chancery or such other court shall deem proper.

(c)   To the extent that a present or former director or officer of a corporation has been successful on the merits or otherwise in defense of any action, suit or proceeding referred to in subsections (a) and (b) of this section, or in defense of any claim, issue or matter therein, such person shall be indemnified against expenses (including attorneys' fees) actually and reasonably incurred by such person in connection therewith.

(d)   Any indemnification under subsections (a) and (b) of this section (unless ordered by a court) shall be made by the corporation only as authorized in the specific case upon a determination that indemnification of the present or former director, officer, employee or agent is proper in the circumstances because the person has met the applicable standard of conduct set forth in subsections (a) and (b) of this section. Such determination shall be made, with respect to a person who is a director or officer of the corporation at the time of such determination,

(1)   By a majority vote of the directors who are not parties to such action, suit or proceeding, even though less than a quorum, or

(2)   By a committee of such directors designated by majority vote of such directors, even though less than a quorum, or

(3)   If there are no such directors, or if such directors so direct, by independent legal counsel in a written opinion, or

(4)   By the stockholders.

(e)   Expenses (including attorneys' fees) incurred by an officer or director of the corporation in defending any civil, criminal, administrative or investigative action, suit or proceeding may be paid by the corporation in advance of the final disposition of such action, suit or proceeding upon receipt of an undertaking by or on behalf of such director or officer to repay such amount if it shall ultimately be determined that such person is not entitled to be indemnified by the corporation as authorized in this section. Such expenses (including attorneys' fees) incurred by former directors and officers or other employees and agents of the corporation or by persons serving at the request of the corporation as directors, officers, employees or agents of another corporation, partnership, joint venture, trust or other enterprise may be so paid upon such terms and conditions, if any, as the corporation deems appropriate.

(f)   The indemnification and advancement of expenses provided by, or granted pursuant to, the other subsections of this section shall not be deemed exclusive of any other rights to which those seeking indemnification or advancement of expenses may be entitled under any bylaw, agreement, vote of stockholders or disinterested directors or otherwise, both as to action in such person's official capacity and as to action in another capacity while holding such office. A right to indemnification or to advancement of expenses arising under a provision of the certificate of incorporation or a bylaw shall not be eliminated or impaired by an amendment to the certificate of incorporation or the bylaws after the occurrence of the act or omission that is the subject of the civil, criminal, administrative or investigative action, suit or proceeding for which indemnification or advancement of expenses is sought, unless the provision in effect at the time of such act or omission explicitly authorizes such elimination or impairment after such action or omission has occurred.

(g)   A corporation shall have power to purchase and maintain insurance on behalf of any person who is or was a director, officer, employee or agent of the corporation, or is or was serving at the request of the corporation as a director, officer, employee or agent of another corporation, partnership, joint venture, trust or other enterprise against any liability asserted against such person and incurred by such person in any such capacity, or arising out of such person's status as such, whether or not the corporation would have the power to indemnify such person against such liability under this section.

(h)   For purposes of this section, references to "the corporation" shall include, in addition to the resulting corporation, any constituent corporation (including any constituent of a constituent) absorbed in a consolidation or merger which, if its separate existence had continued, would have had power and authority to indemnify its directors, officers, and employees or agents, so that any person who is or was a director, officer, employee or agent of such constituent corporation, or is or was serving at the request of such constituent corporation as a director, officer, employee or agent of another corporation, partnership, joint venture, trust or other enterprise, shall stand in the same position under this section with respect to the resulting or surviving corporation as such person would have with respect to such constituent corporation if its separate existence had continued.

(i)   For purposes of this section, references to "other enterprises" shall include employee benefit plans; references to "fines" shall include any excise taxes assessed on a person with respect to any employee benefit plan; and references to "serving at the request of the corporation" shall include any service as a director, officer, employee or agent of the corporation which imposes duties on, or involves services by, such director, officer, employee or agent with respect to an employee benefit plan, its participants or beneficiaries; and a person who acted in good faith and in a manner such person reasonably believed to be in the interest of the participants and beneficiaries of an employee benefit plan shall be deemed to have acted in a manner "not opposed to the best interests of the corporation" as referred to in this section.

(j)   The indemnification and advancement of expenses provided by, or granted pursuant to, this section shall, unless otherwise provided when authorized or ratified, continue as to a person who has ceased to be a director, officer, employee or agent and shall inure to the benefit of the heirs, executors and administrators of such a person.

(k)   The Court of Chancery is hereby vested with exclusive jurisdiction to hear and determine all actions for advancement of expenses or indemnification brought under this section or under any bylaw, agreement, vote of stockholders or disinterested directors, or otherwise. The Court of Chancery may summarily determine a corporation's obligation to advance expenses (including attorneys' fees).

§ 146. Submission of Matters for Stockholder Vote

A corporation may agree to submit a matter to a vote of its stockholders whether or not the board of directors determines at any time subsequent to approving such matter that such matter is no longer advisable and recommends that the stockholders reject or vote against the matter.

§ 151. Classes and Series of Stock; Redemption; Rights

(a)   Every corporation may issue 1 or more classes of stock or 1 or more series of stock within any class thereof, any or all of which classes may be of stock with par value or stock without par value and which classes or series may have such voting powers, full or limited, or no voting powers, and such designations, preferences and relative, participating, optional or other special rights, and qualifications, limitations or restrictions thereof, as shall be stated and expressed in the certificate of incorporation or of any amendment thereto, or in the resolution or resolutions providing for the issue of such stock adopted by the board of directors pursuant to authority expressly vested in it by the provisions of its certificate of incorporation. Any of the voting powers, designations, preferences, rights and qualifications, limitations or restrictions of any such class or series of stock may be made dependent upon facts ascertainable outside the certificate of incorporation or of any amendment thereto, or outside the resolution or resolutions providing for the issue of such stock adopted by the board of directors pursuant to authority expressly vested in it by its certificate of incorporation, provided that the manner in which such facts shall operate upon the voting powers, designations, preferences, rights and qualifications, limitations or restrictions of such class or series of stock is clearly and expressly set forth in the certificate of incorporation or in the resolution or resolutions providing for the issue of such stock adopted by the board of directors. The term "facts," as used in this subsection, includes, but is not limited to, the occurrence of any event, including a determination or action by any person or body, including the corporation. The power to increase or decrease or otherwise adjust the capital stock as provided in this chapter shall apply to all or any such classes of stock.

(b)   Any stock of any class or series may be made subject to redemption by the corporation at its option or at the option of the holders of such stock or upon the happening of a specified event; provided however, that immediately following any such redemption the corporation shall have outstanding 1 or more shares of 1 or more classes or series of stock, which share, or shares together, shall have full voting powers. Notwithstanding the limitation stated in the foregoing proviso:

(1)   Any stock of a regulated investment company registered under the Investment Company Act of 1940 [15 U.S.C. § 80a–1 et seq.], as heretofore or hereafter amended, may be made subject to redemption by the corporation at its option or at the option of the holders of such stock.

(2)   Any stock of a corporation which holds (directly or indirectly) a license or franchise from a governmental agency to conduct its business or is a member of a national securities exchange, which license, franchise or membership is conditioned upon some or all of the holders of its stock possessing prescribed qualifications, may be made subject to redemption by the corporation to the extent necessary to prevent the loss of such license, franchise or membership or to reinstate it.

Any stock which may be made redeemable under this section may be redeemed for cash, property or rights, including securities of the same or another corporation, at such time or times, price or prices, or rate or rates, and with such adjustments, as shall be stated in the certificate of incorporation or in the resolution or resolutions providing for the issue of such stock adopted by the board of directors pursuant to subsection (a) of this section.

(c) The holders of preferred or special stock of any class or of any series thereof shall be entitled to receive dividends at such rates, on such conditions and at such times as shall be stated in the certificate of incorporation or in the resolution or resolutions providing for the issue of such stock adopted by the board of directors as hereinabove provided, payable in preference to, or in such relation to, the dividends payable on any other class or classes or of any other series of stock, and cumulative or noncumulative as shall be so stated and expressed. When dividends upon the preferred and special stocks, if any, to the extent of the preference to which such stocks are entitled, shall have been paid or declared and set apart for payment, a dividend on the remaining class or classes or series of stock may then be paid out of the remaining assets of the corporation available for dividends as elsewhere in this chapter provided.

(d) The holders of the preferred or special stock of any class or of any series thereof shall be entitled to such rights upon the dissolution of, or upon any distribution of the assets of, the corporation as shall be stated in the certificate of incorporation or in the resolution or resolutions providing for the issue of such stock adopted by the board of directors as hereinabove provided.

(e) Any stock of any class or of any series thereof may be made convertible into, or exchangeable for, at the option of either the holder or the corporation or upon the happening of a specified event, shares of any other class or classes or any other series of the same or any other class or classes of stock of the corporation, at such price or prices or at such rate or rates of exchange and with such adjustments as shall be stated in the certificate of incorporation or in the resolution or resolutions providing for the issue of such stock adopted by the board of directors as hereinabove provided.

(f) If any corporation shall be authorized to issue more than 1 class of stock or more than 1 series of any class, the powers, designations, preferences and relative, participating, optional, or other special rights of each class of stock or series thereof and the qualifications, limitations or restrictions of such preferences and/or rights shall be set forth in full or summarized on the face or back of the certificate which the corporation shall issue to represent such class or series of stock, provided that, except as otherwise provided in § 202 of this title, in lieu of the foregoing requirements, there may be set forth on the face or back of the certificate which the corporation shall issue to represent such class or series of stock, a statement that the corporation will furnish without charge to each stockholder who so requests the powers, designations, preferences and relative, participating, optional, or other special rights of each class of stock or series thereof and the qualifications, limitations or restrictions of such preferences and/or rights. Within a reasonable time after the issuance or transfer of uncertificated stock, the registered owner thereof shall be given a notice, in writing or by electronic transmission, containing the information required to be set forth or stated on certificates pursuant to this section or § 156, § 202(a), § 218(a) or § 364 of this title or with respect to this section a statement that the corporation will furnish without charge to each stockholder who so requests the powers, designations, preferences and relative participating, optional or other special rights of each class of stock or series thereof and the qualifications, limitations or restrictions of such preferences and/or rights. Except as otherwise expressly provided by law, the rights and obligations of the holders of uncertificated stock and the rights and obligations of the holders of certificates representing stock of the same class and series shall be identical.

(g) When any corporation desires to issue any shares of stock of any class or of any series of any class of which the powers, designations, preferences and relative, participating, optional or other rights, if any, or the qualifications, limitations or restrictions thereof, if any, shall not have been set forth in the certificate of incorporation or in any amendment thereto but shall be provided for in a resolution or resolutions adopted by the board of directors pursuant to authority expressly vested in it by the certificate of incorporation or any amendment thereto, a certificate of designations setting forth a copy of such resolution or resolutions and the number of shares of stock of such class or series as to which the resolution or resolutions apply shall be executed, acknowledged, filed and shall become effective, in accordance with § 103 of this title. Unless otherwise provided in any such resolution or resolutions, the number of shares of stock of any such series to which such resolution or resolutions apply may be increased (but not above the total number of authorized shares of the class) or decreased (but not below the number of shares thereof then outstanding) by a certificate likewise executed, acknowledged and filed setting forth a statement that a specified increase or decrease therein had been authorized and directed by a resolution or resolutions likewise adopted by the board of directors. In case the number of such shares shall be decreased the number of shares so specified in the certificate shall resume the status which they had prior to the adoption of the first resolution or resolutions. When no shares of any such class or series are outstanding, either because none were issued or because no issued shares of any such class or series remain outstanding, a certificate setting forth a resolution or resolutions adopted by the board of directors that none of the authorized shares of such class or series are outstanding, and that none will be issued subject to the certificate of designations previously filed with respect to such class or series, may be executed, acknowledged and filed in accordance with § 103 of this title and, when such certificate becomes effective, it shall have the effect of eliminating from the certificate of incorporation all matters set forth in the certificate of designations with respect to such class or series of stock. Unless otherwise provided in the certificate of incorporation, if no shares of stock have been issued of a class or series of stock established by a resolution of the board of directors, the voting powers, designations, preferences and relative, participating, optional or other rights, if any, or the qualifications, limitations or restrictions thereof, may be amended by a resolution or resolutions adopted by the board of directors. A certificate which:

(1) States that no shares of the class or series have been issued;

(2) Sets forth a copy of the resolution or resolutions; and

(3) If the designation of the class or series is being changed, indicates the original designation and the new designation, shall be executed, acknowledged and filed and shall become effective, in accordance with § 103 of this title. When any certificate filed under this subsection becomes effective, it shall have the effect of amending the certificate of incorporation; except that neither the filing of such certificate nor the filing of a restated certificate of incorporation pursuant to § 245 of this title shall prohibit the board of directors from subsequently adopting such resolutions as authorized by this subsection.

§ 152. Issuance of Stock; Lawful Consideration; Fully Paid Stock

The consideration, as determined pursuant to § 153(a) and (b) of this title, for subscriptions to, or the purchase of, the capital stock to be issued by a corporation shall be paid in such form and in such manner as the board of directors shall determine. The board of directors may authorize capital stock to be issued for consideration consisting of cash, any tangible or intangible property or any benefit to the corporation, or any combination thereof. The resolution authorizing the issuance of capital stock may provide that any stock to be issued pursuant to such resolution may be issued in 1 or more transactions in such numbers and at such times as are set forth in or determined by or in the manner set forth in the resolution, which may include a determination or action by any person or body, including the corporation, provided the resolution fixes a maximum number of shares that may be issued pursuant to such resolution, a time period during which such shares may be issued and a minimum amount of consideration for which such shares may be issued. The board of directors may determine the amount of consideration for which shares may be issued by setting a minimum amount of consideration or approving a formula by which the amount or minimum amount of consideration is determined. The formula may include or be made dependent upon facts ascertainable outside the formula, provided the manner in which such facts shall operate upon the formula is clearly and expressly set forth in the formula or in the resolution approving the formula. In the absence of actual fraud in the transaction, the judgment of the directors as to the value of such consideration shall be conclusive. The capital stock so issued shall be deemed to be fully paid and nonassessable stock upon receipt by the corporation of such consideration; provided, however, nothing contained herein shall prevent the board of directors from issuing partly paid shares under § 156 of this title.

§ 153. Consideration for Stock

(a)   Shares of stock with par value may be issued for such consideration, having a value not less than the par value thereof, as determined from time to time by the board of directors, or by the stockholders if the certificate of incorporation so provides.

(b)   Shares of stock without par value may be issued for such consideration as is determined from time to time by the board of directors, or by the stockholders if the certificate of incorporation so provides.

(c)   Treasury shares may be disposed of by the corporation for such consideration as may be determined from time to time by the board of directors, or by the stockholders if the certificate of incorporation so provides.

(d)   If the certificate of incorporation reserves to the stockholders the right to determine the consideration for the issue of any shares, the stockholders shall, unless the certificate requires a greater vote, do so by a vote of a majority of the outstanding stock entitled to vote thereon.

§ 154. Determination of Amount of Capital; Capital, Surplus and Net Assets Defined

Any corporation may, by resolution of its board of directors, determine that only a part of the consideration which shall be received by the corporation for any of the shares of its capital stock which it shall issue from time to time shall be capital; but, in case any of the shares issued shall be shares having a par value, the amount of the part of such consideration so determined to be capital shall be in excess of the aggregate par value of the shares issued for such consideration having a par value, unless all the shares issued shall be shares having a par value, in which case the amount of the part of such consideration so determined to be capital need be only equal to the aggregate par value of such shares. In each such case the board of directors shall specify in dollars the part of such consideration which shall be capital. If the board of directors shall not have determined (1) at the time of issue of any shares of the capital stock of the corporation issued for cash or (2) within 60 days after the issue of any shares of the capital stock of the corporation issued for consideration other than cash what part of the consideration for such shares shall be capital, the capital of the corporation in respect of such shares shall be an amount equal to the aggregate par value of such shares having a par value, plus the amount of the consideration for such shares without par value. The amount of the consideration so determined to be capital in respect of any shares without par value shall be the stated capital of such shares. The capital of the corporation may be increased from time to time by resolution of the board of directors directing that a portion of the net assets of the corporation in excess of the amount so determined to be capital be transferred to the capital account. The board of directors may direct that the portion of such net assets so transferred shall be treated as capital in respect of any shares of the corporation of any designated class or classes. The excess, if any, at any given time, of the net assets of the corporation over the amount so determined to be capital shall be surplus. Net assets means the amount by which total assets exceed total liabilities. Capital and surplus are not liabilities for this purpose. Notwithstanding anything in this section to the contrary, for purposes of this section and §§ 160 and 170 of this title, the capital of any nonstock corporation shall be deemed to be zero.

§ 155. Fractions of Shares

A corporation may, but shall not be required to, issue fractions of a share. If it does not issue fractions of a share, it shall (1) arrange for the disposition of fractional interests by those entitled thereto, (2) pay in cash the fair value of fractions of a share as of the time when those entitled to receive such fractions are determined or (3) issue scrip or warrants in registered form (either represented by a certificate or uncertificated) or in bearer form (represented by a certificate) which shall entitle the holder to receive a full share upon the surrender of such scrip or warrants aggregating a full share. A certificate for a fractional share or an uncertificated fractional share shall, but scrip or warrants shall not unless otherwise provided therein, entitle the holder to exercise voting rights, to receive dividends thereon and to participate in any of the assets of the corporation in the event of liquidation. The board of directors may cause scrip or warrants to be issued subject to the conditions that they shall become void if not exchanged for certificates representing the full shares or uncertificated full shares before a specified date, or subject to the conditions that the shares for which scrip or warrants are exchangeable may be sold by the corporation and the proceeds thereof distributed to the holders of scrip or warrants, or subject to any other conditions which the board of directors may impose.

§ 156. Partly Paid Shares

Any corporation may issue the whole or any part of its shares as partly paid and subject to call for the remainder of the consideration to be paid therefor. Upon the face or back of each stock certificate issued to represent any such partly paid shares, or upon the books and records of the corporation in the case of uncertificated partly paid shares, the total amount of the consideration to be paid therefor and the amount paid thereon shall be stated. Upon the declaration of any dividend on fully paid shares, the corporation shall declare a dividend upon partly paid shares of the same class, but only upon the basis of the percentage of the consideration actually paid thereon.

§ 157. Rights and Options Respecting Stock

(a) Subject to any provisions in the certificate of incorporation, every corporation may create and issue, whether or not in connection with the issue and sale of any shares of stock or other securities of the corporation, rights or options entitling the holders thereof to acquire from the corporation any shares of its capital stock of any class or classes, such rights or options to be evidenced by or in such instrument or instruments as shall be approved by the board of directors.

(b) The terms upon which, including the time or times which may be limited or unlimited in duration, at or within which, and the consideration (including a formula by which such consideration may be determined) for which any such shares may be acquired from the corporation upon the exercise of any such right or option, shall be such as shall be stated in the certificate of incorporation, or in a resolution adopted by the board of directors providing for the creation and issue of such rights or options, and, in every case, shall be set forth or incorporated by reference in the instrument or instruments evidencing such rights or options. A formula by which such consideration may be determined may include or be made dependent upon facts ascertainable outside the formula, provided the manner in which such facts shall operate upon the formula is clearly and expressly set forth in the formula or in the resolution approving the formula. In the absence of actual fraud in the transaction, the judgment of the directors as to the consideration for the issuance of such rights or options and the sufficiency thereof shall be conclusive.

(c) The board of directors may, by a resolution adopted by the board, authorize 1 or more officers of the corporation to do 1 or both of the following: (i) designate officers and employees of the corporation or of any of its subsidiaries to be recipients of such rights or options created by the corporation, and (ii) determine the number of such rights or options to be received by such officers and employees; provided, however, that the resolution so authorizing such officer or officers shall specify the total number of rights or options such officer or officers may so award. The board of directors may not authorize an officer to designate himself or herself as a recipient of any such rights or options.

(d) In case the shares of stock of the corporation to be issued upon the exercise of such rights or options shall be shares having a par value, the consideration so to be received therefor shall have a value not less than the par value thereof. In case the shares of stock so to be issued shall be shares of stock without par value, the consideration therefor shall be determined in the manner provided in § 153 of this title.

§ 158. Stock Certificates; Uncertificated Shares

The shares of a corporation shall be represented by certificates, provided that the board of directors of the corporation may provide by resolution or resolutions that some or all of any or all classes or series of its stock shall be uncertificated shares. Any such resolution shall not apply to shares represented by a certificate until such certificate is surrendered to the corporation. Every holder of stock represented by certificates shall be entitled to have a certificate signed by, or in the name of the corporation by any 2 authorized officers of the corporation representing the number of shares registered in certificate form. Any or all the signatures on the certificate may be a facsimile. In case any officer, transfer agent or registrar who has signed or whose facsimile signature has been placed upon a certificate shall have ceased to be such officer, transfer agent or registrar before such certificate is issued, it may be issued by the corporation with the same effect as if such person were such officer, transfer agent or registrar at the date of issue. A corporation shall not have power to issue a certificate in bearer form.

§ 159. Shares of Stock; Personal Property, Transfer and Taxation

The shares of stock in every corporation shall be deemed personal property and transferable as provided in Article 8 of subtitle I of Title 6. No stock or bonds issued by any corporation organized under this chapter shall be taxed by this State when the same shall be owned by nonresidents of this State, or by foreign corporations. Whenever any transfer of shares shall be made for collateral security, and not absolutely, it shall be so expressed in the entry of transfer if, when the certificates are presented to the corporation for transfer or uncertificated shares are requested to be transferred, both the transferor and transferee request the corporation to do so.

§ 160. Corporation's Powers Respecting Ownership, Voting, etc., of Its Own Stock; Rights of Stock Called for Redemption

(a) Every corporation may purchase, redeem, receive, take or otherwise acquire, own and hold, sell, lend, exchange, transfer or otherwise dispose of, pledge, use and otherwise deal in and with its own shares; provided, however, that no corporation shall:

(1) Purchase or redeem its own shares of capital stock for cash or other property when the capital of the corporation is impaired or when such purchase or redemption would cause any impairment of the capital of the corporation, except that a corporation other than a nonstock corporation may purchase or redeem out of capital any of its own shares which are entitled upon any distribution of its assets, whether by dividend or in liquidation, to a preference over another class or series of its stock, or, if no shares entitled to such a preference are outstanding, any of its own shares, if such shares will be retired upon their acquisition and the capital of the corporation reduced in accordance with §§ 243 and 244 of this title. Nothing in this subsection shall invalidate or otherwise affect a note, debenture or other obligation of a corporation given by it as consideration for its acquisition by purchase, redemption or exchange of its shares of stock if at the time such note, debenture or obligation was delivered by the corporation its capital was not then impaired or did not thereby become impaired;

(2) Purchase, for more than the price at which they may then be redeemed, any of its shares which are redeemable at the option of the corporation; or

(3)a. In the case of a corporation other than a nonstock corporation, redeem any of its shares, unless their redemption is authorized by § 151(b) of this title and then only in accordance with such section and the certificate of incorporation, or

    b. In the case of a nonstock corporation, redeem any of its membership interests, unless their redemption is authorized by the certificate of incorporation and then only in accordance with the certificate of incorporation.

(b) Nothing in this section limits or affects a corporation's right to resell any of its shares theretofore purchased or redeemed out of surplus and which have not been retired, for such consideration as shall be fixed by the board of directors.

(c)   Shares of its own capital stock belonging to the corporation or to another corporation, if a majority of the shares entitled to vote in the election of directors of such other corporation is held, directly or indirectly, by the corporation, shall neither be entitled to vote nor be counted for quorum purposes. Nothing in this section shall be construed as limiting the right of any corporation to vote stock, including but not limited to its own stock, held by it in a fiduciary capacity.

(d)   Shares which have been called for redemption shall not be deemed to be outstanding shares for the purpose of voting or determining the total number of shares entitled to vote on any matter on and after the date on which written notice of redemption has been sent to holders thereof and a sum sufficient to redeem such shares has been irrevocably deposited or set aside to pay the redemption price to the holders of the shares upon surrender of certificates therefor.

§ 161.   Issuance of Additional Stock; When and by Whom

The directors may, at any time and from time to time, if all of the shares of capital stock which the corporation is authorized by its certificate of incorporation to issue have not been issued, subscribed for, or otherwise committed to be issued, issue or take subscriptions for additional shares of its capital stock up to the amount authorized in its certificate of incorporation.

§ 162.   Liability of Stockholder or Subscriber for Stock Not Paid in Full

(a)   When the whole of the consideration payable for shares of a corporation has not been paid in, and the assets shall be insufficient to satisfy the claims of its creditors, each holder of or subscriber for such shares shall be bound to pay on each share held or subscribed for by such holder or subscriber the sum necessary to complete the amount of the unpaid balance of the consideration for which such shares were issued or are to be issued by the corporation.

(b)   The amounts which shall be payable as provided in subsection (a) of this section may be recovered as provided in § 325 of this title, after a writ of execution against the corporation has been returned unsatisfied as provided in said § 325.

(c)   Any person becoming an assignee or transferee of shares or of a subscription for shares in good faith and without knowledge or notice that the full consideration therefor has not been paid shall not be personally liable for any unpaid portion of such consideration, but the transferor shall remain liable therefor.

(d)   No person holding shares in any corporation as collateral security shall be personally liable as a stockholder but the person pledging such shares shall be considered the holder thereof and shall be so liable. No executor, administrator, guardian, trustee or other fiduciary shall be personally liable as a stockholder, but the estate or funds held by such executor, administrator, guardian, trustee or other fiduciary in such fiduciary capacity shall be liable.

(e)   No liability under this section or under § 325 of this title shall be asserted more than 6 years after the issuance of the stock or the date of the subscription upon which the assessment is sought.

(f)   In any action by a receiver or trustee of an insolvent corporation or by a judgment creditor to obtain an assessment under this section, any stockholder or subscriber for stock of the insolvent corporation may appear and contest the claim or claims of such receiver or trustee.

§ 163.   Payment for Stock Not Paid in Full

The capital stock of a corporation shall be paid for in such amounts and at such times as the directors may require. The directors may, from time to time, demand payment, in respect of each share of stock not fully paid, of such sum of money as the necessities of the business may, in the judgment of the board of directors, require, not exceeding in the whole the balance remaining unpaid on said stock, and such sum so demanded shall be paid to the corporation at such times and by such installments as the directors shall direct. The directors shall give written notice of the time and place of such payments, which notice shall be mailed at least 30 days before the time for such payment, to each holder of or subscriber for stock which is not fully paid at such holder's or subscriber's last known post-office address.

§ 164. Failure to Pay for Stock; Remedies

When any stockholder fails to pay any installment or call upon such stockholder's stock which may have been properly demanded by the directors, at the time when such payment is due, the directors may collect the amount of any such installment or call or any balance thereof remaining unpaid, from the said stockholder by an action at law, or they shall sell at public sale such part of the shares of such delinquent stockholder as will pay all demands then due from such stockholder with interest and all incidental expenses, and shall transfer the shares so sold to the purchaser, who shall be entitled to a certificate therefor.

Notice of the time and place of such sale and of the sum due on each share shall be given by advertisement at least 1 week before the sale, in a newspaper of the county in this State where such corporation's registered office is located, and such notice shall be mailed by the corporation to such delinquent stockholder at such stockholder's last known post-office address, at least 20 days before such sale.

If no bidder can be had to pay the amount due on the stock, and if the amount is not collected by an action at law, which may be brought within the county where the corporation has its registered office, within 1 year from the date of the bringing of such action at law, the said stock and the amount previously paid in by the delinquent stockholder on the stock shall be forfeited to the corporation.

§ 165. Revocability of Preincorporation Subscriptions

Unless otherwise provided by the terms of the subscription, a subscription for stock of a corporation to be formed shall be irrevocable, except with the consent of all other subscribers or the corporation, for a period of 6 months from its date.

§ 166. Formalities Required of Stock Subscriptions

A subscription for stock of a corporation, whether made before or after the formation of a corporation, shall not be enforceable against a subscriber, unless in writing and signed by the subscriber or by such subscriber's agent.

§ 167. Lost, Stolen or Destroyed Stock Certificates; Issuance of New Certificate or Uncertificated Shares

A corporation may issue a new certificate of stock or uncertificated shares in place of any certificate theretofore issued by it, alleged to have been lost, stolen or destroyed, and the corporation may require the owner of the lost, stolen or destroyed certificate, or such owner's legal representative to give the corporation a bond sufficient to indemnify it against any claim that may be made against it on account of the alleged loss, theft or destruction of any such certificate or the issuance of such new certificate or uncertificated shares.

§ 168. Judicial Proceedings to Compel Issuance of New Certificate or Uncertificated Shares

(a) If a corporation refuses to issue new uncertificated shares or a new certificate of stock in place of a certificate theretofore issued by it, or by any corporation of which it is the lawful successor, alleged to have been lost, stolen or destroyed, the owner of the lost, stolen or destroyed certificate or such owner's legal representatives may apply to the Court of Chancery for an order requiring the corporation to show cause why it should not issue new uncertificated shares or a new certificate of stock in place of the certificate so lost, stolen or destroyed. Such application shall be by a complaint which shall state the name of the corporation, the number and date of the certificate, if known or ascertainable by the plaintiff, the number of shares of stock represented thereby and to whom issued, and a statement of the circumstances attending such loss, theft or destruction. Thereupon the court shall make an order requiring the corporation to show cause at a time and place therein designated, why it should not issue new uncertificated shares or a new certificate of stock in place of the one described in the complaint. A copy of the complaint and order shall be served upon the corporation at least 5 days before the time designated in the order.

(b) If, upon hearing, the court is satisfied that the plaintiff is the lawful owner of the number of shares of capital stock, or any part thereof, described in the complaint, and that the certificate therefor has been lost, stolen or destroyed, and no sufficient cause has been shown why new uncertificated shares or a new certificate should not be issued in place thereof, it shall make an order requiring the corporation to issue and deliver to the plaintiff new uncertificated shares or a new certificate for such shares. In its order the court shall direct that, prior to the issuance and delivery to the plaintiff of such new uncertificated shares or a new certificate, the plaintiff give the corporation a bond in such form and with such security as to the court appears sufficient to indemnify the corporation against any claim that may be made against it on account of the alleged loss, theft or destruction of any such certificate or the issuance of such new uncertificated shares or new certificate. No corporation which has issued uncertificated shares or a certificate pursuant to an order of the court entered hereunder shall be liable in an amount in excess of the amount specified in such bond.

§ 169. Situs of Ownership of Stock

For all purposes of title, action, attachment, garnishment and jurisdiction of all courts held in this State, but not for the purpose of taxation, the situs of the ownership of the capital stock of all corporations existing under the laws of this State, whether organized under this chapter or otherwise, shall be regarded as in this State.

§ 170. Dividends; Payment; Wasting Asset Corporations

(a) The directors of every corporation, subject to any restrictions contained in its certificate of incorporation, may declare and pay dividends upon the shares of its capital stock either:

(1) Out of its surplus, as defined in and computed in accordance with §§ 154 and 244 of this title; or

(2) In case there shall be no such surplus, out of its net profits for the fiscal year in which the dividend is declared and/or the preceding fiscal year. If the capital of the corporation, computed in accordance with §§ 154 and 244 of this title, shall have been diminished by depreciation in the value of its property, or by losses, or otherwise, to an amount less than the aggregate amount of the capital represented by the issued and outstanding stock of all classes having a preference upon the distribution of assets, the directors of such corporation shall not declare and pay out of such net profits any dividends upon any shares of any classes of its capital stock until the deficiency in the amount of capital represented by the issued and outstanding stock of all classes having a preference upon the distribution of assets shall have been repaired. Nothing in this subsection shall invalidate or otherwise affect a note, debenture or other obligation of the corporation paid by it as a dividend on shares of its stock, or any payment made thereon, if at the time such note, debenture or obligation was delivered by the corporation, the corporation had either surplus or net profits as provided in (a)(1) or (2) of this section from which the dividend could lawfully have been paid.

(b) Subject to any restrictions contained in its certificate of incorporation, the directors of any corporation engaged in the exploitation of wasting assets (including but not limited to a corporation engaged in the exploitation of natural resources or other wasting assets, including patents, or engaged primarily in the liquidation of specific assets) may determine the net profits derived from the exploitation of such wasting assets or the net proceeds derived from such liquidation without taking into consideration the depletion of such assets resulting from lapse of time, consumption, liquidation or exploitation of such assets.

§ 171. Special Purpose Reserves

The directors of a corporation may set apart out of any of the funds of the corporation available for dividends a reserve or reserves for any proper purpose and may abolish any such reserve.

§ 172. Liability of Directors and Committee Members as to Dividends or Stock Redemption

A member of the board of directors, or a member of any committee designated by the board of directors, shall be fully protected in relying in good faith upon the records of the corporation and upon such information, opinions, reports or statements presented to the corporation by any of its officers or employees, or committees of the board of directors, or by any other person as to matters the director reasonably believes are within such other person's professional or expert competence and who has been selected with reasonable care by or on behalf of the corporation, as to the value and amount of the assets, liabilities and/or net profits of the corporation or any other facts pertinent to the existence and amount of surplus or other funds from which dividends might properly be declared and paid, or with which the corporation's stock might properly be purchased or redeemed.

§ 173. Declaration and Payment of Dividends

No corporation shall pay dividends except in accordance with this chapter. Dividends may be paid in cash, in property, or in shares of the corporation's capital stock. If the dividend is to be paid in shares of the corporation's theretofore unissued capital stock the board of directors shall, by resolution, direct that there be designated as capital in respect of such shares an amount which is not less than the aggregate par value of par value shares being declared as a dividend and, in the case of shares without par value being declared as a dividend, such amount as shall be determined by the board of directors. No such designation as capital shall be necessary if shares are being distributed by a corporation pursuant to a split-up or division of its stock rather than as payment of a dividend declared payable in stock of the corporation.

§ 174. Liability of Directors for Unlawful Payment of Dividend or Unlawful Stock Purchase or Redemption; Exoneration From Liability; Contribution Among Directors; Subrogation

(a) In case of any wilful or negligent violation of § 160 or § 173 of this title, the directors under whose administration the same may happen shall be jointly and severally liable, at any time within 6 years after paying such unlawful dividend or after such unlawful stock purchase or redemption, to the corporation, and to its creditors in the event of its dissolution or insolvency, to the full amount of the dividend unlawfully paid, or to the full amount unlawfully paid for the purchase or redemption of the corporation's stock, with interest from the time such liability accrued. Any director who may have been absent when the same was done, or who may have dissented from the act or resolution by which the same was done, may be exonerated from such liability by causing his or her dissent to be entered on the books containing the minutes of the proceedings of the directors at the time the same was done, or immediately after such director has notice of the same.

(b) Any director against whom a claim is successfully asserted under this section shall be entitled to contribution from the other directors who voted for or concurred in the unlawful dividend, stock purchase or stock redemption.

(c) Any director against whom a claim is successfully asserted under this section shall be entitled, to the extent of the amount paid by such director as a result of such claim, to be subrogated to the rights of the corporation against stockholders who received the dividend on, or assets for the sale or redemption of, their stock with knowledge of facts indicating that such dividend, stock purchase or redemption was unlawful under this chapter, in proportion to the amounts received by such stockholders respectively.

§ 201. Transfer of Stock, Stock Certificates and Uncertificated Stock

Except as otherwise provided in this chapter, the transfer of stock and the certificates of stock which represent the stock or uncertificated stock shall be governed by Article 8 of subtitle I of Title 6. To the extent that any provision of this chapter is inconsistent with any provision of subtitle I of Title 6, this chapter shall be controlling.

§ 202. Restrictions on Transfer and Ownership of Securities

(a) A written restriction or restrictions on the transfer or registration of transfer of a security of a corporation, or on the amount of the corporation's securities that may be owned by any person or group of persons, if permitted by this section and noted conspicuously on the certificate or certificates representing the security or securities so restricted or, in the case of uncertificated shares, contained in the notice or notices given pursuant to § 151(f) of this title, may be enforced against the holder of the restricted security or securities or any successor or transferee of the holder including an executor, administrator, trustee, guardian or other fiduciary entrusted with like responsibility for the person or estate of the holder. Unless noted conspicuously on the certificate or certificates representing the security or securities so restricted or, in the case of uncertificated shares, contained in the notice or notices given pursuant to § 151(f) of this title, a restriction, even though permitted by this section, is ineffective except against a person with actual knowledge of the restriction.

(b) A restriction on the transfer or registration of transfer of securities of a corporation, or on the amount of a corporation's securities that may be owned by any person or group of persons, may be imposed by the certificate of incorporation or by the bylaws or by an agreement among any number of security holders or among such holders and the corporation. No restrictions so imposed shall be binding with respect to securities issued prior to the adoption of the restriction unless the holders of the securities are parties to an agreement or voted in favor of the restriction.

(c) A restriction on the transfer or registration of transfer of securities of a corporation or on the amount of such securities that may be owned by any person or group of persons is permitted by this section if it:

(1) Obligates the holder of the restricted securities to offer to the corporation or to any other holders of securities of the corporation or to any other person or to any combination of the foregoing, a prior opportunity, to be exercised within a reasonable time, to acquire the restricted securities; or

(2) Obligates the corporation or any holder of securities of the corporation or any other person or any combination of the foregoing, to purchase the securities which are the subject of an agreement respecting the purchase and sale of the restricted securities; or

(3) Requires the corporation or the holders of any class or series of securities of the corporation to consent to any proposed transfer of the restricted securities or to approve the proposed transferee of the restricted securities, or to approve the amount of securities of the corporation that may be owned by any person or group of persons; or

(4) Obligates the holder of the restricted securities to sell or transfer an amount of restricted securities to the corporation or to any other holders of securities of the corporation or to any other person or to any combination of the foregoing, or causes or results in the automatic sale or transfer of an amount of restricted securities to the corporation or to any other holders of securities of the corporation or to any other person or to any combination of the foregoing; or

(5) Prohibits or restricts the transfer of the restricted securities to, or the ownership of restricted securities by, designated persons or classes of persons or groups of persons, and such designation is not manifestly unreasonable.

(d)   Any restriction on the transfer or the registration of transfer of the securities of a corporation, or on the amount of securities of a corporation that may be owned by a person or group of persons, for any of the following purposes shall be conclusively presumed to be for a reasonable purpose:

(1)   Maintaining any local, state, federal or foreign tax advantage to the corporation or its stockholders, including without limitation:

a.   Maintaining the corporation's status as an electing small business corporation under subchapter S of the United States Internal Revenue Code [26 U.S.C. § 1371 et seq.], or

b.   Maintaining or preserving any tax attribute (including without limitation net operating losses), or

c.   Qualifying or maintaining the qualification of the corporation as a real estate investment trust pursuant to the United States Internal Revenue Code or regulations adopted pursuant to the United States Internal Revenue Code, or

(2)   Maintaining any statutory or regulatory advantage or complying with any statutory or regulatory requirements under applicable local, state, federal or foreign law.

(e)   Any other lawful restriction on transfer or registration of transfer of securities, or on the amount of securities that may be owned by any person or group of persons, is permitted by this section.

§ 203.   Business Combinations With Interested Stockholders

(a)   Notwithstanding any other provisions of this chapter, a corporation shall not engage in any business combination with any interested stockholder for a period of 3 years following the time that such stockholder became an interested stockholder, unless:

(1)   Prior to such time the board of directors of the corporation approved either the business combination or the transaction which resulted in the stockholder becoming an interested stockholder;

(2)   Upon consummation of the transaction which resulted in the stockholder becoming an interested stockholder, the interested stockholder owned at least 85% of the voting stock of the corporation outstanding at the time the transaction commenced, excluding for purposes of determining the voting stock outstanding (but not the outstanding voting stock owned by the interested stockholder) those shares owned (i) by persons who are directors and also officers and (ii) employee stock plans in which employee participants do not have the right to determine confidentially whether shares held subject to the plan will be tendered in a tender or exchange offer; or

(3)   At or subsequent to such time the business combination is approved by the board of directors and authorized at an annual or special meeting of stockholders, and not by written consent, by the affirmative vote of at least 66 2/3% of the outstanding voting stock which is not owned by the interested stockholder.

(b)   The restrictions contained in this section shall not apply if:

(1)   The corporation's original certificate of incorporation contains a provision expressly electing not to be governed by this section;

(2)   The corporation, by action of its board of directors, adopts an amendment to its bylaws within 90 days of February 2, 1988, expressly electing not to be governed by this section, which amendment shall not be further amended by the board of directors;

(3)   The corporation, by action of its stockholders, adopts an amendment to its certificate of incorporation or bylaws expressly electing not to be governed by this section; provided that, in addition to any other vote required by law, such amendment to the certificate of incorporation or

bylaws must be adopted by the affirmative vote of a majority of the outstanding stock entitled to vote thereon. In the case of a corporation that both (i) has never had a class of voting stock that falls within any of the 2 categories set out in paragraph (b)(4) of this section, and (ii) has not elected by a provision in its original certificate of incorporation or any amendment thereto to be governed by this section, such amendment shall become effective upon (i) in the case of an amendment to the certificate of incorporation, the date and time at which the certificate filed in accordance with § 103 of this title becomes effective thereunder or (ii) in the case of an amendment to the bylaws, the date of the adoption of such amendment. In all other cases, an amendment adopted pursuant to this paragraph shall become effective (i) in the case of an amendment to the certificate of incorporation, 12 months after the date and time at which the certificate filed in accordance with § 103 of this title becomes effective thereunder or (ii) in the case of an amendment to the bylaws, 12 months after the date of the adoption of such amendment, and, in either case, the election not to be governed by this section shall not apply to any business combination between such corporation and any person who became an interested stockholder of such corporation on or before (A) in the case of an amendment to the certificate of incorporation, the date and time at which the certificate filed in accordance with § 103 of this title becomes effective thereunder; or (B) in the case of an amendment to the bylaws, the date of the adoption of such amendment. A bylaw amendment adopted pursuant to this paragraph shall not be further amended by the board of directors;

(4) The corporation does not have a class of voting stock that is: (i) Listed on a national securities exchange; or (ii) held of record by more than 2,000 stockholders, unless any of the foregoing results from action taken, directly or indirectly, by an interested stockholder or from a transaction in which a person becomes an interested stockholder;

(5) A stockholder becomes an interested stockholder inadvertently and (i) as soon as practicable divests itself of ownership of sufficient shares so that the stockholder ceases to be an interested stockholder; and (ii) would not, at any time within the 3-year period immediately prior to a business combination between the corporation and such stockholder, have been an interested stockholder but for the inadvertent acquisition of ownership;

(6) The business combination is proposed prior to the consummation or abandonment of and subsequent to the earlier of the public announcement or the notice required hereunder of a proposed transaction which (i) constitutes 1 of the transactions described in the second sentence of this paragraph; (ii) is with or by a person who either was not an interested stockholder during the previous 3 years or who became an interested stockholder with the approval of the corporation's board of directors or during the period described in paragraph (b)(7) of this section; and (iii) is approved or not opposed by a majority of the members of the board of directors then in office (but not less than 1) who were directors prior to any person becoming an interested stockholder during the previous 3 years or were recommended for election or elected to succeed such directors by a majority of such directors. The proposed transactions referred to in the preceding sentence are limited to (x) a merger or consolidation of the corporation (except for a merger in respect of which, pursuant to § 251(f) of this title, no vote of the stockholders of the corporation is required); (y) a sale, lease, exchange, mortgage, pledge, transfer or other disposition (in 1 transaction or a series of transactions), whether as part of a dissolution or otherwise, of assets of the corporation or of any direct or indirect majority-owned subsidiary of the corporation (other than to any direct or indirect wholly-owned subsidiary or to the corporation) having an aggregate market value equal to 50% or more of either that aggregate market value of all of the assets of the corporation determined on a consolidated basis or the aggregate market value of all the outstanding stock of the corporation; or (z) a proposed tender or exchange offer for 50% or more of the outstanding voting stock of the corporation. The corporation shall give not less than 20 days' notice to all interested stockholders prior to the consummation of any of the transactions described in clause (x) or (y) of the second sentence of this paragraph; or

(7) The business combination is with an interested stockholder who became an interested stockholder at a time when the restrictions contained in this section did not apply by reason of

any of paragraphs (b)(1) through (4) of this section, provided, however, that this paragraph (b)(7) shall not apply if, at the time such interested stockholder became an interested stockholder, the corporation's certificate of incorporation contained a provision authorized by the last sentence of this subsection (b).

Notwithstanding paragraphs (b)(1), (2), (3) and (4) of this section, a corporation may elect by a provision of its original certificate of incorporation or any amendment thereto to be governed by this section; provided that any such amendment to the certificate of incorporation shall not apply to restrict a business combination between the corporation and an interested stockholder of the corporation if the interested stockholder became such before the date and time at which the certificate filed in accordance with § 103 of this title becomes effective thereunder.

(c)   As used in this section only, the term:

(1)   "Affiliate" means a person that directly, or indirectly through 1 or more intermediaries, controls, or is controlled by, or is under common control with, another person.

(2)   "Associate," when used to indicate a relationship with any person, means: (i) Any corporation, partnership, unincorporated association or other entity of which such person is a director, officer or partner or is, directly or indirectly, the owner of 20% or more of any class of voting stock; (ii) any trust or other estate in which such person has at least a 20% beneficial interest or as to which such person serves as trustee or in a similar fiduciary capacity; and (iii) any relative or spouse of such person, or any relative of such spouse, who has the same residence as such person.

(3)   "Business combination," when used in reference to any corporation and any interested stockholder of such corporation, means:

(i)   Any merger or consolidation of the corporation or any direct or indirect majority-owned subsidiary of the corporation with (A) the interested stockholder, or (B) with any other corporation, partnership, unincorporated association or other entity if the merger or consolidation is caused by the interested stockholder and as a result of such merger or consolidation subsection (a) of this section is not applicable to the surviving entity;

(ii)   Any sale, lease, exchange, mortgage, pledge, transfer or other disposition (in 1 transaction or a series of transactions), except proportionately as a stockholder of such corporation, to or with the interested stockholder, whether as part of a dissolution or otherwise, of assets of the corporation or of any direct or indirect majority-owned subsidiary of the corporation which assets have an aggregate market value equal to 10% or more of either the aggregate market value of all the assets of the corporation determined on a consolidated basis or the aggregate market value of all the outstanding stock of the corporation;

(iii)   Any transaction which results in the issuance or transfer by the corporation or by any direct or indirect majority-owned subsidiary of the corporation of any stock of the corporation or of such subsidiary to the interested stockholder, except: (A) Pursuant to the exercise, exchange or conversion of securities exercisable for, exchangeable for or convertible into stock of such corporation or any such subsidiary which securities were outstanding prior to the time that the interested stockholder became such; (B) pursuant to a merger under § 251(g) of this title; (C) pursuant to a dividend or distribution paid or made, or the exercise, exchange or conversion of securities exercisable for, exchangeable for or convertible into stock of such corporation or any such subsidiary which security is distributed, pro rata to all holders of a class or series of stock of such corporation subsequent to the time the interested stockholder became such; (D) pursuant to an exchange offer by the corporation to purchase stock made on the same terms to all holders of said stock; or (E) any issuance or transfer of stock by the corporation; provided however, that in no case under items (C)–(E) of this subparagraph shall there be an increase in the interested stockholder's proportionate share of the stock of any class or series of the corporation or of the voting stock of the corporation;

(iv) Any transaction involving the corporation or any direct or indirect majority-owned subsidiary of the corporation which has the effect, directly or indirectly, of increasing the proportionate share of the stock of any class or series, or securities convertible into the stock of any class or series, of the corporation or of any such subsidiary which is owned by the interested stockholder, except as a result of immaterial changes due to fractional share adjustments or as a result of any purchase or redemption of any shares of stock not caused, directly or indirectly, by the interested stockholder; or

(v) Any receipt by the interested stockholder of the benefit, directly or indirectly (except proportionately as a stockholder of such corporation), of any loans, advances, guarantees, pledges or other financial benefits (other than those expressly permitted in paragraphs (c)(3)(i)–(iv) of this section) provided by or through the corporation or any direct or indirect majority-owned subsidiary.

(4) "Control," including the terms "controlling," "controlled by" and "under common control with," means the possession, directly or indirectly, of the power to direct or cause the direction of the management and policies of a person, whether through the ownership of voting stock, by contract or otherwise. A person who is the owner of 20% or more of the outstanding voting stock of any corporation, partnership, unincorporated association or other entity shall be presumed to have control of such entity, in the absence of proof by a preponderance of the evidence to the contrary; Notwithstanding the foregoing, a presumption of control shall not apply where such person holds voting stock, in good faith and not for the purpose of circumventing this section, as an agent, bank, broker, nominee, custodian or trustee for 1 or more owners who do not individually or as a group have control of such entity.

(5) "Interested stockholder" means any person (other than the corporation and any direct or indirect majority-owned subsidiary of the corporation) that (i) is the owner of 15% or more of the outstanding voting stock of the corporation, or (ii) is an affiliate or associate of the corporation and was the owner of 15% or more of the outstanding voting stock of the corporation at any time within the 3-year period immediately prior to the date on which it is sought to be determined whether such person is an interested stockholder, and the affiliates and associates of such person; provided, however, that the term "interested stockholder" shall not include (x) any person who (A) owned shares in excess of the 15% limitation set forth herein as of, or acquired such shares pursuant to a tender offer commenced prior to, December 23, 1987, or pursuant to an exchange offer announced prior to the aforesaid date and commenced within 90 days thereafter and either (I) continued to own shares in excess of such 15% limitation or would have but for action by the corporation or (II) is an affiliate or associate of the corporation and so continued (or so would have continued but for action by the corporation) to be the owner of 15% or more of the outstanding voting stock of the corporation at any time within the 3-year period immediately prior to the date on which it is sought to be determined whether such a person is an interested stockholder or (B) acquired said shares from a person described in item (A) of this paragraph by gift, inheritance or in a transaction in which no consideration was exchanged; or (y) any person whose ownership of shares in excess of the 15% limitation set forth herein is the result of action taken solely by the corporation; provided that such person shall be an interested stockholder if thereafter such person acquires additional shares of voting stock of the corporation, except as a result of further corporate action not caused, directly or indirectly, by such person. For the purpose of determining whether a person is an interested stockholder, the voting stock of the corporation deemed to be outstanding shall include stock deemed to be owned by the person through application of paragraph (9) of this subsection but shall not include any other unissued stock of such corporation which may be issuable pursuant to any agreement, arrangement or understanding, or upon exercise of conversion rights, warrants or options, or otherwise.

(6) "Person" means any individual, corporation, partnership, unincorporated association or other entity.

(7) "Stock" means, with respect to any corporation, capital stock and, with respect to any other entity, any equity interest.

(8) "Voting stock" means, with respect to any corporation, stock of any class or series entitled to vote generally in the election of directors and, with respect to any entity that is not a corporation, any equity interest entitled to vote generally in the election of the governing body of such entity. Every reference to a percentage of voting stock shall refer to such percentage of the votes of such voting stock.

(9) "Owner," including the terms "own" and "owned," when used with respect to any stock, means a person that individually or with or through any of its affiliates or associates:

    (i) Beneficially owns such stock, directly or indirectly; or

    (ii) Has (A) the right to acquire such stock (whether such right is exercisable immediately or only after the passage of time) pursuant to any agreement, arrangement or understanding, or upon the exercise of conversion rights, exchange rights, warrants or options, or otherwise; provided, however, that a person shall not be deemed the owner of stock tendered pursuant to a tender or exchange offer made by such person or any of such person's affiliates or associates until such tendered stock is accepted for purchase or exchange; or (B) the right to vote such stock pursuant to any agreement, arrangement or understanding; provided, however, that a person shall not be deemed the owner of any stock because of such person's right to vote such stock if the agreement, arrangement or understanding to vote such stock arises solely from a revocable proxy or consent given in response to a proxy or consent solicitation made to 10 or more persons; or

    (iii) Has any agreement, arrangement or understanding for the purpose of acquiring, holding, voting (except voting pursuant to a revocable proxy or consent as described in item (B) of subparagraph (ii) of this paragraph), or disposing of such stock with any other person that beneficially owns, or whose affiliates or associates beneficially own, directly or indirectly, such stock.

(d) No provision of a certificate of incorporation or bylaw shall require, for any vote of stockholders required by this section, a greater vote of stockholders than that specified in this section.

(e) The Court of Chancery is hereby vested with exclusive jurisdiction to hear and determine all matters with respect to this section.

§ 204. Ratification of Defective Corporate Acts and Stock

(a) Subject to subsection (f) of this section, no defective corporate act or putative stock shall be void or voidable solely as a result of a failure of authorization if ratified as provided in this section or validated by the Court of Chancery in a proceeding brought under § 205 of this title.

(b)(1) In order to ratify 1 or more defective corporate acts pursuant to this section (other than the ratification of an election of the initial board of directors pursuant to paragraph (b)(2) of this section), the board of directors of the corporation shall adopt resolutions stating:

    (A) The defective corporate act or acts to be ratified;

    (B) The date of each defective corporate act or acts;

    (C) If such defective corporate act or acts involved the issuance of shares of putative stock, the number and type of shares of putative stock issued and the date or dates upon which such putative shares were purported to have been issued;

    (D) The nature of the failure of authorization in respect of each defective corporate act to be ratified; and

    (E) That the board of directors approves the ratification of the defective corporate act or acts.

Such resolutions may also provide that, at any time before the validation effective time in respect of any defective corporate act set forth therein, notwithstanding the approval of the ratification of such defective corporate act by stockholders, the board of directors may abandon the ratification of such defective corporate act without further action of the stockholders. The quorum and voting requirements applicable to the ratification by the board of directors of any defective corporate act shall be the quorum and voting requirements applicable to the type of defective corporate act proposed to be ratified at the time the board adopts the resolutions ratifying the defective corporate act; provided that if the certificate of incorporation or bylaws of the corporation, any plan or agreement to which the corporation was a party or any provision of this title, in each case as in effect as of the time of the defective corporate act, would have required a larger number or portion of directors or of specified directors for a quorum to be present or to approve the defective corporate act, such larger number or portion of such directors or such specified directors shall be required for a quorum to be present or to adopt the resolutions to ratify the defective corporate act, as applicable, except that the presence or approval of any director elected, appointed or nominated by holders of any class or series of which no shares are then outstanding, or by any person that is no longer a stockholder, shall not be required.

(2)   In order to ratify a defective corporate act in respect of the election of the initial board of directors of the corporation pursuant to § 108 of this title, a majority of the persons who, at the time the resolutions required by this paragraph (b)(2) of this section are adopted, are exercising the powers of directors under claim and color of an election or appointment as such may adopt resolutions stating:

(A)   The name of the person or persons who first took action in the name of the corporation as the initial board of directors of the corporation;

(B)   The earlier of the date on which such persons first took such action or were purported to have been elected as the initial board of directors; and

(C)   That the ratification of the election of such person or persons as the initial board of directors is approved.

(c)   Each defective corporate act ratified pursuant to paragraph (b)(1) of this section shall be submitted to stockholders for approval as provided in subsection (d) of this section, unless:

(1)(A)   No other provision of this title, and no provision of the certificate of incorporation or bylaws of the corporation, or of any plan or agreement to which the corporation is a party, would have required stockholder approval of such defective corporate act to be ratified, either at the time of such defective corporate act or at the time the board of directors adopts the resolutions ratifying such defective corporate act pursuant to paragraph (b)(1) of this section; and

(B)   Such defective corporate act did not result from a failure to comply with § 203 of this title; or

(2)   As of the record date for determining the stockholders entitled to vote on the ratification of such defective corporate act, there are no shares of valid stock outstanding and entitled to vote thereon, regardless of whether there then exist any shares of putative stock.

(d)   If the ratification of a defective corporate act is required to be submitted to stockholders for approval pursuant to subsection (c) of this section, due notice of the time, place, if any, and purpose of the meeting shall be given at least 20 days before the date of the meeting to each holder of valid stock and putative stock, whether voting or nonvoting, at the address of such holder as it appears or most recently appeared, as appropriate, on the records of the corporation. The notice shall also be given to the holders of record of valid stock and putative stock, whether voting or nonvoting, as of the time of the defective corporate act, (or, in the case of any defective corporate act that involved the establishment of a record date for notice of or voting at any meeting of stockholders, for action by written consent of stockholders in lieu of a meeting, or for any other purpose, the record date for notice of or voting at such meeting, the record date for action by written consent, or the record date for such other action, as the case may be), other than holders whose identities or addresses cannot be determined from the records of the corporation. The notice shall contain a copy of the resolutions adopted by the board of directors pursuant to paragraphs (b)(1) of this section or the information required by paragraph (b)(1)(A) through (E) of this section and a statement that any claim that the defective corporate act or putative stock ratified hereunder is void or voidable due to the failure of authorization, or that the Court of Chancery should declare in its discretion that a ratification in accordance with this section not be effective or be effective only on certain conditions must be brought within 120 days from the applicable validation effective time. At such meeting, the quorum and voting requirements applicable to ratification of such defective corporate act shall be the quorum and voting requirements applicable to the type of defective corporate act proposed to be ratified at the time of the approval of the ratification, except that:

(1) If the certificate of incorporation or bylaws of the corporation, any plan or agreement to which the corporation was a party or any provision of this title in effect as of the time of the defective corporate act would have required a larger number or portion of stock or of any class or series thereof or of specified stockholders for a quorum to be present or to approve the defective corporate act, the presence or approval of such larger number or portion of stock or of such class or series thereof or of such specified stockholders shall be required for a quorum to be present or to approve the ratification of the defective corporate act, as applicable, except that the presence or approval of shares of any class or series of which no shares are then outstanding, or of any person that is no longer a stockholder, shall not be required;

(2) The approval by stockholders of the ratification of the election of a director shall require the affirmative vote of the majority of shares present at the meeting and entitled to vote on the election of such director, except that if the certificate of incorporation or bylaws of the corporation then in effect or in effect at the time of the defective election require or required a larger number or portion of stock or of any class or series thereof or of specified stockholders to elect such director, the affirmative vote of such larger number or portion of stock or of any class or series thereof or of such specified stockholders shall be required to ratify the election of such director, except that the presence or approval of shares of any class or series of which no shares are then outstanding, or of any person that is no longer a stockholder, shall not be required; and

(3) In the event of a failure of authorization resulting from failure to comply with the provisions of § 203 of this title, the ratification of the defective corporate act shall require the vote set forth in § 203(a)(3) of this title, regardless of whether such vote would have otherwise been required.

Shares of putative stock on the record date for determining stockholders entitled to vote on any matter submitted to stockholders pursuant to subsection (c) of this section (and without giving effect to any ratification that becomes effective after such record date) shall neither be entitled to vote nor counted for quorum purposes in any vote to ratify any defective corporate act.

(e) If a defective corporate act ratified pursuant to this section would have required under any other section of this title the filing of a certificate in accordance with § 103 of this title, then, whether or not a certificate was previously filed in respect of such defective corporate act and in lieu of filing the certificate otherwise required by this title, the corporation shall file a certificate of validation with respect to such defective corporate act in accordance with § 103 of this title. A separate certificate of validation shall be required for each defective corporate act requiring the filing of a certificate of validation under this section, except that (i) 2 or more defective corporate acts may be included in a single certificate of validation if the corporation filed, or to comply with this title would have filed, a single certificate under another provision of this title to effect such acts, and (ii) 2 or more overissues of shares of any class, classes or series of stock may be included in a single certificate of validation, provided that the increase in the number of authorized shares of each such class or series set forth in the certificate of validation shall be effective as of the date of the first such overissue. The certificate of validation shall set forth:

(1)   Each defective corporate act that is the subject of the certificate of validation (including, in the case of any defective corporate act involving the issuance of shares of putative stock, the number and type of shares of putative stock issued and the date or dates upon which such putative shares were purported to have been issued), the date of such defective corporate act, and the nature of the failure of authorization in respect of such defective corporate act;

(2)   A statement that such defective corporate act was ratified in accordance with this section, including the date on which the board of directors ratified such defective corporate act and the date, if any, on which the stockholders approved the ratification of such defective corporate act; and

(3)   Information required by 1 of the following paragraphs:

a.   If a certificate was previously filed under § 103 of this title in respect of such defective corporate act and no changes to such certificate are required to give effect to such defective corporate act in accordance with this section, the certificate of validation shall set forth (x) the name, title and filing date of the certificate previously filed and of any certificate of correction thereto and (y) a statement that a copy of the certificate previously filed, together with any certificate of correction thereto, is attached as an exhibit to the certificate of validation;

b.   If a certificate was previously filed under § 103 of this title in respect of the defective corporate act and such certificate requires any change to give effect to the defective corporate act in accordance with this section (including a change to the date and time of the effectiveness of such certificate), the certificate of validation shall set forth (x) the name, title and filing date of the certificate so previously filed and of any certificate of correction thereto, (y) a statement that a certificate containing all of the information required to be included under the applicable section or sections of this title to give effect to the defective corporate act is attached as an exhibit to the certificate of validation, and (z) the date and time that such certificate shall be deemed to have become effective pursuant to this section; or

c.   If a certificate was not previously filed under § 103 of this title in respect of the defective corporate act and the defective corporate act ratified pursuant to this section would have required under any other section of this title the filing of a certificate in accordance with § 103 of this title, the certificate of validation shall set forth (x) a statement that a certificate containing all of the information required to be included under the applicable section or sections of this title to give effect to the defective corporate act is attached as an exhibit to the certificate of validation, and (y) the date and time that such certificate shall be deemed to have become effective pursuant to this section.

A certificate attached to a certificate of validation pursuant to paragraph (e)(3)b. or c. of this section need not be separately executed and acknowledged and need not include any statement required by any other section of this title that such instrument has been approved and adopted in accordance with the provisions of such other section.

(f)   From and after the validation effective time, unless otherwise determined in an action brought pursuant to § 205 of this title:

(1)   Subject to the last sentence of subsection (d) of this section, each defective corporate act ratified in accordance with this section shall no longer be deemed void or voidable as a result of the failure of authorization described in the resolutions adopted pursuant to subsection (b) of this section and such effect shall be retroactive to the time of the defective corporate act; and

(2)   Subject to the last sentence of subsection (d) of this section each share or fraction of a share of putative stock issued or purportedly issued pursuant to any such defective corporate act shall no longer be deemed void or voidable and shall be deemed to be an identical share or fraction of a share of outstanding stock as of the time it was purportedly issued.

(g) In respect of each defective corporate act ratified by the board of directors pursuant to subsection (b) of this section, prompt notice of the ratification shall be given to all holders of valid stock and putative stock, whether voting or nonvoting, as of the date the board of directors adopts the resolutions approving such defective corporate act, or as of a date within 60 days after such date of adoption, as established by the board of directors, at the address of such holder as it appears or most recently appeared, as appropriate, on the records of the corporation. The notice shall also be given to the holders of record of valid stock and putative stock, whether voting or nonvoting, as of the time of the defective corporate act, other than holders whose identities or addresses cannot be determined from the records of the corporation. The notice shall contain a copy of the resolutions adopted pursuant to subsection (b) of this section or the information specified in paragraphs (b)(1)(A) through (E) or paragraphs (b)(2)(A) through (C) of this section, as applicable, and a statement that any claim that the defective corporate act or putative stock ratified hereunder is void or voidable due to the failure of authorization, or that the Court of Chancery should declare in its discretion that a ratification in accordance with this section not be effective or be effective only on certain conditions must be brought within 120 days from the later of the validation effective time or the time at which the notice required by this subsection is given. Notwithstanding the foregoing, (i) no such notice shall be required if notice of the ratification of the defective corporate act is to be given in accordance with subsection (d) of this section, and (ii) in the case of a corporation that has a class of stock listed on a national securities exchange, the notice required by this subsection and the second sentence of subsection (d) of this section may be deemed given if disclosed in a document publicly filed by the corporation with the Securities and Exchange Commission pursuant to § 13, § 14 or § 15(d) [15 U.S.C. § 78m, § 77n or § 78o(d)] of the Securities Exchange Act of 1934, as amended, and the rules and regulations promulgated thereunder, or the corresponding provisions of any subsequent United States federal securities laws, rules or regulations. If any defective corporate act has been approved by stockholders acting pursuant to § 228 of this title, the notice required by this subsection may be included in any notice required to be given pursuant to § 228(e) of this title and, if so given, shall be sent to the stockholders entitled thereto under § 228(e) and to all holders of valid and putative stock to whom notice would be required under this subsection if the defective corporate act had been approved at a meeting other than any stockholder who approved the action by consent in lieu of a meeting pursuant to § 228 of this title or any holder of putative stock who otherwise consented thereto in writing. Solely for purposes of subsection (d) of this section and this subsection, notice to holders of putative stock, and notice to holders of valid stock and putative stock as of the time of the defective corporate act, shall be treated as notice to holders of valid stock for purposes of §§ 222 and 228, 229, 230, 232 and 233 of this title.

(h) As used in this section and in § 205 of this title only, the term:

(1) "Defective corporate act" means an overissue, an election or appointment of directors that is void or voidable due to a failure of authorization, or any act or transaction purportedly taken by or on behalf of the corporation that is, and at the time such act or transaction was purportedly taken would have been, within the power of a corporation under subchapter II of this chapter (without regard to the failure of authorization identified in § 204(b)(1)(D) of this title), but is void or voidable due to a failure of authorization;

(2) "Failure of authorization" means: (i) the failure to authorize or effect an act or transaction in compliance with (A) the provisions of this title, (B) the certificate of incorporation or bylaws of the corporation, (C) or any plan or agreement to which the corporation is a party or the disclosure set forth in any proxy or consent solicitation statement, if and to the extent such failure would render such act or transaction void or voidable; or (ii) the failure of the board of directors or any officer of the corporation to authorize or approve any act or transaction taken by or on behalf of the corporation that would have required for its due authorization the approval of the board of directors or such officer;

(3) "Overissue" means the purported issuance of:

a. Shares of capital stock of a class or series in excess of the number of shares of such class or series the corporation has the power to issue under § 161 of this title at the time of such issuance; or

b. Shares of any class or series of capital stock that is not then authorized for issuance by the certificate of incorporation of the corporation;

(4) "Putative stock" means the shares of any class or series of capital stock of the corporation (including shares issued upon exercise of options, rights, warrants or other securities convertible into shares of capital stock of the corporation, or interests with respect thereto that were created or issued pursuant to a defective corporate act) that:

a. But for any failure of authorization, would constitute valid stock; or

b. Cannot be determined by the board of directors to be valid stock;

(5) "Time of the defective corporate act" means the date and time the defective corporate act was purported to have been taken;

(6) "Validation effective time" with respect to any defective corporate act ratified pursuant to this section means the latest of:

a. The time at which the defective corporate act submitted to the stockholders for approval pursuant to subsection (c) of this section is approved by such stockholders or if no such vote of stockholders is required to approve the ratification of the defective corporate act, the time at which the board of directors adopts the resolutions required by paragraph (b)(1) or (b)(2) of this section;

b. Where no certificate of validation is required to be filed pursuant to subsection (e) of this section, the time, if any, specified by the board of directors in the resolutions adopted pursuant to paragraph (b)(1) or (b)(2) of this section, which time shall not precede the time at which such resolutions are adopted; and

c. The time at which any certificate of validation filed pursuant to subsection (e) of this section shall become effective in accordance with § 103 of this title.

(7) "Valid stock" means the shares of any class or series of capital stock of the corporation that have been duly authorized and validly issued in accordance with this title.

In the absence of actual fraud in the transaction, the judgment of the board of directors that shares of stock are valid stock or putative stock shall be conclusive, unless otherwise determined by the Court of Chancery in a proceeding brought pursuant to § 205 of this title.

(i) Ratification under this section or validation under § 205 of this title shall not be deemed to be the exclusive means of ratifying or validating any act or transaction taken by or on behalf of the corporation, including any defective corporate act, or any issuance of stock, including any putative stock, or of adopting or endorsing any act or transaction taken by or in the name of the corporation prior to the commencement of its existence, and the absence or failure of ratification in accordance with either this section or validation under § 205 of this title shall not, of itself, affect the validity or effectiveness of any act or transaction or the issuance of any stock properly ratified under common law or otherwise, nor shall it create a presumption that any such act or transaction is or was a defective corporate act or that such stock is void or voidable.

§ 205. Proceedings Regarding Validity of Defective Corporate Acts and Stock

(a) Subject to subsection (f) of this section, upon application by the corporation, any successor entity to the corporation, any member of the board of directors, any record or beneficial holder of valid stock or putative stock, any record or beneficial holder of valid or putative stock as of the time of a defective corporate act ratified pursuant to § 204 of this title, or any other person claiming to be substantially and adversely affected by a ratification pursuant to § 204 of this title, the Court of Chancery may:

(1) Determine the validity and effectiveness of any defective corporate act ratified pursuant to § 204 of this title;

(2) Determine the validity and effectiveness of the ratification of any defective corporate act pursuant to § 204 of this title;

(3) Determine the validity and effectiveness of any defective corporate act not ratified or not ratified effectively pursuant to § 204 of this title;

(4) Determine the validity of any corporate act or transaction and any stock, rights or options to acquire stock; and

(5) Modify or waive any of the procedures set forth in § 204 of this title to ratify a defective corporate act.

(b) In connection with an action under this section, the Court of Chancery may:

(1) Declare that a ratification in accordance with and pursuant to § 204 of this title is not effective or shall only be effective at a time or upon conditions established by the Court;

(2) Validate and declare effective any defective corporate act or putative stock and impose conditions upon such validation by the Court;

(3) Require measures to remedy or avoid harm to any person substantially and adversely affected by a ratification pursuant to § 204 of this title or from any order of the Court pursuant to this section, excluding any harm that would have resulted if the defective corporate act had been valid when approved or effectuated;

(4) Order the Secretary of State to accept an instrument for filing with an effective time specified by the Court, which effective time may be prior or subsequent to the time of such order, provided that the filing date of such instrument shall be determined in accordance with § 103(c)(3) of this title;

(5) Approve a stock ledger for the corporation that includes any stock ratified or validated in accordance with this section or with § 204 of this title;

(6) Declare that shares of putative stock are shares of valid stock or require a corporation to issue and deliver shares of valid stock in place of any shares of putative stock;

(7) Order that a meeting of holders of valid stock or putative stock be held and exercise the powers provided to the Court under § 227 of this title with respect to such a meeting;

(8) Declare that a defective corporate act validated by the Court shall be effective as of the time of the defective corporate act or at such other time as the Court shall determine;

(9) Declare that putative stock validated by the Court shall be deemed to be an identical share or fraction of a share of valid stock as of the time originally issued or purportedly issued or at such other time as the Court shall determine; and

(10) Make such other orders regarding such matters as it deems proper under the circumstances.

(c) Service of the application under subsection (a) of this section upon the registered agent of the corporation shall be deemed to be service upon the corporation, and no other party need be joined in order for the Court of Chancery to adjudicate the matter. In an action filed by the corporation, the Court may require notice of the action be provided to other persons specified by the Court and permit such other persons to intervene in the action.

(d) In connection with the resolution of matters pursuant to subsections (a) and (b) of this section, the Court of Chancery may consider the following:

(1)   Whether the defective corporate act was originally approved or effectuated with the belief that the approval or effectuation was in compliance with the provisions of this title, the certificate of incorporation or bylaws of the corporation;

(2)   Whether the corporation and board of directors has treated the defective corporate act as a valid act or transaction and whether any person has acted in reliance on the public record that such defective corporate act was valid;

(3)   Whether any person will be or was harmed by the ratification or validation of the defective corporate act, excluding any harm that would have resulted if the defective corporate act had been valid when approved or effectuated;

(4)   Whether any person will be harmed by the failure to ratify or validate the defective corporate act; and

(5)   Any other factors or considerations the Court deems just and equitable.

(e)   The Court of Chancery is hereby vested with exclusive jurisdiction to hear and determine all actions brought under this section.

(f)   Notwithstanding any other provision of this section, no action asserting:

(1)   That a defective corporate act or putative stock ratified in accordance with § 204 of this title is void or voidable due to a failure of authorization identified in the resolution adopted in accordance with § 204(b) of this title; or

(2)   That the Court of Chancery should declare in its discretion that a ratification in accordance with § 204 of this title not be effective or be effective only on certain conditions, may be brought after the expiration of 120 days from the later of the validation effective time and the time notice, if any, that is required to be given pursuant to § 204(g) of this title is given with respect to such ratification, except that this subsection shall not apply to an action asserting that a ratification was not accomplished in accordance with § 204 of this title or to any person to whom notice of the ratification was required to have been given pursuant to § 204(d) or (g) of this title, but to whom such notice was not given.

§ 211.   Meetings of Stockholders

(a)(1)   Meetings of stockholders may be held at such place, either within or without this State as may be designated by or in the manner provided in the certificate of incorporation or bylaws, or if not so designated, as determined by the board of directors. If, pursuant to this paragraph or the certificate of incorporation or the bylaws of the corporation, the board of directors is authorized to determine the place of a meeting of stockholders, the board of directors may, in its sole discretion, determine that the meeting shall not be held at any place, but may instead be held solely by means of remote communication as authorized by paragraph (a)(2) of this section.

(2)   If authorized by the board of directors in its sole discretion, and subject to such guidelines and procedures as the board of directors may adopt, stockholders and proxyholders not physically present at a meeting of stockholders may, by means of remote communication:

a.   Participate in a meeting of stockholders; and

b.   Be deemed present in person and vote at a meeting of stockholders, whether such meeting is to be held at a designated place or solely by means of remote communication, provided that (i) the corporation shall implement reasonable measures to verify that each person deemed present and permitted to vote at the meeting by means of remote communication is a stockholder or proxyholder, (ii) the corporation shall implement reasonable measures to provide such stockholders and proxyholders a reasonable opportunity to participate in the meeting and to vote on matters submitted to the stockholders, including an opportunity to read or hear the proceedings of the meeting substantially concurrently with such proceedings, and (iii) if any stockholder or proxyholder votes or takes other action at the meeting by means of remote communication, a record of such vote or other action shall be maintained by the corporation.

(b)   Unless directors are elected by written consent in lieu of an annual meeting as permitted by this subsection, an annual meeting of stockholders shall be held for the election of directors on a date and at a time designated by or in the manner provided in the bylaws. Stockholders may, unless the certificate of incorporation otherwise provides, act by written consent to elect directors; provided, however, that, if such consent is less than unanimous, such action by written consent may be in lieu of holding an annual meeting only if all of the directorships to which directors could be elected at an annual meeting held at the effective time of such action are vacant and are filled by such action. Any other proper business may be transacted at the annual meeting.

(c)   A failure to hold the annual meeting at the designated time or to elect a sufficient number of directors to conduct the business of the corporation shall not affect otherwise valid corporate acts or work a forfeiture or dissolution of the corporation except as may be otherwise specifically provided in this chapter. If the annual meeting for election of directors is not held on the date designated therefor or action by written consent to elect directors in lieu of an annual meeting has not been taken, the directors shall cause the meeting to be held as soon as is convenient. If there be a failure to hold the annual meeting or to take action by written consent to elect directors in lieu of an annual meeting for a period of 30 days after the date designated for the annual meeting, or if no date has been designated, for a period of 13 months after the latest to occur of the organization of the corporation, its last annual meeting or the last action by written consent to elect directors in lieu of an annual meeting, the Court of Chancery may summarily order a meeting to be held upon the application of any stockholder or director. The shares of stock represented at such meeting, either in person or by proxy, and entitled to vote thereat, shall constitute a quorum for the purpose of such meeting, notwithstanding any provision of the certificate of incorporation or bylaws to the contrary. The Court of Chancery may issue such orders as may be appropriate, including, without limitation, orders designating the time and place of such meeting, the record date or dates for determination of stockholders entitled to notice of the meeting and to vote thereat, and the form of notice of such meeting.

(d)   Special meetings of the stockholders may be called by the board of directors or by such person or persons as may be authorized by the certificate of incorporation or by the bylaws.

(e)   All elections of directors shall be by written ballot unless otherwise provided in the certificate of incorporation; if authorized by the board of directors, such requirement of a written ballot shall be satisfied by a ballot submitted by electronic transmission, provided that any such electronic transmission must either set forth or be submitted with information from which it can be determined that the electronic transmission was authorized by the stockholder or proxy holder.

§ 212. Voting Rights of Stockholders; Proxies; Limitations

(a)   Unless otherwise provided in the certificate of incorporation and subject to § 213 of this title, each stockholder shall be entitled to 1 vote for each share of capital stock held by such stockholder. If the certificate of incorporation provides for more or less than 1 vote for any share, on any matter, every reference in this chapter to a majority or other proportion of stock, voting stock or shares shall refer to such majority or other proportion of the votes of such stock, voting stock or shares.

(b)   Each stockholder entitled to vote at a meeting of stockholders or to express consent or dissent to corporate action in writing without a meeting may authorize another person or persons to act for such stockholder by proxy, but no such proxy shall be voted or acted upon after 3 years from its date, unless the proxy provides for a longer period.

(c)   Without limiting the manner in which a stockholder may authorize another person or persons to act for such stockholder as proxy pursuant to subsection (b) of this section, the following shall constitute a valid means by which a stockholder may grant such authority:

(1)   A stockholder may execute a writing authorizing another person or persons to act for such stockholder as proxy. Execution may be accomplished by the stockholder or such

stockholder's authorized officer, director, employee or agent signing such writing or causing such person's signature to be affixed to such writing by any reasonable means including, but not limited to, by facsimile signature.

(2)   A stockholder may authorize another person or persons to act for such stockholder as proxy by transmitting or authorizing the transmission of a telegram, cablegram, or other means of electronic transmission to the person who will be the holder of the proxy or to a proxy solicitation firm, proxy support service organization or like agent duly authorized by the person who will be the holder of the proxy to receive such transmission, provided that any such telegram, cablegram or other means of electronic transmission must either set forth or be submitted with information from which it can be determined that the telegram, cablegram or other electronic transmission was authorized by the stockholder. If it is determined that such telegrams, cablegrams or other electronic transmissions are valid, the inspectors or, if there are no inspectors, such other persons making that determination shall specify the information upon which they relied.

(d)   Any copy, facsimile telecommunication or other reliable reproduction of the writing or transmission created pursuant to subsection (c) of this section may be substituted or used in lieu of the original writing or transmission for any and all purposes for which the original writing or transmission could be used, provided that such copy, facsimile telecommunication or other reproduction shall be a complete reproduction of the entire original writing or transmission.

(e)   A duly executed proxy shall be irrevocable if it states that it is irrevocable and if, and only as long as, it is coupled with an interest sufficient in law to support an irrevocable power. A proxy may be made irrevocable regardless of whether the interest with which it is coupled is an interest in the stock itself or an interest in the corporation generally.

§ 213.   Fixing Date for Determination of Stockholders of Record

(a)   In order that the corporation may determine the stockholders entitled to notice of any meeting of stockholders or any adjournment thereof, the board of directors may fix a record date, which record date shall not precede the date upon which the resolution fixing the record date is adopted by the board of directors, and which record date shall not be more than 60 nor less than 10 days before the date of such meeting. If the board of directors so fixes a date, such date shall also be the record date for determining the stockholders entitled to vote at such meeting unless the board of directors determines, at the time it fixes such record date, that a later date on or before the date of the meeting shall be the date for making such determination. If no record date is fixed by the board of directors, the record date for determining stockholders entitled to notice of and to vote at a meeting of stockholders shall be at the close of business on the day next preceding the day on which notice is given, or, if notice is waived, at the close of business on the day next preceding the day on which the meeting is held. A determination of stockholders of record entitled to notice of or to vote at a meeting of stockholders shall apply to any adjournment of the meeting; provided, however, that the board of directors may fix a new record date for determination of stockholders entitled to vote at the adjourned meeting, and in such case shall also fix as the record date for stockholders entitled to notice of such adjourned meeting the same or an earlier date as that fixed for determination of stockholders entitled to vote in accordance with the foregoing provisions of this subsection (a) at the adjourned meeting.

(b)   In order that the corporation may determine the stockholders entitled to consent to corporate action in writing without a meeting, the board of directors may fix a record date, which record date shall not precede the date upon which the resolution fixing the record date is adopted by the board of directors, and which date shall not be more than 10 days after the date upon which the resolution fixing the record date is adopted by the board of directors. If no record date has been fixed by the board of directors, the record date for determining stockholders entitled to consent to corporate action in writing without a meeting, when no prior action by the board of directors is required by this chapter, shall be the first date on which a signed written consent setting forth the action taken or proposed to be taken is delivered to the corporation by delivery to its registered office in this State, its principal place of business or an officer or agent of the corporation having custody of the book in which proceedings of meetings of stockholders are recorded. Delivery made to a corporation's registered office shall be by hand or by certified or registered mail, return receipt requested. If no record date has been fixed by the board of directors and prior action by the board of directors is required by this chapter, the record date for determining stockholders entitled to consent to corporate action in writing without a meeting shall be at the close of business on the day on which the board of directors adopts the resolution taking such prior action.

(c) In order that the corporation may determine the stockholders entitled to receive payment of any dividend or other distribution or allotment of any rights or the stockholders entitled to exercise any rights in respect of any change, conversion or exchange of stock, or for the purpose of any other lawful action, the board of directors may fix a record date, which record date shall not precede the date upon which the resolution fixing the record date is adopted, and which record date shall be not more than 60 days prior to such action. If no record date is fixed, the record date for determining stockholders for any such purpose shall be at the close of business on the day on which the board of directors adopts the resolution relating thereto.

§ 214. Cumulative Voting

The certificate of incorporation of any corporation may provide that at all elections of directors of the corporation, or at elections held under specified circumstances, each holder of stock or of any class or classes or of a series or series thereof shall be entitled to as many votes as shall equal the number of votes which (except for such provision as to cumulative voting) such holder would be entitled to cast for the election of directors with respect to such holder's shares of stock multiplied by the number of directors to be elected by such holder, and that such holder may cast all of such votes for a single director or may distribute them among the number to be voted for, or for any 2 or more of them as such holder may see fit.

§ 215. Voting Rights of Members of Nonstock Corporations; Quorum; Proxies

(a) Sections 211 through 214 and 216 of this title shall not apply to nonstock corporations, except that § 211(a) and (d) of this title and § 212(c), (d), and (e) of this title shall apply to such corporations, and, when so applied, all references therein to stockholders and to the board of directors shall be deemed to refer to the members and the governing body of a nonstock corporation, respectively; and all references to stock, capital stock, or shares thereof shall be deemed to refer to memberships of a nonprofit nonstock corporation and to membership interests of any other nonstock corporation.

(b) Unless otherwise provided in the certificate of incorporation or the bylaws of a nonstock corporation, and subject to subsection (f) of this section, each member shall be entitled at every meeting of members to 1 vote on each matter submitted to a vote of members. A member may exercise such voting rights in person or by proxy, but no proxy shall be voted on after 3 years from its date, unless the proxy provides for a longer period.

(c) Unless otherwise provided in this chapter, the certificate of incorporation or bylaws of a nonstock corporation may specify the number of members having voting power who shall be present or represented by proxy at any meeting in order to constitute a quorum for, and the votes that shall be necessary for, the transaction of any business. In the absence of such specification in the certificate of incorporation or bylaws of a nonstock corporation:

(1) One-third of the members of such corporation shall constitute a quorum at a meeting of such members;

(2) In all matters other than the election of the governing body of such corporation, the affirmative vote of a majority of such members present in person or represented by proxy at the meeting and entitled to vote on the subject matter shall be the act of the members, unless the vote of a greater number is required by this chapter;

(3)   Members of the governing body shall be elected by a plurality of the votes of the members of the corporation present in person or represented by proxy at the meeting and entitled to vote thereon; and

(4)   Where a separate vote by a class or group or classes or groups is required, a majority of the members of such class or group or classes or groups, present in person or represented by proxy, shall constitute a quorum entitled to take action with respect to that vote on that matter and, in all matters other than the election of members of the governing body, the affirmative vote of the majority of the members of such class or group or classes or groups present in person or represented by proxy at the meeting shall be the act of such class or group or classes or groups.

(d)   If the election of the governing body of any nonstock corporation shall not be held on the day designated by the bylaws, the governing body shall cause the election to be held as soon thereafter as convenient. The failure to hold such an election at the designated time shall not work any forfeiture or dissolution of the corporation, but the Court of Chancery may summarily order such an election to be held upon the application of any member of the corporation. At any election pursuant to such order the persons entitled to vote in such election who shall be present at such meeting, either in person or by proxy, shall constitute a quorum for such meeting, notwithstanding any provision of the certificate of incorporation or the bylaws of the corporation to the contrary.

(e)   If authorized by the governing body, any requirement of a written ballot shall be satisfied by a ballot submitted by electronic transmission, provided that any such electronic transmission must either set forth or be submitted with information from which it can be determined that the electronic transmission was authorized by the member or proxy holder.

(f)   Except as otherwise provided in the certificate of incorporation, in the bylaws, or by resolution of the governing body, the record date for any meeting or corporate action shall be deemed to be the date of such meeting or corporate action; provided, however, that no record date may precede any action by the governing body fixing such record date.

§ 216.   Quorum and Required Vote for Stock Corporations

Subject to this chapter in respect of the vote that shall be required for a specified action, the certificate of incorporation or bylaws of any corporation authorized to issue stock may specify the number of shares and/or the amount of other securities having voting power the holders of which shall be present or represented by proxy at any meeting in order to constitute a quorum for, and the votes that shall be necessary for, the transaction of any business, but in no event shall a quorum consist of less than 1/3 of the shares entitled to vote at the meeting, except that, where a separate vote by a class or series or classes or series is required, a quorum shall consist of no less than 1/3 of the shares of such class or series or classes or series. In the absence of such specification in the certificate of incorporation or bylaws of the corporation:

(1)   A majority of the shares entitled to vote, present in person or represented by proxy, shall constitute a quorum at a meeting of stockholders;

(2)   In all matters other than the election of directors, the affirmative vote of the majority of shares present in person or represented by proxy at the meeting and entitled to vote on the subject matter shall be the act of the stockholders;

(3)   Directors shall be elected by a plurality of the votes of the shares present in person or represented by proxy at the meeting and entitled to vote on the election of directors; and

(4)   Where a separate vote by a class or series or classes or series is required, a majority of the outstanding shares of such class or series or classes or series, present in person or represented by proxy, shall constitute a quorum entitled to take action with respect to that vote on that matter and in all matters other than the election of directors, the affirmative vote of the majority of shares of such class or series or classes or series present in person or represented by proxy at the meeting shall be the act of such class or series or classes or series.

A bylaw amendment adopted by stockholders which specifies the votes that shall be necessary for the election of directors shall not be further amended or repealed by the board of directors.

§ 217. Voting Rights of Fiduciaries, Pledgors and Joint Owners of Stock

(a) Persons holding stock in a fiduciary capacity shall be entitled to vote the shares so held. Persons whose stock is pledged shall be entitled to vote, unless in the transfer by the pledgor on the books of the corporation such person has expressly empowered the pledgee to vote thereon, in which case only the pledgee, or such pledgee's proxy, may represent such stock and vote thereon.

(b) If shares or other securities having voting power stand of record in the names of 2 or more persons, whether fiduciaries, members of a partnership, joint tenants, tenants in common, tenants by the entirety or otherwise, or if 2 or more persons have the same fiduciary relationship respecting the same shares, unless the secretary of the corporation is given written notice to the contrary and is furnished with a copy of the instrument or order appointing them or creating the relationship wherein it is so provided, their acts with respect to voting shall have the following effect:

(1) If only 1 votes, such person's act binds all;

(2) If more than 1 vote, the act of the majority so voting binds all;

(3) If more than 1 vote, but the vote is evenly split on any particular matter, each faction may vote the securities in question proportionally, or any person voting the shares, or a beneficiary, if any, may apply to the Court of Chancery or such other court as may have jurisdiction to appoint an additional person to act with the persons so voting the shares, which shall then be voted as determined by a majority of such persons and the person appointed by the Court. If the instrument so filed shows that any such tenancy is held in unequal interests, a majority or even split for the purpose of this subsection shall be a majority or even split in interest.

§ 218. Voting Trusts and Other Voting Agreements

(a) One stockholder or 2 or more stockholders may by agreement in writing deposit capital stock of an original issue with or transfer capital stock to any person or persons, or entity or entities authorized to act as trustee, for the purpose of vesting in such person or persons, entity or entities, who may be designated voting trustee, or voting trustees, the right to vote thereon for any period of time determined by such agreement, upon the terms and conditions stated in such agreement. The agreement may contain any other lawful provisions not inconsistent with such purpose. After delivery of a copy of the agreement to the registered office of the corporation in this State or the principal place of business of the corporation, which copy shall be open to the inspection of any stockholder of the corporation or any beneficiary of the trust under the agreement daily during business hours, certificates of stock or uncertificated stock shall be issued to the voting trustee or trustees to represent any stock of an original issue so deposited with such voting trustee or trustees, and any certificates of stock or uncertificated stock so transferred to the voting trustee or trustees shall be surrendered and cancelled and new certificates or uncertificated stock shall be issued therefore to the voting trustee or trustees. In the certificate so issued, if any, it shall be stated that it is issued pursuant to such agreement, and that fact shall also be stated in the stock ledger of the corporation. The voting trustee or trustees may vote the stock so issued or transferred during the period specified in the agreement. Stock standing in the name of the voting trustee or trustees may be voted either in person or by proxy, and in voting the stock, the voting trustee or trustees shall incur no responsibility as stockholder, trustee or otherwise, except for their own individual malfeasance. In any case where 2 or more persons or entities are designated as voting trustees, and the right and method of voting any stock standing in their names at any meeting of the corporation are not fixed by the agreement appointing the trustees, the right to vote the stock and the manner of voting it at the meeting shall be determined by a majority of the trustees, or if they be equally divided as to the right and manner of voting the stock in any particular case, the vote of the stock in such case shall be divided equally among the trustees.

(b)   Any amendment to a voting trust agreement shall be made by a written agreement, a copy of which shall be delivered to the registered office of the corporation in this State or principal place of business of the corporation.

(c)   An agreement between 2 or more stockholders, if in writing and signed by the parties thereto, may provide that in exercising any voting rights, the shares held by them shall be voted as provided by the agreement, or as the parties may agree, or as determined in accordance with a procedure agreed upon by them.

(d)   This section shall not be deemed to invalidate any voting or other agreement among stockholders or any irrevocable proxy which is not otherwise illegal.

§ 219.   List of Stockholders Entitled to Vote; Penalty for Refusal to Produce; Stock Ledger

(a)   The corporation shall prepare, at least 10 days before every meeting of stockholders, a complete list of the stockholders entitled to vote at the meeting; provided, however, if the record date for determining the stockholders entitled to vote is less than 10 days before the meeting date, the list shall reflect the stockholders entitled to vote as of the tenth day before the meeting date, arranged in alphabetical order, and showing the address of each stockholder and the number of shares registered in the name of each stockholder. Nothing contained in this section shall require the corporation to include electronic mail addresses or other electronic contact information on such list. Such list shall be open to the examination of any stockholder for any purpose germane to the meeting for a period of at least 10 days prior to the meeting: (i) on a reasonably accessible electronic network, provided that the information required to gain access to such list is provided with the notice of the meeting, or (ii) during ordinary business hours, at the principal place of business of the corporation. In the event that the corporation determines to make the list available on an electronic network, the corporation may take reasonable steps to ensure that such information is available only to stockholders of the corporation. If the meeting is to be held at a place, then a list of stockholders entitled to vote at the meeting shall be produced and kept at the time and place of the meeting during the whole time thereof and may be examined by any stockholder who is present. If the meeting is to be held solely by means of remote communication, then such list shall also be open to the examination of any stockholder during the whole time of the meeting on a reasonably accessible electronic network, and the information required to access such list shall be provided with the notice of the meeting.

(b)   If the corporation, or an officer or agent thereof, refuses to permit examination of the list by a stockholder, such stockholder may apply to the Court of Chancery for an order to compel the corporation to permit such examination. The burden of proof shall be on the corporation to establish that the examination such stockholder seeks is for a purpose not germane to the meeting. The Court may summarily order the corporation to permit examination of the list upon such conditions as the Court may deem appropriate, and may make such additional orders as may be appropriate, including, without limitation, postponing the meeting or voiding the results of the meeting.

(c)   For purposes of this chapter, "stock ledger" means 1 or more records administered by or on behalf of the corporation in which the names of all of the corporation's stockholders of record, the address and number of shares registered in the name of each such stockholder, and all issuances and transfers of stock of the corporation are recorded in accordance with § 224 of this title. The stock ledger shall be the only evidence as to who are the stockholders entitled by this section to examine the list required by this section to vote in person or by proxy at any meeting of stockholders.

§ 220.   Inspection of Books and Records

(a)   As used in this section:

(1)   "Stockholder" means a holder of record of stock in a stock corporation, or a person who is the beneficial owner of shares of such stock held either in a voting trust or by a nominee on behalf of such person.

(2) "Subsidiary" means any entity directly or indirectly owned, in whole or in part, by the corporation of which the stockholder is a stockholder and over the affairs of which the corporation directly or indirectly exercises control, and includes, without limitation, corporations, partnerships, limited partnerships, limited liability partnerships, limited liability companies, statutory trusts and/or joint ventures.

(3) "Under oath" includes statements the declarant affirms to be true under penalty of perjury under the laws of the United States or any state.

(b) Any stockholder, in person or by attorney or other agent, shall, upon written demand under oath stating the purpose thereof, have the right during the usual hours for business to inspect for any proper purpose, and to make copies and extracts from:

(1) The corporation's stock ledger, a list of its stockholders, and its other books and records; and

(2) A subsidiary's books and records, to the extent that:

a. The corporation has actual possession and control of such records of such subsidiary; or

b. The corporation could obtain such records through the exercise of control over such subsidiary, provided that as of the date of the making of the demand:

1. The stockholder inspection of such books and records of the subsidiary would not constitute a breach of an agreement between the corporation or the subsidiary and a person or persons not affiliated with the corporation; and

2. The subsidiary would not have the right under the law applicable to it to deny the corporation access to such books and records upon demand by the corporation.

In every instance where the stockholder is other than a record holder of stock in a stock corporation, or a member of a nonstock corporation, the demand under oath shall state the person's status as a stockholder, be accompanied by documentary evidence of beneficial ownership of the stock, and state that such documentary evidence is a true and correct copy of what it purports to be. A proper purpose shall mean a purpose reasonably related to such person's interest as a stockholder. In every instance where an attorney or other agent shall be the person who seeks the right to inspection, the demand under oath shall be accompanied by a power of attorney or such other writing which authorizes the attorney or other agent to so act on behalf of the stockholder. The demand under oath shall be directed to the corporation at its registered office in this State or at its principal place of business.

(c) If the corporation, or an officer or agent thereof, refuses to permit an inspection sought by a stockholder or attorney or other agent acting for the stockholder pursuant to subsection (b) of this section or does not reply to the demand within 5 business days after the demand has been made, the stockholder may apply to the Court of Chancery for an order to compel such inspection. The Court of Chancery is hereby vested with exclusive jurisdiction to determine whether or not the person seeking inspection is entitled to the inspection sought. The Court may summarily order the corporation to permit the stockholder to inspect the corporation's stock ledger, an existing list of stockholders, and its other books and records, and to make copies or extracts therefrom; or the Court may order the corporation to furnish to the stockholder a list of its stockholders as of a specific date on condition that the stockholder first pay to the corporation the reasonable cost of obtaining and furnishing such list and on such other conditions as the Court deems appropriate. Where the stockholder seeks to inspect the corporation's books and records, other than its stock ledger or list of stockholders, such stockholder shall first establish that:

(1) Such stockholder is a stockholder;

(2) Such stockholder has complied with this section respecting the form and manner of making demand for inspection of such documents; and

(3) The inspection such stockholder seeks is for a proper purpose.

Where the stockholder seeks to inspect the corporation's stock ledger or list of stockholders and establishes that such stockholder is a stockholder and has complied with this section respecting the form and manner of making demand for inspection of such documents, the burden of proof shall be upon the corporation to establish that the inspection such stockholder seeks is for an improper purpose. The Court may, in its discretion, prescribe any limitations or conditions with reference to the inspection, or award such other or further relief as the Court may deem just and proper. The Court may order books, documents and records, pertinent extracts therefrom, or duly authenticated copies thereof, to be brought within this State and kept in this State upon such terms and conditions as the order may prescribe.

(d) Any director shall have the right to examine the corporation's stock ledger, a list of its stockholders and its other books and records for a purpose reasonably related to the director's position as a director. The Court of Chancery is hereby vested with the exclusive jurisdiction to determine whether a director is entitled to the inspection sought. The Court may summarily order the corporation to permit the director to inspect any and all books and records, the stock ledger and the list of stockholders and to make copies or extracts therefrom. The burden of proof shall be upon the corporation to establish that the inspection such director seeks is for an improper purpose. The Court may, in its discretion, prescribe any limitations or conditions with reference to the inspection, or award such other and further relief as the Court may deem just and proper.

§ 221. Voting, Inspection and Other Rights of Bondholders and Debenture Holders

Every corporation may in its certificate of incorporation confer upon the holders of any bonds, debentures or other obligations issued or to be issued by the corporation the power to vote in respect to the corporate affairs and management of the corporation to the extent and in the manner provided in the certificate of incorporation and may confer upon such holders of bonds, debentures or other obligations the same right of inspection of its books, accounts and other records, and also any other rights, which the stockholders of the corporation have or may have by reason of this chapter or of its certificate of incorporation. If the certificate of incorporation so provides, such holders of bonds, debentures or other obligations shall be deemed to be stockholders, and their bonds, debentures or other obligations shall be deemed to be shares of stock, for the purpose of any provision of this chapter which requires the vote of stockholders as a prerequisite to any corporate action and the certificate of incorporation may divest the holders of capital stock, in whole or in part, of their right to vote on any corporate matter whatsoever, except as set forth in § 242(b)(2) of this title.

§ 222. Notice of Meetings and Adjourned Meetings

(a) Whenever stockholders are required or permitted to take any action at a meeting, a written notice of the meeting shall be given which shall state the place, if any, date and hour of the meeting, the means of remote communications, if any, by which stockholders and proxy holders may be deemed to be present in person and vote at such meeting, the record date for determining the stockholders entitled to vote at the meeting, if such date is different from the record date for determining stockholders entitled to notice of the meeting, and, in the case of a special meeting, the purpose or purposes for which the meeting is called.

(b) Unless otherwise provided in this chapter, the written notice of any meeting shall be given not less than 10 nor more than 60 days before the date of the meeting to each stockholder entitled to vote at such meeting as of the record date for determining the stockholders entitled to notice of the meeting. If mailed, notice is given when deposited in the United States mail, postage prepaid, directed to the stockholder at such stockholder's address as it appears on the records of the corporation. An affidavit of the secretary or an assistant secretary or of the transfer agent or other agent of the corporation that the notice has been given shall, in the absence of fraud, be prima facie evidence of the facts stated therein.

(c)   When a meeting is adjourned to another time or place, unless the bylaws otherwise require, notice need not be given of the adjourned meeting if the time, place, if any, thereof, and the means of remote communications, if any, by which stockholders and proxy holders may be deemed to be present in person and vote at such adjourned meeting are announced at the meeting at which the adjournment is taken. At the adjourned meeting the corporation may transact any business which might have been transacted at the original meeting. If the adjournment is for more than 30 days, a notice of the adjourned meeting shall be given to each stockholder of record entitled to vote at the meeting. If after the adjournment a new record date for stockholders entitled to vote is fixed for the adjourned meeting, the board of directors shall fix a new record date for notice of such adjourned meeting in accordance with § 213(a) of this title, and shall give notice of the adjourned meeting to each stockholder of record entitled to vote at such adjourned meeting as of the record date fixed for notice of such adjourned meeting.

§ 223.   Vacancies and Newly Created Directorships

(a)   Unless otherwise provided in the certificate of incorporation or bylaws:

(1)   Vacancies and newly created directorships resulting from any increase in the authorized number of directors elected by all of the stockholders having the right to vote as a single class may be filled by a majority of the directors then in office, although less than a quorum, or by a sole remaining director;

(2)   Whenever the holders of any class or classes of stock or series thereof are entitled to elect 1 or more directors by the certificate of incorporation, vacancies and newly created directorships of such class or classes or series may be filled by a majority of the directors elected by such class or classes or series thereof then in office, or by a sole remaining director so elected.

If at any time, by reason of death or resignation or other cause, a corporation should have no directors in office, then any officer or any stockholder or an executor, administrator, trustee or guardian of a stockholder, or other fiduciary entrusted with like responsibility for the person or estate of a stockholder, may call a special meeting of stockholders in accordance with the certificate of incorporation or the bylaws, or may apply to the Court of Chancery for a decree summarily ordering an election as provided in § 211 or § 215 of this title.

(b)   In the case of a corporation the directors of which are divided into classes, any directors chosen under subsection (a) of this section shall hold office until the next election of the class for which such directors shall have been chosen, and until their successors shall be elected and qualified.

(c)   If, at the time of filling any vacancy or any newly created directorship, the directors then in office shall constitute less than a majority of the whole board (as constituted immediately prior to any such increase), the Court of Chancery may, upon application of any stockholder or stockholders holding at least 10 percent of the voting stock at the time outstanding having the right to vote for such directors, summarily order an election to be held to fill any such vacancies or newly created directorships, or to replace the directors chosen by the directors then in office as aforesaid, which election shall be governed by § 211 or § 215 of this title as far as applicable.

(d)   Unless otherwise provided in the certificate of incorporation or bylaws, when 1 or more directors shall resign from the board, effective at a future date, a majority of the directors then in office, including those who have so resigned, shall have power to fill such vacancy or vacancies, the vote thereon to take effect when such resignation or resignations shall become effective, and each director so chosen shall hold office as provided in this section in the filling of other vacancies.

§ 224.   Form of Records

Any records administered by or on behalf of the corporation in the regular course of its business, including its stock ledger, books of account, and minute books, may be kept on, or by means of, or be in the form of, any information storage device, method, or 1 or more electronic networks or databases (including 1 or more distributed electronic networks or databases), provided that the records so kept can be converted into clearly legible paper form within a reasonable time, and, with respect to the stock ledger, that the records so kept (i) can be used to prepare the list of stockholders specified in §§ 219 and 220 of this title, (ii) record the information specified in §§ 156, 159, 217(a) and 218 of this title, and (iii) record transfers of stock as governed by Article 8 of subtitle I of Title 6. Any corporation shall convert any records so kept into clearly legible paper form upon the request of any person entitled to inspect such records pursuant to any provision of this chapter. When records are kept in such manner, a clearly legible paper form prepared from or by means of the information storage device, method, or 1 or more electronic networks or databases (including 1 or more distributed electronic networks or databases) shall be valid and admissible in evidence, and accepted for all other purposes, to the same extent as an original paper record of the same information would have been, provided the paper form accurately portrays the record.

§ 225.   Contested Election of Directors; Proceedings to Determine Validity

(a)   Upon application of any stockholder or director, or any officer whose title to office is contested, the Court of Chancery may hear and determine the validity of any election, appointment, removal or resignation of any director or officer of any corporation, and the right of any person to hold or continue to hold such office, and, in case any such office is claimed by more than 1 person, may determine the person entitled thereto; and to that end make such order or decree in any such case as may be just and proper, with power to enforce the production of any books, papers and records of the corporation relating to the issue. In case it should be determined that no valid election has been held, the Court of Chancery may order an election to be held in accordance with § 211 or § 215 of this title. In any such application, service of copies of the application upon the registered agent of the corporation shall be deemed to be service upon the corporation and upon the person whose title to office is contested and upon the person, if any, claiming such office; and the registered agent shall forward immediately a copy of the application to the corporation and to the person whose title to office is contested and to the person, if any, claiming such office, in a postpaid, sealed, registered letter addressed to such corporation and such person at their post-office addresses last known to the registered agent or furnished to the registered agent by the applicant stockholder. The Court may make such order respecting further or other notice of such application as it deems proper under the circumstances.

(b)   Upon application of any stockholder or upon application of the corporation itself, the Court of Chancery may hear and determine the result of any vote of stockholders upon matters other than the election of directors or officers. Service of the application upon the registered agent of the corporation shall be deemed to be service upon the corporation, and no other party need be joined in order for the Court to adjudicate the result of the vote. The Court may make such order respecting notice of the application as it deems proper under the circumstances.

(c)   If 1 or more directors has been convicted of a felony in connection with the duties of such director or directors to the corporation, or if there has been a prior judgment on the merits by a court of competent jurisdiction that 1 or more directors has committed a breach of the duty of loyalty in connection with the duties of such director or directors to that corporation, then, upon application by the corporation, or derivatively in the right of the corporation by any stockholder, in a subsequent action brought for such purpose, the Court of Chancery may remove from office such director or directors if the Court determines that the director or directors did not act in good faith in performing the acts resulting in the prior conviction or judgment and judicial removal is necessary to avoid irreparable harm to the corporation. In connection with such removal, the Court may make such orders as are necessary to effect such removal. In any such application, service of copies of the application upon the registered agent of the corporation shall be deemed to be service upon the corporation and upon the director or directors whose removal is sought; and the registered agent shall forward immediately a copy of the application to the corporation and to such director or directors, in a postpaid, sealed, registered letter addressed to such corporation and such director or directors at their post office addresses last known to the registered agent or furnished to the registered agent by the applicant. The Court may make such order respecting further or other notice of such application as it deems proper under the circumstances.

§ 226. Appointment of Custodian or Receiver of Corporation on Deadlock or for Other Cause

(a)   The Court of Chancery, upon application of any stockholder, may appoint 1 or more persons to be custodians, and, if the corporation is insolvent, to be receivers, of and for any corporation when:

(1)   At any meeting held for the election of directors the stockholders are so divided that they have failed to elect successors to directors whose terms have expired or would have expired upon qualification of their successors; or

(2)   The business of the corporation is suffering or is threatened with irreparable injury because the directors are so divided respecting the management of the affairs of the corporation that the required vote for action by the board of directors cannot be obtained and the stockholders are unable to terminate this division; or

(3)   The corporation has abandoned its business and has failed within a reasonable time to take steps to dissolve, liquidate or distribute its assets.

(b)   A custodian appointed under this section shall have all the powers and title of a receiver appointed under § 291 of this title, but the authority of the custodian is to continue the business of the corporation and not to liquidate its affairs and distribute its assets, except when the Court shall otherwise order and except in cases arising under paragraph (a)(3) of this § 352(a)(2) of this title.

(c)   In the case of a charitable nonstock corporation, the applicant shall provide a copy of any application referred to in subsection (a) of this section to the Attorney General of the State of Delaware within 1 week of its filing with the Court of Chancery.

§ 227. Powers of Court in Elections of Directors

(a)   The Court of Chancery, in any proceeding instituted under § 211, § 215 or § 225 of this title may determine the right and power of persons claiming to own stock to vote at any meeting of the stockholders.

(b)   The Court of Chancery may appoint a Master to hold any election provided for in § 211, § 215 or § 225 of this title under such orders and powers as it deems proper; and it may punish any officer or director for contempt in case of disobedience of any order made by the Court; and, in case of disobedience by a corporation of any order made by the Court, may enter a decree against such corporation for a penalty of not more than $5,000.

§ 228. Consent of Stockholders or Members in Lieu of Meeting

(a)   Unless otherwise provided in the certificate of incorporation, any action required by this chapter to be taken at any annual or special meeting of stockholders of a corporation, or any action which may be taken at any annual or special meeting of such stockholders, may be taken without a meeting, without prior notice and without a vote, if a consent or consents in writing, setting forth the action so taken, shall be signed by the holders of outstanding stock having not less than the minimum number of votes that would be necessary to authorize or take such action at a meeting at which all shares entitled to vote thereon were present and voted and shall be delivered to the corporation by delivery to its registered office in this State, its principal place of business or an officer or agent of the corporation having custody of the book in which proceedings of meetings of stockholders are recorded.

Delivery made to a corporation's registered office shall be by hand or by certified or registered mail, return receipt requested.

(b)   Unless otherwise provided in the certificate of incorporation, any action required by this chapter to be taken at a meeting of the members of a nonstock corporation, or any action which may be taken at any meeting of the members of a nonstock corporation, may be taken without a meeting, without prior notice and without a vote, if a consent or consents in writing, setting forth the action so taken, shall be signed by members having not less than the minimum number of votes that would be necessary to authorize or take such action at a meeting at which all members having a right to vote thereon were present and voted and shall be delivered to the corporation by delivery to its registered office in this State, its principal place of business or an officer or agent of the corporation having custody of the book in which proceedings of meetings of members are recorded. Delivery made to a corporation's registered office shall be by hand or by certified or registered mail, return receipt requested.

(c)   No written consent shall be effective to take the corporate action referred to therein unless written consents signed by a sufficient number of holders or members to take action are delivered to the corporation in the manner required by this section within 60 days of the first date on which a written consent is so delivered to the corporation. Any person executing a consent may provide, whether through instruction to an agent or otherwise, that such a consent will be effective at a future time (including a time determined upon the happening of an event), no later than 60 days after such instruction is given or such provision is made, if evidence of such instruction or provision is provided to the corporation. Unless otherwise provided, any such consent shall be revocable prior to its becoming effective.

(d)(1)   A telegram, cablegram or other electronic transmission consenting to an action to be taken and transmitted by a stockholder, member or proxyholder, or by a person or persons authorized to act for a stockholder, member or proxyholder, shall be deemed to be written and signed for the purposes of this section, provided that any such telegram, cablegram or other electronic transmission sets forth or is delivered with information from which the corporation can determine (A) that the telegram, cablegram or other electronic transmission was transmitted by the stockholder, member or proxyholder or by a person or persons authorized to act for the stockholder, member or proxyholder and (B) the date on which such stockholder, member or proxyholder or authorized person or persons transmitted such telegram, cablegram or electronic transmission. No consent given by telegram, cablegram or other electronic transmission shall be deemed to have been delivered until such consent is reproduced in paper form and until such paper form shall be delivered to the corporation by delivery to its registered office in this State, its principal place of business or an officer or agent of the corporation having custody of the book in which proceedings of meetings of stockholders or members are recorded. Delivery made to a corporation's registered office shall be made by hand or by certified or registered mail, return receipt requested. Notwithstanding the foregoing limitations on delivery, consents given by telegram, cablegram or other electronic transmission, may be otherwise delivered to the principal place of business of the corporation or to an officer or agent of the corporation having custody of the book in which proceedings of meetings of stockholders or members are recorded if, to the extent and in the manner provided by resolution of the board of directors or governing body of the corporation.

(2)   Any copy, facsimile or other reliable reproduction of a consent in writing may be substituted or used in lieu of the original writing for any and all purposes for which the original writing could be used, provided that such copy, facsimile or other reproduction shall be a complete reproduction of the entire original writing.

(e)   Prompt notice of the taking of the corporate action without a meeting by less than unanimous written consent shall be given to those stockholders or members who have not consented in writing and who, if the action had been taken at a meeting, would have been entitled to notice of the meeting if the record date for notice of such meeting had been the date that written consents signed by a sufficient number of holders or members to take the action were delivered to the corporation as provided in this section. In the event that the action which is consented to is such as would have required the filing of a certificate under any other section of this title, if such action had been voted on by stockholders or by members at a meeting thereof, the certificate filed under such other section shall state, in lieu of any statement required by such section concerning any vote of stockholders or members, that written consent has been given in accordance with this section.

§ 229. Waiver of Notice

Whenever notice is required to be given under any provision of this chapter or the certificate of incorporation or bylaws, a written waiver, signed by the person entitled to notice, or a waiver by electronic transmission by the person entitled to notice, whether before or after the time stated therein, shall be deemed equivalent to notice. Attendance of a person at a meeting shall constitute a waiver of notice of such meeting, except when the person attends a meeting for the express purpose of objecting at the beginning of the meeting, to the transaction of any business because the meeting is not lawfully called or convened. Neither the business to be transacted at, nor the purpose of, any regular or special meeting of the stockholders, directors or members of a committee of directors need be specified in any written waiver of notice or any waiver by electronic transmission unless so required by the certificate of incorporation or the bylaws.

§ 230. Exception to Requirements of Notice

(a) Whenever notice is required to be given, under any provision of this chapter or of the certificate of incorporation or bylaws of any corporation, to any person with whom communication is unlawful, the giving of such notice to such person shall not be required and there shall be no duty to apply to any governmental authority or agency for a license or permit to give such notice to such person. Any action or meeting which shall be taken or held without notice to any such person with whom communication is unlawful shall have the same force and effect as if such notice had been duly given. In the event that the action taken by the corporation is such as to require the filing of a certificate under any of the other sections of this title, the certificate shall state, if such is the fact and if notice is required, that notice was given to all persons entitled to receive notice except such persons with whom communication is unlawful.

(b) Whenever notice is required to be given, under any provision of this title or the certificate of incorporation or bylaws of any corporation, to any stockholder or, if the corporation is a nonstock corporation, to any member, to whom (1) notice of 2 consecutive annual meetings, and all notices of meetings or of the taking of action by written consent without a meeting to such person during the period between such 2 consecutive annual meetings, or (2) all, and at least 2, payments (if sent by first-class mail) of dividends or interest on securities during a 12-month period, have been mailed addressed to such person at such person's address as shown on the records of the corporation and have been returned undeliverable, the giving of such notice to such person shall not be required. Any action or meeting which shall be taken or held without notice to such person shall have the same force and effect as if such notice had been duly given. If any such person shall deliver to the corporation a written notice setting forth such person's then current address, the requirement that notice be given to such person shall be reinstated. In the event that the action taken by the corporation is such as to require the filing of a certificate under any of the other sections of this title, the certificate need not state that notice was not given to persons to whom notice was not required to be given pursuant to this subsection.

(c) The exception in paragraph (b)(1) of this section to the requirement that notice be given shall not be applicable to any notice returned as undeliverable if the notice was given by electronic transmission.

§ 231. Voting Procedures and Inspectors of Elections

(a) The corporation shall, in advance of any meeting of stockholders, appoint 1 or more inspectors to act at the meeting and make a written report thereof. The corporation may designate 1 or more persons as alternate inspectors to replace any inspector who fails to act. If no inspector or alternate is able to act at a meeting of stockholders, the person presiding at the meeting shall appoint 1 or more inspectors to act at the meeting. Each inspector, before entering upon the discharge of the duties of inspector, shall take and sign an oath faithfully to execute the duties of inspector with strict impartiality and according to the best of such inspector's ability.

(b) The inspectors shall:

(1) Ascertain the number of shares outstanding and the voting power of each;

(2) Determine the shares represented at a meeting and the validity of proxies and ballots;

(3) Count all votes and ballots;

(4) Determine and retain for a reasonable period a record of the disposition of any challenges made to any determination by the inspectors; and

(5) Certify their determination of the number of shares represented at the meeting, and their count of all votes and ballots.

The inspectors may appoint or retain other persons or entities to assist the inspectors in the performance of the duties of the inspectors.

(c) The date and time of the opening and the closing of the polls for each matter upon which the stockholders will vote at a meeting shall be announced at the meeting. No ballot, proxies or votes, nor any revocations thereof or changes thereto, shall be accepted by the inspectors after the closing of the polls unless the Court of Chancery upon application by a stockholder shall determine otherwise.

(d) In determining the validity and counting of proxies and ballots, the inspectors shall be limited to an examination of the proxies, any envelopes submitted with those proxies, any information provided in accordance with § 211(e) or § 212(c)(2) of this title, or any information provided pursuant to § 211(a)(2)b.(i) or (iii) of this title, ballots and the regular books and records of the corporation, except that the inspectors may consider other reliable information for the limited purpose of reconciling proxies and ballots submitted by or on behalf of banks, brokers, their nominees or similar persons which represent more votes than the holder of a proxy is authorized by the record owner to cast or more votes than the stockholder holds of record. If the inspectors consider other reliable information for the limited purpose permitted herein, the inspectors at the time they make their certification pursuant to paragraph (b)(5) of this section shall specify the precise information considered by them including the person or persons from whom they obtained the information, when the information was obtained, the means by which the information was obtained and the basis for the inspectors' belief that such information is accurate and reliable.

(e) Unless otherwise provided in the certificate of incorporation or bylaws, this section shall not apply to a corporation that does not have a class of voting stock that is:

(1) Listed on a national securities exchange;

(2) Authorized for quotation on an interdealer quotation system of a registered national securities association; or

(3) Held of record by more than 2,000 stockholders.

§ 232. Notice by Electronic Transmission

(a) Without limiting the manner by which notice otherwise may be given effectively to stockholders, any notice to stockholders given by the corporation under any provision of this chapter, the certificate of incorporation, or the bylaws shall be effective if given by a form of electronic transmission consented to by the stockholder to whom the notice is given. Any such consent shall be revocable by the stockholder by written notice to the corporation. Any such consent shall be deemed revoked if (1) the corporation is unable to deliver by electronic transmission 2 consecutive notices given by the corporation in accordance with such consent and (2) such inability becomes known to the secretary or an assistant secretary of the corporation or to the transfer agent, or other person responsible for the giving of notice; provided, however, the inadvertent failure to treat such inability as a revocation shall not invalidate any meeting or other action.

(b)   Notice given pursuant to subsection (a) of this section shall be deemed given:

     (1)   If by facsimile telecommunication, when directed to a number at which the stockholder has consented to receive notice;

     (2)   If by electronic mail, when directed to an electronic mail address at which the stockholder has consented to receive notice;

     (3)   If by a posting on an electronic network together with separate notice to the stockholder of such specific posting, upon the later of (A) such posting and (B) the giving of such separate notice; and

     (4)   If by any other form of electronic transmission, when directed to the stockholder.

An affidavit of the secretary or an assistant secretary or of the transfer agent or other agent of the corporation that the notice has been given by a form of electronic transmission shall, in the absence of fraud, be prima facie evidence of the facts state therein.

(c)   For purposes of this chapter, "electronic transmission" means any form of communication, not directly involving the physical transmission of paper, including the use of, or participation in, 1 or more electronic networks or databases (including 1 or more distributed electronic networks or databases), that creates a record that may be retained, retrieved and reviewed by a recipient thereof, and that may be directly reproduced in paper form by such a recipient through an automated process.

(d)   [Repealed.]

(e)   This section shall not apply to § 164, § 296, § 311, § 312, or § 324 of this title.

§ 233.   Notice to Stockholders Sharing an Address

(a)   Without limiting the manner by which notice otherwise may be given effectively to stockholders, any notice to stockholders given by the corporation under any provision of this chapter, the certificate of incorporation or the bylaws shall be effective if given by a single written notice to stockholders who share an address if consented to by the stockholders at that address to whom such notice is given. Any such consent shall be revocable by the stockholder by written notice to the corporation.

(b)   Any stockholder who fails to object in writing to the corporation, within 60 days of having been given written notice by the corporation of its intention to send the single notice permitted under subsection (a) of this section, shall be deemed to have consented to receiving such single written notice.

(c)   [Repealed.]

(d)   This section shall not apply to § 164, § 296, § 311, § 312 or § 324 of this title.

§ 241.   Amendment of Certificate of Incorporation Before Receipt of Payment for Stock

(a)   Before a corporation has received any payment for any of its stock, it may amend its certificate of incorporation at any time or times, in any and as many respects as may be desired, so long as its certificate of incorporation as amended would contain only such provisions as it would be lawful and proper to insert in an original certificate of incorporation filed at the time of filing the amendment.

(b)   The amendment of a certificate of incorporation authorized by this section shall be adopted by a majority of the incorporators, if directors were not named in the original certificate of incorporation or have not yet been elected, or, if directors were named in the original certificate of incorporation or have been elected and have qualified, by a majority of the directors. A certificate setting forth the amendment and certifying that the corporation has not received any payment for any of its stock, or that the corporation has no members, as applicable, and that the amendment has been duly adopted in accordance with this section shall be executed, acknowledged and filed in accordance with § 103 of this title. Upon such filing, the corporation's certificate of incorporation shall be deemed to be amended accordingly as of the date on which the original certificate of incorporation became effective, except as to those persons who are substantially and adversely affected by the amendment and as to those persons the amendment shall be effective from the filing date.

(c)   This section will apply to a nonstock corporation before such a corporation has any members; provided, however, that all references to directors shall be deemed to be references to members of the governing body of the corporation.

§ 242. Amendment of Certificate of Incorporation After Receipt of Payment for Stock; Nonstock Corporations

(a)   After a corporation has received payment for any of its capital stock, or after a nonstock corporation has members, it may amend its certificate of incorporation, from time to time, in any and as many respects as may be desired, so long as its certificate of incorporation as amended would contain only such provisions as it would be lawful and proper to insert in an original certificate of incorporation filed at the time of the filing of the amendment; and, if a change in stock or the rights of stockholders, or an exchange, reclassification, subdivision, combination or cancellation of stock or rights of stockholders is to be made, such provisions as may be necessary to effect such change, exchange, reclassification, subdivision, combination or cancellation. In particular, and without limitation upon such general power of amendment, a corporation may amend its certificate of incorporation, from time to time, so as:

(1)   To change its corporate name; or

(2)   To change, substitute, enlarge or diminish the nature of its business or its corporate powers and purposes; or

(3)   To increase or decrease its authorized capital stock or to reclassify the same, by changing the number, par value, designations, preferences, or relative, participating, optional, or other special rights of the shares, or the qualifications, limitations or restrictions of such rights, or by changing shares with par value into shares without par value, or shares without par value into shares with par value either with or without increasing or decreasing the number of shares, or by subdividing or combining the outstanding shares of any class or series of a class of shares into a greater or lesser number of outstanding shares; or

(4)   To cancel or otherwise affect the right of the holders of the shares of any class to receive dividends which have accrued but have not been declared; or

(5)   To create new classes of stock having rights and preferences either prior and superior or subordinate and inferior to the stock of any class then authorized, whether issued or unissued; or

(6)   To change the period of its duration; or

(7)   To delete:

a.   Such provisions of the original certificate of incorporation which named the incorporator or incorporators, the initial board of directors and the original subscribers for shares; and

b.   Such provisions contained in any amendment to the certificate of incorporation as were necessary to effect a change, exchange, reclassification, subdivision, combination or cancellation of stock, if such change, exchange, reclassification, subdivision, combination or cancellation has become effective.

Any or all such changes or alterations may be effected by 1 certificate of amendment.

(b)   Every amendment authorized by subsection (a) of this section shall be made and effected in the following manner:

(1)   If the corporation has capital stock, its board of directors shall adopt a resolution setting forth the amendment proposed, declaring its advisability, and either calling a special meeting of the stockholders entitled to vote in respect thereof for the consideration of such amendment or directing that the amendment proposed be considered at the next annual meeting of the stockholders; provided, however, that unless otherwise expressly required by the certificate of incorporation, no meeting or vote of stockholders shall be required to adopt an amendment that effects only changes described in paragraph (a)(1) or (7) of this section. Such special or annual meeting shall be called and held upon notice in accordance with § 222 of this title. The notice shall set forth such amendment in full or a brief summary of the changes to be effected thereby unless such notice constitutes a notice of internet availability of proxy materials under the rules promulgated under the Securities Exchange Act of 1934 [15 U.S.C. § 78a et seq.]. At the meeting a vote of the stockholders entitled to vote thereon shall be taken for and against any proposed amendment that requires adoption by stockholders. If no vote of stockholders is required to effect such amendment, or if a majority of the outstanding stock entitled to vote thereon, and a majority of the outstanding stock of each class entitled to vote thereon as a class has been voted in favor of the amendment, a certificate setting forth the amendment and certifying that such amendment has been duly adopted in accordance with this section shall be executed, acknowledged and filed and shall become effective in accordance with § 103 of this title.

(2)   The holders of the outstanding shares of a class shall be entitled to vote as a class upon a proposed amendment, whether or not entitled to vote thereon by the certificate of incorporation, if the amendment would increase or decrease the aggregate number of authorized shares of such class, increase or decrease the par value of the shares of such class, or alter or change the powers, preferences, or special rights of the shares of such class so as to affect them adversely. If any proposed amendment would alter or change the powers, preferences, or special rights of 1 or more series of any class so as to affect them adversely, but shall not so affect the entire class, then only the shares of the series so affected by the amendment shall be considered a separate class for the purposes of this paragraph. The number of authorized shares of any such class or classes of stock may be increased or decreased (but not below the number of shares thereof then outstanding) by the affirmative vote of the holders of a majority of the stock of the corporation entitled to vote irrespective of this subsection, if so provided in the original certificate of incorporation, in any amendment thereto which created such class or classes of stock or which was adopted prior to the issuance of any shares of such class or classes of stock, or in any amendment thereto which was authorized by a resolution or resolutions adopted by the affirmative vote of the holders of a majority of such class or classes of stock.

(3)   If the corporation is a nonstock corporation, then the governing body thereof shall adopt a resolution setting forth the amendment proposed and declaring its advisability. If a majority of all the members of the governing body shall vote in favor of such amendment, a certificate thereof shall be executed, acknowledged and filed and shall become effective in accordance with § 103 of this title. The certificate of incorporation of any nonstock corporation may contain a provision requiring any amendment thereto to be approved by a specified number or percentage of the members or of any specified class of members of such corporation in which event such proposed amendment shall be submitted to the members or to any specified class of members of such corporation in the same manner, so far as applicable, as is provided in this section for an amendment to the certificate of incorporation of a stock corporation; and in the event of the adoption thereof by such members, a certificate evidencing such amendment shall be executed, acknowledged and filed and shall become effective in accordance with § 103 of this title.

(4)   Whenever the certificate of incorporation shall require for action by the board of directors of a corporation other than a nonstock corporation or by the governing body of a nonstock

corporation, by the holders of any class or series of shares or by the members, or by the holders of any other securities having voting power the vote of a greater number or proportion than is required by any section of this title, the provision of the certificate of incorporation requiring such greater vote shall not be altered, amended or repealed except by such greater vote.

(c)   The resolution authorizing a proposed amendment to the certificate of incorporation may provide that at any time prior to the effectiveness of the filing of the amendment with the Secretary of State, notwithstanding authorization of the proposed amendment by the stockholders of the corporation or by the members of a nonstock corporation, the board of directors or governing body may abandon such proposed amendment without further action by the stockholders or members.

§ 243. Retirement of Stock

(a)   A corporation, by resolution of its board of directors, may retire any shares of its capital stock that are issued but are not outstanding.

(b)   Whenever any shares of the capital stock of a corporation are retired, they shall resume the status of authorized and unissued shares of the class or series to which they belong unless the certificate of incorporation otherwise provides. If the certificate of incorporation prohibits the reissuance of such shares, or prohibits the reissuance of such shares as a part of a specific series only, a certificate stating that reissuance of the shares (as part of the class or series) is prohibited identifying the shares and reciting their retirement shall be executed, acknowledged and filed and shall become effective in accordance with § 103 of this title. When such certificate becomes effective, it shall have the effect of amending the certificate of incorporation so as to reduce accordingly the number of authorized shares of the class or series to which such shares belong or, if such retired shares constitute all of the authorized shares of the class or series to which they belong, of eliminating from the certificate of incorporation all reference to such class or series of stock.

(c)   If the capital of the corporation will be reduced by or in connection with the retirement of shares, the reduction of capital shall be effected pursuant to § 244 of this title.

§ 244. Reduction of Capital

(a)   A corporation, by resolution of its board of directors, may reduce its capital in any of the following ways:

(1)   By reducing or eliminating the capital represented by shares of capital stock which have been retired;

(2)   By applying to an otherwise authorized purchase or redemption of outstanding shares of its capital stock some or all of the capital represented by the shares being purchased or redeemed, or any capital that has not been allocated to any particular class of its capital stock;

(3)   By applying to an otherwise authorized conversion or exchange of outstanding shares of its capital stock some or all of the capital represented by the shares being converted or exchanged, or some or all of any capital that has not been allocated to any particular class of its capital stock, or both, to the extent that such capital in the aggregate exceeds the total aggregate par value or the stated capital of any previously unissued shares issuable upon such conversion or exchange; or

(4)   By transferring to surplus (i) some or all of the capital not represented by any particular class of its capital stock; (ii) some or all of the capital represented by issued shares of its par value capital stock, which capital is in excess of the aggregate par value of such shares; or (iii) some of the capital represented by issued shares of its capital stock without par value.

(b)   Notwithstanding the other provisions of this section, no reduction of capital shall be made or effected unless the assets of the corporation remaining after such reduction shall be sufficient to pay any debts of the corporation for which payment has not been otherwise provided. No reduction of capital shall release any liability of any stockholder whose shares have not been fully paid.

(c)   [Repealed.]

§ 245.   Restated Certificate of Incorporation

(a)   A corporation may, whenever desired, integrate into a single instrument all of the provisions of its certificate of incorporation which are then in effect and operative as a result of there having theretofore been filed with the Secretary of State 1 or more certificates or other instruments pursuant to any of the sections referred to in § 104 of this title, and it may at the same time also further amend its certificate of incorporation by adopting a restated certificate of incorporation.

(b)   If the restated certificate of incorporation merely restates and integrates but does not further amend the certificate of incorporation, as theretofore amended or supplemented by any instrument that was filed pursuant to any of the sections mentioned in § 104 of this title, it may be adopted by the board of directors without a vote of the stockholders, or it may be proposed by the directors and submitted by them to the stockholders for adoption, in which case the procedure and vote required, if any, by § 242 of this title for amendment of the certificate of incorporation shall be applicable. If the restated certificate of incorporation restates and integrates and also further amends in any respect the certificate of incorporation, as theretofore amended or supplemented, it shall be proposed by the directors and adopted by the stockholders in the manner and by the vote prescribed by § 242 of this title or, if the corporation has not received any payment for any of its stock, in the manner and by the vote prescribed by § 241 of this title.

(c)   A restated certificate of incorporation shall be specifically designated as such in its heading. It shall state, either in its heading or in an introductory paragraph, the corporation's present name, and, if it has been changed, the name under which it was originally incorporated, and the date of filing of its original certificate of incorporation with the Secretary of State. A restated certificate shall also state that it was duly adopted in accordance with this section. If it was adopted by the board of directors without a vote of the stockholders (unless it was adopted pursuant to § 241 of this title or without a vote of members pursuant to § 242(b)(3) of this title), it shall state that it only restates and integrates and does not further amend (except, if applicable, as permitted under § 242(a)(1) and § 242(b)(1) of this title) the provisions of the corporation's certificate of incorporation as theretofore amended or supplemented, and that there is no discrepancy between those provisions and the provisions of the restated certificate. A restated certificate of incorporation may omit (a) such provisions of the original certificate of incorporation which named the incorporator or incorporators, the initial board of directors and the original subscribers for shares, and (b) such provisions contained in any amendment to the certificate of incorporation as were necessary to effect a change, exchange, reclassification, subdivision, combination or cancellation of stock, if such change, exchange, reclassification, subdivision, combination or cancellation has become effective. Any such omissions shall not be deemed a further amendment.

(d)   A restated certificate of incorporation shall be executed, acknowledged and filed in accordance with § 103 of this title. Upon its filing with the Secretary of State, the original certificate of incorporation, as theretofore amended or supplemented, shall be superseded; thenceforth, the restated certificate of incorporation, including any further amendments or changes made thereby, shall be the certificate of incorporation of the corporation, but the original date of incorporation shall remain unchanged.

(e)   Any amendment or change effected in connection with the restatement and integration of the certificate of incorporation shall be subject to any other provision of this chapter, not inconsistent with this section, which would apply if a separate certificate of amendment were filed to effect such amendment or change.

§ 251.   Merger or Consolidation of Domestic Corporations

(a)   Any 2 or more corporations of this State may merge into a single surviving corporation, which may be any 1 of the constituent corporations or may consolidate into a new resulting corporation formed by the consolidation, pursuant to an agreement of merger or consolidation, as the case may be, complying and approved in accordance with this section.

(b)   The board of directors of each corporation which desires to merge or consolidate shall adopt a resolution approving an agreement of merger or consolidation and declaring its advisability. The agreement shall state:

(1)   The terms and conditions of the merger or consolidation;

(2)   The mode of carrying the same into effect;

(3)   In the case of a merger, such amendments or changes in the certificate of incorporation of the surviving corporation as are desired to be effected by the merger (which amendments or changes may amend and restate the certificate of incorporation of the surviving corporation in its entirety), or, if no such amendments or changes are desired, a statement that the certificate of incorporation of the surviving corporation shall be its certificate of incorporation;

(4)   In the case of a consolidation, that the certificate of incorporation of the resulting corporation shall be as is set forth in an attachment to the agreement;

(5)   The manner, if any, of converting the shares of each of the constituent corporations into shares or other securities of the corporation surviving or resulting from the merger or consolidation, or of cancelling some or all of such shares, and, if any shares of any of the constituent corporations are not to remain outstanding, to be converted solely into shares or other securities of the surviving or resulting corporation or to be cancelled, the cash, property, rights or securities of any other corporation or entity which the holders of such shares are to receive in exchange for, or upon conversion of such shares and the surrender of any certificates evidencing them, which cash, property, rights or securities of any other corporation or entity may be in addition to or in lieu of shares or other securities of the surviving or resulting corporation; and

(6)   Such other details or provisions as are deemed desirable, including, without limiting the generality of the foregoing, a provision for the payment of cash in lieu of the issuance or recognition of fractional shares, rights or other securities of the surviving or resulting corporation or of any other corporation or entity the shares, rights or other securities of which are to be received in the merger or consolidation, or for any other arrangement with respect thereto, consistent with § 155 of this title.

The agreement so adopted shall be executed and acknowledged in accordance with § 103 of this title. Any of the terms of the agreement of merger or consolidation may be made dependent upon facts ascertainable outside of such agreement, provided that the manner in which such facts shall operate upon the terms of the agreement is clearly and expressly set forth in the agreement of merger or consolidation. The term "facts," as used in the preceding sentence, includes, but is not limited to, the occurrence of any event, including a determination or action by any person or body, including the corporation.

(c)   The agreement required by subsection (b) of this section shall be submitted to the stockholders of each constituent corporation at an annual or special meeting for the purpose of acting on the agreement. Due notice of the time, place and purpose of the meeting shall be mailed to each holder of stock, whether voting or nonvoting, of the corporation at the stockholder's address as it appears on the records of the corporation, at least 20 days prior to the date of the meeting. The notice shall contain a copy of the agreement or a brief summary thereof. At the meeting, the agreement shall be considered and a vote taken for its adoption or rejection. If a majority of the outstanding stock of the corporation entitled to vote thereon shall be voted for the adoption of the agreement, that fact shall be certified on the agreement by the secretary or assistant secretary of the corporation, provided that such certification on the agreement shall not be required if a certificate of merger or consolidation is filed in lieu of filing the agreement. If the agreement shall be so adopted and certified by each constituent corporation, it shall then be filed and shall become effective, in accordance with § 103 of this title. In lieu of filing the agreement of merger or consolidation required by this section, the surviving or resulting corporation may file a certificate of merger or consolidation, executed in accordance with § 103 of this title, which states:

    (1)   The name and state of incorporation of each of the constituent corporations;

    (2)   That an agreement of merger or consolidation has been approved, adopted, executed and acknowledged by each of the constituent corporations in accordance with this section;

    (3)   The name of the surviving or resulting corporation;

    (4)   In the case of a merger, such amendments or changes in the certificate of incorporation of the surviving corporation as are desired to be effected by the merger (which amendments or changes may amend and restate the certificate of incorporation of the surviving corporation in its entirety), or, if no such amendments or changes are desired, a statement that the certificate of incorporation of the surviving corporation shall be its certificate of incorporation;

    (5)   In the case of a consolidation, that the certificate of incorporation of the resulting corporation shall be as set forth in an attachment to the certificate;

    (6)   That the executed agreement of consolidation or merger is on file at an office of the surviving or resulting corporation, stating the address thereof; and

    (7)   That a copy of the agreement of consolidation or merger will be furnished by the surviving or resulting corporation, on request and without cost, to any stockholder of any constituent corporation.

    (d)   Any agreement of merger or consolidation may contain a provision that at any time prior to the time that the agreement (or a certificate in lieu thereof) filed with the Secretary of State becomes effective in accordance with § 103 of this title, the agreement may be terminated by the board of directors of any constituent corporation notwithstanding approval of the agreement by the stockholders of all or any of the constituent corporations; in the event the agreement of merger or consolidation is terminated after the filing of the agreement (or a certificate in lieu thereof) with the Secretary of State but before the agreement (or a certificate in lieu thereof) has become effective, a certificate of termination or merger or consolidation shall be filed in accordance with § 103 of this title. Any agreement of merger or consolidation may contain a provision that the boards of directors of the constituent corporations may amend the agreement at any time prior to the time that the agreement (or a certificate in lieu thereof) filed with the Secretary of State becomes effective in accordance with § 103 of this title, provided that an amendment made subsequent to the adoption of the agreement by the stockholders of any constituent corporation shall not (1) alter or change the amount or kind of shares, securities, cash, property and/or rights to be received in exchange for or on conversion of all or any of the shares of any class or series thereof of such constituent corporation, (2) alter or change any term of the certificate of incorporation of the surviving corporation to be effected by the merger or consolidation, or (3) alter or change any of the terms and conditions of the agreement if such alteration or change would adversely affect the holders of any class or series thereof of such constituent corporation; in the event the agreement of merger or consolidation is amended after the filing thereof with the Secretary of State but before the agreement has become effective, a certificate of amendment of merger or consolidation shall be filed in accordance with § 103 of this title.

    (e)   In the case of a merger, the certificate of incorporation of the surviving corporation shall automatically be amended to the extent, if any, that changes in the certificate of incorporation are set forth in the agreement of merger.

    (f)   Notwithstanding the requirements of subsection (c) of this section, unless required by its certificate of incorporation, no vote of stockholders of a constituent corporation surviving a merger shall be necessary to authorize a merger if (1) the agreement of merger does not amend in any respect the certificate of incorporation of such constituent corporation, (2) each share of stock of such constituent corporation outstanding immediately prior to the effective date of the merger is to be an identical outstanding or treasury share of the surviving corporation after the effective date of the merger, and (3) either no shares of common stock of the surviving corporation and no shares, securities or obligations convertible into such stock are to be issued or delivered under the plan of merger, or the authorized unissued shares or the treasury shares of common stock of the surviving corporation to be issued or delivered under the plan of merger plus those initially issuable upon conversion of any other shares, securities or obligations to be issued or delivered under such plan do not exceed 20% of the shares of common stock of such constituent corporation outstanding immediately prior to the effective date of the merger. No vote of stockholders of a constituent corporation shall be necessary to authorize a merger or consolidation if no shares of the stock of such corporation shall have been issued prior to the adoption by the board of directors of the resolution approving the agreement of merger or consolidation. If an agreement of merger is adopted by the constituent corporation surviving the merger, by action of its board of directors and without any vote of its stockholders pursuant to this subsection, the secretary or assistant secretary of that corporation shall certify on the agreement that the agreement has been adopted pursuant to this subsection and, (1) if it has been adopted pursuant to the first sentence of this subsection, that the conditions specified in that sentence have been satisfied, or (2) if it has been adopted pursuant to the second sentence of this subsection, that no shares of stock of such corporation were issued prior to the adoption by the board of directors of the resolution approving the agreement of merger or consolidation, provided that such certification on the agreement shall not be required if a certificate of merger or consolidation is filed in lieu of filing the agreement. The agreement so adopted and certified shall then be filed and shall become effective, in accordance with § 103 of this title. Such filing shall constitute a representation by the person who executes the agreement that the facts stated in the certificate remain true immediately prior to such filing.

(g)   Notwithstanding the requirements of subsection (c) of this section, unless expressly required by its certificate of incorporation, no vote of stockholders of a constituent corporation shall be necessary to authorize a merger with or into a single direct or indirect wholly-owned subsidiary of such constituent corporation if: (1) such constituent corporation and the direct or indirect wholly-owned subsidiary of such constituent corporation are the only constituent entities to the merger; (2) each share or fraction of a share of the capital stock of the constituent corporation outstanding immediately prior to the effective time of the merger is converted in the merger into a share or equal fraction of share of capital stock of a holding company having the same designations, rights, powers and preferences, and the qualifications, limitations and restrictions thereof, as the share of stock of the constituent corporation being converted in the merger; (3) the holding company and the constituent corporation are corporations of this State and the direct or indirect wholly-owned subsidiary that is the other constituent entity to the merger is a corporation or limited liability company of this State; (4) the certificate of incorporation and by-laws of the holding company immediately following the effective time of the merger contain provisions identical to the certificate of incorporation and by-laws of the constituent corporation immediately prior to the effective time of the merger (other than provisions, if any, regarding the incorporator or incorporators, the corporate name, the registered office and agent, the initial board of directors and the initial subscribers for shares and such provisions contained in any amendment to the certificate of incorporation as were necessary to effect a change, exchange, reclassification, subdivision, combination or cancellation of stock, if such change, exchange, reclassification, subdivision, combination, or cancellation has become effective); (5) as a result of the merger the constituent corporation or its successor becomes or remains a direct or indirect wholly-owned subsidiary of the holding company; (6) the directors of the constituent corporation become or remain the directors of the holding company upon the effective time of the merger; (7) the organizational documents of the surviving entity immediately following the effective time of the merger contain provisions identical to the certificate of incorporation of the constituent corporation immediately prior to the effective time of the merger (other than provisions, if any, regarding the incorporator or incorporators, the corporate or entity name, the registered office and agent, the initial board of directors and the initial subscribers for shares, references to members rather than stockholders or shareholders, references to interests, units or the like rather than stock or shares, references to managers, managing members or other members of the governing body rather than directors and such provisions contained in any amendment to the certificate of incorporation as were necessary to effect a change, exchange, reclassification, subdivision, combination or cancellation of stock, if such change, exchange, reclassification, subdivision, combination or cancellation has become effective); provided, however, that (i) if the organizational documents of the surviving entity do not contain the following provisions, they shall be amended in the merger to contain provisions requiring that (A) any act or transaction by or involving the surviving entity, other than the election or removal of directors or managers, managing members or other members of the governing body of the surviving entity, that requires for its adoption under this chapter or its organizational documents the approval of the stockholders or members of the surviving entity shall, by specific reference to this subsection, require, in addition, the approval of the stockholders of the holding company (or any successor by merger), by the same vote as is required by this chapter and/or by the organizational documents of the surviving entity; provided, however, that for purposes of this clause (i)(A), any surviving entity that is not a corporation shall include in such amendment a requirement that the approval of the stockholders of the holding company be obtained for any act or transaction by or involving the surviving entity, other than the election or removal of directors or managers, managing members or other members of the governing body of the surviving entity, which would require the approval of the stockholders of the surviving entity if the surviving entity were a corporation subject to this chapter; (B) any amendment of the organizational documents of a surviving entity that is not a corporation, which amendment would, if adopted by a corporation subject to this chapter, be required to be included in the certificate of incorporation of such corporation, shall, by specific reference to this subsection, require, in addition, the approval of the stockholders of the holding company (or any successor by merger), by the same vote as is required by this chapter and/or by the organizational documents of the surviving entity; and (C) the business and affairs of a surviving entity that is not a corporation shall be managed by or under the direction of a board of directors, board of managers or other governing body consisting of individuals who are subject to the same fiduciary duties applicable to, and who are liable for breach of such duties to the same extent as, directors of a corporation subject to this chapter; and (ii) the organizational documents of the surviving entity may be amended in the merger (A) to reduce the number of classes and shares of capital stock or other equity interests or units that the surviving entity is authorized to issue and (B) to eliminate any provision authorized by § 141(d) of this title; and (8) the stockholders of the constituent corporation do not recognize gain or loss for United States federal income tax purposes as determined by the board of directors of the constituent corporation. Neither paragraph (g)(7)(i) of this section nor any provision of a surviving entity's organizational documents required by paragraph (g)(7)(i) of this section shall be deemed or construed to require approval of the stockholders of the holding company to elect or remove directors or managers, managing members or other members of the governing body of the surviving entity. The term "organizational documents", as used in paragraph (g)(7) of this section and in the preceding sentence, shall, when used in reference to a corporation, mean the certificate of incorporation of such corporation, and when used in reference to a limited liability company, mean the limited liability company agreement of such limited liability company.

As used in this subsection only, the term "holding company" means a corporation which, from its incorporation until consummation of a merger governed by this subsection, was at all times a direct or indirect wholly-owned subsidiary of the constituent corporation and whose capital stock is issued in such merger. From and after the effective time of a merger adopted by a constituent corporation by action of its board of directors and without any vote of stockholders pursuant to this subsection: (i) to the extent the restrictions of § 203 of this title applied to the constituent corporation and its stockholders at the effective time of the merger, such restrictions shall apply to the holding company and its stockholders immediately after the effective time of the merger as though it were the constituent corporation, and all shares of stock of the holding company acquired in the merger shall for purposes of § 203 of this title be deemed to have been acquired at the time that the shares of stock of the constituent corporation converted in the merger were acquired, and provided further that any stockholder who immediately prior to the effective time of the merger was not an interested stockholder within the meaning of § 203 of this title shall not solely by reason of the merger become an interested stockholder of the holding company, (ii) if the corporate name of the holding company immediately following the effective time of the merger is the same as the corporate name of the constituent corporation immediately prior to the effective time of the merger, the shares of capital stock of the holding company into which the shares of capital stock of the constituent corporation are converted in the merger shall be represented by the stock certificates that previously represented shares of capital stock of the constituent corporation and (iii) to the extent a stockholder of the constituent corporation immediately prior to the merger had standing to institute or maintain derivative litigation on behalf of the constituent corporation, nothing in this section shall be deemed to limit or extinguish such standing. If an agreement of merger is adopted by a constituent corporation by action of its board of directors and without any vote of stockholders pursuant to this subsection, the secretary or assistant secretary of the constituent corporation shall certify on the agreement that the agreement has been adopted pursuant to this subsection and that the conditions specified in the first sentence of this subsection have been satisfied, provided that such certification on the agreement shall not be required if a certificate of merger or consolidation is filed in lieu of filing the agreement. The agreement so adopted and certified shall then be filed and become effective, in accordance with § 103 of this title. Such filing shall constitute a representation by the person who executes the agreement that the facts stated in the certificate remain true immediately prior to such filing.

(h) Notwithstanding the requirements of subsection (c) of this section, unless expressly required by its certificate of incorporation, no vote of stockholders of a constituent corporation that has a class or series of stock that is listed on a national securities exchange or held of record by more than 2,000 holders immediately prior to the execution of the agreement of merger by such constituent corporation shall be necessary to authorize a merger if:

(1) The agreement of merger expressly:

a. Permits or requires such merger to be effected under this subsection; and

b. Provides that such merger shall be effected as soon as practicable following the consummation of the offer referred to in paragraph (h)(2) of this section if such merger is effected under this subsection;

(2) A corporation consummates an offer for all of the outstanding stock of such constituent corporation on the terms provided in such agreement of merger that, absent this subsection, would be entitled to vote on the adoption or rejection of the agreement of merger; provided, however, that such offer may be conditioned on the tender of a minimum number or percentage of shares of the stock of such constituent corporation, or of any class or series thereof, and such offer may exclude any excluded stock and provided further that the corporation may consummate separate offers for separate classes or series of the stock of such constituent corporation;

a.–d. [Repealed.]

(3) Immediately following the consummation of the offer referred to in paragraph (h)(2) of this section, the stock irrevocably accepted for purchase or exchange pursuant to such offer and received by the depository prior to expiration of such offer, together with the stock otherwise owned by the consummating corporation or its affiliates and any rollover stock, equals at least such percentage of the shares of stock of such constituent corporation, and of each class or series thereof, that, absent this subsection, would be required to adopt the agreement of merger by this chapter and by the certificate of incorporation of such constituent corporation;

(4) The corporation consummating the offer referred to in paragraph (h)(2) of this section merges with or into such constituent corporation pursuant to such agreement; and

(5) Each outstanding share (other than shares of excluded stock) of each class or series of stock of such constituent corporation that is the subject of and is not irrevocably accepted for purchase or exchange in the offer referred to in paragraph (h)(2) of this section is to be converted in such merger into, or into the right to receive, the same amount and kind of cash, property, rights or securities to be paid for shares of such class or series of stock of such constituent corporation irrevocably accepted for purchase or exchange in such offer.

(6) As used in this section only, the term

a. "Affiliate" means, in respect of the corporation making the offer referred to in paragraph (h)(2) of this section, any person that (i) owns, directly or indirectly, all of the outstanding stock of such corporation or (ii) is a direct or indirect wholly-owned subsidiary of such corporation or of any person referred to in clause (i) of this definition;

b. "Consummates" (and with correlative meaning, "consummation" and "consummating") means irrevocably accepts for purchase or exchange stock tendered pursuant to an offer;

c. "Depository" means an agent, including a depository, appointed to facilitate consummation of the offer referred to in paragraph (h)(2) of this section;

d. "Excluded stock" means (i) stock of such constituent corporation that is owned at the commencement of the offer referred to in paragraph (h)(2) of this section by such constituent corporation, the corporation making the offer referred to in paragraph (h)(2) of this section, any person that owns, directly or indirectly, all of the outstanding stock of the corporation making such offer, or any direct or indirect wholly-owned subsidiary of any of the foregoing and (ii) rollover stock;

e. "Person" means any individual, corporation, partnership, limited liability company, unincorporated association or other entity;

f. "Received" (solely for purposes of paragraph (h)(3) of this section) means (a) with respect to certificated shares, physical receipt of a stock certificate accompanied by an executed letter of transmittal, (b) with respect to uncertificated shares held of record by a clearing corporation as nominee, transfer into the depository's account by means of an agent's message, and (c) with respect to uncertificated shares held of record by a person other than a clearing corporation as nominee, physical receipt of an executed letter of transmittal by the depository; provided, however, that shares shall cease to be "received" (i) with respect to certificated shares, if the certificate representing such shares was canceled prior to consummation of the offer referred to in paragraph (h)(2) of this section, or (ii) with respect to uncertificated shares, to the extent such uncertificated shares have been reduced or eliminated due to any sale of such shares prior to consummation of the offer referred to in paragraph (h)(2) of this section; and

g. "Rollover stock" means any shares of stock of such constituent corporation that are the subject of a written agreement requiring such shares to be transferred, contributed or delivered to the consummating corporation or any of its affiliates in exchange for stock or other equity interests in such consummating corporation or an affiliate thereof; provided, however, that such shares of stock shall cease to be rollover stock for purposes of paragraph (h)(3) of this section if, immediately prior to the time the merger becomes effective under this chapter, such shares have not been transferred, contributed or delivered to the consummating corporation or any of its affiliates pursuant to such written agreement.

If an agreement of merger is adopted without the vote of stockholders of a corporation pursuant to this subsection, the secretary or assistant secretary of the surviving corporation shall certify on the agreement that the agreement has been adopted pursuant to this subsection and that the conditions specified in this subsection (other than the condition listed in paragraph (h)(4) of this section) have been satisfied; provided that such certification on the agreement shall not be required if a certificate of merger is filed in lieu of filing the agreement. The agreement so adopted and certified shall then be filed and shall become effective, in accordance with § 103 of this title. Such filing shall constitute a representation by the person who executes the agreement that the facts stated in the certificate remain true immediately prior to such filing.

§ 252. Merger or Consolidation of Domestic and Foreign Corporations; Service of Process Upon Surviving or Resulting Corporation

(a) Any 1 or more corporations of this State may merge or consolidate with 1 or more foreign corporations, unless the laws of the jurisdiction or jurisdictions under which such foreign corporation or corporations are organized prohibit such merger or consolidation. The constituent corporations may merge into a single surviving corporation, which may be any 1 of the constituent corporations, or they may consolidate into a new resulting corporation formed by the consolidation, which may be a corporation of the jurisdiction of organization of any 1 of the constituent corporations, pursuant to an agreement of merger or consolidation, as the case may be, complying and approved in accordance with this section.

(b) All the constituent corporations shall enter into an agreement of merger or consolidation. The agreement shall state:

(1) The terms and conditions of the merger or consolidation;

(2) The mode of carrying the same into effect;

(3) In the case of a merger in which the surviving corporation is a corporation of this State, such amendments or changes in the certificate of incorporation of the surviving corporation as are desired to be effected by the merger (which amendments or changes may amend and restate the certificate of incorporation of the surviving corporation in its entirety), or, if no such amendments or changes are desired, a statement that the certificate of incorporation of the surviving corporation shall be its certificate of incorporation;

(4) In the case of a consolidation in which the resulting corporation is a corporation of this State, that the certificate of incorporation of the resulting corporation shall be as is set forth in an attachment to the agreement;

(5) The manner, if any, of converting the shares of each of the constituent corporations into shares or other securities of the corporation surviving or resulting from the merger or consolidation, or of cancelling some or all of such shares, and, if any shares of any of the constituent corporations are not to remain outstanding, to be converted solely into shares or other securities of the surviving or resulting corporation to be cancelled, the cash, property, rights or securities of any other corporation or entity which the holders of such shares and the surrender of any certificates evidencing them, which cash, property, rights or securities of any other corporation or entity may be in addition to or in lieu of the shares or other securities of the surviving or resulting corporation;

(6) Such other details or provisions as are deemed desirable, including, without limiting the generality of the foregoing, a provision for the payment of cash in lieu of the issuance or recognition of fractional shares, rights or other securities of the surviving or resulting corporation or of any other corporation or entity the shares, rights or other securities of which are to be received in the merger or consolidation, or for some other arrangement with respect thereto, consistent with § 155 of this title; and

(7) Such other provisions or facts as shall be required to be set forth in an agreement of merger or consolidation (including any provision for amendment of the certificate of incorporation (or equivalent document) of a surviving or resulting foreign corporation) by the laws of each jurisdiction under which any of the foreign corporations are organized.

Any of the terms of the agreement of merger or consolidation may be made dependent upon facts ascertainable outside of such agreement, provided that the manner in which such facts shall operate upon the terms of the agreement is clearly and expressly set forth in the agreement of merger or consolidation. The term "facts," as used in the preceding sentence, includes, but is not limited to, the occurrence of any event, including a determination or action by any person or body, including the corporation.

(c)   The agreement shall be adopted, approved, certified, executed and acknowledged by each of the constituent corporations in accordance with the laws under which it is organized, and, in the case of a corporation of this State, in the same manner as is provided in § 251 of this title. The agreement shall be filed and shall become effective for all purposes of the laws of this State when and as provided in § 251 of this title with respect to the merger or consolidation of corporations of this State. In lieu of filing the agreement of merger or consolidation, the surviving or resulting corporation may file a certificate of merger or consolidation, executed in accordance with § 103 of this title, which states:

(1)   The name and jurisdiction of organization of each of the constituent corporations;

(2)   That an agreement of merger or consolidation has been approved, adopted, certified, executed and acknowledged by each of the constituent corporations in accordance with this subsection;

(3)   The name of the surviving or resulting corporation;

(4)   In the case of a merger in which the surviving corporation is a corporation of this State, such amendments or changes in the certificate of incorporation of the surviving corporation as are desired to be effected by the merger (which amendments or changes may amend and restate the certificate of incorporation of the surviving corporation in its entirety), or, if no such amendments or changes are desired, a statement that the certificate of incorporation of the surviving corporation shall be its certificate of incorporation;

(5)   In the case of a consolidation in which the resulting corporation is a corporation of this State, that the certificate of incorporation of the resulting corporation shall be as is set forth in an attachment to the certificate;

(6)   That the executed agreement of consolidation or merger is on file at an office of the surviving or resulting corporation and the address thereof;

(7)   That a copy of the agreement of consolidation or merger will be furnished by the surviving or resulting corporation, on request and without cost, to any stockholder of any constituent corporation;

(8)   If the corporation surviving or resulting from the merger or consolidation is a corporation of this State, the authorized capital stock of each constituent corporation which is not a corporation of this State; and

(9)   The agreement, if any, required by subsection (d) of this section.

(d)   If the corporation surviving or resulting from the merger or consolidation is a foreign corporation, it shall agree that it may be served with process in this State in any proceeding for enforcement of any obligation of any constituent corporation of this State, as well as for enforcement of any obligation of the surviving or resulting corporation arising from the merger or consolidation, including any suit or other proceeding to enforce the right of any stockholders as determined in appraisal proceedings pursuant to § 262 of this title, and shall irrevocably appoint the Secretary of State as its agent to accept service of process in any such suit or other proceedings and shall specify the address to which a copy of such process shall be mailed by the Secretary of State. Process may be served upon the Secretary of State under this subsection by means of electronic transmission but only as prescribed by the Secretary of State. The Secretary of State is authorized to issue such rules and regulations with respect to such service as the Secretary of State deems necessary or appropriate. In the event of such service upon the Secretary of State in accordance with this subsection, the Secretary of State shall forthwith notify such surviving or resulting corporation thereof by letter, directed to such surviving or resulting corporation at its address so specified, unless such surviving or resulting corporation shall have designated in writing to the Secretary of State a different address for such purpose, in which case it shall be mailed to the last address so designated. Such letter shall be sent by a mail or courier service that includes a record of mailing or deposit with the courier and a record of delivery evidenced by the signature of the recipient. Such letter shall enclose a copy of the process and any other papers served on the Secretary of State pursuant to this subsection. It shall be the duty of the plaintiff in the event of such service to serve process and any other papers in duplicate, to notify the Secretary of State that service is being effected pursuant to this subsection and to pay the Secretary of State the sum of $50 for the use of the State, which sum shall be taxed as part of the costs in the proceeding, if the plaintiff shall prevail therein. The Secretary of State shall maintain an alphabetical record of any such service setting forth the name of the plaintiff and the defendant, the title, docket number and nature of the proceeding in which process has been served, the fact that service has been effected pursuant to this subsection, the return date thereof, and the day and hour service was made. The Secretary of State shall not be required to retain such information longer than 5 years from receipt of the service of process.

(e) Section 251(d) of this title shall apply to any merger or consolidation under this section; § 251(e) of this title shall apply to a merger under this section in which the surviving corporation is a corporation of this State; and § 251(f) and (h) of this title shall apply to any merger under this section.

§ 253. Merger of Parent Corporation and Subsidiary Corporation or Corporations

(a) In any case in which: (1) at least 90% of the outstanding shares of each class of the stock of a corporation or corporations (other than a corporation which has in its certificate of incorporation the provision required by § 251(g)(7)(i) of this title), of which class there are outstanding shares that, absent this subsection, would be entitled to vote on such merger, is owned by a corporation of this State or a foreign corporation, and (2) 1 or more of such corporations is a corporation of this State, unless the laws of the jurisdiction or jurisdictions under which the foreign corporation or corporations are organized prohibit such merger, the parent corporation may either merge the subsidiary corporation or corporations into itself and assume all of its or their obligations, or merge itself, or itself and 1 or more of such other subsidiary corporations, into 1 of the subsidiary corporations by executing, acknowledging and filing, in accordance with § 103 of this title, a certificate of such ownership and merger setting forth a copy of the resolution of its board of directors to so merge and the date of the adoption; provided, however, that in case the parent corporation shall not own all the outstanding stock of all the subsidiary corporations, parties to a merger as aforesaid, the resolution of the board of directors of the parent corporation shall state the terms and conditions of the merger, including the securities, cash, property, or rights to be issued, paid, delivered or granted by the surviving corporation upon surrender of each share of the subsidiary corporation or corporations not owned by the parent corporation, or the cancellation of some or all of such shares. Any of the terms of the resolution of the board of directors to so merge may be made dependent upon facts ascertainable outside of such resolution, provided that the manner in which such facts shall operate upon the terms of the resolution is clearly and expressly set forth in the resolution. The term "facts," as used in the preceding sentence, includes, but is not limited to, the occurrence of any event, including a determination or action by any person or body, including the corporation. If the parent corporation be not the surviving corporation, the resolution shall include provision for the pro rata issuance of stock of the surviving corporation to the holders of the stock of the parent corporation on surrender of any certificates therefor, and the certificate of ownership and merger shall state that the proposed merger has been approved by a majority of the outstanding stock of the parent corporation entitled to vote thereon at a meeting duly called and held after 20 days' notice of the purpose of the meeting mailed to each such stockholder at the stockholder's address as it appears on the records of the corporation if the parent corporation is a corporation of this State or state that the proposed merger has been adopted, approved, certified, executed and acknowledged by the parent corporation in accordance with the laws under which it is organized if the parent corporation is a foreign corporation. If the surviving corporation is a foreign corporation:

(1) Section 252(d) of this title or § 258(c) of this title, as applicable, shall also apply to a merger under this section; and

(2) The terms and conditions of the merger shall obligate the surviving corporation to provide the agreement, and take the actions, required by § 252(d) of this title or § 258(c) of this title, as applicable.

(b) If the surviving corporation is a Delaware corporation, it may change its corporate name by the inclusion of a provision to that effect in the resolution of merger adopted by the directors of the parent corporation and set forth in the certificate of ownership and merger, and upon the effective date of the merger, the name of the corporation shall be so changed.

(c) Section 251(d) of this title shall apply to a merger under this section, and § 251(e) of this title shall apply to a merger under this section in which the surviving corporation is the subsidiary corporation and is a corporation of this State. References to "agreement of merger" in § 251(d) and (e) of this title shall mean for purposes of this subsection the resolution of merger adopted by the board of directors of the parent corporation. Any merger which effects any changes other than those authorized by this section or made applicable by this subsection shall be accomplished under § 251, § 252, § 257, or § 258 of this title. Section 262 of this title shall not apply to any merger effected under this section, except as provided in subsection (d) of this section.

(d) In the event all of the stock of a subsidiary Delaware corporation party to a merger effected under this section is not owned by the parent corporation immediately prior to the merger, the stockholders of the subsidiary Delaware corporation party to the merger shall have appraisal rights as set forth in § 262 of this title.

(e) This section shall apply to nonstock corporations if the parent corporation is such a corporation and is the surviving corporation of the merger; provided, however, that references to the directors of the parent corporation shall be deemed to be references to members of the governing body of the parent corporation, and references to the board of directors of the parent corporation shall be deemed to be references to the governing body of the parent corporation.

(f) Nothing in this section shall be deemed to authorize the merger of a corporation with a charitable nonstock corporation, if the charitable status of such charitable nonstock corporation would thereby be lost or impaired.

§ 254. Merger or Consolidation of Domestic Corporations and Joint-Stock or Other Associations

(a) The term "joint-stock association" as used in this section, includes any association of the kind commonly known as a joint-stock association or joint-stock company and any unincorporated association, trust or enterprise having members or having outstanding shares of stock or other evidences of financial or beneficial interest therein, whether formed or organized by agreement or under statutory authority or otherwise and whether formed or organized under the laws of this State or any other jurisdiction, but does not include a corporation, partnership or limited liability company. The term "stockholder" as used in this section, includes every member of such joint-stock association or holder of a share of stock or other evidence of financial or beneficial interest therein.

(b) Any 1 or more corporations of this State may merge or consolidate with 1 or more joint-stock associations, unless the laws of the jurisdiction or jurisdictions under which such joint-stock association or associations are formed or organized prohibit such merger or consolidation. Such corporation or corporations and such 1 or more joint-stock associations may merge into a single surviving corporation or joint-stock association, which may be any 1 of such corporations or joint-stock associations, or they may consolidate into a new resulting corporation of this State or a joint-stock association, pursuant to an agreement of merger or consolidation, as the case may be, complying and approved in accordance with this section. The surviving or resulting entity may be organized for profit or not organized for profit, and if the surviving or resulting entity is a corporation, it may be a stock corporation of this State or a nonstock corporation of this State.

(c) Each such corporation and joint-stock association shall enter into a written agreement of merger or consolidation. The agreement shall state:

    (1) The terms and conditions of the merger or consolidation;

    (2) The mode of carrying the same into effect;

(3)   In the case of a merger in which the surviving entity is a corporation of this State, such amendments or changes in the certificate of incorporation of the surviving corporation as are desired to be effected by the merger (which amendments or changes may amend and restate the certificate of incorporation of the surviving corporation in its entirety), or, if no such amendments or changes are desired, a statement that the certificate of incorporation of the surviving corporation shall be its certificate of incorporation;

(4)   In the case of a consolidation in which the resulting entity is a corporation of this State, that the certificate of incorporation of the resulting corporation shall be as is set forth in an attachment to the agreement;

(5)   The manner, if any, of converting the shares of stock of each stock corporation, the interest of members of each nonstock corporation, and the shares, membership or financial or beneficial interests in each of the joint-stock associations into shares or other securities of a stock corporation or membership interests of a nonstock corporation or into shares, memberships or financial or beneficial interests of the joint-stock association surviving or resulting from such merger or consolidation, or of cancelling some or all of such shares, memberships or financial or beneficial interests, and, if any shares of any such stock corporation, any membership interests of any such nonstock corporation or any shares, memberships or financial or beneficial interests in any such joint-stock association are not to remain outstanding, to be converted solely into shares or other securities of the stock corporation or membership interests of the nonstock corporation or into shares, memberships or financial or beneficial interests of the joint-stock association surviving or resulting from such merger or consolidation or to be cancelled, the cash, property, rights or securities of any other corporation or entity which the holders of shares of any such stock corporation, membership interests of any such nonstock corporation, or shares, memberships or financial or beneficial interests of any such joint-stock association are to receive in exchange for, or upon conversion of such shares, membership interests or shares, memberships or financial or beneficial interests, and the surrender of any certificates evidencing them, which cash, property, rights or securities of any other corporation or entity may be in addition to or in lieu of shares or other securities of the stock corporation or membership interests of the nonstock corporation or shares, memberships or financial or beneficial interests of the joint-stock association surviving or resulting from such merger or consolidation;

(6)   Such other details or provisions as are deemed desirable, including, without limiting the generality of the foregoing, a provision for the payment of cash in lieu of the issuance or recognition of fractional shares, rights, other securities or interests of the surviving or resulting entity or of fractional shares, rights, other securities or interests of any other corporation or entity the securities of which are to be received in the merger or consolidation, or for some other arrangement with respect thereto, consistent with § 155 of this title; and

(7)   Such other provisions or facts as shall be required to be set forth in an agreement of merger or consolidation (including any provision for amendment of the governing documents of a surviving joint-stock association) or required to establish and maintain a joint-stock association by the laws under which the joint-stock association is formed or organized.

Any of the terms of the agreement of merger or consolidation may be made dependent upon facts ascertainable outside of such agreement, provided that the manner in which such facts shall operate upon the terms of the agreement is clearly and expressly set forth in the agreement of merger or consolidation. The term "facts," as used in the preceding sentence, includes, but is not limited to, the occurrence of any event, including a determination or action by any person or body, including the corporation.

(d)   The agreement required by subsection (c) of this section shall be adopted, approved, certified, executed and acknowledged by each of the stock or nonstock corporations in the same manner as is provided in § 251 or § 255 of this title, respectively, and in the case of the joint-stock associations in accordance with the laws of the jurisdiction under which they are formed or organized. The agreement shall be filed and shall become effective for all purposes of the laws of this State when and as provided in § 251 of this title with respect to the merger or consolidation of corporations of this State. In lieu of filing the agreement of merger or consolidation, the surviving or resulting entity may file a certificate of merger or consolidation, executed in accordance with § 103 of this title, which states:

(1)   The name, jurisdiction of formation or organization and type of entity of each of the constituent entities;

(2)   That an agreement of merger or consolidation has been approved, adopted, certified, executed and acknowledged by each of the constituent entities in accordance with this subsection;

(3)   The name of the surviving or resulting corporation or joint-stock association;

(4)   In the case of a merger in which the surviving entity is a corporation of this State, such amendments or changes in the certificate of incorporation of the surviving corporation as are desired to be effected by the merger (which amendments or changes may amend and restate the certificate of incorporation of the surviving corporation in its entirety), or, if no such amendments or changes are desired, a statement that the certificate of incorporation of the surviving corporation shall be its certificate of incorporation;

(5)   In the case of a consolidation in which the resulting entity is a corporation of this State, that the certificate of incorporation of the resulting corporation shall be as is set forth in an attachment to the certificate;

(6)   That the executed agreement of consolidation or merger is on file at an office of the surviving or resulting corporation or joint-stock association and the address thereof;

(7)   That a copy of the agreement of consolidation or merger will be furnished by the surviving or resulting corporation or joint-stock association, on request and without cost, to any stockholder or member of any constituent entity; and

(8)   The agreement, if any, required by § 252(d) of this title.

(e)   Sections 251(d), 251(e) to the extent the surviving entity is a corporation of this State, §§ 251(f), 252(d), 259 through 262 and 328 of this title shall, insofar as they are applicable, apply to mergers or consolidations between corporations and joint-stock associations; the word "corporation" where applicable, as used in those sections, being deemed to include joint-stock associations as defined herein. Where the surviving or resulting entity is a corporation, for purposes of the laws of this State, the personal liability, if any, of any stockholder of a joint-stock association existing at the time of such merger or consolidation shall not thereby be extinguished, shall remain personal to such stockholder and shall not become the liability of any subsequent transferee of any share of stock in such surviving or resulting corporation or of any other stockholder of such surviving or resulting corporation.

(f)   Nothing in this section shall be deemed to authorize the merger of a charitable nonstock corporation or charitable joint-stock association into a stock corporation or joint-stock association if the charitable status of such nonstock corporation or joint-stock association would be thereby lost or impaired, but a stock corporation or a joint-stock association may be merged into a charitable nonstock corporation or charitable joint-stock association which shall continue as the surviving corporation or joint-stock association.

§ 255.   Merger or Consolidation of Domestic Nonstock Corporations

(a)   Any 2 or more nonstock corporations of this State, whether or not organized for profit, may merge into a single surviving corporation, which may be any 1 of the constituent corporations, or they may consolidate into a new resulting nonstock corporation, whether or not organized for profit, formed by the consolidation, pursuant to an agreement of merger or consolidation, as the case may be, complying and approved in accordance with this section.

(b)   Subject to subsection (d) of this section, the governing body of each corporation which desires to merge or consolidate shall adopt a resolution approving an agreement of merger or consolidation. The agreement shall state:

(1)   The terms and conditions of the merger or consolidation;

(2)   The mode of carrying the same into effect;

(3)   In the case of a merger, such amendments or changes in the certificate of incorporation of the surviving corporation as are desired to be effected by the merger (which amendments or changes may amend and restate the certificate of incorporation of the surviving corporation in its entirety), or, if no such amendments or changes are desired, a statement that the certificate of incorporation of the surviving corporation shall be its certificate of incorporation;

(4)   In the case of a consolidation, that the certificate of incorporation of the resulting corporation shall be as is set forth in an attachment to the agreement;

(5)   The manner, if any, of converting the memberships or membership interests of each of the constituent corporations into memberships or membership interests of the corporation surviving or resulting from the merger or consolidation, or of cancelling some or all of such memberships or membership interests, and, if any memberships or membership interests of any of the constituent corporations are not to remain outstanding, to be converted solely into membership or membership interests of the surviving or resulting corporation or to be cancelled, the cash, property, rights or securities of any other corporation or entity which the holders of such memberships or membership interests are to receive in exchange for, or upon conversion of, such memberships or membership interests, which cash, property, rights or securities of any other corporation or entity may be in addition to or in lieu of memberships or membership interests of the surviving or resulting corporation; and

(6)   Such other details or provisions as are deemed desirable, including, without limiting the generality of the foregoing, a provision for the payment of cash in lieu of the issuance or recognition of fractional shares, rights or other securities of any other corporation or entity the shares, rights or other securities of which are to be received in the merger or consolidation, or for some other arrangement with respect thereto, consistent with § 155 of this title.

The agreement so adopted shall be executed and acknowledged in accordance with § 103 of this title. Any of the terms of the agreement of merger or consolidation may be made dependent upon facts ascertainable outside of such agreement, provided that the manner in which such facts shall operate upon the terms of the agreement is clearly and expressly set forth in the agreement of merger or consolidation. The term "facts," as used in the preceding sentence, includes, but is not limited to, the occurrence of any event, including a determination or action by any person or body, including the corporation.

(c)   Subject to subsection (d) of this section, the agreement shall be submitted to the members of each constituent corporation, at an annual or special meeting thereof for the purpose of acting on the agreement. Due notice of the time, place and purpose of the meeting shall be mailed to each member of each such corporation who has the right to vote for the election of the members of the governing body of the corporation and to each other member who is entitled to vote on the merger under the certificate of incorporation or the bylaws of such corporation, at the member's address as it appears on the records of the corporation, at least 20 days prior to the date of the meeting. The notice shall contain a copy of the agreement or a brief summary thereof. At the meeting the agreement shall be considered and a vote, in person or by proxy, taken for the adoption or rejection of the agreement. If the agreement is adopted by a majority of the members of each such corporation entitled to vote for the election of the members of the governing body of the corporation and any other members entitled to vote on the merger under the certificate of incorporation or the bylaws of such corporation, then that fact shall be certified on the agreement by the officer of each such corporation performing the duties ordinarily performed by the secretary or assistant secretary of a corporation, provided that such certification on the agreement shall not be required if a certificate of merger or consolidation is filed in lieu of filing the agreement. If the agreement shall be adopted and certified by each constituent corporation in accordance with this section, it shall be filed and shall become effective in accordance with § 103 of this title. The provisions set forth in the last sentence of § 251(c) of this title shall apply to a merger under this section, and the reference therein to "stockholder" shall be deemed to include "member" hereunder.

(d)   Notwithstanding subsection (b) or (c) of this section, if, under the certificate of incorporation or the bylaws of any 1 or more of the constituent corporations, there shall be no members who have the right to vote for the election of the members of the governing body of the corporation, or for the merger, other than the members of the governing body themselves, no further action by the governing body or the members of such corporation shall be necessary if the resolution approving an agreement of merger or consolidation has been adopted by a majority of all the members of the governing body thereof, and that fact shall be certified on the agreement in the same manner as is provided in the case of the adoption of the agreement by the vote of the members of a corporation, provided that such certification on the agreement shall not be required if a certificate of merger or consolidation is filed in lieu of filing the agreement, and thereafter the same procedure shall be followed to consummate the merger or consolidation.

(e)   Section 251(d) of this title shall apply to a merger under this section; provided, however, that references to the board of directors, to stockholders, and to shares of a constituent corporation shall be deemed to be references to the governing body of the corporation, to members of the corporation, and to memberships or membership interests, as applicable, respectively.

(f)   Section 251 of this title shall apply to a merger under this section.

(g)   Nothing in this section shall be deemed to authorize the merger of a charitable nonstock corporation into a nonstock corporation if such charitable nonstock corporation would thereby have its charitable status lost or impaired; but a nonstock corporation may be merged into a charitable nonstock corporation which shall continue as the surviving corporation.

§ 256. Merger or Consolidation of Domestic and Foreign Nonstock Corporations; Service of Process Upon Surviving or Resulting Corporation

(a)   Any 1 or more nonstock corporations of this State may merge or consolidate with 1 or more foreign nonstock corporations, unless the laws of the jurisdiction or jurisdictions under which such foreign nonstock corporation or corporations are organized prohibit such merger or consolidation. The constituent corporations may merge into a single surviving corporation, which may be any 1 of the constituent corporations, or they may consolidate into a new resulting nonstock corporation formed by the consolidation, which may be a corporation of the jurisdiction of organization of any 1 of the constituent corporations, pursuant to an agreement of merger or consolidation, as the case may be, complying and approved in accordance with this section. The term "foreign nonstock corporation" means a nonstock corporation organized under the laws of any jurisdiction other than this State.

(b)   All the constituent corporations shall enter into an agreement of merger or consolidation. The agreement shall state:

(1)   The terms and conditions of the merger or consolidation;

(2)   The mode of carrying the same into effect;

(3)   In the case of a merger in which the surviving corporation is a corporation of this State, such amendments or changes in the certificate of incorporation as are desired to be effected by the merger (which amendments or changes may amend or restate the certificate of incorporation of the surviving corporation in its entirety), or, if no such amendments or changes are desired, a statement that the certificate of incorporation of the surviving corporation shall be its certificate of incorporation;

(4)   In the case of a consolidation in which the resulting corporation is a corporation of this State, that the certificate of incorporation of the resulting corporation shall be as is set forth in an attachment to the agreement;

(5) The manner, if any, of converting the memberships or membership interests of each of the constituent corporations into memberships or membership interests of the corporation surviving or resulting from the merger or consolidation, or of cancelling some or all of such memberships or membership interests, and, if any memberships or membership interests of any of the constituent corporations are not to remain outstanding, to be converted solely into memberships or membership interests of the surviving or resulting corporation or to be cancelled, the cash, property, rights or securities of any other corporation or entity which the holders of such memberships or membership interests are to receive in exchange for, or upon conversion of, such memberships or membership interests, which cash, property, rights or securities of any other corporation or entity may be in addition to or in lieu of memberships or membership interests of the surviving or resulting corporation;

(6) Such other details or provisions as are deemed desirable, including, without limiting the generality of the foregoing, a provision for the payment of cash in lieu of the issuance or recognition of fractional shares, rights or other securities of any other corporation or entity the shares, rights or other securities of which are to be received in the merger or consolidation, or for some other arrangement with respect thereto, consistent with § 155 of this title; and

(7) Such other provisions or facts as shall be required to be set forth in an agreement of merger or consolidation (including any provision for amendment of the certificate of incorporation (or equivalent document) of a surviving foreign nonstock corporation) by the laws of each jurisdiction under which any of the foreign nonstock corporations are organized.

Any of the terms of the agreement of merger or consolidation may be made dependent upon facts ascertainable outside of such agreement, provided that the manner in which such facts shall operate upon the terms of the agreement is clearly and expressly set forth in the agreement of merger or consolidation. The term "facts," as used in the preceding sentence, includes, but is not limited to, the occurrence of any event, including the determination or action by any person or body, including the corporation.

(c) The agreement shall be adopted, approved, certified, executed and acknowledged by each of the constituent corporations in accordance with the laws under which it is organized and, in the case of a Delaware corporation, in the same manner as is provided in § 255 of this title. The agreement shall be filed and shall become effective for all purposes of the laws of this State when and as provided in § 255 of this title with respect to the merger of nonstock corporations of this State. Insofar as they may be applicable, the provisions set forth in the last sentence of § 252(c) of this title shall apply to a merger under this section, and the reference therein to "stockholder" shall be deemed to include "member" hereunder.

(d) If the corporation surviving or resulting from the merger or consolidation is a foreign nonstock corporation, it shall agree that it may be served with process in this State in any proceeding for enforcement of any obligation of any constituent corporation of this State, as well as for enforcement of any obligation of the surviving or resulting corporation arising from the merger or consolidation and shall irrevocably appoint the Secretary of State as its agent to accept service of process in any suit or other proceedings and shall specify the address to which a copy of such process shall be mailed by the Secretary of State. Process may be served upon the Secretary of State under this subsection by means of electronic transmission but only as prescribed by the Secretary of State. The Secretary of State is authorized to issue such rules and regulations with respect to such service as the Secretary of State deems necessary or appropriate. In the event of such service upon the Secretary of State in accordance with this subsection, the Secretary of State shall forthwith notify such surviving or resulting corporation thereof by letter, directed to such corporation at its address so specified, unless such surviving or resulting corporation shall have designated in writing to the Secretary of State a different address for such purpose, in which case it shall be mailed to the last address so designated. Such letter shall be sent by a mail or courier service that includes a record of mailing or deposit with the courier and a record of delivery evidenced by the signature of the recipient. Such letter shall enclose a copy of the process and any other papers served upon the Secretary of State.

It shall be the duty of the plaintiff in the event of such service to serve process and any other papers in duplicate, to notify the Secretary of State that service is being made pursuant to this subsection, and to pay the Secretary of State the sum of $50 for the use of the State, which sum shall be taxed as a part of the costs in the proceeding if the plaintiff shall prevail therein. The Secretary of State shall maintain an alphabetical record of any such service setting forth the name of the plaintiff and defendant, the title, docket number and nature of the proceeding in which process has been served upon the Secretary of State, the fact that service has been effected pursuant to this subsection, the return date thereof, and the day and hour when the service was made. The Secretary of State shall not be required to retain such information for a period longer than 5 years from receipt of the service of process.

(e) Section 251(e) of this title shall apply to a merger under this section if the corporation surviving the merger is a corporation of this State.

(f) Section 251(d) of this title shall apply to a merger under this section; provided, however, that references to the board of directors, to stockholders, and to shares of a constituent corporation shall be deemed to be references to the governing body of the corporation, to members of the corporation, and to memberships or membership interests, as applicable, respectively.

(g) Nothing in this section shall be deemed to authorize the merger of a charitable nonstock corporation into a nonstock corporation, if the charitable status of such charitable nonstock corporation would thereby be lost or impaired; but a nonstock corporation may be merged into a charitable nonstock corporation which shall continue as the surviving corporation.

§ 257. Merger or Consolidation of Domestic Stock and Nonstock Corporations

(a) Any 1 or more nonstock corporations of this State, whether or not organized for profit, may merge or consolidate with 1 or more stock corporations of this State, whether or not organized for profit. The constituent corporations may merge into a single surviving corporation, which may be any 1 of the constituent corporations, or they may consolidate into a new resulting corporation formed by the consolidation, pursuant to an agreement of merger or consolidation, as the case may be, complying and approved in accordance with this section. The surviving constituent corporation or the resulting corporation may be organized for profit or not organized for profit and may be a stock corporation or a nonstock corporation.

(b) The board of directors of each stock corporation which desires to merge or consolidate and the governing body of each nonstock corporation which desires to merge or consolidate shall adopt a resolution approving an agreement of merger or consolidation. The agreement shall state:

(1) The terms and conditions of the merger or consolidation;

(2) The mode of carrying the same into effect;

(3) In the case of a merger, such amendments or changes in the certificate of incorporation of the surviving corporation as are desired to be effected by the merger (which amendments or changes may amend and restate the certificate of incorporation of the surviving company in its entirety), or, if no such amendments or changes are desired, a statement that the certificate of incorporation of the surviving corporation shall be its certificate of incorporation;

(4) In the case of a consolidation, that the certificate of incorporation of the resulting corporation shall be as is set forth in an attachment to the agreement;

(5) The manner, if any, of converting the shares of stock of a stock corporation and the membership or membership interests of a nonstock corporation into shares or other securities of a stock corporation or membership or membership interests of a nonstock corporation surviving or resulting from such merger or consolidation or of cancelling some or all of such shares or memberships or membership interests, and, if any shares of any such stock corporation or memberships or membership interests of any such nonstock corporation are not to remain

outstanding, to be converted solely into shares or other securities of the stock corporation or memberships or membership interests of the nonstock corporation surviving or resulting from such merger or consolidation or to be cancelled, the cash, property, rights or securities of any other corporation or entity which the holders of shares of any such stock corporation or memberships or membership interests of any such nonstock corporation are to receive in exchange for, or upon conversion of such shares or memberships or membership interests, and the surrender of any certificates evidencing them, which cash, property, rights or securities of any other corporation or entity may be in addition to or in lieu of shares or other securities of any stock corporation or memberships or membership interests of any nonstock corporation surviving or resulting from such merger or consolidation; and

(6)   Such other details or provisions as are deemed desirable, including, without limiting the generality of the foregoing, a provision for the payment of cash in lieu of the issuance or recognition of fractional shares, rights or other securities of the surviving or resulting corporation or of any other corporation or entity the shares, rights or other securities of which are to be received in the merger or consolidation, or for some other arrangement with respect thereto, consistent with § 155 of this title.

Any of the terms of the agreement of merger or consolidation may be made dependent upon facts ascertainable outside of such agreement, provided that the manner in which such facts shall operate upon the terms of the agreement is clearly and expressly set forth in the agreement of merger or consolidation. The term "facts," as used in the preceding sentence, includes, but is not limited to, the occurrence of any event, including a determination or action by any person or body, including the corporation.

(c)   The agreement required by subsection (b) of this section, in the case of each constituent stock corporation, shall be adopted, approved, certified, executed and acknowledged by each constituent corporation in the same manner as is provided in § 251 of this title and, in the case of each constituent nonstock corporation, shall be adopted, approved, certified, executed and acknowledged by each of said constituent corporations in the same manner as is provided in § 255 of this title. The agreement shall be filed and shall become effective for all purposes of the laws of this State when and as provided in § 251 of this title with respect to the merger of stock corporations of this State. Insofar as they may be applicable, the provisions set forth in the last sentence of § 251(c) of this title shall apply to a merger under this section, and the reference therein to "stockholder" shall be deemed to include "member" hereunder.

(d)   Section 251(e) of this title shall apply to a merger under this section; § 251(d) of this title shall apply to any constituent stock corporation participating in a merger or consolidation under this section; and § 251(f) of this title shall apply to any constituent stock corporation participating in a merger under this section.

(e)   Section 251 of this title shall apply to a merger under this section; provided, however, that, for purposes of a constituent nonstock corporation, references to the board of directors, to stockholders, and to shares of a constituent corporation shall be deemed to be references to the governing body of the corporation, to members of the corporation, and to memberships or membership interests, as applicable, respectively.

(f)   Nothing in this section shall be deemed to authorize the merger of a charitable nonstock corporation into a stock corporation, if the charitable status of such nonstock corporation would thereby be lost or impaired; but a stock corporation may be merged into a charitable nonstock corporation which shall continue as the surviving corporation.

§ 258.   Merger or Consolidation of Domestic and Foreign Stock and Nonstock Corporations

(a)   Any 1 or more corporations of this State, whether stock or nonstock corporations and whether or not organized for profit, may merge or consolidate with 1 or more foreign corporations, unless the laws of the jurisdiction or jurisdictions under which such foreign corporation or corporations are organized prohibit such merger or consolidation. The constituent corporations may merge into a single surviving corporation, which may be any 1 of the constituent corporations, or they may consolidate into a new resulting corporation formed by the consolidation, which may be a corporation of the jurisdiction of organization of any 1 of the constituent corporations, pursuant to an agreement of merger or consolidation, as the case may be, complying and approved in accordance with this section. The surviving or resulting corporation may be either a domestic or foreign stock corporation or a domestic or foreign nonstock corporation, as shall be specified in the agreement of merger or consolidation required by subsection (b) of this section. For purposes of this section, the term "foreign corporation" includes a nonstock corporation organized under the laws of any jurisdiction other than this State.

(b)   The method and procedure to be followed by the constituent corporations so merging or consolidating shall be as prescribed in § 257 of this title in the case of Delaware corporations. The agreement of merger or consolidation shall be as provided in § 257 of this title and also set forth such other provisions or facts as shall be required to be set forth in an agreement of merger or consolidation (including any provision for amendment of the certificate of incorporation (or equivalent document) of a surviving foreign corporation) by the laws of the jurisdiction or jurisdictions which are stated in the agreement to be the laws under which the foreign corporation or corporations are organized. The agreement, in the case of foreign corporations, shall be adopted, approved, certified, executed and acknowledged in accordance with the laws under which each is organized.

(c)   The requirements of § 252(d) of this title as to the appointment of the Secretary of State to receive process and the manner of serving the same in the event the surviving or resulting corporation is a foreign corporation shall also apply to mergers or consolidations effected under this section and such appointment, if any, shall be included in the certificate of merger or consolidation, if any, filed pursuant to subsection (b) of this section. Section 251(e) of this title shall apply to mergers effected under this section if the surviving corporation is a corporation of this State; § 251(d) of this title shall apply to any constituent corporation participating in a merger or consolidation under this section (provided, however, that for purposes of a constituent nonstock corporation, references to the board of directors, to stockholders, and to shares shall be deemed to be references to the governing body of the corporation, to members of the corporation, and to memberships or membership interests of the corporation, as applicable, respectively); and § 251(f) of this title shall apply to any constituent stock corporation of this State participating in a merger under this section.

(d)   Nothing in this section shall be deemed to authorize the merger of a charitable nonstock corporation into a stock corporation, if the charitable status of such nonstock corporation would thereby be lost or impaired; but a stock corporation may be merged into a charitable nonstock corporation which shall continue as the surviving corporation.

§ 259.   Status, Rights, Liabilities, of Constituent and Surviving or Resulting Corporations Following Merger or Consolidation

(a)   When any merger or consolidation shall have become effective under this chapter, for all purposes of the laws of this State the separate existence of all the constituent corporations, or of all such constituent corporations except the one into which the other or others of such constituent corporations have been merged, as the case may be, shall cease and the constituent corporations shall become a new corporation, or be merged into 1 of such corporations, as the case may be, possessing all the rights, privileges, powers and franchises as well of a public as of a private nature, and being subject to all the restrictions, disabilities and duties of each of such corporations so merged or consolidated; and all and singular, the rights, privileges, powers and franchises of each of said corporations, and all property, real, personal and mixed, and all debts due to any of said constituent corporations on whatever account, as well for stock subscriptions as all other things in action or belonging to each of such corporations shall be vested in the corporation surviving or resulting from such merger or consolidation; and all property, rights, privileges, powers and franchises, and all and every other interest shall be thereafter as effectually the property of the surviving or resulting corporation as they were of the several and respective constituent corporations, and the title to any real estate vested by deed or otherwise, under the laws of this State, in any of such constituent corporations, shall not revert or be in any way impaired by reason of this chapter; but all rights of creditors and all liens upon any property of any of said constituent corporations shall be preserved unimpaired, and all debts, liabilities and duties of the respective constituent corporations shall thenceforth attach to said surviving or resulting corporation, and may be enforced against it to the same extent as if said debts, liabilities and duties had been incurred or contracted by it.

(b) In the case of a merger of banks or trust companies, without any order or action on the part of any court or otherwise, all appointments, designations, and nominations, and all other rights and interests as trustee, executor, administrator, registrar of stocks and bonds, guardian of estates, assignee, receiver, trustee of estates of persons mentally ill and in every other fiduciary capacity, shall be automatically vested in the corporation resulting from or surviving such merger; provided, however, that any party in interest shall have the right to apply to an appropriate court or tribunal for a determination as to whether the surviving corporation shall continue to serve in the same fiduciary capacity as the merged corporation, or whether a new and different fiduciary should be appointed.

§ 260. Powers of Corporation Surviving or Resulting From Merger or Consolidation; Issuance of Stock, Bonds or Other Indebtedness

When 2 or more corporations are merged or consolidated, the corporation surviving or resulting from the merger may issue bonds or other obligations, negotiable or otherwise, and with or without coupons or interest certificates thereto attached, to an amount sufficient with its capital stock to provide for all the payments it will be required to make, or obligations it will be required to assume, in order to effect the merger or consolidation. For the purpose of securing the payment of any such bonds and obligations, it shall be lawful for the surviving or resulting corporation to mortgage its corporate franchise, rights, privileges and property, real, personal or mixed. The surviving or resulting corporation may issue certificates of its capital stock or uncertificated stock if authorized to do so and other securities to the stockholders of the constituent corporations in exchange or payment for the original shares, in such amount as shall be necessary in accordance with the terms of the agreement of merger or consolidation in order to effect such merger or consolidation in the manner and on the terms specified in the agreement.

§ 261. Effect of Merger Upon Pending Actions

Any action or proceeding, whether civil, criminal or administrative, pending by or against any corporation which is a party to a merger or consolidation shall be prosecuted as if such merger or consolidation had not taken place, or the corporation surviving or resulting from such merger or consolidation may be substituted in such action or proceeding.

§ 262. Appraisal Rights

(a) Any stockholder of a corporation of this State who holds shares of stock on the date of the making of a demand pursuant to subsection (d) of this section with respect to such shares, who continuously holds such shares through the effective date of the merger or consolidation, who has otherwise complied with subsection (d) of this section and who has neither voted in favor of the merger or consolidation nor consented thereto in writing pursuant to § 228 of this title shall be entitled to an appraisal by the Court of Chancery of the fair value of the stockholder's shares of stock under the circumstances described in subsections (b) and (c) of this section. As used in this section, the word "stockholder" means a holder of record of stock in a corporation; the words "stock" and "share" mean and include what is ordinarily meant by those words; and the words "depository receipt" mean a receipt or other instrument issued by a depository representing an interest in 1 or more shares, or fractions thereof, solely of stock of a corporation, which stock is deposited with the depository.

(b)   Appraisal rights shall be available for the shares of any class or series of stock of a constituent corporation in a merger or consolidation to be effected pursuant to § 251 (other than a merger effected pursuant to § 251(g) of this), § 252, § 254, § 255, § 256, § 257, § 258, § 263 or § 264 of this title:

(1)   Provided, however, that, except as expressly provided in § 363(b) of this title, no appraisal rights under this section shall be available for the shares of any class or series of stock, which stock, or depository receipts in respect thereof, at the record date fixed to determine the stockholders entitled to receive notice of the meeting of stockholders to act upon the agreement of merger or consolidation (or, in the case of a merger pursuant to § 251(h), as of immediately prior to the execution of the agreement of merger), were either: (i) listed on a national securities exchange or (ii) held of record by more than 2,000 holders; and further provided that no appraisal rights shall be available for any shares of stock of the constituent corporation surviving a merger if the merger did not require for its approval the vote of the stockholders of the surviving corporation as provided in § 251(f) of this title.

(2)   Notwithstanding paragraph (b)(1) of this section, appraisal rights under this section shall be available for the shares of any class or series of stock of a constituent corporation if the holders thereof are required by the terms of an agreement of merger or consolidation pursuant to §§ 251, 252, 254, 255, 256, 257, 258, 263 and 264 of this title to accept for such stock anything except:

a.   Shares of stock of the corporation surviving or resulting from such merger or consolidation, or depository receipts in respect thereof;

b.   Shares of stock of any other corporation, or depository receipts in respect thereof, which shares of stock (or depository receipts in respect thereof) or depository receipts at the effective date of the merger or consolidation will be either listed on a national securities exchange or held of record by more than 2,000 holders;

c.   Cash in lieu of fractional shares or fractional depository receipts described in the foregoing paragraphs (b)(2)a. and b. of this section; or

d.   Any combination of the shares of stock, depository receipts and cash in lieu of fractional shares or fractional depository receipts described in the foregoing paragraphs (b)(2)a., b. and c. of this section.

(3)   In the event all of the stock of a subsidiary Delaware corporation party to a merger effected under § 253 or § 267 of this title is not owned by the parent immediately prior to the merger, appraisal rights shall be available for the shares of the subsidiary Delaware corporation.

(4)   In the event of an amendment to a corporation's certificate of incorporation contemplated by § 363(a) of this title, appraisal rights shall be available as contemplated by § 363(b) of this title, and the procedures of this section, including those set forth in subsections (d) and (e) of this section, shall apply as nearly as practicable, with the word "amendment" substituted for the words "merger or consolidation", and the word "corporation" substituted for the words "constituent corporation" and/or "surviving or resulting corporation."

(c)   Any corporation may provide in its certificate of incorporation that appraisal rights under this section shall be available for the shares of any class or series of its stock as a result of an amendment to its certificate of incorporation, any merger or consolidation in which the corporation is a constituent corporation or the sale of all or substantially all of the assets of the corporation. If the certificate of incorporation contains such a provision, the provisions of this section, including those set forth in subsections (d), (e), and (g) of this section, shall apply as nearly as is practicable.

(d)   Appraisal rights shall be perfected as follows:

(1)   If a proposed merger or consolidation for which appraisal rights are provided under this section is to be submitted for approval at a meeting of stockholders, the corporation, not less than

20 days prior to the meeting, shall notify each of its stockholders who was such on the record date for notice of such meeting (or such members who received notice in accordance with § 255(c) of this title) with respect to shares for which appraisal rights are available pursuant to subsection (b) or (c) of this section that appraisal rights are available for any or all of the shares of the constituent corporations, and shall include in such notice a copy of this section and, if 1 of the constituent corporations is a nonstock corporation, a copy of § 114 of this title. Each stockholder electing to demand the appraisal of such stockholder's shares shall deliver to the corporation, before the taking of the vote on the merger or consolidation, a written demand for appraisal of such stockholder's shares. Such demand will be sufficient if it reasonably informs the corporation of the identity of the stockholder and that the stockholder intends thereby to demand the appraisal of such stockholder's shares. A proxy or vote against the merger or consolidation shall not constitute such a demand. A stockholder electing to take such action must do so by a separate written demand as herein provided. Within 10 days after the effective date of such merger or consolidation, the surviving or resulting corporation shall notify each stockholder of each constituent corporation who has complied with this subsection and has not voted in favor of or consented to the merger or consolidation of the date that the merger or consolidation has become effective; or

(2) If the merger or consolidation was approved pursuant to § 228, § 251(h), § 253, or § 267 of this title, then either a constituent corporation before the effective date of the merger or consolidation or the surviving or resulting corporation within 10 days thereafter shall notify each of the holders of any class or series of stock of such constituent corporation who are entitled to appraisal rights of the approval of the merger or consolidation and that appraisal rights are available for any or all shares of such class or series of stock of such constituent corporation, and shall include in such notice a copy of this section and, if 1 of the constituent corporations is a nonstock corporation, a copy of § 114 of this title. Such notice may, and, if given on or after the effective date of the merger or consolidation, shall, also notify such stockholders of the effective date of the merger or consolidation. Any stockholder entitled to appraisal rights may, within 20 days after the date of mailing of such notice or, in the case of a merger approved pursuant to § 251(h) of this title, within the later of the consummation of the offer contemplated by § 251(h) of this title and 20 days after the date of mailing of such notice, demand in writing from the surviving or resulting corporation the appraisal of such holder's shares. Such demand will be sufficient if it reasonably informs the corporation of the identity of the stockholder and that the stockholder intends thereby to demand the appraisal of such holder's shares. If such notice did not notify stockholders of the effective date of the merger or consolidation, either (i) each such constituent corporation shall send a second notice before the effective date of the merger or consolidation notifying each of the holders of any class or series of stock of such constituent corporation that are entitled to appraisal rights of the effective date of the merger or consolidation or (ii) the surviving or resulting corporation shall send such a second notice to all such holders on or within 10 days after such effective date; provided, however, that if such second notice is sent more than 20 days following the sending of the first notice or, in the case of a merger approved pursuant to § 251(h) of this title, later than the later of the consummation of the offer contemplated by § 251(h) of this title and 20 days following the sending of the first notice, such second notice need only be sent to each stockholder who is entitled to appraisal rights and who has demanded appraisal of such holder's shares in accordance with this subsection. An affidavit of the secretary or assistant secretary or of the transfer agent of the corporation that is required to give either notice that such notice has been given shall, in the absence of fraud, be prima facie evidence of the facts stated therein. For purposes of determining the stockholders entitled to receive either notice, each constituent corporation may fix, in advance, a record date that shall be not more than 10 days prior to the date the notice is given, provided, that if the notice is given on or after the effective date of the merger or consolidation, the record date shall be such effective date. If no record date is fixed and the notice is given prior to the effective date, the record date shall be the close of business on the day next preceding the day on which the notice is given.

(e)   Within 120 days after the effective date of the merger or consolidation, the surviving or resulting corporation or any stockholder who has complied with subsections (a) and (d) of this section hereof and who is otherwise entitled to appraisal rights, may commence an appraisal proceeding by filing a petition in the Court of Chancery demanding a determination of the value of the stock of all such stockholders. Notwithstanding the foregoing, at any time within 60 days after the effective date of the merger or consolidation, any stockholder who has not commenced an appraisal proceeding or joined that proceeding as a named party shall have the right to withdraw such stockholder's demand for appraisal and to accept the terms offered upon the merger or consolidation. Within 120 days after the effective date of the merger or consolidation, any stockholder who has complied with the requirements of subsections (a) and (d) of this section hereof, upon written request, shall be entitled to receive from the corporation surviving the merger or resulting from the consolidation a statement setting forth the aggregate number of shares not voted in favor of the merger or consolidation (or, in the case of a merger approved pursuant to § 251(h) of this title, the aggregate number of shares (other than any excluded stock (as defined in § 251(h)(6)d. of this title)) that were the subject of, and were not tendered into, and accepted for purchase or exchange in, the offer referred to in § 251(h)(2)), and, in either case, with respect to which demands for appraisal have been received and the aggregate number of holders of such shares. Such written statement shall be mailed to the stockholder within 10 days after such stockholder's written request for such a statement is received by the surviving or resulting corporation or within 10 days after expiration of the period for delivery of demands for appraisal under subsection (d) of this section hereof, whichever is later. Notwithstanding subsection (a) of this section, a person who is the beneficial owner of shares of such stock held either in a voting trust or by a nominee on behalf of such person may, in such person's own name, file a petition or request from the corporation the statement described in this subsection.

(f)   Upon the filing of any such petition by a stockholder, service of a copy thereof shall be made upon the surviving or resulting corporation, which shall within 20 days after such service file in the office of the Register in Chancery in which the petition was filed a duly verified list containing the names and addresses of all stockholders who have demanded payment for their shares and with whom agreements as to the value of their shares have not been reached by the surviving or resulting corporation. If the petition shall be filed by the surviving or resulting corporation, the petition shall be accompanied by such a duly verified list. The Register in Chancery, if so ordered by the Court, shall give notice of the time and place fixed for the hearing of such petition by registered or certified mail to the surviving or resulting corporation and to the stockholders shown on the list at the addresses therein stated. Such notice shall also be given by 1 or more publications at least 1 week before the day of the hearing, in a newspaper of general circulation published in the City of Wilmington, Delaware or such publication as the Court deems advisable. The forms of the notices by mail and by publication shall be approved by the Court, and the costs thereof shall be borne by the surviving or resulting corporation.

(g)   At the hearing on such petition, the Court shall determine the stockholders who have complied with this section and who have become entitled to appraisal rights. The Court may require the stockholders who have demanded an appraisal for their shares and who hold stock represented by certificates to submit their certificates of stock to the Register in Chancery for notation thereon of the pendency of the appraisal proceedings; and if any stockholder fails to comply with such direction, the Court may dismiss the proceedings as to such stockholder. If immediately before the merger or consolidation the shares of the class or series of stock of the constituent corporation as to which appraisal rights are available were listed on a national securities exchange, the Court shall dismiss the proceedings as to all holders of such shares who are otherwise entitled to appraisal rights unless (1) the total number of shares entitled to appraisal exceeds 1% of the outstanding shares of the class or series eligible for appraisal, (2) the value of the consideration provided in the merger or consolidation for such total number of shares exceeds $1 million, or (3) the merger was approved pursuant to § 253 or § 267 of this title.

(h)   After the Court determines the stockholders entitled to an appraisal, the appraisal proceeding shall be conducted in accordance with the rules of the Court of Chancery, including any rules specifically governing appraisal proceedings. Through such proceeding the Court shall determine the fair value of the shares exclusive of any element of value arising from the accomplishment or expectation of the merger or consolidation, together with interest, if any, to be paid upon the amount determined to be the fair value. In determining such fair value, the Court shall take into account all relevant factors. Unless the Court in its discretion determines otherwise for good cause shown, and except as provided in this subsection, interest from the effective date of the merger through the date of payment of the judgment shall be compounded quarterly and shall accrue at 5% over the Federal Reserve discount rate (including any surcharge) as established from time to time during the period between the effective date of the merger and the date of payment of the judgment. At any time before the entry of judgment in the proceedings, the surviving corporation may pay to each stockholder entitled to appraisal an amount in cash, in which case interest shall accrue thereafter as provided herein only upon the sum of (1) the difference, if any, between the amount so paid and the fair value of the shares as determined by the Court, and (2) interest theretofore accrued, unless paid at that time. Upon application by the surviving or resulting corporation or by any stockholder entitled to participate in the appraisal proceeding, the Court may, in its discretion, proceed to trial upon the appraisal prior to the final determination of the stockholders entitled to an appraisal. Any stockholder whose name appears on the list filed by the surviving or resulting corporation pursuant to subsection (f) of this section and who has submitted such stockholder's certificates of stock to the Register in Chancery, if such is required, may participate fully in all proceedings until it is finally determined that such stockholder is not entitled to appraisal rights under this section.

(i) The Court shall direct the payment of the fair value of the shares, together with interest, if any, by the surviving or resulting corporation to the stockholders entitled thereto. Payment shall be so made to each such stockholder, in the case of holders of uncertificated stock forthwith, and the case of holders of shares represented by certificates upon the surrender to the corporation of the certificates representing such stock. The Court's decree may be enforced as other decrees in the Court of Chancery may be enforced, whether such surviving or resulting corporation be a corporation of this State or of any state.

(j) The costs of the proceeding may be determined by the Court and taxed upon the parties as the Court deems equitable in the circumstances. Upon application of a stockholder, the Court may order all or a portion of the expenses incurred by any stockholder in connection with the appraisal proceeding, including, without limitation, reasonable attorney's fees and the fees and expenses of experts, to be charged pro rata against the value of all the shares entitled to an appraisal.

(k) From and after the effective date of the merger or consolidation, no stockholder who has demanded appraisal rights as provided in subsection (d) of this section shall be entitled to vote such stock for any purpose or to receive payment of dividends or other distributions on the stock (except dividends or other distributions payable to stockholders of record at a date which is prior to the effective date of the merger or consolidation); provided, however, that if no petition for an appraisal shall be filed within the time provided in subsection (e) of this section, or if such stockholder shall deliver to the surviving or resulting corporation a written withdrawal of such stockholder's demand for an appraisal and an acceptance of the merger or consolidation, either within 60 days after the effective date of the merger or consolidation as provided in subsection (e) of this section or thereafter with the written approval of the corporation, then the right of such stockholder to an appraisal shall cease. Notwithstanding the foregoing, no appraisal proceeding in the Court of Chancery shall be dismissed as to any stockholder without the approval of the Court, and such approval may be conditioned upon such terms as the Court deems just; provided, however that this provision shall not affect the right of any stockholder who has not commenced an appraisal proceeding or joined that proceeding as a named party to withdraw such stockholder's demand for appraisal and to accept the terms offered upon the merger or consolidation within 60 days after the effective date of the merger or consolidation, as set forth in subsection (e) of this section.

(l) The shares of the surviving or resulting corporation to which the shares of such objecting stockholders would have been converted had they assented to the merger or consolidation shall have the status of authorized and unissued shares of the surviving or resulting corporation.

§ 263.   Merger or Consolidation of Domestic Corporations and Partnerships; Service of Process upon Surviving or Resulting Corporation or Partnership

(a)   Any 1 or more corporations of this State may merge or consolidate with 1 or more partnerships (whether general (including a limited liability partnership) or limited (including a limited liability limited partnership)), unless the laws of the jurisdiction or jurisdictions under which such partnership or partnerships are formed prohibit such merger or consolidation. Such corporation or corporations and such 1 or more partnerships may merge with or into a surviving corporation, which may be any 1 of such corporations, or they may merge with or into a surviving partnership, which may be any 1 of such partnerships, or they may consolidate into a new resulting corporation, which corporation shall be a corporation of this State, or a partnership formed pursuant to an agreement of merger or consolidation, as the case may be, complying and approved in accordance with this section. The term "partnership" as used in this section includes any partnership (whether general (including a limited liability partnership) or limited (including a limited liability limited partnership)) formed under the laws of this State or the laws of any other jurisdiction.

(b)   Each such corporation and partnership shall enter into a written agreement of merger or consolidation. The agreement shall state:

(1)   The terms and conditions of the merger or consolidation;

(2)   The mode of carrying the same into effect;

(3)   In the case of a merger in which the surviving entity is a corporation of this State, such amendments or changes in the certificate of incorporation of the surviving corporation as are desired to be effected by the merger (which amendments or changes may amend and restate the certificate of incorporation of the surviving corporation in its entirety), or, if no such amendments or changes are desired, a statement that the certificate of incorporation of the surviving corporation shall be its certificate of incorporation;

(4)   In the case of a consolidation in which the resulting entity is a corporation of this State, that the certificate of incorporation of the resulting corporation shall be as is set forth in an attachment to the agreement;

(5)   The manner, if any, of converting the shares of stock of each such corporation and the partnership interests of each such partnership into shares, partnership interests or other securities of the entity surviving or resulting from such merger or consolidation or of cancelling some or all of such shares or interests, and if any shares of any such corporation or any partnership interests of any such partnership are not to remain outstanding, to be converted solely into shares, partnership interests or other securities of the entity surviving or resulting from such merger or consolidation or to be cancelled, the cash, property, rights or securities of any other corporation or entity which the holders of such shares or partnership interests are to receive in exchange for, or upon conversion of such shares or partnership interests and the surrender of any certificates evidencing them, which cash, property, rights or securities of any other corporation or entity may be in addition to or in lieu of shares, partnership interests or other securities of the entity surviving or resulting from such merger or consolidation;

(6)   Such other details or provisions as are deemed desirable, including, without limiting the generality of the foregoing, a provision for the payment of cash in lieu of the issuance or recognition of fractional shares, rights, other securities or interests of the surviving or resulting corporation or partnership or of any other corporation or entity the shares, rights, other securities or interests of which are to be received in the merger or consolidation, or for some other arrangement with respect thereto, consistent with § 155 of this title; and

(7)   Such other provisions or facts as shall be required to be set forth in an agreement of merger or consolidation (including any provision for amendment of the partnership agreement and statement of partnership existence or certificate of limited partnership (or equivalent

documents) of the surviving partnership) by the laws of each jurisdiction under which any of the partnerships are formed.

Any of the terms of the agreement of merger or consolidation may be made dependent upon facts ascertainable outside of such agreement, provided that the manner in which such facts shall operate upon the terms of the agreement is clearly and expressly set forth in the agreement of merger or consolidation. The term "facts," as used in the preceding sentence, includes, but is not limited to, the occurrence of any event, including a determination or action by any person or body, including the corporation.

(c)   The agreement required by subsection (b) of this section shall be adopted, approved, certified, executed and acknowledged by each of the corporations in the same manner as is provided in § 251 or § 255 of this title and, in the case of the partnerships, in accordance with their partnership agreements and in accordance with the laws of the jurisdiction under which they are formed. If the surviving or resulting entity is a partnership, in addition to any other approvals, each stockholder of a merging corporation who will become a general partner of the surviving or resulting partnership must approve the agreement of merger or consolidation. The agreement shall be filed and shall become effective for all purposes of the laws of this State when and as provided in § 251 or § 255 of this title with respect to the merger or consolidation of corporations of this State. In lieu of filing the agreement of merger or consolidation, the surviving or resulting corporation or partnership may file a certificate of merger or consolidation, executed in accordance with § 103 of this title, if the surviving or resulting entity is a corporation, or by a general partner, if the surviving or resulting entity is a partnership, which states:

(1)   The name, jurisdiction of formation or organization and type of entity of each of the constituent entities;

(2)   That an agreement of merger or consolidation has been approved, adopted, certified, executed and acknowledged by each of the constituent entities in accordance with this subsection;

(3)   The name of the surviving or resulting corporation or partnership;

(4)   In the case of a merger in which a corporation is the surviving entity, such amendments or changes in the certificate of incorporation of the surviving corporation as are desired to be effected by the merger (which amendments or changes may amend and restate the certificate of incorporation of the surviving corporation in its entirety), or, if no such amendments or changes are desired, a statement that the certificate of incorporation of the surviving corporation shall be its certificate of incorporation;

(5)   In the case of a consolidation in which a corporation is the resulting entity, that the certificate of incorporation of the resulting corporation shall be as is set forth in an attachment to the certificate;

(6)   That the executed agreement of consolidation or merger is on file at an office of the surviving or resulting corporation or partnership and the address thereof;

(7)   That a copy of the agreement of consolidation or merger will be furnished by the surviving or resulting entity, on request and without cost, to any stockholder of any constituent corporation or any partner of any constituent partnership; and

(8)   The agreement, if any, required by subsection (d) of this section.

(d)   If the entity surviving or resulting from the merger or consolidation is a partnership formed under the laws of a jurisdiction other than this State, it shall agree that it may be served with process in this State in any proceeding for enforcement of any obligation of any constituent corporation or partnership of this State, as well as for enforcement of any obligation of the surviving or resulting corporation or partnership arising from the merger or consolidation, including any suit or other proceeding to enforce the right of any stockholders as determined in appraisal proceedings pursuant to § 262 of this title, and shall irrevocably appoint the Secretary of State as its agent to accept service of process in any such suit or other proceedings and shall specify the address to which a copy of such process shall be mailed by the Secretary of State. Process may be served upon the Secretary of State under this subsection by means of electronic transmission but only as prescribed by the Secretary of State. The Secretary of State is authorized to issue such rules and regulations with respect to such service as the Secretary of State deems necessary or appropriate. In the event of such service upon the Secretary of State in accordance with this subsection, the Secretary of State shall forthwith notify such surviving or resulting corporation or partnership thereof by letter, directed to such surviving or resulting corporation or partnership at its address so specified, unless such surviving or resulting corporation or partnership shall have designated in writing to the Secretary of State a different address for such purpose, in which case it shall be mailed to the last address so designated. Such letter shall be sent by a mail or courier service that includes a record of mailing or deposit with the courier and a record of delivery evidenced by the signature of the recipient. Such letter shall enclose a copy of the process and any other papers served on the Secretary of State pursuant to this subsection. It shall be the duty of the plaintiff in the event of such service to serve process and any other papers in duplicate, to notify the Secretary of State that service is being effected pursuant to this subsection and to pay the Secretary of State the sum of $50 for the use of the State, which sum shall be taxed as part of the costs in the proceeding, if the plaintiff shall prevail therein. The Secretary of State shall maintain an alphabetical record of any such service setting forth the name of the plaintiff and the defendant, the title, docket number and nature of the proceeding in which process has been served upon the Secretary of State, the fact that service has been effected pursuant to this subsection, the return date thereof, and the day and hour service was made. The Secretary of State shall not be required to retain such information longer than 5 years from receipt of the service of process.

(e)   Sections 251(d)–(f), 255(c) (second sentence) and (d)–(f), 259–261 and 328 of this title shall, insofar as they are applicable, apply to mergers or consolidations between corporations and partnerships.

(f)   Nothing in this section shall be deemed to authorize the merger of a charitable nonstock corporation into a partnership, if the charitable status of such nonstock corporation would thereby be lost or impaired; but a partnership may be merged into a charitable nonstock corporation which shall continue as the surviving corporation.

§ 264. Merger or Consolidation of Domestic Corporations and Limited Liability Companies; Service of Process upon Surviving or Resulting Corporation or Limited Liability Company

(a)   Any 1 or more corporations of this State may merge or consolidate with 1 or more limited liability companies, unless the laws of the jurisdiction or jurisdictions under which such limited liability company or limited liability companies are formed prohibit such merger or consolidation. Such corporation or corporations and such 1 or more limited liability companies may merge with or into a surviving corporation, which may be any 1 of such corporations, or they may merge with or into a surviving limited liability company, which may be any 1 of such limited liability companies, or they may consolidate into a new resulting corporation, which corporation shall be a corporation of this State, or a limited liability company formed pursuant to an agreement of merger or consolidation, as the case may be, complying and approved in accordance with this section. The term "limited liability company" as used in this section includes any limited liability company formed under the laws of this State or the laws of any other jurisdiction.

(b)   Each such corporation and limited liability company shall enter into a written agreement of merger or consolidation. The agreement shall state:

(1)   The terms and conditions of the merger or consolidation;

(2)   The mode of carrying the same into effect;

(3)   In the case of a merger in which the surviving entity is a corporation of this State, such amendments or changes in the certificate of incorporation of the surviving corporation as are

desired to be effected by the merger (which amendments or changes may amend and restate the certificate of incorporation of the surviving corporation in its entirety), or, if no such amendments or changes are desired, a statement that the certificate of incorporation of the surviving corporation shall be its certificate of incorporation;

(4) In the case of a consolidation in which the resulting entity is a corporation of this State, that the certificate of incorporation of the resulting corporation shall be as is set forth in an attachment to the agreement;

(5) The manner, if any, of converting the shares of stock of each such corporation and the limited liability company interests of each such limited liability company into shares, limited liability company interests or other securities of the entity surviving or resulting from such merger or consolidation or of cancelling some or all of such shares or interests, and if any shares of any such corporation or any limited liability company interests of any such limited liability company are not to remain outstanding, to be converted solely into shares, limited liability company interests or other securities of the entity surviving or resulting from such merger or consolidation or to be cancelled, the cash, property, rights or securities of any other corporation or entity which the holders of such shares or limited liability company interests are to receive in exchange for, or upon conversion of such shares or limited liability company interests and the surrender of any certificates evidencing them, which cash, property, rights or securities of any other corporation or entity may be in addition to or in lieu of shares, limited liability company interests or other securities of the entity surviving or resulting from such merger or consolidation;

(6) Such other details or provisions as are deemed desirable, including, without limiting the generality of the foregoing, a provision for the payment of cash in lieu of the issuance or recognition of fractional shares, rights, other securities or interests of the surviving or resulting corporation or limited liability company or of any other corporation or entity the shares, rights, other securities or interests of which are to be received in the merger or consolidation, or for some other arrangement with respect thereto, consistent with § 155 of this title; and

(7) Such other provisions or facts as shall be required to be set forth in an agreement of merger or consolidation (including any provision for amendment of the limited liability company agreement and certificate of formation (or equivalent documents) of the surviving limited liability company) by the laws of each jurisdiction under which any of the limited liability companies are formed.

Any of the terms of the agreement of merger or consolidation may be made dependent upon facts ascertainable outside of such agreement, provided that the manner in which such facts shall operate upon the terms of the agreement is clearly and expressly set forth in the agreement of merger or consolidation. The term "facts," as used in the preceding sentence, includes, but is not limited to, the occurrence of any event, including a determination or action by any person or body, including the corporation.

(c) The agreement required by subsection (b) of this section shall be adopted, approved, certified, executed and acknowledged by each of the corporations in the same manner as is provided in § 251 or § 255 of this title and, in the case of the limited liability companies, in accordance with their limited liability company agreements and in accordance with the laws of the jurisdiction under which they are formed. The agreement shall be filed and shall become effective for all purposes of the laws of this State when and as provided in § 251 or § 255 of this title with respect to the merger or consolidation of corporations of this State. In lieu of filing the agreement of merger or consolidation, the surviving or resulting corporation or limited liability company may file a certificate of merger or consolidation, executed in accordance with § 103 of this title, if the surviving or resulting entity is a corporation, or by an authorized person, if the surviving or resulting entity is a limited liability company, which states:

(1) The name and jurisdiction of formation or organization of each of the constituent entities;

(2)   That an agreement of merger or consolidation has been approved, adopted, certified, executed and acknowledged by each of the constituent entities in accordance with this subsection;

(3)   The name of the surviving or resulting corporation or limited liability company;

(4)   In the case of a merger in which a corporation is the surviving entity, such amendments or changes in the certificate of incorporation of the surviving corporation as are desired to be effected by the merger (which amendments or changes may amend and restate the certificate of incorporation of the surviving corporation in its entirety), or, if no such amendments or changes are desired, a statement that the certificate of incorporation of the surviving corporation shall be its certificate of incorporation;

(5)   In the case of a consolidation in which a corporation is the resulting entity, that the certificate of incorporation of the resulting corporation shall be as is set forth in an attachment to the certificate;

(6)   That the executed agreement of consolidation or merger is on file at an office of the surviving or resulting corporation or limited liability company and the address thereof;

(7)   That a copy of the agreement of consolidation or merger will be furnished by the surviving or resulting entity, on request and without cost, to any stockholder of any constituent corporation or any member of any constituent limited liability company; and

(8)   The agreement, if any, required by subsection (d) of this section.

(d)   If the entity surviving or resulting from the merger or consolidation is a limited liability company formed under the laws of a jurisdiction other than this State, it shall agree that it may be served with process in this State in any proceeding for enforcement of any obligation of any constituent corporation or limited liability company of this State, as well as for enforcement of any obligation of the surviving or resulting corporation or limited liability company arising from the merger or consolidation, including any suit or other proceeding to enforce the right of any stockholders as determined in appraisal proceedings pursuant to the provisions of § 262 of this title, and shall irrevocably appoint the Secretary of State as its agent to accept service of process in any such suit or other proceedings and shall specify the address to which a copy of such process shall be mailed by the Secretary of State. Process may be served upon the Secretary of State under this subsection by means of electronic transmission but only as prescribed by the Secretary of State. The Secretary of State is authorized to issue such rules and regulations with respect to such service as the Secretary of State deems necessary or appropriate. In the event of such service upon the Secretary of State in accordance with this subsection, the Secretary of State shall forthwith notify such surviving or resulting corporation or limited liability company thereof by letter, directed to such surviving or resulting corporation or limited liability company at its address so specified, unless such surviving or resulting corporation or limited liability company shall have designated in writing to the Secretary of State a different address for such purpose, in which case it shall be mailed to the last address so designated. Such letter shall be sent by a mail or courier service that includes a record of mailing or deposit with the courier and a record of delivery evidenced by the signature of the recipient. Such letter shall enclose a copy of the process and any other papers served on the Secretary of State pursuant to this subsection. It shall be the duty of the plaintiff in the event of such service to serve process and any other papers in duplicate, to notify the Secretary of State that service is being effected pursuant to this subsection and to pay the Secretary of State the sum of $50 for the use of the State, which sum shall be taxed as part of the costs in the proceeding, if the plaintiff shall prevail therein. The Secretary of State shall maintain an alphabetical record of any such service setting forth the name of the plaintiff and the defendant, the title, docket number and nature of the proceeding in which process has been served upon the Secretary of State, the fact that service has been effected pursuant to this subsection, the return date thereof, and the day and hour service was made. The Secretary of State shall not be required to retain such information longer than 5 years from receipt of the service of process.

(e)   Sections 251, (d)–(f), 255(c) (second sentence) and (d)–(f), 259–261 and 328 of this title shall, insofar as they are applicable, apply to mergers or consolidations between corporations and limited liability companies.

(f)   Nothing in this section shall be deemed to authorize the merger of a charitable nonstock corporation into a limited liability company, if the charitable status of such nonstock corporation would thereby be lost or impaired; but a limited liability company may be merged into a charitable nonstock corporation which shall continue as the surviving corporation.

§ 265.   Conversion of Other Entities to a Domestic Corporation

(a)   As used in this section, the term "other entity" means a limited liability company, statutory trust, business trust or association, real estate investment trust, common-law trust or any other unincorporated business including a partnership (whether general (including a limited liability partnership) or limited (including a limited liability limited partnership)), or a foreign corporation.

(b)   Any other entity may convert to a corporation of this State by complying with subsection (h) of this section and filing in the office of the Secretary of State:

(1)   A certificate of conversion to corporation that has been executed in accordance with subsection (i) of this section and filed in accordance with § 103 of this title; and

(2)   A certificate of incorporation that has been executed, acknowledged and filed in accordance with § 103 of this title.

Each of the certificates required by this subsection (b) shall be filed simultaneously in the office of the Secretary of State and, if such certificates are not to become effective upon their filing as permitted by § 103(d) of this title, then each such certificate shall provide for the same effective date or time in accordance with § 103(d) of this title.

(c)   The certificate of conversion to corporation shall state:

(1)   The date on which and jurisdiction where the other entity was first created, incorporated, formed or otherwise came into being and, if it has changed, its jurisdiction immediately prior to its conversion to a domestic corporation;

(2)   The name and type of entity of the other entity immediately prior to the filing of the certificate of conversion to corporation; and

(3)   The name of the corporation as set forth in its certificate of incorporation filed in accordance with subsection (b) of this section.

(4)   [Repealed.]

(d)   Upon the effective time of the certificate of conversion to corporation and the certificate of incorporation, the other entity shall be converted to a corporation of this State and the corporation shall thereafter be subject to all of the provisions of this title, except that notwithstanding § 106 of this title, the existence of the corporation shall be deemed to have commenced on the date the other entity commenced its existence in the jurisdiction in which the other entity was first created, formed, incorporated or otherwise came into being.

(e)   The conversion of any other entity to a corporation of this State shall not be deemed to affect any obligations or liabilities of the other entity incurred prior to its conversion to a corporation of this State or the personal liability of any person incurred prior to such conversion.

(f)   When an other entity has been converted to a corporation of this State pursuant to this section, the corporation of this State shall, for all purposes of the laws of the State of Delaware, be deemed to be the same entity as the converting other entity. When any conversion shall have become effective under this section, for all purposes of the laws of the State of Delaware, all of the rights, privileges and powers of the other entity that has converted, and all property, real, personal and mixed, and all debts due to such other entity, as well as all other things and causes of action belonging to such other entity, shall remain vested in the domestic corporation to which such other entity has converted and shall be the property of such domestic corporation and the title to any real property vested by deed or otherwise in such other entity shall not revert or be in any way impaired by reason of this chapter; but all rights of creditors and all liens upon any property of such other entity shall be preserved unimpaired, and all debts, liabilities and duties of the other entity that has converted shall remain attached to the corporation of this State to which such other entity has converted, and may be enforced against it to the same extent as if said debts, liabilities and duties had originally been incurred or contracted by it in its capacity as a corporation of this State. The rights, privileges, powers and interests in property of the other entity, as well as the debts, liabilities and duties of the other entity, shall not be deemed, as a consequence of the conversion, to have been transferred to the domestic corporation to which such other entity has converted for any purpose of the laws of the State of Delaware.

(g) Unless otherwise agreed for all purposes of the laws of the State of Delaware or as required under applicable non-Delaware law, the converting other entity shall not be required to wind up its affairs or pay its liabilities and distribute its assets, and the conversion shall not be deemed to constitute a dissolution of such other entity and shall constitute a continuation of the existence of the converting other entity in the form of a corporation of this State.

(h) Prior to filing a certificate of conversion to corporation with the office of the Secretary of State, the conversion shall be approved in the manner provided for by the document, instrument, agreement or other writing, as the case may be, governing the internal affairs of the other entity and the conduct of its business or by applicable law, as appropriate, and a certificate of incorporation shall be approved by the same authorization required to approve the conversion.

(i) The certificate of conversion to corporation shall be signed by any person who is authorized to sign the certificate of conversion to corporation on behalf of the other entity.

(j) In connection with a conversion hereunder, rights or securities of, or interests in, the other entity which is to be converted to a corporation of this State may be exchanged for or converted into cash, property, or shares of stock, rights or securities of such corporation of this State or, in addition to or in lieu thereof, may be exchanged for or converted into cash, property, or shares of stock, rights or securities of or interests in another domestic corporation or other entity or may be cancelled.

§ 266. Conversion of a Domestic Corporation to Other Entities

(a) A corporation of this State may, upon the authorization of such conversion in accordance with this section, convert to a limited liability company, statutory trust, business trust or association, real estate investment trust, common-law trust or any other unincorporated business including a partnership (whether general (including a limited liability partnership) or limited (including a limited liability limited partnership)) or a foreign corporation.

(b) The board of directors of the corporation which desires to convert under this section shall adopt a resolution approving such conversion, specifying the type of entity into which the corporation shall be converted and recommending the approval of such conversion by the stockholders of the corporation. Such resolution shall be submitted to the stockholders of the corporation at an annual or special meeting. Due notice of the time, and purpose of the meeting shall be mailed to each holder of stock, whether voting or nonvoting, of the corporation at the address of the stockholder as it appears on the records of the corporation, at least 20 days prior to the date of the meeting. At the meeting, the resolution shall be considered and a vote taken for its adoption or rejection. If all outstanding shares of stock of the corporation, whether voting or nonvoting, shall be voted for the adoption of the resolution, the conversion shall be authorized.

(1)–(4) [Repealed.]

(c) If a corporation shall convert in accordance with this section to another entity organized, formed or created under the laws of a jurisdiction other than the State of Delaware, the corporation shall file with the Secretary of State a certificate of conversion executed in accordance with § 103 of this title, which certifies:

(1) The name of the corporation, and if it has been changed, the name under which it was originally incorporated;

(2) The date of filing of its original certificate of incorporation with the Secretary of State;

(3) The name and jurisdiction of the entity to which the corporation shall be converted;

(4) That the conversion has been approved in accordance with the provisions of this section;

(5) The agreement of the corporation that it may be served with process in the State of Delaware in any action, suit or proceeding for enforcement of any obligation of the corporation arising while it was a corporation of this State, and that it irrevocably appoints the Secretary of State as its agent to accept service of process in any such action, suit or proceeding; and

(6) The address to which a copy of the process referred to in paragraph (c)(5) of this section shall be mailed to it by the Secretary of State. Process may be served upon the Secretary of State in accordance with paragraph (c)(5) of this section by means of electronic transmission but only as prescribed by the Secretary of State. The Secretary of State is authorized to issue such rules and regulations with respect to such service as the Secretary of State deems necessary or appropriate. In the event of such service upon the Secretary of State in accordance with paragraph (c)(5) of this section, the Secretary of State shall forthwith notify such corporation that has converted out of the State of Delaware by letter, directed to such corporation that has converted out of the State of Delaware at the address so specified, unless such corporation shall have designated in writing to the Secretary of State a different address for such purpose, in which case it shall be mailed to the last address designated. Such letter shall be sent by a mail or courier service that includes a record of mailing or deposit with the courier and a record of delivery evidenced by the signature of the recipient. Such letter shall enclose a copy of the process and any other papers served on the Secretary of State pursuant to this subsection. It shall be the duty of the plaintiff in the event of such service to serve process and any other papers in duplicate, to notify the Secretary of State that service is being effected pursuant to this subsection and to pay the Secretary of State the sum of $50 for the use of the State, which sum shall be taxed as part of the costs in the proceeding, if the plaintiff shall prevail therein. The Secretary of State shall maintain an alphabetical record of any such service setting forth the name of the plaintiff and the defendant, the title, docket number and nature of the proceeding in which process has been served, the fact that service has been effected pursuant to this subsection, the return date thereof, and the day and hour service was made. The Secretary of State shall not be required to retain such information longer than 5 years from receipt of the service of process.

(d) Upon the filing in the Office of the Secretary of State of a certificate of conversion to non-Delaware entity in accordance with subsection (c) of this section or upon the future effective date or time of the certificate of conversion to non-Delaware entity and payment to the Secretary of State of all fees prescribed under this title, the Secretary of State shall certify that the corporation has filed all documents and paid all fees required by this title, and thereupon the corporation shall cease to exist as a corporation of this State at the time the certificate of conversion becomes effective in accordance with § 103 of this title. Such certificate of the Secretary of State shall be prima facie evidence of the conversion by such corporation out of the State of Delaware.

(e) The conversion of a corporation out of the State of Delaware in accordance with this section and the resulting cessation of its existence as a corporation of this State pursuant to a certificate of conversion to non-Delaware entity shall not be deemed to affect any obligations or liabilities of the corporation incurred prior to such conversion or the personal liability of any person incurred prior to such conversion, nor shall it be deemed to affect the choice of law applicable to the corporation with respect to matters arising prior to such conversion.

(f) Unless otherwise provided in a resolution of conversion adopted in accordance with this section, the converting corporation shall not be required to wind up its affairs or pay its liabilities and distribute its assets, and the conversion shall not constitute a dissolution of such corporation.

(g) In connection with a conversion of a domestic corporation to another entity pursuant to this section, shares of stock, of the corporation of this State which is to be converted may be exchanged for or converted into cash, property, rights or securities of, or interests in, the entity to which the corporation of this State is being converted or, in addition to or in lieu thereof, may be exchanged for or converted into cash, property, shares of stock, rights or securities of, or interests in, another domestic corporation or other entity or may be cancelled.

(h) When a corporation has been converted to another entity or business form pursuant to this section, the other entity or business form shall, for all purposes of the laws of the State of Delaware, be deemed to be the same entity as the corporation. When any conversion shall have become effective under this section, for all purposes of the laws of the State of Delaware, all of the rights, privileges and powers of the corporation that has converted, and all property, real, personal and mixed, and all debts due to such corporation, as well as all other things and causes of action belonging to such corporation, shall remain vested in the other entity or business form to which such corporation has converted and shall be the property of such other entity or business form, and the title to any real property vested by deed or otherwise in such corporation shall not revert or be in any way impaired by reason of this chapter; but all rights of creditors and all liens upon any property of such corporation shall be preserved unimpaired, and all debts, liabilities and duties of the corporation that has converted shall remain attached to the other entity or business form to which such corporation has converted, and may be enforced against it to the same extent as if said debts, liabilities and duties had originally been incurred or contracted by it in its capacity as such other entity or business form. The rights, privileges, powers and interest in property of the corporation that has converted, as well as the debts, liabilities and duties of such corporation, shall not be deemed, as a consequence of the conversion, to have been transferred to the other entity or business form to which such corporation has converted for any purpose of the laws of the State of Delaware.

(i) No vote of stockholders of a corporation shall be necessary to authorize a conversion if no shares of the stock of such corporation shall have been issued prior to the adoption by the board of directors of the resolution approving the conversion.

(j) Nothing in this section shall be deemed to authorize the conversion of a charitable nonstock corporation into another entity, if the charitable status of such charitable nonstock corporation would thereby be lost or impaired.

§ 267. Merger of Parent Entity and Subsidiary Corporation or Corporations

(a) In any case in which: (1) at least 90% of the outstanding shares of each class of the stock of a corporation or corporations (other than a corporation which has in its certificate of incorporation the provision required by § 251(g)(7)(i) of this title), of which class there are outstanding shares that, absent this subsection, would be entitled to vote on such merger, is owned by an entity, and (2) 1 or more of such corporations is a corporation of this State, unless the laws of the jurisdiction or jurisdictions under which such entity or such foreign corporations are formed or organized prohibit such merger, the entity having such stock ownership may either merge the corporation or corporations into itself and assume all of its or their obligations, or merge itself, or itself and 1 or more of such corporations, into 1 of the other corporations by (a) authorizing such merger in accordance with such entity's governing documents and the laws of the jurisdiction under which such entity is formed or organized and (b) acknowledging and filing with the Secretary of State, in accordance with § 103 of this title, a certificate of such ownership and merger certifying (i) that such merger was authorized in accordance with such entity's governing documents and the laws of the jurisdiction under which such entity is formed or organized such certificate executed in accordance with such entity's governing documents and in accordance with the laws of the jurisdiction under which such entity is formed or organized and (ii) the type of entity of each constituent entity to the merger; provided, however, that in case the entity shall not own all the outstanding stock of all the corporations, parties to a merger as aforesaid, (A) the certificate of ownership and merger shall state the terms and conditions of the merger, including the securities, cash, property, or rights to be issued, paid, delivered or granted by the surviving constituent party upon surrender of each share of the corporation or corporations not owned by the entity, or the cancellation of some or all of such shares and (B) such terms and conditions of the merger may not result in a holder of stock in a corporation becoming a general partner in a surviving entity that is a partnership (other than a limited liability partnership or a limited liability limited partnership). Any of the terms of the merger may be made dependent upon facts ascertainable outside of the certificate of ownership and merger, provided that the manner in which such facts shall operate upon the terms of the merger is clearly and expressly set forth in the certificate of ownership and merger. The term "facts," as used in the preceding sentence, includes, but is not limited to, the occurrence of any event, including a determination or action by any person or body, including the entity. If the surviving constituent party is an entity formed or organized under the laws of a jurisdiction other than this State, (1) § 252(d) of this title shall also apply to a merger under this section; if the surviving constituent party is the entity, the word "corporation" where applicable, as used in § 252(d) of this title, shall be deemed to include an entity as defined herein; and (2) the terms and conditions of the merger shall obligate the surviving constituent party to provide the agreement, and take the actions, required by § 252(d) of this title.

(b) Sections 259, 261, and 328 of this title shall, insofar as they are applicable, apply to a merger under this section, and §§ 260 and 251(e) of this title shall apply to a merger under this section in which the surviving constituent party is a corporation of this State. For purposes of this subsection, references to "agreement of merger" in § 251(e) of this title shall mean the terms and conditions of the merger set forth in the certificate of ownership and merger, and references to "corporation" in §§ 259–261 of this title, and § 328 of this title shall be deemed to include the entity, as applicable. Section 262 of this title shall not apply to any merger effected under this section, except as provided in subsection (c) of this section.

(c) In the event all of the stock of a Delaware corporation party to a merger effected under this section is not owned by the entity immediately prior to the merger, the stockholders of such Delaware corporation party to the merger shall have appraisal rights as set forth in § 262 of this title.

(d) As used in this section only, the term:

(1) "Constituent party" means an entity or corporation to be merged pursuant to this section;

(2) "Entity" means a partnership (whether general (including a limited liability partnership) or limited (including a limited liability limited partnership)), limited liability company, any association of the kind commonly known as a joint-stock association or joint-stock company and any unincorporated association, trust or enterprise having members or having outstanding shares of stock or other evidences of financial or beneficial interest therein, whether formed or organized by agreement or under statutory authority or otherwise and whether formed or organized under the laws of this State or the laws of any other jurisdiction; and

(3) "Governing documents" means a partnership agreement, limited liability company agreement, articles of association or any other instrument containing the provisions by which an entity is formed or organized.

§ 271. Sale, Lease or Exchange of Assets; Consideration; Procedure

(a) Every corporation may at any meeting of its board of directors or governing body sell, lease or exchange all or substantially all of its property and assets, including its goodwill and its corporate franchises, upon such terms and conditions and for such consideration, which may consist in whole or in part of money or other property, including shares of stock in, and/or other securities of, any other corporation or corporations, as its board of directors or governing body deems expedient and for the best interests of the corporation, when and as authorized by a resolution adopted by the holders of a majority of the outstanding stock of the corporation entitled to vote thereon or, if the corporation is a nonstock corporation, by a majority of the members having the right to vote for the election of the members of the governing body and any other members entitled to vote thereon under the certificate of incorporation or the bylaws of such corporation, at a meeting duly called upon at least 20 days' notice. The notice of the meeting shall state that such a resolution will be considered.

(b)   Notwithstanding authorization or consent to a proposed sale, lease or exchange of a corporation's property and assets by the stockholders or members, the board of directors or governing body may abandon such proposed sale, lease or exchange without further action by the stockholders or members, subject to the rights, if any, of third parties under any contract relating thereto.

(c)   For purposes of this section only, the property and assets of the corporation include the property and assets of any subsidiary of the corporation. As used in this subsection, "subsidiary" means any entity wholly-owned and controlled, directly or indirectly, by the corporation and includes, without limitation, corporations, partnerships, limited partnerships, limited liability partnerships, limited liability companies, and/or statutory trusts. Notwithstanding subsection (a) of this section, except to the extent the certificate of incorporation otherwise provides, no resolution by stockholders or members shall be required for a sale, lease or exchange of property and assets of the corporation to a subsidiary.

§ 272.   Mortgage or Pledge of Assets

The authorization or consent of stockholders to the mortgage or pledge of a corporation's property and assets shall not be necessary, except to the extent that the certificate of incorporation otherwise provides.

§ 273.   Dissolution of Joint Venture Corporation Having 2 Stockholders

(a)   If the stockholders of a corporation of this State, having only 2 stockholders each of which own 50% of the stock therein, shall be engaged in the prosecution of a joint venture and if such stockholders shall be unable to agree upon the desirability of discontinuing such joint venture and disposing of the assets used in such venture, either stockholder may, unless otherwise provided in the certificate of incorporation of the corporation or in a written agreement between the stockholders, file with the Court of Chancery a petition stating that it desires to discontinue such joint venture and to dispose of the assets used in such venture in accordance with a plan to be agreed upon by both stockholders or that, if no such plan shall be agreed upon by both stockholders, the corporation be dissolved. Such petition shall have attached thereto a copy of the proposed plan of discontinuance and distribution and a certificate stating that copies of such petition and plan have been transmitted in writing to the other stockholder and to the directors and officers of such corporation. The petition and certificate shall be executed and acknowledged in accordance with § 103 of this title.

(b)   Unless both stockholders file with the Court of Chancery:

(1)   Within 3 months of the date of the filing of such petition, a certificate similarly executed and acknowledged stating that they have agreed on such plan, or a modification thereof, and

(2)   Within 1 year from the date of the filing of such petition, a certificate similarly executed and acknowledged stating that the distribution provided by such plan had been completed,

the Court of Chancery may dissolve such corporation and may by appointment of 1 or more trustees or receivers with all the powers and title of a trustee or receiver appointed under § 279 of this title, administer and wind up its affairs. Either or both of the above periods may be extended by agreement of the stockholders, evidenced by a certificate similarly executed, acknowledged and filed with the Court of Chancery prior to the expiration of such period.

(c)   In the case of a charitable nonstock corporation, the petitioner shall provide a copy of any petition referred to in subsection (a) of this section to the Attorney General of the State of Delaware within 1 week of its filing with the Court of Chancery.

§ 274. Dissolution Before Issuance of Shares or Beginning of Business; Procedure

If a corporation has not issued shares or has not commenced the business for which the corporation was organized, a majority of the incorporators, or, if directors were named in the certificate of incorporation or have been elected, a majority of the directors, may surrender all of the corporation's rights and franchises by filing in the office of the Secretary of State a certificate, executed and acknowledged by a majority of the incorporators or directors, stating: that no shares of stock have been issued or that the business or activity for which the corporation was organized has not been begun; the date of filing of the corporation's original certificate of incorporation with the Secretary of State; that no part of the capital of the corporation has been paid, or, if some capital has been paid, that the amount actually paid in for the corporation's shares, less any part thereof disbursed for necessary expenses, has been returned to those entitled thereto; that if the corporation has begun business but it has not issued shares, all debts of the corporation have been paid; that if the corporation has not begun business but has issued stock certificates, all issued stock certificates, if any, have been surrendered and cancelled; and that all rights and franchises of the corporation are surrendered. Upon such certificate becoming effective in accordance with § 103 of this title, the corporation shall be dissolved.

§ 275. Dissolution Generally; Procedure

(a) If it should be deemed advisable in the judgment of the board of directors of any corporation that it should be dissolved, the board, after the adoption of a resolution to that effect by a majority of the whole board at any meeting called for that purpose, shall cause notice of the adoption of the resolution and of a meeting of stockholders to take action upon the resolution to be mailed to each stockholder entitled to vote thereon as of the record date for determining the stockholders entitled to notice of the meeting.

(b) At the meeting a vote shall be taken upon the proposed dissolution. If a majority of the outstanding stock of the corporation entitled to vote thereon shall vote for the proposed dissolution, a certification of dissolution shall be filed with the Secretary of State pursuant to subsection (d) of this section.

(c) Dissolution of a corporation may also be authorized without action of the directors if all the stockholders entitled to vote thereon shall consent in writing and a certificate of dissolution shall be filed with the Secretary of State pursuant to subsection (d) of this section.

(d) If dissolution is authorized in accordance with this section, a certificate of dissolution shall be executed, acknowledged and filed, and shall become effective, in accordance with § 103 of this title. Such certificate of dissolution shall set forth:

(1) The name of the corporation;

(2) The date dissolution was authorized;

(3) That the dissolution has been authorized by the board of directors and stockholders of the corporation, in accordance with subsections (a) and (b) of this section, or that the dissolution has been authorized by all of the stockholders of the corporation entitled to vote on a dissolution, in accordance with subsection (c) of this section;

(4) The names and addresses of the directors and officers of the corporation; and

(5) The date of filing of the corporation's original certificate of incorporation with the Secretary of State.

(e) The resolution authorizing a proposed dissolution may provide that notwithstanding authorization or consent to the proposed dissolution by the stockholders, or the members of a nonstock corporation pursuant to § 276 of this title, the board of directors or governing body may abandon such proposed dissolution without further action by the stockholders or members.

(f)   Upon a certificate of dissolution becoming effective in accordance with § 103 of this title, the corporation shall be dissolved.

§ 276. Dissolution of Nonstock Corporation; Procedure

(a)   Whenever it shall be desired to dissolve any nonstock corporation, the governing body shall perform all the acts necessary for dissolution which are required by § 275 of this title to be performed by the board of directors of a corporation having capital stock. If the members of a nonstock corporation are entitled to vote for the election of members of its governing body or are entitled to vote for dissolution under the certificate of incorporation or the bylaws of such corporation, such members, shall perform all the acts necessary for dissolution which are contemplated by § 275 of this title to be performed by the stockholders of a corporation having capital stock, including dissolution without action of the members of the governing body if all the members of the corporation entitled to vote thereon shall consent in writing and a certificate of dissolution shall be filed with the Secretary of State pursuant to § 275(d) of this title. If there is no member entitled to vote thereon, the dissolution of the corporation shall be authorized at a meeting of the governing body, upon the adoption of a resolution to dissolve by the vote of a majority of members of its governing body then in office. In all other respects, the method and proceedings for the dissolution of a nonstock corporation shall conform as nearly as may be to the proceedings prescribed by § 275 of this title for the dissolution of corporations having capital stock.

(b)   If a nonstock corporation has not commenced the business for which the corporation was organized, a majority of the governing body or, if none, a majority of the incorporators may surrender all of the corporation rights and franchises by filing in the office of the Secretary of State a certificate, executed and acknowledged by a majority of the incorporators or governing body, conforming as nearly as may be to the certificate prescribed by § 274 of this title.

§ 277. Payment of Franchise Taxes Before Dissolution or Merger

No corporation shall be dissolved, merged, transferred (without continuing its existence as a corporation of this State) or converted under this chapter until:

(a)   All franchise taxes due to or assessable by the State including all franchise taxes due or which would be due or assessable for the entire calendar month during which such dissolution, merger, transfer or conversion becomes effective have been paid by the corporation and

(b)   All annual franchise tax reports including a final annual franchise tax report for the year in which such dissolution, merger, transfer or conversion becomes effective have been filed by the corporation; notwithstanding the foregoing, if the Secretary of State certifies that an instrument to effect a dissolution, merger, transfer or conversion has been filed in the Secretary of State's office, such corporation shall be dissolved, merged, transferred or converted at the effective time of such instrument.

§ 278. Continuation of Corporation After Dissolution for Purposes of Suit and Winding Up Affairs

All corporations, whether they expire by their own limitation or are otherwise dissolved, shall nevertheless be continued, for the term of 3 years from such expiration or dissolution or for such longer period as the Court of Chancery shall in its discretion direct, bodies corporate for the purpose of prosecuting and defending suits, whether civil, criminal or administrative, by or against them, and of enabling them gradually to settle and close their business, to dispose of and convey their property, to discharge their liabilities and to distribute to their stockholders any remaining assets, but not for the purpose of continuing the business for which the corporation was organized. With respect to any action, suit or proceeding begun by or against the corporation either prior to or within 3 years after the date of its expiration or dissolution, the action shall not abate by reason of the dissolution of the corporation; the corporation shall, solely for the purpose of such action, suit or proceeding, be continued as a body corporate beyond the 3-year period and until any judgments, orders or decrees therein shall be fully executed, without the necessity for any special direction to that effect by the Court of Chancery.

Sections 279 through 282 of this title shall apply to any corporation that has expired by its own limitation, and when so applied, all references in those sections to a dissolved corporation or dissolution shall include a corporation that has expired by its own limitation and to such expiration, respectively.

§ 279. Trustees or Receivers for Dissolved Corporations; Appointment; Powers; Duties

When any corporation organized under this chapter shall be dissolved in any manner whatever, the Court of Chancery, on application of any creditor, stockholder or director of the corporation, or any other person who shows good cause therefor, at any time, may either appoint 1 or more of the directors of the corporation to be trustees, or appoint 1 or more persons to be receivers, of and for the corporation, to take charge of the corporation's property, and to collect the debts and property due and belonging to the corporation, with power to prosecute and defend, in the name of the corporation, or otherwise, all such suits as may be necessary or proper for the purposes aforesaid, and to appoint an agent or agents under them, and to do all other acts which might be done by the corporation, if in being, that may be necessary for the final settlement of the unfinished business of the corporation. The powers of the trustees or receivers may be continued as long as the Court of Chancery shall think necessary for the purposes aforesaid.

§ 280. Notice to Claimants; Filing of Claims

(a)(1)   After a corporation has been dissolved in accordance with the procedures set forth in this chapter, the corporation or any successor entity may give notice of the dissolution, requiring all persons having a claim against the corporation other than a claim against the corporation in a pending action, suit or proceeding to which the corporation is a party to present their claims against the corporation in accordance with such notice. Such notice shall state:

a.   That all such claims must be presented in writing and must contain sufficient information reasonably to inform the corporation or successor entity of the identity of the claimant and the substance of the claim;

b.   The mailing address to which such a claim must be sent;

c.   The date by which such a claim must be received by the corporation or successor entity, which date shall be no earlier than 60 days from the date thereof; and

d.   That such claim will be barred if not received by the date referred to in paragraph (a)(1)c. of this section; and

e.   That the corporation or a successor entity may make distributions to other claimants and the corporation's stockholders or persons interested as having been such without further notice to the claimant; and

f.   The aggregate amount, on an annual basis, of all distributions made by the corporation to its stockholders for each of the 3 years prior to the date the corporation dissolved. Such notice shall also be published at least once a week for 2 consecutive weeks in a newspaper of general circulation in the county in which the office of the corporation's last registered agent in this State is located and in the corporation's principal place of business and, in the case of a corporation having $10,000,000 or more in total assets at the time of its dissolution, at least once in all editions of a daily newspaper with a national circulation. On or before the date of the first publication of such notice, the corporation or successor entity shall mail a copy of such notice by certified or registered mail, return receipt requested, to each known claimant of the corporation including persons with claims asserted against the corporation in a pending action, suit or proceeding to which the corporation is a party.

(2)   Any claim against the corporation required to be presented pursuant to this subsection is barred if a claimant who was given actual notice under this subsection does not present the claim to the dissolved corporation or successor entity by the date referred to in paragraph (a)(1)c. of this section.

(3)   A corporation or successor entity may reject, in whole or in part, any claim made by a claimant pursuant to this subsection by mailing notice of such rejection by certified or registered mail, return receipt requested, to the claimant within 90 days after receipt of such claim and, in all events, at least 150 days before the expiration of the period described in § 278 of this title; provided however, that in the case of a claim filed pursuant to § 295 of this title against a corporation or successor entity for which a receiver or trustee has been appointed by the Court of Chancery the time period shall be as provided in § 296 of this title, and the 30-day appeal period provided for in § 296 of this title shall be applicable. A notice sent by a corporation or successor entity pursuant to this subsection shall state that any claim rejected therein will be barred if an action, suit or proceeding with respect to the claim is not commenced within 120 days of the date thereof, and shall be accompanied by a copy of §§ 278–283 of this title and, in the case of a notice sent by a court-appointed receiver or trustee and as to which a claim has been filed pursuant to § 295 of this title, copies of §§ 295 and 296 of this title.

(4)   A claim against a corporation is barred if a claimant whose claim is rejected pursuant to paragraph (a)(3) of this section does not commence an action, suit or proceeding with respect to the claim no later than 120 days after the mailing of the rejection notice.

(b)(1)   A corporation or successor entity electing to follow the procedures described in subsection (a) of this section shall also give notice of the dissolution of the corporation to persons with contractual claims contingent upon the occurrence or nonoccurrence of future events or otherwise conditional or unmatured, and request that such persons present such claims in accordance with the terms of such notice. Provided however, that as used in this section and in § 281 of this title, the term "contractual claims" shall not include any implied warranty as to any product manufactured, sold, distributed or handled by the dissolved corporation. Such notice shall be in substantially the form, and sent and published in the same manner, as described in paragraph (a)(1) of this section.

(2)   The corporation or successor entity shall offer any claimant on a contract whose claim is contingent, conditional or unmatured such security as the corporation or successor entity determines is sufficient to provide compensation to the claimant if the claim matures. The corporation or successor entity shall mail such offer to the claimant by certified or registered mail, return receipt requested, within 90 days of receipt of such claim and, in all events, at least 150 days before the expiration of the period described in § 278 of this title. If the claimant offered such security does not deliver in writing to the corporation or successor entity a notice rejecting the offer within 120 days after receipt of such offer for security, the claimant shall be deemed to have accepted such security as the sole source from which to satisfy the claim against the corporation.

(c)(1)   A corporation or successor entity which has given notice in accordance with subsection (a) of this section shall petition the Court of Chancery to determine the amount and form of security that will be reasonably likely to be sufficient to provide compensation for any claim against the corporation which is the subject of a pending action, suit or proceeding to which the corporation is a party other than a claim barred pursuant to subsection (a) of this section.

(2)   A corporation or successor entity which has given notice in accordance with subsections (a) and (b) of this section shall petition the Court of Chancery to determine the amount and form of security that will be sufficient to provide compensation to any claimant who has rejected the offer for security made pursuant to paragraph (b)(2) of this section.

(3)   A corporation or successor entity which has given notice in accordance with subsection (a) of this section shall petition the Court of Chancery to determine the amount and form of security which will be reasonably likely to be sufficient to provide compensation for claims that have not been made known to the corporation or that have not arisen but that, based on facts known to the corporation or successor entity, are likely to arise or to become known to the corporation or successor entity within 5 years after the date of dissolution or such longer period of time as the Court of Chancery may determine not to exceed 10 years after the date of dissolution. The Court of Chancery may appoint a guardian ad litem in respect of any such proceeding brought under this subsection. The reasonable fees and expenses of such guardian, including all reasonable expert witness fees, shall be paid by the petitioner in such proceeding.

(d)   The giving of any notice or making of any offer pursuant to this section shall not revive any claim then barred or constitute acknowledgment by the corporation or successor entity that any person to whom such notice is sent is a proper claimant and shall not operate as a waiver of any defense or counterclaim in respect of any claim asserted by any person to whom such notice is sent.

(e)   As used in this section, the term "successor entity" shall include any trust, receivership or other legal entity governed by the laws of this State to which the remaining assets and liabilities of a dissolved corporation are transferred and which exists solely for the purposes of prosecuting and defending suits, by or against the dissolved corporation, enabling the dissolved corporation to settle and close the business of the dissolved corporation, to dispose of and convey the property of the dissolved corporation, to discharge the liabilities of the dissolved corporation and to distribute to the dissolved corporation's stockholders any remaining assets, but not for the purpose of continuing the business for which the dissolved corporation was organized.

(f)   The time periods and notice requirements of this section shall, in the case of a corporation or successor entity for which a receiver or trustee has been appointed by the Court of Chancery, be subject to variation by, or in the manner provided in, the Rules of the Court of Chancery.

(g)   In the case of a nonstock corporation, any notice referred to in the last sentence of paragraph (a)(3) of this section shall include a copy of § 114 of this title. In the case of a nonprofit nonstock corporation, provisions of this section regarding distributions to members shall not apply to the extent that those provisions conflict with any other applicable law or with that corporation's certificate of incorporation or bylaws.

§ 281.   Payment and Distribution to Claimants and Stockholders

(a)   A dissolved corporation or successor entity which has followed the procedures described in § 280 of this title:

(1)   Shall pay the claims made and not rejected in accordance with § 280(a) of this title,

(2)   Shall post the security offered and not rejected pursuant to § 280(b)(2) of this title,

(3)   Shall post any security ordered by the Court of Chancery in any proceeding under § 280(c) of this title, and

(4)   Shall pay or make provision for all other claims that are mature, known and uncontested or that have been finally determined to be owing by the corporation or such successor entity.

Such claims or obligations shall be paid in full and any such provision for payment shall be made in full if there are sufficient assets. If there are insufficient assets, such claims and obligations shall be paid or provided for according to their priority, and, among claims of equal priority, ratably to the extent of assets legally available therefor. Any remaining assets shall be distributed to the stockholders of the dissolved corporation; provided, however, that such distribution shall not be made before the expiration of 150 days from the date of the last notice of rejections given pursuant to § 280(a)(3) of this title. In the absence of actual fraud, the judgment of the directors of the dissolved corporation or the governing persons of such successor entity as to the provision made for the payment of all obligations under paragraph (a)(4) of this section shall be conclusive.

(b)   A dissolved corporation or successor entity which has not followed the procedures described in § 280 of this title shall, prior to the expiration of the period described in § 278 of this title, adopt a plan of distribution pursuant to which the dissolved corporation or successor entity (i) shall pay or make reasonable provision to pay all claims and obligations, including all contingent, conditional or unmatured contractual claims known to the corporation or such successor entity, (ii) shall make such provision as will be reasonably likely to be sufficient to provide compensation for any claim against the corporation which is the subject of a pending action, suit or proceeding to which the corporation is a party and (iii) shall make such provision as will be reasonably likely to be sufficient to provide compensation for claims that have not been made known to the corporation or that have not arisen but that, based on facts known to the corporation or successor entity, are likely to arise or to become known to the corporation or successor entity within 10 years after the date of dissolution. The plan of distribution shall provide that such claims shall be paid in full and any such provision for payment made shall be made in full if there are sufficient assets. If there are insufficient assets, such plan shall provide that such claims and obligations shall be paid or provided for according to their priority and, among claims of equal priority, ratably to the extent of assets legally available therefor. Any remaining assets shall be distributed to the stockholders of the dissolved corporation.

(c)   Directors of a dissolved corporation or governing persons of a successor entity which has complied with subsection (a) or (b) of this section shall not be personally liable to the claimants of the dissolved corporation.

(d)   As used in this section, the term "successor entity" has the meaning set forth in § 280(e) of this title.

(e)   The term "priority," as used in this section, does not refer either to the order of payments set forth in paragraph (a)(1)–(4) of this section or to the relative times at which any claims mature or are reduced to judgment.

(f)   In the case of a nonprofit nonstock corporation, provisions of this section regarding distributions to members shall not apply to the extent that those provisions conflict with any other applicable law or with that corporation's certificate of incorporation or bylaws.

§ 282.   Liability of Stockholders of Dissolved Corporations

(a)   A stockholder of a dissolved corporation the assets of which were distributed pursuant to § 281(a) or (b) of this title shall not be liable for any claim against the corporation in an amount in excess of such stockholder's pro rata share of the claim or the amount so distributed to such stockholder, whichever is less.

(b)   A stockholder of a dissolved corporation the assets of which were distributed pursuant to § 281(a) of this title shall not be liable for any claim against the corporation on which an action, suit or proceeding is not begun prior to the expiration of the period described in § 278 of this title.

(c)   The aggregate liability of any stockholder of a dissolved corporation for claims against the dissolved corporation shall not exceed the amount distributed to such stockholder in dissolution.

§ 283.   Jurisdiction

The Court of Chancery shall have jurisdiction of any application prescribed in this subchapter and of all questions arising in the proceedings thereon, and may make such orders and decrees and issue injunctions therein as justice and equity shall require.

§ 284.   Revocation or Forfeiture of Charter; Proceedings

(a)   Upon motion by the Attorney General, the Court of Chancery shall have jurisdiction to revoke or forfeit the charter of any corporation for abuse, misuse or nonuse of its corporate powers, privileges or franchises. The Attorney General shall proceed for this purpose by complaint in the Court of Chancery.

(b)   The Court of Chancery shall have power, by appointment of trustees, receivers or otherwise, to administer and wind up the affairs of any corporation whose charter shall be revoked or forfeited by the Court of Chancery under this section, and to make such orders and decrees with respect thereto as shall be just and equitable respecting its affairs and assets and the rights of its stockholders and creditors.

(c)   No proceeding shall be instituted under this section for nonuse of any corporation's powers, privileges or franchises during the first 2 years after its incorporation.

§ 285.   Dissolution or Forfeiture of Charter by Decree of Court; Filing

Whenever any corporation is dissolved or its charter forfeited by decree or judgment of the Court of Chancery, the decree or judgment shall be forthwith filed by the Register in Chancery of the county in which the decree or judgment was entered, in the office of the Secretary of State, and a note thereof shall be made by the Secretary of State on the corporation's charter or certificate of incorporation and on the index thereof.

§ 291.   Receivers for Insolvent Corporations; Appointment and Powers

Whenever a corporation shall be insolvent, the Court of Chancery, on the application of any creditor or stockholder thereof, may, at any time, appoint 1 or more persons to be receivers of and for the corporation, to take charge of its assets, estate, effects, business and affairs, and to collect the outstanding debts, claims, and property due and belonging to the corporation, with power to prosecute and defend, in the name of the corporation or otherwise, all claims or suits, to appoint an agent or agents under them, and to do all other acts which might be done by the corporation and which may be necessary or proper. The powers of the receivers shall be such and shall continue so long as the Court shall deem necessary.

§ 292.   Title to Property; Filing Order of Appointment; Exception

(a)   Trustees or receivers appointed by the Court of Chancery of and for any corporation, and their respective survivors and successors, shall, upon their appointment and qualification or upon the death, resignation or discharge of any co-trustee or co-receiver, be vested by operation of law and without any act or deed, with the title of the corporation to all of its property, real, personal or mixed of whatsoever nature, kind, class or description, and wheresoever situate, except real estate situate outside this State.

(b)   Trustees or receivers appointed by the Court of Chancery shall, within 20 days from the date of their qualification, file in the office of the recorder in each county in this State, in which any real estate belonging to the corporation may be situated, a certified copy of the order of their appointment and evidence of their qualification.

(c)   This section shall not apply to receivers appointed pendente lite.

§ 293.   Notices to Stockholders and Creditors

All notices required to be given to stockholders and creditors in any action in which a receiver or trustee for a corporation was appointed shall be given by the Register in Chancery, unless otherwise ordered by the Court of Chancery.

§ 294.   Receivers or Trustees; Inventory; List of Debts and Report

Trustees or receivers shall, as soon as convenient, file in the office of the Register in Chancery of the county in which the proceeding is pending, a full and complete itemized inventory of all the assets of the corporation which shall show their nature and probable value, and an account of all debts due from and to it, as nearly as the same can be ascertained. They shall make a report to the Court of their proceedings, whenever and as often as the Court shall direct.

§ 295. Creditors' Proofs of Claims; When Barred; Notice

All creditors shall make proof under oath of their respective claims against the corporation, and cause the same to be filed in the office of the Register in Chancery of the county in which the proceeding is pending within the time fixed by and in accordance with the procedure established by the rules of the Court of Chancery. All creditors and claimants failing to do so, within the time limited by this section, or the time prescribed by the order of the Court, may, by direction of the Court, be barred from participating in the distribution of the assets of the corporation. The Court may also prescribe what notice, by publication or otherwise, shall be given to the creditors of the time fixed for the filing and making proof of claims.

§ 296. Adjudication of Claims; Appeal

(a)   The Register in Chancery, immediately upon the expiration of the time fixed for the filing of claims, in compliance with § 295 of this title, shall notify the trustee or receiver of the filing of the claims, and the trustee or receiver, within 30 days after receiving the notice, shall inspect the claims, and if the trustee or receiver or any creditor shall not be satisfied with the validity or correctness of the same, or any of them, the trustee or receiver shall forthwith notify the creditors whose claims are disputed of such trustee's or receiver's decision. The trustee or receiver shall require all creditors whose claims are disputed to submit themselves to such examination in relation to their claims as the trustee or receiver shall direct, and the creditors shall produce such books and papers relating to their claims as shall be required. The trustee or receiver shall have power to examine, under oath or affirmation, all witnesses produced before such trustee or receiver touching the claims, and shall pass upon and allow or disallow the claims, or any part thereof, and notify the claimants of such trustee's or receiver's determination.

(b)   Every creditor or claimant who shall have received notice from the receiver or trustee that such creditor's or claimant's claim has been disallowed in whole or in part may appeal to the Court of Chancery within 30 days thereafter. The Court, after hearing, shall determine the rights of the parties.

§ 297. Sale of Perishable or Deteriorating Property

Whenever the property of a corporation is at the time of the appointment of a receiver or trustee encumbered with liens of any character, and the validity, extent or legality of any lien is disputed or brought in question, and the property of the corporation is of a character which will deteriorate in value pending the litigation respecting the lien, the Court of Chancery may order the receiver or trustee to sell the property of the corporation, clear of all encumbrances, at public or private sale, for the best price that can be obtained therefor, and pay the net proceeds arising from the sale thereof after deducting the costs of the sale into the Court, there to remain subject to the order of the Court, and to be disposed of as the Court shall direct.

§ 298. Compensation, Costs and Expenses of Receiver or Trustee

The Court of Chancery, before making distribution of the assets of a corporation among the creditors or stockholders thereof, shall allow a reasonable compensation to the receiver or trustee for such receiver's or trustee's services, and the costs and expenses incurred in and about the execution of such receiver's or trustee's trust, and the costs of the proceedings in the Court, to be first paid out of the assets.

§ 299. Substitution of Trustee or Receiver as Party; Abatement of Actions

A trustee or receiver, upon application by such receiver or trustee in the court in which any suit is pending, shall be substituted as party plaintiff in the place of the corporation in any suit or proceeding which was so pending at the time of such receiver's or trustee's appointment. No action against a trustee or receiver of a corporation shall abate by reason of such receiver's or trustee's death, but, upon suggestion of the facts on the record, shall be continued against such receiver's or trustee's successor or against the corporation in case no new trustee or receiver is appointed.

§ 300. Employee's Lien for Wages When Corporation Insolvent

Whenever any corporation of this State, or any foreign corporation doing business in this State, shall become insolvent, the employees doing labor or service of whatever character in the regular employ of the corporation, shall have a lien upon the assets thereof for the amount of the wages due to them, not exceeding 2 months' wages respectively, which shall be paid prior to any other debt or debts of the corporation. The word "employee" shall not be construed to include any of the officers of the corporation.

§ 301. Discontinuance of Liquidation

The liquidation of the assets and business of an insolvent corporation may be discontinued at any time during the liquidation proceedings when it is established that cause for liquidation no longer exists. In such event the Court of Chancery in its discretion, and subject to such condition as it may deem appropriate, may dismiss the proceedings and direct the receiver or trustee to redeliver to the corporation all of its remaining property and assets.

§ 302. Compromise or Arrangement Between Corporation and Creditors or Stockholders

(a) Whenever the provision permitted by § 102(b)(2) of this title is included in the original certificate of incorporation of any corporation, all persons who become creditors or stockholders thereof shall be deemed to have become such creditors or stockholders subject in all respects to that provision and the same shall be absolutely binding upon them. Whenever that provision is inserted in the certificate of incorporation of any such corporation by an amendment of its certificate all persons who become creditors or stockholders of such corporation after such amendment shall be deemed to have become such creditors or stockholders subject in all respects to that provision and the same shall be absolutely binding upon them.

(b) The Court of Chancery may administer and enforce any compromise or arrangement made pursuant to the provision contained in § 102(b)(2) of this title and may restrain, pendente lite, all actions and proceedings against any corporation with respect to which the Court shall have begun the administration and enforcement of that provision and may appoint a temporary receiver for such corporation and may grant the receiver such powers as it deems proper, and may make and enforce such rules as it deems necessary for the exercise of such jurisdiction.

§ 303. Proceeding Under the Federal Bankruptcy Code of the United States; Effectuation

(a) Any corporation of this State, an order for relief with respect to which has been entered pursuant to the Federal Bankruptcy Code, 11 U.S.C. § 101 et seq., or any successor statute, may put into effect and carry out any decrees and orders of the court or judge in such bankruptcy proceeding and may take any corporate action provided or directed by such decrees and orders, without further action by its directors or stockholders. Such power and authority may be exercised, and such corporate action may be taken, as may be directed by such decrees or orders, by the trustee or trustees of such corporation appointed or elected in the bankruptcy proceeding (or a majority thereof), or if none be appointed or elected and acting, by designated officers of the corporation, or by a representative appointed by the court or judge, with like effect as if exercised and taken by unanimous action of the directors and stockholders of the corporation.

(b) Such corporation may, in the manner provided in subsection (a) of this section, but without limiting the generality or effect of the foregoing, alter, amend or repeal its bylaws; constitute or reconstitute and classify or reclassify its board of directors, and name, constitute or appoint directors and officers in place of or in addition to all or some of the directors or officers then in office; amend its certificate of incorporation, and make any change in its capital or capital stock, or any other amendment, change, or alteration, or provision, authorized by this chapter; be dissolved, transfer all or part of its assets, merge or consolidate as permitted by this chapter, in which case, however, no stockholder shall have any statutory right of appraisal of such stockholder's stock; change the location of its registered office, change its registered agent, and remove or appoint any agent to receive service of process; authorize and fix the terms, manner and conditions of, the issuance of bonds, debentures or other obligations, whether or not convertible into stock of any class, or bearing warrants or other evidences of optional rights to purchase or subscribe for stock of any class; or lease its property and franchises to any corporation, if permitted by law.

(c) A certificate of any amendment, change or alteration, or of dissolution, or any agreement of merger or consolidation, made by such corporation pursuant to the foregoing provisions, shall be filed with the Secretary of State in accordance with § 103 of this title, and, subject to § 103(d) of this title, shall thereupon become effective in accordance with its terms and the provisions hereof. Such certificate, agreement of merger or other instrument shall be made, executed and acknowledged, as may be directed by such decrees or orders, by the trustee or trustees appointed or elected in the bankruptcy proceeding (or a majority thereof), or, if none be appointed or elected and acting, by the officers of the corporation, or by a representative appointed by the court or judge, and shall certify that provision for the making of such certificate, agreement or instrument is contained in a decree or order of a court or judge having jurisdiction of a proceeding under such Federal Bankruptcy Code or successor statute.

(d) This section shall cease to apply to such corporation upon the entry of a final decree in the bankruptcy proceeding closing the case and discharging the trustee or trustees, if any; provided however, that the closing of a case and discharge of trustee or trustees, if any, will not affect the validity of any act previously performed pursuant to subsections (a) through (c) of this section.

(e) On filing any certificate, agreement, report or other paper made or executed pursuant to this section, there shall be paid to the Secretary of State for the use of the State the same fees as are payable by corporations not in bankruptcy upon the filing of like certificates, agreements, reports or other papers.

§ 311. Revocation of Voluntary Dissolution; Restoration of Expired Certificate of Incorporation

(a) At any time prior to the expiration of 3 years following the dissolution of a corporation pursuant to § 275 of this title or such longer period as the Court of Chancery may have directed pursuant to § 278 of this title, or at any time prior to the expiration of 3 years following the expiration of the time limited for the corporation's existence as provided in its certificate of incorporation or such longer period as the Court of Chancery may have directed pursuant to § 278 of this title, a corporation may revoke the dissolution theretofore effected by it or restore its certificate of incorporation after it has expired by its own limitation in the following manner:

(1) For purposes of this section, the term "stockholders" shall mean the stockholders of record on the date the dissolution became effective or the date of expiration by limitation.

(2) The board of directors shall adopt a resolution recommending that the dissolution be revoked in the case of a dissolution or that the certificate of incorporation be restored in the case of an expiration by limitation and directing that the question of the revocation or restoration be submitted to a vote at a special meeting of stockholders;

(3) Notice of the special meeting of stockholders shall be given in accordance with § 222 of this title to each of the stockholders.

(4)   At the meeting a vote of the stockholders shall be taken on a resolution to revoke the dissolution in the case of a dissolution or to restore the certificate of incorporation in the case of an expiration by limitation. If a majority of the stock of the corporation which was outstanding and entitled to vote upon a dissolution at the time of its dissolution, in the case of a revocation of dissolution, or which was outstanding and entitled to vote upon an amendment to the certificate of incorporation to change the period of the corporation's duration at the time of its expiration by limitation, in the case of a restoration, shall be voted for the resolution, a certificate of revocation of dissolution or a certificate of restoration shall be executed, acknowledged and filed in accordance with § 103 of this title, which shall be specifically designated as a certificate of revocation of dissolution or a certificate of restoration in its heading and shall state:

a.   The name of the corporation;

b.   The address (which shall be stated in accordance with § 131(c) of this title) of the corporation's registered office in this State, and the name of its registered agent at such address;

c.   The names and respective addresses of its officers;

d.   The names and respective addresses of its directors;

e.   That a majority of the stock of the corporation which was outstanding and entitled to vote upon a dissolution at the time of its dissolution have voted in favor of a resolution to revoke the dissolution, in the case of a revocation of dissolution, or that a majority of the stock of the corporation which was outstanding and entitled to vote upon an amendment to the certificate of incorporation to change the period of the corporation's duration at the time of its expiration by limitation, in the case of a restoration, have voted in favor of a resolution to restore the certificate of incorporation; or, if it be the fact, that, in lieu of a meeting and vote of stockholders, the stockholders have given their written consent to the revocation or restoration in accordance with § 228 of this title; and

f.   In the case of a restoration, the new specified date limiting the duration of the corporation's existence or that the corporation shall have perpetual existence.

(b)   Upon the effective time of filing in the office of the Secretary of State of the certificate of revocation of dissolution or the certificate of restoration, the revocation of the dissolution or the restoration of the corporation shall become effective and the corporation may again carry on its business.

(c)   Upon the effectiveness of the revocation of the dissolution or the restoration of the corporation as provided in subsection (b) of this section, the provisions of § 211(c) of this title shall govern, and the period of time the corporation was in dissolution or was expired by limitation shall be included within the calculation of the 30-day and 13-month periods to which § 211(c) of this title refers. An election of directors, however, may be held at the special meeting of stockholders to which subsection (a) of this section refers and, in that event, that meeting of stockholders shall be deemed an annual meeting of stockholders for purposes of § 211(c) of this title.

(d)   If after the dissolution became effective or after the expiration by limitation any other corporation organized under the laws of this State shall have adopted the same name as the corporation, or shall have adopted a name so nearly similar thereto as not to distinguish it from the corporation, or any foreign corporation shall have qualified to do business in this State under the same name as the corporation or under a name so nearly similar thereto as not to distinguish it from the corporation, then, in such case, the corporation shall not be reinstated under the same name which it bore when its dissolution became effective or it expired by limitation, but shall adopt and be reinstated or restored under some other name, and in such case the certificate to be filed under this section shall set forth the name borne by the corporation at the time its dissolution became effective or it expired by limitation and the new name under which the corporation is to be reinstated or restored.

(e) Nothing in this section shall be construed to affect the jurisdiction or power of the Court of Chancery under § 279 or § 280 of this title.

(f) At any time prior to the expiration of 3 years following the dissolution of a nonstock corporation pursuant to § 276 of this title or such longer period as the Court of Chancery may have directed pursuant to § 278 of this title, or at any time prior to the expiration of 3 years following the expiration of the time limited for a nonstock corporation's existence as provided in its certificate of incorporation or such longer period as the Court of Chancery may have directed pursuant to § 278 of this title, a nonstock corporation may revoke the dissolution theretofore effected by it or restore its certificate of incorporation after it has expired by limitation in a manner analogous to that by which the dissolution was authorized or, in the case of a restoration, in the manner in which an amendment to the certificate of incorporation to change the period of the corporation's duration would have been authorized at the time of its expiration by limitation including (i) if applicable, a vote of the members entitled to vote, if any, on the dissolution or the amendment and (ii) the filing of a certificate of revocation of dissolution or a certificate of restoration containing information comparable to that required by paragraph (a)(4) of this section. Notwithstanding the foregoing, only subsections (b), (d), and (e) of this section shall apply to nonstock corporations.

(g) Any corporation that revokes its dissolution or restores its certificate of incorporation pursuant to this section shall file all annual franchise tax reports that the corporation would have had to file if it had not dissolved or expired and shall pay all franchise taxes that the corporation would have had to pay if it had not dissolved or expired. No payment made pursuant to this subsection shall reduce the amount of franchise tax due under Chapter 5 of this title for the year in which such revocation or restoration is effected.

§ 312. Revival of Certificate of Incorporation

(a) As used in this section, the term "certificate of incorporation" includes the charter of a corporation organized under any special act or any law of this State.

(b) Any corporation whose certificate of incorporation has become forfeited or void pursuant to this title or whose certificate of incorporation has been revived, but, through failure to comply strictly with the provisions of this chapter, the validity of whose revival has been brought into question, may at any time a revival of its certificate of incorporation, together with all the rights, franchises, privileges and immunities and subject to all of its duties, debts and liabilities which had been secured or imposed by its original certificate of incorporation and all amendments thereto, by complying with the requirements of this section. Notwithstanding the foregoing, this section shall not be applicable to a corporation whose certificate of incorporation has been revoked or forfeited pursuant to § 284 of this title.

(c) The revival of the certificate of incorporation may be procured as authorized by the board of directors or members of the governing body of the corporation in accordance with subsection (h) of this section and by executing, acknowledging and filing a certificate in accordance with § 103 of this title.

(d) The certificate required by subsection (c) of this section shall state:

(1) The date of filing of the corporation's original certificate of incorporation; the name under which the corporation was originally incorporated; the name of the corporation at time its certificate of incorporation became forfeited or void pursuant to this title; and the new name under which the corporation is to be revived to the extent required by subsection (f) of this section;

(2) The address (which shall be stated in accordance with § 131(c) of this title) of the corporation's registered office in this State and the name of its registered agent at such address;

(3) That the corporation desiring to be revived and so reviving its certificate of incorporation was organized under the laws of this State;

(4) The date when the certificate of incorporation became forfeited or void pursuant to this title, or that the validity of any revival has been brought into question; and

(5) That the certificate of revival is filed by authority of the board of directors or members of the governing body of the corporation in accordance with subsection (h) of this section.

(e) Upon the filing of the certificate in accordance with § 103 of this title the corporation shall be revived with the same force and effect as if its certificate of incorporation had not been forfeited or void pursuant to this title. Such revival shall validate all contracts, acts, matters and things made, done and performed within the scope of its certificate of incorporation by the corporation, its directors or members of its governing body, officers, agents and stockholders or members during the time when its certificate of incorporation was forfeited or void pursuant to this title, with the same force and effect and to all intents and purposes as if the certificate of incorporation had at all times remained in full force and effect. All real and personal property, rights and credits, which belonged to the corporation at the time its certificate of incorporation became forfeited or void pursuant to this title and which were not disposed of prior to the time of its revival and all real and personal property, rights and credits acquired by the corporation after its certificate of incorporation became forfeited or void pursuant to this title shall be vested in the corporation, after its revival, as if its certificate of incorporation had at all times remained in full force and effect, and the corporation after its revival shall be as exclusively liable for all contracts, acts, matters and things made, done or performed in its name and on its behalf by its directors or members of its governing body, officers, agents and stockholders or members prior to its revival, as if its certificate of incorporation had at all times remained in full force and effect.

(f) If, since the certificate of incorporation became forfeited or void pursuant to this title, any other corporation organized under the laws of this State shall have adopted the same name as the corporation sought to be revived or shall have adopted a name so nearly similar thereto as not to distinguish it from the corporation to be revived or any foreign corporation qualified in accordance with § 371 of this title shall have adopted the same name as the corporation sought to be revived or shall have adopted a name so nearly similar thereto as not to distinguish it from the corporation to be revived, then in such case the corporation to be revived shall not be revived under the same name which it bore when its certificate of incorporation became forfeited or void pursuant to this title, but shall be revived under some other name as set forth in the certificate to be filed pursuant to subsection (c) of this section.

(g) Any corporation that revives its certificate of incorporation under this chapter shall pay to this State a sum equal to all franchise taxes, penalties and interest thereon due at the time its certificate of incorporation became forfeited or void pursuant to this title; provided, however, that any corporation that revives its certificate of incorporation under this chapter whose certificate of incorporation has been forfeited or void for more than 5 years shall, in lieu of the payment of the franchise taxes and penalties otherwise required by this subsection, pay a sum equal to 3 times the amount of the annual franchise tax that would be due and payable by such corporation for the year in which the revival is effected, computed at the then current rate of taxation. No payment made pursuant to this subsection shall reduce the amount of franchise tax due under Chapter 5 of this title for the year in which the revival is effected.

(h) For purposes of this section and § 502(a) of this title, the board of directors or governing body of the corporation shall be comprised of the persons, who, but for the certificate of incorporation having become forfeited or void pursuant to this title, would be the duly elected or appointed directors or members of the governing body of the corporation. The requirement for authorization by the board of directors under subsection (c) of this section shall be satisfied if a majority of the directors or members of the governing body then in office, even though less than a quorum, or the sole director or member of the governing body then in office, authorizes the revival of the certificate of incorporation of the corporation and the filing of the certificate required by subsection (c) of this section. In any case where there shall be no directors of the corporation available for the purposes aforesaid, the stockholders may elect a full board of directors, as provided by the bylaws of the corporation, and the board so elected may then authorize the revival of the certificate of incorporation of the corporation and the filing of the certificate required by subsection (c) of this section. A special meeting of the stockholders for the purpose of electing directors may be called by any officer or stockholder upon notice given in accordance with § 222 of this title. For purposes of this section, the bylaws shall be the bylaws of the corporation that, but for the certificate of incorporation having become forfeited or void pursuant to this title, would be the duly adopted bylaws of the corporation.

(i)　　After a revival of the certificate of incorporation of the corporation shall have been effected, the provisions of § 211(c) of this title shall govern and the period of time during which the certificate of incorporation of the corporation was forfeited or void pursuant to this title shall be included within the calculation of the 30-day and 13-month periods to which § 211(c) of this title refers. A special meeting of stockholders held in accordance with subsection (h) of this section shall be deemed an annual meeting of stockholders for purposes of § 211(c) of this title.

(j)　　Except as otherwise provided in § 313 of this title, whenever it shall be desired to revive the certificate of incorporation of any nonstock corporation, the governing body shall perform all the acts necessary for the revival of the certificate of incorporation of the corporation which are performed by the board of directors in the case of a corporation having capital stock, and the members of any nonstock corporation who are entitled to vote for the election of members of its governing body and any other members entitled to vote for dissolution under the certificate of incorporation or the bylaws of such corporation, shall perform all the acts necessary for the revival of the certificate of incorporation of the corporation which are performed by the stockholders in the case of a corporation having capital stock. Except as otherwise provided in § 313 of this title, in all other respects, the procedure for the revival of the certificate of incorporation of a nonstock corporation shall conform, as nearly as may be applicable, to the procedure prescribed in this section for the revival of the certificate of incorporation of a corporation having capital stock; provided, however, that subsection (i) of this section shall not apply to nonstock corporations.

§ 313.　Renewal of Certificate of Incorporation or Charter of Exempt Corporations

(a)　　Every exempt corporation whose certificate of incorporation or charter has become inoperative and void, by operation of § 510 of this title for failure to file annual franchise tax reports required, and for failure to pay taxes or penalties from which it would have been exempt if the reports had been filed, shall be deemed to have filed all the reports and be relieved of all the taxes and penalties, upon satisfactory proof submitted to the Secretary of State of its right to be classified as an exempt corporation pursuant to § 501(b) of this title, and upon filing with the Secretary of State a certificate of renewal and revival in manner and form as required by § 312 of this title.

(b)　　Upon the filing by the corporation of the proof of classification as required by subsection (a) of this section, the filing of the certificate of revival and payment of the required filing fees, the corporation shall be revived with the same force and effect as provided in § 312(e) of this title for other corporations.

(c)　　As used in this section, the term "exempt corporation" shall have the meaning given to it in § 501(b) of this title. Nothing contained in this section relieves any exempt corporation from filing the annual report required by § 502 of this title.

§ 314.　Status of Corporation

Any corporation desiring to renew, extend and continue its corporate existence, shall upon complying with applicable constitutional provisions of this State, continue for the time stated in its certificate of renewal, a corporation and shall, in addition to the rights, privileges and immunities conferred by its charter, possess and enjoy all the benefits of this chapter, which are applicable to the nature of its business, and shall be subject to the restrictions and liabilities by this chapter imposed on such corporations.

§ 321.　Service of Process on Corporations

(a)　　Service of legal process upon any corporation of this State shall be made by delivering a copy personally to any officer or director of the corporation in this State, or the registered agent of the corporation in this State, or by leaving it at the dwelling house or usual place of abode in this State of any officer, director or registered agent (if the registered agent be an individual), or at the registered office or other place of business of the corporation in this State. If the registered agent be a corporation, service of process upon it as such agent may be made by serving, in this State, a copy thereof on the president, vice-president, secretary, assistant secretary or any director of the corporate registered agent. Service by copy left at the dwelling house or usual place of abode of any officer, director or registered agent, or at the registered office or other place of business of the corporation in this State, to be effective must be delivered thereat at least 6 days before the return date of the process, and in the presence of an adult person, and the officer serving the process shall distinctly state the manner of service in such person's return thereto. Process returnable forthwith must be delivered personally to the officer, director or registered agent.

(b) In case the officer whose duty it is to serve legal process cannot by due diligence serve the process in any manner provided for by subsection (a) of this section, it shall be lawful to serve the process against the corporation upon the Secretary of State, and such service shall be as effectual for all intents and purposes as if made in any of the ways provided for in subsection (a) of this section. Process may be served upon the Secretary of State under this subsection by means of electronic transmission but only as prescribed by the Secretary of State. The Secretary of State is authorized to issue such rules and regulations with respect to such service as the Secretary of State deems necessary or appropriate. In the event that service is effected through the Secretary of State in accordance with this subsection, the Secretary of State shall forthwith notify the corporation by letter, directed to the corporation at its principal place of business as it appears on the records relating to such corporation on file with the Secretary of State or, if no such address appears, at its last registered office. Such letter shall be sent by a mail or courier service that includes a record of mailing or deposit with the courier and a record of delivery evidenced by the signature of the recipient. Such letter shall enclose a copy of the process and any other papers served on the Secretary of State pursuant to this subsection. It shall be the duty of the plaintiff in the event of such service to serve process and any other papers in duplicate, to notify the Secretary of State that service is being effected pursuant to this subsection, and to pay the Secretary of State the sum of $50 for the use of the State, which sum shall be taxed as part of the costs in the proceeding if the plaintiff shall prevail therein. The Secretary of State shall maintain an alphabetical record of any such service setting forth the name of the plaintiff and defendant, the title, docket number and nature of the proceeding in which process has been served upon the Secretary of State, the fact that service has been effected pursuant to this subsection, the return date thereof, and the day and hour when the service was made. The Secretary of State shall not be required to retain such information for a period longer than 5 years from receipt of the service of process.

(c) Service upon corporations may also be made in accordance with § 3111 of Title 10 or any other statute or rule of court.

§ 322. Failure of Corporation to Obey Order of Court; Appointment of Receiver

Whenever any corporation shall refuse, fail or neglect to obey any order or decree of any court of this State within the time fixed by the court for its observance, such refusal, failure or neglect shall be a sufficient ground for the appointment of a receiver of the corporation by the Court of Chancery. If the corporation be a foreign corporation, such refusal, failure or neglect shall be a sufficient ground for the appointment of a receiver of the assets of the corporation within this State.

§ 323. Failure of Corporation to Obey Writ of Mandamus; Quo Warranto Proceedings for Forfeiture of Charter

If any corporation fails to obey the mandate of any peremptory writ of mandamus issued by a court of competent jurisdiction of this State for a period of 30 days after the serving of the writ upon the corporation in any manner as provided by the laws of this State for the service of writs, any party in interest in the proceeding in which the writ of mandamus issued may file a statement of such fact prepared by such party or such party's attorney with the Attorney General of this State, and it shall thereupon be the duty of the Attorney General to forthwith commence proceedings of quo warranto against the corporation in a court of competent jurisdiction, and the court, upon competent proof of such state of facts and proper proceedings had in such proceeding in quo warranto, shall decree the charter of the corporation forfeited.

§ 324. Attachment of Shares of Stock or Any Option, Right or Interest Therein; Procedure; Sale; Title Upon Sale; Proceeds

(a)　The shares of any person in any corporation with all the rights thereto belonging, or any person's option to acquire the shares, or such person's right or interest in the shares, may be attached under this section for debt, or other demands, if such person appears on the books of the corporation to hold or own such shares, option, right or interest. So many of the shares, or so much of the option, right or interest therein may be sold at public sale to the highest bidder, as shall be sufficient to satisfy the debt, or other demand, interest and costs, upon an order issued therefor by the court from which the attachment process issued, and after such notice as is required for sales upon execution process. Except as to an uncertificated security as defined in § 8–102 of Title 6, the attachment is not laid and no order of sale shall issue unless § 8–112 of Title 6 has been satisfied. No order of sale shall be issued until after final judgment shall have been rendered in any case. If the debtor lives out of the county, a copy of the order shall be sent by registered or certified mail, return receipt requested, to such debtor's last known address, and shall also be published in a newspaper published in the county of such debtor's last known residence, if there be any, 10 days before the sale; and if the debtor be a nonresident of this State shall be mailed as aforesaid and published at least twice for 2 successive weeks, the last publication to be at least 10 days before the sale, in a newspaper published in the county where the attachment process issued. If the shares of stock or any of them or the option to acquire shares or any such right or interest in shares, or any part of them, be so sold, any assignment, or transfer thereof, by the debtor, after attachment, shall be void.

(b)　When attachment process issues for shares of stock, or any option to acquire such or any right or interest in such, a certified copy of the process shall be left in this State with any officer or director, or with the registered agent of the corporation. Within 20 days after service of the process, the corporation shall serve upon the plaintiff a certificate of the number of shares held or owned by the debtor in the corporation, with the number or other marks distinguishing the same, or in the case the debtor appears on the books of the corporation to have an option to acquire shares of stock or any right or interest in any shares of stock of the corporation, there shall be served upon the plaintiff within 20 days after service of the process a certificate setting forth any such option, right or interest in the shares of the corporation in the language and form in which the option, right or interest appears on the books of the corporation, anything in the certificate of incorporation or bylaws of the corporation to the contrary notwithstanding. Service upon a corporate registered agent may be made in the manner provided in § 321 of this title.

(c)　If, after sale made and confirmed, a certified copy of the order of sale and return and the stock certificate, if any, be left with any officer or director or with the registered agent of the corporation, the purchaser shall be thereby entitled to the shares or any option to acquire shares or any right or interest in shares so purchased, and all income, or dividends which may have been declared, or become payable thereon since the attachment laid. Such sale, returned and confirmed, shall transfer the shares or the option to acquire shares or any right or interest in shares sold to the purchaser, as fully as if the debtor, or defendant, had transferred the same to such purchaser according to the certificate of incorporation or bylaws of the corporation, anything in the certificate of incorporation or bylaws to the contrary notwithstanding. The court which issued the levy and confirmed the sale shall have the power to make an order compelling the corporation, the shares of which were sold, to issue new certificates or uncertificated shares to the purchaser at the sale and to cancel the registration of the shares attached on the books of the corporation upon the giving of an open end bond by such purchaser adequate to protect such corporation.

(d) The money arising from the sale of the shares or from the sale of the option or right or interest shall be applied and paid, by the public official receiving the same, as by law is directed as to the sale of personal property in cases of attachment.

§ 325. Actions Against Officers, Directors or Stockholders to Enforce Liability of Corporation; Unsatisfied Judgment Against Corporation

(a) When the officers, directors or stockholders of any corporation shall be liable by the provisions of this chapter to pay the debts of the corporation, or any part thereof, any person to whom they are liable may have an action, at law or in equity, against any 1 or more of them, and the complaint shall state the claim against the corporation, and the ground on which the plaintiff expects to charge the defendants personally.

(b) No suit shall be brought against any officer, director or stockholder for any debt of a corporation of which such person is an officer, director or stockholder, until judgment be obtained therefor against the corporation and execution thereon returned unsatisfied.

§ 326. Action by Officer, Director or Stockholder Against Corporation for Corporate Debt Paid

When any officer, director or stockholder shall pay any debt of a corporation for which such person is made liable by the provisions of this chapter, such person may recover the amount so paid in an action against the corporation for money paid for its use, and in such action only the property of the corporation shall be liable to be taken, and not the property of any stockholder.

§ 327. Stockholder's Derivative Action; Allegation of Stock Ownership

In any derivative suit instituted by a stockholder of a corporation, it shall be averred in the complaint that the plaintiff was a stockholder of the corporation at the time of the transaction of which such stockholder complains or that such stockholder's stock thereafter devolved upon such stockholder by operation of law.

§ 328. Effect of Liability of Corporation on Impairment of Certain Transactions

The liability of a corporation of this State, or the stockholders, directors or officers thereof, or the rights or remedies of the creditors thereof, or of persons doing or transacting business with the corporation, shall not in any way be lessened or impaired by the sale of its assets, or by the increase or decrease in the capital stock of the corporation, or by its merger or consolidation with 1 or more corporations or by any change or amendment in its certificate of incorporation.

§ 329. Defective Organization of Corporation as Defense

(a) No corporation of this State and no person sued by any such corporation shall be permitted to assert the want of legal organization as a defense to any claim.

(b) This section shall not be construed to prevent judicial inquiry into the regularity or validity of the organization of a corporation, or its lawful possession of any corporate power it may assert in any other suit or proceeding where its corporate existence or the power to exercise the corporate rights it asserts is challenged, and evidence tending to sustain the challenge shall be admissible in any such suit or proceeding.

§ 330. Usury; Pleading by Corporation

No corporation shall plead any statute against usury in any court of law or equity in any suit instituted to enforce the payment of any bond, note or other evidence of indebtedness issued or assumed by it.

§ 341. Law Applicable to Close Corporation

(a)   This subchapter applies to all close corporations, as defined in § 342 of this title. Unless a corporation elects to become a close corporation under this subchapter in the manner prescribed in this subchapter, it shall be subject in all respects to this chapter, except this subchapter.

(b)   This chapter shall be applicable to all close corporations, as defined in § 342 of this title, except insofar as this subchapter otherwise provides.

§ 342. Close Corporation Defined; Contents of Certificate of Incorporation

(a)   A close corporation is a corporation organized under this chapter whose certificate of incorporation contains the provisions required by § 102 of this title and, in addition, provides that:

(1)   All of the corporation's issued stock of all classes, exclusive of treasury shares, shall be represented by certificates and shall be held of record by not more than a specified number of persons, not exceeding 30; and

(2)   All of the issued stock of all classes shall be subject to 1 or more of the restrictions on transfer permitted by § 202 of this title; and

(3)   The corporation shall make no offering of any of its stock of any class which would constitute a "public offering" within the meaning of the United States Securities Act of 1933 [15 U.S.C. § 77a et seq.] as it may be amended from time to time.

(b)   The certificate of incorporation of a close corporation may set forth the qualifications of stockholders, either by specifying classes of persons who shall be entitled to be holders of record of stock of any class, or by specifying classes of persons who shall not be entitled to be holders of stock of any class or both.

(c)   For purposes of determining the number of holders of record of the stock of a close corporation, stock which is held in joint or common tenancy or by the entireties shall be treated as held by 1 stockholder.

§ 343. Formation of a Close Corporation

A close corporation shall be formed in accordance with §§ 101, 102 and 103 of this title, except that:

(1)   Its certificate of incorporation shall contain a heading stating the name of the corporation and that it is a close corporation; and

(2)   Its certificate of incorporation shall contain the provisions required by § 342 of this title.

§ 344. Election of Existing Corporation to Become a Close Corporation

Any corporation organized under this chapter may become a close corporation under this subchapter by executing, acknowledging and filing, in accordance with § 103 of this title, a certificate of amendment of its certificate of incorporation which shall contain a statement that it elects to become a close corporation, the provisions required by § 342 of this title to appear in the certificate of incorporation of a close corporation, and a heading stating the name of the corporation and that it is a close corporation. Such amendment shall be adopted in accordance with the requirements of § 241 or 242 of this title, except that it must be approved by a vote of the holders of record of at least 2/3 of the shares of each class of stock of the corporation which are outstanding.

§ 345. Limitations on Continuation of Close Corporation Status

A close corporation continues to be such and to be subject to this subchapter until:

(1) It files with the Secretary of State a certificate of amendment deleting from its certificate of incorporation the provisions required or permitted by § 342 of this title to be stated in the certificate of incorporation to qualify it as a close corporation; or

(2) Any 1 of the provisions or conditions required or permitted by § 342 of this title to be stated in a certificate of incorporation to qualify a corporation as a close corporation has in fact been breached and neither the corporation nor any of its stockholders takes the steps required by § 348 of this title to prevent such loss of status or to remedy such breach.

§ 346. Voluntary Termination of Close Corporation Status by Amendment of Certificate of Incorporation; Vote Required

(a) A corporation may voluntarily terminate its status as a close corporation and cease to be subject to this subchapter by amending its certificate of incorporation to delete therefrom the additional provisions required or permitted by § 342 of this title to be stated in the certificate of incorporation of a close corporation. Any such amendment shall be adopted and shall become effective in accordance with § 242 of this title, except that it must be approved by a vote of the holders of record of at least 2/3 of the shares of each class of stock of the corporation which are outstanding.

(b) The certificate of incorporation of a close corporation may provide that on any amendment to terminate its status as a close corporation, a vote greater than 2/3 or a vote of all shares of any class shall be required; and if the certificate of incorporation contains such a provision, that provision shall not be amended, repealed or modified by any vote less than that required to terminate the corporation's status as a close corporation.

§ 347. Issuance or Transfer of Stock of a Close Corporation in Breach of Qualifying Conditions

(a) If stock of a close corporation is issued or transferred to any person who is not entitled under any provision of the certificate of incorporation permitted by § 342(b) of this title to be a holder of record of stock of such corporation, and if the certificate for such stock conspicuously notes the qualifications of the persons entitled to be holders of record thereof, such person is conclusively presumed to have notice of the fact of such person's ineligibility to be a stockholder.

(b) If the certificate of incorporation of a close corporation states the number of persons, not in excess of 30, who are entitled to be holders of record of its stock, and if the certificate for such stock conspicuously states such number, and if the issuance or transfer of stock to any person would cause the stock to be held by more than such number of persons, the person to whom such stock is issued or transferred is conclusively presumed to have notice of this fact.

(c) If a stock certificate of any close corporation conspicuously notes the fact of a restriction on transfer of stock of the corporation, and the restriction is one which is permitted by § 202 of this title, the transferee of the stock is conclusively presumed to have notice of the fact that such person has acquired stock in violation of the restriction, if such acquisition violates the restriction.

(d) Whenever any person to whom stock of a close corporation has been issued or transferred has, or is conclusively presumed under this section to have, notice either:

(1) That such person is a person not eligible to be a holder of stock of the corporation, or

(2) That transfer of stock to such person would cause the stock of the corporation to be held by more than the number of persons permitted by its certificate of incorporation to hold stock of the corporation, or

(3)   That the transfer of stock is in violation of a restriction on transfer of stock, the corporation may, at its option, refuse to register transfer of the stock into the name of the transferee.

(e)   Subsection (d) of this section shall not be applicable if the transfer of stock, even though otherwise contrary to subsection (a), (b) or (c), of this section has been consented to by all the stockholders of the close corporation, or if the close corporation has amended its certificate of incorporation in accordance with § 346 of this title.

(f)   The term "transfer," as used in this section, is not limited to a transfer for value.

(g)   The provisions of this section do not in any way impair any rights of a transferee regarding any right to rescind the transaction or to recover under any applicable warranty express or implied.

§ 348.   Involuntary Termination of Close Corporation Status; Proceeding to Prevent Loss of Status

(a)   If any event occurs as a result of which 1 or more of the provisions or conditions included in a close corporation's certificate of incorporation pursuant to § 342 of this title to qualify it as a close corporation has been breached, the corporation's status as a close corporation under this subchapter shall terminate unless:

(1)   Within 30 days after the occurrence of the event, or within 30 days after the event has been discovered, whichever is later, the corporation files with the Secretary of State a certificate, executed and acknowledged in accordance with § 103 of this title, stating that a specified provision or condition included in its certificate of incorporation pursuant to § 342 of this title to qualify it as a close corporation has ceased to be applicable, and furnishes a copy of such certificate to each stockholder; and

(2)   The corporation concurrently with the filing of such certificate takes such steps as are necessary to correct the situation which threatens its status as a close corporation, including, without limitation, the refusal to register the transfer of stock which has been wrongfully transferred as provided by § 347 of this title, or a proceeding under subsection (b) of this section.

(b)   The Court of Chancery, upon the suit of the corporation or any stockholder, shall have jurisdiction to issue all orders necessary to prevent the corporation from losing its status as a close corporation, or to restore its status as a close corporation by enjoining or setting aside any act or threatened act on the part of the corporation or a stockholder which would be inconsistent with any of the provisions or conditions required or permitted by § 342 of this title to be stated in the certificate of incorporation of a close corporation, unless it is an act approved in accordance with § 346 of this title. The Court of Chancery may enjoin or set aside any transfer or threatened transfer of stock of a close corporation which is contrary to the terms of its certificate of incorporation or of any transfer restriction permitted by § 202 of this title, and may enjoin any public offering, as defined in § 342 of this title, or threatened public offering of stock of the close corporation.

§ 349.   Corporate Option Where a Restriction on Transfer of a Security Is Held Invalid

If a restriction on transfer of a security of a close corporation is held not to be authorized by § 202 of this title, the corporation shall nevertheless have an option, for a period of 30 days after the judgment setting aside the restriction becomes final, to acquire the restricted security at a price which is agreed upon by the parties, or if no agreement is reached as to price, then at the fair value as determined by the Court of Chancery. In order to determine fair value, the Court may appoint an appraiser to receive evidence and report to the Court such appraiser's findings and recommendation as to fair value.

§ 350. Agreements Restricting Discretion of Directors

A written agreement among the stockholders of a close corporation holding a majority of the outstanding stock entitled to vote, whether solely among themselves or with a party not a stockholder, is not invalid, as between the parties to the agreement, on the ground that it so relates to the conduct of the business and affairs of the corporation as to restrict or interfere with the discretion or powers of the board of directors. The effect of any such agreement shall be to relieve the directors and impose upon the stockholders who are parties to the agreement the liability for managerial acts or omissions which is imposed on directors to the extent and so long as the discretion or powers of the board in its management of corporate affairs is controlled by such agreement.

§ 351. Management by Stockholders

The certificate of incorporation of a close corporation may provide that the business of the corporation shall be managed by the stockholders of the corporation rather than by a board of directors. So long as this provision continues in effect:

(1) No meeting of stockholders need be called to elect directors;

(2) Unless the context clearly requires otherwise, the stockholders of the corporation shall be deemed to be directors for purposes of applying provisions of this chapter; and

(3) The stockholders of the corporation shall be subject to all liabilities of directors. Such a provision may be inserted in the certificate of incorporation by amendment if all incorporators and subscribers or all holders of record of all of the outstanding stock, whether or not having voting power, authorize such a provision. An amendment to the certificate of incorporation to delete such a provision shall be adopted by a vote of the holders of a majority of all outstanding stock of the corporation, whether or not otherwise entitled to vote. If the certificate of incorporation contains a provision authorized by this section, the existence of such provision shall be noted conspicuously on the face or back of every stock certificate issued by such corporation.

§ 352. Appointment of Custodian for Close Corporation

(a) In addition to § 226 of this title respecting the appointment of a custodian for any corporation, the Court of Chancery, upon application of any stockholder, may appoint 1 or more persons to be custodians, and, if the corporation is insolvent, to be receivers, of any close corporation when:

(1) Pursuant to § 351 of this title the business and affairs of the corporation are managed by the stockholders and they are so divided that the business of the corporation is suffering or is threatened with irreparable injury and any remedy with respect to such deadlock provided in the certificate of incorporation or bylaws or in any written agreement of the stockholders has failed; or

(2) The petitioning stockholder has the right to the dissolution of the corporation under a provision of the certificate of incorporation permitted by § 355 of this title.

(b) In lieu of appointing a custodian for a close corporation under this section or § 226 of this title the Court of Chancery may appoint a provisional director, whose powers and status shall be as provided in § 353 of this title if the Court determines that it would be in the best interest of the corporation. Such appointment shall not preclude any subsequent order of the Court appointing a custodian for such corporation.

§ 353. Appointment of a Provisional Director in Certain Cases

(a) Notwithstanding any contrary provision of the certificate of incorporation or the bylaws or agreement of the stockholders, the Court of Chancery may appoint a provisional director for a close corporation if the directors are so divided respecting the management of the corporation's business and affairs that the votes required for action by the board of directors cannot be obtained with the consequence that the business and affairs of the corporation can no longer be conducted to the advantage of the stockholders generally.

(b) An application for relief under this section must be filed (1) by at least one half of the number of directors then in office, (2) by the holders of at least one third of all stock then entitled to elect directors, or, (3) if there be more than 1 class of stock then entitled to elect 1 or more directors, by the holders of two thirds of the stock of any such class; but the certificate of incorporation of a close corporation may provide that a lesser proportion of the directors or of the stockholders or of a class of stockholders may apply for relief under this section.

(c) A provisional director shall be an impartial person who is neither a stockholder nor a creditor of the corporation or of any subsidiary or affiliate of the corporation, and whose further qualifications, if any, may be determined by the Court of Chancery. A provisional director is not a receiver of the corporation and does not have the title and powers of a custodian or receiver appointed under §§ 226 and 291 of this title. A provisional director shall have all the rights and powers of a duly elected director of the corporation, including the right to notice of and to vote at meetings of directors, until such time as such person shall be removed by order of the Court of Chancery or by the holders of a majority of all shares then entitled to vote to elect directors or by the holders of two thirds of the shares of that class of voting shares which filed the application for appointment of a provisional director. A provisional director's compensation shall be determined by agreement between such person and the corporation subject to approval of the Court of Chancery, which may fix such person's compensation in the absence of agreement or in the event of disagreement between the provisional director and the corporation.

(d) Even though the requirements of subsection (b) of this section relating to the number of directors or stockholders who may petition for appointment of a provisional director are not satisfied, the Court of Chancery may nevertheless appoint a provisional director if permitted by § 352(b) of this title.

§ 354. Operating Corporation as Partnership

No written agreement among stockholders of a close corporation, nor any provision of the certificate of incorporation or of the bylaws of the corporation, which agreement or provision relates to any phase of the affairs of such corporation, including but not limited to the management of its business or declaration and payment of dividends or other division of profits or the election of directors or officers or the employment of stockholders by the corporation or the arbitration of disputes, shall be invalid on the ground that it is an attempt by the parties to the agreement or by the stockholders of the corporation to treat the corporation as if it were a partnership or to arrange relations among the stockholders or between the stockholders and the corporation in a manner that would be appropriate only among partners.

§ 355. Stockholders' Option to Dissolve Corporation

(a) The certificate of incorporation of any close corporation may include a provision granting to any stockholder, or to the holders of any specified number or percentage of shares of any class of stock, an option to have the corporation dissolved at will or upon the occurrence of any specified event or contingency. Whenever any such option to dissolve is exercised, the stockholders exercising such option shall give written notice thereof to all other stockholders. After the expiration of 30 days following the sending of such notice, the dissolution of the corporation shall proceed as if the required number of stockholders having voting power had consented in writing to dissolution of the corporation as provided by § 228 of this title.

(b) If the certificate of incorporation as originally filed does not contain a provision authorized by subsection (a) of this section, the certificate may be amended to include such provision if adopted by the affirmative vote of the holders of all the outstanding stock, whether or not entitled to vote, unless the certificate of incorporation specifically authorizes such an amendment by a vote which shall be not less than 2/3 of all the outstanding stock whether or not entitled to vote.

(c) Each stock certificate in any corporation whose certificate of incorporation authorizes dissolution as permitted by this section shall conspicuously note on the face thereof the existence of the provision. Unless noted conspicuously on the face of the stock certificate, the provision is ineffective.

§ 356. Effect of This Subchapter on Other Laws

This subchapter shall not be deemed to repeal any statute or rule of law which is or would be applicable to any corporation which is organized under this chapter but is not a close corporation.

§ 361. Law Applicable to Public Benefit Corporations; How Formed

This subchapter applies to all public benefit corporations, as defined in § 362 of this title. If a corporation elects to become a public benefit corporation under this subchapter in the manner prescribed in this subchapter, it shall be subject in all respects to the provisions of this chapter, except to the extent this subchapter imposes additional or different requirements, in which case such requirements shall apply.

§ 362. Public Benefit Corporation Defined; Contents of Certificate of Incorporation

(a) A public benefit corporation is a for-profit corporation organized under and subject to the requirements of this chapter that is intended to produce a public benefit or public benefits and to operate in a responsible and sustainable manner. To that end, a public benefit corporation shall be managed in a manner that balances the stockholders' pecuniary interests, the best interests of those materially affected by the corporation's conduct, and the public benefit or public benefits identified in its certificate of incorporation. In the certificate of incorporation, a public benefit corporation shall:

(1) Identify within its statement of business or purpose pursuant to § 102(a)(3) of this title 1 or more specific public benefits to be promoted by the corporation; and

(2) State within its heading that it is a public benefit corporation.

(b) "Public benefit" means a positive effect (or reduction of negative effects) on 1 or more categories of persons, entities, communities or interests (other than stockholders in their capacities as stockholders) including, but not limited to, effects of an artistic, charitable, cultural, economic, educational, environmental, literary, medical, religious, scientific or technological nature. "Public benefit provisions" means the provisions of a certificate of incorporation contemplated by this subchapter.

(c) The name of the public benefit corporation may contain the words "public benefit corporation," or the abbreviation "P.B.C.," or the designation "PBC," which shall be deemed to satisfy the requirements of § 102(a)(*l*)(i) of this title. If the name does not contain such language, the corporation shall, prior to issuing unissued shares of stock or disposing of treasury shares, provide notice to any person to whom such stock is issued or who acquires such treasury shares that it is a public benefit corporation; provided that such notice need not be provided if the issuance or disposal is pursuant to an offering registered under the Securities Act of 1933 [15 U.S.C. § 77r et seq.] or if, at the time of issuance or disposal, the corporation has a class of securities that is registered under the Securities Exchange Act of 1934 [15 U.S.C. § 78a et seq.].

§ 363. Certain Amendments and Mergers; Votes Required; Appraisal Rights

(a) Notwithstanding any other provisions of this chapter, a corporation that is not a public benefit corporation, may not, without the approval of 2/3 of the outstanding stock of the corporation entitled to vote thereon:

(1) Amend its certificate of incorporation to include a provision authorized by § 362(a)(1) of this title; or

(2) Merge or consolidate with or into another entity if, as a result of such merger or consolidation, the shares in such corporation would become, or be converted into or exchanged for the right to receive, shares or other equity interests in a domestic or foreign public benefit corporation or similar entity.

The restrictions of this section shall not apply prior to the time that the corporation has received payment for any of its capital stock, or in the case of a nonstock corporation, prior to the time that it has members.

(b) Any stockholder of a corporation that is not a public benefit corporation that holds shares of stock of such corporation immediately prior to the effective time of:

(1) An amendment to the corporation's certificate of incorporation to include a provision authorized by § 362(a)(1) of this title; or

(2) A merger or consolidation that would result in the conversion of the corporation's stock into or exchange of the corporation's stock for the right to receive shares or other equity interests in a domestic or foreign public benefit corporation or similar entity;

and has neither voted in favor of such amendment or such merger or consolidation nor consented thereto in writing pursuant to § 228 of this title, shall be entitled to an appraisal by the Court of Chancery of the fair value of the stockholder's shares of stock; provided, however, that no appraisal rights under this section shall be available for the shares of any class or series of stock, which stock, or depository receipts in respect thereof, at the record date fixed to determine the stockholders entitled to receive notice of the meeting of stockholders to act upon the agreement of merger or consolidation, or amendment, were either: (i) listed on a national securities exchange or (ii) held of record by more than 2,000 holders, unless, in the case of a merger or consolidation, the holders thereof are required by the terms of an agreement of merger or consolidation to accept for such stock anything except (A) shares of stock of any other corporation, or depository receipts in respect thereof, which shares of stock (or depository receipts in respect thereof) or depository receipts at the effective date of the merger or consolidation will be either listed on a national securities exchange or held of record by more than 2,000 holders; (B) cash in lieu of fractional shares or fractional depository receipts described in the foregoing clause (A); or (C) any combination of the shares of stock, depository receipts and cash in lieu of fractional shares or fractional depository receipts described in the foregoing clauses (A) and (B).

(c) Notwithstanding any other provisions of this chapter, a corporation that is a public benefit corporation may not, without the approval of 2/3 of the outstanding stock of the corporation entitled to vote thereon:

(1) Amend its certificate of incorporation to delete or amend a provision authorized by § 362(a)(1) or § 366(c) of this title; or

(2) Merge or consolidate with or into another entity if, as a result of such merger or consolidation, the shares in such corporation would become, or be converted into or exchanged for the right to receive, shares or other equity interests in a domestic or foreign corporation that is not a public benefit corporation or similar entity and the certificate of incorporation (or similar governing instrument) of which does not contain the identical provisions identifying the public benefit or public benefits pursuant to § 362(a) of this title or imposing requirements pursuant to § 366(c) of this title.

(d) Notwithstanding the foregoing, a nonprofit nonstock corporation may not be a constituent corporation to any merger or consolidation governed by this section.

§ 364. Stock Certificates; Notices Regarding Uncertified Stock

Any stock certificate issued by a public benefit corporation shall note conspicuously that the corporation is a public benefit corporation formed pursuant to this subchapter. Any notice given by a public benefit corporation pursuant to § 151(f) of this title shall state conspicuously that the corporation is a public benefit corporation formed pursuant to this subchapter.

§ 365. Duties of Directors

(a)   The board of directors shall manage or direct the business and affairs of the public benefit corporation in a manner that balances the pecuniary interests of the stockholders, the best interests of those materially affected by the corporation's conduct, and the specific public benefit or public benefits identified in its certificate of incorporation.

(b)   A director of a public benefit corporation shall not, by virtue of the public benefit provisions or § 362(a) of this title, have any duty to any person on account of any interest of such person in the public benefit or public benefits identified in the certificate of incorporation or on account of any interest materially affected by the corporation's conduct and, with respect to a decision implicating the balance requirement in subsection (a) of this section, will be deemed to satisfy such director's fiduciary duties to stockholders and the corporation if such director's decision is both informed and disinterested and not such that no person of ordinary, sound judgment would approve.

(c)   The certificate of incorporation of a public benefit corporation may include a provision that any disinterested failure to satisfy this section shall not, for the purposes of § 102(b)(7) or § 145 of this title, constitute an act or omission not in good faith, or a breach of the duty of loyalty.

§ 366. Periodic Statements and Third Party Certification

(a)   A public benefit corporation shall include in every notice of a meeting of stockholders a statement to the effect that it is a public benefit corporation formed pursuant to this subchapter.

(b)   A public benefit corporation shall no less than biennially provide its stockholders with a statement as to the corporation's promotion of the public benefit or public benefits identified in the certificate of incorporation and of the best interests of those materially affected by the corporation's conduct. The statement shall include:

(1)   The objectives the board of directors has established to promote such public benefit or public benefits and interests;

(2)   The standards the board of directors has adopted to measure the corporation's progress in promoting such public benefit or public benefits and interests;

(3)   Objective factual information based on those standards regarding the corporation's success in meeting the objectives for promoting such public benefit or public benefits and interests; and

(4)   An assessment of the corporation's success in meeting the objectives and promoting such public benefit or public benefits and interests.

(c)   The certificate of incorporation or bylaws of a public benefit corporation may require that the corporation:

(1)   Provide the statement described in subsection (b) of this section more frequently than biennially;

(2)   Make the statement described in subsection (b) of this section available to the public; and/or

(3)   Use a third party standard in connection with and/or attain a periodic third party certification addressing the corporation's promotion of the public benefit or public benefits

identified in the certificate of incorporation and/or the best interests of those materially affected by the corporation's conduct.

§ 367. Derivative Suits

Stockholders of a public benefit corporation owning individually or collectively, as of the date of instituting such derivative suit, at least 2% of the corporation's outstanding shares or, in the case of a corporation with shares listed on a national securities exchange, the lesser of such percentage or shares of at $2,000,000 in market value, may maintain a derivative lawsuit to enforce the requirements set forth in § 365(a) of this title.

§ 368. No Effect on Other Corporations

This subchapter shall not affect a statute or rule of law that is applicable to a corporation that is not a public benefit corporation, except as provided in § 363 of this title.

§ 371. Definition; Qualification to Do Business in State; Procedure

(a)   As used in this chapter, the words "foreign corporation" mean a corporation organized under the laws of any jurisdiction other than this State.

(b)   No foreign corporation shall do any business in this State, through or by branch offices, agents or representatives located in this State, until it shall have paid to the Secretary of State of this State for the use of this State, $80, and shall have filed in the office of the Secretary of State:

(1)   A certificate, as of a date not earlier than 6 months prior to the filing date, issued by an authorized officer of the jurisdiction of its incorporation evidencing its corporate existence. If such certificate is in a foreign language, a translation thereof, under oath of the translator, shall be attached thereto;

(2)   A statement executed by an authorized officer of each corporation setting forth (i) the name and address of its registered agent in this State, which agent may be any of the foreign corporation itself, an individual resident in this State, a domestic corporation, a domestic partnership (whether general (including a limited liability partnership) or limited (including a limited liability limited partnership)), a domestic limited liability company, a domestic statutory trust, a foreign corporation (other than the foreign corporation itself), a foreign partnership (whether general (including a limited liability partnership) or limited (including a limited liability limited partnership)), a foreign limited liability company or a foreign statutory trust, (ii) a statement, as of a date not earlier than 6 months prior to the filing date, of the assets and liabilities of the corporation, and (iii) the business it proposes to do in this State, and a statement that it is authorized to do that business in the jurisdiction of its incorporation. The statement shall be acknowledged in accordance with § 103 of this title.

(c)   The certificate of the Secretary of State, under seal of office, of the filing of the certificates required by subsection (b) of this section, shall be delivered to the registered agent upon the payment to the Secretary of State of the fee prescribed for such certificates, and the certificate shall be prima facie evidence of the right of the corporation to do business in this State; provided, that the Secretary of State shall not issue such certificate unless the name of the corporation is such as to distinguish it upon the records in the office of the Division of Corporations in the Department of State from the names that are reserved on such records and from the names on such records of each other corporation, partnership, limited partnership, limited liability company or statutory trust organized or registered as a domestic or foreign corporation, partnership, limited partnership, limited liability company or statutory trust under the laws of this State, except with the written consent of the person who has reserved such name or such other corporation, partnership, limited partnership, limited liability company or statutory trust, executed, acknowledged and filed with the Secretary of State in accordance with § 103 of this title. If the name of the foreign corporation conflicts with the name of a corporation, partnership, limited partnership, limited liability company or statutory trust organized under the laws of this State, or a name reserved for a corporation, partnership, limited partnership, limited liability company or statutory trust to be organized under the laws of this State, or a name reserved or registered as that of a foreign corporation, partnership, limited partnership, limited liability company or statutory trust under the laws of this State, the foreign corporation may qualify to do business if it adopts an assumed name which shall be used when doing business in this State as long as the assumed name is authorized for use by this section.

§ 372. Additional Requirements in Case of Change of Name, Change of Business Purpose or Merger or Consolidation

(a) Every foreign corporation admitted to do business in this State which shall change its corporate name, or enlarge, limit or otherwise change the business which it proposes to do in this State, shall, within 30 days after the time said change becomes effective, file with the Secretary of State a certificate, which shall set forth:

(1) The name of the foreign corporation as it appears on the records of the Secretary of State of this State;

(2) The jurisdiction of its incorporation;

(3) The date it was authorized to do business in this State;

(4) If the name of the foreign corporation has been changed, a statement of the name relinquished, a statement of the new name and a statement that the change of name has been effected under the laws of the jurisdiction of its incorporation and the date the change was effected;

(5) If the business it proposes to do in this State is to be enlarged, limited or otherwise changed, a statement reflecting such change and a statement that it is authorized to do in the jurisdiction of its incorporation the business which it proposes to do in this State.

(b) Whenever a foreign corporation authorized to transact business in this State shall be the survivor of a merger permitted by the laws of the state or country in which it is incorporated, it shall, within 30 days after the merger becomes effective, file a certificate, issued by the proper officer of the state or country of its incorporation, attesting to the occurrence of such event. If the merger has changed the corporate name of such foreign corporation or has enlarged, limited or otherwise changed the business it proposes to do in this State, it shall also comply with subsection (a) of this section.

(c) Whenever a foreign corporation authorized to transact business in this State ceases to exist because of a statutory merger or consolidation, it shall comply with § 381 of this title.

(d) The Secretary of State shall be paid, for the use of the State, $50 for filing and indexing each certificate required by subsection (a) or (b) of this section, and in the event of a change of name an additional $50 shall be paid for a certificate to be issued as evidence of filing the change of name.

§ 373. Exceptions to Requirements

(a) No foreign corporation shall be required to comply with §§ 371 and 372 of this title, under any of the following conditions:

(1) If it is in the mail order or a similar business, merely receiving orders by mail or otherwise in pursuance of letters, circulars, catalogs or other forms of advertising, or solicitation, accepting the orders outside this State, and filling them with goods shipped into this State;

(2) If it employs salespersons, either resident or traveling, to solicit orders in this State, either by display of samples or otherwise (whether or not maintaining sales offices in this State), all orders being subject to approval at the offices of the corporation without this State, and all goods applicable to the orders being shipped in pursuance thereof from without this State to the vendee or to the seller or such seller's agent for delivery to the vendee, and if any samples kept

within this State are for display or advertising purposes only, and no sales, repairs or replacements are made from stock on hand in this State;

(3) If it sells, by contract consummated outside this State, and agrees, by the contract, to deliver into this State, machinery, plants or equipment, the construction, erection or installation of which within this State requires the supervision of technical engineers or skilled employees performing services not generally available, and as a part of the contract of sale agrees to furnish such services, and such services only, to the vendee at the time of construction, erection or installation;

(4) If its business operations within this State, although not falling within the terms of paragraphs (a)(1), (2) and (3) of this section or any of them, are nevertheless wholly interstate in character;

(5) If it is an insurance company doing business in this State;

(6) If it creates, as borrower or lender, or acquires, evidences of debt, mortgages or liens on real or personal property;

(7) If it secures or collects debts or enforces any rights in property securing the same.

(b) This section shall have no application to the question of whether any foreign corporation is subject to service of process and suit in this State under § 382 of this title or any other law of this State.

§ 374. Annual Report

Annually on or before June 30, a foreign corporation doing business in this State shall file a report with the Secretary of State. The report shall be made on a form designated by the Secretary of State and shall be signed by the corporation's president, secretary, treasurer or other proper officer duly authorized so to act, or by any of its directors, or if filing an initial report by any incorporator in the event its board of directors shall not have been elected. The fact that an individual's name is signed on a certification attached to a corporate report shall be prima facie evidence that such individual is authorized to certify the report on behalf of the corporation; however the official title or position of the individual signing the corporate report shall be designated. The report shall contain the following information:

(1) The location of its registered office in this State, which shall include the street, number, city and postal code;

(2) The name of the agent upon whom service of process against the corporation may be served;

(3) The location of the principal place of business of the corporation, which shall include the street, number, city, state or foreign country; and

(4) The names and addresses of all the directors as of the filing date of the report and the name and address of the officer who signs the report.

If any officer or director of a foreign corporation required to file an annual report with the Secretary of State shall knowingly make any false statement in the report, such officer or director shall be guilty of perjury.

§ 375. Failure to File Report

Upon the failure, neglect or refusal of any foreign corporation to file an annual report as required by § 374 of this title, the Secretary of State may, in the Secretary of State's discretion, investigate the reasons therefor and shall terminate the right of the foreign corporation to do business within this State upon failure of the corporation to file an annual report within any 2-year period.

§ 376. Service of Process Upon Qualified Foreign Corporations

(a) All process issued out of any court of this State, all orders made by any court of this State, all rules and notices of any kind required to be served on any foreign corporation which has qualified to do business in this State may be served on the registered agent of the corporation designated in accordance with § 371 of this title, or, if there be no such agent, then on any officer, director or other agent of the corporation then in this State.

(b) In case the officer whose duty it is to serve legal process cannot by due diligence serve the process in any manner provided for by subsection (a) of this section, it shall be lawful to serve the process against the corporation upon the Secretary of State, and such service shall be as effectual for all intents and purposes as if made in any of the ways provided for in subsection (a) of this section. Process may be served upon the Secretary of State under this subsection by means of electronic transmission but only as prescribed by the Secretary of State. The Secretary of State is authorized to issue such rules and regulations with respect to such service as the Secretary of State deems necessary or appropriate. In the event that service is effected through the Secretary of State in accordance with this subsection, the Secretary of State shall forthwith notify the corporation by letter, directed to the corporation at its principal place of business as it appears on the last annual report filed pursuant to § 374 of this title or, if no such address appears, at its last registered office. Such letter shall be sent by a mail or courier service that includes a record of mailing or deposit with the courier and a record of delivery evidenced by the signature of the recipient. Such letter shall enclose a copy of the process and any other papers served upon the Secretary of State pursuant to this subsection. It shall be the duty of the plaintiff in the event of such service to serve process and any other papers in duplicate, to notify the Secretary of State that service is being effected pursuant to this subsection, and to pay the Secretary of State the sum of $50 for the use of the State, which sum shall be taxed as a part of the costs in the proceeding if the plaintiff shall prevail therein. The Secretary of State shall maintain an alphabetical record of any such service setting forth the name of the plaintiff and the defendant, the title, docket number and nature of the proceeding in which process has been served upon the Secretary of State, the fact that service has been effected pursuant to this subsection, the return date thereof, and the day and hour when the service was made. The Secretary of State shall not be required to retain such information for a period longer than 5 years from receipt of such service.

§ 377. Change of Registered Agent

(a) Any foreign corporation, which has qualified to do business in this State, may change its registered agent and substitute another registered agent by filing a certificate with the Secretary of State, acknowledged in accordance with § 103 of this title, setting forth:

(1) The name and address of its registered agent designated in this State upon whom process directed to said corporation may be served; and

(2) A revocation of all previous appointments of agent for such purposes.

Such registered agent shall comply with § 371(b)(2)(i) of this title.

(b) Any individual or entity designated by a foreign corporation as its registered agent for service of process may resign by filing with the Secretary of State a signed statement that the registered agent is unwilling to continue to act as the registered agent of the corporation for service of process, including in the statement the post-office address of the main or headquarters office of the foreign corporation, but such resignation shall not become effective until 30 days after the statement is filed. The statement shall be acknowledged by the registered agent and shall contain a representation that written notice of resignation was given to the corporation at least 30 days prior to the filing of the statement by mailing or delivering such notice to the corporation at its address given in the statement.

(c) If any agent designated and certified as required by § 371 of this title shall die or remove from this State, or resign, then the foreign corporation for which the agent had been so designated and certified shall, within 10 days after the death, removal or resignation of its agent, substitute, designate and certify to the Secretary of State, the name of another registered agent for the purposes of this subchapter, and all process, orders, rules and notices mentioned in § 376 of this title may be served on or given to the substituted agent with like effect as is prescribed in that section.

(d)   A foreign corporation whose qualification to do business in this State has been forfeited pursuant to § 132(f)(4) or § 136(b) of this title may be reinstated by filing a certificate of reinstatement with the Secretary of State, acknowledged in accordance with § 103 of this title, setting forth:

(1)   The name of the foreign corporation;

(2)   The effective date of the forfeiture; and

(3)   The name and address of the foreign corporation's registered agent required to be maintained by § 132 of this title.

(e)   Upon the filing of a certificate of reinstatement in accordance with subsection (d) of this section, the qualification of the foreign corporation to do business in this State shall be reinstated with the same force and effect as if it had not been forfeited pursuant to this title.

§ 378.   Penalties for Noncompliance

Any foreign corporation doing business of any kind in this State without first having complied with any section of this subchapter applicable to it, shall be fined not less than $200 nor more than $500 for each such offense. Any agent of any foreign corporation that shall do any business in this State for any foreign corporation before the foreign corporation has complied with any section of this subchapter applicable to it, shall be fined not less than $100 nor more than $500 for each such offense.

§ 379.   Banking Powers Denied

(a)   No foreign corporation shall, within the limits of this State, by any implication or construction, be deemed to possess the power of discounting bills, notes or other evidence of debt, of receiving deposits, of buying and selling bills of exchange, or of issuing bills, notes or other evidences of debt upon loan for circulation as money, anything in its charter or articles of incorporation to the contrary notwithstanding, except as otherwise provided in subchapter VII of Chapter 7 or in Chapter 14 of Title 5.

(b)   All certificates issued by the Secretary of State under § 371 of this title shall expressly set forth the limitations and restrictions contained in this section.

§ 380.   Foreign Corporation as Fiduciary in This State

A corporation organized and doing business under the laws of the District of Columbia or of any state of the United States other than Delaware, duly authorized by its certificate of incorporation or bylaws so to act, may be appointed by any last will and testament or other testamentary writing, probated within this State, or by a deed of trust, mortgage or other agreement, as executor, guardian, trustee or other fiduciary, and may act as such within this State, when and to the extent that the laws of the District of Columbia or of the state in which the foreign corporation is organized confer like powers upon corporations organized and doing business under the laws of this State.

§ 381.   Withdrawal of Foreign Corporation From State; Procedure; Service of Process on Secretary of State

(a)   Any foreign corporation which shall have qualified to do business in this State under § 371 of this title, may surrender its authority to do business in this State and may withdraw therefrom by filing with the Secretary of State:

(1)   A certificate executed in accordance with § 103 of this title, stating that it surrenders its authority to transact business in the state and withdraws therefrom; and stating the address

to which the Secretary of State may mail any process against the corporation that may be served upon the Secretary of State, or

(2)   A copy of an order or decree of dissolution made by any court of competent jurisdiction or other competent authority of the State or other jurisdiction of its incorporation, certified to be a true copy under the hand of the clerk of the court or other official body, and the official seal of the court or official body or clerk thereof, together with a certificate executed in accordance with paragraph (a)(1) of this section, stating the address to which the Secretary of State may mail any process against the corporation that may be served upon the Secretary of State.

(b)   The Secretary of State shall, upon payment to the Secretary of State of the fees prescribed in § 391 of this title, issue a sufficient number of certificates, under the Secretary of State's hand and official seal, evidencing the surrender of the authority of the corporation to do business in this State and its withdrawal therefrom. One of the certificates shall be furnished to the corporation withdrawing and surrendering its right to do business in this State.

(c)   Upon the issuance of the certificates by the Secretary of State, the appointment of the registered agent of the corporation in this State, upon whom process against the corporation may be served, shall be revoked, and the corporation shall be deemed to have consented that service of process in any action, suit or proceeding based upon any cause of action arising in this State, during the time the corporation was authorized to transact business in this State, may thereafter be made by service upon the Secretary of State. Process may be served upon the Secretary of State under this subsection by means of electronic transmission but only as prescribed by the Secretary of State. The Secretary of State is authorized to issue such rules and regulations with respect to such service as the Secretary of State deems necessary or appropriate.

(d)   In the event of service upon the Secretary of State in accordance with subsection (c) of this section, the Secretary of State shall forthwith notify the corporation by letter, directed to the corporation at the address stated in the certificate which was filed by the corporation with the Secretary of State pursuant to subsection (a) of this section. Such letter shall be sent by a mail or courier service that includes a record of mailing or deposit with the courier and a record of delivery evidenced by the signature of the recipient. Such letter shall enclose a copy of the process and any other papers served upon the Secretary of State. It shall be the duty of the plaintiff in the event of such service to serve process and any other papers in duplicate, to notify the Secretary of State that service is being made pursuant to this subsection, and to pay the Secretary of State the sum of $50 for the use of the State, which sum shall be taxed as part of the cost of the action, suit or proceeding if the plaintiff shall prevail therein. The Secretary of State shall maintain an alphabetical record of such service setting forth the name of the plaintiff and defendant, the title, docket number and nature of the proceeding in which the process has been served upon the Secretary of State, the fact that service has been effected pursuant to this subsection, the return date thereof, and the day and hour when the service was made. The Secretary of State shall not be required to retain such information for a period longer than 5 years from receipt of the service of process.

§ 382.   Service of Process on Nonqualifying Foreign Corporations

(a)   Any foreign corporation which shall transact business in this State without having qualified to do business under § 371 of this title shall be deemed to have thereby appointed and constituted the Secretary of State of this State its agent for the acceptance of legal process in any civil action, suit or proceeding against it in any state or federal court in this State arising or growing out of any business transacted by it within this State. If any foreign corporation consents in writing to be subject to the jurisdiction of any state or federal court in this State for any civil action, suit or proceeding against it arising or growing out of any business or matter, and if the agreement or instrument setting forth such consent does not otherwise provide a manner of service of legal process in any such civil action, suit or proceeding against it, such foreign corporation shall be deemed to have thereby appointed and constituted the Secretary of State of this State its agent for the acceptance of legal process in any such civil action, suit or proceeding against it. The transaction of business in this State by such corporation and/or such consent by such corporation to the jurisdiction of any state or federal court in this State without provision for a manner of service of legal process shall be a signification of the agreement of such corporation that any process served upon the Secretary of State when so served shall be of the same legal force and validity as if served upon an authorized officer or agent personally within this State. Process may be served upon the Secretary of State under this subsection by means of electronic transmission but only as prescribed by the Secretary of State. The Secretary of State is authorized to issue such rules and regulations with respect to such service as the Secretary of State deems necessary or appropriate.

(b)   Section 373 of this title shall not apply in determining whether any foreign corporation is transacting business in this State within the meaning of this section; and "the transaction of business" or "business transacted in this State," by any such foreign corporation, whenever those words are used in this section, shall mean the course or practice of carrying on any business activities in this State, including, without limiting the generality of the foregoing, the solicitation of business or orders in this State. This section shall not apply to any insurance company doing business in this State.

(c)   In the event of service upon the Secretary of State in accordance with subsection (a) of this section, the Secretary of State shall forthwith notify the corporation thereof by letter, directed to the corporation at the address furnished to the Secretary of State by the plaintiff in such action, suit or proceeding. Such letter shall be sent by a mail or courier service that includes a record of mailing or deposit with the courier and a record of delivery evidenced by the signature of the recipient. Such letter shall enclose a copy of the process and any other papers served upon the Secretary of State. It shall be the duty of the plaintiff in the event of such service to serve process and any other papers in duplicate, to notify the Secretary of State that service is being made pursuant to this subsection, and to pay the Secretary of State the sum of $50 for the use of the State, which sum shall be taxed as a part of the costs in the proceeding if the plaintiff shall prevail therein. The Secretary of State shall maintain an alphabetical record of any such process setting forth the name of the plaintiff and defendant, the title, docket number and nature of the proceeding in which process has been served upon the Secretary of State, the fact that service has been effected pursuant to this subsection, the return date thereof, and the day and hour when the service was made. The Secretary of State shall not be required to retain such information for a period longer than 5 years from receipt of the service of process.

§ 383. Actions by and Against Unqualified Foreign Corporations

(a)   A foreign corporation which is required to comply with §§ 371 and 372 of this title and which has done business in this State without authority shall not maintain any action or special proceeding in this State unless and until such corporation has been authorized to do business in this State and has paid to the State all fees, penalties and franchise taxes for the years or parts thereof during which it did business in this State without authority. This prohibition shall not apply to any successor in interest of such foreign corporation.

(b)   The failure of a foreign corporation to obtain authority to do business in this State shall not impair the validity of any contract or act of the foreign corporation or the right of any other party to the contract to maintain any action or special proceeding thereon, and shall not prevent the foreign corporation from defending any action or special proceeding in this State.

§ 384. Foreign Corporations Doing Business Without Having Qualified; Injunctions

The Court of Chancery shall have jurisdiction to enjoin any foreign corporation, or any agent thereof, from transacting any business in this State if such corporation has failed to comply with any section of this subchapter applicable to it or if such corporation has secured a certificate of the Secretary of State under § 371 of this title on the basis of false or misleading representations. The Attorney General shall, upon the Attorney General's own motion or upon the relation of proper parties, proceed for this purpose by complaint in any county in which such corporation is doing business.

§ 385. Filing of Certain Instruments With Recorder of Deeds Not Required

No instrument that is required to be filed with the Secretary of State of this State by this subchapter need be filed with the Recorder of Deeds of any county of this State in order to comply with this subchapter.

§ 388. Domestication of Non-United States Entities

(a)   As used in this section, the term:

(1)   "Foreign jurisdiction" means any foreign country or other foreign jurisdiction (other than the United States, any state, the District of Columbia, or any possession or territory of the United States); and

(2)   "Non-United States entity" means a corporation, a limited liability company, a statutory trust, a business trust or association, a real estate investment trust, a common-law trust, or any other unincorporated business or entity, including a partnership (whether general (including a limited liability partnership) or limited (including a limited liability limited partnership)), formed, incorporated, created or that otherwise came into being under the laws of any foreign jurisdiction.

(b)   Any non-United States entity may become domesticated as a corporation in this State by complying with subsection (h) of this section and filing with the Secretary of State:

(1)   A certificate of corporate domestication which shall be executed in accordance with subsection (g) of this section and filed in accordance with § 103 of this title; and

(2)   A certificate of incorporation, which shall be executed, acknowledged and filed in accordance with § 103 of this title.

Each of the certificates required by this subsection (b) shall be filed simultaneously with the Secretary of State and, if such certificates are not to become effective upon their filing as permitted by § 103(d) of this title, then each such certificate shall provide for the same effective date or time in accordance with § 103(d) of this title.

(c)   The certificate of corporate domestication shall certify:

(1)   The date on which and jurisdiction where the non-United States entity was first formed, incorporated, created or otherwise came into being;

(2)   The name of the non-United States entity immediately prior to the filing of the certificate of corporate domestication;

(3)   The name of the corporation as set forth in its certificate of incorporation filed in accordance with subsection (b) of this section; and

(4)   The jurisdiction that constituted the seat, siege social or principal place of business or central administration of the non-United States entity, or any other equivalent thereto under applicable law, immediately prior to the filing of the certificate of corporate domestication; and

(5)   That the domestication has been approved in the manner provided for by the document, instrument, agreement or other writing, as the case may be, governing the internal affairs of the non-United States entity and the conduct of its business or by applicable non-Delaware law, as appropriate.

(d)   Upon the certificate of corporate domestication and the certificate of incorporation becoming effective in accordance with § 103 of this title, the non-United States entity shall be domesticated as a corporation in this State and the corporation shall thereafter be subject to all of the provisions of this title, except that notwithstanding § 106 of this title, the existence of the corporation shall be deemed to have commenced on the date the non-United States entity commenced its existence in the jurisdiction in which the non-United States entity was first formed, incorporated, created or otherwise came into being.

(e) The domestication of any non-United States entity as a corporation in this State shall not be deemed to affect any obligations or liabilities of the non-United States entity incurred prior to its domestication as a corporation in this State, or the personal liability of any person therefor.

(f) The filing of a certificate of corporate domestication shall not affect the choice of law applicable to the non-United States entity, except that, from the effective time of the domestication, the law of the State of Delaware, including this title, shall apply to the non-United States entity to the same extent as if the non-United States entity had been incorporated as a corporation of this State on that date.

(g) The certificate of corporate domestication shall be signed by any person who is authorized to sign the certificate of corporate domestication on behalf of the non-United States entity.

(h) Prior to the filing of a certificate of corporate domestication with the Secretary of State, the domestication shall be approved in the manner provided for by the document, instrument, agreement or other writing, as the case may be, governing the internal affairs of the non-United States entity and the conduct of its business or by applicable non-Delaware law, as appropriate, and the certificate of incorporation shall be approved by the same authorization required to approve the domestication.

(i) When a non-United States entity has become domesticated as a corporation pursuant to this section, for all purposes of the laws of the State of Delaware, the corporation shall be deemed to be the same entity as the domesticating non-United States entity and the domestication shall constitute a continuation of the existence of the domesticating non-United States entity in the form of a corporation of this State. When any domestication shall have become effective under this section, for all purposes of the laws of the State of Delaware, all of the rights, privileges and powers of the non-United States entity that has been domesticated, and all property, real, personal and mixed, and all debts due to such non-United States entity, as well as all other things and causes of action belonging to such non-United States entity, shall remain vested in the corporation to which such non-United States entity has been domesticated (and also in the non-United States entity, if and for so long as the non-United States entity continues its existence in the foreign jurisdiction in which it was existing immediately prior to the domestication) and shall be the property of such corporation (and also of the non-United States entity, if and for so long as the non-United States entity continues its existence in the foreign jurisdiction in which it was existing immediately prior to the domestication), and the title to any real property vested by deed or otherwise in such non-United States entity shall not revert or be in any way impaired by reason of this title; but all rights of creditors and all liens upon any property of such non-United States entity shall be preserved unimpaired, and all debts, liabilities and duties of the non-United States entity that has been domesticated shall remain attached to the corporation to which such non-United States entity has been domesticated (and also to the non-United States entity, if and for so long as the non-United States entity continues its existence in the foreign jurisdiction in which it was existing immediately prior to the domestication), and may be enforced against it to the same extent as if said debts, liabilities and duties had originally been incurred or contracted by it in its capacity as such corporation. The rights, privileges, powers and interests in property of the non-United States entity, as well as the debts, liabilities and duties of the non-United States entity, shall not be deemed, as a consequence of the domestication, to have been transferred to the corporation to which such non-United States entity has domesticated for any purpose of the laws of the State of Delaware.

(j) Unless otherwise agreed or otherwise required under applicable non-Delaware law, the domesticating non-United States entity shall not be required to wind up its affairs or pay its liabilities and distribute its assets, and the domestication shall not be deemed to constitute a dissolution of such non-United States entity. If, following domestication, a non-United States entity that has become domesticated as a corporation of this State continues its existence in the foreign jurisdiction in which it was existing immediately prior to domestication, the corporation and such non-United States entity shall, for all purposes of the laws of the State of Delaware, constitute a single entity formed, incorporated, created or otherwise having come into being, as applicable, and existing under the laws of the State of Delaware and the laws of such foreign jurisdiction.

(k)   In connection with a domestication under this section, shares of stock, rights or securities of, or interests in, the non-United States entity that is to be domesticated as a corporation of this State may be exchanged for or converted into cash, property, or shares of stock, rights or securities of such corporation or, in addition to or in lieu thereof, may be exchanged for or converted into cash, property, or shares of stock, rights or securities of, or interests in, another corporation or other entity or may be cancelled.

§ 389.   Temporary Transfer of Domicile Into This State

(a)   As used in this section:

(1)   The term "emergency condition" shall be deemed to include but not be limited to any of the following:

   a.   War or other armed conflict;

   b.   Revolution or insurrection;

   c.   Invasion or occupation by foreign military forces;

   d.   Rioting or civil commotion of an extended nature;

   e.   Domination by a foreign power;

   f.   Expropriation, nationalization or confiscation of a material part of the assets or property of the non-United States entity;

   g.   Impairment of the institution of private property (including private property held abroad);

   h.   The taking of any action under the laws of the United States whereby persons resident in the jurisdiction, the law of which governs the internal affairs of the non-United States entity, might be treated as "enemies" or otherwise restricted under laws of the United States relating to trading with enemies of the United States;

   i.   The immediate threat of any of the foregoing; and

   j.   Such other event which, under the law of the jurisdiction governing the internal affairs of the non-United States entity, permits the non-United States entity to transfer its domicile.

(2)   The term "foreign jurisdiction" and the term "non-United States entity" shall have the same meanings as set forth in § 388(a) of this title.

(3)   The terms "officers" and "directors" include, in addition to such persons, trustees, managers, partners and all other persons performing functions equivalent to those of officers and directors, however named or described in any relevant instrument.

(b)   Any non-United States entity may, subject to and upon compliance with this section, transfer its domicile (which term, as used in this section, shall be deemed to refer in addition to the seat, siege social or principal place of business or central administration of such entity, or any other equivalent thereto under applicable law) into this State, and may perform the acts described in this section, so long as the law by which the internal affairs of such entity are governed does not expressly prohibit such transfer.

(c)   Any non-United States entity that shall propose to transfer its domicile into this State shall submit to the Secretary of State for the Secretary of State's review, at least 30 days prior to the proposed transfer of domicile, the following:

(1)   A copy of its certificate of incorporation and bylaws (or the equivalent thereof under applicable law), certified as true and correct by the appropriate director, officer or government official;

(2)   A certificate issued by an authorized official of the jurisdiction the law of which governs the internal affairs of the non-United States entity evidencing its existence;

(3)   A list indicating the person or persons who, in the event of a transfer pursuant to this section, shall be the authorized officers and directors of the non-United States entity, together with evidence of their authority to act and their respective executed agreements in writing regarding service of process as set out in subsection (j) of this section;

(4)   A certificate executed by the appropriate officer or director of the non-United States entity, setting forth:

> a.   The name and address of its registered agent in this State;
>
> b.   A general description of the business in which it is engaged;
>
> c.   That the filing of such certificate has been duly authorized by any necessary action and does not violate the certificate of incorporation or bylaws (or equivalent thereof under applicable law) or any material agreement or instrument binding on such entity;
>
> d.   A list indicating the person or persons authorized to sign the written communications required by subsection (e) of this section;
>
> e.   An affirmance that such transfer is not expressly prohibited under the law by which the internal affairs of the non-United States entity are governed; and
>
> f.   An undertaking that any transfer of domicile into this State will take place only in the event of an emergency condition in the jurisdiction the law of which governs the internal affairs of the non-United States entity and that such transfer shall continue only so long as such emergency condition, in the judgment of the non-United States entity's management, so requires; and

(5)   The examination fee prescribed under § 391 of this title.

If any of the documents referred to in paragraphs (c)(1)–(5) of this section are not in English, a translation thereof, under oath of the translator, shall be attached thereto. If such documents satisfy the requirements of this section, and if the name of the non-United States entity meets the requirements of § 102(a)(1) of this title, the Secretary of State shall notify the non-United States entity that such documents have been accepted for filing, and the records of the Secretary of State shall reflect such acceptance and such notification. In addition, the Secretary of State shall enter the name of the non-United States entity on the Secretary of State's reserved list to remain there so long as the non-United States entity is in compliance with this section. No document submitted under this subsection shall be available for public inspection pursuant to Chapter 100 of Title 29 until, and unless, such entity effects a transfer of its domicile as provided in this section. The Secretary of State may waive the 30-day period and translation requirement provided for in this subsection upon request by such entity, supported by facts (including, without limitation, the existence of an emergency condition) justifying such waiver.

(d)   On or before March 1 in each year, prior to the transfer of its domicile as provided for in subsection (e) of this section, during any such transfer and, in the event that it desires to continue to be subject to a transfer of domicile under this section, after its domicile has ceased to be in this State, the non-United States entity shall file a certificate executed by an appropriate officer or director of the non-United States entity, certifying that the documents submitted pursuant to this section remain in full force and effect or attaching any amendments or supplements thereto and translated as required in subsection (c) of this section, together with the filing fee prescribed under § 391 of this title. In the event that any non-United States entity fails to file the required certificate on or before March 1 in each year, all certificates and filings made pursuant to this section shall become null and void on

March 2 in such year, and any proposed transfer thereafter shall be subject to all of the required submissions and the examination fee set forth in subsection (c) of this section.

(e)   If the Secretary of State accepts the documents submitted pursuant to subsection (c) of this section for filing, such entity may transfer its domicile to this State at any time by means of a written communication to such effect addressed to the Secretary of State, signed by 1 of the persons named on the list filed pursuant to paragraph (c)(4)d. of this section, and confirming that the statements made pursuant to paragraph (c)(4) of this section remain true and correct; provided, that if emergency conditions have affected ordinary means of communication, such notification may be made by telegram, telex, telecopy or other form of writing so long as a duly signed duplicate is received by the Secretary of State within 30 days thereafter. The records of the Secretary of State shall reflect the fact of such transfer. Upon the payment to the Secretary of State of the fee prescribed under § 391 of this title, the Secretary of State shall certify that the non-United States entity has filed all documents and paid all fees required by this title. Such certificate of the Secretary of State shall be prima facie evidence of transfer by such non-United States entity of its domicile into this State.

(f)   Except to the extent expressly prohibited by the laws of this State, from and after the time that a non-United States entity transfers its domicile to this State pursuant to this section, the non-United States entity shall have all of the powers which it had immediately prior to such transfer under the law of the jurisdiction governing its internal affairs and the directors and officers designated pursuant to paragraph (c)(3) of this section, and their successors, may manage the business and affairs of the non-United States entity in accordance with the laws of such jurisdiction. Any such activity conducted pursuant to this section shall not be deemed to be doing business within this State for purposes of § 371 of this title. Any reference in this section to the law of the jurisdiction governing the internal affairs of a non-United States entity which has transferred its domicile into this State shall be deemed to be a reference to such law as in effect immediately prior to the transfer of domicile.

(g)   For purposes of any action in the courts of this State, no non-United States entity which has obtained the certificate of the Secretary of State referred to in subsection (e) of this section shall be deemed to be an "enemy" person or entity for any purpose, including, without limitation, in relation to any claim of title to its assets, wherever located, or to its ability to institute suit in said courts.

(h)   The transfer by any non-United States entity of its domicile into this State shall not be deemed to affect any obligations or liabilities of such non-United States entity incurred prior to such transfer.

(i)   The directors of any non-United States entity which has transferred its domicile into this State may withhold from any holder of equity interests in such entity any amounts payable to such holder on account of dividends or other distributions, if the directors shall determine that such holder will not have the full benefit of such payment, so long as the directors shall make provision for the retention of such withheld payment in escrow or under some similar arrangement for the benefit of such holder.

(j)   All process issued out of any court of this State, all orders made by any court of this State and all rules and notices of any kind required to be served on any non-United States entity which has transferred its domicile into this State may be served on the non-United States entity pursuant to § 321 of this title in the same manner as if such entity were a corporation of this State. The directors of a non-United States entity which has transferred its domicile into this State shall agree in writing that they will be amenable to service of process by the same means as, and subject to the jurisdiction of the courts of this State to the same extent as are directors of corporations of this State, and such agreements shall be submitted to the Secretary of State for filing before the respective directors take office.

(k)   Any non-United States entity which has transferred its domicile into this State may voluntarily return to the jurisdiction the law of which governs its internal affairs by filing with the Secretary of State an application to withdraw from this State. Such application shall be accompanied by a resolution of the directors of the non-United States entity authorizing such withdrawal and by a certificate of the highest diplomatic or consular official of such jurisdiction accredited to the United States indicating the consent of such jurisdiction to such withdrawal. The application shall also contain, or be accompanied by, the agreement of the non-United States entity that it may be served with process in this State in any proceeding for enforcement of any obligation of the non-United States entity arising prior to its withdrawal from this State, which agreement shall include the appointment of the Secretary of State as the agent of the non-United States entity to accept service of process in any such proceeding and shall specify the address to which a copy of process served upon the Secretary of State shall be mailed. Upon the payment of any fees and taxes owed to this State, the Secretary of State shall file the application and the non-United States entity's domicile shall, as of the time of filing, cease to be in this State.

§ 390.   Transfer, Domestication or Continuance of Domestic Corporations

(a)   Upon compliance with the provisions of this section, any corporation existing under the laws of this State may transfer to or domesticate or continue in any foreign jurisdiction and, in connection therewith, may elect to continue its existence as a corporation of this State. As used in this section, the term:

(1)   "Foreign jurisdiction" means any foreign country, or other foreign jurisdiction (other than the United States, any state, the District of Columbia, or any possession or territory of the United States); and

(2)   "Resulting entity" means the entity formed, incorporated, created or otherwise coming into being as a consequence of the transfer of the corporation to, or its domestication or continuance in, a foreign jurisdiction pursuant to this section.

(b)   The board of directors of the corporation which desires to transfer to or domesticate or continue in a foreign jurisdiction shall adopt a resolution approving such transfer, domestication or continuance specifying the foreign jurisdiction to which the corporation shall be transferred or in which the corporation shall be domesticated or continued and, if applicable, that in connection with such transfer, domestication or continuance the corporation's existence as a corporation of this State is to continue and recommending the approval of such transfer or domestication or continuance by the stockholders of the corporation. Such resolution shall be submitted to the stockholders of the corporation at an annual or special meeting. Due notice of the time, place and purpose of the meeting shall be mailed to each holder of stock, whether voting or nonvoting, of the corporation at the address of the stockholder as it appears on the records of the corporation, at least 20 days prior to the date of the meeting. At the meeting, the resolution shall be considered and a vote taken for its adoption or rejection. If all outstanding shares of stock of the corporation, whether voting or nonvoting, shall be voted for the adoption of the resolution, the corporation shall file with the Secretary of State a certificate of transfer if its existence as a corporation of this State is to cease or a certificate of transfer and domestic continuance if its existence as a corporation of this State is to continue, executed in accordance with § 103 of this title, which certifies:

(1)   The name of the corporation, and if it has been changed, the name under which it was originally incorporated.

(2)   The date of filing of its original certificate of incorporation with the Secretary of State.

(3)   The foreign jurisdiction to which the corporation shall be transferred or in which it shall be domesticated or continued and the name of the resulting entity.

(4)   That the transfer, domestication or continuance of the corporation has been approved in accordance with the provisions of this section.

(5)   In the case of a certificate of transfer, (i) that the existence of the corporation as a corporation of this State shall cease when the certificate of transfer becomes effective, and (ii) the agreement of the corporation that it may be served with process in this State in any proceeding for enforcement of any obligation of the corporation arising while it was a corporation of this State

which shall also irrevocably appoint the Secretary of State as its agent to accept service of process in any such proceeding and specify the address (which may not be that of the corporation's registered agent without the written consent of the corporation's registered agent, such consent to be filed along with the certificate of transfer) to which a copy of such process shall be mailed by the Secretary of State. Process may be served upon the Secretary of State under this subsection by means of electronic transmission but only as prescribed by the Secretary of State. The Secretary of State is authorized to issue such rules and regulations with respect to such service as the Secretary of State deems necessary or appropriate. In the event of service upon the Secretary of State in accordance with this subsection, the Secretary of State shall forthwith notify such corporation that has transferred out of the State of Delaware by letter, directed to such corporation that has transferred out of the State of Delaware at the address so specified, unless such corporation shall have designated in writing to the Secretary of State a different address for such purpose, in which case it shall be mailed to the last address designated. Such letter shall be sent by a mail or courier service that includes a record of mailing or deposit with the courier and a record of delivery evidenced by the signature of the recipient. Such letter shall enclose a copy of the process and any other papers served on the Secretary of State pursuant to this subsection. It shall be the duty of the plaintiff in the event of such service to serve process and any other papers in duplicate, to notify the Secretary of State that service is being effected pursuant to this subsection and to pay the Secretary of State the sum of $50 for the use of the State, which sum shall be taxed as part of the costs in the proceeding, if the plaintiff shall prevail therein. The Secretary of State shall maintain an alphabetical record of any such service setting forth the name of the plaintiff and the defendant, the title, docket number and nature of the proceeding in which process has been served, the fact that service has been effected pursuant to this subsection, the return date thereof, and the day and hour service was made. The Secretary of State shall not be required to retain such information longer than 5 years from receipt of the service of process.

(6)   In the case of a certificate of transfer and domestic continuance, that the corporation will continue to exist as a corporation of this State after the certificate of transfer and domestic continuance becomes effective.

(c)   Upon the filing of a certificate of transfer in accordance with subsection (b) of this section and payment to the Secretary of State of all fees prescribed under this title, the Secretary of State shall certify that the corporation has filed all documents and paid all fees required by this title, and thereupon the corporation shall cease to exist as a corporation of this State at the time the certificate of transfer becomes effective in accordance with § 103 of this title. Such certificate of the Secretary of State shall be prima facie evidence of the transfer, domestication or continuance by such corporation out of this State.

(d)   The transfer, domestication or continuance of a corporation out of this State in accordance with this section and the resulting cessation of its existence as a corporation of this State pursuant to a certificate of transfer shall not be deemed to affect any obligations or liabilities of the corporation incurred prior to such transfer, domestication or continuance, the personal liability of any person incurred prior to such transfer, domestication or continuance, or the choice of law applicable to the corporation with respect to matters arising prior to such transfer, domestication or continuance. Unless otherwise agreed or otherwise provided in the certificate of incorporation, the transfer, domestication or continuance of a corporation out of the State of Delaware in accordance with this section shall not require such corporation to wind up its affairs or pay its liabilities and distribute its assets under this title and shall not be deemed to constitute a dissolution of such corporation.

(e)   If a corporation files a certificate of transfer and domestic continuance, after the time the certificate of transfer and domestic continuance becomes effective, the corporation shall continue to exist as a corporation of this State, and the law of the State of Delaware, including this title, shall apply to the corporation to the same extent as prior to such time. So long as a corporation continues to exist as a corporation of the State of Delaware following the filing of a certificate of transfer and domestic continuance, the continuing corporation and the resulting entity shall, for all purposes of the laws of the State of Delaware, constitute a single entity formed, incorporated, created or otherwise having come into being, as applicable, and existing under the laws of the State of Delaware and the laws of the foreign jurisdiction.

(f)　When a corporation has transferred, domesticated or continued pursuant to this section, for all purposes of the laws of the State of Delaware, the resulting entity shall be deemed to be the same entity as the transferring, domesticating or continuing corporation and shall constitute a continuation of the existence of such corporation in the form of the resulting entity. When any transfer, domestication or continuance shall have become effective under this section, for all purposes of the laws of the State of Delaware, all of the rights, privileges and powers of the corporation that has transferred, domesticated or continued, and all property, real, personal and mixed, and all debts due to such corporation, as well as all other things and causes of action belonging to such corporation, shall remain vested in the resulting entity (and also in the corporation that has transferred, domesticated or continued, if and for so long as such corporation continues its existence as a corporation of this State) and shall be the property of such resulting entity (and also of the corporation that has transferred, domesticated or continued, if and for so long as such corporation continues its existence as a corporation of this State), and the title to any real property vested by deed or otherwise in such corporation shall not revert or be in any way impaired by reason of this title; but all rights of creditors and all liens upon any property of such corporation shall be preserved unimpaired, and all debts, liabilities and duties of such corporation shall remain attached to the resulting entity (and also to the corporation that has transferred, domesticated or continued, if and for so long as such corporation continues its existence as a corporation of this State), and may be enforced against it to the same extent as if said debts, liabilities and duties had originally been incurred or contracted by it in its capacity as such resulting entity. The rights, privileges, powers and interests in property of the corporation, as well as the debts, liabilities and duties of the corporation, shall not be deemed, as a consequence of the transfer, domestication or continuance, to have been transferred to the resulting entity for any purpose of the laws of the State of Delaware.

(g)　In connection with a transfer, domestication or continuance under this section, shares of stock of the transferring, domesticating or continuing corporation may be exchanged for or converted into cash, property, or shares of stock, rights or securities of, or interests in, the resulting entity or, in addition to or in lieu thereof, may be exchanged for or converted into cash, property, or shares of stock, rights or securities of, or interests in, another corporation or other entity or may be cancelled.

(h)　No vote of the stockholders of a corporation shall be necessary to authorize a transfer, domestication or continuance if no shares of the stock of such corporation shall have been issued prior to the adoption by the board of directors of the resolution approving the transfer, domestication or continuance.

(i)　Whenever it shall be desired to transfer to or domesticate or continue in any foreign jurisdiction any nonstock corporation, the governing body shall perform all the acts necessary to effect a transfer, domestication or continuance which are required by this section to be performed by the board of directors of a corporation having capital stock. If the members of a nonstock corporation are entitled to vote for the election of members of its governing body or are entitled under the certificate of incorporation or the bylaws of such corporation to vote on such transfer, domestication or continuance or on a merger, consolidation, or dissolution of the corporation, they, and any other holder of any membership interest in the corporation, shall perform all the acts necessary to effect a transfer, domestication or continuance which are required by this section to be performed by the stockholders of a corporation having capital stock. If there is no member entitled to vote thereon, nor any other holder of any membership interest in the corporation, the transfer, domestication or continuance of the corporation shall be authorized at a meeting of the governing body, upon the adoption of a resolution to transfer or domesticate or continue by the vote of a majority of members of its governing body then in office. In all other respects, the method and proceedings for the transfer, domestication or continuance of a nonstock corporation shall conform as nearly as may be to the proceedings prescribed by this section for the transfer, domestication or continuance of corporations having capital stock. In the case of a charitable nonstock corporation, due notice of the corporation's intent to effect a transfer, domestication or continuance shall be mailed to the Attorney General of the State of Delaware 10 days prior to the date of the proposed transfer, domestication or continuance.

§ 391. Amounts Payable to Secretary of State Upon Filing Certificate or Other Paper

(a) The following fees and penalties shall be collected by and paid to the Secretary of State, for the use of the State:

(1) Upon the receipt for filing of an original certificate of incorporation, the fee shall be computed on the basis of 2 cents for each share of authorized capital stock having par value up to and including 20,000 shares, 1 cent for each share in excess of 20,000 shares up to and including 200,000 shares, and 2/5 of a cent for each share in excess of 200,000 shares; 1 cent for each share of authorized capital stock without par value up to and including 20,000 shares, 1/2 of a cent for each share in excess of 20,000 shares up to and including 2,000,000 shares, and 2/5 of a cent for each share in excess of 2,000,000 shares. In no case shall the amount paid be less than $15. For the purpose of computing the fee on par value stock each $100 unit of the authorized capital stock shall be counted as 1 assessable share.

(2) Upon the receipt for filing of a certificate of amendment of certificate of incorporation, or a certificate of amendment of certificate of incorporation before payment of capital, or a restated certificate of incorporation, increasing the authorized capital stock of a corporation, the fee shall be an amount equal to the difference between the fee computed at the foregoing rates upon the total authorized capital stock of the corporation including the proposed increase, and the fee computed at the foregoing rates upon the total authorized capital stock excluding the proposed increase. In no case shall the amount paid be less than $30.

(3) Upon the receipt for filing of a certificate of amendment of certificate of incorporation before payment of capital and not involving an increase of authorized capital stock, or an amendment to the certificate of incorporation not involving an increase of authorized capital stock, or a restated certificate of incorporation not involving an increase of authorized capital stock, or a certificate of retirement of stock, the fee to be paid shall be $30. For all other certificates relating to corporations, not otherwise provided for, the fee to be paid shall be $5. In the case of exempt corporations no fee shall be paid under this paragraph.

(4) Upon the receipt for filing of a certificate of merger or consolidation of 2 or more corporations, the fee shall be an amount equal to the difference between the fee computed at the foregoing rates upon the total authorized capital stock of the corporation created by the merger or consolidation, and the fee so computed upon the aggregate amount of the total authorized capital stock of the constituent corporations. In no case shall the amount paid be less than $75. The foregoing fee shall be in addition to any tax or fee required under any other law of this State to be paid by any constituent entity that is not a corporation in connection with the filing of the certificate of merger or consolidation.

(5) Upon the receipt for filing of a certificate of dissolution, there shall be paid to and collected by the Secretary of State a fee of:

a. Forty dollars ($40); or

b. Ten dollars ($10) in the case of a certificate of dissolution which certifies that:

1. The corporation has no assets and has ceased transacting business; and

2. The corporation, for each year since its incorporation in this State, has been required to pay only the minimum franchise tax then prescribed by § 503 of this title; and

3. The corporation has paid all franchise taxes and fees due to or assessable by this State through the end of the year in which said certificate of dissolution is filed.

(6) Upon the receipt for filing of a certificate of reinstatement of a foreign corporation or a certificate of surrender and withdrawal from the State by a foreign corporation, there shall be collected by and paid to the Secretary of State a fee of $10.

(7) For receiving and filing and/or indexing any certificate, affidavit, agreement or any other paper provided for by this chapter, for which no different fee is specifically prescribed, a fee of $115 in each case shall be paid to the Secretary of State. The fee in the case of a certificate of incorporation filed as required by § 102 of this title shall be $25. For entering information from each instrument into the Delaware Corporation Information System in accordance with § 103(c)(8) of this title, the fee shall be $5.

    a.   A certificate of dissolution which meets the criteria stated in paragraph (a)(5)b. of this section shall not be subject to such fee; and

    b.   A certificate of incorporation filed in accordance with § 102 of this title shall be subject to a fee of $25.

(8) For receiving and filing and/or indexing the annual report of a foreign corporation doing business in this State, a fee of $125 shall be paid. In the event of neglect, refusal or failure on the part of any foreign corporation to file the annual report with the Secretary of State on or before June 30 each year, the corporation shall pay a penalty of $125.

(9) For recording and indexing articles of association and other papers required by this chapter to be recorded by the Secretary of State, a fee computed on the basis of 1 cent a line shall be paid.

(10) For certifying copies of any paper on file provided by this chapter, a fee of $50 shall be paid for each copy certified. In addition, a fee of $2 per page shall be paid in each instance where the Secretary of State provides the copies of the document to be certified.

(11) For issuing any certificate of the Secretary of State other than a certification of a copy under paragraph (a)(10) of this section, or a certificate that recites all of a corporation's filings with the Secretary of State, a fee of $50 shall be paid for each certificate. For issuing any certificate of the Secretary of State that recites all of a corporation's filings with the Secretary of State, a fee of $175 shall be paid for each certificate.

(12) For filing in the office of the Secretary of State any certificate of change of location or change of registered agent, as provided in § 133 of this title, there shall be collected by and paid to the Secretary of State a fee of $50, provided that no fee shall be charged pursuant to § 103(c)(6) and (c)(7) of this title.

(13) For filing in the office of the Secretary of State any certificate of change of address or change of name of registered agent, as provided in § 134 of this title, there shall be collected by and paid to the Secretary of State a fee of $50, plus the same fees for receiving, filing, indexing, copying and certifying the same as are charged in the case of filing a certificate of incorporation.

(14) For filing in the office of the Secretary of State any certificate of resignation of a registered agent and appointment of a successor, as provided in § 135 of this title, there shall be collected by and paid to the Secretary of State a fee of $50.

(15) For filing in the office of the Secretary of State, any certificate of resignation of a registered agent without appointment of a successor, as provided in §§ 136 and 377 of this title, there shall be collected by and paid to the Secretary of State a fee of $2 for each corporation whose registered agent has resigned by such certificate.

(16) For preparing and providing a written report of a record search, a fee of $50 shall be paid.

(17) For preclearance of any document for filing, a fee of $250 shall be paid.

(18) For receiving and filing and/or indexing an annual franchise tax report of a corporation provided for by § 502 of this title, a fee of $25 shall be paid by exempt corporations and a fee of $50 shall be paid by all other corporations.

(19) For receiving and filing and/or indexing by the Secretary of State of a certificate of domestication and certificate of incorporation prescribed in § 388(d) of this title, a fee of $165, plus the fee payable upon the receipt for filing of an original certificate of incorporation, shall be paid.

(20) For receiving, reviewing and filing and/or indexing by the Secretary of State of the documents prescribed in § 389(c) of this title, a fee of $10,000 shall be paid.

(21) For receiving, reviewing and filing and/or indexing by the Secretary of State of the documents prescribed in § 389(d) of this title, an annual fee of $2,500 shall be paid.

(22) Except as provided in this section, the fees of the Secretary of State shall be as provided for in § 2315 of Title 29.

(23) In the case of exempt corporations, the total fees payable to the Secretary of State upon the filing of a Certificate of Change of Registered Agent and/or Registered Office or a Certificate of Revival shall be $5 and such filings shall be exempt from any fees or assessments pursuant to the requirements of § 103(c)(6) and (c)(7) of this title.

(24) For accepting a corporate name reservation application, an application for renewal of a corporate name reservation, or a notice of transfer or cancellation of a corporate name reservation, there shall be collected by and paid to the Secretary of State a fee of up to $75.

(25) For receiving and filing and/or indexing by the Secretary of State of a certificate of transfer or a certificate of continuance prescribed in § 390 of this title, a fee of $1,000 shall be paid.

(26) For receiving and filing and/or indexing by the Secretary of State of a certificate of conversion and certificate of incorporation prescribed in § 265 of this title, a fee of $115, plus the fee payable upon the receipt for filing of an original certificate of incorporation, shall be paid.

(27) For receiving and filing and/or indexing by the Secretary of State of a certificate of conversion prescribed in § 266 of this title, a fee of $165 shall be paid.

(28) For receiving and filing and/or indexing by the Secretary of State of a certificate of validation prescribed in § 204 of this title, a fee of $2,500 shall be paid; provided, that if the certificate of validation has the effect of increasing the authorized capital stock of a corporation, an additional fee, calculated in accordance with paragraph (a)(2) of this section, shall also be paid.

(b)(1) For the purpose of computing the fee prescribed in paragraphs (a)(1), (2), (4) and (28) of this section the authorized capital stock of a corporation shall be considered to be the total number of shares which the corporation is authorized to issue, whether or not the total number of shares that may be outstanding at any 1 time be limited to a less number.

(2) For the purpose of computing the fee prescribed in paragraphs (a)(2), (3) and (28) of this section, a certificate of amendment of certificate of incorporation, or an amended certificate of incorporation before payment of capital, or a restated certificate of incorporation, or a certificate of validation, shall be considered as increasing the authorized capital stock of a corporation provided it involves an increase in the number of shares, or an increase in the par value of shares, or a change of shares with par value into shares without par value, or a change of shares without par value into shares with par value, or any combination of 2 or more of the above changes, and provided further that the fee computed at the rates set forth in paragraph (a)(1) of this section upon the total authorized capital stock of the corporation including the proposed change or changes exceeds the fee so computed upon the total authorized stock of the corporation excluding such change or changes.

(c)   The Secretary of State may issue photocopies or electronic image copies of instruments on file, as well as instruments, documents and other papers not on file, and for all such photocopies or electronic image copies which are not certified by the Secretary of State, a fee of $10 shall be paid for the first page and $2 for each additional page. Notwithstanding Delaware's Freedom of Information Act (Chapter 100 of Title 29) or any other provision of this law granting access to public records, the Secretary of State upon request shall issue only photocopies, or electronic image copies of public records in exchange for the fees described in this section, and in no case shall the Secretary of State be required to provide copies (or access to copies) of such public records (including without limitation bulk data, digital copies of instruments, documents and other papers, databases or other information) in an electronic medium or in any form other than photocopies or electronic image copies of such public records in exchange, as applicable, for the fees described in this section or § 2318 of Title 29 for each such record associated with a file number.

(d)   No fees for the use of the State shall be charged or collected from any corporation incorporated for the drainage and reclamation of lowlands or for the amendment or renewal of the charter of such corporation.

(e)   The Secretary of State may in the Secretary of State's discretion permit the extension of credit for the fees required by this section upon such terms as the Secretary of State shall deem to be appropriate.

(f)   The Secretary of State shall retain from the revenue collected from the fees required by this section a sum sufficient to provide at all times a fund of at least $500, but not more than $1,500, from which the Secretary of State may refund any payment made pursuant to this section to the extent that it exceeds the fees required by this section. The fund shall be deposited in the financial institution which is the legal depository of state moneys to the credit of the Secretary of State and shall be disbursable on order of the Secretary of State.

(g)   Secretary of State may in the Secretary of State's discretion charge a fee of $60 for each check received for payment of any fee or tax under Chapter 1 or Chapter 6 of this title that is returned due to insufficient funds or as the result of a stop payment order.

(h)   In addition to those fees charged under subsections (a) and (c) of this section, there shall be collected by and paid to the Secretary of State the following:

(1)   For all services described in subsection (a) of this section that are requested to be completed within 30 minutes on the same day as the day of the request, an additional sum of up to $7,500 and for all services described in subsections (a) and (c) of this section that are requested to be completed within 1 hour on the same day as the day of the request, an additional sum of up to $1,000 and for all services described in subsections (a) and (c) of this section that are requested to be completed within 2 hours on the same day as the day of the request, an additional sum of up to $500; and

(2)   For all services described in subsections (a) and (c) of this section that are requested to be completed within the same day as the day of the request, an additional sum of up to $300; and

(3)   For all services described in subsections (a) and (c) of this section that are requested to be completed within a 24-hour period from the time of the request, an additional sum of up to $150.

The Secretary of State shall establish (and may from time to time alter or amend) a schedule of specific fees payable pursuant to this subsection.

(i)   A domestic corporation or a foreign corporation registered to do business in this State that files with the Secretary of State any instrument or certificate, and in connection therewith, neglects, refuses or fails to pay any fee or tax under Chapter 1 or Chapter 6 of this title shall, after written demand therefor by the Secretary of State by mail addressed to such domestic corporation or foreign corporation in care of its registered agent in this State, cease to be in good standing as a domestic corporation or registered as a foreign corporation in this State on the 90th day following the date of mailing of such demand, unless such fee or tax and, if applicable, the fee provided for in subsection (g) of this section are paid in full prior to the 90th day following the date of mailing of such demand. A domestic corporation that has ceased to be in good standing or a foreign corporation that has ceased to be registered by reason of the neglect, refusal or failure to pay any such fee or tax shall be restored to and have the status of a domestic corporation in good standing or a foreign corporation that is registered in this State upon the payment of the fee or tax which such domestic corporation or foreign corporation neglected, refused or failed to pay together with the fee provided for in subsection (g) of this section, if applicable. The Secretary of State shall not accept for filing any instrument authorized to be filed with the Secretary of State under this title in respect of any domestic corporation that is not in good standing or any foreign corporation that has ceased to be registered by reason of the neglect, refusal or failure to pay any such fee or tax, and shall not issue any certificate of good standing with respect to such domestic corporation or foreign corporation, unless and until such domestic corporation or foreign corporation shall have been restored to and have the status of a domestic corporation in good standing or a foreign corporation duly registered in this State.

(j)   As used in this section, the term "exempt corporation" shall have the meaning given to it in § 501(b) of this title.

§ 393. Rights, Liabilities and Duties Under Prior Statutes

All rights, privileges and immunities vested or accrued by and under any laws enacted prior to the adoption or amendment of this chapter, all suits pending, all rights of action conferred, and all duties, restrictions, liabilities and penalties imposed or required by and under laws enacted prior to the adoption or amendment of this chapter, shall not be impaired, diminished or affected by this chapter.

§ 394. Reserved Power of State to Amend or Repeal Chapter; Chapter Part of Corporation's Charter or Certificate of Incorporation

This chapter may be amended or repealed, at the pleasure of the General Assembly, but any amendment or repeal shall not take away or impair any remedy under this chapter against any corporation or its officers for any liability which shall have been previously incurred. This chapter and all amendments thereof shall be a part of the charter or certificate of incorporation of every corporation except so far as the same are inapplicable and inappropriate to the objects of the corporation.

§ 395. Corporations Using "Trust" in Name, Advertisements and Otherwise; Restrictions; Violations and Penalties; Exceptions

(a)   Except as provided below in subsection (d) of this section, every corporation of this State using the word "trust" as part of its name, except a corporation regulated under the Bank Holding Company Act of 1956, 12 U.S.C. § 1841 et seq., or § 10 of the Home Owners' Loan Act, 12 U.S.C. § 1467a et seq., as those statutes shall from time to time be amended, shall be under the supervision of the State Bank Commissioner of this State and shall make not less than 2 reports during each year to the Commissioner, according to the form which shall be prescribed by the Commissioner, verified by the oaths or affirmations of the president or vice-president, and the treasurer or secretary of the corporation, and attested by the signatures of at least 3 directors.

(b)   Except as provided below in subsection (d) of this section, no corporation of this State shall use the word "trust" as part of its name, except a corporation reporting to and under the supervision of the State Bank Commissioner of this State or a corporation regulated under the Bank Holding Company Act of 1956, 12 U.S.C. § 1841 et seq., or § 10 of the Home Owners' Loan Act, 12 U.S.C. § 1467a et seq., as those statutes shall from time to time be amended. Except as provided below in subsection (d) of this section, the name of any such corporation shall not be amended so as to include the word "trust" unless such corporation shall report to and be under the supervision of the

Commissioner, or unless it is regulated under the Bank Holding Company Act of 1956 or the Savings and Loan Holding Company Act.

(c)　No corporation of this State, except corporations reporting to and under the supervision of the State Bank Commissioner of this State or corporations regulated under the Bank Holding Company Act of 1956, 12 U.S.C. § 1841 et seq., or § 10 of the Home Owners' Loan Act, 12 U.S.C. § 1467a et seq., as those statutes shall from time to time be amended, shall advertise or put forth any sign as a trust company, or in any way solicit or receive deposits or transact business as a trust company.

(d)　The requirements and restrictions set forth above in subsections (a) and (b) of this section shall not apply to, and shall not be construed to prevent the use of the word "trust" as part of the name of, a corporation that is not subject to the supervision of the State Bank Commissioner of this State and that is not regulated under the Bank Holding Company Act of 1956, 12 U.S.C. § 1841 et seq., or § 10 of the Home Owners' Loan Act, 12 U.S.C. § 1467a et seq., where use of the word "trust" as part of such corporation's name clearly:

(1)　Does not refer to a trust business;

(2)　Is not likely to mislead the public into believing that the nature of the business of the corporation includes activities that fall under the supervision of the State Bank Commissioner of this State or that are regulated under the Bank Holding Company Act of 1956, 12 U.S.C. § 1841 et seq., or § 10 of the Home Owners' Loan Act, 12 U.S.C. § 1467a et seq.; and

(3)　Will not otherwise lead to a pattern and practice of abuse that might cause harm to the interests of the public or the State, as determined by the Director of the Division of Corporations and the State Bank Commissioner.

§ 396.　Publication of Chapter by Secretary of State; Distribution

The Secretary of State may have printed, from time to time as the Secretary of State deems necessary, pamphlet copies of this chapter, and the Secretary of State shall dispose of the copies to persons and corporations desiring the same for a sum not exceeding the cost of printing. The money received from the sale of the copies shall be disposed of as are other fees of the office of the Secretary of State. Nothing in this section shall prevent the free distribution of single pamphlet copies of this chapter by the Secretary of State, for the printing of which provision is made from time to time by joint resolution of the General Assembly.

§ 397.　Penalty for Unauthorized Publication of Chapter

Whoever prints or publishes this chapter without the authority of the Secretary of State of this State, shall be fined not more than $500 or imprisoned not more than 3 months, or both.

§ 398.　Short Title

This chapter shall be known and may be identified and referred to as the "General Corporation Law of the State of Delaware."

SECURITIES ACT OF 1933 (15 U.S.C. §§ 77a *et seq.*)—SELECTED PROVISIONS

Table of Sections

---

§ 2.   Definitions; Promotion of Efficiency, Competition, and Capital Formation

(a)   *Definitions.* When used in this subchapter, unless the context otherwise requires—

(1)   The term "security" means any note, stock, treasury stock, security future, security-based swap, bond, debenture, evidence of indebtedness, certificate of interest or participation in any profit-sharing agreement, collateral-trust certificate, preorganization certificate or subscription, transferable share, investment contract, voting-trust certificate, certificate of deposit for a security, fractional undivided interest in oil, gas, or other mineral rights, any put, call, straddle, option, or privilege on any security, certificate of deposit, or group or index of securities (including any interest therein or based on the value thereof), or any put, call, straddle, option, or privilege entered into on a national securities exchange relating to foreign currency, or, in general, any interest or instrument commonly known as a "security", or any certificate of interest or participation in, temporary or interim certificate for, receipt for, guarantee of, or warrant or right to subscribe to or purchase, any of the foregoing.

* * *

(3)   The term "sale" or "sell" shall include every contract of sale or disposition of a security or interest in a security, for value. The term "offer to sell", "offer for sale", or "offer" shall include every attempt or offer to dispose of, or solicitation of an offer to buy, a security or interest in a security, for value. The terms defined in this paragraph and the term "offer to buy" as used in subsection (c) of section 5 of this Act shall not include preliminary negotiations or agreements between an issuer (or any person directly or indirectly controlling or controlled by an issuer, or under direct or indirect common control with an issuer) and any underwriter or among underwriters who are or are to be in privity of contract with an issuer (or any person directly or indirectly controlling or controlled by an issuer, or under direct or indirect common control with an issuer). Any security given or delivered with, or as a bonus on account of, any purchase of securities or any other thing, shall be conclusively presumed to constitute a part of the subject of such purchase and to have been offered and sold for value. The issue or transfer of a right or privilege, when originally issued or transferred with a security, giving the holder of such security the right to convert such security into another security of the same issuer or of another person,

or giving a right to subscribe to another security of the same issuer or of another person, which right cannot be exercised until some future date, shall not be deemed to be an offer or sale of such other security; but the issue or transfer of such other security upon the exercise of such right of conversion or subscription shall be deemed a sale of such other security. Any offer or sale of a security futures product by or on behalf of the issuer of the securities underlying the security futures product, an affiliate of the issuer, or an underwriter, shall constitute a contract for sale of, sale of, offer for sale, or offer to sell the underlying securities. Any offer or sale of a security-based swap by or on behalf of the issuer of the securities upon which such security-based swap is based or is referenced, an affiliate of the issuer, or an underwriter, shall constitute a contract for sale of, sale of, offer for sale, or offer to sell such securities. The publication or distribution by a broker or dealer of a research report about an emerging growth company that is the subject of a proposed public offering of the common equity securities of such emerging growth company pursuant to a registration statement that the issuer proposes to file, or has filed, or that is effective shall be deemed for purposes of paragraph (10) of this subsection and section 5(c) of this title not to constitute an offer for sale or offer to sell a security, even if the broker or dealer is participating or will participate in the registered offering of the securities of the issuer. As used in this paragraph, the term "research report" means a written, electronic, or oral communication that includes information, opinions, or recommendations with respect to securities of an issuer or an analysis of a security or an issuer, whether or not it provides information reasonably sufficient upon which to base an investment decision.

(4) The term "issuer" means every person who issues or proposes to issue any security; except that with respect to certificates of deposit, voting-trust certificates, or collateral-trust certificates, or with respect to certificates of interest or shares in an unincorporated investment trust not having a board of directors (or persons performing similar functions) or of the fixed, restricted management, or unit type, the term "issuer" means the person or persons performing the acts and assuming the duties of depositor or manager pursuant to the provisions of the trust or other agreement or instrument under which such securities are issued; except that in the case of an unincorporated association which provides by its articles for limited liability of any or all of its members, or in the case of a trust, committee, or other legal entity, the trustees or members thereof shall not be individually liable as issuers of any security issued by the association, trust, committee, or other legal entity; except that with respect to equipment-trust certificates or like securities, the term "issuer" means the person by whom the equipment or property is or is to be used; and except that with respect to fractional undivided interests in oil, gas, or other mineral rights, the term "issuer" means the owner of any such right or of any interest in such right (whether whole or fractional) who creates fractional interests therein for the purpose of public offering.

* * *

(10) The term "prospectus" means any prospectus, notice, circular, advertisement, letter, or communication, written or by radio or television, which offers any security for sale or confirms the sale of any security; except that (a) a communication sent or given after the effective date of the registration statement (other than a prospectus permitted under subsection (b) of section 10 of this title) shall not be deemed a prospectus if it is proved that prior to or at the same time with such communication a written prospectus meeting the requirements of subsection (a) of section 10 of this title at the time of such communication was sent or given to the person to whom the communication was made, and (b) a notice, circular, advertisement, letter, or communication in respect of a security shall not be deemed to be a prospectus if it states from whom a written prospectus meeting the requirements of section 10 of this title may be obtained and, in addition, does no more than identify the security, state the price thereof, state by whom orders will be executed, and contain such other information as the Commission, by rules or regulations deemed necessary or appropriate in the public interest and for the protection of investors, and subject to such terms and conditions as may be prescribed therein, may permit.

* * *

(11) The term "underwriter" means any person who has purchased from an issuer with a view to, or offers or sells for an issuer in connection with, the distribution of any security, or participates or has a direct or indirect participation in any such undertaking, or participates or has a participation in the direct or indirect underwriting of any such undertaking; but such term shall not include a person whose interest is limited to a commission from an underwriter or dealer not in excess of the usual and customary distributors' or sellers' commission. As used in this paragraph the term "issuer" shall include, in addition to an issuer, any person directly or indirectly controlling or controlled by the issuer, or any person under direct or indirect common control with the issuer.

* * *

(15) The term "accredited investor" shall mean—

(i)   a bank as defined in section 3(a)(2) of this Act whether acting in its individual or fiduciary capacity; an insurance company as defined in paragraph (13) of this subsection; an investment company registered under the Investment Company Act of 1940 or a business development company as defined in section 2(a)(48) of that Act; a Small Business Investment Company licensed by the Small Business Administration; or an employee benefit plan, including an individual retirement account, which is subject to the provisions of the Employee Retirement Income Security Act of 1974, if the investment decision is made by a plan fiduciary, as defined in section 3(21) of such Act, which is either a bank, insurance company, or registered investment adviser; or

(ii)   any person who, on the basis of such factors as financial sophistication, net worth, knowledge, and experience in financial matters, or amount of assets under management qualifies as an accredited investor under rules and regulations which the Commission shall prescribe.

* * *

(17) The terms "swap" and "security-based swap" have the same meanings as in section 1a of Title 7.

(18) The terms "purchase" or "sale" of a security-based swap shall be deemed to mean the execution, termination (prior to its scheduled maturity date), assignment, exchange, or similar transfer or conveyance of, or extinguishing of rights or obligations under, a security-based swap, as the context may require.

(19) The term "emerging growth company" means an issuer that had total annual gross revenues of less than $1,000,000,000 (as such amount is indexed for inflation every 5 years by the Commission to reflect the change in the Consumer Price Index for All Urban Consumers published by the Bureau of Labor Statistics, setting the threshold to the nearest 1,000,000) during its most recently completed fiscal year. An issuer that is an emerging growth company as of the first day of that fiscal year shall continue to be deemed an emerging growth company until the earliest of—

(A)   the last day of the fiscal year of the issuer during which it had total annual gross revenues of $1,000,000,000 (as such amount is indexed for inflation every 5 years by the Commission to reflect the change in the Consumer Price Index for All Urban Consumers published by the Bureau of Labor Statistics, setting the threshold to the nearest 1,000,000) or more;

(B)   the last day of the fiscal year of the issuer following the fifth anniversary of the date of the first sale of common equity securities of the issuer pursuant to an effective registration statement under this title;

(C)   the date on which such issuer has, during the previous 3-year period, issued more than $1,000,000,000 in non-convertible debt; or

(D)   the date on which such issuer is deemed to be a "large accelerated filer", as defined in Rule 12b–2, or any successor thereto.

(b)   *Consideration of promotion of efficiency, competition, and capital formation.*

Whenever pursuant to this subchapter the Commission is engaged in rulemaking and is required to consider or determine whether an action is necessary or appropriate in the public interest, the Commission shall also consider, in addition to the protection of investors, whether the action will promote efficiency, competition, and capital formation.

§ 3.   Classes of Securities Under This Title

(a)   *Exempted securities.* Except as hereinafter expressly provided, the provisions of this subchapter shall not apply to any of the following classes of securities:

(1)   Reserved.

(2)   Any security issued or guaranteed by the United States or any territory thereof, or by the District of Columbia, or by any State of the United States, or by any political subdivision of a State or territory, or by any public instrumentality of one or more States or territories, or by any person controlled or supervised by and acting as an instrumentality of the Government of the United States pursuant to authority granted by the Congress of the United States; * * *

(3)   Any note, draft, bill of exchange, or banker's acceptance which arises out of a current transaction or the proceeds of which have been or are to be used for current transactions, and which has a maturity at the time of issuance of not exceeding nine months, exclusive of days of grace, or any renewal thereof the maturity of which is likewise limited;

(4)   Any security issued by a person organized and operated exclusively for religious, educational, benevolent, fraternal, charitable, or reformatory purposes and not for pecuniary profit, and no part of the net earnings of which inures to the benefit of any person, private stockholder, or individual, or any security of a fund that is excluded from the definition of an investment company under section 3(c)(10)(B) of the Investment Company Act of 1940;

(5)   Any security issued (a) by a savings and loan association, building and loan association, cooperative bank, homestead association, or similar institution, which is supervised and examined by State or Federal authority having supervision over any such institution; or (b) by (i) a farmer's cooperative organization exempt from tax under section 521 of the Internal Revenue Code of 1954, (ii) a corporation described in section 501(c)(16) of such Code and exempt from tax under section 501(a) of such Code, or (iii) a corporation described in section 501(c)(2) of such Code which is exempt from tax under section 501(a) of such Code and is organized for the exclusive purpose of holding title to property, collecting income therefrom, and turning over the entire amount thereof, less expenses, to an organization or corporation described in clause (i) or (ii);

(6)   Any interest in a railroad equipment trust. For purposes of this paragraph "interest in a railroad equipment trust" means any interest in an equipment trust, lease, conditional sales contract, or other similar arrangement entered into, issued, assumed, guaranteed by, or for the benefit of, a common carrier to finance the acquisition of rolling stock, including motive power;

(7)   Certificates issued by a receiver or by a trustee or debtor in possession in a case under title 11 of the United States Code, with the approval of the court;

(8)   Any insurance or endowment policy or annuity contract or optional annuity contract, issued by a corporation subject to the supervision of the insurance commissioner, bank commissioner, or any agency or officer performing like functions, of any State or Territory of the United States or the District of Columbia;

(9)   Except with respect to a security exchanged in a case under title 11 of the United States Code, any security exchanged by the issuer with its existing security holders exclusively where

no commission or other remuneration is paid or given directly or indirectly for soliciting such exchange;

(10) Except with respect to a security exchanged in a case under title 11 of the United States Code, any security which is issued in exchange for one or more bona fide outstanding securities, claims or property interests, or partly in such exchange and partly for cash, where the terms and conditions of such issuance and exchange are approved, after a hearing upon the fairness of such terms and conditions at which all persons to whom it is proposed to issue securities in such exchange shall have the right to appear, by any court, or by any official or agency of the United States, or by any State or Territorial banking or insurance commission or other governmental authority expressly authorized by law to grant such approval;

(11) Any security which is a part of an issue offered and sold only to persons resident within a single State or Territory, where the issuer of such security is a person resident and doing business within or, if a corporation, incorporated by and doing business within, such State or Territory.

* * *

(b) *Additional exemption—*

(1) *Small issues exemptive authority—*The Commission may from time to time by its rules and regulations, and subject to such terms and conditions as may be prescribed therein, add any class of securities to the securities exempted as provided in this section, if it finds that the enforcement of this subchapter with respect to such securities is not necessary in the public interest and for the protection of investors by reason of the small amount involved or the limited character of the public offering; but no issue of securities shall be exempted under this subsection where the aggregate amount at which such issue is offered to the public exceeds $5,000,000.

(2) *Additional issues—*The Commission shall by rule or regulation add a class of securities to the securities exempted pursuant to this section in accordance with the following terms and conditions:

(A) The aggregate offering amount of all securities offered and sold within the prior 12-month period in reliance on the exemption added in accordance with this paragraph shall not exceed $50,000,000.

(B) The securities may be offered and sold publicly.

(C) The securities shall not be restricted securities within the meaning of the Federal securities laws and the regulations promulgated thereunder.

(D) The civil liability provision in section 12(a)(2) shall apply to any person offering or selling such securities.

(E) The issuer may solicit interest in the offering prior to filing any offering statement, on such terms and conditions as the Commission may prescribe in the public interest or for the protection of investors.

(F) The Commission shall require the issuer to file audited financial statements with the Commission annually.

(G) Such other terms, conditions, or requirements as the Commission may determine necessary in the public interest and for the protection of investors, which may include—

(i) a requirement that the issuer prepare and electronically file with the Commission and distribute to prospective investors an offering statement, and any related documents, in such form and with such content as prescribed by the Commission, including audited financial statements, a description of the issuer's business operations, its financial condition, its corporate governance principles, its use of investor funds, and other appropriate matters; and

(ii) disqualification provisions under which the exemption shall not be available to the issuer or its predecessors, affiliates, officers, directors, underwriters, or other related persons, which shall be substantially similar to the disqualification provisions contained in the regulations adopted in accordance with section 926 of the Dodd-Frank Wall Street Reform and Consumer Protection Act (15 U.S.C. 77d note).

(3) *Limitation*—Only the following types of securities may be exempted under a rule or regulation adopted pursuant to paragraph (2): equity securities, debt securities, and debt securities convertible or exchangeable to equity interests, including any guarantees of such securities.

(4) *Periodic disclosures*—Upon such terms and conditions as the Commission determines necessary in the public interest and for the protection of investors, the Commission by rule or regulation may require an issuer of a class of securities exempted under paragraph (2) to make available to investors and file with the Commission periodic disclosures regarding the issuer, its business operations, its financial condition, its corporate governance principles, its use of investor funds, and other appropriate matters, and also may provide for the suspension and termination of such a requirement with respect to that issuer.

(5) *Adjustment*—Not later than 2 years after the date of enactment of the Small Company Capital Formation Act of 2011 and every 2 years thereafter, the Commission shall review the offering amount limitation described in paragraph (2)(A) and shall increase such amount as the Commission determines appropriate. If the Commission determines not to increase such amount, it shall report to the Committee on Financial Services of the House of Representatives and the Committee on Banking, Housing, and Urban Affairs of the Senate on its reasons for not increasing the amount.

* * *

§ 4.   Exempted Transactions

(a) The provisions of section 5 shall not apply to—

(1) transactions by any person other than an issuer, underwriter, or dealer.

(2) transactions by an issuer not involving any public offering.

(3) transactions by a dealer (including an underwriter no longer acting as an underwriter in respect of the security involved in such transaction), except—

(A) transactions taking place prior to the expiration of forty days after the first date upon which the security was bona fide offered to the public by the issuer or by or through an underwriter,

(B) transactions in a security as to which a registration statement has been filed taking place prior to the expiration of forty days after the effective date of such registration statement or prior to the expiration of forty days after the first date upon which the security was bona fide offered to the public by the issuer or by or through an underwriter after such effective date, whichever is later (excluding in the computation of such forty days any time during which a stop order issued under section 8 of this title is in effect as to the security), or such shorter period as the Commission may specify by rules and regulations or order, and

(C) transactions as to securities constituting the whole or a part of an unsold allotment to or subscription by such dealer as a participant in the distribution of such securities by the issuer or by or through an underwriter.

With respect to transactions referred to in clause (B), if securities of the issuer have not previously been sold pursuant to an earlier effective registration statement the applicable period, instead of forty days, shall be ninety days, or such shorter period as the Commission may specify by rules and regulations or order.

(4)   brokers' transactions executed upon customers' orders on any exchange or in the over-the-counter market but not the solicitation of such orders.

(5)   transactions involving offers or sales by an issuer solely to one or more accredited investors, if the aggregate offering price of an issue of securities offered in reliance on this paragraph does not exceed the amount allowed under section 3(b)(1), if there is no advertising or public solicitation in connection with the transaction by the issuer or anyone acting on the issuer's behalf, and if the issuer files such notice with the Commission as the Commission shall prescribe.

(6)   transactions involving the offer or sale of securities by an issuer (including all entities controlled by or under common control with the issuer), provided that—

(A)   the aggregate amount sold to all investors by the issuer, including any amount sold in reliance on the exemption provided under this paragraph during the 12-month period preceding the date of such transaction, is not more than $1,000,000;

(B)   the aggregate amount sold to any investor by an issuer, including any amount sold in reliance on the exemption provided under this paragraph during the 12-month period preceding the date of such transaction, does not exceed—

(i)   the greater of $2,000 or 5 percent of the annual income or net worth of such investor, as applicable, if either the annual income or the net worth of the investor is less than $100,000; and

(ii)   10 percent of the annual income or net worth of such investor, as applicable, not to exceed a maximum aggregate amount sold of $100,000, if either the annual income or net worth of the investor is equal to or more than $100,000;

(C)   the transaction is conducted through a broker or funding portal that complies with the requirements of section 4A(a) of this Act; and

(D)   the issuer complies with the requirements of section 4A(b) of this Act.

(7)   transactions meeting the requirements of subsection (d).

(b)   Offers and sales exempt under Rule 506 (as revised pursuant to section 201 of the Jumpstart Our Business Startups Act) shall not be deemed public offerings under the Federal securities laws as a result of general advertising or general solicitation.

(c)(1)   With respect to securities offered and sold in compliance with Rule 506 of Regulation D under this Act, no person who meets the conditions set forth in paragraph (2) shall be subject to registration as a broker or dealer pursuant to section 15(a)(1) of this Act, solely because—

(A)   that person maintains a platform or mechanism that permits the offer, sale, purchase, or negotiation of or with respect to securities, or permits general solicitations, general advertisements, or similar or related activities by issuers of such securities, whether online, in person, or through any other means;

(B)   that person or any person associated with that person co-invests in such securities; or

(C)   that person or any person associated with that person provides ancillary services with respect to such securities.

(2)   The exemption provided in paragraph (1) shall apply to any person described in such paragraph if—

(A)   such person and each person associated with that person receives no compensation in connection with the purchase or sale of such security;

(B)   such person and each person associated with that person does not have possession of customer funds or securities in connection with the purchase or sale of such security; and

(C) such person is not subject to a statutory disqualification as defined in section 3(a)(39) of this title and does not have any person associated with that person subject to such a statutory disqualification.

(3) For the purposes of this subsection, the term "ancillary services" means—

(A) the provision of due diligence services, in connection with the offer, sale, purchase, or negotiation of such security, so long as such services do not include, for separate compensation, investment advice or recommendations to issuers or investors; and

(B) the provision of standardized documents to the issuers and investors, so long as such person or entity does not negotiate the terms of the issuance for and on behalf of third parties and issuers are not required to use the standardized documents as a condition of using the service.

(d) The transactions referred to in subsection (a)(7) are transactions meeting the following requirements:

(1) Accredited investor requirement—Each purchaser is an accredited investor, as that term is defined in Rule 501(a) (or any successor regulation).

(2) Prohibition on general solicitation or advertising—Neither the seller, nor any person acting on the seller's behalf, offers or sells securities by any form of general solicitation or general advertising.

(3) Information requirement—In the case of a transaction involving the securities of an issuer that is neither subject to section 13 or 15(d) of the Securities Exchange Act of 1934, nor exempt from reporting pursuant to Rule 12g3–2(b), nor a foreign government (as defined in Rule 405) eligible to register securities under Schedule B, the seller and a prospective purchaser designated by the seller obtain from the issuer, upon request of the seller, and the seller in all cases makes available to a prospective purchaser, the following information (which shall be reasonably current in relation to the date of resale under this section):

(A) The exact name of the issuer and the issuer's predecessor (if any).

(B) The address of the issuer's principal executive offices.

(C) The exact title and class of the security.

(D) The par or stated value of the security.

(E) The number of shares or total amount of the securities outstanding as of the end of the issuer's most recent fiscal year.

(F) The name and address of the transfer agent, corporate secretary, or other person responsible for transferring shares and stock certificates.

(G) A statement of the nature of the business of the issuer and the products and services it offers, which shall be presumed reasonably current if the statement is as of 12 months before the transaction date.

(H) The names of the officers and directors of the issuer.

(I) The names of any persons registered as a broker, dealer, or agent that shall be paid or given, directly or indirectly, any commission or remuneration for such person's participation in the offer or sale of the securities.

(J) The issuer's most recent balance sheet and profit and loss statement and similar financial statements, which shall—

(i) be for such part of the 2 preceding fiscal years as the issuer has been in operation;

(ii) be prepared in accordance with generally accepted accounting principles or, in the case of a foreign private issuer, be prepared in accordance with generally accepted accounting principles or the International Financial Reporting Standards issued by the International Accounting Standards Board;

(iii) be presumed reasonably current if—

(I) with respect to the balance sheet, the balance sheet is as of a date less than 16 months before the transaction date; and

(II) with respect to the profit and loss statement, such statement is for the 12 months preceding the date of the issuer's balance sheet; and

(iv) if the balance sheet is not as of a date less than 6 months before the transaction date, be accompanied by additional statements of profit and loss for the period from the date of such balance sheet to a date less than 6 months before the transaction date.

(K) To the extent that the seller is a control person with respect to the issuer, a brief statement regarding the nature of the affiliation, and a statement certified by such seller that they have no reasonable grounds to believe that the issuer is in violation of the securities laws or regulations.

(4) Issuers disqualified—The transaction is not for the sale of a security where the seller is an issuer or a subsidiary, either directly or indirectly, of the issuer.

(5) Bad actor prohibition—Neither the seller, nor any person that has been or will be paid (directly or indirectly) remuneration or a commission for their participation in the offer or sale of the securities, including solicitation of purchasers for the seller is subject to an event that would disqualify an issuer or other covered person under Rule 506(d)(1) of Regulation D or is subject to a statutory disqualification described under section 3(a)(39) of the Securities Exchange Act of 1934.

(6) Business requirement—The issuer is engaged in business, is not in the organizational stage or in bankruptcy or receivership, and is not a blank check, blind pool, or shell company that has no specific business plan or purpose or has indicated that the issuer's primary business plan is to engage in a merger or combination of the business with, or an acquisition of, an unidentified person.

(7) Underwriter prohibition—The transaction is not with respect to a security that constitutes the whole or part of an unsold allotment to, or a subscription or participation by, a broker or dealer as an underwriter of the security or a redistribution.

(8) Outstanding class requirement—The transaction is with respect to a security of a class that has been authorized and outstanding for at least 90 days prior to the date of the transaction.

(e) Additional requirements

(1) In general—With respect to an exempted transaction described under subsection (a)(7):

(A) Securities acquired in such transaction shall be deemed to have been acquired in a transaction not involving any public offering.

(B) Such transaction shall be deemed not to be a distribution for purposes of section 2(a)(11) of this Act.

(C) Securities involved in such transaction shall be deemed to be restricted securities within the meaning of Rule 144.

(2) Rule of construction—The exemption provided by subsection (a)(7) shall not be the exclusive means for establishing an exemption from the registration requirements of section 5 of this Act.

§ 5.   Prohibitions Relating to Interstate Commerce and the Mails

(a) *Sale or delivery after sale of unregistered securities.* Unless a registration statement is in effect as to a security, it shall be unlawful for any person, directly or indirectly—

(1) to make use of any means or instruments of transportation or communication in interstate commerce or of the mails to sell such security through the use or medium of any prospectus or otherwise; or

(2) to carry or cause to be carried through the mails or in interstate commerce, by any means or instruments of transportation, any such security for the purpose of sale or for delivery after sale.

(b) *Necessity of prospectus meeting requirements of section 10 of this Act.* It shall be unlawful for any person, directly or indirectly—

(1) to make use of any means or instruments of transportation or communication in interstate commerce or of the mails to carry or transmit any prospectus relating to any security with respect to which a registration statement has been filed under this Act, unless such prospectus meets the requirements of section 10 of this Act; or

(2) to carry or cause to be carried through the mails or in interstate commerce any such security for the purpose of sale or for delivery after sale, unless accompanied or preceded by a prospectus that meets the requirements of subsection (a) of section 10 of this Act.

(c) *Necessity of filing registration statement.* It shall be unlawful for any person, directly or indirectly, to make use of any means or instruments of transportation or communication in interstate commerce or of the mails to offer to sell or offer to buy through the use or medium of any prospectus or otherwise any security, unless a registration statement has been filed as to such security, or while the registration statement is the subject of a refusal order or stop order or (prior to the effective date of the registration statement) any public proceeding or examination under section 8 of this Act.

(d) *Limitation.* Notwithstanding any other provision of this section, an emerging growth company or any person authorized to act on behalf of an emerging growth company may engage in oral or written communications with potential investors that are qualified institutional buyers or institutions that are accredited investors, as such terms are respectively defined in Rule 144A and Rule 501(a), or any successor thereto, to determine whether such investors might have an interest in a contemplated securities offering, either prior to or following the date of filing of a registration statement with respect to such securities with the Commission, subject to the requirement of subsection (b)(2).

(e) *Security-based swaps.* Notwithstanding the provisions of section 3 or 4 of this Act, unless a registration statement meeting the requirements of section 10(a) of this Act is in effect as to a security-based swap, it shall be unlawful for any person, directly or indirectly, to make use of any means or instruments of transportation or communication in interstate commerce or of the mails to offer to sell, offer to buy or purchase or sell a security-based swap to any person who is not an eligible contract participant as defined in section 1a(18) of the Commodity Exchange Act.

* * *

§ 11.   Civil Liabilities on Account of False Registration Statement

(a) *Persons possessing cause of action; persons liable.* In case any part of the registration statement, when such part became effective, contained an untrue statement of a material fact or omitted to state a material fact required to be stated therein or necessary to make the statements therein not misleading, any person acquiring such security (unless it is proved that at the time of such acquisition he knew of such untruth or omission) may, either at law or in equity, in any court of competent jurisdiction, sue—

(1) every person who signed the registration statement;

(2) every person who was a director of (or person performing similar functions) or partner in the issuer at the time of the filing of the part of the registration statement with respect to which his liability is asserted;

(3) every person who, with his consent, is named in the registration statement as being or about to become a director, person performing similar functions, or partner;

(4) every accountant, engineer, or appraiser, or any person whose profession gives authority to a statement made by him, who has with his consent been named as having prepared or certified any part of the registration statement, or as having prepared or certified any report or valuation which is used in connection with the registration statement, with respect to the statement in such registration statement, report, or valuation, which purports to have been prepared or certified by him;

(5) every underwriter with respect to such security.

If such person acquired the security after the issuer has made generally available to its security holders an earning statement covering a period of at least twelve months beginning after the effective date of the registration statement, then the right of recovery under this subsection shall be conditioned on proof that such person acquired the security relying upon such untrue statement in the registration statement or relying upon the registration statement and not knowing of such omission, but such reliance may be established without proof of the reading of the registration statement by such person.

(b) *Persons exempt from liability upon proof of issues.* Notwithstanding the provisions of subsection (a) of this section no person, other than the issuer, shall be liable as provided therein who shall sustain the burden of proof—

(1) that before the effective date of the part of the registration statement with respect to which his liability is asserted (A) he had resigned from or had taken such steps as are permitted by law to resign from, or ceased or refused to act in, every office, capacity, or relationship in which he was described in the registration statement as acting or agreeing to act, and (B) he had advised the Commission and the issuer in writing that he had taken such action and that he would not be responsible for such part of the registration statement; or

(2) that if such part of the registration statement became effective without his knowledge, upon becoming aware of such fact he forthwith acted and advised the Commission, in accordance with paragraph (1) of this subsection, and, in addition, gave reasonable public notice that such part of the registration statement had become effective without his knowledge; or

(3) that (A) as regards any part of the registration statement not purporting to be made on the authority of an expert, and not purporting to be a copy of or extract from a report or valuation of an expert, and not purporting to be made on the authority of a public official document or statement, he had, after reasonable investigation, reasonable ground to believe and did believe, at the time such part of the registration statement became effective, that the statements therein were true and that there was no omission to state a material fact required to be stated therein or necessary to make the statements therein not misleading; and (B) as regards any part of the registration statement purporting to be made upon his authority as an expert or purporting to be a copy of or extract from a report or valuation of himself as an expert, (i) he had, after reasonable investigation, reasonable ground to believe and did believe, at the time such part of the registration statement became effective, that the statements therein were true and that there was no omission to state a material fact required to be stated therein or necessary to make the statements therein not misleading, or (ii) such part of the registration statement did not fairly represent his statement as an expert or was not a fair copy of or extract from his report or valuation as an expert; and (C) as regards any part of the registration statement purporting to be made on the authority of an expert (other than himself) or purporting to be a copy of or extract from a report or valuation of an expert (other than himself), he had no reasonable ground to believe and did not believe, at the time such part of the registration statement became effective, that the statements therein were untrue or that there was an omission to state a material fact

required to be stated therein or necessary to make the statements therein not misleading, or that such part of the registration statement did not fairly represent the statement of the expert or was not a fair copy of or extract from the report or valuation of the expert; and (D) as regards any part of the registration statement purporting to be a statement made by an official person or purporting to be a copy of or extract from a public official document, he had no reasonable ground to believe and did not believe, at the time such part of the registration statement became effective, that the statements therein were untrue, or that there was an omission to state a material fact required to be stated therein or necessary to make the statements therein not misleading, or that such part of the registration statement did not fairly represent the statement made by the official person or was not a fair copy of or extract from the public official document.

(c) *Standard of reasonableness.* In determining, for the purpose of paragraph (3) of subsection (b) of this section, what constitutes reasonable investigation and reasonable ground for belief, the standard of reasonableness shall be that required of a prudent man in the management of his own property.

(d) *Effective date of registration statement with regard to underwriters.* If any person becomes an underwriter with respect to the security after the part of the registration statement with respect to which his liability is asserted has become effective, then for the purposes of paragraph (3) of subsection (b) of this section such part of the registration statement shall be considered as having become effective with respect to such person as of the time when he became an underwriter.

(e) *Measure of damages; undertaking for payment of costs.* The suit authorized under subsection (a) of this section may be to recover such damages as shall represent the difference between the amount paid for the security (not exceeding the price at which the security was offered to the public) and (1) the value thereof as of the time such suit was brought, or (2) the price at which such security shall have been disposed of in the market before suit, or (3) the price at which such security shall have been disposed of after suit but before judgment if such damages shall be less than the damages representing the difference between the amount paid for the security (not exceeding the price at which the security was offered to the public) and the value thereof as of the time such suit was brought: Provided, That if the defendant proves that any portion or all of such damages represents other than the depreciation in value of such security resulting from such part of the registration statement, with respect to which his liability is asserted, not being true or omitting to state a material fact required to be stated therein or necessary to make the statements therein not misleading, such portion of or all such damages shall not be recoverable. In no event shall any underwriter (unless such underwriter shall have knowingly received from the issuer for acting as an underwriter some benefit, directly or indirectly, in which all other underwriters similarly situated did not share in proportion to their respective interests in the underwriting) be liable in any suit or as a consequence of suits authorized under subsection (a) of this section for damages in excess of the total price at which the securities underwritten by him and distributed to the public were offered to the public. In any suit under this or any other section of this Act the court may, in its discretion, require an undertaking for the payment of the costs of such suit, including reasonable attorney's fees, and if judgment shall be rendered against a party litigant, upon the motion of the other party litigant, such costs may be assessed in favor of such party litigant (whether or not such undertaking has been required) if the court believes the suit or the defense to have been without merit, in an amount sufficient to reimburse him for the reasonable expenses incurred by him, in connection with such suit, such costs to be taxed in the manner usually provided for taxing of costs in the court in which the suit was heard.

(f) *Joint and several liability; liability of outside director.*

(1) Except as provided in paragraph (2), all or any one or more of the persons specified in subsection (a) of this section shall be jointly and severally liable, and every person who becomes liable to make any payment under this section may recover contribution as in cases of contract from any person who, if sued separately, would have been liable to make the same payment, unless the person who has become liable was, and the other was not, guilty of fraudulent misrepresentation.

(2)(A) The liability of an outside director under subsection (e) shall be determined in accordance with section 21D(f) of the Securities Exchange Act of 1934.

(B) For purposes of this paragraph, the term "outside director" shall have the meaning given such term by rule or regulation of the Commission.

(g) *Offering price to public as maximum amount recoverable.* In no case shall the amount recoverable under this section exceed the price at which the security was offered to the public.

§ 12. Civil Liabilities Arising in Connection With Prospectuses and Communications

(a) *In General.* Any person who—

(1) offers or sells a security in violation of section 5 of this Act, or

(2) offers or sells a security (whether or not exempted by the provisions of section 3 of this Act, other than paragraphs (2) and (14) of subsection (a) of said section), by the use of any means or instruments of transportation or communication in interstate commerce or of the mails, by means of a prospectus or oral communication, which includes an untrue statement of a material fact or omits to state a material fact necessary in order to make the statements, in the light of the circumstances under which they were made, not misleading (the purchaser not knowing of such untruth or omission), and who shall not sustain the burden of proof that he did not know, and in the exercise of reasonable care could not have known, of such untruth or omission, shall be liable, subject to subsection (b), to the person purchasing such security from him, who may sue either at law or in equity in any court of competent jurisdiction, to recover the consideration paid for such security with interest thereon, less the amount of any income received thereon, upon the tender of such security, or for damages if he no longer owns the security.

(b) *Loss Causation.* In an action described in subsection (a)(2), if the person who offered or sold such security proves that any portion or all of the amount recoverable under subsection (a)(2) represents other than the depreciation in value of the subject security resulting from such part of the prospectus or oral communication, with respect to which the liability of that person is asserted, not being true or omitting to state a material fact required to be stated therein or necessary to make the statement not misleading, then such portion or amount, as the case may be, shall not be recoverable.

§ 13. Limitation of Actions

No action shall be maintained to enforce any liability created under section 11 or 12(a)(2) of this Act unless brought within one year after the discovery of the untrue statement or the omission, or after such discovery should have been made by the exercise of reasonable diligence, or, if the action is to enforce a liability created under section 12(a)(1) of this Act, unless brought within one year after the violation upon which it is based. In no event shall any such action be brought to enforce a liability created under section 11 or 12(a)(1) of this Act more than three years after the security was bona fide offered to the public, or under section 12(a)(2) of this Act more than three years after the sale.

§ 14. Contrary Stipulations Void

Any condition, stipulation, or provision binding any person acquiring any security to waive compliance with any provision of this title or of the rules and regulations of the Commission shall be void.

§ 15. Liability of Controlling Persons

(a) *Controlling persons.*—Every person who, by or through stock ownership, agency, or otherwise, or who, pursuant to or in connection with an agreement or understanding with one or more other persons by or through stock ownership, agency, or otherwise, controls any person liable under sections 11 or 12 of this Act, shall also be liable jointly and severally with and to the same extent as such controlled person to any person to whom such controlled person is liable, unless the controlling person had no knowledge of or reasonable ground to believe in the existence of the facts by reason of which the liability of the controlled person is alleged to exist.

(b) *Prosecution of persons who aid and abet violations.*—For purposes of any action brought by the Commission under subparagraph (b) or (d) of section 20 of this Act, any person that knowingly or recklessly provides substantial assistance to another person in violation of a provision of this Act, or of any rule or regulation issued under this Act, shall be deemed to be in violation of such provision to the same extent as the person to whom such assistance is provided.

§ 16.   Additional Remedies; Limitation on Remedies

(a) *Remedies additional.* Except as provided in subsection (b), the rights and remedies provided by this subchapter shall be in addition to any and all other rights and remedies that may exist at law or in equity.

(b) *Class action limitations.* No covered class action based upon the statutory or common law of any State or subdivision thereof may be maintained in any State or Federal court by any private party alleging—

    (1) an untrue statement or omission of a material fact in connection with the purchase or sale of a covered security; or

    (2) that the defendant used or employed any manipulative or deceptive device or contrivance in connection with the purchase or sale of a covered security.

(c) *Removal of covered class actions.* Any covered class action brought in any State court involving a covered security, as set forth in subsection (b), shall be removable to the Federal district court for the district in which the action is pending, and shall be subject to subsection (b).

(d) *Preservation of certain actions.*

    (1) *Actions under State law of State of incorporation.*

        (A) *Actions preserved.* Notwithstanding subsection (b) or (c), a covered class action described in subparagraph (B) of this paragraph that is based upon the statutory or common law of the State in which the issuer is incorporated (in the case of a corporation) or organized (in the case of any other entity) may be maintained in a State or Federal court by a private party.

        (B) *Permissible actions.* A covered class action is described in this subparagraph if it involves—

            (i) the purchase or sale of securities by the issuer or an affiliate of the issuer exclusively from or to holders of equity securities of the issuer; or

            (ii) any recommendation, position, or other communication with respect to the sale of securities of the issuer that—

                (I) is made by or on behalf of the issuer or an affiliate of the issuer to holders of equity securities of the issuer; and

                (II) concerns decisions of those equity holders with respect to voting their securities, acting in response to a tender or exchange offer, or exercising dissenters' or appraisal rights.

    (2) *State actions.*

        (A) *In general.* Notwithstanding any other provision of this section, nothing in this section may be construed to preclude a State or political subdivision thereof or a State pension plan from bringing an action involving a covered security on its own behalf, or as a member of a class comprised solely of other States, political subdivisions, or State pension plans that are named plaintiffs, and that have authorized participation, in such action.

(B) *State pension plan defined.* For purposes of this paragraph, the term "State pension plan" means a pension plan established and maintained for its employees by the government of the State or political subdivision thereof, or by any agency or instrumentality thereof.

(C) *Actions under contractual agreements between issuers and indenture trustees.* Notwithstanding subsection (b) or (c), a covered class action that seeks to enforce a contractual agreement between an issuer and an indenture trustee may be maintained in a State or Federal court by a party to the agreement or a successor to such party.

(D) *Remand of removed actions.* In an action that has been removed from a State court pursuant to subsection (c), if the Federal court determines that the action may be maintained in State court pursuant to this subsection, the Federal court shall remand such action to such State court.

(e) *Preservation of State jurisdiction.* The securities commission (or any agency or office performing like functions) of any State shall retain jurisdiction under the laws of such State to investigate and bring enforcement actions.

(f) *Definitions.* For purposes of this section, the following definitions shall apply:

(1) *Affiliate of the issuer.* The term "affiliate of the issuer" means a person that directly or indirectly, through one or more intermediaries, controls or is controlled by or is under common control with, the issuer.

(2) *Covered class action.*

(A) *In general.* The term "covered class action" means—

(i) any single lawsuit in which—

(I) damages are sought on behalf of more than 50 persons or prospective class members, and questions of law or fact common to those persons or members of the prospective class, without reference to issues of individualized reliance on an alleged misstatement or omission, predominate over any questions affecting only individual persons or members; or

(II) one or more named parties seek to recover damages on a representative basis on behalf of themselves and other unnamed parties similarly situated, and questions of law or fact common to those persons or members of the prospective class predominate over any questions affecting only individual persons or members; or

(ii) any group of lawsuits filed in or pending in the same court and involving common questions of law or fact, in which—

(I) damages are sought on behalf of more than 50 persons; and

(II) the lawsuits are joined, consolidated, or otherwise proceed as a single action for any purpose.

(B) Exception for derivative actions. Notwithstanding subparagraph (A), the term "covered class action" does not include an exclusively derivative action brought by one or more shareholders on behalf of a corporation.

(C) Counting of certain class members. For purposes of this paragraph, a corporation, investment company, pension plan, partnership, or other entity, shall be treated as one person or prospective class member, but only if the entity is not established for the purpose of participating in the action.

(D) Rule of construction. Nothing in this paragraph shall be construed to affect the discretion of a State court in determining whether actions filed in such court should be joined, consolidated, or otherwise allowed to proceed as a single action.

(3) *Covered security.* The term "covered security" means a security that satisfies the standards for a covered security specified in paragraph (1) or (2) of section 18(b) of this title at the time during which it is alleged that the misrepresentation, omission, or manipulative or deceptive conduct occurred, except that such term shall not include any debt security that is exempt from registration under this Act pursuant to rules issued by the Commission under section 4(2) of this Act.

§ 17. Fraudulent Interstate Transactions

(a) *Use of interstate commerce for purpose of fraud or deceit.* It shall be unlawful for any person in the offer or sale of any securities (including security-based swaps) or any security-based swap agreement (as defined in section 3(a)(78) of the Securities Exchange Act of 1934) by the use of any means or instruments of transportation or communication in interstate commerce or by use of the mails, directly or indirectly—

(1) to employ any device, scheme, or artifice to defraud, or

(2) to obtain money or property by means of any untrue statement of a material fact or any omission to state a material fact necessary in order to make the statements made, in light of the circumstances under which they were made, not misleading; or

(3) to engage in any transaction, practice, or course of business which operates or would operate as a fraud or deceit upon the purchaser.

(b) *Use of interstate commerce for purpose of offering for sale.* It shall be unlawful for any person, by the use of any means or instruments of transportation or communication in interstate commerce or by the use of the mails, to publish, give publicity to, or circulate any notice, circular, advertisement, newspaper, article, letter, investment service, or communication which, though not purporting to offer a security for sale, describes such security for a consideration received or to be received, directly or indirectly, from an issuer, underwriter, or dealer, without fully disclosing the receipt, whether past or prospective, of such consideration and the amount thereof.

(c) *Exemptions of section 3 not applicable to this section.* The exemptions provided in section 3 shall not apply to the provisions of this section.

* * *

§ 18. Exemption From State Regulation of Securities Offerings

(a) *Scope of Exemption.* Except as otherwise provided in this section, no law, rule, regulation, or order, or other administrative action of any State or any political subdivision thereof—

(1) requiring, or with respect to, registration or qualification of securities, or registration or qualification of securities transactions, shall directly or indirectly apply to a security that—

(A) is a covered security; or

(B) will be a covered security upon completion of the transaction;

(2) shall directly or indirectly prohibit, limit, or impose any conditions upon the use of—

(A) with respect to a covered security described in subsection (b), any offering document that is prepared by or on the behalf of the issuer; or

(B) any proxy statement, report to shareholders, or other disclosure document relating to a covered security or the issuer thereof that is required to be and is filed with the Commission or any national securities organization registered under section 15A of the

Securities Exchange Act of 1934, except that this subparagraph does not apply to the laws, rules, regulations, or orders, or other administrative actions of the State of incorporation of the issuer; or

(3)   shall directly or indirectly prohibit, limit, or impose conditions, based on the merits of such offering or issuer, upon the offer or sale of any security described in paragraph (1).

(b)   *Covered Securities.* For purposes of this section, the following are covered securities:

(1)   *Exclusive federal registration of nationally traded securities.* A security is a covered security if such security is—

(A)   listed, or authorized for listing, on the New York Stock Exchange or the American Stock Exchange, or listed, or authorized for listing, on the National Market System of the Nasdaq Stock Market (or any successor to such entities);

(B)   listed, or authorized for listing, on a national securities exchange (or tier or segment thereof) that has listing standards that the Commission determines by rule (on its own initiative or on the basis of a petition) are substantially similar to the listing standards applicable to securities described in subparagraph (A); or

(C)   a security of the same issuer that is equal in seniority or that is a senior security to a security described in subparagraph (A) or (B).

(2)   *Exclusive federal registration of investment companies.* A security is a covered security if such security is a security issued by an investment company that is registered, or that has filed a registration statement, under the Investment Company Act of 1940.

(3)   *Sales to qualified purchasers.* A security is a covered security with respect to the offer or sale of the security to qualified purchasers, as defined by the Commission by rule. In prescribing such rule, the Commission may define the term "qualified purchaser" differently with respect to different categories of securities, consistent with the public interest and the protection of investors.

(4)   *Exemption in connection with certain exempt offerings.* A security is a covered security with respect to a transaction that is exempt from registration under this Act pursuant to—

(A)   paragraph (1) or (3) of section 4(a) of this Act, and the issuer of such security files reports with the Commission pursuant to section 13 or 15(d) of the Securities Exchange Act of 1934;

(B)   section 4(a)(4) of this Act;

(C)   section 4(a)(6) of this Act;

(D)   a rule or regulation adopted pursuant to section 3(b)(2) of this Act and such security is—

(i)   offered or sold on a national securities exchange; or

(ii)   offered or sold to a qualified purchaser, as defined by the Commission pursuant to paragraph (3) with respect to that purchase or sale;

(E)   section 3(a) of this Act, other than the offer or sale of a security that is exempt from such registration pursuant to paragraph (4), (10) or (11) of such section, except that a municipal security that is exempt from such registration pursuant to paragraph (2) of such section is not a covered security with respect to the offer or sale of such security in the State in which the issuer of such security is located; or

(F)   Commission rules or regulations issued under section 4(2) of this Act, except that this subparagraph does not prohibit a State from imposing notice filing requirements that are substantially similar to those required by rule or regulation under section 4(2) of this Act that are in effect on September 1, 1996; or

(G)   section 4(a)(7) of this Act.

(c)   *Preservation of Authority.*

(1)   *Fraud authority.* Consistent with this section, the securities commission (or any agency or office performing like functions) of any State shall retain jurisdiction under the laws of such State to investigate and bring enforcement actions in connection with securities or securities transactions.

(A)   with respect to—

(i)   fraud or deceit; or

(ii)   unlawful conduct by a broker, dealer, or funding portal; and

(B)   in connection to a transaction described under section 4(6) of this Act, with respect to—

(i)   fraud or deceit; or

(ii)   unlawful conduct by a broker, dealer, funding portal, or issuer.

(2)   *Preservation of filing requirements.*

(A)   *Notice filings permitted.* Nothing in this section prohibits the securities commission (or any agency or office performing like functions) of any State from requiring the filing of any document filed with the Commission pursuant to this Act, together with annual or periodic reports of the value of securities sold or offered to be sold to persons located in the State (if such sales data is not included in documents filed with the Commission), solely for notice purposes and the assessment of any fee, together with a consent to service of process and any required fee.

(B)   *Preservation of fees.* * * *

(F)   *Fees not permitted on crowdfunded securities.* Notwithstanding subparagraphs (A), (B), and (C), no filing or fee may be required with respect to any security that is a covered security pursuant to subsection (b)(4)(B), or will be such a covered security upon completion of the transaction, except for the securities commission (or any agency or office performing like functions) of the State of the principal place of business of the issuer, or any State in which purchasers of 50 percent or greater of the aggregate amount of the issue are residents, provided that for purposes of this subparagraph, the term "State" includes the District of Columbia and the territories of the United States.

(3)   *Enforcement of requirements.* Nothing in this section shall prohibit the securities commission (or any agency or office performing like functions) of any State from suspending the offer or sale of securities within such State as a result of the failure to submit any filing or fee required under law and permitted under this section.

(d)   *Definitions.* For purposes of this section, the following definitions shall apply:

(1)   *Offering document.* The term "offering document"—

(A)   has the meaning given the term "prospectus" in section 2(a)(10) of this Act, but without regard to the provisions of subparagraphs (a) and (b) of that section; and

(B)   includes a communication that is not deemed to offer a security pursuant to a rule of the Commission.

(2)   *Prepared by or on behalf of the issuer.* Not later than 6 months after October 11, 1996, the Commission shall, by rule, define the term "prepared by or on behalf of the issuer" for purposes of this section.

(3)   *State.* The term "State" has the same meaning as in section 3 of the Securities Exchange Act of 1934.

(4) *Senior security.* The term "senior security" means any bond, debenture, note, or similar obligation or instrument constituting a security and evidencing indebtedness, and any stock of a class having priority over any other class as to distribution of assets or payment of dividends.

§ 27. Private Securities Litigation

(a) *Private class actions.*

(1) *In general.* The provisions of this subsection shall apply to each private action arising under this Act that is brought as a plaintiff class action pursuant to the Federal Rules of Civil Procedure.

(2) *Certification filed with complaint.*

(A) *In general.* Each plaintiff seeking to serve as a representative party on behalf of a class shall provide a sworn certification, which shall be personally signed by such plaintiff and filed with the complaint, that—

(i) states that the plaintiff has reviewed the complaint and authorized its filing;

(ii) states that the plaintiff did not purchase the security that is the subject of the complaint at the direction of plaintiff's counsel or in order to participate in any private action arising under this Act;

(iii) states that the plaintiff is willing to serve as a representative party on behalf of a class, including providing testimony at deposition and trial, if necessary;

(iv) sets forth all of the transactions of the plaintiff in the security that is the subject of the complaint during the class period specified in the complaint;

(v) identifies any other action under this Act, filed during the 3-year period preceding the date on which the certification is signed by the plaintiff, in which the plaintiff has sought to serve, or served, as a representative party on behalf of a class; and

(vi) states that the plaintiff will not accept any payment for serving as a representative party on behalf of a class beyond the plaintiff's pro rata share of any recovery, except as ordered or approved by the court in accordance with paragraph (4).

(B) *Nonwaiver of attorney-client privilege.* The certification filed pursuant to subparagraph (A) shall not be construed to be a waiver of the attorney-client privilege.

(3) *Appointment of lead plaintiff.*

(A) *Early notice to class members.*

(i) *In general.* Not later than 20 days after the date on which the complaint is filed, the plaintiff or plaintiffs shall cause to be published, in a widely circulated national business-oriented publication or wire service, a notice advising members of the purported plaintiff class—

(I) of the pendency of the action, the claims asserted therein, and the purported class period; and

(II) that, not later than 60 days after the date on which the notice is published, any member of the purported class may move the court to serve as lead plaintiff of the purported class.

(ii) *Multiple actions.* If more than one action on behalf of a class asserting substantially the same claim or claims arising under this Act is filed, only the plaintiff or plaintiffs in the first filed action shall be required to cause notice to be published in accordance with clause (i).

(iii) *Additional notices may be required under Federal Rules.* Notice required under clause (i) shall be in addition to any notice required pursuant to the Federal Rules of Civil Procedure.

(B) *Appointment of lead plaintiff.*

(i) *In general.* Not later than 90 days after the date on which a notice is published under subparagraph (A)(i), the court shall consider any motion made by a purported class member in response to the notice, including any motion by a class member who is not individually named as a plaintiff in the complaint or complaints, and shall appoint as lead plaintiff the member or members of the purported plaintiff class that the court determines to be most capable of adequately representing the interests of class members (hereafter in this paragraph referred to as the "most adequate plaintiff") in accordance with this subparagraph.

(ii) *Consolidated actions.* If more than one action on behalf of a class asserting substantially the same claim or claims arising under this Act has been filed, and any party has sought to consolidate those actions for pretrial purposes or for trial, the court shall not make the determination required by clause (i) until after the decision on the motion to consolidate is rendered. As soon as practicable after such decision is rendered, the court shall appoint the most adequate plaintiff as lead plaintiff for the consolidated actions in accordance with this subparagraph.

(iii) *Rebuttable presumption.*

(I) *In general.* Subject to subclause (II), for purposes of clause (i), the court shall adopt a presumption that the most adequate plaintiff in any private action arising under this Act is the person or group of persons that—

(aa) has either filed the complaint or made a motion in response to a notice under Subparagraph (A)(i);

(bb) in the determination of the court, has the largest financial interest in the relief sought by the class; and

(cc) otherwise satisfies the requirements of Rule 23 of the Federal Rules of Civil Procedure.

(II) *Rebuttal evidence.* The presumption described in subclause (I) may be rebutted only upon proof by a member of the purported plaintiff class that the presumptively most adequate plaintiff—

(aa) will not fairly and adequately protect the interests of the class; or

(bb) is subject to unique defenses that render such plaintiff incapable of adequately representing the class.

(iv) *Discovery.* For purposes of this subparagraph, discovery relating to whether a member or members of the purported plaintiff class is the most adequate plaintiff may be conducted by a plaintiff only if the plaintiff first demonstrates a reasonable basis for a finding that the presumptively most adequate plaintiff is incapable of adequately representing the class.

(v) *Selection of lead counsel.* The most adequate plaintiff shall, subject to the approval of the court, select and retain counsel to represent the class.

(vi) *Restrictions on professional plaintiffs.* Except as the court may otherwise permit, consistent with the purposes of this section, a person may be a lead plaintiff, or an officer, director, or fiduciary of a lead plaintiff, in no more than 5 securities class actions brought as plaintiff class actions pursuant to the Federal Rules of Civil Procedure during any 3-year period.

(4) *Recovery by plaintiffs.* The share of any final judgment or of any settlement that is awarded to a representative party serving on behalf of a class shall be equal, on a per share basis, to the portion of the final judgment or settlement awarded to all other members of the class. Nothing in this paragraph shall be construed to limit the award of reasonable costs and expenses (including lost wages) directly relating to the representation of the class to any representative party serving on behalf of the class.

(5) *Restrictions on settlements under seal.* The terms and provisions of any settlement agreement of a class action shall not be filed under seal, except that on motion of any party to the settlement, the court may order filing under seal for those portions of a settlement agreement as to which good cause is shown for such filing under seal. For purposes of this paragraph, good cause shall exist only if publication of a term or provision of a settlement agreement would cause direct and substantial harm to any party.

(6) *Restrictions on payment of attorneys' fees and expenses.* Total attorneys' fees and expenses awarded by the court to counsel for the plaintiff class shall not exceed a reasonable percentage of the amount of any damages and prejudgment interest actually paid to the class.

(7) *Disclosure of settlement terms to class members.* Any proposed or final settlement agreement that is published or otherwise disseminated to the class shall include each of the following statements, along with a cover page summarizing the information contained in such statements:

(A) *Statement of plaintiff recovery.* The amount of the settlement proposed to be distributed to the parties to the action, determined in the aggregate and on an average per share basis.

(B) *Statement of potential outcome of case.*

(i) Agreement on amount of damages. If the settling parties agree on the average amount of damages per share that would be recoverable if the plaintiff prevailed on each claim alleged under this Act, a statement concerning the average amount of such potential damages per share.

(ii) Disagreement on amount of damages. If the parties do not agree on the average amount of damages per share that would be recoverable if the plaintiff prevailed on each claim alleged under this Act, a statement from each settling party concerning the issue or issues on which the parties disagree.

(iii) Inadmissibility for certain purposes. A statement made in accordance with clause (i) or (ii) concerning the amount of damages shall not be admissible in any Federal or State judicial action or administrative proceeding, other than an action or proceeding arising out of such statement.

(C) *Statement of attorneys' fees or costs sought.* If any of the settling parties or their counsel intend to apply to the court for an award of attorneys' fees or costs from any fund established as part of the settlement, a statement indicating which parties or counsel intend to make such an application, the amount of fees and costs that will be sought (including the amount of such fees and costs determined on an average per share basis), and a brief explanation supporting the fees and costs sought.

(D) *Identification of lawyers' representatives.* The name, telephone number, and address of one or more representatives of counsel for the plaintiff class who will be reasonably available to answer questions from class members concerning any matter contained in any notice of settlement published or otherwise disseminated to the class.

(E) *Reasons for settlement.* A brief statement explaining the reasons why the parties are proposing the settlement.

(F) *Other information.* Such other information as may be required by the court.

(8) *Attorney conflict of interest.* If a plaintiff class is represented by an attorney who directly owns or otherwise has a beneficial interest in the securities that are the subject of the litigation, the court shall make a determination of whether such ownership or other interest constitutes a conflict of interest sufficient to disqualify the attorney from representing the plaintiff class.

* * *

§ 28.   General Exemptive Authority

The Commission, by rule or regulation, may conditionally or unconditionally exempt any person, security, or transaction, or any class or classes of persons, securities, or transactions, from any provision or provisions of this Act or of any rule or regulation issued under this Act, to the extent that such exemption is necessary or appropriate in the public interest, and is consistent with the protection of investors.

* * *

SECURITIES EXCHANGE ACT OF 1934
(15 U.S.C. §§ 78a *et seq.*)—SELECTED PROVISIONS

Table of Sections

---

§ 3.   Definitions and Application

(a)   *Definitions*

When used in this Act, unless the context otherwise requires—

(1)   The term "exchange" means any organization, association, or group of persons, whether incorporated or unincorporated, which constitutes, maintains, or provides a market place or facilities for bringing together purchasers and sellers of securities or for otherwise performing with respect to securities the functions commonly performed by a stock exchange as that term is generally understood, and includes the market place and the market facilities maintained by such exchange.

* * *

(10)   The term "equity security" means any stock or similar security; or any security future on any such security; or any security convertible, with or without consideration, into such a security, or carrying any warrant or right to subscribe to or purchase such a security; or any such warrant or right; or any other security which the Commission shall deem to be of similar nature and consider necessary or appropriate, by such rules and regulations as it may prescribe in the public interest or for the protection of investors, to treat as an equity security.

* * *

(13)   The terms "buy" and "purchase" each include any contract to buy, purchase, or otherwise acquire. For security futures products, such term includes any contract, agreement, or transaction for future delivery. For security-based swaps, such terms include the execution, termination (prior to its scheduled maturity date), assignment, exchange, or similar transfer or conveyance of, or extinguishing of rights or obligations under, a security-based swap, as the context may require.

(14) The terms "sale" and "sell" each include any contract to sell or otherwise dispose of. For security futures products, such term includes any contract, agreement, or transaction for future delivery. For security-based swaps, such terms include the execution, termination (prior to its scheduled maturity date), assignment, exchange, or similar transfer or conveyance of, or extinguishing of rights or obligations under, a security-based swap, as the context may require.

(15) The term "Commission" means the Securities and Exchange Commission established by section 4 of this Act.

* * *

(80) *Emerging growth company.*—The term 'emerging growth company' means an issuer that had total annual gross revenues of less than $1,000,000,000 (as such amount is indexed for inflation every 5 years by the Commission to reflect the change in the Consumer Price Index for All Urban Consumers published by the Bureau of Labor Statistics, setting the threshold to the nearest 1,000,000) during its most recently completed fiscal year. An issuer that is an emerging growth company as of the first day of that fiscal year shall continue to be deemed an emerging growth company until the earliest of—

(A) the last day of the fiscal year of the issuer during which it had total annual gross revenues of $1,000,000,000 (as such amount is indexed for inflation every 5 years by the Commission to reflect the change in the Consumer Price Index for All Urban Consumers published by the Bureau of Labor Statistics, setting the threshold to the nearest 1,000,000) or more;

(B) the last day of the fiscal year of the issuer following the fifth anniversary of the date of the first sale of common equity securities of the issuer pursuant to an effective registration statement under the Securities Act of 1933;

(C) the date on which such issuer has, during the previous 3-year period, issued more than $1,000,000,000 in non-convertible debt; or

(D) the date on which such issuer is deemed to be a 'large accelerated filer', as defined in Rule 12b–2, or any successor thereto.

*(80) *Funding portal.*—The term 'funding portal' means any person acting as an intermediary in a transaction involving the offer or sale of securities for the account of others, solely pursuant to section 4(6) of the Securities Act of 1933, that does not—

(A) offer investment advice or recommendations;

(B) solicit purchases, sales, or offers to buy the securities offered or displayed on its website or portal;

(C) compensate employees, agents, or other persons for such solicitation or based on the sale of securities displayed or referenced on its website or portal;

(D) hold, manage, possess, or otherwise handle investor funds or securities; or

(E) engage in such other activities as the Commission, by rule, determines appropriate.

* * *

(h) *Limited exemption for funding portals.*

(1) *In general.*—The Commission shall, by rule, exempt, conditionally or unconditionally, a registered funding portal from the requirement to register as a broker or dealer under section 15(a)(1) of this Act, provided that such funding portal—

---

*   As in original.

(A) remains subject to the examination, enforcement, and other rulemaking authority of the Commission;

(B) is a member of a national securities association registered under section 15A of this Act; and

(C) is subject to such other requirements under this Act as the Commission determines appropriate under such rule.

(2) *National securities association membership.*—For purposes of sections 15(b)(8) and 15A of this Act, the term 'broker or dealer' includes a funding portal and the term 'registered broker or dealer' includes a registered funding portal, except to the extent that the Commission, by rule, determines otherwise, provided that a national securities association shall only examine for and enforce against a registered funding portal rules of such national securities association written specifically for registered funding portals.

§ 6.   National Securities Exchanges

(a) *Registration; application*

An exchange may be registered as a national securities exchange under the terms and conditions hereinafter provided in this section and in accordance with the provisions of section 19(a) of this Act, by filing with the Commission an application for registration in such form as the Commission, by rule, may prescribe containing the rules of the exchange and such other information and documents as the Commission, by rule, may prescribe as necessary or appropriate in the public interest or for the protection of investors.

* * *

§ 9.   Manipulation of Security Prices

(a) *Transactions relating to purchase or sale of security*

It shall be unlawful for any person, directly or indirectly, by the use of the mails or any means or instrumentality of interstate commerce, or of any facility of any national securities exchange, or for any member of a national securities exchange—

(1) For the purpose of creating a false or misleading appearance of active trading in any security other than a government security, or a false or misleading appearance with respect to the market for any such security, (A) to effect any transaction in such security which involves no change in the beneficial ownership thereof, or (B) to enter an order or orders for the purchase of such security with the knowledge that an order or orders of substantially the same size, at substantially the same time, and at substantially the same price, for the sale of any such security, has been or will be entered by or for the same or different parties, or (C) to enter any order or orders for the sale of any such security with the knowledge that an order or orders of substantially the same size, at substantially the same time, and at substantially the same price, for the purchase of such security, has been or will be entered by or for the same or different parties.

(2) To effect, alone or with 1 or more other persons, a series of transactions in any security registered on a national securities exchange, any security not so registered, or in connection with any security-based swap or security-based swap agreement with respect to such security creating actual or apparent active trading in such security, or raising or depressing the price of such security, for the purpose of inducing the purchase or sale of such security by others.

* * *

(f) *Persons liable; suits at law or in equity.* Any person who willfully participates in any act or transaction in violation of subsections (a), (b), or (c) of this section, shall be liable to any person who shall purchase or sell any security at a price which was affected by such act or transaction, and the person so injured may sue in law or in equity in any court of competent jurisdiction to recover the damages sustained as a result of any such act or transaction. In any such suit the court may, in its discretion, require an undertaking for the payment of the costs of such suit, and assess reasonable costs, including reasonable attorneys' fees, against either party litigant. Every person who becomes liable to make any payment under this subsection may recover contribution as in cases of contract from any person who, if joined in the original suit, would have been liable to make the same payment. No action shall be maintained to enforce any liability created under this section, unless brought within one year after the discovery of the facts constituting the violation and within three years after such violation.

* * *

(j) *Regulations relating to security-based swaps.* It shall be unlawful for any person, directly or indirectly, by the use of any means or instrumentality of interstate commerce or of the mails, or of any facility of any national securities exchange, to effect any transaction in, or to induce or attempt to induce the purchase or sale of, any security-based swap, in connection with which such person engages in any fraudulent, deceptive, or manipulative act or practice, makes any fictitious quotation, or engages in any transaction, practice, or course of business which operates as a fraud or deceit upon any person. The Commission shall, for the purposes of this subsection, by rules and regulations define, and prescribe means reasonably designed to prevent, such transactions, acts, practices, and courses of business as are fraudulent, deceptive, or manipulative, and such quotations as are fictitious.

§ 10. Manipulative and Deceptive Devices

It shall be unlawful for any person, directly or indirectly, by the use of any means or instrumentality of interstate commerce or of the mails, or of any facility of any national securities exchange—

(a)(1) To effect a short sale, or to use or employ any stop-loss order in connection with the purchase or sale, of any security other than a government security, in contravention of such rules and regulations as the Commission may prescribe as necessary or appropriate in the public interest or for the protection of investors.

(2) Paragraph (1) of this subsection shall not apply to security futures products.

(b) To use or employ, in connection with the purchase or sale of any security registered on a national securities exchange or any security not so registered, or any securities-based swap agreement, any manipulative or deceptive device or contrivance in contravention of such rules and regulations as the Commission may prescribe as necessary or appropriate in the public interest or for the protection of investors.

(c)(1) To effect, accept, or facilitate a transaction involving the loan or borrowing of securities in contravention of such rules and regulations as the Commission may prescribe as necessary or appropriate in the public interest or for the protection of investors.

(2) Nothing in paragraph (1) may be construed to limit the authority of the appropriate Federal banking agency (as defined in section 1813(q) of Title 12), the National Credit Union Administration, or any other Federal department or agency having a responsibility under Federal law to prescribe rules or regulations restricting transactions involving the loan or borrowing of securities in order to protect the safety and soundness of a financial institution or to protect the financial system from systemic risk.

Rules promulgated under subsection (b) that prohibit fraud, manipulation, or insider trading (but not rules imposing or specifying reporting or recordkeeping requirements, procedures, or standards as prophylactic measures against fraud, manipulation, or insider trading), and judicial precedents decided under subsection (b) and rules promulgated thereunder that prohibit fraud, manipulation, or insider trading, shall apply to security-based swap agreements to the same extent as they apply to securities. Judicial precedents decided under section 17(a) and sections 9, 15, 16, 20, and 21A of this

Act, and judicial precedents decided under applicable rules promulgated under such sections, shall apply to security-based swap agreements to the same extent as they apply to securities.

§ 12.   Registration Requirements for Securities

(a)   *General requirement of registration*

It shall be unlawful for any member, broker, or dealer to effect any transaction in any security (other than an exempted security) on a national securities exchange unless a registration is effective as to such security for such exchange in accordance with the provisions of this Act and the rules and regulations thereunder. The provisions of this subsection shall not apply in respect of a security futures product traded on a national securities exchange. * * *

(g)   *Registration of securities by issuer; exemptions*

(1)   Every issuer which is engaged in interstate commerce, or in a business affecting interstate commerce, or whose securities are traded by use of the mails or any means or instrumentality of interstate commerce shall—

(A)   within 120 days after the last day of its first fiscal year ended on which the issuer has total assets exceeding $10,000,000 and a class of equity security (other than an exempted security) held of record by either—

(i)   2,000 persons, or

(ii)   500 persons who are not accredited investors (as such term is defined by the Commission), and

(B)   in the case of an issuer that is a bank, a savings and loan holding company (as defined in section 1467a of the Home Owners' Loan Act), or a bank holding company, as such term is defined in section 2 of the Bank Holding Company Act of 1956, not later than 120 days after the last day of its first fiscal year ended after the effective date of this subsection, on which the issuer has total assets exceeding $10,000,000 and a class of equity security (other than an exempted security) held of record by 2,000 or more persons,

register such security by filing with the Commission a registration statement (and such copies thereof as the Commission may require) with respect to such security containing such information and documents as the Commission may specify comparable to that which is required in an application to register a security pursuant to subsection (b) of this section. Each such registration statement shall become effective sixty days after filing with the Commission or within such shorter period as the Commission may direct. Until such registration statement becomes effective it shall not be deemed filed for the purposes of section 18 of this Act. Any issuer may register any class of equity security not required to be registered by filing a registration statement pursuant to the provisions of this paragraph. The Commission is authorized to extend the date upon which any issuer or class of issuers is required to register a security pursuant to the provisions of this paragraph.

§ 13.   Periodical and Other Reports

(a)   *Reports by issuer of security; contents*

Every issuer of a security registered pursuant to section 12 of this Act shall file with the Commission, in accordance with such rules and regulations as the Commission may prescribe as necessary or appropriate for the proper protection of investors and to insure fair dealing in the security—

(1)   such information and documents (and such copies thereof) as the Commission shall require to keep reasonably current the information and documents required to be included in or filed with an application or registration statement filed pursuant to section 12 of this Act, except that the Commission may not require the filing of any material contract wholly executed before July 1, 1962.

(2) such annual reports (and such copies thereof), certified if required by the rules and regulations of the Commission by independent public accountants, and such quarterly reports (and such copies thereof), as the Commission may prescribe.

Every issuer of a security registered on a national securities exchange shall also file a duplicate original of such information, documents, and reports with the exchange. In any registration statement, periodic report, or other reports to be filed with the Commission, an emerging growth company need not present selected financial data in accordance with section 301 of title 17, Code of Federal Regulations, for any period prior to the earliest audited period presented in connection with its first registration statement that became effective under this Act or the Securities Act of 1933 and, with respect to any such statement or reports, an emerging growth company may not be required to comply with any new or revised financial accounting standard until such date that a company that is not an issuer (as defined under section 2(a) of the Sarbanes-Oxley Act of 2002) is required to comply with such new or revised accounting standard, if such standard applies to companies that are not issuers.

(b) *Form of report; books, records, and internal accounting; directives*

(1) The Commission may prescribe, in regard to reports made pursuant to this Act, the form or forms in which the required information shall be set forth, the items or details to be shown in the balance sheet and the earnings statement, and the methods to be followed in the preparation of reports, in the appraisal or valuation of assets and liabilities, in the determination of depreciation and depletion, in the differentiation of recurring and nonrecurring income, in the differentiation of investment and operating income, and in the preparation, where the Commission deems it necessary or desirable, of separate and/or consolidated balance sheets or income accounts of any person directly or indirectly controlling or controlled by the issuer, or any person under direct or indirect common control with the issuer; but in the case of the reports of any person whose methods of accounting are prescribed under the provisions of any law of the United States, or any rule or regulation thereunder, the rules and regulations of the Commission with respect to reports shall not be inconsistent with the requirements imposed by such law or rule or regulation in respect of the same subject matter (except that such rules and regulations of the Commission may be inconsistent with such requirements to the extent that the Commission determines that the public interest or the protection of investors so requires).

(2) Every issuer which has a class of securities registered pursuant to section 12 and every issuer which is required to file reports pursuant to section 15(d) of this Act shall—

(A) make and keep books, records, and accounts, which, in reasonable detail, accurately and fairly reflect the transactions and dispositions of the assets of the issuer;

(B) devise and maintain a system of internal accounting controls sufficient to provide reasonable assurances that—

(i) transactions are executed in accordance with management's general or specific authorization;

(ii) transactions are recorded as necessary (I) to permit preparation of financial statements in conformity with generally accepted accounting principles or any other criteria applicable to such statements, and (II) to maintain accountability for assets;

(iii) access to assets is permitted only in accordance with management's general or specific authorization; and

(iv) the recorded accountability for assets is compared with the existing assets at reasonable intervals and appropriate action is taken with respect to any differences.

* * *

(d) *Reports by persons acquiring more than five per centum of certain classes of securities*

(1) Any person who, after acquiring directly or indirectly the beneficial ownership of any equity security of a class which is registered pursuant to section 12 of this Act, or any equity

security of an insurance company which would have been required to be so registered except for the exemption contained in section 12(g)(2)(G) of this Act, or any equity security issued by a closed-end investment company registered under the Investment Company Act of 1940 or any equity security issued by a Native Corporation pursuant to section 1629c(d)(6) of Title 43, or otherwise becomes or is deemed to become a beneficial owner of any of the foregoing upon the purchase or sale of a security-based swap that the Commission may define by rule, and is directly or indirectly the beneficial owner of more than 5 per centum of such class shall, within ten days after such acquisition or within such shorter time as the Commission may establish by rule, file with the Commission, a statement containing such of the following information, and such additional information, as the Commission may by rules and regulations, prescribe as necessary or appropriate in the public interest or for the protection of investors—

(A) the background, and identity, residence, and citizenship of, and the nature of such beneficial ownership by, such person and all other persons by whom or on whose behalf the purchases have been or are to be effected;

(B) the source and amount of the funds or other consideration used or to be used in making the purchases, and if any part of the purchase price is represented or is to be represented by funds or other consideration borrowed or otherwise obtained for the purpose of acquiring, holding, or trading such security, a description of the transaction and the names of the parties thereto, except that where a source of funds is a loan made in the ordinary course of business by a bank, as defined in section 3(a)(6) of this Act, if the person filing such statement so requests, the name of the bank shall not be made available to the public;

(C) if the purpose of the purchases or prospective purchases is to acquire control of the business of the issuer of the securities, any plans or proposals which such persons may have to liquidate such issuer, to sell its assets to or merge it with any other persons, or to make any other major change in its business or corporate structure;

(D) the number of shares of such security which are beneficially owned, and the number of shares concerning which there is a right to acquire, directly or indirectly, by (i) such person, and (ii) by each associate of such person, giving the background, identity, residence, and citizenship of each such associate; and

(E) information as to any contracts, arrangements, or understandings with any person with respect to any securities of the issuer, including but not limited to transfer of any of the securities, joint ventures, loan or option arrangements, puts or calls, guaranties of loans, guaranties against loss or guaranties of profits, division of losses or profits, or the giving or withholding of proxies, naming the persons with whom such contracts, arrangements, or understandings have been entered into, and giving the details thereof.

(2) If any material change occurs in the facts set forth in the statement filed with the Commission, an amendment shall be filed with the Commission, in accordance with such rules and regulations as the Commission may prescribe as necessary or appropriate in the public interest or for the protection of investors.

(3) When two or more persons act as a partnership, limited partnership, syndicate, or other group for the purpose of acquiring, holding, or disposing of securities of an issuer, such syndicate or group shall be deemed a "person" for the purposes of this subsection.

(4) In determining, for purposes of this subsection, any percentage of a class of any security, such class shall be deemed to consist of the amount of the outstanding securities of such class, exclusive of any securities of such class held by or for the account of the issuer or a subsidiary of the issuer.

(5) The Commission, by rule or regulation or by order, may permit any person to file in lieu of the statement required by paragraph (1) of this subsection or the rules and regulations thereunder, a notice stating the name of such person, the number of shares of any equity

securities subject to paragraph (1) which are owned by him, the date of their acquisition and such other information as the Commission may specify, if it appears to the Commission that such securities were acquired by such person in the ordinary course of his business and were not acquired for the purpose of and do not have the effect of changing or influencing the control of the issuer nor in connection with or as a participant in any transaction having such purpose or effect.

(6)   The provisions of this subsection shall not apply to—

(A) any acquisition or offer to acquire securities made or proposed to be made by means of a registration statement under the Securities Act of 1933;

(B) any acquisition of the beneficial ownership of a security which, together with all other acquisitions by the same person of securities of the same class during the preceding twelve months, does not exceed 2 per centum of that class;

(C) any acquisition of an equity security by the issuer of such security;

(D) any acquisition or proposed acquisition of a security which the Commission, by rules or regulations or by order, shall exempt from the provisions of this subsection as not entered into for the purpose of, and not having the effect of, changing or influencing the control of the issuer or otherwise as not comprehended within the purposes of this subsection.

(e)   *Purchase of securities by issuer*

(1)   It shall be unlawful for an issuer which has a class of equity securities registered pursuant to section 12 of this Act, or which is a closed-end investment company registered under the Investment Company Act of 1940, to purchase any equity security issued by it if such purchase is in contravention of such rules and regulations as the Commission, in the public interest or for the protection of investors, may adopt (A) to define acts and practices which are fraudulent, deceptive, or manipulative, and (B) to prescribe means reasonably designed to prevent such acts and practices. Such rules and regulations may require such issuer to provide holders of equity securities of such class with such information relating to the reasons for such purchase, the source of funds, the number of shares to be purchased, the price to be paid for such securities, the method of purchase, and such additional information, as the Commission deems necessary or appropriate in the public interest or for the protection of investors, or which the Commission deems to be material to a determination whether such security should be sold.

(2)   For the purpose of this subsection, a purchase by or for the issuer or any person controlling, controlled by, or under common control with the issuer, or a purchase subject to control of the issuer or any such person, shall be deemed to be a purchase by the issuer. The Commission shall have power to make rules and regulations implementing this paragraph in the public interest and for the protection of investors, including exemptive rules and regulations covering situations in which the Commission deems it unnecessary or inappropriate that a purchase of the type described in this paragraph shall be deemed to be a purchase by the issuer for purposes of some or all of the provisions of paragraph (1) of this subsection.

(3)   At the time of filing such statement as the Commission may require by rule pursuant to paragraph (1) of this subsection, the person making the filing shall pay to the Commission a fee at a rate that, subject to paragraph (4), is equal to $92 per $1,000,000 of the value of securities proposed to be purchased. The fee shall be reduced with respect to securities in an amount equal to any fee paid with respect to any securities issued in connection with the proposed transaction under section 6(b) of the Securities Act of 1933, or the fee paid under that section shall be reduced in an amount equal to the fee paid to the Commission in connection with such transaction under this paragraph.

(4) *Annual adjustment*

For each fiscal year, the Commission shall by order adjust the rate required by paragraph (3) for such fiscal year to a rate that is equal to the rate (expressed in dollars per million) that is applicable under section 6(b) of the Securities Act of 1933 for such fiscal year.

(5) *Fee collections*

Fees collected pursuant to this subsection for fiscal year 2012 and each fiscal year thereafter shall be deposited and credited as general revenue of the Treasury and shall not be available for obligation.

(6) *Effective date; publication*

In exercising its authority under this subsection, the Commission shall not be required to comply with the provisions of section 553 of Title 5. An adjusted rate prescribed under paragraph (4) shall be published and take effect in accordance with section 6(b) of the Securities Act of 1933.

(7) *Pro rata application*

The rates per $1,000,000 required by this subsection shall be applied pro rata to amounts and balances of less than $1,000,000.

* * *

(r) *Disclosure of certain activities relating to Iran.*

(1) *In general.*—Each issuer required to file an annual or quarterly report under subsection (a) shall disclose in that report the information required by paragraph (2) if, during the period covered by the report, the issuer or any affiliate of the issuer—

(A) knowingly engaged in an activity described in subsection (a) or (b) of section 5 of the Iran Sanctions Act of 1996 (Public Law 104–172; 50 U.S.C. 1701 note);

(B) knowingly engaged in an activity described in subsection (c)(2) of section 104 of the Comprehensive Iran Sanctions, Accountability, and Divestment Act of 2010 (22 U.S.C. 8513) or a transaction described in subsection (d)(1) of that section;

(C) knowingly engaged in an activity described in section 105A(b)(2) of that Act; or

(D) knowingly conducted any transaction or dealing with—

(i) any person the property and interests in property of which are blocked pursuant to Executive Order No. 13224 (66 Fed. Reg. 49079; relating to blocking property and prohibiting transactions with persons who commit, threaten to commit, or support terrorism);

(ii) any person the property and interests in property of which are blocked pursuant to Executive Order No. 13382 (70 Fed. Reg. 38567; relating to blocking of property of weapons of mass destruction proliferators and their supporters); or

(iii) any person or entity identified under section 560.304 of title 31, Code of Federal Regulations (relating to the definition of the Government of Iran) without the specific authorization of a Federal department or agency.

(2) *Information required.*—If an issuer or an affiliate of the issuer has engaged in any activity described in paragraph (1), the issuer shall disclose a detailed description of each such activity, including—

(A) the nature and extent of the activity;

(B) the gross revenues and net profits, if any, attributable to the activity; and

(C) whether the issuer or the affiliate of the issuer (as the case may be) intends to continue the activity.

(3) *Notice of disclosures.*—If an issuer reports under paragraph (1) that the issuer or an affiliate of the issuer has knowingly engaged in any activity described in that paragraph, the issuer shall separately file with the Commission, concurrently with the annual or quarterly report under subsection (a), a notice that the disclosure of that activity has been included in that annual or quarterly report that identifies the issuer and contains the information required by paragraph (2).

(4) *Public disclosure of information.*—Upon receiving a notice under paragraph (3) that an annual or quarterly report includes a disclosure of an activity described in paragraph (1), the Commission shall promptly—

(A)   transmit the report to—

(i)   the President;

(ii)   the Committee on Foreign Affairs and the Committee on Financial Services of the House of Representatives; and

(iii)   the Committee on Foreign Relations and the Committee on Banking, Housing, and Urban Affairs of the Senate; and

(B)   make the information provided in the disclosure and the notice available to the public by posting the information on the Internet website of the Commission.

(5) *Investigations.*—Upon receiving a report under paragraph (4) that includes a disclosure of an activity described in paragraph (1) (other than an activity described in subparagraph (D)(iii) of that paragraph), the President shall—

(A)   initiate an investigation into the possible imposition of sanctions under the Iran Sanctions Act of 1996 (Public Law 104–172; 50 U.S.C. 1701 note), section 104 or 105A of the Comprehensive Iran Sanctions, Accountability, and Divestment Act of 2010, an Executive order specified in clause (i) or (ii) of paragraph (1)(D), or any other provision of law relating to the imposition of sanctions with respect to Iran, as applicable; and

(B)   not later than 180 days after initiating such an investigation, make a determination with respect to whether sanctions should be imposed with respect to the issuer or the affiliate of the issuer (as the case may be).

(6) *Sunset.*—The provisions of this subsection shall terminate on the date that is 30 days after the date on which the President makes the certification described in section 401(a) of the Comprehensive Iran Sanctions, Accountability, and Divestment Act of 2010 (22 U.S.C. 8551(a)).

§ 14.   Proxies

(a)(1)   *Solicitation of proxies in violation of rules and regulations*

It shall be unlawful for any person, by the use of the mails or by any means or instrumentality of interstate commerce or of any facility of a national securities exchange or otherwise, in contravention of such rules and regulations as the Commission may prescribe as necessary or appropriate in the public interest or for the protection of investors, to solicit or to permit the use of his name to solicit any proxy or consent or authorization in respect of any security (other than an exempted security) registered pursuant to section 12 of this Act.

(2)   The rules and regulations prescribed by the Commission under paragraph (1) may include—

(A)   a requirement that a solicitation of proxy, consent, or authorization by (or on behalf of) an issuer include a nominee submitted by a shareholder to serve on the board of directors of the issuer; and

(B)   a requirement that an issuer follow a certain procedure in relation to a solicitation described in subparagraph (A).

(b) *Giving or refraining from giving proxy in respect of any security carried for account of customer*

    (1)   It shall be unlawful for any member of a national securities exchange, or any broker or dealer registered under this Act, or any bank, association, or other entity that exercises fiduciary powers, in contravention of such rules and regulations as the Commission may prescribe as necessary or appropriate in the public interest or for the protection of investors, to give, or to refrain from giving a proxy, consent, authorization, or information statement in respect of any security registered pursuant to section 78l of this title, or any security issued by an investment company registered under the Investment Company Act of 1940, and carried for the account of a customer.

    (2)   With respect to banks, the rules and regulations prescribed by the Commission under paragraph (1) shall not require the disclosure of the names of beneficial owners of securities in an account held by the bank on December 28, 1985, unless the beneficial owner consents to the disclosure. The provisions of this paragraph shall not apply in the case of a bank which the Commission finds has not made a good faith effort to obtain such consent from such beneficial owners.

(c) *Information to holders of record prior to annual or other meeting*

Unless proxies, consents, or authorizations in respect of a security registered pursuant to section 12 of this Act, or a security issued by an investment company registered under the Investment Company Act of 1940, are solicited by or on behalf of the management of the issuer from the holders of record of such security in accordance with the rules and regulations prescribed under subsection (a) of this section, prior to any annual or other meeting of the holders of such security, such issuer shall, in accordance with rules and regulations prescribed by the Commission, file with the Commission and transmit to all holders of record of such security information substantially equivalent to the information which would be required to be transmitted if a solicitation were made, but no information shall be required to be filed or transmitted pursuant to this subsection before July 1, 1964.

(d) *Tender offer by owner of more than five per centum of class of securities; exceptions*

    (1)   It shall be unlawful for any person, directly or indirectly, by use of the mails or by any means or instrumentality of interstate commerce or of any facility of a national securities exchange or otherwise, to make a tender offer for, or a request or invitation for tenders of, any class of any equity security which is registered pursuant to section 12 of this Act, or any equity security of an insurance company which would have been required to be so registered except for the exemption contained in section 12(g)(2)(G) of this Act, or any equity security issued by a closed-end investment company registered under the Investment Company Act of 1940, if, after consummation thereof, such person would, directly or indirectly, be the beneficial owner of more than 5 per centum of such class, unless at the time copies of the offer or request or invitation are first published or sent or given to security holders such person has filed with the Commission a statement containing such of the information specified in section 13(d) of this Act, and such additional information as the Commission may by rules and regulations prescribe as necessary or appropriate in the public interest or for the protection of investors. All requests or invitations for tenders or advertisements making a tender offer or requesting or inviting tenders of such a security shall be filed as a part of such statement and shall contain such of the information contained in such statement as the Commission may by rules and regulations prescribe. Copies of any additional material soliciting or requesting such tender offers subsequent to the initial solicitation or request shall contain such information as the Commission may by rules and regulations prescribe as necessary or appropriate in the public interest or for the protection of investors, and shall be filed with the Commission not later than the time copies of such material are first published or sent or given to security holders. Copies of all statements, in the form in which such material is furnished to security holders and the Commission, shall be sent to the issuer not later than the date such material is first published or sent or given to any security holders.

(2)　When two or more persons act as a partnership, limited partnership, syndicate, or other group for the purpose of acquiring, holding, or disposing of securities of an issuer, such syndicate or group shall be deemed a "person" for purposes of this subsection.

(3)　In determining, for purposes of this subsection, any percentage of a class of any security, such class shall be deemed to consist of the amount of the outstanding securities of such class, exclusive of any securities of such class held by or for the account of the issuer or a subsidiary of the issuer.

(4)　Any solicitation or recommendation to the holders of such a security to accept or reject a tender offer or request or invitation for tenders shall be made in accordance with such rules and regulations as the Commission may prescribe as necessary or appropriate in the public interest or for the protection of investors.

(5)　Securities deposited pursuant to a tender offer or request or invitation for tenders may be withdrawn by or on behalf of the depositor at any time until the expiration of seven days after the time definitive copies of the offer or request or invitation are first published or sent or given to security holders, and at any time after sixty days from the date of the original tender offer or request or invitation, except as the Commission may otherwise prescribe by rules, regulations, or order as necessary or appropriate in the public interest or for the protection of investors.

(6)　Where any person makes a tender offer, or request or invitation for tenders, for less than all the outstanding equity securities of a class, and where a greater number of securities is deposited pursuant thereto within ten days after copies of the offer or request or invitation are first published or sent or given to security holders than such person is bound or willing to take up and pay for, the securities taken up shall be taken up as nearly as may be pro rata, disregarding fractions, according to the number of securities deposited by each depositor. The provisions of this subsection shall also apply to securities deposited within ten days after notice of an increase in the consideration offered to security holders, as described in paragraph (7), is first published or sent or given to security holders.

(7)　Where any person varies the terms of a tender offer or request or invitation for tenders before the expiration thereof by increasing the consideration offered to holders of such securities, such person shall pay the increased consideration to each security holder whose securities are taken up and paid for pursuant to the tender offer or request or invitation for tenders whether or not such securities have been taken up by such person before the variation of the tender offer or request or invitation.

(8)　The provisions of this subsection shall not apply to any offer for, or request or invitation for tenders of, any security—

(A)　if the acquisition of such security, together with all other acquisitions by the same person of securities of the same class during the preceding twelve months, would not exceed 2 per centum of that class;

(B)　by the issuer of such security; or

(C)　which the Commission, by rules or regulations or by order, shall exempt from the provisions of this subsection as not entered into for the purpose of, and not having the effect of, changing or influencing the control of the issuer or otherwise as not comprehended within the purposes of this subsection.

(e)　*Untrue statement of material fact or omission of fact with respect to tender offer*

It shall be unlawful for any person to make any untrue statement of a material fact or omit to state any material fact necessary in order to make the statements made, in the light of the circumstances under which they are made, not misleading, or to engage in any fraudulent, deceptive, or manipulative acts or practices, in connection with any tender offer or request or invitation for tenders, or any solicitation of security holders in opposition to or in favor of any such offer, request, or invitation. The Commission shall, for the purposes of this subsection, by rules and regulations define, and prescribe means reasonably designed to prevent, such acts and practices as are fraudulent, deceptive, or manipulative.

(f) *Election or designation of majority of directors of issuer by owner of more than five per centum of class of securities at other than meeting of security holders*

If, pursuant to any arrangement or understanding with the person or persons acquiring securities in a transaction subject to subsection (d) of this section or subsection (d) of section 13 of this Act, any persons are to be elected or designated as directors of the issuer, otherwise than at a meeting of security holders, and the persons so elected or designated will constitute a majority of the directors of the issuer, then, prior to the time any such person takes office as a director, and in accordance with rules and regulations prescribed by the Commission, the issuer shall file with the Commission, and transmit to all holders of record of securities of the issuer who would be entitled to vote at a meeting for election of directors, information substantially equivalent to the information which would be required by subsection (a) or (c) to be transmitted if such person or persons were nominees for election as directors at a meeting of such security holders.

* * *

§ 14A. Shareholder Approval of Executive Compensation

(a) *Separate resolution required*

(1) *In general.* Not less frequently than once every 3 years, a proxy or consent or authorization for an annual or other meeting of the shareholders for which the proxy solicitation rules of the Commission require compensation disclosure shall include a separate resolution subject to shareholder vote to approve the compensation of executives, as disclosed pursuant to section 229.402 of title 17, Code of Federal Regulations, or any successor thereto.

(2) *Frequency of vote.* Not less frequently than once every 6 years, a proxy or consent or authorization for an annual or other meeting of the shareholders for which the proxy solicitation rules of the Commission require compensation disclosure shall include a separate resolution subject to shareholder vote to determine whether votes on the resolutions required under paragraph (1) will occur every 1, 2, or 3 years.

(3) *Effective date.* The proxy or consent or authorization for the first annual or other meeting of the shareholders occurring after the end of the 6-month period beginning on July 21, 2010 shall include—

(A) the resolution described in paragraph (1); and

(B) a separate resolution subject to shareholder vote to determine whether votes on the resolutions required under paragraph (1) will occur every 1, 2, or 3 years.

(b) *Shareholder approval of golden parachute compensation*

(1) *Disclosure.* In any proxy or consent solicitation material (the solicitation of which is subject to the rules of the Commission pursuant to subsection (a)) for a meeting of the shareholders occurring after the end of the 6-month period beginning on July 21, 2010, at which shareholders are asked to approve an acquisition, merger, consolidation, or proposed sale or other disposition of all or substantially all the assets of an issuer, the person making such solicitation shall disclose in the proxy or consent solicitation material, in a clear and simple form in accordance with regulations to be promulgated by the Commission, any agreements or understandings that such person has with any named executive officers of such issuer (or of the acquiring issuer, if such issuer is not the acquiring issuer) concerning any type of compensation (whether present, deferred, or contingent) that is based on or otherwise relates to the acquisition, merger, consolidation, sale, or other disposition of all or substantially all of the assets of the issuer

and the aggregate total of all such compensation that may (and the conditions upon which it may) be paid or become payable to or on behalf of such executive officer.

(2)   *Shareholder approval.* Any proxy or consent or authorization relating to the proxy or consent solicitation material containing the disclosure required by paragraph (1) shall include a separate resolution subject to shareholder vote to approve such agreements or understandings and compensation as disclosed, unless such agreements or understandings have been subject to a shareholder vote under subsection (a).

(c)   *Rule of construction.* The shareholder vote referred to in subsections (a) and (b) shall not be binding on the issuer or the board of directors of an issuer, and may not be construed—

(1)   as overruling a decision by such issuer or board of directors;

(2)   to create or imply any change to the fiduciary duties of such issuer or board of directors;

(3)   to create or imply any additional fiduciary duties for such issuer or board of directors; or

(4)   to restrict or limit the ability of shareholders to make proposals for inclusion in proxy materials related to executive compensation.

(d)   *Disclosure of votes.* Every institutional investment manager subject to section 13(f) of this Act shall report at least annually how it voted on any shareholder vote pursuant to subsections (a) and (b), unless such vote is otherwise required to be reported publicly by rule or regulation of the Commission.

(e)   *Exemption.*

(1)   *In general.*—The Commission may, by rule or order, exempt any other issuer or class of issuers from the requirement under subsection (a) or (b). In determining whether to make an exemption under this subsection, the Commission shall take into account, among other considerations, whether the requirements under subsections (a) and (b) disproportionately burdens small issuers.

(2)   *Treatment of emerging growth companies.*—

(A)   *In general.*—An emerging growth company shall be exempt from the requirements of subsections (a) and (b).

(B)   *Compliance after termination of emerging growth company treatment.*—An issuer that was an emerging growth company but is no longer an emerging growth company shall include the first separate resolution described under subsection (a)(1) not later than the end of—

(i)   in the case of an issuer that was an emerging growth company for less than 2 years after the date of first sale of common equity securities of the issuer pursuant to an effective registration statement under the Securities Act of 1933, the 3-year period beginning on such date; and

(ii)   in the case of any other issuer, the 1-year period beginning on the date the issuer is no longer an emerging growth company.

§ 16.   Directors, Officers, and Principal Stockholders

(a)   *Disclosures Required*

(1)   *Directors, officers, and principal stockholders required to file.* Every person who is directly or indirectly the beneficial owner of more than 10 percent of any class of any equity security (other than an exempted security) which is registered pursuant to section 12 of this title, or who is a director or an officer of the issuer of such security, shall file the statements required by this subsection with the Commission.

(2) *Time of filing.* The statements required by this subsection shall be filed—

(A) at the time of the registration of such security on a national securities exchange or by the effective date of a registration statement filed pursuant to 12(g) of this Act;

(B) within 10 days after he she becomes such beneficial owner, director, or officer, or within such shorter time as the Commission may establish by rule;

(C) if there has been a change in such ownership, or if such person shall have purchased or sold a security-based swap agreement involving such equity security, before the end of the second business day following the day on which the subject transaction has been executed, or at such other time as the Commission shall establish, by rule, in any case in which the Commission determines that such 2-day period is not feasible.

(3) *Contents of statements.* A statement filed—

(A) under subparagraph (A) or (B) of paragraph (2) shall contain a statement of the amount of all equity securities of such issuer of which the filing person is the beneficial owner; and

(B) under subparagraph (C) of such paragraph shall indicate ownership by the filing person at the date of filing, any such changes in such ownership, and such purchases and sales of the security-based swap agreements or security-based swaps as have occurred since the most recent such filing under such subparagraph.

(4) *Electronic filing and availability.* Beginning not later than 1 year after July 30, 2002—

(A) a statement filed under subparagraph (C) of paragraph (2) shall be filed electronically;

(B) the Commission shall provide each such statement on a publicly accessible Internet site not later than the end of the business day following that filing; and

(C) the issuer (if the issuer maintains a corporate website) shall provide that statement on that corporate website, not later than the end of the business day following that filing.

(b) *Profits from purchase and sale of security within six months*

For the purpose of preventing the unfair use of information which may have been obtained by such beneficial owner, director, or officer by reason of his relationship to the issuer, any profit realized by him from any purchase and sale, or any sale and purchase, of any equity security of such issuer (other than an exempted security) or a security-based swap agreement involving any such equity security within any period of less than six months, unless such security or security-based swap agreement was acquired in good faith in connection with a debt previously contracted, shall inure to and be recoverable by the issuer, irrespective of any intention on the part of such beneficial owner, director, or officer in entering into such transaction of holding the security or security-based swap agreement purchased or of not repurchasing the security or security-based swap agreement sold for a period exceeding six months. Suit to recover such profit may be instituted at law or in equity in any court of competent jurisdiction by the issuer, or by the owner of any security of the issuer in the name and in behalf of the issuer if the issuer shall fail or refuse to bring such suit within sixty days after request or shall fail diligently to prosecute the same thereafter; but no such suit shall be brought more than two years after the date such profit was realized. This subsection shall not be construed to cover any transaction where such beneficial owner was not such both at the time of the purchase and sale, or the sale and purchase, of the security or security based swap agreement, or any transaction or transactions which the Commission by rules and regulations may exempt as not comprehended within the purpose of this subsection.

(c) *Conditions for sale of security by beneficial owner, director, or officer*

It shall be unlawful for any such beneficial owner, director, or officer, directly or indirectly, to sell any equity security of such issuer (other than an exempted security), if the person selling the security or his principal (1) does not own the security sold, or (2) if owning the security, does not deliver it against such sale within twenty days thereafter, or does not within five days after such sale deposit it in the mails or other usual channels of transportation; but no person shall be deemed to have violated this subsection if he proves that notwithstanding the exercise of good faith he was unable to make such delivery or deposit within such time, or that to do so would cause undue inconvenience or expense.

(d) *Securities held in investment account, transactions in ordinary course of business, and establishment of primary or secondary market*

The provisions of subsection (b) of this section shall not apply to any purchase and sale, or sale and purchase, and the provisions of subsection (c) of this section shall not apply to any sale, of an equity security not then or theretofore held by him in an investment account, by a dealer in the ordinary course of his business and incident to the establishment or maintenance by him of a primary or secondary market (otherwise than on a national securities exchange or an exchange exempted from registration under section 5 of this Act) for such security. The Commission may, by such rules and regulations as it deems necessary or appropriate in the public interest, define and prescribe terms and conditions with respect to securities held in an investment account and transactions made in the ordinary course of business and incident to the establishment or maintenance of a primary or secondary market.

(e) *Application of section to foreign or domestic arbitrage transactions*

The provisions of this section shall not apply to foreign or domestic arbitrage transactions unless made in contravention of such rules and regulations as the Commission may adopt in order to carry out the purposes of this section.

(f) *Treatment of transactions in security futures products*

The provisions of this section shall apply to ownership of and transactions in security futures products.

(g) *Applicability of other provisions concerning swap agreements*

The authority of the Commission under this section with respect to security-based swap agreements shall be subject to the restrictions and limitations of section 3A(b) of this Act.

* * *

§ 19. Registration, Responsibilities, and Oversight of Self-Regulatory Organizations

(a) *Registration procedures; notice of filing; other regulatory agencies*

(1) The Commission shall, upon the filing of an application for registration as a national securities exchange, registered securities association, or registered clearing agency, pursuant to section 6, 15A, or 17A of this Act, respectively, publish notice of such filing and afford interested persons an opportunity to submit written data, views, and arguments concerning such application. Within ninety days of the date of publication of such notice (or within such longer period as to which the applicant consents), the Commission shall—

(A) by order grant such registration, or

(B) institute proceedings to determine whether registration should be denied. Such proceedings shall include notice of the grounds for denial under consideration and opportunity for hearing and shall be concluded within one hundred eighty days of the date of a publication of notice of the filing of the application for registration. At the conclusion of such proceedings the Commission, by order, shall grant or deny such registration. The

Commission may extend the time for conclusion of such proceedings for up to ninety days if it finds good cause for such extension and publishes its reasons for so finding or for such longer period as to which the applicant consents.

The Commission shall grant such registration if it finds that the requirements of this Act and the rules and regulations thereunder with respect to the applicant are satisfied. The Commission shall deny such registration if it does not make such finding.

* * *

§ 20. Liability of Controlling Persons and Persons Who Aid and Abet Violations

(a) *Joint and several liability; good faith defense*

Every person who, directly or indirectly, controls any person liable under any provision of this Act or of any rule or regulation thereunder shall also be liable jointly and severally with and to the same extent as such controlled person to any person to whom such controlled person is liable (including to the Commission in any action brought under paragraph (1) or (3) of section 21(d)) of this Act, unless the controlling person acted in good faith and did not directly or indirectly induce the act or acts constituting the violation or cause of action.

(b) *Unlawful activity through or by means of any other person*

It shall be unlawful for any person, directly or indirectly, to do any act or thing which it would be unlawful for such person to do under the provisions of this Act or any rule or regulation thereunder through or by means of any other person.

(c) *Hindering, delaying, or obstructing the making or filing of any document, report, or information*

It shall be unlawful for any director or officer of, or any owner of any securities issued by, any issuer required to file any document, report, or information under this Act or any rule or regulation thereunder without just cause to hinder, delay, or obstruct the making or filing of any such document, report, or information.

(d) *Liability for trading in securities while in possession of material nonpublic information*

Wherever communicating, or purchasing or selling a security while in possession of, material nonpublic information would violate, or result in liability to any purchaser or seller of the security under any provisions of this Act, or any rule or regulation thereunder, such conduct in connection with a purchase or sale of a put, call, straddle, option, privilege or security-based swap agreement with respect to such security or with respect to a group or index of securities including such security, shall also violate and result in comparable liability to any purchaser or seller of that security under such provision, rule, or regulation.

(e) *Prosecution of persons who aid and abet violations*

For purposes of any action brought by the Commission under paragraph (1) or (3) of section 21(d) of this Act, any person that knowingly or recklessly provides substantial assistance to another person in violation of a provision of this Act, or of any rule or regulation issued under this Act, shall be deemed to be in violation of such provision to the same extent as the person to whom such assistance is provided.

* * *

§ 20A. Liability to Contemporaneous Traders for Insider Trading

(a) *Private rights of action based on contemporaneous trading*

Any person who violates any provision of this Act or the rules or regulations thereunder by purchasing or selling a security while in possession of material, nonpublic information shall be liable in an action in any court of competent jurisdiction to any person who, contemporaneously with the purchase or sale of securities that is the subject of such violation, has purchased (where such violation is based on a sale of securities) or sold (where such violation is based on a purchase of securities) securities of the same class.

(b) *Limitations on liability*

(1) *Contemporaneous trading actions limited to profit gained or loss avoided*

The total amount of damages imposed under subsection (a) of this section shall not exceed the profit gained or loss avoided in the transaction or transactions that are the subject of the violation.

(2) *Offsetting disgorgements against liability*

The total amount of damages imposed against any person under subsection (a) of this section shall be diminished by the amounts, if any, that such person may be required to disgorge, pursuant to a court order obtained at the instance of the Commission, in a proceeding brought under section 21(d) of this Act relating to the same transaction or transactions.

(3) *Controlling person liability*

No person shall be liable under this section solely by reason of employing another person who is liable under this section, but the liability of a controlling person under this section shall be subject to section 20(a).

(4) *Statute of limitations*

No action may be brought under this section more than 5 years after the date of the last transaction that is the subject of the violation.

(c) *Joint and several liability for communicating*

Any person who violates any provision of this Act or the rules or regulations thereunder by communicating material, nonpublic information shall be jointly and severally liable under subsection (a) of this section with, and to the same extent as, any person or persons liable under subsection (a) of this section to whom the communication was directed.

(d) *Authority not to restrict other express or implied rights of action*

Nothing in this section shall be construed to limit or condition the right of any person to bring an action to enforce a requirement of this Act or the availability of any cause of action implied from a provision of this Act.

(e) *Provisions not to affect public prosecutions*

This section shall not be construed to bar or limit in any manner any action by the Commission or the Attorney General under any other provision of this Act, nor shall it bar or limit in any manner any action to recover penalties, or to seek any other order regarding penalties.

* * *

§ 21A. Civil Penalties for Insider Trading

(a) *Authority to impose civil penalties*

(1) *Judicial actions by Commission authorized*

Whenever it shall appear to the Commission that any person has violated any provision of this Act or the rules or regulations thereunder by purchasing or selling a security or security-based swap agreement while in possession of material, nonpublic information in, or has violated any such provision by communicating such information in connection with, a transaction on or through the facilities of a national securities exchange or from or through a broker or dealer, and which is not part of a public offering by an issuer of securities other than standardized options or security futures products, the Commission—

(A) may bring an action in a United States district court to seek, and the court shall have jurisdiction to impose, a civil penalty to be paid by the person who committed such violation; and

(B) may, subject to subsection (b)(1) of this section, bring an action in a United States district court to seek, and the court shall have jurisdiction to impose, a civil penalty to be paid by a person who, at the time of the violation, directly or indirectly controlled the person who committed such violation.

(2) *Amount of penalty for person who committed violation*

The amount of the penalty which may be imposed on the person who committed such violation shall be determined by the court in light of the facts and circumstances, but shall not exceed three times the profit gained or loss avoided as a result of such unlawful purchase, sale, or communication.

(3) *Amount of penalty for controlling person*

The amount of the penalty which may be imposed on any person who, at the time of the violation, directly or indirectly controlled the person who committed such violation, shall be determined by the court in light of the facts and circumstances, but shall not exceed the greater of $1,000,000, or three times the amount of the profit gained or loss avoided as a result of such controlled person's violation. If such controlled person's violation was a violation by communication, the profit gained or loss avoided as a result of the violation shall, for purposes of this paragraph only, be deemed to be limited to the profit gained or loss avoided by the person or persons to whom the controlled person directed such communication.

(b) *Limitations on liability*

(1) *Liability of controlling persons*

No controlling person shall be subject to a penalty under subsection (a)(1)(B) of this section unless the Commission establishes that—

(A) such controlling person knew or recklessly disregarded the fact that such controlled person was likely to engage in the act or acts constituting the violation and failed to take appropriate steps to prevent such act or acts before they occurred; or

(B) such controlling person knowingly or recklessly failed to establish, maintain, or enforce any policy or procedure required under section 15(f) or section 80b–4a of this Act and such failure substantially contributed to or permitted the occurrence of the act or acts constituting the violation.

(2) *Additional restrictions on liability*

No person shall be subject to a penalty under subsection (a) of this section solely by reason of employing another person who is subject to a penalty under such subsection, unless such employing person is liable as a controlling person under paragraph (1) of this subsection. Section 20(a) of this Act shall not apply to actions under subsection (a) of this section.

(c) *Authority of Commission*

The Commission, by such rules, regulations, and orders as it considers necessary or appropriate in the public interest or for the protection of investors, may exempt, in whole or in part, either unconditionally or upon specific terms and conditions, any person or transaction or class of persons or transactions from this section.

(d) *Procedures for collection*

(1) *Payment of penalty to Treasury*

A penalty imposed under this section shall be payable into the Treasury of the United States, except as otherwise provided in section 7246 of this title and section 21F of this Act.

(2) *Collection of penalties*

If a person upon whom such a penalty is imposed shall fail to pay such penalty within the time prescribed in the court's order, the Commission may refer the matter to the Attorney General who shall recover such penalty by action in the appropriate United States district court.

(3) *Remedy not exclusive*

The actions authorized by this section may be brought in addition to any other actions that the Commission or the Attorney General are entitled to bring.

* * *

(5) *Statute of limitations*

No action may be brought under this section more than 5 years after the date of the purchase or sale. This section shall not be construed to bar or limit in any manner any action by the Commission or the Attorney General under any other provision of this Act, nor shall it bar or limit in any manner any action to recover penalties, or to seek any other order regarding penalties, imposed in an action commenced within 5 years of such transaction.

(e) *Definition*

For purposes of this section, "profit gained" or "loss avoided" is the difference between the purchase or sale price of the security and the value of that security as measured by the trading price of the security a reasonable period after public dissemination of the nonpublic information.

* * *

(g) *Duty of members and employees of congress.*

(1) *In general.*—Subject to the rule of construction under section 10 of the STOCK Act and solely for purposes of the insider trading prohibitions arising under this Act, including section 10(b) and Rule 10b–5 thereunder, each Member of Congress or employee of Congress owes a duty arising from a relationship of trust and confidence to the Congress, the United States Government, and the citizens of the United States with respect to material, nonpublic information derived from such person's position as a Member of Congress or employee of Congress or gained from the performance of such person's official responsibilities.

(2) *Definitions.*—In this subsection—

(A) the term 'Member of Congress' means a member of the Senate or House of Representatives, a Delegate to the House of Representatives, and the Resident Commissioner from Puerto Rico; and

(B) *The term 'employee of congress' means.*—

(i) any individual (other than a Member of Congress), whose compensation is disbursed by the Secretary of the Senate or the Chief Administrative Officer of the House of Representatives; and

(ii) any other officer or employee of the legislative branch (as defined in section 109(11) of the Ethics in Government Act of 1978).

(3) *Rule of construction.*—Nothing in this subsection shall be construed to impair or limit the construction of the existing antifraud provisions of the securities laws or the authority of the Commission under those provisions.

(h) *Duty of other federal officials.*

(1) *In general.*—Subject to the rule of construction under section 10 of the STOCK Act and solely for purposes of the insider trading prohibitions arising under this Act, including section 10(b), and Rule 10b–5 thereunder, each executive branch employee, each judicial officer, and each judicial employee owes a duty arising from a relationship of trust and confidence to the United States Government and the citizens of the United States with respect to material, nonpublic information derived from such person's position as an executive branch employee, judicial officer, or judicial employee or gained from the performance of such person's official responsibilities.

(2) *Definitions.*—In this subsection—

(A) the term 'executive branch employee'—

(i) has the meaning given the term 'employee' under section 2105 of title 5, United States Code;

(ii) includes—

(I) the President;

(II) the Vice President; and

(III) an employee of the United States Postal Service or the Postal Regulatory Commission;

(B) the term 'judicial employee' has the meaning given that term in section 109(8) of the Ethics in Government Act of 1978; and

(C) the term 'judicial officer' has the meaning given that term under section 109(10) of the Ethics in Government Act of 1978.

(3) *Rule of construction.*—Nothing in this subsection shall be construed to impair or limit the construction of the existing antifraud provisions of the securities laws or the authority of the Commission under those provisions.

(i) *Participation in initial public offerings.*

An individual described in section 101(f) of the Ethics in Government Act of 1978 may not purchase securities that are the subject of an initial public offering (within the meaning given such term in section 12(f)(1)(G)(i) of this Act) in any manner other than is available to members of the public generally.

* * *

§ 21D. Private Securities Litigation

(a) *Private class actions*

(1) *In general*

The provisions of this subsection shall apply in each private action arising under this Act that is brought as a plaintiff class action pursuant to the Federal Rules of Civil Procedure.

(2) *Certification filed with complaint*

(A) *In general*

Each plaintiff seeking to serve as a representative party on behalf of a class shall provide a sworn certification, which shall be personally signed by such plaintiff and filed with the complaint, that—

(i) states that the plaintiff has reviewed the complaint and authorized its filing;

(ii)   states that the plaintiff did not purchase the security that is the subject of the complaint at the direction of plaintiff's counsel or in order to participate in any private action arising under this Act;

(iii)   states that the plaintiff is willing to serve as a representative party on behalf of a class, including providing testimony at deposition and trial, if necessary;

(iv)   sets forth all of the transactions of the plaintiff in the security that is the subject of the complaint during the class period specified in the complaint;

(v)   identifies any other action under this Act, filed during the 3-year period preceding the date on which the certification is signed by the plaintiff, in which the plaintiff has sought to serve as a representative party on behalf of a class; and

(vi)   states that the plaintiff will not accept any payment for serving as a representative party on behalf of a class beyond the plaintiff's pro rata share of any recovery, except as ordered or approved by the court in accordance with paragraph (4).

(B)   *Nonwaiver of attorney-client privilege*

The certification filed pursuant to subparagraph (A) shall not be construed to be a waiver of the attorney-client privilege.

(3)   *Appointment of lead plaintiff*

(A)   *Early notice to class members*

(i)   *In general*

Not later than 20 days after the date on which the complaint is filed, the plaintiff or plaintiffs shall cause to be published, in a widely circulated national business-oriented publication or wire service, a notice advising members of the purported plaintiff class—

(I)   of the pendency of the action, the claims asserted therein, and the purported class period; and

(II)   that, not later than 60 days after the date on which the notice is published, any member of the purported class may move the court to serve as lead plaintiff of the purported class.

(ii)   *Multiple actions*

If more than one action on behalf of a class asserting substantially the same claim or claims arising under this Act is filed, only the plaintiff or plaintiffs in the first filed action shall be required to cause notice to be published in accordance with clause (i).

(iii)   *Additional notices may be required under Federal rules*

Notice required under clause (i) shall be in addition to any notice required pursuant to the Federal Rules of Civil Procedure.

(B)   *Appointment of lead plaintiff*

(i)   *In general*

Not later than 90 days after the date on which a notice is published under subparagraph (A)(i), the court shall consider any motion made by a purported class member in response to the notice, including any motion by a class member who is not individually named as a plaintiff in the complaint or complaints, and shall appoint as lead plaintiff the member or members of the purported plaintiff class that the court determines to be most capable of adequately representing the interests of class members (hereafter in this paragraph referred to as the "most adequate plaintiff") in accordance with this subparagraph.

(ii) *Consolidated actions*

If more than one action on behalf of a class asserting substantially the same claim or claims arising under this Act has been filed, and any party has sought to consolidate those actions for pretrial purposes or for trial, the court shall not make the determination required by clause (i) until after the decision on the motion to consolidate is rendered. As soon as practicable after such decision is rendered, the court shall appoint the most adequate plaintiff as lead plaintiff for the consolidated actions in accordance with this paragraph.

(iii) *Rebuttable presumption*

(I) *In general*

Subject to subclause (II), for purposes of clause (i), the court shall adopt a presumption that the most adequate plaintiff in any private action arising under this Act is the person or group of persons that—

(aa) has either filed the complaint or made a motion in response to a notice under subparagraph (A)(i);

(bb) in the determination of the court, has the largest financial interest in the relief sought by the class; and

(cc) otherwise satisfies the requirements of Rule 23 of the Federal Rules of Civil Procedure.

(II) *Rebuttal evidence*

The presumption described in subclause (I) may be rebutted only upon proof by a member of the purported plaintiff class that the presumptively most adequate plaintiff—

(aa) will not fairly and adequately protect the interests of the class; or

(bb) is subject to unique defenses that render such plaintiff incapable of adequately representing the class.

(iv) *Discovery*

For purposes of this subparagraph, discovery relating to whether a member or members of the purported plaintiff class is the most adequate plaintiff may be conducted by a plaintiff only if the plaintiff first demonstrates a reasonable basis for a finding that the presumptively most adequate plaintiff is incapable of adequately representing the class.

(v) *Selection of lead counsel*

The most adequate plaintiff shall, subject to the approval of the court, select and retain counsel to represent the class.

(vi) *Restrictions on professional plaintiffs*

Except as the court may otherwise permit, consistent with the purposes of this section, a person may be a lead plaintiff, or an officer, director, or fiduciary of a lead plaintiff, in no more than 5 securities class actions brought as plaintiff class actions pursuant to the Federal Rules of Civil Procedure during any 3-year period.

(4) *Recovery by plaintiffs*

The share of any final judgment or of any settlement that is awarded to a representative party serving on behalf of a class shall be equal, on a per share basis, to the portion of the final judgment or settlement awarded to all other members of the class. Nothing in this paragraph shall be construed to limit the award of reasonable costs and expenses (including lost wages) directly relating to the representation of the class to any representative party serving on behalf of a class.

(5) *Restrictions on settlements under seal*

The terms and provisions of any settlement agreement of a class action shall not be filed under seal, except that on motion of any party to the settlement, the court may order filing under seal for those portions of a settlement agreement as to which good cause is shown for such filing under seal. For purposes of this paragraph, good cause shall exist only if publication of a term or provision of a settlement agreement would cause direct and substantial harm to any party.

(6) *Restrictions on payment of attorneys' fees and expenses*

Total attorneys' fees and expenses awarded by the court to counsel for the plaintiff class shall not exceed a reasonable percentage of the amount of any damages and prejudgment interest actually paid to the class.

(7) *Disclosure of settlement terms to class members*

Any proposed or final settlement agreement that is published or otherwise disseminated to the class shall include each of the following statements, along with a cover page summarizing the information contained in such statements:

(A) *Statement of plaintiff recovery*

The amount of the settlement proposed to be distributed to the parties to the action, determined in the aggregate and on an average per share basis.

(B) *Statement of potential outcome of case*

(i) *Agreement on amount of damages*

If the settling parties agree on the average amount of damages per share that would be recoverable if the plaintiff prevailed on each claim alleged under this Act, a statement concerning the average amount of such potential damages per share.

(ii) *Disagreement on amount of damages*

If the parties do not agree on the average amount of damages per share that would be recoverable if the plaintiff prevailed on each claim alleged under this Act, a statement from each settling party concerning the issue or issues on which the parties disagree.

(iii) *Inadmissibility for certain purposes*

A statement made in accordance with clause (i) or (ii) concerning the amount of damages shall not be admissible in any Federal or State judicial action or administrative proceeding, other than an action or proceeding arising out of such statement.

(C) *Statement of attorneys' fees or costs sought*

If any of the settling parties or their counsel intend to apply to the court for an award of attorneys' fees or costs from any fund established as part of the settlement, a statement indicating which parties or counsel intend to make such an application, the amount of fees and costs that will be sought (including the amount of such fees and costs determined on an average per share basis), and a brief explanation supporting the fees and costs sought. Such information shall be clearly summarized on the cover page of any notice to a party of any proposed or final settlement agreement.

(D) *Identification of lawyers' representatives*

The name, telephone number, and address of one or more representatives of counsel for the plaintiff class who will be reasonably available to answer questions from class members concerning any matter contained in any notice of settlement published or otherwise disseminated to the class.

    (E) *Reasons for settlement*

A brief statement explaining the reasons why the parties are proposing the settlement.

    (F) *Other information*

Such other information as may be required by the court.

  (8) *Security for payment of costs in class actions*

In any private action arising under this Act that is certified as a class action pursuant to the Federal Rules of Civil Procedure, the court may require an undertaking from the attorneys for the plaintiff class, the plaintiff class, or both, or from the attorneys for the defendant, the defendant, or both, in such proportions and at such times as the court determines are just and equitable, for the payment of fees and expenses that may be awarded under this subsection.

  (9) *Attorney conflict of interest*

If a plaintiff class is represented by an attorney who directly owns or otherwise has a beneficial interest in the securities that are the subject of the litigation, the court shall make a determination of whether such ownership or other interest constitutes a conflict of interest sufficient to disqualify the attorney from representing the plaintiff class.

(b) *Requirements for securities fraud actions*

  (1) *Misleading statements and omissions*

In any private action arising under this Act in which the plaintiff alleges that the defendant—

    (A) made an untrue statement of a material fact; or

    (B) omitted to state a material fact necessary in order to make the statements made, in the light of the circumstances in which they were made, not misleading;

the complaint shall specify each statement alleged to have been misleading, the reason or reasons why the statement is misleading, and, if an allegation regarding the statement or omission is made on information and belief, the complaint shall state with particularity all facts on which that belief is formed.

  (2) *Required state of mind*

    (A) *In general.*—Except as provided in subparagraph (B), in any private action arising under this Act in which the plaintiff may recover money damages only on proof that the defendant acted with a particular state of mind, the complaint shall, with respect to each act or omission alleged to violate this Act, state with particularity facts giving rise to a strong inference that the defendant acted with the required state of mind.

    (B) *Exception.*—In the case of an action for money damages brought against a credit rating agency or a controlling person under this Act, it shall be sufficient, for purposes of pleading any required state of mind in relation to such action, that the complaint state with particularity facts giving rise to a strong inference that the credit rating agency knowingly or recklessly failed—

      (i) to conduct a reasonable investigation of the rated security with respect to the factual elements relied upon by its own methodology for evaluating credit risk; or

      (ii) to obtain reasonable verification of such factual elements (which verification may be based on a sampling technique that does not amount to an audit) from other sources that the credit rating agency considered to be competent and that were independent of the issuer and underwriter.

* * *

(e) *Limitation on damages*

(1) *In general*

Except as provided in paragraph (2), in any private action arising under this Act in which the plaintiff seeks to establish damages by reference to the market price of a security, the award of damages to the plaintiff shall not exceed the difference between the purchase or sale price paid or received, as appropriate, by the plaintiff for the subject security and the mean trading price of that security during the 90-day period beginning on the date on which the information correcting the misstatement or omission that is the basis for the action is disseminated to the market.

(2) *Exception*

In any private action arising under this Act in which the plaintiff seeks to establish damages by reference to the market price of a security, if the plaintiff sells or repurchases the subject security prior to the expiration of the 90-day period described in paragraph (1), the plaintiff's damages shall not exceed the difference between the purchase or sale price paid or received, as appropriate, by the plaintiff for the security and the mean trading price of the security during the period beginning immediately after dissemination of information correcting the misstatement or omission and ending on the date on which the plaintiff sells or repurchases the security.

(3) *"Mean trading price" defined*

For purposes of this subsection, the "mean trading price" of a security shall be an average of the daily trading price of that security, determined as of the close of the market each day during the 90-day period referred to in paragraph (1).

(f) *Proportionate liability*

(1) *Applicability*

Nothing in this subsection shall be construed to create, affect, or in any manner modify, the standard for liability associated with any action arising under the securities laws.

(2) *Liability for damages*

(A) *Joint and several liability*

Any covered person against whom a final judgment is entered in a private action shall be liable for damages jointly and severally only if the trier of fact specifically determines that such covered person knowingly committed a violation of the securities laws.

(B) *Proportionate liability*

(i) *In general*

Except as provided in subparagraph (A), a covered person against whom a final judgment is entered in a private action shall be liable solely for the portion of the judgment that corresponds to the percentage of responsibility of that covered person, as determined under paragraph (3).

(ii) *Recovery by and costs of covered person*

In any case in which a contractual relationship permits, a covered person that prevails in any private action may recover the attorney's fees and costs of that covered person in connection with the action.

(3) *Determination of responsibility*

(A) *In general*

In any private action, the court shall instruct the jury to answer special interrogatories, or if there is no jury, shall make findings, with respect to each covered person and each of the other persons claimed by any of the parties to have caused or contributed to the loss incurred by the plaintiff, including persons who have entered into settlements with the plaintiff or plaintiffs, concerning—

(i)   whether such person violated the securities laws;

(ii)   the percentage of responsibility of such person, measured as a percentage of the total fault of all persons who caused or contributed to the loss incurred by the plaintiff; and

(iii)   whether such person knowingly committed a violation of the securities laws.

* * *

(5)   *Right of contribution*

To the extent that a covered person is required to make an additional payment pursuant to paragraph (4), that covered person may recover contribution—

(A)   from the covered person originally liable to make the payment;

(B)   from any covered person liable jointly and severally pursuant to paragraph (2)(A);

(C)   from any covered person held proportionately liable pursuant to this paragraph who is liable to make the same payment and has paid less than his or her proportionate share of that payment; or

(D)   from any other person responsible for the conduct giving rise to the payment that would have been liable to make the same payment.

* * *

(8)   *Contribution*

A covered person who becomes jointly and severally liable for damages in any private action may recover contribution from any other person who, if joined in the original action, would have been liable for the same damages. A claim for contribution shall be determined based on the percentage of responsibility of the claimant and of each person against whom a claim for contribution is made.

* * *

§ 21E. Application of Safe Harbor for Forward-Looking Statements

(a)   *Applicability*

This section shall apply only to a forward-looking statement made by—

(1)   an issuer that, at the time that the statement is made, is subject to the reporting requirements of section 13(a) or section 15(d) of this Act;

(2)   a person acting on behalf of such issuer;

(3)   an outside reviewer retained by such issuer making a statement on behalf of such issuer; or

(4)   an underwriter, with respect to information provided by such issuer or information derived from information provided by such issuer.

(b)   *Exclusions*

Except to the extent otherwise specifically provided by rule, regulation, or order of the Commission, this section shall not apply to a forward looking statement—

(1)   that is made with respect to the business or operations of the issuer, if the issuer—

(A)   during the 3-year period preceding the date on which the statement was first made—

(i)   was convicted of any felony or misdemeanor described in clauses (i) through (iv) of section 15(b)(4)(B) of this Act; or

(ii)   has been made the subject of a judicial or administrative decree or order arising out of a governmental action that—

(I)   prohibits future violations of the antifraud provisions of the securities laws;

(II)   requires that the issuer cease and desist from violating the antifraud provisions of the securities laws; or

(III)   determines that the issuer violated the antifraud provisions of the securities laws;

(B)   makes the forward-looking statement in connection with an offering of securities by a blank check company;

(C)   issues penny stock;

(D)   makes the forward-looking statement in connection with a rollup transaction; or

(E)   makes the forward-looking statement in connection with a going private transaction; or

(2)   that is—

(A)   included in a financial statement prepared in accordance with generally accepted accounting principles;

(B)   contained in a registration statement of, or otherwise issued by, an investment company;

(C)   made in connection with a tender offer;

(D)   made in connection with an initial public offering;

(E)   made in connection with an offering by, or relating to the operations of, a partnership, limited liability company, or a direct participation investment program; or

(F)   made in a disclosure of beneficial ownership in a report required to be filed with the Commission pursuant to section 13(d) of this Act.

(c)   *Safe harbor*

(1)   *In general*

Except as provided in subsection (b) of this section, in any private action arising under this Act that is based on an untrue statement of a material fact or omission of a material fact necessary to make the statement not misleading, a person referred to in subsection (a) of this section shall not be liable with respect to any forward-looking statement, whether written or oral, if and to the extent that—

(A)   the forward-looking statement is—

(i)   identified as a forward-looking statement, and is accompanied by meaningful cautionary statements identifying important factors that could cause actual results to differ materially from those in the forward looking statement; or

(ii)   immaterial; or

(B)   the plaintiff fails to prove that the forward-looking statement—

(i) if made by a natural person, was made with actual knowledge by that person that the statement was false or misleading; or

(ii) if made by a business entity, was—

(I) made by or with the approval of an executive officer of that entity; and

(II) made or approved by such officer with actual knowledge by that officer that the statement was false or misleading.

(2) *Oral forward-looking statements*

In the case of an oral forward-looking statement made by an issuer that is subject to the reporting requirements of section 13(a) or section 15(d) of this Act, or by a person acting on behalf of such issuer, the requirement set forth in paragraph (1)(A) shall be deemed to be satisfied—

(A) if the oral forward-looking statement is accompanied by a cautionary statement—

(i) that the particular oral statement is a forward-looking statement; and

(ii) that the actual results might differ materially from those projected in the forward-looking statement; and

(B) if—

(i) the oral forward-looking statement is accompanied by an oral statement that additional information concerning factors that could cause actual results to materially differ from those in the forward-looking statement is contained in a readily available written document, or portion thereof;

(ii) the accompanying oral statement referred to in clause (i) identifies the document, or portion thereof, that contains the additional information about those factors relating to the forward-looking statement; and

(iii) the information contained in that written document is a cautionary statement that satisfies the standard established in paragraph (1)(A).

(3) *Availability*

Any document filed with the Commission or generally disseminated shall be deemed to be readily available for purposes of paragraph (2).

(4) *Effect on other safe harbors*

The exemption provided for in paragraph (1) shall be in addition to any exemption that the Commission may establish by rule or regulation under subsection (g) of this section.

(d) *Duty to update*

Nothing in this section shall impose upon any person a duty to update a forward-looking statement.

(e) *Dispositive motion*

On any motion to dismiss based upon subsection (c)(1) of this section, the court shall consider any statement cited in the complaint and any cautionary statement accompanying the forward-looking statement, which are not subject to material dispute, cited by the defendant.

(f) *Stay pending decision on motion*

In any private action arising under this Act, the court shall stay discovery (other than discovery that is specifically directed to the applicability of the exemption provided for in this section) during the pendency of any motion by a defendant for summary judgment that is based on the grounds that—

(1) the statement or omission upon which the complaint is based is a forward-looking statement within the meaning of this section; and

(2)　the exemption provided for in this section precludes a claim for relief.

(g)　*Exemption authority*

In addition to the exemptions provided for in this section, the Commission may, by rule or regulation, provide exemptions from or under any provision of this Act, including with respect to liability that is based on a statement or that is based on projections or other forward-looking information, if and to the extent that any such exemption is consistent with the public interest and the protection of investors, as determined by the Commission.

(h)　*Effect on other authority of Commission*

Nothing in this section limits, either expressly or by implication, the authority of the Commission to exercise similar authority or to adopt similar rules and regulations with respect to forward-looking statements under any other statute under which the Commission exercises rulemaking authority.

(i)　*Definitions*

For purposes of this section, the following definitions shall apply:

(1)　*Forward-looking statement*

The term "forward-looking statement" means—

(A)　a statement containing a projection of revenues, income (including income loss), earnings (including earnings loss) per share, capital expenditures, dividends, capital structure, or other financial items;

(B)　a statement of the plans and objectives of management for future operations, including plans or objectives relating to the products or services of the issuer;

(C)　a statement of future economic performance, including any such statement contained in a discussion and analysis of financial condition by the management or in the results of operations included pursuant to the rules and regulations of the Commission;

(D)　any statement of the assumptions underlying or relating to any statement described in subparagraph (A), (B), or (C);

(E)　any report issued by an outside reviewer retained by an issuer, to the extent that the report assesses a forward-looking statement made by the issuer; or

(F)　a statement containing a projection or estimate of such other items as may be specified by rule or regulation of the Commission.

* * *

§ 27.　Jurisdiction of Offenses and Suits

(a)　*In general*

The district courts of the United States and the United States courts of any Territory or other place subject to the jurisdiction of the United States shall have exclusive jurisdiction of violations of this Act or the rules and regulations thereunder, and of all suits in equity and actions at law brought to enforce any liability or duty created by this Act or the rules and regulations thereunder. Any criminal proceeding may be brought in the district wherein any act or transaction constituting the violation occurred. Any suit or action to enforce any liability or duty created by this Act or rules and regulations thereunder, or to enjoin any violation of such chapter or rules and regulations, may be brought in any such district or in the district wherein the defendant is found or is an inhabitant or transacts business, and process in such cases may be served in any other district of which the defendant is an inhabitant or wherever the defendant may be found. In any action or proceeding instituted by the Commission under this title in a United States district court for any judicial district, a subpoena issued to compel the attendance of a witness or the production of documents or tangible things (or both) at a hearing or trial may be served at any place within the United States. Rule 45(c)(3)

(A) (ii) of the Federal Rules of Civil Procedure shall not apply to a subpoena issued under the preceding sentence. Judgments and decrees so rendered shall be subject to review as provided in sections 1254, 1291, 1292, and 1294 of Title 28. No costs shall be assessed for or against the Commission in any proceeding under this Act brought by or against it in the Supreme Court or such other courts.

(b) *Extraterritorial jurisdiction*

The district courts of the United States and the United States courts of any Territory shall have jurisdiction of an action or proceeding brought or instituted by the Commission or the United States alleging a violation of the antifraud provisions of this Act involving—

(1) conduct within the United States that constitutes significant steps in furtherance of the violation, even if the securities transaction occurs outside the United States and involves only foreign investors; or

(2) conduct occurring outside the United States that has a foreseeable substantial effect within the United States.

Rule 3a11–1.   Definition of the Term "Equity Security"

The term "equity security" is hereby defined to include any stock or similar security, certificate of interest or participation in any profit sharing agreement, preorganization certificate or subscription, transferable share, voting trust certificate or certificate of deposit for an equity security, limited partnership interest, interest in a joint venture, or certificate of interest in a business trust; any security future on any such security; or any security convertible, with or without consideration into such a security, or carrying any warrant or right to subscribe to or purchase such a security; or any such warrant or right; or any put, call, straddle, or other option or privilege of buying such a security from or selling such a security to another without being bound to do so.

Rule 3b–2.   Definition of "Officer"

The term "officer" means a president, vice president, secretary, treasury or principal financial officer, comptroller or principal accounting officer, and any person routinely performing corresponding functions with respect to any organization whether incorporated or unincorporated.

Rule 3b–6.   Liability for Certain Statements by Issuers

(a)   A statement within the coverage of paragraph (b) of this rule which is made by or on behalf of an issuer or by an outside reviewer retained by the issuer shall be deemed not to be a fraudulent statement (as defined in paragraph (d) of this rule), unless it is shown that such statement was made or reaffirmed without a reasonable basis or was disclosed other than in good faith.

(b)   This rule applies to the following statements:

(1)   A forward-looking statement (as defined in paragraph (c) of this rule) made in a document filed with the Commission, in Part I of a quarterly report on Form 10-Q, Rule 308a, or in an annual report to security holders meeting the requirements of Rules 14a–3(b) and (c) or 14c–3(a) and (b) under the Securities Exchange Act of 1934, a statement reaffirming such forward-looking statement after the date the document was filed or the annual report was made publicly available, or a forward-looking statement made before the date the document was filed or the date the annual report was made publicly available if such statement is reaffirmed in a filed document, in Part I of a quarterly report on Form 10-Q or in an annual report made publicly available within a reasonable time after the making of such forward-looking statement; Provided, that

(i)   At the time such statements are made or reaffirmed, either the issuer is subject to the reporting requirements of Section 13(a) or 15(d) of the Securities Exchange Act of 1934 and has complied with the requirements of Rule 13a–1 or 15d–1 thereunder, if applicable, to file its most recent annual report on Form 10-K, Form 20-F or Form 40-F; or if the issuer is not subject to the reporting requirements of Section 13(a) or 15(d) of the Securities Exchange Act of 1934, the statements are made in a registration statement filed under the Securities Act of 1933 offering statement or solicitation of interest written document or broadcast script under Regulation A or pursuant to Section 12(b) or (g) of the Securities Exchange Act of 1934; and

(ii)   The statements are not made by or on behalf of an issuer that is an investment company registered under the Investment Company Act of 1940; and

(2)   Information that is disclosed in a document filed with the Commission, in Part I of a quarterly report on Form 10-Q (Rule 308a) or in an annual report to security holders meeting the requirements of Rules 14a–3(b) and (c) or 14c–3(a) and (b) under the Securities Exchange Act of 1934 and which relates to:

(i)   The effects of changing prices on the business enterprise, presented voluntarily or pursuant to Item 303 of Regulation S–K, "Management's Discussion and Analysis of Financial Condition and Results of Operations," Item 5 of Form 20-F, "Operating and Financial Review and Prospects," Item 302 of Regulation S–K, "Supplementary Financial Information," or Rule 3–20(c) of Regulation S–X, or

(ii)   The value of proved oil and gas reserves (such as a standardized measure of discounted future net cash flows relating to proved oil and gas reserves as set forth in FASB ASC paragraphs 932–235–50–29 through 932–235–50–36 (Extractive Activities—Oil and Gas Topic) presented voluntarily or pursuant to Item 302 of Regulation S–K.

(c)   For the purpose of this rule, the term "forward-looking statement" shall mean and shall be limited to:

(1)   A statement containing a projection of revenues, income (loss), earnings (loss) per share, capital expenditures, dividends, capital structure or other financial items;

(2)   A statement of management's plans and objectives for future operations;

(3)   A statement of future economic performance contained in management's discussion and analysis of financial condition and results of operations included pursuant to Item 303 of Regulation S–K or Item 5 of Form 20-F; or

(4)   Disclosed statements of the assumptions underlying or relating to any of the statements described in paragraphs (c) (1), (2), or (3) of this rule.

(d)   For the purpose of this rule the term "fraudulent statement" shall mean a statement which is an untrue statement of a material fact, a statement false or misleading with respect to any material fact, an omission to state a material fact necessary to make a statement not misleading, or which constitutes the employment of a manipulative, deceptive, or fraudulent device, contrivance, scheme, transaction, act, practice, course of business, or an artifice to defraud, as those terms are used in the Securities Exchange Act of 1934 or the rules or regulations promulgated thereunder.

Rule 3b–7.   Definition of "Executive Officer"

The term "executive officer", when used with reference to a registrant, means its president, any vice president of the registrant in charge of a principal business unit, division or function (such as sales, administration or finance), any other officer who performs a policy making function or any other person who performs similar policy making functions for the registrant. Executive officers of subsidiaries may be deemed executive officers of the registrant if they perform such policy making functions for the registrant.

Rule 10b–5.   Employment of Manipulative and Deceptive Devices

It shall be unlawful for any person, directly or indirectly, by the use of any means or instrumentality of interstate commerce, or of the mails or of any facility of any national securities exchange,

(a)   To employ any device, scheme, or artifice to defraud,

(b)   To make any untrue statement of a material fact or to omit to state a material fact necessary in order to make the statements made, in the light of the circumstances under which they were made, not misleading, or

(c)   To engage in any act, practice, or course of business which operates or would operate as a fraud or deceit upon any person,

in connection with the purchase or sale of any security.

Rule 10b5–1. Trading "on the Basis of" Material Nonpublic Information in Insider Trading Cases

Preliminary Note to Rule 10b5–1: This provision defines when a purchase or sale constitutes trading "on the basis of" material nonpublic information in insider trading cases brought under Section 10(b) of the Act and Rule 10b–5 thereunder. The law of insider trading is otherwise defined by judicial opinions construing Rule 10b–5, and Rule 10b5–1 does not modify the scope of insider trading law in any other respect.

(a)   *General.* The "manipulative and deceptive devices" prohibited by Section 10(b) of the Act and Rule 10b–5 thereunder include, among other things, the purchase or sale of a security of any issuer, on the basis of material nonpublic information about that security or issuer, in breach of a duty of trust or confidence that is owed directly, indirectly, or derivatively, to the issuer of that security or the shareholders of that issuer, or to any other person who is the source of the material nonpublic information.

(b)   *Definition of "on the basis of."* Subject to the affirmative defenses in paragraph (c) of this rule, a purchase or sale of a security of an issuer is "on the basis of" material nonpublic information about that security or issuer if the person making the purchase or sale was aware of the material nonpublic information when the person made the purchase or sale.

(c)   *Affirmative defenses.*

(1)(i)   Subject to paragraph (c)(1)(ii) of this rule, a person's purchase or sale is not "on the basis of" material nonpublic information if the person making the purchase or sale demonstrates that:

(A)   Before becoming aware of the information, the person had:

(1)   Entered into a binding contract to purchase or sell the security,

(2)   Instructed another person to purchase or sell the security for the instructing person's account, or

(3)   Adopted a written plan for trading securities;

(B)   The contract, instruction, or plan described in paragraph (c)(1)(i)(A) of this Rule:

(1)   Specified the amount of securities to be purchased or sold and the price at which and the date on which the securities were to be purchased or sold;

(2)   Included a written formula or algorithm, or computer program, for determining the amount of securities to be purchased or sold and the price at which and the date on which the securities were to be purchased or sold; or

(3)   Did not permit the person to exercise any subsequent influence over how, when, or whether to effect purchases or sales; provided, in addition, that any other person who, pursuant to the contract, instruction, or plan, did exercise such influence must not have been aware of the material nonpublic information when doing so; and

(C)   The purchase or sale that occurred was pursuant to the contract, instruction, or plan. A purchase or sale is not "pursuant to a contract, instruction, or plan" if, among other things, the person who entered into the contract, instruction, or plan altered or deviated from the contract, instruction, or plan to purchase or sell securities (whether by changing the amount, price, or timing of the purchase or sale), or entered into or altered a corresponding or hedging transaction or position with respect to those securities.

* * *

(2) A person other than a natural person also may demonstrate that a purchase or sale of securities is not "on the basis of" material nonpublic information if the person demonstrates that:

(i) The individual making the investment decision on behalf of the person to purchase or sell the securities was not aware of the information; and

(ii) The person had implemented reasonable policies and procedures, taking into consideration the nature of the person's business, to ensure that individuals making investment decisions would not violate the laws prohibiting trading on the basis of material nonpublic information. These policies and procedures may include those that restrict any purchase, sale, and causing any purchase or sale of any security as to which the person has material nonpublic information, or those that prevent such individuals from becoming aware of such information.

Rule 10b5–2. Duties of Trust or Confidence in Misappropriation Insider Trading Cases

Preliminary Note to Rule 10b5–2: This rule provides a non-exclusive definition of circumstances in which a person has a duty of trust or confidence for purposes of the "misappropriation" theory of insider trading under Section 10(b) of the Act and Rule 10b–5. The law of insider trading is otherwise defined by judicial opinions construing Rule 10b–5, and Rule 10b5–2 does not modify the scope of insider trading law in any other respect.

(a) *Scope of Rule.* This rule shall apply to any violation of Section 10(b) of the Act and Rule 10b–5 thereunder that is based on the purchase or sale of securities on the basis of, or the communication of, material nonpublic information misappropriated in breach of a duty of trust or confidence.

(b) *Enumerated "duties of trust or confidence."* For purposes of this rule, a "duty of trust or confidence" exists in the following circumstances, among others:

(1) Whenever a person agrees to maintain information in confidence;

(2) Whenever the person communicating the material nonpublic information and the person to whom it is communicated have a history, pattern, or practice of sharing confidences, such that the recipient of the information knows or reasonably should know that the person communicating the material nonpublic information expects that the recipient will maintain its confidentiality; or

(3) Whenever a person receives or obtains material nonpublic information from his or her spouse, parent, child, or sibling; provided, however, that the person receiving or obtaining the information may demonstrate that no duty of trust or confidence existed with respect to the information, by establishing that he or she neither knew nor reasonably should have known that the person who was the source of the information expected that the person would keep the information confidential, because of the parties' history, pattern, or practice of sharing and maintaining confidences, and because there was no agreement or understanding to maintain the confidentiality of the information.

Rule 10C–1. Listing Standards Relating to Compensation Committees

(a) Pursuant to section 10C(a) of the Securities Exchange Act of 1934 and section 952 of the Dodd-Frank Wall Street Reform and Consumer Protection Act of 2010 (Pub. L. 111–203, 124 Stat. 1900):

(1) National securities exchanges. The rules of each national securities exchange registered pursuant to section 6 of the Securities Exchange Act of 1934, to the extent such national securities

exchange lists equity securities, must, in accordance with the provisions of this rule, prohibit the initial or continued listing of any equity security of an issuer that is not in compliance with the requirements of any portion of paragraph (b) or (c) of this rule.

(2)   National securities associations. The rules of each national securities association registered pursuant to section 15A of the Securities Exchange Act of 1934, to the extent such national securities association lists equity securities in an automated inter-dealer quotation system, must, in accordance with the provisions of this rule, prohibit the initial or continued listing in an automated inter-dealer quotation system of any equity security of an issuer that is not in compliance with the requirements of any portion of paragraph (b) or (c) of this rule.

(3)   Opportunity to cure defects. The rules required by paragraphs (a)(1) and (a)(2) of this rule must provide for appropriate procedures for a listed issuer to have a reasonable opportunity to cure any defects that would be the basis for a prohibition under paragraph (a) of this rule, before the imposition of such prohibition. Such rules may provide that if a member of a compensation committee ceases to be independent in accordance with the requirements of this section for reasons outside the member's reasonable control, that person, with notice by the issuer to the applicable national securities exchange or national securities association, may remain a compensation committee member of the listed issuer until the earlier of the next annual shareholders meeting of the listed issuer or one year from the occurrence of the event that caused the member to be no longer independent.

(4)   Implementation.

(i)   Each national securities exchange and national securities association that lists equity securities must provide to the Commission, no later than 90 days after publication of this rule in the Federal Register, proposed rules or rule amendments that comply with this rule. Each submission must include, in addition to any other information required under section 19(b) of the Securities Exchange Act of 1934 and the rules thereunder, a review of whether and how existing or proposed listing standards satisfy the requirements of this rule, a discussion of the consideration of factors relevant to compensation committee independence conducted by the national securities exchange or national securities association, and the definition of independence applicable to compensation committee members that the national securities exchange or national securities association proposes to adopt or retain in light of such review.

(ii)   Each national securities exchange and national securities association that lists equity securities must have rules or rule amendments that comply with this rule approved by the Commission no later than one year after publication of this rule in the Federal Register.

(b)   Required standards. The requirements of this rule apply to the compensation committees of listed issuers.

(1)   Independence.

(i)   Each member of the compensation committee must be a member of the board of directors of the listed issuer, and must otherwise be independent.

(ii)   Independence requirements. In determining independence requirements for members of compensation committees, the national securities exchanges and national securities associations shall consider relevant factors, including, but not limited to:

(A)   The source of compensation of a member of the board of directors of an issuer, including any consulting, advisory or other compensatory fee paid by the issuer to such member of the board of directors; and

(B)   Whether a member of the board of directors of an issuer is affiliated with the issuer, a subsidiary of the issuer or an affiliate of a subsidiary of the issuer.

(iii) Exemptions from the independence requirements.

(A) The listing of equity securities of the following categories of listed issuers is not subject to the requirements of paragraph (b)(1) of this rule:

(1) Limited partnerships;

(2) Companies in bankruptcy proceedings;

(3) Open-end management investment companies registered under the Investment Company Act of 1940; and

(4) Any foreign private issuer that discloses in its annual report the reasons that the foreign private issuer does not have an independent compensation committee.

(B) In addition to the issuer exemptions set forth in paragraph (b)(1)(iii)(A) of this rule, a national securities exchange or a national securities association, pursuant to section 19(b) of the Securities Exchange Act of 1934 and the rules thereunder, may exempt from the requirements of paragraph (b)(1) of this rule a particular relationship with respect to members of the compensation committee, as each national securities exchange or national securities association determines is appropriate, taking into consideration the size of an issuer and any other relevant factors.

(2) Authority to retain compensation consultants, independent legal counsel and other compensation advisers.

(i) The compensation committee of a listed issuer, in its capacity as a committee of the board of directors, may, in its sole discretion, retain or obtain the advice of a compensation consultant, independent legal counsel or other adviser.

(ii) The compensation committee shall be directly responsible for the appointment, compensation and oversight of the work of any compensation consultant, independent legal counsel and other adviser retained by the compensation committee.

(iii) Nothing in this paragraph (b)(2) shall be construed:

(A) To require the compensation committee to implement or act consistently with the advice or recommendations of the compensation consultant, independent legal counsel or other adviser to the compensation committee; or

(B) To affect the ability or obligation of a compensation committee to exercise its own judgment in fulfillment of the duties of the compensation committee.

(3) Funding. Each listed issuer must provide for appropriate funding, as determined by the compensation committee, in its capacity as a committee of the board of directors, for payment of reasonable compensation to a compensation consultant, independent legal counsel or any other adviser retained by the compensation committee.

(4) Independence of compensation consultants and other advisers. The compensation committee of a listed issuer may select a compensation consultant, legal counsel or other adviser to the compensation committee only after taking into consideration the following factors, as well as any other factors identified by the relevant national securities exchange or national securities association in its listing standards:

(i) The provision of other services to the issuer by the person that employs the compensation consultant, legal counsel or other adviser;

(ii) The amount of fees received from the issuer by the person that employs the compensation consultant, legal counsel or other adviser, as a percentage of the total revenue of the person that employs the compensation consultant, legal counsel or other adviser;

(iii) The policies and procedures of the person that employs the compensation consultant, legal counsel or other adviser that are designed to prevent conflicts of interest;

(iv) Any business or personal relationship of the compensation consultant, legal counsel or other adviser with a member of the compensation committee;

(v) Any stock of the issuer owned by the compensation consultant, legal counsel or other adviser; and

(vi) Any business or personal relationship of the compensation consultant, legal counsel, other adviser or the person employing the adviser with an executive officer of the issuer.

Instruction to paragraph (b)(4) of this rule: A listed issuer's compensation committee is required to conduct the independence assessment outlined in paragraph (b)(4) of this rule with respect to any compensation consultant, legal counsel or other adviser that provides advice to the compensation committee, other than in-house legal counsel.

(5) General exemptions.

(i) The national securities exchanges and national securities associations, pursuant to section 19(b) of the Securities Exchange Act of 1934 and the rules thereunder, may exempt from the requirements of this rule certain categories of issuers, as the national securities exchange or national securities association determines is appropriate, taking into consideration, among other relevant factors, the potential impact of such requirements on smaller reporting issuers.

(ii) The requirements of this rule shall not apply to any controlled company or to any smaller reporting company.

(iii) The listing of a security futures product cleared by a clearing agency that is registered pursuant to section 17A of the Securities Exchange Act of 1934 or that is exempt from the registration requirements of section 17A(b)(7)(A) is not subject to the requirements of this rule.

(iv) The listing of a standardized option, as defined in Rule 9b–1(a)(4), issued by a clearing agency that is registered pursuant to section 17A of the Securities Exchange Act of 1934 is not subject to the requirements of this rule.

(c) Definitions. Unless the context otherwise requires, all terms used in this rule have the same meaning as in the Act and the rules and regulations thereunder. In addition, unless the context otherwise requires, the following definitions apply for purposes of this rule:

(1) In the case of foreign private issuers with a two-tier board system, the term board of directors means the supervisory or non-management board.

(2) The term compensation committee means:

(i) A committee of the board of directors that is designated as the compensation committee; or

(ii) In the absence of a committee of the board of directors that is designated as the compensation committee, a committee of the board of directors performing functions typically performed by a compensation committee, including oversight of executive compensation, even if it is not designated as the compensation committee or also performs other functions; or

(iii) For purposes of this rule other than paragraphs (b)(2)(i) and (b)(3), in the absence of a committee as described in paragraphs (c)(2)(i) or (ii) of this rule, the members of the board of directors who oversee executive compensation matters on behalf of the board of directors.

(3)   The term controlled company means an issuer:

(i)   That is listed on a national securities exchange or by a national securities association; and

(ii)   Of which more than 50 percent of the voting power for the election of directors is held by an individual, a group or another company.

(4)   The terms listed and listing refer to equity securities listed on a national securities exchange or listed in an automated inter-dealer quotation system of a national securities association or to issuers of such securities.

(5)   The term open-end management investment company means an open-end company, as defined by Section 5(a)(1) of the Investment Company Act of 1940, that is registered under that Act.

Rule 13e–3.   Going Private Transactions by Certain Issuers or Their Affiliates

(a)   Definitions.—

Unless indicated otherwise or the context otherwise requires, all terms used in this rule and in Schedule 13E-3 [§ 240.13e–100] shall have the same meaning as in the Act or elsewhere in the General Rules and Regulations thereunder. In addition, the following definitions apply:

(1)   An *affiliate* of an issuer is a person that directly or indirectly through one or more intermediaries controls, is controlled by, or is under common control with such issuer. For the purposes of this rule only, a person who is not an affiliate of an issuer at the commencement of such person's tender offer for a class of equity securities of such issuer will not be deemed an affiliate of such issuer prior to the stated termination of such tender offer and any extensions thereof;

(2)   The term *purchase* means any acquisition for value including, but not limited to, (i) any acquisition pursuant to the dissolution of an issuer subsequent to the sale or other disposition of substantially all the assets of such issuer to its affiliate, (ii) any acquisition pursuant to a merger, (iii) any acquisition of fractional interests in connection with a reverse stock split, and (iv) any acquisition subject to the control of an issuer or an affiliate of such issuer;

(3)   A *Rule 13e–3 transaction* is any transaction or series of transactions involving one or more of the transactions described in paragraph (a)(3)(i) of this rule which has either a reasonable likelihood or a purpose of producing, either directly or indirectly, any of the effects described in paragraph (a)(3)(ii) of this rule;

(i)   The transactions referred to in paragraph (a)(3) of this rule are:

(A)   A purchase of any equity security by the issuer of such security or by an affiliate of such issuer;

(B)   A tender offer for or request or invitation for tenders of any equity security made by the issuer of such class of securities or by an affiliate of such issuer; or

(C)   A solicitation subject to Regulation 14A of any proxy, consent or authorization of, or a distribution subject to Regulation 14C of information statements to, any equity security holder by the issuer of the class of securities or by an affiliate of such issuer, in connection with: a merger, consolidation, reclassification, recapitalization, reorganization or similar corporate transaction of an issuer or between an issuer (or its subsidiaries) and its affiliate; a sale of substantially all the assets of an issuer to its affiliate or group of affiliates; or a reverse stock split of any class of equity securities of the issuer involving the purchase of fractional interests.

(ii)   The effects referred to in paragraph (a)(3) of this rule are:

(A)   Causing any class of equity securities of the issuer which is subject to section 12(g) or section 15(d) of the Act to become eligible for termination of registration under Rule 12g–4 or Rule 12h–6, or causing the reporting obligations with respect to such class to become eligible for termination under Rule 12h–6; or suspension under Rule 12h–3 or section 15(d); or

(B)   Causing any class of equity securities of the issuer which is either listed on a national securities exchange or authorized to be quoted in an inter-dealer quotation system of a registered national securities association to be neither listed on any national securities exchange nor authorized to be quoted on an inter-dealer quotation system of any registered national securities association.

(4)   An *unaffiliated security holder* is any security holder of an equity security subject to a Rule 13e–3 transaction who is not an affiliate of the issuer of such security.

(b)   Application of section to an issuer (or an affiliate of such issuer) subject to section 12 of the Act.

(1)   It shall be a fraudulent, deceptive or manipulative act or practice, in connection with a Rule 13e–3 transaction, for an issuer which has a class of equity securities registered pursuant to section 12 of the Act or which is a closed-end investment company registered under the Investment Company Act of 1940, or an affiliate of such issuer, directly or indirectly

(i)   To employ any device, scheme or artifice to defraud any person;

(ii)   To make any untrue statement of a material fact or to omit to state a material fact necessary in order to make the statements made, in light of the circumstances under which they were made, not misleading; or

(iii)   To engage in any act, practice or course of business which operates or would operate as a fraud or deceit upon any person.

(2)   As a means reasonably designed to prevent fraudulent, deceptive or manipulative acts or practices in connection with any Rule 13e–3 transaction, it shall be unlawful for an issuer which has a class of equity securities registered pursuant to section 12 of the Act, or an affiliate of such issuer, to engage, directly or indirectly, in a Rule 13e–3 transaction unless:

(i)   Such issuer or affiliate complies with the requirements of paragraphs (d), (e) and (f) of this rule; and

(ii)   The Rule 13e–3 transaction is not in violation of paragraph (b)(1) of this rule.

(c)   Application of section to an issuer (or an affiliate of such issuer) subject to section 15(d) of the Act.

(1)   It shall be unlawful as a fraudulent, deceptive or manipulative act or practice for an issuer which is required to file periodic reports pursuant to Section 15(d) of the Act, or an affiliate of such issuer, to engage, directly or indirectly, in a Rule 13e–3 transaction unless such issuer or affiliate complies with the requirements of paragraphs (d), (e) and (f) of this rule.

(2)   An issuer or affiliate which is subject to paragraph (c)(1) of this rule and which is soliciting proxies or distributing information statements in connection with a transaction described in paragraph (a)(3)(i)(A) of this rule may elect to use the timing procedures for conducting a solicitation subject to Regulation 14A or a distribution subject to Regulation 14C in complying with paragraphs (d), (e) and (f) of this rule, provided that if an election is made, such solicitation or distribution is conducted in accordance with the requirements of the respective regulations, including the filing of preliminary copies of soliciting materials or an information statement at the time specified in Regulation 14A or 14C, respectively.

(d)   Material required to be filed.—

The issuer or affiliate engaging in a Rule 13e–3 transaction must file with the Commission:

(1)   A Schedule 13E-3, including all exhibits;

(2)   An amendment to Schedule 13E-3 reporting promptly any material changes in the information set forth in the schedule previously filed; and

(3)   A final amendment to Schedule 13E-3 reporting promptly the results of the Rule 13e–3 transaction.

(e)   Disclosure of information to security holders.

(1)   In addition to disclosing the information required by any other applicable rule or regulation under the federal securities laws, the issuer or affiliate engaging in a Rule 13e–3 transaction must disclose to security holders of the class that is the subject of the transaction, as specified in paragraph (f) of this rule, the following:

(i)   The information required by Item 1 of Schedule 13E-3 (Summary Term Sheet);

(ii)   The information required by Items 7, 8 and 9 of Schedule 13E-3, which must be prominently disclosed in a "Special Factors" section in the front of the disclosure document;

(iii)   A prominent legend on the outside front cover page that indicates that neither the Securities and Exchange Commission nor any state securities commission has: approved or disapproved of the transaction; passed upon the merits or fairness of the transaction; or passed upon the adequacy or accuracy of the disclosure in the document. The legend also must make it clear that any representation to the contrary is a criminal offense;

(iv)   The information concerning appraisal rights required by Regulation M-A (§ 229.1016(f)) of this chapter; and

(v)   The information required by the remaining items of Schedule 13E-3, except for Regulation M-A (§ 229.1016) of this chapter (exhibits), or a fair and adequate summary of the information.

Instructions to paragraph (e)(1):

1.   If the Rule 13e–3 transaction also is subject to Regulation 14A or 14C, the registration provisions and rules of the Securities Act of 1933, Regulation 14D or Rule 13e–4, the information required by paragraph (e)(1) of this rule must be combined with the proxy statement, information statement, prospectus or tender offer material sent or given to security holders.

2.   If the Rule 13e–3 transaction involves a registered securities offering, the legend required by Rule 501(b)(7) of this chapter must be combined with the legend required by paragraph (e)(1)(iii) of this rule.

3.   The required legend must be written in clear, plain language.

(2)   If there is any material change in the information previously disclosed to security holders, the issuer or affiliate must disclose the change promptly to security holders as specified in paragraph (f)(1)(iii) of this rule.

(f)   Dissemination of information to security holders.

(1)   If the Rule 13e–3 transaction involves a purchase as described in paragraph (a)(3)(i)(A) of this rule or a vote, consent, authorization, or distribution of information statements as described in paragraph (a)(3)(i)(C) of this rule, the issuer or affiliate engaging in the Rule 13e–3 transaction shall:

(i)   Provide the information required by paragraph (e) of this rule: (A) In accordance with the provisions of any applicable Federal or State law, but in no event later than 20 days prior to: any such purchase; any such vote, consent or authorization; or with respect to the distribution of information statements, the meeting date, or if corporate action is to be taken by means of the written authorization or consent of security holders, the earliest date on which corporate action may be taken: *Provided, however*, That if the purchase subject to this rule is pursuant to a tender offer excepted from Rule 13e–4 by paragraph (g)(5) of Rule 13e–4, the information required by paragraph (e) of this rule shall be disseminated in accordance with paragraph (e) of Rule 13e–4 no later than 10 business days prior to any purchase pursuant to such tender offer, (B) to each person who is a record holder of a class of equity securities subject to the Rule 13e–3 transaction as of a date not more than 20 days prior to the date of dissemination of such information.

(ii)   If the issuer or affiliate knows that securities of the class of securities subject to the Rule 13e–3 transaction are held of record by a broker, dealer, bank or voting trustee or their nominees, such issuer or affiliate shall (unless Rule 14a–13(a) or 14c–7 is applicable) furnish the number of copies of the information required by paragraph (e) of this rule that are requested by such persons (pursuant to inquiries by or on behalf of the issuer or affiliate), instruct such persons to forward such information to the beneficial owners of such securities in a timely manner and undertake to pay the reasonable expenses incurred by such persons in forwarding such information; and

(iii)   Promptly disseminate disclosure of material changes to the information required by paragraph (d) of this rule in a manner reasonably calculated to inform security holders.

(2)   If the Rule 13e–3 transaction is a tender offer or a request or invitation for tenders of equity securities which is subject to Regulation 14D or Rule 13e–4, the tender offer containing the information required by paragraph (e) of this rule, and any material change with respect thereto, shall be published, sent or given in accordance with Regulation 14D or Rule 13e–4, respectively, to security holders of the class of securities being sought by the issuer or affiliate.

(g)   Exceptions.—This rule shall not apply to:

(1)   Any Rule 13e–3 transaction by or on behalf of a person which occurs within one year of the date of termination of a tender offer in which such person was the bidder and became an affiliate of the issuer as a result of such tender offer: *Provided*, That the consideration offered to unaffiliated security holders in such Rule 13e–3 transaction is at least equal to the highest consideration offered during such tender offer and *Provided further*, That:

(i)   If such tender offer was made for any or all securities of a class of the issuer;

(A)   Such tender offer fully disclosed such person's intention to engage in a Rule 13e–3 transaction, the form and effect of such transaction and, to the extent known, the proposed terms thereof; and

(B)   Such Rule 13e–3 transaction is substantially similar to that described in such tender offer; or

(ii)   If such tender offer was made for less than all the securities of a class of the issuer:

(A)   Such tender offer fully disclosed a plan of merger, a plan of liquidation or a similar binding agreement between such person and the issuer with respect to a Rule 13e–3 transaction; and

(B)   Such Rule 13e–3 transaction occurs pursuant to the plan of merger, plan of liquidation or similar binding agreement disclosed in the bidder's tender offer.

(2)   Any Rule 13e–3 transaction in which the security holders are offered or receive only an equity security *Provided*, That:

(i)   Such equity security has substantially the same rights as the equity security which is the subject of the Rule 13e–3 transaction including, but not limited to, voting, dividends, redemption and liquidation rights except that this requirement shall be deemed to be satisfied if unaffiliated security holders are offered common stock;

(ii)   Such equity security is registered pursuant to section 12 of the Act or reports are required to be filed by the issuer thereof pursuant to section 15(d) of the Act; and

(iii)   If the security which is the subject of the Rule 13e–3 transaction was either listed on a national securities exchange or authorized to be quoted in an interdealer quotation system of a registered national securities association, such equity security is either listed on a national securities exchange or authorized to be quoted in an inter-dealer quotation system of a registered national securities association.

(3)   [Reserved]

(4)   Redemptions, calls or similar purchases of an equity security by an issuer pursuant to specific provisions set forth in the instrument(s) creating or governing that class of equity securities; or

(5)   Any solicitation by an issuer with respect to a plan of reorganization under Chapter XI of the Bankruptcy Act, as amended, if made after the entry of an order approving such plan pursuant to section 1125(b) of that Act and after, or concurrently with, the transmittal of information concerning such plan as required by section 1125(b) of that Act.

(6)   Any tender offer or business combination made in compliance with Rule 802 of the Securities Act of 1933, Rule 13e–4(h)(8) or 14d–1(c) or any other kind of transaction that otherwise meets the conditions for reliance on the cross-border exemptions set forth in Rules 13e–4(h)(8), 14d–1(c) or Rule 802 of the Securities Act of 1933 except for the fact that it is not technically subject to those rules.

Instruction to Rule 13e–3(g)(6): To the extent applicable, the acquiror must comply with the conditions set forth in § 230.802 of this chapter, and Rules 13e–4(h)(8) and 14d–1(c). If the acquiror publishes or otherwise disseminates an informational document to the holders of the subject securities in connection with the transaction, the acquiror must furnish an English translation of that informational document, including any amendments thereto, to the Commission under cover of Form CB (§ 239.800 of this chapter) by the first business day after publication or dissemination. If the acquiror is a foreign entity, it must also file a Form F-X (§ 239.42 of this chapter) with the Commission at the same time as the submission of the Form CB to appoint an agent for service in the United States.

Rule 13e–4.   Tender Offers by Issuers

(a)   Definitions.—Unless the context otherwise requires, all terms used in this rule and in Schedule TO shall have the same meaning as in the Act or elsewhere in the General Rules and Regulations thereunder. In addition, the following definitions shall apply:

(1)   The term *issuer* means any issuer which has a class of equity security registered pursuant to section 12 of the Act, or which is required to file periodic reports pursuant to section 15(d) of the Act, or which is a closed-end investment company registered under the Investment Company Act of 1940.

(2)   The term *issuer tender offer* refers to a tender offer for, or a request or invitation for tenders of, any class of equity security, made by the issuer of such class of equity security or by an affiliate of such issuer.

(3)   As used in this rule and in Schedule TO, the term *business day* means any day, other than Saturday, Sunday, or a Federal holiday, and shall consist of the time period from 12:01 a.m. through 12:00 midnight Eastern Time. In computing any time period under this Rule or Schedule TO, the date of the event that begins the running of such time period shall be included *except that* if such event occurs on other than a business day such period shall begin to run on and shall include the first business day thereafter.

(4)   The term *commencement* means 12:01 a.m. on the date that the issuer or affiliate has first published, sent or given the means to tender to security holders. For purposes of this rule, the means to tender includes the transmittal form or a statement regarding how the transmittal form may be obtained.

(5)   The term *termination* means the date after which securities may not be tendered pursuant to an issuer tender offer.

(6)   The term *security holders* means holders of record and beneficial owners of securities of the class of equity security which is the subject of an issuer tender offer.

(7)   The term *security position listing* means, with respect to the securities of any issuer held by a registered clearing agency in the name of the clearing agency or its nominee, a list of those participants in the clearing agency on whose behalf the clearing agency holds the issuer's securities and of the participants' respective positions in such securities as of a specified date.

(b)   Filing, disclosure and dissemination.—As soon as practicable on the date of commencement of the issuer tender offer, the issuer or affiliate making the issuer tender offer must comply with:

(1)   The filing requirements of paragraph (c)(2) of this rule;

(2)   The disclosure requirements of paragraph (d)(1) of this rule; and

(3)   The dissemination requirements of paragraph (e) of this rule.

(c)   Material required to be filed.—The issuer or affiliate making the issuer tender offer must file with the Commission:

(1)   All written communications made by the issuer or affiliate relating to the issuer tender offer, from and including the first public announcement, as soon as practicable on the date of the communication;

(2)   A Schedule TO, including all exhibits;

(3)   An amendment to Schedule TO reporting promptly any material changes in the information set forth in the schedule previously filed; and

(4)   A final amendment to Schedule TO reporting promptly the results of the issuer tender offer.

Instructions to Rule 13e–4(c):

1.   Pre-commencement communications must be filed under cover of Schedule TO and the box on the cover page of the schedule must be marked.

2.   Any communications made in connection with an exchange offer registered under the Securities Act of 1933 need only be filed under Rule 425 of the Securities Act of 1933 and will be deemed filed under this rule.

3.   Each pre-commencement written communication must include a prominent legend in clear, plain language advising security holders to read the tender offer statement when it is available because it contains important information. The legend also must advise investors that they can get the tender offer statement and other filed documents for free at the Commission's web site and explain which documents are free from the issuer.

4.   See Rules 135, 165 and 166 of the Securities Act of 1933 for pre-commencement communications made in connection with registered exchange offers.

5.   "Public announcement" is any oral or written communication by the issuer, affiliate or any person authorized to act on their behalf that is reasonably designed to, or has the effect of, informing the public or security holders in general about the issuer tender offer.

(d)   Disclosure of tender offer information to security holders.

(1)   The issuer or affiliate making the issuer tender offer must disclose, in a manner prescribed by paragraph (e)(1) of this rule, the following:

(i)   The information required by Item 1 of Schedule TO (summary term sheet); and

(ii)   The information required by the remaining items of Schedule TO for issuer tender offers, except for Item 12 (exhibits), or a fair and adequate summary of the information.

(2)   If there are any material changes in the information previously disclosed to security holders, the issuer or affiliate must disclose the changes promptly to security holders in a manner specified in paragraph (e)(3) of this rule.

(3)   If the issuer or affiliate disseminates the issuer tender offer by means of summary publication as described in paragraph (e)(1)(iii) of this rule, the summary advertisement must not include a transmittal letter that would permit security holders to tender securities sought in the offer and must disclose at least the following information:

(i)   The identity of the issuer or affiliate making the issuer tender offer;

(ii)   The information required by Regulation M-A of this chapter;

(iii)   Instructions on how security holders can obtain promptly a copy of the statement required by paragraph (d)(1) of this rule, at the issuer or affiliate's expense; and

(iv)   A statement that the information contained in the statement required by paragraph (d)(1) of this rule is incorporated by reference.

(e)   Dissemination of tender offers to security holders.—An issuer tender offer will be deemed to be published, sent or given to security holders if the issuer or affiliate making the issuer tender offer complies fully with one or more of the methods described in this rule.

(1)   For issuer tender offers in which the consideration offered consists solely of cash and/or securities exempt from registration under section 3 of the Securities Act of 1933:

(i)   Dissemination of cash issuer tender offers by long-form publication: By making adequate publication of the information required by paragraph (d)(1) of this rule in a newspaper or newspapers, on the date of commencement of the issuer tender offer.

(ii)   Dissemination of any issuer tender offer by use of stockholder and other lists:

(A)   By mailing or otherwise furnishing promptly a statement containing the information required by paragraph (d)(1) of this rule to each security holder whose name appears on the most recent stockholder list of the issuer;

(B)   By contacting each participant on the most recent security position listing of any clearing agency within the possession or access of the issuer or affiliate making the issuer tender offer, and making inquiry of each participant as to the approximate number of beneficial owners of the securities sought in the offer that are held by the participant;

(C)   By furnishing to each participant a sufficient number of copies of the statement required by paragraph (d)(1) of this rule for transmittal to the beneficial owners; and

(D)   By agreeing to reimburse each participant promptly for its reasonable expenses incurred in forwarding the statement to beneficial owners.

(iii)   Dissemination of certain cash issuer tender offers by summary publication:

(A)   If the issuer tender offer is not subject to § 240.13e–3, by making adequate publication of a summary advertisement containing the information required by paragraph (d)(3) of this rule in a newspaper or newspapers, on the date of commencement of the issuer tender offer; and

(B) By mailing or otherwise furnishing promptly the statement required by paragraph (d)(1) of this rule and a transmittal letter to any security holder who requests a copy of the statement or transmittal letter.

> *Instruction to paragraph (e)(1):* For purposes of paragraphs (e)(1)(i) and (e)(1)(iii) of this rule, adequate publication of the issuer tender offer may require publication in a newspaper with a national circulation, a newspaper with metropolitan or regional circulation, or a combination of the two, depending upon the facts and circumstances involved.

(2) For tender offers in which the consideration consists solely or partially of securities registered under the Securities Act of 1933, a registration statement containing all of the required information, including pricing information, has been filed and a preliminary prospectus or a prospectus that meets the requirements of Section 10(a) of the Securities Act, including a letter of transmittal, is delivered to security holders. However, for going-private transactions (as defined by Rule 13e–3) and roll-up transactions (as described by Item 901 of Regulation S-K, a registration statement registering the securities to be offered must have become effective and only a prospectus that meets the requirements of Section 10(a) of the Securities Act may be delivered to security holders on the date of commencement.

Instructions to paragraph (e)(2):

1. If the prospectus is being delivered by mail, mailing on the date of commencement is sufficient.

2. A preliminary prospectus used under this rule may not omit information under Rule 430 or 430A under the Securities Act.

3. If a preliminary prospectus is used under this rule and the issuer must disseminate material changes, the tender offer must remain open for the period specified in paragraph (e)(3) of this rule.

4. If a preliminary prospectus is used under this rule, tenders may be requested in accordance with Rule 162(a) under the Securities Act.

(3) If a material change occurs in the information published, sent or given to security holders, the issuer or affiliate must disseminate promptly disclosure of the change in a manner reasonably calculated to inform security holders of the change. In a registered securities offer where the issuer or affiliate disseminates the preliminary prospectus as permitted by paragraph (e)(2) of this rule, the offer must remain open from the date that material changes to the tender offer materials are disseminated to security holders, as follows:

(i) Five business days for a prospectus supplement containing a material change other than price or share levels;

(ii) Ten business days for a prospectus supplement containing a change in price, the amount of securities sought, the dealer's soliciting fee, or other similarly significant change;

(iii) Ten business days for a prospectus supplement included as part of a post-effective amendment; and

(iv) Twenty business days for a revised prospectus when the initial prospectus was materially deficient.

(f) Manner of making tender offer.

(1) The issuer tender offer, unless withdrawn, shall remain open until the expiration of:

(i) At least twenty business days from its commencement; and

(ii)   At least ten business days from the date that notice of an increase or decrease in the percentage of the class of securities being sought or the consideration offered or the dealer's soliciting fee to be given is first published, sent or given to security holders.

Provided, however, That, for purposes of this paragraph, the acceptance for payment by the issuer or affiliate of an additional amount of securities not to exceed two percent of the class of securities that is the subject of the tender offer shall not be deemed to be an increase. For purposes of this paragraph, the percentage of a class of securities shall be calculated in accordance with section 14(d)(3) of the Act.

(2)   The issuer or affiliate making the issuer tender offer shall permit securities tendered pursuant to the issuer tender offer to be withdrawn:

(i)   At any time during the period such issuer tender offer remains open; and

(ii)   If not yet accepted for payment, after the expiration of forty business days from the commencement of the issuer tender offer.

(3)   If the issuer or affiliate makes a tender offer for less than all of the outstanding equity securities of a class, and if a greater number of securities is tendered pursuant thereto than the issuer or affiliate is bound or willing to take up and pay for, the securities taken up and paid for shall be taken up and paid for as nearly as may be pro rata, disregarding fractions, according to the number of securities tendered by each security holder during the period such offer remains open; *Provided, however,* That this provision shall not prohibit the issuer or affiliate making the issuer tender offer from:

(i)   Accepting all securities tendered by persons who own, beneficially or of record, an aggregate of not more than a specified number which is less than one hundred shares of such security and who tender all their securities, before prorating securities tendered by others; or

(ii)   Accepting by lot securities tendered by security holders who tender all securities held by them and who, when tendering their securities, elect to have either all or none or at least a minimum amount or none accepted, if the issuer or affiliate first accepts all securities tendered by security holders who do not so elect;

(4)   In the event the issuer or affiliate making the issuer tender increases the consideration offered after the issuer tender offer has commenced, such issuer or affiliate shall pay such increased consideration to all security holders whose tendered securities are accepted for payment by such issuer or affiliate.

(5)   The issuer or affiliate making the tender offer shall either pay the consideration offered, or return the tendered securities, promptly after the termination or withdrawal of the tender offer.

(6)   Until the expiration of at least ten business days after the date of termination of the issuer tender offer, neither the issuer nor any affiliate shall make any purchases, otherwise than pursuant to the tender offer, of:

(i)   Any security which is the subject of the issuer tender offer, or any security of the same class and series, or any right to purchase any such securities; and

(ii)   In the case of an issuer tender offer which is an exchange offer, any security being offered pursuant to such exchange offer, or any security of the same class and series, or any right to purchase any such security.

(7)   The time periods for the minimum offering periods pursuant to this rule shall be computed on a concurrent as opposed to a consecutive basis.

(8)   No issuer or affiliate shall make a tender offer unless:

(i)   The tender offer is open to all security holders of the class of securities subject to the tender offer; and

(ii)   The consideration paid to any security holder for securities tendered in the tender offer is the highest consideration paid to any other security holder for securities tendered in the tender offer.

(9)   Paragraph (f)(8)(i) of this rule shall not:

(i)   Affect dissemination under paragraph (e) of this rule; or

(ii)   Prohibit an issuer or affiliate from making a tender offer excluding all security holders in a state where the issuer or affiliate is prohibited from making the tender offer by administrative or judicial action pursuant to a state statute after a good faith effort by the issuer or affiliate to comply with such statute.

(10) Paragraph (f)(8)(ii) of this rule shall not prohibit the offer of more than one type of consideration in a tender offer, provided that:

(i)   Security holders are afforded equal right to elect among each of the types of consideration offered; and

(ii)   The highest consideration of each type paid to any security holder is paid to any other security holder receiving that type of consideration.

(11) If the offer and sale of securities constituting consideration offered in an issuer tender offer is prohibited by the appropriate authority of a state after a good faith effort by the issuer or affiliate to register or qualify the offer and sale of such securities in such state:

(i)   The issuer or affiliate may offer security holders in such state an alternative form of consideration; and

(ii)   Paragraph (f)(10) of this rule shall not operate to require the issuer or affiliate to offer or pay the alternative form of consideration to security holders in any other state.

(12)(i) Paragraph (f)(8)(ii) of this rule shall not prohibit the negotiation, execution or amendment of an employment compensation, severance or other employee benefit arrangement, or payments made or to be made or benefits granted or to be granted according to such an arrangement, with respect to any security holder of the issuer, where the amount payable under the arrangement:

(A)   Is being paid or granted as compensation for past services performed, future services to be performed, or future services to be refrained from performing, by the security holder (and matters incidental thereto); and

(B)   Is not calculated based on the number of securities tendered or to be tendered in the tender offer by the security holder.

(ii)   The provisions of paragraph (f)(12)(i) of this rule shall be satisfied and, therefore, pursuant to this non-exclusive safe harbor, the negotiation, execution or amendment of an arrangement and any payments made or to be made or benefits granted or to be granted according to that arrangement shall not be prohibited by paragraph (f)(8)(ii) of this rule, if the arrangement is approved as an employment compensation, severance or other employee benefit arrangement solely by independent directors as follows:

(A)   The compensation committee or a committee of the board of directors that performs functions similar to a compensation committee of the issuer approves the arrangement, regardless of whether the issuer is a party to the arrangement, or, if an affiliate is a party to the arrangement, the compensation committee or a committee of the board of directors that performs functions similar to a compensation committee of the affiliate approves the arrangement; or

(B)   If the issuer's or affiliate's board of directors, as applicable, does not have a compensation committee or a committee of the board of directors that performs functions similar to a compensation committee or if none of the members of the issuer's or affiliate's compensation committee or committee that performs functions similar to a compensation committee is independent, a special committee of the board of directors formed to consider and approve the arrangement approves the arrangement; or

(C)   If the issuer or affiliate, as applicable, is a foreign private issuer, any or all members of the board of directors or any committee of the board of directors authorized to approve employment compensation, severance or other employee benefit arrangements under the laws or regulations of the home country approves the arrangement.

Instructions to paragraph (f)(12)(ii): For purposes of determining whether the members of the committee approving an arrangement in accordance with the provisions of paragraph (f)(12)(ii) of this rule are independent, the following provisions shall apply:

1.   If the issuer or affiliate, as applicable, is a listed issuer (as defined in Rule 10A–3 of this chapter) whose securities are listed either on a national securities exchange registered pursuant to section 6(a) of the Exchange Act or in an inter-dealer quotation system of a national securities association registered pursuant to section 15A(a) of the Exchange Act that has independence requirements for compensation committee members that have been approved by the Commission (as those requirements may be modified or supplemented), apply the issuer's or affiliate's definition of independence that it uses for determining that the members of the compensation committee are independent in compliance with the listing standards applicable to compensation committee members of the listed issuer.

2.   If the issuer or affiliate, as applicable, is not a listed issuer (as defined in Rule 10A–3 of this chapter), apply the independence requirements for compensation committee members of a national securities exchange registered pursuant to section 6(a) of the Exchange Act or an inter-dealer quotation system of a national securities association registered pursuant to section 15A(a) of the Exchange Act that have been approved by the Commission (as those requirements may be modified or supplemented). Whatever definition the issuer or affiliate, as applicable, chooses, it must apply that definition consistently to all members of the committee approving the arrangement.

3.   Notwithstanding Instructions 1 and 2 to paragraph (f)(12)(ii), if the issuer or affiliate, as applicable, is a closed-end investment company registered under the Investment Company Act of 1940, a director is considered to be independent if the director is not, other than in his or her capacity as a member of the board of directors or any board committee, an "interested person" of the investment company, as defined in section 2(a)(19) of the Investment Company Act of 1940.

4.   If the issuer or affiliate, as applicable, is a foreign private issuer, apply either the independence standards set forth in Instructions 1 and 2 to paragraph (f)(12)(ii) or the independence requirements of the laws, regulations, codes or standards of the home country of the issuer or affiliate, as applicable, for members of the board of directors or the committee of the board of directors approving the arrangement.

5.   A determination by the issuer's or affiliate's board of directors, as applicable, that the members of the board of directors or the committee of the board of directors, as applicable, approving an arrangement in accordance with the provisions of paragraph (f)(12)(ii) are independent in accordance with the

provisions of this instruction to paragraph (f)(12)(ii) shall satisfy the independence requirements of paragraph (f)(12)(ii).

Instruction to paragraph (f)(12): The fact that the provisions of paragraph (f)(12) of this rule extend only to employment compensation, severance and other employee benefit arrangements and not to other arrangements, such as commercial arrangements, does not raise any inference that a payment under any such other arrangement constitutes consideration paid for securities in a tender offer.

(13) Electronic filings.—If the issuer or affiliate is an electronic filer, the minimum offering periods set forth in paragraph (f)(1) of this rule shall be tolled for any period during which it fails to file in electronic format, absent a hardship exemption (§§ 232.201 and 232.202 of this chapter), the Schedule TO, the tender offer material specified in Item 1016(a)(1) of Regulation M-A (§ 229.1016(a)(1) of this chapter), and any amendments thereto. If such documents were filed in paper pursuant to a hardship exemption (*see* § 232.201 and § 232.202 of this chapter), the minimum offering periods shall be tolled for any period during which a required confirming electronic copy of such Schedule and tender offer material is delinquent.

(g) The requirements of section 13(e) (1) of the Act and Rule 13e-4 and Schedule TO thereunder shall be deemed satisfied with respect to any issuer tender offer, including any exchange offer, where the issuer is incorporated or organized under the laws of Canada or any Canadian province or territory, is a foreign private issuer, and is not an investment company registered or required to be registered under the Investment Company Act of 1940, if less than 40 percent of the class of securities that is the subject of the tender offer is held by U. S. holders, and the tender offer is subject to, and the issuer complies with, the laws, regulations and policies of Canada and/or any of its provinces or territories governing the conduct of the offer (unless the issuer has received an exemption(s) from, and the issuer tender offer does not comply with, requirements that otherwise would be prescribed by this rule), *provided that:*

(1) Where the consideration for an issuer tender offer subject to this paragraph consists solely of cash, the entire disclosure document or documents required to be furnished to holders of the class of securities to be acquired shall be filed with the Commission on Schedule 13E-4F and disseminated to shareholders residing in the United States in accordance with such Canadian laws, regulations and policies; or

(2) Where the consideration for an issuer tender offer subject to this paragraph includes securities to be issued pursuant to the offer, any registration statement and/or prospectus relating thereto shall be filed with the Commission along with the Schedule 13E-4F referred to in paragraph (g)(1) of this rule, and shall be disseminated, together with the home jurisdiction document(s) accompanying such Schedule, to shareholders of the issuer residing in the United States in accordance with such Canadian laws, regulations and policies.

Note: Notwithstanding the grant of an exemption from one or more of the applicable Canadian regulatory provisions imposing requirements that otherwise would be prescribed by this rule, the issuer tender offer will be eligible to proceed in accordance with the requirements of this rule if the Commission by order determines that the applicable Canadian regulatory provisions are adequate to protect the interest of investors.

(h) This rule shall not apply to:

(1) Calls or redemptions of any security in accordance with the terms and conditions of its governing instruments;

(2) Offers to purchase securities evidenced by a scrip certificate, order form or similar document which represents a fractional interest in a share of stock or similar security;

(3) Offers to purchase securities pursuant to a statutory procedure for the purchase of dissenting security holders' securities;

(4)   Any tender offer which is subject to section 14(d) of the Act;

(5)   Offers to purchase from security holders who own an aggregate of not more than a specified number of shares that is less than one hundred: *Provided, however,* That:

(i)   The offer complies with paragraph (f)(8)(i) of this rule with respect to security holders who own a number of shares equal to or less than the specified number of shares, except that an issuer can elect to exclude participants in a plan as that term is defined in Regulation M of this chapter, or to exclude security holders who do not own their shares as of a specified date determined by the issuer; and

(ii)   The offer complies with paragraph (f)(8)(ii) of this rule or the consideration paid pursuant to the offer is determined on the basis of a uniformly applied formula based on the market price of the subject security;

(6)   An issuer tender offer made solely to effect a rescission offer: *Provided, however,* That the offer is registered under the Securities Act of 1933, and the consideration is equal to the price paid by each security holder, plus legal interest if the issuer elects to or is required to pay legal interest;

(7)   Offers by closed-end management investment companies to repurchase equity securities pursuant to Rule 23c–3 of the Investment Company Act of 1940;

(8)   Cross-border tender offers (Tier I).—Any issuer tender offer (including any exchange offer) where the issuer is a foreign private issuer as defined in Rule 3b–4 if the following conditions are satisfied.

(i)   Except in the case of an issuer tender offer that is commenced during the pendency of a tender offer made by a third party in reliance on Rule 14d–1(c), U.S. holders do not hold more than 10 percent of the subject class sought in the offer (as determined under Instructions 2 or 3 to paragraph (h)(8) and paragraph (i) of this rule);

(ii)   The issuer or affiliate must permit U.S. holders to participate in the offer on terms at least as favorable as those offered any other holder of the same class of securities that is the subject of the offer; however:

(A)   Registered exchange offers.—If the issuer or affiliate offers securities registered under the Securities Act of 1933, the issuer or affiliate need not extend the offer to security holders in those states or jurisdictions that prohibit the offer or sale of the securities after the issuer or affiliate has made a good faith effort to register or qualify the offer and sale of securities in that state or jurisdiction, except that the issuer or affiliate must offer the same cash alternative to security holders in any such state or jurisdiction that it has offered to security holders in any other state or jurisdiction.

(B)   Exempt exchange offers.—If the issuer or affiliate offers securities exempt from registration under Rule 802 of the Securities Act of 1933, the issuer or affiliate need not extend the offer to security holders in those states or jurisdictions that require registration or qualification, except that the issuer or affiliate must offer the same cash alternative to security holders in any such state or jurisdiction that it has offered to security holders in any other state or jurisdiction.

(C)   Cash only consideration.—The issuer or affiliate may offer U.S. holders cash only consideration for the tender of the subject securities, notwithstanding the fact that the issuer or affiliate is offering security holders outside the United States a consideration that consists in whole or in part of securities of the issuer or affiliate, if the issuer or affiliate has a reasonable basis for believing that the amount of cash is substantially equivalent to the value of the consideration offered to non-U.S. holders, and either of the following conditions are satisfied:

(1)   The offered security is a "margin security" within the meaning of Regulation T and the issuer or affiliate undertakes to provide, upon the request of any U.S. holder or the Commission staff, the closing price and daily trading volume of the security on the principal trading market for the security as of the last trading day of each of the six months preceding the announcement of the offer and each of the trading days thereafter; or

(2)   If the offered security is not a "margin security" within the meaning of Regulation T, the issuer or affiliate undertakes to provide, upon the request of any U.S. holder or the Commission staff, an opinion of an independent expert stating that the cash consideration offered to U.S. holders is substantially equivalent to the value of the consideration offered security holders outside the United States.

(D)   Disparate tax treatment.—If the issuer or affiliate offers "loan notes" solely to offer sellers tax advantages not available in the United States and these notes are neither listed on any organized securities market nor registered under the Securities Act of 1933, the loan notes need not be offered to U.S. holders.

(iii) Informational documents. (A) If the issuer or affiliate publishes or otherwise disseminates an informational document to the holders of the securities in connection with the issuer tender offer (including any exchange offer), the issuer or affiliate must furnish that informational document, including any amendments thereto, in English, to the Commission on Form CB by the first business day after publication or dissemination. If the issuer or affiliate is a foreign company, it must also file a Form F-X with the Commission at the same time as the submission of Form CB to appoint an agent for service in the United States.

(B)   The issuer or affiliate must disseminate any informational document to U.S. holders, including any amendments thereto, in English, on a comparable basis to that provided to security holders in the home jurisdiction.

(C)   If the issuer or affiliate disseminates by publication in its home jurisdiction, the issuer or affiliate must publish the information in the United States in a manner reasonably calculated to inform U.S. holders of the offer.

(iv) An investment company registered or required to be registered under the Investment Company Act of 1940, other than a registered closed-end investment company, may not use this paragraph (h)(8); or

(9)   Any other transaction or transactions, if the Commission, upon written request or upon its own motion, exempts such transaction or transactions, either unconditionally, or on specified terms and conditions, as not constituting a fraudulent, deceptive or manipulative act or practice comprehended within the purpose of this rule.

(i)   Cross-border tender offers (Tier II).—Any issuer tender offer (including any exchange offer) that meets the conditions in paragraph (i)(1) of this rule shall be entitled to the exemptive relief specified in paragraph (i)(2) of this rule, provided that such issuer tender offer complies with all the requirements of this rule other than those for which an exemption has been specifically provided in paragraph (i)(2) of this rule. In addition, any issuer tender offer (including any exchange offer) subject only to the requirements of section 14(e) of the Act and Regulation 14E thereunder that meets the conditions in paragraph (i)(1) of this rule also shall be entitled to the exemptive relief specified in paragraph (i)(2) of this rule, to the extent needed under the requirements of Regulation 14E, so long as the tender offer complies with all requirements of Regulation 14E other than those for which an exemption has been specifically provided in paragraph (i)(2) of this rule:

(1)   Conditions. (i) The issuer is a foreign private issuer as defined in Rule 3b–4 and is not an investment company registered or required to be registered under the Investment Company Act of 1940, other than a registered closed-end investment company; and

(ii)   Except in the case of an issuer tender offer commenced during the pendency of a tender offer made by a third party in reliance on § 240.14d–1(d), U.S. holders do not hold more than 40 percent of the class of securities sought in the offer (as determined in accordance with Instructions 2 or 3 to paragraphs (h)(8) and (i) of this rule).

(2)   Exemptions.—The issuer tender offer shall comply with all requirements of this rule other than the following:

(i)   Equal treatment—loan notes.—If the issuer or affiliate offers loan notes solely to offer sellers tax advantages not available in the United States and these notes are neither listed on any organized securities market nor registered under the Securities Act, the loan notes need not be offered to U.S. holders, notwithstanding paragraph (f)(8) and (h)(9) of this rule.

(ii)   Equal treatment—separate U.S. and foreign offers.—Notwithstanding the provisions of paragraph (f)(8) of this rule, an issuer or affiliate conducting an issuer tender offer meeting the conditions of paragraph (i)(1) of this rule may separate the offer into multiple offers: one offer made to U.S. holders, which also may include all holders of American Depositary Shares representing interests in the subject securities, and one or more offers made to non-U.S. holders. The U.S. offer must be made on terms at least as favorable as those offered any other holder of the same class of securities that is the subject of the tender offers. U.S. holders may be included in the foreign offer(s) only where the laws of the jurisdiction governing such foreign offer(s) expressly preclude the exclusion of U.S. holders from the foreign offer(s) and where the offer materials distributed to U.S. holders fully and adequately disclose the risks of participating in the foreign offer(s).

(iii) Notice of extensions.—Notice of extensions made in accordance with the requirements of the home jurisdiction law or practice will satisfy the requirements of Rule 14e–1(d).

(iv)   Prompt payment.—Payment made in accordance with the requirements of the home jurisdiction law or practice will satisfy the requirements of Rule 14e–1(c).

(v)   Suspension of withdrawal rights during counting of tendered securities.—The issuer or affiliate may suspend withdrawal rights required under paragraph (f)(2) of this rule at the end of the offer and during the period that securities tendered into the offer are being counted, provided that:

(A)   The issuer or affiliate has provided an offer period, including withdrawal rights, for a period of at least 20 U.S. business days;

(B)   At the time withdrawal rights are suspended, all offer conditions have been satisfied or waived, except to the extent that the issuer or affiliate is in the process of determining whether a minimum acceptance condition included in the terms of the offer has been satisfied by counting tendered securities; and

(C)   Withdrawal rights are suspended only during the counting process and are reinstated immediately thereafter, except to the extent that they are terminated through the acceptance of tendered securities.

(vi)   Early termination of an initial offering period.—An issuer or affiliate conducting an issuer tender offer may terminate an initial offering period, including a voluntary extension of that period, if at the time the initial offering period and withdrawal rights terminate, the following conditions are met:

(A)   The initial offering period has been open for at least 20 U.S. business days;

(B)   The issuer or affiliate has adequately discussed the possibility of and the impact of the early termination in the original offer materials;

(C) The issuer or affiliate provides a subsequent offering period after the termination of the initial offering period;

(D) All offer conditions are satisfied as of the time when the initial offering period ends; and

(E) The issuer or affiliate does not terminate the initial offering period or any extension of that period during any mandatory extension required under U.S. tender offer rules.

Instructions to paragraph (h)(8) and (i) of this rule:

1. *Home jurisdiction* means both the jurisdiction of the issuer's incorporation, organization or chartering and the principal foreign market where the issuer's securities are listed or quoted.

2. *U.S. holder* means any security holder resident in the United States. To determine the percentage of outstanding securities held by U.S. holders:

    i. Calculate the U.S. ownership as of a date no more than 60 days before and no more than 30 days after the public announcement of the tender offer. If you are unable to calculate as of a date within these time frames, the calculation may be made as of the most recent practicable date before public announcement, but in no event earlier than 120 days before announcement;

    ii. Include securities underlying American Depositary Shares convertible or exchangeable into the securities that are the subject of the tender offer when calculating the number of subject securities outstanding, as well as the number held by U.S. holders. Exclude from the calculations other types of securities that are convertible or exchangeable into the securities that are the subject of the tender offer, such as warrants, options and convertible securities;

    iii. Use the method of calculating record ownership in Rule 12g3–2(a), except that your inquiry as to the amount of securities represented by accounts of customers resident in the United States may be limited to brokers, dealers, banks and other nominees located in the United States, your jurisdiction of incorporation, and the jurisdiction that is the primary trading market for the subject securities, if different than your jurisdiction of incorporation;

    iv. If, after reasonable inquiry, you are unable to obtain information about the amount of securities represented by accounts of customers resident in the United States, you may assume, for purposes of this definition, that the customers are residents of the jurisdiction in which the nominee has its principal place of business; and

    v. Count securities as beneficially owned by residents of the United States as reported on reports of beneficial ownership that are provided to you or publicly filed and based on information otherwise provided to you.

3. If you are unable to conduct the analysis of U.S. ownership set forth in Instruction 2 above, U.S. holders will be presumed to hold 10 percent or less of the outstanding subject securities (40 percent for Tier II) so long as there is a primary trading market outside the United States, as defined in Rule 12h–6(f)(5) of this chapter, unless:

    i. Average daily trading volume of the subject securities in the United States for a recent twelve-month period ending on a date no more than 60 days before the public announcement of the tender offer exceeds 10 percent (or 40 percent) of the average daily trading volume of that class of securities on a worldwide basis for the same period; or

ii. The most recent annual report or annual information filed or submitted by the issuer with securities regulators of the home jurisdiction or with the Commission or any jurisdiction in which the subject securities trade before the public announcement of the offer indicates that U.S. holders hold more than 10 percent (or 40 percent) of the outstanding subject class of securities; or

iii. You know or have reason to know, before the public announcement of the offer, that the level of U.S. ownership of the subject securities exceeds 10 percent (or 40 percent) of such securities. As an example, you are deemed to know information about U.S. ownership of the subject class of securities that is publicly available and that appears in any filing with the Commission or any regulatory body in the home jurisdiction and, if different, the non-U.S. jurisdiction in which the primary trading market for the subject class of securities is located. You are also deemed to know information obtained or readily available from any other source that is reasonably reliable, including from persons you have retained to advise you about the transaction, as well as from third-party information providers. These examples are not intended to be exclusive.

4. *United States* means the United States of America, its territories and possessions, any State of the United States, and the District of Columbia.

5. The exemptions provided by paragraphs (h)(8) and (i) of this rule are not available for any securities transaction or series of transactions that technically complies with paragraph (h)(8) and (i) of this rule but are part of a plan or scheme to evade the provisions of this rule.

(j)(1) It shall be a fraudulent, deceptive or manipulative act or practice, in connection with an issuer tender offer, for an issuer or an affiliate of such issuer, in connection with an issuer tender offer:

(i) To employ any device, scheme or artifice to defraud any person;

(ii) To make any untrue statement of a material fact or to omit to state a material fact necessary in order to make the statements made, in the light of the circumstances under which they were made, not misleading; or

(iii) To engage in any act, practice or course of business which operates or would operate as a fraud or deceit upon any person.

(2) As a means reasonably designed to prevent fraudulent, deceptive or manipulative acts or practices in connection with any issuer tender offer, it shall be unlawful for an issuer or an affiliate of such issuer to make an issuer tender offer unless:

(i) Such issuer or affiliate complies with the requirements of paragraphs (b), (c), (d), (e) and (f) of this rule; and

(ii) The issuer tender offer is not in violation of paragraph (j)(1) of this rule.

Rule 13p–1. Requirement of Report Regarding Disclosure of Registrant's Supply Chain Information Regarding Conflict Minerals

Every registrant that files reports with the Commission under Sections 13(a) or 15(d) of the Securities Exchange Act of 1934, having conflict minerals that are necessary to the functionality or production of a product manufactured or contracted by that registrant to be manufactured, shall file a report on Form SD within the period specified in that Form disclosing the information required by the applicable items of Form SD as specified in that Form (17 CFR 249b.400).

REGULATION 14A: SOLICITATION OF PROXIES

Rule 14a–1.   Definitions

Unless the context otherwise requires, all terms used in this regulation have the same meanings as in the Act or elsewhere in the general rules and regulations thereunder. In addition, the following definitions apply unless the context otherwise requires:

* * *

(f)   *Proxy.* The term "proxy" includes every proxy, consent or authorization within the meaning of section 14(a) of the Act. The consent or authorization may take the form of failure to object or to dissent.

(g)   *Proxy statement.* The term "proxy statement" means the statement required by Rule 14a–3(a) whether or not contained in a single document.

(h)   *Record date.* The term "record date" means the date as of which the record holders of securities entitled to vote at a meeting or by written consent or authorization shall be determined.

(i)   *Record holder.* For purposes of Rules 14a–13, 14b–1 and 14b–2, the term "record holder" means any broker, dealer, voting trustee, bank, association or other entity that exercises fiduciary powers which holds securities of record in nominee name or otherwise or as a participant in a clearing agency registered pursuant to section 17A of the Act.

* * *

(*l*)   *Solicitation.*

(1)   The terms "solicit" and "solicitation" include:

(i)   Any request for a proxy whether or not accompanied by or included in a form of proxy:

(ii)   Any request to execute or not to execute, or to revoke, a proxy; or

(iii)   The furnishing of a form of proxy or other communication to security holders under circumstances reasonably calculated to result in the procurement, withholding or revocation of a proxy.

(2)   The terms do not apply, however, to:

(i)   The furnishing of a form of proxy to a security holder upon the unsolicited request of such security holder;

(ii)   The performance by the registrant of acts required by Rule 14a–7;

(iii)   The performance by any person of ministerial acts on behalf of a person soliciting a proxy; or

(iv)   A communication by a security holder who does not otherwise engage in a proxy solicitation (other than a solicitation exempt under Rule 14a–2) stating how the security holder intends to vote and the reasons therefor, provided that the communication:

(A)   Is made by means of speeches in public forums, press releases, published or broadcast opinions, statements, or advertisements appearing in a broadcast media, or newspaper, magazine or other bona fide publication disseminated on a regular basis,

(B)   Is directed to persons to whom the security holder owes a fiduciary duty in connection with the voting of securities of a registrant held by the security holder, or

(C)   Is made in response to unsolicited requests for additional information with respect to a prior communication by the security holder made pursuant to this paragraph (*l*)(2)(iv).

Rule 14a–2.   Solicitations to Which Rule 14a–3 to Rule 14a–15 Apply

Rules 14a–3 to 14a–15, except as specified, apply to every solicitation of a proxy with respect to securities registered pursuant to section 12 of the Act, whether or not trading in such securities has been suspended. To the extent specified below, certain of these sections also apply to roll-up transactions that do not involve an entity with securities registered pursuant to section 12 of the Act.

(a)   Rules 14a–3 to 14a–15 do not apply to the following:

(1)   Any solicitation by a person in respect to securities carried in his name or in the name of his nominee (otherwise than as voting trustee) or held in his custody, if such person—

(i)   Receives no commission or remuneration for such solicitation, directly or indirectly, other than reimbursement of reasonable expenses,

(ii)   Furnishes promptly to the person solicited (or such person's household in accordance with § 240.14a–3(e)(1)) a copy of all soliciting material with respect to the same subject matter or meeting received from all persons who shall furnish copies thereof for such purpose and who shall, if requested, defray the reasonable expenses to be incurred in forwarding such material, and

(iii)   In addition, does no more than impartially instruct the person solicited to forward a proxy to the person, if any, to whom the person solicited desires to give a proxy, or impartially request from the person solicited instructions as to the authority to be conferred by the proxy and state that a proxy will be given if no instructions are received by a certain date.

(2)   Any solicitation by a person in respect of securities of which he is the beneficial owner;

(3)   Any solicitation involved in the offer and sale of securities registered under the Securities Act of 1933: Provided, that this paragraph shall not apply to securities to be issued in any transaction of the character specified in paragraph (a) of Rule 145 under that Act;

(4)   Any solicitation with respect to a plan of reorganization under Chapter 11 of the Bankruptcy Reform Act of 1978, as amended, if made after the entry of an order approving the written disclosure statement concerning a plan of reorganization pursuant to section 1125 of said Act and after, or concurrently with, the transmittal of such disclosure statement as required by section 1125 of said Act;

(5)   [Reserved]

(6)   Any solicitation through the medium of a newspaper advertisement which informs security holders of a source from which they may obtain copies of a proxy statement, form of proxy and any other soliciting material and does no more than:

(i)   Name the registrant,

(ii)   State the reason for the advertisement, and

(iii)   Identify the proposal or proposals to be acted upon by security holders.

(b)   Rules 14a–3 to 14a–6 (other than 14a–6(g) and 14a–6(p)), Rules 14a–8, 14a–10, and 14a–12 to 14a–15 do not apply to the following:

(1)   Any solicitation by or on behalf of any person who does not, at any time during such solicitation, seek directly or indirectly, either on its own or another's behalf, the power to act as proxy for a security holder and does not furnish or otherwise request, or act on behalf of a person who furnishes or requests, a form of revocation, abstention, consent or authorization. Provided, however, That the exemption set forth in this paragraph shall not apply to:

(i)   The registrant or an affiliate or associate of the registrant (other than an officer or director or any person serving in a similar capacity);

(ii) An officer or director of the registrant or any person serving in a similar capacity engaging in a solicitation financed directly or indirectly by the registrant;

(iii) An officer, director, affiliate or associate of a person that is ineligible to rely on the exemption set forth in this paragraph (other than persons specified in paragraph (b)(1)(i) of this Rule), or any person serving in a similar capacity;

(iv) Any nominee for whose election as a director proxies are solicited;

(v) Any person soliciting in opposition to a merger, recapitalization, reorganization, sale of assets or other extraordinary transaction recommended or approved by the board of directors of the registrant who is proposing or intends to propose an alternative transaction to which such person or one of its affiliates is a party;

(vi) Any person who is required to report beneficial ownership of the registrant's equity securities on a Schedule 13D (§ 240.13d–101), unless such person has filed a Schedule 13D and has not disclosed pursuant to Item 4 thereto an intent, or reserved the right, to engage in a control transaction, or any contested solicitation for the election of directors;

(vii) Any person who receives compensation from an ineligible person directly related to the solicitation of proxies, other than pursuant to Rule 14a–13;

(viii) Where the registrant is an investment company registered under the Investment Company Act of 1940 an "interested person" of that investment company, as that term is defined in section 2(a)(19) of the Investment Company Act;

(ix) Any person who, because of a substantial interest in the subject matter of the solicitation, is likely to receive a benefit from a successful solicitation that would not be shared pro rata by all other holders of the same class of securities, other than a benefit arising from the person's employment with the registrant; and

(x) Any person acting on behalf of any of the foregoing.

(2) Any solicitation made otherwise than on behalf of the registrant where the total number of persons solicited is not more than ten; * * *

* * *

(6) Any solicitation by or on behalf of any person who does not seek directly or indirectly, either on its own or another's behalf, the power to act as proxy for a shareholder and does not furnish or otherwise request, or act on behalf of a person who furnishes or requests, a form of revocation, abstention, consent, or authorization in an electronic shareholder forum that is established, maintained or operated pursuant to the provisions of Rule 14a–17, provided that the solicitation is made more than 60 days prior to the date announced by a registrant for its next annual or special meeting of shareholders. If the registrant announces the date of its next annual or special meeting of shareholders less than 60 days before the meeting date, then the solicitation may not be made more than two days following the date of the registrant's announcement of the meeting date. Participation in an electronic shareholder forum does not eliminate a person's eligibility to solicit proxies after the date that this exemption is no longer available, or is no longer being relied upon, provided that any such solicitation is conducted in accordance with this regulation.

(7) Any solicitation by or on behalf of any shareholder in connection with the formation of a nominating shareholder group pursuant to Rule 14a–11, provided that:

(i) The soliciting shareholder is not holding the registrant's securities with the purpose, or with the effect, of changing control of the registrant or to gain a number of seats on the board of directors that exceeds the maximum number of nominees that the registrant could be required to include under Rule 14a–11(d);

(ii) Each written communication includes no more than:

(A) A statement of each soliciting shareholder's intent to form a nominating shareholder group in order to nominate one or more directors under Rule 14a–11;

(B) Identification of, and a brief statement regarding, the potential nominee or nominees or, where no nominee or nominees have been identified, the characteristics of the nominee or nominees that the shareholder intends to nominate, if any;

(C) The percentage of voting power of the registrant's securities that are entitled to be voted on the election of directors that each soliciting shareholder holds or the aggregate percentage held by any group to which the shareholder belongs; and

(D) The means by which shareholders may contact the soliciting party.

(iii) Any written soliciting material published, sent or given to shareholders in accordance with this paragraph must be filed by the shareholder with the Commission, under the registrant's Exchange Act file number, or, in the case of a registrant that is an investment company registered under the Investment Company Act of 1940, under the registrant's Investment Company Act file number, no later than the date the material is first published, sent or given to shareholders. Three copies of the material must at the same time be filed with, or mailed for filing to, each national securities exchange upon which any class of securities of the registrant is listed and registered. The soliciting material must include a cover page in the form set forth in Schedule 14N (§ 240.14n–101) and the appropriate box on the cover page must be marked.

(iv) In the case of an oral solicitation made in accordance with the terms of this rule, the nominating shareholder must file a cover page in the form set forth in Schedule 14N (§ 240.14n–101), with the appropriate box on the cover page marked, under the registrant's Exchange Act file number (or in the case of an investment company registered under the Investment Company Act of 1940, under the registrant's Investment Company Act file number), no later than the date of the first such communication.

(8) Any solicitation by or on behalf of a nominating shareholder or nominating shareholder group in support of its nominee that is included or that will be included on the registrant's form of proxy in accordance with Rule 14a–11 or for or against the registrant's nominee or nominees, provided that:

(i) The soliciting party does not, at any time during such solicitation, seek directly or indirectly, either on its own or another's behalf, the power to act as proxy for a shareholder and does not furnish or otherwise request, or act on behalf of a person who furnishes or requests, a form of revocation, abstention, consent or authorization;

(ii) Any written communication includes:

(A) The identity of each nominating shareholder and a description of his or her direct or indirect interests, by security holdings or otherwise;

(B) A prominent legend in clear, plain language advising shareholders that a shareholder nominee is or will be included in the registrant's proxy statement and that they should read the registrant's proxy statement when available because it includes important information (or, if the registrant's proxy statement is publicly available, advising shareholders of that fact and encouraging shareholders to read the registrant's proxy statement because it includes important information). The legend also must explain to shareholders that they can find the registrant's proxy statement, other soliciting material, and any other relevant documents at no charge on the Commission's Web site; and

(iii) Any written soliciting material published, sent or given to shareholders in accordance with this paragraph must be filed by the nominating shareholder or nominating shareholder group with the Commission, under the registrant's Exchange Act file number, or, in the case of a registrant that is an investment company registered under the Investment Company Act of 1940, under the registrant's Investment Company Act file number, no later than the date the material is first published, sent or given to shareholders. Three copies of the material must at the same time be filed with, or mailed for filing to, each national securities exchange upon which any class of securities of the registrant is listed and registered. The soliciting material must include a cover page in the form set forth in Schedule 14N (§ 240.14n–101) and the appropriate box on the cover page must be marked.

Rule 14a–3.   Information to Be Furnished to Security Holders

(a)   No solicitation subject to this regulation shall be made unless each person solicited is concurrently furnished or has previously been furnished with:

(1)   A publicly-filed preliminary or definitive proxy statement, in the form and manner described in § 240.14a–16, containing the information specified in Schedule 14A (§ 240.14a–101);

(2)   A preliminary or definitive written proxy statement included in a registration statement filed under the Securities Act of 1933 on Form S-4 or F-4 (§ 239.25 or § 239.34 of this chapter) or Form N-14 (§ 239.23 of this chapter) and containing the information specified in such Form; or

(3)   A publicly-filed preliminary or definitive proxy statement, not in the form and manner described in Rule 14a–16, containing the information specified in Schedule 14A, if:

(i)   The solicitation relates to a business combination transaction as defined in Rule 165 under the Securities Act of 1933, as well as transactions for cash consideration requiring disclosure under Item 14 of Schedule 14A.

(ii)   The solicitation may not follow the form and manner described in Rule 14a–16 pursuant to the laws of the state of incorporation of the registrant;

(b)   If the solicitation is made on behalf of the registrant, other than an investment company registered under the Investment Company Act of 1940, and relates to an annual (or special meeting in lieu of the annual) meeting of security holders, or written consent in lieu of such meeting, at which directors are to be elected, each proxy statement furnished pursuant to paragraph (a) of this rule shall be accompanied or preceded by an annual report to security holders as follows:

* * *

Rule 14a–4.   Requirements as to Proxy

(a)   The form of proxy

(1)   shall indicate in bold-face type whether or not the proxy is solicited on behalf of the registrant's board of directors or, if provided other than by a majority of the board of directors, shall indicate in bold-face type on whose behalf the solicitation is made;

(2)   Shall provide a specifically designated blank space for dating the proxy card; and

(3)   Shall identify clearly and impartially each separate matter intended to be acted upon, whether or not related to or conditioned on the approval of other matters, and whether proposed by the registrant or by security holders. No reference need be made, however, to proposals as to which discretionary authority is conferred pursuant to paragraph (c) of this rule.

Note to paragraph (a)3 (Electronic filers):

Electronic filers shall satisfy the filing requirements of Rule 14a–6(a) or (b) with respect to the form of proxy by filing the form of proxy as an appendix at the end of the proxy statement. Forms of proxy shall not be filed as exhibits or separate documents within an electronic submission.

(b)(1)   Means shall be provided in the form of proxy whereby the person solicited is afforded an opportunity to specify by boxes a choice between approval or disapproval of, or abstention with respect to each separate matter referred to therein as intended to be acted upon, other than elections to office and votes to determine the frequency of shareholder votes on executive compensation pursuant to Rule 14a–21(b). A proxy may confer discretionary authority with respect to matters as to which a choice is not specified by the security holder provided that the form of proxy states in bold-face type how it is intended to vote the shares represented by the proxy in each such case.

(2)　A form of proxy that provides for the election of directors shall set forth the names of persons nominated for election as directors, including any person whose nomination by a shareholder or shareholder group satisfies the requirements of Rule 14a–11, an applicable state or foreign law provision, or a registrant's governing documents as they relate to the inclusion of shareholder director nominees in the registrant's proxy materials. Such form of proxy shall clearly provide any of the following means for security holders to withhold authority to vote for each nominee:

(i)　A box opposite the name of each nominee which may be marked to indicate that authority to vote for such nominee is withheld; or

(ii)　An instruction in bold-face type which indicates that the security holder may withhold authority to vote for any nominee by lining through or otherwise striking out the name of any nominee; or

(iii)　Designated blank spaces in which the security holder may enter the names of nominees with respect to whom the security holder chooses to withhold authority to vote; or

(iv)　Any other similar means, provided that clear instructions are furnished indicating how the security holder may withhold authority to vote for any nominee.

Such form of proxy also may provide a means for the security holder to grant authority to vote for the nominees set forth, as a group, provided that there is a similar means for the security holder to withhold authority to vote for such group of nominees. Any such form of proxy which is executed by the security holder in such manner as not to withhold authority to vote for the election of any nominee shall be deemed to grant such authority, provided that the form of proxy so states in bold-face type. Means to grant authority to vote for any nominees as a group or to withhold authority for any nominees as a group may not be provided if the form of proxy includes one or more shareholder nominees in accordance with Rule 14a–11, an applicable state or foreign law provision, or a registrant's governing documents as they relate to the inclusion of shareholder director nominees in the registrant's proxy materials.

(3)　A form of proxy which provides for a shareholder vote on the frequency of shareholder votes to approve the compensation of executives required by section 14A(a)(2) of the Securities Exchange Act of 1934 shall provide means whereby the person solicited is afforded an opportunity to specify by boxes a choice among 1, 2 or 3 years, or abstain.

(c)　A proxy may confer discretionary authority to vote on any of the following matters:

(1)　For an annual meeting of shareholders, if the registrant did not have notice of the matter at least 45 days before the date on which the registrant first sent its proxy materials for the prior year's annual meeting of shareholders (or date specified by an advance notice provision), and a specific statement to that effect is made in the proxy statement or form of proxy. If during the prior year the registrant did not hold an annual meeting, or if the date of the meeting has changed more than 30 days from the prior year, then notice must not have been received a reasonable time before the registrant sends its proxy materials for the current year.

(2)　In the case in which the registrant has received timely notice in connection with an annual meeting of shareholders (as determined under paragraph (c)(1) of this rule), if the registrant includes, in the proxy statement, advice on the nature of the matter and how the registrant intends to exercise its discretion to vote on each matter. However, even if the registrant includes this information in its proxy statement, it may not exercise discretionary voting authority on a particular proposal if the proponent:

(i) Provides the registrant with a written statement, within the time-frame determined under paragraph (c)(1) of this rule, that the proponent intends to deliver a proxy statement and form of proxy to holders of at least the percentage of the company's voting shares required under applicable law to carry the proposal;

(ii) Includes the same statement in its proxy materials filed under Rule 14a–6; and

(iii) Immediately after soliciting the percentage of shareholders required to carry the proposal, provides the registrant with a statement from any solicitor or other person with knowledge that the necessary steps have been taken to deliver a proxy statement and form of proxy to holders of at least the percentage of the company's voting shares required under applicable law to carry the proposal.

(3) For solicitations other than for annual meetings or for solicitations by persons other than the registrant, matters which the persons making the solicitation do not know, a reasonable time before the solicitation, are to be presented at the meeting, if a specific statement to that effect is made in the proxy statement or form of proxy.

(4) Approval of the minutes of the prior meeting if such approval does not amount to ratification of the action taken at that meeting;

(5) The election of any person to any office for which a bona fide nominee is named in the proxy statement and such nominee is unable to serve or for good cause will not serve.

(6) Any proposal omitted from the proxy statement and form of proxy pursuant to Rule 14a–8 or 14a–9 of this chapter.

(7) Matters incident to the conduct of the meeting.

(d) No proxy shall confer authority:

(1) To vote for the election of any person to any office for which a bona fide nominee is not named in the proxy statement,

(2) To vote at any annual meeting other than the next annual meeting (or any adjournment thereof) to be held after the date on which the proxy statement and form of proxy are first sent or given to security holders,

(3) To vote with respect to more than one meeting (and any adjournment thereof) or more than one consent solicitation or

(4) To consent to or authorize any action other than the action proposed to be taken in the proxy statement, or matters referred to in paragraph (c) of this rule. A person shall not be deemed to be a bona fide nominee and he shall not be named as such unless he has consented to being named in the proxy statement and to serve if elected. Provided, however, That nothing in this Rule 14a–4 shall prevent any person soliciting in support of nominees who, if elected, would constitute a minority of the board of directors, from seeking authority to vote for nominees named in the registrant's proxy statement, so long as the soliciting party:

(i) Seeks authority to vote in the aggregate for the number of director positions then subject to election;

(ii) Represents that it will vote for all the registrant nominees, other than those registrant nominees specified by the soliciting party;

(iii) Provides the security holder an opportunity to withhold authority with respect to any other registrant nominee by writing the name of that nominee on the form of proxy; and

(iv) States on the form of proxy and in the proxy statement that there is no assurance that the registrant's nominees will serve if elected with any of the soliciting party's nominees.

(e)   The proxy statement or form of proxy shall provide, subject to reasonable specified conditions, that the shares represented by the proxy will be voted and that where the person solicited specifies by means of a ballot provided pursuant to paragraph (b) of this rule a choice with respect to any matter to be acted upon, the shares will be voted in accordance with the specifications so made.

(f)   No person conducting a solicitation subject to this regulation shall deliver a form of proxy, consent or authorization to any security holder unless the security holder concurrently receives, or has previously received, a definitive proxy statement that has been filed with the Commission pursuant to Rule 14a–6(b).

Rule 14a–5.   Presentation of Information in Proxy Statement

(a)   The information included in the proxy statement shall be clearly presented and the statements made shall be divided into groups according to subject matter and the various groups of statements shall be preceded by appropriate headings. The order of items and sub-items in the schedule need not be followed. Where practicable and appropriate, the information shall be presented in tabular form. All amounts shall be stated in figures. Information required by more than one applicable item need not be repeated. No statement need be made in response to any item or sub-item which is inapplicable.

(b)   Any information required to be included in the proxy statement as to terms of securities or other subject matter which from a standpoint of practical necessity must be determined in the future may be stated in terms of present knowledge and intention. To the extent practicable, the authority to be conferred concerning each such matter shall be confined within limits reasonably related to the need for discretionary authority. Subject to the foregoing, information which is not known to the persons on whose behalf the solicitation is to be made and which it is not reasonably within the power of such persons to ascertain or procure may be omitted, if a brief statement of the circumstances rendering such information unavailable is made.

(c)   Any information contained in any other proxy soliciting material which has been furnished to each person solicited in connection with the same meeting or subject matter may be omitted from the proxy statement, if a clear reference is made to the particular document containing such information.

(d)(1)   All printed proxy statements shall be in roman type at least as large and as legible as 10-point modern type, except that to the extent necessary for convenient presentation financial statements and other tabular data, but not the notes thereto, may be in roman type at least as large and as legible as 8-point modern type. All such type shall be leaded at least 2 points.

(2)   Where a proxy statement is delivered through an electronic medium, issuers may satisfy legibility requirements applicable to printed documents, such as type size and font, by presenting all required information in a format readily communicated to investors.

(e)   All proxy statements shall disclose, under an appropriate caption, the following dates:

(1)   The deadline for submitting shareholder proposals for inclusion in the registrant's proxy statement and form of proxy for the registrant's next annual meeting, calculated in the manner provided in Rule 14a–8(e) (Question 5);

(2)   The date after which notice of a shareholder proposal submitted outside the processes of Rule 14a–8 is considered untimely, either calculated in the manner provided by Rule 14a–4(c)(1) or as established by the registrant's advance notice provision, if any, authorized by applicable state law; and

(3)   The deadline for submitting nominees for inclusion in the registrant's proxy statement and form of proxy pursuant to Rule 14a–11, an applicable state or foreign law provision, or a registrant's governing documents as they relate to the inclusion of shareholder director nominees in the registrant's proxy materials for the registrant's next annual meeting of shareholders.

(f)   If the date of the next annual meeting is subsequently advanced or delayed by more than 30 calendar days from the date of the annual meeting to which the proxy statement relates, the registrant shall, in a timely manner, inform shareholders of such change, and the new dates referred to in paragraphs (e)(1) and (e)(2) of this rule, by including a notice, under Item 5, in its earliest possible quarterly report on Form 10-Q (§ 249.308a of this chapter), or, in the case of investment companies, in a shareholder report under Rule 30d–1 of this chapter under the Investment Company Act of 1940, or, if impracticable, any means reasonably calculated to inform shareholders.

Rule 14a–6.   Filing Requirements

(a)   *Preliminary proxy statement.* Five preliminary copies of the proxy statement and form of proxy shall be filed with the Commission at least 10 calendar days prior to the date definitive copies of such material are first sent or given to security holders, or such shorter period prior to that date as the Commission may authorize upon a showing of good cause thereunder. A registrant, however, shall not file with the Commission a preliminary proxy statement, form of proxy or other soliciting material to be furnished to security holders concurrently therewith if the solicitation relates to an annual (or special meeting in lieu of the annual) meeting, or for an investment company registered under the Investment Company Act of 1940 or a business development company, if the solicitation relates to any meeting of security holders at which the only matters to be acted upon are:

(1)   The election of directors;

(2)   The election, approval or ratification of accountant(s);

(3)   A security holder proposal included pursuant to Rule 14a–8;

(4)   A shareholder nominee for director included pursuant to Rule 14a–11, an applicable state or foreign law provision, or a registrant's governing documents as they relate to the inclusion of shareholder director nominees in the registrant's proxy materials.

(5)   The approval or ratification of a plan as defined in paragraph (a)(6)(ii) of Item 402 of Regulation S–K (§ 229.402(a)(6)(ii) of this chapter) or amendments to such a plan;

(6)   With respect to an investment company registered under the Investment Company Act of 1940 or a business development company, a proposal to continue, without change, any advisory or other contract or agreement that previously has been the subject of a proxy solicitation for which proxy material was filed with the Commission pursuant to this rule;

(7)   With respect to an open-end investment company registered under the Investment Company Act of 1940, a proposal to increase the number of shares authorized to be issued; and/or

(8)   A vote to approve the compensation of executives as required pursuant to section 14A(a)(1) of the Securities Exchange Act of 1934 and Rule 14a–21(a) of this chapter, or pursuant to section 111(e)(1) of the Emergency Economic Stabilization Act of 2008 and Rule 14a–20 of this chapter, a vote to determine the frequency of shareholder votes to approve the compensation of executives as required pursuant to Section 14A(a)(2) of the Securities Exchange Act of 1934 and Rule 14a–21(b) of this chapter, or any other shareholder advisory vote on executive compensation.

This exclusion from filing preliminary proxy material does not apply if the registrant comments upon or refers to a solicitation in opposition in connection with the meeting in its proxy material. * * *

(c)   *Personal solicitation materials.* If part or all of the solicitation involves personal solicitation, then eight copies of all written instructions or other materials that discuss, review or comment on the merits of any matter to be acted on, that are furnished to persons making the actual solicitation for their use directly or indirectly in connection with the solicitation, must be filed with the Commission no later than the date the materials are first sent or given to these persons. * * *

(g)   *Solicitations subject to Rule 14a–2(b)(1)*

(1)   Any person who:

(i) Engages in a solicitation pursuant to § 240.14a–2(b)(1), and

(ii) At the commencement of that solicitation owns beneficially securities of the class which is the subject of the solicitation with a market value of over $5 million,

shall furnish or mail to the Commission, not later than three days after the date the written solicitation is first sent or given to any security holder, five copies of a statement containing the information specified in the Notice of Exempt Solicitation (§ 240.14a–103) which statement shall attach as an exhibit all written soliciting materials. Five copies of an amendment to such statement shall be furnished or mailed to the Commission, in connection with dissemination of any additional communications, not later than three days after the date the additional material is first sent or given to any security holder. Three copies of the Notice of Exempt Solicitation and amendments thereto shall, at the same time the materials are furnished or mailed to the Commission, be furnished or mailed to each national securities exchange upon which any class of securities of the registrant is listed and registered.

(2) Notwithstanding paragraph (g)(1) of this Rule, no such submission need be made with respect to oral solicitations (other than with respect to scripts used in connection with such oral solicitations), speeches delivered in a public forum, press releases, published or broadcast opinions, statements, and advertisements appearing in a broadcast media, or a newspaper, magazine or other bona fide publication disseminated on a regular basis.

* * *

Rule 14a–7. Obligations of Registrants to Provide a List of, or Mail Soliciting Material to, Security Holders

(a) If the registrant has made or intends to make a proxy solicitation in connection with a security holder meeting or action by consent or authorization, upon the written request by any record or beneficial holder of securities of the class entitled to vote at the meeting or to execute a consent or authorization to provide a list of security holders or to mail the requesting security holder's materials, regardless of whether the request references this rule, the registrant shall:

(1) Deliver to the requesting security holder within five business days after receipt of the request:

(i) Notification as to whether the registrant has elected to mail the security holder's soliciting materials or provide a security holder list if the election under paragraph (b) of this rule is to be made by the registrant;

(ii) A statement of the approximate number of record holders and beneficial holders, separated by type of holder and class, owning securities in the same class or classes as holders which have been or are to be solicited on management's behalf, or any more limited group of such holders designated by the security holder if available or retrievable under the registrant's or its transfer agent's security holder data systems; and

(iii) The estimated cost of mailing a proxy statement, form of proxy or other communication to such holders, including to the extent known or reasonably available, the estimated costs of any bank, broker, and similar person through whom the registrant has solicited or intends to solicit beneficial owners in connection with the security holder meeting or action;

(2) Perform the acts set forth in either paragraphs (a)(2)(i) or (a)2(ii) of this rule, at the registrant's or requesting security holder's option, as specified in paragraph (b) of this rule:

(i) Send copies of any proxy statement, form of proxy, or other soliciting material, including a Notice of Internet Availability of Proxy Materials (as described in § 240.14a–16), furnished by the security holder to the record holders, including banks, brokers, and similar entities, designated by the security holder. A sufficient number of copies must be sent to the banks, brokers, and similar entities for distribution to all beneficial owners designated by the security holder. The security holder may designate only record holders and/or beneficial owners who have not requested paper and/ or e-mail copies of the proxy statement. If the registrant has received affirmative written or implied consent to deliver a single proxy statement to security holders at a shared address in accordance with the procedures in Rule 14a–3(e)(1), a single copy of the proxy statement or Notice of Internet Availability of Proxy Materials furnished by the security holder shall be sent to that address, provided that if multiple copies of the Notice of Internet Availability of Proxy Materials are furnished by the security holder for that address, the registrant shall deliver those copies in a single envelope to that address. The registrant shall send the security holder material with reasonable promptness after tender of the material to be sent, envelopes or other containers therefore, postage or payment for postage and other reasonable expenses of effecting such distribution. The registrant shall not be responsible for the content of the material; or

(ii)   Deliver the following information to the requesting security holder within five business days of receipt of the request:

(A)   A reasonably current list of the names, addresses and security positions of the record holders, including banks, brokers and similar entities holding securities in the same class or classes as holders which have been or are to be solicited on management's behalf, or any more limited group of such holders designated by the security holder if available or retrievable under the registrant's or its transfer agent's security holder data systems;

(B)   The most recent list of names, addresses and security positions of beneficial owners as specified in Rule 14a–13(b), in the possession, or which subsequently comes into the possession, of the registrant;

(C)   The names of security holders at a shared address that have consented to delivery of a single copy of proxy materials to a shared address, if the registrant has received written or implied consent in accordance with Rule 14a–3(e)(1); and

(D)   If the registrant has relied on Rule 14a–16, the names of security holders who have requested paper copies of the proxy materials for all meetings and the names of security holders who, as of the date that the registrant receives the request, have requested paper copies of the proxy materials only for the meeting to which the solicitation relates.

* * *

(c)   At the time of a list request, the security holder making the request shall:

(1)   If holding the registrant's securities through a nominee, provide the registrant with a statement by the nominee or other independent third party, or a copy of a current filing made with the Commission and furnished to the registrant, confirming such holder's beneficial ownership; and

(2)   Provide the registrant with an affidavit, declaration, affirmation or other similar document provided for under applicable state law identifying the proposal or other corporate action that will be the subject of the security holder's solicitation or communication and attesting that:

(i)   The security holder will not use the list information for any purpose other than to solicit security holders with respect to the same meeting or action by consent or authorization for which the registrant is soliciting or intends to solicit or to communicate with security holders with respect to a solicitation commenced by the registrant; and

(ii)   The security holder will not disclose such information to any person other than a beneficial owner for whom the request was made and an employee or agent to the extent necessary to effectuate the communication or solicitation.

(d)   The security holder shall not use the information furnished by the registrant pursuant to paragraph (a)(2)(ii) of this Rule for any purpose other than to solicit security holders with respect to the same meeting or action by consent or authorization for which the registrant is soliciting or intends to solicit or to communicate with security holders with respect to a solicitation commenced by the registrant; or disclose such information to any person other than an employee, agent, or beneficial owner for whom a request was made to the extent necessary to effectuate the communication or solicitation. The security holder shall return the information provided pursuant to paragraph (a)(2)(ii) of this rule and shall not retain any copies thereof or of any information derived from such information after the termination of the solicitation.

(e)   The security holder shall reimburse the reasonable expenses incurred by the registrant in performing the acts requested pursuant to paragraph (a) of this rule.

Note 1 to Rule 14a–7. Reasonably prompt methods of distribution to security holders may be used instead of mailing. If an alternative distribution method is chosen, the costs of that method should be considered where necessary rather than the costs of mailing.

Note 2 to Rule 14a–7. When providing the information required by Rule 14a–7(a)(1)(ii), if the registrant has received affirmative written or implied consent to delivery of a single copy of proxy materials to a shared address in accordance with Rule 14a–3(e)(1), it shall exclude from the number of record holders those to whom it does not have to deliver a separate proxy statement.

Rule 14a–8.   Shareholder Proposals

This section addresses when a company must include a shareholder's proposal in its proxy statement and identify the proposal in its form of proxy when the company holds an annual or special meeting of shareholders. In summary, in order to have your shareholder proposal included on a company's proxy card, and included along with any supporting statement in its proxy statement, you must be eligible and follow certain procedures. Under a few specific circumstances, the company is permitted to exclude your proposal, but only after submitting its reasons to the Commission. We structured this rule in a question-and-answer format so that it is easier to understand. The references to "you" are to a shareholder seeking to submit the proposal.

(a)   Question 1: What is a proposal? A shareholder proposal is your recommendation or requirement that the company and/or its board of directors take action, which you intend to present at a meeting of the company's shareholders. Your proposal should state as clearly as possible the course of action that you believe the company should follow. If your proposal is placed on the company's proxy card, the company must also provide in the form of proxy means for shareholders to specify by boxes a choice between approval or disapproval, or abstention. Unless otherwise indicated, the word "proposal" as used in this rule refers both to your proposal, and to your corresponding statement in support of your proposal (if any).

(b)   Question 2: Who is eligible to submit a proposal, and how do I demonstrate to the company that I am eligible?

(1)   In order to be eligible to submit a proposal, you must have continuously held at least $2,000 in market value, or 1%, of the company's securities entitled to be voted on the proposal at the meeting for at least one year by the date you submit the proposal. You must continue to hold those securities through the date of the meeting.

(2)   If you are the registered holder of your securities, which means that your name appears in the company's records as a shareholder, the company can verify your eligibility on its own, although you will still have to provide the company with a written statement that you intend to continue to hold the securities through the date of the meeting of shareholders. However, if like many shareholders you are not a registered holder, the company likely does not know that you are a shareholder, or how many shares you own. In this case, at the time you submit your proposal, you must prove your eligibility to the company in one of two ways:

(i)   The first way is to submit to the company a written statement from the "record" holder of your securities (usually a broker or bank) verifying that, at the time you submitted your proposal, you continuously held the securities for at least one year. You must also include your own written statement that you intend to continue to hold the securities through the date of the meeting of shareholders; or

(ii)   The second way to prove ownership applies only if you have filed a Schedule 13D, Schedule 13G, Form 3, Form 4 and/or Form 5, or amendments to those documents or updated forms, reflecting your ownership of the shares as of or before the date on which the one-year eligibility period begins. If you have filed one of these documents with the SEC, you may demonstrate your eligibility by submitting to the company:

(A)   A copy of the schedule and/or form, and any subsequent amendments reporting a change in your ownership level;

(B)   Your written statement that you continuously held the required number of shares for the one-year period as of the date of the statement; and

(C)   Your written statement that you intend to continue ownership of the shares through the date of the company's annual or special meeting.

(c)   Question 3: How many proposals may I submit: Each shareholder may submit no more than one proposal to a company for a particular shareholders' meeting.

(d)   Question 4: How long can my proposal be? The proposal, including any accompanying supporting statement, may not exceed 500 words.

(e)   Question 5: What is the deadline for submitting a proposal?

(1)   If you are submitting your proposal for the company's annual meeting, you can in most cases find the deadline in last year's proxy statement. However, if the company did not hold an annual meeting last year, or has changed the date of its meeting for this year more than 30 days from last year's meeting, you can usually find the deadline in one of the company's quarterly reports on Form 10-Q or in shareholder reports of investment companies under Rule 30d–1 of this chapter of the Investment Company Act of 1940. In order to avoid controversy, shareholders should submit their proposals by means, including electronic means, that permit them to prove the date of delivery.

(2)   The deadline is calculated in the following manner if the proposal is submitted for a regularly scheduled annual meeting. The proposal must be received at the company's principal executive offices not less than 120 calendar days before the date of the company's proxy statement released to shareholders in connection with the previous year's annual meeting. However, if the company did not hold an annual meeting the previous year, or if the date of this year's annual meeting has been changed by more than 30 days from the date of the previous year's meeting, then the deadline is a reasonable time before the company begins to print and send its proxy materials.

(3)   If you are submitting your proposal for a meeting of shareholders other than a regularly scheduled annual meeting, the deadline is a reasonable time before the company begins to print and send its proxy materials.

(f)   Question 6: What if I fail to follow one of the eligibility or procedural requirements explained in answers to Questions 1 through 4 of this rule?

(1)   The company may exclude your proposal, but only after it has notified you of the problem, and you have failed adequately to correct it. Within 14 calendar days of receiving your proposal, the company must notify you in writing of any procedural or eligibility deficiencies, as well as of the time frame for your response. Your response must be postmarked, or transmitted electronically, no later than 14 days from the date you received the company's notification. A company need not provide you such notice of a deficiency if the deficiency cannot be remedied,

such as if you fail to submit a proposal by the company's properly determined deadline. If the company intends to exclude the proposal, it will later have to make a submission under Rule 14a–8 and provide you with a copy under Question 10 below, Rule 14a–8(j).

(2) If you fail in your promise to hold the required number of securities through the date of the meeting of shareholders, then the company will be permitted to exclude all of your proposals from its proxy materials for any meeting held in the following two calendar years.

(g) Question 7: Who has the burden of persuading the Commission or its staff that my proposal can be excluded? Except as otherwise noted, the burden is on the company to demonstrate that it is entitled to exclude a proposal.

(h) Question 8: Must I appear personally at the shareholders' meeting to present the proposal?

(1) Either you, or your representative who is qualified under state law to present the proposal on your behalf, must attend the meeting to present the proposal. Whether you attend the meeting yourself or send a qualified representative to the meeting in your place, you should make sure that you, or your representative, follow the proper state law procedures for attending the meeting and/or presenting your proposal.

(2) If the company holds its shareholder meeting in whole or in part via electronic media, and the company permits you or your representative to present your proposal via such media, then you may appear through electronic media rather than traveling to the meeting to appear in person.

(3) If you or your qualified representative fail to appear and present the proposal, without good cause, the company will be permitted to exclude all of your proposals from its proxy materials for any meetings held in the following two calendar years.

(i) Question 9: If I have complied with the procedural requirements, on what other bases may a company rely to exclude my proposal?

(1) Improper under state law: If the proposal is not a proper subject for action by shareholders under the laws of the jurisdiction of the company's organization;

Note to paragraph (i)(1)

Depending on the subject matter, some proposals are not considered proper under state law if they would be binding on the company if approved by shareholders. In our experience, most proposals that are cast as recommendations or requests that the board of directors take specified action are proper under state law. Accordingly, we will assume that a proposal drafted as a recommendation or suggestion is proper unless the company demonstrates otherwise.

(2) Violation of law: If the proposal would, if implemented, cause the company to violate any state, federal, or foreign law to which it is subject;

Note to paragraph (i)(2)

We will not apply this basis for exclusion to permit exclusion of a proposal on grounds that it would violate foreign law if compliance with the foreign law would result in a violation of any state or federal law.

(3) Violation of proxy rules: If the proposal or supporting statement is contrary to any of the Commission's proxy rules, including Rule 14a–9, which prohibits materially false or misleading statements in proxy soliciting materials;

(4) Personal grievance; special interest: If the proposal relates to the redress of a personal claim or grievance against the company or any other person, or if it is designed to result in a benefit to you, or to further a personal interest, which is not shared by the other shareholders at large;

(5) Relevance: If the proposal relates to operations which account for less than 5 percent of the company's total assets at the end of its most recent fiscal year, and for less than 5 percent of

its net earnings and gross sales for its most recent fiscal year, and is not otherwise significantly related to the company's business;

(6) Absence of power/authority: If the company would lack the power or authority to implement the proposal;

(7) Management functions: If the proposal deals with a matter relating to the company's ordinary business operations;

(8) Director elections: If the proposal:

(i) Would disqualify a nominee who is standing for election;

(ii) Would remove a director from office before his or her term expired;

(iii) Questions the competence, business judgment, or character of one or more nominees or directors;

(iv) Seeks to include a specific individual in the company's proxy materials for election to the board of directors; or

(v) Otherwise could affect the outcome of the upcoming election of directors.

(9) Conflicts with company's proposal: If the proposal directly conflicts with one of the company's own proposals to be submitted to shareholders at the same meeting.

Note to paragraph (i)(9)

A company's submission to the Commission under this rule should specify the points of conflict with the company's proposal.

(10) Substantially implemented: If the company has already substantially implemented the proposal

Note to paragraph (i)(10)

A company may exclude a shareholder proposal that would provide an advisory vote or seek future advisory votes to approve the compensation of executives as disclosed pursuant to Item 402 of Regulation S–K (§ 229.402 of this chapter) or any successor to Item 402 (a "say on-pay vote") or that relates to the frequency of say-on-pay votes, provided that in the most recent shareholder vote required by Rule 14a–21(b) of this chapter a single year (*i.e.,* one, two, or three years) received approval of a majority of votes cast on the matter and the company has adopted a policy on the frequency of say-on-pay votes that is consistent with the choice of the majority of votes cast in the most recent shareholder vote required by Rule 14a–21(b) of this chapter.

(11) Duplication: If the proposal substantially duplicates another proposal previously submitted to the company by another proponent that will be included in the company's proxy materials for the same meeting;

(12) Resubmissions: If the proposal deals with substantially the same subject matter as another proposal or proposals that has or have been previously included in the company's proxy materials within the preceding 5 calendar years, a company may exclude it from its proxy materials for any meeting held within 3 calendar years of the last time it was included if the proposal received:

(i) Less than 3% of the vote if proposed once within the preceding 5 calendar years;

(ii) Less than 6% of the vote on its last submission to shareholders if proposed twice previously within the preceding 5 calendar years; or

(iii) Less than 10% of the vote on its last submission to shareholders if proposed three times or more previously within the preceding 5 calendar years; and

(13) Specific amount of dividends: If the proposal relates to specific amounts of cash or stock dividends.

(j)   Question 10: What procedures must the company follow if it intends to exclude my proposal?

(1)   If the company intends to exclude a proposal from its proxy materials, it must file its reasons with the Commission no later than 80 calendar days before it files its definitive proxy statement and form of proxy with the Commission. The company must simultaneously provide you with a copy of its submission. The Commission staff may permit the company to make its submission later than 80 days before the company files its definitive proxy statement and form of proxy, if the company demonstrates good cause for missing the deadline.

(2)   The company must file six paper copies of the following:

(i)   The proposal;

(ii)   An explanation of why the company believes that it may exclude the proposal, which should, if possible, refer to the most recent applicable authority, such as prior Division letters issued under the rule; and

(iii)   A supporting opinion of counsel when such reasons are based on matters of state or foreign law.

(k)   Question 11: May I submit my own statement to the Commission responding to the company's arguments?

Yes, you may submit a response, but it is not required. You should try to submit any response to us, with a copy to the company, as soon as possible after the company makes its submission. This way, the Commission staff will have time to consider fully your submission before it issues its response. You should submit six paper copies of your response.

(*l*)   Question 12: If the company includes my shareholder proposal in its proxy materials, what information about me must it include along with the proposal itself?

(1)   The company's proxy statement must include your name and address, as well as the number of the company's voting securities that you hold. However, instead of providing that information, the company may instead include a statement that it will provide the information to shareholders promptly upon receiving an oral or written request.

(2)   The company is not responsible for the contents of your proposal or supporting statement.

(m)   Question 13: What can I do if the company includes in its proxy statement reasons why it believes shareholders should not vote in favor of my proposal, and I disagree with some of its statements?

(1)   The company may elect to include in its proxy statement reasons why it believes shareholders should vote against your proposal. The company is allowed to make arguments reflecting its own point of view, just as you may express your own point of view in your proposal's supporting statement.

(2)   However, if you believe that the company's opposition to your proposal contains materially false or misleading statements that may violate our anti-fraud rule, Rule 14a–9, you should promptly send to the Commission staff and the company a letter explaining the reasons for your view, along with a copy of the company's statements opposing your proposal. To the extent possible, your letter should include specific factual information demonstrating the inaccuracy of the company's claims. Time permitting, you may wish to try to work out your differences with the company by yourself before contacting the Commission staff.

(3)   We require the company to send you a copy of its statements opposing your proposal before it sends its proxy materials, so that you may bring to our attention any materially false or misleading statements, under the following timeframes:

(i)   If our no-action response requires that you make revisions to your proposal or supporting statement as a condition to requiring the company to include it in its proxy materials, then the company must provide you with a copy of its opposition statements no later than 5 calendar days after the company receives a copy of your revised proposal; or

(ii)   In all other cases, the company must provide you with a copy of its opposition statements no later than 30 calendar days before its files definitive copies of its proxy statement and form of proxy under Rule 14a–6.

Rule 14a–9.   False or Misleading Statements

(a)   No solicitation subject to this regulation shall be made by means of any proxy statement, form of proxy, notice of meeting or other communication, written or oral, containing any statement which, at the time and in the light of the circumstances under which it is made, is false or misleading with respect to any material fact, or which omits to state any material fact necessary in order to make the statements therein not false or misleading or necessary to correct any statement in any earlier communication with respect to the solicitation of a proxy for the same meeting or subject matter which has become false or misleading.

(b)   The fact that a proxy statement, form of proxy or other soliciting material has been filed with or examined by the Commission shall not be deemed a finding by the Commission that such material is accurate or complete or not false or misleading, or that the Commission has passed upon the merits of or approved any statement contained therein or any matter to be acted upon by security holders. No representation contrary to the foregoing shall be made.

(c)   No nominee, nominating shareholder or nominating shareholder group, or any member thereof, shall cause to be included in a registrant's proxy materials, either pursuant to the Federal proxy rules, an applicable state or foreign law provision, or a registrant's governing documents as they relate to including shareholder nominees for director in a registrant's proxy materials, include in a notice on Schedule 14N (§ 240.14n–101), or include in any other related communication, any statement which, at the time and in the light of the circumstances under which it is made, is false or misleading with respect to any material fact, or which omits to state any material fact necessary in order to make the statements therein not false or misleading or necessary to correct any statement in any earlier communication with respect to a solicitation for the same meeting or subject matter which has become false or misleading.

Note:

The following are some examples of what, depending upon particular facts and circumstances, may be misleading within the meaning of this rule.

a.   Predictions as to specific future market values.

b.   Material which directly or indirectly impugns character, integrity or personal reputation, or directly or indirectly makes charges concerning improper, illegal or immoral conduct or associations, without factual foundation.

c.   Failure to so identify a proxy statement, form of proxy and other soliciting material as to clearly distinguish it from the soliciting material of any other person or persons soliciting for the same meeting or subject matter.

d.   Claims made prior to a meeting regarding the results of a solicitation.

Rule 14a–17.   Electronic Shareholder Forums

(a)   A shareholder, registrant, or third party acting on behalf of a shareholder or registrant may establish, maintain, or operate an electronic shareholder forum to facilitate interaction among the registrant's shareholders and between the registrant and its shareholders as the shareholder or registrant deems appropriate. Subject to paragraphs (b) and (c) of this rule, the forum must comply with the federal securities laws, including Section 14(a) of the Act and its associated regulations, other applicable federal laws, applicable state laws, and the registrant's governing documents.

(b)   No shareholder, registrant, or third party acting on behalf of a shareholder or registrant, by reason of establishing, maintaining, or operating an electronic shareholder forum, will be liable under the federal securities laws for any statement or information provided by another person to the electronic shareholder forum. Nothing in this rule prevents or alters the application of the federal securities laws, including the provisions for liability for fraud, deception, or manipulation, or other applicable federal and state laws to the person or persons that provide a statement or information to an electronic shareholder forum.

(c)   Reliance on the exemption in Rule 14a–2(b)(6) to participate in an electronic shareholder forum does not eliminate a person's eligibility to solicit proxies after the date that the exemption in Rule 14a–2(b)(6) is no longer available, or is no longer being relied upon, provided that any such solicitation is conducted in accordance with this regulation.

Rule 14a–18.   Disclosure Regarding Nominating Shareholders and Nominees Submitted for Inclusion in a Registrant's Proxy Materials Pursuant to Applicable State or Foreign Law, or a Registrant's Governing Documents

To have a nominee included in a registrant's proxy materials pursuant to a procedure set forth under applicable state or foreign law, or the registrant's governing documents addressing the inclusion of shareholder director nominees in the registrant's proxy materials, the nominating shareholder or nominating shareholder group must provide notice to the registrant of its intent to do so on a Schedule 14N (§ 240.14n–101) and file that notice, including the required disclosure, with the Commission on the date first transmitted to the registrant. This notice shall be postmarked or transmitted electronically to the registrant by the date specified by the registrant's advance notice provision or, where no such provision is in place, no later than 120 calendar days before the anniversary of the date that the registrant mailed its proxy materials for the prior year's annual meeting, except that, if the registrant did not hold an annual meeting during the prior year, or if the date of the meeting has changed by more than 30 calendar days from the prior year, then the nominating shareholder or nominating shareholder group must provide notice a reasonable time before the registrant mails its proxy materials, as specified by the registrant in a Form 8-K (§ 249.308 of this chapter) filed pursuant to Item 5.08 of Form 8-K.

Instruction to § 240.14a–18. The registrant is not responsible for any information provided in the Schedule 14N (§ 240.14n–101) by the nominating shareholder or nominating shareholder group, which is submitted as required by this rule or otherwise provided by the nominating shareholder or nominating shareholder group that is included in the registrant's proxy materials.

Rule 14d–2.   Commencement of a Tender Offer

(a)   *Date of commencement.* A bidder will have commenced its tender offer for purposes of section 14(d) of the Act and the rules under that section at 12:01 a.m. on the date when the bidder has first published, sent or given the means to tender to security holders. For purposes of this rule, the means to tender includes the transmittal form or a statement regarding how the transmittal form may be obtained.

(b)   *Pre-commencement communications.* A communication by the bidder will not be deemed to constitute commencement of a tender offer if:

(1)   It does not include the means for security holders to tender their shares into the offer; and

(2)   All written communications relating to the tender offer, from and including the first public announcement, are filed under cover of Schedule TO (§ 240.14d–100) with the Commission no later than the date of the communication. The bidder also must deliver to the subject company and any other bidder for the same class of securities the first communication relating to the transaction that is filed, or required to be filed, with the Commission.

Instructions to paragraph (b)(2):

1.   The box on the front of Schedule TO indicating that the filing contains pre-commencement communications must be checked.

2.   Any communications made in connection with an exchange offer registered under the Securities Act of 1933 need only be filed under Rule 425 under the Securities Act of 1933 and will be deemed filed under this rule.

3.   Each pre-commencement written communication must include a prominent legend in clear, plain language advising security holders to read the tender offer statement when it is available because it contains important information. The legend also must advise investors that they can get the tender offer statement and other filed documents for free at the Commission's web site and explain which documents are free from the offeror.

4.   See Rules 135, 165 and 166 under the securities Act of 1933 for pre-commencement communications made in connection with registered exchange offers.

5.   "Public announcement" is any oral or written communication by the bidder, or any person authorized to act on the bidder's behalf, that is reasonably designed to, or has the effect of, informing the public or security holders in general about the tender offer.

(c)   *Filing and other obligations triggered by commencement.* As soon as practicable on the date of commencement, a bidder must comply with the filing requirements of Rule 14d–3(a), the dissemination requirements of Rule 14d–4(a) or (b), and the disclosure requirements of Rule 14d–6(a).

Rule 14d–3.   Filing and Transmission of Tender Offer Statement

(a)   *Filing and transmittal.* No bidder shall make a tender offer if, after consummation thereof, such bidder would be the beneficial owner of more than 5 percent of the class of the subject company's securities for which the tender offer is made, unless as soon as practicable on the date of the commencement of the tender offer such bidder:

(1)   Files with the Commission a Tender Offer Statement on Schedule TO (§ 240.14d–100), including all exhibits thereto;

(2)   Delivers a copy of such Schedule TO, including all exhibits thereto:

(i)   To the subject company at its principal executive office; and

(ii)   To any other bidder, which has filed a Schedule TO with the Commission relating to a tender offer which has not yet terminated for the same class of securities of the subject company, at such bidder's principal executive office or at the address of the person authorized to receive notices and communications (which is disclosed on the cover sheet of such other bidder's Schedule TO);

(3)   Gives telephonic notice of the information required by Rule 14d–6(d)(2)(i) and (ii) and mails by means of first class mail a copy of such Schedule TO, including all exhibits thereto:

(i)   To each national securities exchange where such class of the subject company's securities is registered and listed for trading (which may be based upon information contained in the subject company's most recent Annual Report on Form 10-K filed with the Commission unless the bidder has reason to believe that such information is not current) which telephonic notice shall be made when practicable before the opening of each such exchange; and

(ii)   To the National Association of Securities Dealers, Inc. ("NASD") if such class of the subject company's securities is authorized for quotation in the NASDAQ interdealer quotation system.

(b)   *Post-commencement amendments and additional materials.* The bidder making the tender offer must file with the Commission:

(1)   An amendment to Schedule TO reporting promptly any material changes in the information set forth in the schedule previously filed and including copies of any additional tender offer materials as exhibits; and

(2)   A final amendment to Schedule TO reporting promptly the results of the tender offer.

Instruction to paragraph (b): A copy of any additional tender offer materials or amendment filed under this rule must be sent promptly to the subject company and to any exchange and/or NASD, as required by paragraph (a) of this rule, but in no event later than the date the materials are first published, sent or given to security holders.

(c)   *Certain announcements.* Notwithstanding the provisions of paragraph (b) of this rule, if the additional tender offer material or an amendment to Schedule TO discloses only the number of shares deposited to date, and/or announces an extension of the time during which shares may be tendered, then the bidder may file such tender offer material or amendment and send a copy of such tender offer material or amendment to the subject company, any exchange and/or the NASD, as required by paragraph (a) of this rule, promptly after the date such tender offer material is first published or sent or given to security holders.

Rule 14d–4.   Dissemination of Tender Offers to Security Holders

As soon as practicable on the date of commencement of a tender offer, the bidder must publish, send or give the disclosure required by Rule 14d–6 to security holders of the class of securities that is the subject of the offer, by complying with all of the requirements of any of the following:

(a)   *Cash tender offers and exempt securities offers.* For tender offers in which the consideration consists solely of cash and/or securities exempt from registration under section 3 of the Securities Act of 1933:

(1)   Long-form publication. The bidder makes adequate publication in a newspaper or newspapers of long-form publication of the tender offer.

(2)   Summary publication.

(i)   If the tender offer is not subject to Rule 13e–3, the bidder makes adequate publication in a newspaper or newspapers of a summary advertisement of the tender offer; and

(ii)   Mails by first class mail or otherwise furnishes with reasonable promptness the bidder's tender offer materials to any security holder who requests such tender offer materials pursuant to the summary advertisement or otherwise.

(3)   Use of stockholder lists and security position listings. Any bidder using stockholder lists and security position listings under Rule 14d–5 must comply with paragraph (a)(1) or (2) of this rule on or before the date of the bidder's request under § 240.14d–5(a).

Instruction to paragraph (a): Tender offers may be published or sent or given to security holders by other methods, but with respect to summary publication and the use of stockholder lists and security position listings under Rule 14d–5, paragraphs (a)(2) and (a)(3) of this rule are exclusive.

(b)   *Registered securities offers.* For tender offers in which the consideration consists solely or partially of securities registered under the Securities Act of 1933, a registration statement containing all of the required information, including pricing information, has been filed and a preliminary prospectus or a prospectus that meets the requirements of section 10(a) of the Securities Act, including a letter of transmittal, is delivered to security holders. However, for going-private transactions (as defined by Rule 240.13e–3) and roll-up transactions (as described by Item 901 of Regulation S–K (17 C.F.R. § 229.901)), a registration statement registering the securities to be offered must have become effective and only a prospectus that meets the requirements of section 10(a) of the Securities Act may be delivered to security holders on the date of commencement.

Instructions to paragraph (b):

1.   If the prospectus is being delivered by mail, mailing on the date of commencement is sufficient.

2.   A preliminary prospectus used under this rule may not omit information under Rule 230.430 430A under the Securities Act of 1933.

3.   If a preliminary prospectus is used under this rule and the bidder must disseminate material changes, the tender offer must remain open for the period specified in paragraph (d)(2) of this rule.

4.   If a preliminary prospectus is used under this rule, tenders may be requested in accordance with Rule 162(a) under the Securities Act of 1933.

(c)   *Adequate publication.* Depending on the facts and circumstances involved, adequate publication of a tender offer pursuant to this rule may require publication in a newspaper with a national circulation or may only require publication in a newspaper with metropolitan or regional circulation or may require publication in a combination thereof: Provided, however, That publication in all editions of a daily newspaper with a national circulation shall be deemed to constitute adequate publication.

(d)   *Publication of changes and extension of the offer.*

(1)   If a tender offer has been published or sent or given to security holders by one or more of the methods enumerated in this rule, a material change in the information published or sent or given to security holders shall be promptly disseminated to security holders in a manner reasonably designed to inform security holders of such change; Provided, however, That if the bidder has elected pursuant to rule 14d–5 (f)(1) of this rule to require the subject company to disseminate amendments disclosing material changes to the tender offer materials pursuant to Rule 14d–5, the bidder shall disseminate material changes in the information published or sent or given to security holders at least pursuant to Rule 14d–5.

(2)   In a registered securities offer where the bidder disseminates the preliminary prospectus as permitted by paragraph (b) of this rule, the offer must remain open from the date that material changes to the tender offer materials are disseminated to security holders, as follows:

(i)   Five business days for a prospectus supplement containing a material change other than price or share levels;

(ii)   Ten business days for a prospectus supplement containing a change in price, the amount of securities sought, the dealer's soliciting fee, or other similarly significant change;

(iii)   Ten business days for a prospectus supplement included as part of a post-effective amendment; and

(iv)   Twenty business days for a revised prospectus when the initial prospectus was materially deficient.

Rule 14d–6.   Disclosure of Tender Offer Information to Security Holders

(a)   *Information required on date of commencement.—*

(1)   Long-form publication. If a tender offer is published, sent or given to security holders on the date of commencement by means of long-form publication under Rule 14d–4(a)(1), the long-form publication must include the information required by paragraph (d)(1) of this rule.

(2)   Summary publication. If a tender offer is published, sent or given to security holders on the date of commencement by means of summary publication under Rule 14d–4(a)(2):

(i) The summary advertisement must contain at least the information required by paragraph (d)(2) of this rule; and

(ii) The tender offer materials furnished by the bidder upon request of any security holder must include the information required by paragraph (d)(1) of this rule.

(3) Use of stockholder lists and security position listings. If a tender offer is published, sent or given to security holders on the date of commencement by the use of stockholder lists and security position listings under Rule 14d–4(a)(3):

(i) The summary advertisement must contain at least the information required by paragraph (d)(2) of this rule; and

(ii) The tender offer materials transmitted to security holders pursuant to such lists and security position listings and furnished by the bidder upon the request of any security holder must include the information required by paragraph (d)(1) of this rule.

(4) Other tender offers. If a tender offer is published or sent or given to security holders other than pursuant to Rule 14d–4(a), the tender offer materials that are published or sent or given to security holders on the date of commencement of such offer must include the information required by paragraph (d)(1) of this rule.

(b) *Information required in other tender offer materials published after commencement.* Except for tender offer materials described in paragraphs (a)(2)(ii) and (a)(3)(ii) of this rule, additional tender offer materials published, sent or given to security holders after commencement must include:

(1) The identities of the bidder and subject company;

(2) The amount and class of securities being sought;

(3) The type and amount of consideration being offered; and

(4) The scheduled expiration date of the tender offer, whether the tender offer may be extended and, if so, the procedures for extension of the tender offer.

Instruction to paragraph (b): If the additional tender offer materials are summary advertisements, they also must include the information required by paragraphs (d)(2)(v) of this rule.

(c) *Material changes.* A material change in the information published or sent or given to security holders must be promptly disclosed to security holders in additional tender offer materials.

(d) *Information to be included.—*

(1) *Tender offer materials other than summary publication.* The following information is required by paragraphs (a)(1), (a)(2)(ii), (a)(3)(ii) and (a)(4) of this rule:

(i) The information required by Item 1 of Schedule TO (Summary Term Sheet); and

(ii) The information required by the remaining items of Schedule TO for third-party tender offers, except for Item 12 (exhibits) of Schedule TO, or a fair and adequate summary of the information.

(2) *Summary Publication.* The following information is required in a summary advertisement under paragraphs (a)(2)(i) and (a)(3)(i) of this rule:

(i) The identity of the bidder and the subject company;

(ii) The information required by Item 1004(a)(1) of Regulation M–A (§ 229.1004(a)(1) of this chapter);

(iii) If the tender offer is for less than all of the outstanding securities of a class of equity securities, a statement as to whether the purpose or one of the purposes of the tender offer is to acquire or influence control of the business of the subject company;

(iv) A statement that the information required by paragraph (d)(1) of this rule is incorporated by reference into the summary advertisement;

(v) Appropriate instructions as to how security holders may obtain promptly, at the bidder's expense, the bidder's tender offer materials; and

(vi) In a tender offer published or sent or given to security holders by use of stockholder lists and security position listings under Rule 14d–4(a)(3), a statement that a request is being made for such lists and listings. The summary publication also must state that tender offer materials will be mailed to record holders and will be furnished to brokers, banks and similar persons whose name appears or whose nominee appears on the list of security holders or, if applicable, who are listed as participants in a clearing agency's security position listing for subsequent transmittal to beneficial owners of such securities. If the list furnished to the bidder also included beneficial owners pursuant to Rule 14d–5(c)(1) and tender offer materials will be mailed directly to beneficial holders, include a statement to that effect.

(3) *No transmittal letter.* Neither the initial summary advertisement nor any subsequent summary advertisement may include a transmittal letter (the letter furnished to security holders for transmission of securities sought in the tender offer) or any amendment to the transmittal letter.

Rule 14d–7.   Additional Withdrawal Rights

(a) *Rights.*

(1) In addition to the provisions of section 14(d)(5) of the Act, any person who has deposited securities pursuant to a tender offer has the right to withdraw any such securities during the period such offer request or invitation remains open.

(2) Exemption during subsequent offering period. Notwithstanding the provisions of section 14(d)(5) of the Act and paragraph (a) of this rule, the bidder need not offer withdrawal rights during a subsequent offering period.

(b) *Notice of withdrawal.* Notice of withdrawal pursuant to this rule shall be deemed to be timely upon the receipt by the bidder's depositary of a written notice of withdrawal specifying the name(s) of the tendering stockholder(s), the number or amount of the securities to be withdrawn and the name(s) in which the certificate(s) is (are) registered, if different from that of the tendering security holder(s). A bidder may impose other reasonable requirements, including certificate numbers and a signed request for withdrawal accompanied by a signature guarantee, as conditions precedent to the physical release of withdrawn securities.

Rule 14d–8.   Exemption From Statutory Pro Rata Requirements

Notwithstanding the pro rata provisions of section 14(d)(6) of the Act, if any person makes a tender offer or request or invitation for tenders, for less than all of the outstanding equity securities of a class, and if a greater number of securities are deposited pursuant thereto than such person is bound or willing to take up and pay for, the securities taken up and paid for shall be taken up and paid for as nearly as may be pro rata, disregarding fractions, according to the number of securities deposited by each depositor during the period such offer, request or invitation remains open.

Rule 14d–9.   Recommendation or Solicitation by the Subject Company and Others

(a) *Pre-commencement communications.* A communication by a person described in paragraph (e) of this rule with respect to a tender offer will not be deemed to constitute a recommendation or solicitation under this rule if:

(1) The tender offer has not commenced under Rule 14d–2; and

(2)   The communication is filed under cover of Schedule 14D-9 (§ 240.14d–101) with the Commission no later than the date of the communication.

Instructions to paragraph (a)(2):

1.   The box on the front of Schedule 14D-9 indicating that the filing contains pre-commencement communications must be checked.

2.   Any communications made in connection with an exchange offer registered under the Securities Act of 1933 need only be filed under Rule 425 of the Securities Act of 1933 and will be deemed filed under this rule.

3.   Each pre-commencement written communication must include a prominent legend in clear, plain language advising security holders to read the company's solicitation/recommendation statement when it is available because it contains important information. The legend also must advise investors that they can get the recommendation and other filed documents for free at the Commission's web site and explain which documents are free from the filer.

4.   See Rules 135, 165 and 166 under the Securities Act of 1933 for pre-commencement communications made in connection with registered exchange offers.

(b)   *Post-commencement communications.* After commencement by a bidder under Rule 14d–2, no solicitation or recommendation to security holders may be made by any person described in paragraph (e) of this rule with respect to a tender offer for such securities unless as soon as practicable on the date such solicitation or recommendation is first published or sent or given to security holders such person complies with the following:

(1)   Such person shall file with the Commission a Tender Offer Solicitation/Recommendation Statement on Schedule 14D-9, including all exhibits thereto; and

(2)   If such person is either the subject company or an affiliate of the subject company,

(i)   Such person shall hand deliver a copy of the Schedule 14D-9 to the bidder at its principal office or at the address of the person authorized to receive notices and communications (which is set forth on the cover sheet of the bidder's Schedule TO filed with the Commission); and

(ii)   Such person shall give telephonic notice (which notice to the extent possible shall be given prior to the opening of the market) of the information required by Items 1003(d) and 1012(a) of Regulation M–A and shall mail a copy of the Schedule to each national securities exchange where the class of securities is registered and listed for trading and, if the class is authorized for quotation in the NASDAQ interdealer quotation system, to the National Association of Securities Dealers, Inc. ("NASD").

(3)   If such person is neither the subject company nor an affiliate of the subject company,

(i)   Such person shall mail a copy of the schedule to the bidder at its principal office or at the address of the person authorized to receive notices and communications (which is set forth on the cover sheet of the bidder's Schedule TO filed with the Commission); and

(ii)   Such person shall mail a copy of the Schedule to the subject company at its principal office.

(c)   *Amendments.* If any material change occurs in the information set forth in the Schedule 14D-9 required by this rule, the person who filed such Schedule 14D-9 shall:

(1)   File with the Commission an amendment on Schedule 14D-9 disclosing such change promptly, but not later than the date such material is first published, sent or given to security holders; and

(2) Promptly deliver copies and give notice of the amendment in the same manner as that specified in paragraph (b)(2) or (3) of this rule, whichever is applicable; and

(3) Promptly disclose and disseminate such change in a manner reasonably designed to inform security holders of such change.

(d) *Information required in solicitation or recommendation.* Any solicitation or recommendation to holders of a class of securities referred to in section 14(d)(1) of the Act with respect to a tender offer for such securities shall include the name of the person making such solicitation or recommendation and the information required by Items 1 through 8 of Schedule 14D-9 or a fair and adequate summary thereof: Provided, however, That such solicitation or recommendation may omit any of such information previously furnished to security holders of such class of securities by such person with respect to such tender offer.

(e) *Applicability.*

(1) Except as is provided in paragraphs (e)(2) and (f) of this rule, this rule shall only apply to the following persons:

(i) The subject company, any director, officer, employee, affiliate or subsidiary of the subject company;

(ii) Any record holder or beneficial owner of any security issued by the subject company, by the bidder, or by any affiliate of either the subject company or the bidder; and

(iii) Any person who makes a solicitation or recommendation to security holders on behalf of any of the foregoing or on behalf of the bidder other than by means of a solicitation or recommendation to security holders which has been filed with the Commission pursuant to this rule or Rule 14d–3.

(2) Notwithstanding paragraph (e)(1) of this rule, this rule shall not apply to the following persons:

(i) A bidder who has filed a Schedule TO pursuant to Rule 14d–3;

(ii) Attorneys, banks, brokers, fiduciaries or investment advisers who are not participating in a tender offer in more than a ministerial capacity and who furnish information and/or advice regarding such tender offer to their customers or clients on the unsolicited request of such customers or clients or solely pursuant to a contract or a relationship providing for advice to the customer or client to whom the information and/or advice is given.

(iii) Any person specified in paragraph (e)(1) of this rule if:

(A) The subject company is the subject of a tender offer conducted under Rule 14d–1(c);

(B) Any person specified in paragraph (e)(1) of this rule furnishes to the Commission on Form CB (17 C.F.R. § 249.480 of this chapter) the entire informational document it publishes or otherwise disseminates to holders of the class of securities in connection with the tender offer no later than the next business day after publication or dissemination;

(C) Any person specified in paragraph (e)(1) of this rule disseminates any informational document to U.S. holders, including any amendments thereto, in English, on a comparable basis to that provided to security holders in the issuer's home jurisdiction; and

(D) Any person specified in paragraph (e)(1) of this rule disseminates by publication in its home jurisdiction, such person must publish the information in the United States in a manner reasonably calculated to inform U.S. security holders of the offer.

(f) *Stop-look-and-listen communication.* This rule shall not apply to the subject company with respect to a communication by the subject company to its security holders which only:

(1) Identifies the tender offer by the bidder;

(2) States that such tender offer is under consideration by the subject company's board of directors and/or management;

(3) States that on or before a specified date (which shall be no later than 10 business days from the date of commencement of such tender offer) the subject company will advise such security holders of (i) whether the subject company recommends acceptance or rejection of such tender offer; expresses no opinion and remains neutral toward such tender offer; or is unable to take a position with respect to such tender offer and (ii) the reason(s) for the position taken by the subject company with respect to the tender offer (including the inability to take a position); and

(4) Requests such security holders to defer making a determination whether to accept or reject such tender offer until they have been advised of the subject company's position with respect thereto pursuant to paragraph (f)(3) of this rule.

(g) *Statement of management's position.* A statement by the subject company of its position with respect to a tender offer which is required to be published or sent or given to security holders pursuant to Rule 14e–2 shall be deemed to constitute a solicitation or recommendation within the meaning of this rule and section 14(d)(4) of the Act.

Rule 14d–10.   Equal Treatment of Security Holders

(a) No bidder shall make a tender offer unless:

(1) The tender offer is open to all security holders of the class of securities subject to the tender offer; and

(2) The consideration paid to any security holder for securities tendered in the tender offer is the highest consideration paid to any other security holder for securities tendered in the tender offer.

(b) Paragraph (a)(1) of this rule shall not:

(1) Affect dissemination under Rule 14d–4 or

(2) Prohibit a bidder from making a tender offer excluding all security holders in a state where the bidder is prohibited from making the tender offer by administrative or judicial action pursuant to a state statute after a good faith effort by the bidder to comply with such statute.

(c) Paragraph (a)(2) of this rule shall not prohibit the offer of more than one type of consideration in a tender offer, Provided That:

(1) Security holders are afforded equal right to elect among each of the types of consideration offered; and

(2) The highest consideration of each type paid to any security holder is paid to any other security holder receiving that type of consideration.

(d)(1) Paragraph (a)(2) of this rule shall not prohibit the negotiation, execution or amendment of an employment compensation, severance or other employee benefit arrangement, or payments made or to be made or benefits granted or to be granted according to such an arrangement, with respect to any security holder of the subject company, where the amount payable under the arrangement:

(i) Is being paid or granted as compensation for past services performed, future services to be performed, or future services to be refrained from performing, by the security holder (and matters incidental thereto); and

(ii)   Is not calculated based on the number of securities tendered or to be tendered in the tender offer by the security holder.

(2)   The provisions of paragraph (d)(1) of this rule shall be satisfied and, therefore, pursuant to this non-exclusive safe harbor, the negotiation, execution or amendment of an arrangement and any payments made or to be made or benefits granted or to be granted according to that arrangement shall not be prohibited by paragraph (a)(2) of this rule, if the arrangement is approved as an employment compensation, severance or other employee benefit arrangement solely by independent directors as follows:

(i)   The compensation committee or a committee of the board of directors that performs functions similar to a compensation committee of the subject company approves the arrangement, regardless of whether the subject company is a party to the arrangement, or, if the bidder is a party to the arrangement, the compensation committee or a committee of the board of directors that performs functions similar to a compensation committee of the bidder approves the arrangement; or

(ii)   If the subject company's or bidder's board of directors, as applicable, does not have a compensation committee or a committee of the board of directors that performs functions similar to a compensation committee or if none of the members of the subject company's or bidder's compensation committee or committee that performs functions similar to a compensation committee is independent, a special committee of the board of directors formed to consider and approve the arrangement approves the arrangement; or

(iii)   If the subject company or bidder, as applicable, is a foreign private issuer, any or all members of the board of directors or any committee of the board of directors authorized to approve employment compensation, severance or other employee benefit arrangements under the laws or regulations of the home country approves the arrangement.

(e)   If the offer and sale of securities constituting consideration offered in a tender offer is prohibited by the appropriate authority of a state after a good faith effort by the bidder to register or qualify the offer and sale of such securities in such state:

(1)   The bidder may offer security holders in such state an alternative form of consideration; and

(2)   Paragraph (c) of this rule shall not operate to require the bidder to offer or pay the alternative form of consideration to security holders in any other state.

(f)   This rule shall not apply to any tender offer with respect to which the Commission, upon written request or upon its own motion, either unconditionally or on specified terms and conditions, determines that compliance with this rule is not necessary or appropriate in the public interest or for the protection of investors.

Rule 14d–11. Subsequent Offering Period

A bidder may elect to provide a subsequent offering period of at least three business days during which tenders will be accepted if:

(a)   The initial offering period of at least 20 business days has expired;

(b)   The offer is for all outstanding securities of the class that is the subject of the tender offer, and if the bidder is offering security holders a choice of different forms of consideration, there is no ceiling on any form of consideration offered;

(c)   The bidder immediately accepts and promptly pays for all securities tendered during the initial offering period;

(d)   The bidder announces the results of the tender offer, including the approximate number and percentage of securities deposited to date, no later than 9:00 a.m. Eastern time on the next business day after the expiration date of the initial offering period and immediately begins the subsequent offering period;

(e)   The bidder immediately accepts and promptly pays for all securities as they are tendered during the subsequent offering period; and

(f)   The bidder offers the same form and amount of consideration to security holders in both the initial and the subsequent offering period.

Note to Rule 14d–11:

No withdrawal rights apply during the subsequent offering period in accordance with Rule 14d–7(a)(2).

Rule 14e–1.   Unlawful Tender Offer Practices

As a means reasonably designed to prevent fraudulent, deceptive or manipulative acts or practices within the meaning of section 14(e) of the Act, no person who makes a tender offer shall:

(a)   Hold such tender offer open for less than twenty business days from the date such tender offer is first published or sent to security holders; provided, however, that if the tender offer involves a roll-up transaction as defined in Item 901(c) of Regulation S–K and the securities being offered are registered (or authorized to be registered) on Form S-4 or Form F-4 under the Securities Act of 1933, the offer shall not be open for less than sixty calendar days from the date the tender offer is first published or sent to security holders;

(b)   Increase or decrease the percentage of the class of securities being sought or the consideration offered or the dealer's soliciting fee to be given in a tender offer unless such tender offer remains open for at least ten business days from the date that notice of such increase or decrease is first published or sent or given to security holders.

Provided, however, That, for purposes of this paragraph, the acceptance for payment of an additional amount of securities not to exceed two percent of the class of securities that is the subject of the tender offer shall not be deemed to be an increase. For purposes of this paragraph, the percentage of a class of securities shall be calculated in accordance with section 14(d)(3) of the Act.

(c)   Fail to pay the consideration offered or return the securities deposited by or on behalf of security holders promptly after the termination or withdrawal of a tender offer. This paragraph does not prohibit a bidder electing to offer a subsequent offering period under Rule 14d–11 from paying for securities during the subsequent offering period in accordance with that rule.

(d)   Extend the length of a tender offer without issuing a notice of such extension by press release or other public announcement, which notice shall include disclosure of the approximate number of securities deposited to date and shall be issued no later than the earlier of: (i) 9:00 a.m. Eastern time, on the next business day after the scheduled expiration date of the offer or (ii), if the class of securities which is the subject of the tender offer is registered on one or more national securities exchanges, the first opening of any one of such exchanges on the next business day after the scheduled expiration date of the offer.

(e)   The periods of time required by paragraphs (a) and (b) of this rule shall be tolled for any period during which the bidder has failed to file electronic format, absent a hardship exemption, the Schedule TO Tender Offer Statement, any tender offer material required to be filed by Item 12 of that Schedule pursuant to paragraph (a) of Item 1016 of Regulation M-A, and any amendments thereto. If such documents were filed in paper pursuant to a hardship exemption, the minimum offering periods shall be tolled for any period during which a required confirming electronic copy of such Schedule and tender offer material is delinquent.

Rule 14e–2.   Position of Subject Company With Respect to a Tender Offer

(a) *Position of subject company.* As a means reasonably designed to prevent fraudulent, deceptive or manipulative acts or practices within the meaning of section 14(e) of the Act, the subject company, no later than 10 business days from the date the tender offer is first published or sent or given, shall publish, send or give to security holders a statement disclosing that the subject company:

    (1)   Recommends acceptance or rejection of the bidder's tender offer;

    (2)   Expresses no opinion and is remaining neutral toward the bidder's tender offer; or

    (3)   Is unable to take a position with respect to the bidder's tender offer. Such statement shall also include the reason(s) for the position (including the inability to take a position) disclosed therein.

(b) *Material change.* If any material change occurs in the disclosure required by paragraph (a) of this rule, the subject company shall promptly publish or send or give a statement disclosing such material change to security holders.

(c) Any issuer, a class of the securities of which is the subject of a tender offer filed with the Commission on Schedule 14D-1F and conducted in reliance upon and in conformity with Rule 14d–1(b) under the Act, and any director or officer of such issuer where so required by the laws, regulations and policies of Canada and/or any of its provinces or territories, in lieu of the statements called for by paragraph (a) of this rule and Rule 14d–9 under the Act, shall file with the Commission on Schedule 14D-9F the entire disclosure document(s) required to be furnished to holders of securities of the subject issuer by the laws, regulations and policies of Canada and/or any of its provinces or territories governing the conduct of the tender offer, and shall disseminate such document(s) in the United States in accordance with such laws, regulations and policies.

(d) *Exemption for cross-border tender offers.* The subject company shall be exempt from this rule with respect to a tender offer conducted under Rule 14d–1(c).

Rule 14e–3.   Transactions in Securities on the Basis of Material, Nonpublic Information in the Context of Tender Offers

(a) If any person has taken a substantial step or steps to commence, or has commenced, a tender offer (the "offering person"), it shall constitute a fraudulent, deceptive or manipulative act or practice within the meaning of section 14(e) of the Act for any other person who is in possession of material information relating to such tender offer which information he knows or has reason to know is nonpublic and which he knows or has reason to know has been acquired directly or indirectly from:

    (1)   The offering person,

    (2)   The issuer of the securities sought or to be sought by such tender offer, or

    (3)   Any officer, director, partner or employee or any other person acting on behalf of the offering person or such issuer, to purchase or sell or cause to be purchased or sold any of such securities or any securities convertible into or exchangeable for any such securities or any option or right to obtain or to dispose of any of the foregoing securities, unless within a reasonable time prior to any purchase or sale such information and its source are publicly disclosed by press release or otherwise.

(b) A person other than a natural person shall not violate paragraph (a) of this Rule if such person shows that:

    (1)   The individual(s) making the investment decision on behalf of such person to purchase or sell any security described in paragraph (a) of this Rule or to cause any such security to be purchased or sold by or on behalf of others did not know the material, nonpublic information; and

    (2)   Such person had implemented one or a combination of policies and procedures, reasonable under the circumstances, taking into consideration the nature of the person's

business, to ensure that individual(s) making investment decision(s) would not violate paragraph (a) of this Rule, which policies and procedures may include, but are not limited to, (i) those which restrict any purchase, sale and causing any purchase and sale of any such security or (ii) those which prevent such individual(s) from knowing such information.

(c)   Notwithstanding anything in paragraph (a) of this Rule to contrary, the following transactions shall not be violations of paragraph (a) of this Rule:

(1)   Purchase(s) of any security described in paragraph (a) of this Rule by a broker or by another agent on behalf of an offering person; or

(2)   Sale(s) by any person of any security described in paragraph (a) of this Rule to the offering person.

(d)(1)   As a means reasonably designed to prevent fraudulent, deceptive or manipulative acts or practices within the meaning of section 14(e) of the Act, it shall be unlawful for any person described in paragraph (d)(2) of this Rule to communicate material, nonpublic information relating to a tender offer to any other person under circumstances in which it is reasonably foreseeable that such communication is likely to result in a violation of this Rule except that this paragraph shall not apply to a communication made in good faith,

(i)   To the officers, directors, partners or employees of the offering person, to its advisors or to other persons, involved in the planning, financing, preparation or execution of such tender offer;

(ii)   To the issuer whose securities are sought or to be sought by such tender offer, to its officers, directors, partners, employees or advisors or to other persons, involved in the planning, financing, preparation or execution of the activities of the issuer with respect to such tender offer; or

(iii)   To any person pursuant to a requirement of any statute or rule or regulation promulgated thereunder.

(2)   The persons referred to in paragraph (d)(1) of this Rule are:

(i)   The offering person or its officers, directors, partners, employees or advisors;

(ii)   The issuer of the securities sought or to be sought by such tender offer or its officers, directors, partners, employees or advisors;

(iii)   Anyone acting on behalf of the persons in paragraph (d)(2)(i) of this Rule or the issuer or persons in paragraph (d)(2)(ii) of this Rule; and

(iv)   Any person in possession of material information relating to a tender offer which information he knows or has reason to know is nonpublic and which he knows or has reason to know has been acquired directly or indirectly from any of the above.

Rule 14e–5.   Prohibiting Purchases Outside of a Tender Offer

(a)   *Unlawful activity.* As a means reasonably designed to prevent fraudulent, deceptive or manipulative acts or practices in connection with a tender offer for equity securities, no covered person may directly or indirectly purchase or arrange to purchase any subject securities or any related securities except as part of the tender offer. This prohibition applies from the time of public announcement of the tender offer until the tender offer expires. This prohibition does not apply to any purchases or arrangements to purchase made during the time of any subsequent offering period as provided for in Rule 14d–11 if the consideration paid or to be paid for the purchases or arrangements to purchase is the same in form and amount as the consideration offered in the tender offer.

* * *

Rule 16a–1.   Definition of Terms

Terms defined in this rule shall apply solely to section 16 of the Act and the rules thereunder. These terms shall not be limited to section 16(a) of the Act but also shall apply to all other subsections under section 16 of the Act.

(a)   The term beneficial owner shall have the following applications:

(1)   Solely for purposes of determining whether a person is a beneficial owner of more than ten percent of any class of equity securities registered pursuant to section 12 of the Act, the term "beneficial owner" shall mean any person who is deemed a beneficial owner pursuant to section 13(d) of the Act and the rules thereunder; provided, however, that the following institutions or persons shall not be deemed the beneficial owner of securities of such class held for the benefit of third parties or in customer or fiduciary accounts in the ordinary course of business * * *

Note to paragraph (a):

Pursuant to this rule, a person deemed a beneficial owner of more than ten percent of any class of equity securities registered under section 12 of the Act would file a Form 3 (17 C.F.R. § 249.103), but the securities holdings disclosed on Form 3, and changes in beneficial ownership reported on subsequent Forms 4 (17 C.F.R. § 249.104) or 5 (17 C.F.R. § 249.105), would be determined by the definition of "beneficial owner" in paragraph (a)(2) of this rule.

(2)   Other than for purposes of determining whether a person is a beneficial owner of more than ten percent of any class of equity securities registered under Section 12 of the Act, the term beneficial owner shall mean any person who, directly or indirectly, through any contract, arrangement, understanding, relationship or otherwise, has or shares a direct or indirect pecuniary interest in the equity securities, subject to the following:

(i)   The term pecuniary interest in any class of equity securities shall mean the opportunity, directly or indirectly, to profit or share in any profit derived from a transaction in the subject securities.

(ii)   The term indirect pecuniary interest in any class of equity securities shall include, but not be limited to:

(A)   Securities held by members of a person's immediate family sharing the same household; provided, however, that the presumption of such beneficial ownership may be rebutted; see also Rule 16a–1(a)(4);

(B)   A general partner's proportionate interest in the portfolio securities held by a general or limited partnership. The general partner's proportionate interest, as evidenced by the partnership agreement in effect at the time of the transaction and the partnership's most recent financial statements, shall be the greater of:

(1)   The general partner's share of the partnership's profits, including profits attributed to any limited partnership interests held by the general partner and any other interests in profits that arise from the purchase and sale of the partnership's portfolio securities; or

(2)   The general partner's share of the partnership capital account, including the share attributable to any limited partnership interest held by the general partner. * * *

(d)   The term equity security of such issuer shall mean any equity security or derivative security relating to an issuer, whether or not issued by that issuer.

(e)   The term immediate family shall mean any child, stepchild, grandchild, parent, stepparent, grandparent, spouse, sibling, mother-in-law, father-in-law, son-in-law, daughter-in-law, brother-in-law, or sister-in-law, and shall include adoptive relationships.

(f)   The term officer shall mean an issuer's president, principal financial officer, principal accounting officer (or, if there is no such accounting officer, the controller), any vice-president of the issuer in charge of a principal business unit, division or function (such as sales, administration or finance), any other officer who performs a policy-making function, or any other person who performs similar policy-making functions for the issuer. Officers of the issuer's parent(s) or subsidiaries shall be deemed officers of the issuer if they perform such policy-making functions for the issuer. In addition, when the issuer is a limited partnership, officers or employees of the general partner(s) who perform policy-making functions for the limited partnership are deemed officers of the limited partnership. When the issuer is a trust, officers or employees of the trustee(s) who perform policy-making functions for the trust are deemed officers of the trust.

Note: "Policy-making function" is not intended to include policy-making functions that are not significant. If pursuant to Item 401(b) of Regulation S–K (§ 229.401(b)) the issuer identifies a person as an "executive officer," it is presumed that the Board of Directors has made that judgment and that the persons so identified are the officers for purposes of Section 16 of the Act, as are such other persons enumerated in this paragraph (f) but not in Item 401(b).

* * *

Rule 16a–2.   Persons and Transactions Subject to Section 16

Any person who is the beneficial owner, directly or indirectly, of more than ten percent of any class of equity securities ("ten percent beneficial owner") registered pursuant to section 12 of the Act, any director or officer of the issuer of such securities, and any person specified in section 30(h) of the Investment Company Act of 1940, including any person specified in Rule 16a–8, shall be subject to the provisions of section 16 of the Act. The rules under section 16 of the Act apply to any class of equity securities of an issuer whether or not registered under section 12 of the Act. The rules under section 16 of the Act also apply to non-equity securities as provided by the Investment Company Act of 1940. With respect to transactions by persons subject to section 16 of the Act:

(a)   A transaction(s) carried out by a director or officer in the six months prior to the director or officer becoming subject to section 16 of the Act shall be subject to section 16 of the Act and reported on the first required Form 4 only if the transaction(s) occurred within six months of the transaction giving rise to the Form 4 filing obligation and the director or officer became subject to section 16 of the Act solely as a result of the issuer registering a class of equity securities pursuant to section 12 of the Act.

(b)   A transaction(s) following the cessation of director or officer status shall be subject to section 16 of the Act only if:

(1)   Executed within a period of less than six months of an opposite transaction subject to section 16(b) of the Act that occurred while that person was a director or officer; and

(2)   Not otherwise exempted from section 16(b) of the Act pursuant to the provisions of this chapter.

Note to Paragraph (b):

For purposes of this paragraph, an acquisition and a disposition each shall be an opposite transaction with respect to the other.

(c)   The transaction that results in a person becoming a ten percent beneficial owner is not subject to section 16 of the Act unless the person otherwise is subject to section 16 of the Act. A ten percent beneficial owner not otherwise subject to section 16 of the Act must report only those transactions conducted while the beneficial owner of more than ten percent of a class of equity securities of the issuer registered pursuant to section 12 of the Act.

(d)(1) Transactions by a person or entity shall be exempt from the provisions of section 16 of the Act for the 12 months following appointment and qualification, to the extent such person or entity is acting as:

(i)   Executor or administrator of the estate of a decedent;

(ii)   Guardian or member of a committee for an incompetent;

(iii) Receiver, trustee in bankruptcy, assignee for the benefit of creditors, conservator, liquidating agent, or other similar person duly authorized by law to administer the estate or assets of another person; or

(iv)   Fiduciary in a similar capacity.

(2)   Transactions by such person or entity acting in a capacity specified in paragraph (d)(1) of this rule after the period specified in that paragraph shall be subject to section 16 of the Act only where the estate, trust or other entity is a beneficial owner of more than ten percent of any class of equity security registered pursuant to section 12 of the Act.

SAMPLE DOCUMENTS

SAMPLE DOCUMENTS

CERTIFICATE OF INCORPORATION

of

INTERNATIONAL BUSINESS MACHINES CORPORATION

As Restated and Filed May 27, 1992

And

As Amended through April 27, 2007

SAMPLE DOCUMENTS

SAMPLE DOCUMENTS

Certificate of Incorporation

of

INTERNATIONAL BUSINESS MACHINES CORPORATION

ONE: The name of the corporation (hereinafter called "the Corporation") is International Business Machines Corporation.

TWO: The purpose of the Corporation is to engage in any lawful act or activity for which corporations may be organized and to exercise powers granted under the Business Corporation Law of the State of New York, provided that the Corporation shall not engage in any act or activity requiring the consent or approval of any state official, department, board, agency, or other body without such consent or approval first being obtained.

THREE: The aggregate number of shares that the Corporation shall have authority to issue is 4,837,500,000 shares, consisting of 4,687,500,000 shares of the par value of $0.20 per share, which shall be designated "capital stock," and 150,000,000 shares of the par value of $.01 per share, which shall be designated "preferred stock."

FOUR: (1) Subject to the provisions of the By-laws, as from time to time amended, with respect to the closing of the transfer books and the fixing of a record date, each share of the capital stock of the Corporation shall be entitled to one vote on all matters requiring a vote of the stockholders and, subject to the rights of the holders of any outstanding shares of preferred stock issued under this Article FOUR, shall be entitled to receive such dividends, in cash, securities, or property, as may from time to time be declared by the Board of Directors. In the event of any liquidation, dissolution, or winding up of the Corporation, either voluntary or involuntary, after payment shall have been made to the holders of preferred stock of the full amount to which they shall be entitled under this Article FOUR, the holders of capital stock shall be entitled, to the exclusion of the holders of the preferred stock of any series, to share ratably, according to the number of shares held by them, in all remaining assets of the Corporation available for distribution.

(2) The Board of Directors is authorized, at any time or from time to time, to issue preferred stock and (i) to divide the shares of preferred stock into series; (ii) to determine the designation for any such series by number, letter, or title that shall distinguish such series from any other series of preferred stock; (iii) to determine the number of shares in any such series (including a determination that such series shall consist of a single share); and (iv) to determine with respect to the shares of any series of preferred stock:

(a) whether the holders thereof shall be entitled to cumulative, noncumulative, or partially cumulative dividends and, with respect to shares entitled to dividends, the dividend rate or rates, including without limitation the methods and procedures for determining such rate or rates, and any other terms and conditions relating to such dividends;

Page 1

836

(b) whether, and if so to what extent and upon what terms and conditions, the holders thereof shall be entitled to rights upon the liquidation of, or upon any distribution of the assets of, the Corporation;

(c) whether, and if so upon what terms and conditions, such shares shall be convertible into, or exchangeable for, other securities or property;

(d) whether, and if so upon what terms and conditions, such shares shall be redeemable;

(e) whether the shares shall be subject to any sinking fund provided for the purchase or redemption of such shares and, if so, the terms of such fund;

(f) whether the holders thereof shall be entitled to voting rights and, if so, the terms and conditions for the exercise thereof, provided that the holders of shares of preferred stock (i) will not be entitled to more than the lesser of (x) one vote per $100 of liquidation value or (y) one vote per share, when voting as a class with the holders of shares of capital stock, and (ii) will not be entitled to vote on any matter separately as a class, except, to the extent specified with respect to each series, (x) with respect to any amendment or alteration of the provisions of this Certificate of Incorporation that would adversely affect the powers, preferences, or special rights of the applicable series of preferred stock or (y) in the event the Corporation fails to pay dividends on any series of preferred stock in full for any six quarterly dividend payment periods, whether or not consecutive, in which event the number of directors may be increased by two and the holders of outstanding shares of preferred stock then similarly entitled shall be entitled to elect the two additional directors until full accumulated dividends on all such shares of preferred stock shall have been paid; and

(g) whether the holders thereof shall be entitled to other preferences or rights and, if so, the qualifications, limitations, or restrictions of such preferences or rights.

FIVE: The town and county within the State of New York in which the office of the Corporation is to be located is the Town of North Castle, County of Westchester.

SIX: The number of directors of the Corporation shall be provided in its By- laws, but not less than 9 nor more than 25.

SEVEN: The Board of Directors may designate from their number an executive committee and one or more other committees, each of which shall consist of three or more directors. All such committees, in the intervals between meetings of the Board of Directors and to the extent provided in the By-laws or the resolution of the Board of Directors establishing such a committee, shall have all the authority and may exercise all the powers of the Board of Directors in the management of the business and affairs of the Corporation to the extent lawful under the Business Corporation Law of the State of New York.

The Board of Directors shall from time to time decide whether and to what extent and at what times and under what conditions and requirements the accounts and books of the Corporation, or any of them, except the stock book, shall be open to the inspection of the stockholders, and no stockholder shall have any right to

Page 2

inspect any books or documents of the Corporation except as conferred by statute of the State of New York or authorized by the Board of Directors.

The Board of Directors may from time to time fix, determine, and vary the amount of the working capital of the Corporation; may determine what part, if any, of surplus shall be declared in dividends and paid to the stockholders; may determine the time or times for the declaration and payment of dividends, the amount thereof, and whether they are to be in cash, securities, or properties; may direct and determine the use and disposition of any surplus or net profits over and above the capital, and in its discretion may use or apply any such surplus or accumulated profits in the purchase or acquisition of bonds or other pecuniary obligations of the Corporation to such extent, and in such manner and upon such terms as the Board of Directors may deem expedient.

Directors shall be stockholders, subject to the power of the Board of Directors from time to time to prescribe a reasonable time after qualification within which newly elected directors must become stockholders.

Each director, in consideration of serving as such, shall be entitled to receive from the Corporation such amount per annum or such fees for attendance at meetings of the stockholders or of the Board of Directors or of committees of the Board of Directors, or both, as the Board of Directors shall from time to time determine, together with reimbursement for the reasonable expenses incurred in connection with the performance of duties. Nothing herein contained shall preclude any director from serving the Corporation or its subsidiaries in any other capacity and receiving compensation therefor.

EIGHT: In the absence of fraud, any director of the Corporation individually, or any firm or association of which any director is a member, or any corporation of which any director is an officer, director, stockholder, or employee, or in which such director is pecuniarily or otherwise interested, may be a party to, or may be pecuniarily or otherwise interested in, any contract, transaction, or act of the Corporation, and

(1) Such contract, transaction, or act shall not be in any way invalidated or otherwise affected by that fact,

(2) Any such director of the Corporation may be counted in determining the existence of a quorum at any meeting of the Board of Directors or of any committee thereof that shall authorize any such contract, transaction, or act, but may not vote thereon, and

(3) No director of the Corporation shall be liable to account to the Corporation for any profit realized by such director from or through any such contract, transaction, or act; provided, however, that if any such director of the Corporation is so interested either individually or as a member of a firm or association, or as the holder of a majority of the stock of any class of a corporation, the contract, transaction, or act shall be duly authorized or ratified by a majority of the Board of Directors who are not so interested and who know of such director's interest therein.

To the extent permitted by law, any contract, transaction, or act of the Corporation or of the Board of Directors or of any committee thereof that shall be ratified, whether before or after judgment rendered in a suit with respect to such

Page 3

contract, transaction, or act, by the holders of a majority of the stock of the Corporation having voting power at any annual meeting or at any special meeting called for such purpose, shall be as valid and as binding as though ratified by every stockholder of the Corporation and shall constitute a complete bar to any such suit or to any claim of execution in respect of any such judgment; provided, however, that any failure of the stockholders to approve or ratify such contract, transaction, or act, when and if submitted, shall not be deemed in any way to invalidate the same or to deprive the Corporation, its directors, officers, or employees of its or their right to proceed with such contract, transaction, or act.

NINE: The Secretary of State of the State of New York is designated as the agent of the Corporation upon whom process in any action or proceeding against it may be served, and the address within the State to which the Secretary of State shall mail a copy of process in any action or proceeding against the Corporation that may be served upon the Secretary of State is Armonk, New York 10504.

TEN: The holders of shares of the Corporation shall have no preemptive or preferential right to subscribe for or purchase any shares of the Corporation or any rights or options to purchase shares of the Corporation or any shares or other securities convertible into or carrying rights or options to purchase shares of the Corporation.

ELEVEN: Pursuant to Section 402(b) of the Business Corporation Law of the State of New York, the liability of the Corporation's directors to the Corporation or its stockholders for damages for breach of duty as a director shall be eliminated to the fullest extent permitted by the Business Corporation Law of the State of New York, as it exists on the date hereof or as it may hereafter be amended. No amendment to or repeal of this Article shall apply to or have any effect on the liability or alleged liability of any director of the Corporation for or with respect to any acts or omissions of such director occurring prior to such amendment or repeal.

TWELVE: At a meeting of stockholders, following all requisite approvals under the Business Corporation Law of the State of New York (BCL), the affirmative vote of a majority of the votes of all outstanding shares entitled to vote thereon shall be required to take any of the following actions:

    a. to adopt a plan of merger or consolidation in accordance with Section 903 of the BCL or any successor provision thereto;

    b. to approve the sale, lease, exchange or other disposition of all or substantially all of the assets of the Corporation in accordance with Section 909 of the BCL or any successor provision thereto;

    c. to adopt a plan for the exchange of shares in accordance with Section 913 of the BCL or any successor provision thereto; and

    d. to authorize the dissolution of the Corporation in accordance with Section 1001 of the BCL or any successor provision thereto.

Page 4

SAMPLE DOCUMENTS

BY-LAWS

of

INTERNATIONAL BUSINESS MACHINES CORPORATION

Adopted April 29, 1958

As Amended Through

October 26, 2009

SAMPLE DOCUMENTS

TABLE OF CONTENTS

SAMPLE DOCUMENTS

ARTICLE V -- OFFICERS

ARTICLE VI -- CONTRACTS, CHECKS, DRAFTS, BANK ACCOUNTS, ETC.

ARTICLE VII -- SHARES

ARTICLE VIII -- OFFICES

- ii -

SAMPLE DOCUMENTS

BY-LAWS

OF

INTERNATIONAL BUSINESS MACHINES CORPORATION

ARTICLE I

DEFINITIONS

In these By-laws, and for all purposes hereof, unless there be something in the subject or context inconsistent therewith:

(a) 'Corporation' shall mean International Business Machines Corporation.

(b) 'Certificate of Incorporation' shall mean the restated Certificate of Incorporation as filed on May 27, 1992, together with any and all amendments and subsequent restatements thereto.

(c) 'Board' shall mean the Board of Directors of the Corporation.

(d) 'stockholders' shall mean the stockholders of the Corporation.

(e) 'Chairman of the Board', 'Vice Chairman of the Board', 'Chairman of the Executive Committee', 'Chief Executive Officer,' 'Chief Financial Officer', 'Chief Accounting Officer', 'President', 'Executive Vice President', 'Senior Vice President', 'Vice President', 'Treasurer', 'Secretary', or 'Controller', as the case may be, shall mean the person at any given time occupying the particular office with the Corporation.

ARTICLE II

MEETINGS OF STOCKHOLDERS

SECTION 1. Place of Meetings. Meetings of the stockholders of the Corporation shall be held at such place either within or outside the State of New York as may from time to time be fixed by the Board or specified or fixed in the notice of any such meeting.

SECTION 2. Annual Meetings. The annual meeting of the stockholders of the Corporation for the election of directors and for the transaction of such other business as may properly come before the meeting shall be held on the last Tuesday of April of each year, if not a legal holiday, or, if such day shall be a legal holiday, then on the next succeeding day not a legal holiday. If any annual meeting shall not be held on the day designated herein, or if the directors to be elected at such annual meeting shall not have been elected thereat or at any adjournment thereof, the Board shall forthwith call a special meeting of the stockholders for the election of directors to be held as soon thereafter as convenient and give notice thereof as provided in these By-laws in respect of the notice of an annual meeting of the stockholders. At such special meeting the

- 1 -

843

stockholders may elect the directors and transact other business with the same force and effect as at an annual meeting of the stockholders duly called and held.

SECTION 3. Special Meetings. Special meetings of the stockholders, unless otherwise provided by law, may be called at any time by the Chairman of the Board or by the Board, and shall be called by the Board upon written request delivered to the Secretary of the Corporation by the holder(s) with the power to vote and dispose of at least 25% of the outstanding shares of the Corporation. Such request shall be signed by each such holder, stating the number of shares owned by each holder, and shall indicate the purpose of the requested meeting. In addition, any stockholder(s) requesting a special meeting shall promptly provide any other information reasonably requested by the Corporation.

SECTION 4. Notice of Meetings. Notice of each meeting of the stockholders, annual or special, shall be given in the name of the Chairman of the Board, a Vice Chairman of the Board or the President or a Vice President or the Secretary. Such notice shall state the purpose or purposes for which the meeting is called and the date and hour when and the place where it is to be held. A copy thereof shall be duly delivered or transmitted to all stockholders of record entitled to vote at such meeting, and all stockholders of record who, by reason of any action proposed to be taken at such meeting, would be entitled to have their stock appraised if such action were taken, not less than ten or more than sixty days before the day on which the meeting is called to be held. If mailed, such copy shall be directed to each stockholder at the address listed on the record of stockholders of the Corporation, or if the stockholder shall have filed with the Secretary a written request that notices be mailed to some other address, it shall be mailed to the address designated in such request. Nevertheless, notice of any meeting of the stockholders shall not be required to be given to any stockholder who shall waive notice thereof as hereinafter provided in Article IX of these By-laws. Except when expressly required by law, notice of any adjourned meeting of the stockholders need not be given nor shall publication of notice of any annual or special meeting thereof be required.

SECTION 5. Quorum. Except as otherwise provided by law, at all meetings of the stockholders, the presence of holders of record of a majority of the outstanding shares of stock of the Corporation having voting power, in person or represented by proxy and entitled to vote thereat, shall be necessary to constitute a quorum for the transaction of business. In the absence of a quorum at any such meeting or any adjournment or adjournments thereof, a majority in voting interest of those present in person or represented by proxy and entitled to vote thereat, or, in the absence of all the stockholders, any officer entitled to preside at, or to act as secretary of, such meeting, may adjourn such meeting from time to time without further notice, other than by announcement at the meeting at which such adjournment shall be taken, until a quorum shall be present thereat. At any adjourned meeting at which a quorum shall be present any business may be transacted which might have been transacted at the meeting as originally called.

- 2 -

844

SAMPLE DOCUMENTS

SECTION 6. Organization. At each meeting of the stockholders, the Chairman of the Board, or in the absence of the Chairman of the Board, the President, or in the absence of the Chairman of the Board and the President, a Vice Chairman of the Board, or if the Chairman of the Board, the President, and all Vice Chairmen of the Board shall be absent therefrom, an Executive Vice President, or if the Chairman of the Board, the President, all Vice Chairmen of the Board and all Executive Vice Presidents shall be absent therefrom, a Senior Vice President shall act as chairman. The Secretary, or, if the Secretary shall be absent from such meeting or unable to act, the person whom the Chairman of such meeting shall appoint secretary of such meeting shall act as secretary of such meeting and keep the minutes thereof.

SECTION 7. Items of Business. The items of business at all meetings of the stockholders shall be, insofar as applicable, as follows:

-- Call to order.

-- Proof of notice of meeting or of waiver thereof.

-- Appointment of inspectors of election, if necessary.

-- A quorum being present.

-- Reports.

-- Election of directors proposed by the Corporation's Board of Directors, as set forth in the Corporation's proxy statement.

-- Other business specified in the notice of the meeting.

-- Voting.

-- Adjournment.

Any items of business not referred to in the foregoing may be taken up at the meeting as the chairman of the meeting shall determine.

No other business shall be transacted at any annual meeting of stockholders, except business as may be: (i) specified in the notice of meeting (including stockholder proposals included in the Corporation's proxy materials under Rule 14a-8 of Regulation 14A under the Securities Exchange Act of 1934), (ii) otherwise brought before the meeting by or at the direction of the Board of Directors, or (iii) a proper subject for the meeting which is timely submitted by a stockholder of the Corporation entitled to vote at such meeting who complies fully with the notice requirements set forth below.

SAMPLE DOCUMENTS

For business to be properly submitted by a stockholder before any annual meeting under subparagraph (iii) above, a stockholder must give timely notice in writing of such business to the Secretary of the Corporation. To be considered timely, a stockholder's notice must be received by the Secretary at the principal executive offices of the Corporation not less than 120 calendar days nor more than 150 calendar days before the date of the Corporation's proxy statement released to stockholders in connection with the prior year's annual meeting.

However, if no annual meeting was held in the previous year, or if the date of the applicable annual meeting has been changed by more than 30 days from the date contemplated at the time of the previous year's proxy statement, a stockholder's notice must be received by the Secretary not later than 60 days before the date the Corporation commences mailing of its proxy materials in connection with the applicable annual meeting.

A stockholder's notice to the Secretary to submit business to an annual meeting of stockholders shall set forth: (i) the name and address of the stockholder, (ii) the number of shares of stock held of record and beneficially by such stockholder, (iii) the name in which all such shares of stock are registered on the stock transfer books of the Corporation, (iv) a representation that the stockholder intends to appear at the meeting in person or by proxy to submit the business specified in such notice, (v) a brief description of the business desired to be submitted to the annual meeting, including the complete text of any resolutions intended to be presented at the annual meeting, and the reasons for conducting such business at the annual meeting, (vi) any personal or other material interest of the stockholder in the business to be submitted, and (vii) all other information relating to the proposed business which may be required to be disclosed under applicable law. In addition, a stockholder seeking to submit such business at the meeting shall promptly provide any other information reasonably requested by the Corporation.

The chairman of the meeting shall determine all matters relating to the efficient conduct of the meeting, including, but not limited to, the items of business, as well as the maintenance of order and decorum. The chairman shall, if the facts warrant, determine and declare that any putative business was not properly brought before the meeting in accordance with the procedures prescribed by this Section 7, in which case such business shall not be transacted.

Notwithstanding the foregoing provisions of this Section 7, a stockholder who seeks to have any proposal included in the Corporation's proxy materials shall comply with the requirements of Rule 14a-8 under Regulation 14A of the Securities Exchange Act of 1934, as amended.

- 4 -

SAMPLE DOCUMENTS

SECTION 8. Voting. Except as otherwise provided by law, each holder of record of shares of stock of the Corporation having voting power shall be entitled at each meeting of the stockholders to one vote for every share of such stock standing in the stockholder's name on the record of stockholders of the Corporation:

(a) on the date fixed pursuant to the provisions of Section 5 of Article VII of these By-laws as the record date for the determination of the stockholders who shall be entitled to vote at such meeting, or

(b) if such record date shall not have been so fixed, then at the close of business on the day next preceding the day on which notice of such meeting shall have been given, or

(c) if such record date shall not have been so fixed and if no notice of such meeting shall have been given, then at the time of the call to order of such meeting.

Any vote on stock of the Corporation at any meeting of the stockholders may be given by the stockholder of record entitled thereto in person or by proxy appointed by such stockholder or by the stockholder's attorney thereunto duly authorized and delivered or transmitted to the secretary of such meeting at or prior to the time designated in the order of business for turning in proxies. At all meetings of the stockholders at which a quorum shall be present, all matters (except where otherwise provided by law, the Certificate of Incorporation or these By-laws) shall be decided by the vote of a majority in voting interest of the stockholders present in person or represented by proxy and entitled to vote thereat. Unless required by law, or determined by the chairman of the meeting to be advisable, the vote on any question need not be by ballot. On a vote by ballot, each ballot shall be signed by the stockholder voting, or by the stockholder's proxy as such, if there be such proxy.

SECTION 9. List of Stockholders. A list, certified by the Secretary, of the stockholders of the Corporation entitled to vote shall be produced at any meeting of the stockholders upon the request of any stockholder of the Corporation pursuant to the provisions of applicable law, the Certificate of Incorporation or these By-laws.

SECTION 10. Inspectors of Election. Prior to the holding of each annual or special meeting of the stockholders, two inspectors of election to serve thereat shall be appointed by the Board, or, if the Board shall not have made such appointment, by the Chairman of the Board. If there shall be a failure to appoint inspectors, or if, at any such meeting, any inspector so appointed shall be absent or shall fail to act or the office shall become vacant, the chairman of the meeting may, and at the request of a stockholder present in person and entitled to vote at such meeting shall, appoint such inspector or inspectors of election, as the case may be, to act thereat. The inspectors of election so appointed to act at any meeting of the stockholders, before entering upon the discharge of their duties, shall be sworn faithfully to execute the duties of inspectors at such meeting, with strict impartiality and according to the best of their ability, and the oath so taken shall be subscribed by them. Such inspectors of election shall take charge of the polls, and, after the voting on any question, shall make a certificate of the results of the

- 5 -

847

vote taken. No director or candidate for the office of director shall act as an inspector of an election of directors. Inspectors need not be stockholders.

ARTICLE III

BOARD OF DIRECTORS

SECTION 1. General Powers. The business and affairs of the Corporation shall be managed by the Board. The Board may exercise all such authority and powers of the Corporation and do all such lawful acts and things as are not by law, the Certificate of Incorporation or these By-laws, directed or required to be exercised or done by the stockholders.

SECTION 2. Number; Qualifications; Election; Term of Office. The number of directors of the Corporation shall be thirteen, but the number thereof may be increased to not more than twenty-five, or decreased to not less than nine, by amendment of these By-laws. The directors shall be elected at the annual meeting of the stockholders. At each meeting of the stockholders for the election of directors at which a quorum is present, the vote required for election of a director shall, except in a contested election, be the affirmative vote of a majority of the votes cast in favor of or against such nominee. In a contested election, a nominee receiving a plurality of the votes cast at such election shall be elected. An election shall be considered to be contested if, as of the record date for such meeting, there are more nominees for election than positions on the Board to be filled by election at the meeting. Each director shall hold office until the annual meeting of the stockholders which shall be held next after the election of such director and until a successor shall have been duly elected and qualified, or until death, or until the director shall have resigned as hereinafter provided in Section 10 of this Article III.

SECTION 3. Place of Meetings. Meetings of the Board shall be held at such place either within or outside State of New York as may from time to time be fixed by the Board or specified or fixed in the notice of any such meeting.

SECTION 4. First Meeting. The Board shall meet for the purpose of organization, the election of officers and the transaction of other business, on the same day the annual meeting of stockholders is held. Notice of such meeting need not be given. Such meeting may be held at any other time or place which shall be specified in a notice thereof given as hereinafter provided in Section 7 of this Article III.

SECTION 5. Regular Meetings. Regular meetings of the Board shall be held at times and dates fixed by the Board or at such other times and dates as the Chairman of the Board shall determine and as shall be specified in the notice of such meetings. Notice of regular meetings of the Board need not be given except as otherwise required by law or these By-laws.

SECTION 6. Special Meetings. Special meetings of the Board may be called by the Chairman of the Board.

SECTION 7. Notice of Meetings. Notice of each special meeting of the Board (and of each regular meeting for which notice shall be required) shall be given by the Secretary as hereinafter provided in this Section 7, in which notice shall be stated the time, place and, if required by law or these By-laws, the purposes of such meeting. Notice of each such meeting shall be mailed, postage prepaid, to each director, by first-class mail, at least four days before the day on which such meeting is to be held, or shall be sent by facsimile transmission or comparable medium, or be delivered personally or by telephone, at least twenty-four hours before the time at which such meeting is to be held. Notice of any such meeting need not be given to any director who shall waive notice thereof as provided in Article IX of these By-laws. Any meeting of the Board shall be a legal meeting without notice thereof having been given, if all the directors of the Corporation then holding office shall be present thereat.

SECTION 8. Quorum and Manner of Acting. A majority of the Board shall be present in person at any meeting of the Board in order to constitute a quorum for the transaction of business at such meeting. Participation in a meeting by means of a conference telephone or similar communications equipment allowing all persons participating in the meeting to hear each other shall constitute presence in person at a meeting. Except as otherwise expressly required by law or the Certificate of Incorporation and except also as specified in Section 1, Section 5, and Section 6 of Article IV, in Section 3 of Article V and in Article XII of these By-laws, the act of a majority of the directors present at any meeting at which a quorum is present shall be the act of the Board. In the absence of a quorum at any meeting of the Board, a majority of the directors present thereat may adjourn such meeting from time to time until a quorum shall be present thereat. Notice of any adjourned meeting need not be given. At any adjourned meeting at which a quorum is present, any business may be transacted which might have been transacted at the meeting as originally called. The directors shall act only as a Board and the individual directors shall have no power as such.

SECTION 9. Organization. At each meeting of the Board, the Chairman of the Board, or in the case of the Chairman's absence therefrom, the President, or in the case of the President's absence therefrom, a Vice Chairman, or in the case of the absence of all such persons, another director chosen by a majority of directors present, shall act as chairman of the meeting and preside thereat. The Secretary, or if the Secretary shall be absent from such meeting, any person appointed by the chairman, shall act as secretary of the meeting and keep the minutes thereof.

SECTION 10. Resignations.

(a) Any director of the Corporation may resign at any time by giving written notice of resignation to the Board or the Chairman of the Board or the Secretary. Subject to Section 10(b), any such resignation shall take effect at the time specified therein, or if the time when it shall become effective shall not be specified therein, then it shall take effect immediately upon its receipt; and unless otherwise specified therein, the acceptance of such resignation shall not be necessary to make it effective.

(b) In an uncontested election, any incumbent nominee for director who does not receive an affirmative vote of a majority of the votes cast in favor of or against such nominee shall promptly tender his or her resignation after such election. The independent directors of the Board, giving due consideration to the best interests of the Corporation and its stockholders, shall evaluate the relevant facts and circumstances, and shall make a decision, within 90 days after the election, on whether to accept the tendered resignation. Any director who tenders a resignation pursuant to this provision shall not participate in the Board's decision. The Board will promptly disclose publicly its decision and, if applicable, the reasons for rejecting the tendered resignation.

SECTION 11. Vacancies. Any vacancy in the Board, whether arising from death, resignation, an increase in the number of directors or any other cause, may be filled by the Board.

SECTION 12. Retirement of Directors. The Board may prescribe a retirement policy for directors on or after reaching a certain age, provided, however, that such retirement shall not cut short the annual term for which any director shall have been elected by the stockholders.

ARTICLE IV

EXECUTIVE AND OTHER COMMITTEES

SECTION 1. Executive Committee. The Board, by resolution adopted by a majority of the Board, may designate not less than four of the directors then in office to constitute an Executive Committee, each member of which unless otherwise determined by resolution adopted by a majority of the whole Board, shall continue to be a member of such Committee until the annual meeting of the stockholders which shall be held next after designation as a member of such Committee or until the earlier termination as a director. The Chief Executive Officer shall always be designated as a member of the Executive Committee. The Board may by resolution appoint one member as the Chairman of the Executive Committee who shall preside at all meetings of such Committee. In the absence of said Chairman, the Chief Executive Officer shall preside at all such meetings. In the absence of both the Chairman of the Executive Committee and the Chief Executive Officer, the Chairman of the Board shall preside at all such meetings. In the absence of the Chairman of the Executive Committee and the Chief Executive Officer and the Chairman of the Board, the President shall preside at all such meetings. In the absence of all such persons, a majority of the members of the Executive Committee present shall choose a chairman to preside at such meetings. The Secretary, or if the Secretary shall be absent from such meeting, any person appointed by the chairman, shall act as secretary of the meeting and keep the minutes thereof.

SECTION 2. Powers of the Executive Committee. To the extent permitted by

- 8 -

law, the Executive Committee may exercise all the powers of the Board in the management of specified matters where such authority is delegated to it by the Board, and also, to the extent permitted by law, the Executive Committee shall have, and may exercise, all the powers of the Board in the management of the business and affairs of the Corporation (including the power to authorize the seal of the Corporation to be affixed to all papers which may require it; but excluding the power to appoint a member of the Executive Committee) in such manner as the Executive Committee shall deem to be in the best interests of the Corporation and not inconsistent with any prior specific action of the Board. An act of the Executive Committee taken within the scope of its authority shall be an act of the Board. The Executive Committee shall render in the form of minutes a report of its several acts at each regular meeting of the Board and at any other time when so directed by the Board.

SECTION 3. Meetings of the Executive Committee. Regular meetings of the Executive Committee shall be held at such times, on such dates and at such places as shall be fixed by resolution adopted by a majority of the Executive Committee, of which regular meetings notice need not be given, or as shall be fixed by the Chairman of the Executive Committee or in the absence of the Chairman of the Executive Committee the Chief Executive Officer and specified in the notice of such meeting. Special meetings of the Executive Committee may be called by the Chairman of the Executive Committee or by the Chief Executive Officer. Notice of each such special meeting of the Executive Committee (and of each regular meeting for which notice shall be required), stating the time and place thereof shall be mailed, postage prepaid, to each member of the Executive Committee, by first-class mail, at least four days before the day on which such meeting is to be held, or shall be sent by facsimile transmission or comparable medium, or be delivered personally or by telephone, at least twenty-four hours before the time at which such meeting is to be held; but notice need not be given to a member of the Executive Committee who shall waive notice thereof as provided in Article IX of these By-laws, and any meeting of the Executive Committee shall be a legal meeting without any notice thereof having been given, if all the members of such Committee shall be present thereat.

SECTION 4. Quorum and Manner of Acting of the Executive Committee. Four members of the Executive Committee shall constitute a quorum for the transaction of business, and the act of a majority of the members of the Executive Committee present at a meeting at which a quorum shall be present shall be the act of the Executive Committee. Participating in a meeting by means of a conference telephone or similar communications equipment allowing all persons participating in the meeting to hear each other shall constitute presence at a meeting of the Executive Committee. The members of the Executive Committee shall act only as a committee and individual members shall have no power as such.

SECTION 5. Other Committees. The Board may, by resolution adopted by a majority of the Board, designate members of the Board to constitute other committees, which shall have, and may exercise, such powers as the Board may by resolution delegate to them, and shall in each case consist of such number of directors as the Board may determine; provided, however, that each such committee shall have at least three directors as members thereof. Such a committee may either be constituted for a

- 9 -

specified term or may be constituted as a standing committee which does not require annual or periodic reconstitution. A majority of all the members of any such committee may determine its action and its quorum requirements and may fix the time and place of its meetings, unless the Board shall otherwise provide. Participating in a meeting by means of a conference telephone or similar communications equipment allowing all persons participating in the meeting to hear each other shall constitute presence at a meeting of such other committees.

In addition to the foregoing, the Board may, by resolution adopted by a majority of the Board, create a committee of indeterminate membership and duration and not subject to the limitations as to the membership, quorum and manner of meeting and acting prescribed in these By-laws, which committee, in the event of a major disaster or catastrophe or national emergency which renders the Board incapable of action by reason of the death, physical incapacity or inability to meet of some or all of its members, shall have, and may exercise all the powers of the Board in the management of the business and affairs of the Corporation (including, without limitation, the power to authorize the seal of the Corporation to be affixed to all papers which may require it and the power to fill vacancies in the Board). An act of such committee taken within the scope of its authority shall be an act of the Board.

SECTION 6. Changes in Committees; Resignations; Removals; Vacancies. The Board shall have power, by resolution adopted by a majority of the Board, at any time to change or remove the members of, to fill vacancies in, and to discharge any committee created pursuant to these By-laws, either with or without cause. Any member of any such committee may resign at any time by giving written notice to the Board or the Chairman of the Board or the Secretary. Such resignation shall take effect upon receipt of such notice or at any later time specified therein; and, unless otherwise specified therein, acceptance of such resignation shall not be necessary to make it effective. Any vacancy in any committee, whether arising from death, resignation, an increase in the number of committee members or any other cause, shall be filled by the Board in the manner prescribed in these By-laws for the original appointment of the members of such committee.

ARTICLE V

OFFICERS

SECTION 1. Number and Qualifications. The officers of the Corporation shall include the Chairman of the Board, and may include one or more Vice Chairmen of the Board, the President, one or more Vice Presidents (one or more of whom may be designated as Executive Vice Presidents or as Senior Vice Presidents or by other designations), the Treasurer, the Secretary and the Controller. Officers shall be elected from time to time by the Board, each to hold office until a successor shall have been duly elected and shall have qualified, or until death, or until resignation as hereinafter provided in Section 2 of this Article V, or until removed as hereinafter provided in Section 3 of this Article V.

SECTION 2. Resignations. Any officer of the Corporation may resign at any

- 10 -

852

time by giving written notice of resignation to the Board, the Chairman of the Board, the Chief Executive Officer or the Secretary. Any such resignation shall take effect at the time specified therein, or, if the time when it shall become effective shall not be specified therein, then it shall become effective upon its receipt; and, unless otherwise specified therein, the acceptance of such resignation shall not be necessary to make it effective.

SECTION 3. Removal. Any officer of the Corporation may be removed, either with or without cause, at any time, by a resolution adopted by a majority of the Board at any meeting of the Board.

SECTION 4. Vacancies. A vacancy in any office, whether arising from death, resignation, removal or any other cause, may be filled for the unexpired portion of the term of office which shall be vacant, in the manner prescribed in these By-laws for the regular election or appointment to such office.

SECTION 5. Chairman of the Board. The Chairman of the Board shall, if present, preside at each meeting of the stockholders and of the Board and shall perform such other duties as may from time to time be assigned by the Board. The Chairman may sign certificates representing shares of the stock of the Corporation pursuant to the provisions of Section 1 of Article VII of these By-laws; sign, execute and deliver in the name of the Corporation all deeds, mortgages, bonds, contracts or other instruments authorized by the Board, except in cases where the signing, execution or delivery thereof shall be expressly delegated by the Board or these By-laws to some other officer or agent of the Corporation or where they shall be required by law otherwise to be signed, executed and delivered; and affix the seal of the Corporation to any instrument which shall require it. The Chairman of the Board, when there is no President or in the absence or incapacity of the President, shall perform all the duties and functions and exercise all the powers of the President.

SECTION 6. Vice Chairman of the Board. Each Vice Chairman of the Board shall assist the Chairman of the Board and have such other duties as may be assigned by the Board or the Chairman of the Board. The Vice Chairman may sign certificates representing shares of the stock of the Corporation pursuant to the provisions of Section 1 of Article VII of these By-laws; sign, execute and deliver in the name of the Corporation all deeds, mortgages, bonds, contracts or other instruments authorized by the Board, except in cases where the signing, execution or delivery thereof shall be expressly delegated by the Board or these By-laws to some officer or agent of the Corporation or where they shall be required by law otherwise to be signed, executed and delivered; and affix the seal of the Corporation to any instrument which shall require it.

SECTION 7. President. The President shall perform all such duties as from time to time may be assigned by the Board or the Chairman of the Board. The President may sign certificates representing shares of the stock of the Corporation pursuant to the provisions of Section 1 of Article VII of these By-laws; sign, execute and deliver in the name of the Corporation all deeds mortgages, bonds, contracts or other instruments authorized by the Board, except in cases where the signing, execution or delivery thereof shall be expressly delegated by the Board or these By-laws to some other officer or agent of the Corporation or where they shall be required by law otherwise to be signed, executed and delivered, and affix the seal of the Corporation to any instrument which shall require it; and, in general, perform all duties incident to the office of President. The President shall in the absence or incapacity of the Chairman of the Board, perform all the duties and functions and exercise all the powers of the Chairman of the Board.

SECTION 8. Designated Officers. (a) Chief Executive Officer. Either the Chairman of the Board, or the President, as the Board of Directors may designate, shall be the Chief Executive Officer of the Corporation. The officer so designated shall have, in addition to the powers and duties applicable to the office set forth in Section 5 or 7 of this Article V, general and active supervision over the business and affairs of the Corporation and over its several officers, agents, and employees, subject, however, to the control of the Board. The Chief Executive Officer shall see that all orders and resolutions of the Board are carried into effect, be an ex officio member of all committees of the Board (except the Audit Committee, the Directors and Corporate Governance Committee, and committees specifically empowered to fix or approve the Chief Executive Officer's compensation or to grant or administer bonus, option or other similar plans in which the Chief Executive Officer is eligible to participate), and, in general, shall perform all duties incident to the position of Chief Executive Officer and such other duties as may from time to time be assigned by the Board. (b) Other Designated Officers. The Board of Directors may designate officers to serve as Chief Financial Officer, Chief Accounting Officer and other such designated positions and to fulfill the responsibilities of such designated positions in addition to their duties as officers as set forth in this Article V.

SECTION 9. Executive Vice Presidents, Senior Vice Presidents and Vice Presidents. Each Executive and Senior Vice President shall perform all such duties as from time to time may be assigned by the Board or the Chairman of the Board or a Vice Chairman of the Board or the President. Each Vice President shall perform all such duties as from time to time may be assigned by the Board or the Chairman of the Board or a Vice Chairman of the Board or the President or an Executive or a Senior Vice President. Any Vice President may sign certificates representing shares of stock of the Corporation pursuant to the provisions of Section 1 of Article VII of these By-laws.

SECTION 10. Treasurer. The Treasurer shall:

(a) have charge and custody of, and be responsible for, all the funds and securities of the Corporation, and may invest the same in any securities, may open, maintain and close accounts for effecting any and all purchase, sale, investment and lending transactions in securities of any and all kinds for and on behalf of the Corporation or any employee pension or benefit plan fund or other fund established by the Corporation, as may be permitted by law;

(b) keep full and accurate accounts of receipts and disbursements in books belonging to the Corporation;

(c) deposit all moneys and other valuables to the credit of the Corporation in such depositaries as may be designated by the Board or the Executive Committee;

(d) receive, and give receipts for, moneys due and payable to the Corporation from any source whatsoever;

(e) disburse the funds of the Corporation and supervise the investment of its funds, taking proper vouchers therefor;

(f) render to the Board, whenever the Board may require, an account of all transactions as Treasurer; and

(g) in general, perform all the duties incident to the office of Treasurer and such other duties as from time to time may be assigned by the Board or the Chairman of the Board or a Vice Chairman of the Board or the President or an Executive or Senior Vice President.

SECTION 11. Secretary. The Secretary shall:

(a) keep or cause to be kept in one or more books provided for the purpose, the minutes of all meetings of the Board, the Executive Committee and other committees of the Board and the stockholders;

(b) see that all notices are duly given in accordance with the provisions of these By-laws and as required by law;

(c) be custodian of the records and the seal of the Corporation and affix and attest the seal to all stock certificates of the Corporation and affix and attest the seal to all other documents to be executed on behalf of the Corporation under its seal;

(d) see that the books, reports, statements, certificates and other documents and records required by law to be kept and filed are properly kept and filed; and

(e) in general, perform all the duties incident to the office of Secretary and such other duties as from time to time may be assigned by the Board or the Chairman of the Board or a Vice Chairman of the Board or the President or an Executive or Senior Vice President.

- 13 -

SECTION 12. Controller. The Controller shall:

(a) have control of all the books of account of the Corporation;

(b) keep a true and accurate record of all property owned by it, of its debts and of its revenues and expenses;

(c) keep all accounting records of the Corporation (other than the accounts of receipts and disbursements and those relating to the deposits of money and other valuables of the Corporation, which shall be kept by the Treasurer);

(d) render to the Board, whenever the Board may require, an account of the financial condition of the Corporation; and

(e) in general, perform all the duties incident to the office of Controller and such other duties as from time to time may be assigned by the Board or the Chairman of the Board or a Vice Chairman of the Board or the President or an Executive or Senior Vice President.

SECTION 13. Compensation. The compensation of the officers of the Corporation shall be fixed from time to time by the Board; provided, however, that the Board may delegate to a committee the power to fix or approve the compensation of any officers. An officer of the Corporation shall not be prevented from receiving compensation by reason of being also a director of the Corporation; but any such officer who shall also be a director shall not have any vote in the determination of the amount of compensation paid to such officer.

ARTICLE VI

CONTRACTS, CHECKS, DRAFTS, BANK ACCOUNTS, ETC.

SECTION 1. Execution of Contracts. Except as otherwise required by law or these By-laws, any contract or other instrument may be executed and delivered in the name and on behalf of the Corporation by any officer (including any assistant officer) of the Corporation. The Board or the Executive Committee may authorize any agent or employee to execute and deliver any contract or other instrument in the name and on behalf of the Corporation, and such authority may be general or confined to specific instances as the Board or such Committee, as the case may be, may by resolution determine.

SECTION 2. Loans. Unless the Board shall otherwise determine, the Chairman of the Board or a Vice Chairman of the Board or the President or any Vice President, acting together with the Treasurer or the Secretary, may effect loans and advances at any time for the Corporation from any bank, trust company or other institution, or from any firm, corporation or individual, and for such loans and advances may make, execute and deliver promissory notes, bonds or other certificates or evidences of indebtedness of the Corporation, but in making such loans or advances no officer or officers shall mortgage, pledge, hypothecate or transfer any securities or other property of the Corporation, except when authorized by resolution adopted by the Board.

- 14 -

856

SECTION 3. Checks, Drafts, etc. All checks, drafts, bills of exchange or other orders for the payment of money out of the funds of the Corporation, and all notes or other evidences of indebtedness of the Corporation, shall be signed in the name and on behalf of the Corporation by such persons and in such manner as shall from time to time be authorized by the Board or the Executive Committee or authorized by the Treasurer acting together with either the General Manager of an operating unit or a nonfinancial Vice President of the Corporation, which authorization may be general or confined to specific instances.

SECTION 4. Deposits. All funds of the Corporation not otherwise employed shall be deposited from time to time to the credit of the Corporation in such banks, trust companies or other depositaries as the Board or the Executive Committee may from time to time designate or as may be designated by any officer or officers of the Corporation to whom such power of designation may from time to time be delegated by the Board or the Executive Committee. For the purpose of deposit and for the purpose of collection for the account of the Corporation, checks, drafts and other orders for the payment of money which are payable to the order of the Corporation may be endorsed, assigned and delivered by any officer, employee or agent of the Corporation.

SECTION 5. General and Special Bank Accounts. The Board or the Executive Committee may from time to time authorize the opening and keeping of general and special bank accounts with such banks, trust companies or other depositaries as the Board or the Executive Committee may designate or as may be designated by any officer or officers of the Corporation to whom such power of designation may from time to time be delegated by the Board or the Executive Committee. The Board or the Executive Committee may make such special rules and regulations with respect to such bank accounts, not inconsistent with the provisions of these By-laws, as it may deem expedient.

SECTION 6. Indemnification. The Corporation shall, to the fullest extent permitted by applicable law as in effect at any time, indemnify any person made, or threatened to be made, a party to an action or proceeding whether civil or criminal (including an action or proceeding by or in the right of the Corporation or any other corporation of any type or kind, domestic or foreign, or any partnership, joint venture, trust, employee benefit plan or other enterprise, for which any director or officer of the Corporation served in any capacity at the request of the Corporation), by reason of the fact that such person or such person's testator or intestate was a director or officer of the Corporation, or served such other corporation, partnership, joint venture, trust, employee benefit plan or other enterprise in any capacity, against judgments, fines, amounts paid in settlement and reasonable expenses, including attorneys' fees actually and necessarily incurred as a result of such action or proceeding, or any appeal therein. Such indemnification shall be a contract right and shall include the right to be paid advances of any expenses incurred by such person in connection with such action, suit or proceeding, consistent with the provisions of applicable law in effect at any time. Indemnification shall be deemed to be 'permitted' within the meaning of the first sentence hereof if it is not expressly prohibited by applicable law as in effect at the time.

- 15 -

857

SAMPLE DOCUMENTS

ARTICLE VII

SHARES

SECTION 1. Stock Certificates. The shares of the Corporation shall be represented by certificates, or shall be uncertificated shares. Each owner of stock of the Corporation shall be entitled to have a certificate, in such form as shall be approved by the Board, certifying the number of shares of stock of the Corporation owned. To the extent that shares are represented by certificates, such certificates of stock shall be signed in the name of the Corporation by the Chairman of the Board or a Vice Chairman of the Board or the President or a Vice President and by the Secretary and sealed with the seal of the Corporation (which seal may be a facsimile, engraved or printed); provided, however, that where any such certificate is signed by a registrar, other than the Corporation or its employee, the signatures of the Chairman of the Board, a Vice Chairman of the Board, the President, the Secretary, and transfer agent or a transfer clerk acting on behalf of the Corporation upon such certificates may be facsimiles, engraved or printed. In case any officer, transfer agent or transfer clerk acting on behalf of the Corporation ceases to be such officer, transfer agent, or transfer clerk before such certificates shall be issued, they may nevertheless be issued by the Corporation with the same effect as if they were still such officer, transfer agent or transfer clerk at the date of their issue.

SECTION 2. Books of Account and Record of Stockholders. There shall be kept at the office of the Corporation correct books of account of all its business and transactions, minutes of the proceedings of stockholders, Board, and Executive Committee, and a book to be known as the record of stockholders, containing the names and addresses of all persons who are stockholders, the number of shares of stock held, and the date when the stockholder became the owner of record thereof.

SECTION 3. Transfers of Stock. Transfers of shares of stock of the Corporation shall be made on the record of stockholders of the Corporation only upon authorization by the registered holder thereof, or by an attorney thereunto authorized by power of attorney duly executed and filed with the Secretary or with a transfer agent or transfer clerk, and on surrender of the certificate or certificates for such shares properly endorsed, provided such shares are represented by a certificate, or accompanied by a duly executed stock transfer power and the payment of all taxes thereon. The person in whose names shares of stock shall stand on the record of stockholders of the Corporation shall be deemed the owner thereof for all purposes as regards the Corporation. Whenever any transfers of shares shall be made for collateral security and not absolutely and written notice thereof shall be given to the Secretary or to such transfer agent or transfer clerk, such fact shall be stated in the entry of the transfer.

SECTION 4. Regulations. The Board may make such additional rules and regulations as it may deem expedient, not inconsistent with these By-laws, concerning the issue, transfer and registration of certificated or uncertificated shares of stock of the Corporation. It may appoint, or authorize any officer or officers to appoint, one or more transfer agents or one or more transfer clerks and one or more registrars and may require all certificates of stock to bear the signature or signatures of any of them.

SECTION 5. Fixing of Record Date. The Board shall fix a time not exceeding sixty nor less than ten days prior to the date then fixed for the holding of any meeting of the stockholders or prior to the last day on which the consent or dissent of the stockholders may be effectively expressed for any purpose without a meeting, as the time as of which the stockholders entitled to notice of and to vote at such meeting or whose consent or dissent is required or may be expressed for any purpose, as the case may be, shall be determined, and all persons who were holders of record of voting stock at such time, and no others, shall be entitled to notice of and to vote at such meeting or to express their consent or dissent, as the case may be. The Board may fix a time not exceeding sixty days preceding the date fixed for the payment of any dividend or the making of any distribution or the allotment of rights to subscribe for securities of the Corporation, or for the delivery of evidences of rights or evidences of interests arising out of any change, conversion or exchange of capital stock or other securities, as the record date for the determination of the stockholders entitled to receive any such dividend, distribution, allotment, rights or interests, and in such case only the stockholders of record at the time so fixed shall be entitled to receive such dividend, distribution, allotment, rights or interests.

SECTION 6. Lost, Destroyed or Mutilated Certificates. The holder of any certificate representing shares of stock of the Corporation shall immediately notify the Corporation of any loss, destruction or mutilation of such certificate, and the Corporation may issue a new certificate of stock in the place of any certificate theretofore issued by it which the owner thereof shall allege to have been lost or destroyed or which shall have been mutilated, and the Corporation may, in its discretion, require such owner or the owner's legal representatives to give to the Corporation a bond in such sum, limited or unlimited, and in such form and with such surety or sureties as the Board in its absolute discretion shall determine, to indemnify the Corporation against any claim that may be made against it on account of the alleged loss or destruction of any such certificate, or the issuance of such new certificate. Anything to the contrary notwithstanding, the Corporation, in its absolute discretion, may refuse to issue any such new certificate, except pursuant to legal proceedings under the laws of the State of New York.

SECTION 7. Inspection of Records. The record of stockholders and minutes of the proceedings of stockholders shall be available for inspection, within the limits and subject to the conditions and restrictions prescribed by applicable law.

SECTION 8. Auditors. The Board shall employ an independent public or certified public accountant or firm of such accountants who shall act as auditors in making examinations of the consolidated financial statements of the Corporation and its subsidiaries in accordance with generally accepted auditing standards. The auditors shall certify that the annual financial statements are prepared in accordance with generally accepted accounting principles, and shall report on such financial statements to the stockholders and directors of the Corporation. The Board's selection of auditors shall be presented for ratification by the stockholders at the annual meeting. Directors and officers, when acting in good faith, may rely upon financial statements of the Corporation represented to them to be correct by the officer of the Corporation having charge of its books of account, or stated in a written report by the auditors fairly to reflect the financial condition of the Corporation.

ARTICLE VIII

OFFICES

SECTION 1. Principal Office. The principal office of the Corporation shall be at such place in the Town of North Castle, County of Westchester and State of New York as the Board shall from time to time determine.

SECTION 2. Other Offices. The Corporation may also have an office or offices other than said principal office at such place or places as the Board shall from time to time determine or the business of the Corporation may require.

ARTICLE IX

WAIVER OF NOTICE

Whenever under the provisions of any law of the State of New York, the Certificate of Incorporation or these By-laws or any resolution of the Board or any committee thereof, the Corporation or the Board or any committee thereof is authorized to take any action after notice to the stockholders, directors or members of any such committee, or after the lapse of a prescribed period of time, such action may be taken without notice and without the lapse of any period of time, if, at any time before or after such action shall be completed, such notice or lapse of time shall be waived by the person or persons entitled to said notice or entitled to participate in the action to be taken, or, in the case of a stockholder, by an attorney thereunto authorized. Attendance at a meeting requiring notice by any person or, in the case of a stockholder, by the stockholder's attorney, agent or proxy, shall constitute a waiver of such notice on the part of the person so attending, or by such stockholder, as the case may be.

SAMPLE DOCUMENTS

ARTICLE X

FISCAL YEAR

The fiscal year of the Corporation shall end on the thirty-first day of December in each year.

ARTICLE XI

SEAL

The Seal of the Corporation shall consist of two concentric circles with the IBM logotype appearing in bold face type within the inner circle and the words 'International Business Machines Corporation' appearing within the outer circle.

ARTICLE XII

AMENDMENTS

These By-laws may be amended or repealed or new By-laws may be adopted by the stockholders at any annual or special meeting, if the notice thereof mentions that amendment or repeal or the adoption of new By-laws is one of the purposes of such meeting. These By-laws, subject to the laws of the State of New York, may also be amended or repealed or new By-laws may be adopted by the affirmative vote of a majority of the Board given at any meeting, if the notice thereof mentions that amendment or repeal or the adoption of new By-laws is one of the purposes of such meeting.

UBS

Record of resolutions of the annual general meeting of UBS AG on Wednesday, 15 April 2009, 10:00 a.m., at Hallenstadion, Zurich

Formalities

Chair: Peter Kurer, Chairman of the Board of Directors
Minutes: Luzius Cameron, Secretary to the Board of Directors

Notary providing official certification of the resolutions passed in respect of amendments to the Articles of Association: Daniel Allemann, Oerlikon-Zurich

Scrutineer: BDO Visura, Solothurn

Independent proxy pursuant to Art. 689c of the Swiss Code of Obligations: Altorfer Duss & Beilstein AG, Zurich.

Auditors: Ernst & Young Ltd., Basel, represented by Andrew McIntyre and Andreas Blumer.

The invitation to the general meeting was published in the Swiss Commercial Gazette on 20 March 2009 and in an abridged form in various daily newspapers. In addition, printed copies of the invitation were sent to all shareholders listed in the share register. The general meeting was thus quorate.

Voting on all items on the agenda was conducted electronically.
The annual general meeting was transmitted live on the Internet in German and English.

Attendance:
At 10:04 a.m. 4,985 shareholders are present, representing 925,014,053 votes (48.15% of shares eligible to vote),

of which
Independent proxies	503,355,673 votes
Corporate proxies	286,923,292 votes
Custody proxies	91,925,155 votes
UBS represents a total of	378,769,719 votes

The Chairman of the Board of Directors reports on the main events of the last 12 months and explains which measures were taken:
- risk control was redefined and the bank's risks reduced;
- a strategic repositioning of the bank was conducted;
- the balance sheet was drastically reduced and at the same time the bank was recapitalized;
- the operating costs were brought down from 35.5 to 27.6 billion francs;
- corporate governance was fundamentally redefined;
- nearly all members of the Board of Directors and management were replaced;
- key legal problems were solved;
- a new compensation model was devised;
- and the bank had to learn how to cope with direct government influence on its business activities.

The text of the Chairman's speech is available on the UBS Internet http://www.ubs.com/agm.

In contrast, Oswald J. Gruebel, Group CEO, addresses the current situation in his speech and summarizes the planned cost-savings measures. He reports a loss attributable of almost 2 billion Swiss francs. Due to a reduction of the balance sheet and risk-weighted assets, UBS expects, despite this loss, to have a tier 1 capital ratio of roughly 10%.

In terms of net new money, UBS will close the quarter with an overall net outflow.

To protect and strengthen the bank's capital base, UBS will avoid loss-making businesses and is compelled to drastically cut costs. Considerable job cuts are inevitable. Oswald Gruebel states that the business areas are being reviewed and UBS will reduce its size.

The speech of the Group CEO is available on the UBS Internet http://www.ubs.com/agm.

The Chairman moves onto Item 1.

Item 1
Annual report, Group and Parent Bank accounts for financial year 2008
1.1.   Approval of the annual report and Group and Parent Bank accounts

The Board of Directors proposes that the annual report and Group and Parent Bank accounts for the financial year 2008 be approved.
In its reports to the annual general meeting, Ernst & Young Ltd., Basel, as a statutory audit, recommended without qualification that the Group and Parent Bank accounts for the financial year 2008 be approved.

The Chairman gives reason for the decision to postpone the discharge of the members of the Board of Directors and the Executive Boards to a later point in time, when all internal and external examinations with regard to the US subprime crisis and their impact on UBS are closed.

A lengthy discussion is held in which 23 shareholders voices their opinion.

The general assembly approves the Group and Parent Bank accounts for the financial year 2008 with the following vote totals:

Votes cast	924,099.384	
Absolute majority	462,049,693	
Votes in favor	**885,721,284**	**95.84%**
Votes against	25,095,923	2.72%
Abstentions	13,282,177	1.44%

1.2.   Advisory vote on principles and fundamentals of the new compensation model for 2009

The Chairman describes the events and measures taken for the business year 2008 and briefly presents the new compensation model:

The Board of Directors proposes that the principles and fundamentals of the new model for 2009 be ratified in a non-binding advisory vote. In the discussion nine shareholders address the item.

The general assembly approves the principles and fundamentals of the new compensation model for 2009 with the following vote totals:

Votes cast	922,403,669	
Absolute majority	461,201,835	
Votes in favor	**808,442,394**	**87.65%**
Votes against	96,674,449	10.48%
Abstentions	17,286,826	1.87%

Item 2
Appropriation of results

The Board of Directors proposes that the Parent Bank UBS AG loss for the period 2008 of CHF 36,489 million to be set off against the general statutory profit reserve and other reserves.

Thereof a total of CHF 2,472 million shall be set off against the general statutory profit reserve and CHF 11,901 million shall be set off against the general statutory capital reserve. The remaining loss of CHF 22,115 million shall be set off against other reserves.

No further comments were made on the proposal. The general assembly approves the proposal with the following vote totals:

Votes cast	922,110,175	
Absolute majority	461,055,088	
Votes in favor	**904,419,858**	**98.08%**
Votes against	8,668,520	0.94%
Abstentions	9,021,797	0.98%

Item 3
Elections
3.1. Re-election of members of the Board of Directors

Due to the newly introduced one-year term of office, adopted at the annual general assembly in 2008, all Board members who are still available will stand for re-election. Exceptions are Sergio Marchionne and Helmut Panke, who will stand for re-election in 2010.
The Board of Directors proposes that Peter R. Voser, David Sidwell, Sally Bott, Rainer-Marc Frey, Bruno Gehrig and William G. Parrett be re-elected for a one-year term. In a generic discussion five shareholders express their thoughts and opinion.

3.1.1. Peter R. Voser

The Board of Directors proposes that Peter R. Voser be re-elected for an additional one-year term of office.
No further comments were made on the proposal. The general assembly approves the proposal with the following vote totals:

Votes cast	921,671,925	
Absolute majority	460,835,963	
Votes in favor	**899,326,623**	**97.58%**
Votes against	16,597,178	1.80%
Abstentions	5,748,124	0.62%

3.1.2. David Sidwell

The Board of Directors proposes that David Sidwell be re-elected for an additional one-year term of office.
No further comments were made on the proposal. The general assembly approves the proposal with the following vote totals:

Votes cast	921,703,849	
Absolute majority	460,851,925	
Votes in favor	**893,797,941**	**96.97%**
Votes against	21,216,181	2.30%
Abstentions	6,689,727	0.73%

3.1.3. Sally Bott

The Board of Directors proposes that Sally Bott be re-elected for an additional one-year term of office.
No further comments were made on the proposal. The general assembly approves the proposal with the following vote totals:

Votes cast	919,168,812	
Absolute majority	459,584,407	
Votes in favor	**894,981,081**	**97.37%**
Votes against	17,387,128	1.89%
Abstentions	6,800,603	0.74%

3.1.4. Rainer-Marc Frey

The Board of Directors proposes that Rainer-Marc Frey be re-elected for an additional one-year term of office.
No further comments were made on the proposal. The general assembly approves the proposal with the following vote totals:

Votes cast	921,609,620	
Absolute majority	460,804,811	
Votes in favor	**879,093,494**	**95.39%**
Votes against	30,358,230	3.29%
Abstentions	12,157,896	1.32%

3.1.5. Bruno Gehrig

The Board of Directors proposes that Bruno Gehrig be re-elected for an additional one-year term of office.
One shareholder comments on the re-election of Bruno Gehrig. The general assembly approves the proposal with the following vote totals:

Votes cast	921,626,199	
Absolute majority	460,813,100	
Votes in favor	**896,346,762**	**97.25%**
Votes against	19,234,963	2.09%

Abstentions	6,044,474	0.66%

3.1.6. William G. Parrett

The Board of Directors proposes that William G. Parrett be re-elected for an additional one-year term of office.
No further comments were made on the proposal. The general assembly approves the proposal with the following vote totals:

Votes cast	921,541,436	
Absolute majority	460,770,719	
Votes in favor	**897,945,061**	**97.44%**
Votes against	16,683,180	1.81%
Abstentions	6,913,195	0.75%

3.2. Election of four new candidates for the Board of Directors

The Chairman bids farewell to the retiring Board members Ernesto Bertarelli, Gabrielle Kaufmann-Kohler and Joerg Wolle. Then he leads into the discussion of the election of the new candidates.

3.2.1 Kaspar Villiger

The Board of Directors proposes that Kaspar Villiger be elected as a non-independent member of the Board of Directors for a one-year term of office.

After a discussion of six shareholders the general assembly approves the election of Kaspar Villiger with the following vote totals:

Votes cast	919,831,034	
Absolute majority	459,915,518	
Votes in favor	**897,114,171**	**97.53%**
Votes against	11,564,862	1.26%
Abstentions	11,152,001	1.21%

3.2.2. Michel Demaré

The Board of Directors proposes that Michel Demaré be elected as an independent member of the Board of Directors for a one-year term of office.

One shareholder comments on the proposal. The general assembly approves the election of Michel Demaré with the following vote totals:

Votes cast	917,975,229	
Absolute majority	458,987,615	
Votes in favor	**899,392,138**	**97.98%**
Votes against	6,517,596	0.71%
Abstentions	12,065,495	1.31%

3.2.3. Ann F. Godbehere

The Board of Directors proposes that Ann F. Godbehere be elected as an independent member of the Board of Directors for a one-year term of office.

No further comments were made on the proposal. The general assembly approves the election of Ann F. Godbehere with the following vote totals:

Votes cast	917,926,723	
Absolute majority	458,963,362	
Votes in favor	**889,865,869**	**96.94%**
Votes against	9,247,139	1.01%
Abstentions	18,813,715	2.05%

3.2.4. Axel P. Lehmann

The Board of Directors proposes that Axel P. Lehmann be elected as an independent member of the Board of Directors for a one-year term of office.

No further comments were made on the proposal. The general assembly approves the election of Axel P. Lehmann with the following vote totals:

Votes cast	917,875,137	
Absolute majority	458,937,569	
Votes in favor	**893,468,600**	**97.34%**
Votes against	6,403,075	0.70%
Abstentions	18,003,462	1.96%

In his speech Kaspar Villiger expresses his gratitude toward the newly elected directors for making themselves available and thanks Oswald Gruebel for his willingness to take over the helm of UBS in these difficult times. In addition, he thanks the retiring Board members and Peter Kurer for dealing with an incredible workload and having set the wheels in motion for the transformation process.

The speech of Kaspar Villiger is available on the UBS Internet http://www.ubs.com/agm.

3.3. Re-election of the auditors (Ernst & Young Ltd., Basel)

The Board of Directors proposes that Ernst & Young Ltd, Basel, be re-elected for an additional one-year term of office as auditors for the financial statements of UBS AG and the consolidated financial statements of the UBS Group.
After two comments by shareholders the general assembly approves the proposal with the following vote totals:

Votes cast	909,743,351	
Absolute majority	454,871,676	
Votes in favor	**881,328,161**	**96.88%**
Votes against	513,922,622	1.53%
Abstentions	14,492,568	1.59%

3.4. Re-election of the special auditors (BDO Visura, Zurich)

The Board of Directors proposes that BDO Visura, Zurich, be re-elected for a three-year term of office as a special auditor.
No further comments were made on the proposal. The general assembly approves the proposal with the following vote totals:

Votes cast	909,595,784	
Absolute majority	454,797,893	
Votes in favor	**895,267,363**	**98.42%**
Votes against	6,996,721	0.77%
Abstentions	7,331,700	0.81%

Item 4
Creation of conditional capital
Approval of Article 4a para. 5 of the Articles of Association

The Board of Directors proposes the creation of conditional capital in a maximum amount of CHF 10,000,000 by means of an addition to the Articles of Association.

The Chairman illustrates the background of the transaction with the Swiss National Bank and explains the necessity of creating earmarked conditional capital.
No further comments were made on the proposal. The general assembly approves the proposal with the following vote totals:

Votes cast	910,578,181	
2/3 majority of votes cast	607,052,121	
Votes in favor	**885,741,633**	**97.27%**
Votes against	17,919,125	1.97%
Abstentions	6,167,338	0.68%
Non delivered, empty and invalid votes	750,085	0.08%

Item 5
Creation of authorized capital
Approval of Article 4b para. 2 of the Articles of Association

The Board of Directors proposes the creation of authorized capital in an amount not to exceed 10% of the issued share capital by means an addition to the Articles of Association.
The Chairman illustrates the necessity of creating authorized capital and explains the need for UBS to have the flexibility to potentially raise capital in the future.
One shareholder comments on the proposal. The general assembly approves the proposal with the following vote totals:

Votes cast	910,504,664	
2/3 majority of votes cast	607,003,110	
Votes in favor	**850,201,658**	**93.38%**
Votes against	52,958,913	5.82%
Abstentions	6,481,627	0.71%
Non delivered, empty and invalid votes	862,466	0.09%

The general meeting closes at 4:45 p.m.

Zurich, 23 April 2009

On behalf of the Board of Directors:

Peter Kurer
Chairman

Luzius Cameron
Company Secretary

SAMPLE DOCUMENTS

Sample of Board Meeting Minutes

Name of Organization
(Board Meeting Minutes: Month Day, Year)
(time and location)

Board Members:

Present: Mollie Martin, Elliott Hatzan, Jerry Gold, George Spears, Thomas Smith and George Jones

Absent: Melody Jones

Quorum present? Yes

Others Present:

Chief Operating Officer Lynda Johnson

Other: Suzette Foley, outside counsel

Proceedings:

* _Meeting called to order_ at 7:00 p.m. by Chair, Mollie Martin

* Last month's meeting minutes were amended and approved

Chief Executive's Report: Elliott Hatzan

— Recommends a study to determine the costs of an upgraded computer system.

— Employee bonuses were set by management at five percent of base salary.

Finance Committee report provided by Chair, Mollie Martin:

— Hatzan explained that outside counsel reviewed the company's insider trading program and found it to be satisfactory.

— Hatzan reviewed highlights, trends and issues from the balance sheet, income statement and cash flow statement. Issues include increased material costs. After brief discussion of the issues and suggestions on how to reduce other costs, MOTION to accept financial statements; seconded and passed.

Board Development Committee's report provided by Chair, Mollie Martin:

— Martin reminded the Board of the scheduled retreat coming up in three months, and provided a drafted retreat schedule for board review. MOTION to accept the retreat agenda; seconded and passed.

— Martin presented members with a draft of the reworded By-laws paragraph that would allow members to conduct actions over electronic mail. Martin suggested review by counsel and a resolution at the next meeting to change the By-laws accordingly.

Other business:

— George Jones announced that he had recently hired a new secretary, Glenda Bottin.

There being no further business.

Minutes submitted by Secretary, George Spears.